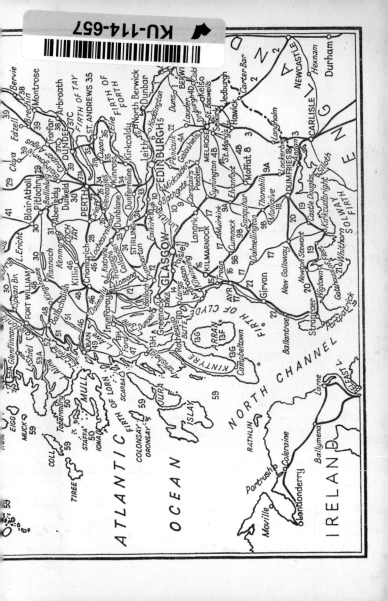

SCOTLAND

THE BLUE GUIDES

SCOTLAND

Edited by
L. RUSSELL MUIRHEAD
M.A., F.S.A.

*With a Complete Atlas of Scotland
and 34 other Maps and Plans*

FOURTH EDITION

LONDON
ERNEST BENN LIMITED
1959

First Edition	.	.	.	1927
Second Edition	.	.	.	1932
Third Edition	.	.	.	1949
Fourth Edition	.	.	.	1959

DISTRIBUTED IN THE U.S.A. BY

RAND McNALLY & COMPANY, CHICAGO

PREFACE

SCOTLAND is a small country, but its appeal is so manifold that it is difficult to catalogue its attractions. Its wonderful and varied scenery of mountain, sea, and loch, of Highland glen and Lowland dale, is the appropriate setting of a wild and romantic history, while over all is cast the fascinating glamour of poetry, legend, and romance. At the same time it is the home of an interesting and virile people, retaining many idiosyncrasies while playing a prominent part in the general progress of the world. The BLUE GUIDE TO SCOTLAND, now in its fourth edition, neglects none of these aspects, while it aims at making the way smooth for the visitor by describing the country in a series of carefully planned routes, by paying special attention to the practical details of travel, and by providing an adequate equipment of maps and plans (including a complete ATLAS) with the appropriate map-reference at the head of every page. A full INDEX (showing the county of each place) is an instantaneous key to every point in the volume.

In the present edition almost all the landward routes are based on the road system, for the better guidance of the independent traveller by road ; but the requirements of the railway traveller have not been forgotten ; and special attention has been paid to the widespread network of public motor transport, which, thanks to the great improvement in roads throughout the country, now penetrates to many of the remoter crofts and hamlets. Furthermore, the provision of convenient air services, bringing remote communities into touch with the main centres of traffic, has been taken into account.

As a winter resort Scotland offers a comparatively mild and not infrequently sunny climate on its western coasts, while the central and north-eastern districts have entered the lists as centres for winter sports.

Hotels in Scotland have maintained the improvement of recent years, a special feature being the conversion to the use of travellers of many country houses, large and small. Such establishments, often with fine grounds and sporting rights, have opened up many remote districts. Hotel charges are seldom excessive, especially considering the shortness of the season and the present-day difficulties of operation. Charges are stated in accordance with tariffs authorised by the hotels themselves, supplemented by the personal experience of the Editor and his Staff and by hotel bills kindly submitted by travellers, but a small increase must now and then be expected.

The cordial and generous assistance which the Editor received in the preparation of the earlier editions of this volume has in many instances been repeated. For the present edition special thanks are due to *Miss Joan Hitchcox*, who was responsible for rewriting a great part of the account of the Western Highlands, the Borders, and the S.W., the result of several journeys made expressly on behalf of the volume; to *Mr. Marryat R. Dobie*, for innumerable suggestions concerning Edinburgh; to *Miss Louie B. Russ*, of Glasgow, for further suggestions and improvements, notably concerning the sections dealing with Glasgow and its environs; to *Mr. E. J. P. Raven*, of Aberdeen, for guidance in the revision of information on Roman and other antiquities; and to *Dr. W. Douglas Simpson*, also of Aberdeen, for help with early-Christian and other survivals. Further acknowledgements are due to the numerous officials of museums, Government departments, burghs, and transport companies, as well as the owners and factors of estates who gave willing and valuable co-operation. General assistance was received, also, from the Scottish National Tourist Board, the Scottish Youth Hostels Association, the National Trust for Scotland, and the British Travel and Holidays Association; and a special word of thanks is due to the staff of the Royal Automobile Club, the Automobile Association, and the Cyclists' Touring Club for general advice in connection with roads and ferries.

No one is better aware than the Editor and his Staff of the difficulty of avoiding errors; and suggestions for the correction or improvement of the Guide will be most gratefully welcomed.

Advertisements of every kind are rigorously excluded from this and every other volume of the Blue Guide Series.

EXPLANATIONS

TYPE. The main routes are described in large type. Smaller type is used for branch-routes and excursions, for historical and preliminary paragraphs, and (speaking generally) for descriptions of minor importance.

ASTERISKS indicate points of special interest or excellence.

POPULATIONS are given according to the census of 1951.

ABBREVIATIONS. In addition to generally accepted and self-explanatory abbreviations the following occur in the Guide:

B. = Breakfast.	Pl. = Plan.
c. = circa (about).	R. = Room.
D. = Dinner.	Rfmts. = Refreshments.
Dec. = Decorated.	Rte. = Route.
E.E. = Early English.	S.Y.H.A. = Scottish Youth Hostels
fl. = floruit (flourished).	Association.
gs. = guineas.	T. = High tea or meat tea.
L. = Luncheon.	temp. = temperance.
N.T. = (Scottish) National Trust.	U.F. = United Free (Church).
P. = pension (board and lodging).	unlic. = unlicensed.
Perp. = Perpendicular.	Y.H. = Youth Hostel.

TABLE OF CONTENTS

II. STIRLING, PERTH, AND THE PERTHSHIRE HIGHLANDS

III. FIFE, ABERDEEN, AND EASTERN SCOTLAND

IV. OBAN AND WESTERN SCOTLAND

V. NORTHERN SCOTLAND AND ITS ISLANDS

MAPS AND PLANS

MAPS

TOWN PLANS

GROUND PLANS

INDEX OF ARCHITECTS
IN SCOTLAND

AN INTRODUCTION TO THE STUDY OF SCOTTISH MONUMENTS

By W. Mackay Mackenzie, M.A., D.Litt.

Late Secretary to the Royal Commission on the Ancient and Historical Monuments of Scotland

SYDNEY SMITH characterised Scotland as the " knuckle-end " of England. It is true that only one island is in question, yet it must not be inferred that the relics and monuments of the northern part are but an extension or reflection of those in the greater southern area. Scotland had other avenues of access than that from the south. Ireland on the west was always an influence in that quarter. The Scandinavian countries at one stage profoundly affected the culture of the islands and the northern districts. Both in early and historic times currents of culture flowed across the North Sea from the Rhine lands ; and the special links between Scotland and France in later historic times are familiar. Yet beyond these infiltrations of culture, the area to be known as Scotland had at all stages something of its own to contribute either by modification or by invention ; and thus certain objects and structures are peculiar to that country.

Prehistoric Monuments. We are not here concerned with relics as such, these for the most part having found a resting-place either in the great collection of the National Museum of Antiquities at Edinburgh or in local museums. The earliest known type of structure, which can be seen only *in situ*, is the CHAMBERED CAIRN. This consists of a great pile of stones composing a structure of elongated, quadrate, oval, or circular shape, having usually one burial chamber, but occasionally two or even three chambers, each entered by a passage from one end or from a side. Or there was a great central chamber with cells opening off it. The chambers are constructed of long slabs laid horizontally and converging or set upright and packed with smaller building to·support a roof of slabs. In length such cairns may run to 240 feet and, where fairly well preserved, rise to a height of about 20 feet. Examples in Caithness and Sutherland, called ' horned cairns,' have the special feature of a crescentic finish at each end. In the Stewartry of Kirkcudbright such horns, where they appear, are at one end only. The horned cairn is peculiar to Scotland. In Argyll and the Outer Isles the Chambered Cairns are approximately circular ; in the latter region they are sometimes known as ' barps,' a good example being *Langass Barp*, about five miles out from

Lochmaddy, North Uist, near the road going west. A unique example is *Maeshowe* (p. 419), between Kirkwall and Stromness, which alone among these structures in Scotland was provided with a practicable door of stone. Such erections are usually regarded as places for successive burials by a people in the Neolithic stage of culture, i.e. using polished stone implements and familiar with the art of making pottery, having domesticated animals, and practising a primitive agriculture. A date about 1500 B.C. may serve as a convenient reference in time but must not be taken too literally. The location of these cairns either on the coast lands and islands or in places not far from the sea suggests a migration coastwise to avoid the forests and marshes that obstructed penetration overland. Many if not most of these monuments occupy conspicuous positions and have had their stones, especially those of any size, brought from some distance ; all which implies a considerable amount of concerted labour.

The presence of tall stones set upright in the chamber or on the margin of these cairns, and the obvious importance attached to the service of the dead, link them with later erections, much more numerous and widespread, viz. the STONE CIRCLES or CROMLECHS, which are almost wholly composed of such stones, set ordinarily in rings but in a comparatively few cases in rows. In some circles a stone cairn lies within the ring, in others an exposed chamber or kist, formed of broad slabs set on end which have been closed with a cover slab or slabs—the dolmen or ' table stone ' construction. These monuments can be roughly classified in three great groups ; one, which is general, composed of a single irregular ring or of concentric rings ; another, represented by those at *Clava* (p. 368), seven miles E. of Inverness, having within the circle a round chambered cairn entered by a passage ; and a third, in Aberdeenshire and adjoining counties, in which a stone recumbent on its side is found between two of the uprights. The most remarkable setting, however, is that at *Callanish* (p. 392), in Lewis, within easy range of three circles of the simpler type. In this great setting the total number of stones is 47 and the full length N. and S. 400 feet. Stones arranged in roughly parallel lines are to be found only in Caithness and in the Strath of Kildonan in Sutherland. The best example is in Caithness, on the hill slope N.W. of *Mid-Clyth* (near Lybster, p. 402), where are 22 rows comprising 192 stones still in position but with no stone exceeding 3 feet in height. These stone rows may be paralleled with some examples in England and Wales and the great rows in Brittany.

Chambered cairns and stone settings are included in a megalithic (' great-stone ') culture, i.e. a civilisation of which a feature is the handling of tall, unwieldy stones for a special purpose—the handsome interment of the dead. Whether this practice implies ideas of a religious nature and whether the standing stones were places of religious ceremonial are matters for conjecture. At every stage occur examples of both direct burial and cremation. As the chambered cairns are Neolithic, so the free standing stone settings, from relics and other considerations, can be attributed to the epoch in which bronze was the dominant material. But cultures overlapped ; there was no clean break-away at any stage. Bronze was introduced to these islands about 1800 B.C. The culture rooted itself in Scotland, as evidence of the local fabrication of tools, weapons, and ornaments shows. The appearance of the clay vessel known as the ' beaker ' among the earliest relics of the period probably indicates a migration from the Rhine lands, where such vessels are associated with the transition from a Neolithic to a metal culture. In the course of this epoch the mode of burial seems to have changed from that of successive interments in one great monument to that of independent burial, with or without superimposed cairn.

Knowledge of metals meant an enrichment of culture in the more efficient nature of implements made from the new material. But of the ordinary houses of the people not much can be said. Scattered over the country, on hill-top or brae-face, on rocky outcrop or shut off on a small peninsula by the sea, are the numerous enclosures known somewhat crudely as HILL FORTS. These are formed by ramparts of earth or walls of dry stone with a ditch outside, or by successive lines or cunning combinations of ramparts and ditches, within which stood the huts, whose stony foundations sometimes survive as ' hut circles,' once crowned with structures of turf or of clay and wattle. Such 'forts' indeed were protected or defensive villages. Probably some of them go back to the Bronze Age, but the bulk of the relics recovered from such sites belong to the time when iron was in use. This Early Iron Age may be limited to the period between about 100 B.C. and, say, A.D. 400. The great fort on *Traprain Law* (p. 6), earlier called Dumpeldar or Dunpender, an isolated hill rising to over 700 feet above the plain of East Lothian, bears witness to an occupation of the site even in the later Stone Age, though its phases of fortification are subsequent to that time. Relics of the Bronze and Early Iron Ages have been recovered at different levels, and the presence of Roman pottery, glass, and coins brings the history of the site down to the beginning of the 5th cent. A.D. Two of the coins accompanied a unique hoard of looted silver plate of Roman fashion, now in the National Museum of Antiquities (p. 68). It must still have been to hill-villages of this type that, as Bede tells us, St. Cuthbert, the apostle of the Lothians in the 7th cent., dared to make his way in his preaching tours. About fifty hill-forts throughout the stretch of country between the Moray Firth and the Solway show evidence of having had less or more of their stone walling subjected to a process of vitrifaction or fusing of the material with fire. Of these ' Vitrified Forts ' *Knock Farrel* (p. 372), above Strathpeffer, is a well-known example ; there is a good one at *Dunnideer* (p. 310), in Aberdeenshire ; another at *Carradale* (p. 154), on the east side of Kintyre.

BROCHS. But the most significant memorials of the time about the beginning of the Christian era are the Brochs. The name is Norse, the Gaelic name for all kinds of strong places being ' Dun.' As a Celtic-speaking people settled in Britain not later than the period defined above as the Early Iron Age, it is probably correct to attribute these buildings to members of that stock in the northern part of the island who were called Picts or Cruithne, that is, Britons. For the brochs are unknown elsewhere and are preponderantly numerous in the most northerly districts of Scotland and in the islands. South of the Forth and Clyde only some half-dozen sporadic examples exist. Though articles of both bronze and iron have been found within them, the character of the relics as a whole is that of the Early Iron Age. In the broch of *Torwoodlee* (p. 15), in Selkirkshire, relics occurred which may be assigned to the close of the 1st cent. A.D. A structurally complete example occurs only at *Mousa* (p. 426), in the Shetland Isles, but a fairly satisfactory specimen is found at *Carloway* in the west of Lewis, whilst two others in about the same state are situated in *Glenelg* (p. 375), in Inverness-shire. The number of more imperfect examples, many little better than stony mounds, runs to several hundreds. Avoiding differences of detail we may say that a broch is a structure composed of concentric walls of hammer-dressed or undressed stone, without mortar, bonded together at heights of 5 feet or less by close-set slabs and rising to a height of 30 to 40 feet. The inner wall is perpendicular but the outer wall shows a bell-like curve. The interior court is from 20 to 35 feet in diameter. Small apartments or cells—in some cases also a gallery—are formed in the lowest section of wall, where it is otherwise of solid construction, and there is usually a cell opening on or just inside the passage from the low entrance, which may have a projection or check for a door with bar-holes behind. From the level a stair winds upwards to the top. The binding slabs between the walls form galleries, which lessen upwards in height and width, and openings in the height of the inner wall occur in perpendicular succession, where enough is left to show this feature. The broch is indeed a triumph of thought and skill in the art of dry stone building, a marvel in the economic use of intractable material. A few examples in the Western Isles give evidence of an outer court of no great area, possibly for cattle. But the towered compactness of the structure, the accommodation sufficient for but a single household, the entrance with its adjacent cell for watch over visitors, and the occasional but rare occurrence of a second entrance or postern, all suggest an analogy with the feudal castles of the Middle Ages as the quarters of a dominant aristocracy.

Another form of residence or retreat was the EARTH HOUSE, or underground corridor-like construction, not easily discernible even now. The example in a field at *Crichton Mains*, in Midlothian, is in part built of stones dressed in the Roman manner, while the underside of one of the roofing slabs displays the forepart of a Pegasus or winged horse, the symbol of the Second Legion (Augusta). This then gives a date subsequent to the 2nd cent. for the construction, but such places seem to have been of earlier age, while in the Western Isles they were still being put to use in the middle of the 16th century, Similarly the CRANNOG, or lake dwelling, was in occupation in the west at an even later time.

Roman Remains. The arrival of the Romans in Scotland (A.D. 80) and their subsequent short-lived occupation may be taken to mark the close of the prehistoric period. This was but an intrusive episode. Its principal contribution was the so-called *Wall of Antonine* (p. 106), dating from c. A.D. 140. This is a line of turf-built wall or rampart (vallum) on a stone foundation—but E. of Falkirk the core was of earth faced with clay —with a ditch out in front and a military way behind, which ran from Old Kilpatrick on the Clyde to Carriden on the Forth, 36 miles in all. At intervals of roughly two miles were forts, each enclosing a headquarters building (principia), barracks, and store-houses, and having an annexed enclosure for traders and civilians. The rampart has in many places disappeared and is nowhere now more than 5 feet high at the best. A good portion of rampart and ditch may be seen at *Hillfoot*, near Bearsden (p. 132), Glasgow, and another section may be followed over the rough or wooded ground west of *Falkirk* (p. 107). Temporary camps are found as far north as *Auchinhove*, at Grange, 4 m. E. of Keith, in Banffshire. But the most impressive occupied site beyond the Forth is that of *Ardoch* (p. 219), in Perthshire, with its complex series of ramparts and ditches unlike any Roman work elsewhere. At *Birrenswark* (p. 97), in Dumfriesshire, the lines of a temporary camp exist on each side of the hill, on which had been a British fortified settlement. The great fort at *Newstead* (p. 24), near Melrose, was covered over after excavation ; its remarkable group of relics is to be seen in the National Museum. The Agricolan legionary fort at *Inchtuthill* (p. 229), and the smaller fort at *Fendoch* (p. 227), both in Perthshire ;

and the recently discovered forts in the S.W. (*e.g.* at *Glen-lochar* and at *Dalswinton*) are further tokens of the Roman penetration.

Celtic Ecclesiastical Buildings.   Of greater significance and more lasting effect than anything Roman was the migration of people and culture from Ireland. The Gaelic kingdom of Dalriada was consolidated in what is now Argyll (i.e. ' coast land of the Gael ') early in the 6th cent., and in 563 Columba entered upon the mission which extended to northern Pictland. The Celtic Church was monastic in organisation; its supreme seat in Scotland was in Iona; and its original buildings were of timber or of dry stone, roofed by projecting each course of slabs beyond that beneath till the sides sufficiently converged. From their circular shape such small structures are known as BEE-HIVE CELLS, and some can still be seen in the more inaccessible islands of the west. In the Western Isles, too, the original influence can be discerned also in the numerous, less or more destroyed, examples of TEAMPULLS (Lat. templum) or CILLS (Lat. cella), small oblong churches built with shell lime and having usually in the east gable a rectangular window, narrow outside but widely splayed internally. After 664, however, the Celtic Church came under the direction of the Roman Church, and its character fundamentally changed. By the middle of the 9th cent. the Gaelic kingdom had absorbed Pictland and become Alba, later known as Scotia. By the 11th cent. it had extended itself over Cumbria or Strathclyde, in the west lowlands, and Lothian in the east : annexing in the former case a Welsh district, in the latter a district that had for some time belonged to Northumbria. As a result influences from England through Northumbria crossed those from Ireland. Survivals of this stage are the lofty narrow ROUND TOWERS existing at *Brechin* (p. 286) and *Abernethy* (p. 274). These are but reproductions of similar towers in Ireland, and so cannot be earlier than the Dalriadic conquest of Pictland in the second half of the 9th cent., while they precede the new foundations of the early 12th century. They are in origin bell-towers, detached from the accompanying church or group of small churches, and so of the class of the free-standing campanili of Italy. Late in the 10th cent. Kenneth II granted Brechin " to the Lord," and this is the earliest date that can be assigned to these erections : more probably they are of the century following. Their original pointed roofs are gone—the roofing of Brechin is later—but the four large windows at the summit clearly define their purpose ; consecrated bells were conceived to have a magic influence upon tempests and the innumerable demons of the air.

Sculptured Slabs and Crosses.   Northumbrian and Irish models contributed to the treatment of the sculptured slabs and crosses so distinctive of the British Isles. But Northumbria opened the long series, passing on from Continental practice the knotwork pattern prevalent in the west of Europe from the 7th to the 12th century. The great cross at *Ruthwell* (p. 100), in Dumfriesshire, with its Biblical and other figures and particularly the lines from an old Northumbrian poem inscribed in Runic letters, is the most interesting and impressive of all such monuments. The date of its production is almost certainly in the first half of the 8th century. Northumbrian practice inevitably inspired the crosses of the south country. In Scotia proper a distinction may be made. Slabs carved with a cross in relief, knotwork, conventionalised foliage, zoömorphic figures and animals or personages, often illustrating subjects from the Bible or the early medieval bestiaries, or any combination of these, are distinctive of the E. side of Scotland, the main part of old Pictland. They appear to continue an earlier Pictish form inscribed with symbols of unknown significance but presumably Christian, which must, as wholly peculiar to Pictland, antedate the Dalriadic conquest of the 9th century. Of these slabs some have crosses in addition, some not. The later work, in its convoluted patterns and crowded detail, betrays its origin in the ornament and illustration of the manuscript page as produced by Gaelic monastic scribes. On the west the prevailing type is the free-standing cross, following the Irish model, and such crosses closely carved in a similar manner continued to be erected there as memorials to the distinguished dead down to the eve of the Reformation. Examples of these four classes are so numerous that a detailed description is here out of the question. Norse art, based on wood carving, also made its contribution, particularly in the field of animal interlacements. Only two Irish OGAM STONES survive (in Argyll—the area first occupied by the invaders from Ireland) ; those in N.E. Scotland are late examples of Pictish origin.

Romanesque Buildings. The great dividing line in Scottish structural history, as in other departments, comes with the late 11th and the 12th cent., the time of Queen Margaret and her immediate descendants. The queen's ecclesiastical reforms made for the removal of the last vestiges of the old Celtic Church. With David I Anglo-Norman direction came into play and thereafter it steadily strengthened. This process is reflected in the buildings of the late 11th and the 12th centuries. Round-headed windows appear. Bell-towers are square and are absorbed in the later churches : that at *Dunblane Cathedral* (p. 202), from the usual door above ground level and the awkward way in which the tower is fitted to the 13th cent. nave, may be judged to have once stood alone. The 12th cent. saw the full establishment of the Norman or, more properly.

Romanesque style. The lofty tower of St. Regulus (p. 271), or St. Rule. at *St. Andrews*, is placed axially between the eastern and western parts of a narrow church, the latter division or nave no longer existing. Gone too is the apse or circular termination of the east end, a fashion limited to this time, with surviving examples in the Romanesque part of the church at *Leuchars* (p. 264), in Fife, and the complete Romanesque church of *Dalmeny* (p. 82), as well as in fragments elsewhere. The apse is angular, not round, revived in Scotland in some erections of the late 15th or early 16th cent., such as, in the latter period, the parish church of *Stirling* (p. 208) and the collegiate church at *Biggar* (p. 92). Features of Romanesque 12th cent. building, besides the round-headed arch and the apse, are the adornment of arches by the cutting of designs such as the chevron or chequers or the regular broken sections of rounded moulding known as ' billets ' or, as on the faces of the arch of the fine door at *Dalmeny*, grotesque animal figures, some of which are signs of the Zodiac. The nave of the church of *Dunfermline Abbey* (p. 252) provides on a greater scale a good example of the structural methods and decoration of the massive Romanesque manner.

Gothic Architecture. In the second half of the 12th cent. a cardinal change was introduced into the architecture of Britain, which ushers in the Gothic style. This was the pointed arch, at first constructional to facilitate the new form of vaulting and then extended to arcades and windows. The old tunnel or barrel vault of masonry, being heavy in itself and also exercising a powerful outward thrust upon its supports, required massive walls of no great height with few open spaces. The intersection of two such simple vaults originated a form in which the vault in four fan-shaped sections or groins rested on supports at the four corners only. The edges of the groins could be strengthened by the attachment of single arches or ribs. The pressures on the walls were now concentrated on the parts where the vault corners rested, and these alone had to be made strong enough ; the intermediate walling carried no roof weight. The wall could therefore be thinned, and the sections bearing the vault load and thrust specially strengthened by the addition of an external buttress with internal wall shafts to receive the ribs. The construction of the vault itself was further developed by articulating it by means of the ribs and making these carry an infilling of fitted stones instead of solid building, whereby the weight of the structure was very greatly lessened. But to secure a level crown for the vaulting it was necessary to carry arching upwards to a point—whereby also thrust and weight were better concentrated—whence arose pointed arch construction and all its cunning structural developments, with the adaptation of other features of the building to fit into or harmonise with the general principle. Such in essence was Gothic architecture, the manifold applications of which can be followed out only in detail and by inspection of individual examples. The style is not in full swing till the 13th cent., and even at the beginning of that period we still have an overlap or Transitional style, in which the round arch and its construction mingle with the pointed arch. At *Jedburgh Abbey* we have from that time Transitional work of two stages, that of the choir being rather earlier than that in the nave. The nave of *Glasgow Cathedral*, mainly of the last part of the same century, is wholly Gothic with the narrow pointed or ' lancet ' windows of the time. It must be observed, however, that in Scotland, as in England, the principles of Gothic construction were not necessarily carried to their logical conclusion, since nave or choir, even if designed for a vaulted roof, were quite often finished with a roof of timber. Further, it is well to keep in mind that Gothic was not confined to ecclesiastical structures ; it was the manner of building of the time for edifices of every sort. It just happens that the survivals are for the most part of an ecclesiastical character.

A Gothic church, however, was planned for its particular purposes. Thus a cathedral or collegiate church had its own features, as for example a place where the clergy sang the service in choir ; a parish church with but a single priest screened off the altar end only as a chancel ; while a monastic church was intended to serve the special needs of the monastic community. To secure place for minor altars in chapels aisles or transepts were projected from the sides, giving the building a cross-like or cruciform shape. At *Glasgow Cathedral* the construction is unique in that the transepts do not extend beyond the line of the outer wall. Another way of providing room for altars was to construct or add side aisles. The outer walls would then rise but one story high, while the wall of the loftier nave would rest upon an arcade of massive piers. Over the arcade was usually a gallery with no opening to the outside and so known as a blind-story or triforium, while above was the ' clerestory ' (' clear story '), lighting the upper part of the church. The triforium, however, tended to be merged in the arcade proper, as at *Jedburgh*, or in the clerestory, as at *Glasgow*, or to shrink to insignificant dimensions, as at *Dryburgh*, or wholly to disappear, as at *Sweetheart Abbey*. Windows appear first as single, tall pointed openings or lancets, but these are grouped later in twos or threes under a common arch. The wall space between this arch and the heads of the windows was pierced with a geometrical curvilinear opening, giving plate-tracery. Next, the divisions between the windows were thinned down to small columns or mullions, and the tracery is added to until it expands by the close of the 13th cent. in a general design made up of trefoils, quatrefoils, etc. In the course of the 14th cent. these openings are cut in more flowing curvilinear patterns. At the same time windows increase in size, until in the late 15th cent. we get a window occupying most of the east gable at *Melrose*. But in Scotland this fashion did not reach the extent it did in England, and in Scotland, too, mullions and tracery—of which but little has survived—are on a heavier scale. Tracery is one guide to date but in Scotland may deceive : that in the nave of *Melrose*, which looks to be of about the middle of the 14th cent., is really of the end of the 15th. Other indications of date are given by the character of the mouldings on the arches and capitals of the piers, or the foliage on the capitals, which, beginning with a stiff upright treatment in the 13th cent., clustered horizontally in the 14th, and later exhibits a naturalistic treatment, as in the oak and acorn foliage on the 15th cent. W. doorway at *Elgin* or the flowers and shells on the cloister arcading at *Melrose*, though at the same time appearing also in a general or conventionalised form.

The two great building periods of Scotland are the 13th and 15th centuries. If what is of an earlier stage, as described above, be put aside, it may be said broadly that building of any extent or consequence will belong to one or other of these periods. In the earlier century development and features are fairly according to rule, and the models followed are still those of England. Cathedral organisation and order of service were copied from English establishments, as monasteries had been settled from English houses. The W. front of *Kelso Abbey Church* was modelled on that of Ely Cathedral. *Glasgow Cathedral* followed that of Salisbury. A characteristic 13th cent. ornament was the small pyramidal figure of four projecting leaf-shaped sides known as the ' dog-tooth.' It is much in evidence in *Elgin Cathedral*. The bases of piers or shaft are round and are moulded with some variety of a shaped hollow between two rolls. The piers at *Sweetheart Abbey* (1275) show the change to three rolls, distinctive of this and a brief succeeding period, though sometimes there are only two. When the bases become octagonal, spread less and rise in height, and display a double curve or ogee it may be inferred that the work is of the 15th cent. or later. During this other important era of building English influence is no longer marked ; the political relations between the two countries had long been hostile or strained. What external elements can be discerned point to France. But in the reconstruction of work destroyed, or in expansion, or new foundations, Scottish builders trusted much to their own resources, whence there is a resurrection of older features among the new, as noted above. The round-arched doorway recovers importance. The apse, probably as a contribution from France, reappears with three sides, and the barrel vault is used with a pointed crown. A square-headed window or one with a very depressed arch, having short mullions in the upper part, seems to have been in favour. During the 15th cent., too, were raised most of the collegiate churches, originating in chantries and served by a staff of clergy or prebendaries under a provost. These are generally cruciform, are built with a facing of ashlar or dressed stone, and have a pointed barrel roof. The most remarkable example is that now known as *Roslin Chapel* (p. 79), of which only the choir was ever completed but that with a lavishness of decoration unparalleled in the whole island. It was being built in 1447. At *Corstorphine* (p. 72) the collegiate church, built about the same time as Roslin, became the parish church; at *Dunglass* (p. 4), in East Lothian, the building, also of the middle of the century, was long used as a barn but has now been cleared and conserved. The greater parish churches also are in the main reconstructions of this time, and that of *Haddington* (p. 89) illustrates one Scottish feature in the blank east walls of its transepts and choir aisles.

Monastic Houses. Monastic establishments suffered a particular severity of treatment at the Reformation and thereafter, the popular wrath being specially directed against them, while their buildings were not generally adaptable for use in the new order. Their remains are therefore very limited in amount and fragmentary in character. Of friars' houses and churches practically nothing survives, names such as Greyfriars (Franciscans) or Blackfriars (Dominicans) alone testifying to their former presence, as well as to the fact that their sphere of activity was in the towns. The monastic orders of Western Europe followed the rule of St. Benedict, but in the course of the centuries sterner souls found this rule being relaxed in various ways, and reformed organisations sprang up. The more notable of the few Benedictine establishments in Scotland were at *Dunfermline* and *Coldingham*. An early reform was that inaugurated in the 10th cent., which sought improvement by subjecting all houses to the control of the original foundation at Cluny. Cluniac houses of a later date existed at *Paisley, Iona*, and *Crossraguel*. A more drastic and severely puritanic reform was that of the Cistercians or White Monks, who adopted this colour of habit in contrast to the black of the Benedictines proper. They flourished exceedingly for a time, planted their houses in uncultivated land, became great farmers, and supplied several of the more famous houses of Scotland—*Melrose, Newbattle, Deer, Sweetheart*. A small order of Valliscaulians, derived from France but unknown in England, was usually reckoned as Cistercian. Their three Scottish houses were *Beauly, Pluscarden*, and *Ardchattan*. Tironensian

Benedictines, again, having but one proper house in England, had four in Scotland, including *Kelso* and *Arbroath*. Monks were in original intention laymen living under a rule (regula) and so 'regulars,' but tended in an ever-increasing degree to take orders. But canons or clergy also in certain cases constituted themselves as a community of regulars as opposed to secular canons in the great churches. They followed a version of a rule modelled on the terms of a letter by St. Augustine or Austin of Hippo, and there were communities of Austin Canons at *Holyrood*, *Jedburgh*, *Inchcolm*, etc., while of Premonstratensian or White Canons, akin to the Cistercians, the best-known house was at *Dryburgh*. Most monastic houses were abbeys, having an abbot as head of the community, but some held lower rank as priories, though the distinction of status weakened in course of time.

Monasteries and houses of regular canons had as their nucleus the cloister or arrangement of buildings round a central court or garth, which was normally placed S. of the church. Where convenient drainage (as at *Melrose*) or some other characteristic of the site was in question the cloister may be found on the N. side. This group, however, and the other buildings for different purposes were enclosed within a great outer court (curia) or precinct, marked off by a wall with an imposing gatehouse. Portions of such a wall, constructed of massive stones laid without mortar, are to be seen at *Sweetheart Abbey*, Dumfriesshire. Within the court stood the Hospitium or guest-house, the abbot's lodging and various domestic offices, while, usually to the E. of the church, was the Infirmary for the sick. The buildings constituting the cloister were common in character with some minor differences ; the only standardised plan was that of the Cistercians. The E. range was in two stories, the lower rooms being devoted to administrative purposes, with the Chapter House for general meetings as the most important and most handsomely built portion. Above was the monks' Dorter or dormitory, connected with a Reredorter or sanitary provision and with a ' night-stair ' at the end abutting on the church (normally at the S. transept), by which the inmates descended to the services at night. The S. range contained the Refectory or Frater, the common dining hall, and in Cistercian houses this was flanked on the E. by a room with a fireplace or ' warming-house,' at the W. end by the kitchen. In other monasteries, however, the warming-house was usually under the dorter and the kitchen detached. Cistercian planning was determined by the fact that the servants and craftsmen of the monastery were also under the rule as conversi. Therefore again these had their own dorter within the cloister in the upper floor of the W. range and their own refectory below, adjacent to the cellarage or store-houses common to all in this part, though the rest of this set of buildings served different ends in houses not Cistercian. In developed Cistercian houses, too, the refectory was placed at right angles to the line of the S. range instead of, as elsewhere, in a parallel position.   The cloistral arrangements may be studied at *Dryburgh* (Premonstratensian Canons), where a comparatively fair amount of structure remains.   A good example of the abbey gateway with some of its adjacent buildings is to be seen at *Arbroath* (Tironensians).   A complete plan of a Cluniac monastery as rebuilt in the late 15th and the 16th cent. with its gatehouse exists at *Crossraguel*.   Of *Sweetheart Abbey* (Cistercian) there is a nearly complete though roofless church of the last quarter of the 13th century.   The church at *Melrose*, as it has survived, is of the late 15th and the early 16th centuries.   It has preserved its stone-built galleried screen with central doorway, the Pulpitum, that marked the W. limit of the choir.   *Inchcolm* (Augustinian Canons) is peculiar in so far as the cloister walk, instead of being a mere covered verandah round the front of the buildings, is carried back under the first floor.   The cloister walk normally—but there are Cistercian exceptions—ended at a door at each end of the S. wall of the church, which was used for processions.

The Castles.   The feudal castle came to Scotland in the same 12th cent. as had witnessed the appearance of the Romanesque type of cathedral and as part of the same general movement which was to substitute a Norman for an Irish influence upon the country.   It came with the new Norman (and Flemish) ruling class.   At first it was a combination of earthworks and timber or timber and clay structures.   In its most regular form it presented a conical mound of earth, the Mote, upon which stood a tower, and which was surrounded by a ditch ; while annexed to the mound was an enclosure defined by a palisaded rampart with a ditch—the Bailey with its buildings.   Or there might be a single large mound and ditch, the mound palisaded and enclosing the buildings, which in this case might include as its principal residence not a tower but a hall.   Of the mote-and-bailey type many examples survive in their earthworks, particularly the mound, such as the conspicuous mote at *Hawick* (p. 13) and the greater one of *Inverurie* (p. 309) in Aberdeenshire.   A good number may be observed in the W. and S.W. Lowlands.   The earlier stone castles broadly repeated the lines of such structures, following a similar development in England and France, but much later in time.   The great stone castles of the 13th and 14th cent. are essentially of this enclosure and tower or towers class.   The simplest case of such reproduction may be seen at *Castle Duffus* (p. 316), a few miles N. of Elgin, which, however, is among the latest of its kind in date.   Of the examples from the second half of the 13th cent. *Bothwell Castle*

(p. 127) on the Clyde has still some parts of its original work, particularly the inner half of its great tower and its independent ditch, but the rest is building or rebuilding of a later time. *Dirleton Castle* (p. 86), in East Lothian, also shows, at the S.W. corner, an impressive section of 13th cent. work. But these as well as other then existing places suffered severe damage or destruction in the wars of that and the following century. Castles of this tower and walled enclosure type, having other buildings within, were erected even in later times in the remoter parts of the country. *Edinburgh Castle*, too, which from the 14th cent. was in a state of intermittent construction and reconstruction, was fundamentally a castle of the enclosure type, having towers on its fore-wall and buildings of different kinds scattered on the summit of the rock ; such too was Stirling Castle. Many castles, of course, were affected in plan and structure by the nature of the chosen site, as is very obvious in the case of *Caerlaverock* (p. 182).

It is towards the end of the 14th cent. that we find indications of a departure from the strict mote-and-bailey plan ; at *Tantallon* (p. 87) and *St. Andrews* (p. 272) the chief residential tower is placed in a forward position, with the courtyard behind and not in front of it and the entrance carried through the base of the tower. More significant, however, is the plan of *Doune* (p. 203), where alongside the great tower is placed a building in two stories, which is of the kind known as the ' Hall,' until now to be found only as an independent building within the enclosure, but in this case actually itself forming part of the enclosure. As we traverse the 15th cent. we find the hall to a steadily increasing extent determining the general plan of new structures as well as changes in old ones, so that one side of a castle after another becomes at once building and enclosure, the curtain wall goes out, and the tower shrinks in importance till it may disappear. In Scotland a building of this hall type in contrast with a tower was known also as a Palatium or palace. A castle in the general sense, of which only one side, as the principal residence, was so built, could still be called a palace, as was *Kinneil* (p. 106) in West Lothian and *Fyvie* (p. 321), in Aberdeenshire, both of the later 16th century. In some cases we have two sides so built with the rest courtyard, and when all four sides are built round in this style we get the fully developed and now understood palace. *Linlithgow Palace* was described by an early 17th cent. writer as "built castlewise." But in Scotland the name signified the style of building, whether that belonged to a laird, an earl, an abbot, a bishop, or a king. Hence the number of ' palaces ' on record in Scotland, by which writers were puzzled since so many were neither royal nor episcopal. When the N. side of *Crichton Castle* (p. 10), in Midlothian, was erected c. 1585 to complete the quadrangle, it was built in this manner, but finished on the inner face with rusticated building and an arcade after the fashion of an Italian palazzo.

Castles were the residences of the nobility, but in conformity with the spirit of the times were equipped with defensive features in addition to their plain power of resistance in lofty walls and towers. The gateway was usually approached over a drawbridge and could be blocked by a portcullis of wood pointed and banded with iron, the groove for which can easily be discerned. Parapets might crown the summits of structures, and when these were carried forward on stone brackets or corbels the interspaces of the corbels could be left open as machicolation to give command of the face of the wall, but such stone machicolation on a complete scale does not occur in Scotland before the late 14th cent., while the corbelling out of the parapet begins to be treated as ornament by the close of the century following. As in the case of the churches this 15th cent. was a great period for building, rebuilding, or adding to castles, and most of what we see surviving is of that time or the century following. Naturally the building of castles outlasted the building of monasteries or cathedrals.

A particular class of castles, so called, from the earliest time to the late 17th cent. was the Tower, to which was attached normally an enclosure for service buildings known as a Barmkin. These were the typical homes of the lairds or lesser nobility. Almost all are of a date subsequent to the 14th cent., though *Threave* (p. 186), near Castle Douglas, existed before 1400. By the 16th cent. they were being embellished with turrets to provide fuller or more private accommodation. Others have a wing or wings attached, either for a vertical set of rooms or for a staircase. The impressive castle of *Borthwick* (p. 15), in Midlothian, erected in the first half of the 15th cent., has two wings on one side; elsewhere and later they may be at diagonal corners. A handsome turreted tower is that of *Amisfield* (p. 184), in Dumfriesshire, built in 1600. Border towers are in current speech styled ' Peles,' but this usage is of quite recent date; a pele in its proper sense was a timber palisade, such as frequently accompanied a tower in early times. In the later towers, as in later castles generally, what had been defensive features are treated to an increasing degree as ornaments, whence arose what has been called ' the baronial style ' with its skyline of turreted projections, a style characteristic of the late 16th and the 17th centuries.

A SUMMARY OF SCOTTISH HISTORY

SCOTLAND, with a population of 5,096,000 (England 41,148,000) and an area of 30,405 sq. m. (England 50,874), has a stirring and romantic history of her own, of whose most important events the following summary is a brief record. Many of the most familiar incidents in Scotland's story, interesting in themselves though unimportant as historical landmarks, will be found described in the text of this volume, under the localities in which their scenes were laid.

Before the Roman invasion Scotland was inhabited by the Picts (Celts with a possible admixture of pre-Celtic stock) and the Britons (Brythonic Celts), the former occupying roughly the territory N. of the Firths of Forth and Clyde, the latter extending S. from that boundary into what afterwards became England.

A.D. 83 or 84. Defeat of the Caledonians at the battle of Mons Graupius by Julius Agricola, who with his Roman legions had outflanked their central stronghold from the east.

138–142. The wall of Antoninus built from the Forth to the Clyde.

397. Christian church founded at Whithorn by St. Ninian.

C. 410. Departure of the Romans from Britain.

498. Invasion and settlement of Dalriada (Argyll) by the Scots (Christian Goidelic Celts from Ireland).

547. Foundation by Ida the Angle of the kingdom of Bernicia, which later extended from the Tees to the Forth.

563. Landing of St. Columba in Iona, followed by the conversion of the Picts to Christianity.

597–717. Roman Christianity, supported by the powerful kings of Northumbria, gradually displaces the system of Columba.

794. Appearance of the Norsemen in the Hebrides.

843–60. Kenneth Macalpine, a Scot of Dalriada, king of the united Picts and Scots N. of the Forth (Kingdom of Alba or Albany).

875–90. Incursions of the Norsemen under Thorstein the Red and Sigurd of Orkney.

c. 945. Strathclyde united to Albany by Malcolm I.

10th cent. Struggles between Macalpine's successors and the Norsemen for supremacy.

1018. Lothian united to Albany by Malcolm II. First appearance of the name Scotia or Scotland for the kingdom.

1040. Duncan I murdered by Macbeth, who is in turn defeated and slain (1057) by Malcolm III (Canmore).

1057–93. Introduction of English language and customs into Scotland by Malcolm III under the influence of his wife Margaret (St. Margaret), sister of Edgar Atheling.

1102. Formal grant of the Western Isles to Magnus of Orkney.

1124–53. David I, the 'sair sanct for the crown.' Foundation of many abbeys and royal burghs; extensive lands granted to Norman nobles, including Robert de Brus and Bernard de Balliol.

1174. William the Lion, taken prisoner by Henry II of England, is forced to acknowledge his supremacy.

1189. In return for a large money payment Richard I of England abandons the claim to supremacy.

1196. Subjugation of Caithness and Sutherland; the Norsemen driven from the mainland.

1200. Negotiations between William the Lion and Philip Augustus of France; the beginning of the 'Auld Alliance' against England.

1214. Alexander II. The beginning of the 'golden age of Scottish history.'

1263. Battle of Largs. Defeat of Hakon of Norway by Alexander III, leading to the annexation of the Western Isles.

1286. Death of Alexander III. The kingdom passes to his grand-daughter, Margaret, Maid of Norway.

1290. Death of the Maid of Norway on her way to Scotland.

1291–2. Arbitration of Edward I of England between the rival claimants to the throne: John Balliol, Robert Bruce, and John Hastings. Accession of Balliol.

1296. Balliol renounces his crown in favour of Edward.

1297–8. Rebellion of William Wallace, suppressed at Falkirk.

1305. Capture and execution of Wallace.

1306. Robert Bruce, grandson of the claimant, slays John Comyn, regent of Scotland, and is crowned at Scone.

1307. Death of Edward I.

1314. Battle of Bannockburn. Bruce acknowledged master of Scotland.

1320. Declaration of Arbroath, asserting full independence of the English Crown, addressed to the Pope by the Estates.

1326. First Scottish Parliament held at Cambuskenneth.

1328. Bruce acknowledged an independent sovereign by Edward III.

1333. Battle of Halidon Hill. Defeat of David Bruce by Edward Balliol, supported by Edward III. Surrender of Berwick-upon-Tweed to England.

1346. Battle of Neville's Cross. David II taken prisoner by the English.

1371. Robert, High Steward of Scotland and son of Marjory, daughter of Robert Bruce, ascends the throne as Robert II and founds the House of Stewart.

1406–24. Captivity of James I. Regency of the Dukes of Albany.

1406. James Resby, the Lollard, burned at Perth.

1411. Battle of Harlaw, leading ultimately to the domination of the Lowlands.

1412. Foundation of the first Scottish university at St. Andrews.

1436. Marriage of Margaret, James I's daughter, to the Dauphin of France (Louis XI).

1450–55. Struggle for supremacy between the Stewarts and the Douglases. The Douglases are crushed by James II.

1469. Orkney and Shetland given to James III as a pledge for the dowry of his wife, Margaret of Denmark. The pledge is still unredeemed.

1472. Creation of the Metropolitan See of St. Andrews.

1489. Supremacy of the Scottish fleet established by Sir Andrew Wood.

1495–6. Perkin Warbeck's claim to the English throne supported by James IV.

1503. Marriage of James IV and Margaret, daughter of Henry VII.

1511. Sea-warfare between Andrew Barton and the fleet of Henry VIII.

1513. Battle of Flodden. Defeat and death of James IV. Regency of the Duke of Albany. Serious troubles on the Border between the houses of Douglas (Earl of Angus) and Hamilton (Earl of Arran).

1528. Burning of Patrick Hamilton at St. Andrews for heresy by Archbp. Beaton.

1537. Marriage of James V and Madeleine of France, in whose train is the poet Ronsard. Death of the queen two months later.

1538. Marriage of James V and Mary of Guise. Discord with Protestant England fomented by the queen and Cardinal Beaton.

1542. Declaration of war on England at the request of France. Rout of the Scots at Solway Moss. Death of James V and accession of his infant daughter Mary. Regency of Arran.

1544–5. Invasion of Scotland by Earl of Hertford in revenge for Arran's support of France and the Catholics. Burning of Edinburgh and ravaging of the Lothians and Border ; defeat of the English at Ancrum Moor.

1546. Beginning of the Religious Revolution ; burning of George Wishart and murder of Cardinal Beaton.

1547. Scots defeated by Hertford (now Duke of Somerset) at the battle of Pinkie.

1554. Regency of Mary of Guise.

1557. Signing of the first Protestant Covenant.

1558. Marriage of Queen Mary and the Dauphin of France (Francis II).

1559. John Knox preaches the Reformation.

1560. Queen Elizabeth sends an army to support the Reformers.

1565. Marriage of Mary and Henry Stewart, Lord Darnley.

1566. Birth of Prince James, assuring the English succession to the House of Stewart. Murder of Rizzio.

1567. Murder of Darnley. Marriage of Mary and James Hepburn, Earl of Bothwell. Mary, defeated at Carberry Hill, is imprisoned in Lochleven Castle, where she abdicates.

1568. Battle of Langside. Mary, defeated by the Earl of Moray, quits Scotland. Successive regencies of Moray, Lennox (1570), Mar (1571), and Morton (1572), the last appointment ensuring the establishment of Protestantism in Scotland.

1578. James VI assumes the government.

1580. Formal condemnation of Episcopacy by the Church Assembly.

1587. Execution of Mary.

1596. Rescue of Kinmont Willie from Carlisle Castle—the last of the Border raids.

1600. Gowrie Conspiracy. The last attempt of the noble families to gain possession of the king's person.

1603. Accession of James VI to the throne of England. Re-establishment of Episcopacy in Scotland.

1606–17. Pacification of the Highlands, Islands, and Borders.

1610. Plantation of Ulster.

1637. Attempt by Charles I to introduce Laud's Liturgy into Scotland. Riot against the bishops in Edinburgh.

1638. Signing of the National League and Covenant to uphold the Presbyterian form of worship. Successful rebellion against Charles led by the Earls of Argyll and Montrose.

1643. Signing of the Solemn League and Covenant, recognised by the English Parliament. Montrose changes sides and leads the Royalist army, at first successfully.

1645. Battle of Philiphaugh. Defeat of Montrose by Leslie and the Covenanters.

1646. Surrender of Charles to the Scottish army.

1649. Execution of Charles I ; Charles II proclaimed king in Scotland.

1650. Signing of the Covenants by Charles II. Invasion of Scotland by Cromwell and defeat of the Royalists and Covenanters at Dunbar.

1651. Invasion of England by the Scots defeated at Worcester. Union of governments proposed by Cromwell.

1653. United Parliament at Westminster.

1660. Restoration of Charles II.

1662. Renunciation of the Covenants by the king and re-establishment of Episcopacy.

1666. The Pentland Rising. Battle of Rullion Green, followed by persecution of the Covenanters. Coercive administration of Lauderdale.

1679. Murder of Archbp. Sharp. New insurrection, quelled by the Royalists at Bothwell Bridge.

1680–89. Increased persecution of the Covenanters carried on by Graham of Claverhouse.

1688. James VII attempts to romanise the country. Deposition of James and accession of William and Mary.

1689. Revolt of Highlanders under Claverhouse (Viscount Dundee) ends at Killiecrankie.

1692. Massacre of the Macdonalds of Glencoe.

1698–9. Failure of the Darien Colony. Increased disaffection against England.

1707. Union of Parliaments, ill-received in Scotland.

1715. Rebellion in favour of James Stewart, son of James VII.

1725–35. Attempted pacification of the Highlands by means of Gen. Wade's four military roads.

1736. The Porteous Riot, an expression of the Scottish people's dislike of English rule.

1745–6. Second Jacobite Rebellion, led by 'Bonnie Prince Charlie,' though nearly successful, is crushed at Culloden.

1746–90. Reduction of the Highlands to order, partly by repressive measures, partly by the construction of further new roads.

1760–1830. Great expansion of the industrial and agricultural resources of Scotland.

1775–1805. Benevolent despotism of Henry Dundas, Lord Melville, who controlled the policy of Scotland by means of a corrupt electorate and a widespread system of patronage.

1768–1822. Construction of the Forth and Clyde and Caledonian Canals.

1812. First Scottish railway built (Kilmarnock to Troon).

1840. The Highland Clearances : forced emigration of crofters
to make way for sheep farms, which were later succeeded
by deer forests.

1843. The Disruption : secession of one-third of the ministers
and members of the Established Church to form the Free
Church of Scotland.

1845–6. Extensive Irish immigration following the severe
potato famines in Ireland.

1847. Chloroform first used as an anæsthetic by Simpson in
Edinburgh.

1865. Lister introduces antiseptic surgery in Glasgow.

1879. Tay Bridge disaster.

1890. Opening of the Forth Bridge.

1902. Amalgamation of the two principal seceding churches
(the Free Church and the United Presbyterian Church) to
form the United Free Church of Scotland.

1914–18. Scotland in the First World War. The four entirely
Scottish divisions were the 9th, 15th, 51st, and 52nd.

1929. Amalgamation of the Established Church and the
United Free Church to form the United Established
Church of Scotland.

1935–47. Inauguration of hydro-electric schemes in the
Highlands, with the partial aim of attracting population
and prosperity.

1939–45. Scotland in Second World War. Re-constitution of
the 15th, 51st, and 52nd Divisions.

1954. Atomic energy plant begun at Dounreay.

RULERS OF SCOTLAND

from the Union of the Picts and Scots

843–860. KENNETH I
(Macalpine).

863–879. CONSTANTINE I.

900–943. CONSTANTINE II.

943–954. MALCOLM I.

971–995. KENNETH II.

1005–1034. MALCOLM II.

1034–1040. DUNCAN I.

1040–1057. MACBETH.

1057–1093. MALCOLM III
(Canmore).

1093–1094. DONALD BANE.

1094. DUNCAN II.

1094–1097. DONALD BANE
(restored) and EDMUND.

1097–1107. EDGAR.

1107–1124. ALEXANDER I.

1124–1153. DAVID I.

1153–1165. MALCOLM IV
(The Maiden).

1165–1214. WILLIAM I (The
Lion).

B

1214–1249. ALEXANDER II.
1249–1286. ALEXANDER III.
1286–1290. MARGARET.
[1290–1292. INTERREGNUM.]
1292–1296. JOHN BALLIOL.
[1296–1306. INTERREGNUM.]
1306–1329. ROBERT I (Bruce).
1329–1371. DAVID II.

Stewarts.

1371–1390. ROBERT II.
1390–1406. ROBERT III.
1406–1437. JAMES I.
1437–1460. JAMES II.
1460–1488. JAMES III.
1488–1513. JAMES IV.
1513–1542. JAMES V.
1542–1567. MARY, Queen of Scots.
1567–1625. JAMES VI (James I of England from 1603).
1625–1649. CHARLES I.
1649–1651. CHARLES II.
[1651–1660. Commonwealth.]

1660–1685. CHARLES II (restored).
1685–1688. JAMES VII (II OF ENGLAND).
1688–1694. WILLIAM III and MARY II.
1694–1702. WILLIAM III.
1702–1714. ANNE.

Hanoverians.

1714–1727. GEORGE I.
1727–1760. GEORGE II.
1760–1820. GEORGE III.
1820–1830. GEORGE IV.
1830–1837. WILLIAM IV.
1837–1901. VICTORIA.

House of Saxe-Coburg.

1901–1910. EDWARD VII.

House of Windsor.

1910–1936. GEORGE V.
1936. EDWARD VIII.
1936–1952. GEORGE VI.
1952–   ELIZABETH II.

GLOSSARY OF LOWLAND SCOTS

Standard English is the same in Scotland as in England; but the following is a brief list of words occurring in Lowland Scots that may possibly present themselves to the 'Southron' visitor.

Aiblins, perhaps.
Arles, earnest-money.
Ashet, meat-dish.

Bailie, alderman.
Bairn, child.
Bannock, flat cake, generally of oatmeal.
Bap, breakfast roll.
Bawbee, halfpenny.
Beadle, church officer, verger.
Ben, see *But and Ben*.
Bien, well-to-do, prosperous.
Biggin, a building; *big*, to build.
Bing, slag-heap.
Birk, birch-tree.

Blate, shy; timid.
Blether, to talk nonsense.
Bothy, farm-hands' barrack.
Brae, rising ground, hill.
Bramble, blackberry.
Branks, scold's bridle (comp. ' jougs ').
Braw, fine, handsome.
Breeks, trousers.
Brig, bridge.
Bubblyjock, turkey.
Burn, stream.
But and Ben, two-roomed cottage.
Byre, cowhouse.

Ca', to set in motion; also, to call; *ca' canny*, be cautious.

Caller, fresh, cool (of air).
Canny, cautious, gentle.
Clarty, dirty.
Close, common entry to a tenement-house.
Clout, to patch ; a cloth.
Clype, a tell-tale.
Corbie, a crow.
Coup, to upset ; a rubbish-heap or dump.
Crack, to converse.
Creel, basket, usually large.
Croft, small-holding, often with a common grazing, peat-bog, fishery, etc.
Cuddy, donkey.
Cutty, short ; *cutty-stool*, stool of repentance.

Daft, mentally deranged ; silly.
Daunder, to stroll.
Ding, to smash, to worst.
Doo, dove.
Douce, sober, quiet, prudent.
Dreigh, tedious, dull.
Drumly, muddy (of water).

Factor, bailiff, land-steward, agent.
Farl, segment of oatcake.
Fash, to trouble, to vex.
Feu, to let (house or land).
Fey, under mystic influence.
Flesher, butcher.
Flype, to turn a stocking inside out.
Forbye, besides.
Fou, intoxicated.
Fushionless, insipid, weak-kneed.

Gab, the mouth ; incessant talk.
Gey, very ; ' pretty.'
Gigot, leg of mutton.
Girdle, round iron baking-plate.
Glaur, mud.
Gleg, ready, sharp.
Gowan, daisy.
Gowk, cuckoo ; foolish person.
Greet, to weep.
Grieve, farm-overseer.
Grozet, gooseberry.

Haar, drizzling rain ; hoar-frost ; mist.
Haggis, " Great chieftain o' the puddin' race."
Hansel, gift for luck.
Hantle, a small amount.
Harl, to roughcast a wall.
Haugh, alluvial plain.
Haver, to talk nonsense.
Heugh, a low hill.
Hog, unshorn lamb.
Hogmanay, New Year's Eve.
Howe, a hollow or sheltered place.
Howff, meeting-place, resort.
Howk, to dig.
Howm, a dell.
Huntygowk, fool's errand (Apr. 1st).

Hurl, to wheel (a barrow).

Ilk, the same ; ' of that ilk ' indicates that a landowner's surname and the name of his property are the same.
Ilka, each, every.

Jink, to dodge.
Jougs, scold's bridle (comp. ' branks ').
Jouk, to duck (e.g. to avoid a blow).

Kail, cabbage.
Keek, to peep.
Keelie, street-arab.
Kelpie, water-sprite ; river-horse.
Kenspeckle, conspicuous ; well-known.
Kitchin, relish or seasoning.
Knowe, a knoll ; head.
Kye, cows.

Laigh, low ; south.
Laird, landed proprietor.
Land, a tenement-house.
Lave, the rest, remainder.
Law, conical hill.
Leal, loyal.
Lift, the sky.
Limmer, rogue.
Links, sand-dunes.
Lith, section (of an orange).
Loan, loaning, lane.
Lug, ear.
Lum, chimney.

Mair, more ; *maist*, most, almost.
Manse, clergyman's official residence.
March, boundary.
Mavis, song-thrush.
Meikle, great, much.
Minister, clergyman.
Muckle, large.

Neeps, turnips.

Outwith, outside.

Partan, crab.
Pawky, shrewd, sly, arch.
Philabeg, kilt.
Pickle, small quantity.
Pig, earthenware pot.
Plenishing, furniture.
Ploy, enterprise, something to do.
Poke, a bag.
Policy, private pleasure-grounds.
Provost, mayor.
Puddock, frog.

Quaich, two-eared drinking-cup.

Reek, smoke.
Rig, a ridge.
Roup, auction-sale.

Sark, shirt.
Saugh, willow.
Scunner, dislike.
Sheriff, county court judge.
Shieling, hut.
Shinty, hockey.

Sicker, sure, certain.
Siller, money, silver.
Skail, dispersal of a meeting.
Skelp, to whip.
Smeddum, mettle, sense.
Smiddy, smithy.
Sneck, snib, latch, hasp.
Sonsie, jolly, good-looking.
Sort, to arrange, to put right.
Soutar, shoemaker.
Speir, to ask.
Spunk, a match (for lighting).
Steek, to shut.
Stey, steep.
Stour, dust.
Stravaig, to wander aimlessly.
Sumph, dunderhead.
Sweer, averse.
Swither, to vacillate, to hesitate.
Syne, ago ; since.

Tassie, small cup.
Tawse, leather strap used for corporal punishment.
Teinds, tithes.
Tent, heed ; *tak' tent*, take care.

Thole, to bear ; to put up with, bear with.
Thrang, crowded, busy.
Thrawn, stubborn, misshapen.
Threap, to assert.
Tine, to lose ; *tint*, lost.
Tocher, dowry, marriage-portion.
Tod, a fox.
Toom, empty.
Tow, a rope.
Trews, trousers.
Twine, to part.

Unco', strange, monstrous : very.
Usquebaugh, whisky.

Vennel, an alley.

Wale, to choose.
Wame, belly.
Wean, child.
W'haup, curlew.
Wight, Wicht, strong, powerful.
Wynd, an alley.
Wyte, blame.

Yett, gate.

GLOSSARY OF GAELIC ROOTS

The following short list of Gaelic (and Norse) roots that occur in place-names in Scotland is intended to aid the traveller in interpreting these names as they are spelt in the ordinary maps, etc.

Aber, mouth or confluence of a river.
Aird, ard, height, promontory.
Allt, ault, stream.
An, a diminutive, as lochan.
An, of the.
Aros, dwelling.
Auch, ach, field.
Auchter, see *uachdar*.
Ay, island.

Ba, bo, cow.
Bal, baile, town, homestead.
Ban, white, fair.
Barr, promontory, top.
Beag, beg, little.
Bealach, balloch, mountain pass.
Bean, woman.
Ben, beann, beinn, mountain.
Bhlair, blar, plain.
Bhuidhe, bui, vuie, yellow.
Bister, busta, bost, dwelling.
Bo, ba, cow, cattle.
Brae, braigh, bread, upper part.
Breac, vrackie, speckled, variegated.

Cailleach, nun, old woman.
Cam, cambus, crooked.
Caolas, a strait, a firth.
Car, a bend or winding.
Carn, cairn, heap of stones.
Ceann, ken, kin, head, end.
Cil, kil, church.
Clach, cloich, stone.
Clachan, place of stones, helmet.
Cladach, shore, beach.
Cnoc, hill, knoll.
Coille, killie, wood.
Coire, corrie, hollow.
Creag, rock, cliff.
Cruach, rick, stack.
Cul, coul, back, recess.

Dal, dail, field.
Dair, valley.
Damph, damh, ox, stag.
Darach, an oak.
Dearg, red.
Dour, water.
Droichead, drochit, bridge.

Druim, drum, ridge, back.
Dubh, dhu, black, dark.
Dun, hill fort.
Dysart, desert (i.e. hermitage).

Eaglais, church.
Eas waterfall, ravine.
Eilean, island.
Ey, island.

Fada, long.
Fail, rock, cliff.
Fear, fir, fhir, man.
Fetter, fothir (for), field or wood.
Fionn, fyne, white, shining.
Froach, heather.

Gabhar, gower, goat.
Garbh, garve, rough, rugged.
Gart, an enclosed place.
Gearr, gair, short.
Geo, gia, gio, chasm, rift.
Gil, ravine.
Gille, lad ; pl. *gillean.*
Glass, grey.
Gleo, gloe, mist.
Gobha, gowan, blacksmith.
Gorm, blue or green.

Holm, uninhabited island.
Hope, small bay.
How, haugr, burial mound.

Inch, innis, island.
Inver, inbhir, mouth of a river.

Ken, kin, head, promontory.
Kil, church, burying-place.
Knock, knoll.
Kyle, a strait, a firth.

Lag, laggan, hollow.
Larach, site of an old ruin.
Larig, pass, mountain track.
Leac, flagstone.
Leana, a plain.
Learg, pass, hill-slope.
Liath, grey.
Linn, linne, pool.

Lis, lios, fortress, now a garden.
Loch, lake ; *lochan,* lakelet.

Machar, plain by the sea.
Maol, meal, mam, bald headland.
Mon, monadh, moorland.
Mor, more, great, extensive.
Mov, a plain.
Muc, muic, sow.
Muli, mull, promontory.

Na, nam, nan, of the.

Ob, oba, oban, bay.
Ochter, high-lying.
Oe, island.

Pit, pet, homestead, hollow.
Poll, pool.

Quoich, cuach, cup.

Rath, fort.
Reidh, smooth.
Riach, riahhach, brindled.
Ross, peninsula, forest.
Ru, rhu, row, rudha, point.

Sgeir, skerry, sea rock.
Sgor, scuir, sgurr, sharp rock.
Slochd, sloc, hollow, a grave.
Spideal, spittal, hospice
Stob, point.
Strath, broad valley.
Strone, sron, nose, promontory.
Struan, struth, stream.

Tarbert, tarbet, isthmus.
Tigh, tay, house.
Tir, land.
Tobar, well.
Tom, hillock, bush.
Torr, round hill, heap.
Tulloch, tilly, tully, knoll.

Uachdar, ochter, high-lying, upper
Uamh, cave, ' weem.'
Uig, nook, sheltered bay.
Uisge, esk, water.

Voe, narrow bay.

Wick, vik, bay or creek.

BOOKS ABOUT SCOTLAND

The following list gives the names of books that may be found useful by the average traveller, if not by the specialist.

GENERAL DESCRIPTION AND TRAVEL. *Daniell (William):* 'Picturesque Voyage Round Great Britain,' 8 vols. (1812–25). *Defoe (Daniel):* 'Tour Through the Whole Island of Great Britain' (1724–26). *Drummond (Robert J.):* 'All Around Scotland' (1947). *Finlay (Ian):* 'The Young Traveller in Scotland' (1954). *Geikie (Prof. A.):* 'The Scenery of Scotland for Country and Climate' (1865). *Hall (Tom S.):* 'Walking Tours in Scotland' (1935). *Holmes (W. Kerslev):* 'Tramping Scottish Hills' (1946). *Meikle (H.)* (ed. by): 'Scotland' (1947).

Morton (H. V.): 'In Search of Scotland' (1929), 'In Scotland Again' (1933). *Muir (Augustus):* 'Scottish Portrait' (1948). *Pennant (Thomas):* 'Tour in Scotland in 1769' (1771–75). *Wordsworth (Dorothy):* 'Recollections of a Tour in 1803' (1874).

LOWLANDS. *Crockett (W. S.):* 'The Scott Country' (1905). *Dick (C. H.):* 'Highways and Byways in Galloway and Carrick' (1938). *Grant (Will):* 'Tweed-dale' (1948). *Hammerton (J. A.):* 'Barrieland: a Thrums Pilgrimage' (1929). *Lang (Andrew and J.):* 'Highways and Byways in the Border' (1913). *Mack (J. L.):* 'The Border Line' (from the Solway to the North Sea) (1925). *Scott (Sir Walter):* 'Minstrelsy of the Scottish Border' (1802–03). *Scott-Moncrieff (George):* 'The Lowlands of Scotland' (new ed. 1949). *Veitch (John):* 'History and Poetry of the Scottish Border' (1893).

HIGHLANDS AND ISLANDS. *Baikie (James):* 'Things Seen in the Scottish Highlands' (1932). *Barnett (T. Ratcliffe):* 'Autumns in Skye, Ross and Suther-land' (reprinted 1946). *Boswell (James) and Johnson (Samuel):* 'Journal of a Tour with Dr. Johnson' (1773), 'A Journey to the Western Isles' (1775) (1 vol.). *Carslaw (R. B.):* 'Leaves from Rowan's Logs' (1945). *Darling (F. Fraser):* 'West Highland Survey' (1955). *Gordon (Seton):* 'Afoot in the Hebrides' (1950), 'The Cairngorm Hills of Scotland' (1925), 'Highways and Byways in the West Highlands' (1935), 'Highways and Byways in the Central Highlands' (1948). *Gunn (J.):* 'Orkney: The Magnetic North' (reprinted 1946). *Gunn (N.):* 'Off in a Boat' (1938). *Livingstone (W. P.):* 'Shetland and the Shetlanders' (1947). *Manson (Thomas):* 'Guide to Shetland' (1940). *Martin (Martin):* 'Description of the Western Islands of Scotland' (1695, reprinted 1934). *Macdonald (Colin):* 'Highland Journey' (1943) and other works. *MacGregor (A. A.):* 'Summer Days Among the Western Isles' (Barra) (1929). *Mackenzie (O. H.):* 'A Hundred Years in the Highlands' (1921). *Mackenzie (W. C.):* 'The Book of the Lews' (1919), 'The Highlands and Islands of Scotland' (1937). *Maclean (Norman):* 'The Former Days' (Skye) (1945). *Palmer (W. T.):* 'The Verge of the Scottish Highlands' (Dumbarton to Inverness) (1947). *Perry (Richard):* 'In the High Grampians' (1948). *Poucher (W. A.):* 'A Camera in the Cairngorms' (1947). *Scott-Moncrieff (G.):* 'The Scottish Islands' (1952). *Smith (Alexander):* 'A Summer in Skye' (1865).

HISTORICAL AND SOCIAL ASPECTS. *Adam (Frank):* 'The Clans, Septs and Regiments of the Scottish Highlands' (1934). *Bain (Robert):* 'The Clans and Tartans of Scotland' (new edn. 1953). *Barr (James):* 'Scottish Covenanters' (1947). *Brown (P. Hume):* 'History of Scotland to the Present Time' (i.e. 1910) 3 vols. (reprinted 1929). *Darling (F. Fraser):* 'The Story of Scotland' (1942). *Ferguson (Thos.):* 'The Dawn of Scottish Social Welfare' (to 1863) (1948). *Graham (H.G.):* 'Social Life in Scotland in the 18th Century' (reprinted 1937). *Grant (I. F.):* 'Everyday Life in Old Scotland' (1931), 'The Economic History of Scotland' (1934), 'The Lordship of the Isles' (1935). *Kermack (W. R.):* 'Historical Geography of Scotland' (1926). *Mackenzie (Agnes Mure):* 'The Kingdom of Scotland' (reprinted 1947), 'Scotland in Modern Times' (1720–1939) 6 vols. (reprinted 1947). *Mackenzie (D. A.):* 'Scotland the Ancient Kingdom' (to c. 1290) (1930). *Mackenzie (W. C.):* 'The Western Isles: Their History, Traditions and Place-Names' (1932). *Mackinnon (James):* 'Social and Industrial History of Scotland' (from the Union) (1921). *Murray (C. de B.):* 'How Scotland is Governed' (1938). *Rait (Sir Robert) and Pryde (G. S.):* 'Scotland' (Nations of the Modern World ; 1954). *Ramsay (Dean):* 'Reminiscences of Scottish Life and Character' (reprinted 1947). *Ritchie (Robert):* 'The Normans in Scotland' (1954). *Salmond (J. B.):* 'Wade in Scotland' (1934). *Scott (Sir Walter):* 'Tales of a Grandfather' (1828–30). *Terry (C. S.):* 'History of Scotland' (from the Roman Evacuation to the Disruption) (1920), 'The Forty-Five' (1922), 'The Jacobites and the Union' (1922). *Thomson (G. M.):* 'Short History of Scotland' (1930). *Todd (George Eyre):* 'Famous Scottish Burghs' (1923). *Tytler (Patrick Fraser):* 'History of Scotland' (to the Union) 4 vols. (1873–77). *Wainwright (F. T.; ed.):* 'The Problem of the Picts' (1955). *Watson (W. J.):* 'The Celtic Place-Names of Scotland' (1951).

ARCHÆOLOGY, ARCHITECTURE AND ART. *Anderson (G. Reid):* 'Abbeys of Scotland' (1939). *Black (G. F.):* 'The Surnames of Scotland' (1946). *Finlay (Ian):* 'Art in Scotland' (1948). *Hay (George):* 'The Architecture of Scottish Post-Reformation Churches' (1957). *Hannah (Ian C.):* 'Story of Scotland in Stone' (1934). *Johnston (J. B.):* 'Place-Names of Scotland' (1934). *Lacaille*

(A. D.) : ' The Stone Age in Scotland ' (1954). *Lindsay (I. G.)* : ' Cathedrals of Scotland ' (1926). *Maxwell (Sir John Stirling)* : ' Shrines and Homes of Scotland' (new edn. 1958). *Macgibbon* and *Ross* : ' Castellated and Domestic Architecture of Scotland ' (1887–92), ' Ecclesiastical Architecture of Scotland ' (1906). *Mackenzie (W. Mackay)* : ' The Mediaeval Castle in Scotland ' (1927). *Piggott (Stuart)* : ' Scotland before History ' (1958). *Scott-Moncrieff (George)* : ' Stones of Scotland ' (1938). Various volumes : British Calendar Customs : Folk Lore Society Publications ; Royal Commission on Historical Monuments.

EDINBURGH. *Bone (James)* : ' Perambulator in Edinburgh ' (1926). *Cockburn (Lord)* : ' Memorials of His Time ' (1909). *Scott (Sir Walter)* : ' Heart of Midlothian ' (1818), ' Chronicles of the Canongate ' (1827–8). *Lindsay (Ian G.)* : ' Old Edinburgh ' [The Royal Mile] (1944), ' Georgian Edinburgh ' (1948). *Scott-Moncrieff (George)* : ' Edinburgh ' (1947). *Stevenson (R. L.)* : ' St. Ives ' and ' Edinburgh : Picturesque Notes ' (1878). *Stewart (Mary D.)* : ' Romance of Edinburgh Streets ' (1925). *Watt (Francis)* : ' Edinburgh and the Lothians ' (1921). Works by : *Robert Chambers ; James Grant ;* and *Alex. Smith.*

GLASGOW. *Bell (J. J.)* : ' Wee Macgreegor ' (1903). *Gunn (J.)* and *Newbegin (Marion I.)* (ed. by) : ' City of Glasgow ' (1921). *Malloch (D. Macleod)* : ' The Book of Glasgow Anecdote ' (1912). *MacGill (Patrick)* : ' Children of the Dead End ' (1914), and ' Rat Pit ' (1915). *Oakley (C. A.)* : ' The Second City ' (1947). *Renwick (R.), Lindsay (Sir J.),* and *Eyre-Todd (G.)* : ' History of Glasgow ', 3 vols. (1921–34).

FICTION. The following are among the best authors of Scottish fiction : *Alexander (W.)* : ' Johnny Gibb of Gushetneuk ' (1881). *Black (W.)* : ' A Princess of Thule ' (1874). *Crockett (S. R.)* : ' The Raiders ' (1894). *Galt (John)* : ' Annals of the Parish ' (1821). *Scott (Sir Walter)* : ' Antiquary ' (Arbroath) (1815), ' The Black Dwarf ' (Lowlands) (1816), ' Rob Roy ' (1817), ' Legend of Montrose ' and ' Bride of Lammermoor ' (1819), ' Monastery ' (Melrose) (1820), ' Pirate ' (Shetland) (1821), ' St. Ronan's Well ' (Firth of Forth) (1823), ' The Fair Maid of Perth ' (1828), ' Castle Dangerous ' (Ayrshire and Lanarkshire) (1832), and many others. *Stevenson (R. L.)* : ' The Master of Ballantrae ' (1889), ' Kidnapped ' (1886) and its sequel ' Catriona ' (1893). Also the works of the following : *Anderson (H. M.) ; Barrie (Sir J. M.) ; Blake (George)* (Greenock) ; *Buchan (John) ; Gunn (Neil) ; Macdonald (George)* (Aberdeenshire) ; *Maclaren (Ian) ; Munro (Neil) (Hugh Foulis) ; Niven (Frederick)* (Glasgow).

MISCELLANEOUS. *Darling (F. Fraser)* : ' Crofting Agriculture ' (1945). *Haldane (A. R. B.)* : ' The Drove Roads of Scotland ' (1952). *Harker (Alfred)* : ' The West Highlands and the Hebrides : A Geologist's Guide for Amateurs ' (1941). *Holden (A. E.)* : ' Plant Life in the Highlands ' (1953). *Miller (Hugh)* : ' Old Red Sandstone ' (1841), and ' My Schools and Schoolmasters ' (1854). *MacNeill (Nigel)* : ' Literature of the Highlanders ' (1929). *Murray (W. H.)* : ' Mountaineering in Scotland ' (1947). *St. John (Charles)* : ' Wild Sport of the Highlands ' (1846), and ' Natural History and Sport in Moray ' (1863). *Scottish Tourist Board* (ed.) : ' Scotland for Fishing ' (pub. yearly).

Maps. A clear and accurate map ($\frac{1}{2}$ inch to 1 m.) perhaps the most practical for motorists is published by *Messrs. John Bartholomew & Son, Ltd.,* of Edinburgh (24 sheets ; paper 3/, mounted 5/, dissected 10/), who issue also maps on the scale of $\frac{1}{8}$ in. to 1 m. (3 sheets, 3/ each), a general road map ($\frac{1}{12}$ in. to 1 m. ; 3/, 6/), as well as a new (1958) motoring atlas of Great Britain ($\frac{1}{4}$ in. to 1 m. ; 7/6).

The *Ordnance Survey* issues a number of useful maps. The 7th series (National Grid) is on a scale of 1 inch to 1 m. (78 sheets ; paper 3/6, 4/6, mounted 7/6 ; where these sheets have not yet been issued the ' Popular ' series is still available at the same prices. More detailed, and useful for walkers, is the new series, first issued in 1948, on a scale of $2\frac{1}{2}$ in. to 1 m. (paper 3/, mounted 4/6 ; at present available only for S., E., and Central Scotland). Climbers may have occasion to use the map on the scale of 6 in. to 1 m. (quarter sheets, 4/). The Ordnance Survey publishes also maps (3/6, 5/6, 8/) on the scale of $\frac{1}{4}$ inch to 1 m. (9 sheets). *Messrs. Gall & Inglis* publish a useful series on the scale of 2 m. to the inch (12 sheets ; 1/6–4/). *Messrs. Johnston and Bacon, Ltd.* publish a touring map on the scale of 8 m. to the inch (6/), and sectional maps on the scale of 3 m. to the inch (1/ each ; 9 sections ; from the Border to Cromarty) and 2 m. to the inch (5/, 3/ ; 3 sections : Central Scotland only).

PRACTICAL INFORMATION

I. RAILWAYS AND OTHER CONVEYANCES

Railways. Since their nationalisation on Jan. 1st, 1948, the railways of Scotland have been amalgamated as the Scottish Region of the British Railways. Previously they were worked by two great private companies, the London, Midland and Scottish, and the London and North-Eastern.

Passengers are left much more to their own initiative than on the Continent. They should therefore make sure that they are in their proper train and compartment. A seat is regarded as ' taken ' if a hat, suitcase, or other article is placed upon it; in the chief express trains seats may be booked in advance (fee 2/). The control of the window is by custom conceded to the passenger seated next to it, facing the engine; considerate travellers, in this position, take the sense of the company on the subject of ventilation. It is forbidden to enter a moving train, or to walk across the metals when a bridge or subway is provided. The railway officials are usually civil in answering questions, and enquiry offices and train-indicators will be found at most of the larger stations.—Americans may be reminded that the ticket-office is called the ' booking-office,' that the conductor is addressed as ' guard,' and that baggage is better known as ' luggage.'

On the longer routes 'corridor' or 'vestibule' carriages, with lavatory accommodation, are general, and restaurant cars (B. 7/6 or 4/, L. 9/6, T. 7/6 or 3/, D. 10/6) are attached to the principal long-distance trains. Sleeping cars are included in the chief night trains (extra charges: 1st cl., between England and Scotland, single-berth 40/; within Scotland, 30/; 2nd cl., between England and Scotland, single berth 35/, two-berth 22/6, four-berth 14/; within Scotland, 20/, 12/). Berths should be reserved well in advance. Most stations of any importance have refreshment rooms. Telegrams ordering refreshments, rooms at railway hotels, etc., are sent free of charge from any station, and meals packed for the journey can be obtained from the refreshment rooms (2/–3/6). Smoking is restricted to the compartments so labelled. Compartments ' for ladies only ' are often provided, or will be so labelled on request. Except for a scanty service on the main lines, no trains run on Sunday in Scotland, a fact to be noted by passengers starting for distant destinations on Saturday. Special services are in force on holidays.

FARES AND TICKETS. The standard 2nd class single fare is c. 2d. per mile (1st class, 3d. per mile); return tickets, available for three months, are issued at double the single fare. These ordinary single and return tickets permit the journey to be broken as often as desired. ' Cheap day return ' tickets, ' circular tour ' tickets, ' holiday runabout ' tickets (in summer), and excursion tickets are also obtainable. Children under 3 years travel free, under 14 years at half-fares.—At many stations persons not travelling by train are not admitted to the platforms without a platform ticket (2d.; obtained from an automatic machine or at the booking office).

LUGGAGE. The maximum allowance of free luggage is 150 lbs. for 1st class passengers, 100 lbs. for 2nd class ; for amounts in excess of this a small extra charge is made. Passengers with luggage should take care that each package is clearly addressed and should see that it is properly labelled and put into the luggage van. The railway porter who conveys luggage between cab and train expects a tip (from 1/ for a light bag upwards). Special tickets are required for dogs, bicycles, baby-carriages, etc. Luggage may be left in the *Cloak Room* or *Left Luggage Office* (at small stations in the booking office) for a fee of 9*d.* for the first day and 4½*d.* per day after (bicycles 1/ and 6*d.*). The British Railways collect passenger's luggage, forward it ' in advance,' and deliver it at a charge of 5/ per package, but the passenger ticket must be bought previously and delays often occur.

Time-Tables. *Murray's Time Tables* (monthly editions for Edinburgh and E. Scotland and for Glasgow and W. Scotland, in A.B.C. form, 6*d.* each), familiarly known as ' Diaries,' give all the Scottish services ; the *British Railways* also issue a regional time-table twice yearly (1/). Local time-tables (2*d.*–6*d.*) are published in every town of importance.

Car Sleeper Services.

In summer (roughly May–Sept.) British Railways convey their passengers overnight between England and Scotland on special trains (2nd cl. only).

(a) *London* (King's Cross) to *Perth* nightly except Fri. (less often in Apr. & Oct.).

(b) *London* (Marylebone) to *Glasgow* (St. Enoch) on Tues., Thurs., & Sun., returning Mon., Wed. & Sat.

(c) *Sutton Coldfield* (Birmingham) to *Stirling* every Sun. & Wed., returning Mon. & Thurs.

FARES. £18 10/ ret. for car and driver, £6 for each extra adult, £3 15/ for a child (from Sutton Coldfield £16 10/, £5, £3).

Out of season (Oct.–Apr.) accompanied cars are carried at higher charges on certain regular night trains between London (King's Cross), Edinburgh, Perth, Aberdeen, and Inverness. On these seating and sleeping accommodation (1st or 2nd cl.) can be reserved. Passengers for Perth and Inverness change at Edinburgh.

Steamers.

Steamers in Scotland are much more important in the tourist's programme than steamers in England. No one can know the full beauty of the splendidly irregular West Coast or of the islands who has not seen them from the sea, while to take a trip in a Clyde steamboat (e.g. to Arran, Campbeltown, or Inveraray) is almost one of the ' classic ' things to do in Scotland. Steamers ply also on some of the larger inland lochs (Loch Lomond, Loch Awe, etc.), and their services, like those of many of the coast steamers, are pleasant links in various through or circular tours.—The regular West Coast tourist steamers, comfortable and well found, have two classes : 1st class (' saloon ' or ' cabin '), situated aft, and 2nd class (' steerage '), situated forward. Ample meals (incl. breakfast) are provided, and some steamers are licensed.

Tickets are usually issued by the purser on board ; but for cruises of more than a day berths should be secured at the steamboat office.

Steamers on the *Clyde* and to *Ardrishaig* and *Inveraray*, see Rte. 13 ; to *Oban* and the *Western Highlands* see Rte. 47c ; to *Mull* and *Iona*, see Rte. 50 ; to *Skye*, *Lewis*, and the *Hebrides*, see Rtes. 58, 59 ; to *Orkney* and *Shetland*, see Rte. 65.

Air Services. Public air transport within Scotland has developed considerably of late years, and has brought many remote parts of the country, hitherto inaccessible except by long and tedious journeys by land and sea, into close touch with the chief centres of population. All services within Scotland are now worked by British European Airways. The chief airport for these services is at Renfrew (Glasgow), with connections to the Hebrides and to Orkney and Shetland, while the Northern Islands have connections also with Inverness, Aberdeen, and Edinburgh. Other services of the B.E.A. connect Edinburgh (Turnhouse) and Aberdeen with London Airport, and Glasgow (Renfrew) with London Airport, the Isle of Man, and Belfast.

There are two categories of service : first-class flights and 'tourist' flights. Fares in the latter are c. 20 per cent. cheaper. Excursion return fares, valid 15 days, and week-end fares are valid out of season (Nov.–May). An Irish service (Aer Lingus) plies between Renfrew and Dublin (Collinstown) ; but the airport for long-distance overseas services is at Prestwick, which is especially suited to flying on account of its fog-free climate.

Motor-Buses. Motor transit by road has been enormously developed within recent years, and practically the whole country S. of Inverness is now traversed in all directions by regular long-distance and short-distance motor-bus services, linking up the principal towns and centres and bringing many beautiful districts within easy reach of the traveller by road. In some regions the motor-bus is the only public means of transport. Comprehensive tours from point to point may be planned with the aid of these services, though their connections are not always convenient and comparatively little luggage can be conveyed. The vehicles are usually comfortable covered single-deckers, and the fares are generally cheaper than the corresponding 2nd class railway fares. Return fares, at a reduced rate, are usually available.

The chief companies operating in Scotland, each of which issues a time table (4d.), are : *Scottish Omnibuses* (Edinburgh), for Edinburgh and S.E. Scotland ; *Central S.M.T. Co.* (Motherwell), for Glasgow, Dunbartonshire, Lanarkshire, and Peebles ; *Western S.M.T. Co.* (Kilmarnock), for Glasgow and S.W. Scotland ; *W. Alexander & Sons* (Falkirk), for Stirling, Fife, and E. Scotland ; *Highland Omnibuses* (Inverness), for much of N.E. Scotland.

Long-Distance Services. A network of long-distance motor-coaches, some plying regularly all the year round, others during the summer season only, connects the chief towns in England and Scotland. The coaches run daily or oftener (in some cases, two or three times a week only ; some of the longer services run also at night) and carry a reasonable quantity of luggage (generally c. 28 lb. or a small suitcase per passenger). They are much faster than the ' service ' motor-buses, and pick up passengers at fixed points only (' limited stop ' service). On the longer routes halts are made at convenient hotels for meals, but other intermediate halts are brief. The fares (especially return fares) are cheaper than the corresponding 2nd class railway fares, but railway transit is, of course, quicker. Seats are usually reserved at a booking-office, and in summer (especially at week-ends) should be secured in good time ; for return tickets the precise date of return should be fixed in advance. Particulars of the principal services are given in the *ABC Coach Guide* (5/ ; from book-stalls), and booking-offices and starting-points are advertised also in the local press.

PUBLIC MOTOR TOURS. An easy if rather superficial method of seeing the country is offered by the longer circular motor-coach tours organised in the season by the *Scottish Motor Traction Co.* (45 Princes St., Edinburgh), *W. Alexander & Sons* (473 Cathedral St., Glasgow), etc. These tours, generally starting from Edinburgh or Glasgow, take from 3 to 14 days at an average charge of 45/–60/ per day, which covers all fares, meals, and hotel accommodation. Similar tours, including Scotland and taking of course longer, start also from London and the larger English provincial towns. Luggage should not exceed the limit of a medium-sized flat suitcase.

II. POSTAL INFORMATION

	United Kingdom.	Commonwealth.	Foreign Countries.
LETTERS . .	3*d.* for 1 oz., 4½*d.* for 2 oz., then 1½*d.* per 2 oz.	3*d.* for 1 oz., then 1½*d.* per oz.	6*d.* for 1 oz., then 4*d.* per oz.
POST CARDS	2½*d.*	2½*d.*	4*d.*
NEWSPAPERS (per copy)	2½*d.* for 6 oz., then 1½*d.* per 6 oz. up to 2 lb.	1½*d.* for 2 oz., then 1*d.* per 2 oz.	1½*d.* for 2 oz., then 1*d.* per 2 oz.
PRINTED PAPERS	2*d.* for 2 oz., 4*d.* for 4 oz., then 1*d.* per 2 oz. up to 2 lb.	2*d.* for 2 oz., then 1*d.* per 2 oz.	2*d.* for 2 oz., then 1*d.* per 2 oz.
TELEGRAMS .	3/ for 12 words (3/6 to Irish Republic), then 3*d.* per word	See below	See below

Full particulars will be found in the *Post Office Guide* (yearly, 2/6, with several supplements, gratis), obtainable at any Post Office.

Post Offices are usually open from 8.30 or 9 a.m. to 5.30 or 6 p.m. on week-days, but most of the smaller offices are closed from 1 p.m. on ' early closing days ' (Wed., Thurs., or Sat.). On Sun. and holidays head offices and many country sub-offices remain open from 9 to 10 a.m. for telegraph business and the sale of stamps ; all others are closed.—There is no Sunday delivery of letters or parcels in Scotland.

International Reply Coupons (9*d*. each), exchangeable abroad for stamps, are convenient for franking replies to letters sent abroad, and *Commonwealth Reply Coupons* (3*d*. each) may be used for prepaying replies to letters sent to any part of the British Commonwealth.

POST CARDS. Picture post cards, etc., may be sent at the ' printed paper ' rate provided the words ' printed paper ' be substituted for ' post card ' and nothing appear in writing except date, addresses, and a formula of courtesy not exceeding five words.

PARCELS. Great Britain and Ireland: 2 lb. 1/6, 3 lb. 1/9, 4 lb. 2/, 5 lb. 2/3, 6 lb. 2/6, 7 lb. 2/9, 8 lb. 3/, 11 lb. 3/3, 15 lb. (max.) 3/6. Parcels must be handed in at a Post Office. Parcels heavier than the above limits of weight must be sent by railway or through a goods agent. No compensation for the loss of a parcel sent by post is payable unless a certificate of posting is obtained.

The rates for Imperial and Foreign parcels vary according to the country of destination ; to the U.S.A., 3 lb. 7/ ; 7 lb. 11/6 ; 11 lb. 17/6 ; 22 lb. 30/ ; to New Zealand, 6/6, 10/, 14/6, 23/ ; to Canada, 8/6, 11/, 15/, 21/ ; to Australia, 1 lb. 3/, then 1/9 per lb. up to 22 lb. ; to South Africa, 2/ per lb. up to 11 lb. only. Various forms have to be filled in for the despatch of Imperial and Foreign parcels.

AIR MAIL. Letters to Canada, South Africa, and the U.S.A., 1/3 per oz., to Australia and New Zealand 1/6 per oz. Further information in the Air Mail Leaflet, copies of which may be obtained free of charge at any Post Office.

REGISTRATION. Letters and parcels for inland post may be registered for 1/-2/8 (according to value), foreign letters for 1/. Money should be enclosed in the special ' registered letter envelopes ' sold at all Post Offices, as otherwise compensation may be refused. Parcels and valuable letters for abroad may be insured (fee 1/2-6/8).

POSTE RESTANTE. Correspondence marked ' to be called for ' or ' poste restante ' may be addressed to any Post Office except town sub-offices. Letters are kept for a fortnight (if from abroad, two months). Travellers may not use the poste restante for more than three months.

MONEY ORDERS. Within the United Kingdom money may be transmitted by postal orders (up to £5) or money orders (up to £50), on both of which a small poundage is charged. The name and address of the sender of a money order must be given by the payee. For foreign and colonial money orders the maximum varies from £10 to £40.—*Telegraph Money Orders* are issued at the same rate, plus the cost of the telegram of advice and a fee of 6*d*. for inland and 1/6 for foreign orders.

Telegrams. Inland : Replies may be prepaid up to a maximum of 12/. Priority can be obtained on payment of additional fee of 1/.

The charges for imperial and foreign telegrams (minimum 5 words) vary between 5½d. and 1/ per word to places in the European System and between 1/5 and 4/11 per word outside it. There is a maximum rate of 1/10 per word to places in the British Commonwealth. Reduced rates are available for 'deferred' and 'letter' telegrams.

Radiotelegrams are accepted at any telegraph office for transmission to ships at sea through British coast-stations at the following charges; 1/6 a word (standard); 9d. a word (for short-voyage ships).

Telephones. Public telephone call-office facilities are provided at many Post Offices, railway stations and shops; and in kiosks. The minimum charge for the use of a call office is 4d. Trunk (and toll) calls (including personal calls) may be effected from practically all public call offices. Reduced rates are charged for trunk (and toll) calls made between 6 p.m. and 6 a.m. (Sun. from 2.30 p.m.).

III. HOTELS

Scottish hotels have the reputation, not wholly deserved, of being expensive. At some isolated tourist and anglers' hotels in the Highlands, at some of the smaller summer resorts where hotel accommodation is limited, and at the favourite tourist centres that are annually overcrowded in the season, charges seem high in comparison with the accommodation provided; but the fair-minded traveller will make allowance for the shortness of the period within which the expenses of the whole year must be recovered, and the astute traveller will avoid, if possible, the most crowded months. In parts of the country where more general conditions prevail charges are not above the average, though perhaps, speaking generally, Scottish hotels may be described as less luxurious than their English counterparts. Large first-class hotels, however, with all modern comforts and conveniences, are found in Edinburgh, Glasgow, and the leading tourist and golfing centres; elsewhere the better hotels are comfortable if not luxurious, and less pretentious but clean and adequate quarters may be found everywhere. There has recently been a large increase in the number of '*Country-House*' *Hotels*, many of which occupy large mansions surrounded by fine estates, often including shooting and fishing rights. Many excellent hotels are unlicensed, though they send out for any alcoholic refreshment required. A number of these describe themselves as 'Private' Hotels, though in fact they are usually open to non-residents. The *Temperance Hotels*, in which alcohol is not consumed, rank higher in the scale of comfort than the temperance hotels of England; even among the smaller houses, to be found in practically every town, the economical traveller will find excellent quarters at moderate prices.— Except in large first-class hotels, and especially in *Commercial Hotels*, the place of the evening table-d'hôte dinner is often taken by an excellent high-tea or meat-tea, though dinner will be served if desired.

In the text of this volume the hotels in each town are named approximately in the order of their generally accepted standing, the cheaper houses being mentioned last. The lists, making no claim to be exhaustive, are intended to offer the traveller a reasonable choice of accommodation; and the omission to name a hotel implies no derogatory judgment.

Before taking possession of his rooms at a hotel, the traveller should have a precise understanding as to the charge. Bills should be paid at short intervals as mistakes are then more easily checked. Notice of departure should be given before noon, as otherwise an extra day may be charged for. Valuables should be kept carefully locked up in the owner's suitcase or deposited with the hotel manager in exchange for a receipt. Most hotels make, on application, an inclusive 'en pension' charge for a stay of more than a day or two; but this arrangement is not always convenient for sightseers, who may prefer to take luncheon or tea elsewhere. The hours at which meals are served are much more rigid than formerly, as the Catering Wages Act (in operation since 1948) strictly regulates the hours of employment of hotel staff. Many inns, indeed, have been obliged to abandon the serving of meals owing to the cost of maintaining an adequate staff. The restriction of hours for the sale of liquor and tobacco does not apply to travellers within their hotels, but alcoholic drinks ordered otherwise than at meal-times are usually paid for on the spot.

CHARGES. The figures quoted in the text, though they give a general idea of the charges at different types of hotel, are to a certain extent approximate and relative only; the lowest terms for single rooms in summer are quoted, but it may not infrequently happen that bedrooms at these terms are not available, and in Edinburgh and most resorts the price of accommodation varies with the season, the highest charges being effective in July–Aug. and at the Christmas and Easter holidays, the lowest in Nov.–March. The cost of meals varies but little; luncheon in a good average hotel costs 7/–9/, dinner slightly more, high tea 5/–6/6. The regular 'bed-&-breakfast' charge includes a bath and an 'English' breakfast; a reduction may be arranged where only a light 'Continental' breakfast is desired. In some hotels morning tea is included in the bed-&-breakfast charge; in most, but not all, a cup of after-dinner coffee is counted as an extra (6d.–1/). There are, however, no fixed rules, the custom varying from house to house. For the larger and more fashionable hotels the daily rate may be estimated at about 45/–55/; for less pretentious houses and good country hotels at 30/–40/; while even in village inns it can seldom be less than about 25/.

Bedroom fires and the serving of meals in private rooms are always extra. The usual charge for private sitting-rooms is relatively high.—In most hotels a 'double bedded room' means a bedroom with a large double bed, not a room with two single beds.

GRATUITIES. The award of gratuities to the staff is still a universal custom. Gratuities may be presented individually—to the waiter or waitress, the porter, and the chambermaid—or they may be paid at the hotel office in the form of a percentage on the bill (10–15 per cent.). At a hotel of moderate class 12/–15/ on a bill of £5 is ample, but a one-night visitor will give proportionately more. An occasional 6d. is enough for the page or lift-boy.

Restaurants in the usual sense of the word are found only in Edinburgh and the other large cities in Scotland. In the average town substantial meals are best taken at a hotel, though luncheon-rooms and, still more universally, tea-rooms, which supply lighter refreshments, abound everywhere, and are found even in some remote country districts.

Boarding Houses. Visitors who propose to spend more than a day or two at any of the chief resorts will find boarding-houses or 'guest-houses' considerably cheaper than hotels. The charges at these range from 5 gs. per week upwards. The most satisfactory guide in choosing such quarters is a recommendation from someone who knows both the house and the traveller; but enquiry of the stationmaster, postmaster, or other local source often yields good results. Similar accommodation may be found in country districts in farmhouse hotels.

Youth Hostels. The cheapest way of seeing Edinburgh and the surrounding countryside is to travel on foot or bicycle from Youth Hostel to Youth Hostel. The *Scottish Youth Hostels Association* (head office, 7 Bruntsfield Crescent, Edinburgh 10) owns c. 95 hostels (including two in Edinburgh itself), occupying buildings of many different characters, each in charge of a warden. Some of these are closed in winter, and all are closed from 11 a.m. to 3 p.m. in summer, except in really bad weather. Membership of the Association costs 10/ per annum for those of 21 or over (5/, 16–20; 2/, 5–15). The Association publishes an annual handbook (1/) in which arrangements about meals, sleeping accommodation, etc., are detailed, and also publishes guide-books for hostellers for various districts. Hostels are open only to members of the Scottish Y.H.A. or of an association affiliated to the International Youth Hostel Federation. In holiday seasons and at week-ends accommodation should be booked in advance.

IV. MOTORING IN SCOTLAND

Communicated by the Automobile Association

Motor-cars and motor-cycles entering the United Kingdom are subject to customs duty and purchase tax which vary not only according to value but to country of manufacture. Visiting motorists wishing to make only a temporary stay, not exceeding one year, need not pay customs duty or purchase tax. They may obtain international documents from the motoring association in their own country or, if there is no such organisation, from the Automobile Association, the Royal Scottish Automobile Club, or the Royal Automobile Club in the United Kingdom. The documents required, which permit free entry, are: (*a*) Triptyque or Carnet de Passages en Douanes; (*b*) International Certificate for Motor Vehicles (with nationality plaque); (*c*) International Driving Permit.

No one under 17 years of age may drive a motor-car in Great Britain, and no one under 16 may ride a motor-cycle. If a visiting motorist holds a valid International Driving

Permit, the A.A. or R.A.C. Port Officer will issue a ' Free Licence to Drive ' (RF 30). If the motorist arrives from a country where International Driving Permits are unobtainable (such as the U.S.A. or Canada), or is otherwise unable to produce a permit, the Port Officer will issue a visitor's British licence for 5/ upon a declaration that the motorist is the holder of a valid licence in his own country. No test is necessary. The Association can also arrange tests for visitors without a valid licence who cannot prove that they hold such a licence in their own country. Similarly, a temporary Registration Card will be issued on production of an International Certificate for Motor Vehicles. If the certificate cannot be produced, temporary registration numbers will have to be taken out at the port. The cost is 27/6.

Whether the car has entered under an International Certificate or temporary British registration arrangements, the Port Officer will issue an International Circulation Permit entitling the motorist to 90 days' tax-free circulation in the United Kingdom. This permit must be exhibited on the windscreen of the vehicle in a special holder, which can be supplied for 7/6. The issue of an International Circulation Permit is subject to the production by the visitor of a valid Insurance Certificate, known as a ' green card.' Visitors using their vehicles in the United Kingdom beyond the initial 90 days' tax-free period must license them with a local Council and pay a proportion of the £12 10/ annual tax. The rate of taxation for motor-cycles is considerably lower.

In hiring a car, visitors must present a valid driving licence to the hire firm. The hirer of a self-driven car must be between the ages of 21 and 60.

The rule of the road throughout the United Kingdom is ' keep to the left and overtake on the right,' which is the reverse of the custom in most parts of Europe and in America. There is a speed limit of 30 miles per hour on roads in built-up areas. These roads are defined as those on which there is a system of street lighting with lamp posts at intervals of not more than 200 yards. There are exceptions to this rule ; some roads which are technically ' built-up ' according to the above definition are not restricted, and others which are not ' built-up ' are restricted. On many arterial roads a differential speed limit of 40 m.p.h. may be found to operate. Other speed limits, of less than 30 m.p.h., are in force on a number of roads, bridges, parks, etc. The boundaries of built-up areas and special speed limits are marked by appropriate signs.

During the hours of darkness motor-cars must show two white lights to the front, indicating the width of the vehicle. In addition, there must be two rear lamps exhibited not more than 16 inches from each of the outer edges of the vehicle and placed between 15 and 42 inches from the ground and not more than 30 inches from the rear of the vehicle. The rear number-plate must also be illuminated.

In towns road crossings are provided for pedestrians, who have the right of way unless a police officer is in control. These crossings are identified by alternate black and white stripes, by studs on the road surface, and by lighted yellow beacons at the roadside. On the approach side to the crossing a double line of studs indicates the prohibited area for parking a motor vehicle. It is an offence not to give precedence to a pedestrian on a crossing or to leave a vehicle within the prescribed area.

The controlling body in matters relating to motoring movement in Scotland is the *Royal Scottish Automobile Club* (over 7500 members), which has a commodious club-house at No. 11 Blythswood Square, Glasgow ; but motorists whose tours are likely to extend into other parts of Great Britain may join one of the larger associations, with headquarters in England mentioned below. Town members of the R.S.A.C. (i.e. those living within 25 miles of the club-house) pay an entrance fee of £21 and an annual subscription of £7 7/ ; country members pay an entrance fee of £5 5/ and an annual subscription of £3 3/.

The *Royal Automobile Club*, which was founded in 1897, is the oldest British motoring organisation. It is the national motoring authority and a constituent member of the Fédération Internationale de l'Automobile. The annual subscription for associate members resident in the British Isles is £2 2/ per annum (motor-cyclists £1 11/6) ; reduced subscription are payable by members living abroad. The headquarters are at 85 Pall Mall, London, S.W.1, and there are offices at 23 Charlotte Sq., Edinburgh, and 16 Sandyford Place, Sauchiehall St., Glasgow.

The *Automobile Association of Great Britain* is the largest single motoring organisation in the world and has a membership exceeding 1,750,000. The full subscription for motorists resident in Great Britain or Ireland is £2 2/ a year ; motorcyclists and the owners of three-wheeled cars may pay £1 11/6, but free breakdown service is then excluded. Visiting motorists who are members of overseas motoring associations and clubs federated or allied with the A.A. may join at a reduced subscription. The head office is at Fanum House, New Coventry St., London, W.1, and there are offices at 20 Melville St., Edinburgh, and 247 W. George St., Glasgow.

Among the benefits enjoyed by members of these organisations are : road patrols, mounted on motor-cycle road service outfits, on all important roads ; roadside telephone boxes ; free breakdown service from garages ; emergency and radio-controlled breakdown services ; free legal defence and advice ; technical advice and assistance, including the inspection of used vehicles ; road routes at home and abroad ; an annual handbook containing particulars of appointed hotels, garages and agents, maps, and much other useful information ; and various special publications of interest and value to car and motor-cycle owners.

Roads in Scotland. Although Scotland is a hilly, not to say a mountainous country, the roads in common use are well adapted to motoring, though the surface is not always up to the English standard. The gradients are long rather than steep and breakneck hills are rare. Highland roads are often narrow and winding, sometimes skirting precipitous slopes with sudden turnings, but the surface is often surprisingly good and long stretches of finely engineered road are often met with. Much has recently been done (and is still being done) to widen and straighten them, or to supersede them by new roads, but they still demand careful and experienced driving. On the narrowest roads passing-places at frequent intervals, sometimes marked by posts, are provided. Bridges, which are frequently at right angles to the road, should be approached slowly, and, owing to the ubiquity of the motor-bus, the motto (' gang warily ') of the R.S.A.C. should never be forgotten. The usual charge for garage is c. 1/6–2/6 per night.

Tours in the Western Highlands must be planned with some care on account of the number of sea-lochs and freshwater-lochs, some of which have to be ferried. The charges (not cheap) and the Sunday services at the ferries are liable to vary ; The ferries to Skye do not ply at all on Sundays. In some cases ferries are difficult to approach for large cars and a long wait is often necessary owing to the state of the tide. Some of the higher passes are occasionally snow-bound for a few days even in late spring.

Cycling (roads, see above). In Scotland the cyclist has several advantages over the motorist. His machine can readily be carried on steamers and ferry-boats and may, without much effort, be taken across many fine moorland paths. The Larig Ghru, Glen Tilt, and Corrieyarrick are, however, for the inveterate ' pass-stormer ' only. In the remoter Highlands the distances between inns or hotels are often great and the rutted state of the by-roads is often trying. Cycles must show a white light in front and a red light behind from 1 hr. after sunset. The *Cyclists' Touring Club* (3 Craven Hill, London, W.2 ; subscription 21/ per annum, entrance free 1/) issues a useful handbook.

V. GENERAL HINTS

Season. The travelling season in Scotland, when tourist facilities are in full operation and the weather is at its best, lasts from the middle of June to the middle of September. Hotels and transport are, however, then apt to be crowded and it is essential to secure quarters well in advance. In May and early June travelling is more comfortable, though some tourist-services have not yet begun; on the other hand hill-walkers will suffer less interference from gamekeepers before the stalking season starts. October is often a beautiful month, but the evenings begin to 'draw in.' A fine Scottish summer is one of the most delightful seasons in the world, but Scotland has an uncertain climate and a raincoat is indispensable at all seasons. The drizzling rain known as a 'Scots mist' is not a rare phenomenon. The west coast has a milder and a moister climate than the east coast.

Travellers are advised to arm themselves with "D.M.P." (dimethylphthalate) anti-midge cream against the attacks of 'midges,' which are very troublesome in the late summer evenings, especially near water.

The sporting seasons are as follows: grouse-shooting Aug. 12th–Dec. 10th; deer-stalking, for stags Aug. 12th–Oct. 12th, for hinds Nov. 10th–March 31st; salmon-fishing Feb. 10th–Nov. 1st; trout-fishing March 1st–Oct. 15th.

Plan of Tour. A motor tour, allowing divergences at will, is the best method of seeing the country. The following hints are for travellers without motors.—The '*Scott Country*' (Rte. 8) may be taken on the way from the South to Edinburgh, the '*Burns Country*' (Rtes. 16–18) on the way to Glasgow, or they may be visited in special excursions from these cities. A visit to *Galloway* (the 'Crockett Country'; Rtes. 19–21) involves a considerable divergence from the direct route to Glasgow.—With EDINBURGH (Rte. 5) or Glasgow (Rte. 11) as starting-points, a round tour including some of the finest points in Scotland and requiring a fortnight or more (according to the time spent in halts and in side-excursions) may be planned as follows. From Edinburgh viâ *Stirling, Dunblane, Callander*, and the *Trossachs* (Rtes. 23–25) to GLASGOW (the Clyde, Rte. 13); from Glasgow by steamer or motor coach viâ Ardrishaig (Rte. 47c) or by railway viâ Crianlarich (Rte. 12) to OBAN (Rte. 49), a centre for many excursions (Staffa and Iona; Glen Coe, etc.). From Oban by steamer (p. 349) or by railway viâ Crianlarich (Rtes. 46, 51) to *Fort William* (p. 354; Ben Nevis), and on by the Great Glen (Rte. 52) to INVERNESS (Rte. 54; Culloden).—From Inverness we return south by the picturesque 'Highland Railway' (Rte. 30) viâ *Aviemore* (the Cairngorms), *Blair Atholl* (Glen Tilt), *Pitlochry* (Killiecrankie; Loch Rannoch), *Dunkeld*, to PERTH (Crieff; Loch Earn), and thence viâ *Kinross* (Lochleven Castle) and *Dunfermline* to Edinburgh.

From this round many extensions may be made. From Fort William the West Highland Railway (Rte. 53A) runs on to *Mallaig* for SKYE (Rte. 58), and after exploring that island we strike E. across the mainland from *Kyle of Lochalsh* by the fine 'Dingwall and Skye' railway (Rte. 55) viâ *Achnasheen* (Loch Maree; Gairloch) and *Dingwall* to *Inverness*. From Inverness we may travel N. (Rte. 61) to *Wick* and *Thurso* (and so to *Orkney* and *Shetland*, Rtes. 65–67), or E. (Rte. 43) to *Elgin* and ABERDEEN (Rte. 39), whence a charming excursion (Rte. 40) may be made to *Ballater* and *Braemar* (and on viâ Glenshee to *Blairgowrie* and *Perth*, see Rte. 29). From Aberdeen the direct line (Rtes. 38, 35) to Edinburgh follows the E. coast, viâ *Montrose*, *Arbroath*, *Dundee*, and Fife (St. Andrews).

The **Scottish Tourist Board**, 2 Rutland Place, West End, Edinburgh, 1 (affiliated with the British Travel and Holidays Association), founded with the object of increasing the number and promoting the comfort of visitors to Scotland, issues annually a *National Register of Accommodation* (2/6), and periodic announcement of coming events, and willingly supplies other convenient and useful information.

The **National Trust for Scotland** FOR PLACES OF HISTORIC INTEREST AND NATURAL BEAUTY (5 Charlotte Square, Edinburgh, 2), the counterpart of the National Trust in England, acts as trustee of properties acquired by the nation to be preserved intact for posterity. It preserves from destruction and damage an ever increasing number of national treasures. The minimum subscription is 10/ per annum. Members have free access to all properties owned by the Trust and by the National Trust in England. Many other historic monuments have been scheduled for preservation by Act of Parliament, and numerous ancient buildings are under the efficient care of the **Ministry of Works** (Ancient Monuments Dept.).

Gardens. Many Scottish gardens and houses of great interest are open to visitors on certain days during the summer (in connection with Scotland's Gardens Scheme, 26 Castle Terrace, Edinburgh 1) in aid of the Queen's Institute of District Nursing. Admission usually 1/.

Sale of Tobacco and Liquor.

Tobacconists' shops are not now open for longer hours and are all closed on Sundays; but tobacco, cigars, and cigarettes may be purchased in restaurants and public-houses during permitted hours. Alcoholic liquor is not sold on weekdays before 11 a.m. nor after 11 p.m., nor during three hours in the afternoon. These 'prohibited hours' do not apply to travellers within their hotels. On Sundays 'bona fide travellers' may obtain alcoholic refreshment at all reasonable hours.

Banks

are open 9.30–12.30 and 1.30–3; on Sat. 9–11.30. Scottish banks issue notes (for £1, £5, and £10) which, especially the pound-notes, freely circulate in addition to the ordinary British currency, but are not accepted in England.

Public Holidays.

New Year's Day is a universal holiday in Scotland, and most towns and villages have also their own spring, summer, or autumn holidays, when shops, etc., are shut, as they are, in the Highlands, on 'fast days' (always a Thurs.) and 'trades' holidays,' which are irregular and vary from town to town. The 'Common Ridings' and similar festivals, in the Border towns, are also whole holidays. BANK HOLIDAYS are New Year's Day, Good Friday, the first Monday in May, the first Monday in August, and Christmas Day.—Quarter-days (terms) are Candlemas (Feb. 2nd), Whitsunday (May 15th), Lammas (Aug. 1st) , and Martinmas (Nov. 11th).—Special festivals are *Hallowe'en* (Oct. 31st), now mainly a children's festival, with dipping for apples and burning of nuts ; *St. Andrew's Day* (Nov. 30th), perhaps more piously observed by the Scot abroad than in Scotland ; and *Hogmanay* (Dec. 31st), when the New Year is 'brought in' with jollity. *Burns's Birthday* (Jan. 25th) is celebrated by dinners, concerts, and speeches.—*Saturday* is a business half-holiday in the towns, but shops are closed usually on Wednesday or Thursday after 1 p.m.

SUNDAY IN SCOTLAND, though no longer so austere an occasion as it used to be, is still a quiet day and travellers must be prepared for a relaxation in their activities. Transport services are much restricted ; on most railway lines there are no Sunday trains at all. Places of entertainment, shops, and restaurants, even in the towns, are closed, so that meals must be obtained at hotels or boarding-houses ; shooting and fishing are suspended ; and 'Sunday golf' is far from being universal. Many of the motor-bus services and excursions, however, run on Sundays, and the picture galleries in the towns are open on Sunday afternoons.

Churches in Scotland. The national *Church of Scotland* or *Established Church* (' the Establishment,' ' the Auld Kirk ') is PRESBYTERIAN, and most Scottish Presbyterians now belong to it. After the final triumph of Presbyterianism at the Revolution of 1688, secessions from the Established Church took place from time to time, not, however, on points of faith, but mainly on the question of the practical relation between Church and State. Some of the seceding bodies, all strictly Presbyterian, split later into smaller bodies, and, though occasionally two or more united, the union almost invariably left a dissatisfied remnant to perpetuate minute shades of difference and to perplex the student of ecclesiastical history. The *Secession Church*, founded in 1740 by Ebenezer Erskine, divided in 1747, on the question of the lawfulness of the burgess oath required in certain towns, into *Burghers* and *Antiburghers*. The Burghers split in turn (1799) into *New Light* and *Old Light Burghers*, and the Antiburghers (1806) into *New Light* and *Old Light Antiburghers* ; but in 1820 the two New Light sections coalesced under the name *United Secession Church*, while the Old Lights combined in 1842 as the *Original Seceders*—the ' Auld Lichts ' of Sir J. M. Barrie's books. In 1847 the United Secession joined the *Relief Church* (which had left the Established Church in 1761) to form the *United Presbyterian Church* (the ' U.P.s '). Meanwhile, at the ' Disruption ' of 1843, the Established Church had suffered a severe blow when, on the question of ' patronage,' 451 ministers headed by Dr. Thomas Chalmers resigned their livings and constituted the *Free Church of Scotland* (the ' Free Kirk '). In 1876 the Free Church absorbed the *Reformed Presbyterian Church*, or Cameronians, a body that had existed independently since 1706. For many years after the Disruption there were at least three unconnected Presbyterian churches in nearly every town and parish : the Church of Scotland, the Free Kirk, and the U.P. Church. In 1900, however, the Free Church and U.P. Church coalesced to form the *United Free Church*, although a few Free Church congregations (chiefly in the Highlands) remain outside this union and retain the name of Free Church (colloquially ' the Wee Frees '). At length, in Oct., 1929, the Church of Scotland and the United Free Church combined to form the *United Established Church of Scotland*, thus uniting the overwhelming majority of Presbyterians in Scotland ; and a further, and almost final, act of union occurred in June, 1956, when the Original Seceders rejoined the Church of Scotland after 200 years.

ROMAN CATHOLICS. At the Reformation a considerable part of the population, especially in the Highlands, remained faithful to the ' old religion,' and still so remain, while their number has been swelled by the immigration of Irish and Lithuanian labourers and miners. A new Roman Catholic hierarchy was established in 1878, and now includes two archbishops (St. Andrews and Edinburgh ; Glasgow) and six bishops (Aberdeen ; Argyll and the Isles ; Dunkeld ; Galloway ; Motherwell ; and Paisley).

The later Stewart kings were foiled in their attempts to establish Episcopacy in Scotland, but the EPISCOPAL CHURCH IN SCOTLAND survived. It is quite independent of the Episcopal Church of England, though allied with it. It has seven bishops (Aberdeen and Orkney ; Argyll and the Isles ; Brechin ; Edinburgh ; Glasgow and Galloway ; Moray, Ross, and Caithness ; and St. Andrews, Dunkeld, and Dunblane), who elect their own Primus.

Golf is ubiquitous in Scotland, and most courses admit visitors to play at moderate green fees (2/6–4/ per round, 4/–10/ per day ; usually more on Sun.), though on the more famous links and on some courses owned by private clubs the fees are higher. A letter from the secretary of the visitor's home club, stating his handicap, is a pleasant introduction, but is not essential. On some popular courses the starting-hours are allotted by ballot, and strict punctuality is exacted.

Sunday play is much more usual than formerly, rather more than half the courses in Scotland being open (some in the forenoon or afternoon only). At St. Andrews only one course is open on Sundays, and in the Hebrides and north of Inverness the only available courses are Port Ellen (Islay), Tain and Kirkwall (Orkney). The majority of the Fife courses are likewise closed on Sunday.

As a rule golf links beside the sea are better than those inland.—The ' championship courses ' in Scotland are *St. Andrews*, *Prestwick*, *Muirfield*, *Troon*, and *Carnoustie*. At the first four a personal introduction is required by strangers, and the same is true of some private courses near the large towns. There are, however, many courses, little if at all inferior to these, to which strangers are admitted on payment ; on the West Coast : *Troon* (several courses), *Prestwick St. Nicholas*, *Gailes*, *Machrihanish*, *Islay* (Port Ellen) ; on the East Coast : *North Berwick*, *Gullane*, *Aberlady*, *Dunbar*, *Montrose*, *Cruden Bay*, *Nairn*, *Dornoch*, *Gleneagles*, though inland, has two of the most sporting courses in Scotland. The ' Book of Scottish Golf Courses ' (annual ; 2/6) gives particulars of golf-courses and their green fees, etc.

Ski-ing in Scotland is supervised by the Scottish Ski Club (15 Hope St., Edinburgh, 2), founded in 1907. It provides maps and information to members, and possesses several club huts. The Club emphasises that ski-ing is rather a spring sport than a winter sport in Scotland, the best snow conditions being found from the end of February to mid-April, often extending even into May ; but there is no guarantee that every winter will bring a sufficient snowfall, and conditions vary greatly from year to year. Generally speaking the best snow and the most suitable weather are to be found in the Eastern Highlands, the preferred areas being the Cairngorms, the Cairnwell district, and the mountains around Drumochter and Loch Tay ; though the Ben Nevis range often affords wonderful opportunities. Ski-ing in Scotland is a much more strenuous and uncomfortable sport than in Switzerland ; short and light ski are preferable, as much carrying has to be done, and steel edges should be used.

Curling, the national winter game of Scotland, may be very roughly described as a variety of bowls played upon ice. It has been practised in Scotland for over 400 years, the oldest dated curling stone, the Stirling Stone, bearing the date 1511. Even more primitive stones, however, have been found in rivers and lochs. Present-day stones, weighing about 40 lb., are made from Ailsa Craig or Burnock Water granite. Originally entirely an open-air game, dependent upon icy winter conditions, curling received a great impetus in 1877 when the first indoor rink was opened at Crossmyloof, Glasgow.

A team or 'rink' of players consists of four members, controlled by a 'skip'; the general idea is to place the stones (two to each player) as near as possible to a bottle-shaped 'tee' which performs the function of the 'jack' at bowls. The length of the rink is 42 yds.; the tees at either end are 38 yds. apart. Players are permitted to control the passage of the stone by 'sooping,' i.e. sweeping the ice with brooms.

The most famous open-air rink is at Carsebreck Loch, Perthshire, where the match between teams from N. and S. of the Forth is played each winter when weather conditions permit. The senior club, to which most clubs are now affiliated, is the Royal Caledonian Curling Club, founded at Edinburgh in 1838.

Camping is organised by the *Camping Club of Great Britain and Ireland* (Scottish secretary, Miss I. F. Anderson, Balnagowan, Bridge of Weir, Renfrewshire), which provides members (subscription 25/, entrance fee 10/) with a list of approved camp-sites, privately owned (with fixed charges for a stay), and issues a useful handbook. Visitors to Britain from overseas are entitled to three months' temporary membership of the club.

There are also public camping sites in the National Forest Parks (Glentrool, Ardgartan, Rothiemurchus) and elsewhere.

Camping Coaches (corridor coaches with room for six persons) and 'camping apartments' (in disused stations), fully equipped with furniture, crockery, and linen, are let by the week or fortnight in April–Oct. by British Railways. Apply to the Chief Commercial Manager, 87 Union St., Glasgow, C.1.

Canoeing. Scotland presents the canoe tourist with some of the finest water in Europe, varying from fast rivers to tranquil canals. Sea and inland lochs provide ideal settings for cruising through the unsurpassed grandeur of the Scottish Highlands and the islands of the West. The rivers Tay, Spey and Tweed give excellent sport, though there are a number of shorter but equally exciting runs. Loch Lomond and Loch Awe are but two of the many freshwater lochs which make ideal centres for canoeing holidays, while for the more venturesome there are the Western Islands and the Great Glen, the latter combining tidal and fresh water with canal and river amid glorious scenery.

Canoe clubs in Scotland are organised in the Scottish Canoe Association, which is the Scottish Division of the British Canoe Union, and members may fly the B.C.U. pennant and compete in national and international regattas as members of the B.C.U. Other information and advice are obtainable through the secretary of the S.C.A. (J. H. Cuthill, 2 Merchiston Bank Av., Edinburgh, 10).

VI. ROUTES TO SCOTLAND

1. From England

A. Road Routes

The principal roads from England to Scotland lead from Berwick, from Carlisle and from Newcastle; and the approaches to these towns from the South are given in detail in the *Blue Guide to England*.

BERWICK-UPON-TWEED may be reached from London direct (338 m.) viâ the Great North Road or viâ York (344–361 m. according to route chosen).—Thence to (57 m.) *Edinburgh* by Dunbar and Haddington, see Rte. 1.

To CARLISLE there are four main routes from London: (*a*)

viâ Grantham and Appleby (303 m. ; the fastest though not the shortest route) ; (b) viâ Grantham and Skipton (311½ m.) ; (c) viâ Warrington and Lancaster (298½–304½ m.) ; (d) viâ the Lake District (315½–328½ m.).—From Carlisle to *Glasgow* (117 or 94 m. ; alternative routes), see Rte. 9 ; to *Edinburgh* (94, 96, or 93 m.), see Rte. 3.

From NEWCASTLE, 275 m. from London by the Great North Road, one of the most picturesque approaches to Scotland leads viâ (7½ m.) *Ponteland* and (31 m.) *Otterburn* (Percy Arms) and up the wild green valley of *Redesdale* in the Cheviot Hills to (46½ m.) *Carter Bar*, ¼ m. beyond the Border. Thence viâ Jedburgh to *Edinburgh* (105 m. from Newcastle), see Rte. 2.

MOTOR COACHES every evening from London to (c. 15¼ hrs.) *Edinburgh* and to (c. 15½ hrs.) *Glasgow* (in each case, 40/] ; day-service also in June–Sept.—In summer there are also two-day services to Edinburgh by the W. or E. coast, the nights being spent at Chester or Buxton and York respectively (42/6, 82/6).

B. RAILWAY ROUTES

On the following routes restaurant and sleeping cars run as required. Seats may be reserved (2/) on the principal trains.

1. From London (King's Cross) to *Edinburgh* (Waverley) viâ York, Newcastle, and Berwick, 393 m. in 5–8 hrs., with through sleeping cars to Fort William, Dundee, and Aberdeen.

2. From London (Euston) to *Glasgow* (Central) viâ Crewe and Carlisle, 401½ m. in 6¾–9 hrs. Through sleeping cars also by this route (avoiding Glasgow) from London to Perth, Aberdeen or Inverness, and to Oban.

3. From London (St. Pancras) to *Edinburgh* (Waverley) viâ Sheffield, Leeds, Carlisle, and Galashiels, 409 m. in 9¾–10 hrs.

4. From London (St. Pancras) to *Glasgow* (St. Enoch) viâ Sheffield, Leeds, Carlisle, Dumfries, and Kilmarnock, 423½ m. in 9½ hrs.

Through sleeping car services also connect Birmingham, Liverpool, and Manchester with Glasgow viâ Carlisle.

C. AIR ROUTES

1. From London Airport to *Edinburgh* (Turnhouse), 3 or 4 times daily in summer in 1½ hr. ; once or twice daily in winter. The morning services goes on to Aberdeen and Orkney.

2. From London Airport to *Glasgow* (Renfrew) 5–7 times on weekdays in 1 hr. 35 min.

There are also services daily or oftener from Manchester and Birmingham to *Glasgow* (Renfrew ; 65–75 min.) ; in summer from the Isle of Man to *Renfrew* (1 hr.) or to *Stranraer* (25 min.) and thence by coach ; and from Jersey to *Renfrew* (daily in c. 3½ hrs.) and to *Turnhouse* (at week-ends ; 3½ hrs.).

2. From Ireland

A. SEA ROUTES

1. From Larne to *Stranraer*, British Railways steamer daily (twice daily July–Sept.) except Sun. in c. 2¼ hrs. (open sea

passage c. 1¼ hr.). Berths should be booked in advance from the Steamship Superintendent, 24 Donegall Place, Belfast, and sailing tickets (free) may be necessary at the height of the holiday season. Cycles, motor-cycles, and motor-cars are conveyed at varying rates.

2. From Belfast to *Glasgow* (Lancefield Quay), Burns & Laird Lines steamer nightly every weekday in 9½ hrs. In summer daylight service also every weekday to *Ardrossan* (Montgomerie Pier) in 4 hrs. with rail connection to Glasgow.

3. From Londonderry to *Glasgow* (Broomielaw), Burns & Laird Lines steamer on Wed. and Sat. in c. 12 hrs. In summer on Tues., Thurs., Sat. viâ Greenock.

4. From Dublin to *Glasgow* (Anderston Quay), Burns & Laird Lines steamer on Wed. and Sat. in c. 16 hrs. In summer on Tues. and Fri. also. On certain days a call is made at Greenock (enquire at company's offices).

B. Air Routes

1. From Belfast (Nutt's Corner) to *Glasgow* (Renfrew), 4–7 times daily in 1 hr.

2. From Dublin (Collinstown) to *Glasgow* (Renfrew), 2–4 times daily in 85 min.

3. From Europe and America

A. Sea Routes

1. From Copenhagen to *Leith*, Currie Line steamer on alternate Fri. in 48–56 hrs.

2. From Reykjavik (Iceland) to *Leith* in 3–4 days, going on to Copenhagen, Iceland Steamship Co's steamer c.fortnightly.

3. From Montreal (in winter from St. John, N.B.) to *Glasgow* (Princes Dock), Donaldson Line steamer c. every 3 weeks. Steamers of the C.P.R. also call c. every 3 weeks at the Tail of the Bank (Greenock) ; and several transatlantic cargo vessels, carrying a few passengers between New York, Boston, and Glasgow, are likewise available.

B. Air Routes

Prestwick Airport is served by Air Liners from Hamburg, Copenhagen, and Oslo or Bergen (daily) ; from Stockholm and Oslo viâ Stavanger (weekly) ; from Amsterdam (2–3 times daily) ; from Paris viâ Birmingham or Manchester (twice every weekday) ; from Reykjavik (Thurs., Sun.) ; from Luxembourg (Thurs., Sun.), etc.

There are also air services from Montreal (Mon. & Sat.), viâ Goose Bay or Gander ; from New York (B.O.A.C.) viâ Boston or direct (6 times weekly) ; from Chicago and Detroit (B.O.A.C. ; Tues., Thurs., Sat.) ; and a daily service from New York (K.L.M.) direct.

I. EDINBURGH, GLASGOW, AND SOUTHERN SCOTLAND

1. FROM BERWICK TO EDINBURGH

ROAD (A 1), 57 m., commanding fine sea-views for many miles.—30 m. **Dunbar** (by-passed).—41 m. **Haddington.**—52 m. *Musselburgh.*—We enter (57 m.) **Edinburgh** by London Road (Pl. 13, 14).—MOTOR-BUS in 2¼ hrs. direct or in 2½ hrs. viâ Ayton or Eyemouth.

RAILWAY, 57½ m. in 1–2 hrs.—This is part of the 'East Coast Route' from London (King's Cross) to Scotland viâ York and Newcastle: to *Edinburgh,* 393 m. in 6⅔–8 hrs., with restaurant car or sleeping car. Comp. the *Blue Guide to England.*—Principal stations : 5½ m. *Burnmouth* (junction for Eyemouth, 3 m.). —11¼ m. *Reston.*—28½ m. **Dunbar.**—39¾ m. *Drem* (junction for North Berwick, 4¾ m.).—44¼ m. *Longniddry.*—48 m. *Prestonpans.*—57½ m. **Edinburgh** (Waverley).

Berwick-on-Tweed (*King's Arms*, RB. from 25/6, P. 16 gs. ; *Castle*, RB. from 30/, P. from 14½ gs. ; *Salmon*, RB. 17/6), a seaport and fishing town (12,550 inhab.), lies at the mouth of the Tweed, on its N. bank.

This ancient Border town, alternately English and Scottish for centuries, was finally surrendered to England in 1482, and was then organised as a kind of extra-territorial community, with a government of its own, as a bastion against the Scots. It is now regarded as included in Northumberland.

The most interesting monument of Berwick is its Elizabethan **Ramparts* (begun c. 1558), which are, with those of Verona (1523), Antwerp (1545), and Lucca (1561), the earliest example of the new military engineering afterwards developed by Vauban. They enclose a much smaller area than Edward I's wall, only traces of which survive. Of the *Castle* in which that king gave judgment in 1291 in favour of Balliol's claim to the Scottish crown, some fragments remain W. of the station, which stands on the site of the great hall (tablet). The *Parish Church* (1648–52) is one of the few built in England during the Commonwealth ; the *Town Hall,* too tall for its width, was completed in 1754. Characteristic of Berwick are its bridges. The famous *Old Bridge* of 15 arches only 17 ft. wide (1611–34) was supplemented in 1928 by the high concrete bridge, with a main span of 361½ ft., that now carries the Great North Road across the Tweed. Farther upstream is the Royal Border Bridge of the railway (126 ft. high, 2000 ft. long).

At *Halidon Hill* (537 ft.), 2 m. N.W., a Scottish army under the Regent Archibald Douglas, endeavouring to raise the siege of Berwick, was defeated with great slaughter by the English in 1333. The Regent and many Scottish noblemen fell in this revenge for Bannockburn.

FROM BERWICK TO KELSO. A 699 (23 m.) runs direct viâ *Swinton,* where the church contains the tomb of Alan Swinton of Swinton (c. 1200), and *Eccles* with a church of 1774. Near the last are slight remains of the Cistercian nunnery founded by Earl Gospatric in 1156. A more interesting route bears l. after 7 m. for (9½ m.) *Ladykirk,* where the stone-vaulted church, built by James IV in 1500, is said to commemorate his escape from drowning in the Tweed. This route joins the main Tweedside road (A 698) at (16½ m.) *Coldstream.* Both roads are served by motor-buses (1½ hr.), and there is another bus-route viâ Cornhill (to Kelso 65 min.; p. 30).

Motor-buses from Berwick also to *Galashiels* (2¼ hrs.) viᴀ Duns, Greenlaw, Earlston, and Melrose ; and to *Coldingham* (½ hr.) and *St. Abb's* (¾ hr.).

About 3 m. N. of Berwick, at *Lamberton Bar*, where the toll-keeper performed the same good offices for runaway couples as the blacksmith at Gretna Green, we pass from the ' Liberties of Berwick ' into Scotland proper, and enter Berwickshire.

Berwickshire, the most S.E. county of Scotland, taking its name from a town now included in England, embraces the three vaguely defined districts of the *Merse*, in the S., extending into Roxburghshire to form the largest plain in Scotland, *Lammermuir*, to the N.W., with the hills of that name, and *Lauderdale* to the S.W. The county is agricultural and pastoral; its coast is rocky and inhospitable ; and on the S. it is bounded for 20 m. by the Tweed. Its county town is Duns ; its only royal burgh is Lauder ; and in the extreme S.W. corner is Dryburgh Abbey. The Gospatrics, the Humes or Homes, the Hepburns, and the Douglases were prominent in the early restless history of this Border county.

The ruined church of *Lamberton* (l.) figures in the marriage contract between James IV and Margaret, daughter of Henry VII, in 1502, which laid the foundation for the union of the two countries. The coast is lined by lofty cliffs.—5½ m. *Burnmouth*, a fishing village at the foot of a steep descent.— 8 m. *Ayton* (Red Lion, RB. 19/6, P. 9½ gs.), on the Eye, has a sandstone castle of 1851, the successor of a stronghold destroyed by Surrey in 1498 as recorded in Ford's ' Perkin Warbeck '.

Eyemouth (*Home Arms*, RB. 22/6, P. 8 gs.), a fishing village (2270 inhab.) and summer resort, is 2 m. N.E. of Ayton. Thence A1107 leads N.W. for 3½ m. to **Coldingham** (*Anchor*, RB. 21/6, P. 7 gs.), the *Urbs Coludi* of Bede. This large village, with a market cross, is noted for the ruins of its Benedictine *Priory* (before 1139), the successor of the nunnery of St. Ebba founded in the 7th cent. on St. Abb's Head and burned by the Danes c. 870. The priory was much damaged by the Earl of Hertford in 1545 and most of its domestic buildings were demolished by Cromwell in 1648 ; the choir has been restored as a parish church. The discovery, early in the 19th cent., of the skeleton of a woman immured upright in the walls has been turned to account in Scott's ' Marmion.' The visitor should notice, on the outside, the Romanesque arcade and string courses surmounted by lancet windows at the E. end, and, within the church, the E.E. arcade, with foliated columns, that forms a gallery round the N. and E. walls. Fragments of the S. transept and ruins of the monastic refectory remain.

St. Abb's Head (310 ft. ; lighthouse), a bold and rocky promontory, projects from the magnificent coast 2½ m. N.E., beyond (1¼ m.) the village of St. Abb's with its little harbour.—About 3½ m. farther along the coast, in a striking position on a projecting cliff, are the battered fragments of *Fast Castle*, popularly accepted as the original of ' Wolf's Crag ' (in the ' Bride of Lammermoor '), where the poverty-stricken household of the Master of Ravenswood was administered by the capable Caleb Balderstone. The gloomy castle, ' fitter to lodge prisoners than folk at liberty,' was a fortress of the Homes, and later belonged to Logan of Restalrig, one of the Gowrie conspirators, whose corpse was tried and condemned for high treason.

FROM AYTON TO EARLSTON (Melrose), 30 m. (B· 6355, A 6105), at first traversing the fertile Merse.—5 m. *Chirnside* has a 12th cent. S. doorway in its church. Ninewells House, S. of the village, is the successor of the ancestral home of David Hume (1711–76) and his occasional residence. ˙We cross the Whitadder, which is joined 2 m. downstream by the Blackadder.—7½ m. *Edrom* church preserves a fine Norman doorway, rebuilt outside the church, and, in the 15th cent. Blackadder aisle, the tomb of Patrick Home (1553).—12 m. **Duns** (*Black Bull*, RB. 18/6, P. 8 gs.; *Waverley*, temp., RB. 17/6, P. 7 gs.; *White Swan*, similar charges) is an agricultural centre (2025 inhab.) and an anglers' resort, with a big square, at the foot of *Duns Law* (700 ft.). The original town stood on the S.W. slopes of the Law, but was destroyed by the English in 1545; the present Duns that ' dings a' ' was founded in 1588. In Market Square is the conspicuous *Town Hall* of 1816, now a factory, while to the S. lies the attractive *Park* in which stands the Mercat Cross of 1792.

Duns was the birthplace of Thomas Boston (1676–1732), author of ' The Fourfold State ' (house in Newtown St.; tablet) and of Thomas McCrie (1772–1835), biographer of Knox; but its claim upon Duns Scotus (1265 ?–1308), the schoolman, is disputed by Down, in Ulster, and by Dunstane, in Northumberland. The Covenanters' Stone, on the top of Duns Law, commemorates the encampment in 1639 of the Covenanting army under Gen. Leslie, with whom the hollow Pacification of Berwick was patched up the same year. *Duns Castle*, ½ m. N.W., a 19th cent. mansion, includes an old tower said to have been built by Randolph, Earl of Moray; the beautiful grounds are open to the public on application to Messrs. Ferguson & Petrie, Market Square.

At *Abbey St. Bathans* (7 m. N.; motor-bus), reached by a delightful road and situated on a lovely stretch of the Whitadder, the parish church incorporates parts of the E. and W. walls and a prioress's tomb from the nunnery church (13th cent.) dedicated to St. Baothen of Tiree, cousin and successor of Columba. —About 2 m. S.E. of St. Bathans, at the foot of Cockburn Law (1065 ft.) yet 200 ft. above the Whitadder, is the ruined broch of *Edin's Hall*, notable for its size (90 ft. in diameter).—*Cranshaws Castle*, 9 m. N.W. of Duns, a fine example of a Border tower (still inhabited), stands ½ m. W. of Cranshaws church on the road over the Lammermuirs to (18 m.) Gifford, which rises to 1346 ft.—About 1 m. W. of Duns a pleasant road (r.), passing the golf course (9 holes), ascends the moors to Hardens Hill (1056 ft.; view) and then descends to (7 m.) *Longformacus* (Hot. Rathburne, RB. from 17/6, P. 9 gs.) in the valley of the Dye (motor-bus on Tues. & Sat.). The road (rough) goes on through the Lammermuir to join the Gifford road.—Other buses run from Duns to Kelso viâ Swinton or Greenlaw.

15¾ m. *Polwarth*. In the grounds of Marchmont House, famous for its tall oaks, is Polwarth church, built in 1703 by Sir Patrick Hume, who, as an adherent of Argyll in 1685, lay hid in its earlier vaults for a month, fed at night by his heroic young daughter, afterwards Lady Grisell Baillie.— 20 m. *Greenlaw* (Castle, RB. 21/, P. 8 gs.), a small town on the Blackadder, has a church dating from 1675 with a tall square tower (1696) and a court house of 1834. About 3 m. S., on a rocky eminence, is *Hume Castle* (13th cent.), once the seat of the earls of Home, captured in 1651 by Cromwell. The ruins (a mere shell), restored in 1794 as a kind of sham antique, command a wide view.—24 m. *Gordon* (Gordon Arms, RB. 15/, P. 6 gs.), the original seat of the ancestors of the Duke of Richmond and Gordon.—*Greenknowe*, 1 m. N. on the Lauder road, is a well-preserved fortified house (1581). *Mellerstain* (Earl of Haddington), 3 m. S. on the Kelso road, is a stately mansion, begun probably by William Adam about 1725 for Lady Grisell Baillie and completed in 1773–78 by his son Robert, with graceful interiors and interesting paintings (adm. 2/6; June–Sept. 2–5.30 daily exc. Sat.; garden 1/; teas available).—30 m. **Earlston** (*Red Lion*, RB. 17/6, P. 7 gs.; *White Swan*, RB. 15/, P. 6 gs.), formerly *Ercildoune*, was the abode of Thomas Learmont (fl. 1220?–1294?), known also as Thomas of Ercildoune, Thomas the Rhymer, and True Thomas, famous for his 'prophecies' and for his adventures in fairyland. The Russian poet Lermontof (1814–41) claimed descent from this early Scottish poet. A fragment of the *Rhymer's Tower* lingers between the town and the Leader, and a stone on the wall of the church records that 'Auld Rymer's race lies in this place.' We join A 68 (see Rte. 2) about 5 m. N.E. of Melrose.

The Edinburgh road ascends the valley of the Eye and crosses the hilly district of Lammermuir.—20 m. An old tower (r.) is the supposed original of 'Ravenswood Castle', Lucy Ashton's home, in the 'Bride of Lammermoor'. Beyond the railway is the *Pease Dean*, with its lofty old bridge, where Leslie had a skirmish with Cromwell's cavalry just before the battle of Dunbar (1650).—21½ m. *Cockburnspath* (pron. Coburnspath; Hotel, RB. 19/6, P. 7 gs.) has an old manor house in its street, and a good village cross, well restored. The church has a 16th cent. round 'beacon' tower, while 2 m. E. are the shattered ruins of St. Helen's church (? 11th cent.). Beyond the railway a steep track descends to the fine sands and tiny harbour of *Cove*. The magnificent rocky cliffs of this coastline are well seen. At the bridge (1932) across the Dunglass Burn we enter East Lothian. In the grounds of *Dunglass House* is a beautiful collegiate church, founded c. 1443 by Sir Alex. Home and partially restored (adm. free), with fine sedilia.

East Lothian or **Haddingtonshire** has for centuries been noted for the richness of its arable land and for the skill of its farmers. In 1650 Cromwell's soldiers found here " the greatest plenty of corn they ever saw, not one of the fields being fallow." On the slopes of the Lammermuir Hills, which culminate in this county (Lammer Law, 1733 ft.), are extensive sheep-walks. The N. seaboard, about North Berwick (off which lies the Bass Rock), is a famous golfing country, rivalling the coast of Ayrshire. East Lothian is the county of John Knox, of William Dunbar, and of George Heriot, and amongst its famous families were the Fletchers of Salton, the Hamiltons of Preston, and the Maitlands of Lethington.

LOTHIAN, or THE LOTHIANS, a district extending from the Lammermuirs to the Firth of Forth, at one time belonged to the Kingdom of Northumbria, and includes, besides East Lothian, also Midlothian or Edinburghshire and West Lothian or Linlithgowshire.

About 6 m. farther on we cross the Broxburn, and, leaving the Dunbar by-pass on the left, reach the field of the *Battle of Dunbar* (Sept. 3rd, 1650), where Cromwell defeated the Covenanting supporters of Charles II.

Cromwell's army, enfeebled by famine and disease, was posted between this point and Belhaven, with its back to Dunbar and the sea. The Scottish army under Leslie occupied an almost impregnable position on high ground (Doon Hill, 582 ft.) along the right flank of the deeply sunk Broxburn effectually barring the roads to England. Giving way, however, to the urgent exhortations of the Covenanting clergy in his army, Leslie descended from his vantage ground and pushed forward his right wing to occupy the flat ground near the mouth of the Broxburn Glen. Cromwell and Lambert at once seized their opportunity, and with a large force of cavalry charged through Leslie's right wing and drove it in disorder back upon the Scottish infantry, which, not having room to deploy between the Broxburn and the hills, was broken and utterly routed. About 3000 Scots were slain, 10,000 made prisoners.

30 m. **DUNBAR,** an ancient seaport, a royal burgh, and a summer and golfing resort (4115 inhab.), consists mainly of one long street.

Hotels. Bellevue, RB. 25/, P. from 11 gs. ; **Roxburghe-Marine,** RB. from 24/, P. 11½–14 gs. ; **Craig-en-Gelt,** RB. 21/, P. 10–11½ gs. ; **Bayswell,** RB. 21/, P. 11 gs. ; **St. George,** RB. 20/, P. 9 gs. ; **Royal,** RB. 17/6, P. 9 gs. **Motor-Buses** run to *Edinburgh* (1½ hr.) ; *Newcastle* (4 hrs.) ; *North Berwick* (¾ hr.) ; *Eyemouth* (1 hr.) ; *Duns* (65 min.), etc.

In the main street is the quaint 17th cent. *Town House,* and at the end is *Lauderdale House* (now barracks), once a residence of the Earls of Lauderdale. The *Church* (rebuilt in 1821) contains a huge marble monument to George Home, Earl of Dunbar and Lord Treasurer (d. 1611). A 16th cent. dovecot at the W. end of the town is really the tower of a Trinitarian friary church, founded in 1240–48 by Cristiana de Brus. On a rock above the *Harbour* are the shapeless ruins of the ancient *Castle,* formerly of great strength. There is a good swimming-pool on the rocky shore W. of the harbour.

In 1314 Edward II, fleeing after Bannockburn, here hastily embarked for England. In 1339 ' Black Agnes,' Countess of March and Dunbar, daughter of Randolph, Earl of Moray, successfully defended the fortress for six weeks against the Earl of Salisbury. Queen Mary fled hither with Darnley in 1566, two days after the murder of Rizzio, and a month or so later appointed the Earl of Bothwell governor of the castle, to which she paid two further visits in 1567 ; once when she was carried off from Edinburgh by Bothwell, three weeks before their marriage, and again when the honeymoon was interrupted at Borthwick Castle. A few days later she surrendered at Carberry Hill, and Dunbar Castle was destroyed by the Regent Moray.

Beyond Dunbar the route lies through the famous farming district of East Lothian. On our right the Bass Rock rises in the sea, and on the right front appears North Berwick Law.

To the left, on either side of the Biel Water, are the mansions of *Belton,* noted for its fir-woods, and *Biel,* birthplace of William Dunbar (1465 ?–1530 ?), with charming grounds (no adm.).

A 198 diverges N. (r.), 2 m. beyond the W. end of the by-pass, for North Berwick.—1 m. *Tyninghame House* (r.) is a seat of the Earl of Haddington, with noted hollies in the woods. Part of the 12th cent. church, with a fine chevron-moulded arch, survives in the grounds as a family burial-chapel. On the shore beyond it is a cape with a rock called St. Baldred's Cradle (see p. 87) and a large cairn of the Bronze Age.—2¾ m. *Whitekirk* has a fine pre-Reformation church, injured by suffragettes in 1914, and a two-storeyed barn, partly 16th cent. Thence we may go on to North Berwick either viâ Tantallon (5¾ m.) or by a pleasant inland road (4½ m.) ; see Rte. 6.

36½ m. *East Linton* (Crown, RB. 16/6 ; Linton Lodge, RB. 16/, P. 7 gs.), with a 16th cent. bridge on the Tyne, is by-passed

by the main road, and is in the parish of *Prestonkirk*,
where Gavin Douglas, Bp. of Dunkeld, was priest. The
church (1770) has a 13th cent. E. end and a 17th cent. square
tower. *Preston Mill* (N.T.), a charming 17th cent. relic,
restored in 1760, is probably the oldest water-mill still working in Scotland. *Phantassie*, ½ m. E., is the mansion in which
Sir John Rennie (1761–1821), the engineer, was born.

On the Tyne, 2 m. above East Linton, are the extensive ruins of *Hailes Castle*
(adm. 6*d.* ;   10–7, winter 10–4, Sun. from 2), dating from the 13th–15th cent.,
with a 16th cent. window in the chapel. It was a fortified manor of the Hepburns,
and it was to Hailes that Bothwell brought Queen Mary on their flight from
Borthwick. Near it rises *Traprain Law* (734 ft.), a conspicuous hill on which
a remarkable hoard of Gallo-Roman silver was discovered in 1919. Here was
a Celtic township of 300 years' occupation, having trading relations with the
Romans down to their departure from Britain. Farther S.E. is *Whittingehame*
(1817 ; by Smirke), birthplace of the Earl of Balfour (1848–1930), in the grounds
of which (open on Wed. and Fri.) are his tomb, a 15th cent. tower, and an old
yew-tree beneath which the murder of Darnley is said to have been planned.

41 m. **Haddington** (by-pass), and thence to (57 m.) **Edinburgh,** see Rte. 6.

2. FROM CARTER BAR (NEWCASTLE) TO EDINBURGH

Road (A 68), 59 m., a fine motor route, part of the shortest road from Newcastle
to Edinburgh (105 m.).—10½ m. **Jedburgh.**—19 m. *St. Boswells.*—31½ m. *Lauder.*
—52 m. *Dalkeith.*—59 m. **Edinburgh,** entered by Clerk St. or St. Leonard's
St. (Pl. 41, 42). From Newcastle viâ Otterburn to Carter Bar, see the *Blue
Guide to England.*—Motor-Bus daily in 5 hrs. ; more frequently from Jedburgh
in 2¼ hrs.

Carter Bar (1371 ft. ; fine view), where A 68 crosses the
Border and enters Roxburghshire, is on the site of the Raid
of the Reidswire (1575), the last Border battle between Scots
and English.

Roxburghshire is perhaps the most characteristic of the Scottish Border
counties, with its varied scenery of upland and wooded dale, its lovely streams
famed in song and ballad, its ruined pele-towers with their memories of the rough
old Border " life of spur, spear, and snaffle," its shattered abbeys (Melrose,
Jedburgh and Kelso), recalling the sterner struggle with ' our auld enemies of
England,' and its lordly mansions and prosperous farms, witnesses to more
peaceful times. Liddesdale extends N. into the county, but the Teviot, whose
course of 37 m. lies wholly within it, makes Teviotdale almost synonymous
with Roxburghshire, and there are many lesser streams—Gala, Allan Water, the
' crystal Jed '—not less in fame. Roxburgh is the county of Thomas the Rhymer,
James Thomson of ' The Seasons ' and John Leyden ; and, in another sense,
of Scott, whose house of Abbotsford overshadows the statelier mansions of Floors
Castle and Minto House.

Just N. of the Border a road diverges on the left for (16 m.) Hawick, passing
(4 m.) the ruin of *Southdean Church* (' Souden '), the rendezvous of the Scottish
leaders before the Battle of Otterburn in 1388, where a memorial service is held
yearly on Aug. 13th. James Thomson, the poet, spent his boyhood in his father's
manse here. We cross the Rule Water at (8½ m.) *Bonchester Bridge* (Horse &
Hound Inn, RB. 17/6 ; Wolfelee, 2 m. S., RB. 22/6, P. 9 gs.).

About 4½ m. from the Border we cross the Jed Water and
descend its valley, leaving a road to Oxnam (see p. 9) on
the right.—8½ m. *Ferniehirst Castle* (r.), the 16th cent. seat of

the Kers, has been lent to the S.Y.H.A. for use as a hostel ; a mile farther (l.) is the ' Capon Tree,' a venerable relic of Jed Forest.

10½ m. **JEDBURGH** (*Royal*, RB. from 25/, P. 11 gs. ; *Spread Eagle*, RB. 18/6), a royal burgh (4075 inhab.), pleasantly situated on the Jed, is a quiet little town, famous for its beautiful abbey. The town was completely destroyed in the English raids of the 16th century. Industry is represented by a large rayon factory.

Jedburgh Castle (on the site occupied by the disused prison of 1823) was one of the five fortresses surrendered to England by the treaty of Falaise in 1174 as security for the ransom of William the Lion. It later became a favourite royal residence, but was pulled down in 1409 as being of more use to the invading English than to the Scots. Malcolm IV died here in 1165. It was in this castle that, at the marriage feast of Alexander III in 1285, a grisly spectre appeared, afterwards interpreted as a presage of the king's death (p. 259).—Mary, Queen of Scots, who had come to open the Justice Ayres (circuit court), lodged in the town from Oct. 9th to Nov. 9th, 1566.

' Jeddart Justice,' like Lydford Law, consisted in hanging a man first and trying him afterwards. The ' Jeddart Staff,' a shaft 7 or 8 ft. long with a head shaped like a hook or an axe, was a well-known Border weapon that did good service in the Raid of the Reidswire (see p. 6), when the men of Jedburgh with their war-cry ' Jeddart's here ' contributed largely to victory. Mrs. Somerville (Mary Fairfax ; 1780–1872), the mathematician, and Sir David Brewster (1781–1868) were born at Jedburgh, the former in the old manse (now pulled down), where her father-in-law, Dr. Somerville, was minister from 1774 to 1830. Samuel Rutherford and James Thomson were scholars at Jedburgh school. At Candlemas a riotous game of handball is played in the streets, between the ' uppies ' and the ' doonies ' i.e. those born above and below the Mercat Cross. Jethart Snails, a local confection, are said to derive from a recipe brought here by a French prisoner in the Napoleonic Wars.

Facing Market Place are the 18th cent. *New Gate*, with the Town Steeple, and the adjoining *County Buildings* (1812). From High St. Smith's Wynd (r.) leads to **Queen Mary's House** (in Queen St.), the old bastel house in which Queen Mary nearly died after her exhausting ride to visit Bothwell at Hermitage Castle in 1566. The house (adm. 6*d.* ; 10–12, 1–8, Sun. 1–5), built after 1544, probably belonged to the Kers of Ferniehirst ; it is now a museum with interesting relics of the queen and her time, including Mary's Communion set, and her thimble-case and watch, the latter having been found in a bog 200 years after her arduous ride. The queen's tiny bedroom, the room in which her four Marys slept, the kitchen with an ancient roasting-jack, etc., are shown. The garden, with public tennis courts, is attractively laid out.

Canongate leads from Market Place to the old bridge with three-ribbed arches, said to be coeval with the abbey. In it is the house (No. 40) in which Sir David Brewster, son of the grammar-school master, was born. Prince Charles Stewart lodged at No. 11 Castlegate in 1745, on his march to England, and No. 27 Canongate (demolished) was visited by Burns in 1787. Wordsworth in 1803 occupied lodgings at No. 5 Abbey Close, where he found in his hostess ' the picture of a life well-spent,' and was visited by Scott.

*Jedburgh Abbey, an impressive building of red sandstone dating mainly from 1150–1225, stands above the river down

c

to which its conventual buildings extended. It is entered from Abbey Close, off Castlegate (adm. 1/; 10–4 or 7, Sun. from 2).

History. The priory founded c. 1138 on this site by David I, for Austin canons brought from the abbey of St. Quentin at Beauvais, became an abbey in 1147. In 1285 Alexander III was married in the church to Yolande, daughter of the Count of Dreux. The abbey suffered severely from the invasions of the English, notably in 1523, when it was bombarded by the Earl of Surrey, and in 1544 and 1545 when it was sacked by the Earl of Hertford. At the Reformation (1560) its property passed into the possession of the Kers of Ferniehirst. Subsequently part of the nave of the church was used by the parish until 1875, when a new parish church was built by the Marquess of Lothian.

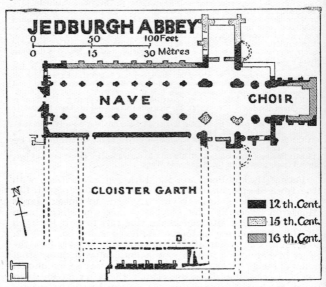

In the W. front (c. 1180–1200), the striking Norman doorway is surmounted by three gables, then by a large window amid arcading, and that again by a beautiful 14th cent. wheel-window. The long *Nave* (130 ft.) of nine bays is one of the finest examples of Transition in Scotland, with three tiers of arches remarkable for grace and lightness. The main arcade, with clustered pillars, is pointed and supports a triforium of round arches, each enclosing two pointed arches, while above is a clerestory of pointed arches. In the S. aisle is the tomb of Lord Chancellor Campbell (1779–1861), who lived at Hartrigge House, N.E. of the town. The transepts and crossing, ruined in the 15th cent., were rebuilt after 1478 by Abbots Hall and Cranston, both of whose names appear on the new work. The Tower (86 ft. ; view), rebuilt in 1500, is supported on round arches. At the N. end of the N. transept is the 15th cent. *Lothian Chapel* (adm. on application to the custodian), with a fine window, containing the tombs of the Kers and a recumbent effigy, by G. F. Watts, of the 8th marquess (d. 1870), while the ashes of the 11th marquess (d. 1941) were brought hither from America for interment. The *Choir*, now of two bays only, has massive round piers carried up to include the triforium in a semicircular arch embracing two smaller arches (comp. Oxford cathedral), with a beautifully designed clerestory above. The chapel on the S. side, still entire, with a good window, was likewise built by Abbot Hall and was at one time used as the parish school.—The elaborate but weather-worn exterior decoration of the Norman door on the S. side of the nave is repeated in facsimile on a modern doorway farther W. The foundations of the cloister, the chapter house (with central pillar), and other buildings have been laid bare S. of the church ; and a small museum contains fragments from the abbey.

Excursions may be made from Jedburgh to *Dunian Hill* (1095 ft. ; 2 m. S.W.) and to the *Waterloo Monument* (5½ m. N.), as well as to the chief points in the Scott Country (Rte. 4).—An unfrequented road leads S.E. to (4½ m.) *Oxnam* and thence to the remote upper valley of the Kale Water, a favourite haunt of the persecuted Covenanters. *Dere Street*, a drove road which ascends almost to the head of the Kale Water, is part of the Roman road from Yorkshire to the Lothians viâ Newstead. At *Cappuck*, where it crosses Oxnam Water (1½ m. N. of Oxnam), is a Roman fort.—From Jedburgh by road to *Hawick* and to *Kelso*, see p. 14.

The Edinburgh road (A 68) descends the Jed Water, turning to the left short of (12½ m.) *Jedfoot Station*, and then to the right, beyond *Bonjedward* (l.), mentioned in the ' Raid of the Reidswire.' We cross the Teviot.—14 m. *Ancrum* (l.), on the Ale, has a 13th cent. cross. In the steep sandstone banks of the river, above Ancrum, are several caves, in one of which James Thomson, the poet, has carved his name.—To the right, on Penielheugh (741 ft.), above *Nisbet*, birthplace of Samuel Rutherford (1600–61), rises the Waterloo Monument, raised in 1815 by the Marquess of Lothian and his tenants.—The Edinburgh road next crosses *Ancrum Moor*, where in 1545 the English, under Sir Ralph Eure and Sir Bryan Latoun (both of whom were killed), were defeated with great slaughter as they were returning laden with booty from a raid. Ancrum Moor is known also as *Lilliard's Edge*, from Lilliard, a legendary Scottish maiden, who fought and fell in this contest.

We now enter the ' Scott Country,' and (19 m.) *St. Boswells Green*, (20 m.) *Newtown St. Boswells*, and (21¾ m.) *Leaderfoot*, where we cross the Tweed 2 m. E. of Melrose, are fully described in Rte. 4. A 68 ascends the Leader, passing (24 m.) *Earlston* (Rte. 1) and enters Lauderdale.—31½ m. **Lauder** (*Black Bull* RB. from 15/, P. 7 gs. ; *Lauderdale*, unlic., RB. 18/6, P. 6½ gs., closed in winter), a little royal burgh (625 inhab.) with an old town hall, is an angling centre. The church (1673 ; by Sir Wm. Bruce), with an octagonal steeple, is built on the plan of a Greek cross. On the right is the stately *Thirlestane Castle*, the ancestral home of the Maitlands (adm., for large parties only, 2/6 ; June–Sept.). The present building, begun c. 1575, was extended by Bruce for the Duke of Lauderdale a century later, and again in the 19th century.

The nucleus of the mansion is *Lauder Fort*, built probably in the time of Edward I, and rebuilt and strengthened by Edward II in 1324. The castle was taken by Protector Somerset in 1548 and was visited by Prince Charles in 1745 after Prestonpans. The fine collection of family portraits includes Maitland of Lethington, the Duke of Lauderdale (by *Lely*), the 7th earl and countess (by *Reynolds*), the 8th countess (by *Romney*), and the 6th earl (by *Aikman*). Prince Charles' Bedroom and the Panelled Room (part of the original tower-house) are specially interesting. The first Scottish residence of the Maitlands was Thirlestane Tower, which lies in ruins some 2 m. E., S. of the Kelso road, the original name having been transferred to the ' new ' mansion.

In 1482 James III with his army halted here on his way to invade England. His nobles, jealous of Cochrane, the king's architect and minister, and of other humbly-born royal favourites, seized them and forthwith hanged them from the bridge of Lauder. Archibald Douglas, Earl of Angus, as leader in this action, won the title of ' Bell-the-Cat.' The site of the old bridge, of which no vestige remains, is in the grounds of the castle.

Beyond (35½ m.) *Carfraemill* (Hotel, RB. 21/, P. 10 gs.) we begin the fine ascent over Soutra Hill, a noted view-point, and enter Midlothian. Just beyond (c. 40 m.) the summit level of the road (1131 ft.) B 6368 leads left to *Soutra Aisle*, a fragment (? 15th cent.) of a hospital for poor men founded by Malcolm IV (1164) and attached in 1460 to Trinity College, Edinburgh. Thence the road descends viâ (43 m.) *Black-shiels* (Juniper Lea, RB. 15/, P. 6 gs. ; Johnstounburn, 1 m. N.E., with fine grounds, P. 10–14 gs.) and (47 m.) *Pathhead* (Stair Arms, ½ m. nearer Dalkeith, RB. from 25/, P. 10 gs.).

About 2 m. S. of Pathhead is **Crichton,** with its plain little naveless collegiate church (1449), with typical barrel vaults and tower, ½ m. from the road to Tynehead Station. *Crichton Castle* (adm. 6d. ; 10–4 or 7, Sun. from 2, closed Fri.), ¼ m. by path from the church, belonged to Sir William Crichton, chancellor under James II and adversary of the Douglases. The narrow keep dates from the 14th cent. ; the remainder (15–17th cent.) is in a more elaborate and ornamented style than was usual in Scottish castles. Notable are a tall internal wall adorned with projecting bosses in an Italian style, built by the 5th earl of Bothwell in 1581–91 and (high up) an admirable example of the round arch. Marmion was here entertained by Sir David Lyndsay for two days on his way to Edinburgh as English envoy.

52 m. *Dalkeith*, and thence to (59 m.) **Edinburgh,** see p. 77.

3. FROM CARLISLE TO EDINBURGH
Via Hawick and Galashiels

ROAD (A 7), 94 m., for the most part a moorland road with several steep hills. — 20 m. *Langholm.*—43 m. **Hawick.**—54¾ m. **Selkirk.** Thence to Edinburgh, see Rte. 4A (reversed).—MOTOR-BUS in 4½–5 hrs. ; to *Hawick* in 2 hrs. ; frequent service between Hawick and Edinburgh (2¾ hrs.).

RAILWAY, 98¼ m. in 2¾–3¼ hrs. This is part of the ' Midland ' and ' Waverley Route ' from London (St. Pancras) to Scotland viâ Sheffield and Leeds : to *Edinburgh*, 408¾ m. in 9½–11 hrs. Comp. the *Blue Guide to England.*—Principal stations : 14 m. *Riddings*, junction for Langholm (7 m.).—21 m. *Kershopefoot*, the last station in England.—24 m. *Newcastleton.*—45½ m. **Hawick.**—58 m. *St. Boswells.*—61 m. **Melrose.**—65 m. **Galashiels.**—98¼ m. **Edinburgh** (Waverley).

Carlisle (*Crown & Mitre*, RB. from 22/6 ; *County & Station*, RB. 25/ ; *Red Lion, Central*, RB. 22/), the ' merrie Carlisle ' of many a Border ballad, is the county town (67,900 inhab.) of Cumberland (see the *Blue Guide to England*). Leaving the city by the Eden bridge and Scotland Rd., we traverse the plain between the Eden and the Esk and cross the Lyne at (5¼ m.) *Westlinton.*—8 m. *Longtown* (Graham Arms, RB. 18/6) is an ancient Border town on the Esk, just outside of which is the old parish church of *Arthuret* (early 17th cent.).

To the W. of Longtown extends *Solway Moss*, the scene of a crushing defeat of the Scots in 1542, said to have hastened the death of James V.—On the E. bank of the Esk, 2 m. N., stands *Netherby Hall*, whence Young Lochinvar carried off his bride.

We enter Scotland a little below the confluence of the Esk and the Liddel, and follow the Esk.—14 m. *Canonbie* (Cross Keys, RB. 21/6) is charmingly situated on the Esk. The Augustinian abbey founded here c. 1220 was suppressed by Henry VIII in 1544, as being in the ' debatable land,' and destroyed in 1620. The church was built (1822) by Wm. Atkinson, the Abbotsford architect.

FROM CANONBIE TO HAWICK (motor-bus to Newcastleton on Sat. and Sun.). The road ascends *Liddesdale*, the home of the Elliots and the Armstrongs and the country of Dandie Dinmont, following the N. bank of the Liddel, which for seven miles here divides England from Scotland. Ruined towers on the green hills recall the stirring times of the past, sung in many ballads.—Beyond (7 m.) *Kershopefoot* the view narrows and the grey tablelands that skirt the Cheviots appear on the right now largely covered by conifer forest.—10 m. *Newcastleton* (Liddesdale, RB. 18/ ; Grapes), where a car may be hired for Hermitage Castle (6 m.). *Mangerton Tower*, an old Border hold, lies 1½ m. S., and on the opposite hill dwelt John of the Syde (' a greater thief did never ride '), whose rescue from the men of Liddesdale by his cousins of Mangerton—the Laird's Jock and the Laird's Wat—is the theme of a stirring ballad.

The Liddesdale route to Hawick (35 m. ; B 6357) passes (16 m.) *Larriston*, once a stronghold of the Elliots as celebrated in a stirring ballad by Hogg, and (18 m. ; r.) *Thorlieshope*, the home of Dandie Dinmont and his famous terriers (' *Guy Mannering* '). Crossing the pass called the Note o' the Gate (c. 1250 ft.), it descends to Bonchester Bridge (p. 6).

Another route to Hawick (B 6399) ascends the Hermitage Water, a tributary of the Liddel.—17 m. **Hermitage Castle*, on this stream, ¾ m. left of road, stands in a bleak, lonely open plain, encircled by rounded hills. It was the grand stronghold of the Douglases more or less continually from 1341 to 1492 (adm. 6d. ; 10–4 or 7, Sun. from 2). The original 13th cent. castle belonged to the families of Bolbec and Soulis ; and William, Lord Soulis, surnamed ' the Wizard ' is said to have forfeited the lands in 1320 for conspiring against Bruce. In 1341 the castle was taken by Sir William Douglas, ' the Knight of Liddesdale,' a natural son of the good Lord James. Here in 1342 Sir Alexander Ramsay was starved to death by Douglas, though the unhappy prisoner supported life for seventeen days on corn that trickled through the roof of his dungeon from a granary above. In 1492 the castle was exchanged by the Douglases for Bothwell Castle on the Clyde, and here, in 1566, Queen Mary paid a flying visit to the 4th earl of Bothwell riding from Jedburgh and back (50 miles in all) in one day, a feat which cost her ten days of fever.—The castle, much restored outside, consists of a rectangular block of the late 14th cent. with four corner towers (c. 1400) joined by huge arches at the E. and W. ends, the whole being surmounted by a corbelled parapet. The S.W. tower was extended in the 15th century. In the ruined interior survive remains of the original tower around which the later walls were built.—To the E. is *Nine Stane Rig,* a hill with a stone circle, where the cruel Lord Soulis is said to have been boiled alive by his infuriated vassals. In reality Lord Soulis died in prison at Dumbarton Castle.

Beyond Hermitage the road is very lonely ; the summit (1200 ft.) is reached at (22¼ m.) Limekiln Edge, part of the ridge of hills along which runs the *Catrail* or *Pict's Work.* Most of this work lies off to the left, under the curiously shaped Maiden Paps (1677 ft.). The *Catrail* is a ditch, over 20 ft. wide and rarely more than 3–4 ft. deep, with the excavated earth piled usually on the lower side of the slopes which it skirts. It runs from Peel Fell on the Border N.W. to Borthwick Water and thence to the neighbourhood of Galashiels. Its purpose is still a subject of controversy.

The road descends rapidly into the valley of the Slitrig, passing (26 m.) *Shank-end* and (29 m.) *Stobs,* with its military camp.—30 m. *Hawick,* see below.

From Canonbie A 7 ascends a beautiful stretch of the Esk, passing (16 m.) *Holehouse* or *Hollows Tower,* a stronghold of Armstrong of Gilnockie (see below), and, near (16¾ m.) *Gilnockie,* a rock known as ' Gilnockie's Garden,' a favourite haunt of his.—20 m. **Langholm** (2400 inhab. ; *Crown,* RB. 18/6, P. 8 gs.; *Ashley Bank,* RB. 18/, 8 gs. ; *Eskdale,* RB. 17/, P. 8 gs.), with woollen manufactures and a Town House of 1811, is a good angling centre where the Esk is joined by the Wauchope and Ewes Waters. An obelisk on the hill to the E. commemorates Sir John Malcolm of Burnfoot (1769–1833), Indian administrator, most famous of the four brother " Knights of Eskdale." It was the birthplace of William Mickle (1734–88), translator of Camoens and author of ' There's nae luck aboot the hoose.'

In 1455 James II finally crushed the power of the Douglases in a battle here. The neighbourhood is closely associated with Johnny Armstrong of Gilnockie, a noted Border reiver, who in the days of James V levied blackmail as far as Newcastle and ' rode ever with 24 able gentlemen well horsed ; yet he never molested any Scottishman.' James V, feigning a hunting party, enticed Armstrong to Caerlanrig (see below) and there hanged him and his followers.

From Langholm B 709 goes on N.W., up the lovely dale of the Esk, viâ (6 m.) the solitary hamlet of *Westerkirk,* birthplace of Thomas Telford (1757–1834), the engineer son of a shepherd on the banks of the Megget (memorial ; 1928), to (14 m.) *Eskdalemuir* church. At Craighaugh Ford, just beyond, the ancient Craikmuir Road crosses the Esk, beside the Roman fort of *Raeburnfoot,* and traverses the hills N.E. in the direction of the Roman station of Trimontium (Newstead).—17 m. *Eskdalemuir Observatory,* a noted meteorological station. Crossing the watershed at 1096 ft., B 709 descends to Ettrick, and (29 m.) *Tushielaw Inn* (p. 19).

The main road ascends Ewes Water to (31 m.) the *Mosspaul Hotel* (RB. 16/6; 850 ft.) and enters Roxburghshire ; then descends to (35 m.) *Teviothead*, with a memorial stone in the churchyard to Johnny Armstrong (see above), who was hanged at *Caerlanrig*, ½ m. up the valley.

The conspicuous cairn on the left is a memorial to Henry Scott Riddell of Sorbie (1798–1870), song-writer, who lived and is buried at Teviothead.

37 m. *Teviotdale Lodge* (RB. 23/6, P. 10 gs.) is seen across the river.—39½ m. *Branxholm* or *Branksome Tower*, the key of upper Teviotdale, has been held by the Scotts, barons of Buccleuch, since 1420. The chief scene of the 'Lay of the Last Minstrel' is laid in this fine castle, where 'nine-and-twenty knights of fame hung their shields.' The old castle was blown up in 1570 and the oldest part of the present house (tower and S. front) was built in 1571–76.—41½ m. *Goldielands*, at the mouth of the Borthwick Water, is a well-preserved keep, whose last laird is said to have been hanged over his own gateway for reiving.

43 m. **Hawick** (16,720 inhab. ; *Tower*, RB. 24/6. P. 12 gs.; *Buccleuch*, RB. 19/6, P. 9 gs. ; *Crown*, RB. 25/, P. 12 gs.), attractively situated at the junction of the Slitrig with the Teviot and surrounded by hills, is the largest town in Roxburghshire. It is the chief seat of the Scottish manufacture of woollens, tweeds and hosiery, knitting mills being first introduced in 1771. In 1570 the town was burned down by Sussex. The lone survivor of this disaster is the old tower (now part of the Tower Hotel), in High Street, which was the residence of the Douglases of Drumlanrig and afterwards of Anne Scott, later Duchess of Monmouth (comp. p. 77). *St. Mary's Church* (1764 ; restored), on a hillock, replaces the church in which Sir Alexander Ramsay was seized by Douglas in 1342. *Mote Hill* (reached by Howegate), 30 ft. high and 300 ft. round, was the ancient meeting-place of the Court of the Manor. In High St., beyond the town buildings (1887), is the equestrian monument to the 'callants' of Hawick, bearing their ancient pagan war-cry. Thence North Bridge St. leads to the Post Office and the Station. At the other end of the town, on the N. bank of the Teviot, are the delightful grounds of *Wilton Lodge Park*.

In 1514, immediately after Flodden, the 'callants' (i.e. youths) of Hawick defeated a body of English soldiers at *Hornshole*, c. 1¼ m. N.E. of the town, and captured their banner. The victory is annually celebrated by the callants under their 'cornet' at the 'Riding of the Marches' at the beginning of June.

Harden House, the ancient seat of the Scotts of Harden, stood c. 4 m. W. of Hawick, above the Borthwick Water (p. 20). 'Auld Wat' of Harden, who married Mary Scott, the 'Flower of Yarrow,' in 1576, used to subsist on the spoils of his freebooting until a clean pair of spurs was served on a dish to remind him that the larder was low and another raid was required. His son married 'mucklemou'd Meg' and was the ancestor of 'Beardie' and of Sir Walter Scott.

FROM HAWICK TO JEDBURGH AND KELSO, 21 m., motor-bus in 1½ hr. down the valley of the Teviot. (The direct road to Kelso, 18 m., omits Jedburgh.) *Cavers House* (c. 1400), built by the son of the Douglas who fell at Otterburn, lies off the road to the right. In the old church (1662) is the burial aisle of the

Eliotts.—5 m. *Denholm*, with a big square green and a church (1831) by W. H. Playfair, was the birthplace of John Leyden (1775–1811), poet and orientalist, of John Scott (1836–80), botanist, and of Sir James Murray (1837–1915), of the Oxford English Dictionary. About 2 m. S. rises dark *Ruberslaw* (1392 ft.), a retreat of the Covenanters, to whom Alexander Peden used to preach from 'Peden's Pulpit,' a crag near the top, while 2 m. E. is *Bedrule*, the birthplace of Bp. Turnbull, founder of Glasgow University.—About 1½ m. beyond Denholm we see, on our left, across the Teviot, *Minto House* (now a school) with Minto Crags, surmounted by *Fatlips Castle*, to the N.E. Jane Elliot (1727–1805), author of a version of 'The Flowers of the Forest' lived here in an earlier house. —Our road now turns to the E. (r.) to make the detour viâ Jedburgh and, crossing the Rule, ascends over the shoulder of *Dunian Hill* (1095 ft. ; *View).— 11 m. **Jedburgh**, see Rte. 2.—We descend along the Jed Water to (13 m.) *Jedfoot*, where we rejoin the Teviot and the direct road from Hawick. The monument on Penielheugh (p. 9) is conspicuous.—15 m. *Crailing*.—17 m. *Eckford Church*, on which still hang the 'jougs' or scold's bridle, stands near the mouth of the Kale Water.—21 m. *Kelso*, see p. 28.

The by-road from Hawick to Melrose (B 6359 ; 16½ m. ; buses on Thurs. and Sat.) runs viâ (4½ m.) *Hassendean*, recalling the lively song 'Jock o' Hazeldean,' and (9 m.) *Lilliesleaf* (i.e. Lilla's cliff), a village of one long street.

The Edinburgh road ascends N. from Hawick, with a magnificent retrospect of the whole range of the Cheviots from the Cheviot to Carter Fell, with Ruberslaw, the Minto Hills and Penielheugh to the E. We enter Selkirkshire, and cross the Ale water at (49 m.) *Ashkirk*.—54½ m. **Selkirk,** and thence to (94 m.) **Edinburgh,** see Rte. 4A.

4. THE SCOTT COUNTRY

The chief centres of the **Scott Country**, i.e. the district personally associated with Sir Walter Scott, which is at the same time the scene of some of his best-known works, are *Galashiels, Selkirk,* and *Melrose*, from each of which motor-buses ply in the season to the surrounding points of interest. *St. Boswells* is the station nearest to Dryburgh and the junction for Jedburgh and Kelso. For a stay of a day or two Melrose, convenient both for Abbotsford and for Dryburgh Abbey, is the best general centre. Galashiels, Melrose, and St. Boswells are stations on the 'Waverley Route' to the South (comp. Rte. 3) ; and most of these places have also direct motor-bus connection with Edinburgh and with Glasgow.

MOTOR COACHES, starting from Edinburgh and from Glasgow in the season, make the round of all the chief places of interest in one long day.

A. Edinburgh to Galashiels, Selkirk and Melrose

ROAD. (i) A 7 to (34 m.) **Galashiels** and (40 m.) **Selkirk**, see below.—A 6091 runs from Galashiels S.E. to (38 m. from Edinburgh) **Melrose**.—(ii) A 68, less direct and more hilly, quitting Edinburgh viâ St. Leonard's St. (Pl. 41, 42), leads over *Soutra Hill*, as detailed in Rte. 2 (reversed). After crossing (35½ m.) the Tweed we turn to the right for (37½ m.) **Melrose** or keep straight on for St. Boswells and (48 m.) **Jedburgh**.—MOTOR-BUSES to *Galashiels* direct (1½ hr.) or viâ Peebles (2 hrs.) ; to *Melrose* viâ Earlston (2 hrs.) ; to *Selkirk* viâ Galashiels (1¾–2½ hrs.).

RAILWAY to *Galashiels*, 33½ m. in 50 min.–1½ hr. ; to *Melrose*, 37¼ m. in 1–1¾ hr. This is part of the main route (Rte. 3) to the South.

We leave Edinburgh by Nicolson St. (Pl. 34) and Newington. Thence to (7 m.) *Eskbank* (Dalkeith), see Rte. 5A. A 7 crosses the S. Esk at (8½ m.) *Lothianbridge*, whence B 704 leads r. to *Cockpen Church* and *Dalhousie Castle* (c. 1450 ; later additions), a seat of the Ramsays since the 13th century. Near the castle once stood the abode of the Laird of Cockpen, whose wooing Lady Nairne has celebrated in song. He was one of the Carse family, who held the estate in 1635–1733.— 11¼ m. *Gorebridge* (Kirkhill, RB. 20/, P. 9 gs.): the village lies mostly to the left.

B 6372 leads S.E., passing *Arniston*, the seat of the Dundas family, notable for its statesmen and lawyers, to (2 m.) *Temple*, where the roofless low-lying church (14th cent.) was the principal seat of the Knights Templar in Scotland. To the N. (1 m. r.) is *Carrington*, where the charming little church-tower (1710) serves as a dovecot.—From (3 m.) *Rosebery*, a plain house from which the Earl of Rosebery takes his title, we skirt the Moorfoot Hills, with three reservoirs, to join A 703 (8½ m. ; p. 91).

Beyond *Fushiebridge* (13 m.) a lane leads left for **Borthwick,** in the manse of which William Robertson (1721–93) was born. The church preserves some Romanesque features, a 15th cent. aisle with Borthwick tombs, and Dundas memorials in the former sacristy. **Borthwick Castle* (adm. on written application only), a massive gloomy double tower built by Sir William Borthwick beside the Gore Water in 1430 and recently restored as a residence, is of extraordinary strength, and contains a magnificent great hall with a huge chimney-piece, a withdrawing-room fitted up as an oratory, and other features of interest.

Queen Mary and Bothwell were here alarmed in 1567, about a month after their marriage, by the approach of the hostile Scottish lords. Bothwell fled to Dunbar and Mary is said to have followed two days later in the disguise of a page. In 1650 the castle surrendered to Cromwell, after a very brief bombardment.

The ascent into the lonelier Moorfoot Hills soon starts, and after reaching the summit (16 m.) at 891 ft., the road begins to descend the valley of the Gala, celebrated in the old song, (re-edited by Burns), ' The braw, braw lads of Gala water.' It was at one time known as Wedale or ' vale of woe.'—From (18 m.) *Heriot* B 709 crosses the Moorfoots to Innerleithen viâ Glentress.—27 m. *Stow* (Royal, RB. 16/6, P. 8 gs.), on the Gala, has an old church and bridge.—Passing (30 m.) *Bowland* we enter Selkirkshire. At *Torwoodlee* (r.), 1 m. farther, is a ruined broch commanding a fine view.

Selkirkshire or *Ettrick Forest*, a beautiful Border county of peaceful hills and lonely valleys, remote from railways, was once a royal hunting ground, but has long since been given over to pastoral solitude and quiet with only the scattered pele-towers of the moss-troopers to recall its romantic past recorded in many a stirring or pathetic ballad. The ' Flowers of the Forest,' the most pathetic of all, is a lament for Flodden. Yarrow, descending from St. Mary's Loch, and Ettrickdale, parallel on the S., are its famous valleys, while the Tweed flows for a space across its N. part. Scott, sheriff-depute (' Shirra ') of the county for 33 years (1799–1832), lived at Ashiestiel in 1804–12 ; Wordsworth visited and revisited Yarrow ; and James Hogg, the ' Ettrick Shepherd,' was a link between the romance of Scott and the joviality of ' Christopher North,' who brought Tibbie Shiel's into fame. Thomas Boston, of the ' Fourfold Estate,' was minister of Ettrick. Galashiels and Selkirk are the only towns in the county.

At (34 m.) **Galashiels** (see below), the roads to Selkirk and to Melrose separate. The Melrose road (A 6091) keeps straight on, crossing the Tweed 1¾ m., before (38 m.) **Melrose** (Rte. 4c).

B. Galashiels and Selkirk

GALASHIELS (12,500 inhab.), on both banks of the Gala, is noted for the manufacture of tweeds and woollen hosiery, and its largest buildings are the woollen mills.

Hotels. Douglas, RB. 21/, P. 10 gs. ; **Royal,** RB. 20/, P. 9 gs., both in Channel St. ; **Maxwell,** RB. 21/, P. 9 gs., Bridge St. ; **King's,** RB. 17/6, P. 9 gs., near the station.

Post Office, Channel St.

Motor-Buses to *Selkirk* (20 min.), *Hawick* (1 hr.), and Carlisle ; to *Edinburgh* (1½–2 hrs.) viâ Heriot or viâ Peebles and Penicuik or Auchen-dinny ; viâ *Melrose* (½ hr.) to *Earlston* (for Newcastle) or to *St. Boswells* (for Jedburgh) and *Kelso* (65 min.) ; to *Greenlaw* and *Berwick* (2¼ hrs.) ; viâ Peebles and Biggar to *Glasgow* (3¾ hrs.) ; etc.

Golf Courses at *Ladhope* (municipal) to the N.W., and *Torwoodlee* (9 holes), 1 m. N.

Galashiels is a long grey, modern town, with good shops and a spacious market-place. In Corn Mill Square rises the effective *_War Memorial_ (1925), consisting of a clock-tower (by Sir Robt. Lorimer), in front of which is a spirited figure of a mounted moss-trooper by T. J. Clapperton. Opposite is a bust of Scott, also by Clapperton, and at the foot of the Lawyer's Brae, beside the Municipal Buildings, is a bust of Burns. The *Mercat Cross* (1695) is the centre of the gathering of the 'Braw Lads' at midsummer, and near the market square is the *Scottish Woollen Technical College* (1909). The *Old Church* (1813) preserves an aisle of its 17th cent. pre-decessor. *Old Gala House,* originally the home of the Pringles, contains ceiling-paintings dating from c. 1635. It is now the home of an Arts Club and visitors are admitted on application.

The ROAD to Melrose and Abbotsford (A 6091) leads S.E., parallel with the railway. Opposite (1 m.) Langlee House a tablet commemorates Scott's last journey home to Abbotsford (July 11th, 1832). On the opposite bank of the Tweed is the hamlet of Bridgend, beside the ford where Father Philip met the White Lady of Avenel ('The Monastery'). We cross (1¾ m.) the *Allan Water,* the narrow glen of which is the 'Glendearg' of Scott's 'Monastery'; then pass over (2¼ m.) Melrose Bridge and turn to the left for (4 m.) *Melrose,* to the right for (3½ m.) *Abbotsford.*

From GALASHIELS TO PEEBLES, 18½ m., road (motor-bus) or railway. A 72 follows the N. bank of the Tweed, but there is a by-road on the S. bank, viâ Ashiestiel and Traquair.—At (2½ m.) *Clovenfords* (Hotel, RB. 16/), a village at which Leyden was schoolmaster in 1792, are the well-known Tweed Vineries (visitors admitted), showing a vast expanse of profitable glass.—About 2½ m. farther, we join the road from Selkirk. On the opposite bank of the Tweed appears **Ashiestiel,** the house tenanted by Sir Walter Scott in 1804–12, before he went to Abbotsford. This was the period of the 'Lay,' the 'Lady of the Lake,' and 'Marmion.'—We enter Peeblesshire. 6½ m. *Thornilee.* *Elibank Tower,* the ruined seat of the Murrays, is seen across the river, about 2½ m. short of (10½ m.) *Walkerburn,* a textile-manufacturing village.

12 m. **Innerleithen** (*Traquair Arms,* RB. 17/6, P. 8 gs. ; *Tighnuilt,* unlic., 1 m. W., RB. 18/6, P. 9 gs.), a little town (2360 inhab.), prettily placed at the junction of Leithen and the Tweed, has mineral springs and passes for the

original, so far as there is any one original, of ' St. Ronan's Well.' About 1½ m. S., on the Quair Water, is **Traquair** (adm. 2/6 daily exc. Fri. in May–Sept., 2–5.30), a somewhat gaunt 17th cent. mansion, including a much more ancient tower, one of the oldest inhabited mansions in Scotland. The avenue gates, flanked by stone figures of bears supposed to have suggested the bears of Bradwardine at Tully-Veolan in ' Waverley,' have never been opened since they were closed in 1796 on the death of the seventh (and, as it proved, last) countess of Traquair ' until an eighth countess should enter.' Originally a royal hunting-seat, it was visited by Alexander I and William the Lion, and Mary and Darnley stayed here in 1566. Historical relics are on view within, together with 16th cent. painted beams, recently uncovered.

The road going up the glen (B 709), the scene of Laidlaw's ' Lucy's Flittin',' may be followed passing Traquair church, the ' Bush aboon Traquair,' sung by Robert Crawford in 1724, and (2 m.; r.) the road to *Glen*, the mansion of Lord Glenconner, early home of the Countess of Oxford and Asquith (d. 1945). It continues to (9 m.) the Gordon Arms, and was the route by which the Ettrick Shepherd led Wordsworth when Yarrow was ' visited ' in 1814. To the E. of this road rises the heather-clad *Minchmuir* (1856 ft.), across which runs the old road from Selkirk to Peebles, by which Montrose fled after Philiphaugh, drawing bridle first at Traquair House.

On the right, beyond Innerleithen, above Glenormiston House, rises the peaked *Lee Pen* (1647 ft.). The road passes between the shattered remnant of *Horsburgh Castle* (r.), and, on the S. bank, the ruins of *Kailzie Church*.—18½ m. *Peebles*, see Rte. 7.

FROM GALASHIELS TO SELKIRK, 6½ m., road (A 7), affording a glimpse of Abbotsford, on the left.—The road crosses the Tweed, and then the Ettrick at (4¼ m.) *Lindean Bridge*, where B 6300 turns left for Abbotsford and Melrose.

6½ m. **SELKIRK** (*County*, RB. 18/6, P. 8 gs., in the square ; *Heatherliehill*, unlic., RB. 18/6, P. 8½ gs., closed Oct.–Feb. ; *Station*, RB. 17/6), a tweed-making royal burgh (5850 inhab.) with numerous mills, is strikingly situated on a hilly site overlooking the Ettrick, 2 m. below its junction with the Yarrow. In the triangular market-place is the *Town Hall*, with its lofty spire, in front of which is a statue of Scott. Some 17th cent. cottages in Halliwell's Close, off the S. end, house an interesting *Museum of Ironmongery* (adm. free). At the other end of High St. is a statue of Mungo Park, and farther on, in front of Victoria Hall, is a memorial (1913) of Flodden (' O Flodden field '). Andrew Lang (1844–1912) was born in the house now named *Viewfield*. A tablet in the West Port marks the house where Montrose spent the night before Philiphaugh.

The old tag, " Up wi' the sutors of Selkirk and doon wi' the Earl of Home," commemorates the former fame of the town for its shoemakers (sutors). Tradition has it that the sutors greatly distinguished themselves at Flodden and captured an English banner, which is still preserved by the corporation. The town, however, was burned by the English after the battle.

The ceremony of ' licking the birse ' still prevails at the admission to the dignity of burgess of the town ; three or four bristles such as shoemakers use, attached to the seal on the burgess ticket, are dipped in wine and passed through the mouth of the candidate.

Abbotsford may be visited from Selkirk viâ the road (5¼ m.) down the valleys of the Ettrick and the Tweed ; and a direct road (A 699) leads E. from Selkirk to (9½ m.) St. Boswells (for *Dryburgh*), passing (6½ m.) near *Bowden Church* ; while A 707 descends the opposite bank of the Ettrick and then ascends the Tweed to join (7½ m.) the road from Galashiels to Peebles, crossing the Tweed at (4½ m.)

the old *Yair Bridge*, with a fine view of the narrow glen. *Fairnilee*, just beyond the bridge, is a modern mansion adjoining the partly ruined home of Alison Cockburn (1712–94), author of ' The Flowers of the Forest ' (comp. p. 14). The principal excursions from Selkirk, however, are those to the valleys of the Yarrow and the Ettrick, which may be combined on one long round (c. 40 m. in all).

MOTOR-BUSES run to *Galashiels* (20 min.) and Edinburgh ; to *Hawick* (30 min.) and Carlisle ; to *Ettrickbridge End* ; to *Tushielaw* and *Ettrick* (Sat.).

FROM SELKIRK TO ST. MARY'S LOCH, 19 m. (motor-bus in summer). The road (A 708), crossing the Ettrick and turning to the left, ascends the *VALLEY OF THE YARROW, noted for quiet beauty and famous in song, from the ' Dowie Dens of Yarrow,' downwards. Hamilton of Bangour (1704–54) wrote ' The Braes of Yarrow ' (' Busk ye, busk ye, my bonny, bonny bride ') ; Wordsworth devoted three poems (' Yarrow Unvisited,' ' Yarrow Visited,' and ' Yarrow Revisited ') to this lovely valley, which inspired also Scott, Hogg, Shairp, Veitch, and many lesser singers.—The name of (3 m.) *Philiphaugh* (r.), a mansion with fine gardens, recalls the battle on the neighbouring ' haugh ' or flatland, where in **1645** Montrose was disastrously defeated by the Covenanters under Leslie. A little farther on the General's Bridge, built by General Mackay, leads to *Bowhill*, a residence of the Duke of Buccleuch, which contains Raeburn's portrait of Sir Walter Scott as a young man and portraits of the Duke and Duchess of Monmouth by Kneller. Visitors to Newark Castle cross this bridge, but we keep on the left bank.—4 m. *Foulshiels*, with the humble cottage in which Mungo Park (**1771**–1806?), the African explorer, was born. On our left, across the river, the massive 15th cent. ruin of **Newark Castle** '' looks out from Yarrow's birchen bower.'' Newark was originally a royal hunting seat and shows the arms of James I on its W. side. It was afterwards granted to the Scotts, and here the ' Last Minstrel ' recited his famous Lay to the Duchess of Buccleuch. In the courtyard Leslie barbarously shot the prisoners taken at Philiphaugh.—5 m. *Broadmeadows Hotel* (RB. 18/, P. 9 gs.). Hence the Minch Road, a drovers' track, crosses *Minchmuir* (**1856** ft.) to Traquair (8 m. N.W.).

Near (6 m.) the modern mansion of *Hangingshaw* are a few fragments of the old castle of the Outlaw Murray, celebrated in an ancient ballad. The scenery changes its character ; the woods cease and the hills are smooth and bare.—9 m. *Yarrow Church* ('restored' within after a fire in 1922) took the place in 1635 of the ruined church of St. Mary on St. Mary's Loch (see below). Four isolated upright stones close by are said to commemorate the fight described in the ' Dowie Dens ' (' gloomy glens ' ; see above), but really date back (according to Prof. Rhys) to the 5th or 6th century. A rough road (practicable for motors) leads hence to *Kirkhope*

(3 m.) in Ettrick.—13 m. *Gordon Arms* (RB. 21/, P. 8 gs.), an anglers' hotel, stands at the divergence of a road N. to Innerleithen (9 m.). On our right is the farm of *Mount Benger*, 'a gey cauld place,' of which James Hogg was the unsuccessful tenant in 1821–30. B 709, diverging on the left, leads past the farm of *Altrive Lake*, now Eldinhope, where Hogg died, to Tushielaw Inn in Ettrick (6½ m.).

We cross (14 m.) the Douglas Burn, flowing down from the ruined *Blackhouse Tower*, the stronghold of Sir James Douglas, the friend of Bruce, and the scene of the elopement of the lovers in the 'Douglas Tragedy.' Scott met Laidlaw, his future amanuensis, at the farm of Blackhouse, and was introduced by him to Hogg.—15½ m. *Dryhope Tower*, on the right, is the alleged birthplace of Mary Scott, the 'Flower of Yarrow,' who wedded 'Auld Wat of Harden.' We have now reached the N.E. end of **St. Mary's Loch** (Rte. 8), the N.W. bank of which we skirt, noting the old churchyard of *St. Mary* on the hillside, to (18 m.) *Rodono Hotel*, above the road and (19 m.) *Tibbie Shiel's*. Thence to Moffat, see Rte. 8.

The return to Selkirk may be made viâ the Gordon Arms and Ettrickdale, see below. To Tweedsmuir, see p. 95.

FROM SELKIRK TO TUSHIELAW BY ETTRICK, 15 m. This beautiful road (B 7009) leads S.W. from Selkirk, up the right bank of the Ettrick.—3 m. *Carterhaugh*, where the Ettrick is joined by the Yarrow, is the scene of the fairy ballad of 'Tamlane.'—4½ m. *Oakwood Tower*, actually an early-17th cent. building, was chosen by Scott as the home of Michael Scot the Wizard, and it is supposed to have seen the 'three lords birling at the wine' in the ballad of the 'Dowie Dens of Yarrow.' Near by (S.E.) is a Roman fort, of Agricolan origin but reoccupied in the 2nd century. We cross to the left bank at (7 m.) *Ettrick Bridge*, and beyond (7½ m.) *Kirkhope*, whence a road leads (r.) to Yarrow Church, we enter a pastoral valley. Kirkhope Tower, on the hillside (r.), was a stronghold of Wat of Harden.—At (10 m.) *Hyndhope* the burn-foot was a gathering-place of Scottish armies, and here were made two treaties between England and Scotland (1384 and 1497).—12 m. *Deloraine*, home of William of Deloraine, 'good at need.'—15 m. *Tushielaw Inn* (P. 8 gs.), an anglers' hotel.

B 709, diverging N. about ½ m. short of the inn, leads over to (6½ m.) the Gordon Arms (see above), whence the return to Selkirk may be made down the Yarrow.

FROM TUSHIELAW TO MOFFAT, 19 m., an interesting road for robust walkers, following the upper Ettrick. We pass (¼ m.) *Tushielaw Castle*, the retreat of Adam Scott, 'King of the Border,' who was hanged in his own courtyard by James V on his famous raid against raiders (1528).—2½ m. *Thirlestane Castle*, the seat of Lord Napier and Ettrick, adjoins the ruins of the tower of John Scott, a follower of James V. About 1 m. farther on B 709 diverges (l.) for *Eskdalemuir* (12 m.) and Langholm (26 m.), see p. 12.—Between Ettrick school and (4 m.)

Ettrick Church a monument indicates the site of the cottage where James Hogg (1770–1835) was born. He is buried in the churchyard, where lie also Tibbie Shiel (1783–1878) and Thomas Boston (1676–1732), minister of the parish and author of the ' Fourfold Estate,' who preached his last sermons from the window of the neighbouring manse. Track to the Loch of the Lowes and Chapelhope, see p. 94.—Farther on Ettrickdale the road crosses (6 m.) the *Back Burn*, descending from *Androwhinnie Hill* (2220 ft.) ; 4 m. beyond which a rough road (for pedestrians only) strikes right, S. of *Bodesbeck Law* (2173 ft.) for (13½ m.) *Capplegill*, in Moffatdale, 5½ m. N.E. of (19 m.) *Moffat* (Rte. 8).

B 711, leading S.E. from Tushielaw Inn over the moors to (16 m.) Hawick, passes (3 m.) *Buccleuch Farm*, near the site of the tower whence the Duke of Buccleuch takes his title, and (7½ m.) *Alemoor Loch*, and descends the Borthwick Water.

C. Melrose and Abbotsford

MELROSE (2150 inhab.), famous for its beautiful abbey and charming surroundings, is the best centre for the exploration of the ' Scott Country.'

Hotels. **George & Abbotsford,** RB. from 30/, P. 15 gs. ; **Waverley Hydro** (1 m. N.W.), RB. 21/, P. 9 gs. ; **Burt's,** RB. 23/, P. 9 gs. ; **King's Arms,** RB. 21/, P. 10 gs. ; **Bon-Accord,** RB. 19/6, P. 9 gs.

Post Office, Buccleuch Street.

Motor-Buses to *Galashiels* (¼ hr.) ; to *Edinburgh* (c. 2 hrs.) viâ Earlston ; to *Kelso* (50 min.) ; to *Jedburgh* (35 min.) viâ St. Boswells, etc. Many circular tours in the ' Scott Country.'

Golf Course on Dingleton Common, ¼ m. S. of the station.

The little town, the ' Kennaquhair' of Scott's ' Monastery' and ' Abbot,' is in a sheltered position at the foot of the Eildon Hills on the S. bank of the Tweed. From the market-place, with its cross (dated 1642) bearing the arms of Scotland, diverge the three main streets, many of the older houses in which show carved stones pillaged from the abbey. A foot-bridge (1826) connects Melrose with *Gattonside* and its river-side walk, but Melrose Bridge is c. 1 m. W. of the town.

In the evening of Dec. 27th (St. John's Day) or the 28th (if the 27th is a Sun.) occurs the Masons' Walk, when members of the ancient Masonic Lodge of Melrose march by torchlight from the Mercat Cross to the Abbey and back. The procession dates from 1746.

**Melrose Abbey is the beautiful ruined church of the Cistercian abbey of St. Mary (adm. 1/ ; 10–4 or 7, Sun. from 2). On moonlight nights it is possible to ' view fair Melrose aright' from the road. It is said that Scott himself never saw the ruins by moonlight.

History. In 1136 David I founded and richly endowed a monastery at Melrose, filling it with Cistercian monks from Rievaulx in Yorkshire, as a successor to the ancient Culdee monastery at Old Melrose (see p. 25). Alexander II was buried here in 1249, probably in the choir. The new abbey lay in the direct forthright of English invasion, and was wrecked again and again, notably in 1322 and 1385. Robert Bruce restored it in 1326 and bequeathed his heart to it ; but the present remains represent a later rebuilding of c. 1385 and the mid-15th cent. ; only a small portion is older. In 1545 the abbey was plundered and seriously damaged in the Earl of Hertford's invasion and it was probably never thoroughly restored. The Reformers did little injury, but the ruins came to be freely used as a quarry for building materials and wind and weather did the rest. In 1566 Queen Mary made Bothwell commendator of the abbey, and after his proscription in 1568 it passed through many hands, until in 1918 it was presented to the nation by the Duke of Buccleuch.

The present ruin represents the E. part of the nave of the abbey church (into which the monks' choir projects for three bays), the transepts, with remains of the central tower, and the chancel as well as much of the S. nave aisle. Every part of the church will repay careful study. The remains of stone vaulting are very elaborate, and the bosses and the capitals of the columns display in their intricate and delicate foliage, especially in the leaves of 'curly kale', the proverbial skill

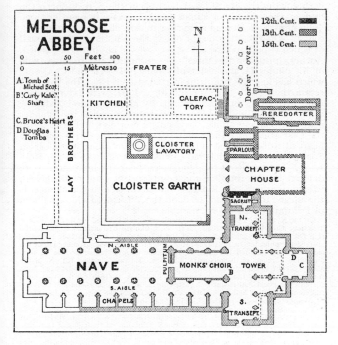

and fancy of the Scottish stone-carvers. Visitors should not omit to view the outside, especially the fine window of the S. transept.

The S. aisle was flanked in 1503–07 by a series of chapels (of which eight remain), each used as the burial-place of some distinguished family and with windows showing beautiful mid-15th cent. tracery. The N. aisle, which is remarkably narrow, had no side chapels, as it here abuts upon the cloister. A stone choir screen separates the central aisle from the monks' choir, the elegant pointed arches of which are obscured on the N. side by heavy piers and arches erected in 1618, when it was fitted up as a Presbyterian church (until 1810).—At the crossing the two W. piers of the TOWER remain ; the capitals of the clustered shaft on the S.W. pier are amongst the finest carvings in the church.—Both the TRANSEPTS have E. aisles. The Dec. *Window of five lights, 24 ft. high and 16 ft. wide, with flowing tracery of great beauty, in the S. transept, is the best in the abbey. A tablet in this transept mentions one John Morow or Moreau as master mason of Melrose (mid-15th cent.).—Off the N. transept opens the SACRISTY, the N. wall of which is perhaps the oldest part of the church (12th cent.). An inscription on the threshold commemorates Joanna, wife of Alexander II and sister of Henry III.—In the CHANCEL, which has kept its beautiful fretted stone * Roof, the windows retain their early-Perp. design of c. 1387, with later tracery (mid-15th cent.) inserted perhaps by Morow. The E. window of five lights divided by a cross transom, with its ' slender shafts of shapely stone,' is vividly described in the ' Lay of the Last Minstrel.' Immediately beneath it lies (it is said) the heart of Robert Bruce, interred here when brought back from Spain, whither Douglas had carried it on the way to the Holy Land. The tombs of the Douglases, near the high altar, were defaced by Sir Ralph Eure (comp. p. 9), who, nevertheless, was buried here. In a chapel on the S. side of the chancel is the alleged tomb of Michael Scot, the Wizard, to which William of Deloraine paid his memorable visit.

On the N. are the CLOISTERS, the S. walk of which is noted for its fine shallow arcading, while the earlier arcade on the E. is likewise attractive. It was by the rich Dec. circular-headed doorway at the E. end of the S. walk that Deloraine entered the church. In 1921 excavations revealed the whole ground-plan of the cloisters and identified the foundations of the chapter house (on the E. side) and other portions of the monastic buildings. Beyond Cloisters Rd., N. of the abbey precinct, further foundations of the conventual buildings have been revealed, including the water-supply conduit. A 15–16th cent. house here, perhaps the guest-house, has been fitted up as an *Abbey Museum* and contains fragments found in and around the abbey, including the base of the Shrine of St. Waltheof, the second abbot (d. 1159), from the chapter house.

The *Graveyard* should be visited. Beneath the fifth window from the W. end of the abbey lies Sir David Brewster (1781–1868), who died at Allerly, near Gattonside. Just beyond the line of the S. transept, to the right of the path, is a little old red tombstone (1761) with a quaint moralised inscription beginning ' The earth goeth on the earth Glistring like gold.' Farther S.E. (r.) in the third row beyond a white Gothic tomb, is the red stone erected by Sir Walter Scott on the grave of Tom Purdie (d. 1829), his favourite henchman, wood-forester at Abbotsford, and in the extreme S.W. corner is the grave of Peter Matheson (d. 1852, aged 84), Scott's coachman.

Abbotsford

The house is open to visitors from 10 to 5 every weekday between March 31st and mid-Oct. ; also Sun. (from 2) in June–Sept. (adm. 2/). It stands 2½ m. W. of Melrose and is conveniently visited also from Galashiels or Selkirk.

From Melrose we follow the pretty Selkirk road to the W. viâ (1 m.) the village of *Darnick*, with its pele tower rebuilt in 1569 (no adm.).

Scott's interest in the tower, which has belonged to the Heitons since it was built in 1425, earned him the sobriquet of 'Duke of Darnick.'—A road diverging here to the left leads to *Chiefswood*, the summer cottage of J. G. Lockhart, the son-in-law of Scott. The Huntly Burn descends from the *Rhymer's Glen*, where True Thomas met the Queen of the Fairies. Higher up is *Cauldshiels Loch.*

Beyond Darnick we see (r.) *Skirmish Hill*, a name recalling a fight between the Scotts and the Elliots for the custody of the young James V in 1526. Farther on we turn to the left (B 6360), and reach (2½ m.) the postern in the wall by which tourists are admitted to Abbotsford.

Abbotsford, the home of Sir Walter Scott, where he died in 1832, is a mansion of many turrets and gables, somewhat ill-placed, close below the road, on a slope descending to the Tweed. Like the surrounding estate, on which he planted nearly every tree, it is the creation of Scott, and it contains many personal memorials of its famous founder besides numerous interesting historical relics collected by him.

Scott purchased the farm (c. 100 acres) of Clarty or Cartley Hole in 1811, improved and enlarged the house, afterwards (1816–23) erecting a much more ambitious mansion, begun by Blore and completed by Wm. Atkinson. When financial disaster overtook him the house and library were presented to him by his creditors (1830), and their possession was ensured to his family by a subscription of friends at his death (1832). Scott's elder and last surviving son died childless in 1847, and the property passed to Scott's grandson, Walter Lockhart, younger brother of the 'Littlejohn' for whom the 'Tales of a Grandfather' were written. Since then it has descended three more times in the female line, the name 'Scott' being assumed by each holder.

The ENTRANCE HALL has panelling from the old kirk of Dunfermline, and round the cornice are armorial bearings of Scottish Border families. The fire-grate belonged to Archbishop Sharp. A glass case contains the last suit of clothes worn by Scott. Here are also 15th cent. armour, a sword presented to Montrose by Charles I, hunting knives of Prince Charlie, relics from Waterloo, and the keys of the old Edinburgh Tolbooth and of Selkirk jail. Outside is the door of the Tolbooth, built into the W. end of the house. The STUDY, little altered, contains Scott's desk and arm-chair. The light gallery opens on a staircase leading to Sir Walter's bedroom. In the small adjacent turret-room is a death mask of Scott.

The LIBRARY (20,000 books) has a carved ceiling with designs from Roslin Chapel and Scott's reading desk. Over the fireplace is a military portrait of Sir Walter's son, by Sir

W. Allan. The bust, by Chantrey (1820), is considered to be the best likeness of Scott. A cabinet-table in the bay window contains historical relics : Queen Mary's seal, Balfour of Burley's snuff-box and that of the Old Pretender, Charles Stewart's quaich, purse made by Flora Macdonald, Rob Roy's purse, Napoleon's pen and writing-case, Burns's toddy tumbler, Scott's knife, fork, and snuff-box ; etc.

In the DRAWING ROOM, with a writing cabinet given to Scott by George IV, are portraits of Scott (by Raeburn), and of his parents ; also a Head of Queen Mary painted an hour after her execution. The cornice reproduces the ' curly kale ' carving of Melrose.

In the DINING ROOM Sir Walter died. His bed was put near the window within sight of the Tweed. The silver urn was a present from Byron.

The ARMOURY contains Scottish weapons of all periods ; also pistols of Napoleon and Claverhouse ; Swiss and German heading-swords; Rob Roy's claymore, sporran, and dirk ; claymore used in ' the '45 ' ; one of the seven sets of keys in Scotland claiming to be the authentic set thrown into Loch Leven when Queen Mary escaped. On the wall hang caricatures and other pictures.

The three conspicuous summits of the **Eildon Hills** (S. summit 1215 ft. ; middle 1385 ft. ; N.E. 1327 ft.), to the S. of Melrose, may be ascended from the Dingleton road in 1 hr. From the highest summit (topographical indicator) Scott could " point out forty-three places famous in war and verse." There are traces of a prehistoric settlement on the N. summit ; and to the E. of Newstead (see below) is a typical example of a strong Roman fort, identified as *Trimontium* (from the shape of the Eildons). It was built c. A.D. 80 and finally abandoned a century later, having been rebuilt in two sections after a temporary desertion c. 100–140.

Eildon Hill, once a single cone, was split into three in a single night at Michael Scot's command by a demon for whom the wizard was bound to find constant employment. The building of the cauld or weir across the Tweed at Kelso took no longer, but the endless task of making ropes out of sea-sand finally vanquished the importunate spirit. Thomas the Rhymer spent more than three years in the enchanted country within the Eildons after his capture by the Queen of the Fairies.

The road goes on to join (c. 3 m.) the Selkirk and St. Boswells road, not far from the church of *Bowden*, many times rebuilt since its foundation in 1128, with the interesting Cavers loft-front (1661).

FROM MELROSE TO DRYBURGH. This excursion is most directly made via St. Boswells (see below).—A more attractive route (6 m.) runs E. via *Newstead* (see above), crosses the Tweed and immediately afterwards turns right at (2 m.) *Leaderfoot* across the Leader, and then turns right again. The road ascends to a commanding point known as ' Sir Walter's View ' (indicator). In a loop of the

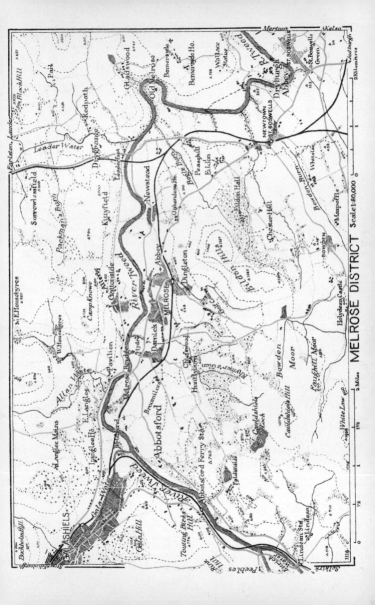

Tweed below us (r.) lies Old Melrose (see below) and in the distance rise the Eildons. Descending the hill we pass *Bemersyde*, seat of the Haigs, who have held it for 800 years, according to a prophecy of Thomas the Rhymer:

> " Tyde what may betide
> Haig shall be Haig of Bemersyde."

The mansion was purchased by national subscription and presented in 1921 to Earl Haig (d. 1928). The house is mostly 18th cent., but with a 16th cent. tower containing personal relics of the Field-Marshal (adm. 2/; 10–6 on Wed., Sat. & Sun., May–Sept.). We keep right for (6 m.) *Dryburgh Abbey*, see below.

Smailholm Tower (60 ft. high), the scene of Scott's ' Eve of St. John ' and described in the 3rd canto of ' Marmion,' is about 5½ m. E. of Melrose, and lies 1 m. S. of the road from Leaderfoot to Kelso. Close to the tower is the farmhouse of *Sandyknowe*, where Scott as a child used to visit his paternal grandfather.

From Melrose to *Earlston* (Edinburgh) and to *Jedburgh*, see Rte. 2.

D. Melrose to St. Boswells, Dryburgh, and Kelso

ROAD, 13¾ m. (A 6091, 699).—3¼ m. *Newtown St. Boswells.*—4½ m. *St. Boswells Green* (l. for *Dryburgh*).—13¾ m. *Kelso.*—Motor-bus direct or viâ Earlston. Alternative route viâ Leaderfoot, see above.

RAILWAY from St. Boswells, 11½ m. in 25 min. viâ (8½ m.) *Roxburgh*. This line goes on beyond Kelso to Coldstream and (35 m.) Berwick.

From Melrose A 6091 rounds the N.E. slope of the Eildons, passing Eildon Hall (Earl of Dalkeith).—2⅔ m. **St. Boswells Station** (*Railway Hotel*, RB. 17/6, P. 8 gs. ; *Dryburgh Arms*, RB. 15/6, P. 7 gs.), in the village of *Newton St. Boswells.*—3½ m. *St. Boswells Green* (Buccleuch Arms, RB. from 21/, P. 11 gs.), with its spacious common, lies at the junction of the road from Selkirk. It is adjoined by the old village of *St. Boswells,* or *Lessudden,* taking its name from St. Boisil, prior of *Old Melrose,* a monastery founded by St. Aidan (7th cent.) which lay in a loop of the Tweed, 2 m. N.E. St. Cuthbert, born in the district c. 625, became a monk at Old Melrose in 651.

Dryburgh Abbey is 1¼ m. E. of the station, on the other side of the Tweed. A lane diverging on the left c. ½ m. S. of the station leads to a footbridge over the river, on the farther side of which is a monument to James Thomson, the poet, erected by the 11th Earl of Buchan. The lane leads right for the abbey, while a track to the left passes the huge sandstone statue (1814) of William Wallace, also erected by Buchan, now hidden by trees. Motors (for the abbey) should make a detour (4 m.) by the bridge beyond St. Boswells village, passing near the fine woods of *Mertoun House*, begun by Sir Wm. Bruce in 1703 for Sir Wm. Scott of Harden, and now a seat of the Earl of Ellesmere. The former 17th cent. house and the dovecot (1576) still stand in the policies. Mertoun church retains its 17th cent. tower and jougs. *Dryburgh Abbey Hotel* (RB. from 27/6, P. 13 gs., open May–Oct.) is close to the abbey.

*Dryburgh Abbey, the burial-place of Sir Walter Scott, was never of great size or wealth but occupies a most beautiful position in a loop of the Tweed, amid splendid trees. The remains include the ruined church and considerable portions of the conventual buildings (adm. 1/; 10–4 or 7, Sun. from 2).

History. On a spot once occupied by the 6th cent. sanctuary of St. Modan, the Abbey of St. Mary was founded in 1150 for Premonstratensians probably by Hugh de Morville, constable of Scotland. In 1322 and again in 1385 it was ruined by the English, and after a more complete destruction by the Earl of Hertford

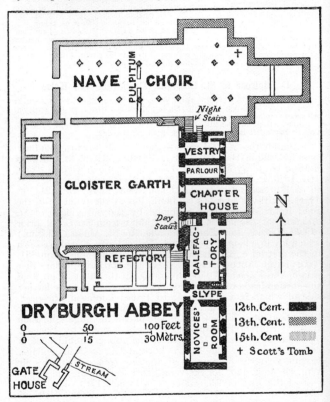

NAVE CHOIR

PULPITUM

Night Stairs

VESTRY

PARLOUR

CLOISTER GARTH

CHAPTER HOUSE

N

Day Stairs

REFECTORY

CALEFAC-TORY

SLYPE

DRYBURGH ABBEY

0   50   100 Feet
0   15   30 Mètres

NOVICES' ROOM

12th. Cent.
13th. Cent.
15th. Cent.
+ Scott's Tomb

GATE HOUSE   STREAM

in 1544 it seems never to have been rebuilt. After the Reformation the abbey lands passed through various hands. About 1700 they belonged to Thomas Haliburton, great-grandfather of Scott, but in the next generation they passed from his heirs (of whom Scott was in the direct line), leaving them only the right to 'stretch their bones' in the abbey. In 1786 the estate was acquired by the Earl of Buchan. It was finally purchased by Lord Glenconner, who, in 1919, presented it to the nation.

Of the CHURCH, originally 190 ft. long and 75 ft. wide across the transepts, there remain the W. front, with a 13th cent. doorway of Romanesque design, fragments of the nave of six bays, the E. aisle of the N. transept, and parts of the choir and S. transept. In the beautiful E. aisle of the N. transept, which opens towards the choir by two pointed arches surmounted by seven-foil openings and a triforium gallery, Sir Walter Scott was interred on Sept. 26th, 1832, and here rest also his wife, his son, and his son-in-law, John Gibson Lockhart (1794–1854). Adjoining is the burial-place of the Erskines and of the Haigs of Bemersyde, with the grave of Field-Marshal Lord Haig (1861–1928) and Lady Haig (1879–1939). At the E. end a tablet commemorates De Morville (d. 1162 ; see above). From the S. transept a night stair ascends to the remains of the dormitory.

The cloister garth with the CONVENTUAL BUILDINGS, on the S. side of the church, is on a lower level, to which steps descend from the nave through a fine Norman arch. On the E. side are the *Sacristy*, the so-called ' Chapel of St. Modan ' (burial-place of the Earls of Buchan), and a small parlour. Entered by a beautiful portal, the *Chapter House*, still entire, has barrel vaulting and retains part of its arcading as well as traces of 12th cent. painting. Adjoining is the *Calefactory*, with its large fireplace and remains of the elegant vaulting columns. Farther S. is the *Novices' Room*. On the S. the garth is bounded by the *Refectory*, the W. gable of which exhibits a large rose window of great beauty. Just S. of the cloisters are the remains of a *Gatehouse*.

From St. Boswells Green A 699 descends the S. bank of the Tweed.—6½ m. *Maxton* retains the shaft of its old cross. The ruined *Littledean Tower*, a hold of the Kers, lies above the river, 1 m. N.E., while conspicuous in the distance (N.) is *Smailholm Tower*. The scenery is attractive, with beautiful views of the valley below us and, farther on, of Floors and its woods.—11 m. *Barns.*

Here B 6400 ascends the Teviot, for Ancrum, passing (1¾ m.) *Roxburgh*, prettily placed near the river. In the churchyard is buried Andrew Gemmels (d. 1793 ; aged 106), the original of Edie Ochiltree, the bedesman in Scott's ' Antiquary ' ; the church dates from 1752. Roxburgh Castle, 2 m. downstream, is reached by a fine walk on the left bank of the Teviot ; the steep right bank abounds in caves. At *Kirkbank* (2 m. upstream) a chain-bridge crosses the river to Kalemouth and Eckford Church.

12½ m. *Roxburgh Castle*, on a grassy knoll between the Tweed and Teviot, has left scanty remains, though it was a place of strength since the 12th cent. and a royal residence that saw the marriage of Alexander II and the birth of Alexander III (1241). Nothing remains of the once important town of Roxburgh beside it, though in the 13th cent. this was one of the four royal burghs (Edinburgh, Stirling, Berwick,

Roxburgh) that established a convention or court. Both castle and town had long been English possessions when they were destroyed by the Scots after the death of James II.— The road crosses the Teviot and then the Tweed.

13¾ m. **KELSO** (4120 inhab.), somewhat partially described by Scott as " the most beautiful if not the most romantic village in Scotland," lies ¾ m. from its station on the other side of the Tweed, at its junction with the Teviot. It is a busy little market town, with a fine abbey.

Hotels. Ednam House, RB. 25/, P. 14 gs., in the dower-house of the Dukes of Roxburghe ; **Cross Keys,** RB. 21/, P. 10 gs. ; **Queen's Head,** RB. 19/6, P. 10 gs. ; **Border Temperance,** RB. 15/, P. 7 gs.

Motor-Buses to *Berwick* (c. 1–1½ hr.) viâ Coldstream, Cornhill, or Swinton ;

to *Yetholm* (25 min.) ; to *Melrose* (¾ hr.) and *Galashiels* (1 hr.) ; to *Jedburgh* (40 min.) and *Hawick* (1½ hr.) ; to *Edinburgh* ; to *Newcastle*, etc.

Golf Course, 9 holes.—RACECOURSE, 1 m. N. (meetings Mar., May and Oct.).

History. Kelso, known in the 12th cent. as Calkou or Calchoh (i.e. ' Chalkheugh '), underwent its share of affliction at the hands of English invaders, notably in 1522, 1544, and 1545. It received various royal visits, and several treaties between the English and Scots were arranged here, while it was frequently a rendezvous for Scottish armies on their way to the south. James III was crowned here in 1460. Queen Mary spent two nights at Kelso in 1566. In 1715 the rebel forces proclaimed James VIII in the market-place, and in 1745 Prince Charles Stewart stayed two nights here on his northward retreat. Walter Scott in 1783 was for six months a school-fellow of James and John Ballantyne (natives of the town) at the old grammar school, which stood on the site of the abbey nave ; and at Kelso, in 1802, the Ballantyne Press issued the first two volumes of his ' Minstrelsy of the Scottish Border.' Famous Free Kirk ministers here were Horatius Bonar (1808–89), the hymn-writer, and Robertson Nicoll (1851–1923), founder of the ' British Weekly.' Sir William Fairbairn (1789–1874), friend of the Stephensons and part-designer of the Menai Tubular Bridge, began life as a labourer on Kelso bridge.

A ' Kelso convoy ' is a bare civility from host to parting guest : ' a step and a half ower the door-stane.'

We approach the town by a fine bridge, by Rennie (1803), affording a justly famous view of the abbey close by. In the wide and dignified Square is the *Town Hall* with a tablet expressing the gratitude of the Polish Forces for the town's hospitality in 1942–43.

In Roxburgh St. (opposite No. 34), N. of the Square, a horshoe in the roadway marks the spot where Prince Charlie's horse cast a shoe. Chalkheugh Terrace (l.) commands a delightful view. The octagonal *Parish Church* (1793), with family pews of the Duke of Roxburghe and of the Douglases of Springwood, lies S.E. of the Square.

*Kelso Abbey, a Norman and E.E. structure with a conspicuous tower, long passed for the remains of a comparatively small abbey church. Recent investigations, however, based upon a description of the church in 1517 (preserved in the Vatican Library), have totally altered this view, and the venerable building is now considered to represent only the extreme W. end of the largest and perhaps the finest of the Border abbeys. Adm. free weekdays, 10–4 or 7, Sun. from 2.

History. The abbey, one of the earliest completed by David I, was founded in 1128, and was occupied by monks from Tiron in Picardy, who had previously been settled at Selkirk in 1113. In 1152 it received the body of its founder's son, Henry, Earl of Northumberland. Profiting by royal favour, the abbey rose to wealth and influence, and its abbots, mitred since 1165, claimed precedence over even St. Andrews until a decision was given against them by the king in 1420. When the Earl of Hertford entered Kelso in 1545 the abbey was garrisoned as a fortress and was taken only at the point of the sword ; the garrison of 100 men, including 12 monks, were slaughtered, and the building was almost entirely razed. From 1649 till 1771 the existing transept was used as a parish church, but in 1805 the unsightly additions were removed. At the Reformation the abbey with its lands was conferred upon Sir Robert Ker of Cessford, ancestor of the Duke of Roxburghe, its last private owner, who presented it to the nation in 1919.

The abbey church (250–300 ft. long) seems to have consisted originally of a long aisled nave of 7 or 8 bays, with transepts at each end (unique in Scotland) and a tall tower above each crossing. At the W. end projected a square Galilee porch, partly preserved, and at the E. end the choir, perhaps prolonging the nave by 1 or 2 bays, terminated in a corresponding projecting presbytery. Of all this only the W. façade, the W. transepts, the injured W. tower, and two bays of the nave remain, though the line of the nave-walls has been traced. Beyond the W. porch, entered by a deeply moulded doorway of good design, rises the tower, which was supported by four magnificent arches, 45 ft. high, of which two remain. The piers of the nave were circular ; above are a triforium of small arches, with delicate shafts, and a clerestory with similar arcades. The façade of the N.W. transept has remained unaltered for 800 years. The beautiful doorway is surmounted by an ornamental arcade and a diapered gable ; above are two stories of Norman windows ; still higher is a round window ; and at the top between two turrets is a gable-like structure with round-headed openings. Around the walls of the church, both inside and out, ran an elegant interlaced arcade, on the ground level. An ancient Gothic arch, S. of the church, has been employed as entrance to a small cloister in the Romanesque style, erected as a memorial to the 8th Duke and Duchess of Roxburghe (d. 1932, 1937).

Rosebank, a small house on the left bank of the Tweed just below Kelso, was a favourite resort of the boy Walter Scott, to whose uncle it belonged. At *Garden Cottage* (now Waverley Lodge ; bust over the door), in the Knowes (E. of the abbey), he stayed with his " kind and affectionate Aunt Janet." ' Beardie,' Scott's great-grandfather, who refused to shave till the restoration of the Stewarts, lived in The Butts.

In the neighbourhood of Kelso are several dignified residences, the chief of which is **Floors Castle** (Duke of Roxburghe), " so situated as to combine the ideas of ancient baronial grandeur with those of modern taste." It was built by Vanbrugh in 1718 and altered to its present Tudor aspect by Playfair about 1849. The grounds and fine gardens are open to the public on Wed. 10–4 (permit at the National Bank of Scotland, 10 The Square, Kelso) ; the plain dignified lodges (1929) are at the end of Roxburgh St. A holly tree in the park is said to mark the spot where James II, besieging Roxburgh Castle in 1460, was killed by the bursting of a cannon, which he was inspecting " with more curiosity than became a king."

James Thomson (1700–48), author of 'The Seasons,' was born in the former manse of *Ednam*, an ancient village c. 2 m. N. of Kelso, and H. F. Lyte (1793–1847), author of ' Abide with Me,' was born at Ednam West Mains.

About 8 m. S.E. of Kelso (by B 6352) lies **Yetholm** (*Border*, at Kirk Yetholm, RB. 20/, P. 27/6 ; *Plough*, RB. 17/6 ; *White Swan*, RB. 15/, both plain, at Town Yetholm), once noted as the headquarters of the Scottish gipsies and the residence of their ' King.' It is divided by the Bowmont Water into two villages, ¼ m. apart : Town Yetholm and Kirk Yetholm, the old gipsy resort. The old gipsy dynasty of the Faas is, however, extinct ; Esther Faa Blyth, the last ' queen,' was buried here in 1883, and her ' palace ' is pointed out in the village. Yetholm lies 1½ m. W. of the English border, and c. 7 m. S.E. as the crow flies is the *Cheviot* (2676 ft.), the highest point of the Cheviot Hills.

A pleasant excursion S. may be made from Kelso (by B 6436) to (6 m.) *Linton* church (Norman ; restored) with its original font and tympanum ; the latter is said to show Sir John Somerville, who was knighted by William the Lion, slaying a ' ravening beast '. About 2½ m. S.W. of *Morebattle* (1 m. S.), in a fine position on the Eckford-Yetholm road, stands the keep of *Cessford Castle*, a stronghold of the Kers. The best return is viâ Eckford church (p. 14), 4½ m. W. of Morebattle on A 698.

FROM KELSO TO COLDSTREAM AND BERWICK, 23¼ m. by the S. bank of the Tweed ; A 698 along the N. bank is an alternate route to Coldstream (9 m.) ; railway in 50 min. From 5 m. below Kelso the river marks the Border.—B 6350, keeping left at (2¼ m.) *Sprouston*, enters England before (6 m.) *Carham*.—7¾ m. *Wark-on-Tweed*, with the scanty remains of the once formidable Wark Castle, defended against David II by the Countess of Salisbury. Edward III hastened to its relief, and, according to Froissart, fell in love with its beautiful defender.—10 m. *Cornhill* (Collingwood Arms, RB. 30/, P. 14½ gs.), with the station of Coldstream, lies in Northumberland. Here Adm. Duncan died in 1804 returning from London to Scotland.—**Coldstream** (*Newcastle Arms*, RB. 25/, P. 13 gs. ; *Crown*, RB. 17/6, P. 6 gs.), a little town (1295 inhab.), 1½ m. N. beyond the Tweed, is in Scotland. Coldstream, like Gretna Green, was once noted for irregular marriages, and here Lord Brougham was married in 1819. The Coldstream Guards were originally raised here by General Monk in 1660.

About 3 m. S.E. is the battlefield of **Flodden,** where the Scots under James IV were disastrously defeated in 1513 by the English under the Earl of Surrey. A monument ' to the brave of both nations ' stands on a hill near *Branxton* church, on the spot where James IV is believed to have fallen. The so-called ' Sybil Grey's Well ' (see ' Marmion ') lies just below the church.

The road leading N. from Coldstream to (9½ m.) *Duns* (Rte. 1) passes (1 m. ; left) *The Hirsel*, seat of the Earl of Home (adm. free to grounds and at (4½ m.) *Swintonmill* intersects the road from Berwick to Kelso, 2¼ m. W. of Swinton (comp. p. 1).

At (13¼ m.) *Twizel* (Tillmouth Park, RB. 27/6–40/, P. 13–18 gs.), with its ruined castle, the Berwick road (A 698) crosses the deep glen of the sluggish but treacherous Till by the single-span bridge over which James IV, from an infatuated sense of chivalry, permitted the English vanguard to pass unmolested before the battle of Flodden.—16¾ m. **Norham** lies

1¾ m. N.W., of the main road. The ruined *Castle* (adm. 1/ daily, Sun. from 2), in which Scott places the opening scenes of 'Marmion,' was originally a Border stronghold of the prince-bishops of Durham. The splendid Norman keep dates from Bp. Puiset (c. 1160). In the *Church* (partly Norman) Edward I opened the fateful convention of 1291 to weigh the contesting claims of Bruce and Balliol to the Scottish crown. 23¼ m. *Berwick*, see p. 1.

5. EDINBURGH AND ITS ENVIRONS

EDINBURGH (466,750 inhab.), the capital of Scotland, the seat of the chief Scottish law-courts, and of a university and many noted schools, is famous alike for its romantic history and the surpassing beauty of its natural situation. Arthur's Seat (823 ft.), like a couchant lion, flanked by the ramparts of Salisbury Crags, guards the city on the E. ; to the W. is Corstorphine Hill; to the S. Blackford Hill and the Braid Hills, with the Pentland range beyond ; and to the N. is the Firth of Forth. Edinburgh's claim to be ' the Modern Athens ' rests not only on its intellectual record but also on several points of physical resemblance between its landscape and that of the beautiful capital of Greece. R. L. Stevenson suggests that its more homely name of ' Auld Reekie ' was given by the Fifeshire people, watching the distant smoke of its chimneys. The characteristic industries of Edinburgh are law, education, printing, and brewing ; and, compared with Glasgow and other opulent manufacturing towns, it has been likened to a " penniless lass wi' a lang pedigree," whose face is her fortune. Since 1920 the official bounds of the city have been widely extended, so as to include Leith and Portobello on the coast, besides Corstorphine, Colinton, Liberton, Gilmerton, and many other villages on the west and south ; but the historic Edinburgh occupies a comparatively small area. The OLD TOWN is built upon the long sloping ridge that descends from the rock crowned by the Castle to the Palace of Holyroodhouse, 1 m. away. The main thoroughfares here, the High Street and the Canongate, are flanked with tall tenement houses, some of them nine stories high, and off them open steep narrow closes, wynds or alleys, and dingy courts, once the abode of rank and fashion, but now for the most part teeming hives of less prosperous citizens. Divided from the Old Town by the valley, occupied once by the Nor' Loch and now by public gardens, is the NEW TOWN, dating only from the end of the 18th cent., with its broad and regular streets and its dignified if somewhat frigid squares, and its handsome public buildings.

Old and New Town are connected by the lofty viaduct of the North Bridge at the E. end of Princes St., by the Waverley Bridge, a little farther west, and by the Mound, about the middle. It is convenient to remember that the principal streets, the High St. as well as Princes St., George St., and Queen St., run from E. to W.

Railway Stations. *Waverley Staion* (Pl. 26), at the E. end of Princes St., for the E. coast route to England; for Glasgow viâ Falkirk; for Carlisle viâ Galashiels; for the W. Highland line to Mallaig; for Aberdeen viâ Dundee, etc.—*Princes Street Station* (Pl. 24), at the W. end of Princes St., for the W. coast route to England viâ Carstairs; for Glasgow viâ Holytown; for Callander and Oban; for Aberdeen viâ Perth, etc.

Airport at *Turnhouse*, 6 m. W., for services to Aberdeen (for Shetland), Orkney, Birmingham, London, Glasgow, and Dublin. Booking office, 133 George St.; coach to airport 2/6.

Hotels, George (g; 18), first class, 21 George St., RB. 45/; **Caledonian** (b; 24), at the W. end of Princes St., RB. 45/; **North British Station** (a; 19), at the E. end of Princes St., RB. 45/, two large railway hotels, with restaurants and grill-rooms; **Roxburghe** (e; 24), 38 Charlotte Square, RB. 35/; **Queen** (h; 17), 2 St. Colme St., RB. 32/; **Royal British** (d; 19), 20 Princes St., RB. 35/; **Carlton**, T.H., North Bridge (Pl. 26), RB. 30/; **Royal** (c; 18), 53 Princes St., RB. 27/6; **Bruntsfield**, 69 Bruntsfield Place (beyond Pl. 39), **Braid Hills**, Braid Rd., 2½ m. S., at these RB. from 30/; **Grosvenor**, Grosvenor St. (Pl. 30) RB. 25/6; **County**, **Abercromby**, Abercromby Place, **Scotia**, Gt. King St. (all Pl. 11), RB. 25/; **Buckingham**, Buckingham Terr. (Pl. 16), RB. 25/; **Adelphi**, Cockburn St. (Pl. 26), RB. 24/6; **Rutland** (k; 24), 3 Rutland St., near Princes St. station, RB. 24/; **Imperial**, 143 Leith St., RB. 22/6; **Dorchester**, Clarendon Cres. (Pl. 16), RB. 23/6; **Learmonth**, Learmonth Terr. (Pl. 16), RB. 21/. *Unlicensed and Temperance Hotels*: **Old Waverley** (m; 19), 43 Princes St.; **Darling's Regent**, 21 Waterloo Pl. (Pl. 19), at both, RB. 27/6, P. 13 gs.; **St. Andrew**, 10 S. St. Andrew St., RB. 25/, P. 10 gs.; **Cockburn** (f; 26), Cockburn St., RB. 24/6, P. 10½ gs.; **Shelbourne**, Hart St. (Pl. 12), 105 R., RB. 23/6, P. 12 gs.; **Murrayfield**, Murrayfield Rd. (beyond Pl. 29), RB. 26/, P. 9½ gs.;

Forres, 9 Forres St. (Pl. 17), RB. 21/6, P. 10 gs.; **Green's**, 24 Eglinton Cres. (Pl. 22), RB. 25/, P. 10 gs.; **Royal Circus** (Pl. 10), RB. 23/, P. 11 gs.; **Royal Stuart**, 18 Abercromby Pl. (Pl. 11), RB. 21/, P. 8 gs.; **Suttie's**, South Bridge, RB. 20/, P. 10 gs.; **Menzies**, RB. 22/6, and many others in Royal Terrace (Pl. 13–14) and Regent Terrace (Pl. 21). *Boarding Houses* are numerous.

Restaurants at the principal hotels; also *Apéritif*, 24 Frederick St.; *Albyn*, 77 Queen St.; *Athenian*, 24 Howe St. (Pl. 11), these three first-class. *Beehive* 20 Grassmarket, in an 18th cent. building with interesting decorations; *Café Royal*, West Register St.; *White Cockade*, 55 Rose St.; *Epicure*, West End, 19 and 22 Shandwick Place; *Grand*, 3 South St. Andrew St.; *Garrick*, 7–11 Spittal St.; *Bon Accord*, 21 Rose St.; *Beresford*, Coates Gardens, Haymarket; *National* 24 Nicolson St.; *Brown Derby*, 1 Hanover St.; *Berkeley*, 25 Lothian Rd.; *Wee Windaes*, plain, 142 High St.—TEA ROOMS AND CAFÉS (closed at 5). *Crawford*, *Mackie*, *Fuller's*, *Macvitties & Guest*, *Alexander Ferguson*, 70, 108, 120B, 136, and 144 Princes St.; etc. Also at the large department stores of *Jenner*, *Wm. Small*, and *Binns*, 45, 106, and 146 Princes St., and *Patrick Thomson*, North Bridge.—RESTAURANTS IN THE OUTSKIRTS. *House o' Hill*, 222 Queensferry Road, Blackhall; *Zoological Park* (L. and tea only); *Cramond Inn* at Cramond; *Open Arms* at Dirleton, etc.

General Post Office (Pl. 19), at E. end of Princes St., always open for telegrams; *West End Post Office*, Hope St. (Pl. 24).

Scottish National Tourist Beard 2, Rutland Place (adjoining Princes St. Station).—TOURIST AGENTS; *Thomas Cook*, *American Express*, 126 and 139 Princes St.; *Mackay Bros.*, 33 Hanover St.; *Lawrie*, 5 Antigua St., etc.

American Consul, 3 Regent Terrace (Pl. 21).—*English-Speaking Union*,

32 Heriot Row; *Overseas League*, 100 Princes St.

Taxicabs, 2/6 per mile or per 17 min. waiting; 4*d*. each additional ⅛ mile or 3⅛ min.; each passenger beyond 4, 6*d*.; luggage carried outside 2*d*. per package.—Horse-Drawn Cabs, 1/6 up to 1¼ m., 9*d*. each additional ½ m.; each passenger beyond 4, 6*d*.; by time 4/ per hr.; each additional ¼ hr. 1/; each passenger beyond 4, 6*d*.

Motor-Buses. Most of the routes start and end in the suburbs and pass through the centre, the most important 'picking up' places being in Princes St. (West End, Waverley Bridge, or Post Office) and at the Tron Church at the intersection of High Street and 'the Bridges'. Special service **32** in June–Sept. (not Sun. morning) every ¼ hr. from *Waverley Bridge* to the *Castle*. Important regular services: **1.** *Corstorphine*–Gorgie – *Tron* – Holyrood – *Leith*. **3.** *Saughton Rd.*–Gorgie–*West End–Post Office*–Surgeons' Hall–Newington–*Gilmerton*. **4.** *Bingham Rd.* (Duddingston)–Leith Walk–*Waverley–West End*–Colinton–*Fairmilehead*. **5.** *Morningside*–Surgeons' Hall–*Tron–Post Office*–Leith Walk–*Restalrig*. **8.** *Silverknowes*–Granton–*Post Office–Tron*–Newington–*Gilmerton*. **9, 10.** *Granton–Post Office–West End*–Craiglockhart–*Colinton*. **11.** from *Newhaven* and **15.** from *Joppa* and Portobello to Leith Walk–*Waverley* – *West End* – Morningside – Braid Hills–*Fairmilehead*. **12, 25, 26.** *Corstorphine* – Zoo – Murrayfield–*West End* – *Waverley* – Craigentinny – *Portobello*. **16.** *Granton*–Leith–*Waverley–West End*–Morningside–*Oxgangs*. **18.** *Burdiehouse* –Liberton–Tollcross–*West End* (Charlotte Sq.)–Blackhall–*Barnton*. **21.** *Leith Walk*–Holyrood–*Tron*–Castle Hill–Viewforth–Corstorphine–*Clermiston* (returning viâ House o' Hill and Arboretum Rd.). **23.** *Morningside*–Bruntsfield–*George IV Bridge*–Mound – Canonmills – *Inverleith* (for Botanic Gdns.). **24, 29.** *Craigleith*–Frederick St.–*West End*–Tollcross–Surgeons' Hall–*Post Office*–Frederick St.–*Craigleith*. **31.** *Gilmerton* (Hyvot Drive) – Liberton – Newington – Surgeons' Hall–*Waverley–West End*–Murrayfield–Zoo–*Corstorphine*. **33.** *Saughton Rd.*–Gorgie–*West End–Post Office–Tron* – Surgeons' Hall – Craigmillar – *Little France* (Fernieside Drive). **39.** *Silverknowes*–Lauriston Castle–Comely Bank–*West End* (Charlotte Sq.)–*George IV Bridge*–Grange–*Morningside* (Greenbank). **41.** *Waverley–West End* (Charlotte Sq.)–Craigleith–Lauriston Castle–Cramond–*Barnton*. **44.** *Eastfield*–Duddingston–Leith Walk–*Waverley–West End*–Slateford–*Juniper Green*. **45.** *Portobello*–Duddingston–Holyrood –*Tron–George IV Bridge*–Bruntsfield–Colinton–*Juniper Green*.

Country Buses, operated by Scottish Omnibuses, Ltd. (45 Princes St.), and starting from *St. Andrew Sq.* bus terminal (Pl. 19), run daily in all directions. The fares listed below are for single journeys; reduction in return fares. To *Turnhouse Airport* in 23 min., 10*d*.; to *Roslin* in ½ hr., 11½*d*.; to *Dalkeith* in ½ hr., 10½*d*.; viâ Cramond Bridge to *South Queensferry* (Forth Bridge) in ½ hr., 1/, and *Bo'ness* in 1 hr., 2/; viâ Musselburgh, Prestonpans, and Gullane to *North Berwick* in 65 min., 2/5; to *Linlithgow* in ¾ hr., 1/9, going on viâ Falkirk to *Stirling* (1¾ hr., 3/2); viâ Stirling to *Callander* (2¾ hrs., 4/7) and *Crieff* (3 hrs., 5/3); viâ Stirling to *Perth* (3 hrs., 6/9), *Dundee* (3¾ hrs., 8/9) and *Aberdeen* (7 hrs., 15/1); viâ Stirling and Perth to *Inverness* (19/9; summer only); to *Glasgow* viâ Bathgate (2½ hrs., express service in 1¾ hr., 4/6), also viâ Bellshill (4/8) and viâ Shotts (5/2) in 2½ hrs.; to *Haddington* (55 min., 1/10) and *Berwick-upon-Tweed* (2½ hrs., 6/), going on to *Newcastle upon Tyne* (5½ hrs., 11/9); viâ Dalkeith and St. Boswells to *Jedburgh* (2¼ hrs., 5/10), going on to *Newcastle* (5¼ hrs., 11/9); viâ Coldstream to *Newcastle* in 5½ hrs., 11/9; viâ Stow to *Galashiels* in 1¾ hr., 3/7; viâ Peebles to *Galashiels* in 2½ hrs., 4/11; viâ Stow and Galashiels to *Selkirk* (3 hrs., 4/6), *Hawick* (2¾ hrs., 5/9), and *Carlisle* (4½ hrs., 11/1). Other services to *London*, *Liverpool*, etc., see p. xlii.

Motor-Coach Excursions in summer. 'Round Edinburgh' tours (June–Sept.) start daily from Waverley Bridge, at 10.30 a.m. and 2 p.m. (Sun. at 2 only), visiting the Old Town, Holyrood and Arthur's Seat (10/, children 5/; incl. adm. fees); shorter tours at 10.30 and 2.30 (5/). Longer tours covering the outskirts, and extended tours (2–8 days), are arranged by Scottish Omnibuses, Ltd., (5 S. St. David St.) and the chief tourist agents.

Suburban Railways (weekdays only) From Waverley Station. A. Circular Line to *Abbeyhill*, *Piershill*,

Portobello, Duddingston, Newington, Blackford Hill, Morningside Road, Craiglockhart, Gorgie, Haymarket, and *Waverley.* To *Balgreen* (for Murrayfield ground), *Pinkhill,* and *Corstorphine.*—From PRINCES ST. STATION. To *Dalry Road, Murrayfield, Craigleith, East Pilton, Granton Rd., Newhaven,* and *Leith.*

Steamers from *Leith* (p. 74), the port of Edinburgh, to *Aberdeen* and *Orkney* and *Shetland,* see Rte. 65 ; to *Copenhagen* and other Danish ports ; to *Reykjavik,* and to the *Faeroe Islands* ; to *Antwerp, Rotterdam,* and *Amsterdam* ; and *viâ* Grangemouth to *Hamburg* and *Bremen.* In summer excursion steamers to *Inchcolm, Aberdour, North Berwick, Largo, Elie,* etc.

Amusements. THEATRES. *King's*

(Pl. 38, 39), Leven St. ; *Lyceum* (Pl. 31), Grindlay St. ; *Empire* (Pl. 34). Nicolson St. ; *Little,* Pleasance (Pl. 34) ; *Gateway,* 41 Elm Row (Pl. 13), managed by the Church of Scotland ; *Palladium,* E. Fountainbridge (Pl. 31) ; *Open-Air* (5500 seats), Braidburn Valley.—CINEMAS in Princes St., Lothian Rd., Nicolson St., etc. ; *Cameo,* Tollcross for Continental films ; *Monseigneur News,* Princes St., W. end, etc.—DANCING. In the *Caledonian Hotel* ; *Palais,* Fountainbridge, etc.—GOLF. Public courses at the *Braid Hills* and at *Carrickknowe,* opposite the Zoo (3/ per round) ; and (9-hole) at *Craigentinny* and *Portobello* (1/6 per round) ; private clubs abound (4/–5/ per day on introduction).—SWIMMING POOL at Portobello (June–Sept. 10–8 or 9 ; 1/).

History. The history of Edinburgh is at first the history of the Castle, and although Holyrood Abbey was founded in 1128 and the Blackfriars' monastery in the 13th cent., the communities that grew up beside these and the Castle remained of comparatively small importance until c. 1450, a few years after the murder of James I at Perth (1437), when Edinburgh superseded Perth as the real capital of Scotland. In 1456 was built the first town-wall, of which the Wellhouse Tower (p. 38) is a relic. The Scottish army before Flodden assembled on the Borough Muir in 1513, and when the news of the stricken field reached the capital the dismayed citizens hastily encircled the S. side of their city with a wall (the Flodden Wall, pp. 57, 50). Henry VIII, baulked in his plan of marriage between his son, Edward, and Mary, the young Queen of Scots, devastated Edinburgh in 1544 and again, after the battle of Pinkie, in 1547. Mary returned from France to Edinburgh in 1561 to begin her troubled reign. In 1566 Rizzio was slain at Holyrood and James VI was born in the Castle. Next year saw the murder of Darnley at the Kirk o' Field and Mary's marriage to Bothwell, followed by her departure from the city, which she saw only once again, as a prisoner on her way to Loch Leven Castle in 1567. Under James VI Edinburgh University was founded, but when he went S. to ascend the throne of England in 1603, the court and nobility followed him and Edinburgh's importance waned. The capital had its full share in the struggle for religious and civil liberty that began in this reign and lasted until the Revolution of 1688. Within this period falls the erection of the bishopric of Edinburgh (1633–39). Jenny Geddes's protest against episcopacy (1637), the enthusiastic signing of the National Covenant at Greyfriars (1638) the occupation of Edinburgh by Cromwell after the battle of Dunbar (1650), the executions of the Marquess of Montrose (1650) and of the Marquess of Argyll (1661), the martyrdom of many Covenanters in the Grassmarket, the confinement in Greyfriars Churchyard of the Covenanting prisoners taken at the battle of Bothwell Bridge (1679), and the execution of the Earl of Argyll (1685). In 1707 the Act of Union between England and Scotland was settled at Edinburgh and the Scottish Parliament ceased to have a separate existence (' the end o' an auld sang '). The outbreak known as the Porteous Riot in 1736 was evidence of the smouldering discontent with which the ancient capital accepted its now subordinate position. In 1745 Prince Charles Edward Stewart held his brief court at Holyrood, though the Castle remained in the hands of the Hanoverian government. Towards the end of the 18th cent. and the beginning of the 19th Edinburgh, which already knew Allan Ramsay (d. 1758), enjoyed a period of great literary brilliancy, when David Hume (d. 1776), Adam Smith (d. 1790), Principal Robertson (d. 1793) and Tobias Smollett (d. 1771) were succeeded by James Hogg (d. 1835), Francis Jeffrey (d. 1850), Professor Wilson (d. 1854), and the greatest of them all, Sir Walter Scott (d. 1832). Robert Burns visited Edinburgh in 1786 and 1787, and Dickens in 1834 and 1841, staying, on the second occasion, at the Royal Hotel and receiving the Freedom of the city, while Chopin lived at 10 Warriston Crescent, beyond Canonmills, in 1848 (tablet). In the 18th cent. the city began to extend southwards beyond the Flodden Wall and in 1769 was built the first house in the now widespread New Town. Expansion since then has been steady, and since the municipal extension in 1920 it has been, in area, the largest city in Great Britain, except London and Birmingham. The city was attacked from the air in 1916 and again in 1940, but material damage was happily negligible.

The **Edinburgh International Festival of Music and Drama,** started in 1947, is now established as one of the world's foremost annual artistic events. It is held for three weeks at the end of August and beginning of September, and includes musical, dramatic, operatic, and ballet performances. Concerts (see above) are given in the Usher Hall and Freemasons' Hall, opera in the King's Theatre, drama in the Lyceum Theatre and, on an apron stage, in the Assembly Hall, and ballet in the Empire Theatre. The *Festival Office,* Synod Hall, Castle Terrace, deals with applications for tickets, and arranges accommodation for visitors (booking opens in April). The *Festival Club,* at the Music Hall, George St., with restaurant and reading rooms, is open to all visitors. A feature of the Festival is the military searchlight tattoo on the Esplanade of Edinburgh Castle, with the floodlit castle as backcloth.

PRINCES STREET

The centre of Edinburgh, for both visitor and native, is **Princes Street* (Pl. 24, 25, 19), one of the beautiful streets of the world, which runs from E. to W. between the two principal railway stations and is the animated and favourite promenade at all hours of the day. This famous street, c. ¾ m. long, has continuous buildings on the N. side only—shops, hotels, clubs, and offices, miscellaneous, and of no architectural importance—its distinction is the wonderful views it commands, especially that across the dip of the valley on the S. to the Castle on its abrupt rock and the long romantic line of the Old Town. Once known as the Lang Gait, it received its present name in honour of Prince George (later George IV).

At the E. end of Princes St., on either side of the approach to the North Bridge, are the *General Post Office* (Pl. 19; 1861) and the large North British Station Hotel. Opposite, with a statue of the Duke of Wellington, by Sir John Steell, in front (1852; 'The Iron Duke, in bronze, by Steell'), stands the **General Register House,** a fine building with a central cupola, by Robert Adam (1772; adm. free weekdays 10–4, Sat 10–1).

The Register House is the public record office of Scotland, in which all public documents relating to Scotland are kept. Among the valuable and interesting State papers usually on view in show-cases are the Articles of Union (1707), with the parallel signatures and seals of the Scottish and English commissioners; the Arbroath Declaration (1320) of the Scottish barons to the Pope; the signed oaths to maintain the Presbyterian religion taken by each successive monarch since Queen Anne; letters, autographs and papers relating to Mary, Queen of Scots; the Newbattle copy of the National Covenant; the warrant of execution of James Stewart 'of the Glens'; and documents extending back to 1171. In the Register House is also the *Court of the Lord Lyon King of Arms* (11–3, Sat. 11–1), the Scottish Government office for armorial bearings and genealogies, of which the registers are open to public inspection. Authoritative sets of clan tartans are likewise preserved. The Lyon Court is one of the few surviving courts of heraldry in Europe and functions as a Scottish court of law. Besides the Lord

Lyon, there are three Heralds (Marchmont, Albany, Rothesay), and four Pursuivants (Carrick, Falkland, Unicorn, Kintyre).

The steep East Register St., beside the Register House, ascends to *St. James's Square*, a characteristic and little altered relic of 18th cent. Edinburgh, where Robert Burns lived in 1787 ; and where also St. Ives and Rowley lodged with Mrs. McRankine.—In or near West Register St. was the tavern in which Christopher North held his Noctes Ambrosianæ.

Beyond the North British Station Hotel is the flat roof (laid out with flower-beds) of the *Waverley Market*, now used for flower shows, etc., beside which opens the wide approach to the *Waverley Bridge* (rebuilt in 1896) and to *Waverley Station* (Pl. 19, 26). From this point westward Princes St. is flanked on its S. side by attractive public gardens, which descend into the valley once occupied by the old *Nor'* or *North Loch* (finally drained in 1816) and are embellished at the street level with monuments to distinguished Scotsmen. In East Princes Street Gardens are statues of Dr. Livingstone (1813–73), Prof. John Wilson (Christopher North, 1785–1854) and Adam Black (1784–1874) and the *Scott Monument,* a graceful Gothic spire, 200 ft. high, forming a canopy over a statue of Sir Walter Scott (1771–1832) with his dog, Maida, by Steell. The monument, in the niches of which are figures of characters in Scott's works, was erected in 1840–44 from the design of George Kemp, an architect of humble birth who did not live to see his plans completed. An interior staircase (adm. 3*d.* ; weekdays 10–7, in winter 10–3) ascends to the top (view), passing a chamber with a few relics of Scott.

The **Mound** (Pl. 25), which separates East and West Princes Street Gardens, was made with the earth dug from the foundations of the New Town and affords the most convenient approach from Princes St. to the Castle and the Old Town. At its foot are two important classical edifices by W. H. Playfair. Nearest to Princes St., in a Doric building originally known as the *Royal Institution* (founded in 1823), are the galleries of the **Royal Scottish Academy,** whose exhibition is held annually from April to August (adm. 1/). The *Diploma Collection* and the collection of the *Scottish Modern Arts Association*, entered by the door at the S.W. corner, are open free daily (10–4 or 5 ; closed on Sun. and during the Academy's exhibition).

Immediately behind is the *National Gallery (Pl. 25), erected in 1850–58 in the Ionic style, which contains an important though not large collection of paintings, embracing fine examples of the Italian, Dutch, and French schools as well as an admirable survey of British and especially Scottish art. Open free 10–4 or 5, Sun. 2–5.

Room I (left) contains the earlier paintings, including some good Italian work : *Bernardo Daddi*, Triptych ; *Filippino Lippi*, Holy Family and angels, a small work on panel ;

Perugino, Figures from a classical composition ; *Spanish School* (15th cent.), St. Michael ; *Clouet,* Mme de Canaples ; *Iac. del Sellaio,* Coronation procession ; *Van Orley,* Before the Crucifixion, Portrait of a Lady.—On stands in this room (and in R. XII, opposite) are exhibited the valuable Flemish *Paintings by *Hugo van der Goes,* formerly at Holyrood, and originally part of the altarpiece of Trinity College church (p. 50) : The Holy Trinity, and on the other side, James III and his son, James IV (c. 1474) ; St. Cecilia (a portrait of Mary of Gueldres) with Sir Edward Boncle, first Provost of Trinity College, and on the other side, Margaret of Denmark, consort of James III.—R. II. Later Italian Schools. *Iac. Bassano,* Adoration of the Magi, Portrait of a gentleman ; *Veronese,* Mars and Venus, Madonna with St. Joseph and a donor, Venetian gentleman with St. Anthony Abbot ; *Tiepolo,* Finding of Moses ; *Tintoretto,* *Venetian family presented to the Madonna by St. Lawrence and a bishop ; *Guardi,* Views in Venice ; *Scorza,* Landscapes with figures. In a case : Bronzes after *Michelangelo.*

R. III. Dutch and Flemish Schools. Outstanding here are two *Portraits by *Frans Hals* and the *Portrait of Hendrikje Stoffels, by *Rembrandt.* Noteworthy also are : *Van Dyck,* The Lomellini family, Italian nobleman ; *J. Ruisdael,* River scenes ; *Rembrandt,* Portrait of the artist ; *Rubens,* Feast of Herod, *Head of St. Ambrose.—*El Greco,* *Salvator Mundi, St. Jerome ; *Velazquez,* *Old woman frying eggs, painted when the artist was 19 ; *Zurbarán,* Immaculate Conception.— R. IV. *Nic. Poussin,* The Seven Sacraments (from the Bridgewater Collection, see below).—R. V. The 17th and 18th centuries. *W. van de Velde,* Boats in a calm ; several examples of *Greuze* ; *Pater,* Ladies bathing ; *Poussin* (after Giov. Bellini), Feast of the gods ; *Lancret,* Toy windmill ; *Van Goyen,* Dutch river scene ; *Dirck van Deelen,* Architectural subject ; *David Teniers,* Peasants playing at skittles ; *Du Jardin,* Halt at winehouse ; *Vermeer,* *Christ in the house of Martha and Mary ; *Goya,* El medico ; *Jan Steen,* Physician and patient ; *Chardin,* Vase of flowers ; *Watteau,* Fête champêtre ; *Boucher,* Madame de Pompadour.—R. VI. French and Dutch schools of the 19th century. Examples of *Corot, Daubigny, Monticelli, Boudin, Mauve,* and *J.* and *W. Maris. Monet,* Poplars on the Epte ; *Boudin,* Port of Bordeaux ; *Degas,* Diego Martelli ; *Van Gogh,* Olive grove ; *Corot,* The artist's mother ; *C. Pissarro,* The Marne at Chennevières ; *Gauguin,* Jacob wrestling with the angel, Vision after the sermon ; *Fantin-Latour,* Flower paintings.— An anteroom contains paintings by Scots artists, including : *Sir David MacNee,* Lady in grey ; *D. O. Hill,* Leith Pier.

R. VII contains *Paintings on loan from the Bridgewater

Collection (lent by the Earl of Ellesmere), including out-standing examples of *Raphael* (*Holy Family with the palm tree, *Bridgewater Madonna), *Titian* (*Three Ages of Man), *Lor. Lotto*, *Rembrandt*, *Terborch*, *Jan Steen* (The schoolroom), *Poussin*, and *Claude*.—R. VIII. Scottish Painters 1800–50. *Andrew Geddes*, Summer, The artist's mother; *Patrick Nasmyth*, Landscapes; *R. S. Lauder*, *Portrait of Henry Lauder; *Wilkie*, Pitlessie Fair, Irish whiskey still, The artist's sister.—R. IX. *Portraits by *Sir Henry Raeburn* (1756–1823), a distinguished collection. Among the most attractive are those of *Rev. Robert Walker skating on Duddingston Loch, Mrs. R. Scott-Moncrieff, Mrs. Campbell of Balliemore, Mrs. Hamilton, Dr. Adam Rolland, Lady Dunbar, and Lord Newton.—R. X is devoted to exhibitions of prints and drawings.—R. XI. English Painters. *Gains-borough*, *Mrs. Graham, a delightful portrait, Suffolk land-scape; *Reynolds*, *The Ladies Waldegrave, Lady Frances Scott; *Hogarth*, Sarah Malcolm; *Hoppner*, Adm. Duncan; *Richard Wilson*, Italian landscape; *Cotman*, Buildings on a river; *Constable*, *Dedham Vale, Noon on Hampstead Heath; *Bonington*, Estuary, Grand Canal at Venice; characteristic examples of *Morland* and *Turner*.—R. XII. 17–18th cent. Scottish Schools. *Geo. Jamesone* (d. 1644), Lady Mary Erskine, Countess Marischal; examples of *John Alexander* and his son *Cosmo*, *David Allan*, and the brothers *Alex.* and *John Runciman*; *Allan Ramsay*, Portraits of *Mrs. David Cunyngham, Lady Robert Manners, J. J. Rousseau, *The Artist's wife, Mrs. Bruce of Arnot, and others; *Wm. Aikman*, Self-portrait.

The UPPER FLOOR is devoted to paintings by recent Scottish artists, notably *Wm. MacTaggart* (1835–1910), who revolutionised Scottish landscape painting; *Horatio McCulloch* (1805–67); the Glasgow School (*MacGregor*, *Guthrie*, *Hornel*); the Edinburgh painters, *Sir David Cameron*, *Pryde*, and *Peploe*; and others.

In West Princes St. Gardens the *Floral Clock*, just E. of the Mound, is an attractive summer feature. Allan Ramsay (1686–1758), the poet, Sir James Simpson (1811–70), who introduced the use of chloroform as an anæsthetic in 1847, and Dr. Thomas Guthrie (1803–73), the apostle of ragged schools, are honoured by statues. Here also, below street level, is the *Scottish American Memorial* (' The Call, 1914 '; by R. Tait McKenzie of Philadelphia) from men and women of Scottish blood and sympathies in the United States. Near the S.E. corner of the gardens, against the high ground of the Mound, is the *Royal Scots Memorial* (1952) by Sir Frank Mears. At the foot of the Castle rock (beyond the railway) is the ruined *Wellhouse Tower*, a relic of the town-wall of 1456.—An Iona Cross commemorates Dean Ramsay (1793–1872), long incumbent of the adjoining episcopal church of *St. John*, which has a ' Gothic revival ' nave of 1817, by William Burn. The choir was added in 1882, the Lady Chapel in 1935. Sir Henry Raeburn (1756–1823) is buried in the roofless mortuary chapel outside the E. end. Behind St. John's is the church of *St. Cuthbert* (Pl. 24), or the ' West Kirk,' an ancient foundation, rebuilt by Hippolyte Blanc in 1894 but retaining its tower of 1790. The vestibule contains a monument to John Napier of Merchiston (d. 1617). In its churchyard are the graves of Thomas de Quincey (1785–1859), George Kemp (1795–1844), architect of Scott's monument, Alex. Nasmyth (1758–1840), the painter, and many Edinburgh celebrities besides.—At the W. end of Princes St. is *Princes Street Station* (Pl. 24), with the Caledonian Hotel.

THE OLD TOWN : CASTLE, HIGH STREET, HOLYROOD

From Princes St. the direct approach to the Old Town is by the Mound (Pl. 25), which the visitor ascends in full view of the Castle and the towering ' lands ' of the ancient city. From the Black Watch Monument at the top of the Mound cars must make a detour viâ Bank St. (l.) and the Lawnmarket (r.) to reach the Castle Esplanade. Pedestrians may either follow the steps straight ahead, which afford a characteristic approach to the ' Royal Mile ' through Milne's Court (1690) ; or they may turn to the right, passing *New College* and the *Assembly Hall of the Church of Scotland*. In the quadrangle is a statue of John Knox (1505–72) by J. Hutchison. The two towers of the college are skilfully disposed so as to blend, architecturally, when seen from a distance, with the tall spire of the Tolbooth Church behind.

The General Assembly, the supreme court of the United Established Church, meets here annually for c. 10 days in May. The Sovereign is represented at its deliberations by a Lord High Commissioner (usually a Scottish nobleman, except when a Labour Government is in power), whose progresses, attended by a military escort, to and from Holyrood Palace, where he resides, provide one of the popular sights of Edinburgh.

The college (now occupied by the divinity faculty of the University) and the hall were originally founded after the Disruption of 1843 (p. 65) for the Free Church ; and until the final union of 1929 the Assembly of the Established Church met in the Tolbooth Church. In 1929 the first united General Assembly was held in a large hall in Annandale St., but since 1930 it has met here.

Farther on, Ramsay Lane ascends steeply to the Castle Esplanade, passing on the right a striking group of gabled and turreted buildings (1894) incorporating *Ramsay Lodge,* Allan Ramsay's last home, which was familiarly known as ' Goose-pie Lodge ' from its octagonal shape, and may still be made out on the S. side of the enclosing pile.

The original house, built by Allan Ramsay the elder in 1740 and occupied by his son until his death in 1784, was enlarged to form a University Hall of Residence, and is now a hostel and training centre for the Commercial Bank.

D

The *Castle Esplanade* (views), or parade ground, the spacious sloping approach to the Castle, was in ancient days the scene of many executions, and is embellished with military monuments, including an equestrian statue of Field-Marshal Earl Haig, presented by Sir Dunjibhoy Bomanji of Bombay. The ' Witches' Well ' here is a bronze fountain marking the place where witches were burnt in 1479–1722. The flight of steps at the S.E. corner descends to Johnston Terrace and so to the Grassmarket.

*Edinburgh Castle (Pl. 25) occupies a position of vantage at the W. extremity of the old town ridge, where it attains a height of 445 ft. above the sea and drops suddenly down on three sides in rocky precipices.

Admission. The precincts and War Memorial are open free in June–Aug. 9.30–9, Sept. 9.30–6, Feb.–May & Oct. 10–5, Nov.–Jan. 10–4 ; the Historical Apartments (Argyll Tower, St. Margaret's Chapel, Crown Room, Queen Mary's Room, Banqueting Hall, and United Services Museum) are open (adm. 1/, children 6d.) on weekdays at the same hours (except June–Aug when they close at 6), on Sun., in June–Aug. only, 11–6.

History. The Castle rock was no doubt the site of a very early settlement ; in monkish legends the spot appears as the Castrum Puellarum, or Maiden Castle, the safe retreat for the daughters of Pictish kings. The original, and very descriptive, name was *Duneadain* (fort on a slope) of which the present form is a translation ; its position as an outpost of Edwin's kingdom of Northumbria doubtless influenced the later spelling. Here Malcolm Canmore's sainted Queen Margaret died in 1093, soon after hearing of her husband's death at Alnwick ; and hence, to escape Donald Bane, who was besieging the castle, her body was stealthily conveyed away to Dunfermline by the West Sally Port (see below) and down the cliffs on the west. The Castle was one of the five fortresses surrendered by William the Lion to Henry II by the Treaty of Falaise in 1174. In 1296 it was taken by Edward I and it was held by the English until Randolph, Earl of Moray, recaptured it in 1313 by a daring escalade up the sheer southern face of the rock. The Castle, dismantled by Bruce, was given back to the English by Edward Balliol and re-fortified in 1337 by Edward III, but it was again taken by the Scots under Sir William Douglas in 1341. David II greatly strengthened the fortress, and died in 1371 in the keep he had begun. In 1439 James II, when a child of seven, is said to have been smuggled out of the Castle in a box by his mother, who feared the overweening influence of the Chancellor Crichton ; but he was present in 1440 when the young Earl of Douglas, invited to a banquet in the Castle, was seized and summarily executed. The appearance of a black bull's head upon the board was the intimation to the earl of his doom ; whence the murder is known as the ' Black Dinner.' In 1566 James VI was born in the Castle. Kirkcaldy of Grange held the Castle for Mary, Queen of Scots, in 1573, but after a desperate resistance in which much damage was wrought was forced to capitulate to the Regent Morton and his English auxiliaries, and was forthwith hanged. After the battle of Dunbar in 1650 Cromwell took the fortress after a brief siege, his threat of mining and blowing up the rock being effectual. He wrote to Speaker Lenthall : " I need not speak of the strength of the place which, if it had not come in as it did, would have cost very much blood to have attained, if at all to be attained." In 1745 the Castle refused to open its gates to Prince Charles Stewart, who was unable either to reduce or blockade it. During the Napoleonic wars French military prisoners were confined in the Castle, as described in Stevenson's ' St. Ives.' The 15th cent. office of Governor of Edinburgh Castle, in abeyance since 1860, was revived in 1936.

The entrance is across the moat and through an outer gateway (1888), flanked by figures of Bruce (l.) and Wallace (r.), to the *Portcullis Gate,* a vaulted archway beneath the

Constable's Tower, later called *Argyll's Tower*. The old state prison here, built by David II in 1369, was destroyed in the siege of 1573. The present gateway, begun after 1574, contains the dungeon in which the Marquess of Argyll was confined before his execution (1661), but is mainly a reconstruction of 1890. The flight of steps on the left is a direct approach to the highest part of the Castle, but we continue to follow the sloping carriage-way. Beyond the Argyll Battery (r.), named after the victor at Sheriffmuir (1715) and overlooking Princes St., are the hospital, governor's house, and barracks, behind which (but not shown) is the *West Sally Port*, through which Queen Margaret's body was carried (see above). Hither Claverhouse, the Bonny Dundee of Scott's stirring ballad, proudly leading his men from hostile Edinburgh to rouse the Highlands for James VII in 1689, climbed the rock for a last interview with the Duke of Gordon, who commanded the Castle. Turning to the left, we reach the *King's Bastion*, the highest platform of the Castle, on which stand Queen Margaret's Chapel and Mons Meg, with the Scottish National War Memorial to the right.

The *View from this point is famous. Ranging over the New Town of Edinburgh it extends E. down the Forth, N. to the Lomonds in Fife, the Forth Bridge, and the Ochils, W. to Ben Ledi and Ben Lomond.

St. Margaret's Chapel, whether used as an oratory by Queen Margaret (d. 1093) or founded in her honour by her son, David I (d. 1153), is one of the oldest ecclesiastical structures in Scotland. The tiny building (16½ ft. by 10½ ft.), the only Norman work in Edinburgh except the scanty survivals at Holyrood (p. 55), has a chancel arch with good zigzag mouldings and lozenge patterns. It was restored in 1853 by Queen Victoria (and again in 1887), and its windows (1921) show figures of St. Margaret, St. Andrew, St. Columba, St. Ninian, and William Wallace.

Mons Meg, regarded as a kind of Scottish palladium, is a huge piece of antique artillery made of long iron bars hooped together. One tradition asserts that it was made in 1486 at Mons in Hainault, another that it was forged at Castle Douglas by a blacksmith named McKim, who presented it to James II at the siege of Threave Castle in 1455 and received in return the lands of Mollance, whence the name 'Mollance Meg.' It was employed at the siege of Norham Castle in 1497, and the 'great iron murderer called Muckle-Meg' was among the captured guns listed by Cromwell as taken in the Castle in 1650. Mons Meg is referred to in Scott's 'Bonnie Dundee,' but by that time (1689) it was incapable of speaking even 'twa words or three,' for it had burst in 1682 while firing a salute in honour of the Duke of York, afterwards James VII. In 1754 it was removed to the Tower of London, but it was restored to Edinburgh in 1829 at the request of Sir Walter Scott, to the joy of the Scottish people. The gun-carriage is a reproduction of that used at Norham.

To the S. of the chapel is *Palace Yard* or *Crown Square*, a quadrangle surrounded by the most interesting buildings in the Castle. On its N. side, on the site of the ancient Castle church, rises the ***Scottish National War Memorial*** (opened in

1927), a dignified but not ornate building designed by Sir Robert Lorimer, incorporating some of the walls of the barracks that succeeded the church on this site. On the exterior are round-headed recesses in the random-coursed wall, with figures of the virtues, and stone panels with service badges and the insignia of the four Scottish divisions that fought in the First World War. Beyond the porch as we enter the Gallery of Honour extends on either hand. Facing us is the octagonal *Shrine*, entered through iron gates beneath a lofty sculptured archway. Here, on an outcrop of the Castle rock, stands the Stone of Remembrance, a block of green Italian marble, showing the Cross of Sacrifice, and bearing a wrought steel casket, containing records. The seven windows are filled with stained glass (by Douglas Strachan), depicting War as a mysterious element in the destiny of man ; below are reliefs (by Morris and Alice Meredith Williams) showing types of all who served in the war—men and women, animals, and even carrier pigeons. The *Gallery of Honour*, with a bay at each end, is divided by octagonal columns into recesses devoted to the twelve Scottish regiments, each with inscribed and carved panels and a record of battle-honours on the entablature. The stained-glass windows are representations of the war as seen at home at the different seasons of the year (S. wall) and service memorials. In the W. bay Women's War Services and the Air Force are commemorated, in the E. bay the Navy, Cavalry and Yeomanry, Artillery and Engineers.

The bronze medallion portrait of Earl Haig (1861–1928) in the E. bay is the sole individual commemoration that is to be admitted.

On the E. side of Crown Square is the old *Palace*, which probably dates from the 15th cent., with additions made in 1566 and 1615. A stairway ascends to the **Crown Room,** a bomb-proof vault in which the *Regalia,* the ' Honours of Scotland,' are shown within an iron cage.

The crown may be as old as the days of Bruce but was refashioned for James V before 1540, when the mound and cross at the top were added. It was last used for the coronation of Charles II at Scone (1651). The sceptre (1494, refashioned 1536), a gift from Pope Alexander VI, shows figures of the Madonna, St. James, and St. Andrew. The sword, a rich Italian work, was presented to James IV by Pope Julius II in 1507. The following objects were bequeathed by Cardinal York, the last of the Stewarts (d. 1807), to the Prince of Wales (afterwards George IV) ; the Collar and George of the Order of the Garter presented by Elizabeth I to James VI, James VI's badge of the Thistle, and a ring given by him to Charles I.—After their adventures at Dunnottar Castle (p. 288) the regalia were returned to Edinburgh, and on the Union of the parliaments in 1707 they were deposited in a strong chest (preserved here) and forgotten. A search made in 1818, at Sir Walter Scott's instigation, rediscovered them, safe and sound, to the relief of Scott and his countrymen.

In the S.E. corner of the square are **Queen Mary's Apartments,** containing furniture, plans, etc. In a small room on the ground floor James VI was born on June 19th, 1566. On the ceiling are his own initials and those of his mother, Mary, surmounted by a crown. The erroneous story that the infant James VI was lowered in a basket to the foot of the cliff from the window of this room is probably a confused reminiscence of the possible experience of his ancestor James II.

On the floor above these apartments is the E. section of the **Scottish United Services Museum,** comprising an entrance hall with Jacobite relics (and a fine view), the medal room and the Royal Air Force room. The W. section of the museum, of greater interest, is housed on the opposite side of Crown Square. The interesting and varied exhibits include the remarkable Colville Collection of Highland weapons, and a fine series of statuettes illustrating the changes in Scottish military uniform from 1633 to 1945. In the naval section are models of the 'Great Michael' (1511), the 'Yellow Caravel' (1468), and other famous Scottish warships. A reference collection of tartans, ancient and modern, is likewise included in the museum.

The **Old Parliament Hall,** or *Banqueting Hall,* on the S. side of the square, a handsome room 84 ft. long, 33 ft. wide and 45 ft. high, with an open timber roof, is mainly a rebuilding by James IV of an early-15th cent. structure. It was occasionally the meeting-place of the Estates of the Realm. It was the scene of the 'Black Dinner' in 1440 (p. 40), and here the Earl of Leven entertained Cromwell in 1648. Thereafter it fell into oblivion for c. 200 years, being subdivided into stories and used as a military hospital, but in 1892 it was restored at the expense of Wm. Nelson, publisher, and now contains ancient armour and weapons and similar historical relics.

To the right of Crown Square, and facing E., is the *Halfmoon Battery,* erected after the destruction of David's Tower in 1573, the remains of which it covers. From this battery royal salutes are fired and a time-gun is discharged daily (Sun. excepted) at 1 p.m., by the clock (i.e. following and changing with 'summer time'). A large ball, hoisted on a mast on the top of the Nelson Monument on the Calton Hill, is dropped, for the benefit of navigators at sea, at 1 p.m. mean time all the year round.

Behind the Halfmoon Battery is the entrance to the remains of **David's Tower** (no adm. at present). This formidable tower, the ancient royal keep, begun by David II in 1367, was battered down by English cannon during Kirkcaldy of Grange's famous defence; its ruins were completely masked by the Halfmoon Battery, and all but the name was forgotten until its remains were located in 1912 by a Royal Commission. The ruins, which are of several stories, include a casemate with a gun emplacement commanding the Lawnmarket, chambers used by Cromwell as water-tanks, the dungeon whence the Duke of Albany made a daring escape (1479), and the pitch-dark dungeon in which the beautiful Countess of Glamis was pent in 1537.

The dungeons below the Banqueting Hall, in one of which the 9th Earl of Argyll was confined before his execution in 1685, are not shown to visitors; nor are the quarters of the French prisoners, whence, as described in Stevenson's exciting romance, St. Ives and his companions escaped down the sheer face of the precipice.

We may quite the Castle by the flight of steps descending beside the Portcullis Gate.

That part of Edinburgh extending from the Castle by way of High Street and the Canongate to Holyrood is familiarly known as the **Royal Mile.** Extensive and sympathetic reconstruction along its route is gradually approaching completion. A traditional way of covering the distance is to take an open horse-drawn cab (occasionally on hire during the summer), with calls at St. Giles's and the Parliament House ; but no adequate exploration of High Street and the Canongate, with their ' closes,' can be made except on foot.

On the right, at the corner of Castle Hill, where it quits the Esplanade, is a house of 1630 with a cannon ball (said to date from 1745) in its gable and, behind, curious stone grooves or 'runnels' for outside shutters. On the left rises the *Outlook Tower* (adm. 2/, children 6*d.*, 10–6 or 8, Sun. 11.30–6), with an exhibition of Scottish crafts and a fine Camera Obscura. Just below is Milne's Court (p. 39) adjoining the site of a house occupied by Mary of Guise, mother of Queen Mary ; and on the right is *Tolbooth St. John's,* called 'the Highland Church,' built in 1842–44 by Gillespie Graham and A. W. N. Pugin, with a noble tower and spire (240 ft.) attr. to Thos. Hamilton.

The *Free Church Assembly* meets in St. Columba's, at the head of the Upper Bow, which led down (r.) to the West Bow and the Grassmarket. In the West Bow (much changed) once lived Lord Ruthven, one of the murderers of Rizzio, and also Major Weir, a notorious criminal and reputed warlock, who was burned with his sister in 1670.

We now enter the LAWNMARKET, the W. part of High St., once crowded with the stalls and booths of linen-sellers. On the left rises the lofty **Gladstone's Land** (No. 483 ; 1631), with its unique arcaded ground floor and fine painted ceilings. It now belongs to the National Trust and is leased to the patriotic Saltire Society (adm. free, weekdays 2–6 on application to caretaker ; occasional exhibitions held). Also on this side is *James's Court,* with a flat occupied by David Hume and afterwards by James Boswell, who entertained Paoli here in 1771 and Dr. Johnson in 1773. Opposite is the double *Riddle's Close.* In the outer court Hume began his 'History of England,' and in the inner, or *Macmorran's Close,* is the fine late-16th cent. house of Bailie Macmorran, who was shot while quelling a barring-out of High School boys in 1595. His son entertained James VI here in 1598. Between this and Fisher's Close a restored late-16th cent. tenement is occupied by the *Scottish Central Library* (opened 1953) ; and on the same side is *Brodie's Close,* where lived the hypocritical Brodie, 'Deacon of the Wrights' and reputable citizen by day but a burglar by night, who was hanged in 1788 by a drop improved by himself and has provided material for a play by W. E. Henley and R. L. Stevenson. In *Lady Stair's Close,* opposite (l.), is **Lady Stair's House** (10–4, Sat. 10–1 ; adm. 6*d.*), with prints and autographs of Scott, Burns, and Stevenson, antiquities, etc. The house (1622), built by Sir

William Gray and restored and presented to the City by Lord
Rosebery, his descendant, was occupied by the Countess
Dowager of Stair (d. 1731), a leader of society whose history
as Lady Primrose (during her first marriage) is the basis of
Sir Walter Scott's story of 'My Aunt Margaret's Mirror.'
Burns lodged in 1786 in a house (now gone) in the same close.

At the foot of the Lawnmarket is a busy crossroads. On the left Bank St.
comes in from the Mound ; on the right Melbourne Place leads S. to George IV
Bridge and the National Library (p. 49).

We proceed down the HIGH STREET proper, passing (r.) the
County Buildings (1902–3) and (l.) the new *Sheriff Court*
(1936) and *Advocates' Close*, with a picturesque turret, which
leads down to Waverley Bridge. Just beyond the statue of the
5th Duke of Buccleuch (d. 1884), note a heart-shaped design
in the causeway and a line of white 'setts' marking the site
of the *Old Tolbooth*, or prison, the 'Heart of Midlothian,'
which plays its part in Scott's famous romance.

Built about 1466, perhaps as a chapter house or provost's house for St. Giles's,
and extended by the New Tolbooth (after 1561) behind, the building was used
by the parliament, the law courts, and the town council, but later degenerated
into a prison, which was stormed by the Porteous Mob in 1736. Here were
exposed the heads of the Regent Morton (1581), the Marquess of Montrose (1650),
and the Marquess of Argyll (1661). The Tolbooth was pulled down in 1817 and
its doorway and keys are now at Abbotsford. The same year saw the demolition
of the **Luckenbooths** (i.e. locked shops), a picturesque but obstructive block in
the middle of the street farther E. At the E. end was Allan Ramsay's famous
shop. The passage between the Luckenbooths and St. Giles's was known as the
Krames, from the numerous little booths built against the wall of the church.

No. 347 High St. was the first home of the '*Scotsman*' newspaper (1817–55) ;
the first daily issue appeared from No. 257 in the latter year. In 1864 the office
removed to Cockburn St.

The Gothic ***Church of St. Giles** (Pl. 26), the principal
church in Edinburgh, has lost much of its once great architectural beauty through alterations and unhappy restorations,
but its square central tower still raises unspoiled the famous
'Crown of St. Giles,' while the interior has been restored to
dignity and beauty. The church, usually entered by the N.
door, is open daily, 10–5 (adm. to the Thistle Chapel, 3*d.*).
Services on Sun. at 11 a.m. and 6.30 p.m. ; on weekdays at
12 noon.

History. A church of St. Giles is supposed to have existed here in the 9th
cent. and was replaced by a Norman structure c. 1120, which was destroyed
by Richard II of England in 1385. The present building was erected by degrees
between c. 1387 and the middle of the 15th cent., the tower dating from c. 1495.
In 1466 it was made a collegiate church, of which the poet Gavin Douglas became
the provost. After the Reformation the forty-four altars of the church were
removed, the statue of St. Giles was thrown into the Nor' Loch, and John
Knox became minister of St. Giles (1559–72). Subsequently the building was
divided by partitions, at first into two, then into four, and finally (until the
restoration of 1872) into three churches. In 1633, under Charles I, a short-lived
bishopric of Edinburgh was established, with St. Giles's as the cathedral. Here,
on July 23rd, 1637, occurred a legendary incident, when Jenny Geddes, a market-
woman, incensed at hearing Laud's service book being read from the pulpit,
threw her stool at the head of Dean Hannay, the officiating minister, and so
" struck the first blow in the great struggle for freedom of conscience, which after

a conflict of half a century ended in the establishment of civil and religious liberty." St. Giles's was again a cathedral under Charles II, but lost that title when episcopacy was disestablished in Scotland at the Revolution of 1688. In 1829–33 a disastrous restoration ruined the W. parts of the church and demolished many of the ancient side chapels ; but the operations of 1872–83, carried on mainly at the expense of Dr. William Chambers, publisher (d. 1883), have had happier results, especially in the interior. In 1911 the elaborate little chapel of the Order of the Thistle was added at the S.E. angle of the church.

INTERIOR. The interior, though somewhat sombre, is dignified and impressive in a way differing from most other Presbyterian churches. The church contains numerous memorials to famous Scots, the colours of Scottish regiments hang in the nave, and many of the stained-glass windows are interesting. The vaulted stone roof of the choir deserves notice ; the two E. bays, with fluted columns, are of later date than the rest. Entering by the N. door, we first cross the church to the **Preston Aisle,** S. of the S. choir aisle, founded in honour of Sir William Preston of Gorton, who presented the church with an arm-bone of St. Giles (1454). The royal pew, by the S. wall, is occupied by the Lord High Commissioner when he attends service.

To the S. of the ante-chapel is the small but highly ornate **Chapel of the Thistle** (adm. 3*d.*), designed by Sir Robert Lorimer and opened in 1911. The lofty groined roof, the elaborate canopies of the carved oak stalls, the heraldic windows, and the other embellishments are very effective. The old Gothic entrance doorway (1387) was the original S.W. doorway of St. Giles's. The Most Ancient and Most Noble Order of the Thistle, the premier Order in Scotland, consists of the sovereign and sixteen knights. The chapel was erected from funds originally bequeathed by the 11th Earl of Leven for restoring Holyrood Abbey, the former chapel of the Order, which, however, was found impracticable.

In the S.W. angle of the Preston aisle is the **Chepman Aisle,** founded by Walter Chepman (d. 1532), the ' Scottish Caxton.' Beneath its floor are the remains of the Marquess of Montrose (d. 1650), whose monument is on the E. wall.

From the Preston Aisle we cross the S. transept and enter the *Side Chapel,* in which a daily service is held. On the W. wall is a monument in bronze relief to Robert Louis Stevenson (1850–94) by Augustus St. Gaudens ; on the S. wall are medallions to Dr. John Brown (1810–82), Mrs. Oliphant (1828–97), Dr. Thomas Chalmers (1780–1847), and others. On the pavement at the entrance from this chapel into the nave is a tablet marking the traditional spot whence Jenny Geddes launched her missile (see above). Opening off the S.E. corner of the chapel is the **Moray Aisle** (formerly the Holy Blood Aisle), with a modern monument (1864) to the Regent Moray (? 1531–70), bearing a Latin inscription by George Buchanan. The window, by Sir Noël Paton, depicts the murder of Moray at Linlithgow, and John Knox preaching his funeral sermon. The font, near the W. end of the S. aisle, is a reproduction of Thorwaldsen's well-known work at Copenhagen. The bronze statue of John Knox is by MacGillivray (1906).

We cross the nave to the **Albany Aisle** (in the N.W. angle of the church), said to have been founded by the Duke of Albany in expiation of the murder of the Duke of Rothesay (1402; p. 262), and rededicated in 1951 as a memorial to members of the congregation who died in the Second World War. On the walls are military memorials, including one to Scottish soldiers who fell in France in 1914–18, placed by the French colony in Edinburgh.

To the E., near the N. door of the church, is *St. Eloi's* or the *Hammermen's Chapel*, in which was dedicated the famous

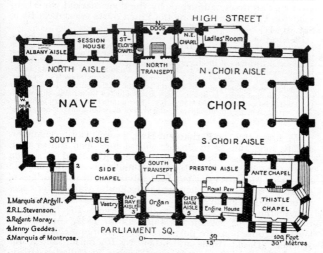

1. Marquis of Argyll.
2. R.L. Stevenson.
3. Regent Moray.
4. Jenny Geddes.
5. Marquis of Montrose.

'Blue Blanket,' the craftsmen's banner which was presented by James III and accompanied the burgesses to Flodden. The name is said to have been first used, in contempt, by James VI. In this chapel is the handsome monument of the covenanter Marquess of Argyll, beheaded in 1661. The *N.E. Chapel*, on the other side of the N. entrance, restored as a memorial to William Chambers, is now used as a Chapel of Youth. In the N. choir aisle is a tablet to Dr. Elsie Inglis (1864–1917), founder of the Scottish Women's Hospital in the Balkans. The reredos at the E. end was a gift (1953) of the Merchant Company.

Upon the pillars of the crossing, which date from the 12th cent., are memorial brasses to Gavin Douglas (Provost in 1501), who 'died in exile at London 1522,' Abp. Leighton (Principal of the University, 1653–62), and other noted Scots.

PARLIAMENT SQUARE, once *Parliament Close*, behind St.
Giles's, was originally part of the churchyard, and here a
small inscription in its pavement, nearly opposite the S.
transept, marks the *Grave of John Knox* (I.K. 1572). Close
by is a leaden equestrian statue of Charles II, erected in 1685.

The **Parliament House** (Pl. 26), on the S. side of the square,
was completed in 1640, but the original Gothic façade was
replaced in 1808–14 by the present façade in the Italian taste.
The building, in which the Scottish Parliament met until
the Union in 1707, is now used by the Courts of Justice, and
strangers are freely admitted, by the door marked No. 11, to
visit the Parliament Hall or the Law Courts (weekdays 10–5,
Sat. 10–1).

The Court of Session, the supreme civil court of Scotland, with 13 judges,
includes the Outer and Inner House. The five Lords Ordinary sit singly in
the courts of the Outer House, which are courts of first instance, while the First
and Second Divisions of the Inner House (equal in authority), have each four
judges, presided over respectively by the Lord President and the Lord Justice-
Clerk, and hear appeals from the Lords Ordinary and from Sheriffs of counties.
The judges of the Court of Session form also the High Court of Justiciary, or
supreme criminal court, in which causes are conducted by a public prosecutor,
the Lord Advocate or one of his deputies. The number of the jury is fifteen;
a majority is sufficient to decide; and the verdict may be ' guilty,' ' not guilty,'
or ' not proven.'

We first enter the **Parliament Hall,** a noble Gothic chamber,
122 ft. long and 49 ft. broad, with a fine open timber roof.
This is now the waiting hall of the courts, and in session
time (mid-May to mid-July and mid-Oct. to mid-March;
except on Mon.) is crowded with advocates in wig and gown,
' writers ' and other solicitors, and clients, waiting for cases
to be called. The large window of Munich glass at the S. end
(where the throne used to stand) represents the Institution
of the Court of Session by James V in 1532. Among the
legal portraits here are portraits of Sir George Mackenzie, by
Kneller ; David Hume and others by Raeburn ; and a fine
statue, by Roubillac, of Duncan Forbes of Culloden (1685–
1747). The law courts are entered from the corridor adjoining
the S. end of the hall. Sir Walter Scott was clerk of the First
Division ; beside the library entrance is his statue (1831) by
Greenshields.

A glass door on the W. side of the Parliament Hall admits
to the *Advocates' Library*, founded c. 1682, when Sir George
Mackenzie (' Bluidy Mackenzie ') was Dean of the Faculty of
Advocates, and formally opened as a law library in 1689.

The library soon developed into a general library, and from 1709 was given
the right to claim a copy of every book published in Britain. Thanks to the
enlightened policy of the Faculty of Advocates and the efforts of distinguished
Keepers of the Library (including Ruddiman and Hume) the library became an
intellectual centre and was, in fact, a national library long before the Faculty,
in 1922, offered it to the nation (reserving for themselves the specifically legal
works). This generous offer, supplemented by a donation of £100,000 from
Sir Alex. Grant of Forres as an endowment, was accepted in 1925, and the library

was transferred to the State under the name of the National Library of Scotland. The call for new buildings was met by a further £100,000 from Sir Alex. Grant ; and plans were approved in 1936.—A new use for the Laigh Hall, in which the treasures of the library were formerly exhibited, has yet to be decided upon.

The ***National Library of Scotland** (open weekdays 9.30–4.30, Sat. 9.30–12.30, Thurs. also 5.30–8.30; closed last week of July and first week of Aug.) occupies a building to the W. of Parliament House, entered from George IV Bridge (Pl. 26). Designed by *Reginald Fairlie* (d. 1952), the building was begun in 1937 and opened in 1956. The main façade is adorned with statues by Hew Lorimer typifying seven branches of learning. Behind them is the long and lofty Reading Room, lit only from above. The books are stacked in seven lower floors, descending to the level of the Cowgate.

The Reading Room is normally open to holders of tickets for which a written application accompanied by a suitable recommendation must be sent in advance. Persons wishing to use the library for a single day may apply at the counter for permission.

The library possesses fine illuminated MSS. and specimens of early printing. The Department of Printed Books is especially strong in Scottish material. Among the MSS. which illustrate Scottish history, literature, and life, are the last letter of Mary, Queen of Scots, written on the eve of her execution, a copy of the National Covenant of 1638, the order for the Massacre of Glencoe, documents relating to the Jacobite risings, letters of Hume, Boswell, Burns, and Stevenson, and rich collections of letters and manuscripts of Scott and Carlyle. Some of these and other treasures are exhibited in the exhibition rooms on the right of the entrance.

We now resume our descent of the High Street. The **Mercat Cross,** a restoration at the expense of W. E. Gladstone (1885), incorporating part of the ancient shaft, stands between St. Giles's and the Police Office, which occupies the site of Old Fishmarket Close, once the abode of George Heriot (p. 61). Royal proclamations are made by the heralds from the gallery at the base of the shaft. On the left side of the street are the *City Chambers*, or *Municipal Buildings*, originally erected as the Royal Exchange in 1753–1761, with entrance-archways rebuilt in 1902.

In the quadrangle stands a group of Alexander and Bucephalus by Steell. Within (gratuity) are shown a good statue of Prince Charles Edward, engraved portraits of the Lord Provosts since 1557, and historical mural paintings by Wm. Hole.—In *Anchor Close* (No. 243 ; l.) the original ' Encyclopædia Britannica ' (1768–71) and the first Edinburgh edition of Burns were printed by Wm. Smellie. At the top of Cockburn St. (l. ; coming from Waverley Bridge), a tablet marks the site of the house in which Queen Mary spent the night of June 15th, 1567, after her surrender at Carberry Hill.

The **Tron Church** (Pl. 26 ; 1637–63), where the High St. intersects ' the Bridges,' received its name from a neighbouring public ' tron ' or weighing beam. Its wooden steeple was burned in 1824 and the present stone steeple was erected in 1828. Outside this church, which was closed in 1952 and is threatened with demolition in the interests of planning, the populace assemble on Hogmanay (Dec. 31st) to ' bring in '

the New Year. On either side of the church two parallel
streets—Blair St. and Niddrie St.—descend to the Cowgate
(Pl. 26). Allan Ramsay's first shop stood on the N. side of
High St., near *Carrubbers Close*, where he opened his unsuccessful theatre in 1736. *Old St. Paul's* in this close (entered
usually from Jeffrey St.) is the successor of the first episcopal
church in the city (1689), originally a wool store, and rebuilt
in 1882. Raeburn and Samuel Seabury (1729–96), first bishop
of the American church, were worshippers here. No. 107 High
St. is *Bailie Fyfe's Close*, with a good escutcheon. No. 101, with
the head of a boy on its front, is the 'Heave awa' House. A
tenement on this site collapsed in 1861, with great loss of life;
among those pinned down by the wreckage was a lad who
encouraged the rescuers by his plucky shout of " Heave awa'
Chaps ; I'm no deid yet."—Farther on the **John Knox House**
(Pl. 27 ; adm. weekdays 10–5, 6*d*.) dating from c. 1550,
projects into the street. On the W. side, just above the
ground floor, appears the inscription ' Lufe God abufe al and
yi nychtbour as yi self.' The house contains some memorials
of Knox, and 17th cent. painted panels, but the attribution
to the great reformer goes back only to 1784. His ' manse '
stood in Warriston Close, near the present City Chambers.
In Hyndford's Close, nearly opposite, is the *Museum of
Childhood* (adm. weekdays 10–5, 6*d*., children 3*d*.), a collection
of Victorian and later toys, schoolbooks, etc. The former
Moray-Knox church (l.) is now the *Art Centre*.

The entry below this admits to the cottage (to the left at the end) of the
caretaker of *Trinity College Church*. A collegiate church, founded in 1460 by
Mary of Gueldres, widow of James II, was taken down in 1849 to make way for
Waverley Station, and its stones were numbered for re-erection on a new site.
Litigation delayed the reopening until 1877, and the fine late-Gothic fragment
which forms an aisle at the E. end of the present church represents only a portion
of the original building.

Just below John Knox's House stood the *Netherbow*, the lower gate of the
city, which was removed in 1764 (site indicated in roadway). It was by this gate
(and not by the West Port) that Bonnie Dundee quitted the city in 1689, and it
was by this gate that Prince Charlie's Highlanders rushed the city in 1745.

To the left diverges *Jeffrey St.*, leading to the fruit and vegetable market ;
it has obliterated Leith Wynd, in which the ' Waverley Novels ' were first printed.
—*St. Mary's St.*, diverging to the right for the Cowgate, follows the line of the old
city boundary and of the Flodden Wall. At the White Horse Inn in Boyd's
Close, on its E. side, Dr. Johnson put up in 1773 before his tour to the Hebrides.

We now pass from the High Street into the **Canongate,**
the famous street that runs through the former burgh of
that name. The burgh (absorbed in 1856) was created by
charter of David I as the property of the abbey of Holyrood,
and this street was trod by the canons on their way to and
from their kirk in the Castle. Later many of the most eminent
of the Scots nobility built houses in the street, which, under
the sympathetic hand of the restorer, has regained much of
its former grandeur.

In fulfilment of the project for the rehabilitation of the Royal Mile (see p. 44) extensive works were begun in 1952 in the Canongate. Sections of modern buildings, with shops and flats, are being combined with those of old structures deemed worthy of survival.

In *Chessel's Court* (r. ; reconstructed) was the Excise Office, the burgling of which was Deacon Brodie's last crime ; and on the same side is *Playhouse Close,* named from the first theatre in Edinburgh, in which Home's ' Douglas ' was produced in 1747. *Little Jack's Land,* where David Hume lived in 1753–62 has gone ; but Nos. 176–184 Canongate and No. 1 St. John St. (r.) preserve the façade of the house where Smollett stayed with his sister in 1756. James Ballantyne, Scott's printer, was frequently visited by the ' Great Unknown ' at No. 10 St. John St.—**Moray House** (now a training college ; adm. free), on the right, was built by the Countess of Home in 1628–30, and passed to the Countess of Moray in 1645. It contains some interesting rooms with good ceilings, and beneath the large window is a balcony from which in 1650, ten years before his own execution, Argyll at his son's wedding-party beheld Montrose carried in a cart to his death at the Old Tolbooth.

Cromwell occupied this house in 1648 and 1650. At the date of the Union (1707) the Chancellor Seafield resided here, and the Treaty of Union was at least arranged in a small summer-house still shown in the garden, although for the actual signing the Commissioners are said, in fear of the populace, to have betaken themselves to a cellar beneath the present National Bank, at 179 High St. In fact, the articles were signed at Whitehall, in London.

On the opposite side of the street new blocks incorporate the façades of the 17th cent. *Bible Land* and the 18th cent. *Shoemakers' Land,* with their interesting carvings, and a reproduction of the 17th cent. *Morocco Land.* Just below is the *Canongate Tolbooth,* with its projecting clock, built in 1591. Over the door is the motto ' pro patria et posteris.' It is now part of the City Museum (open weekdays 10–5, 6*d.*) and includes an early 17th cent. ceiling from Nisbet of Dirleton's House in the Canongate. Next door is **Canongate Church,** beside which is a replica of the Old Canongate Cross. The church was built in 1688 by James Smith to house the parishioners ejected from Holyrood by James VII. It was well restored in 1947–50 ; the early-19th cent. pulpit was used by Dr. Chalmers in the old West Port kirk.

In the churchyard, in the first side-path on the left, N. of the church, is the simple tombstone raised by Robert Burns over the grave of Robert Fergusson (1751–74), the poet. Adam Smith (1723–1790) lies in the S.W. corner of the cemetery near the Tolbooth ; beside him, Dr. Gregory (1753–1821). On the E. cemetery wall, almost opposite Fergusson's grave, is the tomb, with portrait-bust, of Burns's ' Clarinda ' (Mrs. Agnes Maclehose ; d. 1841). Dugald Stewart (1753–1828) lies in a vault near the foot of the churchyard, where a red granite cross commemorates soldiers who died in the garrison of Edinburgh between 1692 and 1886.

On the other side of the street is HUNTLY HOUSE, or the *Speaking House* (1570), the only timber-fronted house remaining in the city, with four Latin aphorisms on its façade (copies ; originals preserved inside). This has been restored to receive the ***City Museum** (Pl. 27 ; weekdays 10–5, Wed. also in June–Sept. 6–9, adm. 6*d.*), with collections of great interest and value to the student of the history of the city, including panelling from demolished houses in the Cowgate, as well as important Burns and Scott collections (MSS. and relics).

On the opposite side of Bakehouse Close, from which Huntly House is entered, is *Acheson House* (1633), with a picturesque courtyard, well seen from the outside stair in the close. The house has been well restored and is now the *Scottish Craft Centre* (Mon.–Fri. 10–12.30, 2–5.30, Sat. 10–12.30). Just below it, in the Canongate, is an old doorway, with quaint inscription, removed from Anchor Close. *Panmure House*, opposite, where Adam Smith lived in 1778–90, has been restored (1958) to house a boys' club. Lower down (r.) is the 17th cent. *Queensberry House*, dismantled in 1801 by ' Old Q,' and now a home for the aged. The poet Gay (1685–1732) visited here as secretary to the wife of the 3rd Duke of Queensberry, while boarding at an inn across the street. Within Galloway's Entry, nearly opposite, was *Whitefoord House*, once belonging to the Earl of Winton, now the Naval and Military Veterans' Residence and Workshops. It occupies the site of ' the Lord Seyton's Lugeing ' into which Roland Graeme (in ' The Abbot ') followed Catherine Seyton with such headlong haste. *White Horse Close* (l.), well restored, is a picturesque survival. The White Horse Inn here, dating from c. 1623, was a famous inn at which journeys in the 17th and 18th cent. between Edinburgh and London usually began and ended ; and here Captain Waverley (in ' Waverley ') put up.—Opposite the foot of the Canongate stands Holyrood Palace, with Holyrood Abbey behind it.

At the foot of the Canongate the ' Girth Cross ' once marked the W. bounds of the ' Sanctuary ' of Holyrood, which until the abolition of imprisonment for debt in 1880 furnished a refuge for insolvent debtors. In 1816 the sanctuary sheltered 116 of these ' abbey lairds,' who dwelt in some old houses (demolished in 1857), S. of the palace. The sanctuary limits included the grounds to the E. of the Palace, Salisbury Crags and Arthur's Seat, a circuit of at least four miles.— To the left, near what was once the Watergate, is a curious little turreted lodge called *Queen Mary's Bathroom*, by which the murderers of Rizzio are supposed to have left the Palace. A dagger found in the roof many years ago is conjectured to have belonged to one of them.

The ***Palace of Holyroodhouse,** or *Holyrood Palace* (Pl. 21), the chief royal palace in Scotland and the residence of Mary, Queen of Scots, for six tragic years, is a somewhat unimposing building in a French style surrounding a quadrangle.

Admission. In the absence of the Court or the Lord High Commissioner it is open to visitors in June–Sept. on weekdays 9.30–6, Sun. 11–6 ; other times on weekdays 10–4 or 5, Sun. 1–4 or 2–5 ; adm. 1/, children 6d. In summer there is a tea room at the Abbey Strand, by the main gate.

History. Holyrood Palace was begun c. 1500 by James IV, and James V is said to have built the N.W. pavilion or tower partly in front of the abbey church in order to command a view up the Canongate. It bears his badge and that of his queen, Mary of Guise. Completed in its first state by James V, the palace was burned down (all but the N.W. portion) by the Earl of Hertford in 1544 and again injured in 1547. Mary, Queen of Scots, spent only six years at Holyrood, but from these years dates its halo of tragic romance. Hither the young widowed queen came from France in 1561, here took place her famous interview with John Knox, the murder of Rizzio, and her hasty marriage with Bothwell. Since the departure of James VI in 1603 to ascend the English throne, Holyrood has never been the residence for any length of time of any British crowned head. Cromwell occupied it in 1650 and restored it after a fire. In the reign of Charles II the palace was enlarged to its present extent by the autocratic Duke of Lauderdale, who, carrying back the line of James V's N.W. tower, ruthlessly destroyed the S.W. tower of the abbey church to make room for additions designed by Sir Wm. Bruce of Balcaskie. The S.W. tower, matching James V's tower, was likewise added. In 1745, from Sept. 17th till Oct. 31st, Prince Charles Stewart held his gay court at Holyrood, beneath the guns of the hostile Castle, though he often passed the night with his troops at Duddingston. In the following January the Duke of Cumberland is said to have slept in the bed once occupied by the Young Chevalier. The Comte d'Artois (afterwards Charles X of France) occupied a suite of rooms in the palace for some years after 1795, and again, as an exiled monarch, in 1830–32. Queen Victoria occasionally used the palace on her journeys to and from Balmoral ; Edward VII, as a boy, spent some months here in 1859 when studying in Edinburgh ; and the visits of his successors have been more frequent. In 1947 the Order of St. John of Jerusalem was revived in Scotland at Holyroodhouse, after a lapse of 414 years.

The spacious FORECOURT in front of the Palace is enclosed by fine wrought-iron gates, which, together with the statue of the King in his robes as Knight of the Thistle in its N. part, form the *National Memorial to Edward VII*. The fountain in the centre of the square is a reproduction (1859) of one in Linlithgow Palace. The low buildings opposite the Palace are the Guardhouse and Royal Stables and the Abbey Court-house.

On entering the Palace we turn to the left and ascend to the **Historical Apartments** on the first floor, entering first the PICTURE GALLERY, 150 ft. long, hung with the portraits of over 100 Scottish kings, who, as Sir Walter Scott observes, " if they ever existed, lived several hundred years before the invention of oil-painting." These were a government commission executed in 1684–86 by Jacob de Wet, of Haarlem. In this hall, in 1567, Queen Mary was married to Bothwell, within three months of Darnley's death. It was the scene of the ball given in 1745 by the Young Chevalier, as described in Scott's ' Waverley,' and is used for the banquets of the Lord High Commissioner and for the election of Scottish representative peers to Parliament. In a glass case by the windows are objects found in the course of excavations in the abbey grounds ; in the central case is a 15th cent. MS. copy of the Holyrood Ordinale, the service book used in the chapel royal.

On this same floor are DARNLEY'S APARTMENTS, comprising an audience chamber, bedroom, and dressing-room, and communicating by a private stair in the thickness of the wall with the Queen's apartments above. They contain tapestry, several portraits, old furniture, etc.—In QUEEN MARY'S APARTMENTS, on the second floor, we first enter the *Audience Chamber*, where Knox had his famous interview with the young queen in 1561. A small oratory opens into the thickness of the wall. The coffered ceiling, its panels decorated with heraldic achievements or with the crowned initials J.R. and M.R. (for James V and his queen) is original, as are portions of the painted frieze, and the horn windows (over the entrance-door). In a window recess is a facsimile of Mary's last letter, written to her brother-in-law, Henri III of France, on the eve of her execution. A brass plate on the floor at the door indicates the spot where Rizzio's body was left by his murderers. The alleged indelible stain of his blood is (if it exist) concealed by the floor covering. In the *Queen's Bedroom*, where the initials on the coffered ceiling are repeated, is an ancient bed shown, on very doubtful authority, as Queen Mary's ; the workbox is more probably hers. A painted plaster frieze was uncovered in 1957. Opening off this room are two tower-cabinets, one being the *Queen's Dressing Room*, the other the *Queen's Supper Room* (near the head of the privy staircase).

On March 9th, 1566, Mary and a small party, including David Rizzio or Riccio, an accomplished Italian secretary and skilful musician, were at supper here, when they were surprised by Darnley, Ruthven, and other conspirators. Suspecting their purpose, Rizzio threw himself behind the Queen, grasping her robe. Darnley, seizing the Queen, held her fast in his arms, while her wretched favourite was torn from his hold, dragged through the two outer rooms, and left a corpse with fifty-six dagger wounds at the head of the staircase. Jealousy of Rizzio's political influence with the Queen, and perhaps a darker suspicion in Darnley's mind, are the motives ascribed for the crime.

From the end of the Picture Gallery parties are admitted every ½ hr. to view the STATE APARTMENTS. These rooms, used by the Sovereign when in residence, were panelled in Scottish oak, redecorated, and appropriately refurnished in 1932–33. There are several fine 17th cent. ceilings, and tapestries of the same period, and overmantels by Jacob De Wet. The rooms are usually shown in the following order: *Queen Victoria's Breakfast Room* ; *Prince Albert's Dressing Room* ; *Queen Victoria's Bedroom* ; *Ante-Room* ; with a portrait of Queen Mary by David Jagger ; *Morning Drawing Room*, with chairs covered with sewn or embroidered work executed by noble ladies for Queen Mary (1921–23) ; *Evening Drawing Room* ; *Throne Room*, with the throne of George IV and several portraits, including a magnificent equestrian group of Charles I and the Comte de St-Antoine, by *Van Dyck*. In the *Ante-room* beyond are George III and Queen Charlotte, by Reynolds; in the *West Drawing Room*, portraits of Mary of Gueldres, Margaret Tudor, and others.

On the *Grand Staircase* stands Lady Nairne's sedan chair. The *Household Dining Room* was used as a private chapel by Charles X.

Holyrood Abbey, the Chapel Royal, of which only the ruined nave remains, is entered from the N.E. angle of the Palace inner quadrangle.

History. Holyrood Abbey, the Abbey of the Holy Cross, was founded in 1128 for Augustinian Canons by David I, that 'sair sanct for the crown' as James I called him. The king's motive is said to have been gratitude for his escape, through the miraculous interposition of a cross, from being gored to death by a stag while hunting; but more matter-of-fact authorities connect the name of the abbey with a fragment of the True Cross which once belonged to St. Margaret, his mother. The abbey, mitred in 1379, was a regular residence of the court under the first three Jameses, who probably preferred it to their bleaker quarters in the Castle. It suffered severely in 1544 when Hertford burned it, and again in 1547. James II was born (1430) and crowned at Holyrood, and he, James III, and James IV, were married in the church, where, likewise, Mary was wedded to Darnley in 1565. David II, James II, James V, and Darnley now rest in the royal vault here, whither the remains of Mary of Gueldres were brought from Trinity College Church in 1849. Rizzio is also buried in the chapel. In 1633 the building was sumptuously fitted up by Charles I, who was crowned here. Though under Charles II it became a chapel royal, it was deprived of one of its W. towers by Lauderdale. Under James VII it was the chapel of the Order of the Thistle, 'revived' by him in 1687. At the Revolution in 1688 the church was sacked though not materially damaged by the Presbyterian mob; the present ruinous state of the church is mainly due to the collapse in 1768 of an over-heavy stone roof which had been erected during a 'restoration' in 1758.

The finest portion of the church is the West Front, which, before the destruction of the S.W. tower, was the widest in Scotland, next to that of St. Giles. The existing N.W. tower (with the tomb of Viscount Belhaven, 1639) is small but richly arcaded, and near it is a doorway composed of six shafts and orders of mouldings with foliage exquisitely undercut, though now much blackened. The flying buttresses on the N. wall should be noted. The nave consisted of eight bays with aisles; the blind arcading on each side (later on the N.) is noteworthy. A Norman doorway to the cloisters, at the S.E. end, is a fragment of the original building of David I; the remainder dates from the early part of the 13th century. After the destruction of the choir, the vault at the S.E. end of the nave was used as the royal sepulchre. Recent excavations have revealed the foundations of the E. parts of the church and also of the chapter-house.

To the S.E. of Holyrood extends the KING'S PARK, 4 m. round, embracing **Arthur's Seat** (823 ft.; view), a hill of volcanic origin, the ascent of which is nowhere difficult (easiest from Dunsappie Loch). The name is probably a corruption of ' Archers' Seat ' and has no connection with King Arthur. The base of the hill is encircled by the *Queen's Drive*, commanding interesting views. Joining this road to the S. of the Palace, we turn to the left (E.), passing the pretty Gothic *St. Margaret's Well*, which dates from James IV's days and was brought from Restalrig. On the hill, to the right, is *St. Anthony's Chapel*, a small ruin beside a spring, W. of which a path leads to the top of Arthur's Seat. Beyond the little *St. Margaret's Loch* a branch diverges (l.) towards an exit from the park, beside which is *Muschat's Cairn*, the scene of a murder in 1720, where Jeanie Deans met Robertson, her sister's seducer ('Heart of Midlothian'). The drive sweeps round the W. side of the hill, passing *Dunsappie Loch* and *Duddingston*

Loch, a skating resort, now public property and a bird sanctuary. The pretty village of **Duddingston**, reached by a lower road, has a church with a Norman S. door and chancel arch ; at its gate are a ' loupin'-on stane,' to assist riders to the saddle, and the jougs. The N., or Prestonfield, aisle was added c. 1730–40. John Thomson (1778–1840), the landscape painter (' Thomson of Duddingston '), was minister here from 1805, when the Curling House Tower beside the loch served as his studio. Scott was an elder here, and *Peffermill House*, across the valley, is claimed as the original of ' Dumbiedykes.' Duddingston House, E. of the village, was built in 1768 by Sir Wm. Chambers for the Earl of Abercorn. Passing above the precipice known as ' Samson's Ribs,' the road descends to St. Leonard's Gate, to the N.W. of which is St. Leonard's Hill, with Davie Deans's Cottage. Skirting the base of *Salisbury Crags*, the bold W. front of Arthur's Seat, behind which lies the Hunter's Bog (now a rifle range), where David Balfour's naïve courage disarmed Lieut. Duncansby, we complete the circle at Holyrood again. The high path at the immediate foot of the rocks of Salisbury Crags is known as the ' Radicals' Road,' and was made or improved in 1819 by the unemployed, on the suggestion of Sir Walter Scott, who is said often to have walked here.

The Old Town : Grassmarket, Greyfriars, University

Quitting the W. end of Princes St. by Lothian Road (Pl. 24) and skirting St. Cuthbert's cemetery, we follow the drab King's Stables Road, once a tilting ground, to the Grassmarket. High above us, on the Castle rock, on our left, we note the West Sally Port of the fortress. The **Grassmarket** (Pl. 32), where no markets are held now, is a large oblong open space, occupying a hollow at the S. base of the Castle rock. It was the starting-point for many local carriers, including Jock Noble, of ' Rab and his Friends,' whose howff was the Harrow Inn at the Cowgatehead. Burns and Wordsworth were among the patrons of the old White Hart Inn on the N. side ; and some old houses farther E., at the foot of the West Bow have been well restored.

For over a century after 1660 the Grassmarket was the place of execution, and here most of the Covenanting martyrs for conscience' sake suffered, or, in the scoffing phrase of the Earl of Rothes, ' glorified God in the Grassmarket.' The site of the gallows is marked by a cross in the pavement at the E. end of the open space, close to the spot where the West Bow, the shortest route from the Tolbooth, debouches ; hence the distich quoted by Scott :

" Up the Lawnmarket and down the West Bow,
Up the big ladder and down the short tow."

Here, too, culminated the **Porteous Riot** in 1736. The execution of a man named Wilson, who had been condemned for no heinous crime in the eyes of the populace (see p. 267), and had won admiration by his self-devotion in assisting the escape of his comrade, Robertson, was followed by disorder, in which missiles were hurled at the executioner and his guards. Captain Porteous, the unpopular commander of the City Guards, fearing a riot, injudiciously ordered his men to fire, and a number of spectators at windows overlooking the scene were killed. Porteous was thereupon tried for murder and unanimously found guilty, but was reprieved by Queen Caroline. A well-organised mob, however, broke into the Tolbooth where he was confined, and dragging him to the Grassmarket hanged him on a dyer's pole immediately opposite the place of the gallows.

The *West Port*, the street leading from the S.W. angle of the Grassmarket, was the old W. exit from Edinburgh, where, however, the gate was not unhooked for Bonnie Dundee (see p. 50). In Tanner's Close (now gone), on its N. side, close to the Grassmarket, was the den of the Irish monsters, Burke and Hare, whither in 1827–28 they enticed their victims in order to suffocate them and sell their bodies to the doctors. Eighteen men and women (mostly poor tramps) were thus murdered.

The Flodden Wall (p. 34) descending from the Castle, crossed the Grassmarket, and important remains of it, including a bastion, may be seen in the *Vennel*, which ascends to the S. in steps, and leads to Heriot's Hospital.

At the end of the Grassmarket three streets diverge. On the left, Victoria St. winds up to George IV Bridge (p. 62) ; on the right is Candlemaker Row (see below) ; in the middle is the Cowgate.

The **Cowgate** (Pl. 26, 27), fashionable in Mary's reign, is now one of the poorest parts of Edinburgh, though recent improvements have diminished both its squalor and its picturesque interest. It was in this depressing street that the cheery remark of a poor old woman furnished the title and subject of Ballantyne's graceful lyric, ' Ilka blade o' grass keps its ain drap o' dew.' The Cowgate passes under George IV and South Bridges to St. Mary's St., and is continued thence by Holyrood Road, the old South Back of Canongate, to (c. ¾ m.) Holyrood.

Near the beginning of the Cowgate, on the right, is the interesting old *Magdalen Chapel (adm. daily). It is now within the premises of the Livingstone Dispensary of the University, entered from No. 39 Cowgate. Just beyond is the old entrance, surmounted by a 17th cent. pediment with the insignia of the Hammermen's Incorporation, which united all the workers in metal except the goldsmiths, and was a very influential guild in the 16–17th centuries. The chapel and hospital of St. Mary Magdalene were founded in 1547 for a chaplain and seven bedesmen by Michael MacQueen and Janet Rhynd (d. 1553 ; tomb in the chapel), his widow, and placed under the patronage of the Hammermen, who retained it until they sold the building in 1857. The steeple was added in 1618–28. Although the bedesmen lingered until 1665, the chapel was chiefly used after the Reformation (1560) for the meetings of the Hammermen's guild, as its present arrangement indicates. The ' brods ' or boards on the N. and E. walls record donations for the benefit of the poor members of the craft, from 1686 onwards ; and below the dais is a fine wrought-iron railing, with the craft insignia in the middle (a hammer surmounted by a crown). The stained glass in the central window is the only important pre-Reformation stained glass in Scotland. The four roundels display the arms of Scotland, of Mary of Guise, and of the founders.

In the 17–18th cent. the chapel was used as a mortuary, perhaps in connection with the neighbouring gallows ; and hither in 1685 the body of the Earl of Argyll was brought after his execution.

Farther along the Cowgate, near the point where it passes under the South Bridge, Blair St. and Niddry St., descending from the Tron, come in on the left. At the foot of Niddry St. is *St. Cecilia's Hall*, built in 1762, on the model of the Teatro Farnese at Parma, by Robert Mylne, and used by the Musical Society of Edinburgh until 1802. It then became a Baptist chapel, and in 1809–49 was a Freemasons' Hall. It is now used as a hall for entertainments.

We return along the Cowgate to the Grassmarket and thence ascend Candlemaker Row. At the top of this street, on the right, is the entrance to Greyfriars Churchyard, with its church (Pl. 33). The name is derived from the Franciscan Observantines, whose friary here, a favoured retreat of James IV, was founded c. 1455 and destroyed in 1559.

Greyfriars Churchyard (weekdays 8–4 or 5, Sat. 8–12 ; Sun. 10–4 or 6), a sacred spot in Scottish religious history, is partly surrounded with dwelling-houses, on which R. L. Stevenson suitably moralises. Here in 1638, in a tide of popular enthusiasm, was signed the National Covenant, some of the names being written in blood. Legend has it that the parchment was spread for signature on the through-stone, or flat tombstone, of Boswell of Auchinleck, at the S.E. corner of the church, but the signing must have taken place inside the church, as the occasion was late on a winter afternoon. On the wall near the N.E. corner of the cemetery is the *Martyrs' Memorial* (1771 ; original slab in the City Museum), bearing a noteworthy inscription. In this churchyard were penned for five months the 1200 Covenanters taken prisoners at the battle of Bothwell Bridge in 1679 ; without shelter, rigorously guarded, and poorly fed, except for the compassion of the citizens. At that time the cemetery extended much farther to the S. and W. of the small enclosure in the S.W. corner that is now usually indicated as the Covenanters' prison.

Within the enclosure is the tomb of Sir George Mackenzie (d. 1691), Lord Advocate under James VII. It was popularly believed that ' Bluidy Mackenzie ' would not remain quiet in his grave ; and the boys of Edinburgh used to consider it a heroic deed to shout into the tomb ' Bluidy Mackenzie, come out if you dare.' Among other noted men buried here are the Regent Morton (d. 1581), George Buchanan (1582), Alex. Henderson (1646), William Carstares (1715), Captain Porteous (1736), Colin Maclaurin (1746), Forbes of Culloden (1747), Allan Ramsay (1758), William Robertson (1793), James Hutton (1797 ; ' the father of modern geology '), Henry Mackenzie (1831), and Duncan Ban MacIntyre (1812).

The church of **Greyfriars**, long divided into two parts, between two congregations, was restored as a single church in 1936. Old Greyfriars was originally erected in 1612–14, but in 1721 a dividing wall was built at the fourth bay, and two new bays added to the W. (' New Greyfriars '). In 1845 the older part was restored after a damaging fire. Above the pillars hang copies of the Covenanters' flags. Principal Robertson, the historian, was minister of Old Greyfriars in 1762.

A fountain at the corner of Candlemaker Row and George IV Bridge commemorates ' *Greyfriars Bobby*,' a terrier that in 1858 watched his master's grave until his own death. American lovers of ' Bobby ' erected a red granite tombstone on the grave (on the left side of the cemetery walk leading N.).

Almost opposite the gate of Greyfriars Cemetery opens the broad *Chambers Street* (Pl. 33), which leads to the South Bridge and the older University Buildings. On its N. (l.) side are the *Heriot-Watt Technical College* (much enlarged in

1954–56), in front of which is a statue of James Watt, and *Minto House*, now the University Department of English and Modern Languages, but formerly the hospital of ' Rab and his Friends.' Near the E. end is Guthrie St., the successor of College Wynd, in which Sir Walter Scott (1771–1832) was born. On its S. side rises the **Royal Scottish Museum** (Pl. 33), a spacious edifice in a ' Venetian ' style, designed by Capt. Fowke and opened in 1866, and considerably extended since. Archaeology, applied art, ethnology, natural history, geology, and technology are amply illustrated in its important and valuable collections. The museum is open free daily 10–5; Sun. 2–5. In front is a statue of William Chambers (1800–83), publisher and Lord Provost.

DEPARTMENT OF ART, ARCHAELOGY AND ETHNOLOGY. The remarkable collection of Silverware includes the most representative collection of Scottish work in any museum, including the *Watson Mazer, a ' standing ' mazer made in the early 16th cent., probably in Edinburgh, and the unique Freedom Box, by John Rollo of Edinburgh (1736). Here are also the *Lennoxlove Toilet Service, presented by Charles II to Frances, Duchess of Richmond and Lennox (' La Belle Stuart ') ; made in Paris c. 1675, it lay concealed in a travelling-chest at Lennoxlove until c. 1900. English silverware of Henry VIII's reign is represented by a *Chalice and Paten, perhaps the finest of their kind, and a Font Cup, unique except for one at the Victoria and Albert Museum. The *Glass* includes Roman and 16–18th cent. Venetian glass, English sweetmeat glasses, rare Jacobite Amen glass, and two 14th cent. enamelled mosque lamps. *Textiles* : 16th cent. curtains said to have come from Queen Mary's bed at Lochleven Castle ; the Murthly Castle panels of 16th cent. embroidery ; Ayrshire needle-work. *Woodcarving* : 13th cent. S. French Madonna ; two pieces in the style of Tilmann Riemenschneider. *French Ivories. *Arms and Armour* : *Pembridge Helm, *Sword of Battle Abbey, 15th cent. hauberk of mail, Highland weapons. In the *Coin Collection* is a ' Petition crown ' of Charles II. *Oriental Section* : Chinese lacquer, including an *Imperial Throne ; *Gordon-Munro Collection of prehistoric Japanese antiquities ; and the largest Indian collection outside London. *Egyptian Collection*, largely from the excavations of the 19th cent. antiquary Alex. Rhind : Edinburgh bilingual papyri, poem on a royal war chariot inscribed on a flake of limestone, toilet casket of Amenophis II. The *Ethnological Collections*, among the most important in Britain, include Hawaiian feather cloaks and capes ; Maori carved boxes ; gold *Beaker, stone carvings, and pottery and textiles from Peru and Mexico ; carvings from the N.W. Pacific Coast ; sculpture from Africa.

DEPARTMENT OF NATURAL HISTORY. Two halls are devoted to *British Fauna*, with numerous habitat groups, among them one of golden eagles at their eyrie ; and three to *Foreign Mammals*, including the collection of Antarctic seals brought back by the Scottish explorer W. S. Bruce, and the skeleton of a blue whale stranded at North Berwick in 1831. The **Children's Gallery* has many fine habitat groups.—DEPARTMENT OF GEOLOGY. Models, including one of the Edinburgh district and another of Arthur's Seat ; **Heddle-Dudgeon Collection* of Scottish minerals, the most complete in existence ; *Hugh Miller Collection* of fossils.

DEPARTMENT OF TECHNOLOGY. *Hall of Mining and Metallurgy*, with scale models of coal mining and related industrial processes. *Hall of Power* : *' Wylam Dilly ', one of the original colliery locomotives built by Wm. Hedley at Wylam (Northumberland) in 1813 ; Parsons's turbo-alternator of 1890 ; *Aero-engine used by the Wright Brothers in 1906 ; Newcomen's atmospheric steam engine (1735) ; scale models of locomotives of various periods. *Civil Engineering Gallery* : Working model of a rolling-lift bascule bridge, made in the museum workshops. The *Lighthouse Gallery* contains the original drafts of Smeaton's Eddystone Lighthouse, etc. Among the *Science Collections* is laboratory apparatus used by the chemists Lyon Playfair (1818–98), Joseph Black (1728–99), and Justus von

Liebig (1803–73). The rich collection of early scientific instruments includes the *Hieronymus Hamilthon Watch (1595), engraved with the earliest known view of Edinburgh Castle. In the *Hall of Shipping* are ship models.

The **University** (Pl. 33, 34), i.e. the old University building, entered from the South Bridge by a triple archway, is a massive structure in a classic style, designed by Robert Adam in 1789 and completed by W. H. Playfair in 1827. The dome, surmounted by a figure of Youth, by J. Hutchison, was added in 1883. At the end of the quadrangle, under the arcade, is the University War Memorial, with an inscription by Kipling. To the right open the class-rooms, and on the left is the *Library* (adm. daily 9–5, Sat. 9.30–1 ; small fee), which includes the library of Drummond of Hawthornden and many interesting early books and MSS. In the N.E. angle of the quadrangle were the rooms of the *Speculative Society*, a students' debating society, with memorials of famous students.

Edinburgh University, the youngest of the Scottish Universities, was founded in 1582 as the ' town's college ' by the town council, who appointed Robert Rollock as the first principal. When James VI graciously extended his patronage to it, it became known as the College of King James. It has faculties of theology, law, arts, medicine, science, and music, a teaching staff of over 50 professors besides lecturers, and over 4000 students, of whom some 1250 are women. It was one of the first universities to admit women to classes and degrees. Its medical school has long enjoyed a high reputation, attracting students from every country, and large new medical buildings were erected at the close of last century, while more recently new scientific laboratories, the King's Buildings, have been built c. ½ m. E. of Blackford Hill. Latterly, the University's work in agriculture and forestry has been noted, and the training facilities of the University Farm (at Boghall, near Glencorse) were supplemented in 1947 by the purchase of the neighbouring estates of The Bush and Dryden (farther E., near Roslin), while in 1951 the *Royal (Dick) Veterinary College*, founded 1823, was embodied in the university.

The old university stands partly on ground once belonging to the collegiate church of **Kirk o' Field**, i.e. St. Mary in the Fields, a name recalling a famous crime. In Feb. 1567, a house here, in which Henry Darnley was lying ill, was mysteriously blown up by gunpowder early one morning, and the dead bodies of Darnley and his page were found in an adjoining garden, showing marks of strangulation but no other injuries. Queen Mary, apparently reconciled to her husband after the murder of Rizzio, had tended his sick bed, but on the night before the explosion had retired to Holyrood to be present at the marriage of a favourite servant. About three months later she was married to Bothwell.

In Infirmary Street (Pl. 34), opposite Chambers St., is the University Geographical Department, occupying the *Old Infirmary*, in which R. L. Stevenson and W. E. Henley met in 1875. Adjacent, in 1578–1829, stood the Old High School, the High School of Scott's time.

South College St., skirting the S. side of the Old University, is continued by Lothian St. (in which Thomas de Quincey died at No. 42 in 1859) to the **New University Buildings** (Pl. 33), an imposing academic group, designed by Sir Rowand Anderson in 1884. At its E. end is the handsome *McEwan Hall*, the University graduation hall, opened in 1897. To the left is the *Students' Union* (by Sydney Mitchell) opened in 1889 and since enlarged, and behind the McEwan Hall is the *Music Class Room* (1860). To the W., facing Teviot Place, is the **Medical College,** a huge pile by Rowand Anderson. Still farther

W., in Lauriston Place and separated from the W. façade of the Medical College by the Meadow Walk, is the magnificent **Royal Infirmary** (Pl. 33, 40), designed by David Bruce in the Scottish Baronial style, and opened in 1879. The infirmary, which has about 1300 beds, is built on the pavilion system and spreads over about 19½ acres. The Simpson Memorial wing, a large new extension on the W., stands on the former site of George Watson's College.

On the opposite side of Lauriston Place stands ***Heriot's Hospital**, founded for the maintenance and education of the sons of poor freemen of the city by George Heriot (1563–1624), the ' Jingling Geordie ' of Scott's ' Fortunes of Nigel,' jeweller and banker to James VI. The fine building, one of the handsomest and most original in Edinburgh, is open free to visitors on weekdays 10–4 (Sat. 10–12).

The architect was William Wallace, the King's master-mason, who died in 1631 and was succeeded by Wm. Aytoun. The building, begun in 1628, was used by Cromwell as a military hospital, and it was not opened for its intended purpose until 1659, when General Monk removed the patients. It was not completed until 1693, when Robert Mylne added the N. gate-tower. The gateway is by W. H. Playfair (1819). Heriot's original endowment has more than doubled in value since his death and the scope of his trust has been extended. The hospital is now a modern and technical fee-paying day school with no boarders, though there are a certain number of foundationers, to whom an allowance for board is made. In addition the trust contributes to the maintenance of the Heriot-Watt College and has established a considerable number of bursaries at the schools and university of the city. Raeburn is the most distinguished pupil.

The Hospital, the main façade of which is on the N. side, is a square building in a mixed Gothic and Palladian style with towers at the corners. Mylne's gate-tower, with a statue of Heriot on its inner side, admits to a quadrangle, 94 ft. square, not unlike that of an English college. Of the windows, over 200 in number, no two are said to be alike in ornament. The examination hall, on the W. side, was added in 1894. The Gothic chapel and various rooms, with portraits, etc., are shown on application.

Heriot Place (r.) leads to the Vennel, which skirts the grounds of the Hospital and descends to the Grassmarket. Lauriston Place goes on to Tollcross, but we diverge to the right into Lady Lawson Street (Pl. 32), in which is the *College of Art* (1907), and viâ Castle Terrace (Pl. 31) regain the W. end of Princes St.

THE SOUTH SIDE

To the immediate S. suburbs of Edinburgh—Newington, Grange, Morningside, Merchiston, etc.—which are commonly grouped together as ' the South Side,' with the customary vagueness as to definite limits, there are three main routes from Princes St., starting respectively from the Mound, from the E. end, and from the W. end, and all served by buses.

From Bank St., at the top of the Mound, we cross the ' Royal Mile ' and proceed S. by Melbourne Place, at the corner of which are the *County Buildings*. GEORGE IV BRIDGE (Pl. 26 ; 1825–36) leads straight on. Facing Victoria St. (diverging on the right for the Grassmarket, p. 56) is the new National Library (p. 49) and opposite are the *Public Libraries*, a building in the French Renaissance style by Washington Browne (1890), on the site of Hope House, built in 1616 by Sir Thomas Hope, the King's Advocate. We cross the Cowgate and see on the right the little tower of Magdalen Chapel. Passing the entrance to Greyfriars Churchyard (r.), we follow Forrest Road to the *Meadow Walk*, a fine avenue, for pedestrians only, which intersects the flat grassy public park known as *The Meadows* (Pl. 39, 40).

The Meadows were formerly occupied by the Burgh Loch, which later degenerated into a marsh, but was drained after 1722 and became a highly fashionable promenade at the end of the 18th century. ' Under these trees,' writes Lord Cockburn (d. 1854), ' walked and talked and meditated all our literary and scientific, and many of our legal worthies of the last and beginning of the present century.'

The first turning on the left in the Meadow Walk leads to ***George Square** (Pl. 40), an old-world square dating from c. 1770, when the gentry began to quit the Old Town. Sir Walter Scott lived with his father at No. 25 (W. side) from the year after his birth (1772) until his marriage in 1797, and Thomas Carlyle courted Jane Welsh at No. 22 in 1821–23. At No. 5 (N. side) is *George Watson's Ladies' College* (comp. p. 64), In 1951 the University obtained powers to develop the buildings round the square, the outward appearance of which, however, is to be preserved as far as possible. Lord Jeffrey (1773–1850) was born at No. 7 Charles St., to the N.E. of George Square, and in 1802, in his elevated residence on the second floor of No. 18 Buccleuch Place (tablet) to the S.W., he, with Henry Brougham, Sydney Smith, and others, founded the ' Edinburgh Review ' in 1802, rejecting the motto proposed by Smith, ' tenui musam meditamur avena ' (we cultivate literature on a little oatmeal) on the ground that it was too near the truth. In Buccleuch St., just to the S., is *Archers' Hall* (Pl. 41 ; no adm.), the headquarters of the Royal Company of Archers, built in 1776 and since extended.

The Company of Archers, constituted by the Privy Council in 1676, chartered under Queen Anne (1704), and formally appointed the King's Bodyguard in Scotland by Geroge IV in 1822, with high rights of precedence, consists of c. 500 noblemen and gentlemen of good social position, commanded by a captain-general, who is invariably a distinguished Scottish peer. They maintain the ancient art of archery and shoot for a number of prizes annually. When the monarch holds court in Edinburgh they are on duty as escort, guards, and gentlemen-in-waiting. The full-dress uniform is very elaborate, but there is also a simpler field dress or shooting dress.

The S. part of the Meadow Walk is adjoined, on the E., by an enclosure where the Royal Company of Archers are sometimes to be seen at practice. On the S.W. the Meadows are continued by Bruntsfield Links. The line of the Meadow

Walk goes on due S. to the *Grange Cemetery*, in which are buried Dr. Chalmers, Hugh Miller, Dr. Duff, Professor Masson (all in the main N. walk), and other noted men. Thence we may turn E. for Newington (see below) or W. for Morningside (p. 64), or push on S., viâ Kilgraston Road and Oswald Road, to (c. ¾ m. more) **Blackford Hill,** the viewpoint so eloquently described in Scott's 'Marmion,' whence we look N. over the city (' mine own romantic town ') and across the Forth, with its islands " like emeralds chased in gold," to the Ochils. On the hill, now a public park, stands the *Royal Observatory* (1896). We may either descend W. to the Braid Hills Road or follow West Mains Road, leading E. past the new *King's Buildings* of the University, to (c. 1 m.) the line of the Liberton buses.

FROM THE E. END OF PRINCES ST. we turn to the S. viâ the NORTH BRIDGE (first built in 1764 ; entirely rebuilt in 1897), which spans Waverley Station. On the right rise the offices of 'The Scotsman.' Reaching the High St. at the Tron we hold S., crossing the SOUTH BRIDGE (1785-87) over the Cowgate and passing the University (r.). The classical building on the left in Nicolson St., beyond the University, is *Surgeon's Hall*, containing the *Museum of the Royal College of Surgeons* (open free, Mon. and Wed. 12-4, Sat. 10-1). An uninteresting street of shops follows. From St. Patrick's Square (Pl. 41) an archway leads W. to Buccleuch Place and George Square (Pl. 40), and the name of Hope Park Terrace (Pl. 41) will recall the beginning of David Balfour's affair with the truculent Lieut. Duncansby (comp. p. 56). The main road follows Minto St. through the residential district of *Newington* and goes on to Liberton and Burdiehouse (p. 78).

In 1787 in *Sciennes Hill House* (tablet on No. 7 Braid Place, opening off Causewayside, parallel with Minto St. on the E.), Burns (aged 28) and Scott (a boy of 15) had their only meeeting. Scott alone of the company could identify a quotation from Langhorne on a print that interested Burns (see p. 92).

FROM THE W. END OF PRINCES ST. Lothian Road (Pl. 24, 31) leads off to the S., passing between St. Cuthbert's Church and Princes St. Station. On the left are the *Usher Hall* (1914), a magnificent hall for public meetings and concerts, and the *Lyceum Theatre* (Pl. 31). On the right farther on is *Lothian House,* a massive block of Government offices (1936). From Tollcross (Pl. 38) Lauriston Place leads (l.) to Heriot's Hospital, but we bear r. into Home St. and Leven St. Beyond the *King's Theatre* (Pl. 38, 39) we skirt the W. side of *Bruntsfield Links* (Pl. 39), once a favourite golfing ground of the citizens. The links formed part of the *Burgh Muir*, which extended S.W. from the old Burgh Loch (see p. 62) and was a frequent gathering place for Scottish armies (see p. 64). On their E. side, in Whitehouse Loan, is the old mansion of

Bruntsfield House. We are now in Merchiston, a district taking its name from an estate that belonged since **1483** to the family of Neper, Napair, or Napier, several of whose heads were provosts of Edinburgh. A little farther on Colinton Road diverges on the right.

Near the beginning of this road is **Merchiston Castle,** in which John Napier (1556O–1617), inventor of logarithms, was born (tablet). The mansion, with its old gateway and square tower, probably dates from the 16th cent. with alterations of the 17th. Montrose spent his college vacations in the castle, then the residence of his brother-in-law Lord Napier. Occupied from 1833 until 1930 by the well-known Merchiston Castle School (now at Colinton), the house is being incorporated in a new Polytechnic College. On the opposite side of the road, farther on, are the spacious buildings (opened in 1932) of *George Watson's College,* one of the chief boys' schools in Edinburgh, founded by bequest of George Watson (d. 1723), a banker's accountant, and adminstered by the Merchant Company. The road goes viâ (1¾ m.) *Redford Barracks* to (2½ m.) *Colinton.*

In Churchhill, diverging on the left, Dr. Chalmers died at No. 1 in 1847 ; Clinton Rd., with *East Morningside House* (1726), leads on E. to the Grange (p. 63).—In the wall at No. 69 Morningside Road, just above Morningside Church, is preserved the *Bore Stone,* wrongly said to be the stone on which the royal standard was planted while the Scottish army was mustering on the Burgh Muir before Flodden. Beyond *Morningside Road Station,* Braid Hills Road diverges l. for the *Braid Hills,* now a public park, with two frequented golf courses. The main road goes on, past the *Open Air Theatre* in Braidburn Valley Park, to Fairmilehead, 1 m. S. (p. 78).

THE NEW TOWN AND WEST END

The NEW TOWN, in its narrower signification, embraces Princes St. and the rectangularly planned region to the N., with its squares and streets, those " draughty parallelograms," as Stevenson with perfect propriety calls them ; but in common usage it means N. Edinburgh generally. The WEST END includes the Victorian residential district W. of Princes St. Station and Queensferry St. (Pl. 23, 24).

The original plan of the New Town, devised by James Craig in 1767, was extended N. and W. by Robert Reid in 1802, E. by Archibald Elliot in 1815 and by Wm. Playfair in 1819, and finally N.W. by James Gillespie Graham in 1822, and beyond the Water of Leith by Raeburn up to 1823.

Princes St., the principal street of the New Town, has already been described. From its W. end South Charlotte St., No. 16 in which was the birthplace of Alex. Graham Bell (1847–1922), pioneer of the telephone, leads N. into **Charlotte Square** (Pl. 17, 24), a beautiful square, with the *Albert Memorial* (by Steell ; 1876) in the middle and the ponderous domed church of *St. George* (1810–14 ; by Reid) on the W. side. The *N. side, restored to its original state by the late

Lord Bute, is Robert Adam's most charming composition (1791). Lord Haig (1861–1928) was born at No. 34, Lord Lister (1827–1912) lived at No. 9 (tablet). **George St.** (Pl. 17, 18), running thence to the E., is a fine street whose spacious dignity successfully rivals the very different attractions of Princes Street. In its medial line statues of Chalmers, by Steell, and of William Pitt and George IV, both by Chantrey, stand at its intersection with the side streets ascending from Princes St. On the W. side of Castle St., the first turning on the left, Kenneth Grahame (1859–1932) was born at No. 30, while opposite is ' poor No. 39,' Scott's House (Pl. 17) in 1802–26, where many of the Waverley Novels were written. On quitting it Scott wrote that it had sheltered him ' from the prime of life to its decline.' Previously, in 1799–1802 he had occupied No. 10 South Castle St.; soon after his marriage in 1797 he lived for a time at No. 107 George St.; and Shelley and Harriet Westbrook lodged in this street after their runaway marriage in 1811. On the S. side of the street is the *Music Hall* (1843), containing a concert hall and assembly rooms ; and at No. 45 is ' Blackwoods,' the famous publishing house. The *Royal Society of Edinburgh*, the leading scientific society in Scotland, incorporated in 1783, has had its seat at No. 22 George St. since 1909. Its list of presidents includes Scott and Kelvin. The church of *St. Andrew*, at the E. end of George St., by Andrew Fraser, was the first in the New Town (1782–85 ; steeple by Sibbald, 1789). It is notable as the church where the actual ' Disruption ' took place in 1843, when 450 ministers, seceding from the Established Church for conscience' sake, marched thence in a body to Tanfield Hall at Canonmills (Pl. 4) to found the dissenting Free Church of Scotland.—**St. Andrew Square** (Pl. 19), a pendant to Charlotte Square, is notable for the fine mansion of 1772 (now a bank) on its E. side. Lord Brougham (1778–1868) was born at No. 21 and David Hume, in 1771–76, occupied the house (rebuilt) at the corner of South St. David St., where he entertained Benjamin Franklin. In the central garden rises the *Melville Monument*, a fluted column, 150 ft. high (incl. the statue), supporting a statue of Henry Dundas, 1st Viscount Melville (1742–1811). On the E. side is the entrance to the *Bus Station*.

Parallel with George St. on the N., and cutting across the face of the slope that descends steeply towards the Forth is **Queen St.** (Pl. 17, 18), one-sided like Princes St., and skirted by pleasant gardens. At its E. end, in a tall building of red sandstone, dedicated by the munificence of J. R. Findlay, a proprietor of ' The Scotsman,' to ' the illustration of Scottish history,' are the ***Scottish National Portrait Gallery** and the ***Museum of Antiquities.** The building, in a 13th cent. Gothic style, designed by Sir Rowand Anderson, is embellished on the exterior with statues of illustrious Scotsmen by Scottish sculptors. The collections are open free on week-days 10–4 or 5 (Sun. 2–5).

The **National Portrait Gallery** occupies the right wing of the building. The importance of this interesting and valuable collection is chiefly historical, though it contains some works of high artistic value. The arrangement is chronological, the earliest portraits being on the ground floor. Only a selection of the paintings is exhibited, the less important works, stored for reference, being accessible on application. Except where they are included in groups, no portraits of living persons are admitted. The *Reference Section*, on the first floor, contains c. 20,000 engraved portraits and a rapidly expanding collection of photographs, with a valuable subject-index.

CENTRAL HALL. Murals of events in, and frieze depicting the principal figures of, Scottish history, by *Wm. Hole*. Portrait of the founder, *J. R. Findlay* (d. 1898), by Sir George Reid. Marble statues of *Robert Burns* (d. 1796), by Flaxman, and of *Thomas Carlyle* (d. 1881), by Sir Joseph Boehm.— We turn to the right for ROOM I. *James I* (murdered 1437) ; *James II* (accidentally killed 1460) ; *James III* (murdered 1488) ; *James IV* (killed at Flodden, 1513) ; *James V* (d. 1542) and his queen *Mary of Guise* (d. 1560 ; attr. to Corneille de Lyon). *Mary, *Queen of Scots* (d. 1587), by Oudry, dated 1578, the ' Cobham ' version of the ' Sheffield ' portrait ; also the Queen in white mourning for her first husband Francis I of France. *James VI and I* (d. 1625), two portraits ; his daughter *Queen Elizabeth of Bohemia* (d. 1662) ; *Marquess of Hamilton* (d. 1625), studio of Mytens ; *Charles I* at his trial, by Edward Boyer (1649) ; *Charles I* and his consort *Henrietta Maria*, after Van Dyck ; *Henry, Prince of Wales* (d. 1612) ; *Charles II (d. 1685) as a boy, with his page, by Dobson ; *Gen. Monk* (d. 1670), *Gen. David Leslie* (d. 1682), both by Lely ; *George Buchanan* (d. 1582) ; *James Graham, Marquess of Montrose* (d. 1650), after Honthorst ; *Marquess of Argyll* (d. 1661), by David Scougal.

On the STAIRCASE are numerous busts : *W. E. Henley* (d. 1903), by Rodin ; *R. B. Cunninghame Graham* (d. 1936) and *Ramsay Macdonald* (d. 1937), by Epstein ; *Sir George Henschel* (d. 1934), by Onslow Ford. Also many smaller portraits, including : *Thomas Campbell* (d. 1844), by Maclise ; *Thomas Carlyle* (d. 1881), by Linnell ; *John Wilson* (Christopher North ; d. 1854), by Thos. Duncan ; *Samuel Smiles* (d. 1904), by Sir George Reid ; *Sir James Barrie* (d. 1937), by Sir Wm. Nicholson ; *Earl Haig* (d. 1928), *Lord Milne* (d. 1948), and other generals of the First World War, by Sargent ; *Sir C. Grant Robertson* (d. 1948), by Meredith Frampton ; and self-portraits of *Allan Ramsay* (d. 1784), *William Strang* (d. 1922), and *S. J. Peploe* (d. 1935).

FIRST FLOOR. R. II. *James VII and II* (d. 1701) and *Anne Hyde* (d. 1671), his first wife, both by Lely ; *Mary of Modena* (d. 1718), his second wife ; *William III* (d. 1702) ; *Duke of Hamilton* (d. 1712), by Kneller ; *Queen Anne* (d. 1714). *Mary II* (d. 1694). Portraits by Sir John Baptiste de Medina : *Earl of Melville* (d. 1707), *Earl of Leven* (d. 1728), *Sir William*

Bruce (d. 1710). *Robert Carr*, or *Ker* (d. 1645), favourite of James VI ; *John Graham of Claverhouse* (' Bonnie Dundee'; d. 1689). *George II* (d. 1760), by John Shackleton, signed and dated 1755 ; **James*, the ' Old Pretender ' (d. 1766), by De Troy ; his wife *Princess Clementina Sobieska* (d. 1765) ; and their sons *Charles Edward* (' Bonnie Prince Charlie,' the ' Young Pretender ' ; d. 1788), and *Henry* (Cardinal York, the last of the Stewarts ; d. 1807) ; *Charlotte, Duchess of Albany* (d. 1789), daughter of Charles Edward ; *Flora Macdonald* (d. 1790), by Richard Wilson. Portraits by Allan Ramsay : *David Hume* (d. 1776), *Lord Elchies* (d. 1754), *Lord Prestongrange* (d. 1764). *William Hamilton of Bangour* (d. 1754), by Gavin Hamilton ; *James Boswell* (d. 1795), by Geo. Willison ; *Allan Ramsay*, the poet (d. 1758), by Wm. Aikman ; *Elizabeth Gunning, Duchess of Hamilton* (d. 1790), by Gavin Hamilton ; *James Bruce*, the explorer (d. 1794), by Pompeo Batoni. Portraits by Reynolds : *Earl of Dunmore*, Governor of New York and Virginia (d. 1809), *Rev. Wm. Robertson* (d. 1793). *David Allan* (d. 1796), by John de Medina after a self-portrait. In this room also is a bust, in coloured wax, of *William III*, by Lorenz Strauch.

SECOND FLOOR. R. III. Portraits by Raeburn : *Lord Braxfield* (d. 1797), *Adm. Inglis* (d. 1791), *Lord Eldin* (d. 1832), *Francis Horner* (d. 1817), **Sir Walter Scott* (d. 1832), *Prof. John Bruce* (d. 1826), *Mrs. Elizabeth Hamilton* (d. 1816). *Neil Gow* (d. 1807). *Lord Brougham* (d. 1868) ; *Andrew Geddes* (d. 1844), by himself ; *Sir David Wilkie* (d. 1841), by Geddes ; *George IV* (d. 1830), by Lawrence ; *William IV* (d. 1837), by Wilkie ; **4th Duke of Argyll* (d. 1770), by Gainsborough ; *Gen. James Stuart* (d. 1793), by Romney ; *Sir John More* (d. 1809), by Northcote. Portraits by Reynolds : *Sir John Macpherson* (d. 1821), Governor-General of India, **Sir William Forbes* (d. 1805). *Adm. Lord Duncan* (d. 1804) ; *Gen. Abercromby* (d. 1801), and *William Dundas* (d. 1845), by Hoppner ; *Joseph Hume* (d. 1855) ; *Henry Mackenzie* (d. 1831) ; *George Watson* (d. 1837), first president of the Royal Scottish Academy, a self-portrait ; two portraits of *Robert Burns* (d. 1796), by Nasmyth ; *James Hogg* (d. 1835), the ' Ettrick Shepherd,' by Wm. Nicholson.—R. IV. *Sir James Mackintosh* (d. 1832), *Viscount Melville* (d. 1851), by Colvin Smith ; *Earl of Aberdeen* (d. 1860), by Archer Shee ; *Queen Victoria* (d. 1901), by Winterhalter ; *Thomas Carlyle* (d. 1881), by Walter Greaves ; *W. E. Gladstone* (d. 1898) ; *Adm. Sir Charles Napier* (d. 1860) ; *Prof. J. S. Blackie* (d. 1895), by Sir George Reid ; *Lord Kelvin* (d. 1907) ; *Andrew Lang* (d. 1912), by W. B. Richmond ; *Earl Beatty* (d. 1936), by Orpen ; *J. Keir Hardie* (d. 1915), by J. J. Dobson ; *J. Ramsay Macdonald* (d. 1937), by A. McEvoy ; *James Maxton* (d. 1946), by Lavery ; *R. L. Stevenson* (d. 1894), by Count Nerli (1892) ; *Mrs. Kennedy Fraser* (d. 1930), by John Duncan ; and some good works by Watson Gordon, Sir George Reid, and R. S. Lauder.

The **National Museum of Antiquities of Scotland** occupies the left wing. On the ground floor, reached from the Central Hall (see above), is the *Historic Gallery* ; on the first floor is the *Prehistoric Gallery* ; on the second floor are the *Roman Gallery* and the *Reference Library* (adm. free during the hours of opening).

HISTORIC GALLERY. Besides personal relics this room contains a remarkable collection of medieval antiquities and later objects, which throw a welcome light upon allusions in Burns, Scott, and other Scottish authors. Round the walls are flags, including a Covenanters' banner from Drumclog (1679), and the Cavers Standard, said to have been carried by Douglas at the battle of Otterburn (1388).—On the left is a notable series of originals and casts of 6–11th cent. sculptured stones, particularly Anglian and Pictish, including the *Hilton of Cadboll Stone, from Easter Ross, with a carving of a lively hunting party. Many of the stones bear symbols of unknown meaning, peculiar to Scotland. Here also are the 16th cent. Montrose Panels, and other examples of woodwork.—The chief surviving relics of the Celtic Church in Scotland include the bell and crozier of St. Fillan (c. 800) ; bells of characteristic quadrangular shape ; the *Monymusk Reliquary, or Brecbennoch of St. Columba, a casket of wood adorned with silver, bronze, enamel, and gilding (c. 700), which was carried at Bannockburn in 1314. Of later date are a stool and gown of repentance, communion vessels, and the gold oil-vial used at the coronation of Charles I at Holyrood (1633).—In the next bay : *Weapons of all kinds, notably Highland pistols, targes, and broadswords ; jewellery and other relics of Mary, Queen of Scots ; targe of Bonnie Prince Charlie ; the fine Clanranald Collection of Jacobite relics ; Scott's helmet as a trooper in the Midlothian Volunteer Yeomanry.

At the end of the gallery is the Maiden, or guillotine, by which were beheaded Regent Morton (1581), the Marquess of Argyll (1661), and the Earl of Argyll (1685). To the left are objects connected with trades and corporations, and an interesting collection of *Personal Relics : baby basket used by Sir Walter Scott's mother ; Wat o' Harden's horn and spurs ; Lady Grisell Baillie's three-cornered lantern ; lantern and skeleton keys of Deacon Brodie ; Burns's pistols ; snuff-mull of the Ettrick Shepherd ; Neil Gow's punch ladle.—To the right, in a recess, are instruments of punishment, including jougs and branks ; sea chest of Alexander Selkirk, the original of ' Robinson Crusoe ' ; late-17th cent. clothing (in remarkable condition) found in peat mosses in Caithness (1920) and Shetland (1951).—We return by the right side of the hall.

Here are objects of domestic and culinary use ; quaichs ; spinning and weaving machines ; lighting appliances ; snuff-mulls, shoes, and ornaments ; golf balls of leather stuffed with feathers (19th cent.) ; and 12th cent. ivory *Chessmen from Lewis. Among the musical instruments are the Lamont and ' Queen Mary ' clarsachs (15–16th cent.) and Highland and Lowland bagpipes. Here too are the Galloway *Mazer (by James Gray of the Canongate, 1569) ; the Ballochyle Brooch, a large silver talisman (late 16th cent.) ; and the 13th cent. Eglinton Casket, of whalebone with bronze mounts.

On the way up to the first floor we pass examples of medieval West Highland sculpture. The PREHISTORIC GALLERY illustrates the earlier stages in the development of Scotland. By the windows is the Torrs Chamfrein (200 B.C.), some sort of pony-harness but probably rearranged since its discovery in 1820. It once belonged to Scott. Other cases contain early Celtic ornamental metalwork ; *Gold Ornaments of the Bronze Age ; massive silver chains of double rings (Pictish) occurring only in Scotland, and typical Celtic ring brooches, notably the *Hunterston Brooch from Ayrshire (post-Roman); Viking objects from the village at Jarlshof, Shetland, and silver ornaments from Orkney ; implements and weapons of the Stone and Bronze Ages ; carved stone balls, of a kind almost peculiar to Scotland ; necklaces of jet ; pottery, mainly from burials ; and objects of everyday life from Skara Brae, Orkney.

ROMAN GALLERY. In the centre is a noteworthy collection of objects found in Traprain Law, near Haddington, a hill settlement which was occupied from at least the late 1st cent. A.D. and flourished under the Roman occupation until the 4th century. The *Treasure of Traprain, a hoard of Christian and pagan silver plate (770 oz.), mainly domestic, discovered in 1919 in a crushed and broken condition, represents the proceeds of a 5th cent. raid southwards, possibly into Gaul ; the workmanship is Roman, chiefly of the 4th century. On the left are *Finds from forts excavated on the Wall of Antoninus, as well as from Roman stations in S. Scotland ; on the right, hoard of coins from Falkirk, and the colossal leg of a bronze statue, from near Hawick. Farther on, important and varied series of finds from Newstead (Melrose), and discoveries from Inveresk and Cramond and the northerly forts of Ardoch and Inchtuthill.

Eastwards Queen St. is continued to Leith Walk by York Place and Picardy Place. A tablet on No. 32 York Place commemorates Sir Henry Raeburn's residence. No. 47 was built by Alex. Nasmyth in 1786, and was the birthplace of his sons Patrick, the painter (1787), and James, the engineer (1808). Sir Arthur Conan Doyle (1859–1930), creator of ' Sherlock Holmes,' was born at No. 11 Picardy Place. This name recalls a settlement of French weavers in the employ of the British Linen Company.

Proceeding W. along Queen St., now very largely occupied by offices, we pass the *Royal College of Physicians* (No. 9), with its imposing front, and the *Mary Erskine School* (No. 70), a leading girls school, founded in 1695 by the Merchant Company. Sir Henry Bishop (1786–1853) lived at No. 22 in 1842 ; Sir James Y. Simpson died at No. 52 in 1870 ; Christopher North lived for a time at No. 53 and Lord Jeffrey at No. 62.

To the N. and N.W. of Queen St. extends a more or less fashionable residential district with quiet grey streets and substantial houses, conspicuous among which is *Moray Place* (Pl. 17), a spacious circle of fine large mansions, in one of which (No. 24) Lord Jeffrey died in 1850. No. 17 Heriot Row, which runs thence E., skirting the N. side of Queen St. Gardens, was the home of Robert Louis Stevenson, during the 'Sturm und Drang' of his Edinburgh life, from 1857 until 1879, while, at No. 6 Gloucester Place (leading W. from India St.), Christopher North lived from 1836 till his death in 1854 (tablets). As we descend N. the houses become simpler, and beyond Moray Place and Royal Circus is the humbler district of *Stockbridge* (Pl. 10). David Roberts (1796–1864) was born at No. 8 Church St., Stockbridge (tablet).

From Princes St. buses Nos. 23 and 27, coming from the Mound, run along Hanover St., intersecting George St. and Queen St. They then descend the steep Dundas St. and Pitt St. to *Canonmills* (Pl. 4), where they cross the Water of Leith, going on viâ Howard Place and Inverleith Row to Granton. In Henderson Row, which diverges to the left at the foot of Pitt St., is the *Edinburgh Academy* (Pl. 3), a leading boys' school, founded in 1823. Warriston Road, short of the bridge, leads, on the right, to *Warriston Cemetery*. A tablet on No. 10 Warriston Cres., just beyond the bridge on the right, marks Chopin's lodging in 1848. No. 8 Howard Place, where Robert Louis Stevenson (1850–94) was born, is now the ***Stevenson Memorial House** (Pl. 4 ; adm. weekdays 10–4 or 5, Sat. 10–1, 1/), with a most interesting collection of personal relics, letters, and MSS. ; books by or about R. L. S. ; portraits ; photographs and views. There is also a collection of articles that belonged to 'Cummy' (Alison Cunningham, "my second Mother, my first Wife ") and a linen-press made by Deacon Brodie and used by R. L. S. and W. E. Henley.

In Inverleith Row, a few yards farther on, is the entrance to the ***Royal Botanic Garden** and **Arboretum** (9 till dusk ; Sun. 11 till dusk ; plant-houses, 1–4 or 5), founded in 1670 on the site of Waverley Station and moved here in 1823. It is an admirably arranged and beautiful domain (c. 60 acres), notable both for its scientific value and for its fine views of Edinburgh.

The Arboretum has an exit into Arboretum Road, separating it from *Inverleith Public Park* (Pl. 2). At No. 4 Inverleith Terrace (Pl. 3) died William Nicol (1786–1851), inventor of the polarising prism. We follow Arboretum Avenue to Stockbridge (Pl. 10). Raeburn Place (Pl. 9), diverging on the right, is named after Sir Henry Raeburn (1756–1823), who was born in the vicinity, and later designed some of the neighbouring streets, including **Ann Street* (Pl. 9, 16), which is named after his wife. De Quincey stayed with Christopher North at No. 29 Ann

Trinity 1 m.

ARBORETUM

Royal Botanic Gardens

Fettes College

Glencorse Ho.

INVERLEITH PUBLIC PARK

Moredun Ho.

Ch. Tanfield

Women's Missy College

Printing Works

Bowling Greens

1

2

3

Edinburgh Academy

Deaf & Dumb Inst.

Baths

St Bernards

Grange Cricket Gr.

Ancient Bow Butt

Edin. Academy Sports Gr.

Coates Curling Pond

Comely Bank Rd.

Raeburn Pl.

Ch.

School

Ch.

Wes. Meth.

Sch.

Fettes Stephens

8

9

10

STOCKBRIDGE

Bank Gro.

St Barnabas

St Learmonth

DEAN

DANUBE ST.

ROYAL

CIRCUS

GREAT

Learmonth

Tennis

HERIOT

Buckingham

CLARENDON TER.

St Bernards Ch.

Public Footpath

Queen

QUEENSFERRY ROAD

Bristo Chapel

Gardens

Epis.

16

17

Dean Ch.

Stewarts Cemetery

Colls.

15

Gardens

Water of Leith

CHARLOTTE

R.C. Ch.

Dean Cemetery

Sch.

Baths

St George

24

Dean Orphanage

BELFORD ROAD

DRUMSHEUGH GAR.

Ch.

West Princes

Melville Coll.

QUEENSBERRY ST.

St Cuthberts Ch.

22

DRUMSHEUGH GAR.

23

MELVILLE STR.

RANDOLPH

Bells Mills

Belford Bridge

COATES CRES.

PRINCES STR. STATION

Mill Lead

The Haugh

DOUGLAS CRES.

MANOR

ATHOLL

Ush

Synod Hall

LYCEUM THEATRE

Donaldsons Hospital

GLENCAIRN CRES.

Epis. Theo. Coll.

Ch.

Cinema

29

COATES

30

TORPHICHEN ST.

Electric Light Sta.

31

Hall

Hebrew

Mem.

MORRISON STR.

MORRISON ST.

BREAD ST.

HAYMARKET TER.

HAYMARKET

Lothian House

R.C. Ch.

Flour Mills

Coal Depot

Bakery

Haymarket Station

Devon Pl.

Caledonian Distillery

Grove

Ch.

37

Brandfield

FOUNTAIN

Mound

38

D A L R Y

36

Brewery

Rubber Works

KINGS THEATRE

Dalry Rd.

Teller Subway

Ch.

Sch.

Drill Hall

Brunt

Copyright Midcalder

Carlops

Queensferry, Forth Bridge

Zoological Park, Stirling, Glasgow

Scale of ½ Mile

0   100   200   300   400   500   600   700   800   880 Yards

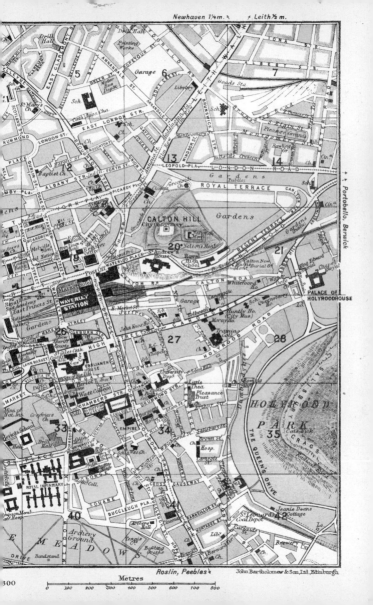

St. before 1840. Raeburn Place is continued by *Comely Bank*, where, at No. 21 (tablet), Thomas Carlyle spent the first eighteen months of his married life (1826–28). The elaborate building, with tower and spire, on the hill to the right is *Fettes College* (Pl. 1), an important public school for boys, administered on the lines of the great English public schools. It was opened in 1870 from funds bequeathed in 1836 by Sir William Fettes, a wealthy banker.

WEST END. From the W. end of Princes St. Queensferry St. (Pl. 24, 25) leads N.W. to the Dean Bridge. The broad Melville St., in which is a monument to the 2nd Viscount Melville (1802–61), diverges on the left for the episcopal **Cathedral of St. Mary** (Pl. 23), designed by Sir Gilbert Scott, one of the largest Gothic churches erected in Britain since the Reformation.

Begun in 1874, with funds bequeathed by the Misses Barbara and Mary Walker of Coates, it was consecrated in 1879, though the W. towers were not completed until 1917. The height of the central spire is 276 ft. and the length of the building is 260 ft. The interior, severe but impressive, contains paintings by Mateo Cerezo and Parmigianino. The chapter house was added in 1890. To the N. of the cathedral is *Easter Coates House* (c. 1615), now the choir-school and library. From the W. end of the church Palmerston Place leads S. towards Haymarket.

The ***Dean Bridge** (Pl. 16), 106 ft. high, is one of Telford's best designs (1832). It spans the *Water of Leith*, once a polluted stream, but now as clear as a Highland burn, with banks prettily laid out.

Upstream, far below the bridge, is seen the little hamlet of *Dean*, with its mills, where Catriona lived with Lady Allardyce. We may descend to the stream by the road to the left of the bridge, and follow its banks downwards to Stockbridge passing *St. Bernard's Well* (Pl. 16), a little Doric domed temple, built by Alex. Nasmyth in 1789 and restored in 1887. The statue of Hygieia is by D. W. Stevenson.

Beyond the N. end of the bridge we enter the broad Queensferry Road, which skirts the N. side of the *Dean Cemetery* (Pl. 15). In this beautiful burial-ground, opened in 1845, rest many men of note : Lord Jeffrey, Lord Cockburn, Prof. John Wilson, James Nasmyth, inventor of the steam hammer, and many more.—Beyond the cemetery are the buildings (1849–53) of *Daniel Stewart's College* (Pl. 15), in a 16th cent. style, by David Rhind.

Opened in 1854 as a free school, or ' hospital ', under the will of Daniel Stewart (1741–1814), a shepherd lad who amassed a fortune in the Indies, it was taken over by the Merchant Company in 1860 and is now a boys' public day school.

To the S.W. Princes St. is prolonged by Shandwick Place, at No. 18 in which is the *Branch Museum* of the Nat. Museum of Antiquities (adm. free weekdays 10–5) containing a highly popular selection of medieval and later exhibits, notably costumes.—Beyond Coates Crescent (r.) with the Gladstone Memorial by McGillivray (1917), and *Haymarket Station* (Pl. 30), we keep r. for *Donaldson's Hospital* (Pl. 29), another of the educational foundations by wealthy citizens, in a fine building by W. H. Playfair.

James Donaldson (d. 1830) bequeathed nearly £200,000 for the upbringing of poor children ; the establishment is now exclusively devoted to the education of the deaf.

E

Beyond *Murrayfield Station* Roseburn St. diverges left for the football ground of the *Scottish Rugby Union*, where international and other important matches are played. *Roseburn House*, on the right of this street, is a fine old mansion of c. 1562.—The road crosses the Water of Leith at *Coltbridge*. A body of dragoons stationed here to oppose Prince Charles Stewart in 1745 were so alarmed by the approach of the Highlanders that they incontinently fled, dashing down the Lang Gait (Princes St.) and not drawing bridle till they reached Prestonpans, c. 9 m. distant, a flight that is known as the ' Canter of Coltbridge.'—About ½ m. farther, on the right, is the ***Zoological Park** (*Rfmts.*), the attractive gardens of the Royal Scottish Zoological Society, laid out on the slope of Corstorphine Hill, with a good collection of animals, exhibited as far as possible under natural conditions. The penguins, of many varieties, are especially famous. The park is open on weekdays from 9 to 7 or dusk, on Sun. from 12 (adm. 2/6, Sat. 3/, children half price ; aquarium 6*d*. extra).

The road goes on (½ m. more) to **Corstorphine** (*Harp*, RB. 25/, P. 12 gs.), an ancient village now within the city boundary. The interesting church, founded after 1376 by Sir Adam Forrester as a votive chapel (now the chancel, with sedilia and family tombs) was extended westwards in 1429 by his son Sir John. On the S.W. is a belfry tower, with an octagonal spire, and the unrestored portions have roofs of flagstones. An old dovecot, adjoining the workshops of the Edinburgh Tapestry Company, is the sole relic of the Forresters' castle. *Corstorphine Hill* (520 ft.), on the N., now a public park, is crowned by the *Clermiston Tower*, erected in 1871–2 in honour of Scott (adm. 3*d*. ;   10–3 or 6). A by-way, passing behind the Zoological Park, crosses the hill to Ravelston ; at the point known as *Rest and be Thankful*, noted for its view of Edinburgh and the Forth, David Balfour and Alan Breck parted on the last page in ' Kidnapped,' though they met again in ' Catriona.'

EASTERN EDINBURGH

From the General Post Office, at the E. end of Princes St., we follow Waterloo Place (Pl. 19, 20), which, crossing Low Calton by the *Regent Bridge*, an imposing structure of 1815 by Archibald Elliot, with well-designed arches above and below, is continued by Regent Road. On the right, immediately beyond the bridge, an inconspicuous flight of steps ascends from a doorway in the retaining wall to the *Old Calton Burying Ground*, in which are the tombs of David Hume (1711–76) and other Scottish worthies. The Obelisk, or ' Martyrs' Monument,' commemorates five political reformers who were sentenced to transportation for sedition in 1793–94, at a time when the Government was alarmed by the Reign of Terror and other events in France. The fine Lincoln Monument here, the earliest monument (1893) to Lincoln on this side of the Atlantic, is dedicated also to the Scottish-American soldiers who fell in the American Civil War (1861–65). Farther on is *St. Andrew's House* (by T. S. Tait; 1937–39), a long block housing the principal Government offices for Scotland.

Opposite rises the ***Calton Hill** (c. 350 ft.), which, with its monuments, effectively fills in the vista from Princes St., while itself commanding magnificent views. " Of all places for a view," remarks Stevenson, " the Calton Hill is perhaps the best ; since you can see the Castle, which you lose from the Castle ; and Arthur's Seat, which you cannot see from Arthur's Seat." The hill is accessible by a flight of steps opposite St. Andrew's House or by a road farther E., which is continued around the crown of the hill. Near the top of the steps a reproduction of the monument of Lysicrates (' the Lantern of Demosthenes ') at Athens commemorates Prof. Dugald Stewart (1753–1828), and farther N. are a monument to Prof. John Playfair (1748–1819), the mathematician, and the buildings of the *City Observatory* by Wm. Playfair (1818), with James Craig's castle-like *Old Observatory* (1774) near by. Both are now disused. The Portuguese cannon (1624) near by was captured at Mandalay in 1886. The tallest structure on the hill is *Nelson's Monument* (102 ft. high ; open daily 10–7, in winter 10–3 ; adm. 3d.), built in 1807–15, which it is customary to liken to a ' spy glass on a butter-churn ' (time-ball, see p. 43) ; but the most prominent is the unfinished *National Monument*, commemorating the fallen in the Peninsular and Waterloo campaigns. This building, intended to be a reproduction of the Parthenon, was begun in 1822, but after the erection of the present twelve columns (each of which is said to have cost £1000) funds gave out. The descent on the N. side of the hill (walkers only) leads to Greenside and Leith Walk.

Farther on Regent Road passes below the ***Royal High School,** the finest of the many fine classical buildings in Edinburgh, which occupies a commanding position on the S. slope of the Calton Hill. The original building, of 1825–29, by Thomas Hamilton, an old High School boy, is a happy adaptation of the temple of Theseus at Athens. The school claims to trace its history back to the 12th cent., and before 1829 it stood in the Old Town (p. 60).

The roll of former pupils includes Alex. Graham Bell, George Borrow, James Boswell, Dr. John Brown, Lord Cockburn, Henry Dundas (Lord Melville), Lord Jeffrey, and Allan Ramsay the younger.

The view opens on the right, across the valley to Arthur's Seat. *Burns's Monument*, on the right, is another classical design by Hamilton (1830), apparently inspired by the Lysi-crates monument. On the slope below lies the New Calton Burying Ground.—Abbey Mount diverges on the right for Holyrood just before we join the old London road (l.), which we follow to *Piershill*, an important road junction where Restalrig Road strikes off on the left for **Restalrig Church** (apply at the house beside the churchyard gate).

The parish church, destroyed in 1560 as ' a monument of idolatry,' was restored in 1837 and again in 1910. Adjoining is a small hexagonal chapel, with a groined roof supported by a central pillar. This was the chapel of a college founded by James III in 1478 ; it was restored in 1908, but the new pavement was burst by a water spring below it, and the building is identified as the successor of the *Chapel of St. Triduana*, whose spring was once resorted to for diseases of the eye. There is no such saint as Triduana (or Tredwall) ; the name refers to the three-days' fast practised in the old Celtic church.—Overlooking the lake in *Lochend Park*, a pleasant oasis in a dismal area (reached from Restalrig Rd. by Sleigh Drive), is old Lochend House, part of the mansion of Logan of Restalrig (p. 86).

On the left of the Portobello road, just beyond Restalrig Avenue (l.) there is seen on the left the tall isolated tomb of William Henry Miller of Craigentinny (1789–1848), founder of the famous Britwell Library. On the sides are two bas-reliefs by Alfred Gatley (d. 1863), known as the *Craigentinny Marbles* and representing the Overthrow of Pharaoh in the Red Sea and the Song of Moses and Miriam. About ½ m. farther on is *Portobello*.

LEITH. NEWHAVEN. GRANTON

Leith, officially the ' Port of Leith,' one of the chief seaports in Scotland, is situated on the Forth, at the mouth of the Water of Leith, which divides it into North Leith and South Leith. Immediately contiguous to Edinburgh, with no apparent line of division, it was included within the extended boundaries of that city in 1920. It has preserved a few memorials of antiquity.

History. From the days of Robert the Bruce until 1832 Leith was under the ' superiority ' of Edinburgh, a relationship that was the cause of frequent friction ; but from the Reform Bill of 1832 until 1920 it had a municipality of its own. As the port of the capital Leith is prominent both in Scottish history and Scottish song. It was frequently attacked by the English, and was devastated by them in 1544 and 1547. Several of the Stewart kings welcomed their brides at the shore of Leith. Mary, Queen of Scots, landed here in 1561 on her return from France, a maiden of nineteen. George IV, who landed here in 1822, was the first Hanoverian king to visit Scotland. Leith was the headquarters of Mary of Guise during her struggle with the Lords of the Congregation, and in 1559 beat off their attack, in which they were aided by the English. Of the citadel, erected by Cromwell in 1650 and seized by a Highland Jacobite force in 1715, there are practically no remains.

Leith Street (Pl. 19), which descends steeply N.E. from the E. end of Princes St., skirting the W. base of the Calton Hill, is continued by the broad *Leith Walk* (Pl. 13, 7). On the left we pass the Roman Catholic *Cathedral of St. Mary* (by Gillespie Graham ; 1813–14), then Picardy Place (p. 69) and the quarter of Pilrig, mentioned in ' Catriona.' Thomas Carlyle lodged near Leith Walk about 1823.

From the foot of Leith Walk three streets radiate towards

the N. Constitution St., the most easterly, is a busy commercial street in which are the old *Town Hall* (seriously damaged by enemy action in 1941) and the *Post Office*. A little to the E. of it are *Leith Links*, on which Charles I was playing golf when the news of the Irish rebellion in 1641 reached him. The first known ' gouf house ' was built on these links in 1768. Kirkgate is the old main street of Leith. On the right is the church of *St. Mary*, dating from the 15th cent. but much restored. John Logan, a claimant to be the author of the ' Ode to the Cuckoo ' (comp. p. 257), was minister of this church (1773–86). Nearly opposite the church is the *Trinity House*, founded in 1555 as a hospital or almshouse, but rebuilt in 1817 as the seat of a corporation which until 1913 licensed pilots for the North Sea and the Firth, but is now solely a charitable trust for the Merchant Navy. It contains four portraits (including Adm. Duncan) by Raeburn, and a picture of Vasco da Gama rounding the Cape, by David Scott. In Water St., which continues Kirkgate to Bernard St., or in one of the parallel streets, stood the house of Mary of Guise. Tolbooth Wynd, leading W. from the foot of Kirkgate, recalls the ancient tolbooth (demolished in 1819) in which Secretary Lethington (c. 1528–73) is said to have poisoned himself, but both the place and the deed are doubtful. The wynd debouches on the Water of Leith between the Coal Hill (l.) and the Shore (r.). The father and grandfather of W. E. Gladstone were corn-merchants in the Coal Hill, before the first removed to Liverpool. The Shore was the old landing place and a stone on the quay wall records the landing of George IV in 1822. In Water Close is a 16th cent. merchant's house, perhaps *Andrew Lamb's House*, where Queen Mary spent the first day after her landing in 1561. It is the property of the Nat. Trust and may be restored as an old people's home. In Quality St., between Water St. and Constitution St., No. 38 is another fine old house, and at No. 29 was born John Home (1722–1808), author of ' Douglas ' (buried in the churchyard).

The **Port of Leith** comprises an outer and inner harbour (used by coasting vessels), six enclosed docks, and a new western harbour protected by two breakwaters, 2800 ft. and 3600 ft. long. In addition it has six dry docks and two small graving docks. Ample facilities are provided for the loading and discharging of cargoes, and there are extensive warehouses (capacity 36,000 tons). The principal imports are grain and timber ; coal is the main export.

From the N. end of Constitution St., Bernard St. (r.) and Commercial St. skirt the *Docks*. Near the W. end of Commercial St., on the left, is an entrance of the citadel of 1650. *Leith Fort*, erected in 1779, a little farther on, is to be demolished and built over.

To the W. of Leith is **Newhaven,** a fishing port, once noted for its fish dinners and for the conservative peculiarities of its fishing population, alleged to be of Dutch or Danish origin. A few pleasant old houses with outside stairs survive. The Newhaven fishers seldom marry outside their own ranks ; the men are distinguished for hardy daring, and the women for their physical strength, testified by the heavy loads of fish they bear in their creels. Clad in a peculiar costume of many heavy petticoats, Newhaven fishwives are still occasionally to be seen in the streets of Edinburgh.

Newhaven is adjoined on the W. by *Trinity*, a pleasant residential suburb, and farther W. is *Granton*, a creation of the Duke of Buccleuch, who began the construction of the spacious harbour in 1835.—To Cramond by the shore, see p. 81.—To the W. of Granton (reached by a turning off W. Granton Rd. just before the gas works) is *Caroline Park*, built by Sir George Mackenzie (Viscount Tarbat) in 1685–96. It is remarkable for its balconies and has painted ceilings by Nicholas Heyde (adm. only on written application to Messrs. A. B. Fleming & Co., Ltd.). Originally called Roystoun, its name was changed in 1740 by the 2nd Duke of Argyll in honour of the queen of George II.

Excursions from Edinburgh

Opportunities for excursions from Edinburgh, long or short, are innumerable, and are very visibly pressed upon the attention of the summer visitor. The motor-bus services and the railways provide convenient access to many interesting points in the environs.

Midlothian, or *Edinburghshire*, is one of the smaller Scottish counties and its interest, certainly its historic interest, centres mainly in the capital which now occupies 50 sq. m. in the N., including almost the entire seaboard of c. 12 miles. On the S. Edinburgh is girt by a pleasant zone of attractive country, with some of the best agricultural land in Britain, and further S., where the Pentlands rise in the S.W. and the Moorfoots to the S.E., we find ourselves among the lonely hills. Midlothian farms and farming are famous, and paper-making and sea-fishing are other chief industries, while coal-mining (often open-cast) is of growing importance. The battlefields of Pinkie (1547), Carberry Hill (1567), and Rullion Green (1666) are in this county ; among its ancient castles are Craigmillar Roslin, Borthwick, and Crichton.

A. FROM EDINBURGH TO DALKEITH, 7 m. (frequent buses from St. Andrew Sq. in 25 min. ; $10\frac{1}{2}d$.). The Old Dalkeith Road, the direct continuation of St. Leonard's St. (Pl. 41, 42), passes within $\frac{1}{4}$ m. of Craigmillar Castle, but the New Dalkeith Road, which continues the line of ' the Bridges,' Nicolson St., and Clerk St. (Pl. 41) to Newington and (2 m.) the suburb of *Nether Liberton*, is more usually chosen, though it passes 1 m. S.W. of Craigmillar. At Nether Liberton we diverge to the left along Gilmerton Road and ascend to (c. 3 m.) the former U.F. church of Liberton, beside the golf course.

Kingston Avenue strikes hence left to join ($\frac{1}{2}$ m.) the Old Dalkeith Road, where we turn right, then left, to reach (c. 1 m.) the picturesque ruin of ***Craigmillar Castle** (adm. 6*d*. 10–4 or 7, Sun. from 2), a favourite residence of Mary, Queen of Scots. This is a lofty square keep of the 14th cent., to which large additions were afterwards made. Visitors inspect the vaulted halls, the small chamber known as Queen Mary's, and the dungeons, and ascend the staircase (1661) to the top, which commands a renowned view. The castle belonged to the Preston family until 1760. Here the Earl of Mar, brother of James III, was imprisoned in 1477 on a charge of treason, and here (or in Edinburgh) he is said to have been bled to death. James V as a boy spent some time at Craigmillar when the pest was raging in Edinburgh. Mary came hither to recruit in 1566 after her illness at Jedburgh, and here before the year closed she held the secret conference with Bothwell, Argyll, Huntly, and Maitland that led to the murder of Darnley. A group of houses on the Old Dalkeith Road is known as *Little France*, recalling the quarters there of some of Mary's French attendants.— About $\frac{1}{2}$ m. N.E. of the castle lies the suburb of *Craigmillar*. To the S. of the road returning thence to Newington is the *Thistle Foundation Settlement* for disabled ex-servicemen (1950), an attractive quadrangle of cottages with the Robin Memorial Chapel (1953) by John Matthew.

From (3¼ m.) *Greenend* Stenhouse Rd. leads right to the restored *Stenhouse Mansion* (1623 ; N.T.), with fine plaster ceilings.—Beyond (4¼ m.) *Gilmerton* we cross the North Esk.—At (6½ m.) *Eskbank*, an important road-junction, we turn left.

7 m. Dalkeith (*Lothian Arms*, RB. 19/6 ; *Cross Keys*, RB. 16/6), a little town (8790 inhab.), with a considerable grain market, is situated between the North and South Esk. Half-way down the main street, which extends to (½ m.) the gates of Dalkeith House, is the old church of *St. Nicholas*, made collegiate in 1406, and latterly used mainly as a parish church. In the roofless E. apse, the burial chapel of the Douglases and Buccleuchs, is the tomb of Anne, Duchess of Buccleuch (1651–1732), to whom the ' last minstrel ' sang his lay at **Newark**.

Dalkeith House, or *Dalkeith Palace*, was a former Scottish residence of the Dukes of Buccleuch and Queensberry. Its fine collection of paintings and furniture have now been removed to other seats of the family. The large park, in which the North and South Esk meet, is no longer open to the public.

The mansion, mainly rebuilt for Duchess Anne c. 1700 by James Smith, is a heavy imitation of the palace of Het Loo in Holland. The original stronghold was given in the 12th cent. by David I to the Grahams, from whom it passed to the Douglases of Liddesdale. In 1642 the estate was sold to Francis Scott, 2nd Earl of Buccleuch, who left two daughters. General Monk, as the custodier of the elder sister (d. 1661), resided at Dalkeith House for five years (1654–59), and here the Restoration is said to have been planned. Anne, the younger sister, married the Duke of Monmouth (executed in 1685), and in 1663 the pair were created Duke and Duchess of Buccleuch. Froissart visited Dalkeith for a fort-night in 1364 (he spells it Alvest) ; other noted visitors were James VI (1581 and 1617), Charles I (1633), and Prince Charlie (1745).

The scene of ' The Gray Brother,' an unfinished ballad by Scott, was Burndale, afterwards named Gilmerton Grange, near Dalkeith ; and in the poem many of the famous spots in the pretty valley of the Esk are lovingly recalled :

> " Who knows not Melville's beechy grove
> And Roslin's rocky glen,
> Dalkeith, whom all the virtues love,
> And classic Hawthornden ? "

On the S. Esk, ¾ m. S. of Eskbank, is *Newbattle* church (by Alex. McGill, 1727), which contains the pulpit of Archbp. Leighton, minister here in 1641–53. Opposite is the entrance to **Newbattle Abbey,** a mansion surrounded by trees in a fine park, presented to the nation by the Marquess of Lothian and opened as a college for adult education in 1937 (reopened, after use as an Army College, in 1949). Visitors are admitted on application to the Bursar (preferably not at week-ends). The house succeeds a Cistercian abbey founded in 1140 and burned down by Hertford in 1544 ; it contains a few good paintings, notably an equestrian portrait of Charles I, by Van Dyck, and a family group by Allan Ramsay. The crypt and chapel in the basement are a relic of the abbey buildings.

The last abbot, Mark Ker, changed his opinions in 1560, and in 1564 was made commendator of the abbey's possessions, which remained the property of his descendants. The gardens are exceptionally attractive, with two remarkable sundials and the recently restored ' Maiden Bridge.'

Melville Castle, rebuilt by James Playfair in 1786, once the seat of Viscount Melville, with its ' beechy grove,' lies 1 m. N.W. of Eskbank, on the N. Esk, and is now a hotel (RB. 27/6, P. 14 gs.).

From Dalkeith, the Penicuik bus may be taken S.W., viâ (1½ m.) the colliery village of *Bonnyrigg* (5430 inhab., with Lasswade), to (2 m.) **Lasswade,** which has a direct bus service from Edinburgh viâ Liberton. This village, pleasantly placed in the N. Esk valley, is perhaps the prototype of the ' Gandercleuch ' of ' Tales of my Landlord,' for here, opposite the gate of Dunesk House (l. bank of the Esk), is the cottage (much enlarged) in which Scott passed six happy years after his marriage (1797). Beside the ruins of the Norman church, and of the later church (designed by Robert Adam in 1793, but probably built by his brother-in-law John Clerk), are the graves of Drummond the poet (see below; tablet), and of Henry Dundas (1742–1811), 1st Viscount Melville, who was practically ' King of Scotland ' from 1775 to 1805.—Near *Polton,* with its paper mills, 1 m. S.W., is Mavisbush (now De Quincey Cottage) occupied by Thomas de Quincey in 1840–59. Mavisbank is a mansion completed in 1724 by William Adam. From Polton a pleasant path leads up the Esk to (2½ m.) Roslin, passing Hawthornden.

Hawthornden (no adm.), a mansion grafted on to an old tower in 1638 by William Drummond (1585–1649), a poet of the Spenserian school, sometimes spoken of as ' the Scottish Petrarch,' is 3½ m. from Dalkeith by B 6094. It is planted on the edge of a red cliff looking sheer down into the glen or ' den ' of the N. Esk and surrounded by pretty gardens and woods. Drummond here entertained Ben Jonson for about a fortnight in 1618–19, and the sycamore tree under which ' royal Ben' was welcomed by ' Hawthornden ' still exists.

B. FROM EDINBURGH TO ROSLIN, 7½ m. (frequent buses viâ Loanhead or Lothianburn in c. ½ hr. ; 11½d.). The most direct route follows the Dalkeith road to *Nether Liberton,* whence we proceed straight on uphill to (3 m.) *Liberton* with its conspicuous square pinnacled church tower. Liberton House has an attractive 17th cent. dovecot ; and in the village is a 15th cent. tower of the Dalmahoys, which may be ascended.— 4½ m. *Burdiehouse* is said to take its name ('Bordeaux House ') from a settlement of Queen Mary's French attendants in 1561.—5 m. *Straiton.* At (6½ m.) *Bilston Inn* turn left for (7½ m.) *Roslin.*

A slightly longer but preferable route leads from the W. end of Princes St. past the Braid Hills to (3½ m.) the populous new suburb of *Fairmilehead.* From the cross-roads at the bus terminus the branch on the left leads to Liberton, the branch on the right to Colinton (2 m.), see p. 81.

Half-a-mile along the road to Colinton and a few yards short of the white-washed ' Hunters' Tryst,' the rendezvous of the Six Foot Club mentioned in ' St. Ives,' a by-road diverges on the left for (½ m. more) **Swanston,** the Pentland village with *Swanston Cottage,* which R. L. Stevenson loved so dearly and which plays its romantic part in ' St. Ives.' From 1867 till 1881 this simple cottage was the holiday home of the Stevenson family : it now belongs to the city of Edinburgh and contains some relics of R. L. S., but is not open to the public. From the village we regain the Roslin road by a path skirting the N. side of Lothianburn golf course.—Beyond the Hunters' Tryst we take the first turning on the left and reach *Colinton,* where the manse is another Stevenson shrine.

Beyond Fairmilehead are Lothianburn Golf Course, and (5 m.) *Hillend Park,* a pleasant public park on the breezy

slopes of the Pentlands (see below). For Roslin we keep
straight on by A 703, joining the Penicuik road a little S. of
Bilston Inn, but soon diverging again from it (l.) on B 7008.

8 m. **Roslin** (*Royal*, RB. 21/, P. 9 gs.) is a miners' village,
famous for its chapel and its castle. ***Roslin Chapel** (adm. 1/6
on weekdays, 10–1, 2–5 ; services on Sun. at 9, 11.30, 3.30) is
the choir of a church of which the nave was never built and
the transepts only begun. Its glory is the rich profusion of its
sculptural decoration, in which Spanish or Portuguese
influence seems traceable. The carvings, flying buttresses,
and pinnacles on the exterior should be noted.

History. The chapel, founded in 1446 by William Sinclair, 3rd Earl of Orkney
(and subsequently Earl of Caithness), was intended as the church of a college,
which was not, however, established until c. 1521 by Sir William Sinclair, for a
provost and four prebendaries. The chapel became the burial-place of the
Sinclairs, and the ballad of ' Rosabelle ' (in the ' Lay of the Last Minstrel ')
recalls the legend that on the night before the death of any of the family it
seemed to be all on fire within.

> " Blazed battlement and pinnet high
> Blazed every rose-carved buttress fair—
> So still they blaze when fate is nigh
> The lordly line of high St. Clair.

The barons were (it is said) interred in full armour until 1650, when the widow
of that year departed from the ancestral custom, " thinking it beggarly to be
buried in that manner." The chapel was damaged by the Edinburgh mob in
1688, but after being partly repaired in the next century, was thoroughly restored
in 1862 by the Earl of Rosslyn for Episcopalian services. A baptistery and organ
chamber were added at the W. end in 1881.

The central aisle, of 5 bays, 15 ft. wide, is separated from
the side aisles by clustered columns, the capitals of which
are richly carved. It is barrel-vaulted with transverse ribs,
and the roof of each bay is carved with a different flower.
Between the columns and the outer walls the side aisles are
crossed by straight stone transoms covered on both sides
with elaborate bas-reliefs. On one are represented the Seven
Deadly Sins and, on the other side, the Seven Cardinal
Virtues ; on another is a Dance of Death with many figures ;
on a third are the words ' Forte est vinum, fortior est rex,
fortiores sunt mulieres, super omnia vincet veritas.' At the
E. end of the S. aisle is the **Prentice Pillar*, adorned with
spirals of flowers and foliage more elaborately carved than
the rest. It receives its name from the story (by no means
peculiar to Roslin) that it was carved by an apprentice in the
absence of his master, who slew him in a fit of jealousy on
his return. Three carved heads at the S.W. end of the chapel
pass for those of the 'prentice, his mourning mother, and his
master. An incised slab in the pavement (E. end of N. aisle),
showing a knight in armour with a dog at his feet, is said to
represent the founder of the castle, but is probably later.

The story goes that Sir William Sinclair wagered his head against the lands
of Pentland that his two hounds, ' Help ' and ' Hold,' would pull down, before

it reached a certain burn, a deer that had often baffled the royal huntsmen on
the Pentland Hills. The deer was killed exactly at the burn and Robert Bruce
awarded the estate to Sinclair, who in gratitude built a chapel to St. Katherine in
the Hopes, now covered by the waters of Glencorse Reservoir.

Behind the altar is a Lady Chapel, only 15 ft. high, one step
above the pavement of the choir. It is vaulted and groined
in four bays, and carved pendants descending from the
central ribs give a rich effect.—At the S.E. angle of the choir
a flight of steps descends to a chamber or ' crypt ' projecting
beyond the E. end of the chapel and, owing to the slope of
the ground, only partly subterranean. The altar and piscinæ
show that it was a chapel, while the fireplace and other secular
conveniences suggest that it was later used as a vestry or as a
priest's residence. On the N. wall is an incised plan of one of
the bays of the Lady Chapel.

Roslin Castle (adm. 6*d.* daily, 10–6 ; tea-room), a little
below the chapel to the S., is built on the edge and against the
face of a cliff overhanging the North Esk. It is approached
by a short bridge over a gully on the N.E. side, and the ruins
are impressive only when seen from the side next the river,
where three stories descend to the living rock. The oldest
part was founded by Sir William Sinclair, who was a contemporary of Robert Bruce, and was killed in Spain fighting
the Moors (1330). The keep or S.W. tower, built by his
grandson, was enlarged by the founder of Roslin Chapel.
Destroyed in 1544 by the Earl of Hertford, the castle was
restored c. 1580, and the 16–17th cent. apartments are still
habitable. The great hall, with the Sinclair arms, serves as a
restaurant; and various retainers' rooms, dungeons, kitchen,
etc., are shown.

A little to the N. of Roslin is the moor where, in 1303, the Scottish army under
the Regent Comyn fought and won three battles in one day against three successive divisions of the invading English.—To the S., on the other bank of the
N. Esk, are the slight remains of *Woodhouselee Castle* ('haunted Woodhouselee '),
once the property of Hamilton of Bothwellhaugh, the assassin of the Regent
Moray.—A pleasant footpath leads from Roslin down the Esk to (2⅓ m.) *Polton*,
passing within sight of Hawthornden (p. 78).

C. THE PENTLANDS. From Edinburgh either the Biggar
road (A 702) or the Lanark road (A 70) affords a convenient
approach to the slope of the **Pentland Hills,** which are traversed
by footpaths, affording opportunities for many delightful
walks. The range, the highest point of which is *Scald Law*
(1898 ft.), begins c. 3 m. S. of Edinburgh and stretches S.W.
for c. 16 m. with an average breadth of c. 4½ m. Its streams
feed many reservoirs. The Lanark road (bus to Juniper Green
and Balerno) skirts its N.W. side ; the Biggar road (bus to
Carlops) is at its S.E. foot.

The BIGGAR ROAD follows the Roslin route (see above) to (5 m.) Hillend Park,
then bears right. On our right rises *Caerketton Hill* (1500 ft.) and we pass the
University farm of *Boghall* and (6¼ m.) the entrance to *New Woodhouselee*,

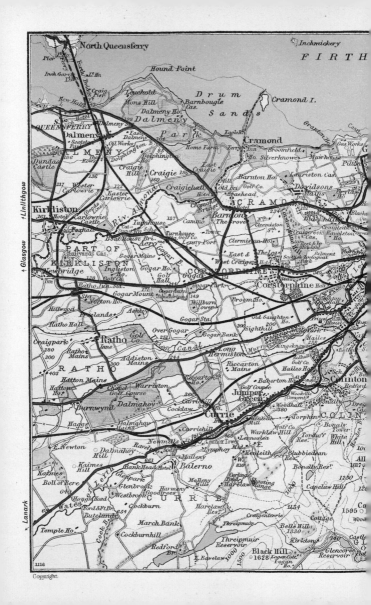

ENVIRONS OF
EDINBURGH

FORTH

LEITH

EDINBURGH

PORTOBELLO
Joppa

MUSSELBURGH
Fisherrow

INVERESK

Holyrood Park
Arthurs Seat
Duddingston

DALKEITH

Liberton

Braid
Hills

Gilmerton

Lasswade

Loanhead

Bonnyrig

Roslin

COCKPEN

Peebles

John Bartholomew & Son, Ltd. Edinburgh

but not the 'haunted Woodhouselee' of Scott's ballad. From (7¼ m.) *Flotter-stone Bridge* a road ascends, on the right, to *Glencorse Reservoir* (¾ m.), in the lower part of which lies engulfed the church of St. Katherine in the Hopes. On *Castlelaw* (1595 ft.), N. of Glencorse Reservoir, are remains of a Celtic fort (c. A.D. 100) and a rather later earth-house.—On the lower slopes of Carnethy Hill (1890 ft.), beyond the bridge, lies (r.) the battlefield of *Rullion Green* where the Western Covenanters, marching on Edinburgh, were defeated by Gen. Thomas Dalyell in Nov. 1666. At c. 9¼ m. a path diverges on the right, which leads over the pass (1456 ft.) between Scald Law and Carnethy to *Loganlee Reservoir*, 1½ m. S.W. of Glencorse Reservoir, and 2 m. E. of Bavelaw (see below). From the top of the pass either of these hills (views) may be ascended in ¼ hr.— Beyond (12 m.) *Ninemileburn*, where a road from Penicuik comes in, stands (l.) *Newhall House*, amid the scenery of Allan Ramsay's ' Gentle Shepherd.' *Habbie's Howe*, "where a' that's sweet in spring and summer grow," is usually identified (but not without dissidents) in a dell reached viâ the first turning on the left beyond the gates of Newhall. Here the visitor may look for the "flowery howm between twa verdant braes," the little waterfall that "maks a singin' din," and the "pool, breast deep, beneath, as clear as glass."—Beyond (14 m.) **Carlops** (*Allan Ramsay*, plain, RB. 15/6) the road goes on to West Linton (16½ m.) and Biggar or Carnwath.

The direct LANARK ROAD, viâ Gorgie and (2¼ m.) *Slateford*, birthplace of the artist John MacWhirter (1839–1911), is to be avoided. A pleasanter route follows Colinton Road (p. 64) past Merchiston Castle, to (3½ m.) *Colinton*, on the Water of Leith, where R. L. Stevenson spent many happy days at his grandfather's manse. It is now a centre of suburban development. *Bonaly Tower*, 1 m. S., was the residence of Lord Cockburn, a famous judge, from 1811 to 1854. Before (5 m.) *Juniper Green* we join the main road. About ¾ m. N.W. is *Baberton House* (1622, with additions of 1765), occupied by Charles X of France in 1830–32.— Between (6 m.) *Currie* and (7¼ m.) *Balerno*, with its paper mills, we pass *Lennox Tower*. From Balerno a track runs S. to (2¼ m.) *Threipmuir Reservoir* and (2¾ m.) *Bavelaw Castle* (1624), whence a path goes S.E. to Loganlee reservoir (see above), 2 m. farther.—From Balerno to Carnwath, Carstairs and *Lanark*, see Rte. 9A.

D. From Edinburgh to the Forth Bridge and South Queensferry (frequent buses ; half-hourly viâ Dalmeny).— Crossing the Dean Bridge we follow Queensferry Road (Pl. 15) to the W.—Beyond (1½ m.) *Craigleith Quarry* (r. ; abandoned), whence emerged much of the New Town of Edinburgh, we pass the entrance to *Ravelston House* (l. ; not seen), whose old-fashioned garden supplied some of the features for Tully Veolan in 'Waverley.' Beyond (2¼ m.) *Blackhall* the main road from Leith comes in on the right.

Craigcrook Castle, the residence of Lord Jeffrey from 1815 until his death in 1850, lies ¾ m. to the left, beautifully situated under Corstorphine Hill.

A road to the right leads past *Davidson's Mains* (formerly Muttonhole), another suburb, to the charming old village of **Cramond** (*Inn*) at the mouth of the Almond, passing (½ m.) *Lauriston Castle*, the early home of John Law (1671–1729), founder of the first bank in France and author of the disastrous Mississippi scheme (1717–20). The grounds (adm. 3*d.*) and castle (adm. 1/ extra), now public property, are open on weekdays, except Fri., in summer (grounds 11–dusk ; castle 2–5, in winter Sat. & Sun. only, 2–4). The grounds of the adjacent *Barnton House* are now a public recreation park and contain also the course of the Royal Burgess Golfing Society. Close by is the course of the Bruntsfield Links Golfing Society. *Cramond Tower* (c. 1400), N.W. of the existing mansion, is a relic of a palace of the Bishops of Dunkeld. A fort at Cramond (? A.D. 142) was the N. end of the Roman Dere Street, which ran from York viâ Newstead. The Emperor Severus landed here, c. 210, and made an attack on Fife and N.E. Scotland. A riverside promenade (for pedestrians) connects Cramond with Granton (2 m.), skirting the new golf course. A parallel motor-road at a higher level is under construction. —At Cramond St. Ives dined with the senatus of the University of Cramond, whose device was Plain Living and High Drinking. A private foot-ferry (6*d.* ; 9–1, 2–7 ; in winter 10–½ hr. before dusk) crosses the Almond to a shore path through the grounds of Dalmeny Park (see below), along which, by courtesy of the Earl of Rosebery, we may walk, past the rebuilt *Barnbougle Castle,* to Queensferry. Ferry and path are closed two days in the year (usually in Feb.).

Beyond (4 m.) *Barnton* (Hotel, RB. 25/, P. 11 gs.) we cross the Almond, a mile above its mouth, by Cramond Bridge (Cramond Brig Hotel, RB. 15/6) and enter West Lothian.

Old Cramond Bridge (1619) is a little lower down, and it was on a predecessor of this that James V, while wandering incognito as the ' guidman of Ballengeich ' was rescued by Jock Howieson, the miller, from footpads. James presented Howieson with the estate of Braehead, on condition that the holders should ever present a basin and ewer for the king's use whenever he should visit Holyrood or cross Cramond Bridge. The service was duly rendered to George IV in 1822, to Queen Victoria in 1842, and to George V in 1927.

On the left is *Craigiehall,* a 17th cent. mansion which is now an anti-aircraft headquarters ; on the right is the Earl of Rosebery's seat, *Dalmeny Park* (1819 ; no adm.). To the left, c. 2 m. farther on, is the village of **Dalmeny,** with its beautiful little Romanesque *Church.

This church, dating probably from the 12th cent., ranks with Leuchars church (Fife) among the finest specimens of Romanesque in Scotland. The S. door, with its arch of double mouldings, much worn, is surmounted by an interlaced arcade of five arches. The stone-vaulted chancel and apse alone remain in their original state and show two richly sculptured circular arches. The windows are round-headed with chevron mouldings. The W. tower, which fell in the 15th cent., has been rebuilt. On the N. side of the nave an addition has been made for the Rosebery pew and burial vault.

The *Royal Elizabeth Yard* at Dalmeny (1948), named after the queen of George VI, is the first permanent naval victualling yard to be built since the Royal William Yard (1833) at Plymouth.

Returning to the main road we descend the steep Hawes Brae and, passing under the viaduct approach to the Forth Bridge, reach the old *Hawes Inn,* at New Halls, on the outskirts of South Queensferry. Here Jonathan Oldbuck and Lovell foregathered in the first chapter of Scott's ' Antiquary ' ; and here, in ' Kidnapped,' Ebenezer Balfour and Capt. Hoseason plotted the abduction of David Balfour. A steam ferry-boat plies to North Queensferry c. every ½ hr. (5*d.*, cycle 6*d.* motor-cycle 1/6, motor-car from 3/6).

9 m. **South Queensferry** (*Hawes Inn,* RB. 20/, P. 9 gs. ; *Sealscraig,* RB. 19/6), a quaint little royal burgh (2490 inhab.), derives its name from Queen Margaret, wife of Malcolm Canmore, who frequently passed here on her journeys between Edinburgh and Dunfermline. The chapel of a Carmelite friary, founded by James Dundas in 1440, served as parish church c. 1583–1630, and was restored in 1890 as an Episcopalian church. The existing dark building dates from the late 15th cent., the finest portion being the E. wall, with its charming little niche.

The Burgh Chambers house a *Museum* of local antiquities (weekdays, 10–12, 2–4 ; Sat. 10–12), including the Queensferry copy of the National Covenant, and papers relating to the construction of the Forth Bridge.—*Plewlands House* (no adm.), a fine town house of 1643 in the main street, was saved from demolition on its acquisition by the National Trust in 1952.

At Queensferry the Firth of Forth (here 218 ft. deep) contracts to a width of 1¼ m. and here it is spanned by the ***Forth Bridge** (1883–90), one of the engineering wonders of the world. In midchannel, and affording a stepping-stone for the bridge, lies *Inchgarvie*, an islet on which a fort, originally built c. 1491, opposed Cromwell in 1650 and was restored in 1779 when Paul Jones was in the offing. The bridge, exclusively for railway traffic, is built on the canti-lever system, with three massive steel towers or piers, from each of which extends an arm or bracket on both sides to meet the arm of its neighbour or the approach-viaduct, as the case may be. This huge yet graceful and striking structure is best viewed from the ferry, and even then it is difficult to realise its enormous proportions, except perhaps, when an apparently toy train is seen puffing across the gigantic network of girders.

The length of the bridge and its approaches is c. 1¾ m. (2765½ yds. to be exact), of which the bridge proper represents 1 m. and 23 yds. There are two main spans of 1710 ft. each and two side spans of 689¾ ft. each. The railway track is 157 ft. and the top of the bridge 361 ft. above high water level, and the headway under each span is 150 ft. In the construction 54,000 tons of steel were used and 6½ million rivets, and at the busiest time 5000 men were employed. The painted surface represents 135 acres. The cost of the bridge was about £2,750,000 ; the engineer was Sir John Fowler, assisted by Sir Benjamin Baker, with Sir William Arrol as contractor.

The great railway bridge will be rivalled, and in some ways surpassed, by the Forth Road Bridge, which will start c. ¾ m. upstream and will cross to the site of the ferry slip at N. Queensferry. In summer 1958 work began on this sus-pension bridge, which, with a span of 3300 ft. between the main piers (each with a tower 150 ft. high), and a total length over water of more than a mile, will be the largest suspension bridge in Europe and the fourth largest in the world.

Beyond South Queensferry the main road goes on to Linlithgow (9 m.) ; but the coast road, passing *Port Edgar* with its naval establishments, and the oddly named hamlet of *Society*, turns inland to cross the park of *Hopetoun House*, the splendid mansion of the Marquess of Linlithgow (adm. 2/6 daily 2–6 in May–Sept. exc. Thurs. & Fri. ; grounds only 1/6 ; teas). Built in 1699–1703 by Sir William Bruce and much enlarged in 1721–54 by William Adam and his sons, the house contains relics connected with the Hope family, paintings, and good furniture. Just beyond the park (r.) is the secluded old church of **Abercorn,** the seat of a short-lived Northumbrian bishopric (early 7th cent.). Though over-restored in 1839, the building preserves a blocked 12th cent. doorway, and, in the vestry, a fine cross-shaft with interlaced pattern and a hog-backed tombstone. The Hopetoun loft (c. 1700) is a particularly fine and complete example. In an adjoining vault is buried Thomas Dalyell of the Binns (see below), though legend says that his body was carried off by the devil, and in the churchyard are several tombstones with emblems of the trade of the deceased.—Beyond the church the lane ascends to the main road, passing the 16th cent. *Midhope Tower,* fast falling to decay.

Westward from the Abercorn turn, A 904 skirts the grounds of Philpstoun, and then those of *The Binns,* seat of the Dalyells since 1612 and home of the long-bearded Gen. Thomas Dalyell (c. 1605–85), who defeated the Covenanters at Rullion Green in 1666 and raised the Scots Greys in 1681. In 1944 it was presented to the National Trust and it is shown on Sat. & Sun. at 2, 3, 4, and 5 ; adm. 2/, car 1/. Among the relics of ‘General Tam’ are his Bible, jack-boots, and sword, the last a gift from Tsar Alexis of Russia. The conspicuous tower on the hill above is a ‘ folly ’ of 1823. About 1½ m. N. on the Forth, is *Blackness,* once an important port, with a 15th cent. castle (adm. 6*d.* 10–4 or 7, Sun. from 2), which was used as a state-prison in Covenanting times, and was one of the four fortresses which, by the Articles of Union, were to be left fortified. About 1870 it was converted into a powder magazine.

6. FROM EDINBURGH TO NORTH BERWICK AND TO HADDINGTON

A. To North Berwick

ROAD, 23½ m., A 1 viâ (6 m.) *Musselburgh* to (7½ m.) *Levenhall* ; thence A 198.—9½ m. *Prestonpans.*—16 m. *Aberlady.*—18½ m. *Gullane.*—23½ m. **North Berwick.** MOTOR-BUSES every ½ hr. from Clyde St. in 1½ hr.

RAILWAY from Waverley Station, 22½ m. in 40–50 min., on weekdays only, viâ (17¾ m.) *Drem,* where carriages are sometimes changed.

Leaving Edinburgh by Regent Rd. (Pl. 14) and London Rd., we bear right at (1¾ m.) *Jock's Lodge* to avoid the crowded streets of Portobello.

The old road (A 1140, A 199) keeps to the left. 3 m. **Portobello** (*Milton House,* on A 1, RB. 25/ ; *Gray's,* at Joppa, RB. 16/6, P. 7½ gs.), now part of Edinburgh, is a popular seaside resort, with broad sands, crowded in summer. Hugh Miller (1802–56) shot himself in Tower St., in a fit of insanity. Sir Harry Lauder (1870–1950) was born at Portobello. The name was given by a sailor who had served under Adm. Vernon at the capture of Portobello in Panama (1739) and built the first house here.—3¾ m. *Joppa,* another seaside resort, is the E. extension of Portobello. The former Marine Gardens here are now occupied by a Home for Dogs and Cats.

Old and new roads converge before reaching (5½ m.) *Fisherrow,* the W. suburb of Musselburgh, and cross the Esk.—6 m. **Musselburgh** (*Woodside,* RB. 21/ ; *Drummore Motel,* near Levenhall)) is an “ old-world, old-fashioned, half fishing, half manufacturing town ” (17,000 inhab.), at the mouth of the Esk. By the Esk bridge is a statue of David Moir (1798–1851), the ‘ Delta ’ of ‘ Blackwood's Magazine ’ and author of ‘ Mansie Wauch,’ who was born here. Randolph, Earl of Moray, Bruce's faithful lieutenant, died here in 1332. Golf has long been played on the links N.E. of the town, where Cromwell camped after the battle of Dunbar and where the

Edinburgh race-meeting is held in autumn. Between town and links is *Loretto*, a public school founded in 1829 near the site of a chapel of Our Lady of Loretto, a famed pilgrim resort, the stones of which were sacrilegiously used to build the *Tolbooth* in the High St. in 1590.

Prince Charlie spent the night after the battle of Prestonpans at *Pinkie House* (no adm.), a Jacobean mansion with a fine fountain, S.W. of Musselburgh. To the S. lies **Inveresk,** a quiet suburb on the site of a Roman station, with a charming 17–18th cent. street, a church (1806) with a steeple by Sibbald, and well-known paper mills. To the E. is the battlefield of *Pinkie* where the Earl of Hertford defeated the Scots under Arran in 1547. The road goes on from Inveresk to (1¾ m.) *Carberry Tower*, above which lies *Carberry Hill*, where Mary, Queen of Scots, after a brief skirmish, surrendered in 1567 to the rebel lords, by whom she was immediately sent to Lochleven Castle.

Beyond (7½ m.) *Levenhall* we bear left on A 198 and enter East Lothian. 9¼ m. **Prestonpans,** with 2900 inhab., was once noted for its salt pans. The main street lies along the shore, ½ m. N.; the old village of Preston, inland, by-passed by the main road, preserves several notable buildings. *Hamilton House* (1628), well restored, stands opposite *Northfield* (before 1607). Both are N.T. property but are not open to view. Farther E. is *Preston Tower*, a 15th cent. stronghold of the Hamiltons, burned by accident in 1663 and later raised two stories, with its old dovecot adjoining. Just beyond it is a very fine *Cross of the 17th century. Beyond the village, between the main road and the coast road, is the battlefield where Prince Charles Stewart, on his southward march, defeated Sir John Cope in Sept. 1745.

The Highlanders, approaching from Tranent across a morass, surprised the royal forces at the break of day and by their furious charge decided the action in ten minutes, losing only 30 men and slaying 400. The victory is celebrated in the lively Jacobite song, ' Hey, Johnnie Cope, are ye wauken yet ? ' A monument in the grounds of the 17th cent. *Bankton House* (now a farm beyond the railway nearer Preston) commemorates Col. Gardiner of Bankton, mortally wounded in the battle.

On the coast road, E. of Prestonpans, are the fishing villages of *Cockenzie* and *Port Seton* (together 3175 inhab.), with a holiday camp at Seton Sands beyond.

On the main road 1½ m. farther, just beyond *Seton Castle* (1790), is the early 15th cent. collegiate church of **Seton** (adm. 1/ ; 10–4 or 7, Sun. from 2). Though never completed beyond the chancel, the transepts, and the truncated spire, it incorporates details of great interest.

There are niches for 14 statues on the buttresses, while within, the ribbed stone vault, the capitals of the crossing, and the piscina are notable. The tomb of James, Earl of Perth (d. 1611), has an epitaph by Drummond of Hawthornden, and there are recumbent effigies of the 3rd Lord Seton (slain at Flodden) and his lady ; the Seton arms—three crescents—are much in evidence. Foundations of the nave and of domestic buildings (N.W. of the church) have been excavated.

It was to Seton Palace, the once splendid home of the great family of Seton (demolished to make way for the ' castle ') that Queen Mary and Darnley rode, the night after Rizzio's murder in 1566, on their way to Dunbar ; and in 1567, a week after Darnley's murder, Mary and Bothwell spent a week here in amusement. The 5th Lord Seton or Seyton, who figures in Scott's ' Abbot,' was one of

Mary's most devoted adherents. James VI and Charles I were likewise entertained here. The last of the Seton family, the 5th Earl of Winton, was attainted
in 1716, and the title has since become merged in that of Eglinton.

At (13 m.) *Longniddry* John Knox was a private tutor
in 1643–47. We turn left and follow the flat sandy coast,
skirting the park of *Gosford House*, long a seat of Lord
Wemyss.—16 m. *Aberlady* (Golf Hotel) has two good golf
links, a restored village cross, and a 15th cent. church tower,
on a wide sandy bay. On the right is seen the 16th cent.
Saltcoats Castle, with its dovecot.—18¼ m. **Gullane** (*Greywalls*,
RB. 35/, P. 16 gs. ; *Bisset's*, RB. 21/, P. 12 gs. ; *Queen's*,
RB. 37/6, P. 12 gs. ; *Linga*, unlic., P. 8 gs.) is noted for its
three public golf courses on the springy turf of its sandy
dunes. The championship course of *Muirfield*, ½ m. N., is the
headquarters of the Hon. Company of Edinburgh Golfers.

It was from the sandy shore at Gullane that Alan Breck made his exciting
final escape (in ' Catriona '), and the stunted trees of Archerfield are the ' Graden
sea-wood ' of ' The Pavilion on the Links.'

21 m. *Dirleton* (Open Arms, RB. 25/, P. 12 gs.) is one of the
prettiest villages in Scotland, with a 17th cent. church and
the massive ruins of a castle (adm. 1/ ; 10–4 or 7, Sun. from 2)
which held out for some time in 1298 for Wallace against
Edward I and was dismantled by Gen. Lambert in 1650. The
' clustered ' donjon is 13th cent. work ; and the garden
encloses a 17th cent. bowling-green. It is said to have been
the bribe that induced Logan of Restalrig to join the Gowrie
Conspiracy.

23½ m. **NORTH BERWICK** (4000 inhab.), a royal burgh
and fishing village on the Firth of Forth, is one of the most
attractive and fashionable seaside resorts of Scotland, with
golf as the absorbing interest. The view seaward is diversified
by a chain of islets : from W. to E., Fidra, the Lamb, Craigleith, the Bass Rock.

Hotels. Marine, a large first-class
hotel, W. of the station, RB. 32/6,
P. 17 gs. ; **Westerdunes,** similar
charges, these two closed Dec.–Feb. ;
Royal, at the station, RB. 27/6, P. 13½
gs. ; **Redcroft, Golf, Dalrymple,** at
these three, P. 10 gs. ; **Imperial,** P.
9½ gs. *Private :* **King's Knoll,** P. 10
gs. ; **Seabank,** P. 8 gs. ; and many
others.—**St, Ann's,** for children and
their attendants, P. 11 gs., summer
only.

   Amusements. Golf. *West Course,*
7/ per day, 30/ per week in summer ;
Burgh Course, 5/ per day (Sun. 7/6),

25/ per week ; *Tantallon Club,* 10/ per
week.—Tennis Courts (E. Links) and
Bowling Greens (Clifford Rd.) are
available.—Bathing Pool (adm.
9d.) at the harbour, adjoined by an
Entertainment Pavilion.

   Motor-Buses to the golf courses at
Muirfield, Gullane, Aberlady, etc. ;
to *Haddington, Dunbar,* etc.—Motor
Launches make excursions in summer
around the *Bass Rock,* to *Fidra,* etc. ;
and arrangements can be made with
boatmen for trips to the *Bass Rock,
Isle of May,* etc. (c. 40/ for 8–10 pers.
with landing).

North Berwick has two sandy bays—West and East—
separated by a spit on which is the fishing harbour. Near
the last is a 16th cent. porch of the ' Auld Kirk ', the founda-

tions of which (12th cent.) have been uncovered. The town, mainly one street with good shops, is on the W. bay; the E. bay is surrendered to villas, which are let in the season. In private grounds S.W. of the station is a fragment of a Cistercian nunnery founded by Duncan, earl of Fife, c. 1150. The town and district are charmingly sketched in Stevenson's essay ' The Lantern Bearers.'

North Berwick Law (612 ft.), a conical hill of felsite ⅔ m. to the S., commands a splendid panorama of sea and land. On the top are the ruins of a watch-tower, built during the last war with France, and the jawbones of a whale. The walk may be continued to (2 m.) the 16th cent. *Fenton Tower.*

Off the coast lie a number of rocky islets, the chief of which is the **Bass Rock**, a precipitous mass of basalt (350 ft. high) about 1 m. in circumference, 3 m. N.E. of North Berwick and 1¼ m. from the shore at *Canty Bay.* It may be visited by boat from North Berwick (see above); landing is a little difficult except in very calm weather. The precipitous cliffs are the home of innumerable noisy sea-birds, mainly gannets. There was a castle on the island from very early times, and traces of fortifications and of a chapel connected with the name of St. Baldred are still to be seen. After 1671 the island was used as a prison for Covenanters, including Blackadder (who died here) and Prophet Peden. A few Jacobite prisoners succeeded in 1691 in seizing the fort and maintained it until 1694, when it was destroyed. David Balfour (in ' Catriona ') was a later captive.— On *Fidra*, farther E., are remains of a chapel of St. Nicholas, served by canons from Dryburgh before 1240.

About 2¾ m. E. of North Berwick are the extensive ruins of ***Tantallon Castle** (adm. 1/; 10 -4 or 7, Sun. from 2), the famous and romantic stronghold of the Douglases across the drawbridge of which Marmion made a hair's-breadth escape after bearding the Douglas in his hall. The castle occupies a position of great strength on a headland washed on three sides by the sea and protected on the land side by a double moat; so that to ' ding doon Tantallon and mak a brig to the Bass ' were, proverbially, feats of equal improbability. Tantallon dates from the 14th cent., and although it withstood a regular siege by James V in 1528, it was eventually destroyed by General Monk.—About 1 m. E. of Tantallon, in the grounds of Seacliffe House, are the remains of a small monastery called *Auldhame Castle*, and said to have been St. Baldred's place of abode and death (8th cent.).—To Whitekirk and Tyninghame, see Rte.I.

At the mouth of the Firth of Forth, c. 12 m. N.E. of North Berwick and 4½ m. S.E. of the coast of Fife (to which county it belongs), lies the **Isle of May** (1 m. long by ¼ m. broad), with its lighthouse and bird-watching station. It contains the ruins of a Benedictine priory founded by David I c. 1153, and abandoned, c. 1318, for Pittenweem. It has a shadowy connection with St. Adrian, a missionary from Hungry murdered by the Danes (c. 870), whose stone coffin is said to have floated across to Anstruther Wester.

B. To Haddington

ROAD, 17½ m., A 1.—5 m. *Musselburgh.*—10 m. *Tranent.*—17½ m. **Haddington.**—MOTOR-BUS direct in 55 min.; less frequently viâ Pencaitland or viâ Gifford.

To (7½ m.) Levenhall crossroads viâ Musselburgh, see Rte. 6A. A 1 keeps straight on and enters East Lothian.— 10 m. *Tranent* (5600 inhab.; Crown, RB. 18/6) is a colliery town. Col. Gardiner (see p. 85) died in the manse, and is buried in the church, which contains good 18th cent. memorials to the Seton and Scott families. The direct road to Haddington passes (13½ m.) *Gladsmuir*, where Principal Robertson (1721–93) was minister in his youth (1743–58) and

wrote his 'History of Scotland.' More interesting is the
detour viâ Ormiston and Pencaitland.

Falside Castle, 2 m. S.W. of Tranent, is a conspicuous 15–16th cent. ruin of a
Seton stronghold, burnt after the battle of Pinkie. More interesting is *Elphinstone Tower*, 2 m. S. of Tranent, an unusually strong 15th cent. fortalice (fine
view) where George Wishart was imprisoned by Card. Beaton in 1546 after his
arrest by the Bothwells at Ormiston Hall (see below).

Leaving Tranent by the Pencaitland road, we soon bear r.
for (12¼ m.) *Ormiston*, a pleasant village with an old cross
and a monument to Robert Moffat (1795–1883), the African
missionary. At Ormiston Hall (1 m. S.), held by the Cockburns
from 1368 to 1748 (since enlarged), George Wishart took
refuge in Dec. 1545 with Alex. Cockburn.—Beyond Ormiston
we turn l. on A 6093.—14¾ m. *Pencaitland*, a charming village
divided by the Tyne, preserves the 13th cent. N. choir aisle
in its church, with a good 'laird's loft' and a 17th cent.
pulpit. Wester Pencaitland has a village cross, and the
bridge dates from 1510.

Two 17th cent. buildings N.E. of the bridge are all that remains of Pencaitland
House, but farther on is *Winton House*, the seat of the Earls of Winton until
1716, a fine Renaissance mansion (1620) spoilt by additions. *Fountainhall* or
Penkaet Castle, c. 1 m. S.W. of the village, is a very complete small 17th cent.
house. Originally known as Woodhead, its name was changed in 1685 by Sir
John Lauder (1646–1722), jurist and chronicler, created Lord Fountainhall in
1689.—B 6093 leads direct to (19 m.) *Haddington* (see below).

FROM PENCAITLAND TO GIFFORD, 6½ m. B 6355 turns right from the Haddington road.—1½ m. *Saltoun Hall* was the birthplace of Andrew Fletcher (Fletcher
of Saltoun ; 1653–1716), the Scottish patriot, especially remembered for his
obiter dictum that ' if a man were permitted to make all the ballads, he need not
care who should make the laws of a nation.' Fletcher's tutor was Gilbert Burnet,
minister of Saltoun in 1665–69 and afterwards bishop of Salisbury.—At (2½ m.)
East Saltoun we branch left.—6½ m. **Gifford** (*Goblin Ha'*, RB. 21/, P. 8 gs. ;
Tweeddale Arms, RB. 18/6, P. 8 gs.) is a neat village with a Dutch-looking
church at the end of its street. It was removed bodily in the late 17th cent.
from the earlier site near Yester House, 1 m. S.E. A tablet near the church
commemorates the Rev. John Witherspoon (1723–94), born at Gifford, principal
of Princeton and the only cleric to sign the U.S. Declaration of Independence.
A broad avenue of limes links the village with the gates of *Yester House*, the seat
of the Marquess of Tweeddale. Passing through these, we turn l. at the bridge
on approaching the house, beyond which cars should not proceed. Walkers
may ascend the track up the Hopes Water through fine woods; on the right
is the dark little collegiate church of *Yester* or *Bothans* (1421–43 ; refaced), the
burial place of the Hay family since 1710. Taking the path (r.) between the third
and fourth bridge, we ascend to (2 m. from Gifford) the romantic ruin of **Yester
Castle**. Not much of the castle remains above ground, but rough steps descend to
the extraordinary underground chamber called **Goblin Ha'*, with its massive
ribbed stone vaulting and low exit passage, built in the 13th cent., with supernatural aid, it is said, by Hugo of Yester, the warlock of Gifford. Here Alexander
III had a mysterious encounter with an elfin knight, as related in ' Marmion '
(Canto 3). A stile leads out of the woods to Castle Mains farm, whence Gifford
may be regained by by-road viâ Long Yester (3 m.). *Lammer Law* (1733 ft.),
most prominent of the Lammermuir Hills, rises to the S.

B 6369 leads direct from Gifford to Haddington (5 m.), but a pleasant detour
may be made by following B 6370 to (4 m. E.) *Garvald*, a retired village with
scanty traces of 12th cent. work in its church. The 16th cent. mansion of *Nunraw*,
¾ m. S.E., on land that once belonged to the Cistercian nuns of Haddington, was
acquired by Trappists in 1946.

Haddington (*George*, RB. 21/, P. 9 gs. ; *Tyne House*, RB. 17/6 ; *Black Bull*, RB. 14/6), the pleasant county town (4500 inhab.) of East Lothian, is noted for its grain market. Made a royal burgh by David I and later a royal residence (for Alexander II was born here in 1198), it was several times burned by the English. John Knox (1505–72) was born either at Haddington or at *Morham* (2 m. S.E.), and a statue of the Reformer stands on the *Knox Memorial Institute* (1879), the successor of the ancient school at which Knox and William Dunbar (1465 ?–1530 ?), the poet, were educated. The mathematical school, at which Edward Irving taught in 1810–12, is likewise absorbed in the present school. The *Town House* in High St. was designed by William Adam (1748 ; enlarged 1830). *Haddington House*, in the Poldrate (S. of the town on the Gifford road), is one among many dignified 17th cent houses ; but the chief building of interest is the Abbey, really a collegiate church near the river, a mainly Dec. edifice of the 13th or 14th cent., of which only the nave and stately tower (90 ft.) are intact, while the choir and transepts are roofless. The tower was once crowned by a lantern (' the Lamp of the Lothians ') like St. Giles. On the N. wall of the choir is a chamber (seen through a wicket) with coloured heraldry and effigies of John, Lord Maitland of Thirlestane (d. 1595) and of the 1st Earl of Lauderdale (d. 1645). Near the E. end of the choir is the tomb of Jane Welsh (1801–66), a native of Haddington and wife of Thomas Carlyle. Samuel Smiles (1812–1904) was likewise born in Haddington (tablets on 51 and 62 High St.). Abbey Bridge, across the Tyne, is of the 16th cent., while Nungate Bridge, downstream, recalls the Cistercian nunnery founded by the Countess of Northumberland, c. 1159.

About 1 m. S. of Haddington is the 15th–17th cent. mansion of **Lennoxlove**, a 14th cent. tower with a 17th cent. wing (adm. 2/, daily 2–5 Apr.–Sept.), so named after Frances, Duchess of Lennox, ' la belle Stuart,' who bought the estate in 1682. Originally called Lethington, it was the seat of ' Secretary Lethington ' (Wm. Maitland ; d. 1573) and birthplace of his grand-nephew the first Duke of Lauderdale (1616–82), and contains fine family portraits and furniture.—In the churchyard of *Bolton*, farther on, are the graves of Burns's mother, brother, and sister ; a tablet marks the site of the house (Grant's Braes) where they lived. The road goes on viâ Humbie to (11 m.) Blackshiels (p. 10).

To the N. of Haddington rise the *Garleton Hills* (590 ft.) with the conspicuous monument to the 4th Earl of Hopetoun (1766–1823), a Peninsular hero. On their slopes lies *Athelstaneford*, where John Hume (1722–1808) was constrained to resign the living on account of having written the tragedy of ' Douglas.' At *East Fortune*, 1½ m. farther on, a monument marks the starting-point of the first double air-crossing of the Atlantic (by airship R 34 ; July 1919).—From Haddington to *Dunbar* and *Berwick*, see Rte. 1.

7. FROM EDINBURGH TO PEEBLES (MOFFAT)

Road (A 703), 56 m. 10 m. *Penicuik*.—23 m. **Peebles.**—41 m. *Tweedsmuir*.— 56 m. **Moffat**. Motor-Buses to *Penicuik* in 32 min. ; to *Peebles* viâ Penicuik or Howgate in 65 min. ; to *Moffat* viâ Penicuik and Broughton in 2¼ hrs.

RAILWAY, to *Peebles*, 27 m. in c. 1 hr. Principal stations : 8 m. *Eskbank* —
11¼ m. *Rosewell & Hawthornden.*—12½ m. *Rosslynlee*, 1¾ m. from Roslin.—
27 m. **Peebles.** The trains go on to Innerleithen and Galashiels.

From Edinburgh to (7 m.) Bilston inn, see Rte. 5B. We
fork right, just beyond, for (8¼ m.) *Glencorse*, with its barracks,
the depot of the Royal Scots in 1875–1951 and 1954–58 ; and
since then of the Lowland Brigade. The church, in which R. L.
Stevenson worshipped, is now an ivied ruin.

The left fork leads direct to Leadburn, viâ (8½ m. from Edinburgh) *Auchen-
dinny*, with the residence of Henry Mackenzie, ' the Man of Feeling ' (1745–1831),
and (10¼ m.) *Howgate*, whence Rab (of ' Rab and his Friends ') came daily to
Edinburgh with his master, the carrier.

10 m. **Penicuik** (*Royal*, RB. 13/6) is a papermaking town
(4250 inhab.) pleasantly situated on the N. Esk near the base
of the Pentlands, which may be explored from here.

The ancestors of the Clerks, owners of *Penicuik House* (1¼ m. S.W. ; burned
in 1899), were bound by their tenure to receive the king when he came to Edinburgh with three blasts of the horn at the Bore Stone, and their motto was
' Free for a blast.' In the grounds is an obelisk in memory of Allan Ramsay the
poet (1686–1758), and about 1 m. farther up the Esk are the ruins of *Brunstane
Castle*, formerly a stronghold of the Crichtons.

FROM PENICUIK TO BIGGAR, 19½ m. A 766 runs S.W., joining the Edinburgh–
Biggar road (A 702) before (5 m.) *Carlops* (Rte. 5c), in the country of Allan
Ramsay's ' Gentle Shepherd.'—8 m. **West Linton** (*Gordon Arms, Raemartin*,
RB. 17/6, P. 7 gs.) was once a town of some little impoitance, whose masons
were renowned for their skill in carving tombstones. In the village is Lady
Gifford's Well (re-erected 1861) surmounted by her figure, carved in 1666 by her
husband. A curious bas-relief on a house nearly opposite shows the dates 1678
and 1660, and figures representing ' the six progenitors of James Gifferd, his
awne portract and eldest sone.' *Halmyre House* (16th cent.), 2¾ m. S.E., is an old
residence of the Gordon family. The fine drovers' pass (1430 ft.) of *Cauld Stane
Slap* leads over the Pentlands to (13 m. ; 4 hrs.) Midcalder.—At (12½ m.) *Dolphinton* we are in Lanarkshire.—19½ m. Biggar, see below.

A 701 offers an alternative route (20 m.) from Penicuik to Biggar, passing
(9¾ m.) *Romanno Bridge* (Hotel, RB. 15/, P. 6 gs.) and (17¾ m.) *Skirling*, with a
hilltop church (1720) and the house of Lord Carmichael, in which is preserved the
embroidered cap worn by Charles I on the scaffold.—From Romanno Bridge
B 7059 descends the Lyne to Peebles (9¼ m.) passing Newlands church and
(3 m. r.) *Drochil Castle*, half fortress, half manor-house, begun by the Regent
Morton ; his execution in 1581, however, abruptly arrested its completion.

13 m. *Leadburn* (862 ft. ; Hotel, RB. 17/6) is in Peeblesshire. *Whim*, 1½ m. S.W., is a charming 18th cent. mansion,
now a hotel, (RB. 22/6, P. 8 gs.) *Lamancha House* (1663), 1½ m.
farther, was so called by an Earl of Dundonald after his
estates in Spain.

Peeblesshire, an inland county lying between Selkirkshire and Midlothian,
is sometimes called *Tweeddale*, from the fact that the Tweed rises and has nearly
half its course within it, with almost all the Peeblesshire streams as its tributaries.
It is, in the main, a hilly pastoral and agricultural region, pleasant and well
cultivated rather than strikingly picturesque, with rounded hills and numerous
streams that make it the best angling county in S. Scotland. Though more
secluded than the other Border counties it did not escape the Border unrest, as
is witnessed not more clearly by numerous pele-towers than by the pathetic
' Border Widow's Lament,' the beautiful ballad-dirge for a reiver executed in
1529. Peeblesshire is the county of Allan Ramsay's ' Gentle Shepherd ' and of
Scott's ' St. Ronan's Well ' and ' The Black Dwarf ' ; as well as of Crawford's

' Bush aboon Traquhair,' Laidlaw's ' Lucy's Flittin',' and several poems by Hogg. It may also be called the ' John Buchan country,' for his youthful holidays were spent in and around Broughton, and his first long novel ' John Burnet of Barns' centres round an old Peeblesshire mansion. The largest recorded salmon in Britain (69¾ lb.) was taken in the Tweed by the Earl of Home in 1730.

On the left extend the *Moorfoot Hills,* culminating in Black-hope Scar (2136 ft.).—18½ m. *Eddleston,* with the Black Barony Hotel (RB. 25/, P. 12½ gs.) occupying *Darnhall,* a 17th cent. mansion with fine grounds. On the high ground 1 m. S.E. are the pear-shaped *Milkieston Rings,* the largest fort in the county, with a detached rampart on the slope of the hill below. The road runs by the Eddleston Water, passing a memorial to G. M. Kemp, architect of the Scott Monument, who here served apprentice to a wheelwright.

23 m. **PEEBLES** (6020 inhab.), a royal burgh with woollen mills and an environment of pleasant villas, is charmingly situated on the Tweed. It is a quiet town, but, if the attractions of a pastoral hilly country, many historical associations, and excellent angling in the neighbouring streams appeal to the visitor, the sarcastic old tag, ' Peebles for pleasure,' is not so sarcastic after all.

Hotels. Peebles Hydro, on the slope of Ven Law, ½ m. E., RB. 30/, P. 14 gs.; **Minden,** Innerleithen Rd., with garden, RB. 25/, P. 10½ gs.; **Tontine,** High St., RB. 24/, P. 11 gs.; **Cross Keys,** Northgate, RB. 21/6, P. 9 gs.; **Green Tree,** E. end of High Street, RB. 19/6, P. 8½ gs.; **County,** High St., RB. 17/6, P. 8 gs.; **Venlaw Castle,** RB. 22/6, P. 10½ gs.; **Waverley,** unlic., High St., RB. 19/6, P. 8½ gs.

Post Office, Northgate.

Motor-Buses to *Biggar* (1 hr.), *Lanark* (1½ hr.) and *Glasgow* (2¾ hrs.); *Penicuik* (35 min.) and *Edinburgh* (1¼ hr.); *Innerleithen* (18 min.) and *Galashiels* (1 hr.), etc.

History. Peebles is of ancient foundation and its castle (now vanished) was a favourite hunting lodge of the early Scottish kings, particularly of Alexander III. The humours of its ancient fair or feast of Beltane are the subject of ' Peblis to the Play,' a poem ascribed both to James I and to James V. Though less harassed than towns nearer the border, Peebles was burned by the English more than once. It was occupied by Cromwell in 1649 and by the Pretender in 1745. Only a few fragments of the town walls remain. ' Old Q,' the notorious 4th Duke of Queensberry (1725–1810), and Robert Chambers (1802–71), publisher and author, are the most famous natives of the town. Mungo Park was a surgeon in Peebles (1801–2) between his African journeys.

We enter the town by Northgate, passing the 17th cent. *Cross Keys Inn,* formerly the town house of the Williamsons of Cardrona, claiming to be the original of the ' Cleikum Inn ' of which Meg Dods was the masterful hostess (' St. Ronan's Well '). Mungo Park lived at No. 7 in the Bridgegate, which leads to the right to the Eddleston Water. The shaft of the old *Town Cross* has been set up at the S. end of Northgate, nearly opposite the *Chambers Institution* (adm. free 10–7, closed Wed. at 12), a library and museum presented to the town by William Chambers (1800–83), brother and partner of Robert.

The older part (bearing the date 1644) was the town house of the Hays of Yester and afterwards of the Queensberry family. ' Old Q' (see above), who was born in the house, sold it in 1781. In the museum are the trowel of the Black Dwarf (see below), an axe used by Gladstone, and other relics, including the small print ' Affliction ' before which Burns and Scott had their only meeting (p. 63).

From the farther end of High St. an ancient bridge (15th cent. ; widened in 1834 and 1900) crosses the Tweed. The ' old town ' is reached by crossing the Cuddy Brig over the Eddleston Water at the W. end of High St. Here, in Biggies-knowe, were born the brothers Chambers (see above) at No. 18 and Prof. Veitch (1829–94), philosopher and poet, at No. 14. A little N. are the ruins of the *Cross Kirk*, built by Alexander III, on the spot where in 1261 a fine old cross was found ; the church, to which was attached a Trinitarian friary, served as the parish church until 1784.

From the old tower of the church of *St. Andrew* (founded in 1195), 1 m. W. of the Cross Kirk, we may follow the road (or, preferably, the agreeable path by the river ; gate opposite the tower) to the ruins of ***Neidpath Castle** (adm. *6d.*), beautifully situated on the left bank of the Tweed, c. 1¼ m. above Peebles. This stronghold passed from the Frasers to the Earls of Tweeddale, whose crest (a goat's head) surmounts the gateway of the courtyard. The 2nd earl held it for Charles II, but the old tower, to which a later castle had been united, was battered by Cromwell's cannon and taken after an obstinate resistance. The castle was purchased in 1686 by the 1st Duke of Queensberry, whose worthless successor, ' Old Q,' was denounced in a sonnet by Wordsworth as ' degenerate Douglas,' for wantonly cutting down the fine timber surrounding it.

A road, diverging to the left c. 1 m. beyond Neidpath and crossing the Tweed, ascends the lovely valley of the Manor Water (pron. ' mayner ') to (3½ m.) *Manor* church, and then (by the second turning on the left) to (4½ m.) the *Black Dwarf's Cottage* (rebuilt). Near the church is *Hallyards*, where Scott stayed with Prof. Adam Ferguson (1797) when he visited David Ritchie, the original black dwarf. Peebles may be regained by following the road round the S. side of the *Cademuir*. —Walkers may keep up the Manor Water between *Black Law* (2285 ft.) and *Dollar Law* (2680 ft. ; r.), then cross the watershed to strike the Megget Water and (c. 17 m. from Peebles) *St. Mary's Loch* (Rte. 8).

From Peebles to Symington, 20 m., by road ascending Tweeddale for 10 m. On the left (3 m.) is the ivy-covered tower of *Barns*, the residence in the 16th cent. of William Burnet, who on account of his propensity for marauding expeditions at night was nicknamed ' the howlet.' *Lyne Church* (1 m. N.W. on A 72 ; c. 1645) contains a contemporary pulpit and two canopied pews. B 712 follows the Tweed to the left.—5½ m. *Stobo Church* has some Norman work (13th cent.) at the doorway and in the nave and chancel. The whole upper portion of the Gothic window in the chancel from the spring of the arch is in one piece. The jougs still hang by the porch. Beyond Stobo Castle (r. ; 1805) the main road crosses the Tweed (p. 96) ; a more interesting but hilly route keeps N. of the Tweed, then, parting company with the river, commands a fine view of Upper Tweeddale.—11 m. *Broughton* stands at the crossing of the Edinburgh–Moffat road (A 701). The village is associated with John Buchan, Lord Tweedsmuir (1875–1940), who spent many holidays with his grandparents at their house, The Green, and located his first novel ' John Burnet of Barns ' at the neighbouring mansion of Barns (see above).

B 7016 runs W. and enters Lanarkshire.—16 m. **Biggar** (*Hartree*, 1 m. S.W., RB. 22/6, P. 14 gs. ; *Toftcombs*, ½ m. N.W., RB. 21/, P. 9 gs. ; *Elphinstone*, RB. 17/6, P. 8 gs. ; *Clydesdale*, RB. 16/6, P. 7½ gs.), a country town (1440 inhab.) of one wide street, was the birthplace of Dr. John Brown (1810–82), author of ' Rab and his Friends.' Beside the collegiate church of St. Mary, the last pre-Reformation foundation in Scotland (by Lord Fleming ; 1546), are the graves of the Gledstanes or Gladstones, ancestors of the statesman, whose grandfather left Biggar for Leith about 1756. Only one small tower remains of *Boghall Castle*

(½ m. S.), the seat of the Flemings.—17 m. We cross the Clyde.—20 m. *Symington,* see Rte. 9A.

From Peebles to *Innerleithen, Galashiels,* and the *Scott Country,* see Rte. 4B; to Upper Tweeddale and *Moffat,* see Rte. 8.

8. MOFFAT AND ITS ENVIRONS

Moffat stands on the main Dumfries–Edinburgh road (A 701), 2 m. from its crossing of the Carlisle–Glasgow road at Beattock. MOTOR-BUSES, see below.

MOFFAT (345 ft.), a clean and thriving little town (2110 inhab.), with one of the broadest High Streets in Scotland, is a favourite summer resort, a noted angling centre, and convenient for walks among the mountains and glens of the Border, interesting also for their associations with the Covenanters.

Hotels. Moffat House, with pleasant grounds, RB. 22/6, P. 10½ gs.; **Buccleuch Arms,** RB. 18/6, P. 10 gs.; **Annandale Arms,** RB. 21/, P. 8 gs.; **Balmoral, Star,** RB. 15/6, P. 8½ gs.; **Bankfoot,** unlic., in the N. suburb of Beechgrove, P. 7½ gs.

Motor-Buses to *Edinburgh* (2¼ hrs.); *Beattock* (5 min.) and *Dumfries* (55 min.); *Lochmaben* and *Annan* (1¾ hr.); in the season to *St. Mary's Loch* and *Selkirk* (Tues., Fri., Sat.); to the *Devil's Beef Tub* and *Broughton* (for Peebles).

In the High St., opposite a fountain with the figure of a ram, by Brodie, are the former *Bath Buildings,* now council offices. Close by is *Moffat House* (now occupied as a hotel), the mansion in which James Macpherson was a tutor when he published his first translation of the Ossianic fragments (1759). The sulphur spring, 1½ m. to the N.E. (with pavilion), was discovered in 1630, and in the 18th cent. Moffat was a kind of miniature Bath, and was visited by Hume, Blair, Boswell, and Burns.

John Macadam (1756-1836), the inventor of macadamised roads, died in the neighbouring mansion of Dumcrieff and is buried in the old churchyard; and John Locke (1805–60), the railway engineer, died here on holiday.—*Gallow Hill* (832 ft.), with pleasant wooded walks, rises N. of the town.

EXCURSIONS. *Bell Craig Glen,* 4 m. S.E., a picturesquely wooded and fern-clad ravine, is reached by a road crossing (2 m.) the Moffat Water, with Dumcrieff House on the left and a view (right) of the *Three Waters Meet,* where the Moffat, Evan, and Annan unite.—*Garpol Glen,* c. 2 m. S.W. (1 m. N. of Beattock), is another pretty glen, with the striking ruin of *Auchencass Castle,* a 14th cent. rectangular fort, probably the work of a follower of Edward I.—*Lochfell* (2256 ft.) c. 7 m. E., commanding the most central hill view in the district, is easily ascended viâ the valley of the Cornal Burn. The descent may be made viâ the Craigmichan Scaurs and the Selcoth Burn (see below) to Shortwoodend, c. 4 m. from Moffat.—The combined ascent of *White Coomb* (2695 ft.) and *Hartfell* (2651 ft.), the highest hills in the neighbourhood, is best begun by taking the Selkirk bus to the Grey Mare's Tail and thence ascending to Loch Skeen (see below). This route leads S.W. to the top of White Coomb and then over boggy hills W. to Hartfell. The descent thence may be made viâ the *Auchencat Burn* to Granton House, on the old Edinburgh road, 3 m. N. of Moffat. This is a round of c. 7 hrs., after quitting the bus.

FROM MOFFAT TO ST. MARY'S LOCH, 15 m. This fine road (A 708) leads at first S.E. and beyond (1 m.) *Hunterheck Hill* (retrospective view) descends to the Moffat Water, where it turns N.E., following the stream up Moffat Dale all the way to the Grey Mare's Tail. We cross (2 m.) the Craigie Burn (left) amid woods where " sweet fa's the eve on Craigieburn," but *Craigieburn House*, birthplace of Jean Lorimer, Burns's ' Chloris,' is not seen. 3 m. *Burns's Cottage* stands on the site of an inn in which Burns wrote his jovial song, ' O Willie brewed a peck o' maut.' We enjoy a fine view up Moffat Dale, with Bodesbeck Law prominent on the right.—4 m. *Shortwoodend.*

On the right are seen the *Craigmichan Scaurs*, of great interest to geologists, c. 2 m. up the Selcoth Burn (comp. above).

At (5½ m.) *Capplegill* the Blackshope Burn comes down from Hartfell, through a wild glen, a refuge of the Covenanters, with the curious double-peaked *Saddleyoke* (2412 ft.) on the right. To the right of the main road is *Bodesbeck Law* (2173 ft.), associated with Hogg's ' Brownie of Bodesbeck ' (comp. p. 20). Another wild glen opens on the left at (7 m.) *Carrifran* and 3 m. farther is the stream on which, to the left, is the ***Grey Mare's Tail** (over 200 ft. high), one of the highest waterfalls in Scotland. A path leads in 10 min. to the foot of the fall, " white as the snowy charger's tail," described in Scott's ' Marmion.'

Good walkers may ascend the steep hillside, on the left of the fall, and follow the stream to (1 hr.) its source in dark **Loch Skeen** (1750 ft.), a wild and solitary little ' lochan ' or tarn, situated under *Lochcraig Head* (2625 ft.). Ascent of White Coomb, see above.—A path, not easy to follow though marked by cairns, strikes off E., a few yards below Loch Skeen, and leads viâ Dobb's Linn, a Covenanter's hiding-place, to (1 hr.) Birkhill (see below).

At (11 m.) *Birkhill* (1080 ft.), close to the watershed between the Moffat and the Yarrow, we pass from Dumfriesshire into Selkirkshire. The road now descends.—14 m. *Chapelhope* was the home of the ' Brownie of Bodesbeck,' until the imprudent benevolence of his host set him wandering again.

The path ascending the Riskinhope Burn, where James Renwick, the last of the Covenanting martyrs, preached almost his last sermon, leads S. over to (4 m.) Ettrick Church.

We now skirt the little *Loch of the Lowes* (i.e. of the lakes), once probably part of St. Mary's Loch, from which it is now separated by a narrow neck of land. Here stands *Tibbie Shiel's Inn* (RB. 21/, P. 8½ gs.), long kept by Tibbie Shiel (Isabella Richardson ; 1783–1878), the famous scene of one of the ' Noctes Ambrosianæ ' of Christopher North (Prof. Wilson) and Hogg. De Quincey, Aytoun, Brewster, Lockhart, and many other eminent people have visited the once humble little anglers' inn. To the left of the main road is a seated statue, by A. Currie, of James Hogg, the Ettrick Shepherd.

15 m. ***St. Mary's Loch,** c. 3 m. long by ¼ m. broad, idyllically situated in a surrounding of smooth green hills, is " the lone St. Mary's silent lake " of ' Marmion,' on which the swan " floats double, swan and shadow," while " not a feature of those hills is in the mirror slighted " (Wordsworth).—16 m. *Rodono Hotel* (RB. 21/, P. 9 gs.), delightfully situated above the road and overlooking the lake, takes its name from the ancient barony of Rodonna, which comprised the valley of the Megget Water and was granted to the monks of Melrose in 1236.

On the hillside, 1¾ m. farther on and c. 1 m. from the foot of the loch whence issues the Yarrow, are the scanty ruins of *St. Mary's Chapel* and its peaceful graveyard, " where the shepherds of Yarrow are sleeping." Many traditions cling around this remote spot, where a service is annually held in August. The lovers in the ' Douglas Tragedy ' were buried in the chapel, with the customary appearance of briar roses from their graves. The chapel is the scene of Hogg's ballad of ' Mary Scott,' and his ' Mess John ' has its scenes in the vicinity.

From the Rodono Hotel to *Selkirk*, see Rte. 4B ; to *Tweedsmuir*, see below.

FROM MOFFAT VIÂ THE DEVIL'S BEEF TUB TO PEEBLES, 33 m. (A 701). Proceeding N. we leave the old Edinburgh road on the right and cross the Annan. The road mounts steadily, with views behind us over Moffat to Birrenswark, and to Skiddaw in Cumberland.—5½ m. The **Devil's Beef Tub** is a large semicircular hollow among the hills to the right of the road, forming the head of Annandale. In this out-of-the-way retreat the Johnstones are said to have hidden the cattle ' lifted ' in their raids. The sensational escape of the Laird of Summertrees in ' Redgauntlet ' was suggested by the daring feat of a rebel in 1746 who eluded his guards by plunging head over heels into the Beef Tub, then filled with mist.—A short distance farther we reach the watershed where ' Tweed, Annan, Clyde, Rise out o' ae hillside,' and the road begins to descend beside the infant Tweed, the source of which (*Tweeds Well* ; 1500 ft.) lies a little to the right.—From (14¾m.) *Tweedsmuir*, near the church of which is a standing stone, 5 ft. high, a fair road leads up the valley of the Talla, passing the great Talla Reservoir of the Edinburgh water supply, and then down the Megget Water to St. Mary's Loch, ½ m. N. of the Rodono Hotel.

16 m. *Crook Inn* (RB. 22/6, P. 12 gs.), once a famous posting house on the old high-road from Edinburgh to Dumfries, whence *Broad Law* (2754 ft.), second only to Merrick among Scottish hills S. of the Forth, may be ascended in 2 hrs. viâ the Hearthstane Burn.—At (21½ m.) *Rachan Mill* we turn right on B 712 and cross the Tweed. The main road goes on to Broughton and Penicuik.—23 m. *Drumelzier*, where Merlin's grave is pointed out between the Tweed and the Powsail. Thomas the Rhymer foretold that " When Tweed and Pausayl meet at Merlin's grave,

England and Scotland shall one monarch have"; and it is said that on the day of James VI's coronation the Tweed overflowed into the Powsail. Drumelzier Castle, now in ruins, was a fortress of the Tweedie family in the 16th century. A little farther on are the conspicuous ruins of *Tinnis Castle* (i.e. Thane's Castle).—Beyond the finely timbered park of *Dawyck* (r.) we recross the Tweed.—26½ m. *Stobo*, and thence to (33 m.) **Peebles,** see p. 92.

9. FROM CARLISLE TO GLASGOW

A. Viâ Lockerbie and Lanark

Road (A 74), 101 m.—24¾ m. **Lockerbie.**—38 m. *Beattock.*—57¼ m. *Abington* (alternative route thence, 94 m. viâ *Lesmahagow*; A 74).—A 73. 63¼ m. *Symington.*—73 m. **Lanark.**—A 72. 86½ m. *Hamilton.*—102 m. **Glasgow,** entered by Dalmarnock Bridge and Gt. Hamilton St. (Pl. 42).—Motor-Bus (viâ Lesmahagow) twice daily in 3¾–4¼ hrs.; from Symington to Glasgow (viâ Motherwell) in 1¾ hr.

Railway, 102¼ m., viâ Lockerbie and Carstairs in 2½–4 hrs. This is part of the 'West Coast Route' from London (Euston) to Scotland viâ Crewe and Preston: to Glasgow, 401½ m. in 8¾–10½ hrs. Principal stations: 20¼ m. *Ecclefechan.*—25¾ m. *Lockerbie.*—39¾ m. *Beattock* (for *Moffat*, 2 m.), beyond which the railway runs to over 1000 ft.—55¼ m. *Crawford.*—66¾ m. *Symington* (for *Biggar*, 3½ m.).—73½ m. **Carstairs,** junction for *Midcalder* and **Edinburgh** (Princes St.; 28½ m.).—89½ m. *Motherwell*, junction for *Hamilton* (4 m.).—102¼ m. **Glasgow** (Central).

Carlisle, see Rte. 2. We soon bear left, away from A 7. Beyond (6 m.) *Metal Bridge Inn* we cross the Esk and enter the Debatable Land, a Border tract long disputed by the adjacent countries until a boundary line was agreed upon in 1552. The tract, c. 8 m. long by 4 m. broad, extends N. to the Sark and was held by Border robbers and, indeed, until the time of James VI was "no other thing but theft, reiff, and slaughter."

On the left lies the **Solway Firth,** an estuary fed by the Eden, Esk, Annan, and Nith, and notorious for its dangerous tides, which sometimes rise with extraordinary rapidity, forming a bore 3 or 4 ft. high. Strangers should remember the caution given to Darsie Latimer (in 'Redgauntlet'), that "he who dreams in the bed of the Solway will wake up in the next world."

At (8 m.) *Sark Bridge* we enter Scotland (Dumfriesshire) and fork right.

Dumfriesshire, stretching N. from the Solway Firth to the wild hills on the borders of Peeblesshire, consists mainly of the parallel valleys of Nithsdale, Annandale, and Eskdale, with many smaller dales, such as Moffatdale, Dryfesdale, and Ewesdale. It has its own share in Border minstrelsy and its own memories of Border warfare. Sanquhar is a prominent name in the history of the Covenanters. Among the historic families of the county are the Bruces, the Comyns, the Johnstones, the Maxwells, the Jardines, and the Kirkpatricks; and the haughty Douglases were long its overlords. Robert Burns was a gauger and died at Dumfries, Thomas Carlyle was born at Ecclefechan; Ellisland and Craigenputtock, both in the county, are, in their way, scarcely less famous than Horace's 'Sabine farm.'

10 m. **Gretna Green** (*Gretna Hall*, unlic., RB. 18/6, P. 9 gs. ; *Greenlaw*, unlic., RB. 17/6, P. 8 gs.) was formerly the goal of runaway couples from England eager to take advantage of the Scottish law by which a declaration before two witnesses made a man and woman husband and wife. Since 1856, however, Scottish law required a residential qualification for at least one of the parties and in 1940 marriage ' by declaration ' was declared illegal. Some curios are shown in the once-famous smithy.—13 m. *Kirkpatrick Fleming*.

A narrow road crossing the railway (l.) ¾ m. farther on leads to *Cove House* (rfmts.), overlooking the Kirtle Glen. In the face of the sheer cliff above the river is *Bruce's Cave* (now made accessible by a gallery), where Robert Bruce was hidden for c. 3 months by Irving of Bonshaw. The cavern is man-made ; neolithic implements have been unearthed in the glen below.

From the main road we see (l.) the old tower of *Robgill*, the home of Gen. Sir Paulus Æmilius Irving (1751–1828 ; captured at Saratoga), and then the tower of *Bonshaw* and reach (16 m.) *Kirtlebridge* (Hotel, RB. 19/6).

In the churchyard of the ruined church of *Kirkconnell*, 2½ m. N., are the graves of ' Fair Helen of Kirkconnell Lee ' and her lover, Adam Fleming, who were waylaid at their trysting-place here by Bell of Middlebie, the suitor favoured by the lady's parents. Helen received the bullet intended for her lover. Fleming slew the assassin and fled abroad, but returned hither to die.

A fine view is obtained over Annandale, on the left, as we approach (19 m.) **Ecclefechan** (*Ecclefechan*, RB. 20/, P. 10 gs. ; *Cressfield*, *Kirkconnel Hall*, both unlic., RB. 17/6, P. 8 gs.), a little town famous as the birthplace of Thomas Carlyle (1795–1881) and as the ' Entepfuhl ' of ' Sartor Resartus.' In a house (the ' Arched House '), built by Carlyle's father and uncle, near the middle of the single street, easily identified by the archway or ' pend ' though it, are shown the room in which Carlyle was born, furniture brought from his study at Chelsea, and personal relics (N.T. ; adm. 6d., weekdays 10–dusk). At the top of the town is a replica of Boehm's statue of Carlyle at Chelsea. In the churchyard is his simple tomb, where he is buried with his parents and his brother.

About 3 m. N. is the hill of *Birrenswark* or *Burnswark* (920 ft. ; wide view) with four entrenched works at its foot and two more on top. This is the most probable site of the battle of Brunanburh (937), immortalised in an Anglo-Saxon poem, where Athelstan defeated the allied Scots (under Constantine I) and Dublin Danes (under Olaf Guthfrithson).—The Roman station of *Blatobulgium*, at *Birrens*, 1¾ m. E., between Middlebie and Kirtlebridge station, was occupied c. A.D. 80–300, with an intermission as at Newstead (p. 24).

On the hill above *Hoddam Castle* (1437–84), 2½ m. S.W. of Ecclefechan, is the watch-tower of *Trailtrow*. The word ' Repentance ', carved over the door, is said to commemorate the remorse of a Lord Herries for having pulled down a church to build Hoddam Castle or for having thrown his prisoners overboard during a storm while returning from a sea-raid on England.

Crossing the Water of Milk, we reach (24¾ m.) **Lockerbie** (*Lockerbie House*, N. of the town, with pleasant grounds, RB. 25/6, P. 12½ gs. ; *King's Arms*, RB. 21/, P. 10½ gs. ;

Dryfesdale House, unlic., N. on A 74, RB. 20/, P. 9 gs. ; *Blue Bell*, RB. 18/6, P. 9½ gs.; *Queen's*, RB. 25/; *Crown*, RB. 18/6), a Border town (2620 inhab.) noted for its lamb fairs. The phrase ' a Lockerbie lick ' refers to the cruel slaughter inflicted by the Johnstones upon the Maxwells, after defeating them at *Dryfe Sands*, N. of the Lochmaben road, in 1593.

Near Lockerbie is a ruined castle of the Johnstones, and ' Maxwell's Thorns,' on the W. side of the Dryfe, mark the spot where (traditionally) a lady of the Johnstones brained a Lord Maxwell with the great key of the castle, which she was pretending to surrender.

FROM LOCKERBIE TO DUMFRIES, 12 m. (motor-bus in 40 min.). A 709 crosses the Annan and skirts the Castle Loch.—4 m. **Lochmaben** (*Balcastle*, RB. 15/, P. 7 gs.), an ancient royal burgh (1125 inhab.), has a broad main street with a statue of Robert Bruce (1879), and is surrounded by five small lochs. The vendace (*Coregonus vandesius*), a small fish resembling smelt, which rejects all bait and is captured in nets, is peculiar to three of these lochs, including the *Castle Loch* (¾ m. square), to the S. Its introduction was probably due to the monks of some neighbouring convent, though tradition characteristically prefers Mary, Queen of Scots. At the S. end of the Castle Loch are the ruins of *Lochmaben Castle*, once of great extent and strength. This, or an earlier castle which stood on the W. side of the loch, disputes with Turnberry the honour of being the birthplace of Robert Bruce in 1274. Much of the land in this vicinity is held by the so-called ' kindly tenants of Lochmaben ' on a very ancient kind of copyhold tenure. *Elshieshields*, 1½ m. N., is one of the oldest Border towers still inhabited. —6 m. (r.) *Skipmire* was the birthplace of William Paterson (1658–1719), loosely called the founder of the Bank of England.—8 m. *Torthorwald*, commanding fine views of Nithsdale, preserves an old keep of the Carlyles and an 18th cent. thatched crutch cottage (to be opened as a folk museum).—12 m. *Dumfries*, see Rte. 18.

Soon after quitting Lockerbie the road crosses the Dryfe and enters ANNANDALE, the patrimony of the Bruces, abounding in memories of Border warfare. The Johnstones and the Jardines were other powerful families of Annandale. Ben Jonson claimed descent from the former.—28¾ m. On the left are *Jardine Hall* and, beyond the Annan, *Spedlin's Tower* (1605), once a Jardine residence.—31 m. We cross the Annan by the picturesque *Johnstone Bridge* (Dinwoodie Lodge, RB. 22/6, P. 11–14 gs.) beside Johnstone church (1733).

Approaching (38 m.) *Beattock*, we have a fine view up Moffatdale ; then, as we climb the vale of the Evan Water, the hills draw in, and the scenery becomes wilder. On the left is the pretty Garpol Glen (p. 93) and the 19th cent. Auchen Castle, now a hotel (RB. 25/, P. 13 gs.). Short of the summit (1014 ft.) we pass into Lanarkshire, and beyond it we descend into CLYDESDALE.—At (51½ m.) *Elvanfoot* the Elvan joins the Clyde, while in the glen of the Daer Water to the S. is a huge reservoir with a dam ½ m. long (completed in 1955) supplying industrial Lanarkshire with water.

FROM ELVANFOOT TO SANQUHAR, 15¾ m.—The road (B 7040) ascends the Elvan.—5¾ m. **Leadhills** (1350 ft. ; *Hopetoun Arms*, RB. 18/6, P. 9 gs.), once described by Dr. John Brown as " a dreary unexpected little town," was the birthplace of Allan Ramsay (1686–1758), author of ' The Gentle Shepherd,' and of William Symington (1763–1831), pioneer of steam navigation (p. 134).—

7¼ m. *Wanlockhead* (1380 ft.), in a bleak situation. The mines of these two mining villages, the highest villages in Scotland, have produced more lead than any others in the country, besides some gold and silver from the 13th cent. onwards, but the industry is now extremely intermittent. The fine road (B 797) goes on over the *Mennock Pass* (1409 ft.) to (13½ m.) *Mennock*, on the Nith, 2¼ m. S.E. of Sanquhar (Rte. 9B).—From either Leadhills or Wanlockhead a track may be followed, viâ the W. shoulder of *Lowther Hill* (2377 ft.), to (c. 8 m. from Wanlockhead) *Enterkinfoot* (p. 102), on the Nith, passing through the short, deep, narrow, and sudden **Enterkin Pass*, with its smooth vertical sides. Here as graphically described by Defoe in his ' Memoirs of the Church of Scotland,' a party of dragoons was trapped by Covenanters holding the heights, and was forced to surrender its prisoners.

From Elvanfoot by the Dalveen Pass to *Carronbridge*, see Rte. 9B.

54¼ m. *Crawford* (Crawford, RB. from 22/6, P. 10 gs.; *West End*, unlic., RB. 18/6, P. 8 gs., closed in winter), with a golf course, retains a fragment of Tower Lindsay, an old seat of the Lindsays, Earls of Crawford.—57¼ m. *Abington* (Abington, RB. 26/6, P. 12 gs.) is the starting-point of Dr. John Brown's charmingly described expedition up the Glengonnar Burn to Leadhills and thence by the Enterkin Pass to Mennock.

Here also A 74, the shortest route to Glasgow, diverges left, and, crossing rather featureless moorland, runs viâ (66 m.) *Douglas Mill* and (72 m.) *Lesmahagow* or *Abbey Green*, a village taking one name from St. Machute or Mahego, a Culdee misionary (6th cent.), the other from a vanished abbey (1144), colonised by Tironensian monks from Kelso ; and suggesting in its turn the name of Capt. Lismahago in ' Humphry Clinker.' It was the birthplace of John Greenshields (1795–1835), the sculptor.—At (84 m.) *Hamilton* the route described below is rejoined.

About 2 m. N. of Abington A 702 (r.) crosses the Clyde, for (10 m.) Biggar.—1¾ m. *Wandell Bower* was once a strong fortress guarded on three sides by the Clyde.—More remains of the late 16th cent. tower of (4 m.) *Lamington*, where the church (1721), once visited by Burns, who thought little of the sermon; retains a fine and elaborate Norman doorway. Sir William Wallace married the heiress of Lamington, and his chair is preserved in Lamington House.

On the left rises the isolated *Tinto Hill* (2335 ft.), a dull climb (best from Symington), rewarded by a view ranging from Goatfell to Arran, on the W., to the Bass Rock, on the E.

A cynical rhyme has it that " Be a lassie ne'er so black, Gin she hae the penny siller, Set her up on Tinto tap, The wind will blaw a man till her." To carry a stone to the top of Tinto was once a common form of penance. On the E. side of the hill are the ruins of *Fatlips Castle*, a seat of the Lockharts.

We enjoy a fine view (r.) of the hills at the head of Tweeddale as we approach (66¼ m.) **Symington** (*Tinto*, RB. 22/6, P. 10 gs.), junction of the road to Biggar (A 72).—On the opposite bank of the Clyde rises *Quothquhan Law* (1097 ft.). The Clyde makes a wide bend to the N.E., returning to the road at (70 m.) *Hyndford Bridge*, an important road-crossing (see below). A 73 runs N.W., past Lanark racecourse.—73 m. **Lanark,** and thence to (86½ m.) **Hamilton** and (102 m.) **Glasgow,** see Rte. 11.

FROM HYNDFORD BRIDGE TO EDINBURGH, 26 m. (A 70).—3 m. **Carstairs** (*Carstairs Arms*, RB. 17/6 ; *Station*, RB. 15/6) is an important railway junction where the lines from Carlisle to Edinburgh and Glasgow separate. A mile S. of Carstairs village is the Roman fort of *Castledykes*, occupied in the 1st and 2nd cent. (80–185), with the usual intermission. A brick with the emblem of the IInd Legion was found in excavation in 1950.—At (6 m.) *Carnwath* (Old Bush, RB. 16/6) part of a transept of the collegiate church, founded in 1424 by Thos. Somerville, adjoins the parish church ; little remains of the Somervilles' once-famous stronghold of *Cowthally Castle* (to the N. beyond the railway). On the right a road leads to (9½ m.) *Dolphinton* viâ (6½ m.) *Dunsyre*, with memories of the Covenanters. Skirting the rather dreary N.W. side of the Pentlands, with the large *Cobbinshaw Reservoir* (pike-fishing) 1½ m. off to the left, we enter the upper valley of the Water of Leith.—18¾ m. *Balerno*, and thence to Edinburgh, see Rte. 5c.

B. Viâ Dumfries and Kilmarnock

ROAD, 117 m. This pleasant route avoids the Clyde coalfield.—A 75 : 17 m. *Annan*.—33 m. **Dumfries**.—A 76 : 60 m. *Sanquhar*.—76 m. *Cumnock*.—83 m. *Mauchline*.—92 m. **Kilmarnock**.—A 735 : 100 m. *Dunlop*.—A 736 : 109 m. *Barrhead*.—117 m. **Glasgow**, entered viâ Pollokshaws and Eglinton St. (Pl. 40).

Motorists bound for the Highlands by this route may avoid Glasgow by striking W. from Kilmarnock to *Irvine* and proceeding thence viâ *Largs* to *Gourock* ; or by going from Barrhead to *Paisley* and *Erskine Ferry*.

RAILWAY, 115½ m. in 2¾–3¾ hrs. This is part of the 'Midland Route' from London (St. Pancras) to Scotland viâ Sheffield and Leeds : to *Glasgow*, 423½ m. in 9½–12 hrs. Principal stations : 17½ m. *Annan*.—33 m. **Dumfries**.—47¼ m. *Thornhill*.—59¼ m. *Sanquhar*.—70 m. *New Cumnock*.—81¾ m. *Mauchline*.—91½ m. **Kilmarnock**.—115½ m. **Glasgow** (St. Enoch).

From Carlisle to (8 m.) *Sark Bridge*, see Rte. 9A.—We fork left on A 75, through *Gretna*, and soon cross the Kirtle Water.

17 m. **Annan** (*Queensberry Arms*, RB. 21/6, P. 11 gs. ; *Central*, similar charges ; *Firth*, unlic., RB. 17/6, P. 10 gs.), a pleasant little royal burgh (4630 inhab.), once noted for shipbuilding, stands on the Annan, 2 m. from its mouth. No trace remains of the castle owned by Robert Bruce. Edward Irving (1792–1834), the friend of Carlyle and the founder of the Catholic Apostolic Church, was born here (at the corner of Butt St. and High St.) and was here deposed for heresy from the Scottish Church by the Presbytery of Annan. Hugh Clapperton (1788–1827), African explorer, was another native. Annan school is the 'Hinterschlag Gymnasium' of 'Sartor Resartus.'

Motor-buses to *Carlisle*; *Dumfries* (viâ Cummertrees) ; *Lockerbie* (viâ Ecclefechan) ; *Canonbie* and *Langholm* ; and *Lochmaben* and *Moffat*.—At *Chapelcross*, 3 m. N.E., are four atomic reactors built in 1955–60.

The direct road to Dumfries is dull ; it is more interesting, and only 1 m. longer, to turn left on crossing the Annan. At (20½ m.) *Cummertrees* (Powfoot Golf, RB. 21/6, P. 10 gs. ; *Richmond*, unlic., RB. 18/6, P. 8 gs.), a village on the Pow Water, we are in the neighbourhood of many of the scenes described in ' Redgauntlet.'—23 m. *Ruthwell* (pron. ' Rivvel ') is noted for the remarkable *Ruthwell Cross*, since 1887 preserved in the church (1800), to the right of the road (key at Glebe Cottage).

Ruthwell Cross, 18 ft. high, dates most probably from the early 8th century. It bears (in Runic characters) the earliest known specimen of written English, a poem on the Passion, in Northumbrian speech. The principal faces bear expressive carvings of scenes from the life of Christ, with Latin inscriptions, partly from the Vulgate. On the sides is foliage interlaced with birds and beasts devouring

fruit. The cross lay under the church floor from 1642 to 1790 and in 1823 was
erected in the manse garden. Dr. Henry Duncan (1774–1846), founder of the
savings bank movement (1810), was minister of Ruthwell in 1799–1843.

Comlongan Castle, a well-preserved ruin ½ m. W. of (24 m.)
Clarencefield, was a residence of the Warden of the Western
Marches, and is regarded by some as the scene of Wandering
Willie's tale in ' Redgauntlet.'—We skirt Lochar Moss (l. ;
10 m. long), with Criffel conspicuous on the left.

33 m. **Dumfries**, see Rte. 18. We cross the Nith and turn
right on the Glasgow road (A 76), ascending the broad and
well-cultivated valley of NITHSDALE, the country of the
Maxwells, the Crichtons, and the Comyns (comp. p. 181). At
(35 m.) *Newbridge* (Embassy, RB. 36/, P. 14 gs.) we cross the
Cluden Water.—At (40¾ m.) *Auldgirth* (Inn, RB. 17/6, P. 8 gs.)
the Nith is spanned by a bridge that Carlyle's father helped
to build. The ruined tower of *Lag* stands 2½ m. W. An
important Roman fort has been located N. of the park.

On a small lake in the park of *Dalswinton*, 2½ m. S.E. of Auldgirth, Patrick
Millar in 1788 first used steam to propel a small vessel. Burns was a passenger
on the trip and Lord Brougham witnessed it from the bank.

45 m. *Closeburn* has a castle, the old seat of the Kirkpatricks from whom the Empress Eugénie (1826–1920)
traced her descent. About 2½ m. N., on a little stream in a
remarkable ravine, is *Crichope Linn*, described in ' Old Mortality ' as the hiding-place of Balfour of Burley, when he
was visited by Morton—48 m. **Thornhill** (*Buccleuch and
Queensberry*, RB. 22/6, P. 11 gs. ; *George*, RB. 17/6, P. £8),
with a broad main street, is a neat and well-built little town
(1260 inhab.) ; the town cross, blown down in 1955 and now
restored, was erected in 1714 by the Duke of Queensberry.

The Buccleuch Hotel is on the site of the souter's shop where Burns (from
Ellisland) had his shoes repaired. Joseph Thomson (1858–94), the African
explorer, was born at Thornhill, and Kirkpatrick Macmillan (1813–78), inventor
of the bicycle in 1839, was born at *Keir*, 2 m. S.W., in Courthill Smithy (tablet).

Motor-buses run from Thornhill to the railway station ; to Penpont and
Moniaive (see p. 184) ; to *Sanquhar* ; viâ the Dalveen Pass and Crawford to
Biggar and *Edinburgh* ; to *Dumfries* viâ Dalswinton, etc.

50 m. *Carronbridge* stands at the foot of the Roman road
over the Dalveen Pass.

This road (A 702) ascends the Carron Water. To the right (4 m. from Carronbridge) is the charming little church of *Durisdeer* (1699) containing a fine *Monument, by Van Nost, to the second duke of Queensberry (d. 1711) and his duchess
(d. 1709). The road ascends gradually through the *Dalveen Pass*, one of the
finest passes in the Lowlands, and after reaching a height of 1105 ft. it descends
by the Powtrail Water to (15 m.) *Elvanfoot*, p. 98.

Morton Castle, 2½ m. N.E. of Carronbridge, on a small loch, was occupied by
Randolph, Earl of Moray, as Regent for David II. It afterwards passed to the
Douglases, a branch of whom became earls of Morton, and is now a ruin.

Drumlanrig Castle (no adm.), a seat of the Duke of Buccleuch, on the right
bank of the Nith, 1½ m. N.W., is a stately château of red stone, forming a hollow
square with corner turrets. It was built in 1675–88 by the first duke of Queensberry, who was so horrified by the expense that he spent only one night in the

completed castle. In 1745 it was occupied by the Young Chevalier on the retreat from Derby, when his followers wrought considerable damage. In the finely wooded park stands *Tibber's Castle*, the ruin of an Edwardian tower.

The road affords a view of Drumlanrig (l.) and follows the left bank of the Nith, with fine river scenery amid splendid oak woods.—54 m. *Enterkinfoot*. Beyond (58 m.) *Mennock*, on the opposite bank, lies *Eliock*, claiming to be the birth-place of the Admirable Crichton (1560–85? ; but comp. Clunie Castle).

For the track by the Enterkin Pass and the road by the Mennock Pass, both leading to Wanlockhead and Leadhills, see Rte. 9A.

60 m. **Sanquhar** (*Commercial* ; *Nithsdale*, both plain ; 2380 inhab.), famous in the history of the Covenanters, has been a royal burgh since 1484 and is a trim little town, with a tolbooth dating from 1735. A granite monument (1864) marks the site of the town cross to which in 1680 an armed band of Covenanters under Richard Cameron (p. 175) affixed the first ' Declaration of Sanquhar,' renouncing allegiance to Charles II. In 1685 a second Declaration was similarly affixed by James Renwick (see below), protesting against the ' usurpa-tion ' of James VII. The ruined castle to the S. was the refuge of the first duke of Queensberry on his retreat from Drumlanrig Castle.

The COVENANTS that played so important a part in Scottish history, especially in the 17th cent., were solemn national agreements of which a principal object was the maintenance of the Presbyterian form of worship as opposed to popery and prelacy. Two are of especial importance. The *National Covenant* of 1637, a renewal of an earlier Covenant of 1580, repelled the attempt of Charles I to impose prelacy and the Laudian service book upon Scotland. This was the Covenant enthusiastically signed in 1638 at Greyfriars Church in Edinburgh, and copies for subscription were sent all over the country. The *Solemn League and Covenant* of 1643, confirmed in 1646, was virtually a treaty between Scotland and England for the suppression of prelacy. The Covenanters were at first dominant and Charles II accepted both Covenants on landing in Scotland in 1650 and again at his coronation at Scone in 1651. At the Restoration, however, in 1660, he abjured them, and in 1662 they were declared illegal. The deprivation of ministers and other persecutions followed. In 1665 the Covenanters took up arms ; their resistance soon swelled into rebellion ; and in 1679 Claverhouse was defeated at Drumclog (p. 169). Repressive measures grew sterner and more ruthless as the struggle became embittered ; in 1685 adherence to the Covenants was declared treasonable ; and during the ' Killing Time,' which lasted from Aug. 1684 or Feb. 1685 (authorities differ) until the Revolution, the Covenanters, martyrs for conscience' sake, were mercilessly hunted down and too often slain with scant trial. Renwick, executed at Edinburgh on Feb. 17th, 1688, was the last Covenanting martyr.—Though all adherents of the Covenants were, of course Covenanters, that name is frequently used to mean specifically the persecuted Covenanters—the men of the moss-hags—between the Restoration and the Revolution.

Motor-buses from Sanquhar to *Dumfries*, and to *Ayr* viâ Cumnock.

63½ m. *Kirkconnel*, on the edge of the Ayrshire coalfield, is not to be confounded with the more famous Kirkconnell in S.E. Dumfriesshire.—We pass from Dumfriesshire into Ayr-shire and approach the Ayrshire coalfield.—71 m. *New*

Cumnock (Crown, plain) is at the junction of the Nith and the
' Sweet Afton ' of Burns. We leave the Nith and cross the
watershed (659 ft.).—76 m. **Cumnock** (4600 inhab. ; *Dumfries
Arms*, RB. 19/6, P. 10 gs. ; *Royal*, RB. 17/6, P. 8 gs. ; *Black
Bull*, RB. 15/), on the Lugar water, is a not unattractive coal-
mining town, once famous for its iron and for wooden snuff-
boxes (comp. p. 170). The cross in the square dates from
1703. Outside the Town Hall is a bust (by Benno Schotz) of
James Keir Hardie (1856–1915), who, born near Holytown,
spent most of his life in Cumnock.

At Bello Mill, in the village of *Lugar*, 2½ m. E. of Cumnock, was born William
Murdoch (1754–1839), the pioneer of coal-gas lighting (tablet). A cave here,
where he carried out his early experiments, is still a local curiosity.

From Cumnock to *Ayr* and to *Lanark*, see Rte. 17.

77½ m. *Auchinleck* (Railway Hotel). Auchinleck House,
3 m. W., was built by Lord Auchinleck (d. 1782), father of
James Boswell. Dr. Johnson, who visited it in 1733, was
" less delighted with the elegance of the modern mansion than
with the sullen dignity of the old castle," which adjoins.
Boswell (1740–95) is buried in the church.—83 m. **Mauchline,**
and thence viâ (92 m.) **Kilmarnock** to (117 m.) **Glasgow,** see
Rte. 16B.

10. FROM EDINBURGH TO GLASGOW

Edinburgh and Glasgow are connected by three distinct road routes and two
direct railway routes. The roads are described below ; the railways run as follows :
(A) viâ *Linlithgow*, 47¼ m., from *Waverley Station* to *Queen St. Station* in 1–1¼ hr.,
passing Polmont and Falkirk, an interesting route affording views of the hills to
the N. ; (B) viâ *Midcalder*, 46¼ m., from *Princes St. Station* to *Central Station* in
1¼–1¾ hr., passing through the oil-shale area and affording glimpses of the
Scottish ' Black Country '.

Of the road routes, the main trunk road, A 8, is the most rapid, but by-passes
all places of interest. Of the older roads, that viâ Midcalder and Holytown is
the shortest, but the longer route viâ Linlithgow is more interesting and commands the finest views northward. Parts of the new arterial road may be
combined with the routes viâ Bathgate or Midcalder.—Express Motor-Bus
hourly to Glasgow (Buchanan St.) in 1 hr. 40 min.

A. Viâ Linlithgow and Falkirk

47 m.—Motor-Bus to *Linlithgow* in ¾ hr. ; to *Falkirk* in 1 hr. ; from Falkirk
to *Glasgow* (Buchanan St.) viâ Cumbernauld in 1¼ hr. ; to *Glasgow* (Dundas St.)
viâ Kilsyth in 1⅓ hr.

We leave Edinburgh on A 8, viâ Haymarket Terrace (Pl. 29)
and Corstorphine, and, bearing r. on A 9, reach (7 m., l.)
Turnhouse airfield, with a terminal building (1953–55) by
R. H. Matthew. We cross the Almond, to enter West Lothian.

West Lothian or **Linlithgowshire,** the smallest Scottish county but two, has
a coast-line of c. 15 m. on the estuary of the Forth, with Bo'ness as its chief
harbour. It shares the reputation of the other Lothians for good farming, but its
mineral wealth (coal, oil-shale, iron) is more important. Linlithgow, Blackness
and Barnbougle Castles, Dalmeny and Abercorn, with their fine churches, and

F

Torphichen, with its memories of the Knights of St. John, are among its historic sites. The Forth Bridge unites the county with Fife.

8½ m. *Kirkliston* (Newliston Arms, RB. 15/6) has a well-sited church preserving a notable Romanesque doorway. Here are the tombs of the first Countess of Stair (the stern Lady Ashton of ' The Bride of Lammermoor ') and the second Earl of Stair (1673–1747). The latter is said to have planted the trees around his residence of *Newliston* (1 m. S.W.) to represent the formation of his regiment at the battle of Dettingen. The house, rebuilt in 1789–93 by Robert Adam, has wings by Bryce (1845). Round (10½ m.) *Winchburgh* vast heaps of reddish shale announce our approach to the oil-shale district, though the industry has diminished in importance in recent years. About ¾ m. S.E. is *Niddry Castle*, a 15th cent. tower of the Setons with 17th cent. additions, where Queen Mary passed the first night after her escape from Lochleven. On the right is a road to Abercorn and The Binns (Rte. 5D).

17 m. **LINLITHGOW** (*Star and Garter*, RB. 18/6, P. 9 gs. ; *Bonsyde*, 1¾ m. N. near the golf links, RB. 21/, P. 9 gs.), the county town of West Lothian, is an ancient little place (3930 inhab.) with a long High Street, steep-pitched roofs and numerous fountains (' Lithgow for wells, Glasgow for bells '), besides one of the most interesting churches in Scotland and the ruins of one of the finest palaces. In a park to the N. is Linlithgow Loch (c. 1 m. long), a favourite resort of skaters.

History. Linlithgow was one of David I's royal burghs and early a place of some importance. Edward I, who encamped beside the town the night before the first battle of Falkirk (1298), wintered in Linlithgow in 1301, and in 1302 built a tower or pele, afterwards incorporated in the palace that was long a favourite royal residence. James V was born in the palace in 1512 and his daughter Mary in 1542. In 1570 the Regent Moray, as he rode through " old Linlithgow's crowded town," was shot from a balcony by James Hamilton of Bothwellhaugh, who escaped on a horse held in readiness at the back of the house, as related in Scott's ballad of ' Cadyow Castle.' The house was immediately burned and its owner, John Hamilton, Archbishop of St. Andrews, captured at Dumbarton Castle in 1571, was put to death. The legend of the Regent's previous ill-treatment of the assassin's wife and child has been disproved, though adopted by Scott. Edinburgh University temporarily transferred its seat to Linlithgow in 1645–46, when plague was raging in the capital. In 1651–59 the town was garrisoned by Cromwell ; and in 1745 Prince Charles Stewart passed through it.

Several late 16th cent. houses survive in the High St. Here also is the *Fountain of St. Michael*, bearing the inscription ' 1720 St. Michael is kinde to strangers.' Near the present *Town Hall* (r.) is the *Cross Well*, with its quaint figures of burghers and others, a reproduction (1807) of an earlier fountain said to have dated from James V's reign. The *County Buildings*, on the S. side of the High St., stand on the site of the house from which Moray was shot (tablet). Ascending the Kirkgate hill we pass the old *Town House* (l.)

and the *County Hall* (r.) and reach the precincts of the palace and church, which are entered through an embattled and vaulted *Gateway* erected by James V c. 1535.

Over the entrance are the (restored) insignia of four orders of knighthood to which James V belonged : the Garter, of England (three lions), St. Andrew, of Scotland (one lion), the Golden Fleece, of Spain (castles and lions), and St. Michael, of France (fleurs de lys).

The ***Church** *of St. Michael*, in the Scottish Dec. style showing marked French influence, is one of the finest parish churches in Scotland. It is open daily 10–12, 1–5.

The church was consecrated in 1242 by Bp. David de Bernham, of St. Andrews, but the present edifice is due to a rebuilding after a fire in 1424. The chancel (c. 1497) and tower are later than the nave, and the apse was not completed until 1531. Until 1821 the tall pinnacled tower was surmounted by an open crown, like that of St. Giles, added by James IV. Beneath the tower is a fine doorway, and there is another entrance on the S. side, under an elegant porch with a priest's chamber and an unusual oriel above it. The image of St. Michael, at the S.W. angle, is the only image that survived the Reformation.

The stately and wide NAVE has five bays, with pointed arches resting on clustered piers. The triforium and the clerestory, each with a main arch enclosing two smaller lights, deserve note. The window tracery is very varied and graceful, especially that of the Flamboyant window in the S. transept. It was in this transept, called St. Catherine's Aisle, that just before Flodden an apparition warned James IV against war with England. The chancel continues the general design, but the triforium is blank. At the E. end of the church is a three-sided apse of tall windows with austere tracery. The stalls and reredos date from 1956. In the vestry is a stone altarpiece, representing the Passion and Betrayal of Christ.

The ***Palace** (adm. 1/, weekdays 10–4 or 7, Sun. from 2) is a fine example of a fortified palace, externally somewhat heavy and severe, but with a more attractive inner quadrangle. The original entrance was on the E. side, approached by a drawbridge (now removed) over the moat. We now enter by a low portal, flanked with turrets, on the S. side, but it is well worth while to walk round the exterior, noting the N.W. oriel.

There was probably a royal dwelling here in the time of David I, but the earliest work seen to-day is the tower of Edward I (1302) at the S.W. angle. The W. side of the quadrangle dates partly from James I, the real founder of the present palace ; the S. and E. sides, architecturally the richest, from the reign of James V. The N. side collapsed in 1607 and was rebuilt after 1618. The capture of Edward I's castle in 1313 by a handful of Scots who entered concealed in a load of hay is one of the romantic feats that abound in Scottish history. The later palace was a favourite abode of several queens, and here James IV's Queen Margaret " all lonely sat and wept the weary hour," vainly awaiting his return from Flodden. Henry VI of England, a refugee after Towton, found shelter here in 1461–62. Charles I was the last monarch to sleep in the palace (1633). The palace remained perfect until 1746, when it was burned, probably accidentally, by General Hawley's troops who were quartered here a fortnight after the second battle of Falkirk.

In the midst of the quadrangle is a richly and boldly sculptured fountain, built for James V (reproduced at Holyroodhouse). At each angle is a round staircase-tower, and on the N. side there is a fifth (octagonal) tower, dated 1620. The chief apartments are on the first floor : on the E. side is the *Great Hall*, 94 ft. long, lighted by tall windows on each side, with a huge fireplace and ornamented mantelpiece at one end, while at the other it communicates with the *Kitchen*. In the S. wing are the *Chapel*, which has five lancet windows, and a large hall. On the W. side of the quadrangle are the *Royal Apartments*, comprising the *King's Hall*, the *Presence Chamber* and the *Bedchamber*. Two beautifully carved recesses in the N. wall are the remains of the *King's* and the *Queen's Oratories*. The room in which Mary, Queen of Scots, was born on Dec. 7th, 1542, while James V, her father, was lying on his deathbed at Falkland, may have been in the rebuilt N. wing. The N.W. tower staircase ascends to a little octagonal turret with a groined roof, known as *Queen Margaret's Bower*, where that queen kept her sad vigil.

Bo'ness (contracted from **Borrowstounness**), 3½ m. N., is an industrial town (9950 inhab.) connected by bus with Falkirk, Linlithgow, and Edinburgh (viâ S. Queensferry). *Kinneil House* (S.W. of the town ; adm. 6*d.* ; 10–7, or 12–4 ; Sun. from 2), a 16–17th cent. seat of the dukes of Hamilton, contains wall-paintings and a large Crucifixion found in 1951 beneath the ruins of the old parish church. The mansion was occupied by Dugald Stewart (p. 171) and earlier by John Roebuck (1718–94), co-founder of the Carron Ironworks in 1760 (tomb in Carriden churchyard, E. of the town). In the grounds, now a public park, is the outhouse in which James Watt (invited by Roebuck) developed his invention of the condensing steam engine, his first engine being erected at the adjacent Burn Pit colliery in 1765. A large iron cylinder, cast to Watt's design for the mine pump at Schoolyard Pit, was set up alongside, in 1946, as a memorial.

The **Antonine Wall,** the Roman fortification extending from the Forth at Bridgeness, 1 m. E. of Bo'ness, to Old Kilpatrick on the Clyde, a distance of 36 m., was a turf rampart with a parallel ditch on the N. and a military road on the S. It dates from A.D. 138–142, when Lollius Urbicus reoccupied a line of posts set up by Agricola in A.D. 80–81, and was strengthened by 17 forts, of which nine have been excavated, with at least two outlying forts to the W., S. of the Clyde. Only intermittent portions of the wall, formerly known as Graham's or Grim's Dyke, are visible, and of three of the forts there is no trace above ground. The site of the easternmost fort, at *Carriden*, ¾ m. S.E. of the E. end of the wall, has been almost certainly identified as *Velunias*, from an inscription discovered near Bo'ness in 1955. This, with a good collection of other inscriptions and sculptures found along the wall, is in the Museum of Antiquities in Edinburgh ; but no other fort can yet be certainly named. The wall was abandoned within a few years of the end of the 2nd cent. A.D.

Linlithgow is connected by bus also with *Grangemouth*, with *Stirling* viâ Falkirk, with *Blackness*, and with *Bathgate* ; Torphichen is 4½ m. S.

We cross the Avon and enter Stirlingshire at (17¾ m.) *Linlithgow Bridge*, in 1526 the scene of a battle between the Earls of Angus and Lennox for the custody of the youthful James V.—Beyond (22 m.) *Polmont* (Inchyra Grange, RB. 20/, P. 10 gs.) A 905 diverges on the right for Kincardine Bridge (10 m. ; p. 255).

This road, in 1½ m., traverses the W. outskirts of **Grangemouth** (*Lea Park*, RB. 25/6, P. 14 gs. ; *Queen's*, RB. 16/6, P. 7 gs.), an active and growing seaport

(15,430 inhab.) with oil-refining and chemical works, and large docks extending for 2 m. N.E. at the mouth of the Carron and the Forth–Clyde Canal.

25 m. **Falkirk** (*Royal*, High St., RB. 17/6, P. 7 gs.), an irregular old town (37,530 inhab.) with narrow and sometimes steep streets (one-way traffic), is a centre of the light castings industry. Entering High St. we reach Callendar Riggs (approached from Glasgow viâ Newmarket St. and Princes St.), the principal bus station of Falkirk. In High St. are a well-head (1817), on the probable site of the town cross, and *Falkirk Steeple* (1814), opposite which a bootmaker's shop occupies the site of the house in which Prince Charles Edward slept in 1746. The *Cross Keys Inn* on the right, farther on, was visited by Burns. In *Dollar Park* is a small but excellent local museum (9–12.30, 2–5, 6 or 9 ; closed Sun. & Mon.).

Falkirk gives name to two important battles. In the first, fought on the S. side of Callendar Wood in 1298, Edward I defeated William Wallace ; in the second, at Bantaskyne, S.W. of the town, Prince Charles Edward, retreating N., inflicted a severe repulse on General Hawley in Jan. 1746.

Falkirk was formerly noted for its *Trysts*, or cattle-fairs, held monthly from April to Nov. on Stenhouse Muir, c. 3 m. N. of the town. Immense quantities of live-stock congregated here from far and near, including cattle from the Western Isles, sheep from Ross and Sutherland, even ponies from Shetland, and after sale found their way farther S. by the great drove roads. About 1 m. beyond the N. quarter of Grahamston are the well-known Carron Ironworks, founded in 1760, where carronades (an old type of naval gun) were first made.

A well-preserved portion of the rampart of the Antonine Wall may be seen at Watling Lodge, 1¼ m. W. of Falkirk ; and ¾ m. farther on is *Rough Castle*, the best preserved of all the forts on the wall, in a commanding site, with 'civilian' annexes. The rampart is well seen also at Callendar House (no adm.), just S.E. of Falkirk, and in Seabegs Wood, ½ m. W. of Bonnybridge (see below).

After quitting Falkirk we have pleasing views to the N. of the Ochil Hills and the rich vale of the Forth, with Ben Ledi and Ben Vorlich behind. The road crosses and then runs parallel with the Forth and Clyde Canal, and follows for a time the line of the Roman Wall, through the industrial villages of (26¼ m.) *Camelon*, (29 m.) *Bonnybridge*, and (30 m.) *Dennyloanhead*, beyond which we bear left on A 80.—31¾ m. *Castlecary* is near one of the forts on the Antonine Wall, and there are others on the low hills (Croy Hill, Bar Hill, etc.) overlooking the Kelvin valley beyond the railway on the right. 33 m. *Cumbernauld* (by-pass), at the divergence of the Carlisle road, is to be the centre of a 'new town.'—At (37 m.) *Mollins-burn* we enter *Lanarkshire* and run viâ (39½ m.) *Muirhead* and the suburban areas of Stepps, Barlinnie (with its prison), and Alexandra Park, to enter (47 m.) **Glasgow** by Garngad Rd. (Pl. 21).

B. From Edinburgh to Glasgow viâ Bathgate

44½ m.—MOTOR-BUS to *Glasgow* (Buchanan St.) in 2¼ hrs.

From Edinburgh to (7 m.) *Turnhouse*, see Rte. 10A. Thence we follow the arterial road (A 8), passing (r.) the site of the

Royal Highland Show at *Ingliston*, and crossing the Almond at (9 m.) *Newbridge* (Norton, to the left, RB. 30/, P. 15 gs.) to enter West Lothian. The new road by-passes the mining villages of (11 m.) *Broxburn* and (13 m.) *Uphall*. Uphall church (12–13th cent., with the Shairp aisle of 1620) contains the graves of Lord Chancellor Erskine (1750–1823), Henry Erskine (1746–1817), and Principal Shairp (1819–85 ; born at *Houston*, a 16th cent. mansion with crow-stepped gables just S. of the village). The arterial road bears off to the left, 1½ m. short of Bathgate, to join the route via Midcalder (Rte. 10c).

18½ m. **Bathgate** (*Dreadnought, Kaimpark*, at both RB. 21/) is a pleasantly situated little town (11,300 inhab.) depending on the coal and mineral oil industries. Sir James Y. Simpson (1811–70), who introduced the use of chloroform in 1847, was the son of a baker of Bathgate.

At *Torphichen*, the birthplace of Henry Bell (1767–1830), pioneer of steamboat transport, c. 2½ m. N., is the curious church (c. 1450) of the Knights of St. John of Jerusalem, who from c. 1153 had their Scottish seat here (adm. *3d.* ; 10–4 or 7, Sun. from 2). It consists simply of a gabled tower and transepts, the latter vaulted with an upper chamber above. A Romanesque W. arch survives ; the nave, rebuilt in 1765, is now the parish church.—The Bathgate Hills rise to 1017 ft. E. of the road to Torphichen. On *Cairnpapple*, N. of the highest summit, is a fine late Bronze Age burial cairn (adm. *3d.*), built on top of two earlier sanctuaries (c. 1800 B.C.–c. 200 A.D.).

21¼ m. *Armadale* is a high-lying little burgh (5800 inhab.). About 5 m. farther on we enter *Lanarkshire*, with the Hillend reservoir (641 ft.) on our right. We descend into the Scottish ' Black Country ' at (33 m.) *Airdrie*, a mining town of 30,300 inhabitants.—35 m. *Coatbridge* (47,550 inhab.), the chief centre of the Scottish iron trade.—44½ m. **Glasgow,** see Rte. 11.

C. From Edinburgh to Glasgow via Midcalder

44 m.—MOTOR-BUS to *Glasgow* (Carlton Place) via Bellshill in 2¼ hrs. ; via Shotts and Hamilton to *Glasgow* (Buchanan St.) in 2⅔ hrs.

We leave Edinburgh by Dalry Rd. (Pl. 36) and Gorgie, and in 5¼ m. cross the little used Union Canal, passing (l.) *Riccarton*, a mansion of 1621, used in 1940–54 as Scottish Anti-Aircraft Command H.Q.—7½ m. *Dalmahoy*, an estate famous for its trees.—12 m. **Midcalder** is a little town, 1½ m. N.W. of its railway station. The church (enlarged) has a choir rebuilt by Sir James Sandilands in 1541 and restored in 1932. Abp. Spottiswood (1565–1639) was born in the manse.

Linhouse, to the S., is a fine late-16th cent. mansion ; while *Calder House*, to the W., is memorable as the mansion in which, in 1556, the Communion was first administered after the Protestant rite by John Knox. Here also Chopin stayed, as the guest of Lord Torphichen, for a brief holiday during his triumphant tour of Britain in 1848. The two legal Erskines (comp. above) died at their country house of *Amondell*, 1¾ m. N.E.

From Midcalder A 71 runs S.W. via (5 m.) *Westcalder*, through an oil-shale area, to (14 m.) *Shotts*, once noted for its ironworks, and (20 m.) *Wishaw*.

The Glasgow road (A 705) ascends the Almond valley to (15 m.) *Livingston* and (21 m.) *Whitburn* (Road House, RB. 17/6), with a police training college, where the arterial road (A 8) comes in on the right. Crossing a dreary moor, we enter Lanarkshire at (23½ m.) *Harthill*, and farther on is the television station of *Kirk o' Shotts*. At (30 m.) *Newhouse* (Hotel, RB. 25/) the old and new roads again separate. The new road (r.) avoids the worst of the industrial area, and crosses the Glasgow–Coatbridge road at (37 m.) *Baillieston*, approaching (44 m.) **Glasgow** by Alexandra Park.

The old road from Newhouse runs through (32 m.) *Holytown* (1½ m. N. of *Carfin*, p. 131) and (33¾ m.) *Bellshill*, with huge disused sandstone quarries. Passing (36 m.) *Uddingston*, we enter (45 m.) **Glasgow** by Gallowgate (Pl. 35).

11. GLASGOW AND ITS ENVIRONS

GLASGOW (1,089,770 inhab.), by far the most populous town and most important seaport of Scotland and the third city for population in Great Britain, is a busy, strenuous, and opulent commercial community and the centre of an industrial district, in which almost no manufacture in the United Kingdom is unrepresented. The shipbuilding yards on the Clyde between Glasgow and Greenock are renowned all over the globe ; scarcely less noted are its chemical works, its engineering works, its iron works, and its textile factories. Ships from every part of the world enter and clear at its spacious docks. Glasgow, mainly in Lanarkshire though it has overflowed into Renfrewshire and Dunbartonshire, is situated on the Clyde, 14 m. above Dumbarton, where the Firth of Clyde begins. It is the seat of the oldest university in Scotland after St. Andrews, and it contains a fine cathedral, a notable gallery of art, and many splendid public buildings, though the relics of its antiquity have almost disappeared. The Corporation of Glasgow enjoys a special reputation for the efficiency and variety of its municipal activities : tramways, illumination, parks, libraries, markets, and watersupply (introduced in 1859 from Loch Katrine), as well as the Art Gallery are under its direct control. The rise of the ' Glasgow School ' of painting at the end of the 19th cent. is a testimony to the city's love of art.

Railway Stations. *Central* (Pl. 26), for Carlisle, London, Edinburgh, Greenock, etc., with ' Low Level ' station for Balloch (Loch Lomond), etc.—*St. Enoch* (Pl. 34), for Carlisle, and S.W. Scotland.—*Buchanan Street* (Pl. 20), at the N. end of Buchanan St., for the North.—*Queen Street* (Pl. 27), for Edinburgh and the North, West Highland Line, England by the East Coast route, etc., with ' Low Level ' suburban station.

Airport at *Renfrew*, 7 m. W., for services to Aberdeen, Inverness, Orkney, and Shetland, Campbeltown and the Western Isles ; also to Belfast, Dublin, Manchester, London, Paris, etc. Booking office, St. Enoch Square ; coach to airport 2/6.—*Prestwick Airport* for international services, is 30 m. S.W. (see p. 167).

Hotels. Central (a ; 26), at the Central Station, RB. 51/; **More's** (e ; 25), 18 India St., RB. 39/6 ; **St. Enoch** (b ; 33, 34), at St. Enoch Station, RB. 37/6 ; **North British** (c ; 27), at Queen St. Station, RB. 42/; **George** (k ; 27), RB. 35/, **Ivanhoe**, RB. 30/, 235 and 185 Buchanan St.; **Blythswood**, 320 Argyle St., RB. 28/6 ; **Bath** (h ; 19, 26), 152 Bath St., RB. 27/6.— Unlicensed : **Green's**, 22 Woodlands Terr. (Pl. 17), RB. 25/, P. 9 gs. ; also, in the W. district (beyond Pl. 2), **Cleveden Court**, 61 Cleveden Drive, RB. 30/, P. 11 gs. ; **Belhaven**, 23 Belhaven Terr., Gt. Western Rd., RB. 25/, P. 8 gs. ; **Grosvenor**, 1 Grosvenor Terr., **Cavendish, Devonshire**, 1 and 5 Devonshire Gdns., P. from 8–8½ gs., and many others.

Restaurants. *Malmaison*, at the Central Hotel ; *Rogano*, 11 S. Exchange Place (noted for sea-food) ; *One-o-one*, 101 Hope St. ; *Copacabana*, 60 Bath St. ; *Guy's*, 196 Hope St. ; *Ferrari*, 174 W. Nile St. and 10 Sauchiehall St.; *Whitehall*, West Regent St. ; *Grosvenor*, 74 Gordon St.; *Berkeley*, North St., Charing Cross (Pl. 18 ; T. and D. only); *His Lordship's Larder*, 4 St. Enoch Place ; *Adelphi*, St. Enoch Sq. ; *Ivy*, 111 St. Vincent St. ; *Sloan's*, Argyle Arcade ; *Wendy's* (unlic.), 245 Sauchiehall St., 104 W. George St. ; *Lang's*, 83 W. George St. and 73 Queen St. (sandwiches, etc. ; customers help themselves ; open till 6) ; *Reid's*, 34 Gordon St. and 286 Buchanan St. (unlic. ; open till 9) ; *Fuller's*, Buchanan St. & Gordon St. (L. & T. ; unlic.). Also at the larger cinemas and department stores.

General Post Office (Pl. 27), George Square, open 6–10, Sun. 9 or 10–4 or 5 ; telegraph office always open.

Municipal Information Bureau, St. Enoch Sq. (9–5, Sat. 9–12.30).

American Consulate, 7 Woodside Terrace, C.3 (Pl. 18).

Taxicabs, 2/ per mile, 4*d.* each additional mile ; waiting 4*d.* per 3 min. after the first six min. ; each passenger beyond 2, 6*d.* ; luggage above 56 lb., 6*d.*

Tramways and **Trolley-Buses** traverse the principal streets and serve outlying suburbs. The trams are being gradually replaced by motor-buses. The focal point of the system is the junction of Argyle St. and Union St. (Pl. 33). Enquiries to 46 Bath St.

Motor-Buses. Practically every town and village within a wide radius around Glasgow may be conveniently reached by motor-bus services, the chief starting-places of which are : Buchanan St. & Killernont St., just S. of Buchanan St. Station (Pl. 20) ; Carlton Place (Pl. 33, 40) ; Clyde St. (Pl. 33) ; Dundas St. (Pl. 27) ; 46 Parliamentary Rd. (Pl. 20) ; St. Enoch Sq. (Pl. 33) ; and Waterloo St. (Pl. 26).—MOTOR-COACH EXCURSIONS in summer from 194 Buchanan St. or 46 Parliamentary Rd. to all parts of the Highlands and Lowlands. A popular afternoon excursion is the *'Three Lochs'* (Loch Lomond, Gareloch, Loch Long) from Buchanan St. (6/).

LONG-DISTANCE SERVICES to *Edinburgh* viâ Bathgate (2¼ hrs. ; 4/6) ; *Aberdeen* viâ Stirling, Perth, and Dundee or Forfar (6¾–7 hrs. ; 14/6) ; *Dunfermline* (2 hrs. ; 4/), with connections for the Fife Coast ; *St. Andrews* (4 hrs. ; 7/9) ; *Inverness* in summer viâ Stirling, Perth, and Pitlochry (8½ hrs. ; 23/6) ; *Oban* (4½ hrs. ; 10/7) ; *Ayr* viâ Kilmarnock or Troon (1¾–2¼ hrs. ; 3/5 or 4/) *Dumfries* (3¾ hrs. ; 8/2) ; etc. Also to *London* (16 hrs. ; 40/), *Liverpool* or *Manchester* (25/2), etc.

Underground Railway (frequent service on a circular route). *St. Enoch* (subway station), *Buchanan St., Cowcaddens, St. George's Cross, Kelvin Bridge, Hillhead, Partick Cross, Merkland St., Govan Cross, Copland Road, Cessnock, Kinning Park, Shields Road, West Street, Bridge St., St. Enoch.*—**Suburban Railways**, CATH-CART CIRCLE. *Central* (High Level), *Eglinton St., Pollokshields* (*West*), *Maxwell Park, Shawlands, Pollokshaws* (*East*), *Langside, Cathcart, Mount Florida, Crosshill, Queen's Park, Pollokshields* (*East*), *Eglinton St., Central.*—RUTHERGLEN TO POSSIL. *Rutherglen, Dalmarnock, Bridgeton Cross, Glasgow Green, Glasgow Cross, Central* (Low Level), *Anderston Cross, Stobcross, Partick* (*Central*), *Partick* (*West*), *Crow Road, Maryhill,* and *Possil.*

Ferries (free) cross the Clyde at *Finnieston* (Pl. 31), *Kelvinhaugh* (Pl. 22 ; foot passengers), *Govan, Meadowside* (foot), and *Whiteinch.* No vehicular ferries on Sunday.

Steamers from Glasgow to places down the Clyde start from Clyde Place (Pl. 33), on the S. bank (but see p. 141). The packets for *Belfast* and

Derry start from the Broomielaw (N. bank); for *Dublin* from Anderston Quay (N. bank). Long-distance liners berth at George V Dock, Shieldhall.

Amusements. THEATRES. *King's* (Pl. 18), Bath St.; *Citizen's*, Gorbals St. (Pl. 41), repertory; *Alhambra*, 105 Hope St. (Pl. 26); *Empire*, Sauchiehall St. (Pl. 26); *Pavilion*, Renfield St. (Pl. 19); *Metropole*, Stockwell St. (Pl. 34).—CINEMAS. *Gaumont*, *La Scala*, *Regal*, 140, 155, and 326 Sauchiehall St.; *Green's Playhouse*, *Odeon*, Renfield St.; *Cosmo* (continental films a specialty), Rose St. (Pl. 19); *Gaumont*, 1544 Gt. Western Rd. (Anniesland Cross); news theatre at 17 Renfield St.—CONCERTS. *Scottish National Orchestra*, on Sat. evenings in winter (Nov.–Feb.), in St. Andrew's Hall (Pl. 18), on Sun. evenings in Green's Playhouse or Odeon cinema; data about other concerts from Cuthbertson, 226 Sauchiehall St.—DANCING. *Majestic Ballroom*, Hope St. and Renfrew St.; *Astoria*, *Locarno*, 490, 506 Sauchiehall St. (Charing Cross).—GREYHOUND RACING at Shawfield Stadium, Rutherglen.—ICE SKATING AND CURLING at the rink adjoining Crossmyloof station.—GOLF. Eight public courses in the environs (2/–3/ per 18 holes; Sun. play); also 8 private courses for which an introduction is not necessary. —RUGBY FOOTBALL at the High School ground, Old Anniesland (Dumbarton Rd.), etc.—ASSOCIATION FOOTBALL at Hampden Park (international matches, Queen's Park club), Ibrox Park, on the Paisley Rd. (' Rangers '), Celtic Park, Bridgeton (' Celtic '), etc.

Glasgow Fair is an old-established public holiday, in the 2nd or 3rd week in July, when the factories, etc., are closed, but no fair is now held.

History. St. Kentigern (d. 603), alias St. Mungo (' dear one '), is the patron saint of Glasgow, and *Glascau* (' green hollow ') is believed to describe the spot on the bank of the Molendinar where he dwelt and died, after coming from Culross to convert the Britons of Strathclyde. The name of his mother Thenew persists in Glasgow in the form ' St. Enoch,' and his miracles figure in the arms of the city: the tree is the frozen branch with which he rekindled the monastery fire, the bird is the decapitated redbreast he restored to life, the salmon with a lost ring in its belly was a miraculous capture to save the honour of a princess, the bell was brought from Rome by the saint in his later years. The city motto—in its fuller form, ' Let Glasgow flourish by the preaching of the Word '—is carried back to him. Glasgow relapsed into paganism, but in 1115 David I restored the bishopric and c. 1180 William the Lion granted a charter making Glasgow a burgh ot barony holding of the bishops, whose palace, first mentioned in 1290, became a strong castle. The first cathedral was finished in 1136. In 1300 Wallace won the battle at ' Bell o' the Brae.' In 1450 the University was founded; in 1454 Glasgow was created a royal burgh ; and in 1492 the bishopric became an archbishopric, under Robert Blacader. Pepys, visiting Glasgow in 1682, described it as " a very extraordinary town indeed for beauty and trade, much superior to any in Scotland." Though between the Reformation and the Revolution of 1688 there were fifteen Protestant archbishops of Glasgow (among whom was Robert Leighton, 1670–74), the city was opposed to Episcopacy, and in 1638 an important General Assembly here abjured that form of Church government. Montrose entered the city after the battle of Kilsyth in 1645 and raised a forced loan. In 1650 and in 1651 Cromwell was in Glasgow. In 1678 Glasgow beheld the ' Highland Host,' sent from the North to overawe the Covenanters, whose response was at the battles of Drumclog and Bothwell Bridge. Both in 1715 and 1745 the city remained loyal to the Hanoverian government. Prince Charles Stewart spent ten days here on his northward retreat in 1745 and levied contributions on the city, whose trade had grown steadily in importance since the Union of 1707. In 1651 the Clyde at the Broomielaw was a fordable stream, and for more than a century after that Glasgow was still dependent on its foreports at Irvine and later at Port Glasgow. The first attempts to deepen the river at Glasgow date from c. 1768, and the last hundred and fifty years have seen the development of this shallow stream into the present harbour, where the largest ocean steamers can enter the docks. The earliest dock dates from 1867, the latest (at Shieldhall) was opened in July 1931.

The four principal railway stations are all situated near the centre of the city, which may be placed about BUCHANAN

STREET (Pl. 26, 27), the most fashionable shopping centre. At its S. end is *St. Enoch Station* (Pl. 34), at the N. end, *Buchanan St. Station* (Pl. 20) ; Gordon St., coming from the *Central Station* (Pl. 26), a little to the W., joins it opposite the *Royal Bank*, passages on either side of which lead into ROYAL EXCHANGE SQUARE, facing Queen St., which leads N. to George Square and *Queen St. Station* (Pl. 27). The *Royal Exchange*, in front of which is a statue of Wellington, by Marochetti, is a dignified classical building by David Hamilton (1829), in a monumental setting by Archd. Elliot.

It incorporates an 18th cent. mansion and now contains *Stirling's Library*, founded in 1791, and the *Commercial Library* (weekdays 9.30–8.30, Sat. to 5.30).

EASTERN GLASGOW

At the N.W. corner of Buchanan St. and St. Vincent St. is the *Western Club*, a leading club in Glasgow, adjoined on the N. side by the *Stock Exchange*, in a Moorish style of architecture. From the club St. Vincent Place leads E. (r.) to the spacious **George Square** (Pl. 27), surrounded by important buildings and notable for its numerous statues.

In the centre rises a Doric column, 80 ft. high (1837), surmounted by a colossal statue of Scott, by Greenshields. The plaid is worn on the ' wrong ' shoulder, as was characteristic of Sir Walter. This is flanked by equestrian figures (by Marochetti) of Queen Victoria and Prince Albert. In the other statues (Watt, by Chantrey, Sir John Moore, by Flaxman, Lord Clyde, by Foley, etc.), all of Scotsmen except that of Sir Robert Peel (by Mossman), may be traced the admirations of Glasgow during the past century.—At the E. end is the noble *Cenotaph*, the War Memorial for 1914–18, by Sir John Burnet.

The W. side of George Square is occupied by the Bank of Scotland and the *Merchants' House*, whose hall, adorned with the customary civic portraits, is the meeting place of the Chamber of Commerce. On the N. side are Queen St. Station and its hotel. The *General Post Office* (1876–78), in the Italian style, is on the S. side. The whole of the E. side is taken up by the **City Chambers** (Pl. 27), an elaborate but not wholly successful edifice in the Venetian Renaissance style, by William Young (1889), with a good extension to the E. by John Watson (1923). The tower is 240 ft. high. Visitors are admitted on weekdays except Thurs. 10–12 and 2–4, Sat. 10–12.

The interior is very magnificent, and the vistas obtained of and from the staircases are striking. Marble, alabaster, mosaics, majolica, and choice woods are all laid under contribution. Colossal statues of Knowledge and Power guard the council staircase, statues of Purity and Honour the main staircase. In the Library and the Lord Provost's room are good tapestries ; and the Council Chamber is panelled with mahogany from San Domingo. The splendid Banqueting Hall (120 ft. long, 50 ft. wide) contains four painted historical panels by Glasgow artists, and there are other interesting paintings in the Satinwood Salon.

From the N.E. corner of George Square, GEORGE STREET (Pl. 27) runs E., passing the huge *Royal College of Science and*

Technology (1903), the successor of Anderson's College, founded in 1795 by Prof. John Anderson, where Livingstone studied medicine. The medical classes, removed in 1889, now occupy Anderson's Medical College, in the Dumbarton Road. Colin Campbell, Lord Clyde (1792–1863), was born at No. 246 George St., and Thomas Campbell (1777–1844), the poet, in a house (demolished) that stood near the foot of the steep Balmanno St. (on the left).

Beyond High St. the line of George St. is continued eastwards by the long Duke Street (Pl. 28), which leads to the residential suburb of *Dennistoun*, lying to the N., and the poorer districts of *Camlachie, Parkhead,* and *Shettleston.*

George St. joins High St. at its curved N. portion, known as ' Bell o' the Brae,' where in 1300, on the evidence of Blind Harry, William Wallace is said to have defeated and slain Earl Percy in a sharp encounter for the possession of the bishops' castle (see below), then occupied by Percy as English governor. The name is said to refer to a bell in a turret at the top of the hill, which was tolled at funerals. We ascend the hill, noting, on the left, the steep Rottenrow, and on the right, the Drygate, both once among the aristocratic streets of Glasgow, and soon come in sight of the cathedral with the Necropolis behind it, High St. ends at the *Barony Church,* by Burnet (1896–1900) ; opposite stands a lively equestrian statue of William III (1735 ; attr. to Sir H. Cheere). More to the left is a statue of Norman Macleod (1812–72), near the site of the old church of which he was minister from 1851 to 1872. Hereabouts was the house in which Darnley is said to have lain sick, just before his removal to Kirk o' Field in Edinburgh (p. 60).— High St. is continued by Castle St., No. 3 in which (l.) is *Provand's Lordship,* probably the only pre-Reformation house now left in Glasgow.

Built in 1471 by Bp. Andrew Muirhead of Durisdeer, whose arms appear on the lowest step of the S. gable, this old house is part of the Hospital of St. Nicholas, founded for a priest and 12 old men, and claims to have been occupied by James IV, as an honorary canon of the cathedral, and by Mary, Queen of Scots, while visiting Darnley in 1567. It afterwards belonged to the Baillies, lords of Provand, and it is now occupied by a society, which has furnished it in the style of c. 1700, with early Scottish oak furniture, four Flemish tapestries, and some 16th cent. window-glass. Admission (6d.) daily except on Sun. and Thurs. ; 10–1 and 2–5 in April–Sept. 11–1 and 2–4 in winter.

Conspicuous in front of us rises the large *Royal Infirmary,* founded in 1792 on the site of the old bishops' castle, and repeatedly enlarged, a late extension involving the destruction of the ward in which Lister developed his antiseptic treatment.

Castle Street goes on northward, past *Barony Church North* (by Honeyman, 1880), to *St. Rollox* and *Springburn,* industrial districts with extensive locomotive works. *Sighthill Cemetery* (Pl. 7) and *Springburn Park* (1½ m. N. of the Infirmary) command fine views.—Another viewpoint is *Alexandra Park,* 1 m. E. of the Infirmary, reached viâ Alexandra Parade (Pl. 21), which is continued thence N.E. by Cumbernauld Road to (1¾ m. more) *Hogganfield Loch* (½ m. long ; boats for hire.)—About 1½ m. N., beyond *Robroyston* station, a monument marks the site of the house in which Wallace was betrayed by Sir John Menteith in 1305.

*Glasgow Cathedral (Pl. 28), dedicated to St. Mungo, the
only unmutilated survivor of the great Gothic churches of
South Scotland, is mainly in the E.E. style of the 13th cent.,
though several periods are represented in its architecture. It
is smaller than any of the great English cathedrals, being
(319 ft. long, 63 ft. wide) almost exactly the same size as
Southwell Minster, though having a lofty central spire (225 ft.).
Striking peculiarities are the very slight projection of the
transepts and the construction of the E. end in two stories,
permitted or prescribed by the sloping character of the
site, so that the crypt is really the 'Laigh Kirk' or Lower
Church. The windows on the N. side are plain Early English;
those on the S., with trefoil heads, are later. The best view
of the smoke-blackened exterior is from the S.E. or from
the Bridge of Sighs (see below). The church is now used as a
parish church (the High Church), with services on Sun. at
11 and 6.30. On weekdays the cathedral is open from 10 to
4 or 5.30.

" Ah," says Andrew Fairservice in ' Rob Roy ', " it's a brave kirk—name o'
yere whigmaleeries and curliewurlies and open-steek hems about it—a' solid
weel-jointed masonwark, that will stand as long as the warld—keep hands and
gunpowther aff it."

History. St. Kentigern (p. 111) is said to have dwelt and been buried by
the banks of the Molendinar, the stream (now covered) that flows through the
valley to the E. The church built above his grave in 1123–36 by Bp. Achaius,
under David I, was burned in 1192. Bp. Jocelin began the present church, and
his beautiful crypt was consecrated in 1197, though only a small pillar and part
of the vaulting in the S.W. corner now remain of that date. The choir was
completed under Bp. Bondington (1233–58), to whom is ascribed also the tower.
The stone spire was added nearly 200 years later, by Bp. Lauder (1408–25),
who finished the chapter house or crypt below the sacristy. Bp. Cameron (1425–
47) completed the sacristy and perhaps also raised the beautiful choir screen,
though that has been attributed alternatively to Abp. Robert Blacader (1483–
1508), who constructed the stair from the nave to the crypt and founded the
Blacader Aisle. The nave, begun early in the 14th cent., was not finished until
1480. In 1560 James Beaton, the last Roman Catholic archbishop of Glasgow,
carried off the treasure and the archives of the Cathedral to France, whence they
have never returned. At the Reformation the church was ' purged ' of all ' monuments of idolatry,' but the building was preserved from destruction by the
energetic action of the trade guilds of the city (1578), and it was later divided
among three distinct congregations (in the nave, in the choir, and in the crypt).
In 1650 Oliver Cromwell sat in the nave to hear himself denounced as a ' sectary
and blasphemer ' in a sermon of two hours by Zachary Boyd (d. 1653), rector of
the university and minister of the Barony kirk, but his only revenge was to
invite the bold preacher to dinner and to conclude the entertainment with a
prayer that lasted for three hours. When the crypt ceased to be used as a church,
in 1801, it was partly filled with earth and used as a cemetery. The church
was repaired in 1829 and a more thorough restoration took place in 1846, during
which a belfry tower on the N.W. side of the façade and a consistory house on
the S.W. were pulled down.

Interior. We enter the cathedral by the S.W. porch, to
the right of which (outside) is the monument of Thomas
Hutcheson, one of the founders of Hutcheson's Hospital
(p. 118). The NAVE is stately and well proportioned, with
a triforium of two arches to each bay and a clerestory. The

clustered columns separating it from the aisles have plain capitals. On the walls are numerous monuments and regimental flags and on the easternmost column on the N. side of the nave hangs a 17th cent. Italian Nativity. The Victorian stained glass was of poor quality, but good modern glass (1950–58) has replaced it in most of the windows; the great W. window, with the Creation, is by Francis Spear (1958). The *CHOIR, a beautiful example of E.E. Gothic, now used as the High Church, is raised 3 ft. above the nave and is entered by a low elliptic-arched doorway in the fine *Rood Screen (see above), on the corbels of which appear the

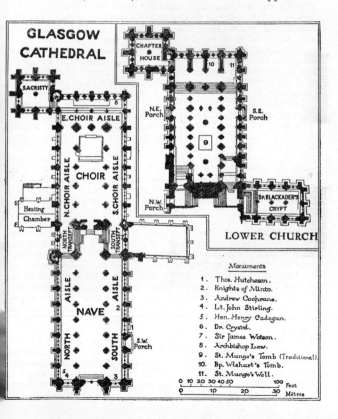

GLASGOW CATHEDRAL

SACRISTY

E. CHOIR AISLE

CHAPTER HOUSE

10   11

N.E. Porch

S.E. Porch

N. CHOIR AISLE

S. CHOIR AISLE

CHOIR

9

Heating Chamber

N.W. Porch

NORTH TRANSEPT

SOUTH TRANSEPT

Bp. BLACKADER'S CRYPT

LOWER CHURCH

NORTH AISLE

SOUTH AISLE

NAVE

2

1

S.W. Porch

5 4   3

Monuments

1. Thos. Hutcheson.
2. Knights of Minto.
3. Andrew Cochrane.
4. Lt. John Stirling.
5. Hon. Henry Cadogan.
6. Dr. Crystal.
7. Sir James Watson.
8. Archbishop Law.
9. St. Mungo's Tomb (Traditional).
10. Bp. Wishart's Tomb.
11. St. Mungo's Well.

0 10 20 30 40 50   100 Feet
0   10   20   30 Métres

Seven Deadly Sins. It is separated from its aisles by clustered columns with flowered capitals, and has a peculiarly fine triforium. A window is the S. aisle shows the arms of the fourteen incorporated trades. The E. end has four slender lancet windows instead of the more usual three or five, and its arrangement is interesting. Here is a double aisle, the W. half forming an ambulatory, while on the E. are chapels, separated by elegant shafts supporting the vaulted roof. In the S.E. chapel is the tomb of Abp. Law (d. 1632). Adjoining the choir on the N.E. is the *Sacristy*, a square chamber with its original oak door, and a central shaft on which appear the arms of the founder, Bp. Cameron (d. 1446).—From the S. transept steps descend to the BLACADER CHAPEL, founded by Abp. Blacader (d. 1508), a fine vaulted crypt the top of which rises only a little above the level of the choir pavement. This crypt, intended no doubt to support a S. transept, is sometimes known as the ' Aisle of St. Fergus,' or the ' Aisle of Car Fergus,' and on the roof is a rude carving of the two-wheeled car constructed by St. Mungo to bring St. Fergus's body to burial at Glasgow.

The splendid 12th cent. *CRYPT, or *Laigh Kirk*, to which steps descend from the nave on both sides of the choir, is the chief glory of the cathedral. " There is a solidity in its architecture, a richness in its vaulting, and a variety of perspective in the placing of its pillars, which make it one of the most perfect pieces of architecture in these islands." The fine vault is illumined by wrought-iron lamps. Its E. end repeats the arrangement of the E. end of the choir above, but here the chapels are separated by solid walls instead of by columns. In the centre is the traditional tomb of St. Mungo (d. 603), but of the monument only the base remains. In the S.E. chapel is St. Mungo's Well, and in that adjoining is the tomb of Bp. Robert Wishart (d. 1316), the determined adherent of Robert the Bruce, whom he crowned. Near the N.E. porch a brass plate marks the grave of Edward Irving (1792–1834), whose portrait (as John the Baptist) appears in the window above, by Bertini of Milan. A pillar, near the S.W. angle, with a capital differing from those of the others, is regarded as a relic of Bp. Jocelin's crypt (p. 114) ; and another pillar passes for ' Rob Roy's Pillar,' from behind which that outlaw whispered his warning to Francis Osbaldistone in ' Rob Roy.'—At the N.E. angle of the crypt is the *Chapter House* (13–15th cent.), founded by Bp. de Bondington, and connected by a turret staircase with the sacristy immediately above. Here are preserved a bell of 1594, recast in 1790, and a gravestone (removed in 1897 from the graveyard on the N. side of the cathedral) commemorating nine martyred Covenanters in a quaint rhymed inscription.

The churchyard around the cathedral is paved with the tombstones of the forefathers of the city, and on the hill behind, reached by the ' Bridge of Sighs ' spanning the valley of the Molendinar, is the *Necropolis*, the old Fir Park of the bishops. The most conspicuous monument is a Doric column erected in 1825 to the memory of the Reformers and crowned by a statue of John Knox.

From the cathedral we return to the Bell o' the Brae (p. 113) and descend the High Street (largely rebuilt). Wm. Motherwell (1798–1835) was born at No. 117. The goods station on the left occupies the site of the Old University (see p. 123), in the grounds behind which took place the duel between Francis and Rashleigh Osbaldistone (in ' Rob Roy '). At the S. end of High St., is ' the Cross,' with the now isolated *Cross Steeple* (Pl. 34) the sole relic of the old Tolbooth (c. 1628), the prison described in ' Rob Roy.' Here the Gallowgate and London Rd. diverge to the E., the Saltmarket to the S., and the Trongate to the W.—all important names in the commercial annals of the city, when the ' tobacco lords ' and other merchants used to meet in the piazzas of the old Tontine Buildings W. of the Tolbooth.

The GALLOWGATE (Pl. 35) traverses the poor district of *Calton*. No. 203, c. ¼ m. from the Cross, marks the site of the Saracen Inn, where Johnson and Boswell lodged on their return from the Hebrides (1773), and where Wordsworth and his sister Dorothy put up in 1803. *Kent St.*, at No. 34 in which (tablet) Edward Irving lived and was visited by Carlyle, leads on the right to *Moncur St.*, the scene of a popular market on Saturdays. The Cattle Market (best visited on Wed.) lies to the left of Gallowgate a little farther on.

The SALTMARKET (Pl. 34), running from the Cross to the Clyde, was long a fashionable part of the town, and here Bailie Nicol Jarvie, Rob Roy's Lowland cousin, enjoyed ' a ' the comforts o' the Sautmarket ' in the early part of the 18th century. James VII lodged here when Duke of York, and here the 18th cent. printers, Robert and Andrew Foulis, held their book auctions. To the E., in St. Andrew's Square, is *St. Andrew's* (1739–56), by Allan Dreghorn, with the finest 18th cent. church interior in Scotland ; and farther S., facing Glasgow Green, is the *Court House*, seat of the High Court. The Fishmarket, to the W., is built round the ' *Briggate Steeple* ', a relic of the old Merchants' House, probably designed by Sir Wm. Bruce (1665). Clyde St., with the Roman Catholic *St. Andrew's Cathedral* (1866), meets Stockwell St. at the *Victoria Bridge.* Here was the medieval Clyde bridge, at the S. end of which stood a leper hospital. No. 27 Stockwell St. was the birthplace of James McGill (1744–1813), founder of McGill University (tablet).

Glasgow Green (Pl. 41, 42), a flat riverside park of 136 acres, the frequent scene of popular demonstrations, stretches E. from the Saltmarket. In 1745 Prince Charles Stewart reviewed his troops on the Fleshers' Haugh, at the S. end of the Green, before resuming his retreat to the North. The ' Unlucky Brig ' crosses the Clyde from the Fleshers' Haugh to Richmond Park. Once damaged by fire and thrice condemned as unsafe, it was considered unlucky to have been built of wood instead of stone. Last demolished in 1953, it was reopened in 1955 as the *Kay Bridge.* The *McLennan Arch* (the Charlotte St. entrance to the park) was built by Robert Adam for the Assembly Rooms in Ingram St. (1796 ; demolished 1888). Opposite *Monteith Row*, a pleasant early-19th cent. terrace, is the **People's Palace** (adm. free 10–5, Sun. 2–5, on Sat. in May–Sept., 10–9), containing the OLD GLASGOW MUSEUM. The collections include views of Glasgow by Jules Lessore (d. 1892) and others, portraits commissioned by the Corporation, maps and documents. Of special interest are Abp. Beaton's Bible, the remarkable and elaborate orrery made in 1823–33 by John Fulton, shoemaker of Fenwick in Ayrshire ; and the collection relating to Sir Thomas Lipton and his racing yachts (all named ' Shamrock '). Adjoining is a Palm House.—The conspicuous edifice to the E., in a Venetian style, is a carpet factory. To the E. of Glasgow Green extends the densely populated district of *Bridgeton*, with large cotton mills.

We follow Trongate (Pl. 34) westwards. No. 32 was the site of a workshop of James Watt; Sir John Moore (1761–1809) was born at No. 90 (demolished). The *Tron Steeple* (126 ft. high), on the left, survives from a church of 1637, burned down in 1793. In the *New Tron Church*, by Robt. Adam (now a municipal workshop), Dr. Chalmers was minister for five years (1815–19). No. 188 Trongate stands on the site of Shawfield House, where Prince Charles Stewart lodged in 1745. Farther W. the busy Trongate is continued by Argyle St. to St. Enoch Square and Buchanan St. We, however, diverge to the right viâ Candleriggs (Pl. 34), a street leading N. past the large *City Hall*, built partly above the fruit market, to INGRAM STREET (Pl. 27). Here, facing us, is the church of *St. David*, whose curious sobriquet, ' the Ram's Horn Kirk,' has been explained as a reference to the collapse of a monastery before the attack of the Reformers, as the walls of Jericho collapsed when the priests of the Israelites blew their trumpets of rams' horns. On the back wall is the gravestone of Prof. Anderson (d. 1796), while the initials R.F. and A.F. on the pavement in front indicate the graves of the Foulis brothers, the famous University printers (see p. 117). A little to the W. (l.) in Ingram St. is *Hutcheson's Hospital*, founded in 1641 by George and Thomas Hutcheson, whose 17th cent. statues appear on the building (by David Hamilton; 1803–05). In Hutcheson St., opening opposite the hospital, are the *County Buildings*, or law courts, an extensive block with a Corinthian portico. At the corner of Ingram St. and Glassford St. is the *Savings Bank*, adjoined by the *Trades' House*, a domed building by Robert Adam (1794), occupied by the fourteen Incorporated Trades, who administer large charitable funds. The Adam ceiling in the main hall was replaced in 1955 by a panelled ceiling by Walter Underwood. Ingram St. ends at Queen St., opposite the Royal Exchange.

WESTERN GLASGOW

Both E. and W. of Buchanan St. lies a region of well-built and regularly planned business streets, which, with their attractive shops, substantial offices, banks, churches, and institutions, are expressive of the wealth of a great commercial city. The central E.–W. thoroughfare of this quarter is ST. VINCENT STREET, which eventually converges with Argyle St.

A tablet on No. 79 Renfield St. (now an insurance office) records De Quincey's visits to Glasgow in 1846–47.—In the pleasant Blythswood Square (Pl. 26), between St. Vincent St. and Sauchiehall St., No. 18 is *Baillie's Library* (9.30–5), a free public reference library founded in 1865.—In Elmbank St., farther W., is the *High School* (Pl. 25), a very ancient foundation, at which J. G. Lockhart, Sir John Moore, Campbell-Bannerman, and Bonar Law were pupils.

To those parts of Western Glasgow, however, that are more especially interesting to the visitor, the most convenient approaches are Argyle St. and Sauchiehall St., which, leading respectively from the S. and the N. end of Buchanan St., converge c. 1½ m. farther W., beside the Art Galleries.

ARGYLE STREET (Pl. 16–34), leaving Jamaica St. on the left, passes under a broad railway viaduct (' the Highlandman's Umbrella ') and traverses the poor district of *Anderston*, where, at Anderston Cross (Pl. 25), Stobcross St. goes off on the left for Queen's Dock. Beyond *St. Vincent Street Church* (Pl. 24), a dominating building of 1857–59 by ' Greek ' Thomson, Argyle St. approaches Kelvingrove Park.

SAUCHIEHALL STREET (Pl. 17–19), the E. part of which is one of the chief shopping streets in Glasgow, farther on traverses a residential neighbourhood, and towards its W. end is flanked by terraces of substantial houses. At its E. end is the Empire Theatre ; at No. 270 are the *McLellan Galleries*, in which the annual exhibitions of the Institute of Fine Arts are held. Almost immediately behind these galleries, in Renfrew St., is the *School of Art* (1897–1907), an original building by C. R. Mackintosh. Sauchiehall St. skirts *Garnethill* (r.), an eminence once known as Highlandman's Hill, as the camping ground of the Highland Host. At *Charing Cross* (Pl. 18), we reach a busy cross-roads.

A few yards down North St., which leads hence S. to Argyle St., stands the large **Mitchell Library** (Pl. 18), an imposing domed building by W. B. Whitie (1911), the chief public library in the city, with over 300,000 vols. (open free daily, 9.30 a.m. to 9 or 10 p.m.). Originally established in 1874 in Miller St. by bequest of Stephen Mitchell, tobacco manufacturer, the library includes a large reading room, a magazine room showing 800 periodicals, a music room, the Jeffrey collection of rare books on art, and a special section devoted to Scottish poetry, with an important Burns collection.—Immediately behind (chief entrance in Granville St.) are the **St. Andrew's Halls** (by James Sellars ; 1873–77), where the principal concerts and public meetings take place (remarkably good acoustics).

St. George's Road (Pl. 18–11) leads N.E. from Charing Cross to Great Western Road, Woodlands Road N.W., towards Hillhead and the University. In Lynedoch Place is *Trinity College* (Pl. 17, 18), the former Free Church college, a fanciful building of 1856 by Charles Wilson (view from the tower). At 17 Woodside Place, to the S., Joseph Lister lived for nine years from 1860 (tablet). Sir William Ramsay (1852–1916), the chemist, was born at 2 Clifton St., off Woodside Terrace. Between Woodlands Rd. and Kelvingrove Park is a once-fashionable quarter of imposing mid-19th cent. mansions.

The turnings on the right as we proceed lead from Sauchiehall St. to Kelvingrove Park (p. 122).

The ***Art Gallery and Museum** (Pl. 16) occupy a palatial red sandstone building of two stories with many towers, by J. W. Simpson and Milner Allan, situated in Kelvingrove Park and opened in 1901 at a cost of c. £250,000. The collection of paintings, one of the most important in the kingdom, is rich in Dutch works, and includes notable examples of Rembrandt, Titian, and Giorgione, besides an interesting representation of the modern French and Scottish schools. The museum, in addition to its scientific departments, includes a fine assemblage of ship-models, and collections of applied art; while selections from the enormously rich and varied Burrell Collection, the bequest of Sir William Burrell (1861–1958) are always on view, pending the acquisition of a permanent home for the collection, which is to be in the neighbourhood of Glasgow. The galleries are open free on weekdays 10–5, on Sun. 2–5 (occasionally also in the evening). Tea-room on the first floor.

GROUND FLOOR. The large Central Hall is devoted to temporary exhibitions, usually including works of art from the Burrell Collection (see above). The main hall on the left contains the remarkable collection of *Ship Models*, which includes Drake's ' Golden Hind ', a contemporary model of Henry Bell's ' Comet ', (1811), and the ' Charlotte Dundas ' (1801–02), the first steamship, as well as modern vessels. The outer galleries on this side (starting from the entrance) are devoted to *Armour*, with a Covenanters' banner of 1689, Scottish arms, the *Churburg Harness, an Italian armour of 1450 (helmet not original), a horse armour made for the Earl of Pembroke (1550), and other fine suits; *Clyde Navigation*; *Engineering*, a particularly well-arranged display; *History*; and *Archaeology*. In the last, four early Bronze Age *Cists, with their contents as discovered, and the Egyptian and Cypriot antiquities are of outstanding interest.—The large hall on the other side of the central court illustrates *Zoology*, with good habitat groups. The outer galleries are devoted to *Ethnography* (l.), *Zoology* (centre), and *Geology and Palaeontology* (r.).

FIRST FLOOR. The galleries overlooking the main courts accommodate the valuable and varied collection of *Applied Art*, notably glass and crystal, silverware, bronzes, costume, and ceramics. Here also is a selection from the museum's collection of *Sculpture*, and in the side galleries are *Prints* and *Drawings*.

The *Picture Gallery* occupies the W. and E. wings of this floor, the foreign schools on the W. and the British schools on the E. Staircases ascend from the vestibule and from the outer ends of the side halls.

W. wing. ROOM I. ITALIAN SCHOOLS. *Botticelli*, Annunciation; *Giov. Bellini*, Madonna; *School of Botticelli*, *Madonna with St. John and angels; *Carlo Dolci*, Adoration of the Magi; *Palma Vecchio*, Holy Family; *Correggio*, Angel's head (fresco); *Giorgione*, *The woman taken in adultery, one of the few paintings certainly attributed to this master; *School of Bassano*, St. Joachim and the angel; *Bonifazio Veronese*, Holy Family; *Dosso Dossi*, Virgin and saints; *Francia*,

GLASGOW

Scale of ½ Mile

0   1   2   3   4 Furlongs

Nativity ;   *Gaudenzio Ferrari*, Nativity and Flight into Egypt ;   *Dom. Veneziano*, Judgment of Paris ;   views of Venice by *Canaletto* and *Guardi*.

FLEMISH SCHOOLS. *Master of Moulins*, *St. Victor and a donor (15th cent.) ;   *B. van Orley*, Virgin by the fountain ; *Lambert Lombard*, Jesus takes leave of his Mother ;   *Cornelis de Vos*, Portrait ; *Jordaens*, Fruit-seller ;   *Rubens*, Boar-hunt, Nature adorned by the Graces, Fight with Amazons ; *Hieronymus Bosch*, Christ and the money-changers ;   *Jan Brueghel*, Triumph of Bacchus, Offering to Venus.

DUTCH SCHOOLS. *Rembrandt*, Portraits of the artist, *Man in armour, *Entombment, Slaughterhouse ;   *Jacob van Ruysdael*, Egmond-on-Sea, Brederode Castle, and other good examples ;   *Hobbema*, Wooded landscape ;   *J. V. Strij*, Pastoral landscape ;   *Caspar Netscher*, Lady in white satin ; *Hals*, *Boys' heads ;   *Bart. van der Helst*, Admiral ;   typical landscapes by *Wouwerman* and seascapes by *W. van de Velde* ; poultry and flowers by *Hondecoeter* and *Rachel Ruysch*.

The central piece in the next room is the Christ of St. John of the Cross, by *Salvador Dali*, an amazing tour-de-force of perspective, of which the artistic merits have been variously judged. Here are also important paintings from the Burrell Collection, changed from time to time.

FRENCH SCHOOLS. Here are classical landscapes by *Poussin* and two camp scenes by *Watteau*, but the room is specially notable for its fine selection of 19th cent. works especially *Impressionist and Post-Impressionist (many from the Burrell Collection). *Corot* is represented by portraits as well as landscapes, and there is a fine *Delacroix* (Expulsion from Paradise). There are characteristic works by *Boudin* (Trouville jetty in stormy weather, and others) and *Monticelli* ; landscapes by *Harpignies*, *Théodore Rousseau*, and *Cam. Pissarro* ;   outstanding examples of *Millet*, *Daumier* (The good Samaritan), *Manet*, *Monet* (Vintimille, Vétheuil), *Sisley*, *Courbet*, *Fantin-Latour*, *Degas* (portrait of Duranty), *Renoir*, *Van Gogh*, *Gauguin* (Landscape), *Cézanne*, *Signac*, *Vuillard*, *Utrillo*, *Derain* (St. Paul's), *Matisse*, *Picasso*, and *Rouault*.

The galleries of the other (E.) wing are devoted to the British Schools of painting. The first room covers the earlier paintings, mainly 18th cent., but including a portrait of Mary, Queen of Scots (1580). The portraits are excellent :   *Raeburn*, William Urquhart, *Mrs. Wm. Urquhart, *Mrs. Anne Campbell, Mr. & Mrs. Robert Campbell ;   *Allan Ramsay*, Countess of Stafford ;   *Romney*, Gen. Sir Charles Stuart ; *Nasmyth*, Robert Burns (the ' Auchendrane ' portrait) ; *Geddes*, Jeremiah Greatrex ;   *Reynolds*, Countess of Erroll, Angelica Kaufmann ;   *Hoppner*, Mrs. Errington ;   *David Martin*, Provost Murdoch.—*Richard Wilson*, Convent at twilight; *Zoffany*, Minuet; *Nasmyth*, Windsor Castle, Falls of Clyde; *Gawen Hamilton*, The vicar's visit; *Gainsborough*, Landscape near Bath; *Constable*, *Hampstead Heath.

The next room is occupied mainly by painters of the Glasgow School: *Horatio McCulloch*, Glencoe; *Wm. McTaggart*, Kilbrennan Sound, Paps of Jura; *McGregor*, Durham at evening; *Wm. Strang*, The café; *Stanley Cursiter*, Authors in session. The 19th century occupies the following large room: outstanding are *Whistler's* Thomas Carlyle, a celebrated portrait acquired by the gallery in 1891, in face of much opposition; *Turner*, Modern Italy (The Pifferari); *Wilkie*, The Cottar's Saturday Night; *Ford Madox Brown*, Wyclif on trial; good examples of *McEvoy* (Portrait), *Lavery* (Pavlova), and *Wilson Steer*. The last room is devoted to contemporary painting, with good examples of *Augustus John* (W. B. Yeats), *Feliks Topolski* (G. B. Shaw), *Paul Nash*, *L. S. Lowry*, *Stanley Spencer*, *Graham Sutherland*, *James Morrison*, *Ian Fleming*, *Margaret Hislop*, *Carel Weight*, *Wyndham Lewis*, *John Piper*, *Edward Wadsworth*, and *Matthew Smith*.

In Dumbarton Road, opposite the Art Galleries, is *Kelvin Hall* (Pl. 16; rebuilt after a destructive fire in 1926), the largest building of its kind in Britain, for exhibitions, carnivals, etc. Behind it is the *Sick Children's Hospital* on Yorkhill. Dumbarton Road, crossing the Kelvin, passes (r.) *Anderson's College Medical School* (comp. below), near the S. entrance to the conspicuous *Western Infirmary*, and goes on to PARTICK, which is largely inhabited by workers in its great ship-yards (free car ferry to Govan on weekdays). Farther on, 1¾ m. from the Art Galleries, is *Whiteinch*, with Victoria Park, in which is a remarkable fossil grove, and a free ferry to Linthouse (Renfrew; not on Sun. and not after 4 on Sat.).

Kelvingrove Park (Pl. 16, 17, 10), through which the Kelvin flows, is a beautiful ornamental park of c. 90 acres, originally laid out by Sir Joseph Paxton. It contains a war memorial to the Scottish Rifles by P. Lindsay Clark (1924), monuments to Carlyle, Lister, Kelvin, and Lord Roberts, besides tennis-courts and an amphitheatre on the bank of the river, in which concerts are given several times weekly in summer.

We cross the park to the *University* (Pl. 9), which occupies a commanding situation on Gilmorehill. This striking edifice, the most prominent feature of which is a tower and spire 300 ft. high, has a frontage of 525 ft. and was designed by Sir Gilbert Scott in a Gothic style with characteristic Scottish details. The main buildings, begun in 1868 and first occupied in 1870, form two quadrangles, separated by a cloister of granite pillars, which support the great Bute Hall, for graduation and other university functions, added in 1882 by the munificence of the 3rd Marquess of Bute. The tower, which commands a wide view, the Bute Hall (110 ft. long, 74 ft. high), and the smaller Randolph Hall (for examinations, etc.), are shown on application to the porter (at the foot of the tower; daily 10–5, Sat. 10–2; gratuity).

Glasgow University was founded in 1451, in the reign of James II, mainly through the exertions of Bp. Turnbull, its first principal. The classes met at first in the crypt of the cathedral, then in a house, ' the auld pedagogy,' in Rottenrow, but after c. 1460 in High St., where, however, the accommodation was very humble until 1632, when the chief parts of the Old College were begun. " Here Adam Smith taught doctrines which have changed the policy of nations, and Watt perfected discoveries that have subdued the elements to be the ministers of mankind." In 1870 the University was transferred to the new buildings in Gilmorehill. It has faculties of Arts, Science, Engineering, Medicine, Law, and Theology, a teaching staff of 50 professors (besides lecturers), and, with over 7000 students, claims to be the largest university in Britain. *Anderson's College of Medicine*, founded in 1799, and *St. Mungo's College* (likewise medical), founded in 1889, were incorporated in the University in 1947.—The undergraduates wear short red gowns, and in voting for the election of their Lord Rector are divided into Nationes : *Natio Glottiana*, those born in Lanarkshire, *Transforthana*, those born N. of the Forth, *Rothseiana*, those born in the counties of Renfrew, Bute, and Ayr, *Loudoniana*, all others.

Opposite the N.E. entrance to the University, in University Avenue (Pl. 10), stands the *Students' Union*, a massive building in the Scottish baronial style. At the University entrance is the *Pearce Lodge*, incorporating the main 17th cent. gateway of the old college. The ceremonial gates, farther W., by Graham Henderson (1951), celebrate the fifth centenary of the University. Leaving on our left the large science buildings added in 1907, we enter the E. quadrangle. A handsome staircase in the N.W. angle ascends to the Randolph and Bute Halls, which are separated by an imposing wooden screen, and on the same staircase is the entrance to the **Hunterian Museum and Library,** the nucleus of which was the valuable collection of anatomical preparations, coins and medals, antiquities, paintings, and books, bequeathed by Dr. William Hunter (1718–83), the distinguished physician, brother of the famous surgeon John Hunter. The museum is open daily, 10–5, Sat. 10–12.

ENTRANCE HALL. *Case I* (r.). Illuminated MSS. ; papyri ; early and fine editions of Latin and Greek books ; at the end, synagogue roll. *Case II.* Autographs, medals and decorations. Bindings and fine editions. *Cases III. & IV.* Illuminated MSS. and early printed works. Above the standard cases, Portraits of eminent Scotsmen ; portrait of F.-M. Montgomery by Augustus John, and an interesting little portrait of Constanza Weber, wife of Mozart. The sculptures include some fine busts and statues of Watt (by Chantrey) and Adam Smith (by Gasser) ; an electromagnetic clock patented by Alex. Bain (1810–1877) ; and a model of Newcomen's steam engine, in repairing which Watt discovered the principle of the separate condenser.—ANTE ROOM. Microscopes and other souvenirs of the Hunters and Lister. *Paintings*, including examples (l. to r.) of *Chardin, G. Reni, Jan Steen, Rembrandt, Reynolds, P. Veronese, Titian, Millet, Whistler*, and others. Above are medical portraits.—MAIN HALL. The ground floor is mainly devoted to *Archaeology* (interesting prehistoric and Roman collections, the latter with special reference to the Antonine Wall) and *Ethnology* (case of specimens collected by Capt. Cook). In the gallery are very rich *Geological Collections*.

On the N. side of the W. quadrangle is the **University Library** (305,000 vols.), which includes the library of Sir William Hamilton (1788–1856), the philosopher, and a unique collection of Bibles and other rare books (c. 15,000 vols.), bequeathed to the University by William Euing. Visitors are admitted daily on application, 10–5 (Sat. 10–1) ; in vacation (July and Aug.), 10–2, except on Sat. The W. side of this quadrangle is occupied by a *War Memorial Chapel* (service on Sun. in term at 11), from the S.W. end of which we may descend the *Lion and Unicorn Staircase*, another relic of the old college, to a group of houses built for the ' college professors,' i.e. those whose chairs were established before 1800. Opposite the N.W. exit stands the *Women's Union*, which preserves the name of Queen Margaret College, a separate college for women in the period 1883–1914. The circular *Reading Room* across the road, on the site of Hillhead House, accommodates 5000.

Modern science buildings separate the older part of the University from the *Western Infirmary* (p. 122), on the W. ; and new buildings are springing up to the N. towards HILLHEAD (Pl. 9), a favourite residential district. On the N. **Great Western Road** (Pl. 2–11), flanked by terraces and mansions, extends N.W. in a straight line, past *Gartnavel* mental hospital (l.) to (2 m.) *Anniesland*, whence its line is continued by a new boulevard, affording fine views of the Clyde estuary, viâ Duntocher to *Bowling* (p. 133).—Entered from Great Western Road are the *Botanic Gardens* (Pl. 2 ; adm. free ; closed at dusk), on the bank of the Kelvin, originally laid out by Sir Joseph Hooker, and containing the large Kibble Palace (transported from Coulport, Loch Long, in 1871) and other hothouses. Facing the E. end is *Broadcasting House*, the Scottish headquarters of the B.B.C., an enlarged reconstruction of the former Queen Margaret College (see above), opened in 1938. *Kelvinside*, to the W. of the Botanic Gardens, with its fine terraces, is perhaps the most fashionable suburb of Glasgow. To the N., beyond the Kelvin, lie the long-drawn-out tenements of *Maryhill*, with the ingenious R. C. church of the *Immaculate Conception* (by T. S. Cordiner ; 1958), with its triangular front and lavish marble decoration.

Going citywards (E.), Great Western Road passes (l.) *Glasgow Academy* (Pl. 3), a well-known boys' school, attended by Sir James Barrie when he lived at 5 Burnbank Terrace, near by. Farther on, beyond the Kelvin, is the graceful episcopal cathedral of *St. Mary* (Pl. 11 ; open 9–6). At St. George's Cross (Pl. 11), where St. George's Road diverges on the right (see p. 119), it changes its name to **New City Road**, which in turn is continued to the N. end of Buchanan St. by *Cowcaddens* (Pl. 19), a busy and somewhat squalid street, taking its name from the old common pasture of the citizens' cattle. To the N. of Cowcaddens is the picturesque canal-side district of *Port Dundas* (Pl. 19), beyond which is (½ m.) *Possilpark*, with large foundries.

SOUTHERN GLASGOW

The few special attractions for the tourist on the S. side of the Clyde are easily accessible by bus, tram, or local train (Cathcart Circle, p. 110). From Argyle St., near the S. end of Buchanan St., Jamaica St. (Pl. 33), a name recalling Glasgow's West Indian trade, leads S. to **Glasgow Bridge**, a massive structure, known also as *Broomielaw Bridge* and *Jamaica Bridge*, opened in its present form in 1899. The first bridge on this site was erected in 1767–72, a second, by Telford, in 1833–36. The large *George V Bridge*, only a few yards downstream, was opened in 1928. Between these road bridges the river is spanned by the railway bridge approaching Central Station.

From the S. end of the bridge the long Eglinton St. (Pl. 40) leads due S., between *Tradeston*, on the W., and *Gorbals* and *Hutchesontown*, on the E.

The once notorious slums of Gorbals are being replaced by modern dwellings (1957–59), and the burial ground, where Burns's ' Dr. Hornbook ' (John Wilson, d. 1839) is interred, has become a rose-garden. In Hutchesontown is *Caledonia Road Church* (1855), Alex. Thomson's most characteristic building.

Beyond Maxwell Road, which leads off on the W. to the villas of *Pollokshields*, Pollokshaws Road runs S.W. viâ *Strathbungo*, *Crossmyloof*, and *Shawlands* (where the Kilmarnock road diverges left), to the old burgh of *Pollokshaws*. **Queen's Park,** on the left 1½ m. from the river, is an attractive park of c. 150 acres, part of which was laid out by Paxton in 1862. *Camphill House*, on the W. side of the park, is now a museum and art gallery (11–5, Sun. 2–5, Sat. in summer 11–9).

A memorial column, erected in 1887, at the S. gate of the park, marks the site of the battle of *Langside* (May, 1568), fatal to the cause of Mary, Queen of Scots. Here, eleven days after her escape from Lochleven Castle, Mary's adherents, seeking to convey her to the shelter of Dumbarton, were signally defeated by Moray. The queen is said to have watched the battle from the ' Queen's Knowe,' near the ruined castle of *Cathcart*, 1 m. S. Three days later she crossed the Solway into England.—To the E. of Cathcart is *King's Park* (68 acres), bequeathed to the city in 1930, with the mansion of *Aikenhead* (1806–23), now a museum of costume and royal portraits (adm. as for Camphill).

In Pollokshaws, 3 m. from Glasgow Bridge, is **Pollok House* (adm. 2/6 daily, exc. Fri., in Apr.–Sept., 2.30–6, on Sun. in mid-May–mid-Aug. 2.30–9), a mansion built in 1747–52 by William Adam for Sir John Maxwell (2nd baronet). It stands in delightful and secluded grounds near the N. bank of the White Cart, with a pleasant garden created by Sir John Stirling Maxwell (10th bart. ; 1866–1956), for whom Rowand Anderson added the entrance hall and wings. The fine collection of paintings, notably Spanish, was made by Sir William Stirling Maxwell (9th bart. ; d. 1878).

APPROACHES. Buses Nos. 21, 23, 39, 48 from Broomielaw to Cowglen Golf Club (Barrhead Rd.), whence the house is approached across meadows by a bridge over the Cart.—Tramways Nos. 14, 25, 31 from Central Glasgow to Pollokshaws Burgh Hall, whence there is a pleasant walk of ¾ m. through the wooded park.

The pictures are displayed in 12 rooms with appropriate furniture, **Silverware*, and china, and, in the Drawing Room, good plasterwork by Clayton, Adam's plasterer. Outstanding among the paintings of the Spanish School are : *Juan Carreño*, Charles II of Spain ; *Sánchez Coello*, Don John of Austria ; *El Greco*, Unknown Man, and **The Artist's Daughter (so-called)*, a magnificent portrait of his early Spanish period ; *Goya*, Boys playing (two small subjects) ; *Murillo*, SS. Justa and Rufina ; *Navarrete*, Christ bearing the Cross ; *Morales*, Pietà ; *Alonso Cano*, Adam and Eve ; *Valdés Leal*, *Murillo*, Madonnas ; *Luis Tristán*, Adoration of the Magi ; *Herrera el Mozo*, Doctors of the Church ; *Sch. of Berruguete*, St. Ildefonso receiving the chasuble ; *Velazquez*, Small landscapes with figures ; *Eugenio Caxes*, St. Julian of Cuenca ; *Esteban March* (Valencian School), Portrait of a painter ; *Carducho*, Self-portrait.

The Italian Schools are represented by a portrait of Pope Clement VII by *Seb. del Piombo*, a Pietà by *Signorelli* ; there are good works by *Antonis Mor*, *Jan Steen*, and *Jacob Jordaens* ; while, in the British School, there are four fine works by *Wm. Blake*, *Vision of the Last Judgment, Entombment, Adam naming the Beasts, The Canterbury Pilgrims ; two not very effective *Hogarths* ; portraits by *Reynolds* (John, Duke of Roxburgh), *Isaac Oliver* (Arabella Stuart), *Kneller* (Mrs. Masham), *Etty* (Lady Stirling Maxwell), *W. Nicholson* (Anne Stirling Maxwell), *Raeburn* (Sir John Maxwell, 8th bart.; crayon), and (?) *Lely* (Sir John Maxwell, 2nd bart.). In the dining-room are interesting sporting pictures by *G. Malleyn* (1753–1816).

The Kilmarnock Road goes on S. from Shawlands (see above) to the residential suburb of *Giffnock*, W. of which is *Rouken Glen*, a picturesque public estate with a waterfall, a boating lake and a golf course.

Excursions from Glasgow

Glasgow has been cynically described as an excellent place to get away from, and it is certainly a convenient starting-point for many attractive short excursions as well as for longer expeditions. Of the out-and-home excursions for one day the favourites are those to the beautiful estuary of the Clyde (Rte. 13), to the Falls of Clyde (p. 130) and to Loch Lomond and the Trossachs (Rte. 25). The innumerable tram and bus services to points in the nearer environs and the motor-coach excursions in summer have already been referred to (p. 110).

Lanarkshire, extending from Glasgow and the black and busy industrial district in the N. to the pastoral solitudes near the sources of the Clyde, 50 m. to the S., lies mainly in the basin of the Clyde, and its alternative name might well be Clydesdale. The most populous county in Scotland, though only tenth in point of size, it is divided into three 'wards.' The Upper Ward, in the S., with Lanark as its chief town, comprises more than half the county ; the Middle Ward has Hamilton as its capital ; in the small Lower Ward is Glasgow. The supreme economic asset of Lanarkshire is the great Glasgow coal and iron basin, with all its varied industries. The Upper Ward, covered in the S. with rolling rounded hills, is almost entirely pastoral and agricultural. The orchards in the vale of Clyde about Lanark and Bothwell have been celebrated for ages ; and the famous Clydesdale draught horses were first bred in this ward. This county was the scene of William Wallace's early exploits against the English at Lanark, of the final collapse of the cause of Mary, Queen of Scots, at Langside, and of the alternate victory and defeat of the Covenanters at Drumclog and Bothwell Bridge.

From Glasgow to Hamilton

Hamilton may be reached by railway (11¾ m. in 35 min.) from Central Station ; or by motor-bus at frequent intervals from Killermont St. or Waterloo St. viâ Uddingston and Bothwell or viâ Cambuslang and Blantyre.

(a) Viâ Uddingston. Leaving Glasgow by the long and dreary Gallowgate A 721 passes (3 m.) *Tollcross*, with a

Children's Museum (open 11–5, Sun. 2–5) in Tollcross Park.—
5½ m. *Calderpark*. On the left is the Glasgow **Zoological Park**
(open on weekdays 9.30–dusk, Sun. from 1.30 ; adm. 1/,
children 6*d*.), opened in 1947, with a growing collection of
animals, in pleasant grounds left as far as possible in their
natural state. Crossing the W. Calder, we bear r. on A 724,
through *Uddingston*.—9¼ m. **Bothwell** (*Silvertrees*, RB. 25/,
P. 12½ gs.), on a height above the Clyde, lies in a pleasant
region of villas. The church, founded in 1398 by Archibald the
Grim, Earl of Douglas (whose daughter was here married in
1400 to the ill-fated Duke of Rothesay), preserves its original
choir, with stone-slab roof and large buttresses. Within, the
sedilia are notable, also some capitals from an earlier (Norman)
church, the grave-slab of Walter de Moravia (Murray),
builder of Bothwell Castle, and monuments to the first two
Earls of Forfar (d. 1712, 1715), flanking the Burne-Jones E.
window. A door beside the elaborate monument to the 3rd
Duke of Hamilton (d. 1694) admits to the 14th cent. sacristy.
Nave and tower were added by David Hamilton in 1833.
Joanna Baillie (1762–1851), the poet, was born in the manse.
A footbridge, ½ m. W., crosses the Clyde to Blantyre (see
below).

To the N.W. (c. 1 m.), beyond the golf course, amid beautiful grounds stretching
down to the Clyde, are the picturesque red ruins of *****Bothwell Castle**, perhaps the
finest 13th cent. castle in Scotland (adm. 6*d*. ; 10–4 or 7, Sun. from 2). The great
13th cent. donjon, standing half-wrecked at the S.W. corner, is round without
and octagonal within. From it a lofty and massive curtain wall, running S.E.
to the prison tower and postern, was extended in the early 15th cent. to the S.E.
tower. At the E. end of the court, on the first floor, was the banqueting hall, and
in the S.E. corner are the scanty remains of the chapel. The castle was begun
c. 1278 by the Murrays, but it was held by the English from 1296 until Bannockburn, and again in 1331–37. In 1361 it passed by marriage to the ' Black '
Douglases, and after their forfeiture in 1455 was eventually granted in 1488 to
Patrick Hepburn, created Earl of Bothwell, who exchanged it for Hermitage
four years later with Archibald, Earl of Angus, the ' Red ' Douglas. Thus the
earls of Bothwell had a very brief connection with the castle. In the adjoining
18th cent. mansion, now demolished, Scott wrote ' Lochinvar '.

We cross the Clyde at (10 m.) *Bothwell Bridge*, the scene of
the battle (June 22nd, 1679), described in ' Old Mortality,' in
which the royal troops under Monmouth and Claverhouse,
approaching from the N., routed with great slaughter the
Covenanters who were strongly posted on the S. The bridge,
at that time only 12 ft. wide, with a steep rise to the centre,
where it was barred with a gate, was rebuilt in 1826.—11½ m.
Hamilton, see below.

(*b*) Viâ Blantyre. From Glasgow Cross we follow London
St. and Great Hamilton St. (Pl. 43) and cross the Clyde by
Dalmarnock Bridge. At Shawfield Stadium A 749 bears r. for
Rutherglen, while our road (A 74) keeps to the left.

3½ m. **Rutherglen** (familiarly ' Ruglen ' ; 24,200 inhab.), a royal burgh since
the 12th cent., is of greater antiquity than Glasgow, incorporation with which
it has successfully resisted. A low steeple is all that remains of the ancient church

in which, according to Blind Harry, a truce between Scotland and England was made in 1297, and in which Sir John Menteith agreed to betray Wallace to the English. Its ancient royal castle, burned by the Regent Moray after the battle of Langside (fought 2 m. W.), has disappeared. A seditious 'declaration' affixed by Covenanters to the town cross in 1679 was the immediate cause of the affrays at Drumclog and Bothwell Bridge.

Beyond Rutherglen A 749 goes on to (4¾ m.) *Burnside*, above which lies *Cathkin Braes*, an attractive woodland public park commanding fine views over Glasgow.—8 m. **East Kilbride**, notable as the scene of the first Scottish meeting of the Society of Friends (1653), was selected as the site of the first new 'satellite' town in Scotland. Building is mainly to the S. of the old village, and the new town includes a Mechanical Engineering Research Station and an episcopal church (St. Mark's) of triangular elevation (by Noad and Wallace; 1956). To the N. is the ruined *Mains Castle* (13th cent.) recently restored. The house of *Long Calderwood*, 1¼ m. E., was the birthplace of William and John Hunter, the 18th cent. anatomists.—A 726, passing *Torrance House* (partly 14th cent.), now the headquarters of the East Kilbride Development Corpn., goes on S. to (17 m.) *Strathaven* (p. 169), while B 764 leads S.W. towards Kilmarnock viâ (13 m.) *Eaglesham*, a 'model' village laid out in 1769 by the Earl of Eglinton, near which Rudolf Hess made his sensational landing from the air in 1941.

A 74 goes on through (5 m.) *Cambuslang*.—9 m. **Blantyre** is a mining village with cotton-mills, famous as the birthplace of David Livingstone (1813–73), explorer and missionary, who as a boy, worked as a 'piecer' in the mills. The tenement in which he was born, in a 'one-room' dwelling, and the adjoining houses have been restored as a National Memorial (adm. 1/, 10–dusk, Sun. 2–6 or dusk), and now contain a highly interesting museum of his career, including a workman's room of 1813, illuminated groups of coloured statuary by Pilkington Jackson, personal relics (pocket Bible, medicine case, MS maps), collections illustrative of the African slave-trade, a 'shrine,' etc. There are also a tea-room (closed Sun.) and a pleasant garden. The buses from Glasgow to Blantyre pass c. ½ m. from the memorial. On the Clyde c. 1 m. downstream is a fragment of a priory founded by Alexander II in 1249 for Austin canons from Jedburgh. Footbridge to Bothwell, see above.

11½ m. **Hamilton** (40,175 inhab. ; *Commercial*, RB. 20/ ; *Royal*, RB. 19/6) lies in a mining district about a mile from the junction of the Clyde and Avon, and is regarded as the centre of local government in Lanarkshire.

Mary, Queen of Scots, on her way to Langside, rested at Queenzie Neuk in the town. Cromwell fixed his headquarters at Hamilton for a time in 1651. After Drumclog the victorious Covenanters marched to Hamilton ; and after their defeat at Bothwell Bridge in 1679 many of them sought refuge in the woods of the palace, and the Duchess Anne requested Monmouth not to disturb the game in her coverts. Sir Harry Lauder (1870–1950) is buried in Bent Cemetery.

The handsome *Municipal Buildings* (1914) stand beside the bridge over the Cadzow by which the Bothwell road enters the town. The centrally-planned *Old Church* (1732) is by William Adam (1732). Before it stands the ancient *Cross* from Netherton (see below). *Hamilton Palace*, long the imposing seat of the

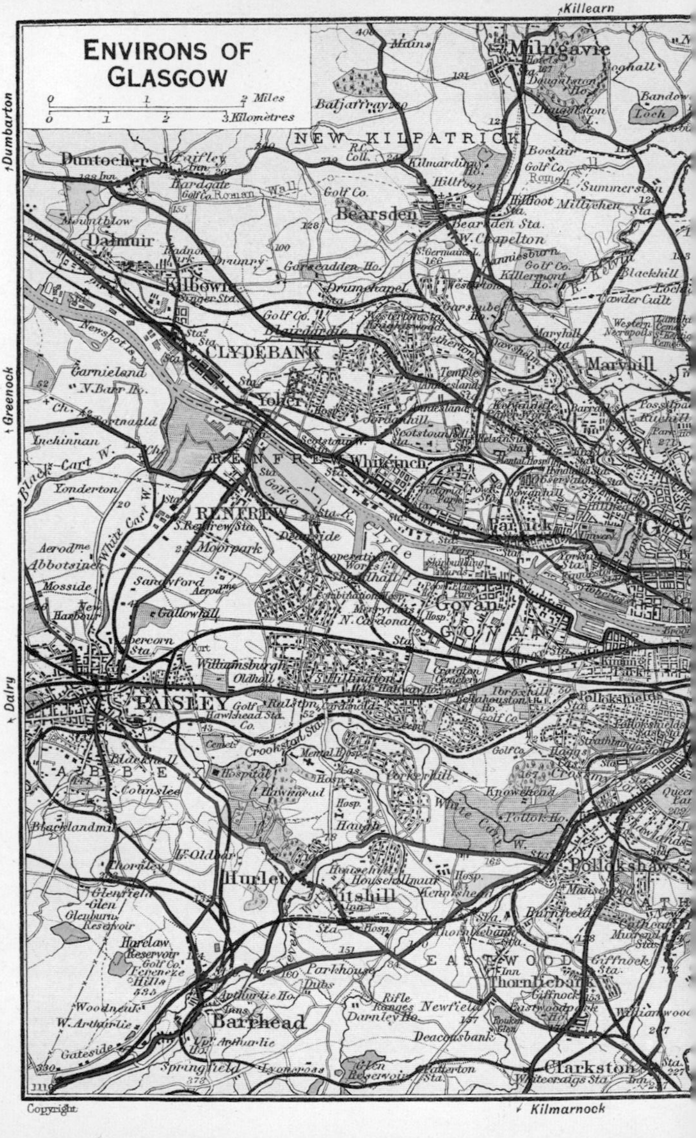
ENVIRONS OF GLASGOW
0 1 2 Miles
0 1 2 3 Kilomètres
Killearn
Dumbarton
Greenock
Dalry
Kilmarnock
Milngavie
Mains
Baljaffray
NEW KILPATRICK
Duntocher
Faifley
Hardgate
Roman Wall
Golf Co.
Bearsden
Kilmardinny Ho.
Boclair
Summerston
Millichen
Bearsden Sta.
W. Chapelton
Canniesburn
Killermont Ho.
R. Kelvin
Blackhill
Cawder Cuilt
Mountblow
Dalmuir
Radnor Park
Drumry
Garscadden Ho.
Drumchapel
Kilbowie
Singer Sta.
Garscube Ho.
Westerton
Blairdardie
Knightswood
Netherton
Maryhill Sta.
Dawsholm
Maryhill
Western Necropolis
Newshot Is.
CLYDEBANK
Temple
Anniesland
Yoker
Jordanhill
Scotstounhill
Scotstoun
Garnieland
N. Barr Ho.
Portnauld
Inchinnan
Black Cart W.
Yonderton
RENFREW
Whiteinch
Victoria Park
Partick
Dowanhill
Hyndland Sta.
Possilpark
Ruchill
White Cart W.
S. Renfrew Sta.
Moorpark
Deanside
Aerodme
Abbotsinch
Mosside
New Harbour
Sandyford
Gallowhill
Abercorn Sta.
Shieldhall
Govan
GOVAN
N. Cardonald
Williamsburgh
Oldhall
Hillington
Craigton Cemetery
Ibrox
Bellahouston
Kinning Park
Pollokshields
PAISLEY
Golf
Ralston
Cardonald
Hawkhead Sta.
Crookston Sta.
Cemet.
Blackhall
ABBEY
Colinslee
Hospital
Hawkhead
Hosp.
Corkerhill
Haggs Cas.
Crossmyloof
Strathbungo
Knowehead
Pollok Ho.
Queen's Park
Blacklandmill
Thornley
Glenfield
Glen
Glenburn Reservoir
Oldbar
Hurlet
Househillmuir
Nitshill
Hosp.
Pollokshaws
Shawlands
Mansewood
Burnfield
Cathcart
Harelaw Reservoir
Golf Co.
Fereneze Hills
Parkhouse
Dubs
EASTWOOD
Thornliebank
Giffnock
Giffnock Sta.
Muirend Sta.
Woodneuk
W. Arthurlie
Arthurlie Ho.
Barrhead
Up. Arthurlie Ho.
Rifle Ranges
Newfield
Darnley Ho.
Eastwoodpark
Rouken Glen
Williamwood
Deaconsbank
Gateside
Springfield
Lyoncross
Glen Reservoir
Patterton Sta.
Clarkston
Whitecraigs Sta.

Copyright

Kilsyth

KIRKINTILLOCH

Stirling

Edinburgh

E. Carleton
W. Carleton
Torrance
Haughton Ho.
Tintock
Gartshore
W. Gartshore
Merkland
Waterside
Sauchenhall
Barbeth
E. Cadder
Roman Wall
Gallowhill
Oxgang
Mental Hosp.
Cadder
Lenzie
Boghead
Jellyhill
Loch
Myremailing
Auchinloch
Chryston
Beglay
Bedcow Ho.
Springfield
Auchinairn
Mollinsburn
Hornshill
Gartshirrie
Mount Harriet
Blenheim
Gartsherrie
Robroyston
Robroyston Ho.
Stepps
Lochend Ho.
Johnston
Garnkirk
Springburn
Millerston
Stepps Sta.
Craigendmuir
Cardowan
Gartcosh Sta.
Hogganfield
Hogganfield Loch
Frankfield
Gartloch
Gartloch
Mental Hosp.
Lethamhill
Garthamlock
Gartloch
Bishop L.
Lochwood
Prison
Craigend
Gardowan
Provanhall
Lochend L.
Alexandra Park
Garterauggie
Monkland
Blairtummock
Maryston Sta.
Cumbrae
Carntyne
Springboig
Bartonhall
Easterhouse
Barlanark
Shettleston
Baillieston
Carntyne Park
Mount Vernon Sta.
Bredisholm
Tollcross
Fullarton
Calderbank
Newlands
Easterdale
North Calder Water
Aitkenhead
Kennmuir
Thorniewood
Camtyle
Daldowie
River Clyde
Mary
RUTHERGLEN
Eastfield
Westburn
Newton
Uddingston
Stonelaw
Blantyre
Cambuslang
Cairns Ho.
Hallside
Drumsagard
Flemington
Rutherglen
Caldergien
Bothwell Castle
Springhill
Gilbertfield
Dalton
Hardykes Rows
Blantyre
Cathkin
CAMBUSLANG
Dechmont Hill
Stonefield
Bothwell
CARMUNNOCK
Greenlees
Reservoir
Cathkin Braes
Public Park
Dechmont
Barnhill
Milheugh Ho.

John Bartholomew & Son, Ltd. Edinburgh

dukes of Hamilton, was pulled down in 1927 on account of subsidence caused by coal-workings beneath, but its parks still repay a visit. The 17th cent. *Tolbooth* was demolished in 1954 for the same reason.

The Low Parks (adm. weekdays 10–5 6*d.*, including mausoleum) which included the palace, and extend towards the Clyde, are entered from the Bothwell road by a gateway a little above the Municipal Buildings. They were purchased by the town in 1922. Within their bounds are Hamilton racecourse (race meeting in July) and a mote-hill indicating the site of *Netherton*, the original village removed to the site of the present Hamilton in the 15th century. Here also is the ducal *Mausoleum* (key at the neighbouring cottage), a tall square edifice with a stone cupola in the classic style, by David Bryce, erected by the 10th duke at a cost of £130,000. The interior is a solemn octagonal chapel, where voices arouse a long-drawn-out and beautiful echo. The vaults beneath the floor of inlaid marble are now empty. The bronze doors (now kept inside, because of the damage caused by underground workings), are copied from Ghiberti's doors at the Baptistery in Florence. On the E. façade of the basement are three stone masks by A. H. Ritchie, representing Life, Death, and Eternity, and two lions, by the same sculptor, guard the approach-steps.

The High Parks lie S. of the town. They are now owned by the Hamilton and Kinneil Estates, Ltd., and permits are granted by the factor (A. D. L. McDonald) at the Estate Office in Muir St. Near the entrance, c. ½ m. from the Central Station, is *Barncluith*, a modest mansion with quaint Dutch gardens overhanging the Avon, laid out c. 1583. The High Parks are traversed by the Avon, about a mile up which are the romantically situated ruins of **Cadzow Castle**, a royal abode under Alexander II and Alexander III, and later the cradle of the Hamilton family. Queen Mary on her way to Langside visited the castle, which was destroyed after the battle by the Regent Moray. The secular stag-headed oaks in the surrounding woods are held to be relics of the great Caledonian Forest of S. Scotland ; several of them are estimated to be over 500 years old. The herd of wild white cattle in the parks was originally of the same breed as the herd at Chillingham in Northumberland, and is now the only remnant in Scotland of the native wild white cattle of Britain to which Scott refers in his ballad of ' Cadyow Castle.' On the right bank of the Avon stands the building called *Chatelherault*, copied in 1732 from the château of Châtellerault (near Poitiers), from which the duke takes his French title of Duke of Chatelherault.

From Hamilton to Lanark (motor-bus hourly in 50 min.), we continue to follow A 74, skirting the High Parks for 2½ m., then diverge l. on A 72 from the road to the S. viâ Lesmahagow, to descend to the Clyde near Dalserf.—6½ m. *Rosebank* (Popinjay Inn, RB. 18/6).—9 m. *Crossford* and thence to (14 m.) *Lanark*, see below.

From Hamilton to *Kilmarnock*, see pp. 170, 169.

From Glasgow to Lanark and the Falls of Clyde

Railway to *Lanark*, 32¼ m. in 70–80 min. from Central Station viâ Motherwell and Carluke.—Road, 24¾ m., viâ Hamilton, see above.—Motor-Buses from Waterloo St.: No. 240, frequent service viâ Wishaw and Carluke to *Lanark* in 1¼ hr.; No. 44 viâ Bellshill and New Stevenston to *Carfin* and *Wishaw*.

Lanark (*Clydesdale*, RB. 21/, P. 10 gs.; *Caledonian*, RB. 19/, P. 9 gs.; *Royal Oak*, RB. 16/6, P. 7 gs.), plain), on an upland nearly 700 ft. above sea-level, is a plain little town (6220 inhab.) retaining little evidence of the antiquity of which it can boast. The wide High Street, with the parish church of 1774–77, is embellished by an ungainly statue of Wallace by a self-taught artist. Wallace is said to have lived in the Castlegate (leading left from the church to the site of the old castle), and may possibly have been married in the ancient church of *St. Kentigern* (12th cent.), of which some arches remain in the graveyard S.E. of the station.

According to the story, Wallace, having slain a soldier of the English garrison in a quarrel in 1297, fled to Cartland Crags (see below) while his wife was put to death. Returning with a band, Wallace overpowered the garrison and slew William Hazelrig, their leader, and therewith began his warlike career.

On *Lanark Moor*, c. 1 m. E. of the town, are a small loch (tea-room ; skating), a racecourse (with meetings in July and Sept.), and a golf course. The 'Declaration of Lanark,' affixed to the cross in 1682, was a confirmation of the first declaration of Sanquhar. 'Lanimer Day' (i.e. 'land-march' or beating the bounds), in the first week of June, is celebrated with pageantry and processions through the town.

The FALLS OF CLYDE, three in number, occur on a stretch of the river less than 4 m. long. The falls of Cora Linn and Bonnington Linn, above Lanark, are most conveniently (and perhaps best) seen from the right (W.) bank (the ' Bonnington side '), but may be viewed also from the opposite or ' Corehouse side ' by a detour (see below). The fall of Stonebyres, below Lanark, is viewed from the l. bank. The whole area is best visited on foot or bicycle. The utilisation of the Falls for hydro-electric power affects their volume at certain seasons, and permits to view the falls (and power-stations) must be obtained from the South of Scotland Electricity Board, 168 Broomhill Drive, Glasgow, W.1.

Quitting Lanark by Wellgate, diverging S. from High St., we descend by a zigzag road (short cut for walkers) to (1 m.) *New Lanark*, a group of textile mills and tall houses on the right bank of the Clyde, founded in 1784 by David Dale and Richard Arkwright, and famous as the scene of the socialistic experiments of Robert Owen (1771–1858), Dale's son-in-law, who was manager from 1800 to 1828. Near the N. end of New Lanark is *Braxfield*, the home of Lord Braxfield (Robert Macqueen ; 1722–99), the 'hanging judge' drawn by Stevenson as 'Weir of Hermiston.—From the lodge of the ruined Bonnington House, c. ½ m. farther on, the road leads to a power-station, beyond which a path ascends along the bank of the Clyde, here bordered by cliffs and rocks alternating with fine hanging woods, to (½ m. more) *Cora Linn* (86 ft. high), the finest of the falls, in a magnificent amphitheatre of rocks. On the verge of the cliff on the opposite bank is the ruined Cora Castle, the 'time-cemented tower' of Wordsworth's apostrophe to the fall. The path goes on to a narrow part of the river channel, with Wallace's Cave, and to (c. ¾ m. more) *Bonnington Linn* (30 ft.), where the river, sweeping round a curve, descends in two foaming branches separated by a rocky island.

About 1¼ m. W. of Lanark are the **Cartland Crags,** precipitous cliffs 200–400 ft. high, flanking a remarkable chasm (¾ m. long) on the *Mouse*, reached by a poor path. We take A 73, the Carluke road, which crosses the defile by one of Telford's elegant bridges, 120 ft. high ; the path descends to the r. on the farther side. About 1 m. up the Mouse glen lies *Jerviswood*, the home of Robert Baillie, the ' Scottish Sidney,' hanged for high treason in 1684.—Downstream from Telford's bridge the Mouse is crossed by a low bridge beside a very narrow older bridge called a Roman bridge.

FROM LANARK TO TILLIETUDLEM, 6½ m. Passing to the right of the church and keeping to the left at (½ m.) a fork we descend a steep hill and cross the Clyde by a new bridge (1958) alongside the 17th cent. bridge to (1¼ m.) *Kirkfieldbank*, a pretty village, beyond which are extensive orchards.

By turning to the left immediately on crossing the bridge we may ascend a by-road to (1¾ m.) the West Lodge of Corehouse, where walkers are admitted (by permit) to view the falls of Cora Linn and Bonnington from a path ascending the left bank of the Clyde.

At (2½ m.) *Cairniepark* a road (r.) descends, and crosses the river to a large power-house (permits shown here). Thence a path leads up the right bank of the Clyde to *Stonebyres Fall* (originally 60–70 ft.), seen to best advantage from this side. The road may be regained by crossing the tilting-weir, a little above the falls.—The road goes on through orchards. On the left is the old keep of *Stonebyres*, and, above that, *Blackhill* (N.T.), a good viewpoint.—Beyond (4½ m.) *Crossford* the road crosses the Nethan and goes on to (13¼ m.) Hamilton, but a path, diverging on the left short of the bridge, leads up the stream to (½ m.) *Craignethan Castle* (16th cent.), accepted as the original of *Tillietudlem Castle* in ' Old Mortality,' and enthusiasts may perhaps identify the window out of which Jenny soused the hot broth over Cuddy Headrigg. This fortified manor-house of the great Evandale branch of the Hamilton family is now reduced to two towers with portions of the walls and a vaulted hall.

An alternative route from Glasgow to Lanark (followed by the motor-buses) traverses the heart of the Lanarkshire coal-field, now approaching exhaustion. The road to Hamilton is followed as far as (5½ m.) *Calderpark* ; then, crossing the Calder, we bear left on A 721 for (9 m.) *Bellshill*, with its huge red sandstone quarry.—12½ m. *Motherwell* and (15¼ m.) *Wishaw*, surrounded by coal-pits and steelworks, form a single burgh (68,150 inhab.), and Motherwell since 1947 has been the seat of a Roman Catholic bishop. Carfin (see below) is 2 m. N.E. of Motherwell, and near *Flemington* (between Motherwell and Wishaw) is Dalzell House (no adm.), incor-porating a 15th cent. tower. J. G. Lockhart (1794–1854) was born in the manse of *Cambusnethan*, ½ m. E. of Wishaw.

Carfin, a mining village 2 m. N. of Motherwell with a population largely of Irish or Polish extraction, is noted for a *Grotto* dedicated in 1922 to Our Lady of Lourdes and visited annually by thousands of pilgrims (entrance in Newarthill Road, between two railway bridges and opposite the church of St. Francis). The original shrine, to the left, is modelled on that at Lourdes. The surrounding area has been beautifully laid out as a garden, and several other shrines have been constructed.

Beyond (20 m.) *Carluke* (Crown, RB. 21/) we quit the colliery district. A plaque at Miltonhead marks the birthplace of Gen. William Roy (1729–90), ' father of the Ordnance Survey.'—22 m. *Braidwood*, with limestone quarries, is

connected with Crossford (2½ m.) by a downhill road passing the ancient *Halbar Tower*, possibly of 11th cent. foundation.—
26 m. *Lanark*, see above.

The Lee, a castellated mansion on the left of the road between Braidwood and Lanark, was long the seat of the Lockharts ; but the ' Lee Penny ', a jewel set in a shilling of the time of Edward I, is now preserved elsewhere. This talisman, which suggested Scott's story of ' The Talisman ' was brought from the East by the Sir Simon Lockhart of Bruce's day, and the water in which it is dipped is supposed to have wonderful medicinal virtue. Its use was permitted by the General Assembly of the Church about 1628, when other amulets were condemned, and it was actually used as late as 1824.

From Lanark to *Douglas* and *Ayr*, see Rte. 17A ; to *Carlisle* and to *Edinburgh* viâ Carstairs, see Rte. 9A.

FROM GLASGOW TO PROVAN HALL, c. 5 m. E. There are two alternative ROAD routes : (*a*) by motor-bus No. 90 from Dundas St. viâ Garngad Road and Riddrie to (4¼ m. in 25 min.) *Blackfaulds Cottages* at Cardowan ; thence by lanes, first to the r. beyond a quarry, then l. and r. again ; (*b*) by the main Edinburgh road (A 8) from St. Rollox (Pl. 21) to (3 m.) *Lightburn Hospital*, turning l. about 1¼ m. farther on.—RAILWAY from Queen St. (Low Level) viâ High St. and Shettleston to (6 m. in 20 min.) *Easterhouse*, whence the Hall is 1¾ m. N.W.

Provan Hall, or *Old Mailing* (N.T.), standing in 10 acres of woodland near the bank of the derelict Monkland Canal, is one of the finest extant 15th cent. mansions in Scotland. It was restored in 1938 (adm. 6*d*. daily, exc. Mon. & Fri. ; in May–Sept., weekdays 10–8, Sun. 2–8 ; Oct.–Apr. 10–4, Sun. 2–4 ; tea can be arranged by telephone to Baillieston 1538). The hall was the country home of the prebendary of Barlanark or Balernock (at one time James IV), whose town house was *Provand's Lordship* (p. 113). It consists of two buildings on opposite sides of a picturesque courtyard ; the original building has a turret and a corbie-stepped gable ; the other (now the caretaker's residence) was added in the 17–18th cent. ; and an attractive walled garden adjoins.

FROM GLASGOW TO DRYMEN, 16¼ m., by road through moorland country N.W. of Glasgow (motor-bus hourly from Killermont St. in 1 hr.). From St. George's Cross (Pl. 11) *Canniesburn*, 3½ m. N.W., may be reached either viâ Maryhill Road (tramway route) or viâ Great Western Road to Anniesland Station and then to the right over Temple Bridge. Between the two roads lies the pleasant *Dawsholm Park*, in the Kelvin valley. At Canniesburn we follow A 809 to the left.

The road to the right leads to (2 m.) *Milngavie* (pron. Milguy), a small town (7890 inhab.) in Dunbartonshire, the terminus of a short branch railway from Glasgow, with pretty surroundings. Above the town are the Mugdock and Craigmaddie reservoirs of the Glasgow water-works. *Mugdock Castle*, with an ancient tower, 1½ m. N., was formerly the principal seat of the Montrose family. Road to *Strathblane* and *Aberfoyle*, see Rte. 25B.

4½ m. *Bearsden* or *New Kilpatrick*, on the line of the Roman Wall, is a community of pleasant villas, with a station on the Milngavie branch railway.—Skirting the Kilpatrick Hills, on the left, we follow the Stockiemuir road to the N.W., and (9 m.), crossing the Allander, pass from Dunbartonshire into Stirlingshire. Bailie Nicol Jarvie and his companions passed this way on their route to Aberfoyle, and (9¼ m.) the Halfway Inn is supposed to represent the alehouse in which they dined. About 1½ m. beyond the inn a path diverges on the left for *Auchineden Hill* (1171 ft. ; view of Loch Lomond, etc.), on the N. slope of which, c. 1 m. from the road, is the curious chasm known as *The Whangie* (no adm.).—The road farther on crosses (13½ m.) the Carnock Burn, flowing down from the pretty *Finnich Glen*, into which a path descends from the bridge. From the next fork B 834 leads r. to *Killearn* (2 m. ; p. 217). Our road crosses the Endrick for (16¼ m.) *Drymen* (p. 210).

From Glasgow to *Ayr*, see Rtes. 15, 16 ; to *Balloch*, see Rte. 12 ; to the *Clyde*, see Rte. 14 ; to *Dumbarton* and *Helensburgh*, see Rte. 12 ; to *Edinburgh*, see Rte. 10 ; to *Fort William* and *Mallaig*, see Rte. 48 ; to *Greenock, Gourock* and *Wemyss Bay*, see Rte. 14 ; to *Oban*, see Rte. 47 ; to *Stirling* and *Callander*, see Rte. 23 ; to the *Trossachs*, see Rte. 25.

12. FROM GLASGOW BY ROAD TO HELENSBURGH AND LOCH LOMOND

A. To Helensburgh, Arrochar and Crianlarich

ROAD, 60½ m.—16½ m. *Dumbarton.*—25 m. **Helensburgh.**—42 m. *Arrochar.*—60½ m. **Crianlarich.** MOTOR-BUSES : frequent service from Glasgow (Waterloo St.) to *Helensburgh* in 1½ hr. ; once or twice daily from Glasgow (Dundas St.) to *Arrochar* (2 hrs.) and *Crianlarich* (3 hrs.) going on to *Tyndrum, Dalmally,* and *Oban* (see Rte. 47).

RAILWAY, 59 m., from Queen St. Station to *Crianlarich* in 2¼ hrs. ; to *Dumbarton*, 15¼ m. in 30–40 min. ; to *Helensburgh*, 23½ m. in ¾ hr. ; to *Arrochar* and *Tarbet*, 42 m. in 1½–2 hrs. Dumbarton is reached also from Central Station (low level) in 40–50 mins. Helensburgh has two stations, one the terminus of local trains from Glasgow, which diverge at Craigendoran, the other (Upper Helensburgh) on the main West Highland Line, which goes on viâ Crianlarich to Fort William and Mallaig (see Rte. 48).

Out of Glasgow the new Duntocher Boulevard, a continuation of Great Western Road (Pl. 2, 3 ; A 82) runs N.W. to (8½ m.) *Duntocher* and (10 m.) *Old Kilpatrick*, with shipyards, long claimed to be the birthplace of St. Patrick (but comp. below). The Clyde is here crossed by *Erskine Ferry* (car 1/6, motor-cycle 6*d.*, cycle or passenger 2*d.*).

An alternative route (9½ m. ; followed by the Helensburgh buses), viâ Dumbarton Road, Whiteinch, Yoker and (7 m.) Clydebank, has very heavy traffic. *Clydebank* (44,640 inhab.) is a shipbuilding burgh of recent growth, which suffered heavily from enemy aircraft in 1941. Beyond the Forth and Clyde Canal are the extensive works of the Singer Sewing-Machine Company.

Our route traverses **Dunbartonshire**, once known as Lennox, which includes the industrial Vale of Leven, and many favourite coast-resorts on the Clyde, the Gareloch and Loch Long, as well as the romantic beauties and associations of Loch Lomond. This is the country of Tobias Smollett.

At (12 m.) *Bowling*, a shipbuilding place with a large dock where Clyde steamers are laid up in winter, Smeaton's *Forth and Clyde Canal* (1768–90) enters the Clyde. On the right are the *Kilpatrick Hills* (1313 ft.; *Views), now studded with small reservoirs.

This canal, 38 m. long, crosses Scotland at its narrowest point, following roughly the line of the Roman Wall (p. 106), which began at Dunglass Point and had a fort at Old Kilpatrick, and another at Duntocher. The tug 'Charlotte Dundas', engined by Symington, the first practical steamboat, appeared on this canal in 1802.

On the left, just beyond Bowling, is *Dunglass Point*, with the ivy-covered ruins of a castle in front of which is an obelisk to Henry Bell. Near the base of the isolated *Dumbuck* (view) we turn left on A 814, crossing the railway.

14½ m. **DUMBARTON** (*Dumbuck*, RB. 18/6, P. 10 gs., 1 m. E. of the town), a busy industrial town and royal burgh (23,700 inhab.) near the mouth of the Leven, with shipbuilding yards, is of interest mainly for its historic and conspicuous castle.

History. Dumbarton (Dun Bretane, 'hill of the Britons') has been identified with the *Alcluyth* of Bede and the *Balclutha* of Ossian. St. Patrick (373–463), originally named Sucat, who c. 389 was kidnapped in the vicinity by raiders and sold into captivity in Ireland, and St. Gildas (c. 516–c. 570), the historian, were probably born here. The castle became a royal hold in the 13th cent., but frequently changed hands. Sir John Menteith, the treacherous captor of Sir William Wallace in 1305, was governor of the castle, whither perhaps the hero was carried before being sent to his execution in London. It was from this castle that, in 1548, Mary, Queen of Scots, then a child of six, was secretly sent to France (landing at Roscoff in Brittany) in a French fleet which, in order to elude the cruisers of Henry VIII, sailed N. about Scotland by the Pentland Firth to receive her. The Treaty of Union (1707) undertook to maintain the castle as one of the chief national fortresses of Scotland.—In 1658 a proposal that the harbour should be developed as a foreport of Glasgow was rejected by the magistrates on the ground that "the influx of mariners would tend to raise the price of butter and eggs to the inhabitants." Since then a more far-sighted policy has prevailed.

***Dumbarton Castle** (adm. free, 10–4 or 7, Sun. from 2) is built upon an isolated basaltic rock (240 ft.), c. 1 m. round, which rises abruptly from the edge of the Clyde, and is cleft into two summits, the higher of which is known as 'Wallace's Seat.' It consists now of a group of modern barracks with an ancient dungeon or brine-pit. It is entered from the seaward side, the landward entrance having been destroyed. The sundial at the foot of the rock was presented by Mary, Queen of Scots. From the former governor's house (1735–1832) a long flight of steps ascends in the cleft between the peaks, passing 'Wallace's Guardhouse,' with a gable terminating in rude heads of Wallace and Sir John Menteith, the latter with his finger in his cheek, the signal of betrayal. Higher up we pass through a 12th cent. archway, grooved for a portcullis. Dorothy Wordsworth (1803) was of opinion that the views from the summit were "sufficient recompense for the trouble of climbing the Rock of Dumbarton."

In 1571 the castle was sensationally captured from the adherents of Queen Mary by 100 men under Thomas Crawford of Jordanhill, who at dead of night climbed the least accessible side of the rock by means of scaling ladders and ropes, and fell upon the astonished garrison. At a critical moment one of the assailants was seized with a fit and could move neither up nor down. He was accordingly lashed to the ladder, the ladder was turned round, and his comrades ascended over his body. None of the attackers was killed and only four of the garrison. John Hamilton, Archbp. of St. Andrews, was captured in the castle and four days later was hanged at Stirling for alleged complicity in the murders of Darnley and the Regent Moray.

In Church St., opposite the Academy, a tower-arch of the collegiate church of *St. Mary*, founded by the Duchess of Albany in 1454, was re-erected in 1850.

The Helensburgh road crosses the Leven to (15¾ m.) *Dalreoch*, a suburb of Dumbarton, leaving a road to Balloch on the right.—At (17½ m.) *Cardross*, with its bridge of 1688, Robert Bruce died in 1329. A cairn with a portrait-medallion (by A. Proudfoot) on the Castle Hill (N.T.) is a memorial to R. B. Cunninghame Graham (1852-1936), author and traveller, who lived at Ardoch, near by. On the hillside, 1 m. N., is the keep of *Kilmahew*, near a 19th cent. mansion. The little Kilmahew Chapel was dedicated in 1467 to St. Mahew, a companion of St. Patrick. Derelict since c. 1840, it was restored to use in 1955. Across the Clyde appear Port Glasgow and Greenock, and beyond the mile-long peninsula of *Ardmore* a fine view of the Argyll mountains opens on the left.—24½ m. **Craigendoran** (l.) is a busy centre of passenger steamer traffic.

Steamers ply hence to *Kilcreggan, Kirn, Dunoon, Innellan,* and *Rothesay* (Rte. 13D) ; to *Blairmore, Lochgoilhead,* and *Arrochar* (Rte. 13B).

25 m. **Helensburgh** (*Queen's*, E. end, RB. 25/, P. 10½ gs. ; *Cairndhu*, W. end, RB. 30/, P. 11 gs. ; *Kingsclere*, RB. 21/, P. 8 gs.) is an agreeable residential town (8760 inhab.) and summer resort, named after the wife of Sir James Colquhoun of Luss, who laid out the older part of the town on the draughtboard plan at the end of the 18th century. It was the birthplace of J. L. Baird (1888-1946), pioneer of television. An obelisk commemorates Henry Bell, provost in 1807-9, who in 1812 launched the ' Comet ' (3 h.p.) on the Clyde, the first practical passenger-steamer in Europe, five years later than Fulton's ' Clermont ' on the Hudson.

Helensburgh, the farthest up the river of the Clyde watering-places, lies at the mouth of the *Gareloch* (220 yds. wide). This loch, Loch Long, Loch Lomond, and Glen Fruin may be visited by road in a round of 35 miles.

A 814 skirts the E. shore of the **Gareloch,** which stretches N. for c. 4½ m. with a breadth of less than a mile. During the war this sheltered loch was used as a base for combined operations.—At (27½ m.) *Rhu* (Rhuellen, RB. 25/, P. 9 gs. ; Ardencaple, RB. 21/, P. 9½ gs.), with its seaside villas and the club-house of the Royal Northern Yacht Club, Henry Bell (see above) is buried beside the church. This quiet little resort lies sheltered by charming woods.

Beyond (30 m.) *Shandon* is the unsightly shipbreaking station at (31 m.) *Faslane Bay*, where the road from Balloch

viâ Glen Fruin comes in on the right.—32 m. *Garelochhead*
(Hotel, RB. 18/6, P. 9 gs.) is connected by road (B 833) down
the W. side of the Gareloch with Rosneath and (10 m.)
Kilcreggan (Rte. 13c).—33½ m. *Whistlefield Roadhouse* lies
on the watershed between the Gareloch and Loch Long,
whence we may catch a glimpse of the entrance to Loch Goil
and of Carrick Castle.   The scenery becomes wilder as we
descend to (35 m.) *Finnart*, on Loch Long, which is being
developed as an oil port.   On the left, across Loch Long
(Rte. 13B), which we now skirt, appears the rugged sky-line
of Argyll's Bowling Green and the Cobbler comes into view
ahead.   From (38½ m.) *Gorten* a rough road leads E. viâ Glen
Douglas to *Inverbeg Inn* (5 m.), on Loch Lomond.   Above
Glen Croe, on the opposite bank, towers *Ben Arthur* (2891 ft.)
or *The Cobbler* (see p. 143), with *Ben Narnain* (3036 ft.) and
A' Chrois (2785 ft.) to the N., making a splendid group.

42 m. **Arrochar,** at the head of Loch Long, see Rte. 13B.
We turn right on A 83 at the entrance to the village, and a
beautiful view of the head of Loch Lomond opens as we
descend to the station of *Arrochar and Tarbet*, midway
between Loch Long and Loch Lomond, here less than 2 m.
apart.—43½ m. **Tarbet** (p. 140) is in full view of Ben Lomond
opposite, while to the right appears Duncryne (462 ft.),
a conical hill at the S. end of the loch, 15 m. away.   The road
now skirts the W. bank of Loch Lomond.—At (46½ m.)
Inveruglas, with its power-station, almost opposite Inversnaid
and its waterfall, we cross the Inveruglas Water descending
from *Loch Sloy*, between *Ben Vane* (3004 ft. ; r.) and *Ben
Vorlich* (3092 ft.).   About 1½ m. farther is the Pulpit Rock,
once used for preaching.

The Loch Sloy scheme was the first project of the North of Scotland Hydro-
Electric Board ; the waters of the loch, doubled in volume by the erection of a
dam 1160 ft. long and 160 ft. high, are transmitted through a tunnel 1¾ m. long
beneath Ben Vorlich to the Inveruglas power-house.   The loch is approached by
two roads (cars by permit only from the N. of Scotland Hydro-Electric Board),
one from Inveruglas, the other from below Rest and be Thankful on the Arrochar-
Inveraray road.

Beyond (52 m.) **Ardlui** (p. 140) the road quits Loch Lomond
and ascends the charming tree-clad *Glen Falloch*, with the
river on the right.   At (54 m.) *Inverarnan House* (RB. 18/,
P. 8 gs., unlic.) we cross the Arnan which divides Dunbartonshire from *Perthshire*.   Next we bridge the gorge of the Dubh
Eas, with the railway viaduct higher up on the left.   The
Falls of Falloch, with Rob Roy's Bath, are seen on the right,
about 1½ m. farther on, and we enter a bleak mountain
district, dotted with a few stunted survivors of the great
Caledonian Forest.   From the head of Glen Falloch the road
descends to Strathfillan.—60½ m. **Crianlarich,** and thence to
Oban, or to Killin and Callander, see Rte. 46.

B. To Balloch and Loch Lomond

ROAD (A 82) to Crianlarich, 54 m., keeping close to the W. shore of Loch Lomond.—19 m. **Balloch.**—27 m. *Luss.*—38 m. *Tarbet.*—54 m. **Crianlarich.**
MOTOR-BUSES. Frequent service from Waterloo St. to *Balloch* viâ Dumbarton n 1¼ hr. ; thence to *Luss* several times daily in 25 min. There is also a service on Sat. & Sun. from Buchanan St. to *Balmaha* (1¼ hr.).
RAILWAY from Queen St. to *Balloch* viâ Anniesland, 20 m. in ¾–1 hr. ; from Central Station viâ Clydebank, 19 m. in 1 hr.

From Glasgow to (12 m.) *Bowling*, see Rte. 12A. We keep to the right at the foot of Dumbuck and ascend the valley of the Leven, which flows from Loch Lomond. Since the middle of the 18th cent. this short valley has been devoted to dyeing, bleaching, and calico-printing, the chief centres (14,900 inhab. together) being *Renton* and *Alexandria* (named after an Alexander Smollett), both on the W. bank, and the river is no longer quite the " pure stream in whose translucent wave" Tobias Smollett (1721–71), the novelist, used to lave his youthful limbs. A monument at Renton, with an inscription partly by Dr. Johnson, commemorates Smollett, who was born at the old house of *Dalquharn* (pron. ' Dalwhan '), ½ m. S. Our road ascends the E. bank to (17 m.) *Bonhill*, near which was the ancestral home of the Smolletts, and then crosses by a suspension bridge to (17½ m.) *Alexandria*, 1¼ m. N. of Renton.—19 m. **Balloch** (*Lomond Castle*, 2 m. along the Luss road, RB. 32/6, P. 16 gs. ; *Tulliechewan*, RB. 21/, P. 11 gs. ; *Woodbank*, RB. 24/, P. 11 gs. ; *Glenroy*, RB. 25/6, P. 12 gs. ; *Balloch*, RB. 20/, P. 9 gs.), continuous with Alexandria, lies ½ m. from the S. end of Loch Lomond. A footpath leads to the pier from which the steamers start. The banks of the Leven above the bridge are lined in summer with gay cabin-cruisers—an unusual feature in Scotland— and beside its outflow from the loch is an attractive public park, belonging to Glasgow, in which a mound marks the site of old Balloch Castle (luncheons in the modern castle).

FROM BALLOCH TO GARELOCHHEAD, 10½ m. We follow A 82 up the W. shore of Loch Lomond, but at 3½ m. we turn left on B 831, and cross the Fruin, with *Bannachra*, a ruined stronghold of the Colquhouns, on the left. Beyond B 832 (the Helensburgh–Luss road) our road becomes rougher as it ascends to the head of **Glen Fruin** (' the glen of sorrow '), which extends for about 5 m. N.W. This glen was the scene in 1603 of a bloody battle between the MacGregors and the Colquhouns (pron. ' Co-hoon '), in which 200 of the latter were slain, while a number of onlookers (sons of the gentry of the district), who had been shut up in a barn for safety by the Colquhouns, were massacred in cold blood by the victors. This latter accusation, however, was denied. Sixty widows of the Colquhouns appeared before James VI at Stirling, each with the bloody shirt of her husband in her hand, and the king was so moved that he outlawed the MacGregors and proscribed their very name. The act of outlawry was reversed in 1663 by Charles II, as a reward for services rendered to Montrose, but it was renewed in 1693 by William III, and full legal rights were not finally restored until 1755, under George II.—From the head of the glen our road crosses a steep ridge and descends to the Gareloch at (9 m.) *Faslane Bay* (p. 135).

A motor-bus runs from Balloch to *Drymen* (9 m.) viâ (4 m.) *Gartocharn* (Hotel, RB. 20/, P. 9 gs.), a quiet holiday resort at the foot of *Duncryne* (462 ft. ; view) and 1 m. from the S. shore of Loch Lomond at *Ross Priory*, once visited by Sir Walter Scott.

From Balloch to the *Trossachs* and *Callander*, see Rte. 25 ; to *Stirling* viâ Buchlyvie, see Rte. 24.—Steamers on *Loch Lomond*, see below ; road to *Tarbet* and *Crianlarich*, see p. 140.

*Loch Lomond (23 ft.), 24 m. long by ¾–5 m. wide, is the largest lake in Great Britain, and makes high claims to be the most beautiful. Stretching in its long narrow N. reach between ranges of fine and lofty mountains (Ben Vorlich, Ben a Chroin, Ben Lomond), it expands in the S. to embrace a charming group of wooded islands, while its banks exhibit a delightful variety of pastoral and wooded scenery. Smollett, speaking as Mr. Mathew Bramble in ' Humphry Clinker,' remarks : " I have seen the Lago di Gardi, Albano, De Vico, Bolsena, and Geneva, and on my honour I prefer Loch Lomond to them all." Dr. Johnson, however, visiting the loch on a rainy October day in 1773, seems to have thought little of it, and Wordsworth, whose first visit with Coleridge was paid in 1803, was not greatly impressed, holding that " the proportion of diffusêd water was too great." Of the thirty islets in the loch, six small ones lie N. of Ross Point, while the remaining twenty-four form an archipelago (to quote Smollett again) of " verdant islands that seem to float on its surface, affording the most enchanting objects of repose to the excursive view." The W. bank of the loch is skirted throughout by the Crianlarich road (A 82 ; see below) ; on the E. bank there is no road N. of Rowardennan.

Loch Lomond divides Dunbartonshire (W.) from Stirlingshire (E.), but the Stirlingshire bank extends only from about 2 m. S. of the head of the loch to the mouth of the Endrick, 16 m. S. The ancient name was Loch Leven, whence the surrounding country came to be known as Levenax or Lennox. The leading clans on the shores of the loch were the MacGregors and the Colquhouns, who in 1603 met in deadly conflict in Glen Fruin, near the S.W. angle. Magnus, King of Man, son-in-law of Hakon, is said to have dragged his galleys across the narrow isthmus from Loch Long (Arrochar) in 1263 and to have harried the startled loch. Robert Bruce is supposed to have sought refuge in Rob Roy's Cave near Inversnaid in 1306. In 1715 the MacGregors, as ardent Jacobites, seized all the boats on the loch and assembled them at Inversnaid, where, however, they were speedily recaptured by a Hanoverian force that had dragged some armed boats up the Leven to the loch. Rob Roy was the presiding genius in the early 18th cent., and the whole district around Imversnaid is Rob Roy's country.

Steamers (rfmts.). Daily service in summer (twice on Sat. in July–mid-Sept.) from *Balloch Pier* to (2¼ hrs.) *Ardlui*, at the N. end of the lake, with intermediate piers at *Balmaha*, *Rowardennan*, *Tarbet* (for Loch Long), and *Inversnaid* (for the Trossachs ; comp. Rte. 25).

As the steamer quits Balloch Pier numerous more or less ambitious modern residences are visible on both banks. On the right are Balloch Park and Boturich Castle, occupying the site of an ancient seat of the Lennox family ; on the left opens Glen Fruin (see above). In the middle of the loch lies at the S. end of which are the ruins of old *Lennox Castle*,

Inchmurrin (' isle of the spear '), the largest of the islands, whither the Duchess of Albany retired after the execution of her husband, sons, and father in 1425. Both this island and Inchlonaig (see below) used to be places of internment for drunken and insane persons. Keeping E. of Inchmurrin, with Ross Priory on the right, the steamer touches at (½ hr.) **Balmaha,** prettily situated, whence a narrow road (coming from Drymen, p. 210, 4 m. S.E.) goes on through the Pass of Balmaha and along the loch-side to (6½ m.) Rowardennan.

Immediately opposite is *Inchcailleoch*, the ' island of old women,' the burial-place of the MacGregors, who took oaths ' upon the halidome of him that sleeps beneath the grey stone at Inchcailleoch.' The yew trees of this sacred island furnished the wood for the fiery cross of ' The Lady of the Lake.' It is now a site of the Camping Club. The Buchanans took their slogan from the adjacent islet of *Clairinch*, now a sanctuary for wild life.

The other chief islands in this part of the loch are *Inchfad* (' long isle '), *Inch-cruim* (' round isle '), *Inchmoan* (' peat isle '), *Inchconnachan* (' dog isle '), *Inch-tavanach* (' monk's isle '), and N. of the steamer track, *Inchlonaig* (' marsh isle ').

From Balmaha the steamer, passing the islands, steers up the loch to (1 hr. 10 min.) **Rowardennan** (*Hotel*, RB. 21/, P. 10 gs.), the terminus of the road on the E. bank and the usual starting-point for the ascent of Ben Lomond. Walk to *Aberfoyle*, see p. 217 ; to *Inversnaid*, see p. 140.

Ben Lomond (3192 ft.), which is covered with grass to the top, can be easily ascended before the return of the steamer (up 2–3 hrs., down 1½ hr.). An easy track, beginning opposite the hotel, leads all the way to the top, but demands caution in misty weather. After gaining the ridge (c. 1250 ft.) it crosses an extensive moor (small cairns) and then ascends steeply near an impressive corrie. The descent may be made on the N.W. to Rowchoish (see below). The *View is varied and extensive. Far to the S.W. are the peaks of Arran ; farther N. the Cowal hills (beyond which the Paps of Jura are sometimes visible) extend up to the Cobbler, Ben Ime, and Ben Vorlich, behind which (N.W.) are the twin peaks of Ben Cruachan. Nearer and to the right is Ben Lui, beyond which the top of Ben Nevis is sometimes seen. To the N.E. are Ben More and Stobinian, more distant Ben Lawers, and nearer and to the right Ben Vorlich, Ben Ledi, and close at hand Ben Venue. In the lowlands we see the Ochils, the Wallace Monument, Stirling Castle, and Edinburgh Castle and the Pentlands, to the right of which is Tinto, appearing beyond the smoke of the Glasgow district.

As we steam N., Ben Lomond (r.) dominates the scene. Between it and the loch rises Ptarmigan (2398 ft.), whose slopes—the *Craigroyston*, at one time the shelter of Rob Roy—descend steeply to the shore. Amid the broken masses of rock W. of Ptarmigan is a kind of cavern known as *Rob Roy's Prison*.—The next pier is at (1½ hr.) **Tarbet** (see below), whence the steamer crosses to the E. bank. Ahead we enjoy a beautiful view up Glen Falloch at the head of the loch ; to the W., Ben Narnain and the rugged Cobbler are well seen ; S.E., Ben Lomond presents an unfamiliar aspect.— At (1 hr. 50 min.) **Inversnaid** (*Hotel*, RB. 24/, P. 14 gs.) the route from the Trossachs comes in (see Rte. 25). Just S. of the pier, on the Arklet Water, is the waterfall where in 1803 Wordsworth met ' the Highland Girl ' of his charming poem, to whom he again alludes in his ' Three Cottage Girls,' written twenty years later.

A path leads N. by the loch-side to (1 m.) *Rob Roy's Cave*, among rocks which, as Dorothy Wordsworth remarks, " are in fact no caves, but some fine rocks on the brink of the lake, in the crevices of which a man might hide himself cunningly enough." Bruce is said to have sought refuge here in 1306 after the battle of Dalry. The track goes on to (3½ m. more) the head of the loch, and thence some distance up Glen Falloch before it joins the high-road.—To the S. a very up-and-down track leads through Craigroyston to (7½ m.) *Rowardennan* viâ (3 m.) *Rowchoish*, whence Ben Lomond may be ascended.

Opposite Inversnaid the Loch Sloy transmission pipes are conspicuous ; then Rob Roy's Cave may be seen on the right, and a little farther on is *Eilean Vow*, an islet with a ruined castle of the Macfarlanes. The residence here of a hermit-scion of this family furnished Wordsworth with the subject of his poems on ' The Brownie ' and ' The Brownie's Cell.' Yews are said to have been planted on the islet by Bruce to provide bows for his successors.—At (2¼ hrs.) **Ardlui** (*Colquhoun Arms*, RB. 19/6, P. 10 gs.) the steamer reaches its terminus. Thence to *Crianlarich* (motor-bus or railway), see p. 136.

FROM BALLOCH TO CRIANLARICH BY ROAD, 34 m. on A 82, following the W. bank of Loch Lomond, with delightful views. We pass (2 m.) the Loch Lomond youth hostel (l.) in the mock-baronial mansion of Auchindennan, and (3½ m.) leave the Garelochhead road on the left, soon afterwards crossing the Fruin. At 4½ m. the road from Helensburgh comes in on the left, while on the right, a little farther on, the beautiful woods of *Rossdhu*, the seat of the Colquhouns, intervene between the road and the loch.—8 m. **Luss** (*Colquhoun Arms*, RB. 25/6, P. 12½ gs.) is a village enjoying one of the loveliest sites on Loch Lomond. Here Wordsworth with his sister and Coleridge spent a night in 1803. In the church is an 14–15th cent. effigy of St. Kessog, the evangelist of Lennox in the 6th century. —The loch narrows, with Ross Point opposite, as we approach (11½ m.) *Inverbeg* (Hotel, RB. 18/6, P. 9 gs.), with its youth hostel at the foot of Glen Douglas, up which a rough road runs to join the Loch Long road 2½ m. S. of Arrochar. Ben Lomond, with its buttress Ptarmigan, dominates the view across the loch.—17 m. **Tarbet** (*Hotel*, RB. 25/, P. 13 gs.) is a summer resort, with a pier, and a station (Arrochar and Tarbet) ¾ m. W., on the road crossing the narrow isthmus between Loch Lomond and Loch Long over which Magnus, King of Man, dragged his ships in 1263. We join the road from Arrochar. Thence to (25½ m.) *Ardlui* and (34 m.) *Crianlarich*, see p. 133.

13. THE CLYDE

The **Clyde,** rising among the hills of Tweeddale, 80 m. from Glasgow, and descending the headlong falls at Lanark in its N.W. course, reaches Glasgow as a broad and shallow stream, but has thence been made navigable by an expenditure of millions.

Below Dumbarton it becomes the Firth of Clyde, which, turning S. beyond Gourock, expands into a wide and beautiful estuary between Kintyre and the Ayrshire coast, embracing the islands of Bute, the Cumbraes, and Arran, and sending many narrow sea-lochs northwards deep into the Argyllshire highlands. It is this estuary, with its picturesque and varied scenery, its shores dotted with summer resorts and the mansions of the wealthy, and its admirable steamer services, that is ' the Clyde ' in tourist parlance, a glorious outlet for the people of Glasgow and for their visitors.

Steamer Services. In summer the Clyde is covered by a busy network of excellent steamer services. No one service touches at all, or at nearly all, the piers, but the connections in most cases are fairly convenient. Tickets are taken on board. *Gourock, Wemyss Bay, Fairlie,* and *Craigendoran,* reached from Glasgow by railway (Rtes. 12, 14), are the points at which the Clyde steamers are usually joined ; but the descent of the river, all the way from Glasgow (see below), is of considerable interest, though it entails an early start and adds c. 2 hrs. to the voyage. Refreshments may be obtained on all the steamers, and meals (B., L., or T. 5/6–6/6) are served on the well-equipped steamers that ply on the longer routes. Tickets for a seat at table should be secured in good time. Many of the steamers proudly exhibit brass plates with a record of their war services.

In summer extra boats run on Sat., and also daily during the Glasgow Fair holidays in July (p. 111), when the Clyde is better avoided except by students of popular life. Moonlight cruises are occasionally arranged (see the newspapers), with trains in connection from Glasgow. On Sun. there are no services except to Dunoon, Innellan, Rothesay, Tighnabruaich, and Millport. The summer services ply from May 31st to Sept. 30th, but enquiries as to exact hours, etc., are prudent about the beginning and end of the season. In winter the services are much curtailed.

At most piers (except in the larger places) an annoying toll of 3d.–6d. is exacted from passengers in addition to the fare ; at ' boat stations ' passengers land and embark in small boats for a similar charge.

A. From Glasgow to Gourock and Dunoon by the River

Below Glasgow the " clamorous and sombre stream," as Conrad calls it, is full of interest as an approach to a great seaport. with its bold and skilful engineering, its docks and shipping, the crowded industrial towns and suburbs on its banks, and all its strenuous activities, characterised in good times by the machine-gun clatter of the shipbuilders' hammers.

Leaving *Bridge Wharf* (Pl. 33), we pass, on the S., the quays for the coasting steamers to England, Ireland, and the Continent and, on the N., those used by the boats to the Highlands and Islands and the packet-boats for Ireland. Below *Finnieston* (Pl. 24), with its ferry and subway, Queen's Dock (17 acres ; 1872–80) lies on the right, Prince's Dock (35 acres ; 1892–97) on the left. We are soon off (l.) the ship-

yards of **Govan,** long an independent burgh but now included
in Glasgow and best visited by tramway or by underground
railway. The modern parish church, on the site of an ancient
Celtic monastery, stands amid early Christian monuments,
and in the chancel is the alleged sarcophagus of St. Constantine.
Opposite Govan is the mouth of the *Kelvin* (ferry to *Partick*)
and inland appear the Sick Children's Hospital on Yorkhill
and, more distant, the University on Gilmorehill. The N.
bank is lined with cattle wharves, a huge granary, and the
shipyards of *Whiteinch*; on the S. bank (ferry) at *Linthouse* are
sewage works and timber-yards, followed by the King George V
Dock (20 acres) at *Shieldhall*. On the N. bank is *Scotstoun*.
Beyond the huge Braehead power station (l.), **Renfrew** is
connected by vehicle ferry with *Yoker*, on the N. bank. Also on
the N. bank, opposite the mouth of the Cart, lies the busy
town of *Clydebank*; in the distance are seen the *Kilpatrick
Hills*. *Dalmuir* and *Old Kilpatrick*, with engineering works, are
likewise on the N. bank. Beyond Erskine Ferry (vehicles) is
Erskine House (l. ; see p. 161).—The next reach, as the river
expands into an estuary, is fine. Ahead, on the right bow,
rises the isolated Dumbarton Rock, while Ben Lomond
appears in clear weather far to the N.—11 m. *Bowling* and
Dunglass Castle, among oil stores, on the N. bank. Across the
river from (14 m.) **Dumbarton** is *Langbank*, 2 m. W. of which
is *Finlayston*, once the residence of Lord Glencairn, the patron
of Burns.—18 m. *Port Glasgow* (S.).—On the N. bank is
Cardross, with *Ardmore Point* beyond it ; and as we look
N. we see the beautiful entrance to the *Gareloch*, backed by
rugged mountains.—Passing (21 m.) **Greenock** (S.), we cross
Gourock Bay to (23 m.) **Gourock** (p. 162) or go on to (27 m.)
Dunoon (p. 145), opposite Cloch Point.

B. From Glasgow to Loch Goil and Loch Long

RAILWAY from Glasgow (Queen St.) to *Craigendoran* in 45 min or from Glasgow
(Central) to *Gourock* in 50 min. STEAMER thence on Tues. and Thurs. at c. 10 a.m.
or every weekday c. 11.45 a.m. viâ Gourock and Dunoon to Lochgoilhead and
(3¼ hrs.) *Arrochar* (day return fare 13/8, 11/11). This service permits a stay of
2¼–3 hrs. at Lochgoilhead or ½–1 hr. at Arrochar. Passengers from Rothesay,
Innellan, and Kilcreggan change boats at Dunoon.

From *Craigendoran* we steer S.W. to *Gourock*, then cross
the Firth of Clyde to *Dunoon* and *Kirn* (Rte. 13D). Thence
we steam N. across the mouth of the Holy Loch to *Blairmore*
(Creggandarroch, RB. 17/6, P. 9 gs., with good grounds), a
favourite resort on the W. bank of Loch Long. The villas of
Blairmore stretch S. to meet those of *Strone* (Argyll, RB. 14/6,
P. 6 gs.) on the point at the entrance to the Holy Loch.
A road ascends the shore to (5 m.) *Ardentinny* (Hotel, RB. 24/6, P. 10½ gs.),
the home of Tannahill's 'Sweet Lass o' Arranteenie,' at the mouth of *Glen*

Finart, which is traversed by a rough road to Whistlefield Inn on Loch Eck (5 m. more).

From Blairmore we ascend **Loch Long**, one of the longest, deepest, and most beautiful fjords in Scotland, which separates Argyllshire with its fine mountains (W.), from Dunbartonshire (E.), passing Ardentinny (l.). A few miles N. we diverge (l.) into **Loch Goil**, a loch about 6 m. long, in an impressive mountain setting (not the Loch Gyle of ' Lord Ullin ' ; p. 342). On the E. it is separated from upper Loch Long by the rugged peninsula of *Ardgoil*—' Argyll's Bowling Green '—a magnificent natural mountain park belonging to Glasgow, which, with the estate of Ardgartan to the N., makes up the N. portion of the Argyll National Forest Park. Passing *Carrick Castle* (Hotel, RB. 17/6, P. 160/), on the W. shore, with a ruined stronghold of the Argylls, burnt in 1685 by the men of Atholl, we go on to *Lochgoilhead* (Hotel, RB. 18/6, P. 8½ gs.), a quiet Highland village finely situated at the mouth of the Goil. The church, well restored in 1955, has the remains of a chantry-altar founded by Campbell of Ardkinglas in 1512 ; a 17th cent. memorial to that family frames the E. door (the entrance to a vault destroyed in 1849) ; and a 17th or 18th cent. pulpit from the disused church of Kiltearn, Easter Ross.

FROM LOCHGOILHEAD TO ST. CATHERINE'S (Inveraray), 9 m. The road (B 839) ascends the valley of the Goil and, after passing (2½ m.) a branch leading E. to ' Rest and be Thankful ' in Glen Croe (see below ; 5¾ m.), climbs steeply through the wild rock-strewn *Hell's Glen* (summit-level 719 ft.) and then descends in steep zigzags to the shores of Loch Fyne.—At 6½ m. the road round the head of the loch to Inveraray (12½ m.) diverges on the right.—9 m. *St. Catherine's* is on the S.E. shore of Loch Fyne, connected by ferry (2/, cycle 6d.) with (1½ m.) Inveraray (see p. 158).—Motor-buses run to Arrochar, also down the W. bank of the loch to Carrick Castle (4¾ m.).

The steamer returns to the mouth of Loch Goil and, doubling the S. end of Argyll's Bowling Green, enters the narrow upper reach of Loch Long. High up on the E. shore runs the West Highland Railway. About 2 m. from the head of the loch we have a fine view (l.) up Glen Coe. At the foot of the glen is *Ardgartan* with a large camping-site.

Arrochar (*Arrochar*, RB. 25/, P. 10½ gs. ; *The Ross*, RB. 21/6, P. 9 gs. ; *Arrochar House*, unlic., RB. 20/, P. 180/), at the head of Loch Long, lies in the heart of the Macfarlane country. Here Coleridge parted from Wordsworth and his sister Dorothy (Aug. 29th, 1803). Tarbet, on Loch Lomond, lies 1½ m. E. and midway is the station common to them both. The return to Glasgow may be made by rail, by road viâ Garelochhead (Rte. 12A), or by lake-steamer to Balloch and thence by rail.

Arrochar is a good centre for excursions. To the W., and ascended from Ardgartan or from Sugach farm in Glen Loin, rises *Ben Arthur* (2891 ft.), better known as the **Cobbler** from the Gaelic *An Gobaileach*, i.e. the forked peak. The adjoining summit (N.) is the cobbler's wife and the S. peak his daughter (good rock-climbing on all three). *Ben Ime* (3318 ft. ; *View) is 2 m. N. of the

Cobbler.—Pedestrians may make their way up *Glen Loin*, at the head of the loch, to 4½ m.) *Loch Sloy*.

FROM ARROCHAR TO INVERARAY viâ Glen Croe, 22 m., motor-bus twice daily. After rounding the head of Loch Long the road strikes N.W. up the wild and desolate *Glen Croe*, which ascending steadily to the summit of the pass (860 ft.) is marked by a rude stone seat inscribed ' *Rest and be Thankful*,' an admonition that Wordsworth at least regarded as superfluous (" Who . . . rests not thankful ? "). To the left diverges a road for Lochgoilhead (see above), but our road descends straight on past the little *Loch Restil*, with *Ben-an-Lochan* (2955 ft.) on the left, to the pastoral *Glen Kinglas*.— We reach the shores of Loch Fyne, at (12 m.) *Cairndow*. Thence around the head of the loch to (22 m.) **Inveraray** see Rte. 13H.

C. Gourock to Kilmun

STEAMER several times on weekdays in summer from Gourock to *Kilcreggan*, *Hunter's Quay*, and *Kilmun* in 45–60 min. calling at *Blairmore* either before or after Hunter's Quay. Fare to Kilcreggan 1/1, beyond 2/, cycle 10*d*.

From *Gourock* we steer due N. across the Clyde to *Kilcreggan* (St. Helen's, RB. 20/, P. 10 gs.), which adjoins *Cove* (Clevedon, RB. 20/, P. 8 gs.) at the mouth of Loch Long.

On the E. bank of Loch Long a road (B 833) runs N. to (5½ m.) *Coulport*, viâ (2 m.) Cove and (3 m.) *Knockderry Castle*, which stands on the dungeons of an ancient tower and figures as ' Knock Dunder ' in the closing scenes of the ' Heart of Midlothian.' About 1 m. short of Coulport a hill road strikes off on the right for (1½ m.) *Rahane*, on the Gareloch.—In the opposite direction B 833 serves the E. bank of the Gareloch, reaching its shore at Rosneath Bay. To the right are *Old Rosneath Castle*, on a promontory, and the remains of *Rosneath House*. To the left is (2¾ m.) *Rosneath* village, with the holy well of St. Modan. The road goes on to (8 m.) *Garelochhead*, passing *Clynder* (Auchmar, RB. 21/, P. 9 gs.) and Rahane (see above).

From Kilcreggan the steamer crosses Loch Long to *Blairmore* (p. 142) or *Hunter's Quay* (p. 145) before entering the *Holy Loch*, a short loch owing its name either to St. Mun or to the traditional wreck of a shipload of earth from the Holy Land destined for the foundations of Glasgow Cathedral. **Kilmun,** on the N.E. bank, has a well-decorated church (1841) by Thos. Burns, but of the collegiate church founded here by Sir Duncan Campbell of Lochow in 1441 the tower alone remains. In a domed vault are buried the Marquess of Argyll (beheaded in 1661), nicknamed ' Gillespie Grumach ' and the ' gleed-eyed marquess,' and the wife of the 5th duke (one of ' the beautiful Miss Gunnings ' ; d. 1790). Elizabeth Blackwell (1821–1910), the first woman to be inscribed in the British Medical Register, lies in the churchyard. To the N.W. are fine woods, with great thickets of rhododendrons, part of the S. portion of the Argyll National Forest Park.

The road leading N.W. connects with the Dunoon–Loch Eck road (see below); in the other direction are Strone and Blairmore.

D. Glasgow to Dunoon and Rothesay

STEAMERS. *Dunoon* and *Rothesay* are on the routes of the large tourist steamers to Ardrishaig, Inveraray, and Campbeltown (see pp. 154, 152); and they are served also by various local steamers. The quickest route to Dunoon is viâ Gourock; to Rothesay, viâ Wemyss Bay.—In the following account the places are named in order from north to south, but no one steamer calls at them all.

From GOUROCK to *Dunoon*, 20–25 min.; to *Innellan*, 35–45 min.; to *Rothesay*, c. 1 hr.; to *Tighnabruaich*, 1¾–2 hrs.—From WEMYSS BAY to *Rothesay*, ½ hr.—From CRAIGENDORAN to *Dunoon*, 40 min.—There are Sunday services to Dunoon, Innellan, and Rothesay from Gourock, Wemyss Bay, and Craigendoran; and from Glasgow direct to Dunoon, Rothesay, and Tighnabruaich.—Cars are ferried on certain services between Gourock and Dunoon (24/9–33/ return) and between Wemyss Bay and Rothesay (36/3–44/ return); accommodation should be reserved from the Caledonian Steam Packet Co., Gourock.

From Glasgow to *Gourock* or to *Craigendoran*, see Rtes. 14 and 12. Thence the steamers proceed W. to the Cowal shore of the Firth of Clyde. On this coast S. of the Holy Loch lie *Hunter's Quay* (Royal Marine, RB. 27/6, P. 14 gs. closed Nov.–March; many private hotels, named after the Hunters of Hafton House, ¾ m. N.W., *Kirn* (Queen's, RB. 27/6, P. 11 gs.; and many private hotels), and *Dunoon*—each with a steamboat pier but forming practically one long community, especially animated in the regatta season. At Hunter's Quay are the headquarters of the Royal Clyde Yacht Club.

DUNOON, the 'capital of Cowal' and one of the most popular of the Clyde resorts (9940 inhab.), is an excellent centre for excursions by land and water, and has many attractions in itself.

Hotels. McColl's, RB. 32/6, P. 15 gs.; **Argyll,** RB. 22/6, P. 10 gs.; **Wellington,** RB. 21/, P. 9½ gs.; **Crown,** RB. 15/; **Blarevhin,** P. 9 gs., closed Nov.–Feb.; **Glenmorag,** P. 8½ gs.; **Esplanade,** P. 7½ gs., these three unlic. Many other private hotels.

Motor-Buses in summer to *Innellan* and *Toward*; to *Kilmun* and *Ardentinny*; to *Strachur* and *Inveraray*; daily to *Glendaruel* and *Dunans Castle.* Motor-coach tours to all parts of the S.W. Highlands.—MOTOR-BOAT SERVICE to *Gourock* on summer afternoons in ½ hr.

Amusements. *Golf Course,* behind Kirn. *Tennis Courts,* Bogleha' and Castle Gardens. *Swimming* at the Lido, West Bay; Port Riddell, East Bay; and Kirn.—*Cowal Highland Gathering* (last Fri. and Sat. in August); *Clyde Yachting Fortnight* (early July) at Hunter's Quay; *Sheep-Dog Trials* in July.

Though the modern 'Castle' of Dunoon (now the Council Chambers and Library), dates only from 1822, on a conical rock above the pier are traces of an ancient castle, formerly the seat of the Lord High Steward of Scotland, and since 1370 a royal palace, the hereditary keeper of which is the Duke of Argyll. At the foot is a statue of Burns's 'Highland Mary' who was born on the farm of Auchnamore, 1 m. from the town. Morag's Fairy Glen, behind the Lido, is a pretty public pleasance.

FROM DUNOON TO STRACHUR AND INVERARAY ('Loch Eck Tour'), 36½ m., motor coach on Tues. and Thurs. in summer in c. 2¼ hrs. The coach quits Dunoon c. 9.30 a.m. after the arrival of the Inveraray steamer, and returns from Inveraray in time to catch it at Dunoon c. 6.45 p.m. on the return voyage.—The road, running N. past Loch Loskin, reaches the shore of the Holy Loch just short of (3 m.) *Sandbank*, well known for its yacht-building industry. We leave on the left the Glendaruel road and a road to Benmore (see below) viâ Glen Masson ; then, crossing the Eachaig, we pass (5 m.) *Cothouse Inn* (RB. 17/6, P. 7 gs.) to join the road from Kilmun. The road now traverses the southern and most interesting part of the *Argyll National Forest Park* (58,500 acres ; 15,000 acres planted) which offers fine opportunities for rambling and camping.—6 m. *Puck's Glen* (r.) is a charming rocky glen, ascending to a good point of view.—7 m. *Benmore House*, on the opposite bank of the river, is now a Forestry Training School. Its gardens (daily, Apr.–Sept., 1/) are noted for rhododendrons and other flowering shrubs, and for exotic trees.—Beyond (7½ m.) *Inverchapel* (not included in the Park) we reach the lonely **Loch Eck** (6¼ m. long, c. ½ m. broad), set among hills rising from the water's edge. The road follows the E. bank, passing (9 m.) *Coylet Hotel* and (11¾ m.) *Whistlefield Hotel* (RB. 17/6, P. 7½ gs.), where a hill road to Ardentinny diverges on the right. Beyond (13¾ m.) the head of Loch Eck we cross the watershed and descend to (16½ m.) **Strachur**, a village and summer resort on Loch Fyne, with the *Creggans Hotel* (RB. 21/, P. 9 gs.) a mile farther on. For the road thence to Inveraray, see Rte. 13H.

A fine but narrow road, diverging from this route c. 1 m. short of Cothouse Inn, runs W. through the hills of Cowal, passing (r.) *Loch Tarsan*, a power-reservoir with dams in Glen Lean and Glen Tarsan, to (13½ m. from Dunoon) the head of Loch Striven (see below). The road goes on into Glendaruel, the glen N. of *Loch Riddon*, joining a road which descends that sea-loch to Colintraive (8 m. ; ferry to Bute, p. 147).—17 m. *Glendaruel Hotel* (RB. 18/6, P. 8 gs.) adjoins *Kilmodan* church, where there is a memorial to Colin Maclaurin (1698–1746), the mathematician who organised the defence of Edinburgh against the Jacobites in 1745. Beyond the river is the *Ormidale Hotel* (P. 20 gs., with sporting rights). A fine pass (1026 ft.) leads W. to Otter Ferry (6 m.) on Loch Fyne, and a fair road ascends the glen to reach Loch Fyne-side at Strathlachlan (10 m.).

Steamers from Dunoon to *Ardrishaig* or *Inveraray* see Rte. 13H.

Off Dunoon lie the *Gantock Rocks*, marked by a beacon ; and across the firth, here 2 m. wide, is the white lighthouse on *Cloch Point*. Steaming S., we skirt the Cowal coast, with its villas, to **Innellan** (*Royal*, RB. 27/6, P. 12½ gs. ; *Braemar*, RB. 18/6, P. 8½ gs. ; *Springfield*, RB. 15/6, P. 7 gs., these two unlic.), a favourite resort with a sandy beach, 4 m. from Dunoon by road and opposite Wemyss Bay. About 3 m. farther S. is *Toward Point*, with its lighthouse and Castle Toward (1821), now a school for convalescent children.

From the point a road, passing the ruined *Toward Castle*, a stronghold of the Lamonts, and *Knockdow*, their present mansion, runs up the E. shore of *Loch Striven*, a naval testing-area, to (c. 10 m.) the *Craig*, whence a path goes on to join (13 m.) the road at the head of the loch (see above).

From Toward Point we cross the strait between Bute and the mainland and enter Rothesay Bay.

ROTHESAY (10,140 inhab.), the capital of Bute and an ancient royal burgh giving the title of duke to the Prince of Wales, is perhaps the most popular resort on the Clyde, and the animated summer crowd that throngs the pier to meet the steamers is a highly characteristic sight. Though with only a poor beach, it lies at the head of a fine bay commanding beautiful views, described with enthusiasm in Mrs. Craik's song ' Sweet Rothesay Bay,' and on either side extends a crescent of pleasant houses—E. to Craigmore, W. towards Ardbeg.

Hotels. Glenburn, E. side, RB. 35/, P. 15 gs.; **Grand Marine,** W. side, RB. 25/, P. 12½ gs.; **Victoria,** near the pier, RB. 21/, P. 12 gs.; **Royal,** at the pier, RB. 21/, P. 10 gs.; **Bute Arms,** at the pier, RB. 25/, P. 12½ gs.; **George,** 3 min. from the pier, RB. 16/6, P. 8 gs.—Unlicensed: **Craigaird, Madeira, Bell-Trees,** P. 7 gs.; and many other private hotels, boarding houses, and apartments.

Motor-Buses to (2 m.) *Port Bannatyne* and *Ettrick Bay* (20 min.); to *Kilchattan Bay*; to *Kerrycroy*, for Mount Stuart, returning viâ *Kingarth* and *Loch Fad*; to *Rhubodach Ferry*,

for Colintraive; to *Kilmichael*, beyond Ettrick Bay; to *Dunagoil*; round the island; etc.

Steamers to *Ardrishaig, Inveraray, Wemyss Bay, Dunoon, Gourock, Greenock, Craigendoran, Glasgow,* etc.

Amusements. *Pavilion* and *Winter Gardens* for concerts, etc., and dancing nightly.—*Cinemas.* *Palace, Regal,* E. and W. of the pier.—*Putting Greens,* in the Esplanade Gardens.

Golf Course, 2 m. N.W. of the town. —*Tennis Courts* at the Meadows; several *Bowling Greens.—Swimming.* Outdoor bathing station, Ardbeg (W.); indoor baths, Battery Place (E.).

In the old town, c. 3 min. above the pier, by Tower St., is the **Castle** (adm. 1/, 10–4 or 7, Sun. from 2), which first appears in history when stormed by the Norsemen in 1230; their breach can still be detected. The existing remains date mainly from the 'palace' of Robert II, in which Robert III died in 1406, eight years after creating his ill-fated son David (p. 262) the first duke of Rothesay. Enlarged by James IV and James V, the castle, battered in the Civil War, was burned by a brother of the Earl of Argyll in 1685. We enter across the moat by the 16th cent. fore-tower on the N. side. The castle is circular in plan (unique in Scotland) and is flanked by four round towers (of which three have fallen). Behind the roofless chapel of St. Michael is the 'Bluidy Stair,' on which, according to tradition, the daughter of a High Steward stabbed herself to escape from an unwelcome bridegroom.

In High St., E. of the castle, are the County Buildings and the *Bute Museum* (adm. 6*d.*; weekdays 2.30–4.30 or 5; in summer also 11–1), and the 17th cent. *Mansion House* (Bute Estate Office); and ½ m. farther up, beside the *High Kirk* (1796) is the ruined chancel of the old church of *St. Mary* (adm. on application at the castle), containing two canopied tombs of the Stewarts of Menteith (13–14th cent.), including Walter, High Steward of Scotland (d. 1326), and his wife Marjory Bruce, ancestors of the Stewart kings. Here also are buried five 14th cent. bishops of Sodor and Man (no tombs).

The island of **Bute** (12,550 inhab.), giving name to *Buteshire*, which embraces Bute, Arran (p. 149), and the Cumbraes (p. 148), is c. 15 m. long and c. 3 m. broad. Various pleasant excursions, on foot or by motor-coach, may be made from Rothesay in its hilly and pretty interior .

Barone Hill (530 ft.), 1½ m. S.W., is a good view-point overlooking the group of lakes S. of Rothesay.—On the W. shore of the narrow inland *Loch Fad*, S. of the town, is *Kean's Cottage*, built by Edmund Kean, the actor (1787–1833), in 1827, during his temporary unpopularity, and later occupied by the minor dramatist Sheridan Knowles (1784–1862). A 844 (bus) runs N. from Rothesay to (2 m.) *Port Bannatyne* (Kyles of Bute Hydro, unlic., RB. 27/6, P. 13½ gs.), a large village and summer resort on Kames Bay, at whose head is the picturesque tower of *Kames Castle* (said to date from the 14th cent.). John Sterling (1806–44), whose biography was written by Carlyle, was born in " the dilapidated baronial residence," at that time rented with the adjoining farm by his father. In the grounds is the tower house of *Wester Kames* (17th cent.; rebuilt 1900). A coast road goes on N. from Port Bannatyne to (8 m.) *Rhubodach Ferry* crossing the Kyles of Bute to (½ m.) *Colintraive* (car 7/6–9/6, motor-cycle 2/6, cycle 6*d.*, passenger 6*d.*). The main road, however, turns W. at Port Bannatyne and crosses the island to (5 m.) *Ettrick* or *Etterick Bay,* a beautiful sandy expanse with fine views, but somewhat spoiled by " attractions ' for trippers. At *Kilmichael* about 4 m. N.W. of this bay, are the remains of an ancient chapel ; while on *St. Ninian's Point*, 3½ m. S., facing the island of *Inchmarnock*, is a similar chapel (within a cashel) which may be associated with St. Ninian's mission.

FROM ROTHESAY TO KILCHATTAN BAY in S. Bute, 8 m., motor-bus, see above. The road skirts the E. side of Rothesay Bay viâ Craigmore and beyond (1 m.) Bogany Point turns S.—2½ m. *Ascog*.—At (4 m.) the model village of *Kerrycroy* is the avenue-gate of *Mount Stuart*, seat of the Marquess of Bute. A permit to visit the lavishly decorated modern Gothic mansion (1877) and its grounds may be obtained, in the absence of the family, at the Estate Office, Rothesay.—The main road strikes inland, with a grand view of Arran, to (7 m.) *Kingarth* (Inn) and thence runs S.W. to the shore and the quiet watering-place of (8 m.) *Kilchattan Bay* (St. Blane's, RB. 15/6, P. 8½ gs.).

From Kingarth we may return N. to (7½ m.) Rothesay by A 845 ; or may extend our excursion by the rough road leading S. past (1¼ m.) the *Standing Stones of Lubas* to (2 m.) the ruined *St. Blane's Chapel*. N. of the chapel are traces of a curious circular structure, c. 32 ft. wide, known as the Devil's Cauldron, and on the shore, ⅓ m. W., is the vitrified fort of *Dunagoil*. Garroch Head, the S. point of Bute, lies 1 m. S.

E. Glasgow to Largs and Millport

The Clyde route from Glasgow to *Largs* and *Millport* is viâ Wemyss Bay, whence steamers ply 3 or 4 times daily. Railway or road to Wemyss Bay, see Rte. 14c. There is a bus between Wemyss Bay and (6 m.) Largs, but no railway. Millport is served also by occasional steamers from Fairlie, see Rte. 13G.

On leaving Wemyss Bay the steamer steers S. along the Ayrshire coast, on which appear the red houses of Skelmorlie against a background of hills, while ahead we have a fine view of Arran. Farther on, on the left, are the conspicuous spires of (½ hr.) **Largs** (p. 163). Beyond Largs the steamer holds its southward course, with Great Cumbrae on the starboard side. On the mainland appears Kelburn Castle, with Fairlie pier beyond it.

We cross the channel to the **Cumbraes,** two small islands lying 1½ m. off the Ayrshire coast and c. 2½ m. E. of Bute. Beside *Keppel Pier*, at the S. end of *Great Cumbrae* (3½ m. long by 3 m. broad), is a Marine Biological Station, with a museum and aquarium (adm. 6*d.* weekdays 9.30–1, 2.30–5.30). The pier here is the port of call in bad weather, and for through steamers proceeding west.

Most steamers round Farland Point and enter the wide Millport Bay. On the mainland to the S. the reactors of the atomic power station at *Hunterston* are conspicuous.

Millport (2010 inhab. ; *Royal George*, RB. 19/6, P. 10 gs. ; *MacGillivray Arms*, similar charges ; many unlic. hotels), curving round its bay for c. 1½ m., is one of the favourite family resorts on the Clyde, with good golf and bathing. The episcopal collegiate church, begun by Butterfield in 1849 and still incomplete, was in 1876 consecrated as the episcopal *Cathedral of Argyll and the Isles*, but Millport is more famous as the cure of the Rev. Jas. Adam, parish minister in the early 19th cent., who used to pray for " the Great and Little Cumbrae and the adjacent islands of Great Britain and

Ireland.'' A motor-coach plies round the island in summer and horse-drawn victorias may be hired for drives.

On *Little Cumbrae* (1¾ by ¾ m.) the only dwellings are a farm and a lighthouse. An islet (Castle Island), off the E. shore, bears the remains of a tower, occupied by Robert II in 1375 and 1384 and destroyed by Cromwell in 1653. On the N. slope are the remains of a chapel of St. Vey.

After leaving Millport some steamers steer W. to Lochranza in Arran on their way to Campbeltown (Rte. 13G).

F. Arran

Approaches. (A) From ARDROSSAN, steamer 3 or 4 times daily (except Sun.), in connection with trains from Glasgow, to *Brodick* (50 min.) and *Whiting Bay* (1¼ hr.). This is the direct and quickest approach.—(B) From FAIRLIE, ferry-steamer twice daily to *Brodick* (65 min.).—(C) From GOUROCK, DUNOON, and ROTHESAY, turbine steamer on Mon., Wed., Fri. to *Brodick* and *Whiting Bay.*—(D) By CAMPBELTOWN STEAMER (Rte. 13G) FROM FAIRLIE daily to *Lochranza* (whence a motor in connection runs to *Brodick*).—MOTORS meet the Ardrossan steamers at Brodick for *Corrie*, 6 m. N., and *Lochranza*, 14 m. N.; for *Lamlash*, 3½ m. S., and *Whiting Bay*, 6¾ m. S.; for *Machrie*, 9½ m. W., and *Pirnmill*, 15½ m. N.W.; and for *Shedog* and *Blackwater Foot*, 11 m. S.W.; and at Whiting Bay for *Kildonan, Lagg,* and *Corriecravie*, 11¼ m. S.W.

CARS may be ferried to Brodick from Ardrossan (summer only) or Fairlie on weekdays, by previous arrangement with the Caledonian Steam Packet Co., Gourock. Fare 47/–80/; Motor-cycle 7/6. Passenger 5/, cycle 1/7.

ARRAN (4650 inhab.), c. 20 m. long and c. 10 m. wide, mainly occupied by uncultivated mountains (several over 2600 ft. high), is the largest island in the estuary of the Clyde, and its noble sky-line, culminating in Goatfell (see below), near its N. end, is one of the finest features of that beautiful region. It lies c. 12 m. off the Ayrshire coast and, on the W., is separated from Kintyre by Kilbrennan Sound, 4–6 m. wide. The island is of peculiar interest to geologists (comp. Bryce's ' Geology of Arran '; 1859). The policy of its proprietors has spared Arran conventional ' development ' as a summer resort, but its simple and limited accommodation is usually taxed to the utmost in the season by lovers of an unsophisticated life amid beautiful scenery, tempered by bathing, boating, fishing, golf (18-hole courses at Brodick, Lamlash, and Whiting Bay), and climbing. Many of the hotels are closed from Nov. to March.

History. Arran, which was wrested from Norway by Somerled, Lord of the Isles (d. 1164), was for centuries a royal domain and hunting ground. Robert Bruce, fired by the example of the famous spider in the Irish island of Rathin, landed in Arran in 1306 and thence made the descent upon Turnberry (1307) to strike another blow for Scotland. Hogg's ballad poetically but unhistorically describes how the island and the hand of James III's eldest sister was won in a tournament by Sir James Hamilton of Cadzow, ancestor of the dukes of Hamilton. In fact he was awarded the island by royal charter in 1503 for political services. With the exception of the small estate of Kilmichael, in Glen Cloy (held by the Fullartons, the oldest proprietors in Arran), and a few farms, the island belongs to the Hamilton family.

Brodick (*Douglas*, RB. 22/6, P. 12 gs.; *Ormidale, Invercloy,* P. 10 gs.; *Ennismoor, Kingslay,* P. 9½ gs., the last three unlic.), perhaps the best tourist centre in the island, lies at the point where Glen Rosa (descending from Goatfell), Glen Shurig, and Glen Cloy converge upon the beautiful Brodick Bay, about the middle of the E. coast. The village, whose real name is *Invercloy*, lies c. ½ m. E. of the pier.

In a commanding position 1½ m. N. (bus 1/6 return) is BRODICK CASTLE (N.T., open weekdays May–Sept. 12.45–5 ; adm. to castle 1/6, to gardens 1/ ; tea-room), the ancestral mansion of the Hamiltons until 1957. Like many of the larger baronial mansions, the castle is a mixture of ancient and (comparatively) modern. The centre block was built in the 16th cent., the N. wing may well date back to the 13th cent., and contains the prison-like ' Bruce's Room,' while the larger portion was added c. 1845 by Gillespie Graham.

The original castle was seized by Edward I and held by Sir John Hastings, whom Scott represents as having been expelled by Douglas. It was afterwards garrisoned by Cromwell, whose soldiers, however, were massacred by the islanders. On the death of the Duchess of Montrose (daughter of the 12th duke of Hamilton) in 1957, the house, with 600 acres, was offered to the Treasury in lieu of death duties, and by them in turn to the National Trust.

The rooms on view contain family treasures and some good paintings (*Lely*, Anne, Duchess of Hamilton ; *Gainsborough*, Earl of Rochford ; sporting water-colours by *Rowlandson*, *Pollard*, and *Reinagle*).—The gardens are noted for subtropical shrubs.

The ascent of *Goatfell (2866 ft., c. 3 hrs.), Scott's ' Ben Ghoil, the Mountain of the Wind,' is usually made from Brodick. We follow the road N.W. for 1½ m. from the pier and, after the second bridge is crossed, we pass through the planta-tions behind the castle and emerge on the moor. Thence there is a path to the top, and any temptation not to keep to the right shoulder but to take a direct course should be resisted. Only the last 20 min., up a steep rocky staircase, are trying. The *View embraces the Firth of Clyde and Ailsa Craig to the E. and S., the Irish coast to the S.W., Islay and the Paps of Jura N.W., Loch Fyne and Ben Cruachan N., and Ben Lomond to the N.E.—We may descend to *Corrie* direct (c. 3 m. E.) ; practised climbers may descend into *Glen Rosa*, or (more difficult) to the saddle between Glen Rosa and Glen Sannox (see below).

FROM BRODICK BY GLEN ROSA TO CORRIE, 11½ m., a fine walk. We follow the road N.W. for 1½ m., turn left just before the second bridge, and at the church pass through a wood to (3 m.) the lower part of the glen. The road is continued by a path which c. 1½ m. farther on, beyond a wooden bridge, becomes wet and boggy. From the head of the romantic glen we mount (7 m.) the saddle joining Goatfell (right) to Cir Mhor (Keer Vore). Thence a rock-chimney leads down into the short but wild *Glen Sannox*. On reaching (10 m.) the coast road at the foot of Glen Sannox we turn right for (11½ m.) *Corrie* (see below).

Lamlash (*White House*, RB. 15/6, P. 8 gs. ; *Lamlash*, RB. 18/, P. 9 gs.), the largest village in Arran, lies 3⅓ m. S. of Brodick by road, or 4½ m. by an agreeable path (views) diverging from the road c. ½ m. from the pier and passing the ancient fort of *Dun Fionn*. Lamlash Bay, a well-known harbour of refuge, in which Hakon assembled his shattered fleet after the battle of Largs, is protected by *Holy Island* (1030 ft. ; c. 2 m. long, with farm guest-house, P. 7 gs.). From *Kingscross Point*, the S. horn of Lamlash Bay, Bruce embarked for his descent on Carrick in 1307.

Holy Island owes its name to St. Molaise, a disciple of St. Comhgall, who is said to have died at the age of 120 and to be buried at Shiskine (p. 152). His cave, on the W. shore of the island, contains some Runic inscriptions, supposed to refer to those who fell at the battle of Largs.

From Lamlash the ' Ross Road,' attaining the height of 974 ft., leads S.W. up *Monamore Glen* and down *Glen Scorradale*, to (9½ m.) Sliddery.—A fine moorland walk diverging from this road a little beyond the Whiting Bay turn, leads viâ Loch Urie, *Tighvein* (1497 ft. ; *View) and Auchareoch to (8 m.) Lagg.

Whiting Bay (*Whiting Bay*, RB. 22/6, P. 11 gs. ; *Royal*, RB. 17/6, P. 7½ gs. ; *Burlington*, unlic., P. 7 gs.), with a steamer-pier, is a popular resort, 3¼ m. S. of Lamlash, near the mouth of Glen Ashdale, with its pretty waterfall.

Round Arran by the Coast Road

The road (55 m.) is very fair all the way, and walkers and cyclists will find sufficient if humble accommodation at tolerably convenient distances apart. Shorter rounds may be planned by using the ' String Road ' between Blackwaterfoot and Brodick or the ' Ross Road ' between Sliddery and Lamlash.—Motor-bus tour from Brodick or Lochranza, 7/6.

From Brodick Pier the road runs N., passing between the castle and the sea.—6 m. **Corrie** (*Corrie*, RB. 20/, P. 11 gs. ; *Blackrock House*, unlic., P. 6 gs.) is a picturesque collection of cottages, with a golf course, close to the foot of Goatfell.—About 1½ m. farther we enjoy a fine view up Glen Sannox and the road quits the coast to follow North Glen Sannox, passing through a charming piece of Highland scenery.

A path diverging from the road leads by the coast to (1¾ m. N.) the *Fallen Rocks*, a favourite excursion from Corrie.

At 9½ m. we cross North Glen Sannox, and after a steep ascent to 654 ft. we begin the descent of *Glen Chalmadale* to (14 m.) **Lochranza** (*Lochranza*, RB. 22/6, P. 8½ gs. ; *Westwood*, unlic., P. 7 gs.), on a beautiful inlet of the sea, c. 1 m. long, a favourite summer resort with a steamer-pier and a golf course. The castle with two square towers on a promontory in the loch was erected in the 14th cent. as a hunting seat.

Bruce landed in Loch Ranza on his return from Rathlin (1306), but of the nunnery in which, according to Scott's ' Lord of the Isles,' his sister Isobel found refuge, no traces are left.—The *Cock of Arran*, the extreme N. point of the island, lies 1¾ m. N.E.

Rounding *Coillemore Point* and turning S. we reach (16½ m.) *Catacol Bay* and pass (18 m.) the lonely little church of *Lenimore*.

High on the slopes of *Ben Vrackie* (2333 ft. ; 2 m. S.E.) is the solitary loch *Coire an Lochain*, in grim surroundings, well worth a visit.

As we follow the road S. along the W. coast of the island, passing the hamlets of (20¾ m.) *Pirnmill*, and (23 m.) *Imachar*, we have fine views across Kilbrennan Sound towards Kintyre, amongst whose mountains Ben-an-Tuirc (1491 ft.) is conspicuous.—At (25¼ m.) *Dougrie Lodge* we cross the mouth of the lonely *Glen Iorsa*.—From (27 m.) *Auchagallon* a road strikes E. to join the ' String Road ' to Brodick (9½ m.).—28 m. *Machrie* (Hotel, unlic., P. 7 gs.), with a golf course.

About 1 m. up the Machrie Water, on the left bank, are the celebrated *Standing Stones of Tormore*, showing remains of at least ten circles, with some upright stones 12–18 ft. high. —At 28¾ m., where the road trends inland, a path diverges towards the coast and leads in 1¼ m. to the *King's Caves*.

The last and largest of these, called the *King's Cave*, is said to have been occupied by Fingal (Finn MacCoul), leader of the Fenians, and later by Bruce. On the walls are rough sketches of the chase, ascribed with the greatest improbability to the leisure hours of Bruce and his companions. The coast path goes on to (2 m.) Blackwaterfoot.

The road regains the coast at (31½ m.) *Blackwaterfoot* (Kinloch, RB. 18/, P. 7 gs. ; Blackwaterfoot, unlic., P. 7½ gs. ; Greannan, unlic., P. 7 gs.), with a golf course, on Drumadoon Bay.

A road here strikes N.E. for (2 m.) *Shiskine* (Shedog Inn, small), and crosses (7¾ m.) the ' *String*,' a pass 768 ft. high, to (11 m.) *Brodick*. In Shiskine church is a rudely figured tombstone from the old burial ground, said to have covered the remains of St. Molaise (p. 150).

To the right at (36 m.) *Corriecravie* is *Tor Chaistel*, or ' Castle Hill,' an oblong barrow on which are two stone circles.— 37 m. *Sliddery*, at the S. end of the ' Ross Road.'—38¼ m. *Lagg Hotel* (RB. 24/, P. 10 gs.), at the village of *Kilmory*, is prettily situated in a wooded dell. On the right, farther on, appears *Bennan Head.*—The hamlet of *Kildonan* (Hotel, RB. 17/6, P. 8 gs.), with a golf course, lies on the shore ½ m. S. of the main road, near *Kildonan Castle*, a ruined keep. The small isle of *Pladda*, with a lighthouse, lies 1 m. offshore. The fine *Dippin Rocks* extend N. to Dippin Head, which we cross before reaching (46¼ m.) *Glen Ashdale.*—47 m. *Whiting Bay* and thence viâ (50¼ m.) *Lamlash* to (55 m.) *Brodick*, see above.

G. From Glasgow to Campbeltown

STEAMERS. (A) Turbine steamer from Gourock in summer every weekday at 9.25 a.m. (day return from Glasgow 19/2, 16/10), calling at *Dunoon, Rothesay, Fairlie* and *Lochranza* ; also at *Millport* (not Sat.). The steamers reach Campbeltown c. 1.40 p.m. and leave again c. 3.15 p.m.—Another route to Campbeltown is by steamer to *Tarbert* (see Rte. 13H) and thence by motor-bus.

AIR SERVICE twice every weekday in summer (once in winter) from *Renfrew Airport* (motor leaves St. Enoch Station 45 min. before starting time), reaching *Machrihanish Airport*, 4 m. W.N.W. of Campbeltown, in 40 min. Motor thence to Campbeltown in 25 min. (return fare 79/).

ROAD ROUTE, 135 m. From Glasgow to (38 m.) *Arrochar*, see p. 133. Thence (A 83) we climb Glen Croe to (44½ m.) *Rest and be Thankful* and descend to (50 m.) *Cairndow*, on Loch Fyne. Rounding the head of the loch (r.) we skirt its shores for the next 40 miles.—60 m. *Inveraray*.—68 m. *Furnace*.—77 m. *Lochgair*. —84 m. **Lochgilphead**.—86 m. *Ardrishaig*.—97 m. *Tarbert*.—From (102½ m.) *Redhouse* we have a choice of routes (comp. p. 156). The W. coast route runs viâ (116 m.) *Tayinloan* and (125 m.) *Bellochantuy*.—135 m. **Campbeltown**.— MOTOR-BUS every afternoon from Parliamentary Rd. in 5¾ hrs. (return 32/).

On quitting Gourock the steamer crosses the Firth to *Dunoon*, passing (l.) Cloch Point with its lighthouse. We round Toward Point before calling at *Rothesay*, then call at *Fairlie* and pass between the Cumbraes and Bute, with fine views of Arran ahead. Rounding the Cock of Arran we touch at *Lochranza*, then sail down Kilbrennan Sound, between Arran and the long narrow peninsula of Kintyre. On the Arran shore we note the solitary little church of Lenimore, beyond which we cross to Kintyre and pass the fishing-village of *Carradale*.—We soon draw abreast of the lighthouse on Davaar Island, and enter the fine harbour of *Campbeltown Loch.*

Campbeltown (*Royal*, RB. 21/, P. from 11 gs. ; *Argyll Arms*, RB. 21/, P. 10 gs. ; *White Hart*, RB. 21/, P. 9 gs. ; *Ardshiel*, RB. 17/6, P. 7 gs.) is a plain little royal burgh (7175 inhab.), with a few whisky distilleries, and some fishing boats. Renewed activity was brought to the town by the sinking of the Argyll pit in 1946, to replace the old Drumlemble colliery (3 m. W.). In the main street is a *Cross* (c. 1500), with elaborate ornamentation and an inscription in Lombardic letters.

Originally known as *Kinlochkerran*, after the Irish St. Kieran or Ciaran (6th cent.), a forerunner of Columba, the town takes its present name from the Campbells of Argyll, to whom James V transferred it from the Macdonalds. Castlehill church, above the town, was the rallying-place of Argyll's rebellion in support of Monmouth (1685). In 1774 Flora Macdonald, emigrating with her family to Carolina, set sail from the harbour. Norman Macleod (1812–72), the divine, Sir William Mackinnon (1823–93), founder of the British India line, and William McTaggart (1835–1910), the painter, were born at Campbeltown.

A boat may be taken to *Davaar Island* at the mouth of the loch, on the E. side of which is a cave with a Crucifixion painted by Archibald Mackinnon, a local artist, in 1887.

Motor-buses to *Machrihanish*, to *Southend*, and to *Tarbet* viâ Carradale and the E. Kintyre coast or viâ the main W. coast road.

From Campbeltown a road crosses the fertile ' laggan ' or ' hollow ' of Kintyre, with the airfield on the right, to (5½ m.) **Machrihanish** (*Ugadale Arms*, RB. 35/, P. 14 gs. ; *Warren*, unlic., P. 11–11¼ gs.), a hamlet with a famous golf course on the sand dunes that fringe the wide bay facing the open Atlantic.

FROM CAMPBELTOWN TO THE MULL OF KINTYRE. As far as Southend there are two roads ; an inland road, 9½ m., diverging from the Machrihanish road and leading S. through Conie Glen, and a more interesting but very much hillier coast road, 13½ m.—Following the latter we reach (1 m.) *Kilkerran*, perhaps the landing-place of St. Kieran (see above). The ruined castle near the shore was intended by James V to overawe the Macdonalds, who, however, captured it and hanged the governor before the king was well out of sight. About 1½ m. farther on a spit of gravel offers a passage dryshod at low tide to *Davaar Island* (see above).—At (4½ m.) *Achinhoan Head* is **St. Kieran's Cave**, 25 ft. above high water and difficult of access, which recent interesting discoveries tend to identify as perhaps the earliest Christian chapel in Scotland.—10½ m. *Macharioch*, an estate of the Duke of Argyll.—13½ m. **Southend** (*Argyll Arms*, RB. 20/, P. 9 gs. ; *Keil House*, 1 m. W., RB. 19/6, P. 9½ gs.), with a golf course, is the traditional landing-place of St. Columba on his first mission to Scotland. On a precipitous rock, near the golf course, is the site of *Dunaverty Castle*, a stronghold of the Macdonalds, where Edward Bruce once lay in hiding. In 1647 about 300 men, chiefly Irish, of Montrose's forces were here besieged by General Leslie and the

Covenanters, who, when thirst compelled surrender, put them ruthlessly to death. The island of *Sanda*, 2 m. offshore, was a hiding-place of Bruce in 1306.

Beyond Southend the road (which soon deteriorates) runs close to the sea at (14½ m.) *Keil* with the ruins of a church perhaps founded by St. Columba. A little to the W. it turns inland and ascends to high ground whence a breakneck descent (1200 ft. in 1½ m.) leads to the lighthouse on the **Mull of Kintyre**, identified by some authorities with the Epidium Promontorium of the Romans. Ireland is only 13 m. distant and the *View extends along its N. coast, off which lies the island of Rathlin, to the cliffs of Donegal. To the W. is the open Atlantic ; N.W. is Islay.

From Campbeltown to Tarbert there are two roads. (A) The Glasgow motor-bus follows the route (37½ m.) by the W. coast of Kintyre, described on p. 156.—(B) The picturesque but hillier E. coast road (B 842 ; 38 m.) runs close to the shore of Kilbrennan Sound for most of the way, with fine views of Arran on the right. Beyond (5 m.) the mouth of the romantic *Glen Lussa* we pass (7¼ m.) *Ugadale*, a small estate presented to an ancestor of the Macleans by Robert Bruce in gratitude for guidance across the hills of Kintyre on his flight to Ireland. The upper part of Glen Lussa has been dammed to form a loch 2 m. long for hydro-electric power. The power station is c. 2 m. upstream from the shore.— At (9 m.) *Saddell*, one of the most attractive places on the road, are a half-ruined castle (1508), and the scanty remains of a Cistercian monastery (fine grave-slabs), founded before 1207 by Reginald, son of Somerled, and handed over to the bishop of Lismore in 1508.

The glen may be ascended to *Beinn-an-Tuirc* (1490 ft.), the highest peak in Kintyre, where Diarmuid the Fenian hero slew a fierce wild boar.

Beyond (12 m.) *Torrisdale* and (13 m.) *Dippen*, a road diverges for (1½ m. r.) the little harbour of **Carradale** (*Hotel*, unlic., RB. 16/, P. 8 gs.), a simple summer resort with the ruins of Aird Castle.—From Saddell Church our road runs N. to (17½ m.) *Grogport* (Inn) and (26½ m.) *Claonaig*, where it quits the coast to strike N.W. across the peninsula, joining the W. coast road at (31½ m.) *Redhouse*, 6½ m. S. of (38 m.) *Tarbert* (p. 155).

About 2 m. N.E. of Claonaig is *Skipness*, near the mouth of Loch Fyne, with remains of a substantial castle and the ruined church of St. Columba. It commands the finest general *View of Arran.

H. From Glasgow to Ardrishaig or to Inveraray

To Ardrishaig. MacBrayne's steamer from Gourock every weekday in summer at 9.30 a.m., calling at *Dunoon, Innellan, Rothesay, Tighnabruaich,* and *Tarbert,* and reaching *Ardrishaig* at 12.45 p.m. (day return fare from Glasgow 17/, 15/). Return from Ardrishaig at 1 p.m. and reaching Gourock at 4.25. This is part of a through-route to Oban (see Rte. 47). Passengers from Glasgow, leaving by train, may embark at Gourock or Rothesay (viâ Wemyss Bay) ; passengers from Edinburgh, travelling viâ Craigendoran, join at Dunoon by steamer in connection.

To Inveraray. British Railways steamer from Gourock at 8.55 in summer on Tues. and Thurs., calling at *Dunoon, Wemyss Bay* (9.40), *Rothesay,* and *Tighnabruaich,* and reaching *Inveraray* at 1.30 p.m. (from Glasgow, day return,

1st cl. and saloon 19/2, 2nd cl. and saloon, 17/5). Return from Inveraray at 3 p.m. reaching Gourock at 7.40 p.m.—Passengers may quit the steamer at Dunoon, proceed to Inveraray by motor coach in connection viâ Loch Eck, and return to Gourock thence by steamer (return fares from Glasgow, 21/6 or 20/). Or they may reverse this route, returning from Inveraray by coach leaving at 2 p.m. for Dunoon.

A MOTOR COACH (MacBrayne's), starting at 46 Parliamentary Rd., runs in the season twice daily from Glasgow to *Inveraray* (2¾ hrs. ; 8/) and *Ardrishaig* (4 hrs. ; 11/). The route is viâ *Alexandria* (comp. Rte. 12) and the W. bank of Loch Lomond to *Arrochar* and thence viâ Glen Croe to *Inveraray* and by the W. shore of Loch Fyne to *Ardrishaig*.

From Gourock to (c. 1 hr.) *Rothesay*, see Rte. 13D.—Leaving Rothesay the steamer steers N., with *Port Bannatyne* and *Kames Bay* on the left and the mouth of *Loch Striven* on the right, and enters the famous ***Kyles of Bute,** the long and beautiful strait that curves round the N. end of Bute.—At *Colintraive* (Hotel, RB. 21/, P. 8 gs. ; car ferry, p. 147), the 'strait of swimming' for cattle on their way to and from Bute, we approach the most beautiful part of the Kyles, where the steamer threads its way amid the low rocky *Burnt Islands*. As we emerge from the narrows the picturesquely situated mansion of Glen Caladh appears ahead and *Loch Riddon* (3½ m. long) opens on the right.

On *Eilean Dearg*, one of the islets, a fort was built by the Earl of Argyll in co-operation with the Duke of Monmouth's rebellion ; but the fort was reduced by an English fleet and its builder was beheaded in Edinburgh (1685).—A road ascends the W. bank of Loch Riddon to (8 m.) *Glendaruel* (p. 146).

The Kyles now bend sharply to the left. On the hillside in Bute (l.) are a couple of rocks usually kept painted to resemble two 'Maids of Bute.'—**Tighnabruaich** (*Royal*, RB. 19/6, P. 9 gs. ; *Chalet*, unlic., P. 7½ gs. ; *Wellpark*, unlic. P. 7 gs.), 'the house on the brae,' with its attractive villas and distant view of Arran, is one of the favourite family summer resorts on the Clyde.—Inland from *Kames* (Hotel, RB. 15/6, P. 7 gs.), ¾ m. S.W., are large disused powder-mills. —Rounding Ardlamont Point we enter *Loch Fyne* (c. 40 m. long), one of the largest sea-lochs in Scotland, famous for its herrings, though the fishing is no longer so prolific as formerly. The Ardrishaig and the Inveraray steamers now follow different courses.

The ARDRISHAIG STEAMER steams diagonally across the loch to **Tarbert** (*Tarbert*, RB. 21/6, P. 10 gs. ; *Victoria*, *Columba*, RB. 18/–18/6, P. c. 8½ gs. ; *Castle*, RB. 21/, P. 11 gs. —*Stonefield Castle* with grounds, 2½ m. N., RB. 25/, P. 11 gs.), the headquarters of the Loch Fyne fishing industry. The village (¾ m. from the pier) lies picturesquely at the head of the short *East Loch Tarbert* (1 m.), which is overlooked by a ruined 14th cent. castle, once the residence of Bruce and of James II.. About 1¾ m. S.W. (motor-bus) is *West Tarbert*

(Campbell Arms, RB. 19/6, P. 8½ gs.) at the head of *West Loch Tarbert*, which stretches 10 m. S.W. to the Atlantic between lovely wooded banks, and separates the districts of Knapdale (N.W.) and Kintyre (S.E.). Both villages are summer resorts.

Across the narrow isthmus between the lochs King Magnus Barfod (11th cent.) is said to have been dragged in his galley, because a treaty had assigned to him all the lands he could circumnavigate. Robert Bruce carried out the same manoeuvre 300 years later.

From West Tarbert to *Gigha, Islay,* and *Jura,* see Rte. 59A.

FROM TARBERT TO CAMPBELTOWN, 37½ m., motor-bus daily in connection with the steamer. Beyond (1¾ m.) *West Tarbert* we skirt the S.E. bank of West Loch Tarbert (see above). At (6½ m.) *Redhouse* B 8001 diverges l. to join the road on the E. side of the Kintyre peninsula (Rte. 13G).—At (12 m.) *Clachan* (Inn), a prettily situated village with a sandy beach, we reach the Atlantic coast.—From (20 m.) *Tayinloan* (Macdonald Arms, RB. 15/, P. 7 gs.), a ferry crosses the Sound of Gigha to Gigha (Rte. 59A).—Near (23 m.) *Killean Church* are the ruins of a primitive older church, showing a double window with toothed moulding. The road commands fine seaward views : S.W. to Fair Head and the Giant's Causeway in Ireland with Rathlin Island in front, W. to Islay, N.W. to Cava and Gigha, with the Paps of Jura conspicuous in the background. From the moors above may be seen Colonsay and Oronsay, and even Mull in clear weather.—26½ m. *Glenbarr* (Temperance Inn) near the ancient but modernised Glenbarr Abbey.—29½ m. *Bellochantuy* (Argyll, RB. 18/6, P. 7½ gs.). About 4 m. farther on we have a picturesque glimpse of Tangy Glen, and in another ¾ m. we quit the Atlantic coast to strike S.E. across the 'laggan' past the ancient cemetery of *Kilchenzie,* to (37½ m.) *Campbeltown* (p. 153).

On quitting Tarbert the steamboat skirts the Knapdale coast, affording fine views up Loch Fyne. Entering *Loch Gilp* it reaches its terminus at (73 m.) **Ardrishaig** (*Royal,* RB. 21/6, P. 9½ gs. ; *Anchor,* RB. 18/, P. 8½ gs. ; *Auchendarroch,* unlic., RB. 18/6, P. 8 gs.). Thence to *Oban,* see Rte 47.

FROM TARBERT TO ARDRISHAIG AND INVERARAY by road (A 83), 38 m., motorbus several times daily. A longer road to Ardrishaig (33 m.) makes a circuit of the hills of *Knapdale.* The direct road skirts the W. shore of Loch Fyne, and at (9½ m.) *Inverneill* is joined by the Knapdale loop-road.—12 m. **Ardrishaig** (see above).—Our road rounds Loch Gilp, and at (14 m.) **Lochgilphead** (see Rte. 47) leaves the Oban road on the left. Thence we keep fairly near the Loch Fyne coast, with a view of Otter Ferry (r.).—21 m. *Lochgair* (Hotel, RB. 21/, P. 10 gs.) is charmingly situated at the head of a little inlet. Skirting the woods of Minard, we descend to the shore at (26 m.) *Crarae,* with a granite quarry and the lovely *Gardens of Crarae Lodge* (Sir George Campbell of Succoth, Bart. ; adm. 1/ daily, all day, Apr.–Oct.), noted for azaleas, conifers, and ornamental shrubs. —At (30 m.) *Furnace,* so called from an abandoned smelting-work, but now dependent on its huge quarry, we quit the coast but rejoin it 5 m. farther on.— 38 m. *Inveraray,* see below.

The INVERARAY STEAMER, after rounding Ardlamont Point, steers directly up Loch Fyne and, passing (r.) the remarkable Oitir sand-spit, near the base of which is *Otter Ferry* (no ferry), it enters the narrow upper part of the loch with its picturesque views. On the left are the little *Loch Gair* and *Minard Castle*, a conspicuous 19th cent. mansion. Opposite (r.) is *Castle Lachlan*, and 3 m. farther on is *Furnace* (l.). On the right is seen Creggans or Strachur pier, and we reach Inveraray about 1.30 p.m.

Inveraray (*Argyll Arms*, RB. 25/6, P. 13 gs.; *George*, RB. 25/. P. 11 gs.; *MacBride's*, S. of the town, RB. 21/, P. 9 gs.), a very small but historic royal burgh (503 inhab.), situated c. 8½ m. from the head of Loch Fyne, is famous as the ancestral abode of the Duke of Argyll, the Highlanders' ' MacCailean Mor ' (' son of great Colin '), a title popularly corrupted (even by Scott) into ' MacCallum More.' The town, with its attractive buildings facing the loch, is delightfully situated, and the surrounding woods are unsurpassed in Scotland.

The town originally clustered around the old castle (where the site of the church is marked by a Tiree Cross, E. of the present mansion), and was rebuilt on its present site after 1743. Its history is the history of the Campbells. The 'great Colin', founder of the fortunes of this powerful and politically astute family, was Sir Colin Campbell of Lochow (d. 1296), whose son married Mary, sister of Robert Bruce, and whose descendants became earls in 1457 and dukes in 1701. Archibald, 8th earl (beheaded in 1661), leader of the Covenanters, who became a marquess in 1641, figures in Scott's ' Legend of Montrose.' His son, who supported Monmouth's rebellion, was likewise beheaded (1685). The 2nd duke (d. 1743) was the duke of ' The Heart of Midlothian.' The 8th duke (d. 1900) was a distinguished author and Liberal statesman. The 9th (d. 1914) married Princess Louise, a daughter of Queen Victoria.—Dr. Johnson was duly entertained at the castle in 1773 by the 5th duke; but Burns, at Inveraray in 1787, expressed his pique at ducal inattention by scratching some bitter satirical lines on the window of his inn. The town, in the reign of the 3rd duke, plays a graphic part in the closing scenes of Stevenson's ' Catriona.' Neil Munro (1864–1930), a native of the town, laid part of the plot of ' John Splendid ' and ' The New Road ' at Inveraray, and his ' Doom Castle ' is close by (see below).

At one end of the main street is the severe *Church* (1794), by Robert Mylne, the spire of which was taken down in the Second World War. At the other end is a fine *Cross* from Iona. A large gateway on the left of the Argyll Arms (c. 1780) admits to an avenue which passes the Episcopalian church of All Saints with its conspicuous tower. The 17th cent. beech avenue was felled in 1956. Attractive 18th cent. bridges cross the Aray and, farther N., the Shira.

Inveraray Castle (adm. 2/6, grounds only 1/, May–Sept. 10.30–12, 2–6; closed Fri. and on Sun. morning) stands c. ½ m. N. of the town in a park through which flows the Aray. The present ' massive and uniform mansion ' (as Scott describes it), a square edifice with round towers at the four corners and a central tower, replaces a 15th cent. castle (some ruins of which remain) and was begun for the 3rd duke in

1746 by *Roger Morris* assisted by *Wm. Adam* ; the interior decoration was completed by *Robert Mylne* in 1772–82 for the 5th duke ; while the top story and the conical caps to the towers are due to a rebuilding after a fire in 1877.

The splendidly decorated interior, including murals by *Biagio Rebecca* in the Dining Room, contains family portraits by *Gainsborough, Ramsay, Raeburn, Hoppner, Cosway, Opie,* and others ; and historical relics such as Rob Roy's dirk-handle and sporran and the cap worn by the Marquess of Argyll at his execution. The table-plate and the Beauvais tapestries (in the room where Johnson was received) are noteworthy. The Central Hall, with stands of arms, dates from the rebuilding of 1877. The mantelpieces and doorcases in the S.W. Drawing Room, brought back from Rosneath in 1952, are by *James Adam*. In the basement are the great kitchen and a refreshment room.

A pleasant walk through the castle grounds leads N. to (1 m.) the 17th cent. dovecot at *Carlunan,* and (3¼ m.) the pretty *Falls of Aray.*—**Duniquoich** (850 ft.), the conical hill "wooded to the chin" and surmounted by a watch tower, N. of Inveraray, is approached through the castle grounds or by steps over the wall a little beyond the first milestone on the Strachur road. A direct steep path and a longer winding ascent lead to the top (c. 2 hrs. there and back).

Ferry on weekdays to *St. Catherine's* (see below ; 2/, cycle 6*d.*).

FROM INVERARAY TO CAIRNDOW AND STRACHUR, 20 m., road round the head of Loch Fyne. Beyond Duniquoich opens (1½ m. ; l.) the pretty GLEN SHIRA, in which the stream forms the little *Dhu Loch,* ½ m. above its mouth.

Roads run up both banks of the Shira, meeting and ending at a point c. 7 m. from Inveraray and c. ¼ m. below *Rob Roy's House,* a ruin on the farm of Benbuie, where that outlaw is said to have lived for some time. *Ben Buie* (3106 ft. ; *View) may be easily ascended hence in c. 2½ hrs. by following the ridge behind the ruined cottage. Dams farther up the glen, N.W. of Ben Buie, have formed two small power-reservoirs, the waters of which are conducted by tunnel to a generating station above Clachan at the head of Loch Fyne.

Farther on our road passes (4½ m.) the old tower-house of *Dunderave* (restored in 1912), the 'Doom Castle' of Neil Munro, occupied in 1685 by McNaughton, sheriff of Argyll. It bears the date 1598 and an inscription : " IM.AN. Behald the end. Be nocht Vyser nor the Biestes. I hoip in God,"— We cross *Glen Fyne* at (8½ m.) the head of the loch and descend the E. bank.—10 m. *Cairndow* (Hotel, RB. 21/, P. 10 gs.) is near the foot of Glen Kinglas, up which runs the road to Arrochar (Rte. 13c). We turn sharp r. and, beyond the road through Hell's Glen to Lochgoilhead, reach (16 m.) *St. Catherine's* (Hotel, RB. 18/6, P. 8 gs.), opposite Inveraray. —20 m. *Strachur* (p. 146) is at the junction of the road to Loch Eck and Dunoon.

From Strachur A 886 goes on down the wooded E. bank of Loch Fyne.—From (4 m.) *Strathlachlan* B 836 crosses the hills S.E. to Glendaruel (p. 146 ; 10 m.). —15 m. *Otter Ferry* (hill road to Glendaruel, p. 146).—Thence our road strikes S.E. for (18½ m.) *Kilfinan* (Hotel) and eventually descends to the Kyles of Bute at (26 m.) *Kames,* 1½ m. S.W. of Tighnabruaich.

FROM INVERARAY TO DALMALLY (Oban), 15 m., motor coach daily. This fine road ascends the beautifully wooded *Glen Aray,* passing close to the Falls of Aray (see above).

From (7½ m.) the summit level (673 ft.), among the moors, we command a magnificent view of Loch Awe, overshadowed by Ben Cruachan. A series of steep descents lead to (9 m.) *Cladich*, where we join the road from Portsonachan and Ford. Thence to (15 m.) *Dalmally*, see Rte. 49.

14. FROM GLASGOW TO GREENOCK, GOUROCK, AND WEMYSS BAY

ROADS. (i) A 8 viâ Govan, Renfrew, and Langbank, and thence along the coast viâ Port Glasgow to (22 m.) *Greenock*, (25 m.) *Gourock*, and (32 m.) *Wemyss Bay*. (ii) A 737 to (7 m.) *Paisley*. (iii) A 761 thence viâ (17½ m.) *Kilmacolm* to (24 m.) *Greenock*, joining A 8 at Port Glasgow. MOTOR-BUSES from St. Enoch Station viâ Renfrew to Greenock, *Gourock* in 1¼ hr. and *Wemyss Bay* in 1¾ hr., going on to *Largs* (2 hrs.) ; also from Clyde St. viâ Paisley and Kilmacolm to Greenock and *Gourock* (1⅜ hr.).
There are three routes by RAILWAY from Glasgow to Greenock, all of which touch Paisley and take ¾–1 hr. Passengers who propose to join a steamer at Gourock should take Rte. B. Rte. C (to Wemyss Bay) calls at Upper Greenock, some distance from the river.
    A. From St. Enoch Station to (7½ m.) *Paisley* (Gilmour St. or Canal)., (13¾ m.) *Bridge of Weir*, (17½ m.) *Kilmacolm*, and **Greenock** (24 m. Lynedoch St.; 25½ m. Princes Pier).
    B. From Central Station to (7¼ m.) *Paisley* (Gilmour St.), (20¼ m.) *Port Glasgow*, (23 m.) **Greenock** (Central), and (26¼ m.) **Gourock**.
    C. From Central Station, as Rte. B. to *Port Glasgow*, thence viâ (23 m.) *Upper Greenock* and (28¾ m.) *Inverkip* to (31 m.) **Wemyss Bay**.
    STEAMER to *Greenock* and *Gourock*, see Rte. 13A.
The following routes lie wholly within **Renfrewshire**, on the Clyde estuary, one of the smallest but one of the most populous of the Scottish counties. Within its bounds are Paisley, Greenock, Renfrew, and Port Glasgow, with their busy industries, and it is one of the dormitories of Glasgow, a portion of which it includes. In this county, the N.W. part of which was once known as Strathgryfe, Somerled met his fate in 1164 (p. 161). Renfrew is the county of Sir William Wallace, Capt. Kidd, James Watt, ' Christopher North', and of Robert Tannahill and many minor singers.

A. To Paisley and Greenock

We leave Glasgow by Paisley Road (A 737 ; Pl. 36), which runs nearly due W. through *Ibrox*, *Bellahouston*, and the trading-estate of *Hillington*.—7 m. **PAISLEY** (*Brabloch*, Renfrew Rd., RB. 23/; *Garthland*, unlic., 7 Glasgow Rd., RB. 16/, excellent), an ancient burgh on the White Cart (no longer white), is a busy industrial town (93,700 inhab.) with a remarkable Abbey Church, besides many imposing public buildings.

Paisley was noted c. 1805–70 for its gauzes and fine ' Paisley shawls ' with Oriental patterns, but it is now known mainly as the largest thread-producing town in the world, with the immense factories of the Coats-Clark Company. It was the birthplace of Alexander Wilson (1766–1813), poet and American ornithologist ; of Robert Tannahill (1774–1810), the weaver poet ; and of Professor John Wilson (1785–1854), the genial 'Christopher North' of Blackwood's Magazine. A Roman Catholic bishopric was established here in 1947. At the harbour on the Cart, 1 m. N. of the centre, were landed the first American troops to touch British soil in the Second World War (1942).

On the E. side of the Cart, opposite the classical *Town Hall* (1879–82), is the ***Abbey,** a fine Decorated structure, the nave of which is used as the parish church. It is open free on weekdays 10–4.30, in winter 10–3. In the grounds are statues of Alexander Wilson and Robert Tannahill.

The priory of Pasletum was founded c. 1163 by Walter Fitz Alan, who brought hither 13 Cluniac monks from Wenlock in Shropshire, his native county. The relics of St. Mirren or Merinus (8th cent. ?), whose cell had stood here, were transferred to the church, and his shrine became a place of pilgrimage. The priory rapidly became a wealthy house and was made an abbey in 1219, but it was destroyed by the English under Pembroke in 1307, and though favoured by the Stewart kings it was not rebuilt until after 1450, to which date the present building mainly belongs. The tower seems to have collapsed after the Reformers' ravages in 1561, destroying the choir in its fall. The church, with the exception of the nave and one chapel, fell into decay, and though the lower parts of the choir walls are original, the design above, with that of the tower, is the work of Sir Robert Lorimer (1902–28).

Adjoining the church on the S. is a part of the abbey buildings, restored in 1956 to parochial use ; in the 17th cent., as ' the Place of Paisley,' it was the town house of the Earl of Dundonald (d. 1686) ; and either here or in the church his granddaughter, Jean Cochrane, was married to Claverhouse in 1684.

The West Front is a graceful composition, with a deeply recessed E.E. doorway flanked by two blind arches and surmounted by three traceried windows.—The NAVE is remarkable for a richly developed triforium of broad round arches. The N. TRANSEPT has a finely traceried window. The place of the S. transept is occupied by *ST. MIRREN'S CHAPEL (1499), formerly called the ' Sounding Aisle ' from the echoes, which, however, ceased in 1862 with the opening up of the arches communicating with the nave. The interesting but incomplete sculptures beneath the N.E. window, depicting the life of St. Mirren, may have decorated his original cell. —The CHOIR is paved with slabs from the basement of Hamilton Palace. The recumbent effigy (found in fragments in the abbot's garden in 1778) passes for that of Marjory (d. 1317), daughter of Robert Bruce, the ' lass ' by whom the crown came to the Stewart line. She was fatally injured while hunting at Knock, just N. of the town. Here also were buried the wives of Robert II and Robert III (d. 1337), who himself probably also lies here.

To the W. of the Cross is High Street, with the birthplace of ' Christopher North ' (No. 63 ; rebuilt), and the *Museum* (adm. free weekdays 10–5, Tues. and Sat. 10–8). The latter contains a well-arranged series of local history rooms and ' interiors ', with Paisley shawls and relics of Alex. Wilson and Tannahill.

Perhaps the most conspicuous building in Paisley is the *Thomas Coats Memorial Church* (by Hippolyte Blanc ; 1894), the cruciform ' cathedral ' of the Baptist community with a central tower and elaborate alabaster adornment. No. 8 Castle St., ½ m. W. of the church, was the birthplace of Tannahill, who wrote most of his ballads in a thatched cottage surviving in Queen St. (still farther W.).

About 1¾ m. S. of Paisley is the old corbelled keep of *Stanley Castle*, beyond which B 775 climbs to the *Braes o' Gleniffer*, sung by Tannahill, whence we have lovely views over the Firth to the Highland hills.—*Crookston Castle*, 2½ m. S.E. of Paisley, reached by B 770 from S. Hillington, retains one tower of a 14th cent. stronghold of the Stewarts of Darnley (adm. 6*d.* daily ; May–Sept. 10–8 ; Oct.– Apr. 10–4.30, Sat. and Sun. 2–4.30). This was the legendary scene of the betrothal of Darnley and Queen Mary. The estate passed to the Maxwells in 1757, and the castle was presented to the National Trust, as its first property, by Sir John Stirling Maxwell in 1931. Ross Hall, at Crookston, is the first complete ' hotel school ' in Britain (1946).

A 741 leads N.E. to (3 m.) *Renfrew* (see below), while A 726 runs N.W., passing St. James's Park, to (5 m.) *Erskine Ferry* (car 1/6) on the Clyde opposite Old Kilpatrick (p. 133).—From Paisley to *Ardrossan, Ayr*, etc., see Rte. 15.

A 737 goes on through the straggling W. suburbs of Paisley, and in less than 2 m. we turn right on A 761.—14 m. *Bridge of Weir* (Gryffe Arms, plain) is a golfing resort with the two Ranfurly courses, and tanneries.—17½ m. *Kilmacolm* (350 ft. ; Hydro, RB. 30/, P. 14 gs.) is another old-fashioned holiday resort. A gradual rise to 404 ft. is followed by a steep descent (*View) to (21 m.) *Port Glasgow* c. 3 m. E. of Greenock (see below).

To the E. of A 767 (1½ m. from Bridge of Weir) lies *Houston*, a ' model ' village of 1781–82, with an old cross surviving from the earlier settlement. On the Langbank road, 1½ m. N., is the *Barochan Cross*, a fine culptured Celtic cross 11 ft. high.

B. To Renfrew, Greenock, Gourock, and Wemyss Bay

Skirting Princes Dock (Pl. 30) on the S. side of the Clyde, A 8 traverses Govan.—6 m. **Renfrew** (17,100 inhab.), an ancient royal burgh, with shipyards, gives the title of baron to the Prince of Wales. Somerled, Lord of the Isles, was defeated and slain here by Malcolm IV in 1164. To the S. extends the *Airport* for internal services, with buildings by W. H. Kininmonth (1954). The lowest continuous ferry on the Clyde crosses from Renfrew to Yoker (cars 1/). Near the bridge, which crosses the White Cart and the Black Cart near their junction, the ' Argyll Stone ' marks the spot where the Earl of Argyll was arrested in 1685. In the churchyard of *Inch-innan* here are interesting Celtic stones and Templar grave-stones, and, on the S. wall, ' mortsafes ' recalling the days of the resurrectionists.—We cross the road leading (r.) to Erskine Ferry (see above) for Helensburgh and the North.— From (11¼ m.) *Bishopton* another road (r.) leads to the ferry, passing *Erskine Church* (1814), by David Hamilton, and *Erskine House* (1828), now a hospital for the disabled ; Smirke designed its gallery. From (15¼ m.) *Langbank* (Eastbank, RB. 27/6, P. 11 gs.) the road skirts the Clyde, here fringed with pools for the seasoning of timber. We pass *Parklea Farm* (N.T.) on the riverside and then, beyond the railway, *Newark Castle* (adm. free) of the 16–17th cent., a turreted mansion of the Maxwells incorporating an ancient tower.—Amid ship-yards, we reach (19¼ m.) *Port Glasgow* (21,620 inhab. ; Star,

RB. 16/), founded in 1668 to be the harbour of Glasgow, before the Clyde was deepened. An uninterrupted succession of houses, factories, docks, and shipyards now fringes the river.

22 m. GREENOCK (*Tontine*, Ardgowan Square at the W. end of the town, RB. 25/, P. 12 gs. ; *Trinidad*, unlic., 38 Eldon St., RB. 20/), birthplace of James Watt (1736–1819), of the scholar brothers Caird (John, 1820–98 ; Edward, 1835–1908), of Hamish MacCunn (1868–1916), the composer, and of Capt. Kidd (d. 1701), the pirate, is a busy seaport (76,300 inhab.) and an important industrial town, with large shipyards, sugar refineries, engineering works, worsted mills, etc. ; the docks of c. 100 acres include the only non-tidal dock in the Clyde. Immediately off Greenock lies the important roadstead known as the ' Tail of the Bank.'

From the Central Station, Cathcart St., beyond the *Post Office*, leads to the *Municipal Buildings* (1886) with its lofty *Victoria Tower* (245 ft.) ; a tablet at the corner of William St. and Dalrymple St. records the birthplace of Watt. Beyond the *Mid Kirk* (1757–87), the classical steeple of which recalls that of St. Andrew's in Edinburgh, Hamilton St. runs N.W. to cross West Burn St. and Nicolson St. John Galt (p. 166) died in West Burn St. (plaque) and is buried in the old grave-yard in Inverkip St., its continuation up the hill. In Nicolson St. is the *West Kirk* (1841–53), the masterpiece of David Cousin. Argyle St., parallel with Nicolson St., leads left to George Sq. and Union St., in which is the building (1835 ; by Blore), erected as a memorial to James Watt by his son, and containing his statue by Chantrey ; here are also the *Watt Library*, *Art Gallery* and *McLean Museum* housing a miscellaneous collection of model ships, natural history, and paintings by Sir James Guthrie (1859–1930), a native of Greenock, and others. Farther on, in Campbell St. (r.), is the *Arts Guild* with its two theatres.

Nicolson St. (see above) ascends to the picturesque *Cemetery*, in which are the remains and tombstone of Burns's ' Highland Mary ' (p. 171), removed from the graveyard of the old West Kirk (see below). From the point where the main approach avenue in the cemetery divides the path on the right ascends (beside the wall) to the spot.—The old *West Kirk* (1591), the first church built after the Reformation and the first Presbyterian church confirmed by the National Parliament, taken down for industrial development in 1920, has been carefully re-erected on the Esplanade, W. of Princes Pier. It has stained-glass windows by Burne-Jones, Morris, Rossetti, and F. M. Brown.—In 1940–45 Greenock was the chief French naval base in Britain, and a granite Cross of Lorraine and anchor, on Lyle Hill, is a monument (1946) to Free French sailors who died in the Battle of the Atlantic.

The heights above Greenock command fine *Views of the Highland hills and sea-lochs and of the Clyde and its shipping.

Beyond Greenock we pass *Fort Matilda*, with the Royal Naval Torpedo Factory and Research Station.—**25 m. Gourock** (*Bay*, RB. 25/6, P. 12½ gs. ; *Queen's*, RB. 22/6, P. 9–11 gs. ; *Ashton*, RB. 18/6, P. 8½ gs. ; *Levanne House*,

1½ m. S.W., P. 8½ gs., unlic.), a highly popular summer resort (9100 inhab.) with a good open-air swimming-pool and a fine quay on the E. side of Kempock Point, is one of the chief centres for passenger steamers on the Clyde. About 2 m. S.W. of the pier, on the pleasant coast road to (8 m.) *Wemyss Bay* (see below ; motor bus), is the ruined tower of *Levan Castle*, and 1 m. farther on is the low white *Cloch Lighthouse*, where the open firth, running N. and S., may be said to begin.

Steamers from Gourock, see Rte. 13. Car Ferry to *Dunoon* (Sun. incl.) 8–10 times daily in 20 min. (16/6–22/, ret. 24/9–33/). Tidal ferries to *Craigendoran* (2/7, cycle 10*d*.; motor cycle 3/6) and to *Kilmun* (2/, cycle 10*d*., motor cycle 3/3).

C. From Glasgow to Wemyss Bay, Largs, and Ardrossan

ROAD to *Greenock*, see Rtes. 14A and B ; thence viâ Gourock (A 78), see above. The direct road, climbing inland, with fine views, is 2 m. shorter. STEAMERS, see Rte. 13.

The two roads from Greenock unite a little short of (29 m.) *Inverkip*, a seaside village beautifully situated.—32 m. **Wemyss Bay** (*Hotel*, RB. 20/–25/, P. 10–12 gs.), another of the chief centres of passenger steamers on the Clyde, is separated by the county boundary from **Skelmorlie** (*The Hydro*, RB. 33/, P. 14 gs. ; *Heywood*, RB. 25/, P. 12 gs. ; *Manor Park*, 2 m. S., RB. 27/6, P. 14 gs.), the two together making a pleasant summer resort. To the N. is the 19th cent. Castle Wemyss, and conspicuous above the station are the ruins of Kelly House, a modern mansion destroyed by fire and never restored. Beyond Skelmorlie Castle, dating from 1502, the road hugs the coast on the edge of agreeable country to Largs, 2½ m. short of which is Knock Castle.

38 m. **Largs**, sheltered from the E. by the Mistylaw Hills (p. 165), is a pleasant town (8600 inhab.) and a popular holiday resort with numerous parks.

Hotels. Near Broomfields : **Castle**, RB. 30/, P. 15½ gs. ; **Curlinghall**, RB. from 27/6, P. 14 gs. ; **Marine**, similar charges ; **Elderslie**, RB. 23/, P. 11 gs. ; **Mackerston**, unlic., P. 11 gs. ; **South Bay**, P. from 9 gs. ; **Largs**, RB. 21/, P. 12 gs. ; **Victoria**, P. 10 gs. ; **Queen's, Springfield**, P. 9 gs., these four on the Esplanade ; **George**, Main St., RB. 16/6, P. 8½ gs. ; **Haylie**, unlic., Irvine Rd., P. 9 gs.

Motor-Buses to *Glasgow* viâ Wemyss Bay and Gourock (2 hrs.) or Lochwinnoch and Paisley (1¾ hr.) ; to

Kilmarnock (1¾ hr.) ; to *Saltcoats* (50 min.) viâ Fairlie and West Kilbride.

Motor Boat at frequent intervals in summer to *Millport* ; also regular ferry service in June–Sept. in 35 min. —STEAMERS, see Rte. 13E.

Amusements. *Bathing Station*, North Bay ; *Golf Courses*, N. and S. of the town ; *Tennis Courts, Bowling* and *Putting Greens* ; *Regattas* in late June and in early August.—*Concert Parties* at Barrfields Pavilion, North Shore.

History. In 1263 Alexander III engaged Haco or Hakon, king of Norway, at the *Battle of Largs*, as a result of which the Hebrides and the Isle of Man, held by the Norsemen for 400 years, were ceded to Scotland. A round tower erected on the shore at Bowen Craig, S. of the town, marks the probable site of the spot where part of the Norse fleet was driven ashore.—Dr. John Cairnie, founder of the Royal Caledonian Curling Club, built the first open-air artificial rink in the grounds of Curlinghall Hotel in 1813.

On the Esplanade, skirting Largs Bay, are the *Pier* and the conspicuous parish church of *St. Columba* (1877) by Alex. Ross, while on South Bay, facing the Great Cumbrae, is the green space of the *Broomfields*. From the pier Main St., the principal shopping centre, goes inland to be prolonged by Irvine Road. In Bellman's Close, leading out of Main St. on the left (below the station), is the *Skelmorlie Aisle (open daily exc. Wed. 10–5.30, Sun. 2–5), the N. transept of the old church, transformed by Sir Robert Montgomery of Skelmorlie. It has a wooden barrel-vault, elaborately painted by Stalker (1638), and contains the rich Renaissance monument (1639) of Sir Robert and his wife. Here is said to be buried also Sir Hew Montgomery, a hero of Chevy Chase (1388). *Douglas Park*, above the town off Irvine Rd., commands a fine view across the Firth.

In the valley of the Noddsdale Water, on the N.E. are (c. 1 m.) Netherhall, long the summer residence of Lord Kelvin (1824–1907), the physicist, and (1½ m.) Brisbane House, birthplace of Sir Thomas Brisbane (1773–1860), governor of New South Wales (1821–25), after whom the city of Brisbane was named.

Beyond Largs we pass *Kelburn Castle* (16th cent. ; altered), a seat of the Earl of Glasgow.—41 m. **Fairlie** (*Fairlieburne*, with good grounds, unlic., RB. 25/, P. 9 gs. ; *Kelburn Arms*, RB. 18/6, P. 8½ gs.), a pleasant seaside and bathing resort, once noted for yacht-building, is the starting-point of the Campbeltown steamers (Rte. 13G). In a pretty glen to the E. stand the ruins of Fairlie Castle, not built until 1521, though Lady Wardlaw (1677–1727), places in this tower the scene of her ballad of 'Hardyknute,' which refers to the battle of Largs.—Thence to (49½ m.) **Ardrossan,** see p. 166.

15. FROM GLASGOW TO ARDROSSAN (Largs) AND TO AYR

ROAD, A 737.—7 m. *Paisley.*—19 m. *Beith.*—At (28 m.) *Kilwinning* A 78 branches r. for (33½ m.) **Ardrossan** and l. for (42 m.) **Ayr.**

MOTOR-BUSES from Waterloo St. to *Ardrossan* in 2 hrs. ; to *Ayr* viâ Troon in 2 hrs. 20 min.

RAILWAYS. To AYR, 41½ m. from St. Enoch Station in 1–1½ hr. ; to *Kilwinning*, 26¾ m. in ¾ hr. This is the route of the through expresses to Stranraer. A less direct route, interesting to the Burns pilgrim, runs viâ Kilmarnock or Mauchline, see Rte. 16.

To ARDROSSAN (¾–1½ hr.) and LARGS (1½–2 hrs.) from St. Enoch. Principal stations : 8 m. *Paisley* (Gilmour St. or Canal Station). Thence either viâ (11 m.) *Johnstone* or viâ (17 m.) Lochwinnoch and (20½ m.) Kilbirnie to (23½ m.) *Dalry.*— 26¾ m. **Kilwinning,** where the lines diverge. The Ayr line runs viâ (30¼ m.) *Irvine,* (34½ m.) *Troon,* and (38¼ m.) *Prestwick* ; the Ardrossan–Largs line serves

(30¾ m.) *Saltcoats* and (32 m.) **Ardrossan** (South Beach, Town, or Winton Pier).—
36 m. *West Kilbride.*—40 m. *Fairlie* (Fairlie Pier for boat-trains).—43 m. **Largs**.

To (7 m.) *Paisley*, see Rte. 14A.—9 m. *Elderslie* (3900 inhab.),
the traditional birthplace of William Wallace (? 1272).—10 m.
Johnstone, mainly to the right, is a busy town (15,650 inhab.)
with cotton mills and engineering works.

On the town steeple (1755) of **Kilbarchan**, once known as a tartan-weaving
town (2 m. W.), is a restored figure of Habbie Simpson, a famous 17th cent.
town piper referred to in the song of ' Maggie Lauder.' The 18th cent. *Weaver's
Cottage* (N.T. ; open daily, 1/), restored since 1955, is typical of the dwellings
in which the craft of hand-loom weaving was pursued till 1940. The *Old Kirk*
(1724) is now used as a hall.

At (13 m.) *Howwood* a road on the right diverges for Lochwinnoch (3½ m. W.), skirting the park of *Castle Semple*, long
the seat of the lords Sempill. Their burial aisle, near the
mansion, is a fragment of a collegiate church founded in 1504.

Lochwinnoch, on the Kilmacolm road at the S.W. end of Castle Semple Loch,
is a small textile and furniture-making town (1950 inhab.), where Wilson
the ornithologist was once a journeyman weaver. About ½ m. S. is the lofty
loopholed tower of *Barr Castle*, and on the S. side of the loch are the ruins of
Peel Castle (16th cent.), formerly on an island.—4½ m. *Kilbirnie*, W. of Kilbirnie
Loch, is connected by road with Dalry (see below). Kilbirnie Place (14th cent. ;
burned in the 18th cent.) was a seat of the Earls of Crawford. The church (adm.
2–4), on the Glengarnock road, contains a carved pulpit and a Renaissance
carved gallery with 18 coloured coats-of-arms from the lineage of the first Viscount
Garnock, who built the church in 1654.—A 760, passing Kilbirnie Place, ascends
past Camphill Reservoir to nearly 800 ft. ; then descends above the grounds of
Kelburn Castle to (13½ m.) Largs (see below).—The *Mistylaw Hills*, which rise
to the N. of this road, reach a height of 1711 ft. at the *Hill of Stake* (c. 6 m.
N.W. of Lochwinnoch, 5 m. E. of Largs), which is little visited but commands
a magnificent view.

19 m. *Beith* (Saracen's Head, RB. 15/), a little furniture-
making town (4350 inhab.) in Ayrshire, is by-passed by the
main road. The corbie-stepped Old Kirk dates from 1807–10,
while the Town House was erected in 1817. Alexander
Montgomery (c. 1556–c. 1610), James VI's poet laureate and
author of ' The Cherrie and the Slae ', was probably born in
the family mansion of *Hessilhead*, 2 m. E.—24 m. *Dalry* (King's
Arms, Royal, RB. 15/6) is a centre of the Ayrshire coalfield,
with 4025 inhabitants.

28 m. **Kilwinning** (6550 inhab.) claims to be the first home
of Scottish freemasonry, introduced by the foreign builders
of the priory, and ' Mother Lodge Kilwinning ' ranks as the
parent lodge of the craft in Scotland. *Kilwinning Abbey* was
founded by Richard de Morville c. 1162 on the site of a church
built by the Irish St. Wynnin (6th cent.). The most striking
part of the scanty remains is the S. transept gable with its
three lancets ; also extant are the doorway into the E. cloister
walk, the chapter house entrance, and part of the W. front.
The parish church has a detached Gothick tower of 1815.

In the evening of the first Sat. in July, the Kilwinning Papingo, a 17th cent.
silver ' bird,' set out on top of the town steeple, is shot at by the Ancient Society

of Kilwinning Archers.—In *Eglinton Park*, S.E. of the town, was held the
'Eglinton Tournament' (1839), a romantic attempt to revive on a large scale
the forms and ceremonies of ancient chivalry. Lady Seymour, a granddaughter
of Sheridan, was 'Queen of Beauty' and Napoleon III figured among 'the
knights.' The castle (1798) lies derelict.

The ROAD TO ARDROSSAN AND LARGS parts company with
the Ayr road at Kilwinning, passing at first through a region
of factories and coal-mines.—30½ m. (from Glasgow) *Stevenston*,
like the two following towns, can be by-passed on the N.—
32 m. **Saltcoats** (13,100 inhab. ; *Osborne*, unlic., RB. 17/6,
P. 7 gs.), where saltworks were established by James V, has
a harbour and a bathing beach. The *North Ayrshire Museum*
(adm. 6*d.* ; June–Aug., weekdays 10–9 ; other times Mon.,
Tues., Thurs., Sat. 11–5), in the former parish church, illustrates the industrial development of the region and includes
early 19th cent. interiors.—33½ m. **Ardrossan** (*Eglinton Arms*,
at the harbour, RB. 21/, P. 9 gs. ; *Kilmeny, Ingledene*, RB.
19/6, P. 8½ gs.), a port and sea-bathing place (8800 inhab.),
laid out on a regular plan by Peter Nicholson in 1806, is of
tourist importance only as a port of departure for steamers to
Arran, to Belfast, and to the Isle of Man. Off the coast lies
Horse Island. The road affords good views of Arran.—Beyond
(37 m.) *Seamill* (Hotel, RB. 21/, P. 10 gs. ; Glenbryde, RB.
20/, P. 8½ gs. ; Hydro, unlic., P. 9 gs. ; Beach House, unlic.,
P. 8 gs.), a summer resort, the tiny town of *West Kilbride*
(Wellington Inn) lies 1 m. inland with an ancient tower known
as Law Castle. The mansion of Crosbie (partly 17th cent.),
1 m. N.E., is a youth hostel, while c. 2 m. W. are the ruins of
Portincross Castle, off which one of the ships of the Spanish
Armada is believed to have foundered. The road goes on
through pretty country to (42 m.) *Fairlie* and (45 m.) **Largs**,
see p. 163.

ROAD TO AYR (continued). With Eglinton grounds on the
left, we have *Bogside* racecourse on the right, beyond the
railway.—31 m. **Irvine** (*Redburn*, Kilwinning Rd., RB. 21/,
P. 10 gs.), a royal burgh (14,750 inhab.), once the foreport of
Glasgow, has large chemical works and a coal-port at the
mouth of the Irvine.

James Montgomery (1771–1854), the poet, and John Galt (1779–1839), the
novelist, were natives of Irvine, and Burns was a flax-dresser here for a year
and a half (1781–83) before his shop was burned down (a tablet marks his lodgings
in Glasgow Vennel). J. B. Dunlop (1840–1921), inventor of the pneumatic tyre,
was born at *Dreghorn*, 2 m. E. (tablet).

The flat seaboard is bordered by a succession of golf courses
and abandoned camps. At 34½ m. a road on the right leads to
Troon (2 m. ; *Marine*, RB. from 35/, P. 15–22 gs. ; *South
Beach*, RB. 25/–30/, P. 10–12 gs. ; *Craiglea*, RB. 22/6, P. 11 gs.

Ardneil, P. 10 gs. ; *Welbeck*, *Mar Lodge*, unlic., P. 9 gs.), one
of the three leading ports (10,050 inhab.) of Ayrshire, with
shipbuilding and shipbreaking yards. It is also a highly
popular summer resort on account of its extensive sandy
beach and its many golf courses, both private (introduction
necessary) and municipal. Off the coast lies *Lady Isle*, a bird
sanctuary. The main road may be rejoined ½ m. N. of Monkton.

Dundonald Castle, a rough ruin on a hill 4 m. N.E. (½ m. S. of the Kilmarnock
road), was the abode of Robert II before his accession, and here he died in 1390 ;
Robert III also died here in 1406. Dr. Johnson, who visited the castle in 1773,
" was very jocular on the homely accommodation of King Bob, and roared and
laughed till the ruins echoed." *Auchans House* (16th cent.), near the main road,
was also visited by Johnson.

Fullarton House (now flats), between Troon and the main road, was occupied
in 1801 by Louis Philippe, afterwards King of the French.

Above the Dutch House Motel (RB. 20/), just short of
(88 m.) *Monkton* (Park, RB. 17/6, P. 8½ gs.), where the ruined
old kirk preserves a Romanesque doorway, is a monument to
James Macrae (d. 1744), a poor Ayrshire boy who became
Governor of Madras.—39½ m. **Prestwick** (11,400 inhab. ;
Queen's, RB. 25/–30/, P. 12–14 gs. ; *Parkstone*, RB. 23/6,
P. 11 gs., both on the Esplanade ; *Towans*, RB. 25/, P. 12 gs. ;
Links, RB. 21/, P. 11 gs. ; *St. Nicholas*, Ayr Rd., RB. 21/6,
P. 9 gs.), now practically a suburb of Ayr, with an old market
cross, has long been known as one of the classic homes of golf,
and latterly has won new fame as the seat of the principal
airport of Scotland. Bruce's Well, in the bungalow estate of
Kingcase, recalls the story that Bruce was said to have been
here cured of a skin disease.

For the full use of the ' championship ' links of Prestwick Golf Club, one of
the finest golf courses in Scotland, an introduction is necessary, but for a fee of
5/ per day visitors may play over the course on Mon.–Friday. There are two other
good courses to which a lower fee obtains admission.

Prestwick Airport (*Hotel*, for air travellers and their friends, RB. 22/6), N.E.
of the town, is one of the chief international airports of the world,'with services
to New York, Montreal, Stockholm, Copenhagen, etc., as well as Ireland and
London (p. lviii). In 1936–39 it served as a training-school for R.A.F. pilots,
and during the war years it was used as the H.Q. of R.A.F. Ferry Command
(the first transatlantic plane landing on Nov. 29th, 1940) and later as a main
centre for U.S. Transport Command (1943–45), many of the buildings being
occupied as the chief Transit Evacuation Hospital between France and U.S.A.
Some 40,000 transatlantic planes landed at Prestwick during the war.

42 m. **Ayr**, see Rte. 17.

16. FROM GLASGOW TO AYR VIÂ KILMARNOCK

ROADS. (i) Viâ A 77, direct, 33 m. We quit Glasgow viâ Eglinton St. (Pl. 40).—
7 m. *Newton Mearns*.—17 m. *Fenwick*.—21 m. **Kilmarnock**, entering viâ Wellington St., leaving viâ Titchfield St.—29 m. *Monkton*.—30½ m. *Prestwick*.—33 m.
Ayr, entering by Main St. (A 2). (ii) Another route (A 736, 735).—26 m. to
Kilmarnock (entering viâ Hill St.) runs viâ *Pollokshaws*, *Barrhead* (8 m.) and
Dunlop (17 m.). From Kilmarnock we may proceed to Ayr (45 m.) viâ Mauchline
and Tarbolton.—MOTOR-BUSES from Waterloo St. viâ Fenwick to *Kilmarnock*
in 1 hr. 5 min. and *Ayr* in 1 hr. 40 min. ; viâ Barrhead to *Kilmarnock* in 1½ hr.

H

RAILWAY to *Kilmarnock*, 24½ m. in ½–1 hr. ; to *Mauchline*, 33¾ m. in 1¼–1½ hr.
This line, less direct than Rte. 15 but introducing us to an important part of the
' Burns Country,' is a section of the main route between Glasgow and Dumfries.
There is a branch line from Kilmarnock to Ayr.—Principal stations :   7½ m.
Barrhead.—14½ m. *Lugton.*—16¾ m. *Dunlop.*—19 m. *Stewarton.*—22¼ m. *Kilmaurs.*

A. Direct

The DIRECT ROAD (A 77) ascends rapidly through the S.W.
outskirts of Glasgow to (7 m.) *Newton Mearns* and joins the
old road (viâ Clarkston) at (9 m.) a monument to Robert
Pollok (1798–1827), a minor poet born at the neighbouring
farm of Moorhouse. Traversing moorland country praised by
' Christopher North,' we enter Ayrshire just before reaching
(13 m.) the summit-level (c. 775 ft.) a little S. of Drumboy
Hill (876 ft.).

Ayrshire is primarily the ' Land of Burns,' and although it is of no striking
beauty, its streams, its hills, its vales, and even its villages are touched with the
magic of a poetry that has made their names familiar the world over. The county,
which has a sea-front fringed with noted golf-links, is divided by the Irvine and
the Doon into the districts of Cunningham (N.), Kyle (centre), and Carrick (S.),
all mainly agricultural though manufacturing industries are not absent :

" Kyle for a man, Carrick for a coo,
    Cunninghame for butter and cheese, and Galloway for woo'."

This county, which saw the battle of Largs, was later the scene of Wallace's
early exploits and the starting-point of Bruce's final triumph. On its inland
borders are the wild moorlands of the Covenanters. Ayrshire claims both Robert
Bruce and Burns (" there was a lad was born in Kyle ") as sons ; among lesser
lights are James Boswell, John Galt, the novelist, and John Macadam, the road-
maker. The earldom of Carrick, once held by Bruce, is an appanage of the
Prince of Wales. The art of embroidery, or ' flooerin,' introduced from France
c. 1815 by Lady Mary Montgomerie, flourished until the American Civil War
and was revived in the 1950's.

On the descent the main road by-passes (17 m.) *Fenwick*
(King's Arms) and leaves on the left the ruined castle of
(18½ m.) *Craufurdland* and (20 m.) *Dean Castle*, formerly a
seat of Lord Howard de Walden. Kilmarnock may be avoided
by a ' ring road ' on the right.

21 m. **Kilmarnock** (*Ossington*, unlic., RB. 19/6 ;   *Station*,
RB. 17/6), a manufacturing town (42,125 inhab.) of importance,
with factories for carpets, shawls, boots, and engineering
works, has few attractions for the tourist beyond its associations with Robert Burns. The Kilmarnock bonnet is well
known as a soldier's headgear. The first edition of Burns's
poems here issued from the press of John Wilson in 1786, and
among the people of Kilmarnock were some of the poet's most
generous friends. The *Laigh Kirk* figures in Burns's poem
' The Ordination ' ;   and the Angel Hotel is the ' Begbie's '
of that satire, but only the 17th cent. tower of the church of
his time survives ; the rest dates from 1802. In the churchyard are several Covenanters' monuments and an epitaph by
Burns on ' Tam Samson.' The *Old High Kirk* is a typical
building of 1732–40. In Kay Park stands the *Burns Monument*

(1879), a temple of red sandstone on a raised platform,
surmounted by a tower 80 ft. high. The statue of the poet
beneath the canopy is by W. G. Stevenson. Within is a Burns
Museum (open 12.30–4, 5–9; in winter 10–12, 1–5) with books
and MSS. of Burns, his draught-board, and other relics.

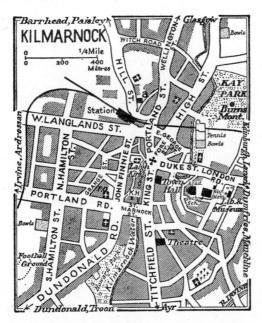

Alexander Smith (1830–67), author of 'Dreamthorp,' was born at Kilmarnock,
and William Boyd, the last Earl of Kilmarnock, was beheaded on Tower Hill
in 1746, after Culloden. William Wallace is said to have spent many of his
younger days at his uncle's farm at *Riccarton*, 1 m. S. of Kilmarnock.

FROM KILMARNOCK TO STRATHAVEN, 20 m., motor-bus hourly in 50 min. on
A 71.—1½ m. *Hurlford.*—5½ m. *Galston* (4560 inhab.), N. of which is *Loudoun
Castle* (15th cent.) surrounded by a later building of 1811 and badly damaged
by fire in 1941. The Irvine valley, hence to Darvel, is noted for machine-made
lace.—7 m. *Newmilns* (4050 inhab.) is noted for muslins.—9 m. *Darvel* (3240
inhab.) was the birthplace of Sir Alexander Fleming (1881–1955), discoverer of
penicillin (monument at Lochfield Farm).—11¾ m. *Loudounhill.* Here, in May
1306, Bruce defeated the Earl of Pembroke and laid the foundation of his
ultimate success.—We enter Lanarkshire.—14½ m. **Drumclog.** An obelisk 1½ m.
N.W. commemorates Sun. June 1st, 1679, when Claverhouse, marching with a
troop of lifeguards and some dragoons to disperse an armed conventicle, was
signally routed by 200 Covenanters commanded by Hackston of Rathillet,
Balfour of Kinloch, and other experienced officers.—20 m. **Strathaven** (*Buck's*

Head, RB. 25/ ; *Sun*, RB. 18/6 ; pron. Strayven), a small place (4300 inhab.) with an old quarter containing the ruins of *Avondale Castle* (15th cent.), has bus connection viâ East Kilbride or Hamilton with Glasgow, and with Airdrie. Sir Harry Lauder (1870–1950) died here at Lauder Ha'.

MOTOR-BUSES run from Kilmarnock to *Ayr* viâ Dundonald and Troon, or viâ Symington ; to Irvine, Ardrossan, and *Largs* ; to *Muirkirk* viâ Mauchline and Cumnock ; to *Beith* viâ Kilmaurs and Dunlop ; to *Girvan* ; to *Dumfries* (see Rte. 9B), etc.

Leaving Kilmarnock by the Irvine bridge and Riccarton (see above), A 77 passes (26 m. ; r.) *Symington* (Half-Way, RB. 22/6, P. 10 gs.), a pleasant village, with some Norman work in its (rebuilt) church.—29 m. *Monkton*, and thence to (33 m.) **Ayr,** see Rte. 15.

B. Viâ Barrhead and Mauchline

Leaving Glasgow by *Pollokshaws* we follow A 736 (r.) to (7½ m.) *Barrhead* (Hotel, RB. 25/), a busy manufacturing town (12,975 inhab.) on the Levern, the birthplace of John Davidson (1857–1909), the poet.—The route becomes pretty as we approach (12 m.) *Loch Libo* (r.), beyond which we enter Ayrshire.—At (14½ m.) *Lugton* we turn l. on A 735.—17 m. *Dunlop* gives name to the cheese for which the district is noted.—19 m. *Stewarton* has woollen manufactures (it was once famous for its bonnets), and remains of an ancient tower of the Cunninghames.—22 m. **Kilmaurs,** an old burgh, has an attractive Tolbooth (still with the jougs outside) and Mercat Cross, and remains of the mansion of the Cunninghames, earls of Glencairn, the last of whom died in 1796. The church, a collegiate foundation of 1413 (rebuilt 1888), contains the tomb of the 8th earl (d. 1600), by Scougal, in the 17th cent. Glencairn aisle. *Rowallan Castle* (mainly c. 1560), 1 m. E., was once the residence of the Mures of Rowallan, a daughter of which family was the first wife of Robert II. The present Lord Rowallan is Chief Scout.—We enter (25 m.) **Kilmarnock** (see above) by Hill St. and leave by London Road.

Turning S. at (26¾ m.) *Hurlford* on A 76, we pass the Burns Memorial (see below).—34 m. **Mauchline** (*Poosie Nansie's Inn*, RB. 15/6 ; *Loudoun Arms*, RB. 15/), a straggling little town (2990 inhab.), noted c. 1830–60 for its wooden snuff-boxes and similar small wooden ware, was closely associated with Burns during his stay at Lochlea and Mossgiel (see below). The churchyard was the scene of 'The Holy Fair,' but the church has been rebuilt (1829) since Burns's time. A plan just within the churchyard gate indicates the position of the graves of Gavin Hamilton, four of Burns's children, and other contemporaries of Burns, many of whom figure in the satiric poem. The Mary Morison mentioned on the plan is, however, not the 'lovely Mary Morison' of Burns's song. William

Fisher, the ' Holy Willie ' of the famous ' Prayer,' was an elder and ' Daddy Auld ' was minister at Mauchline. Opposite the churchyard gate, in Loudoun St., is the cottage of ' Poosie Nansie ' (Ann Gibson), the scene of the ' Jolly Beggars,' separated from which by a lane is the former Whitefoord Arms Inn, once kept by John Dove, the subject of Burns's epitaph on ' Johnny Pigeon.' Jean Armour, daughter of a Mauchline mason, lived with her father a little farther up the lane. On the other side of the churchyard, in Castle St., was ' Auld Nanse Tinnock's '; and between the churchyard and the tower of the ' Castle ' (really a grange of Melrose abbey, c. 1450) is the house of Gavin Hamilton, Burns's friend and landlord, with the room in which the poet was married in 1788.

About ½ m. N. is the *Burns Memorial* (1896–97), a tall red tower (adm. 6*d.*) with a good Burns museum, and some model cottages (tea-room) beside it, and 1 m. farther (to the left at the tower) is **Mossgiel**, with the " very field where Burns ploughed up the Daisy." The farm (118 acres) was rented by Robert Burns and his brother Gilbert in 1784–1788; here most of the poet's first volume was written ; and hence he set out in 1786 on his celebrated first visit to Edinburgh. The house was almost entirely rebuilt in 1859.—About 1½ m. farther on a road diverging on the right leads to *Lochlea*, the farm that was the home of the Burns family from 1777–1784, where the poet's life, combined, in his own words, " the cheerless gloom of a hermit with the unceasing moil of a galley-slave."

Motor-buses run from Mauchline to (3½ m.) *Catrine*, a village noted for a huge water-wheel in one of its mills, near which is *Ballochmyle House*, the scene of two of Burns's songs : ' The Braes of Ballochmyle,' written to express the sorrow of Miss Whiteford when her father was obliged to part with the old family place, and ' The Lass o' Ballochmyle,' composed in honour of Miss Alexander, whose brother had purchased the property. *Catrine House*, to the S.W. of the village, was the residence of Prof. Dugald Stewart (1753–1828), as whose guest Burns " dinner'd wi' a lord " before going to Edinburgh in 1786.— We may go on, up the Ayr valley, to (5¾ m.) *Sorn*, an attractive village with an old bridge, and the ' jougs ' still hanging on the wall of the church (1658). Sorn Castle dates in part from the 15th cent. Alexander Peden (1626 ?–86) was born at the farm of Auchencloich and spent his last days, a fugitive, in a cave on the moors near by. The road (B 743) goes on E. to (14 m.) Muirkirk (see Rte. 17).

From Mauchline to *Dumfries* and *Carlisle*, see Rte. 9B.

The direct road to Ayr (A 758) leads W. from Mauchline, but it is better to return to the Burns Monument and bear left on B 744, which passes Mossgiel and commands good views.— 38 m. **Tarbolton** (*Black Bull*, RB. 15/). Here in 1781 Burns became a freemason (memorials in the Masonic Hall), and here in 1780 he founded the Bachelors' Club in a 17th cent. house (N.T. ; key on application), still used by a literary society. ' Willie's Mill,' mentioned in ' Death and Dr. Hornbook,' is identified with the mill a little to the E. of the village. The ' Castle o' Montgomery,' where Mary Campbell, Burns's ' Highland Mary,' was in service, rises ½ m. S.W. of Tarbolton. A monument on A 758 near the junction of the Water of Fail and the Ayr marks the spot where the poet parted from her. The mansion, now known as *Montgomerie Castle*, was then named Coilsfield, from the tradition that ' auld

King Coil ' was slain in battle by Fergus, King of Scots.—We rejoin A 758 before (40¼ m.) *Annbank*, surrounded by collieries. —42½ m. *Auchincruive House* (l.) is now the West of Scotland Agricultural College, and opposite is the Hannah Dairy Research Institute. Wallace is said to have hidden in the Laighland or·Leglen Wood here before burning the Barns of Ayr (see below) and Burns visited the wood " with as much devout enthusiasm as ever pilgrim did the shrine of Loretto." A cairn (1929) marks the site, while the Barnweil Monument, a tall tower (c. 1860) 2 m. N. of Tarbolton, stands on the spot from which Wallace is said to have watched the burning.— 45½ m. **Ayr,** see Rte. 17.

17. AYR AND ITS ENVIRONS

A. Ayr and Alloway

AYR (42,375 inhab.), famous as the centre of the ' Burns Country,' is a pleasant royal burgh with a small harbour at the mouth of the Ayr and a popular racecourse. It is also a summer resort with good sands and an esplanade.

Hotels. Station (a ; C 3), RB. 30/, P. 14 gs. ; **Dalblair** (b ; C 2), 42 Alloway St., similar charges ; **County,** Wellington Sq. (B 1), RB. from 21/, P. 12 gs. ; **Berkeley,** Barns St. (C 2), RB. 25/, P. 11 gs. ; **Ayrshire & Galloway,** Burns Statue Sq. (C 3), RB. 27/6, P. 14 gs. ; **Gartferry, Savoy Park,** both in Racecourse Rd., RB. from 25/, P. from 11 gs. ; **Burns Monument,** see p. 174 ; **Elms Court,** Miller Rd. (C 2), RB. 25/, P. 12½ gs. ; **Beresford,** in the town, RB. 21/ ; **Benalt,** Racecourse Rd., RB. 21/, P. 10 gs. ; **Belleisle House,** unlic., in pleasant grounds, Doonfoot Rd., P. 9 gs. ; **Durward,** Prestwick Rd., RB. 21/ ; **Clifton, Parkdene,** Miller Rd., unlic., P. 8–9 gs., and other modest houses.

Post Office (B 2), Sandgate.

Motor-Buses from Fullarton St. (B 2) to *Glasgow* (1¾ hr.) ; *Troon* (25 min.) ; *Kilmarnock* (65 min.) ; *Kirkoswald* (½ hr.) ; *Girvan* (1–1¼ hr.) by several routes ; *Stranraer* (2½ hrs.) ; *Castle Douglas* (2½ hrs.) ; *Sanquhar* (1¾ hr.) ; *Muirkirk* (80 min.) ; *Cumnock* (1 hr.) ; etc.

Steamers. EXCURSION STEAMERS in summer, from South Quay, to the Clyde.

Amusements. *Pavilion,* Low Green (C 1 ; variety) ; *Gaiety,* Carrick St. (B 2).—GOLF, S. of the town.— RACECOURSE at Craigie, E. of the town, meetings in April, July and Sept. (Gold Cup).

History. Ayr, which received its first charter from William the Lion c. 1203, played a part in the wars of independence. One of Wallace's early exploits (1297) was the burning, with 500 inmates, of the ' Barns of Ayr,' a number of temporary barracks erected by Edward I ; and the castle near the mouth of the Ayr was destroyed by Bruce in 1298 to prevent its occupation by the English. The castle was, however, repaired and is said to have existed until Cromwell's time. The harbour in the Middle Ages was of both commercial and strategic importance; Perkin Warbeck sailed thence in 1497, to encounter his final defeat ; and James IV's fleet lay there in 1513. In 1315 the parliament which settled the succession of the Scottish crown in the event of Robert Bruce's death met at Ayr in the 12th cent. church of St. John the Baptist. This church was afterwards absorbed in the great fort (enclosing 12 acres) established by Cromwell in 1652, of which almost the only memorials are the church tower and the names of the streets (Fort St., Citadel Place) tha t mark its site.—The more recent interest of

Ayr centres in its associations with Burns, and the inhabitants never forgot his reference to—

> " Auld Ayr, wham ne'er a town surpasses
> For honest men and bonnie lasses."

John L. Macadam (1756–1836), the road-maker, was a less conspicuous native of Ayr.

Beyond the conspicuous statue of Burns (by Lawson ; 1891), outside the railway station (C 3), we turn to the right to enter Alloway St., which is continued by High Street. The little *Tam o' Shanter Inn* (B C 3) is the accepted starting-point of the exciting ride so graphically described by Burns ; it is now a museum (adm. 6*d.*) of the poet's relics. The *Wallace Tower* farther on, built in 1832, is popularly supposed to occupy the site of an older tower from which William Wallace made a daring escape. It displays the " drowsy dungeon clock " (referred to in the ' Twa Brigs ') from the old jail pulled down in 1826, and has, in a niche in front, a statue of Wallace, by the local sculptor James Thom (d. 1850), who afterwards worked in Trinity Church, New York. By the Kirk Port, on the same side, we may diverge to visit the *Auld Kirk*, where Burns was baptized. The church, erected with its kirkyard gateway in 1654–56 from funds supplied by the Common-wealth in payment for the earlier church of St. John (see above), was restored (as a war memorial) in 1952 ; it preserves three lofts (merchants', traders', and sailors') and the panelling of its original pulpit. The next turning on the right, beyond the site of the Old Tolbooth, leads from High St. to the **Auld Brig** (A B 2), which dates from the latter part of the 13th cent. and was for 500 years the only bridge of the town, though but a " poor narrow footpath of a street Where twa wheelbarrows tremble when they meet."

The *New Bridge* (A 2), the other interlocutor in Burns's famous dialogue the ' Twa Brigs,' was built in 1788 a little lower down the river. Its abutments, adorned with allegorical figures, roused the ire of the Auld Brig, whose prophecy that it would not last has come true. It was replaced in 1877 by a newer bridge of five arches, which has been repaired more than once.

At the end of High St. rises the tall spire of the *Town Buildings* (B 2 ; 1820–28) by Thos. Hamilton. Near the river, in Boat Vennel, is the 16th cent. *Loudoun Hall,* beautifully restored. In Fort St., close by, stands *Ayr Academy,* a school dating its origin from 1233. A little farther on Citadel Place (r.) leads to *Fort Castle* (B 1 ; adm. 6*d.,* 10–5), the restored tower of the church of St. John the Baptist. Beyond the tower Cassillis St. leads S. viâ Wellington Square, with the *County Buildings,* by Robt. Wallace (c. 1820–22 ; extended 1931). The *Low Green* (C 1) is a pleasant common where a band plays on summer evenings. Farther S. are Racecourse Road, and the municipal estate of *Belleisle,* with a golf course and hotel.

Inland from the station, the S. bank of the river Ayr is skirted by the pleasant river walk, while on its N. bank is the municipal estate of *Craigie*, with the racecourse.

FROM AYR TO BURNS'S MONUMENT AND THE BRIG O' DOON, 2¼ m. (bus). From Burns's statue we follow Beresford Terrace, prolonged by Carrick Rd., and then by Monument Road. Farther on the road follows the general line of Tam o' Shanter's memorable ride, but it has been somewhat straightened and some of the points mentioned in the poem lie a little aside.— Just before reaching Rozelle Woods we cross (1½ m.) a stream on which, a little above the bridge was " the ford Whare in the snaw the chapman smoored," and on the right, less than 100 yds. farther, is the cottage in the garden of which stood " the meikle stane Whare drucken Charlie brak's neck-bane." In the centre of (2 m.) **Alloway** village is *Burns's Cottage (C 2 ; adm. daily 6d., Sun from 2), in which Robert Burns (1759–1796) was born. Originally a ' clay biggin',' it was rebuilt by the poet's father with his own hands, and, after being an ale-house until 1880, it has been restored to its ' original aspect.' Visitors are shown the room where " a blast of Januar wind blew hansel in on Robin." The Burns family occupied their humble thatched abode from 1757 till 1766, afterwards removing to *Mount Oliphant*, a farm c. 1½ m. to the S.E., where they stayed until 1777. Adjoining is a museum, with a most interesting collection of Burns relics, including Burns's family Bible (bought for £1700), many MSS., letters, editions of the works, engravings, and illustrations.

The Cottage stood on the left side of the old road, and some distance to the right lies *Cambusdoon*, in the park of which was " the cairn Whare hunters fand the murder'd bairn."

About ⅓ m. farther on stands (left) old *Alloway Kirk* (C 2), a ruin long before Burns's day and now reduced to four bare walls with gables and a bell-cote. Through the E. window Tam o' Shanter here beheld the witches' orgy. In the church-yard is buried Burns's father (1721–84 ; tombstone re-erected in 1881). Opposite the *Burns Monument Hotel* (RB. 25/, P. 11 gs.) rises the **Burns Monument** (adm. daily 6d., Sun. from 2), built in 1820 by Hamilton, an inappropriate Grecian round temple like a choragic monument with nine fluted Corinthian columns. Within are preserved the Bibles exchanged by Burns and ' Highland Mary,' Jean Armour's wedding ring, and many other relics. In a grotto in the garden are rude but spirited figures of ' Tam o' Shanter ' and ' Souter Johnnie ' by Thom (p. 173).—Close by the Doon is spanned by two bridges. The bridge with a single arch is the *Auld Brig o' Doon*, the keystone of which was won barely in time by Tam's stout nag ' Meg,' in their flight from the witches, who, of course, dared not cross running water. In a cottage garden on a small tributary of

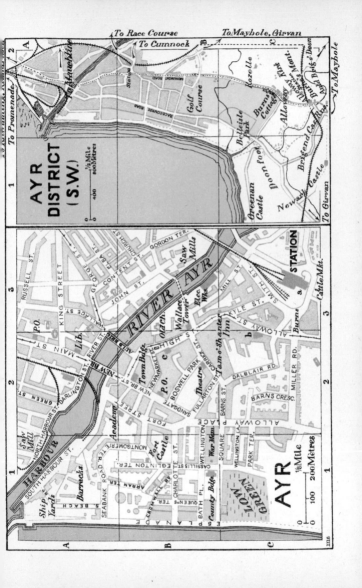

the Doon is " the thorn aboon the well, Whare Mungo's mither hanged hersel'." After crossing the Doon Tam had a ride of c. 12 m. viâ Maybole and Kirkoswald to his farm of Shanter (p. 176).

Between the bridges is the *Banks o' Doon Tea Garden* (adm. 6*d*.), the pleasant grounds of which extend to the river and contain a shell grotto.

FROM AYR TO HYNDFORD BRIDGE (Lanark, Edinburgh), 45 m. (A 70), motor-bus to Muirkirk in 1⅓ hr. and thence to Lanark in 70 min. The road runs due E.—3¾ m. (l.) *Sundrum Castle Hotel* (RB. 24/, P. 12 gs.), in pleasant grounds overlooking the Coyle Water, preserves its 14th cent. tower.— At (5 m.) *Coylton* we enter the productive Ayrshire coalfield, destined for further development.—11½ m. *Ochiltree* (Inn) is the ' Barbie ' of ' The House with the Green Shutters,' by George Douglas Brown (1869–1902) who was born in the village. John Knox, at the age of 60 (1564), married the 17-year-old heiress of Ochiltree House (demolished). Auchinleck House (Rte. 9B) lies 1 m. N.

Beyond (16 m.) *Cumnock* and (18½ m.) *Lugar* (Rte. 9B) our route skirts the dreary *Airds Moss* (l.), where, in a sharp skirmish between Covenanters and Royalists in 1680, Richard Cameron was slain, " leaving his name to a religious sect and to a renowned regiment in the British Army."—26 m. *Muirkirk* (Eglinton Arms) has large ironworks. To the S. rises *Cairntable* (1944 ft.).

A cairn at Muirkirk marks the site of Macadam's tar works (1756–1827).— In the hills c. 5 m. N.E. is *Priesthill*, the farm where John Brown the Covenanter was shot in the presence of his wife and family by Claverhouse in 1685 (monument).

We now enter Lanarkshire and soon enjoy a good view (r.) of the Douglas valley.—36 m. **Douglas** (*Douglas Arms*, RB. 18/, P. 8 gs. ; 2260 inhab.) is a quaint little town, with collieries of increasing importance.

To the N.E. stood *Douglas Castle* (permit for the grounds from the Estates Office, Springhill), rebuilt in 1759 and demolished, except for the chapel and porch, in 1938–48 when a new coal-seam was opened beneath it. Of Scott's ' Castle Dangerous ' there remains but a small fragment close by.

In the churchyard is the chancel of the *Church of St. Bride*, founded by the 12th cent. and containing (N. side) the canopied tombs (with effigies) of " the good Sir James of Douglas, killed in battle with the moors in Spain while on his way to the Holy Land " with the heart of Bruce (1330), and of Archibald, 5th Earl of Douglas (d. 1439). On the S. side is the canopied tomb (with effigies) of James, Earl of Douglas (d. 1443) and his wife, Beatrice Sinclair, daughter of the Earl of Orkney ; along the base are the upright figures of their ten children. In the centre is the tomb, with a figure in pink and white alabaster, of Lucy Elizabeth Douglas of Douglas, Countess of Home (1805–77). E. of it are the hearts, in leaden caskets, of the Good Sir James and of Archibald, Earl of Angus, ' Bell the Cat ' (d. 1514, see p. 10). To the S.W. of the building is a tower of 1618 containing a clock dated 1565, traditionally gifted by Mary, Queen of Scots. Near by, overlooking the river, is a monument commemorating the 200th anniversary (1889) of the raising, by James, Earl of Angus (statue), of the 26th or Cameronian Regiment. He fell in command at Steinkirk (1692).

At (38 m.) *Castle Mains* we join A 74, but soon bear r., following the Douglas water.—45 m. *Hyndford Bridge* (Rte. 9A). Here A 73 bears l. for Lanark (3 m.), while A 70 leads N. to Carstairs and Edinburgh.

B. From Ayr to Girvan by the Coast

COAST ROAD (A 719 and A 77), 21½ m., affording charming sea-views (Arran ; Ailsa Craig). Motor-bus viâ Maybole and Maidens (1 hr.) ; and to Maybole viâ Dunure.

Quitting Ayr by Racecourse Road we cross the Doon at (2 m.) *Doonfoot*. To the left is *Newark Castle* and to the right the ruined *Greenan Castle*. Farther on the former naval station, H.M.S. *Scotia*, has been fitted up as a holiday camp (view of Ayr), beyond which is the grassy cape called *Heads of Ayr*.—8 m. *Dunure*, a small seaside resort and fishing village below the road, retains a fragment of its old castle, in which an earl of Cassillis is said to have roasted the commendator of Crossraguel Abbey (p. 198) over a slow fire until the victim consented to surrender the abbey lands.

Brown Carrick (940 ft.), due E. of Dunure, commands one of the widest views in S. Scotland.

The view opens across Culzean Bay to Culzean Castle, then, traversing the ' Electric Brae ' where an optical illusion makes a downhill seem an uphill, we are joined by the Maybole road at (11 m.) *Pennyglen*.—13 m. **Culzean Castle** (N.T. ; pron. ' Cullean ') is a Gothic structure built for the 10th Earl of Cassillis by Robert Adam in 1771–92 around an ancient tower of the Kennedys. The public may visit the beautiful policies and the castle (adm. 1/6 to each, children 6*d*., cars 1/ ; castle closed Dec.–Feb.), the notable features of which are the Round Drawing Room with its circular carpet and special furniture (also by Adam), the fine plaster ceilings (restored in 1954), and the magnificent Oval Staircase. In 1946 the top flat of the castle was presented to Gen. Eisenhower as a Scottish residence ; a group of houses for ex-service men has been erected in the grounds. The garden (tea-room) contains rare shrubs and plants.

Culzean has been, ever since the 15th cent., in the hands of the Kennedys, who succeeded the earls of Carrick and afterwards became earls of Cassillis. It is still the residence of the Marquess of Ailsa. Of this powerful family the popular rhyme goes—

> " 'Twixt Wigtown and the town of Ayr
> Portpatrick and the Cruives of Cree,
> No man may think for to bide there
> Unless he court St. Kennedie."

At the foot of the rock on which the castle stands are the Coves of Culzean, rock caves used as hiding-places in troublous times and the rendezvous of fairies on Hallowe'en.

15¼ m. *Maidens*, a popular little village with a harbour, lies 1½ m. W. of Kirkoswald (p. 198) and c. 1 m. N. of Shanter farm, though Tam's house no longer stands. 16½ m. **Turnberry** (*Hotel*, with indoor swimming pool, RB. from 45/, P. 20–22½ gs.) is a noted golfing centre, with two full courses (6/–7/6 per day). Remains of its war-time airfield are still visible. Robert Bruce (1274–1329), son of a lord of Annandale whose wife was a countess of Carrick, is said to have been born in *Turnberry Castle*, the scanty ruins of which adjoin the lighthouse, probably built on its courtyard (but comp. p. 98). According to the story Bruce, lured from his retreat in Arran by a false (or mystic) signal-fire at Turnberry, landed here in 1307 to begin the fight for freedom that ended at Bannockburn (1314). —21½ m. **Girvan,** see Rte. 22.

C. From Ayr to Dalmellington and Dalry

22 m. Motor-Bus in 1½ hr. viâ Carsphairn (A 713) going on to New Galloway and Castle Douglas ; the hilly old road (B 729, 7000) viâ Kendoon Loch has better views.—Railway on weekdays as far as (15 m.) Dalmellington (35 min.).

Beyond (6½ m.) *Hollybush* (Hollybush House, with fine grounds and fishing, RB. 25/, P. 12 gs.) A 713 approaches the Doon, the valley of which it ascends all the way to Dalmellington.—At (9½ m.) *Patna* the hills begin to close in and we enter a coal-mining region.—15 m. **Dalmellington** (*Eglinton*, RB. 16/), ¾ m. from the river, is a colliery town (4700 inhab.) with a lofty mote-hill near the site of Dalmelling Priory, the only Gilbertine house in Scotland (1221–35), founded by Walter II Stewart.

The Doon, issuing from Loch Doon, 3 m. S. (by road), threads the narrow and romantic *Ness Glen*, which is open to visitors on Sat. (entrance at the S. end only). —**Loch Doon,** one of the largest lochs in the south of Scotland, offers pleasant though not grand scenery, especially toward its S. end. The loch, now 5½ m. long and ½–1 m. wide, has been enlarged since its conversion into a power reservoir. The ruins of *Doon Castle*, formerly on an islet at the S. end, have been re-erected beside the road which skirts the W. bank for 5 m. A new road leading W. from Loch Doon to (2½ m.) *Loch Riccur* is continued by a footpath to *Balloch Lodge* and thence by road to (8 m.) *Craiglure*, on the moorland road 4 m. S. of *Tairlaw* bus terminus and 7 m. S. of *Straiton* (p. 198).—The country S. of Loch Doon is wild and difficult, and as lonely as any in Scotland. By ascending the stream of Gala Lane for c. 3 m., then diverging to the right to reach (c. 3 m. more) the summit ridge of *Mullwharchar* (2270 ft.) we may descend to (2 m. more) *Loch Enoch*, below the slopes of Merrick. Thence to Loch Trool, see p. 192. To the E. of Gala Lane lie the mountains known as the *Rhinns of Kells*, of which *Corserine* (2668 ft.), *Carlin's Cairn* (2650 ft.), and *Meikle Millyea* (2446 ft.) are the highest points.

Quitting Dalmellington the road ascends alongside the Muck Water, passing (17 m.) the turning for Loch Doon. Beyond (19 m.) *Polnaskie Bridge*, beside the little *Loch Muck*, we are in Kirkcudbrightshire. On the right appears Loch Doon. We cross the Deugh at (24 m.) *Lagwine Well*.—25 m. **Carsphairn** (*Salutation*, RB. 27/6, P. 11 gs.), a small village, is a good starting-point for ascents in the Rhinns of Kells

c. 6 m. S.W. (see above), and for *Cairnsmore of Carsphairn* (2612 ft.), 3 m. N.E.

> " There's Cairnsmore of Fleet, there's Cairnsmore of Dee,
> But Cairnsmore of Carsphairn is the highest of a' three."

Two roads lead from Carsphairn to Dalry. The hillier road on the E. may be used for the return (see below); we now turn right across the Deugh on A 713 and traverse the region known as the *Glenkens*, noted for mountain scenery and pastoral farming. At (28½ m.) the confluence of the Polmaddy Burn the scanty ruins of *Dundeugh Castle* rise on the left beyond the Deugh, and farther on we skirt *Garsfad Loch* and *Earlston Loch*, two power-reservoirs on the Ken. Below the dam at the foot of the second loch we cross the Ken by (32½ m.) *Allangibbon Bridge*; A 762 diverges r. before the bridge for New Galloway (3¼ m.) avoiding Dalry. Just to the right is *Earlston Tower* (1655).—34 m. *Dalry*, and thence to New Galloway, Castle Douglas, and the south, see Rte. 20.

Returning from Dalry, we turn left on B 7000, off the Moniaive road (A 702) and follow a hilly course on the E. side of the Glenkens, with the reservoirs and Kendoon power-station below us on the left.—Beyond (6 m.) the *High Bridge of Ken*, in a charming site, we join A 729 and skirt the new *Kendoon Loch*, at the confluence of Ken and Deugh, which has submerged the narrow gorge called the Tinkler's Loup.— A pile of boulders in *Knockgray Park*, ½ m. short of Carsphairn, is said to mark the spot where the last wild deer in S. Scotland was killed.—10 m. *Carsphairn*, see above.

From Ayr to *Glasgow*, see Rtes. 15, 16; to *Girvan* and *Stranraer*, see Rte. 22; to *Kilmarnock* and to *Mauchline*, see Rte. 16.

18. DUMFRIES AND ITS ENVIRONS

DUMFRIES (26,325 inhab.), the ancient chief town of the S.W. Border counties, addressed by Burns, to whom it owes much of its fame, as " Maggie by the Banks o' Nith, A dame with pride eneuch," is well situated on the left bank of the Nith, about 7 m. from its mouth. *Maxwelltown*, on the opposite (Kirkcudbrightshire) side of the river, was incorporated with Dumfries in 1929.

Hotels. Station (a; 3), RB. 31/6, D. from 12/6, P. daily 50/6; **County** (b; 5), RB. 30/, P. 12 gs.; **Cairndale,** English St., RB. 35/, P. 15 gs.; **King's Arms** (c; 5), High Street, RB. 24/6, P. 12 gs.; **Nithsdale,** St. Mary's St., near the station, RB. 21/, P. 9 gs.; **Eden,** English St., RB. 17/6, P. 10 gs.; **Newton House,** 1½ m. N.W. on A 76, with fishing, RB. 21/ P. 10 gs.—*Oughton's Restaurant*, Church Place.

Post Office (Pl. 2), Gt. King Street.

Motor-Buses. Local services to *Maxwelltown, Lincluden, Locharbriggs,* etc. Also daily to *Annan* (50 min.) and *Carlisle* (1¾ hr.); to *Thornhill* (½ hr.) and *Sanquhar* (1 hr.); to *New Abbey* (25 min.), *Carsethorn,* and *Southwick* (55 min.), going on to

Rockcliffe or *Southerness* (65 min.) ;
to *Corsock* ;   to *Lochmaben* and
Lockerbie (40 min.) ;   to *Moffat* (1
hr.) ;   to *Moniaive* (50 min.) ;   to
Dalbeattie (40 min.) and *Kippford*
(1 hr.) ;   to *Castle Douglas* (55 min.)
and *Kirkcudbright* (1¼ hr.) or *Stranraer* (3¾ hrs.) ; to *Kilmarnock* (2¾ hrs.)

and *Glasgow* (3 hrs. 50 mins.) ;   to
Edinburgh (3 hrs. 20 min.) ; etc.
   Boating on the Nith, between the
New Bridge and Lincluden.—FISHING
in the Nith (salmon and trout) and in
Glenkiln Reservoir (trout) ;   rates
on application to the Municipal
Chambers.

History. Dumfries was made a royal burgh by David I in the 12th cent. and
seems to have grown with some rapidity. In 1300 Edward I seized and added
to the castle (now vanished) beneath which the original village grew up. In

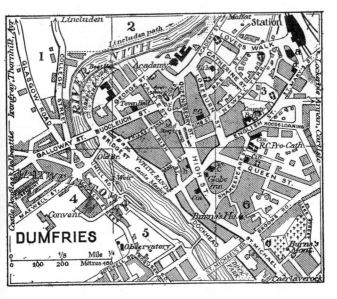

1306 the murder of Comyn by Bruce (see below) rekindled the War of Independence. Dumfries, burned by the English in 1448 and 1536 and sacked in 1570,
had its share also in the trials of Scotland under Charles I and Charles II. In
1745 Prince Charles Stewart, on his retreat from Derby, halted in Dumfries and
treated the town with severity on account of its hostility to him on his southward
march. Robert Burns removed from Ellisland (p. 181) to Dumfries in Dec. 1791,
and there served as an excise officer and wrote nearly a hundred of his songs.
His first house was in the Wee Vennel (now Bank St.), but he removed in 1793 to
Mill Vennel (now Burns St.), where he died in 1796. In 1940–45 Dumfries was
the headquarters of the Norwegians in Britain, an event commemorated by a
tablet in St. Michael's church, and a font in the suburban church of Troqueer,
as well as by a model Viking ship in the Municipal Chambers.

   In the High St. is the *County Hotel*, formerly the Commercial Hotel, where Charles Stewart held a council in the

panelled room now used as a sitting-room. A little farther down (S.) a narrow passage on the left leads to the *Globe Tavern* (Pl. 5), a favoured ' howff ' of Burns, in which his chair, punch-bowl, jug, and ladle are exhibited. High St. is continued S. by St. Michael's St., off which (left) runs Burns St., leading to **Burns's House** (Pl. 6 ; adm. 6*d.* ; 10–5 or 9 daily). The upper room, in which Burns died, contains numerous personal relics and memorials of the poet, besides MSS. and books presented to the collection by Sir James Barrie.—Farther on in St. Michael's St. is the church of St. Michael (Pl. 6), built in 1745–54 on the site of an older edifice. A tablet on a pillar near the entrance marks Burns's pew. The path immediately to the left as we enter its pre-cincts leads straight to the corner in which Burns was at first buried. Thence conspicuous (to the right) is **Burns's Tomb**, a mausoleum in the form of a Grecian temple, to which his remains were transferred in 1815. It contains a sculptured group (by Turnerelli) depicting the Muse of Poetry finding Burns at the plough (adm. daily in summer ; gratuity). Here rest also Jean Armour (d. 1834), Burns's wife, and several of his children. A grey granite pyramid near the mausoleum marks the tomb of three Covenanters executed, two in 1667, one in 1685.

We return to High St., which leads N. to Greyfriars church, passing the *Mid Steeple* (1707), the former Town House, now occupied by shops. Beyond is Queensberry Square and farther on, on the right, is the ' Hole i' the Wa',' another tavern with relics of Burns. *Greyfriars Church* (Pl. 2), a red building (1866–67) with a tall spire, in front of which is a statue of Burns, by Mrs. D. O. Hill (1882), stands on the site of the old castle, to the W. and S. of which extended the Greyfriars' house.

In the 13th cent. Franciscan friary founded by Alan, lord of Galloway, or his daughter Devorguilia (see below), Duns Scotus is believed to have taken the habit in 1278. It was in the old church of the friary, in 1306, that Robert Bruce quarrelled with John, ' the Red Comyn,' and stabbed him before the altar. To his exclamation as he rushed out, " I doubt I have slain the Comyn," his retainer Roger Kirkpatrick replied, " I'll mak siccar," and entered the church to finish the bloody deed. A tablet on a wine shop in Castle St. marks the site.—A little to the N.E. are the imposing red buildings (Pl. 2 ; 1897) of *Dumfries Academy*, at which Sir James Barrie was a pupil.

Friars' Vennel and the parallel Buccleuch St. (Pl. 2) descend W. from Castle St. to the bus station on the banks of the Nith, the most attractive point in Dumfries. The *Municipal Chambers* in Buccleuch St. contain a portrait of Wm. Stothert by Raeburn, in the reception room, in the window of which appears St. Michael, patron saint of Dumfries, with ' A Loreburn,' the old war-cry, below.

Four bridges cross the Nith to Maxwelltown, called Bridgend until 1810 and an independent municipality until 1929, in which are hosiery mills, a large

Roman Catholic nunnery, and an *Observatory and Museum* (Pl. 5 ; adm. free, 10–7 or 11–5 ; Sun. 2–7 Apr.–Oct.), with a round tower containing a camera obscura (6*d.*) and a collection of strong local interest, including the ' Siller Gun ' presented as a ' challenge ' trophy by James VI to encourage the use of firearms. The *New Bridge*, erected in 1792, was widened in 1893. The *Old Bridge* (Pl. 4 ; for foot passengers only), built in the 13th cent. by Devorguilla Balliol (p. 182), originally with nine arches, now has six. The *Suspension Bridge*, farther down, dates from 1876. *St. Michael's Bridge*, still lower, was opened in 1927.

EXCURSIONS FROM DUMFRIES

*Lincluden Abbey (adm. 3*d.*, 10–4 or 7, Sun. from 2) is a picturesque ruin at the junction of the Cluden and the Nith, still delightfully situated in spite of the near-by suburb (bus from Queensberry Sq.). The abbey, founded before 1174 by Uchtred, lord of Galloway, for Benedictine nuns and converted into a collegiate foundation in 1389 by Archibald the Grim, 3rd Earl of Douglas, is now represented by the choir and part of the S. transept of its small but beautiful church (15th cent.). The choir is entered through a stone screen, noteworthy for its carvings from the Life of Christ with angels above. On the N. side is the richly decorated canopied tomb (1409–24) of Margaret, Countess of Douglas (d. about 1430) and daughter of Robert III, with a mutilated effigy. Opposite are three fine sedilia. The carved doorway beside Margaret's tomb, with the Douglas heart and chalices above it, admits to the sacristy. The window-tracery is almost wholly gone, but the mouldings throughout the church are bold and rich. Of the domestic buildings (15–16th cent.) to the N. little remains but to the E. the terraces of the garden survive. Lincluden was a favourite resort of Burns, who here beheld his ' Vision of Libertie.'

Ellisland, the farm (170 acres) by the bank of the Nith which Robert Burns, making " a poet's choice but not a farmer's," rented in 1788–91 from Patrick Millar of Dalswinton, lies 6 m. N. of Dumfries, by the Glasgow road, and is best visited thence by road (Penpont or Kilmarnock bus). The road passes (3½ m.) *Holywood*, where the church (r. ; near the railway) is built of the stones of the Premonstratensian priory of Dercongal founded here before 1225.—Less than ½ m. short of the cart road diverging on the right for the farm we pass the site of *Old Dunscore Church*, with the grave of Grierson of Lag (see p. 184).—At Ellisland Burns's room is shown (gratuity) and the stackyard, where ' Mary in Heaven ' was composed, and the ' Tam o' Shanter Walk ' by the river may be visited. The farm has been presented to Dumfries as a national possession.

CAERLAVEROCK CASTLE, 8 m. S. of Dumfries, near the marshy shore of the Solway between the Nith and the Lochar, may be reached by either of two roads (bus on Sat., or daily to Glencaple, 2 m. N.). The upper (l.) road passes (5½ m.) just to the W. of the church of *Caerlaverock* ; in the churchyard lies Robert Paterson (1715–1801), Scott's ' Old Mortality ' a humble stonecutter who for forty years wandered over Scotland, repairing the scattered tombs of Covenanters.

The alias is said to be the ' happy thought ' of a young lady of Galloway who was entertaining a young advocate, named Walter Scott, in the parlour when the stonecutter happened to call at the back-door. Lockhart states that the only actual meeting between Scott and ' Old Mortality ' occurred in Dunnottar churchyard in 1793.

The lower road (r. ;   B 725), passing (1½ m.) the *Crichton Royal Institute*. a mental hospital founded in 1835 instead of a contemplated university, skirts for its last five miles the estuary of the Nith, viâ (5½ m.) *Glencaple* (Nith, RB. 17/6, P. 10 gs.), a little bathing place, sometimes regarded as the ' Portanferry ' of ' Guy Mannering ' (but comp. p. 189).

Caerlaverock Castle, the 'Ellangowan' of 'Guy Mannering', is a fine ruin dating from c. 1290.

The castle belonged to the Maxwells, afterwards Earls of Nithsdale. From their descendants the Lords Herries, it passed to the Duke of Norfolk who in 1946 placed it in the care of the Ministry of Works. Caerlaverock was captured in 1300 by Edward I after a siege of two days, minutely described in ' The Roll of Caerlaverock,' a rhymed Norman-French chronicle by an eye-witness. In 1312 Sir Eustace Maxwell, keeper of the castle, supported Bruce who ordered it to be partly dismantled. The castle, once more taken by the English, was captured in 1355 by Sir Roger Kirkpatrick, who seems to have destroyed much of the building. Caerlaverock changed hands again and in 1570 the Earl of Sussex took it with little damage. Repaired by Lord Maxwell in 1593 and extended in 1634 by the first earl of Nithsdale, the castle capitulated to the Covenanters in 1640 after a siege of thirteen weeks, and was thereafter suffered to fall into ruin.—Adm. 6d., 10–4 or 7, Sun. from 2.

The castle (mostly of the 15th cent.) is triangular in plan, an unusual ·design, with machicolated round towers at the angles, that on the S.W. being called Murdoch's Tower (1347) as the prison of Murdoch, Duke of Albany, in 1425 (p. 217), while that on the S.E. is ruinous. Over the gateway between two splendid towers (at the N. apex) is the Maxwell crest and motto. The interior dates from the 17th cent. and preserves fine carving over the windows.

The road (A 710) to SWEETHEART ABBEY (bus in 25 min.), runs due S. from Maxwelltown, following the valley of the Nith at some distance from the river. From (5¾ m.) *Whinny-hill* we have a fine view of Dumfries and the valley. In front of us the bulky mass of Criffel is conspicuous, at the foot of which lies (7½ m.) the pleasant village of *New Abbey* (Abbey Arms, RB. 17/, P. 7 gs. ; Criffel Inn, RB. 17/6, P. 8 gs.), with a tall Waterloo Monument on the height beyond it.

Incorporated in a cottage, on the left, is a stone from the abbey representing three ladies in a boat, who, according to tradition, are supposed to have brought the stone for the abbey across the Nith.

*Sweetheart Abbey or **New Abbey** (adm. 6d., 10–4 or 7, Sun. from 2) was founded in 1273 for Cistercians from Dundrennan by Devorguilla, foundress of Balliol College, Oxford, and widow of John Balliol, father of the Scottish king. With Devorguilla, who was buried in front of the high altar, was interred her husband's heart, carefully treasured by her ; whence the abbey obtained its name of Dulce Cor or Sweetheart Abbey. Fragments of her desecrated grave have been incorporated in a reconstructed tomb in the S. transept. The ruined church (E.E. with some Dec. alterations) retains all the main arches and part of the clerestory of the nave (oddly combined with an inside passage to form a triforium), besides considerable remains of the transepts and choir, and a central tower 90 ft. high. The tracery of the main E. window is fairly intact. The great W. window, strengthened by masonry in the 14th cent., consists of three lights surmounted by a fine wheel. High in the gable is a trefoil. The aisle of the S. transept alone retains the roof, which is groined, with shields at the intersections. On one of these appear two pastoral staves, surmounted by a heart ; on another is the inscription ' Chus tim of nid ' (choose time of need). The plain W. door of the cloister, and the window erected on the site of the chapter house (probably from the refectory) are about all that is left of the domestic buildings.

FROM DUMFRIES TO DALBEATTIE VIA NEW ABBEY (A 710), a beautiful round of 26 m. This road encircles **Criffel** (1866 ft.), a conspicuous object in all this region, easily ascended in 2 hrs. by following up the Glen Burn. The wide view from the top includes the summits of the Lake District, the Isle of Man, the Dumfriesshire and Galloway hills, and the valley of the Nith.—Beyond (7½ m.) *New Abbey* the road turns S. to (12½ m.) *Kirkbean*, where the church contains a memorial font to Paul Jones, presented by the U.S. Navy. *Carsethorn* (Steamboat Inn), a fishing village, lies 1 m. E., while 2½ m. S.E. is *Arbigland*, the estate on which was born John Paul, later known as Paul Jones (1747–92), the gardener's son and slave trader who founded the American navy. Best reached by the lane (to Powillimount) on the left of A 710 beyond the Arbigland lodge (l.). A little farther on we leave on the left a road to *Southerness* (Paul Jones, RB. 22/6, P. 9½ gs.), 2¼ m. S., a seaside hamlet (properly Satterness) with extensive sands, golf links, and a disused lighthouse.—16½ m. *Southwick* is the junction of an inland road to Dalbeattie (A 745), affording charmingly varied views, passes *Sandyhills Bay* and just N. of *Portling*, with its rocky cliffs, S.W. of which is *Port o' Warren*, another little bay.—21 m. *Colvend* is 1½ m. E. of *Rockcliffe* (Baron's Craig, RB. 25/, P. 11 gs.), a sheltered seaside resort on the Urr estuary. *Rough Island* (N.T.), a tidal islet, is a bird sanctuary.—Thence it is 5 m. to *Dalbeattie* (Rte. 19).

FROM DUMFRIES TO MONIAIVE, 17½ m. (bus in 50 min.) by a road diverging left from A 76 at (1½ m.) Newton House (see p. 178) and ascending the valleys of the Cluden and the Cairn.

To the left, c. 1 m. farther, is a road to **Terregles** (1½ m.), the mansion of Lord Herries (rebuilt 1789). This was probably the last resting-place of Queen Mary in 1568 before her ill-fated journey south into England (comp. p. 188). Built on to the late 18th cent. parish church is *Terregles Choir* (1583, restored 1878), an interesting example of 16th cent. Gothic work. It contains two 16th cent. Maxwell tombs, two stalls from Lincluden, and a medieval panel part of the Blessed Virgin.

In the churchyard of (5 m.) *Irongray* a stone erected by the author of ' Waverley ' in 1831 commemorates Helen Walker (d. 1791), from whom the character of Jeannie Deans in ' The Heart of Midlothian ' was drawn. On a knoll about ¼ hr. W. of the church is the tomb of two Covenanters with a characteristic inscription (1685). From Irongray we can ascend either side of the stream.—10½ m. *Dunscore* (George, RB. 14/) gives name to the parish in which are both the famous farms of Craigenputtock and Ellisland.

About 1½ m. N.E. of the village is the ruined tower of *Lag*, seat of Sir Robert Grierson (1650–1736), the noted ' persecutor ' of the Covenanters and Scott's Sir Robert Redgauntlet.—The road to (6 m.) Craigenputtock leads W. from the village and passes (3 m.) the ruined tower of *Bogrie*. **Craigenputtock,** a moorland farm of 773 acres inherited by Mrs. Carlyle, was in 1828–34 the home of Thomas Carlyle and Jane Welsh, his wife. Here ' Sartor Resartus ' was written and Lord Jeffrey and Emerson entertained. The estate was bequeathed by Carlyle (d. 1881) to Edinburgh University for the purpose of founding ten bursaries or scholarships. —The road goes on to (11 m.) *Corsock*.—For *Ellisland*, see p. 181.

Beyond a road-fork for Thornhill, on the right, appears *Maxwelton House*, birthplace of ' Annie Laurie ' (1682–1761), the subject of perhaps the most popular song in the language. The house incorporates part of the old castle of Glencairn, and was built after 1611 by Annie's great-grandfather.

The original song was written about 1700 by William Douglas of Fingland ; the more modern version by Lady John Scott in 1835.—Annie Laurie, who married Alexander Fergusson, died at *Craigdarroch*, c. 2½ m. W. of Moniaive, and is said to be buried in Glencairn Church (see below). At Craigdarroch is preserved ' The Whistle,' of Burns's ballad.

We join A 702, passing *Glencairn Church*.—17½ m. **Moniaive** (*Craigdarroch Arms*, RB. 17/6, P. 8 gs.), with an old cross (1638), is situated in quiet pastoral scenery at the junction of the three streams that form the Cairn. Above the village is a monument, erected near his birthplace, to James Renwick (1662–88), the last Covenanter martyr.

FROM MONIAIVE TO THORNHILL, A 702 (8 m. ; motor-bus in ½ hr.). We descend the Shinnel Water, leaving on our left (4⅔ m.) *Tynron Doon*, a conical hill once bearing a fortalice in which Bruce sought temporary refuge after the murder of Comyn (p. 180). We cross the Scar Water near its junction with the Shinnel.—6 m. *Penpont* (Volunteer Arms, RB. 16/6, P. 8½ gs.).—8 m. *Thornhill*, see p. 101.

FROM DUMFRIES TO MOFFAT, 21½ m. (A 701). The road is unattractive as far as (4½ m.) *Amisfield*, to the left of which is Amisfield Tower (c. 1600), a well-preserved stronghold of the Charteris family.—7½ m. *Bridge of Ae*. To the left is the village of *Ae* (2½ m.), founded by the Forestry Commission in 1947.— Beside a bridge over the Garrel or Garvald Water (10½ m.) are the remains of *Garvald* church ; the ruins called Wallace's House (in the forest), ¾ m. upstream, are said to represent a tower garrisoned by Wallace in 1297, while Blue Cairn, on the S.E. slope of *Queensberry* (2285 ft.), the S. outpost of the Lowther Hills, is supposed to mark the site of a victory of his.—At (13½ m.) *St. Ann's* we cross the Kinnel Water which flows through the charming *Raehills Glen*.—16 m. To the right is *Lochwood Tower*, a ruined hold of the Johnstones, situated in a wood of ancient oaks and formerly so protected by bogs that James VI declared that its builder must have been " a knave at heart." The burning of Lochwood **by** the Maxwells in 1592 was avenged at Dryfe Sands in 1593. Only a couple of va lted rooms remain.—19¼ m. *Beattock* (Rte. 9A).—21½ m. *Moffat* (Rte. 8).

19. FROM DUMFRIES TO NEWTON STEWART
BY DALBEATTIE AND KIRKCUDBRIGHT

Road, 56 m.—A 711. 13½ m. **Dalbeattie.**—A 745. 19½ m. **Castle Douglas.**—
A 75, A 711. 29½ m. **Kirkcudbright.**—A 755, A 75. 38 m. *Gatehouse of Fleet.*—
50 m. *Creetown.*—56 m. **Newton Stewart.**

Railway to Kirkcudbright, 30 m. in 70 min. Principal Stations : 14¼ m.
Dalbeattie.—19¾ m. **Castle Douglas.**—26½ m. *Tarff.*—30 m. **Kirkcudbright.** To
Newton Stewart and *Stranraer*, see Rte. 20.

Dumfries, see Rte. 18. The road crosses the Nith to *Maxwelltown*, and enters Kirkcudbrightshire, bearing left on to
A 711. At (6 m.) *Lochanhead*, where the scenery assumes a
moorland character, a lane on the right passes *Hills Tower*
(1527), still inhabited, with its contemporary yett. As we
approach (8½ m.) *Beeswing* we have a fine view of Criffel, with
Lotus Hill in the foreground. Loch Arthur lies ½ m. E. on
the New Abbey road.—10½ m. *Kirkgunzeon* (pron. Kirk-
gunnion), i.e. the church of St. Wynnin, lies near the ruined
towers of *Drumcoltran* (16th cent. ; 1½ m. N.) and *Corra*, the
latter an old seat of the Maxwells.

13½ m. **Dalbeattie** (*Maxwell Arms*, RB. 25/, P. £14 ; *Galloway
Arms*, RB. 19/6, P. 8 gs. ; *Crown*, RB. 14/6), a prettily
situated little town (3285 inhab.) on the Urr, is built of grey
granite from the quarries that form its main wealth. It has a
golf course and is a starting-point for several pretty excursions.

Near the tower called Buittle Place, c. 1¼ m. W. of Dalbeattie, stood the old
castle of *Buittle*, birthplace of John Balliol (1249–1315), where his mother
Devorguilla (p. 182) signed the charter of Balliol College in 1282.

The *Mote of Urr* (78 ft. high), c. 2½ m. N. of Dalbeattie, consisting of an almost
circular mound (91 by 76 ft.) surrounded by a deep trench and standing on a
platform (500 by 216 ft.) likewise within a foss, is one of the finest examples in
Britain of this variety of Saxon and early Norman fortification. The road goes
on, beside the picturesque Urr Water, viâ *Haugh of Urr* (Inn) and (6 m.) the Old
Bridge of Urr, to (11 m.) *Corsock* (p. 184).

From Dalbeattie to Dundrennan Abbey, 13 m. (motor-bus in 35 min.
going on to Kirkcudbright). The road (A 711), after crossing the Urr, runs S.
to (3½ m.) *Palnackie*, passing (r.) a curious rock known as the ' Lion's Face.'
At 4½ m. the right-hand road (B 736) goes to Castle Douglas (5 m.), while ours
on the left diverges for the 12th cent. tower of *Orchardton*, the only round tower
in Galloway (key at farm).—Conspicuous on our right is Screel Hill (1120 ft.).
We pass *Screel House* (r.) and (l.) *Orchardton House*, now a hotel (P. 7 gs., unlic.),
to reach (8 m.) *Auchencairn* (Auchencairn Arms ; Balcary House, 1½ m. S.E.,
RB. from 18/6, P. 8 gs.), a village of some size on a bay of the Solway, visited for
bathing. The hilly road goes on S.W. to (13 m.) *Dundrennan Abbey* (p. 187).
—*Hestan Island*, at the mouth of Auchencairn Bay, is the ' Isle Rathan ' of
Crockett's ' Raiders.'

Motor-buses from Dalbeattie to (4 m.) *Kippford* (Anchor, P. 10 gs. ; Glencairn Rest., unlic., P. 20/), a charming yachting and golfing resort, in ¼ hr. ;
and to Castle Douglas (½ hr.) viâ Haugh of Urr (see above).

We cross Buittle Bridge and turn right (A 745).—19½ m.
Castle Douglas (*King's Arms*, RB. 21/, P. 10 gs. ; *Douglas
Arms*, RB. 20/, P. 9 gs. ; *Imperial*, similar charges ; *Crown*,
RB. 19/6, P. 8½ gs. ; *Royal, Victoria*, RB. 18/6.—*Ernespie*

House, ¾ m. N., RB. 24/, P. 10 gs.), a busy country town
(3325 inhab.) of comparatively recent growth, is well situated
near the N. end of *Carlingwark Loch* (¾ m. long, ¼ m. broad).
The town, originally known as Causewayend, from an old
causeway leading to one of the wooded islets in the loch, and
then as Carlingwark, received its present name in 1789 from
a manufacturer named Douglas, who bought the town. The
Gallows Plot, at the S. end of the loch, recalls the stern rule
of the Douglases of Threave. In winter the notable wildfowl
of the loch remain undisturbed by the main-road traffic. The
marshes of Threave are also noted for their geese.

On an island in the Dee, 2½ m. W. off A 75 (10 min, walk from farmhouse to
ferry), is **Threave Castle** (adm. 6*d.*; 10–7, Sun. from 2; closed Thurs. Apr.–Sept.),
long the headquarters of the Douglases, then that of the Earls of Nithsdale.
This gloomy tower, a typical example of its period and notable for its large
bretêche, was built in the 14th cent. by Archibald the Grim, third earl of Douglas.
Outside is a 15th cent. curtain wall. Over the doorway projects the 'hanging stone'
or 'gallows knob,' which the Douglases used to boast, "never wanted its tassel."
In 1452 William, eighth earl (p. 207), here imprisoned Sir Patrick MacLellan
the 'tutor of Bombie,' and when Sir Patrick Gray, MacLellan's uncle, arrived
with a royal order of release, Douglas insisted upon dining before opening the
king's letter and meanwhile gave orders for the immediate murder of his prisoner.
In 1455 it was the last of the Douglas strongholds to surrender to James II, who
employed 'Mons Meg' (p. 41) against it. In 1640 the interior was wrecked by
the Covenanters. In 1948 the whole estate was gifted to the National Trust.

FROM CASTLE DOUGLAS TO NEW GALLOWAY, 12 m. (motor-bus in ¾ hr.). A 713
running parallel with the railway, goes N.W. up the Dee valley. At 2 m. (l.) is
Glenlochar, where the site of a large Roman fort adjoins the barrage constructed
in 1934, by which *Loch Ken* was considerably enlarged (1000 acres; 10¾ m. long).
Opposite (3¼ m.) *Crossmichael* (Culgruff House, RB. 22/6, P. 10 gs.), Balmaghie
church (p. 188) is seen on the other side of the loch. Beyond (6¾ m.) *Parton* we
part company with the railway, and skirt Loch Ken to Ken Bridge, ½ m. N.E.
of New Galloway.

The railway strikes off to the left, crossing a narrow part of Loch Ken, through
roadless country, and enters a wild and desolate region. Between Parton and
Creetown, roads are touched only at the stations of *New Galloway*, 5 m. S. of its
village, and *Gatehouse of Fleet*, 6 m. N. of its town.

The road (motor-bus) skirts the loch and crosses the Dee.
We bear left on to A 711 and skirt the W. bank of the reservoir,
passing the site of *Queen Mary's Bridge*, by which she crossed
the Dee on her way from Langside to Dundrennan (see below),
and a power-station, to (28 m.) *Tongland*, near the church of
which is the site of a Premonstratensian abbey founded in
1218 by Alan, lord of Galloway. A 711 crosses the Dee on
Telford's bridge of 1804–8, near its confluence with the Tarff.

29½ m. **Kirkcudbright** (pron. Kir-coó-bry; *Selkirk Arms*,
RB. 22/6, P. 10 gs.; *Royal*, RB. 25/, P. 12 gs.; *Mayfield*,
unlic., P. 8½ gs.; *Commercial*, RB. 15/), delightfully situated
on the estuary of the Dee, is the ancient capital (2500 inhab.)
of the Stewartry, a town of wide streets and dignified houses,
with a quay on the river. Its name means 'Kirk of Cuthbert,'
its ancient church having been dedicated to that saint.

A Franciscan friary was founded at Kirkcudbright in the first half of the
13th cent., and the friary church was used as the parish church in 1569–1730.
Only a fragment of it now survives in Greyfriars church. The town was made

a royal burgh in 1455 by James II. Kirkcudbright is said to have been agreed upon by Philip II and Lord Maxwell as a landing-place for the Spanish Armada in 1588.

Near the main square are the ruins of *McLellan's Castle* (adm. 6*d.* ; 10–4 or 7, Sun. from 2), a turreted mansion built after 1577 by Sir Thomas McLellan of Bombie, ancestor of the barons of Kirkcudbright, a title now extinct. *Greyfriars Episcopal Church* (19th cent.), near by, incorporates a 16th cent. aisle of the old church with the fine tomb (1597) and effigy of Sir Thomas. The old royal castle of Kirkcudbright, where Henry VI took refuge after Towton in 1461, has entirely disappeared. A pleasant walk leads to its site, the Castledykes, W. of the town. *Broughton House*, an early 18th cent. mansion in High St., parallel to Castle St., contains a collection of paintings and curios. Bequeathed to the town by E. A. Hornel (d. 1933), artist, the house also contains a good library (open Mon.–Fri. 2–4, Apr.–Sept. ; in winter Tues. and Thurs. 2–4). At the end of High St. is the *Tolbooth* (16–17th cent.), on the steps of which stands the Mercat Cross (1610). In St. Mary's St. is the *Museum* (adm. 9–6, 6*d.*). *St. Cuthbert's Church of Scotland* (19th cent.), at the cross-roads, has a huge empty churchyard ; the old churchyard, where three Covenanting martyrs, executed at Kirkcudbright in 1684–85, are buried, is ¼ m. N.E. up the hill, near the golf course.

About 1 m. S. of the town the peninsula of *St. Mary's Isle* stretches into the estuary of the Dee. It is occupied by private grounds (no adm.), once the property of the Douglases, earls of Selkirk, one of whom Paul Jones (comp. p. 183) made a daring attempt to abduct (1778). The earl was not at home, so the privateer had to content himself with looting the plate, which, however, he afterwards returned to the countess. The old heronry in the grounds contains many hundreds of birds. The modern house embodies some portions of a priory (a cell of Holyrood) founded c. 1220.

The principal short excursion from Kirkcudbright is that to DUNDRENNAN ABBEY, 6 m. S.E. by a road (A 711 ; motor-bus in 25 min.) passing (2 m. ; l.) the site of Bombie Castle, the early residence of the McLellans (comp. p. 186). The hawthorns which grow luxuriantly here, gave to the place the name of Dun-nan-draighnean (Hill of the Thorn Bushes). *Dundrennan* village (Crown and Anchor, RB. 18/6, P. £8), at the head of a pretty valley, is partly built of the stones of the Abbey.

*Dundrennan Abbey (adm. 6*d.* ; 10–4 or 7, Sun. from 2) was built in 1142 by David I, or, according to some authorities, by Fergus, lord of Galloway, for Cistercian monks perhaps from Rievaulx in Yorkshire. In 1606 it came into the possession of John Murray, later earl of Annandale. For many years it was utterly neglected and used as a quarry, until in 1842 the Commissioners of Woods and Forests stopped the depredations. Queen Mary is said to have ridden hither from Langside viâ Dumfries and to have passed her last night (May 15th, 1568) in Scotland either here or at *Terregles*, the mansion of Lord Herries, near Dumfries.

On the W. side are the cellars and the entrance to the garden. We enter by the W. door (E.E.), all that remains of the nave. The transepts, with roofless aisles on the E. side, are the most beautiful remnant of the church. The pointed arches are surmounted in the N. transept by fine blind arcading, and in the S. by a triforium of pointed arches ; above these are round-headed windows. An exquisite pointed doorway (13th cent.) with an elegant window on either side was the entrance to the chapter house. Of the chancel, with its plain round windows, only the N. and S. walls remain. In the N. transept is a monument to Alan, lord of Galloway, grandson of Fergus and Constable of Scotland in 1233, while at the W. end is an unusual effigy of an abbot.

The Abbey Burn may be descended for c. 2 m. to *Burnfoot*, whence a cliff-walk brings us to *Port Mary* to the E. Here is shown the rock from which Queen Mary stepped on the boat which bore her across the Solway to Workington.

FROM KIRKCUDBRIGHT TO NEW GALLOWAY VIÂ RINGFORD, 18½ m. The road (A 762) goes N., crosses the Dee, and follows the Tarff and railway to (4 m.) *Ringford*. Roads on the left lead to *Twynholm* (1½ m. ; Star Inn), where a grave in the churchyard is said to be that of the minstrel 'Wandering Willie' (d. 1816). —Thence the road passes through beautiful scenery to (6 m.) *Kirkconnell*. On the moor to the left is the Martyrs' Monument, commemorating the massacre of five Covenanters by Grierson of Lag in 1685. About 3 m. N.E. of (9 m.) *Laurieston* is *Balmaghie*, where Crockett, 'minister of the Gospel and novelist,' is buried. John MacMillan, first minister of the Reformed Presbyterian church (1706 ; 'Cameronians'), was previously parish minister of Balmaghie. 11½ m. *Little Duchrae* was the birthplace of Samuel Rutherford Crockett (1860–1914), author of 'The Raiders.' Beyond (13 m.) *New Galloway* station the road, passing under the fir-clad slopes of Cairn Edward (1066 ft.), skirts for some distance **the W. bank of *Loch Ken*.** Overlooking the head of the loch is *Kenmure Castle* (15–17th cent.), long the seat of the Gordons of Lochinvar, Viscounts Kenmure. The sixth viscount was executed for his part in the '15 Rebellion ; the seventh (d. 1840) was a friend of Burns. The title, afterwards revived, became extinct in 1847. 18½ m. *New Galloway*, see Rte. 20.

From Kirkcudbright a pleasant detour (c. 15 m. ; bus) to Gatehouse follows B 727 (on the left beyond the Dee bridge) to (5½ m.) *Borgue*, the scene of Stevenson's 'Master of Ballantrae.' William Nicholson (1783–1849), author of 'The Brownie o' Blednoch,' was born here and is commemorated by a monument. Thence we may gain the coast at (7½ m.) *Kirkandrews Bay*, with a charming view of the Isles of Fleet.—9½ m. *Knockbrex* is 1½ m. S.E. of *Carrick Shore* (N.T.), a lovely headland. The main road is rejoined 3 m. short of Gatehouse.

The main road (A 755) crosses the Dee and climbs to (33 m.) the hamlet of *High Borgue*, where a road diverges on the left for (2 m.) *Borgue*. About 3½ m. farther on, c. 1 m. left of the road, are the ruins of the old church (c. 1625 ; with medieval fragments) of *Girthon* the name of the parish in which Gatehouse chiefly lies. We pass (l.) *Cally Hotel*, with fine grounds through which there is a public right of way.— 38 m. **Gatehouse of Fleet** (*Cally*, RB. from 25/, P. 9–15 gs. ; *Murray Arms*, RB. 19/6, P. 8–12 gs. ; *Anwoth*, RB. 21/, P. 11 gs. ; *Angel*, RB. 21/, P. 9 gs.), the 'Kippletringan' of 'Guy Mannering,' is an unassuming town (877 inhab.) on the Water of Fleet.

About ¾ m. W. of the village a footpath leads to the ruins of **Anwoth Church** (1626), where Samuel Rutherford (1600–61) was minister in 1627–39. A granite obelisk (1842) to his memory crowns a neighbouring hill.—*Rusko Castle*, 3½ m. N.W. up the Water of Fleet, was a seat of the Kenmures and bears the date 1514 in archaic Arabic numerals.

We now descend the Water of Fleet, passing (39 m.) the ruins of *Cardoness Castle* (r. ; adm. 6*d.* ; 10–4 or 7, Sun. from 2), a splendid 15th cent. tower (*View) with its stone benches and elaborate fireplaces. This beautiful road touches the shore at Skyreburn Bay, then skirts the base of *Cairnharrow* (1497 ft.). Beyond (44 m.) *Ravenshall Point*, whence we have a fine sea-view, we reach the bridge over the Kirkdale Burn at a lovely bend of the road. On the shore, c. 250 yds. E. of the mouth of the burn, is the very narrow entrance to *Dirk Hatteraick's Cave*, the largest of several ; up the glen lies *Cairnholy*, where Meg Merrilees's gypsies had their encampment. Near the entrance to the glen (E. side) are the remains of *Barholm Castle*, and farther on below the road is the ruined 16th cent. tower-house of *Carsluith*, both claimants to be ' Ellangowan.' About 1½ m. farther on is the manse of *Kirkmabreck*, where Dr. Thomas Brown (1778–1820), moral philosopher, was born. Passing some large granite quarries, we reach (r.) *Cassencary*, a mansion claiming to possess the original of ' Dominie Sampson's ' library, books and all. Another ½ m. brings us to (50 m.) **Creetown** (*Ellangowan*, RB. 20/–25/, P. 9 gs. ; *Barholm Arms*, RB. 18/, P. 7½ gs.). The little town and port, near the mouth of the Cree in Wigtown Bay, lies 1 m. S. of the station. Creetown is usually identified as the ' Portan-ferry ' of ' Guy Mannering ' (but comp. p. 182).—At (53 m.) *Palnure Bridge* we cross the foot of the picturesque and popular *Bargaly Glen*.—56 m. **Newton Stewart,** see Rte. 20.

20. FROM DUMFRIES TO STRANRAER VIÂ NEW GALLOWAY

Road, 67 m.—A 75. 9 m. *Crocketford*.—A 712. 24 m. *New Galloway*.—A 712. 42 m. **Newton Stewart.**—A 75. 57 m. *Glenluce*.—67 m. **Stranraer.**

Railway, 73 m. in 2¼–2¾ hrs. ; to (49½ m.) *Newton Stewart* in 1¼–1¾ hr. This line is part of the express route from London (Euston) to Ireland viâ Stranraer and Larne (Belfast) : to *Stranraer Harbour*, 406 m. in 9¾ hrs., to *Belfast*, 14¼ hrs. The voyage between Stranraer and Larne is the shortest sea passage between Great Britain and Ireland. Principal stations : to (19¾ m.) **Castle Douglas,** see Rte. 19.—28¾ m. *New Galloway*, 5 m. S. of its village.—43¼ m. *Creetown*.—49½ m. **Newton Stewart.**—55¾ m. *Kirkcowan*.—69¼ m. *Glenluce*.—67½ m. *Dunragit*.—73 m. **Stranraer** (Town).

The route, passing through some of the finest and wildest scenery in southern Scotland traverses the district of **Galloway**, which comprises both Kirkcudbrightshire and Wigtownshire, and, until the end of the 12th cent., included also Carrick in Ayrshire (p. 168). The name is derived from ' Gallgaidhel ' or ' Gallwyddel ' (' stranger Gaels '), a term applied to the Celtic Gauls of this region, an independent race (the Novantae or Attecotti of the Romans), because they fraternised with the Scandinavian rovers who made many settlements here, after the latter part of the 9th century. Though the Picts of Galloway supported Kenneth Macalpine as king, and won from him the honour of leading the van of the Scottish armies, they professed no allegiance to the Scottish crown until the reign of Malcolm Canmore (c. 1060), and even thereafter they maintained a quasi-independence under native 'lords' or 'kings' until the death of the last in 1234. The mysterious *Deil's Dyke*, long supposed to mark the boundary of a 5th or 6th cent. Gallovidian kingdom, is now reckoned as merely a series of detached earthworks of dubious origin. In the 14th cent. the chief Galloway families were the Balliols and Comyns, who naturally opposed the Bruce, and after the overthrow of Edward Balliol the lordship of Galloway was bestowed (c. 1370) upon the Douglases, who exercised a haughty and somewhat lawless dominion until their deprivation c. 1450. Galloway then passed to the crown, but was administered by hereditary sheriffs until 1747. The Covenants (p. 102) were obstinately supported in Galloway and the 'wild western whigs' were largely recruited from that region.—The dark Galloway cattle are indigenous, and the small but hardy horses known as 'Galloways' were supposed to have partly sprung from horses that had swum ashore from wrecked vessels of the Spanish Armada.

Between 1929 and 1936 was developed the GALLOWAY POWER SCHEME, using the waters of the Dee and Ken for the generation of electric power. Five power-stations—Kendoon, Garsfad, Earlston, Glenlee, and Tongland—were erected. Of these the first three, in the hills between Carsphairn and Dalry, are supplied from reservoirs created by damming the Ken. Glenlee is supplied from Clatteringshaws Loch, a storage reservoir, to the W., made by a dam on the Black Water of Dee, the waters being piped through a tunnel; while Tongland, on the Dee estuary, utilises its own headpond, and storage water from Loch Ken, which has been raised in level by a barrage at Glenlochar to form a reservoir. In addition, Loch Doon (which drains naturally northward) is employed as an extra storage reservoir, and is also connected, by a reversible-flow aqueduct and tunnel with the Water of Deugh and Bow Burn. Fish-passes for salmon have been built at Tongland (70 ft.), Earlston, and Garsfad, as well as a special regulated-level pass at Loch Doon. The total cost of construction was about £3,000,000.

Kirkcudbrightshire or *East Galloway* is known also as the 'Stewartry of Kirkcudbright,' because, on the deprivation of the Balliols, their lordship was placed under a royal steward. From 1526 till 1747 this office was hereditary in the family of Maxwell. The county has a bold and picturesque coast-line on the Solway, which plays its part in 'Guy Mannering' and in many smugglers' tales. In the N.W. is the desolate and wild hill country described in Crockett's romances. The four most N. parishes, in the basin of the Ken—Carsphairn, Dalry, Balmaclellan, and Kells—form the district of Glenkens.

Wigtownshire or *West Galloway*, the S.W. extremity of Scotland, comprises the Rhinns of Galloway, i.e. the double peninsula on the W., the Machars or low lands in the triangle between Wigtown and Luce Bays, and the Moors, in the N. It is a grazing and agricultural county with a much indented coast-line with many 'smugglers' caves.' Stranraer is the principal town. At Whithorn Christianity was first introduced into Scotland by St. Ninian (4th cent.) and the county is notable for the number of ancient Christian crosses surviving.

We quit Dumfries (Maxwelltown) viâ Buccleuch St. (Pl. 2) by A 75 and at (9 m.) *Crocketford* (Galloway Arms, RB. 27/6, P. 14 gs.) diverge right (A 712); the main road bears left for Castle Douglas, skirting Auchenreoch Loch and crossing the Urr. Our road is hilly but affords fine views of wild Galloway. At (22 m.) *Balmaclellan* (Inn), a monument commemorates 'Old Mortality' (p. 181), whose wife kept a school here for twenty years (1765–85). In the churchyard rests Robert Grierson (d. 1685), a Covenanting martyr, beneath a stone with an inscription in the usual impassioned style.

24 m. **New Galloway** (*Cross Keys*, RB. 22/, P. 10 gs.; *Kenmure Arms*, RB. 17/6, P. 8 gs.; *Ken Bridge*, 1 m. N.E., RB. 18/, P. 8½ gs.) on the Ken, a village (305 inhab.) which has the dignity of being a royal burgh, is a good centre for angling

and for the exploration of an interesting and somewhat little known country. It lies in the parish of *Kells*, in the churchyard of which, ½ m. N.W., is the grave of a Covenanter shot in 1685.—**Dalry** (*Lochinvar*, RB. 19/6, P. 9–12 gs.; *Milton Park*, 1 m. N., similar charges; *Commercial, St. John's*, unlic., RB. 15/), a similar centre, 3½ m. N. of New Galloway (motor-buses), is known also as *St. John's Town of Dalry*, from a former church of the Knights Templar, and is to be distinguished from Dalry in Ayrshire.

About 3 m. E. of Dalry a cart-track, diverging left from the road to (13 m.) Moniaive, leads N. to (2 m.), *Lochinvar*, a small lake with an islet bearing a ruined castle, the home of the 'Young Lochinvar' of the song (comp. p. 11).

From Dalry to *Carsphairn* and *Dalmellington* (Ayr), see Rte. 17c.

Running W. from New Galloway the road (A 712), one of the wildest in the south of Scotland, ascends steeply beside a stream, with *Cairnsmore of Dee* (1600 ft.) on the left. From (c. 28½ m.) the summit level (653 ft.) we descend rapidly past the *Clatteringshaws Reservoir* to (31 m.) the Upper Bridge of Dee, spanning the Black Water of Dee. Bruce's Stone, near the E. shore of the reservoir, marks the scene of a successful skirmish against the English in 1307.

A route for good walkers strikes off N.W., immediately beyond the bridge, for (8 m. or more) Loch Dee and (13 m.) Loch Trool (p. 192).

The next 4 or 5 miles are the wildest on the route. 35 m. *Murray's Monument*, an obelisk on the hill on the right, commemorates Dr. Alexander Murray (1775–1813), who, reared a shepherd boy on these hillsides, became professor of Oriental Languages at Edinburgh. The *Grey Mare's Tail*, a waterfall by the Black Loch, is reached by a steep path near the monument. *Cairnsmore of Fleet* (2331 ft.), on the left, is one of the loftiest hills in Galloway. We pass (36½ m.) a rocking stone and, farther on, a road on the left diverges into the Bargaly Glen (see p. 189).—Our road descends steadily passing Larg Tower (l.), and joins the Creetown road, where we turn to the right.—Crossing the Cree at *Creebridge*, the E. suburb of Newton Stewart, we enter Wigtownshire.

42 m. **NEWTON STEWART** (2000 inhab.), a small town consisting mainly of one long street, is situated amid fine hill scenery. It is a gateway to interesting environs rather than interesting in itself. Important cattle markets are held here.

Hotels. Galloway Arms, RB. 22/6–27/6, P. 10–12 gs.; **Crown**, RB. 21/6–26/, P. from 10 gs.; **Creebridge House**, with garden, RB. 22/6, P. from 9 gs.; **Kirroughtree House**, similar charges; **Black Bull**, RB. 17/6, P. 7–8½ gs.

Motor-Buses to *Kirkcudbright* (1½ hr.) viâ Gatehouse of Fleet, going on to *Dumfries* (2¾ hrs.); to *Wigtown* (20 min.); to *Isle of Whithorn* (1½ hr.); to *Girvan* (1½ hr.), etc.

The bridge across the Cree has a monument to the ninth earl of Galloway at its W. end; a little higher upstream is a suspension bridge—both bridges being fine view-points. To the W. of the main bridge is the parish church of *Penninghame* (1840 ; by Wm. Burn), with a lofty spire.

To the N. of Creebridge, on the E. bank of the Cree, is *Minnigaff* ; the parish church (1836 ; also by Wm. Burn) and its churchyard are pleasantly situated above the Penkill Burn. A road leads up the burn to (2 m.) *Cumloden*, a seat of the Earl of Galloway, in the woods beyond which are the ruins of *Garlies Castle*.

The chief excursion from Newton Stewart is that to LOCH TROOL (13 m. ; motor coaches), one of the most beautiful spots in South Scotland. Roads lead N. up both ' Banks of the Cree,' immortalised by Burns ; the hilly road on the left bank is perhaps the more attractive, but we here describe that on the right (W.) bank. At (2 m.) *Challoch*, where B 7027 to Girvan diverges to the left, stands the episcopal church of *All Saints*, and a little farther on the small ruin of *Castle Stewart* is seen on the left. Beyond (3½ m.) *Penninghame House* (now a prison) the road skirts the expansion of the river, known as *Loch Cree*, or the *Cruives of Cree*, with finely wooded banks. We pass (r. ; 6½ m.) the mouth of the Minnoch, spanned c. 1 m. upstream by a so-called Roman bridge of unknown origin. At (8 m.) *Bargrennan*, where A 714 leads left for *Barrhill* (see below ; 9 m.), we keep to the right (entering Kirkcudbrightshire) viâ the House o' Hill Inn (RB. 15/), about 1¼ m. beyond which we turn to the right for Glen Trool, crossing the Minnoch. For the road to *Straiton*, see p. 198.—13 m. The narrow
*Loch Trool (1½ m. long), with banks broken by wooded promontories and embosomed in lofty hills that rise precipitously to the N.E., is one of the gems of Scottish scenery. Just before we reach its S.W. end a track leads to the right, crossing the Trool, to a Covenanters' monument commemorating a skirmish in 1685, and to the house of *Caldons* (see below). We follow the N. bank of the loch, passing (c. 14 m.) *Glentrool Lodge*, and crossing the Buchan Burn. At the N. end of the loch Robert Bruce (in hiding after the murder of Comyn), with a small following, routed a much superior English force by hurling down rocks upon them from the heights of Mulldonach (1306).

A *National Forest Park* has been established at Glen Trool, with S.E. extensions on either side of the New Galloway–Newton Stewart road, c. 100,000 acres in all. The main area extends from Loch Dee and Loch Trool N. to Loch Doon and Barr, including Merrick and the wild country to the N.W. An organised camping site is provided at Caldons, S.W. of Loch Trool (see above).

From Loch Trool good walkers may push E. over the hills to (5 m.) *Loch Dee* (p. 191) and (18 m.) *New Galloway* (p. 190) ; or they may explore the wild mountainous district to the N.E., graphically described in Crockett's ' Raiders.' —**Merrick** (2764 ft. ; view), the highest summit on the mainland of Scotland south of the Clyde, c. 5 m. N. of Loch Trool, may be ascended viâ the Buchan Burn (see above), leaving *Loch Neldricken*, with its ' murder hole,' on the right. To the E. of the savage escarpments of Merrick lie *Loch Enoch* (1650 ft.), famous for its scythe sand, and several smaller lochs and tarns, including the *Round Loch of the Dungeon*, in a wild environment of mountain, moss-hag, and rock.

FROM NEWTON STEWART TO GIRVAN there are two roads, separating at Challoch and joining at Barrhill. One of these (31 m.) leaves the Glen Trool route at Bargrennan, and the other (30 m.) goes viâ The Snap Inn and passes between Loch Maberry and Loch Dornal. From (17 m.) *Barrhill* (Commercial) we descend the pretty valley of the Duisk to (22 m.) *Pinwherry* on the inland road from Ballantrae to Girvan (Rte. 22).

From Newton Stewart to Wigtown and Whithorn, see Rte. 21.

For some distance beyond Newton Stewart the road traverses uninteresting country.—From a little beyond (46 m.) *Bladnoch Bridge* a road diverges left for (1¼ m.) *Kirkcowan* (Craiglaw Arms, RB. 18/6), with woollen mills.—About 4 m. farther on, to the N. of the railway, are seen the ruins of *Carscreugh*, seat of Lord Stair (1619–95), President of the Court of Session, whose daughter Janet (d. 1669) was the unhappy prototype of the ' Bride of Lammermoor.'—57 m.

Glenluce (Judge's Keep, RB. 18/, P. 8 gs. ; King's Arms, RB. 16/, P. 7 gs.), at the head of Luce Bay, lies 1½ m. S.E. of **Glenluce Abbey** (adm. 6*d.* ; 10–4 or 7, Sun. from 2).

The abbey, founded in 1192 by Roland, lord of Galloway, as a daughter-house of Dundrennan, originally covered a considerable area, and its gardens are still the glebe of the parish. Of the E.E. church little remains but the foundations, with the exception of the gable of the S. transept. The walls of the cloister still stand. One of the few entire in Scotland, the vaulted chapter house (1470), with a central pillar, has some Dec. windows and is entered by a round-arched doorway with fine ornamentation ; part of the vaulting has been restored. Perhaps unique are the interlocking red clay water pipes ; pieces of lead-piping and some glazed tiles also remain. Michael Scot, the Wizard, who resided here in the 13th cent., is said to have locked up the plague in a vault, while his books are still buried in the ground.

New Luce, where Prophet Peden was minister in 1659–62 prior to his ejection, is 3½ m. N. of the abbey. Thence rough tracks lead N.W. to Ballantrae and N. to Barrhill.

From Glenluce to *Port William* and *Whithorn*, see pp. 197, 196.

The road crosses the Luce beside a lofty viaduct. To the right is *Castle of Park* (1590), a good type of the Scottish mansion of the period.—64 m. *Castle Kennedy* is 1½ m. S. of *Lochinch Castle* (1870), the stately Scots-French château of the Earl of Stair. In front of the mansion, on a peninsula between the White Loch and Black Loch, are the ruins of **Castle Kennedy,** built in the reign of James VI and destroyed by fire in 1715. Long a seat of the earls of Cassillis, Castle Kennedy passed to the Stair family in the 17th century. The beautiful *Gardens and grounds (adm. 2/6 ; Wed. and Sun. 2.30–5.30, mid-April–July) are specially noted for the pinetum, the first in Scotland. The gardens, at one time neglected, were restored c. 1847 to their original 17th cent. form. The manse of Inch, S.W. of the village, occupies the site of *Soulseat Abbey* (' sedes animæ '), founded for Premonstratensians, perhaps by Fergus, lord of Galloway (d. 1161).

67 m. **STRANRAER** (8620 inhab.), a seaport at the head of Loch Ryan, is the largest town in Galloway and the starting-point of the shortest sea-passage to Ireland (35 m.). The boat-trains run to and from the *Harbour Station.*

Hotels.   George, RB. from 25/, P. 14 gs. ; **Auld King's Arms,** similar charges ; **Buck's Head,** RB. 21/–24/, P. 10 gs.
Motor-Buses viâ Ballantrae and Girvan to *Ayr* (2½ hrs.) ; to *Drummore* (1 hr.) ; to *Portpatrick* (½ hr.) ; to

Isle of Whithorn (1¾ hr.) once daily viâ Glenluce ; to *Newton Stewart* (1¼ hr.) ; to *Kirkcudbright* (2½ hrs.) ; to *Dumfries* (3¾ hrs.).
Steamer to Larne every weekday (two passages in summer) in 2¼–2¾ hrs. (open sea passage, 70 min.).

Stranraer has little to offer the tourist. The *Castle*, in the middle of the town, built about the beginning of the 16th cent. and afterwards used as the town jail, was occupied for a time in 1682 by Claverhouse. A house known as *North-West Castle* was the residence of Sir John Ross (1777–1856), the Arctic explorer (comp. below), and has a dining-room modelled on a ship's cabin.

The **Rhinns of Galloway** is the name given to the peninsula or double peninsula (once, no doubt, an island) that forms the S.W. extremity of Wigtownshire and terminates on the S. in the Mull of Galloway.—In the N. part, 5¾ m. N.W. of Stranraer, stands *Lochnaw Castle*, the ancient seat of the Agnews, who were hereditary sheriffs of Galloway from 1451 until the abolition of heritable jurisdictions in 1747 except for the years 1681–88, when Claverhouse superseded them.—The road skirting the W. side of Loch Ryan leads to (6 m.) *Wig Bay*, used in 1939–45 as a repair base for flying boats, and to (6½ m.) *Kirkcolm* (Corsewall Arms, RB. 20/), 3 m. W. of which is *Balsarroch*, birthplace of Sir John Ross (see above). Farther N. are the ruined castle of *Corsewall* and Corsewall Point, with a lighthouse.

FROM STRANRAER TO DRUMMORE, 17½ m. (motor-bus daily ; viâ Port Logan on Sat.). The road (A 716) traverses the S. part of the Rhinns, passing (3½ m.) *Garthland Tower* and (8 m.) *Sandhead*, a coast village. A mile farther on, beside a church, a by-road diverges (r.) for the old church of *Kirkmadrine*, with two remarkable ancient inscribed stones in a niche. The inscriptions in Roman capitals, dating perhaps from the late 5th cent., commemorate three priests or bishops, and point to the early establishment of Christianity in this remote quarter, within a generation or so of the death of St. Ninian.—About 1 m. beyond (10½ m.) *Ardwell* is the entrance (r.) to *Logan House* (18th cent.), the home of the MacDoualls from remote antiquity until 1940 ; the magnificent sub-tropical garden is open on Mon., Wed. and Fri. 2–6 (April–Oct.), 2/6. Farther on a road diverges (r.) for *Port Logan* (2 m.), a little decayed port. On the N. side of the lovely bay is a tidal *Sea-fish Pond* (adm. 1/6 ; 12.30–6.30 on Mon., Wed., Fri. and Sat.), remarkable for the tameness of the fish confined in it ; the pond, opened in 1800, was closed in 1939–55 after damage by a mine.—17½ m. *Drummore* (Queen's, RB. 18/6, P. 8 gs.), with a small harbour, is in the parish of *Kirkmaiden*, the most southerly parish in Scotland, recalling Burns's line " Frae Maidenkirk to Johnny Groats." The road (rough for last 2 m.) may be followed S. to (5 m.) the *Mull of Galloway* (210 ft. ; lighthouse), which commands an extensive view. Near (3½ m.) Mull Farm, at the foot of the cliff on Luce Bay, is the *Chapel of St. Medan*, a mere fragment, the oldest church in Galloway. The Double Dykes, an entrenchment across the W. end of the Mull, was traditionally the last defence of the Picts against the Scots pressing in from the N. The Celtic tragedy of the Secret of the Heather Ale is sometimes located here (comp. the poem by R.L.S.).

FROM STRANRAER TO PORTPATRICK, 7½ m. **Portpatrick** (*Portpatrick*, RB. from 22/6, P. 11½–17 gs. ; *Crown*, RB. 21/, P. 9 gs. ; *Roslin*, unlic., similar charges), now frequented as a summer resort, was until 1849 the port of departure of a mail service to Donaghadee in Ireland.—a distance of only 21 m., once taken in his stride by St. Patrick. With the development of steam, Stranraer was found more convenient and the harbour works at Portpatrick, constructed c. 1843 at enormous expense, have been suffered to fall into ruin. About ½ m. S. of the town, on a bold promontory, are the ruins of *Dunskey Castle*, dating from about 1510, while c. 2 m. N. is *Killantringan* lighthouse.

The North Channel was swum for the first time (from Donaghadee to Portpatrick) in July 1947 by Mr. Thomas Blower of Nottingham in 16 hrs. 7 min.

21. FROM NEWTON STEWART TO WIGTOWN AND WHITHORN

ROAD, 17 m. (A 714), traversing the Machars of Wigtownshire, see Rte. 20.—
MOTOR-BUS in 1¼ hr., going on to Isle of Whithorn or Port William.

Newton Stewart, see p. 191. We cross (3½ m.) Bishop Burn
after passing the site of Penninghame Hall, once a residence
of the bishops of Galloway.

6½ m. **Wigtown** (*Commercial*, RB. 15/, plain), the county
town (1375 inhab.) and a royal burgh since 1457, is a shabby
little place on a hill, with a disused harbour at the mouth of
the Bladnoch. In the middle of the broad main street are
the old (1738) and new (1816) Burgh *Crosses*. The bowling
green and tennis courts occupy the site of an enclosure in
which cattle, driven into the town for safety, used to be
penned at night. A projecting house, near the crosses, marks
the position of the old West Port. Half-way down the hill,
beyond the *County Buildings* is the parish churchyard in
which rest the Wigtown martyrs, Margaret Lachlan, aged 63,
and Margaret Willson, a girl of 18, who, it is alleged, were tied
to a stake and left to drown in the rising tide at the river
mouth (1685). Three other Covenanting martyrs are buried
here. Opposite the church a post points to the traditional site
of the martyrdom. The *Martyrs' Monument*, an obelisk
erected in 1858, stands on high ground above the town (view).
Near the river-mouth (by the railway track) a grassy mound
marks the site of the old castle, but there is now no trace of
the Dominican priory founded by Devorguilla Balliol.

About 3 m. W. of the town, on the left of a road leading to (8 m.) Kirkcowan
(p. 192), are the *Standing Stones of Torhouse*, a complete circle, 60 ft. in diameter,
consisting of 19 stones, the two largest 5½ and 5 ft. high.—Beyond the Bladnoch
bridge B 7005 runs W. to join (10½ m.) the coast road between Glenluce and
Port William. A turning on the right of it after 8 m. leads to the *Old Place of
Mochrum*, with two 15th cent. towers at the N. end of Mochrum Loch (2 m.).—
The lane on the left beyond the bridge leads to the ruins of *Baldoon Castle*, the
home of David Dunbar, who was the original of the unfortunate bridegroom
in the ' Bride of Lammermoor.'

About 1 m. beyond the Bladnoch A 714 forks right for
Port William (8 m.), while our road (A 746) forks left to
(10 m.) *Kirkinner*, where there is a Celtic cross in the churchyard, S.W. of the not unhandsome church (1828).—From
(13 m.) *Sorbie* the direct road goes S. to Whithorn, while a
left-hand turning, passing (l.) the *Old Place of Sorbie*, now a
ruin, leads to the small port of **Garlieston** (2½ m.; *Queen's Arms*,
RB. 19/6, P. 10 gs.) on a bay of the same name. To the S.
are the fine grounds of *Galloway House*. Farther S. (2 m.),
almost hidden by trees and surrounded by a high stone wall
(stile), is *Cruggleton Church* (key at Cruggleton Farm to the N.),

one of the few examples of Norman architecture in Galloway. Near the shore are the ruins of the *Castle*, a fortress of the Comyns. The road (B 7063) goes on to (6 m.) Isle of Whithorn (see below).

17 m. **Whithorn** (1070 inhab. ; *Grapes*, RB. 16/6, P. 7½ gs. ; *Station*, similar charges), a pleasant little town and a royal burgh since the days of Bruce, derives its name from the A.S. *Hvit-aern* (a white house ; Lat. *Candida Casa*), because here St. Ninian built the first stone church in Scotland.

St. Ninian (called also St. Ringan) was born on the shores of the Solway towards the middle of the 4th cent., and in 397, on his return from a pilgrimage to Rome, built his church and dedicated it to his master, St. Martin of Tours, who had sent masons to shape the walls after the Roman fashion. Excavations at the beginning of the 20th cent., E. of the later church, revealed the walls of an ancient building, with a coat of light-coloured plaster over its masonry, making it almost certain that here indeed was the site of the 'white house' of St. Ninian. For many generations the shrine was visited by pilgrims of all ranks and of many nationalities. The Celtic see, continued by a Northumbrian bishopric in the 8th cent., was revived c. 1125, and c. 1175 a Premonstratensian priory was founded here to serve it and to tend the shrine. Among famous pilgrims of later days were Robert Bruce (1329), and James III, IV, and V. James IV was especially devoted, visiting the shrine almost annually. After the Dissolution, the nave of the church was adapted as a cathedral for the Protestant bishop, and from the 18th cent. until 1822 it served as the parish church.

All that remains above ground is the 13th cent. nave of the *Priory Church* (adm. 6*d.* ; 10–4 or 7, Sun. from 2), with 17–18th cent. alterations. It is approached from the main street by a 17th cent. arch, called *The Pend*, flanked by 15th cent. pillars with sculptured coats of arms and surmounted by a panel with the Scottish arms as borne before the Union. On the S. side of the church are two reset doorways, that at the W. end, with handsome mouldings, dating from the 12th cent., while the other is of the 13th cent., with a rich outer archway of c. 1500. On the N. side, within, are two canopied tombs (c. 1300) and a 17th cent. arched recess. To the E., beneath the sanctuary and S.E. chapel of the priory church, is a barrel-vaulted crypt (c. 1200 ; key at the museum) ; the cloister and domestic buildings lay to the N.

In the *Museum*, at the churchyard gate, have been collected a remarkable series of early Christian *Crosses and other fragments. Outstanding are the *St. Peter Stone* with lettering of a type normally found in Merovingian Gaul (7th cent.) ; and the *Latinus Stone* of the 5th cent., the earliest Christian memorial in Scotland.

About 3½ m. S.E. of Whithorn (motor-bus in ¼ hr.) is **Isle of Whithorn**, a tiny port on a rocky coast c. 2 m. from *Burrow Head*. The ruined chapel of c. 1300 was probably used by pilgrims from overseas, Excavations revealed foundations of an earlier building, though no early Christian relics have been discovered here.—**St. Ninian's Cave,** said to have served the saint for an oratory, lies 3 m. S.W. of Whithorn and W. of Physgill Glen. On the W. wall and on the rocks outside are small votive crosses dating from the 8th century.

From Whithorn to Glenluce, 22 m. A 746 leads S.W. to (1½ m.) *Glasserton Church* with quaint early Victorian outbuildings. Thence A 747 (r.) descends to the shore at (6 m.) *Monreith Bay*, with good sands. Near the golf course is the ancient church (restored) of *Kirkmaiden-in-Fernis*, the burial chapel of the Maxwells. *Monreith House* (Sir Aymer Maxwell), 1½ m. N., has interesting gardens (adm. on application to the Estate Office). In the park is the White Loch of Myrton " one half whereof doth freeze by natural congelation as other pooles and plashes, but the other is never seene to bear anie yce all " (Boece) ; here also is a fine Cross of the Whithorn school.—8½ m. **Port William** (*Monreith Arms*, RB. from 21/, P. 10 gs.; *Eagle*, RB. 18/6, P. 8 gs.) is a little seaside resort with a quay. Our road hugs the coast as far as (17 m.) *Auchenmalg Bay* and thence strikes inland to (22 m.) *Glenluce* (p. 193).

22. FROM STRANRAER TO AYR VIÂ MAYBOLE

Road, 52 m. (A 77).—17 m. *Ballantrae.*—42 m. *Maybole.*—52 m. **Ayr.** The road keeps near the coast as far as Turnberry, except for the digression through Glen App. The sea-views are fine, especially on the section beyond Ballantrae, whence Ailsa Craig and Arran are prominent.—Motor-Bus in 2½ hrs.

Railway, 59¼ m. in 1¾–2 hrs. Principal stations : 6 m. *Dunragit.*—12¾ m. *New Luce.*—25¾ m. *Barrhill.*—29¾ m. *Pinwherry.*—33 m. *Pinmore.*—38 m. **Girvan.**—50¼ m. *Maybole.*—59¼ m. **Ayr.**

For 9 m. the road skirts the E. shore of **Loch Ryan,** the *Rerigonius Sinus* of the Romans. Off the coast near its mouth the Irish mail packet, ' *Princess Victoria*', was sunk with great loss of life in 1953.—The 13th cent. foundations of (3 m.) *Craigcaffie Castle* are said to have been laid on bags of wool, on account of the boggy nature of the ground.—Beyond (6 m.) *Cairn Ryan* we cross (8 m.) the Galloway Burn and enter Ayrshire. During the war Cairn Ryan was a port of some importance and latterly controlled by the Americans ; components of the Mulberry Harbour were made here.—From (9 m.) *Finnart Bay*, nearly opposite Milleur Point, the N. extremity of the Rhinns of Galloway, the road, temporarily leaving the coast, ascends for four miles through *Glen App*. Crossing the Stinchar, we regain the coast at (18 m.) **Ballantrae** (*King's Arms*, RB. 19/6, P. 9 gs. ; *Royal*, RB. 17/6, P. 8 gs.), a small fishing port, with golf links. The church contains a good pulpit (c. 1819) and the Cassillis aisle with the monument of Gilbert Kennedy (d. 1601). Though R. L. Stevenson visited Ballantrae in 1876 (and, according to his own account, was stoned by the populace for the eccentricity of his costume), this village is not the scene of the ' Master of Ballantrae ' (comp. p. 188). Near the village is the shell of *Ardstinchar Castle*, which commanded the pass below.

A motor-bus runs from Ballantrae, up the beautiful valley of the Stinchar, viâ (5¼ m.) *Colmonell* (Queen's) to (9 m.) *Pinwherry* (Daljarrock House, RB. 17/6, P. 8 gs.), and thence viâ (12 m.) *Pinmore* to (17 m.) Girvan. To the left, 2½ m. from Ballantrae, is the prominent hill of *Knockdolian* (869 ft.). A monument above Colmonell commemorates John Snell (1629–59), founder of the exhibitions at Balliol College open to Scottish students. *Craigneil Castle* (13th cent.), opposite, was a stronghold of the Kennedys, as was *Kirkhill*, nearer the village.   About 1¾ m. beyond Pinwherry, B 734 diverges r. up the Stinchar valley for *Barr* (Inns), an anglers' resort about 5¼ m. E.   Thence a poor hill-road leads E., and S.E. to the Minnoch valley, 9 m. by road N. of Bargrennan (p. 192).

The road from Ballantrae to Girvan closely hugs the coast, which at many points is exceedingly bold, especially at (20 m.) *Bennane Head*, and near (24 m.) *Lendalfoot*.   The ruined *Carleton Castle*, on the hill to the right, is famed in ballad as the seat of a baron who got rid of seven wives by pushing them over the cliff, but was himself similarly disposed of by the adroit ' May Cullean,' his eighth wife.

30 m. **Girvan** (*King's Arms*, RB. 23/, P. 11 gs. ; *Hamilton Arms*, RB. 21/, P. 9 gs.; *Ailsa Arms*, similar charges; *Royal*, RB. 21/) is a busy little town (5990 inhab.) and holiday resort, with a harbour, small fishing fleet, and good sands.   In the centre of the town is the green plot called Knockusion (' Hill of Justice ') where Bruce granted a charter and held his courts (tablet).

About 10 m. off the coast here, a sentinel at the mouth of the Clyde, stands the lonely pyramidal islet of **Ailsa Craig** (1114 ft. ; c. 2 m. round), known as ' Paddy's Milestone,' as half-way between Belfast and Glasgow.   It is the haunt of in-numerable sea-fowl, and is noted for its granite quarries which yield excellent curling stones.   A motor boat is usually available from Girvan in summer in favourable weather, and visitors may ascend a steep winding path, passing an ancient tower, to the top of the islet (view), which is precipitous on its W. side. Both Wordsworth and Keats have written sonnets on Ailsa Craig.

Penkill Castle, 3 m. E. of Girvan on the road to Barr (B 734), was the home of the painter Wm. Bell Scott (1811–90), who ' castellated ' the old house of the Boyds, and entertained Rossetti, then at his most melancholy, in 1868–69.

FROM GIRVAN TO DALMELLINGTON, 19½ m. (B 741).   We ascend the right bank of Girvan Water, passing (3 m.) *Killochan Castle* (adm. 2/6 ; 2–6 daily exc. Sat. in summer), the 16th cent. mansion of the Cathcarts.   Near (6 m.) *Dailly*, with a church of 1766, are the old (15th cent.) and new (1790) castles of *Dalquharran*, standing picturesquely by the waterside.   About 3½ m. farther on we keep right for (13½ m.) *Straiton*, where the church preserves a medieval aisle.   B 741 goes on to Dalmellington (p. 177) ;   B 7045 offers an attractive route to Maybole (7 m.), high above the Girvan valley viâ *Kirkmichael* with its 18th cent. church ; while a lonely moorland road runs S. to the Minnoch glen and *Bargrennan* (21 m.), with good views of the W. side of the Merrick range, *Shalloch on Minnoch* (2520 ft.) and *Kirriereoch Hill* (2562 ft.).

From Girvan to *Ayr* by the coast road, see Rte. 17B.

About 5 m. farther on, just before Turnberry, A 77 strikes inland, passing (36½ m.) *Ballochniel* where Burns lodged with his mother's friends the Browns in 1777 while learning surveying at Kirkoswald.   His mother was born at Craigenton farm, on the hill to the S.—38 m. **Kirkoswald** (*Shanter*, RB. 17/6, P. 8 gs. ; *Kirkton Arms*, RB. 21/, P. 8 gs.) is a pleasant village, in the churchyard of which are the graves of ' Tam o' Shanter ' (Douglas Graham) and ' Souter Johnnie ' (John Davidson).   *Souter Johnnie's Cottage* (N.T. ; adm. 1/, 10–dusk, Sun. 2.30–dusk) has, in its garden, life-sized figures by James Thom.—40 m. **Crossraguel Abbey** (adm. 1/; 10–4 or 7, Sun. from 2) was founded in 1244 by Duncan, Earl of

Carrick, for Cluniac monks from Paisley, who remained in occupation till 1592, probably later than any other abbey in Scotland ; the monks ran their own mint. The interesting and attractive ruins are approached by a turreted *Gatehouse*. The *Church* consists of nave and choir, terminating in a triple apse (15th cent.), in which are fine sedilia, unusually with four seats ; the original church had transepts, part of the foundations of which are seen. The N. doorway is noteworthy, likewise the rough tracery of a window in the nave.   The *Chapter House*, rebuilt 1460–91, retains its roof vaulted from a central column ; the *Sacristy* (15th cent.) also preserves its vault. Among the remains of the conventual buildings are the 16th cent. *Abbot's House* and *Dovecot.*—We pass (r.) *Baltersan Tower* (16th cent.) before reaching (42 m.) **Maybole** (*King's Arms*, RB. 18/), a town (4770 inhab.) manufacturing agricultural implements and shoes. The *Tolbooth* preserves the 17th cent. tower of the town mansion of the Kennedys of Bargany, and the *Castle* (restored) was that of the Lords Cassilis, hereditary bailiffs of Carrick (p. 168).   In the steep John Knox St. a plaque marks the site of the provost's house where John Knox and Quentin Kennedy, abbot of Crossraguel, waged a memorable theological contest for three days in 1561. At the foot of the hill farther on are the 15th cent. ruins of the *Collegiate Church* (key with caretaker), founded in 1373, later a burial chapel of the Kennedys. The old graveyard close by is on the site of a church founded by Duncan, earl of Carrick, before 1196.

Macadam was a schoolboy at Maybole when his family were living at *Blair-quhan*, 5½ m. S.E., and, in 1783–98, he resided at *Sauchrie House*, 2½ m. N.— In the grounds of *Cassilis House*, c. 2¾ m. N.E. of Maybole on B 742, are the ' Cassillis Downans ' where fairies dance, as mentioned in Burns's ' Hallowe'en.' *Culzean Castle* lies 4 m. W., see Rte. 17B.

Thence either A 77 or B 7024 leads us to (52 m.) **Ayr,** see Rte. 17.

I

II. STIRLING, PERTH, AND THE PERTHSHIRE HIGHLANDS

23. FROM GLASGOW OR EDINBURGH TO STIRLING AND CALLANDER

A. Glasgow to Callander

ROAD. 45½ m. A 803. 7½ m. *Kirkintilloch.*—12 m. *Kilsyth.*—19 m. *Dennyloanhead.*—A 80. 28 m. **Stirling**, and thence to **Callander,** see Rte. 23B.—MOTOR-BUS hourly viâ Cumbernauld in 2¼ hrs. ; to *Stirling* in 78 min. ; also hourly viâ *Kirkintilloch* to *Stirling* in 1½ hr.

For an alternative route (A 80) to Dennyloanhead viâ Cumbernauld, see Rte. 10A.

RAILWAY from Buchanan St. Station, 46½ m. in 1½ hr. Principal Stations : 22 m. *Larbert.*—30¼ m. **Stirling.**—33¼ m. *Bridge of Allan.*—35 m. *Dunblane.*—39 m. *Doune.*—46½ m. **Callander.**

We quit Glasgow viâ Sighthill (Pl. 7) and follow A 803 to (7½ m.) **Kirkintilloch** (14,825 inhab ; *Kincaid House*, RB. 22/6, P. 10 gs., on the Milton road), an ancient town on the Roman Wall and the Forth and Clyde Canal. *Old St. Mary's,* a Gothic church of 1644, is to be restored as a museum.

FROM KIRKINTILLOCH TO CALLANDER viâ the Crow Road, 27½ m. A by-road goes N. to (1¾ m.) *Milton of Campsie,* with print-works, where A 891 leads W. to (3½ m.) *Lennoxtown,* a small town with print-works and mines. Norman Macleod (p. 113), whose father was parish minister, is buried in the churchyard.—On the road to Strathblane, 1¾ m. W., is **Campsie,** a village with the ruins of an old church, at the entrance of *Campsie Glen,* one of the prettiest glens near Glasgow. The path up the glen, passing the falls, joins the Crow Road (see below). To the N.W. rises *Earl's Seat* (1896 ft.), the highest of the Campsie Fells. Half way to Strathblane, S. of the (disused) railway, is *Craigend,* where Sir Thos. Mitchell (1792–1855), the Australian-explorer, was born. Dunglass, a volcanic vent on the left, displays columnar basalt similar to Staffa.

From the W. road of Lennoxtown, the Crow Road (r.) steadily climbs, with magnificent views over the Clyde valley, to 1064 ft. and then drops to (10½ m.) *Fintry* (Clachan Inn, RB. 25/). On either side are the *Campsie Fells,* whose short grass barely covers igneous rocks " along the S. flank of which the successive sheets of lava may be traced by the eye." With the *Fintry Hills* (1676 ft.) prominent on the right, B 822 goes on viâ (18½ m.) *Kippen* and (22½ m.) *Thornhill* to (27½ m.) *Callander,* see Rte. 23B.

We cross the Kelvin into Stirlingshire.—*Kilsyth* is a mining town (9925 inhab.) near which, on Aug. 15th, 1645, Montrose gained a signal victory over the Covenanters under General Baillie, putting 6000 of them to the sword, and losing hardly 10 of his own men. Relics of the battle are on view at *Colzium,* a mansion ½ m. N.E., now a community centre (adm. week-days, except Thurs., 2–5). To the N. rise the Kilsyth Hills, the highest point of which is Meiklebin (1870 ft.).

A hill road (l.), crossing the Carron at Carronbridge Hotel, offers an alternative approach to Stirling, avoiding the industrial areas.

The Highlands and Lowlands meet in **Stirlingshire,** which stretches from E. to W. across the waist of Scotland, from the industrial region of Falkirk and Grangemouth, on the shores of the Forth, to the moorlands about Ben Lomond and Inversnaid, on the banks of Loch Lomond. Its central position early gave

this county importance, and many decisive battles have been fought within
its bounds : Stirling Bridge (1297), the first battle of Falkirk (1298), Bannockburn
(1314), Sauchieburn (1488), Kilsyth (1645), and the second battle of Falkirk
(1746). Stirling, its ancient capital, looks down from a historic past upon the
fertile Carse of Stirling and the famous Links of the Forth.

Beyond (19 m.) *Dennyloanhead*, a mining village, our route
strikes N. to (20¾ m.) *Denny*, a small manufacturing town on
the Carron (6750 inhab., incl. Dunipace). At (26½ m.) *St.
Ninian's* we join the road from Edinburgh, near the site of
the *Battle of Bannockburn*, on the outskirts of (28 m.) **Stirling,**
see Rte. 24.

B. Edinburgh to Callander

ROAD. 54 m. A 9. To (26¼ m.) *Camelon*, see Rte. 10A.—28 m. *Larbert.*—35¾ m.
Stirling.—39 m. *Bridge of Allan.*—42 m. *Dunblane.*—A 820. 46 m. *Doune.*—A 84.
54 m. **Callander.**—MOTOR-BUS hourly in 2¾ hrs. ; to *Stirling* in 2 hrs. every ½ hr.
   RAILWAY from Princes St. Station, 52¼ m. in 1 hr. 40 min.–2¼ hrs. Principal
Stations : 25½ m. *Falkirk.*—28½ m. *Larbert.*—36½ m. **Stirling.**—39½ m. *Bridge
of Allan.*—41½ m. *Dunblane.*

From Edinburgh viâ Falkirk to (26½ m.) *Camelon*, see Rte.
10A.—A 9 bears r. for (28 m.) **Larbert** (*Red Lion*, RB. 18/6 ;
Station, RB. 14/), an important railway junction. In the
village churchyard an iron pillar marks the grave of James
Bruce (1730–94), the African traveller, who, after surviving
the perils of an adventurous career, met his death by falling
downstairs in his residence, Kinnaird House, 2½ m. N.E.—
Beyond (30¾ m.) *Plean* we have good views of the Ochil Hills
(r.) and of the Wallace Monument, ahead.—33½ m. *Bannockburn*, a coalminers' village, is not convenient for the battlefield.—At (34½ m.) *St. Ninian's* we join the road from Glasgow.
   This neighbourhood (the exact spot is doubtful) witnessed also the *Battle of
Sauchieburn* in 1488, when James III was defeated by his insurgent nobles, with
his son in the midst. The king, grievously wounded, was carried into a near-by
mill house, and there, as the story goes, was stabbed to death by a man calling
himself a priest.

35¾ m. **Stirling,** see Rte. 24.
As it quits Stirling the road crosses the Forth, affording
good views of the Old Bridge (l. ; p. 210) and, in the distance,
of the Campsie Fells, the cone of Ben Lomond, Ben Venue, and
Ben Ledi. On the right is the Abbey Craig with the conspicuous Wallace Monument and beyond the important
crossroads at (37½ m.) *Causewayhead* is Airthrey Castle (1791).

39 m. **Bridge of Allan** (*Allan Water*, RB. 32/6, P. 14½ gs. ;
Royal, RB. 27/, P. 12 gs. ; *Queen's*, RB. 22/6, P. 10 gs. ;
Allangrange, RB. 21/6, P. 10 gs. ; *Carmichael's, Eagleton*,
RB. 18/6–19/, P. 9 gs., these two unlic. ; *Walmer*, RB. 18/6,
P. 7 gs.) is a quiet holiday resort (3175 inhab.), especially
pleasant in spring. The little town is charmingly situated, with
its numerous villas stretching in terraces along the Airthrey

Woods overlooking the Allan Water, and is an admirable centre for walks and drives. The saline waters (antiscorbutic and aperient) are drunk in the Well House, near the Allan Water Hotel.

Lecropt church, 1 m. N.W. on the Doune road, contains the Keir loft, dating from 1826. It stands at the approach to *Keir*, formerly the seat of Sir William Stirling Maxwell (d. 1878), the authority on Spanish art, where Chopin was a guest in 1848.—*Dunmyat* (1375 ft.), a conical hill, c. 3 m. E. of Bridge of Allan, commands one of the finest low-ascent views in Scotland.

The Dunblane road crosses the Allan Water on a bridge of 1957–58 and enters Perthshire passing Keir on the left. A more attractive road diverges to the right at the bridge and leads through Kippenross Glen.

42 m. **DUNBLANE** (*Hotel-Hydro*, P. 15 gs., above the town ; *Stirling Arms*, RB. 23/6, P. 12 gs., beside the 15th cent. bridge ; *Dunkeld House*, RB. 30/, P. 13 gs. ; *Atholl Arms*, RB. 22/6, P. 10 gs. ; *The Neuk*, RB. 16/6, P. 7 gs. ; *Schiehallion*, RB. 16/, P. 6 gs., these two unlic.), the home of Tannahill's ' Jessie, the Flower of Dunblane,' is a charming little ' city ' (2985 inhab.) pleasantly situated on the swift and tawny Allan.

The ***Cathedral**, at the end of High St., is a beautiful Gothic edifice of the 13th cent. with a Norman tower incorporated at an awkward angle with the S. wall of the nave. The W. front, a good example of pure E.E., comprises a deeply recessed portal surmounted by a triplet of tall lancet windows of two lights each. Above (and seen only from the outside) is the so-called ' Ruskin Window,' a vesica adorned with carved foliage enthusiastically praised by John Ruskin. The cathedral is open free on weekdays 10–4 or 7 (Sun. 2–4 or 5.30). Sunday services at 11.15 and 6.30.

History. Dunblane was made a bishopric by David I, who, it is believed, founded the cathedral c. 1150 on the site of a Celtic church built by St. Blane (6th cent.), but only the two lower stories of the tower are David's work, the upper stories being of the 15th century. The existing church, notably the two lower stories of the tower, was mainly erected by Bishop Clement (c. 1233–58), the real founder of the see, but there are alterations and additions of the 15th century. Neglected after the Reformation, the roof of the nave collapsed in the late 16th cent., but the choir continued to be used as the parish church. A thorough and admirable restoration of the nave was completed in 1893, followed by that of the choir in 1914.—The saintly Robert Leighton (1611–84) was bishop of Dunblane from 1662 until his translation to the archbishopric of Glasgow in 1670.

Interior. The noble aisled NAVE of eight bays has a fine clerestory with double arches towards the W., single towards the E. The stained glass and the roof are modern. At the E. end of the S. aisle (behind a curtain) is the effigy of Bishop Ochiltree, who crowned James II in 1437. At the W. end of the nave stand six carved stalls, known as the Bishop's Stalls (early 16th cent.), and to the S. is the entrance to ' Katie Ogie's Hole,' a small vaulted chamber in the W. wall of unknown history (perhaps the prison of a ' witch ' awaiting

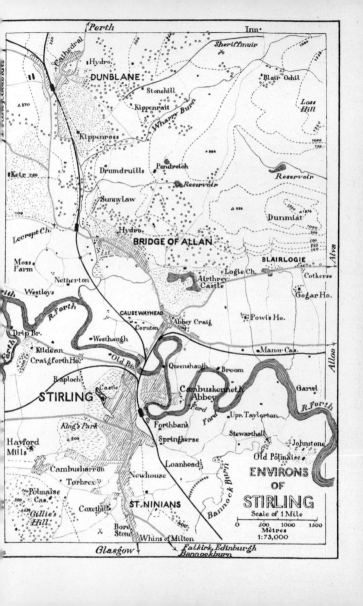

ENVIRONS
OF
STIRLING

Scale of 1 Mile

0   500   1000   1500

Mètres

1:73,000

trial). At the W. end of the N. aisle is a stone showing a Celtic cross and allegorical carvings (c. 900), and farther E. are the recumbent effigies of Malise, 5th Earl of Strathearn, and his countess (1271). The modern pulpit bears figures illustrating the history of the see.—Three blue slabs in the pavement in the centre of the aisleless Choir of six bays commemorate Margaret Drummond, wife but not queen of James IV, and her two sisters, poisoned at Drummond Castle in 1502 by certain nobles who favoured a more influential royal alliance with Princess Margaret of England. An effigy on the N. wall is supposed to represent Bishop Clement (see above) or Bishop Finlay Dermoch, who built the bridge over the Allan. The E. end of the low vaulted Lady Chapel, adjoining the choir on the N., is now a War Memorial by Lorimer, with windows by Strachan.

To the S. of the cathedral are the 17th cent. *Dean's House*, with an interesting little Cathedral Museum ; and *Bp. Leighton's Library*, in a building of 1687–88, marked with his arms, which retains its original fittings and most of his books. This and the museum are open free on weekdays 2–5. The path by the river at the W. end is known as ' the Bishop's Walk ' after Bishop Leighton, and pleasant walks may be enjoyed in the *Beech Walk* and *Wharrie Woods* to the S.E.

About 3 m. E. of Dunblane is **Sheriffmuir**, celebrated for the indecisive battle fought there in 1715, between the Earl of Mar, who commanded the Pretender's forces, and the Duke of Argyll, at the head of the Royal troops, whose object was to prevent Mar from crossing the Forth to join his friends in the South. The right wing on each side was completely victorious, the left wing on each side was completely routed. Both sides claimed the victory, but the fruits of it were with Argyll, for Mar retreated.

> " There's some say that we wan,
> And some say that they wan,
> And some say that nane wan at a', man."

The *Gathering Stone of the Clans* (protected by a grating), upon which the Highlanders are said to have sharpened their dirks before the action, is best reached on foot by following the road up the hill behind the hydropathic, leading past Dykedale farm (numerous sign-posts). Near the stone is a simple Inn past which a rough road crosses the moor to Greenloaning (4 m. N. ; views).

To the N.W., on the right bank of the Ardoch burn, is the attractively situated castle of *Kilbryde* (1460), long a residence of the Earls of Menteith.

From Dunblane to *Perth*, see Rte. 26.

Doune Castle is seen on the left as we cross the Ardoch burn and reach (46 m.) **Doune** (*Deanston House*, to the W. beyond the river, RB. 27/6, P. 12 gs. ; *Woodside*, RB. 21/, P.10 gs.), a large village of 850 inhab., formerly noted for its fairs of Highland cattle and sheep, and in c. 1650–1800 for the manufacture of pistols. The bridge here over the rapid Teith was built in 1535 by Robert Spittal, tailor to James IV.

* **Doune Castle** (adm. daily until sundown ; 1/6), though a ruin, is one of the grandest relics of Scottish baronial architecture. Robert, Duke of Albany (d. 1419), and his son, Murdoch, were the builders, and when Murdoch was executed in 1425 the castle was forfeited to the Crown, to be later settled by

James IV upon his queen, Margaret. Margaret's third husband was Lord Methven, a descendant of the Dukes of Albany, and the office of constable of the castle became hereditary in his family, now represented by the Earl of Moray. In 1745–46 the castle was held for Prince Charles Stewart by Macgregor of Glengyle, and in it were confined not only the hero of Scott's 'Waverley,' but also the prisoners taken at Falkirk, including a number of Edinburgh University Volunteers (among them Home, the author of 'Douglas '), who escaped by means of a rope of twisted bedclothes.—The castle, strongly posted on a triangular site, washed on two sides by the Teith and Ardoch and protected on the third by a deep moat, encloses a large court, with a large square external tower at the N.E. corner and an internal tower of later date at the N.W. corner. We enter through the great tower, in which is the baron's hall, while the other tower contains the kitchen and guest-rooms. Between the towers, both of which command extensive views, is the large dining hall.

Leaving Doune, the road skirts the *Braes of Doune* (r.) the highest point of which, *Uam Var* (2179 ft.), c. 5 m. N., was crossed by the stag in the 'Lady of the Lake.' On the bank of the Teith are seen (47½ m.) *Lanrick Castle* and then (50½ m.) *Cambusmore*, where Sir Walter Scott, collecting ' local colour ' for ' The Lady of the Lake,' was more than once a guest of the Buchanan family. On one occasion he personally timed a gallop from Coilantogle Ford (p. 214) to Stirling. The road now crosses the Keltie, the very name of which reminds the traveller that he is on the borders of the Highlands. Straight in front rises the peak of Ben Ledi.

54 m. **CALLANDER,** a large village (1725 inhab.) and an excellent tourist centre, with ample accommodation for visitors, is situated on the Teith, near its junction with the Leny.

Hotels. Dreadnought, RB. 30/, P. 14 gs.; **Ancaster Arms,** RB. 25/, P. 12 gs.; **Roman Camp,** RB. 35/, P. 15 gs.; **Pinewood,** RB. 23/6, P. 11 gs.; **Caledonian,** RB. 20/, P. 9½ gs.; **Waverley,** unlic., RB. 19/6, P. 9 gs.; **Crown,** RB. 17/6, P. 9 gs.

Motor-Buses to *Stirling* (55 min.) viâ Doune, going on to *Glasgow* (2¼ hrs.) or *Edinburgh* (3 hrs.); to *Crieff* (1¾ hr.) viâ Lochearnhead and St. Fillans; etc.—MOTOR-COACH TOURS (3/–15/) to all points of interest in the vicinity.

As the nearest railway station to the Trossachs, Loch Vennachar, Loch Achray, and Loch Katrine, and to the whole romantic and beautiful region of Scott's ' Lady of the Lake,' Callander is an animated resort in summer. As we look upstream from the bridge over the Teith we have the wooded Callander Craig on the right and in front the grand outline of Ben Ledi, which is nowhere seen to greater advantage. The traditional location of a Roman camp at Callander, long connected with some grassy embankments E. of the town, was confirmed in 1948 near the old farm of *Bochastle*, 1 m. W., between the rivers.

Just W. of Callander on a peninsula, at the confluence of the rivers, is *Little Leny*, the ancestral burial-ground of the Buchanans, with a memorial to Dugald Buchanan (d. 1768), the Gaelic poet.

A pleasant walk, passing the golf course, leads to *Bracklinn Falls* (" Bracklinn's thundering wave ") on the Keltie, c. 1½ m. N.E., above the village.—A track, diverging to the left c. ¼ m. short of the falls, goes on up the Keltie and then across the hills to (8 m.) *Auchinner Lodge*, whence a road descends " lone

Glenartney's hazel shade," the opening scene of 'The Lady of the Lake,' to *Dalginross*, a suburb of (14½ m.) *Comrie* (p. 227).

A picturesque and good road leads W. from Callander, skirting the Leny beyond (1 m.) *Kilmahog* (just short of which the 'Trossachs route' diverges to the left; see Rte. 25), to (2½ m.) the beautiful ***Pass of Leny**, at the foot of Ben Ledi, where road, river, and railway (p. 327) have scarcely room to run. A footpath descends (l.) to the stream and, after skirting for some distance the foaming Leny as it dashes in rapids through a narrow rocky gorge, rejoins the road c. ¾ m. S. of the site of *St. Bride's Chapel* (3¾ m. from Callander), where the fiery cross was thrust into the hands of young Norman on his very marriage morn. The fine road goes on, skirting the E. bank of Loch Lubnaig, to (9 m.) Strathyre.

Ben Ledi (2875 ft.; 'the hill of God') is easily ascended in c. 1½ hr. from (2¼ m.) the farm of *Coilantogle* (p. 214), where a sign post indicates the beginning of the path. The descent may be made to the Pass of Leny (E.) or to Glen Finglas (W.) and Brig o' Turk (p. 214) 4 m. W. of Coilantogle. The *View, like that from many other mountains on the edge of the Highlands, unites a pleasing variety of mountain and lowland scenery.

From Callander to the *Trossachs*, *Loch Katrine*, and *Loch Lomond* (*Glasgow*), see Rte. 25; to the *Lake of Menteith* and *Aberfoyle*, see p. 218; to *Oban*, see Rte. 46; to *Perth* viâ Dunblane, see Rte. 26.

24. STIRLING AND ITS ENVIRONS

STIRLING (26,950 inhab.; *Rfmts.*), an interesting and ancient royal burgh whose name is prominent in the martial and the political annals of Scotland, stands nobly on rising ground, overlooking the river Forth "that bridles the wild Highlandman." Its castle is situated on a precipitous bluff (340 ft.; recalling the Castle Rock at Edinburgh), whence its irregular streets lead down to the plain.

Hotels. Golden Lion (a; 12), 8 King St., RB. 25/6, P. 14½ gs.; **Station** (b; 9), Murray Place, RB. 25/, P. 12½ gs.; **Garfield**, Victoria Sq. (beyond Pl. 10), **King's Park**, Victoria Pl. (Pl. 10), both unlic., RB. 19/6; **Douglas** (f; 9), Commercial, 12 King St., RB. 19/6; **Allan Bank**, 20 Allan Park (Pl. 12), RB. 18/6.

Restaurants. *Gateway*, 6 Maxwell Pl. (Pl. 9; near P.O.); *Cruachan*, 18 Maxwell Place.

Post Office (Pl. 9), in Murray Place.

Motor-Buses from the Bus Station

in Thistle St. (beyond Pl. 12) to *Bannockburn* (10 min.) and *Falkirk* (¾ hr.), *Linlithgow* (1 hr.) and *Edinburgh* (2 hrs.); to *Glasgow* (1–1¼ hr.) viâ Cumbernauld or Kilsyth; to *Kippen*, *Buchlyvie* and *Balfron* (1 hr.); to *Aberfoyle* (1 hr.); to *Bridge of Allan* (8 min.), *Dunblane* (14 min.), *Perth* (1½ hr.), and *Dundee* (2¼ hrs.); to *Dollar* (40 min.), *Kinross* (1¼ hr.), *Cupar* (2¼ hrs.) and *St. Andrews* (2¾ hrs.); to *Alloa* (50 min.); to *Dunfermline* (1½ hr.), etc.

Theatre. *Little*, at the foot of Upper Craigs (beyond Pl. 12).

History. The history of "the bulwark of the North, Grey Stirling," the key of the main passage between the N. and S. of Scotland, is substantially the history of its castle, an ancient name for which (perhaps poetical only) was *Snawdon* or *Snowdoun*. Alexander I died in the castle in 1124, William the Lion in 1214. Stirling, surrendered to the English in 1296, but retaken by Sir William Wallace at the battle of Stirling Bridge the next year, was the last place in all Scotland that held out against Edward I, who laid siege to it in person in 1304. When, after an obstinate resistance, the garrison under Sir William Oliphant capitulated, they amounted to only 140 men. It was in order to raise the siege of Stirling, ten years later, that Edward II hazarded the fateful fight of Bannockburn. Under the Stewarts Stirling was a favourite royal residence and played for a time practically the rôle of capital of the kingdom. Within its walls were born James III (1451) and possibly James IV (1472). James V, brought to Stirling for safety in 1513, is styled ' Knight of Snowdoun ' in ' The Lady of the Lake.' The infant Queen Mary was crowned in the High Church at the age of 9 months, and her son, James VI, whose baptism was " performed in a papistical manner " in the castle chapel, spent his boyhood in the castle-palace, with George Buchanan as his tutor. His son, Prince Henry, was born in the castle in 1594. The castle was taken by General Monk in 1651 and unsuccessfully besieged by Prince Charles Stewart in 1746. In Aug. 1787 Burns spent two nights in what is now the Golden Lion hotel.

From the modern centre of the town we make for the castle by ascending King St. (Pl. 12), Baker St., and Bow St. to Broad St. (Pl. 5, 8), in the centre of which is the old *City Cross* (shaft modern). Facing up the street is a 17th cent. house of the Erskines of Mar, bearing the erroneous inscription ' Darnley's House, the nursery of James VI and of his son Prince Henry ' ; and on the W. side is the old *Town House* (1701), replacing that in front of which John Hamilton, last Roman Catholic Archbishop of St. Andrews, was hanged in 1571. Several other reconditioned 17th and early-18th cent. houses survive in this street.

At the upper end of Broad St. stands **Mar's Work** (Pl. 5), a singular fragment of Scottish domestic architecture (1570 ; never finished), in an uncouth sort of Renaissance architecture, with statues and pilasters projecting from the walls.

The royal arms over the main entrance are flanked by those of Mar and his countess. On the front wall are two inscribed tablets (one reading, ' I pray a lvikaris on this lvging vith gentil e to gif thair ivging ') and a third on the back.

Omitting for the present a visit to the High Church (see below), we turn to the right, passing **Argyll's Lodging** (Pl. 5), 'probably the finest specimen of an old town residence remaining in Scotland,' which has several times been occupied by royalty. Since 1799 it has been a military hospital.

It was built in 1632 by Sir William Alexander (1567 ?–1640), the poetic Earl of Stirling, whose arms appear above the doorway, but when he died insolvent in 1640 it passed to the Argyll family, whose crest, a boar's head, may be seen over some of the windows in the attractive court, dating from an enlargement in 1674.

Farther on is the *Castle Esplanade*, on which is a colossal statue of Bruce, in the act of sheathing his sword after Bannockburn. In the gardens below (S.W. side) is a pyramid to the Covenanters.

The ***Castle** (Pl. 1) is in a commanding position, but has been sadly neglected. Its historical buildings long sacrificed to the requirements of a modern barrack, are being slowly restored (adm. 1/, 10–4 or 7, Sun. from 2).

The office of keeper of Stirling Castle, hereditary in the Erskine family from 1370 (with one short break), was forfeited by the Earl of Mar in 1715 after the battle of Sheriffmuir, but was restored to the Earl of Mar and Kellie in 1923.

The *Outworks* at the first moat date from the time of Queen Anne (1709). The stunted drum towers of the *Gatehouse* were erected by James III (1460–88), who built also the square *Princes' Tower* (l.), in which James VI was educated. Two half-drums on either side were reduced in the 18th cent. to their present level. The ramparts to the left command a good view of the King's Knott and King's Garden. As we enter the Outer Court or Lower Square, we have on our left the **Palace**, begun in 1540 by James V and finished by his widow, Mary of Guise.

It is a fantastic building with curious pillars and emblematic figures recalling in some of its features the Manueline style of Portugal. Amongst those on the N. and S. are types of Scottish soldiers of the 14th cent.; on the E. grotesque representations of a king, a queen, a chamberlain, a cook, lust, Venus, etc. Some of the oak carvings of the kings and queens, called the 'Stirling Heads,' which adorned the ceiling of the presence-chamber but were taken down in 1777, are preserved in the Smith Institute.

To the right in Lower Square, near the castle well, are some (re-excavated) vaults that served as the palace kitchens, and lower down is the vaulted entrance (perhaps 13th cent.) to the Nether Bailey, surmounted by a building which served as the *Royal Mint*.

Facing us is the gable end, with two of the original windows of the *Parliament Hall*, 125 ft. long, a Gothic building with details foreshadowing the Renaissance, said to have been designed by Robert Cochrane, the cultured favourite of James III (c. 1475). It is still unhappily divided and converted into dormitories and store-rooms. This and the Palace form respectively the E. and S. sides of the Upper Square. On the N. side is the *Chapel Royal* (no adm.), built in 1501 as a collegiate church by James IV and rebuilt in 1594 by James VI, who had been both christened (1566) and crowned in it. The building on the W. of the square, on the probable site of an older palace, bears a tablet in memory of Sir Wm. Oliphant (see above).

On the left in Upper Square is the entrance to the *Museum of the Argyll & Sutherland Highlanders* (6d.; 10–12.30, 2–4.30).

A passage at the N.W. corner of this court admits to a small garden, whence a flight of steps ascends to an ante-room with relics from excavations in the castle and from the field of Bannockburn, Knox's pulpit and communion table from the Chapel Royal, James VI's tilting lance, etc. Adjoining is the *Douglas Room*, partially rebuilt after a fire in 1856.

In a room on this site William, eighth Earl of Douglas, was stabbed by James II in 1452, and then thrown out of the window. The skeleton of an armed man, supposed to be his, was found in the garden in 1797.

The view from '*Queen Victoria's Look-out*' (420 ft. above the sea) at the N.W. corner of the ramparts above the garden is magnificent. The balustrade bears the initials of royal visitors.

To the W. are the Campsie Fells; from W. to N. Ben Lomond, Ben Venue, Ben Ledi, and Ben Vorlich; N.E. the Ochils, below which are the winding Links o' Forth, with the Wallace Monument and Cambuskenneth Abbey; and S. the field of Bannockburn. In the foreground, N.W., is the rich Carse of Stirling and across it Doune Castle. Below, to the N.E., across Ballengeich, rises the *Gowan* or *Gowlan Hill* (Pl. 2), on which Prince Charles Stewart planted his batteries in

1746, so as to oblige the citizens and spare the town. They were speedily silenced by the Castle guns. Near its N. angle is the *Heading Hill*, the place of execution.

Below the rampart farther on is seen the ancient *Sally-port*, which led to *Ballengeich*, and may have been used as an exit by James V when he went out, disguised as the ' Guidman of Ballengeich,' to seek adventures among his people.

A flight of steps descends from the Esplanade to the valley between the Castle and the High Church, in former days the tilting ground, but now a cemetery and public garden containing a representation of the Wigtown Martyrs, enclosed by glass. Close to the last is the *Ladies' Rock* (view indicator), whence the ladies of the court watched the games in the valley below, but the view (once almost as good as that from the ramparts) is somewhat hidden by foliage.

From the Castle we may return as we came or find our way through the cemetery to the ***Church of the Holy Rude** (Pl. 8 ; adm. daily), a fine Gothic building, 196 ft. long and 55 ft. wide inside, with a choir considerably higher than the nave, which gives it a distinctive external appearance. From 1656 to 1935 it was divided into the W. and E. parish churches, but the dividing wall was removed and the crossing well restored in 1936-40. At the W. end is a plain square battlemented *Tower* (90 ft.), stepped back on the N. and S., on which the shot marks made by the guns during Monk's siege (1651) are still visible. The *Nave* of five bays with massive round pillars was begun c. 1415, and has a contemporary oak roof and vaulted aisles. The *Choir*, with its high-pitched ceiling, was built in 1510-23. The E. end (an addition attributed to Cardinal Beaton) is apsidal, and has a fine window and a notable roof. In the vaulted N. chapel is a piscina from Cambuskenneth (long used as a font). Here and in the choir the consecration crosses are conspicuous.

In this church—long erroneously called ' Greyfriars ' after a Franciscan house which stood near the present High School and was destroyed in 1559—Mary was crowned (1543) at the age of 9 months ; here, in the same year, the Earl of Arran renounced the Reformed faith ; and here, in 1544, Mary of Guise, mother of the infant queen, was appointed regent of Scotland. In 1567 James VI when a year old was crowned in the choir—John Knox preaching the sermon. James Guthrie (1612 ?–1661), the Covenanting martyr, was minister of the E. church ; and Ebenezer Erskine (1680–1754), founder of the Scottish Secession Church, was minister of the W. church.

Close to the church (S.W.) is the **Guildhall** (adm. free May–Sept. 10–8, Sun. 2–6 ; in winter, weekdays 10–4), or *Cowane's Hospital* (Pl. 7), an old charitable institution bearing a statue of its founder, John Cowane (d. 1634) and pious inscriptions.

Its main hall contains Cowane's chest, copiously inscribed, his Bible, old Scots weights and measures, etc. An annual income of some £4000 is now distributed in out-relief.

St. John St. and Spittal St. lead downhill from the church passing (r.) *Erskine Marykirk* (1826), with a memorial to Erskine before it, and the *High School*. At the foot of the street are the old *Burgh Buildings* with a steeple and a figure of Wallace.

Corn Exchange Rd. (Pl. 11, 12), diverging to the r. at the Burgh Buildings, leads past the *Municipal Buildings* (r.) and *Library* (l.), beyond which is a section of the *Town Wall*. To the r. Albert Place leads to the *Albert Halls* and the

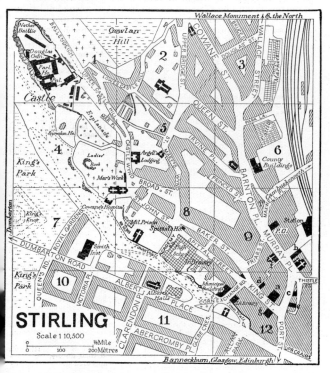

Smith Institute (Pl. 7; adm. 6*d*., weekdays 10–4 or 5), containing a picture gallery, a library, and a museum of local antiquities. Among the last are the 'Stirling Heads' (p. 207), the 'Stirling Jug' (the standard of the old Scots pint), calthrops from Bannockburn, Doune pistols, Highland dirks, the oldest dated curling-stone (1511), etc. The picture gallery includes works by John Phillip and other Scottish artists and Jacob Maris and Fantin Latour; water-colours by Cox, Bonington, and David Muirhead.—Farther on are the grassy terraces of the *King's Garden*, with the mound known as the *King's Knott* (adm. free 10–4 or 7, Sun. 10–4), showing the lay-out of a formal garden, perhaps of James V. Opposite these is the *King's Park*, now a recreation ground and golf course.

Murray Pl. is continued N. by Barnton Place (Pl. 6, 9) and Wallace St. (Pl. 3) to (c. 1 m.) *Stirling Bridge,* a few yards above which is the **Old Bridge** (c. 1400), long the only exit to the N. and still used as a footbridge. The battle of Stirling Bridge, however, at which in 1297 Wallace defeated the Earl of Surrey, is supposed to have been fought at a wooden bridge, of which no trace remains, c. 1 m. farther upstream.

The road to the North crossing Stirling Bridge goes on to (1½ m. from Stirling) *Causewayhead,* situated below the *Abbey Craig* (362 ft.), held by Wallace on the eve of the battle. This is now crowned by the **Wallace Monument** (1869), an elaborate and widely conspicuous tower, 220 ft. high, famous for its *View (adm. 6*d.*). The interior contains Wallace's sword (5½ ft. long) which was stolen in 1936 and replaced in 1941, and marble busts of eminent Scots. Cambuskenneth Abbey lies 1½ m. S.

Cambuskenneth Abbey is ¾ m. E. of Stirling by footbridge and path (r.) reached viâ Maxwell Place (Pl. 9). Founded by David I c. 1140 for Austin canons, the abbey became mitred in 1406. All that now remains above the foundations is a noble detached tower (14th cent.), the W. doorway of the church, and another tall building (? part of the infirmary). A staircase ascends the *Tower* (adm. 6*d.*, 10–4 or 7, Sun. from 2 ; *View) which contains coped gravestones and a dug-out canoe from the Forth. At times the Scottish Parliament met here, but the abbey was given in 1604 to the Earl of Mar, who is said to have reduced it to ruins in order to build Mar's Work (p. 206). James III (d. 1488) and his Queen, Margaret of Denmark, were buried at Cambuskenneth, and in 1864 a monument was erected to their memory by Queen Victoria as a " restoration of the tomb of her ancestors."

FROM STIRLING TO THE FIELD OF BANNOCKBURN. Taking almost any motorbus going S., we alight at the main cross-roads in (1¼ m.) the village of *St. Ninian's.* Thence we proceed to the right by the Glasgow road, to the right again at the next fork, and in c. 8 min. reach the memorial cairn (1957) beside the *Borestone* (protected by a grating). Here Bruce's standard is said to have been planted during the **Battle of Bannockburn** (June 23rd, 1314) fought in the triangular level between the Bannock and the Forth. The exact site of the battle is disputed, but modern research seems to place it considerably E. of the traditional site and on a different alignment. The English army, advancing to raise the siege of Stirling, were greatly superior in numbers and were led by Edward II in person, but Bruce, whose forces were almost entirely pikemen, strengthened his carefully selected position by strewing his front with calthrops and planting sharp stakes in concealed pits, so as to hamper the attack of the English cavalry. The English, though defeated, stood their ground until the Scottish camp-followers, like a fresh army, suddenly appeared over the *Gillies' Hill* on the N.W., now planted with fir trees. The rout was complete, the slaughter of the fleeing foe was immense, and the independence of Scotland was won. Stirling was surrendered to the Scots and Edward II fled, without drawing bridle, to Dunbar. The encounter between Bruce and the impetuous De Bohun, so graphically described by Scott in ' The Lord of the Isles,' took place on the day before the battle. The National Trust owns 58 acres of the battlefield. —*Bannockburn House,* over 1 m. S. beyond the Bannock Burn, was the headquarters of Prince Charles in Jan. 1746, where he first met Clementina Walkinshaw.

FROM STIRLING TO BALLOCH viâ BUCHLYVIE, A 811, 31 m.—This road, connecting the two great central rivers of Scotland, runs in the wide strath between the Gargunnock, Fintry, and Campsie Hills, on the S., and the advance posts of the Highland ranges on the N.—10 m. *Kippen* (Crown, RB. 16/6) claims to possess the largest vine in the world (adm. 6*d.* ; N. end of village), producing c. 2000 bunches of grapes annually. Beyond is the wide *Flanders Moss* (r.), whose depth and shifting character gave the engineers of the railway much trouble. At (12½ m.) *Arnprior* B 8034 leads r. to Port of Menteith (4¾ m.).—14½ m. *Buchlyvie* has a local hand-weaving industry.—From (22½ m.) *Drymen* (Buchanan Arms, RB. 32/, P. c. 14½ gs. ; road to Glasgow, see p. 133) a shady road runs N.W., viâ (l.) the Buchanan Castle estate (golf course) and Balmaha, to Rowardennan (10½ m.; p. 139).—Beyond (25 m.) the bridge over the Endrick Water is *Kilmaronack Church*, near the site of 'Maronnan's Cell,' mentioned in 'The Lady of the Lake.'—After passing (27 m.) *Gartocharn* (p. 137) we reach (31 m.) **Balloch**, see Rte. 12B.

FROM STIRLING TO ABERFOYLE, 19½ m. The road (A 84) runs N.W., crossing the Forth just above the inflow of the Teith to enter the district of Menteith, with the estate of Blair Drummond on the right.—At (5¾ m.) *Kincardine-in-Menteith* we follow A 873 (l.); on the Doune road (A 84; r.) is the church of Kincardine (by Richard Crichton; 1816), containing 17–18th cent. Drummond monuments, including one of the few brasses in Scotland (17th cent.).—At (9½ m.) *Thornhill* (Lion & Unicorn, RB. 21/) the Kippen–Callander road is crossed.—15 m. *Port of Menteith* and thence to Aberfoyle, see Rte. 25.

FROM STIRLING TO ALLOA AND KINCARDINE, 12¾ m.; motor-bus in ¾ hr.—Quitting Stirling, we cross the Forth. Beneath the Wallace Monument we turn right and follow the N. side of the river, which winds tortuously through the *Links of the Forth*, so celebrated for their fertility that the saying runs : ' A crook o' the Forth is worth an earldom o' the North.' Alloa is 5½ m. from Stirling as the crow flies, but 12½ m. by the river.—Crossing the Devon we enter *Clackmannanshire* (55 sq. m.), the smallest county in Scotland, and reach (5 m.) *Tullibody*, birthplace of Robert Dick (1811–66), the geologist. Of the small Pre-Reformation church John Knox records that the French troops sent to aid Mary of Guise, "expert enough in such feats, tuke down the roof to make ane brig over the Devon," and so escaped to Stirling.

7 m. **Alloa** (*Station*, RB. 17/6), the largest town (13,450 inhab.) in Clackmannanshire, is noted for its manufactures of yarn, glass, ale, and whisky. It has a small harbour on the Forth. The parish church (1817–19) retains a tower of 1680. *Alloa Tower* (13th cent.), E. of the town, was a stronghold of the earls of Mar, with walls 13 ft. thick. Queen Mary, her son, James VI, and his son, Prince Henry, all spent part of their youth here ; and Mary revisited it in 1566 with Darnley. David Allan (1744–96), the 'Scottish Hogarth,' illustrator of Burns's poems, was son of the piermaster of Alloa. Above Alloa the Forth is crossed by a long railway bridge.

9½ m. *Clackmannan* (Tower, RB. 17/6), the ancient county town (2350 inhab.), lies above the road to the right. Grouped in the central square are the tower of the Tolbooth, the old Town Cross, and the stone or 'clach' of Mannan, of unknown origin. On the hill to the W. is a tall 15th cent. tower. In a house (now gone) beside the tower Robert Burns was ' knighted ' in 1787 with the sword of Bruce by Mrs. Bruce of Clackmannan.—At (11 m.) *Kilbagie* crossroads A 977 bears r. for (12¾ m.) *Kincardine Bridge* (Rte. 33).

A 907 keeps straight on at Kilbagie for (22 m.) *Dunfermline*, passing (17 m.) the modern ' model ' colliery of *Comrie*; while A 977 on the left leads to (29¼ m.) *Kinross* viâ Crook of Devon.

FROM STIRLING TO KINROSS, 21½ m.; motor-bus viâ Yetts of Muckhart in 1¼ hr.—We leave Stirling as above, keep left of the Wallace Monument on A 91, and pass Dunmyat (p. 202) on the left.

5 m. *Menstrie* is a small furniture-making town, the birth-place of Sir Ralph Abercromby (1734–1801). The 16th cent. castle, the home of Sir Wm. Alexander (? 1567–1640), founder of Nova Scotia, has been reconditioned.—7 m. **Alva** (4100 inhab. ; *Alva Glen*, RB. 15/), a wool-weaving town. The striking *Alva Glen* (with a waterfall at its head) is called the 'Silver Glen' from the former silver mines. The ascent of *Ben Cleuch* (2363 ft. ; wide view), the highest of the Ochils, may be combined with a visit to the glen by following the first large tributary from the E. (in all c. 3½ m. from Alva). The descent may be made to Tillicoultry or to Dollar.—9 m. *Tillicoultry*, a small town (3820 inhab.) with tartan and other woollen manufactures, has a handsome church.—As we follow the winding Devon we see the 19th cent. Harviestoun Castle (l.), sung by Burns.

12 m. **Dollar** (1385 inhab. ; *Castle Campbell*, RB. 16/6, P. 9 gs.) is best known for *Dollar Academy*, a school founded by John McNabb (d. 1802), a poor boy of the town who became a wealthy sea-captain. Opened in 1818, the school rose to fame under its first rector, Andrew Mylne (d. 1853). Conspicuous on the left above the village are the ruins of **Castle Campbell**, occupying an isolated position on the steep hill-side, and guarded by deep gorges which meet 300 yards below the fortress (N.T. with 60 acres ; adm. 6*d*., 10–4 or 7, Sun. from 2).

It is reached by a pleasant walk of c. 1 m., following the left bank of the burn from the main street. After crossing a field the glen is reached. When the glen forks, keep to the right up the E. gorge, or 'Burn of Care,' to the castle. The castle, at one time called 'Castle Gloom,' situated in the parish of 'Dolour' (Dollar), beside the waters of 'Grief' (Griff), and surrounded by the 'Glen of Care,' came by marriage to the Campbell family in the 15th cent., and the present building was begun after 1481 by the first Earl of Argyll, who gave it its new name in 1489. In 1556 John Knox preached here for a short time before going to Geneva ; in 1645 Montrose, on his way to Kilsyth, ravaged the surrounding country ; but the burning of the castle is due to the Cromwellians (c. 1654). It remained in the possession of the Argyll family until 1805.

The castle is entered through a vaulted pend (c. 1600) admitting to a court or barmkin. The square N.E. tower (15th cent.), the chief feature, is joined to the 16th cent. S. wing by a 17th (or late-16th) cent. range with an open loggia. On the first floor of the tower was the great hall, with the entrance to a pit-prison on the right of the fireplace ; the second floor is roofed over, while the third floor is covered by a great ribbed barrel-vault, an early-17th cent. addition. The view from the top is extensive rather than interesting.—We may return by the other stream—the 'Burn of Sorrow'—which flows through the *Windy Edge Pass*, an extraordinary and romantic chasm, in one place less than 10 ft. wide, with steep walls of bare rock some 80 ft. high.

From Dollar the ascent of *Ben Cleuch* (see above) is a walk of 6½ m. N.W. passing Castle Campbell.

Beyond Dollar we enjoy a splendid view of the Devon valley, where the woods in July are unequalled in their beauty. In 2 m. we turn r. on a by-road, at Muckhart golf course [The main road goes on to Yetts of Muckhart and

Milnathort, p. 257]. We cross (15½ m.) A 823 just N. of
Rumbling Bridge (p. 255), and cross the Devon to enter
Kinross-shire, the county of Loch Leven, a small shire lying
between the Ochils, on the W., and the Lomond Hills, on the
E.—16½ m. *Crook of Devon*, a village so called from its position
at a point where the river doubles back on itself, is on A 977.
On the right is *Tullibole Castle*, an interesting old tower,
bearing the date 1608.—21½ m. **Kinross,** see Rte. 34.

From Stirling to *Crieff* viâ Gleneagles, see Rte. 26 ; to *Edinburgh* or *Glasgow*,
see Rte. 23 ; to *Perth*, see Rte. 26 ; to the *Trossachs* viâ Callander, see Rte. 25.

25. THE TROSSACHS TOUR

The Trossachs.   Loch Katrine

The famous **Trossachs Tour,* one of the most popular in
Scotland, takes the traveller through a region of beautiful
and varied scenery—the lovely setting for the romantic
episodes of ' The Lady of the Lake ' as well as for some of the
dramatic scenes of ' Rob Roy.' This tour, in its traditional
form, leads from Callander viâ the Trossachs to Loch Katrine
and thence by steamers on Loch Katrine and Loch Lomond
to Balloch at the lower end of Loch Lomond. Travellers are
recommended to join one of the round tours organised by the
road transport companies or by tourist agents and beginning
at *Edinburgh* or *Glasgow*, which, though they entail an early
start, are easily made in one day.

The complete Trossachs tour, interrupted by two lakes, cannot be made by motor car. Determined cyclists, however (not
motor cyclists), may make their way from the Trossachs to
Stronachlachar and Inversnaid by the paths (N. bank) round
the head of Loch Katrine and return viâ Loch Ard, Aberfoyle
and the hill road thence.

A. From Edinburgh to the Trossachs viâ Callander

RAILWAY to *Callander*, 52½ m. in 2 hrs. from Princes St. viâ Larbert, or ROAD
(61 m.) viâ Larbert, Stirling, and Callander, see Rtes. 10B, 23B. The alternative
road approach viâ Stirling and Port of Menteith to Aberfoyle (see p. 211) may
be kept for the return. Thence MOTOR COACH to (9½ m.) *Trossachs Pier*. STEAMER
on Loch Katrine daily in summer to (7 m.) *Stronachlachar* and back. MOTOR
COACH thence to (5 m.) *Inversnaid*. STEAMER on Loch Lomond to Tarbet or
(18½ m.) *Balloch*.

From Edinburgh to (54 m.) *Callander*, see Rte. 23. At
Callander station a fleet of motor coaches awaits the train,
and seats are taken at once.—The Trossachs road (A 892)
crosses the Teith and turns right (W.) along its S. bank for
1½ m., then recrosses to the N. side. We approach and follow

the N. bank of **Loch Vennachar** (4 m. long), at the base of
Ben Ledi, where already the followers in Fitz-James's famous
chase had begun to tail off. At its E. end was *Coilantogle Ford*
" far past Clan-Alpine's outmost guard," the scene of the
combat between Fitz-James and Roderick Dhu, now occupied
by the sluices of the Glasgow waterworks. On the farther bank
of the loch appears Invertrossachs House, and Ben Venue is
well seen ahead of us. On the flats at the W. end of the loch
is *Lanrick Mead*, the muster-place of the Clan Alpine, i.e. the
MacGregors, but the road, quitting the loch, mounts to the
clachan of *Duncraggan*, where " Angus, heir of Duncan's line,"
left his father's funeral to speed the fiery cross to St. Bride's
(p. 205), and then descends to the *Brig o' Turk*, where " the
headmost horseman rode alone," Fitz-James having out-
distanced the rest of the hunt.

The picturesque bridge spans the Turk or Finglas water, descending from
Glen Finglas, the scene of Scott's weird ballad, ' Glenfinlas, or Lord Ronald's
Coronach.' By following the Finglas the pedestrian will find a choice of three
routes, viz. Glen Finglas, with a reservoir, to the W., leading over high hills to
Loch Doine and Loch Voil ; *Glen Main*, up which a track leads to Glen Buckie
and (11 m.) Balquhidder ; and *Glen Casaig*, whence he may proceed over *Ben
Vane* (2685 ft.) to Strathyre.

Beyond the Brig o' Turk the road, made entirely since Sir
Walter Scott's day, passes the small but lovely ***Loch Achray,**
whose shores are clothed with copse to the water's edge. On
the N. bank stands the *Trossachs Hotel* (RB. 27/6, P. 16 gs.).
At the W. end of the loch is the *Loch Achray Hotel* (RB. 27/6,
P. 12 gs.).

The Trossachs Hotel succeeds an inn known in Gaelic as ' Ardcheanocrochan '
(' head height of the knoll '). A path beginning behind the hotel ascends *Ben
A'an* (1750 ft. ; *View) ; the descent (steep) may be made to Loch Katrine.
Fine views are obtained also from the hill behind the hotel or from the road
which runs round the W. end of Loch Achray and over to (6¼ m.) *Aberfoyle*.—
Bealach-nam-Bo (see below) is within an hour's walk of the hotel.

The gorge of the ***Trossachs** (' bristly country '), where in a
' rugged dell ' Fitz-James's chase ended with the death of his
' gallant grey,' extends from Loch Achray to Loch Katrine,
between Ben A'an, on the right, and Ben Venue, on the left.
The ' old pass ' diverges to the right from the present road
just beyond the head of Loch Achray, and in Scott's time there
was no exit from the defile " excepting by a sort of ladder
composed by the branches and roots of trees." This whole
region is a rugged labyrinth of rocks and mounds covered with
a luxuriant vegetation of oak, birch, hazel, and rowan, heather,
bog-myrtle, and foxgloves, amid which the road winds in and
out, up and down, at each turn presenting fresh views of the
crags of Ben Venue or Ben A'an—" so wondrous wild the
whole might seem the scenery of a fairy dream." Important
afforestation has been undertaken since 1929, especially on
the Aberfoyle side, due care being taken not to harm the

scenic beauty, and 41,450 acres are now included in a National Forest Park.

A road diverging on the left, about half-way through the pass, leads beside the Achray water to the massive sluices of the Glasgow waterworks, on the far side of which lies **Bealach-nam-Bo**, the 'pass of the cattle,' through which the MacGregors used to drive their plunder from the lowlands. Here is some of the grandest scenery in the district. About ¾ m. above the sluices we reach the pass, which "yawns like a gash on warrior's breast," on the rough slopes of *Ben Venue* (2393 ft.), which may be ascended thence.

Our first view of ***Loch Katrine** surveys only a contracted but very beautiful reach, for a projecting crag conceals the main basin. A short descent brings us to (9 m.) the pier whence a little steamer (return fare 4/; cycle 1/) plies 2–4 daily (once on Sun.) in summer to Stronachlachar. To enjoy the full beauty of the loch and shore, however, we should follow the road on the N. bank (cars by permit only) to (1 m.) the site of the *Silver Strand* (now submerged), the scene of the meeting of Fitz-James and fair Ellen Douglas, the Lady of the Lake. Here, opposite Ellen's Isle, is the 'airy point' whence Fitz-James beheld the *View, eloquently described in the poem.

Loch Katrine, 9 m. long and 1 m. broad at its widest, derives its name, according to Scott, from the caterans or freebooters who frequented its shores. Its beauties were known even before the appearance of 'The Lady of the Lake' (1810), and Dorothy Wordsworth (1804) gives a graphic description of it in her diary. Since 1859 Loch Katrine has been one of the chief sources of the water supply of Glasgow (34 m. distant), of which fact there are numerous reminders in the neighbourhood, indicating the course of the subterranean aqueduct. The level of the lake has been raised 17 ft.

The road on the N. bank goes on to (8½ m.) *Glengyle* and is continued on the S. shore to (10½ m.) *Stronachlachar* (see below). The steamer makes an evening cruise (2/6) on Tues., Wed., Thurs., & Sun.

The little bay at the E. end of the loch is lovely in the extreme, and though farther on the banks become tamer, there is a charming view as the steamer makes its way through the narrow channel into the open loch. On the right is the site of the Silver Strand, on the left is the Bealach-nam-Bo and lower down the *Goblin's Cave*, where Douglas hid his daughter when he took her from the island. In front is *Ellen's Isle*, once the cattle-pen and larder of the Macgregors, who hid here their stolen herds and guarded them with a flotilla, but playing a more romantic part in Scott's poem. The massive peak of Ben Lomond comes into sight (l.) and there is a splendid view of the mountains beyond Loch Lomond as we approach the pier at **Stronachlachar,** 'the point of the mason,' where coaches meet the steamer to convey passengers to Inversnaid.

A road (no cars) leads N.W. from Stronachlachar to (2 m.) *Glengyle*, at the head of the loch, birthplace of Robert MacGregor or Campbell (1671–1734), better known as 'Rob Roy,' i.e. 'red Robert' (from the colour of his hair). Rob Roy, grazier and cattle-lifter, represented by tradition and Sir Walter Scott as a romantic and genial outlaw on the lines of Robin Hood, was a scion of the fierce clan of MacGregors, whose very name was proscribed in 1603 (comp. p. 137). In 1712, with £1000 belonging to his creditors, he retired to the hills behind Inversnaid to adopt the career of a freebooter. He was present as a Jacobite at the battle of Sheriffmuir (1715), but abstained from assisting either side. Later, under the wing of the Duke of Argyll, he established himself at Craigroyston (p. 139) and lived largely by blackmailing the lowland farmers. He submitted to General Wade in 1722 and was imprisoned in Newgate, but was pardoned in 1727. He died at Inverlochlaraig and is buried at Balquhidder.

The picturesque road to Inversnaid (5 m.), from which the road to Aberfoyle (see below) diverges (l.) almost immediately, enters Stirlingshire and rises quickly to **Loch Arklet** (507 ft.), a lake doubled in size since its inclusion in the Glasgow waterworks system. Helen MacGregor, Rob Roy's wife, is said to have been born in a cottage in Glen Arklet, c. 4 m. from Stronachlachar. The greater part of the descent to Loch Lomond, which is only 27 ft. above sea-level, is concentrated in one great zigzag at the W. end. Near the top of this descent a farm, still called ' the Garrison,' incorporates the remains of a fort, built in 1713 (and once commanded by General Wolfe) to overawe the clan MacGregor.

At **Inversnaid** (*Hotel*, RB. 24/, P. 14 gs.) we reach the "bonny, bonny banks of Loch Lomond" (p. 139). The steamer crosses the loch to *Tarbet* (railway to Glasgow), then descends to **Balloch** (1¾–2 hrs. ; p. 137) calling in the evening at Rowardennan and Balmaha; or the return may be varied by taking the road to Aberfoyle from the E. end of Loch Arklet (Rte. 25B).

B. From Glasgow to the Trossachs viâ Aberfoyle

ROAD (32 m.) viâ Strathblane. MOTOR COACH from Aberfoyle to *Trossachs Pier*, 6 m. ; thence as in Rte. 25A. MOTOR-BUS daily from Glasgow to Aberfoyle viâ Drymen in 1¾ hr.

From Glasgow on A 81 viâ Canniesburn to (5½ m.) *Milngavie*, see p. 132. The pleasant road leads past the reservoir (l.) and castle (r.) of (7½ m.) *Craigmaddie*, with an old moated tower. On *Blairskaith Muir*, behind the castle, are the curious boulders known as the *Auld Wives' Lifts*. We descend into the Blane valley, at the head of which is (10 m.) the prettily situated *Strathblane* (Kirkhouse Inn, small, RB. 15/6).

1 m. N.E. is the *Spout of Ballagan*, a series of cascades falling over a very fine example of stratification, where a great number of layers of sandstones, clays, and slates succeed each other with unusual regularity.

11 m. *Blanefield* (Blane Valley, RB. 35/, P. 14 gs., with grounds) is a small place with print-works. On the right rises the conical *Dumgoyne* (1401 ft.) ; on the left is *Duntreath Castle* (partly 15th cent.), preserving the dungeons and stocks of its ancient feudal jurisdiction.—Beyond the Blane, c. 2 m.

LOCH LOMOND AND THE TROSSACHS

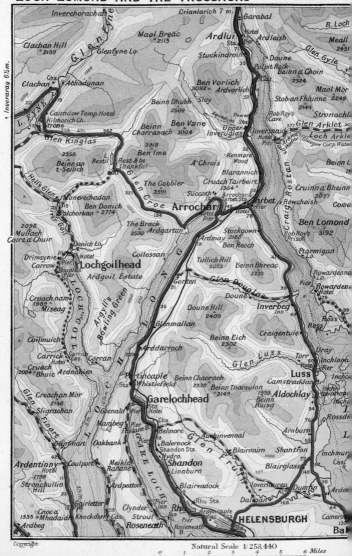

Natural Scale 1 : 253,440

0   1   2   3   4   5   6 Miles

0   2   4   6   8   10 Kilometres

Copyright

Height of Land in Feet

0   500   1000   1500   2000   3000

John Bartholomew & Son, Ltd, Edinburgh

N.W., is *Moss*, the birthplace of George Buchanan (1506–82), humanist, reformer, and historian, and tutor of James VI.

A 875 bears r. for (16 m. from Glasgow) *Killearn* (Black Bull, RB. 20/, P. 9 gs.) where Buchanan is commemorated by an obelisk.—19 m. *Balfron*, a prettily situated village, is said to owe its name ('town of sorrow') to the tradition that all its children were once destroyed by wolves.

At 15½ m. B 834 leads W. in 1 m. to the interesting Finnich Glen (p. 133). *Gartness House*, to the left, in a loop of the Endrick, belonged to the family of John Napier, inventor of logarithms, who lived here for some time. We cross the Endrick, pass under the Loch Katrine aqueduct, and cross the Balloch–Stirling road. Beyond (22 m.) the ruin of *Gartfarran*, not now considered to be a Roman outpost, we enter Perthshire and cross the Forth. To the left of the road is *Gartmore House*, now an 'approved' school, once the home of R. B. Cunninghame Graham.

26 m. **Aberfoyle** (*Bailie Nicol Jarvie*, RB. 32/6, P. 17½ gs. ; *Covenanters' Inn*, in a fine situation, RB. 26/, P. 12 gs. ; *Clachan*, unlic., RB. 16/), now a rather suburban-looking village (1150 inhab.), is a favourite summer resort for visitors from Glasgow. Of the 'clachan' whither Frank Osbaldistone and Bailie Nicol Jarvie repaired to meet Rob Roy there are scant remains, but a plough coulter hanging from a tree opposite the hotel recalls the spirited conduct of the bailie on that occasion. The surrounding scenery, without being grand, is very broken and romantic, and the district is a favourite with walkers.

Motor-buses daily to *Kinlochard* in ¼ hr. ; to *Stirling* viâ Port of Menteith in 1 hr. ; to *Buchlyvie* in ¼ hr. ; to *Balfron* in ½ hr.

FROM ABERFOYLE TO INVERSNAID, 15 m., a good hill road. About 1½ m. W. of Aberfoyle is the lovely **Loch Ard**, a beautiful and placid basin embedded in woods over which rises the graceful form of Ben Lomond (l.). The best view is obtained at first when only a small portion of the loch, nearly separated from the main body by a wooded promontory, is seen. A perpendicular rock over the road gives a remarkable echo. The road follows the N. bank, traverses the *Pass of Aberfoyle*, where Helen MacGregor discomfited the king's troops, and c. ¾ m. farther on reaches the margin of the main part of the loch. On a tiny island near the S. bank are the foundations of a castle owned by Murdoch, the 2nd Duke of Albany (beheaded in 1425). *St. Malloch's* (or *Gorm*), another small island, in the S.W. corner, had a chapel.—Half a mile up the last burn crossed before the road divides are the *Falls of Ledard*, the first about 12 ft. in height, and the second 50 ft. From these Sir Walter Scott took his description of the waterfall, in 'Waverley,' beside which Flora M'Ivor sang to her harp.—At (4½ m.) *Kinlochard* (Forest Hills, RB. 27/6, P. 12 gs. ; Altskeith House, RB. 22/6, P. 8 gs.) the Inversnaid road keeps to the right, while the road on the left, making a wide sweep to the S. of Loch Ard, viâ the Duchray and (8 m.) *Duchray Castle*, returns to Aberfoyle. A path diverging to the right, near the beginning of this latter road, leads to Rowardennan (p. 139), a fine hill walk of 9½ m. from Aberfoyle (c. 5 hrs.).

The Inversnaid road runs N.W. from the fork, past the little *Loch Dhu* to (6 m.) **Loch Chon**, which is rockier and wilder than Loch Ard and beautifully wooded with birch, ash, and other trees. On the S.W. rises a precipitous outlier of Ben Lomond.—Beyond Loch Chon our road crosses (9 m.) the culvert of the Glasgow waterworks, with a view of Loch Arklet in front, and in 2 m. more joins the road leading from *Stronachlachar* (½ m. to the right) to (15 m. ; l.) *Inversnaid* (see Rte. 25A).

FROM ABERFOYLE TO THE LAKE OF MENTEITH AND CALLANDER, 10½ m., by a good road (A 81) along the S. edge of the Highland fault, whose direction is very marked in the ridging of the Menteith Hills.—4 m. **Port of Menteith** (*Lake Hotel*, RB. 28/6, P. 12½ gs.), a quiet holiday resort, lies on the N. shore of its lake, with a church, beside which is the mausoleum of the Grahams of Gartmore. Boats may be hired at the hotel to visit the islands. Our road diverges to the left from the Stirling road (Rte. 24) c. 1½ m. beyond the hotel, and crosses a moor, with *Loch Rusky* on the right, to (10½ m.) *Callander*, which it enters by the bridge over the Teith.

The Lake of Menteith (1½ m. long by 1 m. broad) has three islands, on the largest of which are the beautifully placed ruins of the Priory of *Inchmahome* ('Isle of St. Colmoc or Macholmoc,' called also the ' Isle of Rest '), founded for Austin canons after 1238 by Walter Comyn, earl of Menteith. Like Cambuskenneth Abbey, it passed at the Reformation to the Earl of Mar. Adm., incl. ferry, 1/6, 10–4 or 7, Sun. from 2.—Of the 13th cent. church, in which David II was married in 1362 to his second wife, Margaret, daughter of Sir John Logie, there remain part of the choir, the tower arch, and two arches of the nave. The mouldings of the W. entrance, which is deeply recessed, are exceedingly beautiful. In the chancel is the tomb of Sir John Drummond (d. 1390) and in the chapter house, partly rebuilt in the 17th cent. are those of Walter Stewart, earl of Menteith (d. 1295) and his wife (d. 1286), with another late 13th cent. Stewart knight alongside. R. B. Cunninghame-Graham (1852–1936) is also buried here.

After the battle of Pinkie in Sept. 1547 (p. 85), and in consequence of the English invasion, Mary, Queen of Scots, then aged five, was sent to this secure place and stayed on the isle until July 1548. She was then stealthily removed to Dumbarton, where she embarked for France (see p. 134). A little garden called Queen Mary's Bower, said to have been tended by herself and to have remained as she left it, is shown.—The ruined castle on *Inch Talla* was the principal residence of the earls of Menteith, 1227–1694. The date of its erection is unknown. The small *Dog Island* was used for kennels.

FROM ABERFOYLE TO THE TROSSACHS, 6 m. The picturesque but hilly road, running N. from Aberfoyle (A 821), was formerly known as the ' Duke's Road ' or ' Toll Road.' From the initial steep zigzag ascent we have fine views of Loch Ard and Ben Lomond, and near the top we pass the large slate quarries. From the summit (796 ft.) *Loch Drunkie* and Loch Vennachar are well in view, and from a sharp bend farther on walkers may descend direct, through newly-planted forests, to Brig o' Turk. Our road strikes the S. bank of Loch Achray, passes Loch Achray Hotel, and rounds the W. end of the lake to join (5¾ m.) the road to the *Trossachs Pier* (p. 215), c. ½ m. W. of the Trossachs Hotel.

26. FROM STIRLING TO PERTH

ROAD, 34 m. A 9.—6 m. *Dunblane.*—12 m. *Greenloaning.*—19 m. *Gleneagles.*— 21 m. *Auchterarder.*—34 m. **Perth**, see Rte. 27.—MOTOR-BUS (hourly service) in c. 1½ hr.

RAILWAY, 33 m. in ¾–1¼ hr. Principal Stations : 5 m. *Dunblane.*—17¼ m. *Gleneagles*, junction for Crieff and Comrie.—33 m. **Perth**.

Stirling, see Rte. 24. Thence to (6 m.) *Dunblane*, where we diverge from the road to Callander, see Rte. 23B. The road runs N.E., up the valley of the Allan with Sheriffmuir on the slopes of the Ochils to the right.—12 m. *Greenloaning* (Allanbank, RB. 15/, P. 6 gs.), whence a rough road leads over Sheriffmuir, and another road (A 822) goes N. to (11 m.) Crieff.

Just beyond (1½ m.) *Braco* (Hotel, RB. 15/6, P. 6½ gs.) the road to Crieff crosses the Knaik and skirts the W. side of the large Roman station of ***Ardoch**, the most perfect example of the kind in Britain. We enter from beside the lodge of Ardoch House, in whose grounds the remains lie. The central area (420 ft. by 375 ft.) is on the customary Roman rectangular plan, with sides nearly facing the cardinal points, but on the N. and E., instead of the usual rampart and ditch, there are five trenches with strong earthen ramparts between them. The W. and S. sides are less well preserved. The camp-buildings were probably of wood ; the stone foundations discovered in the middle of the area are those of a medieval chapel and its churchyard wall. A little farther N.W. the Crieff road intersects the *Great Camp* (2800 ft. by 1950 ft.), to the W. of which is a smaller camp, partly within it and crossing its ramparts. These camps, estimated to accommodate 26,000 and 12,000 troops respectively, were defended by a single entrenchment with entrances protected by straight traverses, but little now remains to be seen. The latest coins found at Ardoch belong to the reign of Hadrian (A.D. 117–138), but the station probably continued in use as an outpost even after the completion of the Roman Wall farther S. (p. 106).

After traversing the Muir of Orchill, we join the road from Gleneagles (see below), and soon enjoy a magnificent view of W. of Ben Vorlich (3224 ft.) and Stuc-a-Chroin (3189 ft.).—7½ m. *Muthill* (Drummond Arms, RB. 16/6, P. 6 gs.) has ruins of a 15th cent. church with a square 12th cent. tower, 70 ft. high, and effigies of Sir Muriel Drummond (d. 1362) and his wife. A little farther on is *Drummond Castle*, with a fine avenue (l.). We cross the Earn on the outskirts of *Crieff* (Rte. 28).

High on the right beyond (16½ m.) *Blackford* (Blackford RB. 19/ ; Moray Arms, RB. 17/6) are the remains of *Ogilvie Castle*, once a place of great strength.—19 m. **Gleneagles** (from ' eaglais '—church), a station with no village. Conspicuous on the left is the palatial *Gleneagles Hotel* (RB. 67/6, P. 27½ gs.; open Easter to October), a fashionable resort, especially for golf, with two first-class courses. On the Glendevon road (r.) is the house of *Gleneagles*, built in 1624, with stones from the former castle, the ancestral home of the Haldanes, who have been in possession of the estate for over 700 years.

Farther up *Glen Eagles*, on the right, is *St. Mungo's Chapel*, dating from 1149, with ancient and modern memorials of the Haldanes. Viscount Haldane of Cloan (1856–1928) is buried in the churchyard.

FROM GLENEAGLES TO CRIEFF, 11 m., A 823.—2½ m. *Tullibardine* gives the courtesy title of marquis to the eldest sons of the dukes of Atholl, who were earls of Tullibardine before they became dukes. The castle is now only a site. The old chapel (1446) here, with a remarkable open roof, formerly the mausoleum of the dukes of Atholl, is now that of the Strathallan family.—5½ m. We join the road from Greenloaning, see above.

From Gleneagles to *Rumbling Bridge* and *Dunfermline*, see p. 255.

21 m. **Auchterarder** (*Crown*, RB. 19/6, P. 10 gs. ; *Coll-Earn*, RB. 17/6, P. 8 gs. ; *Ruthven Towers*, RB. 17/6, P. 7 gs.), a village (2435 inhab.) mainly of one long street, figures in Scottish church history as the scene in 1834 of the first of the disputes as to ' patronage ' that led to the Disruption in 1843. Its status as a royal burgh, dating back to the 13th cent., fell into abeyance in the 17th, but was revived in 1951. With

Dunning and other places in the neighbourhood it was burnt by the Earl of Mar in 1716 after the battle of Sheriffmuir.

About 1¼ m. S. on the banks of the Ruthven Water is the modern *Kincardine Castle*, beyond which, on a strong site, is a fragment of the old castle, the original seat of the Grahams, dismantled in 1645.

From Auchterarder to *Perth* viâ Forteviot, see Rte. 27.

Beyond (24 m.) *Aberuthven* are the ruins of *St. Kattan's Chapel* and the mausoleum of the dukes of Montrose.—We cross the Earn by the new Dalreoch Bridge ; on the hill to the left is the mansion of *Gask* (1801), beside which are the scanty remains of the 'Auld House' (1666), of Lady Nairne's song. Prince Charles Stewart breakfasted here in 1745, and Lady Nairne (1766–1845) was named Carolina in his honour. The Oliphants of Gask were devoted Jacobites, and the mansion preserves many relics of Prince Charlie. On the road between Gask and *Dupplin Loch* (2 m. E.) was a Roman station. *Dupplin Castle* (1832), the seat of Lord Forteviot, in a finely wooded estate is on the S. side of our road. A stone cross marks the site of the battle of Dupplin (1332) in which Edward Balliol and the 'disinherited barons' defeated the Regent Mar.—34 m. **Perth,** see Rte. 27.

27. PERTH AND ITS ENVIRONS

PERTH (40,500 inhab.), surnamed 'the Fair City,' is a royal burgh of great antiquity with cattle-markets, dye-works, distilleries, etc., and a small but active harbour on the Tay, downstream ; but its chief attractions for the tourist are its convenient railways, its fine old church, and its associations with 'The Fair Maid of Perth.' It is charmingly situated between its green 'Inches' on the right bank of the Tay in attractive country.

Hotels. Station (a ; C 1), RB. 32/, P. 17 gs. ; **Royal George** (b ; A 3), George St., RB. 23/, P. 13½ gs. ; **Salutation** (c ; B 3), 34 South St., RB. 27/6 ; **Royal British** (d ; C 1), Leonard St., RB. 22/6 ; **Waverley** (e ; B 1), 31 York Place, RB. 18/6, P. 8½ gs. ; **County** (g ; B 2), County Place, RB. 17/6, P. 7 gs. ; **Queen's** (h ; C 1), Leonard St., unlic., RB. 21/, P. 10 gs. ; **Atholl,** St. Leonard's Bank, private, RB. 17/6, P. 7½ gs. ; **Laidlaw,** Leonard St., temperance, RB. 15/6.

Post Office (B 2), High Street.

Motor-Buses. Frequent service to all suburban districts. Also from the Railway Station to *Blairgowrie* (viâ Meikleour, 50 min., viâ Coupar Angus, 1 hr.) ; *Cupar* and *St. Andrews* (1¾ hr.); *Leven* (2 hrs.) ; *Kirkcaldy* (viâ Newburgh or Strathmiglo, 1¾ hr.); *Dunkeld* and *Pitlochry* (1½ hr.).—From Tay St. to *Stirling* (1½ hr.), going on to *Glasgow* (3 hrs.) ; *Dundee* (1 hr.) ; *Kirkcaldy* viâ Glenfarg (1¾ hr.) ; *Leven* (2 hrs.).

Amusements. *Theatre* (repertory), High St., opposite Post Office.— *Golf* at North Inch (municipal), Moncreiffe Island, and Craigie Hill (1 m. S.W.).—*Bowls* and *Putting,* North and South Inch.—*Tennis,* Murray Crescent, Craigie.—*Swimming Baths,* Dunkeld Road.—*Boats* for hire on the Tay, North Inch.

History. Perth on its present site dates from the foundation of the royal burgh by William the Lion in 1210 ; an older town, destroyed by a disastrous flood in that year, lay a little N. As capital of Scotland until c. 1452 Perth was a civil and religious centre of importance and it contained the large monasteries of the Black Friars, the Grey Friars, the White Friars, and the Carthusians, all of which have vanished. From its church of St. John (see below) it was at one time known also as St. John's Town or St. Johnstoun, and the phrase, a 'St. Johnstoun's tippet,' meaning (like 'Bridport dagger') a hangman's halter, dates from 1559, when 300 Perth citizens marched with halters round their neck to oppose Mary of Guise to the death. In 1311 Bruce captured the city, which had been fortified by Edward I, but after the battle of Dupplin in 1332 it fell to Edward Balliol, and from 1335 until 1339 it was again in English hands. From the garden of the Blackfriars Monastery Robert III and his queen witnessed in 1396 the extraordinary combat on the North Inch, and in the same monastery James I was assassinated in 1437. The destruction of this and the other great monasteries in Perth was the first fruits of Knox's famous iconoclastic sermon in St. John's church in 1559. In 1600 the city was the scene of the Gowrie Conspiracy (p. 222). Montrose occupied Perth after his victory at Tippermuir in 1644, and Claverhouse seized it in 1689. Perth surrendered to Cromwell after a day's siege in 1651, and it was occupied by the Jacobite insurgents in 1715 and again in 1745.—St. William, martyred in 1201, whose shrine is venerated in Rochester Cathedral, is said to have been a baker of Perth. It was from the plague in Perth in 1645 that Allan Ramsay's 'Bessie Bell and Mary Gray' fled into the country, where, however, the infection was carried to them by their lover. Wm. Soutar (1898–1943), the vernacular poet, was born in Perth; a tablet marks the house in Wilson St. where he died.

When Agricola's soldiers (c. A.D. 80) came into sight of the Tay and the South Inch they are said to have shouted "Ecce Tiberis, ecce Campus Martius!" Sir Walter Scott's comment was:

> "Behold the Tiber! the vain Roman cried,
> Viewing the ample Tay from Baiglie's side;
> But where's the Scot that would the vaunt repay
> And hail the puny Tiber for the Tay?"

From the railway station (C 1) to the centre of the city, the most direct route leads viâ Leonard St. and Hospital St. to County Place (B 2), at the W. end of South Street.

On the right in Hospital St. is the *King James VI Hospital*, founded in 1569, destroyed by Cromwell in 1652 to obtain material for his fort (p. 222), and rebuilt in 1750. It stands on the site of the Charterhouse (the only one in Scotland), founded in 1429 by James I, in which he and his queen were buried. The monastery was destroyed in 1559 and James's tombstone removed later to St. John's. The hospital is now let in tenements and the beneficiaries receive outdoor relief.

South Street (B 2, 3), like the parallel High St. farther N., runs E. to the broad avenue flanking the Tay. Between the two are the *City Halls* and the church of **St. John** (B 3), an interesting cruciform structure of various dates, with a square central tower surmounted by a fine 15th cent. steeple. The present choir was built c. 1440, the low nave c. 1490. The entire building was restored in 1923–28 as a War Memorial. It is open on weekdays 11–1 (Sat. 10–12) and 2–4.

History. In 1126 the church was granted by David I to Dunfermline Abbey, and it was freely restored, if not rebuilt, in the early 15th century. An earlier restoration begun by Robert Bruce in 1328 was arrested by his death next year. In 1296 Edward I here kept the feast of the nativity of St. John the Baptist. That Edward III slew his brother, the Earl of Cornwall, before the high altar in St. John's in 1335 is an unauthenticated tradition. In 1541 Queen Margaret Tudor was buried here. John Knox here preached, in 1559, his momentous sermon urging the "purging of the churches from idolatry," which sent an iconoclastic storm over Scotland, drastic and destructive far beyond the preacher's intentions. The interior was divided in 1598 into two churches (East and West), between which a Mid Church was inserted c. 1773, but all these are now again thrown into one. In 1644 800 Covenanters were confined in the church by Montrose after his victory at Tippermuir. Charles I attended service in the church in 1633, Charles II in 1650, and Prince Charles Stewart in 1745. The scene of the ordeal of ' bier-right ' after the death of Oliver Proudfute, as described in ' The Fair Maid of Perth,' is laid in St. John's. The interesting plate includes two late-16th cent. cups and covers of German manufacture and two of the early 17th cent. from London.

The INTERIOR is said once to have contained forty altars dedicated to as many saints. Adjoining the N. transept is the lowest story of the old Halkerston's Tower (1126?), and the staircase to the upper stories has been rediscovered. The N. transept, entirely rebuilt in 1828, has been altered and a special War Memorial chapel, by Sir Robert Lorimer, was opened here in 1928.

At the E. end of South St. the Tay is spanned by the *Victoria Bridge* (B 3, 4), while to the right and left it is skirted by the wide tree-shaded Tay St., with its handsome buildings. The *County Buildings*, on the right, by R. Smirke, were built in 1818–20 on the site of Gowrie House (1520), the scene of the still mysterious Gowrie Conspiracy of 1600. A bronze tablet in one of the blind windows gives a representation of the picturesque old mansion, which was one of the chief ornaments of the city. Within are portraits, including one of Neil Gow, by Sir Henry Raeburn.

The Gowrie Conspiracy seems to have been an attempt by the Earl of Gowrie and his brother Alexander Ruthven to secure the person of James VI and therewith political advantage. The king, lured to Gowrie House by a story of foreign treasure, was skilfully detached from his retinue and led to an upper room by Ruthven, who, after some heated colloquy, attempted to bind the king's hands. James, however, succeeded in giving the alarm through an open window, and his attendants forced their way to his rescue. In the fracas both Gowrie and Ruthven were slain. As a result, the very name of Ruthven was proscribed (comp. p. 224). The ' Ruthven Stone ', marking the site of the former village of that name, is in the housing estate of *Letham*, 2 m. W. of Perth.

The *Greyfriars Cemetery*, behind Tay St. farther S., occupies the site of the Franciscan monastery founded by Lord Oliphant in 1460 and destroyed in 1559.

Passing under the railway bridge at the end of Tay St. we reach the **South Inch** (C 2, 3), a spacious green expanse, once used for archery and witch-burnings. No traces remain of the fort built by Cromwell in 1652 at its N.E. angle. The large building on the far side of the Inch is the *General (Convict) Prison for Scotland*, originally erected in 1812 for French prisoners of war.

The railway bridge (on which there is likewise a footpath) crosses the N. end of the long *Friarton* or *Moncrieffe Island* (C 3, 4) in the Tay, on which is the King James VI Golf Course.

Upstream (N.) from Victoria Bridge, Tay St. is flanked by public buildings, including the *City Chambers* (at the foot

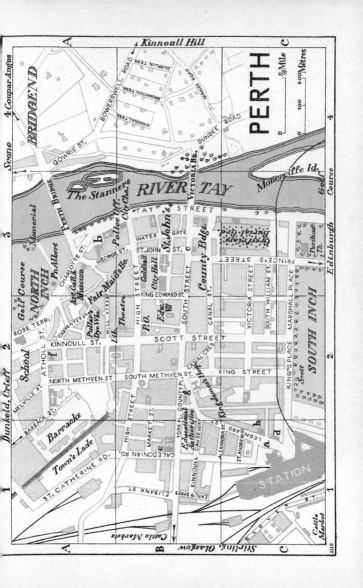

PERTH

⅛ Mile

100   200 Metres

Kinnoull Hill

BRIDGEND

Scone   4 Coupar-Angus

Dunkeld, Crieff   2

DUPPLIN TERR.

BOWERSWELL ROAD

BROMPTON TERR.

KINNOULL TERR.

MANSE ROAD

GOWRIE ST.

DUNDEE ROAD

The Stanners

RIVER TAY

Victoria Br.

Moncrieffe Id.

Golf Course

Memorial

Perth Bridge

P.a Albert

TAY   STREET

St John's   STREET

City Cha.

Police Off.

WATER

ST. JOHN   GATE

ST.

Greyfriars Burial Grd.

PRINCE'S   STREET

Pavilion

Th.

Edinburgh

NORTH INCH

Golf Course

Rose Terr.

Art Gall.   Museum

CHARLOTTE ST.

GEORGE ST.

Fair Maid's Ho.

Guildhall   City Hall

County Bldgs

CANAL ST.

Victoria STREET

South William St.

School

ATHOLL ST.

MELVILLE ST.

Pullar's Dye Wks.

Lib.

Theatre

KING EDWARD ST.

HIGH   STREET

SOUTH   STREET

SOUTH INCH

Marshall PLACE

KING'S PLACE

Scott

Kinnoull St.

CARPENTER ST.

P.O.

Edw.

VII

Edw.

SCOTT   STREET

KING   STREET

BARRACK ST.

NORTH METHVEN ST.

MILL STREET

SOUTH METHVEN ST.

CANAL CRES.

King James's Hosl.

Victoria STREET

Barracks

Town's Lade

ST. CATHERINE RD.

CALEDONIAN RD.

HIGH STREET

MARKET ST.

YORK PL.

COUNTY PL.

Educational

Authorities

CAUSEWAY

ALEXANDRA ST.

ST. ANDREW ST.

LEONARD ST.

STATION

Cattle Market

EARL'S DYKES

ELIBANK ST.

KINNOULL ST.

GLOVER   ST.

Cattle Market

Stirling, Glasgow

me

of High St.), and ends at **Perth Bridge** (A 3), a fine work of nine arches by Smeaton (1766–71), from which there is a magnificent view of the Grampians.

Beyond Perth Bridge lies the **North Inch** (A 2, 3), a fine park of 100 acres, with cricket ground, golf course, bowling greens, etc. At the top of George St. (A 3), as we approach, is the *Art Gallery and Museum* (A 3 ; adm. free 11–5, Sun. 2–4 ; Wed. and Fri. also 6–8), containing not only art and anti-quarian collections, but also well-arranged exhibits illustrating the geology, botany, and zoology of Perthshire. The building (1935) incorporates the façade of the old museum, with a statue of Provost Hay Marshall (1824).

The remarkable judicial combat between the Clan Chattan and the Clan Quhele (Kay), so graphically described in ' The Fair Maid of Perth,' took place on the North Inch in 1396. Thirty champions fought on each side, and as the Clan Chattan were one man short they were assisted by Hal o' the Wynd, a bandy-legged or crooked smith ('Gow Chrom') of Perth, who contributed largely to their victory. This worthy's stout assertion that he fought 'for his own hand' has become proverbial.

In Rose Terrace, on the W. side of the Inch, rises the classic façade of the *Old Academy* (1807). Perth Academy, a well-known boys' school, was moved to a new site W. of the city in 1932.

The North Port, opposite a statue of Prince Albert, leads from the North Inch to Curfew Row, in which stands the **Fair Maid's House** (A 2). The niche on the corner of this house once contained an image of St. Bartholomew, patron saint of the Glovers' Corporation. The small upper rooms are shown (9–dusk ; adm. 3*d.*).

Behind the house and facing the North Inch stood the *Blackfriars Monastery*, founded in 1231 by Alexander II and destroyed in 1559. Here homage was paid to Edward I in 1291, and here James I, the poet-king, long a prisoner in Windsor Castle, was assassinated in 1437 by Sir Robert Graham, in spite of the devotion of one of the queen's ladies who thrust her arm into the staples of the door in place of the missing iron bar. " 'Twas Catherine Douglas sprang to the door, but I fell back Kate Barlass " (*Rossetti*, ' The King's Tragedy '). This brave lady afterwards married Richard Lovell of Ballumbie.

Curfew Row leads on through Pullar's dye-works, and we make our way by narrow lanes to the *High Street* (B 3), which runs parallel with South Street. No. 104 is the old *Guildhall* (1722 ; rebuilt in 1907), and in Parliament Close (No. 77), on the other side of the street, is a Masonic Hall on a site occupied until 1818 by the building in which the Scottish parliaments met down to the reign of James II (1438–60). The area to the W. between High St. and South St. is to be rebuilt, with the 17th cent. Mercat Cross as its centre (1958).

The prominent red stone building a few yards up Kinnoull St., the N. con-tinuation of Scott St., is the *Sandeman Public Library* ; and at the end of N. Methven St., the next parallel street on the left, is *St. Ninian's Cathedral* (A 2), the handsome episcopal cathedral, begun in 1850 for the diocese of St. Andrews, Dunkeld and Dunblane and completed in 1890 (chapter house 1900).—Farther W. are the *Queen's Barracks* (A 1), with the museum (Mon.–Fri. 10–12, 2–5) of the Black Watch, the regiment whose headquarters were at Perth from its formation in 1749 until 1948.

John Ruskin (1819–1900) spent part of his childhood in *Bridgend*, on the E. bank of the Tay. Turning to the left, by Main St., immediately on crossing Perth Bridge, we find the house (tablet) on the left, just beyond a church. Its garden has " a door opening to the water, which ran past it, clear brown over the pebbles, 3 or 4 ft. deep, an infinite thing for a child to look down into." Bowerswell Road (B 4) leads E. to (1 m.) Kinnoull Hill, passing *Bowerswell*, the mansion in which was celebrated the luckless marriage of Ruskin and Effie Gray (1848). The house, with 9½ acres, has been bought by the town council for an old people's home, a war memorial for 1939–45.

*Kinnoull Hill (729 ft.), the S.W. spur of the Sidlaw Hills, rising abruptly from the Tay E. of Perth, is a noted view-point (view-indicators). Most of the hill was presented to the city by Lord Dewar in 1923.—On the opposite side of the Tay, S. of Perth, rises *Moncrieffe Hill* (725 ft.), beneath which, 3 m. downstream, stands *Elcho Castle* (adm. 6*d.*; 10–4 or 7, Sun. from 2), the remarkably well preserved 16th cent. stronghold of the earls of Wemyss.

Scone Palace (no adm.; pron. 'scoon'), seat of the Earl of Mansfield, stands on the left bank of the Tay, c. 2 m. N. of Perth Bridge by the Blairgowrie road. The present castellated mansion (1803–8) is the successor of a 16th cent. house, which itself succeeded the abbey and palace destroyed by John Knox's 'rascal multitude' in 1559. The priory founded by Alexander I c.1120 became an abbey in 1164 and Robert II was buried there in 1390. One aisle survives of a parish church (no adm.) built by Viscount Stormont in 1624; it contains his sumptuous monument (after 1631) and other memorials of the Murrays of Tullibardine.

The importance of Scone dates back to the 8th cent., when its mote-hill was a solemn meeting-place. Kenneth Macalpine (9th cent.) is said to have brought hither from Dunstaffnage the 'Stone of Scone,' which was believed to carry sovereignty with it, and though Edward I carried it off to England in 1297, all the Scottish kings, including Robert Bruce, were crowned at Scone until the days of James I. James IV also was crowned here in 1488, and Charles II in 1651. Traditionally identified with Jacob's pillow at Bethel (afterwards the 'Lia Fail' or 'Stone of Destiny' at Tara in Ireland), or, less improbably, with Columba's pillow on Iona, the stone is held to have vindicated its character when James VI became also James I of England in 1603. The 'Old Pretender' kept royal state in Scone Palace for some weeks in 1716 and Prince Charlie slept there in 1745. David Douglas (1798–1834), discoverer of the Douglas spruce, was once a gardener at Scone Palace.

Huntingtower Castle, named Ruthven until 1600, which stands 3 m. N.W. of Perth, was the scene of the 'Raid of Ruthven' in 1582. James VI, when a youth of 16, accepted the invitation of the Earl of Gowrie to his hunting seat of Ruthven, and on arriving found himself in the hands of a band of nobles whose demands included the dismissal of the royal favourites, the Duke of Lennox and the Earl of Arran. When James attempted to leave the room the Master of Glamis planted his back against the door, at which outrage the King burst into tears and was told roughly, " better bairns greet than bearded men." This 'raid' (not to be confounded with the Gowrie Conspiracy, p. 222) gave the control of the realm to the Ruthven confederates for some months, but the Earl of Gowrie was beheaded in 1584. The castle (adm. 6*d.*; 10–4 or 7, Sun. from 2) has two massive 15th cent. towers, 9½ ft. apart, united by a late-17th cent. building. The space between the towers is known as the 'maiden's leap,' from the tradition that a daughter of the first earl sprang across it to avoid detection in a love affair. Wall and ceiling paintings (c. 1540) decorate the great hall on the first floor. The return to Perth may be made by a footpath skirting the Almond and then the Tay.—*Pitheavlis Castle* (after 1552), a tower-house 1 m. S.W. of Perth station, was restored in 1956.

FROM PERTH TO FORTEVIOT AND AUCHTERARDER, 14½ m. Leaving Perth by York Place (B 1) we follow B 9112 (l.) to (3½ m.) *Aberdalgie*, and beyond Dupplin Castle (r.; p. 220) we cross the Earn.—6½ m. *Forteviot*, now a very small village, was at one time the capital of the Pictish kings of Fortrenn, and Kenneth Macalpine died here in 860.—From (9½ m.) *Dunning*, with an interesting church tower (c. 1210), a road runs S., across the Ochil Hills, to Yetts of Muckhart (p. 212).—14½ m. *Auchterarder*, see Rte. 26.

From Perth to *Aberdeen*, see Rte. 39 ; to *Blairgowrie* and *Braemar*, see Rte. 29 ; to *Dundee*, see Rte. 37 ; to *Edinburgh* viâ Queensferry, see Rte. 34 ; to *Inverness*, see Rte. 30 ; to *Lochearnhead*, see Rte. 28 ; to *Stirling*, see Rte. 26.

28. FROM PERTH TO CRIEFF AND LOCHEARNHEAD

ROAD (A 85), 36¼ m.—6 m. *Methven.*—17½ m. **Crieff.**—23¾ m. *Comrie.*—29 m. *St. Fillans.*—36¼ m. (by the N. bank of Loch Earn) **Lochearnhead.** MOTOR-BUS to Crieff in 55 min. (1½ hr. viâ Auchterarder ; 1 hr. viâ Madderty).

We leave Perth viâ Crieff Road, and, passing Huntingtower Castle on the right, reach (3½ m.) the turning for *Almondbank*, ¾ m. S. of the village.

On the opposite bank of the Almond is (½ m.) *Pitcairngreen* (Inn), one of the most picturesque villages in Scotland, with its large green bordered with high tree-hedges cut to resemble festoons. On Dronach Haugh, c. 2½ m. up the Almond, a stone marks the site of the ' bower ' of Bessie Bell and Mary Gray.

To the left of the Crieff road lies *Tibbermore* or *Tippermuir*, which gave name to the first battle between Montrose and the Covenanters. On *Lamerkin Muir*, to the S.E., on Sept. 1st, 1644, Montrose, with 1100 half-clad Irish and 1300 half-armed Highlanders, defeated a tumultuous mob of about 6000 Covenanters, citizens of Perth and others, hastily gathered together under Lord Elcho to oppose him. The city of Perth was the prize of victory.

6 m. *Methven*, a village with a fragment of a collegiate church of 1433, which serves as a burial-place for the Methven family. To the N. of the village Bruce was defeated in 1306 by the English under the Earl of Pembroke. *Methven Castle* (1½ m. E.), where Queen Margaret Tudor died in 1541, has a fine estate abounding in old timber.

From between the castle and the village a road runs N.E. up GLEN ALMOND to (8½ m.) the *Sma' Glen* (p. 227). It leaves on the r. (3 m.) *Millhaugh*, with its bridge of 1619 leading to *Logiealmond* (Chapelhill Inn, RB. 25/, P. 12 gs.), the ' Drumtochty ' of Ian Maclaren.—4½ m. *Trinity College* (r.) is a public school opened in 1847 and run on English lines.—Beyond (7 m.) *Buchanty* (with a pretty linn), where we join a road from Logiealmond, is the Roman site of *Fendoch* (p. 227), ½ m. short of the Sma' Glen road.

8½ m. *Balgowan House*, the birthplace of Lord Lynedoch (1748–1843), the victor of Barrosa (1811), lies to the left of our road.—10½ m. A road to Madderty, also on the left, passes (¾ m. S.) the scanty ruins of the Augustinian *Inchaffray Abbey*, founded on a Celtic site by Gilbert, Earl of Strathearn, in 1200. Its name signifies ' Isle of Offerings ' and is latinised as Insula Missarum. Its most treasured possession was the silver reliquary of the arm of St. Fillan, with which Abbot Maurice blessed Bruce's army at Bannockburn.—From (12 m.) New Fowlis a road runs N. to (½ m.) *Fowlis Wester*, a quaint village consisting of a church, manse, inn, and school-house, an 8th cent. Cross, with jougs attached, and a few pictur-esque cottages.—15¼ m. *Gilmerton* (Cultoquhey House, RB. 18/, P. 8 gs.).

17¼ m. **CRIEFF** (5475 inhab.), the chief town of *Strathearn*, is built on the S. side of a hill on the left bank of the Earn.

The neighbourhood abounds in fine scenery and historic interest; excursions are numerous; and accommodation is ample.

Hotels. Drummond Arms, James Square, RB. 27/6, P. 10 gs.; **George,** RB. 23/6, P. 10 gs.; **Strathearn Hydro,** unlic., above the town, RB. 24/, P. 8 gs.; **Murray Park,** near golf course, RB. 18/6, P. 8 gs.; **Station,** RB. 17/6, P. 7 gs.; **Ardenmohr,** unlic., RB. 25/, P. 8 gs.; **Aveland, Glenburn, Ancaster,**

Central, and many other unlic. houses (RB. 16/6–18/6, P. 6½–7½ gs.).

Motor-Buses from Church St. to *Comrie* (20 min.), going on to Loch Earn, Strathyre, and *Callander* (1¾ hr.); *Perth* viâ Methven (55 min.), Madderty (1 hr.), or Auchterarder (1½ hr.); *Stirling* (1 hr.), going on to *Edinburgh* (3 hrs.) or *Glasgow* (2½ hrs.).

From James Square with its small tree-shaded boulevard, in the centre of the town, East High St. passes the *Town Hall,* at the entrance to which are the old stocks and the slender octagonal *Cross* of the Burgh of Regality of Drummond (1688). Farther on is (l.) the older *Mercat Cross* of Crieff, of red sandstone with Runic knots but no inscription (perhaps 12th cent.). The road goes on to the *Golf Course,* on which are three large stones with 'cup and ring' markings.—West High St. leads in the opposite direction towards MacRosty Park, on the bank of the Earn, with tennis courts. *Morrison's Academy* (1860) is a well-known school for boys and girls.—The *Knock* (911 ft.), a wooded hill and public park, N. of the town, commands *Views on all sides (indicator). On its S.E. slope is *Ferntower,* where Sir David Baird (1757–1829), the hero of Seringapatam, died—" ill to leeve wi' but waur to want."— On *Gallow Hill,* near the station to the S., once stood the ' Kind Gallows of Crieff,' on which many Highland caterans were hanged by the Stewards of Strathearn. The clans, cherishing in consequence a grudge against the town, burned Crieff in 1716 and wrecked several houses in 1745.—David Mallet (1700–65), the poet and friend of James Thomson, was born at Crieff.

EXCURSIONS FROM CRIEFF

Innerpeffray, on the Earn 4 m. S.E. of Crieff, is approached by B 8062 viâ (1½ m.) *Highlandman* station, to the W. of which are interesting river-terraces. It was once a place of importance at the Roman crossing of the Earn (guarded by a fort at *Strageath* on the S. bank). It is now notable for its *Library* (adm. daily till dusk, exc. Mon.), the oldest public library in Scotland, founded in 1691 by David Drummond, Lord Madderty, and housed in a building begun in 1758. It contains some valuable old Scots volumes. Adjoining is the burial-chapel of the Drummonds, founded in 1508 as a collegiate church on the site of an older chapel; and ¼ m. farther on is a ruined castle (1610).

The road encircling the Knock (6½ m.) passes *Monzie* (pron. ' Monee '), with the fine grounds (no adm.) of Monzie Castle (1684; rebuilt after a fire in 1908), and crosses three wooded glens whose streams form charming waterfalls. A very steep road (no motors) ascends the most westerly of these glens to (6½ m.) *Glenturret Lodge,* at the head of LOCH TURRET (1127 ft.), affording a fine moorland walk of 5½ m. (magnificent retrospective views). From the end of the road *Ben Chonzie* (3048 ft.) may be ascended (c. 3 m.).

COMRIE (see below) is reached by pleasant roads (c. 7 m.) on either bank of the Earn, that on the N. bank being perhaps the more interesting. After crossing the Turret this road skirts the beautiful grounds of *Ochtertyre* (no adm.), in which is a mausoleum on the site of an old church where many of the Murrays with their wives and children were burnt alive by the Drummonds and Campbells (1491).—Beyond (3 m.) *Monzievaird* a road on the left leads viâ (½ m.) *Tomachastle Hill* (view), with a monument to Sir David Baird (see p. 226), to (1 m.) the picturesque *Strowan Bridge*, on a lovely stretch of the Earn, beyond which we join (1½ m.) the S. road to Comrie. The classical mansion of *Lawers*, on the main road 2½ m. from Comrie, is now a farming school for Perthshire.

Drummond Castle with its beautiful gardens (open on special occasions only), the seat of the Earl of Ancaster, is 2 m. S. of Crieff, on the tree-shaded Muthill road. From the gates an avenue, 1 m. long, leads to the castle.

The castle, founded in 1491 by the 1st Lord Drummond, whose descendants became Earls of Perth, was bombarded by Cromwell, fell into neglect at the Revolution, and in 1745 was partly pulled down by the Jacobite Duchess of Perth to prevent its occupation by the King's troops. Only the square tower (containing a small armoury and some interesting relics) is old, all the rest having been rebuilt in the old style. The castle was visited often by James IV and twice in 1566 by Queen Mary.—The beautiful old-fashioned **Garden* behind is laid out formally in a series of natural stepped terraces on the rock. The multiple *Sundial* (1630) was designed by John Mylne for the 2nd Earl of Perth, who laid out the gardens.—On the N. side of the park is *Drummond Pond* (¾ m. long), said to have been made to cover ground 'desecrated' by being allotted to Hanoverian supporters.

FROM CRIEFF TO AMULREE (Aberfeldy, Dunkeld) BY THE SMA' GLEN, 12 m., a fine expedition. We follow the Perth road, with Crieff Knock and the golf course on our left, to (2 m.) *Gilmerton*, where we diverge to the left on A 822. A steep ascent affords a fine view of Strathearn and below (l.), in the valley of the Shaggie, of Monzie Castle.—4½ m. *Foulford Hotel* (RB. 15/6, P. 7 gs.).—We strike (6 m.) the Almond (view), just beyond a road-fork. About ⅓ m. along the road to the right (going on to Glenalmond) is the site of the Roman outpost of *Fendoch*. Keeping l. at the fork, we soon enter the interesting **Sma' Glen**, where the road is carried for c. 2 m. through a stony defile, one of the gates of the Highlands. Near its upper end a huge flat stone (8 by 5 ft.) marks the traditional spot where, as Wordsworth puts it, " in this still place, remote from men, sleeps Ossian in the narrow glen." The tomb was disturbed by the soldiers of Gen. Wade, by whom the road was made in 1746.—From (8½ m.) *Newton Bridge*, where we cross and quit the Almond, our road crosses a bleak moor, viâ (10½ m.) *Corriemuckloch*, to (12 m.) **Amulree** (*Hotel*, RB. 21/, P. 10 gs.), a pleasant hamlet on the Bran, which issues from *Loch Freuchie*, 2 m. W. For the routes to *Aberfeldy* (12 m.), *Kenmore* (11 m.), or *Ardtalnaig* viâ Glen Almond (19 m.), see Rte. 31 ; to *Dunkeld* (9 m.), see Rte. 30.

From Crieff to Comrie we have a choice of roads (see above) on either bank of the Earn.

23¾ m. **Comrie** (*Royal*, RB. 21/, P. 10 gs. ; *Ancaster Arms*, RB. 18/6, P. 8 gs. ; *Comrie*, RB. 17/6, P. 7 gs.), beautifully situated at the meeting of Glen Artney and Glen Lednock with Strathearn, is a summer resort. It stands immediately over the great geological fault which separates the Highlands from the Lowlands and is therefore subject to frequent small earthquakes, seldom violent enough to do more than rattle the crockery on the shelves. The castellated steeple of the *Old Parish Church* (by John Stewart; 1805) is unusually graceful.

A delightful view of the surrounding country is to be had from *Dunmore* (837 ft.), a hill 1 m. N. (footpath passing Comrie House) bearing an obelisk in memory of the 1st Lord Melville (1742–1811). Below it are the FALLS OF LEDNOCK which, though not of great volume, well repay a visit by the grandeur of the ' *Devil's Cauldron*,' a remarkable chasm in the rock through which they force their way.⁑ Above the falls the road ascends the wooded *Glen Lednock* to (4 m.) *Invergeldie Lodge* and (5½ m.) the dam of the new *Loch Lednock* (1958), the waters of which work the power-station of Dalchonzie. *Ben Chonzie* (3048 ft.) may be ascended from Invergeldie by a path up the right bank of the Invergeldie burn (3½ m.), while a path up the main glen crosses the moors to (12 m.) Ardeonaig (p. 248).

From Comrie to *Callander* viâ Glen Artney, see p. 205.

Between Comrie and St. Fillans the road keeps to the N. bank of the Earn. On the S. bank (1½ m. W. of Comrie) *Aberuchill Castle* is seen beneath its rugged hills.—From (26½ m.) *Dalchonzie*, with its power-station, we see *Dunira* (r.), a burnt-out mansion that replaces the cottage to which Lord Melville retired. The green conical hill of Dunfillan (600 ft.) rises on the left as we approach (29 m.) **St. Fillans** (*Drummond Arms*, RB. 27/6, P. 10 gs.; *Achray*, RB. 18/6, P. 8½ gs.; *Colleonard*, unlic., RB. 16/6, P. 7 gs.), a pleasant village at the E. end of Loch Earn. In the cemetery beyond the golf course (S.E.) are the ruins of a chapel (c. 1500) on the site of the cell of St. Fillan, which since 1586 has been the burial-place of the Stewarts of Ardvorlich. Its old font is now in the church.

Loch Earn, a lovely Highland loch, overlooked on the S. by the bold peaks of Ben Vorlich and Stuc-a-Chroin, and on the N. by Sron Mhor (2203 ft.), stretches for 7 m. from St. Fillans to Lochearnhead (boats for hire). There are good roads on both banks ; the longer and hillier road on the S. side is the more varied.

From St. Fillans to Lochearnhead by the S. bank. At the mouth of (4 m.) Glen Vorlich is *Ardvorlich House*, the 'Darnlinvarach' of the 'Legend of Montrose,' with fine grounds. It was here that the MacGregors in 1589, having murdered Stewart, the king's forester, in revenge for a supposed grievance, placed his head on a dish, with a crust between the teeth, and presented it to his sister on her return from preparing food for them. Here is likewise preserved the famous Clach Dearg, a rock-crystal gem, one of the oldest talismans in Scotland. Close by, on the roadside, stands the tombstone of six Macdonalds of Glencoe, killed in an attempt to harry Ardvorlich. At the head of Glen Vorlich rises the peak of **Ben Vorlich** (3224 ft.), easily ascended hence in c. 2½ hrs. The wide view from the summit extends from Ben Ledi and Stirling Castle in the S. to the Ben Lawers range and Ben Nevis in the N. and N.W. The descent may be made into Glen Artney (p. 199) or Glen Ample (see below). *Stuc-a-Chroin* (3189 ft.) may be climbed in 1½ hr. from Ben Vorlich, with a dip of 700 ft. and a steep 'chimney' ascent.—At the mouth of (6 m.) *Glen Ample* there is a pretty cascade, below the road. On the right is *Edinample*, an old castellated house ; and at the S.W. corner of the loch are the ruins of *St. Blane's Chapel*.—8 m. *Lochearnhead*, see below.

The main road follows the N. shore of Loch Earn, commanding a good view of Ben Vorlich, with Ardvorlich at its base. We cross the mouth of (34½ m.) *Glen Beich*, and on the opposite shore see Glen Ample before curving S. across the mouth of Glen Ogle.—36¼ m. **Lochearnhead** (*Lochearnhead*, RB. 25/, P. 11 gs.; *Auchraw*, RB. 17/6, P. 8 gs.) is a charming village on the main road N. from Callander (Rte. 46), where the scarlet tropæolum grows in profusion.

29. FROM PERTH TO BRAEMAR VIÂ BLAIRGOWRIE

ROAD, 51 m., A 93. Motor-Bus viâ Kirkmichael daily in summer in 3¼ hrs.
There is a frequent bus service between Perth and (16 m.) Blairgowrie (50 min.).

From Perth to (2 m.) *Scone*, see p. 224.—The road goes on,
holding at first away from the river, viâ (5½ m.) *Guildtown*,
founded in 1818, where we may notice a cottage (l.) bearing a
curious masonic device dated 1835. Just over 1 m. farther
a lane on the left leads to *Burnmouth Ferry*, on the Tay a little
below *Campsie Linn*, the only cataract on the river and the
scene of Conachar's death in 'The Fair Maid of Perth.'—The
road skirts the grounds of *Stobhall* (Earl of Perth; no
adm.).

This was the seat of Sir John Drummond, whose daughter Annabel married
Robert III (1390–1406), but the present main building was built in 1578. The
Dower House, begun by John, Earl of Perth (d. 1662), was completed in 1671.

Beyond (10 m.) *Cargill* we cross the *Bridge of Isla*, spanning
the Isla a little above its junction with the Tay. Between the
road and the Tay are the grounds of *Meikleour*, celebrated for
its magnificent beech *Hedge, planted in 1746 and now 85 ft.
high, which borders the road for 580 yds. The house is
modern (1873).

At the N. end of the avenue a road (A 984) diverges left for (10½ m.) *Dunkeld*.
Traversing the model village of *Meikleour* (Hotel), with its curious cross (1698),
it leaves on the left, at 2½ m., the lane to the Agricolan legionary camp of
Inchtuthill, the most important Roman station N. of the Antonine Wall. The
traces of it lie 1 m. S., in a bend of the Tay.—At (6 m.) *Caputh* we join a road
from Stanley and thence keep closer to the river.

Traversing the fertile Plain of Stormont, we cross the
Lunan and pass between White Loch (l.) and Black Loch.—
16 m. **Blairgowrie** (*Royal*, RB. 21/, P. 10 gs.; *Queen's*, RB.
23/, P. 9½ gs.; *Angus*, RB. 19/6, P. 8 gs.; *Glen Ericht*, RB.
16/6, P. 7 gs.), a small town (5375 inhab.) surrounded by
raspberry farms, in a sheltered situation on the Ericht, is a
summer resort of no very great interest, but an excellent
centre for tours, with good motor-bus connections. The
Episcopal Church has a painting by Caravaggio.

FROM BLAIRGOWRIE TO DUNKELD, 12 m., a very pleasant road. On the left is
Ardblair Castle (16th cent.), with Stewart relics. Beyond (2 m.) *Kinloch* (Marlee,
unlic., RB. 15/, P. 6 gs.) the road skirts the chain of lochs fed by the Lunan, the
first of which is *Loch Marlee*.—4 m. *Loch Clunie* contains an island on which
stands the ruined *Clunie Castle*, built by Bp. Brown of Dunkeld c. 1500, perhaps
an early home but not the birthplace of the Admirable Crichton (1560; see p. 102).
Farther on we pass the lochs of (8 m.) *Butterstone* and (9 m.) *Craiglush*.—12 m.
Dunkeld, see p. 232.

The Braemar road crosses the Ericht to (16½ m.) *Rattray*,
but soon recrosses to the right bank and enters the lovely
*GORGE OF THE ERICHT, which flows between red sandstone
walls 200 ft. high. High up on the right is seen *Craighall
Rattray*, the seat of the Rattrays since c. 1100 and one of the
mansions claiming to be the original of Tullyveolan in

' Waverley.' Farther upstream, on the same side, are the ruins of *Lady Lindsay's Castle.* The road mounts above the right bank but descends after 3 m. to (22 m.) *Bridge of Cally* (Hotel, unlic., RB. 18/6, P. 8 gs.), on the Ardle, which ¾ m. downstream unites with the Blackwater to form the Ericht.

FROM BRIDGE OF CALLY TO PITLOCHRY, 19 m. The road on the left (A 924) beyond the bridge (views) ascends Strath Ardle to (7 m.) *Kirkmichael* (Kirkmichael, Aldchlappie, at both RB. 18/6, P. 7–8 gs.), served by buses from Blairgowrie and Pitlochry. B 950 here bears r. for Glenshee.—At (9 m.) *Enochdhu,* facing the wooded crag of Kindrogan, we join the track from Spittal of Glenshee (see below). Beyond (10 m.) *Straloch,* at the mouth of Glen Fernait (r.), the road ascends, with views of Ben Vrackie ahead and of the precipices of Ben-y-Gloe, 7 m. N. The road-summit (14¾ m. ; 1260 ft.) commands a magnificent prospect over the Perthshire mountains, among which Schiehallion and Ben Lawers are conspicuous. After a very steep descent we turn sharp to the right (17¼ m.), passing Kinnaird Cottage, and approach (19 m.) *Pitlochry* (p. 234) viâ Moulin.

The Braemar road, on the right beyond the bridge, turns immediately to the left and ascends the right bank of the Blackwater or Shee which flows down GLEN SHEE (*Dalrulzion House,* RB. 18/6, P. 7½ gs., near the junction of B 950 ; *Drumore House,* RB. 18/, P. 8 gs., with private loch, at Blacklunans on the r. farther on). Beyond *Persie* church we join (25 m.) a moorland road from Alyth (9½ m. S.E. ; p. 278), and leave on the left (26½ m.) the road (B 950) leading over to (3 m.) Kirkmichael (see above), across a high moor rich in hut circles and cairns.—Beyond (31 m.) a road (B 951) on the right leading to Glen Isla (p. 278) round the N. slopes of Mount Blair (2441 ft.), the broken and precipitous S. face of Glas Maol (3502 ft.) becomes prominent to the N.E.—35 m. **Spittal of Glenshee** (1125 ft. ; *Dalmunzie House,* RB. 30/6, P. 14½ gs., with private golf course, Easter–Oct. ; *Spittal,* RB. 17/6, P. 7 gs.), perhaps the site of a chapel, is a hamlet standing at the junction of Glen Beg and Glen Lochy, whose streams here unite to form the Shee. On the left bank of the Shee, ½ m. E., is a tumulus known as *Diarmid's Tomb.*

The path leading S.W. across the ridge (2100 ft.) descends to (5¾ m.) *Enochdhu* on the road between Kirkmichael and Pitlochry (see above).

The road ascending Glen Beg becomes gradually steeper and negotiates (41½ m.) a zigzag known as the *Devil's Elbow* (1950 ft.).—42 m. The **Cairnwell Pass** (2199 ft.), between Cairnwell (l. ; 3059 ft.) and Meall Odhar (3019 ft.), a spur of the mighty *Glas Maol* (3502 ft.), is the highest pass on a main road in Great Britain. Here we quit Perthshire and begin to descend *Glen Clunie,* on the Aberdeenshire side of the watershed, less steep than the S. slope. We pass (46 m. ; l.) the mouth of *Glen Baddoch,* and (49 m.) are joined by the Tolmounth track at the foot of *Glen Callater.* Ben Avon (3843 ft.) is conspicuous in front as we approach (51 m.) **Braemar** (Rte. 41).

30. FROM PERTH TO INVERNESS

ROAD, 116 m., A 9.—We quit Perth by the Dunkeld Road (Pl. A 1).—
15 m. *Dunkeld.*—28 m. *Pitlochry.*—35 m. *Blair Atholl.*—53½ m. *Drumochter
Summit* (1500 ft.)—73 m. *Kingussie.*—85 m. *Aviemore.*—92 m. *Carrbridge.*—
116 m. **Inverness,** entered by Kingsmills Rd. (Pl. C 2). This road was laid out by
General Wade in 1726–33, improved in 1830 by Telford, and thoroughly reconstructed in 1925–28. There are few steep hills and the surface is excellent.
MOTOR-BUS daily in summer in 4½–5½ hrs.

RAILWAY, 118 m. in 3¾–4¼ hrs., following practically the same course as the
road, except between Perth and Dunkeld, where a detour is made to the E. The
express trains call at Pitlochry, Blair Atholl, Kingussie, and Aviemore, with
'request' stops at certain intermediate stations. Passengers for Aberfeldy
change at Ballinluig.—This is for the most part a single line which, at *Drumochter*
(1484 ft.), reaches the highest level of any railway in Britain. The scenery is
extremely fine, though perhaps not so varied as that on the West Highland or
Callander and Oban railways. On Sunday, Inverness is reached viâ Forres,
diverging from the direct route at Aviemore (see Rte. 32) : to *Forres,* 119¼ m. in
3½ hrs. ; to *Inverness,* 144 m. in 4¼ hrs.

Perthshire, through which runs the first part of the present route, is, in Sir
Walter Scott's opinion, " the fairest portion of the Northern Kingdom." It is the
largest, almost circular, central county of Scotland, and comprises not only
much of the most beautiful scenery of Scotland, but also many of its most
historic spots. The Grampians, the Sidlaws, and the Ochils are among its mountains ; Lochs Tay, Earn, Rannoch, Ericht, and Katrine are its largest lakes ; the
Tay is its great river. Ruined castles and lordly mansions of historic fame over-
look its straths and glens ; grouse moors, great treeless deer-forests, and salmon
streams abound. There are cathedrals at Dunkeld and Dunblane. The ' Highland Line,' where Highlands and Lowlands meet, runs N.E. from Loch Katrine
viâ Crieff and Dunkeld to Strathardle, and so into Angus ; and the names of
many of the old territorial districts are prominent in Scottish history. *Atholl*
occupies most of the N. and N.E., with Strathardle and Glenshee as subdivisions.
' Atholl Brose,' a mixture of whisky, honey, and eggs, is one of its lesser claims
to fame. *Breadalbane,* including Rannoch, lies on the W. border, S. of Atholl ;
Gowrie, with the fertile Carse of Gowrie, stretches along the Tay on the E.
frontier ; *Menteith* or *Monteith* lies in the basin of the Forth, W. of the Ochils ;
Methven surrounds the town of that name, N.W. of Perth ; *Stormont* runs
westward in a narrow strip, N. of Gowrie ; *Strathearn* is the basin of the Earn
and the country N. of Menteith ; *Strathmore* stretches N. of the Sidlaw Hills N.E.
into Angus.—Within the county were fought the battles of Mons Graupius (A.D.
84), Luncarty (990), Methven (1306), Dupplin (1332), Tippermuir (1644), Killiecrankie (1689), and Sheriffmuir (1715).

Perth, see Rte. 27. The road approaches the Tay, beyond
which are seen the trees of Scone Park, and soon crosses the
Almond (view of Strathearn to the left).—Between (4½ m.)
Luncarty and the Tay is a salmon hatchery.

At the battle of Luncarty (990) Kenneth II is said to have defeated the
Danes, the Scots being rallied at the crucial moment by a peasant named Hay,
armed only with a plough-yoke. Hay was rewarded by a grant of lands, and is
the legendary ancestor of the Hays of Tweeddale ; but several families of the
name of Hay have a peasant with a yoke supporting their coat of arms.

Before reaching (5¼ m.) *Strathord* we cross the Shochie and
the Ordie a little above their confluence with the Tay.

Stanley, 2 m. N.E. on B 9099, is a Tayside village named in the early 18th cent.
after Lady Emily Stanley, mother of the 1st Duke of Atholl. The road goes on to
(6 m.) *Murthly,* with the large county mental hospital and, across the Tay, to
(7¼ m.) *Caputh.* With the wooded grounds of Murthly Castle (l. ; no adm.) are noted
for their avenues of various trees.

8½ m. *Bankfoot* (Bankfoot, RB. 21/6 ; New Inn, RB. 21/)

K

is a long village on the edge of the level Cairnleith Moss. We
approach the Tay again and rejoin the railway at (12 m.)
the *Pass of Birnam*, where the scenery assumes a more
Highland character, and the hills, closing in, contrast delightfully with the fertile banks of the Tay. Near *Birnam House*
(r.) is an old oak, called the hangman's tree, where Highland
marauders were summarily executed before the abolition of
heritable jurisdiction. On the left rises BIRNAM HILL (1324 ft.),
well worth ascending (¾ hr.) for the sake of the view. The path
leaves the road up the right bank of Inchewan burn just
before passing under the railway. *Birnam Wood* is said by
Pennant never to have recovered from the march to Dunsinane ; it has, however, been reinforced by plantations.

The view from the hill includes Ben Lawers (W.), Schiehallion (N.W.), Farragon
above Pitlochry, Ben Vrackie (N.E.), Strathmore and the Sidlaws (including
Dunsinane) to the E., and the Lomonds, the Ochils, and the Campsie Hills to
the S. An ill-marked fort on the S.E. side, known as *Duncan's Castle*, overlooks
the *Pass of Birnam*, between the hill and the river, the ' Mouth of the Highlands '
from which rushed forth the Highland bands of Montrose and of the '45.—On the
Terrace Walk, which follows the right bank of the Tay for more than a mile below
Birnam, are some fine old trees, including an oak and a sycamore said to be the
sole survivors of Birnam Forest.

14 m. **Birnam** (hotels, see below) is a charming village
frequented, like Dunkeld, as a summer resort, and containing
the railway station of Dunkeld. Passing the end of the short
road leading to *Little Dunkeld Church*, with the graveyard
where lies Niel Gow the elder (see below), we leave on the left
the roads to Amulree and Dalguise and cross the Tay.

15 m. **DUNKELD,** an ancient cathedral city (840 inhab.),
lies in a beautiful situation on the left bank of the Tay, here
hemmed in between wooded mountains and crossed by a
bridge erected by Telford in 1809.

Hotels. Birnam, near the station, good, RB. 21/, P. 9½–15 gs. ; **Dunkeld House,** RB. 30/, P. 13 gs. ; **Atholl Arms,** at the bridge, RB. 22/6, P. 10 gs. ; **Royal,** High St., RB. 16/6, P. 7 gs. ; **Merlewood,** private, at Birnam, RB. 14/6, P. 7 gs. ; **Perth Arms,** at Dunkeld, RB. 17/6, P. 7½ gs.

Motor-Buses to *Perth* (50 min.), *Pitlochry* (40 min.), and *Aberfeldy* (55 min.) ; to *Inverness* (3½–4½ hrs.) and to *Glasgow* (c. 3 hrs.) in summer only.

History. Dunkeld owes its name (' Fort of the Celts ') to an ancient abbey
founded in 815 as a home for the Celtic monks who had been driven from Iona
by the Norsemen and as a shrine for the relics of St. Columba. A bishopric said
to have been established here by Alexander I endured until the desecration of
the cathedral in 1560. Gavin Douglas (1474–1522), the poet, was the most
distinguished bishop. In 1689 the cathedral and Dunkeld House were held by
1200 Cameronians, a newly-raised Lowland regiment, against 5000 Highlanders,
victorious after Killiecrankie. Though William Cleland (1661–89), the young
colonel of the Cameronians, was killed, the Highlanders were beaten off with
great loss, and the cause of James VII in Scotland was lost. J. J. R. Macleod
(1876–1935), co-discoverer, with Banting, of insulin, was born at Dunkeld.

On the left of the High St., in a little 18th cent. square, is the
entrance to the venerable *Cathedral (adm. 6d. ; 10–4 or 7,
Sun. from 2), which stands on a tree-studded lawn beside
the river. Parts of the fabric date from the 12th cent., but

most of the remains are 14–15th cent. work. The church was desecrated in 1560, and the nave and the aisles are still roofless. The choir, however, roughly patched up in 1600, was thoroughly restored after 1815 and in 1908.

The NAVE, begun by Bp. Cardney in 1406 and consecrated by Bp. Lauder in 1464, is remarkable for the Flamboyant tracery of the aisle windows. The great W. window is not truly centred in its gable. Above the plain arcade is an ungraceful round-headed triforium surmounted by a clerestory. The massive but graceful tower at the end of the N. aisle dates from 1469–1501, and contains 15th cent. wall-paintings. In the S. aisle is the tomb of Bp. Cardney and in the nave is the gravestone of Count Roehenstart (? 1781–1854), natural son of Charlotte, Duchess of Albany, and probably the last lineal descendant of the Young Pretender.

The aisleless CHOIR, now used as the parish church, was built in 1318–1400. At the E. end are the remains of a statue of its founder Bp. Sinclair (d. 1338), the hero of Donibristle, a recumbent armoured effigy believed to represent Robert II's natural son, Alexander Stewart, the vicious and violent Earl of Buchan (? 1343–94), better known as the ' Wolf of Badenoch,' and two pre-12th cent. grave-slabs. Against the E. wall is a monument to the 42nd Highlanders (the ' Black Watch '), and on the same wall a tablet (1903) commemorates Col. Cleland (see above), who is buried in the nave. On the N. wall is a war memorial to members of the Scottish Horse, a yeomanry regiment raised by the 8th Duke of Atholl (d. 1942), with a monument to him adjoining. A house in the square is occupied by the regimental museum. The CHAPTER HOUSE (1457–65), N. of the choir, is now the ducal tomb-chapel.

The grounds of *Dunkeld House*, for many years the seat of the Duke of Atholl, at the N. end of the town, contain the foundations of a *Palace*, begun on a lavish scale by the 4th duke in 1830 but abandoned soon after.

Craigiebarns (1106 ft.), on the Dunkeld side of the river, is an excellent viewpoint, commanding a fine prospect of Strath Tay. It is approached from the Blairgowrie road (A 923), about 150 yds. along which we take the Calley Lodge avenue on the left. A stile on the left at a gate affords access to the path up the hill. The precipitous slopes were successfully planted in an ingenious way by the Duke of Atholl, who, at the suggestion of Alex. Nasmyth, caused canisters of seeds to be fired at the crags out of small cannon.

By crossing the Tay Bridge and keeping to the right on B 898 we reach the bridge over the Braan, beyond which is *Inver*. Here are tablets to the native fiddlers Niel Gow (1727–1807), Nathaniel Gow (1766–1831), and Niel Gow (1795–1823), with the eldest of whom Burns spent a convivial evening in 1787 ; also commemorated is Charles Macintosh (1839–1922), the ' Perthshire naturalist,' likewise a violinist. The attractive road goes on up the right bank of the Tay to (5 m.) *Dalguise* and (11 m.) *Grandtully* (Rte. 21 ; for Aberfeldy).

A path on the right of the Old Amulree Road (which diverges l. just before the Braan bridge), or a lane on the left just beyond Inver, afford access to the *Hermitage*, a charming spot near a waterfall on the Braan (N.T.) overlooked by a belvedere of 1758 (rebuilt 1952), known as *Ossian's Hall*.—The modern road to *Amulree* (9 m. ; A 822) ascends *Strath Braan*, the valley joining the Tay opposite Dunkeld. From (2 m.) *Rumbling Bridge*, where the Braan in spate roars as it falls into a chasm, a by-road crossing the bridge returns to Dunkeld viâ Inver. Higher up, the strath becomes bare and featureless.

From Dunkeld to *Blairgowrie*, passing (c. 1½ m. N.E.) the group of lochs fed by the Lunan, see p. 229. Cart roads lead N. from these lochs to (6 m.) *Loch Ordie*, whence we may return viâ *Dowally* (see below), 2½ m. S.W.

Beyond Dunkeld the road enters a lovely reach of Strath Tay.—At (19½ m.) *Dowally* the parish church preserves the jougs of an older church. A fine view opens out up the Tay to the left, with the shapely Schiehallion and the round-topped Farragon rising from the valley, as we approach (23 m.) *Ballinluig*, where the road and railway for Aberfeldy diverge (see Rte. 31).—Our route here quits the Tay and follows its tributary the Tummel. *Moulinearn*, 1½ m. N., between the railway and the Tummel, was formerly an inn, patronised by Prince Charlie (1745) and by Queen Victoria (1844).

28 m. **PITLOCHRY** (2380 inhab.), claiming to be the centre of Scotland, is one of the most popular summer resorts in the country, charmingly situated above the Tummel, surrounded by woods and backed by the mass of Ben Vrackie. Extensive hydro-electric development, including the creation of a new loch, has changed the landscape in the neighbourhood, but to the newcomer's eye the glory of the scenery is undiminished.

Hotels (mostly open April–Oct.). **Atholl Palace** (130 R.), first class, grounds incl. tennis courts, 9-hole golf course and swimming-pool, RB. from 37/6, P. 14 gs. ; **Hydro**, RB. 35/, P. 15 gs. ; **Green Park**, on Loch Faskally, RB. 25/6, P. 15 gs. ; **Fisher's**, RB. 27/, P. 13 gs., open always ; **Dundarach**, RB. from 21/, P. 9–12 gs. ; **Pine Trees**, unlic., RB. 23/6, P. 12 gs., open always ; **Moulin**, ¾ m. N., RB. 22/6, P. 10½ gs. ; **Scotland's**, RB. 22/6, P. 10 gs., open always ; **Airdanair**, similar charges ; **Craigower**, **Castlebeigh**, both unlic., RB. 18/6, P. 9 gs. ; **Wellwood**, unlic., RB. 22/6, P. 10½ gs.—**Killiecrankie**, RB. from 21/, P. 10 gs. ; **Old Faskally House**, RB. 21/, P. 12 gs., both 3½ m. N.W.

Hotel Accommodation Bureau (no advance reservations), 43 Atholl Rd.

Festival Theatre, in a semi-perman-

ent building, open from late April or May to Sept. (restaurant closes 11 p.m.), seats 6/–10/6.

Golf Course at the foot of Craigower ; tournaments in July and Aug.— TENNIS. Tournament held in Sept. at Atholl Palace.—BOATING and FISHING on Loch Faskally (2/–2/6 per hr.).— SHEEP DOG TRIALS in late Aug.— HIGHLAND GAMES in early Sept.

Motor-Buses to *Struan* (Calvine ; 40 min.) ; to *Aberfeldy* (¾ hr.) ; to *Kinloch Rannoch* (1½ hr.) ; to *Perth* (1½ hr.) viâ Dunkeld ; to *Braemar* (2 hrs.) and *Balmoral* (3½ hrs.) viâ the Spittal of Glenshee on Tues. and Thurs. in summer. Daily express service in summer to *Inverness* in 3 hrs. (also nightly on Mon., Wed., Fri.) ; to *Edinburgh* and to *Glasgow* in 4 hrs. (also nightly in 3¾ hrs. on Tues., Thurs., Sat.) viâ Perth and Stirling.

To the N.W. of the town lies *Loch Faskally*, a lovely stretch of water 2½ m. long, created from the Tummel in 1949–50. Alongside the *Pitlochry Dam* and *Power Station*, at its S. end, is an extensive *Fish-Ladder* (with an observation chamber), up which pass c. 5000 salmon annually. A footway crosses the dam to the W. bank of the Tummel whence the return may be made viâ the foot suspension-bridge at *Portnacraig*, a little downstream. Alternatively, walkers can go upstream through woods to return by the new aluminium suspension footbridge, replacing the old Clunie bridge. For the hilly road to Loch Tummel, see below ; for the path to Strathtay (Grandtully), see p. 246.

The most famous spot in the neighbourhood of Pitlochry is the **Pass of Killiecrankie** (2½–3 m. N.), the defile through which the Garry forces a way to join the Tummel. From the main road (car-park) a path descends the wooded hillside to the river far below, where the narrowest part of the chasm is known as the *Soldier's Leap ;* thence a footpath goes through the defile to the *Bridge of Garry*, at its lower end, on the Kinloch Rannoch road, 2½ m. from Pitlochry. The woods on the E. side of the pass are Nat. Trust property.

The battle of Killiecrankie, graphically described by Scott and Macaulay, was fought and won for James VII by Graham of Claverhouse, Viscount Dundee, against General Mackay on July 27th, 1689. Mackay's troops had emerged at the upper end of the pass and had formed up facing N. on the plateau above the Haugh of Urrard when the Highlanders received the signal to charge. " It was past 7 o'clock. Dundee gave the word. The Highlanders dropped their plaids. The few who were so luxurious as to wear rude socks of untanned hide spurned them away. It was long remembered in Lochaber that Lochiel took off what possibly was the only pair of shoes in his clan, and charged barefoot at the head of his men. In two minutes the battle was lost and won . . . and the mingled torrent of red coats and tartans went raving down the valley to the gorge of Killiecrankie " (Macaulay). Dundee, fatally wounded, is said to have been carried to *Urrard House*, in the woods near the road. An upright stone marks the spot where he fell.

In 1746 the Hessian troops employed in subduing the Young Pretender's followers refused to traverse the pass, believing that they had reached the last outpost of civilisation.

Beyond the W. end of the *Bridge of Garry* (see above) a path (l.) provides access to the *Falls of Tummel* (N.T. ; 50 acres), ¾ m. S., near the confluence of the Garry and the Tummel ; the falls have been reduced in height by the alteration in the level of the river. Queen Victoria paid a visit here in 1844. The footbridge, a little upstream, provides an attractive return route to Pitlochry (c. 3 m.) along the W. side of Loch Faskally (see above).

The *Black Spout* (1¼ m.), a picturesque fall amid dense woods S.E. of Pitlochry. is reached by a track running (l.) up the left bank of the second stream passed on the Dunkeld road, or by a shorter path through the Atholl Palace grounds.

The favourite short ascent (c. 1 hr.) is that of *Craigower* (N.T. ; 1300 ft.), from which a lovely view is obtained of Loch Tummel, Schiehallion, and the Shepherds of Etive ; it is best reached by the path behind the Moulin Hotel and thence above the golf course. **Moulin**, ¾ m. N. of Pitlochry, is a pleasant village, S.E. of which are the ruins of *Castle Dhu*, once a stronghold of the Campbells. Kinnaird Cottage (tablet), 1 m. farther along the road, was occupied for two months in 1881 by R. L. Stevenson, who here wrote ' Thrawn Janet,' ' The Merry Men,' and other short stories. Moulin was the birthplace of Alexander Duff (1806–78), missionary in India.—*Faskally House* (1831), between the foot of Craigower and the river, is now a Forestry Training School.

The easy ascent of **Ben Vrackie** (*Beinn Bhreac*, ' brindled hill ' ; 2757 ft. ; 2–2½ hrs.) is rewarded by a view including Ben Nevis, the Shepherds of Etive, Ben Lawers, Schiehallion, and the Lomonds. The cairn and view-indicator on top commemorate the sojourn of The Leys School at Pitlochry in 1940–45. The direct path leaves the road behind the hotel at Moulin.

FROM PITLOCHRY TO TUMMEL BRIDGE, 14 m. viâ the S. side of Loch Tummel. This narrow, hilly and charming road is greatly recommended for its delightful views. Near the Atholl Palace we cross Aldour Bridge and turn right ascending above Loch Faskally. We pass the *Clunie Memorial Arch* in memory of five workers killed during the construction of the tunnel (2 m. long ; 1946–50) through which the waters of Loch Tummel are brought from the Clunie Dam (with fish-pass) to Clunie Power Station, near the falls (see above). Above the far end of the loch we bear right on to B 846 for *Tummel Bridge*, see below.

From Aldour Bridge the by-road to the left along the W. bank of the Tummel may be followed, viâ (1 m.) *Dunfallandy* with its interesting sculptured stone, to (4½ m.) *Logierait* (p. 246), ½ m. W, of Ballinluig.

From Pitlochry to Rannoch Station, 38 m., one of the finest drives in Scotland. The by-roads on the S. shores of the lochs offer pleasant alternatives.

Crossing (2½ m.) the Bridge of Garry (p. 235) we pass (4 m.) *Bonskeid House* (leased by the Scottish Y.M.C.A. as a holiday house), with fine woods. After crossing (5 m.) the Fincastle burn the road bends to the left, drawing closer to the Tummel with its new dam (see above). A little farther on (l.) is *Strathtummel Youth Hostel*.—6¾ m. The *Queen's View* (753 ft.), a rocky spur on the left, commands a magnificent prospect of *Loch Tummel* (7½ m. long), Schiehallion, and the Shepherds of Etive. Since 1950 the loch has been extended by 4½ m. and the Queen's View correspondingly altered.

The road runs above the loch to (10 m.) *Loch Tummel Hotel* (RB. 17/6, P. 8 gs.) and joins B 846 at (14 m.) *Tummel Bridge*, opposite the power-station (1933) of the Rannoch hydro-electric scheme. The wildness of the scenery is tempered by the pipes leading to the dam (with fish-pass) and reservoir of *Dunalastair* (2¼ m. long), beside which we are joined by a road from Struan.—21 m. The neat village of **Kinloch Rannoch** (*Dunalastair*, RB. 25/, P. 10 gs. ; *Loch Rannoch*, RB. 25/6, P. 10 gs. ; *Bunrannoch*, RB. 19/6, P. 9 gs. ; motor-buses to Rannoch station and Pitlochry), in an expansion of the valley, stands, in spite of its name, at the foot of *Loch Rannoch*, a beautiful sheet of water 10 m. long and 1 m. broad, now a power-reservoir. In the centre of the village is an obelisk to Dugald Buchanan, " the Rannoch Schoolmaster, Evangelist, and Sacred Poet, d. 1768."

Schiehallion (3547 ft.), the graceful peak which has for so long been dominating the landscape on the left, raises a perfect cone of snowy quartzite to the S.E. of Kinloch Rannoch. It is described by Geikie as " a noble instance of a cone not yet freed from its parent ridge," and it is interesting also as the mountain utilised by Maskelyne in his experiments relating to the specific gravity and weight of the earth (1774). Schiehallion may be ascended most directly and steeply (2–3 hrs.) viâ the course of the Tempar burn, or more easily along the ridge from the *Braes of Foss Farm* (Tigh-an-tSocaich), 6½ m. S.E. of Kinloch Rannoch. Road to *Aberfeldy*, see Rte. 31.

Beyond Kinloch Rannoch there are roads on both banks of the loch. That on the N. bank, keeping close to the loch, has the finer distant views, but the other runs through the magnificent *Black Wood of Rannoch*, whose ancient and finely coloured firs are a relic of the Caledonian Forest. We follow the N. bank, on which are a power-station (1930) and other works of the Rannoch hydro-electric scheme connecting Loch Rannoch and Loch Ericht.—At (29½ m.) *Bridge of Ericht* we cross the Ericht some 5 m. after its outflow from *Loch Ericht* (p. 238).—Just beyond (30½ m.) *Rannoch Lodge* the roads reunite and we see, on the S. bank of the Gaur, a mansion known as *The Barracks*, having been erected for the accommodation of troops after the '45.—Hence we follow the impetuous Gaur through desolate country, past the *Loch Eigheach* reservoir, to (38 m.) **Rannoch Station** on the West Highland Railway (Rte. 48), where the road ends.

From Pitlochry to *Bridge of Cally*, for *Blairgowrie* and *Glenshee*, see p. 230.

Beyond Pitlochry road and railway run beside the Garry through the *Pass of Killiecrankie (see above), of which the best general view is obtained from the train. There is an easy ascent of Ben Vrackie (p. 235) from Killiecrankie station.

35 m. **Blair Atholl** (427 ft. ; *Atholl Arms*, RB. 25/, P. 12 gs. ; *Tilt*, RB. 20/6, P. 10 gs.) stands at the junction of the Tilt with the Garry and is the last village of any size passed for many miles. The old parish church of Kilmaveonaig (1591) was rebuilt in 1794 and is distinguished as having always been

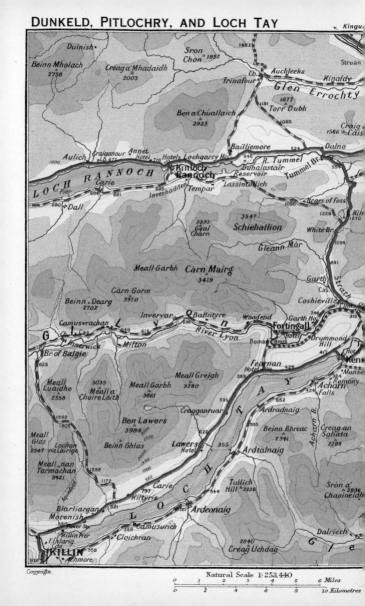

DUNKELD, PITLOCHRY, AND LOCH TAY

Natural Scale 1 : 253,440

0   1   2   3   4   5   6 Miles
0   2   4   6   8   10 Kilometres

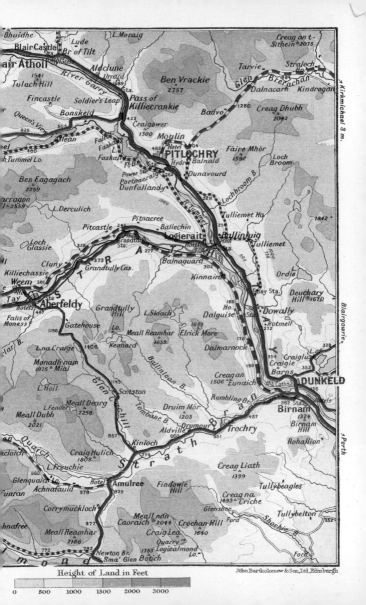

Height of Land in Feet

0   500   1000   1500   2000   3000

John Bartholomew & Son, Ltd., Edinburgh

in the possession of the Scottish Episcopal church. ' Bonnie Dundee ' was buried in the Atholl vault in the churchyard of Old Blair, 1 m. N. *Blair Castle*, seat of the Duke of Atholl, a large white-washed mansion of various dates in the Scottish baronial style, is finely situated in wooded grounds to the N. The castle and its park are open in summer (May–mid-Oct.; weekdays 10–6, Sun. 2–6; adm. 2/6, teas obtainable).

The oldest part of the castle, Cumming's Tower on the N.E., was built c. 1269 by John Comyn of Badenoch, and various alterations and additions were made down to 1903–04. Garrisoned in 1644 by Montrose, stormed in 1652 by Cromwell, and occupied by Claverhouse in 1689, the castle was partly dismantled in 1690 to prevent its occupation by the rebels. Prince Charlie spent three days here in 1745, and paid another visit in 1746; but later that year, just before Culloden, when it was held as an outpost for the Duke of Cumberland, it was successfully defended by Sir Andrew Agnew for 17 days against Lord George Murray, brother of the Duke of Atholl.—The Murrays of Tullibardine and Atholl have been a power in the land since the time of David I (12th cent.), and were at one time sovereigns of the Isle of Man. The title passed to them by marriage in 1629. The first Stewart earl received the earldom from his half-brother, James II, in 1457, and the motto, ' Furth fortune and fill the fetters,' was granted to him by James III in 1475 when he was despatched against a rebellious Lord of the Isles. The Duke is the only British subject permitted to retain a standing army (The Atholl Highlanders), at the head of which he used to march to open the Highland Gathering held in early Sept. in a field near the castle.

The rooms on view contain an interesting collection of family portraits, Jacobite relics, including Lord George's library, Dundee's helmet and breastplate, china and lace, and souvenirs of Queen Victoria's visit to the castle in 1844. Remarkable series of stuccoes were added in 1748–58 by Thos. Clayton, Adam's plasterer; the panels are by Charles Steuart (fl. 1762–90).

Among the shorter excursions are those to the Pass of Killiecrankie, and the Falls of Bruar; and a visit up the left bank of the Tilt to (c. 2½ m.) *Fender Bridge* and the pretty *Falls of Fender* should not be omitted, while from *Tulach Hill* (1541 ft.), 1 m. S., a good view of the neighbourhood may be enjoyed.

From Blair Atholl to *Braemar*, viâ Glen Tilt, see pp. 303–05.

Ben-y-Gloe (3671 ft.; ' mountain of the mist ') is a mountain group N.E. of Blair Atholl with three principal summits: *Cairn Gabhar* or *Gour* (3671 ft.), *Cairn Liath* (3193 ft.), and between these, *Ben-y-Gloe* (3505 ft.). The highest point, well worth ascending, is c. 8 m. from Blair Atholl, and the three peaks can be visited on foot by good walkers in 8–9 hrs. (c. 21 m.). From *Fender Bridge* (see above) we keep up the left bank of the Fender to (3 m.) the N. end of *Loch Moraig*. The track on the left here omits Cairn Liath, and it is preferable to keep straight on for 1½ m. until the top of Cairn Liath is seen quite clearly without any rising ground in front and then ascend straight to the top (1¾ m.; view of Schiehallion). Another 2 m. (¾ hr.), with a dip of 700 ft., takes us to the central cairn (3505 ft.), from which there is a magnificent *View* up Glen Tilt with the distant peaks of Cairn Toul, Braeriach, Ben Macdhui, Lochnagar, Ben Lawers, the Black Mount, and Ben Nevis. Another ¾ hr. (2 m.), with another dip of 700 ft., brings us to Cairn Gabhar (3671 ft.), commanding the Angus and Aberdeenshire mountains. The descent may be made down Glen Girnaig (S.) to (6½ m.) Killiecrankie station.

About 3 m. beyond Blair Castle the road crosses the Bruar, up the glen of which paths ascend to the *Falls of Bruar* with their three cascades.

The fir plantations surrounding the falls were planted by the 4th Duke of Atholl, in response to the ' Humble Petition of Bruar Water ' written by Burns after his visit in 1787.—Thence to Kingussie viâ the Minigaig Pass, see p. 241.

We pass the Falls of Garry with their salmon leap to reach (40 m.) *Calvine* (post office), with the village, Inn (plain), and

railway station of *Struan* on the opposite bank of the
river.

A road (B 847) runs up *Glen Erochy* or *Errochty* to (6 m.) *Trinafour*, where a
rough road strikes due N. for (5 m.) Dalnacardoch (see below). Higher up is *Loch
Errochty* (3¼ m. long), a power-reservoir formed by a dam 1310 ft. long and 127 ft.
high. Our road turns S., and, passing a rough road on the left for (4 m.) Tummel
Bridge, ascends rapidly to 1100 ft., commanding a fine prospect of Schiehallion
in front. A steady descent brings us to (10½ m.) Dunalastair reservoir, 2½ m. E.
of (13 m.) *Kinloch Rannoch*, see p. 236.

Quitting Calvine the road begins the long and steep ascent
(over 800 ft. in 13 m.) of the wild *Glen Garry*, side by side with
the tumbling river. At 46½ m. we pass *Dalnacardoch*, a well-
known inn in coaching days, now a shooting lodge ; it stands
on the site of the hut which was Wade's headquarters when
roadmaking in 1729. Here a rough road diverges N. for
(5½ m.) *Edendon Lodge* ; thence to (19 m.) *Kingussie*, see
p. 241.—Beyond a bridge across the Garry snow-screens testify
to the severity of the winter in these parts, where snow ploughs
are often required to clear the route.—51½ m. *Dalnaspidal*
('field of the hospital' ; 1422 ft.), in a bleak situation, S.W. of
which lies Loch Garry. Two prominent hog-backed hills
on the left are named the *Sow of Atholl* (S.) and the *Boar of
Badenoch* (N.). At (53½ m.) the *Pass of Drumochter* (1484 ft.),
the highest summit on any railway in Britain, we pass from
Perthshire into Inverness-shire and from the Forest of Atholl
into Badenoch. General Wade's stone, on the high-road,
marks the spot where the troops who made the road from
Inverness met those who had worked up from Dunkeld (1729).

Inverness-shire (4120 sq. m.), the largest county in Scotland, stretches
diagonally across the mainland from the Moray Firth, on the N.E., to Loch Eil,
on the S.W., and it includes also Skye and all the Outer Hebrides (Rtes. 58, 59)
except Lewis. Even the distant isles of St. Kilda, 40 m. at sea and 120 m. from
the county town, are within its bounds. Inverness is also the most mountainous
county, emphatically a land of the mountain and the flood, of brown heath and
shaggy wood. The mainland portion is divided into two well-defined sections
by *Glenmore* or the *Great Glen of Alban*, with its chain of lochs linked by the
Caledonian Canal. West of this line, from N. to S., open Strath Glass, Glen
Moriston, and Glen Garry, and on the Sound of Sleat, separated from each other
by deep sea-fjords, lie the districts of Glenelg, Knoidart, Morar, and Moidart.
East of the line, in the S., touching on Argyll, is the famous region of *Lochaber*,
including Glen Spean, Glen Roy, and Glen Nevis. Farther N.E., on the confines
of Perth and Aberdeen, is *Badenoch*, with Glen Truim, Glen Tromie, and Glen
Feshie. Among the clan-names of Inverness are Fraser, Grant, Chisholm,
Macdonald, Cameron, Mackintosh, and Macpherson.

59 m. Dalwhinnie (1180 ft. ; *Loch Ericht*, RB. 21/, P. 9 gs. ;
Grampian, RB. 21/, P. 10 gs.), at the head of Glen Truim, is
a desolate and solitary spot, protected from the cold winds by
a few firs.

On the left lies **Loch Ericht** (good fishing and boats), a dreary loch 15 m. long,
noted for Salmo ferox, girdled by the mountains of the Drumochter and Ben
Alder deer forests. Its waters, which are discharged at the S. end by the Ericht
into Loch Rannoch, have never been known to freeze. This loch has also been
incorporated in the Rannoch hydro-electric scheme. *Cluny's Cage*, which David

Balfour found " hanging like a wasp's nest in a green hawthorn bush," was near the S. foot of *Ben Alder* (3757 ft.), on the W. shore of the loch (⅓ m. N. of Alder Cottage). Here Prince Charlie lay in concealment after Culloden with Cluny Macpherson.

A good road (A 889) runs N from Dalwhinnie to (7 m.) *Laggan Bridge.*

The wild country around Dalwhinnie was a favourite gathering-place of the Highlanders, who often held their own against a far more numerous force of disciplined troops. Here Cromwell's Ironsides received a check from the men of Atholl ; and, on Aug. 26th, 1745, General Cope declining to encounter in their native stronghold the Highlanders, who were descending with Prince Charlie from the Pass of Corrieyarrick, retired to Inverness, leaving open the road to the Lowlands and Edinburgh.

At (65 m.) *Etteridge Bridge* the road crosses the railway near (998 ft.) the *Falls of Truim.* The country now becomes more fertile, with fine views of isolated mountains in front. Below the junction of the Truim and the Spey the battle of *Invernahavon* was fought in 1386 between the clans Cameron and Mackintosh. We cross the Spey.—70¼ m. **Newtonmore** (800 ft. ; *Mains*, RB. 24/, P. 10 gs. ; *Balavil Arms*, RB. 21/6, P. 9 gs., these two open always ; *Lodge*, similar charges ; *Craigerne*, unlic., RB. 25/, P. 9 gs. ; *Craig Mhor*, unlic., RB. 21/, P. 8 gs. ; *Badenoch, Glen*, RB. 18/6, P. 8 gs. ; *Braeriach*, unlic., RB. 16/6), a long village where, in the *Clan Macpherson House* (shown by the curator, weekdays 10–12, 2–6), are preserved the ' Black Chanter ' of the pipes said to have been played at the North Inch of Perth, the clan's invincible green banner, and other relics.

A track hence ascends the Calder, through wild and impressive scenery, to (6¼ m.) Loch Dubh and (7¼ m.) *Cairn Mairg* (3093 ft.), a mountain frequented by eagles. This is the highest summit of the Monadhliath Mountains, and on its N.W. slopes rises the Findhorn. This uninhabited waste is best explored on pony-back (excursions organised by the Balavil Arms).

73 m. Kingussie (745 ft. : pron. ' Kinyewssie ' ; *Duke of Gordon*, first-class, RB. 25/6, P. 10 gs. ; *Star*, RB. 22/6, P. 10 gs. ; *Royal*, RB. 19/6, P. 8 gs. ; *Silverfjord*, RB. 17/6, P. 7 gs.), a pleasant village (1075 inhab.) on the N. bank of the Spey, with a golf course and a Youth Hostel, is frequented for its pure air.

To the right of the main street is *Am Fasgadh (i.e. ' the Shelter '), the *Highland Folk Museum* (open May–Sept. daily 10–1, 2–5 exc. Sun.), founded in 1935 (on Iona) by Miss I. F. Grant, who herself created and is still developing the collection. Since 1954 it has been owned by the Scottish universities. The main building contains a ' Badenoch room ' (1800), examples of Highland dress, furniture, pottery, relics of old crafts, etc. Outside are representative cottages, a mill from Lewis, and obsolete farm implements. Admission is free, but visitors should contribute to the collection box.

The walks in the environs (best in May–June) are delightful, though visitors are discouraged from straying on the mountains, which are preserved as grouse-moors and deer-forests. *Craig Beg* (1593 ft.), behind the village, is a fine view-point ; on its N. side is *Loch Guinach* (⅓ m. long), whence we may return viâ Glen Guinach and the golf course.—Motor-buses to *Grantown* on Tues., Thurs. & Sat. viâ Aviemore.

Ruthven, on the opposite bank of the Spey, was the birthplace of James Macpherson (1736–96), translator and author of the Ossianic poems. The ruined barracks are conspicuous (see below). Kingussie is a good base for visiting the wild district of **Badenoch,** which formerly belonged to the Comyns, and was,

upon their annihilation by Bruce's party, bestowed upon Randolph, Earl of
Moray. Part of it, however, was retained by the Crown, and was subsequently
granted to Alexander, son of Robert II, known as the ' Wolf of Badenoch.' One
of the fortresses by which his power was maintained was on the spot occupied
by the ruins of *Ruthven Barracks*, built in 1718 to keep the Highlanders in check,
but destroyed by them in 1746. Ruthven was the closing scene of the '45 rebellion,
for here many of the Highlanders assembled after the rout at Culloden, in hopes
that Prince Charlie would take the field again. He, however, saw the uselessness
of another attempt and sent a message bidding them farewell.

FROM KINGUSSIE TO FORT WILLIAM, 49 m. by road (A 86) ;
motor-bus on Fri. morning (c. June 20th–Sept. 26th only),
returning in the afternoon, in 2¼ hrs. ; to Loch Laggan in ¾ hr.

We follow A 9 to (3 m.) *Newtonmore*, whence we have a
choice of two routes. A 86, described below, bears to the
right, but an attractive, though rough and hilly, alternative
leaves A 9 2¾ m. farther on and follows the S. bank of the Spey,
rejoining our road at Drumgask.—Our road crosses the Calder
and ascends a narrow valley, one of the prettiest parts of the
route. On the left are the Spey and two lovely little lochs,
while on the right rise the precipitous cliffs of Craig Dhu
(2350 ft.), with a cave where Prince Charlie hid with Cluny
Macpherson. Farther on the valley suddenly opens out,
affording an extensive view with Ben Alder and other mountains in the distance.—8½ m. *Cluny Castle* (r.) was the home of
Cluny, and many chieftains of Clan Macpherson lie buried in
a little churchyard beside the road. At (11 m.) *Laggan Bridge*
we cross the Spey, and at (11½ m.) *Drumgask*, where our route
is joined by a road from Dalwhinnie, we turn (r.) up Strath
Mashie.

From a point ¾ m. W. of Drumgask the old military road made by General
Wade in 1735 (described in Neil Munro's ' The New Road ') strikes off N.W. up
the right bank of the Spey, crossing the river on Wade's bridge at (7 m.) *Garvamore*
(rfmts. at a cottage), where in 1187 William the Lion subdued the local rebels.
Vehicles cannot proceed beyond (11 m.) *Drummin*, where a path diverges
S.W. up the Spey for *Loch Spey* (3½ m.) and for Glen Roy (p. 337). Beyond
Drummin the main track ascends to (15 m.) the **Pass of Corrieyarrick** (2507 ft. ;
*View from the Moray Firth to the peaks of Skye) and then descends to *Glen
Tarff* and (24 m.) *Fort Augustus* (p. 357). Wade's bridge over the Allt Lagan a'
Bhainne, above Glen Tarff, destroyed by floods, is replaced by a suspension
footbridge erected by students of Edinburgh University (1932).

In the angle between Strath Mashie and the Spey rises
Dun-na-Lamb, a fine prehistoric hill-fort, 600 ft. above the
valley. Beyond a bridge over the Mashie Water the watershed
(848 ft.) is imperceptibly crossed, and soon the Pattack
comes rushing down from the left in a picturesque gorge.
The Ben Nevis range comes into view before we reach (18 m.)
Loch Laggan Hotel (RB. 18/6, P. 9 gs., Easter–mid-Oct.), at
the N.E. end of the finely-wooded **Loch Laggan** (7 m. long and
½ m. broad) ; ancient dug-out canoes have been recovered
from the loch. The road runs along the N. shore, passing
(22 m.) the old farm of *Aberarder*, 4 m. above which (1200 ft.
above the loch) is *Corrie Arder*, a desolate corrie with a tarn

partly surrounded by cliffs 1000 ft. high. By climbing N.W. through ' The Window,' a prominent gap in these buttresses of *Craig Meaghaidh* (3700 ft.), we may gain its summit viâ the ridge.—Beyond (25 m.) *Moy Lodge*, at the S.W. end of the loch, the country becomes bleaker as we descend Glen Spean and skirt *Loch Moy*, a reservoir with a dam 180 ft. high and 700 ft. long, and connected by a tunnel with Loch Treig. ' Parallel roads ' (p. 337) are well marked as we descend steeply to (31 m.) *Tulloch*, on the W. Highland railway, which we follow closely viâ Roy Bridge and Spean Bridge to (49 m.) *Fort William* (see Rtes. 48, 52).

FROM KINGUSSIE TO STRUAN, 30 m. (26½ m. viâ the Minigaig Pass), by road and path.—Crossing the Spey to *Ruthven* (see above), whence a path opposite the Barracks, leading direct to Glentromie Lodge, saves 2 miles but misses some attractive scenery, we follow the road on the left to (3 m.) *Tromie Bridge*. Here we turn S., ascending the right bank of the Tromie.—5 m. *Glentromie Lodge* (962 ft.).—From (9½ m.) the near side of an iron bridge across Allt Bhran an alternative path to Struan, shorter but harder, climbs to (14 m.) the *Minigaig Pass* (c. 2600 ft.) and thence descends Glen Bruar to (25 m.) the *Falls of Bruar* and (26½ m.) *Struan*.—The road goes on up the Tromie to (11 m.) the cliff-bound *Loch-an-tSeilich* and ends at (13 m.) *Gaick Lodge* (1500 ft.). The waters of the loch are partly diverted by a dam (fish-pass) to flow 4½ m. W. through a tunnel to Loch-na-Cuaich, whence they are directed, partly by aqueduct, to Loch Ericht for the Rannoch hydro-electric scheme.—We follow the path and c. 1 m. beyond Gaick Lodge we turn to the right, skirting (14½ m.) *Loch Vrotten* and (17 m.) *Loch-an-Duin* (1700 ft.), a miniature Wastwater.—At (18½ m.) *Edendon Lodge* (1500 ft.) we strike a cart road descending to (24 m.) *Dalnacardoch*, 6 m. W. of Struan.

FROM KINGUSSIE TO BRAEMAR, 33½ m. by road and path.—From (3 m.) *Tromie Bridge* (see above) we go ¼ m. N. (walkers may strike through the wood) and then turning sharply to the right follow a rough road across the hills to (7 m.) *Druimcaillich*, where we join the route from Aviemore. Thence we ascend the left bank of the Feshie, crossing the stream ¼ m. short of (10 m.) *Glenfeshie Lodge*, in the finest and wildest part of the glen. We cross (16 m.) the Eidart, and in ½ m. more we leave the Feshie and, keeping to the left, reach the watershed (17 m. ; 1834 ft.), whence the view, though impressive, is restricted. We descend to the E. above the Geldie, passing (19 m.) *Geldie Lodge* on the farther bank, and (22½ m.) join the bridle path from Blair Atholl. We descend by the combined waters of the Geldie and Bynack to (24 m.) their junction with the Dee. Thence by road to (33½ m.) *Braemar*, see p. 302.

FROM KINGUSSIE TO AVIEMORE BY THE S. SIDE OF THE SPEY, 14½ m., a pleasant alternative to the main road. To (3 m.) *Tromie Bridge*, see above.—5 m. *Insh*, 4 m. from its church, see below.—Beyond (7 m.) *Loch Insh* a road crosses the Spey for Kincraig (see below).—We keep to the right and soon after (8½ m.) *Feshiebridge* skirt Rothiemurchus Forest.—From (11¼ m.) *South Kinrara*, just beyond a tiny loch, a path mounts on the right to (¾ m. ; r.) Loch-an-Eilean. About 1 m. beyond (12¼ m.) *Rothiemurchus* we turn sharp left and cross the Spey for (14½ m.) *Aviemore* (see below).

The main road and railway pass, 2¼ m. from Kingussie, an obelisk to James Macpherson (' Ossian '), who built the neighbouring mansion of *Balavil* (formerly Belleville). Sir David Brewster (d. 1868), who married Macpherson's daughter, afterwards resided here. The house occupies the site of *Raits Castle*, a stronghold of the Comyns and the scene of the massacre of their chiefs by Mackintoshes.

The Comyn had invited his Mackintosh enemies to a dinner in pretended reconciliation, but had arranged that each of his clansmen was to slay a

Mackintosh when the boar's head appeared. The Mackintoshes, however, had been warned of the plot, and on the appearance of the boar's head forestalled their treacherous enemies in their murderous intention. The 'Listening Stone,' a large grey rock to the W. of the castle, is said to stand where the plot was overheard.

We leave Loch Insh on our right and reach (79 m.) *Kincraig* (Suie Hotel, RB. 22/6, P. 9 gs.), the station for Feshiebridge. The church of *Insh*, beyond the Spey, is said to be the only church in Scotland on a site continuously used for service since the coming of the Culdee missionaries in the 6th century. —We lose sight of the Spey and pass between *Loch Alvie* (l.) and the *Tor of Alvie* (r.). Sir George Henschel (1850–1934) is buried in *Alvie* churchyard (l.). He made his summer home at Allt-na-Criche, on the hill above. On the shore of the loch is *Lynwilg Hotel* (RB. 25/, P. 10 gs.), frequented by climbers. The Tor (view) is crowned by a Waterloo cairn and a monument to the last Duke of Gordon (d. 1836). In the grounds of *Kinrara* beside the Spey rests the body of the Duchess of Gordon (d. 1812), who helped to raise the Gordon Highlanders (obelisk).

85 m. **Aviemore** (*Cairngorm*, RB. 23/6, P. 10 gs. ; *Aviemore Motel*, RB. 18/6, P. 7½ gs. ; *The Dell*, private, at Rothiemurchus, RB. 21/, P. 9 gs.), a long village above the Spey, attracts many visitors and is a convenient base for exploring the Cairngorms and for winter sports. It is important also as the junction of the direct railway line to Inverness with the line to Forres. The rock of *Craigellachie* above the village was the trysting-place of Clan Grant, whose war-cry was "Stand fast, Craigellachie." The country ' between the two Craigellachies ' extending from this rock to Craigellachie (p. 320) at the foot of Strathspey, 37 m. N.E., was the home of Clan Grant.

The favourite short excursion from Aviemore is that to Loch-an-Eilean, 3½ m. S. Crossing the Spey to (1¼ m.) *Inverdruie* we turn sharp to the right for (2¼ m.) *Rothiemurchus* (see above). Hence a road branching to the left at a monument to Dr. James Martineau, who founded a local school of carving, mounts through a lovely birch avenue to (3½ m.) *Loch-an-Eilean*, famous for its triple echo. On the island, from which the loch is named, are the remains of a stronghold of the Wolf of Badenoch, which was one of the last Scottish nesting-places of the osprey. *Ord Ban* (1405 ft.), N.W. of the loch, commands a fine view. Much felling has thinned the great *Rothiemurchus Forest*, between this loch and Loch Morlich.

A fine moorland walk (bridle path) leaves the Kingussie road 1½ m. S. of Aviemore and crosses the hills N.W. to (6½ m.) the *Dulnain Valley* (p. 244) whose upper reaches, in the desolate *Monadhliath Mountains* (the ' grey hills '), are the haunt of the eagle and the wild cat. The track down the valley leads to (13¾ m.) *Carrbridge*.

FROM AVIEMORE TO NETHYBRIDGE VIÂ THE REVOAN PASS, 16¼ m., by rough road, hardly practicable for driving.—Motor-bus to Glenmore in ½ hr. on Wed., Sat. & Sun. (mid-July–Aug.).—At (1¼ m.) *Inverdruie* (see above) we keep straight on, crossing the Druie at (2¼ m.) *Coylum Bridge*. The road on the left here leads straight to Nethybridge (9½ m.) viâ (4 m.) the little 18th cent. Kincardine church.—Our road mounts to (5¼ m.) *Loch Morlich* (1046 ft.), from whose nearer end a charming by-road (l.) leads over the *Sluggan Pass* (1100 ft.) to (4½ m.) Kincardine church. The *Queen's Park*, or *Glenmore National Forest Park*, occupies 12,500 acres here. A herd of Swedish reindeer, introduced here experimentally since 1952 and now including 11 Scottish-born descendants, can be seen by arrangement with the Reindeer Company's herder at Glenmore, at the E. end of the loch. From (6¼ m.) *Glenmore Lodge*, now the Scottish Centre for Outdoor Training (camping site), starts the usual ascent of Cairngorm. The road, now really bad, ascends steeply to (8¼ m.) the **Revoan Pass** (1197 ft.), a narrow pine-clad gorge with a lovely green tarn on the right, beyond which there is a short ascent to the left before we begin the rapid zigzag descent of the Nethy valley. A forest path on the left (12¾ m.) saves ½ m.—16¼ m. *Nethybridge* (p. 249).

The **Cairngorms**, the group of splendid mountains lying between Aviemore and Braemar, are the highest mountain-mass in Britain (6 peaks over 4000 ft.), though no individual peak comes within 100 ft. of Ben Nevis ; 40,000 acres were designated a nature reserve in 1954. The whole group is of granite and is famous for the transparent crystals of smoked quartz, often of considerable size, known as ' cairngorms.' The lower slopes, though springs are plentiful, lack the rich flora of the western hills ; among the barren boulders of the tops reindeer moss is sometimes found. The golden eagle is often seen and ptarmigan are plentiful. Snowclad in winter, the group is well adapted for ski-ing and other winter sports, with perhaps Braemar as the chief centre.

Ascents. Vexatious restrictions are imposed upon walkers by the owners of the grouse-moors and deer-forests, especially during the stalking season (Aug.–March), but there are three undisputed rights of way in the Cairngorms, viz. from Aviemore to the summit of Cairngorm viâ Loch Morlich ; from Aviemore to Braemar viâ Larig Ghru ; and from Aviemore to Braemar viâ Morlich and Larig Laoigh.

ASCENT OF CAIRNGORM AND BEN MACDHUI, 6¼ m. by road to Glenmore Lodge and 4–5 hrs. thence.—To *Glenmore Lodge*, see above. We diverge to the right from the Revoan Pass road and ascend Allt Mor, a stream descending from Cairngorm. An easy walk of 2–3 hrs. brings us to the summit of **Cairngorm** (4084 ft.), the least interesting of the group, commanding a wide view W. and N. The route thence follows the ridge S.W. and then S.E., never dropping below 3500 ft., to (c. 2 hrs. more) **Ben Macdhui* (4296 ft. ; *Beinn Muic Duibhe*, ' MacDuff's mount '), long believed to be the highest peak in Britain. The summit is a wide almost level plateau of red granite, so that the whole of the magnificent **View* (indicator) cannot be seen at once. To the N. Ben Hope (98 m. distant) is visible and Morven in Caithness ; S.W. is Ben Nevis, and due S. the fine group of Ben-y-Gloe. To the S.E. rises Lochnagar, beyond the Dee valley. The view from the precipitous W. side, across the Larig Ghru pass to the cliffs of Braeriach, Cairn Toul, and the Devil's Point, is the most impressive in the Grampians. The N.E. spur ends in a precipice overlooking Loch A'an. *Lochan Buidhe* (3683 ft.), below the N. slopes, is probably the highest mountain tarn in Britain.

The descent may be made to Braemar viâ Loch Etchachan (p. 305) or viâ Loch A'an. The latter descent (steep) starts from the ridge ½ m. S.W. of Cairngorm, beside a stream which offers the only feasible way down. In less than 1 hr. we reach **Loch A'an* or *Loch Avon* (2450 ft. ; 1½ m. long), surrounded by beautiful beaches of red granite sand in an almost inaccessible corrie. Thence to Braemar, see p. 305. The *Shelter Stone*, beneath which is a cavity with room for c. 8 people, is a huge fallen boulder ¼ m. S.W. of the head of the loch. The return thence to Glenmore Lodge (4 hrs.) leaves the N. shore ½ m. from the E. end and crosses *The Saddle* (2707 ft.) into Glen Nethy. We descend the valley (very rough) for c. 5 m. and then strike N.W. up a stream, rejoining the road at the Revoan Pass.

The ASCENT OF BRAERIACH AND CAIRN TOUL, 9 m. by road to Loch Eunach and 3–4 hrs. thence. Permission to drive to Loch Eunach must be obtained ; in the stalking season objection may be made to the passage even of pedestrians without authority. The road runs S. from (2¼ m.) *Coylum Bridge* (p. 242) and ascends gradually through Rothiemurchus Forest to Glen Eunach.—9 m. *Loch Eunach* (1650 ft.) is a lonely loch over 1 m. long, with a fine corrie at the S. end. From the end of the road near the N. end of the loch we climb a track on the left ascending to the main ridge. The summit of **Braeriach** (4248 ft.), 1½–2 hrs. from the loch, is 2 m. N. and E. **Cairn Toul** (4241 ft.) is c. 2 m. S.E., but the ascent involves an intermediate climb up the *Angel's Peak* (4149 ft.), and a scramble up a staircase of enormous boulders. Each of the two mountains intercepts a great part of the view from the other, but in both cases the prospect westwards is very fine, and the mass of Ben Macdhui towers grimly to the E.

At the head of the corrie (*Garbh Choire*) S.W. of Braeriach are the *Wells of Dee*, attainable by 1 hr.'s scramble down the ridge. In one of the corries is a drift of perpetual snow. Alternative descents lead from Braeriach N.E. to the Larig Ghru track ; down the N.E. shoulder and then N.W. to Glen Eunach 5½ m. S. of Coylum Bridge (short but uninteresting) ; or S.W. and then W. above the corries S. of Loch Eunach to (3¾ m.) *Cairn Ban* (3443 ft.) and (7 m.) *Druim-caillich* in Glen Feshie.

FROM AVIEMORE TO BRAEMAR VIÂ LARIG GHRU, 28 or 30 m., a splendid but fatiguing walk of c. 12 hrs. over one of the wildest and grandest passes of the lofty Cairngorm range. There is no inn or house of shelter on the route, but judicious inquiries at Coylum Bridge, Lui Beg, or Inverey may result in an offer of hospitality. The last 9½ m. are practicable for driving. Unless an early start is made, this expedition should be made in the direction described below, to avoid the chance of being benighted in Rothiemurchus forest. Those making it in the opposite direction enjoy a sudden surprise view from the summit, having laid two-thirds of the walk behind them.

Just before (2¼ m.) *Coylum Bridge* (p. 242) we take the road on the right and after ⅓ m. quit it for a path which follows the left bank of the stream from Loch Eunach for 1¾ m. We cross this stream just before the confluence of a large tributary, high above whose right bank the path runs to (7½ m.) the entrance to the **Larig Ghru** or *Lairig Dhruie* (' Pass of the Dhruie '), which is guarded by a well-marked moraine, between the precipices of Cairngorm and Braeriach. At the summit (2750 ft. ; 10 m.) *Aberdeenshire* is entered. The next mile affords the roughest possible walking over detached boulders, and the ground remains very uneven until we are past (11 m.) the *Pools of Dee*, three clear tarns connected by underground streams. A path on the right, affording access to (1 hr.) *Braeriach*, is the only route to that mountain always open.

We soon see the magnificent corrie into which the Garrochorry burn, the loftiest source of the Dee, leaps from the Wells of Dee, high up on Braeriach. When mist rolls in it, as if boiling in a mighty cauldron, the majesty of the scene is, if possible, enhanced. The *Devil's Point* (3303 ft.) stands out boldly in front. When it is breasted the Dee may be followed, past (20½ m.) *White Bridge*, to (23½ m.) the *Linn of Dee* ; or by keeping high up above the left bank, we may bear round Cairn-a-Mhaim and strike the *Lui Beg* burn, following its left bank past (18 m.) Derry Lodge to (21½ m.) *Linn of Dee*. A half-mile may be saved by striking through the wood at a point ½ m. S. of the bridge over the united Lui waters. From the Linn of Dee to (6½ m. more) *Braemar*, see p. 303.

From Aviemore to *Forres* and to *Craigellachie* (Elgin), see Rte. 32.

The main road to Inverness traverses pleasant wooded country, enjoying a fine retrospect of the Cairngorms, and passes the little *Loch Vaa* (r.) before reaching (89 m.) *Kinveachy*, where A 95 diverges (r.) for) Grantown (Forres, Elgin, etc.).—92 m. **Carrbridge** (*Carr Bridge*, RB. 25/, P. 10 gs. ; *Rowanlea*, RB. 15/, P. 8 gs. ; *Struan House*, unlic., RB. 16/6, P. 8 gs., ski-ing lessons and equipment) is a small village on the charming river Dulnain. Beside the bridge (1928), which replaced an older one, is the arch of one still older (c. 1715 ; damaged by flood in 1829) ; General Wade's bridge lies higher up the river (see below).

The road from the station up the Dulnain valley leaves on the right (2¼ m.) the road to the picturesque *Sluggan Bridge*, built by General Wade, and, at a ford

(2¾ m.), the track to *Inverlaidnan*, now a ruin, where Prince Charlie spent a night on the way to Culloden. At (4½ m.) *Dalnahaitnach* the road, now very rough, crosses the Dulnain. It mounts the left bank to (7½ m.) the point where it is joined by the moorland track from Aviemore (p. 242).—The track opposite the Sluggan Bridge road and a path on the left leading off it after 1½ m. offer a pleasant wooded return to Carrbridge.—A 938 runs downstream viâ (2½ m.) *Duthil* and (6¾ m.) *Dulnain Bridge* to (9½ m.) *Grantown*. The road on the left at Duthil leads to (9 m.) *Loch-in-Dorb* (see Rte. 32).

The road now ascends with a splendid retrospective view of the Cairngorms, and enters the gorge of *Slochd Mor*, with its railway viaduct. Just beyond the viaduct we reach the summit (1217 ft.) and begin a rapid descent into the Findhorn valley. On the left we have a view up *Strath Dearn*, the lonely upper valley of the Findhorn, and soon we cross the river above the railway viaduct (148 ft. high).—101 m. *Tomatin* (Freeburn, c. 1 m. N., RB. 20/, P. 9 gs.) has fir plantations in the neighbourhood. In (105 m.) *Loch Moy* is an island with ruins of an ancient castle and an obelisk in honour of Sir Æneas Mackintosh (d. 1820). *Moy Hall*, the seat of The Mackintosh of Mackintosh, chief of Clan Mackintosh, is near the N. end of the loch.

Moy has been the heart of the race of Mackintosh for over 600 years. The old castle on the island was replaced c. 1700 by a mansion (close to the site of the present hall) but this was burned down in 1800. Its successor was again replaced by a new hall begun in 1955.

In 1745 The Mackintosh remained loyal to the king, but his wife, ' Colonel Anne,' raised the clan for Prince Charlie. Lord Loudoun, the commander at Inverness, hearing that the Prince was visiting her, advanced with 1500 men, but the Mackintoshes were forewarned and Donald Fraser, the Moy blacksmith, and four others approached the army as it was marching at night through the Pass of Moy, on the old military road 2 m. W. of the loch. Firing their guns and shouting stentorian commands to imaginary clansmen they caused a panic known thenceforth as the ' Rout of Moy.'

We pass a little Highland loch (r.) and descend.—From (110 m.) *Daviot* (Meallmore, 2½ m. S.E., RB. 21/6, P. 8 gs.), on the river Nairn, the road leads straight over the Muir of Drummossie, with a superb view in front of Ben Wyvis and of Morven in Caithness, 55 m. away. The road ascending Strath Nairn leads to (20 m.) Inverfarigaig on Loch Ness (p. 358).—The railway descends Strath Nairn, crosses the river on one of the longest and highest viaducts in Scotland (140 ft. high), and turns N.W. to *Culloden Moor* station, 1 m. W. of the Cumberland Stone on the battlefield.—116 m. **Inverness,** see Rte. 54.

31. FROM PITLOCHRY TO KILLIN

ROAD, 36 m. To (4½ m.) *Ballinluig* on A 9, see Rte. 30.—A 827. 14 m. **Aberfeldy.**—20 m. *Kenmore.*—36 m. **Killin.**—MOTOR-BUSES (weekdays only) in 50 min. to *Aberfeldy* ; from Aberfeldy to *Killin* in 70 min. by the N. shore of Loch Tay viâ Fortingall.

RAILWAY from Pitlochry to *Ballinluig*, where trains are changed ; thence viâ Balnaguard and Grandtully to (13¾ m.) *Aberfeldy*.

From Pitlochry to (4½ m.) *Ballinluig*, see Rte. 30. The road and railway cross the Tummel ½ m. above its mouth, the railway soon afterwards bridging the Tay also.—5 m. *Logierait* (Hotel, RB. 19/6, P. 10 gs.), a village situated on the tongue of land separating the Tay from the Tummel, was celebrated as the seat of the regality court where the Lords of Atholl wielded despotic power in a hall that was deemed the ' noblest apartment in Perthshire.'

Rob Roy escaped in 1717 from the gaol, which was later used by Prince Charles to contain 600 prisoners from Prestonpans. The hollow ' Ash Tree of the Boat of Logierait ' is said to be a remnant of the ' dool tree ' on which caterans and robbers were formerly hanged.

A road ascends the right bank of the Tummel to (4½ m.) *Aldour Bridge*, see p. 236.

We ascend the beautiful *Strath Tay* and cross to the S. bank of the river.—9 m. *Strathtay* (Grandtully, RB. 22/6, P. 10 gs.) is the usual base for ascending *Farragon* (2559 ft.), an easy climb of 2½ hrs. rewarded by an extensive view.

The route follows the road on the N. bank of the Tay for 2 m. towards Aberfeldy, and then leads up the left bank of the Derculich burn to (1½ hr.) *Loch Derculich*, whence we approach the summit from the right. The descent (2 hrs.) may be made to *Weem* (see below) viâ Loch Glassie.—At *Dunard*, c. ¾ m. E. of the Derculich burn, is the building of the Free School set up in 1819 by the will of Daniel Stewart, founder of Stewart's Hospital in Edinburgh (p. 71), who was born on this hillside in 1741.

A path ascending N. beside the old golf course crosses the Tullypowrie Burn and leads over the hills (*View) to the Portnacraig bridge at *Pitlochry* in 4 miles.

11½ m. *Grandtully Castle* (1560, enlarged in 1626 and 1893) is one of the suggested originals of ' Tullyveolan ' in ' Waverley.' The old church of *St. Mary's*, ½ m. S.W., the former burial-place of the Stewarts of Grandtully, preserves its painted 17th cent. ceiling (key at farm).

14 m. **Aberfeldy** (*Palace*, RB. 22/6, P. 9½–10½ gs. ; *Breadalbane Arms*, RB. 21/6, P. 8–10 gs. ; *Crown*, RB. 23/6, Apr.–Oct. ; *Moness House*, RB. 23/, P. 11–12 gs., Easter–Sept. ; *Station*, RB. 18/6, P. 8½ gs.), a pleasant little town of 1525 inhab., stands on both sides of the Urlar Burn near its confluence with the Tay. The large cairn near the far end of the *Tay Bridge* (the finest of Gen. Wade's bridges ; built in 1733) commemorates the enrolment of the Frecadan Dubh, or Black Watch (1740), a regiment which had been raised in 1725 to watch the Highlanders. The " birks of Aberfeldy " sung by Burns seem never to have existed, and in the opinion of some the poet intended to describe Abergeldie, where birches are plentiful.

The three *Falls of Moness*, c. 1 m. up the Urlar burn, are approached by a path whose entrance is opposite the Breadalbane Arms. All three falls are beautiful, and the uppermost has a clear leap of 50 ft.

FROM ABERFELDY TO TUMMEL BRIDGE (13½ m.) AND TO KINLOCH RANNOCH (18 m.) by B 846, bus in summer to Coshieville.—We cross the Tay to (1 m.) *Weem* (Hotel, RB. 21/6, P. 10 gs.), a village at the foot of the Rock of Weem

(800 ft.; good view). Wade lived at the hotel in 1733. In the old kirk (disused; 1609) is a curious monument to Sir Alexander Menzies (d. 1624) and other members of his family. Ascent of Farragon, see above.—*Castle Menzies*, on the right farther on in a well-timbered park (no adm.), is a fine example of an old Scottish mansion (1577), with a small door and walls of immense thickness.—3½ m. *Dull*, a village on the right of B 846, preserves an ancient cross, which probably marked the limit of sanctuary of a Celtic monastery founded here, according to some, by St. Adamnan or Eonan c. 700. The broad valley of the Tay is here called the Strath of Appin (i.e. abbey lands).—We approach the Lyon, reaching the river opposite (4½ m.) *Comrie Castle*, a small ruined keep, and joining a road from Kenmore.—At (5¼ m.) *Coshieville Hotel* (RB. 21/, P. 10 gs.), we leave the Lyon on our left and ascend the Keltney Burn. *Garth Castle*, 1 m. farther on, on the opposite side of the valley, was built by the ' Wolf of Badenoch.'—In another mile a track diverging up a glen on the left offers a rough ascent of (4 m.) Schiehallion (p. 236).—Beyond (8¾ m.) *White Bridge* the road divides. The right branch, after rising to 1262 ft., descends to (13¾ m.) *Tummel Bridge* (p. 236).—The left branch passes near Loch Kinardochy (r.) and reaches (10 m.) its summit (1233 ft.), which commands a fine view of Ben-y-Gloe and Glen Tilt beyond Loch Tummel.—11½ m. *Braes of Foss Farm* (Tigh-an-tSocaich) is a starting-point for the ascent of Schiehallion. Thence to (18 m.) *Kinloch Rannoch*, see p. 236.

FROM ABERFELDY viâ GLEN LYON TO BRIDGE OF ORCHY OR TYNDRUM, 44 m., motor-bus in the morning for Glenlyon (Bridge of Balgie ; 2½ hrs.), returning at lunch-time ; more frequent service to Fortingall (25 min.). **Glen Lyon**, the longest glen in Scotland (over 30 m.), is a narrow valley overhung by frowning mountains, between which the beautiful river flows over rocks sparkling with crystals. It was the scene of a fierce battle between the Stewarts of Garth and the MacGregors, in which the latter were almost exterminated. The Campbells of Glenlyon were bitter enemies of the clans to the N. and W., and their chief was a prime mover in organising the massacre of Glencoe. The upper part of the glen has been considerably altered by the Breadalbane hydro-electric scheme.

From Aberfeldy to (5¼ m.) *Coshieville*, see above. Thence the road ascends the left bank of the Lyon.—7 m. *Garth Memorial Youth Hostel* in memory of H.M. Submarine Odin sunk in 1939.—8¼ m. *Fortingall* (429 ft. ; Hotel, RB. 24/, P. 13 gs.) has a yew-tree in its churchyard, said to be 3000 years old and still clinging to life. In 1772, according to Pennant, the trunk was 56 ft. in circumference. On the right beyond the village is *Glenlyon House*, once the stronghold of the Campbells ; on the left is the road to Fearnan. A footpath ascends the right bank of the Lyon from Culdaremore (an old Menzies mansion) to Bridge of Balgie.

Above Fortingall the valley closes in to form the **Pass of Lyon*, a gloomy defile at whose narrowest point is (9¾ m.) *MacGregor's Leap*, a reminder of the battle of the clans. As the valley widens again we catch a glimpse (l.) of *Meall Gruaidh* (3661 ft.), the N. shoulder of Ben Lawers. The range to the N., culminating in *Cairn Mairg* (3419 ft.), commands fine views. We pass a succession of waterfalls, ravines, and corries hollowed out by the headlong tributaries of the Lyon.—12¾ m. *Carnbane Castle* (636 ft.) is a ruined stronghold of the Macnaughtons.—From (19 m.) *Innerwick*, a clachan with a church, a track crosses the hills on the N. side to (7 m.) Loch Rannoch.—20 m. **Bridge of Balgie** (700 ft. ; Glenlyon Post Office), the chief hamlet in the glen, is connected by a rough road with Killin, passing *Lochan-na-Lairige* (c. 5 m.), a new reservoir.—About 1 m. farther a track (l.) descends to *Meggernie Castle*, an attractive whitewashed mansion with an old tower (1579). It rejoins the road at a point whence a track (r.) ascends a side glen for c. 2 m. to the lonely *Loch Giorra* (now a power-reservoir), recently enlarged and united with Loch Dhamh as a result of hydro-electric operations.—We pass Cashlie power station and a small reservoir, formed by the Stronuich dam. *Ben Vannoch* (3125 ft.) comes into view straight ahead as we reach the end of the road at (30 m.) *Lubreoch* dam, at the foot of the greatly enlarged *Loch Lyon* (c. 4 m. long). From Lubreoch a track (l.) leads to *Kenknock* (4½ m.) in Glen Lochay ; or walkers may follow the S. shore of the loch to gain the track between Ben Vannoch (r.) and *Ben Fhuaran* (2632 ft.). Beyond its summit (1250 ft.) it descends between Ben Fhuaran (l.) and *Ben Douran* (3524 ft.), reaching the old road (40½ m.) half-way between (44 m.) Tyndrum (l. ; p. 330) and (44 m.) Bridge of Orchy (r. ; p. 335).

FROM ABERFELDY TO AMULREE (Crieff, Dunkeld), 12 m. The road ascends S.E., with good backward views, to (3½ m.) *Loch-na-Craige*, a small moorland tarn on the watershed (1406 ft.). The much more gradual descent leads down the desolate Glen Cochill, and at 10½ m. joins the road in Strath Bran, coming from *Dunkeld* (r. ; 7 m.). We turn to the right for (12 m.) *Amulree* and (24 m.) *Crieff*.

FROM ABERFELDY TO KENMORE a pretty tree-shaded road ascends above the Tay. From (18 m.) *Croftmoraig* triple stone circle (l.) we enjoy a fine view of Schiehallion. We skirt the S.E. side of *Taymouth Park* with its golf course.—20 m. **Kenmore** (*Breadalbane*, RB. 25/, P. 12 gs., with fishing, Mar.– mid-Oct.) is a pretty little 'model' village on the loch at the outflow of the Tay, with the wooded *Drummond Hill* (c. 1500 ft.) rising to the N. The *Church* (1760) is by Wm. Baker. Burns recorded his pleasure in the view from the *Bridge* (1774) by writing one of his most charming English lyrics over the fireplace in the inn-parlour (1787), though Dorothy Wordsworth gave the palm to the view from the bridge at Killin.

On the island in the loch are the ruins of a priory built by Alexander I in 1122 over the grave of his wife Sibilla, daughter of Henry I of England.

The turreted *Taymouth Castle*, now a civil defence college, in finely wooded grounds, is the early 19th cent. successor of a mansion built c. 1573 by Colin Campbell of Glenorchy. In 1940–46 it was used as a hospital for Polish army officers. In 1837 the Earl of Breadalbane, whose seat it was, reintroduced here from Sweden the capercailzie, which had become extinct in Scotland.

FROM KENMORE TO KILLIN by road along the S. bank of Loch Tay, 17 m.— 1½ m. *Acharn* has a charming cascade on the burn c. ⅓ m. S. of the village.—6¼ m. *Ardtalnaig*, opposite Ben Lawers, near some old copper and lead mines, is the starting-point of a track which ascends Gleinn-a-Chilleine and leads to (4¼ m.) *Dunan* at the head of Glen Almond, 10½ m. above Newton Bridge (p. 227).— From (9½ m.) *Ardeonaig* (Hotel, unlic., RB. 17/6, P. 8½ gs.) a delightful walk ascends the Finglen Burn and crosses (1750 ft.) into Glen Lednock for (12¼ m.) *Comrie* (p. 227).—17 m. *Killin*, see Rte. 46.

FROM KENMORE TO AMULREE, 11 m. The steep rough road running S.E. with fine retrospective views of Ben Lawers, the Glen Lyon range, and Schiehallion, ascends to 1672 ft. in 3 m., and soon afterwards drops even more steeply into *Glen Quaich*, crossing (5 m.) the river.—7 m. *Loch Freuchie*, 2 m. long, lies on our left.—At 10 m. we join the road coming from Crieff viâ the Sma' Glen and turn to the left for (11 m.) *Amulree* (p. 227).

The road from Aberfeldy up Glen Lyon may be joined either viâ Fearnan, 4 m. along the main Killin road, or viâ the road descending the left bank of the Tay and crossing the Lyon at (c. 2 m.) Comrie Castle (p. 242).

From Kenmore to *Killin* by the main road, and for *Loch Tay*, see Rte. 46.

32. FROM AVIEMORE TO FORRES

ROAD, 56 m.—A 9. 4 m. *Kineveachy*.—A 95. 14 m. *Grantown*.—22 m. *Dava*.— A 940. 35½ m. **Forres**.—From Dava A 939 runs N.W. to (37 m.) *Nairn*. MOTOR-BUSES on weekdays (exc. Mon. & Fri.) between Aviemore and Grantown viâ Nethybridge ; on Mon. & Fri. between Nethybridge and Grantown only.

RAILWAY, 35¾ m. in 1–1½ hr. (through trains to Nairn and Inverness). Principal Stations : 5 m. *Boat of Garten*, junction for Grantown East and *Craigellachie* (33¾ m.).—12½ m. **Grantown West**.—35¾ m. **Forres**.

Aviemore, and thence to (4 m.) *Kineveachy*, see Rte. 30.— A 95 runs N.E., affording glorious views of the Cairngorms and

descending gradually towards the Spey. To the right of the
road lies (6½ m.) *Boat of Garten* (Boat of Garten, RB. 23/,
P. 11 gs. ; Craigard, RB. 23/, P. 10 gs.), junction of the
railway to Craigellachie. The ferry on the Spey, from which
the place takes its name, was superseded in 1898 by a bridge.
We are now in STRATH SPEY, the broad lower valley of the
Spey, which has given its name to the 'strathspey,' a dance
in slower time than the reel, which was invented in the
district in the early 18th century. *Tullochgorum* (2½ m. N.E.)
gives its name to one of the best known strathspey tunes,
composed by Hamish Dallasall, an 18th cent. fiddler.

FROM BOAT OF GARTEN TO CRAIGELLACHIE, 31 m. ; bus 4–6 times daily from
Grantown, going on to Elgin. The road crosses the Spey, joins B 970, coming
from Aviemore viâ Coylum Bridge, and soon leaves on the r. a forest road to
Loch Garten (1¾ m.).—4 m. *Nethybridge* (Hotel, RB. 25/6, P. 12 gs. ; Grey House,
unlic., Apr.–Sept., RB. 16/6, P. 8 gs.) is connected by bridge with Broomhill,
¼ m. N. Near *Abernethy* church, ¾ m. N., is *Castle Roy*, a ruined fortress of the
Comyns of a primitive type.—8 m. *Grantown East* station, 1½ m. S. of the town
(see below), is on A 95, which we follow. To the right of (11 m.) *Cromdale* rise the
Cromdale Hills, with the Haughs of Cromdale at their base (see below).—At
21 m.) *Dalnashaugh Inn* (RB. 18/6), where we cross the Avon c. 1 m. from its
mouth, the road from Tomintoul and Glenlivet joins the Speyside road. *Ballindalloch Castle*, ¾ m. downstream, preserves an old square tower. From the station
of Ballindalloch, opposite, a motor-bus (in connection with the Aberdeen trains)
runs to Tomintoul in 1½ hr. The railway crosses the Spey and keeps near the
river. A 95 ascends to 718 ft., but regains Speyside just short of (28½ m.) *Aberlour*
Aberlour, RB. 18/6, P. 10 gs. ; Lour, RB. 19/6, P. 8½ gs.). The *Linn of Ruthie*,
m. S., is a fine fall on the burn descending from the conspicuous *Ben Rinnes*
2755 ft.) ; *View).—31 m. *Craigellachie*, see Rte. 43B.

9 m. *Broomhill Station* (see above).—At (11 m.) *Dulnain
Bridge* we cross the Dulnain and enter Moray. One mile along
the Carrbridge road is the old tower of *Muckrach* (1598).—
4 m. **Grantown-on-Spey** (7000 ft. ; *Grant Arms*, RB. 33/,
P. 14 gs., closed Oct.–Easter ; *Palace*, RB. 25/, P. 13 gs. ;
Craiglynne, RB. 25/, P. 11½ gs. ; *Ben Mhor*, RB. 18/6, P. 8 gs. ;
Seafield Lodge, Garth, P. 9 gs. ; *Coppice*, 8½ gs. ; *Rosehall*, 8 gs.,
these four unlic.), founded by Sir James Grant of Grant in
1776, is a well-kept town (1540 inhab.) with a wide tree-
planted main street and two railway stations (see above).
The charming environs, the swift-flowing Spey, the pine and
birch woods intersected by roads and paths, the bracing air,
and a golf course attract many visitors. The parish church
contains a fine black oak pulpit and some old panelling.

Castle Grant, 1½ m. N., may be visited on application (phone Grantown 125). It
partly derelict, but contains some unusual 17th cent. portraits by R. Waitt,
and ancient weapons.—The CROMDALE HILLS, a fine ridge 9 m. long, rising to
329 ft., are best reached from Grantown viâ *Cromdale*, 4 m. along the road to
Craigellachie (see above) or from the Tomintoul road (see below). A battle
1690) on the *Haughs of Cromdale* (S.E. of the village), commemorated in a fine
ballad, closed the struggle begun by Dundee.
Craigellachie may be reached either by the main road beyond the Spey (see
above), or by B 9102 descending the left bank viâ (16 m.) *Knockando* (see p. 320).
Loch-in-Dorb (see below) may be reached on foot by a hill path (6 m.) ascending
W., high up on the N.E. side of Glen Beag, and bearing to the *left* on approaching the watershed (1252 ft.). The descent passes the little *Loch-an-tSithein*.

FROM GRANTOWN TO TOMINTOUL, RETURNING VIÂ GLEN
LIVET, 41¼ m. by road. After crossing Spey Bridge (1 m. S.E.)
we turn left and then bear right beyond the railway on A 939,
a moorland road requiring care. We rise steadily to (6½ m.)
the pass (1424 ft.) between the Cromdale Hills on the N. and
Baddoch (1863 ft.), and then descend to (9 m.) the picturesque
Bridge of Brown, entering Banffshire.—Beyond another
ridge we cross (11 m.) the Avon and ascend its right bank.
13 m. **Tomintoul** (*Richmond Arms*, RB. 18/, P. 9 gs. ; *Gordon
Arms*, RB. 17/6, P. 8½ gs. ; *Glenavon, Tomnabat*, unlic.), the
highest village in the Highlands (1160 ft.), with a large green,
is a summer and angling resort surrounded by unpopulated
moorlands. The large Roman Catholic church is conspicuous.

Buses run to *Ballindalloch*, and in summer to *Dufftown* in 1¾ hr. From Tomintoul to *Braemar*, see p. 305 ; to *Strathdon*, etc., see p. 308.

The Glen Livet road (B 9008) turns N.E. and crosses the Conglass Water.
Beyond (17½ m.) *Knockandhu* (Pole Inn ; path to Strathdon, p. 308) we enter
Glen Livet and cross the Livet water. From (21 m.) *Glenlivet* church a road runs
through Glen Rinnes to Dufftown (11 m. ; p. 319). In Glen Livet James VI in
person defeated the rebel earls Huntly and Errol in Oct. 1594, afterwards
destroying their strongholds of Huntly and Slains. Across the stream we see the
celebrated distillery and the ruins of *Glenlivet Castle*, and at (23 m.) *Bridgend* are
remains of an old bridge near the junction of the Livet with the Avon.—26¾ m.
Dalnashaugh, and thence to (41¼ m.) *Grantown* viâ Cromdale, see above.

Beyond Grantown the Forres road (A 939) leaves Strathspey, across which the Cromdale Hills stand out, and passes
Castle Grant and, 2 m. farther, a cave where the Marquis of
Huntly hid from the followers of Montrose, both on the
right. We ascend to 1052 ft. and cross a rather dull moor to
(22 m.) *Dava* ; the railway station lies ¾ m. to the right.

A narrow road on the left leads in 3 m. to **Loch-in-Dorb** (2 m. long), on an
island in which is a castle dismantled under James II. Once a mere hunting seat
of the Comyns, it was occupied in person by Edward I in 1303 and greatly
strengthened. In 1336 Edward III raised the siege in which the Countess of
Atholl was beleaguered here by David II's troops ; and in 1372 the castle became
the stronghold of the Wolf of Badenoch.—Hill-path to Grantown, see above.

From Dava A 939 leads N.E. to (15 m.) *Nairn*, crossing the Findhorn at
(6½ m.) *Logie Bridge*. The beautiful valley of the Findhorn, both above and
below this road, is conveniently explored from Forres (p. 316).

We descend on A 940, crossing (26 m.) the Divie, a tributary
of the Findhorn, beside a lofty railway viaduct.—Beyond
(28½ m.) *Dunphail* and (30 m.) the turning for Relugas, near
Randolph's Leap (p. 317), we traverse the fir-woods of
Altyre.—35½ m. **Forres,** see Rte. 43A.

III. FIFE, ABERDEEN, AND EASTERN SCOTLAND

33. FROM EDINBURGH TO DUNFERMLINE

ROAD, 16½ m. viâ the Queen's Ferry across the Forth, and A 823 from North Queensferry. Ferry across the Forth from Hawes Pier (S. Queensferry) c. every ½ hr. (5d., cycle 6d., motor-cycle, 1/6, car from 3/6 ; reduced return fares).—MOTOR-BUSES from Edinburgh (St. Andrew Sq.) to S. Queensferry (Hawes Pier ; 28 min. ; 1/), and from N. Queensferry to Dunfermline (½ hr. ; 10½d.).

RAILWAY, 16½ m. from Waverley Station in 25–40 min. Principal Stations : 9½ m. *Dalmeny.*—11¼ m. *North Queensferry.*—13¼ m. *Inverkeithing.*—16¾ m. **Dunfermline** (Lower Station). The train takes c. 2½ min. to cross the bridge, and there are interesting views on both sides as we look out through the network of girders.

From Edinburgh by A 90 to (8½ m.) *Hawes Pier,* just short of S. Queensferry, see Rte. 5D. Thence we cross the Forth, here only 1¼ m. wide, by the vehicle-ferry, which affords a remarkable view of the Forth Bridge from below.—At the N. end of the bridge is (10½ m.) *North Queensferry* (Albert, RB. 15/), and we enter Fife.

To the left on the estuary is St. Margaret's Hope, a safe anchorage in E. winds, acquired with 1500 acres of land by government in 1903 to form the naval base of **Rosyth**, used in both World Wars. The little dockyard church contains naval memorials of the Second World War. *Rosyth Castle* (for adm. apply at dockyard), a small 16th cent. tower with a fine dovecot, makes a momentary appearance in Scott's ' Abbot.'

Beyond (13 m.) *Rosyth Garden Village* we traverse the site of the battle of *Pitreavie,* where the Cromwellians defeated Charles II's supporters in 1651.

16½ m. **DUNFERMLINE,** a royal burgh with a historic past, the birthplace of many Scottish kings, including Charles I, and the burial-place of many, including Robert the Bruce, is now noted as a centre of the linen industry and as the head-quarters of the Carnegie Trusts. It is a plain grey town (44,720 inhab.) with narrow streets and an interesting abbey church.

Railway Stations. *Lower Station* (D 3), for all important trains.—*Upper Station* (C, D 1) for some trains viâ Lochgelly to the Fife coast, etc.

Hotels. Brucefield, Woodmill Rd., well situated outside the town, RB. 21/, P. 10 gs. ; **Royal** (b ; C 2), 83 High St., RB. 22/6, P. 9 gs. ; **City** (a ; B 1), 18 Bridge St., RB. 18/, P. 8½ gs.

Motor-Buses to *Glasgow* viâ Stirling and Kincardine ; to towns in Fife, Clackmannan, and Kinross ; and to *Crieff* (Sat., Sun., Tues) viâ Rumbling Bridge. All main services start from Carnegie St. (B 1) except those to North Queensferry and to the Fife coast, which start at St. Margaret's (B 2), etc.

History. Dunfermline succeeded Forteviot (p. 224) as a royal residence in the days of Malcolm Canmore, who built the palace, probably about the time of his marriage (1067) with the Saxon princess St. Margaret, sister of Edgar Atheling, and, with her, founded the abbey a little later. The palace became a favourite abode of the Scottish kings, and the abbey superseded Iona as their place of burial. In the ballad of ' Sir Patrick Spens ' the " king sits in Dunfermline town, drinking the bluid-red wine.'' Edward I held his court here during his second invasion of Scotland (1303). Charles II stayed here before his march to Worcester and was forced by the Covenanters to accept the Covenants and to sign the Dunfermline Declaration, in which his parents are condemned in sufficiently strong language.—Among famous natives of Dunfermline, in addition to several kings, are Robert Henryson or Henderson (1430 ?–1506), poet and schoolmaster at the abbey, Sir Noël Paton (1821–1901), artist, and Andrew Carnegie (1835–1919), millionaire and philanthropist.

Dunfermline is the headquarters of the CARNEGIE TRUSTS, including both those whose benevolent scope extends to the entire country, and those which are concerned only with the donor's native city. Mr. Carnegie established a trust-fund of £500,000 in 1903, increased by a further £250,000 in 1911, for the benefit of the inhabitants of Dunfermline, without, however, relieving them of any of their municipal obligations. Other gifts were baths, a library, a public park, a college of hygiene, etc.

From the Lower Station the direct route to the centre of the town is up New Row (C 3, 2), but to reach the Abbey we follow Priory Lane (C 3) and Monastery St. At the corner of Moodie St., passed by the latter route, is the unassuming cottage (No. 4) in which Andrew Carnegie (see above) was born, and adjoining is a memorial building containing public tributes to his munificence. Monastery St., with a war memorial garden on the right, skirts the S. wall of the abbey refectory and passes through a massive Gothic gateway (' *The Pends* '), above which are some restored apartments.

The *Abbey Church (B 2), the sepulchre of Robert Bruce, consists of two diverse parts—a noble Norman nave (1150) and a spacious and successful Gothic choir of 1817–22, by Wm. Burn. The nave, one of the best examples of its style in Scotland, is externally somewhat marred by the great size of the buttresses added in the 16th century. The fine W. doorway is flanked by towers, that on the N. rebuilt c. 1590, with its spire. The S.W. tower was rebuilt after being struck by lightning in 1887. The choir (now a parish church) is sur-mounted by a square tower (100 ft. high), whose lettered balustrade shows the words ' King Robert the Bruce.' The church is open free on weekdays 10–5 or 7, in winter 10–4. We enter by the S. portal, which has some good carving.

A Benedictine priory, founded here c. 1070 by the sainted queen, Margaret, superseded Iona as the royal burial-place. David I raised it in 1128 to the rank of an abbey and began a new church, of which the existing nave is a relic. An elegant choir and transepts added in 1250, but ruined by the Reformers in 1560, were finally swept away in 1818 to make way for the present New Church. Malcolm and Margaret, who both died in 1093, were buried in a special chapel (now gone) built outside the church (see below). Their sons Edgar, Alexander I, and David I, and their descendants Malcolm IV, Alexander III, and Robert Bruce are buried in the church.

The *Nave, 106 ft. long and 54 ft. high, has six bays, with tall round piers and round arches. The arch next the W. door was rebuilt by James VI in the Early Gothic style. The E. piers are grooved with zigzags and spirals, recalling Durham cathedral. The elaborate Norman carving on the inner arch of the N. porch presents a contrast with the groined roof, which is later. The glass of the large ' historical window ' over the W. door was designed by Sir Noël Paton. In the N. aisle are the tomb of Thomas Gillespie (1708–74), founder of the Relief Church, and a memorial to George Durie, the last abbot (1560).—Beneath the pulpit in the New Church is the *Grave of Robert Bruce (1274–1329), marked by a memorial brass. During the excavations for the New Church in 1818 Bruce's body was discovered wrapped in a shroud interwoven with threads of gold and encased in two leaden coverings. It was placed in a new coffin and re-interred. In

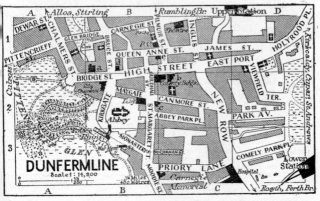

the N. transept is the front of the old royal gallery (17th cent.), and in the S. transept is a monument to Lady Augusta Stanley (d. 1876), a daughter of Bruce of Broomhall. Here and in the S. aisle is some good glass of 1937.

In the churchyard we note the tombs of Malcolm and St. Margaret, at the E. end of the church. Close by (N.E.) is the sarcophagus tomb (1875) of Ralph Erskine (1685–1752), minister of the abbey (1711–37) and one of the leaders of the Secession movement. Of the monastic buildings (adm. free), which stood S. of the church, with foundations at a considerably lower level, the chief remains are those of the *Frater* or *Refectory*, showing a large window of seven lights, with the upper parts filled with quatrefoils, and a reader's pulpit.

Opposite the W. door of the abbey is an entrance to **Pittencrieff Glen,** an attractive ornamental estate presented to the town by Andrew Carnegie in 1903 as a public park, with one of the finest flower-gardens in Scotland. The 17th cent. mansion contains a museum of local antiquities. The burn that runs through the glen encircles a mound bearing the remains of ' *Malcolm's Tower*,' attributed to Malcolm Canmore whence comes the name of Dunfermline (' fort of the crooked linn '). Immediately on our left as we enter the grounds are the ruins of the **Palace** (B 3; adm. free), originally the guest-house of the abbey and a favourite abode of the Scottish kings. It was reconstituted as a palace after the Dissolution, and the monastic kitchen is its chief relic.

Here were born Maud, wife of Henry I of England, and her brothers (after-wards kings) Edgar, Alexander, and David I. David II (1324) and James I (1394) also were born at Dunfermline. The building, which had been destroyed by fire in 1304, when Edward I quitted it, was rebuilt by James IV in 1500, and it was occupied by Mary, Queen of Scots, in 1561. Her son, James VI, subscribed the Covenant here, and here in 1600 his son, Charles I, was born, and his daughter Elizabeth, afterwards Queen of Bohemia, in 1596.

Kirkgate, passing Maygate, in which are the offices of the Carnegie Trusts (including the 16th cent. Abbot House), ascends from the abbey gate to the turreted *Municipal Buildings* (B 2; 1880), whose great bell daily sounds the ' factory bell ' and the ' curfew bell.' Within is a cartoon by Sir Noël Paton. Bridge St., built on a bridge of 1770, leads hence, to the left, to another entrance to Pittencrieff Glen. High St. leads to the right. Outside the *County Buildings* (C 2 ; 1808), with their tall spire, is the shaft of the old town cross. Opposite the *Post Office* (B 1), in the parallel Queen Anne St., a church (formerly U.F.) occupies the site of the original church (1741), built by the Seceders of 1733–40, whose leaders were Ebenezer and Ralph Erskine.

On the Forth shore 3 m. S. of Dunfermline (motor-bus) lies *Limekilns*, " a place that sits near in by the waterside and looks across the Hope to the town of the Queen's Ferry," where David Balfour and Alan Breck found means of crossing the Forth (' Kidnapped '). Adjoining on the W. is the small coal-port of *Charles-town* (Elgin Hotel), and just N. of Limekilns is *Broomhall*, the home of Lord Bruce (to whom applications to visit it should be addressed). Here is preserved Bruce's helmet ; and the mantelpiece in the dining-room is made of the bedstead in which Charles I was born.

From Dunfermline to Culross and Falkirk, 17 m., motor-bus in 65 min., to Culross in 25 min. Following Pitten-crieff St. (A 1), we reach the Forth at (5 m.) *Torryburn*, a small coal-port, and keep left alongside the railway. The main road to Kincardine (A 985) keeps right viâ High Valley-field ' garden ' village.

7 m. **Culross** (*Dundonald Arms*, RB. 19/6, P. 7 gs.), a decayed royal burgh (575 inhab.), is the most perfect example of a small Scots town of the 17–18th cent. The lower town, beside the Forth, is connected with the upper—where are the abbey and the laird's house—by steep paved alleys.

Culross is the supposed site of a 5th or 6th cent. religious establishment presided over by St. Serf (Servan), and St. Kentigern (d. 603), the apostle of Glasgow, is said to have been born or educated here. A ruined chapel of 1503, E. of the town, marks his legendary birthplace. Later, Culross was noted for its ' girdles ' for baking oatcakes, and its former salt-pans were visited by James VI, who raised the burgh to royal standing in 1588. Recently many of the older houses have been taken over by the National Trust and are being, or have been, restored, mainly to their original purpose as dwellings.

Culross Abbey was founded for Cistercians by Malcolm, Earl of Fife, in 1217. The church, dating mainly from c. 1300 and rebuilt under James IV, preserves its choir and splendid central tower, with vestibule, intact ; but the nave is in ruins. In a chamber on the N. side are the alabaster effigies of Sir George Bruce of Carnock (d. 1625) and his numerous family (a unique arrangement in Scotland). The monastic buildings (adm. 3d.) are also in ruins, much of their stone having been used by Lord Kinloss to build the fine *Abbey House* just above. Begun in 1608 and altered in 1670, it was remodelled in 1952, and is now the home of the Earl of Elgin, and contains the sword of Robert Bruce. A steep descent leads to the *Mercat Cross* (shaft modern) and the curious corbelled-out turret known as the *Study* of Bishop Leighton (d. 1684). On the main road alongside the river are the pleasant *Tolbooth* (1626), with a tower of 1783 and a tablet recording the long service of a recent provost, and *CULROSS PALACE (adm. 6d., 10–4 or 7, Sun. from 2), a charming example of the smaller Scottish town mansion, built around an open yard, with well-kept terraced gardens behind. It was built by Sir George Bruce (see above), and many of the panelled rooms are painted all over, in the Scottish style, with scenes from the Scriptures, etc., the best of them dated 1597 (W. wing). The N. wing was added in 1611.

Dunimarle Castle, c. ½ m. W., contains notable Dutch and Italian paintings and 18th cent. furniture, etc., but is at present (1959) under reconstruction.

The upper and lower roads join at (10½ m.) *Kincardine-on-Forth*, a small river-port (1830 inhab.) with a good mercat cross. It was the birthplace of Sir John Dewar (1842–1923), inventor of the vacuum flask.

At the N. end of the village is *Tulliallan*, with a church of 1675 (roofless). The castle behind (1824) was occupied by Gen. Sikorski in the Second World War and became a Police College in 1954 ; beyond it extends the chief tree-nursery of the Forestry Commission.

The fine **Kincardine Bridge** (1936), over ½ m. long, with a central swing span of 100 yds., crosses the Forth, replacing an old ferry. On the S. side we join A 905, leading S. to (17 m.) *Falkirk* (to the r. ; Rte. 10A) or to (20½ m.) *Linlithgow*.

On A 905, about 1¼ m. N. of the junction of the new bridge road, lies the old village of *Airth*, with several early 18th cent. houses and a reconstructed village cross. Airth Castle, S. of the village, is a modernised 16th cent. mansion, with an older ' Wallace's Tower.'

A 977, running N.E. from Kincardine, affords rapid access to (8 m.) *Dollar* (p. 212 ; to the left) and (20 m.) *Kinross*.—From Kincardine to *Stirling*, see p. 211.

FROM DUNFERMLINE TO GLENEAGLES, 22½ m., motor-bus at week-ends in 62 min.—A 823 leaves the town by Pilmuir St., crosses the Cleish Hills and descends, leaving the Kinross road on the right.—11 m. **Rumbling Bridge** (*Hotel*, RB. 25/, P. 10 gs.) on the Devon. The river is spanned by three bridges—the present highway, an old narrow arch without parapets, built by a local mason in 1713, and a light footbridge, access to which last and to the path by the river can be gained only through the hotel. The glen above the bridge is particularly striking, especially the *Devil's Mill*, a waterfall so called from the mill-wheel-like sound it makes and because it never rests on Sundays. A pretty path down the left bank leads to (1¼ m.) the *Caldron Linn*, a beautiful spot with a double cascade.

Aldie Castle, 2½ m. S.E., is a fine laird's house of the 16–17th cent. recently restored (1957).—Crossing the Devon, our road enters Perthshire. Beyond (13 m.) *Yetts of Muckhart*, an important road-junction, it traverses the Ochil Hills, ascending the pleasant *Glen Devon* (Castle, RB. 27/6, P. 13 gs.; Tormaukin RB. 19/6, P. 8 gs.) and reaching the summit-level (881 ft.) at 9½ m. *Glendevon Castle* (r.) is a well-preserved ruin. The descent follows the steeper *Glen Eagles* (comp. p. 219) to (22½ m.) *Gleneagles* (Rte. 26).

34. FROM EDINBURGH TO PERTH VIÂ KINROSS

ROAD (A 90), 45½ m. To (10½ m.) *N. Queensferry*, see Rte. 33. We keep right and, at (12½ m.) *Inverkeithing*, bear left.—The Perth road (A 90) runs N. to (17½ m.) *Cowdenbeath*, (25 m.) *Kinross*, and (34½ m.) *Glenfarg*.—At (39½ m.) *Aberargie* A 913 diverges W. for *Abernethy* (1½ m.).—42 m. *Bridge of Earn*.— We enter (45½ m.) **Perth** (Rte. 27) by the South Inch (Pl. C 3).

RAILWAY, 47¾ m. from Waverley Station in 1½–2 hrs.; to (30½ m.) *Kinross* in 1¼ hr. Best views on the right. Through trains from London to Inverness run on this route, and trains from Glasgow (Queen St.) to Perth viâ Larbert and Alloa join this line at Kinross.—Principal Stations : to (16¾ m.) *Dunfermline*, see Rte. 33.—22½ m. *Cowdenbeath*.—30½ m. *Kinross*.—31¼ m. *Milnathort*.— 37½ m. *Glenfarg*.—44¼ m. *Bridge of Earn*.—47¾ m. **Perth**.

From Edinburgh by the Queen's Ferry to (10½ m.) *North Queensferry*, see Rtes. 5D and 33.—12½ m. **Inverkeithing** (3700 inhab.; *Queen's*, RB. 17/6), an old royal burgh, was a residence of David I, and of Annabella Drummond (d. 1462), queen of Robert III. The 15th cent. *Greyfriars' Hospital* has been restored as a public library, and the mercat cross survives outside the *Town House*, with its rather ungainly tower. In the church (1826, with medieval tower) is one of the few ancient fonts in Scotland.

From Inverkeithing to *Kirkcaldy* and *St. Andrews*, see Rte. 35.

The Perth road crosses the productive Fife coalfield, of which (17½ m.) *Cowdenbeath* (13,150 inhab.) is the principal centre, with *Lochgelly* (9100 inhab.), 1½ m. E.—At (20 m.) *Kelty* we quit the mining district and enter the county of Kinross. To the W. is *Blairadam*, a mansion visited by Sir Walter Scott, who described the beauties of the grounds in 'The Abbot.' On the right of the road is *Benarty* (1167 ft.); on the left are the *Cleish Hills* (1241 ft.), at the E. end of which is the ruined Lindsay stronghold of *Dowhill* (adm. on application), reached by B 5097.—A roadside monument at (22½ m.) *Gairney Bridge* commemorates the foundation here of the first Secession presbytery in 1733.

25 m. **Kinross,** a sleepy little town (2500 inhab.) on Loch Leven, beyond which rise the Lomond Hills, is the capital of the small county of Kinross. It is a great angling centre, and national and international championships are held on the loch in late May.

Hotels. Green, RB. 23/6, P. 10 gs.; **Bridgend,** RB. 18/6, P. 8½ gs.; **Kirkland's,** RB. 21/6, P. 8 gs.

Boats. With boatman, from 47/6 per day, without boatman, from 4/ per hr.; apply to the Manager, the Pier, Kinross.

Kinross House, between the town and the lake, was built in 1685–92 by Sir William Bruce, Lauderdale's architect at Holyrood. The old church stood on the tip of the peninsula (*Ceann-ros*) beyond it; the 17th cent. tower of the *Old Tolbooth* was repaired by Robert Adam.

Loch Leven, celebrated for the imprisonment and escape of Mary, Queen of Scots, the main theme of Scott's ' The Abbot,' and for its pink trout, is 3½ m. long by c. 2 m. broad. It contains several islands, on the nearest of which, ½ m. from the shore, is **Lochleven Castle**, a rough square tower of c. 1400, standing in a court surrounded by a curtain wall mainly of later date. Here Queen Mary was imprisoned on the 16th June, 1567, after her surrender at Carberry Hill, and here she remained for 11 months in the custody of Lady Douglas of Lochleven, a woman adapted by temper for a gaoler. The tower was entered at a low round-headed door, half-way up the wall, by a draw-stair or platform. It comprised two vaulted chambers below—a store house and kitchen, with trap-doors in the floors—and three stories above, whose wooden floors are gone. Here dwelt Lady Douglas. Her prisoner was lodged in a round turret in the angle of the rampart, where she occupied a room only 15 ft. in diameter, furnished with a fireplace and one window and entered by a stair from the courtyard. Here, on July 23rd, 1567, by persuasion or compulsion of Lord Lindsay and Robert Melville, Mary signed a deed of abdication in favour of her son, and another appointing her half-brother, Moray, regent. Many attempts to deliver the queen were made, but eventually by her personal charms she succeeded in captivating the heart of George Douglas, the son of her gaoler. His devotion to her caused him to be expelled from the castle, but he left behind a confederate, William Douglas, a lad of 18, who, on the night of May 2nd, 1568, while the inmates of the castle were at prayers, secured the keys, placed the queen in a boat, and having locked the gates behind him threw the keys overboard. At the loch-side she was received by Lord Seton, George Douglas, and Sir James Hamilton, and conveyed to Niddry Castle (p. 104). Thirteen days later she was defeated at Langside and fled to England.—Owing to drainage the waters of the loch have fallen, and boats can no longer land close under the castle walls.

On *St. Serf's Island* (1 m. S.E.) are the ruins of a priory, founded on an earlier settlement of Culdees. David I transferred the property to the Augustinian canons of St. Andrews and ordered the Culdees to conform to the rules of that order or to quit the island. Andrew Wyntoun (d. c. 1420), one of the earliest of the Scots chroniclers, was prior of St. Serf's.

For the road to *Stirling*, see Rte. 24.

Quitting Kinross, the Perth road curves around Loch Leven (good views of the loch and castle) to (26½ m.) *Milnathort* (Royal, RB. 16/6, P. 8 gs.), a small town with woollen mills. Between the town and the loch is the ruined tower, with barbican, of *Burleigh Castle*, once a stronghold of the Balfours, and 4 m. S.E. is *Kinnesswood*, where Michael Bruce (1746–67), author of the ' Ode to the Cuckoo,' was born.

The road to Leslie and Leven (A 911) skirts the E. side of Loch Leven and, at (4 m.) *Portmoak*, passes beneath the steep slope of *Bishop Hill* (the W. outlier of the Lomonds), the Scottish headquarters of gliding.

The road from Milnathort to (19 m.) *Cupar* (A 91) traverses the fertile Howe of Fife, passing the quaint little towns of (8 m.) *Strathmiglo* (Stratheden, RB. 12/6), with its tall town-steeple, and (10 m.) *Auchtermuchty* (Hollies Guest House, RB. 15/, P. 5½ gs.), also with an attractive town-steeple (1728) on the hill. The name of the latter town, which is notable for its thatched roofs (uncommon in Scotland), signifies ' height of the swineherd.' John Glas (1695–1773), founder of the Glassites, was born here.—13 m. *Collessie*, of which Hugh Blair (1718–1800) was parish minister as young man, is 1 m. W. of *Melville House*, a mansion (1692–1702) built for the Earl of Melville by James Smith. It is now a school (adm. by written appointment with the headmaster). In the garden is a tower of a country house of the Abp. of St. Andrews.

We now ascend, with a pleasing view of the Howe of Fife (r.), and pass from Kinross into *Perthshire*.—34½ m. *Glenfarg* (Glenfarg, RB. 21/, P. 9 gs. ; Lomond, RB. 17/6, P. 7 gs.) is situated at the head of a lovely Norwegian-like defile, 4 m. in length. Beyond (37½ m.) *Bein Inn* (RB. 21/) we enjoy a fine view (r.) down the Carse of Gowrie to the Tay Bridge and (l.) up Strathearn. *Balvaird Castle*, 1 m. S. (E. of A 912), is a well-preserved 15–16th cent. tower. At (39½ m.) *Aberargie* (Baiglie Inn) A 913 diverges (r.) for Abernethy, while a by-road (l.) leads in c. 1 m. to *Balmanno*, one of the most perfect examples of the old Scottish mansion.—42 m. *Bridge of Earn* (Moncreiffe Arms, RB. 22/6, P. 14 gs. ; Bridge of Earn, RB. 15/6, P. 8 gs.) is a summer resort, about 1¼ m. W. of which are the mineral wells of *Pitkeathly* or *Pitcaithly*.—Crossing the Earn we pass between Kirkton Hill and *Moncreiffe Hill* and soon have a fine view (r.) of *Kinnoull Hill*, across the Tay, and (ahead) of (45½ m.) **Perth** (Rte. 27).

35. FROM EDINBURGH TO DUNDEE AND TO ST. ANDREWS VIÂ CUPAR

ROAD. To (12½ m.) *Inverkeithing*, see Rte. 34. A 92.—19½ m.. *Burntisland.*—25 m. **Kirkcaldy.**—42½ m. **Cupar.**—49 m. *Balmullo.*—53½ m. *Newport.* Frequent ferry service across the Tay (6d., cycle 6d., motor-cycle 1/2, car from 5/ ; reduced return fares).—55 m. **Dundee.**—About 3½ m. E. of Cupar A 91 bears right for (52½ m.) **St. Andrews.**

RAILWAY to Dundee, 59¼ m. from Waverley Station in 1¾–3 hrs. ; to (26 m.) *Kirkcaldy* in 40 min.–1 hr. ; to (44½ m.) *Cupar* in 1½–2½ hrs. To *St. Andrews*, 56 m. in 1¾–3¼ hrs.—Through trains from London to Aberdeen traverse this route. Principal Stations : to (13¼ m.) *Inverkeithing*, see Rte. 33.—20½ m. *Burntisland.*—26 m. *Kirkcaldy.*—30¾ m. *Thornton*, junction for *Cowdenbeath* (10 m.), and for St. Andrews by the coast (Rte. 36).—36¼ m. *Falkland Road* (2½ m. from *Falkland*).—39 m. *Ladybank.*—44½ m. **Cupar.**—50¾ m. *Leuchars Junc.* (for **St. Andrews**, 5 m.).—59¼ m. **Dundee** (Tay Bridge).

From Edinburgh to (12½ m.) *Inverkeithing*, see Rte. 34. Diverging to the right from the road to Kinross, we have only occasional views of the Forth.—17½ m. **Aberdour** (*Woodside*, RB. 22/6, P. 11 gs. ; *Star*, RB. 17/6) is a popular summer resort with the old church of St. Fillan (Norm. and Dec.) and ruins of a 17th cent. castle.

To the W. of Aberdour is *Donibristle Park* (open to pedestrians 9–6 Tues.–Fri. ; entr. opposite Woodside Hot.), once an R.A.F. station. Farther W., on the shore of Dalgety Bay, is the roofless church of St. Bridget, *Dalgety*, dating from 1244, with a notable 17th cent. laird's loft and burial vault. Still farther is the old castle of *Donibristle*, near which 'the bonnie Earl of Moray' was slain by the Earl of Huntly (1592). Bp. Sinclair's war-cry during an English attack on Donibristle in 1317 is historical : " All ye that love Scotland's honour, follow me."

In the Forth, c. 1½ m. S. of Aberdour, lies the small island of **Inchcolm,** with the ruins of the *Abbey of St. Columba, founded in 1123 by Alexander I in gratitude for the hospitality of the island's hermit when he was shipwrecked. His priory of Austin Canons became an abbey in 1235 and was plundered more than once by the English. The well-preserved remains include a small 13th and

15th cent. church, an octagonal chapter house with a stone roof (c. 1283), and a 14th cent. cloister with vaulted dorter, frater, and guest-house above. Remains of wall-paintings were discovered in the choir in 1926. A primitive cell to the N.W. may have been the hermit's home, on a site traditionally associated with St. Columba. In ' Macbeth,' St. Colme's Inch is mentioned as the burial-place of the defeated forces of Sweno of Norway, and a hog-backed gravestone W. of the church may date from this time. After the expiry of the abbey in 1578, the buildings were used as a dwelling. The islet is conveniently visited by boat from Aberdour (2/6) or, in summer, from Granton. Landing charge 6d. ; 10–4 or 7, Sun. from 2.

19½ m. **Burntisland** (*Greenmount*, RB. 21/) is a royal burgh (5670 inhab.) with considerable shipbuilding trade. Overlooking the shipyards (behind Royal Hotel) is the dismantled *Rossend Castle*, a house grafted upon the 15th cent. castle of the Melvilles in which Queen Mary was lodging in 1563 when Chastelard was found concealed in her bedroom, an offence for which he was brought to the block. A remarkable painted ceiling (c. 1610), discovered by accident in 1957, has been restored. The **Church*, one of the most remarkable post-Reformation churches in Scotland (1592), is octagonal in plan, with an outside stair to the Sailors' Loft and a tower of 1749. The fine canopied central pew (1606) and the carved and painted Trades' Lofts (17th and 18th cent.) are outstanding. In a General Assembly here in 1601 James VI, then a guest of the Melvilles at Rossend, mooted the necessity for a new translation of the Bible, which led to the Authorised Version of 1611. In Somerville St., where Mary Somerville lived in the 1780's, is a good group of 17th cent. houses, with contemporary ceiling-paintings. The town is said to have surrendered to Cromwell in 1651 on the canny condition that he would repair its streets and harbour.

Beyond (21 m.) a monument (1886) marking the spot where Alexander III was killed by a fall from his horse, we cross the promontory of Pettycur to (21¾ m.) *Kinghorn* (2340 inhab. ; Hotel, R.B. 17/6, P. 7 gs.), a royal burgh of Alexander III, whence there is a fine view seawards.

In the Forth, c. 2½ m. S.E., lies the fortified island of **Inchkeith** (c. ¾ m. long) with its lighthouse. James IV is said to have here interned two infants under the care of a dumb woman, in order to investigate man's primitive speech, and found that " they spak very guid Ebrew." In 1547, after the battle of Pinkie, the English planted a fort on the island, but from 1549 until 1567 it was held and garrisoned by the French. Inchkeith was visited in 1773 by Dr. Johnson, and Boswell, who found " very good grass but rather a profusion of thistles." In 1817 Carlyle and Irving rowed to it from Kirkcaldy, and found in the lightkeeper a man whose whole speech and aspect said " Behold the victim of unspeakable ennui."

25 m. **Kirkcaldy** (49,050 inhab. ; *Station*, a, B 1, RB. 22/6 ; *Anthony's*, b, B 1, RB. 22/6, P. 12 gs. ; *Victoria House*, c, C 1, RB. 21/, P. 8 gs.; *Abbotshall*, d, A 3, unlic. RB. 17/6), a royal burgh since 1450, is a coal-shipping port and industrial town, noted especially for linoleum. It is well called the

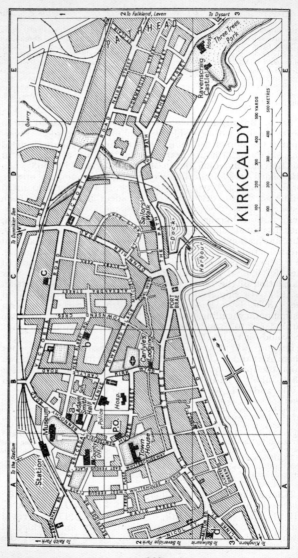

KIRKCALDY

Lang Toun,' for its main street extends for nearly 4 m. from *Invertiel* and *Linktown* (S.W.) through *Pathhead* and *Sinclairtown* to *Gallatown* (N.E.), and it now includes Dysart, to the E. Overlooking the harbour is the *Sailor's Walk* (D 2), a group of 15–17th cent. houses, well restored by the N.T. The Esplanade—the scene, for a week in mid-April, of the great Links Fair—lies seaward of the High St., a tablet in which marks the site of the birthplace of Adam Smith (1723–80), who returned in 1767 to write 'The Wealth of Nations'. Thomas Carlyle (1816–19) and Edward Irving (1812–19) were masters at the burgh school and here laid the foundation of their long friendship. A tablet marks Carlyle's lodging in Kirk Wynd (B 2). Robert Adam (1728–92), the architect, was another famous native.

In the War Memorial Square, higher up, is the imposing *Town House* (1939–56), by Carr and Howard, with mural painting and statues of famous natives. The *Museum and Art Gallery* (B 1 ; adm. 1.30–5, Sun. 2–5) is notable for paintings by MacTaggart and Peploe and for interesting archæological and geological collections, including examples of carving in ' parrot ' coal, a local craft that has only recently died out.

Behind Kirkcaldy is the beautiful *Beveridge Park*, with public access into the extensive park of *Raith House*, and 1 m. N.W. of Pathhead is *Dunnikier Park*, now burgh property, with fine timber and two picturesque wooded ' dens ' (tea-room in the former mansion). Michael Scot, the wizard (c. 1175–c. 1234), was born and resided at *Balwearie*, 1½ m. S.W., in a tower the ruined walls of which are 7 ft. thick ; while in *Abbotshall Cemetery*, N. of Beveridge Park, is a tomb-statue (1930) of Marjory Fleming (1803–11 ; born in High St.), the ' Youngest Immortal ', whose writings and her supposed friendship with Scott are charmingly described by Dr. John Brown.

Overhanging the sea at Pathhead are the picturesque ruins of *Ravenscraig Castle* (E 3 ; 1440), the Ravensheugh of Scott's ' Rosabelle.' It was granted by James III to Wm. Sinclair, Earl of Orkney, on his resignation of that title, and was inhabited until Monk dismantled it in 1651. A fine public park extends E. towards Dysart (p. 265 ; pleasant path).—Motor-Buses connect Kirkcaldy with all points in the neighbourhood and traverse the chief streets. For the Fife coast road, see Rte. 36.

In Pathhead, N. of Kirkcaldy proper, A 92 turns uphill to the left, and runs N., leaving the coast, to (29¼ m.) *Thornton*, a centre of the East Fife coalfield.—31 m. *Glenrothes*, a new town on the Leven, designed to accommodate 30,000 inhab., lies 1 m. S. of *Cadham Cross*, at the junction of the Kinross–Leven road.

Markinch (2300 inhab. ; Laurel Bank, RB. 17/6), 1 m. E., has a well-designed church on a hill, with a spire of 1809 crowning a 12th cent. tower. *Balgonie Castle*, on the Leven 1 m. farther S.E., is a 12th cent. tower with courtyard (key for the tower at the cottage beyond). In Balgonie church rests David Leslie (Lord Newark ; d. 1682), the Covenanting general who was defeated in 1650 by Cromwell at Dunbar.—*Leslie* (Rothes Oak, RB. 17/6), 2½ m. W. of Cadham Cross, is a small town (2600 inhab.), making paper, linen, and plastics, with some interesting old houses and a ' Green ' that is among the claimants to be the scene of ' Christ's Kirk on the Green.' From above the ruins of *Strathendry*

Castle (1¼ m. N.W.) there is a fine view over Loch Leven. Adam Smith, when a child, was kidnapped at Strathendry by tinkers, but was speedily recovered.

Beyond (34 m.) *New Inn* A 912 leads to (2½ m. N.W.) **Falkland** (1025 inhab. ; *Bruce Arms*, RB. 15/6), a royal burgh since 1458, noted for its palace. It is charmingly situated at the N. base of the East Lomond (1471 ft.), while 3½ m. W. is the twin hill of West Lomond (1713 ft. ; *View ; indicator). Richard Cameron (d. 1680), the Covenanter, was born in the village and became its schoolmaster and precentor. Adjoining and opposite the palace some 17th and early-18th cent. houses have been well restored.

*Falkland Palace (N.T. ; adm. 2/, weekdays 11–5, Oct.– Mar., Wed. & Sat. only; gardens 1/, June–Sept. only, 10–5) is an attractive royal pleasance of the 16th cent. The S. wing, the only one in tolerable preservation, presents an elegant ornamental façade with narrow mullioned and grated windows to the village street and has an imposing gatehouse flanked by loopholed round towers.

History. An earlier castle here, mentioned in a charter of 1160, belonged to the Macduffs, the powerful thanes or earls of Fife, and in 1371 passed to Robert III's ambitious brother, the Duke of Albany, who, according to the popular story followed in Scott's ' Fair Maid of Perth,' here starved to death in 1402 his nephew, David, Duke of Rothesay and heir to the throne. The official pronouncement, however, was that that dissolute prince had " died by the visitation of providence and not otherwise." On the attainder and execution of Albany's son and grandsons in 1425 the castle became Crown property.—The *Palace*, begun by James II (c. 1450), became a favourite seat of the Scottish court, and the phrase ' Falkland bred ' implied courtly manners. It owes its present appearance mainly to James V, who completed and embellished it (1525–37). As a boy he fled hence from the tutelage of his guardian, the Earl of Angus, and here he died in 1542, broken-hearted after the defeat at Solway Moss. A few days before his death he was told of the birth of his daughter Mary (the future Queen of Scots) ; his only comment—" God's will be done ; it cam wi' a lass and it'll gang wi' a lass "—referred to the fact that the Stewarts had obtained the throne by marriage. Mary and her son James VI highly appreciated the good hunting in the neighbourhood, and it was from Falkland that James rode to Perth just before the Gowrie Conspiracy (p. 222). Charles I (in 1633) and Charles II (in 1650) visited the palace. In 1715 Rob Roy, after Sheriffmuir, occupied it and levied contributions on the town. In 1887 the Falkland estates were purchased by the 3rd Marquess of Bute, hereditary keeper, who restored the palace.

Approaching by a gateway at the corner of the grounds, we enter the inner court, which was originally enclosed on three sides. The façade (1530–40) of the S. wing on this side is somewhat Italian in character ; it is divided by buttresses, faced with Renaissance columns and entablatures, the upper windows being flanked with medallion heads of kings and queens and dignitaries. The E. wing, burned in 1654 when the palace was occupied by Cromwell's forces, has a similar but less elaborate façade. The foundations on the N. side of the court are those of the great hall begun by James II, and are now laid out as a rose-garden.—In the restored interior

of the S. wing a corridor with 17th cent. Flemish tapestries, a
19th cent. ceiling of oak, and stained glass showing the
escutcheons of Scottish monarchs and their consorts, leads to
the banquet hall (now the Chapel Royal and used for R.C.
services) which retains its original walls and ceiling and
contains an interesting screen. In the damaged E. wing were
the royal apartments, and here are pointed out the door by
which the youthful James V escaped in disguise, his probable
death chamber (redecorated and furnished), and Rothesay's
alleged dungeon.

The *Garden* has been replanted after the design of an old print ; in the middle
are indicated the site of the keep and curtain-wall of the Macduffs' castle. At
the end is a *Royal Tennis Court* (restored), unique in Scotland.

Beyond Falkland A 912 goes on to Strathmiglo, A 983 to Auchtermuchty,
continuing respectively for Glenfarg and Newburgh (for Perth).

From the Falkland road-fork A 92 runs N.E.—36¾ m.
Kingskettle (Annfield House, RB. 25/), to the left, is just over
1 m. S. of the railway junction of *Ladybank*.—38½ m. *Pitlessie*
(George, RB. 15/). Sir David Wilkie (1785–1841) was born in
the manse of *Cults*, c. 1 m. S. His first picture was ' Pitlessie
Fair.'

On the hill to the right farther on is the late-16th cent. tower of *Scotstarvit*
(N.T.; adm. on application), once the residence of Sir John Scot or Scott (1585–
1670), brother-in-law of Drummond of Hawthornden and author of ' The
Staggering State of Scots Statesmen.' Farther W., beyond the Cupar–Leven
road, is *Hill of Tarvit* (N.T.), a 17–19th cent. mansion refaced by Sir R. Lorimer
in 1906. It is now a convalescent home but contains the art-collections of the
last owner, H. F. B. Sharp (adm. Wed. & Sun. in summer 2.30–6). A copy of
Cupar Cross in the grounds marks the alleged spot on which the treaty between
Mary of Guise and the Lords of the Congregation was signed in 1559.

42½ m. **Cupar** (*Royal, Station*, at both, RB. 21/), sometimes
called Cupar-Fife (comp. p. 283), is the county town (5530
inhab.) of *Fife* and a royal burgh of David II. The dignified
main streets retain many good 18th and early-19th cent.
houses, with narrow wynds behind ; at their junction is the
shaft of the old *Town Cross*, reinstated after temporary
removal in 1817 to Hill of Tarvit (see above). A tablet in
Crossgate marks the birthplace of Lord Chancellor Campbell,
a ' son of the manse '. The *Old Parish Church*, on the S.W.
hill, retains a medieval tower (with spire of 1620) and three
bays of 1415 ; in the large churchyard are buried the hands of
Hackston of Rathillet and the heads of two other Covenanters,
dismembered in Edinburgh. The site of the castle, on the N.E.
hill, is occupied by a school.

The Scots phrase, ' He that will to Cupar maun to Cupar ' (i.e. a wilful man
must have his way), refers to the time when Cupar was the seat of the Fife
courts of justice.

About 3¼ m. N.W. an obelisk to the 4th Earl of Hopetoun now crowns *The
Mount*, the property and patrimonial seat of Sir David Lindsay or Lyndsay
(1490–1555), the poet, satirist, and Lyon King of Arms.

L

At (45 m.) *Dairsie* (½ m. r.) the Eden is crossed by a bridge of three arches dating from 1522. On a height by the river are the ruins of *Dairsie Castle,* where David II spent a great part of his minority, and where Archbishop Spottiswood wrote his ' History of the Church and State of Scotland.' The little church, once alluded to as " ane of the beautifulest little pieces of church work that is left to this unhappy country," was built by the archbishop (1621) as part of his great scheme for bringing Scotland into religious conformity with England.

From Dairsie bridge a charming road ascends the wooded *Dura Den,* a glen with a ruined mill, noted for important discoveries of fossil fish in the Old Red Sandstone. Emerging at Pitscottie, we turn right for (3½ m.) **Ceres** (i.e. St. Cyr's), a tiny decayed town, with a green, an ancient bridge, and the medieval mausoleum of the Crawfords adjoining the church of 1806, with an attractive interior. Some of the houses are decorated with sculptured emblems, and at the cross is a strange 17th cent. figure of a church provost by a local artist. Cupar is 3 m. N.W. by a hilly road.

A little farther on the road divides, A 92 going left viâ (49 m.) *Balmullo* to (53½ m.) *Newport* (see below).—A 91 keeps right for St. Andrews, crossing the Eden at (48½ m.) *Guard Bridge,* where a modern bridge has been built alongside the old bridge of c. 1420 (repaired in 1520). Thence it skirts the links for (52½ m.) *St. Andrews* (Rte. 36).

We turn left on A 919, without crossing the bridge, for (50½ m.) **Leuchars,** a village (Commercial Arms Inn) celebrated for its *Church, the E. end of which (12th cent.) is perhaps the most beautiful fragment of Romanesque work in Scotland. The exterior of the apse is arcaded, with blind arches and pilasters showing axe-marking. The octagonal tower (17th cent.) is crowned by a lantern. Within, the mouldings of the arches at the entrances to the choir and apse are very rich ; the corbels at the base of the groining should be noted. Beside the modern door are two carved slabs (formerly in the choir) from the tombs of Lady Bruce of Erleshall (d. 1635) and her husband.—The ancient mansion of *Earlshall* (1546–1607 ; no adm.) is ½ m. E.

A road runs N. from Leuchars (St. Michael's) to (5½ m.) *Tayport* (3225 inhab.), once known as *Ferry Port on Craig* (ferry discontinued). It skirts the sandy waste of *Tents Muir,* with an R.A.F. station (memorial to Norwegian airmen, 1957), forestry plantations, and a hundred-acre nature reserve (N.E. end).

Rejoining A 92 at (52 m.) the *St. Michael's Hotel* (RB. 17/6), we proceed N. to (55½ m.) **Newport-on-Tay** (3275 inhab. ; *Seymour,* unlic., RB. 17/6), a seaside resort commanding a fine view of Dundee across the Firth of Tay. Wormit and the Tay Bridge lie 2 m. upstream, and are well seen from the ferry which crosses the firth to (57 m.) **Dundee** (Rte. 37c).

36. FROM EDINBURGH TO ST. ANDREWS VIÂ THE FIFE COAST

ROAD (A 955), 62 m. To (25 m.) *Kirkcaldy*, see Rte. 35.—35 m. *Leven.*—38 m. *Largo*, whence the direct road runs N.E. to (48 m.) *St. Andrews*. The coast road (A 917), 14 m. longer, passes (43 m.) *Elie* and (48 m.) *Anstruther*, and turns N.W. beyond (52 m.) *Crail.*—62 m. **St. Andrews.**—MOTOR-BUSES half-hourly from Inverkeithing to Leven, and hourly from Leven to St. Andrews.

RAILWAY 65 m. from Waverley Station in 2¾ hrs.; through trains from Glasgow (Buchanan St.) to St. Andrews in 3½ hrs. Most trains terminate at Crail. Principal Stations : To (30¾ m.) *Thornton*, see Rte. 35.—36½ m. *Leven.*—39½ m. *Largo.*—44½ m. *Elie.*—48½ m. *Pittenweem.*—49½ m. *Anstruther.*—53¾ m. *Crail.*—64¾ m. **St. Andrews.**

The county of **Fife, or Fifeshire,** within which the following route lies, occupies the peninsula between the Firths of Forth and Tay, and its most characteristic feature is the series of ancient little burghs and fishing ports that line its S. seaboard. " He that will view the county of Fife must go round the coast," says Defoe, and James VI spoke of the county as " a grey cloth mantle with a golden fringe." The little burghs have for the most part lost their commercial importance, but they retain some of their quaintness, and are popular as summer and golfing resorts. The peninsula has been known since ancient days as the ' Kingdom of Fife,' perhaps because it included Abernethy, an old Pictish capital, or simply because it has always been one of the richest and most self-contained provinces in Scotland. The people have the reputation of cherishing various little peculiarities of manner and custom that differentiate them from other Lowlanders and their country is a land of sudden and surprising contrasts. The flat *Howe of Fife*, in the centre, and the *East Neuk*, the blunt promontory in the S.E., are among the most fertile parts of a fertile county. The linen of Dunfermline and the floorcloth of Kirkcaldy are noted, and the Fife coal-field (W. and S.W.) extending E. across the Leven and threatening more and more farming land with opencast working, now equals that of Lanarkshire in importance. St. Andrews, Dunfermline, and Falkland are prominent names in Scottish history.

From Edinburgh to (25 m.) *Kirkcaldy*, see Rte. 35. The most interesting road keeps near the coast.—27 m. **Dysart,** united with Kirkcaldy in 1930, is an attractive old port, taking its name from the hermit's cell of St. Serf (5th cent.). Near the sea are the ruined church of St. Serf, older than the date 1570 that appears on one of its windows, and the 16th cent. Bay Horse inn ; and in the town is the Tolbooth, with a stumpy Dutch-looking tower of 1576. John M. Stuart (1815–66), the Australian explorer, was born at Dysart.

To the right of our road are (29 m.) *West Wemyss* and (30½ m.) *East Wemyss*, both taking name from the numerous large ' weems ' or caves (some with rude inscriptions) on this coast. Near the modern Wemyss Castle, overlooking the sea between E. and W. Wemyss, is the earlier castle in which Queen Mary first met Darnley in 1565, five months before their marriage. The Erskines of Wemyss claim descent from Macduff, thane of Fife in the reign of Malcolm Canmore, and a ruin a little E. of East Wemyss is known as *Macduff's Castle*. An ancient dovecot stands below it.

32 m. *Buckhaven* and (33½ m.) *Methil* are united coal-ports (20,150 inhab.). There is an attractive modern church (1942) at *Innerleven*, the landward suburb of Methil on the main road.—At (35 m.) **Leven** (*Beach*, RB. 22/6, P. 10 gs. ; *Caledonian*, High St., RB. 18/6, P. 10 gs.), a coaling port and

seaside resort (8870 inhab.), we reach the shores of the Forth.
Letham Glen, E. of the town, is a pleasant public park.—37 m.
Lundin Links (Lundin Links, RB. 25/, P. 10 gs. ; Beach, RB.
18/6, P. 8½ gs.) has a well-known golf course. In a field behind
the station are three large standing stones.—38 m. **Largo**
(*Crusoe*, RB. 17/6, P. 8 gs. ; *Largo Bay*, unlic., P. 7½ gs.) is a
straggling village on Largo Bay, the fame of whose fishing is
recalled in the song ' The Boatie Rows.' Alexander Selkirk
(1676–1721), the prototype of Robinson Crusoe (statue near
the harbour), was the son of a Largo shoemaker. The barony
was granted in 1482 to Sir Andrew Wood (d. 1515), the captain
of the 'Yellow Carvel,' who defeated a marauding English
squadron in the Firth. The parish church (1400 ; much
altered), at Upper Largo, has a typical tower and spire of
1623. In the churchyard is a Pictish cross-slab.

Behind the town are the romantic glen called *Kiels Den* and (1½ m. N.) *Largo
Law*, a conspicuous volcanic hill (*View). A 915, the direct road to St. Andrews
(10¼ m.), runs from Upper Largo viâ (c. 5 m.) *Largoward* (Staghead, RB. 21/ ;
Lathones, RB. 18/6 ; Peat Inn, to the N., RB. 15/) a scattered village.—A 921,
forking left from the coast road at 40 m., offers a direct route to Crail, avoiding
Elie and passing (41 m.) *Colinsburgh* (Balcarres Arms), a 'model' village of 1718,
with a characteristic long street. *Balcarres* (l.), where Lady Anne Lindsay
(1750–1825) wrote 'Auld Robin Gray,' is the seat of the Lindsays, earls of
Crawford and Balcarres, and dates in part from 1595.

41½ m. *Kilconquhar* (pron. Kinnúchar), the 'cell of St.
Conacher,' is a pretty village (l.) near a little loch.—43 m.
Elie (*Marine*, RB. 27/6, P. 12 gs. ; *Golf*, RB. 26/, P. 12 gs. ;
Queen's, RB. 21/, P. 9½ gs. ; *Victoria*, P. 8 gs. ; many unlic.
hotels) and its W. continuation, *Earlsferry* (together 1190
inhab.), are favourite summer resorts, with fine sands and
golf course. Earlsferry, a royal burgh of great antiquity, is
said to take its name from the boatmen who ferried Macduff
across the Firth when he was fleeing from the fury of Macbeth.
A cave at Kincraig Point, to the W., still bears his name.
Elie is known for its 'rubies,' i.e. small garnets, which are
picked up on the beach.—The ruins of *Newark Castle* (17th
cent.) are seen on the right just short of (45¼ m.) *St. Monance*
(May View, P. 6½ gs.). The *Church of St. Monan, built by
David II c. 1362 in gratitude for his recovery at the saint's
shrine from a wound, the transepts and choir of a cruciform
edifice of which the nave was never built, has a short square
tower, surmounted by an octagonal steeple, with characteristic
little belfry windows. The interior, lighted by beautiful Dec.
windows, has a fine groined roof and ogee-headed sedilia.—
At (46¾ m.) **Pittenweem** (1625 inhab. ; *Station*, RB. 17/6), a
royal burgh, are remains of the dormitory and refectory of an
Augustinian priory which in 1318 superseded the Benedictine
house on the Isle of May, 7 m. out at sea. The episcopal
parsonage occupies the 12th cent. priory church ; the parish

church, adjoining, preserves its medieval tower. It was at Pittenweem that Wilson and Robertson robbed the Fife customs-collector (1736), a crime that led to the Porteous Riot in Edinburgh. The 16th cent. *Kellie Castle*, 2¼ m. N.W., was the birthplace of Thomas Erskine, sixth earl of Kellie (1732–81), a distinguished musician.—48 m. **Anstruther** (*Commercial*, RB. 20/, at Anstruther Easter) is the popular name for the small prawn-fishing ports of *Anstruther Wester*, *Anstruther Easter*, and *Cellardyke* (or Nether Kilrenny). The two Anstruthers and *Kilrenny* (all three royal burghs) are now municipally united (3000 inhab.). The churches of both Anstruther Wester and Anstruther Easter (the latter at Upper Kilrenny, 1 m. N.E.) have good towers of local type.

52 m. **Crail** (*Marine*, unlic., RB. 22/6, P. 10 gs. ; *East Neuk*, RB. 21/, P. 9 gs. ; *Balcomie Links*, to the E., RB. 18/6, P. 8 gs.) is a picturesque little fishing town and royal burgh (1140 inhab.) with numerous old houses and a larger number of red-tiled roofs than is usual in Scotland. The interesting *Collegiate Church*, founded in 1517, where Archbp. Sharp was minister before he became an Episcopalian and where Knox preached at the beginning of the Reformation, has a good tower of local pattern. In the entrance lobby are a Celtic cross-slab and the tombstone of Miss Cunningham, who was betrothed to Drummond of Hawthornden during his sojourn at the old house of *Barns* (1 m. W.) but died c. 1619, aged 19. The quaint *Town House*, with a Dutch tower, contains bulls granted to the church by Popes Julius II and Leo X. On leaving Crail the main road turns N.W.

Fife Ness, 2 m. N.E., is the E. promontory of the ' East Neuk ' of Fife. At *Balcomie Castle*, 1½ m. on the way to the headland, Mary of Guise, the future bride of James V, was entertained on her landing in 1538. A beacon and lightship mark the dangerous Carr Rocks to the N.E., beyond which the Bell Rock light is sometimes visible.

62 m. **ST. ANDREWS** (9450 inhab.), one of the historic towns of Scotland, stands on a rocky promontory jutting into the North Sea, with a venerable ruined Cathedral at one end, the famous golf links at the other, and the oldest Scottish University midway between them. In summer it is a fashionable and often crowded seaside resort, and it has acquired by prescription the title of the ' Mecca of golfers.'

Hotels. Rusack's (a ; A 1), The Links, RB. 27/6, P. 15 gs., closed Oct.– Apr.; **Atholl**, Links Cres., RB. 27/6, P. 12½ gs. ; **Station & Windsor** (f ; B 1), Alexandra Place, RB. 27/6, P. 12 gs. ; **Cross Keys** (h ; B 2), Market St., RB. 22/6, P. c. 11½ gs. ; **Rufflets**, on the Cupar road, RB. 25/, P. 10 gs. ; **Scores,** on the Scores (A 2), RB. 25/, P. 10 gs., closed Dec.–Feb. ; **Golf** (e ; A 1), Golf Place, RB. 22/6, P. 11 gs.; **Royal** (c ; B 2), 118 South St., RB. 21/, P. 12 gs. ; **Star** (g ; B 2), Market St., RB. 22/6, P. 9½ gs. ; **West Park**, Market St., unlic., RB. 21/, P. 11½ gs. ; and many others.

Post Office (Pl. B 2), South Street.

Motor-Buses from City Rd. to *Leven* viâ Largoward or Peat Inn (1 hr.), or viâ Crail, Anstruther, and Elie (1¼ hr.) ; to *Newport* (¾ hr.) viâ Leuchars and Tayport ; viâ Ceres to *Cupar*,

Newburgh and *Perth* (1¾ hr.); viâ Dairsie to *Cupar* (½ hr.) and *Kirkcaldy* (1¾ hr.); to *Anstruther* (34 min.) viâ Dunino; to *Glasgow* (4 hrs.) viâ Cupar, Kinross, and Stirling.

Theatre. *Byre*, Abbey St. (B 3).

Sea-Bathing. At the *Bathing Ponds* (A 2 and A 3) and from the *West Sands* (A 1; best) and *East Sands* (C 4).

Golf. The *Royal and Ancient Golf Club* of St. Andrews is the premier golf club in the world and is the ruling authority on the game. The Autumn Golf Meeting at the end of Sept., when the captain for the ensuing year plays himself into office, is the principal event of the year.—There are four Golf Courses (all 18-hole); the *Old Course* (4 m.), still the favourite, starting from the Royal and Ancient Golf Club House (Pl. A 1); the *New Course* (3¾ m.) starting from the shelter beyond the Ladies' Putting Green, across the Swilcan Burn; the *Jubilee Course* (2¾ m.) starting on the dunes to the right of the shelter, at the end of the path leading past the Ladies' Putting Green; the *Eden Course* (3½ m.), reached by a gate on the right in Guardbridge Rd., just beyond the goods station. The links are the property of the town, the Old and New Courses being kept up by the R. & A. Golf Club, the others by the City Corporation. Charges per round are 6/ on the Old Course, 3/ on the New, 3/6 (5/ on Sun.) on the Eden, and 1/6 on the Jubilee Course. In Aug. and Sept. the places in the ballot between 10 and 11.16 a.m. and between 2 and 3.16 p.m. on the Old Course are reserved for members of the ' R. & A.' From July to September ratepayers and members have prior right of starting on the New Course between 9 and 10 a.m. and 1 and 2 p.m. Sunday play on the Eden Course only.

History. That St. Regulus or Rule, bearing the relics of St. Andrew, was shipwrecked at St. Andrews in the 4th cent. is one of the many picturesque legends of Scottish history. It is more likely that these relics were brought hither in the mid-8th cent., and the Culdee settlement, founded then or previously, became a bishopric which by the beginning of the 10th cent. had superseded Abernethy in the primacy of Scotland. In 1124 Robert, prior of the Augustinian house at Scone, was appointed bishop, and from his time the Culdees were gradually superseded by Canons Regular. In 1140 the town became a royal burgh. The cathedral was founded in 1160, and forty years later (1200) the castle was begun as the episcopal residence. The present town church and the university date from 1412. In 1407 John Risby was here burned for heresy, and in 1433 Paul Craw, a Bohemian. In 1472 the see became an archbishopric. Patrick Hamilton suffered in 1527, and the burning of George Wishart was almost immediately followed by the murder of Cardinal Beaton (1546). Another victim was Walter Myln in 1558, the last Reformation martyr.

In 1538 Mary of Guise received a ceremonial welcome here before her marriage. Her daughter Mary, Queen of Scots, visited St. Andrews in 1563 and 1564, and James VI in 1583 escaped hither from the Gowrie family and visited it often again. In the two following centuries many fine dwelling-houses were built, a good number of which still survive in South St. (e.g. Nos. 42, 46) and elswhere.

The **University** of St. Andrews, the oldest but smallest in Scotland, was founded by Bp. Henry Wardlaw in 1412, and now includes three colleges and over 2000 students. The colleges of St. Salvator and St. Leonard, founded respectively in 1450 and 1512, were combined in 1747 to form the *United College of St. Salvator and St. Leonard* with the faculties of arts and science. *St. Mary's College*, founded in 1538, contains the theological faculty and the University library. *University College*, at Dundee, founded in 1880, and now called *Queen's College*, was incorporated with the University in 1897. Each college has its own principal and staff of professors, but there is only one University Court.

The railway station and links are at the W. end of the town, and from that quarter the three principal streets—South St., Market St., and North St.—converge at the ruins of the Cathedral, at the E. end of the town.

To the N. of the station lie the famous *Golf Links* (A 1), with the old *Club House* of the Royal and Ancient Club (founded in 1754), and its new headquarters. As on Sun. golf is played on the Eden Course only, the other links are then safe for walkers. On the green, E. of the links, above a hollow known as the Bow

Butts, stands the *Martyrs' Monument*, commemorating Reformers who were
burned at St. Andrews : Hamilton, Forrest, Wishart, and Myln.—Thence the
road called the Scores skirts the coast E. to the Castle.

South Street, the principal street, is spanned at its W. end
by the *West Port* (B. C 1), a gateway rebuilt in 1589, with
a later (1845) figure of David I on the outside ; the side arches
are 19th cent. additions. On the right side of the street, a
little farther on, is the **Blackfriars Chapel,** a picturesque
fragment (1525) of the church of the Dominican friary, founded
in 1274 by Bp. Wishart and destroyed in 1559 by the ' rascal
multitude.' The chapel stands in the grounds of *Madras
College*, a school for boys and girls, founded in 1832 from a
bequest of Dr. Andrew Bell. The *Post Office* (B 2), on the
opposite side of the street, stands on the site of the house
occupied by Dr. Chalmers when Professor of Moral Philosophy
at the United College 1823–24. Tradition assigns the same
house to ' Kate Dalrymple,' the heroine of the well-known
song. On the S. side we next note the *Town Hall* (B 2), which
contains some interesting portraits and municipal relics,
including the headsman's axe.

In the square, opposite the Town Hall, is **Holy Trinity,**
the large and beautiful town church, founded in 1412 but
many times altered, spoiled by rebuilding in 1799, and
redesigned in 1906–09 by MacGregor Chalmers, who followed
the old lines and retained as much as possible of the original
work. The fine tower, however, is Pre-Reformation. The
church is open daily 10–1 and 2.45–4 ; on Sat. 10–12 only.
John Knox here preached his first public sermon in 1547 ;
and here in 1638 Alex. Henderson delivered a rousing sermon
in support of the Covenant.

The chief object of interest in the interior—somewhat
unexpected in a Presbyterian church—is the elaborate marble
monument in the S. transept to Archbp. Sharp, carved in
Holland and erected by his son, with a fulsome inscription
and a representation of the archbishop's murder. To the S.E.
is the *Memorial Aisle*, with two surviving choir-stalls (c. 1505)
and the silver Book of Remembrance (in a shrine-recess)
made after the Second World War ; and on the N. side is the
Playfair Aisle, with memorials to Sir Nigel Playfair (1874–
1934) and members of his family. The great E. and W.
windows, and 11 others in the church (1910–50), are the work
of Douglas Strachan.

The pulpit, lectern, and font commemorate ' A. K. H. B.' (Dr. Boyd), essayist
and preacher, minister of the church in 1865–99. On the W. wall is a tablet to
Old Tom Morris, the famous golfer.—In the session house (adm. 2*d*., apply to
the church officer), adjoining the S. aisle, are shown a chair of repentance, two
' cutty ' stools, the ' branks ' or scold's bridle, some 17th cent. plate, etc.

On the right is **St. Mary's College** (B 2, 3), founded in 1537
by Archbp. James Beaton, now containing the theological

faculty and the University library. The coats-of-arms on the
street façade are those of Chancellors of the University from
Bp. Wardlaw (1411) to Field-Marshal Earl Haig. The older
buildings form two sides of an attractive quadrangle, in which
a thorn tree planted by Mary, Queen of Scots, still flourishes.
On the E. (l.) side are new library buildings and laboratories,
and on the S. is a Botanic Garden (adm. free). The *Senate
Room* contains historical portraits connected with the college.
In the *Library* (founded by James VI) are shown the Bassan-
dyne Bible, the works of Augustine on vellum, Dr. Duff's
Bible, and a copy of the Solemn League and Covenant, with
interesting signatures. In the lower hall of the old library a
number of the prisoners taken at Philiphaugh were condemned
to death.

Beyond Abbey St., on the right, are the remains of **St. Leonard's College,** which
was founded in 1512, on the site of an older hospital, by Prior John Hepburn and
Abp. Alex. Stewart, natural son of James IV, with whom he died at Flodden
(1513), aged 21. George Buchanan was principal in 1566–70, and John Knox
resided within its walls. Here many of the youthful Reformers studied, and the
phrase ' to have drunk of St. Leonard's well ' meant to have imbibed Protestant
doctrines. The college was united with St. Salvator in 1747, and the domestic
buildings were sold for other purposes. Some of them form part of *St. Leonard's
School*, a well-known school for girls founded in 1877.

Farther on in South St. on the right is the 16th cent. house
of the Scrimgeours (now St. Leonard's school library ; open
Thurs. 2.30–3.30 in term ; adm. 6*d.*) in which Mary, Queen
of Scots, probably (1563–64) and Charles II certainly lodged
(1650). South St. ends almost opposite the cathedral entrance.
On the right are the PENDS, two fine 14th cent. arches once the
chief entrance to the precinct of the priory, which is surrounded by a defensive wall, 20 ft. high and c. 1 m. round,
with towers at intervals. This dates from the 16th cent.,
though on older foundations. There is another gate, the *Teinds
Yett*, in Abbey Walk.

Pends Road descends to the harbour, passing the gateway (r.) of the *Hospitium
Novum* of the priory (once a residence of Abp. Sharp), and ends at the *Mill Port*,
a third gate in the wall.

On the right beyond the Pends is the entrance to **St. Leonard's Chapel** (Mon.–
Fri. 10–4, Sat. 10–12), the early-16th cent. chapel of the college (see above).
After a period as a parish church (1578–1671) the chapel stood neglected until
1910, when the University began a restoration which was successfully completed
in 1948–52. In the choir are the monuments of two principals of the college,
Robert Wilkie (d. 1611) and Peter Bruce (d. 1620), and of Robert Stewart, Earl
of March (d. 1586).

Facing the cathedral entrance is a group of 16–17th cent. houses known as
Dean's Court, the former archdeaconry, restored in 1952 as a residence for
research students. The arms over the old gateway are those of George Douglas
of Loch Leven fame.

The **Cathedral* (B 4 ; adm. free 10–4 or 7, Sun. from 2),
which serves also as the priory church, is by far the largest
cathedral in Scotland though only about the same size as

Chester Cathedral in England. It is 34 ft. longer than Glasgow Cathedral.

History. The cathedral was founded by Bp. Arnold in 1160 but was finished and consecrated only in 1318, in presence of King Robert the Bruce. In this church James V married Mary of Guise ; and within its walls Patrick Hamilton, George Wishart, and Walter Myln were tried and condemned for heresy. John Knox's sermons on the ' Cleansing of the Temple ' on four consecutive days in June 1559 led to the destruction of images and ' popish ' ornaments, but there is no evidence that any damage was done to the fabric at the Reformation. Neglect, co-operating with wind and weather, seem to have reduced it to a ruinous state by 1649, when stones from it were used in fortifying the town, an evil example soon followed by the citizens generally in erecting their houses down to about 1826.

The cathedral when perfect was 355 ft. in length, and about 160 ft. wide across the transepts. The only remains standing are parts of the W. and E. ends, entirely isolated from each other, and part of the S. wall of the nave of eleven bays, pierced with windows of which three, to the E., are round-headed, and all c. 18 ft. from the ground. The plan of the remainder is marked on the ground in lines filled with granite chips. The W. front (1273–79) has a deeply recessed central doorway, surmounted by a blank E.E. arcade and flanked by a turret still propped by a flying buttress. The original front was two bays farther W. In the S. aisle, the W. bays have late-13th cent. windows ; those to the E. are a century earlier. Both doorways to the cloister are bricked up. The 12th cent. E. end wall stands perfect, with its flanking turrets, three narrow windows with round heads below, and a pointed window above, a 15th cent. insertion. On the E. side of the cloister is the triple entrance to the chapter house (c. 1250), which was extended E. by Bp. Lamberton in 1313–21. Between this and the S. transept is a slype, once vaulted, while to the S. is the warming house (now a museum, see below), above which was the dorter. The undercroft of the refectory, on the S. side of the cloister, was reconstructed c. 1899 ; to the S.E. is a detached building, called the prior's house (15th cent.).

Close to the S.E. angle of the cathedral is the remarkable small **Church of St. Rule,** built for Bp. Robert in 1127–44. It is distinguished by its curious square slender *Tower, 108 ft. high, and by a very narrow choir, with its chancel-arch built up. The nave has vanished.

The tower may be ascended. The ticket (6*d.*) admits also to the *Museum* in the cloister which contains notable Early Christian sculptured stones and a fine 10th cent. sarcophagus.

In the *Cemetery* near St. Rule's are buried Samuel Rutherford (p. 9) and Tom Morris (1821–1908).—In the *East Cemetery*, S. of St. Rule's, are the graves of Principal Tulloch, Lord Playfair, Bp. Wordsworth, Dr. Boyd, and Andrew Lang. On the cliff E. of the precinct is the *Kirk Heugh*, perhaps the site of the earliest Culdee settlement, on which are some scanty traces of the church of *St. Mary of the Rock* (c. 1250), once a collegiate church. In the cliff below is *St. Rule's Cave,* " where good St. Rule his holy lay from midnight to the dawn of day sung to the billow's sound." It is better known as *Lady Buchan's Cave*, after a lady who fitted it up as a summer house in the 18th century.

On a rock rising abruptly from the sea, c. 300 yds. N.W. of the cathedral, is the **Castle** (A 3 ; adm. 1/ 10–4 or 7, Sun. from 2), which was also the episcopal palace, now a shattered but picturesque ruin.

History. Founded by Bp. Roger in 1200, the castle was rebuilt after Bannockburn by Bp. Lamberton and has several times been repaired. It was the prison of Gavin Douglas, bishop of Dunkeld, and of many early Reformers, and from its walls Cardinal David Beaton luxuriously watched the burning of George Wishart in March, 1546. In the following May a body of sixteen foes of the cardinal, headed by Norman Leslie, son of the Earl of Rothes, seized the castle, slew the cardinal, and hung his corpse over the battlements to prove that he was dead. Joined by many adherents, including John Knox, they held out until the castle was taken by a French fleet in July, 1547, when Knox and many of the garrison were sent to the galleys at Nantes. The fortress passed into the possession ot the town in the 17th cent. and was suffered to decay.

A modern bridge crosses the moat to the entrance, which is flanked by guard-rooms, beyond which is a courtyard, with the castle well. In the *Sea Tower*, at the N.W. angle, is a curious bottle-shaped dungeon, c. 25 ft. deep, where several Reformers are said to have been confined. Into this the body of Beaton was cast and covered with salt, " to await," says Knox, " what exsequies his brethren the bishops would prepare for him." At the N.E. angle is the *Kitchen Tower*. The strong tower at the S.W. angle is supposed to have contained Beaton's apartments. To the S.E. of the courtyard is the entrance to a *Subterranean Passage*, a unique example of a mine and counter-mine dating from the siege of 1546. Its exploration, though interesting, is not for the elderly.

Castle St. (B 3) runs S. from the castle to North Street, which leads to the right (W.) to the modern buildings of the **United College** OF ST. SALVATOR AND ST. LEONARD (A 2, 3), in which are the University faculties of arts and science. The college of St. Salvator was founded on this site in 1450, by Bp. James Kennedy (c. 1408–65), grandson of Robert III. In 1747 it was united with the college of St. Leonard. Patrick Hamilton was burned before the gate of the college in 1528.— The sole survivor of Kennedy's buildings is the **Church of St. Salvator,** now the University chapel (entered from the cloister on the N. side), with its lofty tower. It contains the beautiful and elaborately decorated tomb of the founder ; and a fine mace of Kennedy's time is preserved in the vestry. John Knox's pulpit, from the town church, is now in St. Salvator's. At the W. end is the tomb-slab of Principal Hugh Spens (d. 1533), and a tablet by the entrance commemorates Andrew Lang (1844–1912), an alumnus of the university.

The other buildings in the quadrangle (1844–46) are competent work by Robert Reid and William Nixon. Close by is the palatial *Younger Graduation Hall* (1929), and behind that, facing the Scores, is *St. Salvator's Hall of Residence*, for men students.

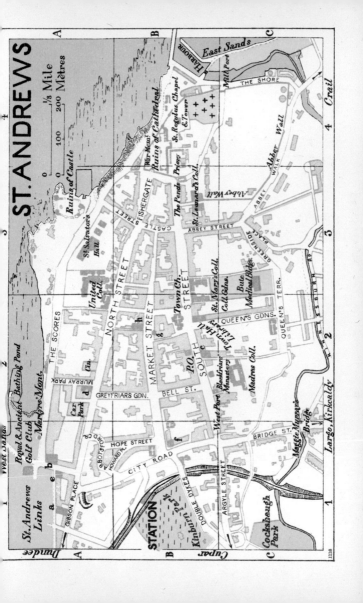

ST. ANDREWS

Scale: 0 — 100 — 200 Mètres — 1/8 Mile

West Sands

Dundee

St. Andrews Links

Royal & Ancient Golf Club

Bathing Pond

Martyrs Mont.

GIBSON PLACE

THE SCORES

Car Park

MURRAY PARK

Fln.

United Coll.

St. Salvator's Hall

Ruins of Castle

East Sands

HARBOUR

MillPort

THE SHORE

War Mem'l

Ruins of Cathedral

St. Regulus Chapel & Tower

The Pends

Priory

St. Leonard's Coll.

FISHERGATE

CASTLE STREET

NORTH STREET

MARKET STREET

ABBEY STREET

ABBEY WALL

Abbey Wall

GREENSIDE PLACE

ABBEY WALK

GREYFRIARS GDN.

HOPE STREET

ABBOTSFORD CR.

MONRO PL.

CITY ROAD

KINBURN PARK

DOUBLE DYKES

STATION

Kinburn Park

BELL ST.

P.O.

SOUTH STREET

Town Ch.

Town Hall

Hol. Trin.

St. Mary's Coll.

Coll. Gdns.

Bute Medical Bldgs.

QUEEN'S GDNS.

QUEEN'S TERR.

Madras Coll.

West Port

Blackfriars Monastery

ARGYLE STREET

BRIDGE ST.

Maggie Murray's Bridge

Cockshough Park

KINNESSBURN RD.

Cupar

Largo, Kirkcaldy

Crail

A   B   C

1   2   3   4

1216

College St., opposite St. Salvator's, leads from North St. to Market St., by which we may return towards the station. A St. Andrew's Cross in the ground marks the site of the old Market Cross, at which Paul Craw was burned (1433) and Chastelard beheaded (1563).

Over 3 m. W., between the two roads to Ceres and Cupar, a cairn within a plantation on the left marks the spot on **Magus Muir** where, on the night of May 3rd, 1679, a party of Covenanters, headed by Balfour of Kinloch and Hackston of Rathillet, waylaid Archbp. Sharp, dragged him from his coach, and butchered him in the arms of his daughter who vainly strove to protect him. Five prisoners taken at Bothwell Bridge (p. 127) were executed and hung in chains.—About 2 m. from St. Andrews on the S. road the fine public *Craigtoun Park* (44 acres) occupies the estate of Mount Melville, once the home of G. J. Whyte-Melville (1821–78), the sporting novelist.

The coast for some miles S.E. of St. Andrews (huge caravan park) is bold and has numerous caves, and the strata visible at low water are much bent and contorted.—About 1¾ m. from the East Sands are *Kinkell Ness* and *Castle*, close to which is the Spindle Rock, a curious example of marine denudation.

From St. Andrews to *Leuchars* (Dundee, Cupar), see Rte. 35.

37. FROM PERTH TO DUNDEE

A. Direct

ROAD (A 85), 22 m. MOTOR-BUS every ½ hr. in 1 hr.
RAILWAY, 21 m. in 30–35 min. viâ (10½ m.) *Errol* and (17½ m.) *Invergowrie*.

Perth, see Rte. 27. After crossing the Tay on Victoria Bridge the road skirts a lovely reach of the river beneath (l.) the precipitous Kinnoull Hill.—From (3¾ m.) *Kinfauns* the ruins of Elcho Castle are visible across the Tay. We traverse the CARSE OF GOWRIE, a level tract between the Sidlaw Hills and the Tay, that has long been noted for its fertility and is especially famous for strawberries. Pennant quotes a proverb to the effect that the inhabitants " want water in summer, fire in winter, and the grace of God all the year round."—6 m. *Glencarse* (Hotel, RB. 21/, P. 7 gs.).

B 958 (r.) passes *Pitfour Castle*, a Gothic-revival house with additions by Wm. Burn (1826), and goes on to Dundee viâ (4 m.) *Errol* (Central, RB. 15/, P. 6 gs.), whence the Earls of Erroll take their title.

13 m. *Inchture* (Hotel, RB. 14/6, P. 5 gs.). Above the village are the extensive grounds of *Rossie Priory* (Lord Kinnaird ; no adm.) and (2 m. W.) *Kinnaird Castle* (12th and 15th cent., restored in 1855).—As we approach (15½ m.) *Longforgan* the stately *Castle Huntly* appears on a lofty rock on the right. The great tower was built on the foundations of an older one by Lord Gray of Foulis, Master of the Household to James II (1452), and additions were made by the 1st Earl of Strathmore (c. 1680), in whose time it was called Castle Lyon.—17½ m. *Invergowrie*, the landing-place of the missionary St. Boniface c. 715 and a favourite residence of Alexander I, preserves two fine though fragmentary 8th cent.

sculptured stones, built into the ruin of the 15th cent. church.—22 m. **Dundee,** see below.

B. Viâ Newburgh

ROAD, 30½ m. A 90 to (6 m.) *Baiglie Inn* (Aberargie).—A 913. 8½ m. *Abernethy.*—12 m. *Newburgh.*—18 m. *Parbroath* cross-roads.—A 914. 27 m. *Wormit.*—29 m. *Newport* (ferry to **Dundee**).—MOTOR-BUS from Perth to *Newburgh* (35 min.) and thence to *Newport* (55 min.) with rail connection at *Wormit* for *Dundee* (70 min.).

To (6 m.) *Baiglie Inn*, see Rte. 34.—8½ m. **Abernethy,** once a Pictish capital and the seat of a Culdee community replaced by Austin Canons in 1272, is now a large village, and the only monument of its early history is its celebrated ROUND TOWER, one of three in Scotland (comp. pp. 286, 422). This isolated tower is 74 ft. high and tapers from 48 ft. to 32 ft. in circumference. At its foot is an incised stone with 'ritual' patterns. The somewhat Norman-looking upper windows and the even masonry, resembling that of St. Rule's Tower at St. Andrews, deserve notice. Ian Hannah ascribes the lower part to the 9th cent., the upper to the 11th or 12th. About 6 ft. from the ground hang the jougs.—We now approach the Tay, beyond which are the Sidlaw Hills.—12 m. **Newburgh** (2360 inhab.; *North British, Commercial,* RB. 17/6), with a small harbour on the Tay, is a prettily situated royal burgh, with a town steeple of 1808 and linoleum factories.

About ¾ m. E. are the scanty remains of **Lindores Abbey,** which was founded in 1191 by David, Earl of Huntingdon (the 'Sir Kenneth' of Scott's 'Talisman'), on his return from Palestine, and became a place of great note before its secularisation in 1600. The unhappy Duke of Rothesay was buried here in 1402, and miracles were wrought at his tomb until his death began to be avenged by James I. John Knox records his visit to Lindores and the burning of the mass-books of the black priests. The remains of the abbey are scattered over a wide area, but the groined arch of the main entrance and a portion of the W. tower are the only important features standing.

Macduff's Cross, on the hill 1½ m. above Newburgh station, is a huge pedestal within a circle of stones, commanding a *View of the Tay.

An alternative by-road from Newburgh to Balmerino (9¾ m.; see below) skirts the S. shore of the firth, passing (2¾ m.) the romantically-placed ruin of *Ballanbreich Castle.*

At 14 m. we leave Lindores Loch (¾ m. long) on the right. The ruined 14th cent. church of *Abdie,* ¼ m. from the N.W. angle of the loch, preserves some interesting monuments.—At (18 m.) *Parbroath* cross-roads we bear left on A 914; A 913 goes on to Cupar, 3½ m. S.E.—21½ m. *Rathillet,* the home of the Covenanter David Hackston (executed 1680), one of the murderers of Archbp. Sharp.—At (23 m.) *Kilmany* Thomas Chalmers was minister in 1803–15.—25½ m. *St. Fort.*

The first road on the left leads to (3½ m.) **Balmerino Abbey** (pron. Bamérnie), founded c. 1227 by Alexander II and his mother Ermengard (buried here in 1234) for a Cistercian colony from Melrose and dedicated to St. Edward. Only the beautiful cloistral entrance to the chapter house and the roofless sacristy remain and the ruins (N.T.) are temporarily closed to visitors. The sixth and last Lord Balmerino was beheaded as a Jacobite in 1746. The charming quadrangle of cottages in the abbey lane was erected by the Earl of Dundee as a memorial to his brother killed in France in 1944.

At (27 m.) *Wormit*, where we reach the shore of the Firth of Tay, begins the **Tay Bridge**. This structure, built in 1883–88, crosses the river in a graceful curve. It is 2 m. long and has 73 pairs of piers, and the double line of rails is 92 ft. above the water. It stands about 20 yards W. of the site of its predecessor (1871–78), the central spans of which were blown over by a gale on Dec. 28th, 1879, while a train was crossing, carrying (it is said) 90 passengers, every one of whom perished. —29 m. *Newport*, and thence by ferry to **Dundee**, see Rte. 35.

C. Dundee and its Environs

DUNDEE (177,350 inhab.), the third city in Scotland for population and shipping and second only to Glasgow for manufactures, stands, in the county of Angus, on the N. shore of the Firth of Tay, here 2 m. wide. It is a busy commercial city, with few antiquities, but well illustrating the modern spirit of progress that reveals itself in handsome public buildings and useful institutions presented by wealthy citizens and in 'improvements' of all kinds. Its staple industry is the manufacture of jute, but engineering, shipbuilding, and the manufacture of preserves (' Dundee marmalade ') are likewise important.

Railway Stations. West (Pl. 13; Rfmts.), for trains to Glasgow, Stirling and Perth.—*Tay Bridge* (Pl. 13; Rfmts.), for trains to Fife and Edinburgh, to Aberdeen viâ Montrose to Arbroath, etc.

Hotels. Royal British (c; 9), 4 Castle St., RB. 25/, P. 13 gs. ; **Queen's** (a; 12), 160 Nethergate, RB. 25/, P. 11 gs. ; **Royal** (b; 13), 5 Union St., RB. 24/, P. 13 gs. ; **Mathers** (d; 13, 14), Whitehall Place, RB. 21/, P. 10½ gs., unlic.

Restaurants. At the hotels. Luncheon rooms : *Nicoll & Smibert*, 2 Nethergate ; *Keiller*, 64 High St. ; *Wilson*, Union St., all closed Sun.

Post Office (Pl. 8), Meadowside.

Motor-Buses, starting from the Dock Gates, traverse the chief streets and serve *Broughty Ferry, Monifieth*, etc.—Country Buses from the Bus Station (N. Lindsay St.) to almost every neighbouring town and village ; and to *Glasgow* (3½ hrs.) and *Edinburgh* (3½ hrs.) viâ *Perth* (¾ hr.) and *Stirling* (2¼ hrs.) ; to *Aberdeen* (2¾ hrs.) ; etc.

Ferry Steamer from Craig Harbour (Pl. 14) to *Newport* every ½ hr. (every hr. on Sun.), 9d., ret. 1/2, motor car from 5/, ret. 7/6.—Occasional excursion steamers in summer to Arbroath, the Bell Rock, etc.

Amusements. *King's Theatre*, Cowgate ; *Palace*, Nethergate (variety) ; *Kinnaird*, Bank St. ; *Repertory*, Nicoll St., off Ward Rd. (Pl. 8) ; *Scala*, Nethergate.—Concerts in the *Caird Hall*.—Tennis, bowls, etc., in the public parks.—Golf in Caird Park.

History. Dundee, the name of which has only a punning connection with its motto ' Dei Donum,' seems to have been made a royal burgh by William the Lion about 1190, and speedily rose to be one of the chief towns in the realm. William Wallace was a pupil at the grammar school but, having fatally avenged an insult with his dagger, was outlawed and so began his revolt against the English.

In the wars with England, Dundee was repeatedly taken and retaken and suffered accordingly. It was the first town in Scotland to adhere whole-heartedly to the Reformed religion, and George Wishart (1513–46) was its prophet (comp. below). In 1547 the forces of Henry VIII held the town for a week and plundered and burned it ; in 1645 it was stormed by the Marquess of Montrose ; and in 1651 it was captured and treated with the utmost severity by General Monk. Though Graham of Claverhouse is the ' Bonnie Dundee ' of Scott, the phrase probably originally referred to the town. Claverhouse was born at *Old Claverhouse Castle* (N.E. of the city), the site of which is marked by a dovecot ; and became hereditary constable of Dundee in 1683, but he was Viscount Dundee for less than a year before his death at Killiecrankie. The Old Pretender spent a night in Dundee in 1716 and the Jacobites held it from Sept. 1745 till after the battle of Culloden. In 1889 Dundee was created a city, and since 1892 its provost has been a lord provost.—Among famous natives of Dundee are Hector Boece (1465 ?– 1536), the historian ; Sir George Mackenzie (1636–91), known as ' Bluidy Mackenzie ' (p. 58) ; and Admiral Lord Duncan (1731–1804).

The centre of Dundee is the CITY SQUARE, an expansion of High St. (Pl. 9). Presenting an effective N. façade of ten Doric columns to the square rises the **Caird Hall** (Pl. 14), a magnificent edifice covering two acres, built in 1914–23, chiefly with a bequest from Sir James Caird (d. 1916), as a new City Hall and Council Chambers. *St. Paul's Episcopal Cathedral* (by Gilbert Scott), to the E., occupies the site of the old Castle of Dundee. Monk while in Dundee occupied a house at the W. end of High St., which was also the birthplace of Anne Scott, Duchess of Monmouth (1651–1732).—In Cowgate, 600 yds. E., beyond *St. Andrew's*, a typical work of Samuel Bell (1774), is the *East Port* or *Wishart Arch* (Pl. 10), from the parapet of which, during the plague of 1544, George Wishart is said to have preached to the plague-stricken without and to the sound within. The present arch, however, is not older than c. 1591.

At the back of the Caird Hall, below which are the City Arcade and Market, Dock St. (Pl. 14–10) connects the railway stations and affords access to the *Docks* (35½ acres), at the entrance to which is the *Royal Arch*, a singular rather than beautiful memorial of Queen Victoria's visit in 1844. The ferry to Newport starts from the little *Craig Harbour*, W. of the docks.

To the W. of the City Square are the **City Churches** (Pl. 8), a large cruciform pile, comprising three parish churches under one roof and dominated by the ***Old Steeple** (156 ft. high). This noble 15th cent. tower is the boast of Dundee, and, with St. Mary's (E. end), is the only part of the building normally open to visitors.

The chapel founded on this site c. 1195 by David, Earl of Huntingdon, in fulfilment of a vow made during a storm at sea, was destroyed by the English in 1296 and 1385, but it was rebuilt before 1480. Although the nave was battered down by an English fleet in 1547, the pile was gradually extended until by 1788 it included the four churches of St. Mary, St. Paul, St. Clement, and St. John. After almost complete destruction by fire in 1841 the churches were rebuilt or restored, but the congregation of St. John's was accommodated elsewhere.—In 1651, when Monk assaulted Dundee, the garrison in the Old Steeple held out against him until burning straw was heaped at the base.

At the S.W. corner of the church enclosure is the *Mercat Cross*, only the octagonal shaft of which is original (1586). From behind the churches Overgate leads W. to the squalid but picturesque Hawkhill.

DUNDEE

Mains Castle, Forfar   Arbroath↑   ↑ **Broughty Ferry**

FIRTH OF TAY

Ferry to Newport

DENS ROAD
COTTON RD.
WILLIAM ST.
WELLINGTON ST.
NELSON ST.
FOREBANK RD.
ANN STREET
DENS BRAE
PRINCES ST.
CONSTABLE ST.
BLACKSCROFT
VICTORIA DOCK
EAST STA.

HILLTOWN

VICTORIA ROAD
KING ST.
COWGATE
East Port
ALLAN ST.
RING PL.
TRADES LANE
SEAGATE
H.M.TR.
KING WILLIAM DOCK
TIDAL HARBOUR

DALLFIELD WALK
ROSE ST.
WELLGATE
MURRAYGATE
PANMURE ST.
ALBERT INST.
COMMERCIAL ST.
CASTLE ST.
HIGH ST.
REFORM ST.
Camp.
Hall
Arch
EARL GREY DOCK
W. DOCK
CAMPERDOWN HARBOUR

Tech. Coll.
BELL ST.
MID ST.
DUDHOPE ST.
The Howff
Meadow
Lby.
BANK ST.
WHITE HALL ST.
UNION ST.
S. UNION ST.

CONSTITUTION ROAD
BARRACK RD.
ROSEBANK RD.
R. Infirm.
Bleach Green
Castle Mill
Peter Mill

WARD ROAD
W. BELL ST.
LINDSAY ST.
OVERGATE
YEAMAN SHORE
NETHERGATE
TAY BR. STA.
WEST STA.

Courts
DUDHOPE CRES. RD.
N. TAY ST.
WEST PORT
S. TAY ST.
RIVERSIDE DRIVE

LOCHEE ROAD
DOUGLAS ST.
BLINSHALL ST.
BROWN ST.
GUTHRIE ST.
HAWKHILL
PARK PLACE
University
PARK WYND
SWALES
College
AIRLIE PL.
Esplanade Sta.

BROOK ST.
Larch ST.
BLACKNESS ROAD
KINCARDINE ST.
ASHFIELD ST.
URE STREET
HAWKHILL
WATT ST.
MILLERS WYND
MID WYND
FREE
NPT. PL.
WESTFIELD PL.
SEAFIELD RD.
PERTH ROAD
THOMSON ST.

Perth ↓

Scale 1:17,000
Miles
200 Métres
100

Balgay Hill Park

1816

Farther W. in Nethergate is **Queen's College,** formed in 1954 by the union of *University College* (Pl. 7) with the *Dundee School of Economics* and the *Medical* and *Dental Schools.* It now has more than 900 students.

University College was endowed by John Boyd Baxter and Miss Baxter of Balgavies, and opened in 1833 in some old houses on this site. It was incorporated with the University of St. Andrews in 1890–95 and again, after a brief separation, in 1897. An extensive building programme is in hand (1958) and the area between Nethergate and Hawkhill extending W. from Park Place to Park Wynd is intended as a university precinct.

Commercial St. and Reform St. lead N. from High St. to the **Albert Institute** (Pl. 9 ; 1867, enlarged 1887), which contains the *Public Library* (open 10–7.30, Thurs. 10–1) and the *Central Museum* and *Art Gallery*, both of considerable interest (open free weekdays ; 11–7.30, Thurs. 11–1). Outstanding in the museum is the oldest known astrolabe (1555) ; in the gallery is Allan Ramsay's portrait of Edward Harvey. In front is a statue of Burns, by Steel. In Euclid Crescent, to the N.W., is the *High School.*—Meadowside, leading W. from the Albert Institute, passes the *Post Office* (Pl. 8) and the **Howff** (Pl. 8), for three centuries (until 1878) the chief burying-ground of the city. The ancient cemetery, full of quaint old tombstones, was originally the orchard of a Franciscan monastery founded by Devorguilla Balliol and was given to the town by Mary, Queen of Scots, in 1564. In Ward Rd. just W. of the Howff, is the *Museum of Local Industry and Shipping*.

The steep Constitution Road (Pl. 3), known as ' Mount Zion' from the number of churches in it, runs N. to **Dundee Law** (571 ft. ; view), crowned by the Dundee War Memorial. About halfway up Constitution Road, Barrack Road diverges on the left for *Dudhope Park* (Pl. 2), surrounding **Dudhope Castle**, built in the late 16th cent. on 15th cent. foundations.

Dudhope Castle was the seat of the Scrimgeours, whom Wallace appointed hereditary constables of Dundee in the 13th century. After passing through several hands both castle and office were acquired in 1683 by Claverhouse, who held them until he set out for Killiecrankie in 1689. In its day the castle has been a wooden mill, infantry barracks, and a technical school ; it is now threatened with demolition.

Among the other fine parks of Dundee are *Baxter Park*, in the N.E. ; *Balgay Park*, in the N.W. with the *Mills Observatory* (adm., weekday afternoons, 2*d.* ; also 5–7 Mon.–Fri. in summer, Mon., Wed., Fri. in winter, 3*d.*) ; and *Caird Park*, in the N., in which are a golf course and the ruined *Mains of Fintry* castle (1582), an ancestral seat of the Grahams.

From Dundee to Alyth (A 927), 17 m. (motor-bus in 55 min.). Quitting Dundee by Lochee Road and the suburb of (2 m.) *Lochee*, we skirt the public grounds of *Camperdown House* (daily 9–5), built after 1824 for the 1st Earl of Camperdown, son of Adm. Lord Duncan (p. 283). About 2 m. W., beyond Liff village, is *Fowlis Easter*, which has a very interesting church of 1453 (restored), with ' jougs ' beside the S.W. door. Within are preserved the door of the original rood screen, four pre-Reformation paintings on oak (quaintly representing the Crucifixion ; the Virgin, St. John the Baptist, and St. Catherine, with an Entombment below ; and eleven saints), a sculptured font, badly mutilated, and a tabernacle adorned with a charming Annunciation. Our road bears right at (5¼ m.) *Muirhead* and ascends, passing 2 m. S.W. of *Auchterhouse Hill* (1400 ft.), with the Sidlaw Sanatorium which commands a fine view N. and S. This, and *Craigowl* (1493 ft.), farther E., are the highest summits of the SIDLAW HILLS, which extend from Perth almost to Arbroath. We traverse the ridge by the *Glack of Newtyle*, a narrow pass overlooked (r.) by the 16th cent. ruins of *Hatton Castle*. 11 m. *Newtyle*.—At (12 m.) *Alyth Junction* (Belmont Arms) we cross the main railway from Perth to Aberdeen and enter Perthshire.—13 m. **Meigle** (*Kinloch Arms*, RB. 17/6, P. 7 gs. ; *Meigle*, RB. 15/, P. 140/). Collected in a small *Museum* (adm. 6*d.* ; 10–4 or 7, closed Sun.) are 21 sculptured *Stones of the Celtic Christian period, found in or near the old church-yard. *Belmont Castle* (½ m. S.), now an ' eventide home ' belonging to the Church of Scotland, was for many years the seat of Sir H. Campbell-Bannerman (1836–1908), who is buried in Meigle churchyard.—We cross the Isla.—23¼ m. **Alyth** (300 ft. ; *Lands of Loyal*, to the N., with grounds, RB. 18/6, P. 8½ gs. ; *Commercial*, RB. 17/6, P. 7½ gs.), a small town (2070 inhab.), lies at the base of the Braes of Angus with the Alyth Burn traversing its main street. In the old upper town is an arcade of the 13th cent. church, with 18th cent. tombs of the Ramsays of Bamff.

FROM ALYTH TO AIRLIE CASTLE, THE SLUG OF AUCHRANNIE, AND THE REEKIE LINN, a pleasant round of c. 15 m. by road.—Going E. from Alyth we pass (2 m., l.) *Barry Hill*, crowned by an Iron Age camp, and cross (4 m.) the Isla. We ascend beside the river to (4¾ m.) *Mains of Airlie*. Thence the castle is approached by a footpath leading into the main avenue. **Airlie Castle**, a historic Ogilvy residence, is commandingly situated above the junction of the Melgam and the Isla ; but save the E. wall, with its portcullis entry, little remains of the ' Bonnie House o' Airlie,' which was plundered and burnt in 1640 by the ' Great Argyll and a' his men,' the royalist Earl of Airlie having left Scotland to avoid signing the Covenant. The injury was avenged by Montrose when he destroyed Castle Campbell (p. 212).—We may cross the Melgam below the castle and follow the left bank of the Isla for c. 2 m. by a path which allows views of the extraordinary sandstone gorge cut by the river. At the *Slug of Auchrannie*, where the path ends, there is a waterfall 60 ft. high. Pedestrians may retrace their steps for c. 1 m. and take the first road on the left, which leads to the Lintrathen road, but motorists must return to the Mains of Airlie and take a road to the left ¾ m. farther on for (8 m.) the *Loch of Lintrathen*, a sheet of water enlarged to supply water to Dundee (motor-bus from Kirriemuir). Hence we follow the road running W. to (10½ m.) *Bridge of Craig*, whence a path leads for 100 yds. down the right bank of the Isla to the *Reekie Linn*, a fine fall named from its ' reek ' or smoke-like spray. Bridge of Craig is 4¾ m. from Alyth by road, or 3¼ m. by a cart road which leads due S. over the *Hill of Alyth* (966 ft. ; view).

FROM ALYTH TO GLEN ISLA, 22 m., B 954, 951 ; motor-bus to Folda in 1¾ hr. From (4¾ m.) *Bridge of Craig* the road runs N., at first at some distance from the Isla, to (10½ m.) *Kirkton of Glenisla* (Glenisla, RB. 15/, P. 6 gs.) in an open vale with wide views.—At (12 m.) *Brewlands Bridge* B 951 crosses the Isla and ascends the right bank to (14½ m.) *Forter Castle*, burnt and ruined at the same time as Airlie (1640). Another road ascends the left bank viâ (14 m.) *Folda* (Inverharity Inn), crossing the river above Forter.—B 951 turns W. for Glen Shee (2½ m.), while a rough road goes on up the Isla to (19½ m.) *Tulchan Lodge* and is continued by a track past (21½ m.) *Bessie's Cairn* to (22 m.) the grand *Canlochan Glen* (l.) on the E. slope of *Glas Maol* (3502 ft.), where the Isla rises in a precipitous corrie noted for rare plants. A right-of-way, keeping to the left of Bessie's Cairn and Monega Hill (2917 ft.), crosses the ridge (c. 3200 ft.) to the right of Glas Maol and descends to the Cairnwell Road at the head of Glen Clunie (p. 230) ; or we may find our way from the head of *Canness Glen* (r. at the cairn) to the path at the head of Glen Doll (p. 286).

FROM DUNDEE TO FORFAR (14 m.) AND TO KIRRIEMUIR (17 m.) ; motor-bus to Forfar in ¾ hr. ; to Kirriemuir viâ Glamis or Forfar in c. 1 hr. The roads, crossing the Sidlaw Hills, separate beyond (5 m.) *Tealing*, where there are a 16th cent. dovecot and a well-preserved earth-house (l.). A 928 leads l. for Glamis and Kirriemuir ; A 929 bears r. for Forfar, passing near (11 m. ; r.) *Fothringham Hill* (761 ft.), the site of the battle of *Nectansmere* (685), in which Ecgfrith of Northumbria was slain by the Picts.—For Forfar and Kirriemuir, see Rte. 39.

38. FROM DUNDEE TO ABERDEEN VIÂ MONTROSE

DIRECT ROAD, 65 m. (A 92). We quit Dundee by Princes St. (Pl. 10).—11 m. *Muirdrum* (for *Carnoustie*, 2 m. r.).—17 m. *Arbroath*.—29 m. *Montrose*.—41 m. *Inverbervie*.—51 m. *Stonehaven*.—65 m. **Aberdeen** (Rte. 39), entered by Welling ton Rd. (Pl. 21).—MOTOR-BUS hourly in 3½ hrs.

RAILWAY, 71¼ m. from *Tay Bridge Station* in 1¾–2 hrs. Principal Stations : 4 m. *Broughty Ferry*.—10¾ m. *Carnoustie*.— 17 m. **Arbroath**.—30¾ m. **Montrose**.— 41½ m. *Laurencekirk*.—55¼ m. *Stonehaven*.—71¼ m. **Aberdeen**. The railway keeps close to the road, except between Montrose and Stonehaven, when it runs inland viâ Laurencekirk.

The main road keeps inland as far as Arbroath. More varied, if slower, is the coast road which runs past factories and shipyards to (4 m.) **Broughty Ferry** (*Taypark*, RB. 21/, P. 9½ gs. ; *Woodlands*, RB. 21/, P. 11 gs. ; *Ballinard*, RB. 19/6, P. 9 gs.), a pleasant seaside suburb of Dundee, with the residences of many Dundee merchants. The *Orchar Gallery*, in Beach Crescent (closed Thurs. aft. and Sun. morning), contains paintings by Scottish artists. The ancient ferry to Tayport in Fife is suspended.

On the point is *Broughty Castle* (15th cent. ; adm. free), occupied by the English in 1547 after their victory at Pinkie, and stormed in 1550 by French auxiliaries in Scots service.—The quaint *Claypots Castle* (c. ¾ m. N.W.) was built c. 1570 ; in defiance of dates it is said to have been the residence of a mistress of Cardinal Beaton (who died in 1546).—*Linlathen*, c. 2 m. N., was the residence of Thomas Erskine (1788–1870), the theologian ; while c. 6 m. N.E., on a turning off B 978 (the Dundee–Letham bus-route), is *Affleck Castle* (adm. 6*d.* ; open every weekday), a late-15th cent. tower-house with solar and oratory in a fine state of preservation.

Beyond (6¼ m.) *Monifieth* (3420 inhab. ; Panmure, RB. 25/6, P. 12 gs. ; Royal, RB. 19/6, P. 11½–12 gs.), where a Culdee community survived until the 13th cent., we skirt the *Barry Links* (r.), on which lies Buddon Camp, with rifle and artillery ranges. On *Buddon Ness* are high and low lighthouses, at the mouth of the Tay, which is obstructed by sandbanks except for a narrow channel.—11 m. **Carnoustie**

(5200 inhab. ; *Bruce*, RB. 35/, P. 15 gs. ; *Glencoe*, RB. 25/6, P. 10 gs. ; *Station*, RB. 19/6, P. 180/ ; *Aboukir*, *Morven*, unlic., P. 8 gs. ; *Kinloch Arms*, RB. 15/6, P. 7 gs.) is a seaside resort with fine sands and a famous golf course.—Turning inland we rejoin the main road at (13 m.) *Muirdrum*.

About 1½ m. N.W. on the Forfar road stood *Panmure House*, built after 1661 and demolished in 1955. The gates, which survive, have not been opened since the 4th Earl of Panmure fled to France in 1715. The original 13th cent. castle, destroyed by Monk, stood about a mile away. The pillar on the hill to the W. commemorates the 1st Lord Panmure of Brechin (d. 1852).

18 m. **ARBROATH** (*Seaforth*, RB. 21/6, P. 11 gs.; *Windmill*, with garden, RB. 22/6, P. 9 gs. ; *Royal*, RB. 18/6, P. 8½ gs. ; *North Sea*, RB. 18/6, P. 9½ gs. ; *Imperial*, similar charges), noted for its fine Abbey Church and as the 'Fairport' of Scott's 'Antiquary,' is an industrial town and seaside resort (19,500 inhab.) overlooking a small harbour. Its main industries are engineering and the manufacture of jute and sailcloth. Its unabbreviated name was *Aberbrothock*, from its position at the mouth of the Brothock Water. It was made a royal burgh by James VI in 1599.

The seashore promenade E. of the town leads to the low grassy cliffs, while to the W. is a large and well-equipped sea-water *Bathing Pool*. Beyond are the sandy West Links, with a miniature railway, and the golf course.

The ***Abbey Church** (adm. 1/, 10–4 or 7, Sun. from 2), at the top of the long High Street, is a beautiful ruin of red sandstone, E.E. in style but showing, like many other buildings of the period in Scotland, many traces of the Romanesque. When Dr. Johnson visited Scotland in 1773 he wrote, " I should scarcely have regretted my journey had it afforded nothing more than the sight of Aberbrothock."

History. The Cluniac priory, dedicated to St. Thomas Becket, was founded in 1178 by William the Lion, and completed in 1233 after two fires during the construction. It was colonised by Tironensian monks from Kelso and became an abbey in 1285. In 1320 an assembly of the Estates of Scotland in the abbey spiritedly asserted their country's independence of the English Crown and sent a letter to Pope John XXII, acknowledging Robert Bruce as their king. The abbey was burned in 1216 and in 1232, but its ultimate ruin was due to neglect after the Reformation. In the 18th cent. the town council had an evil habit of selling the materials of the ruin without accounting for the proceeds. The most famous abbots were Bernard de Linton, the probable author of the declaration of independence ; the three Beatons (Cardinal David, and two Archbishops James, uncle and nephew of the cardinal) ; and Gavin Douglas, Bp. of Dunkeld.

Above the fine semicircular *W. Doorway*, with its deep E.E. mouldings, is an arcade of six pointed arches, but of the fine rose-window only the lower arc remains. Much of the N.W. tower and part of the S.W. survives ; the S. wall and S. transept remain and there are some pier-bases ; but the N. wall has vanished entirely. At the E. end were three rows of deeply embayed lancets emphasising the length of the church ; of these only the lowest now survives. The *S. Transept*, with arcades and triforium intact, has a fine round window called the ' O ' of Arbroath, formerly lighted with a beacon to act as a sea-mark. Next to this transept is a vaulted structure with remarkable acoustics, probably the *Sacristy*, surrounded within by sedilia. The adjoining stone closet was most likely a strong-room.

To the W. and S. stood the domestic buildings, the chief relic of which is the massive *Gatehouse Tower* flanking the *Abbey Pend*, an arch above which was the chamber where the declaration of independence was signed in 1320 (see above). The *Abbot's House*, to the S., has a fine vaulted kitchen, while the hall above retains some original 13th cent. tiles. It has been restored and fitted up as a Museum. Among the monuments preserved in it is a headless effigy with the feet resting on a lion, which is supposed, on this slight foundation, to represent William the Lion, who was buried before the high altar. One of the rooms is called Bruce's bedroom. Adjoining is the *Guest House*, with a reconstructed vault.

Hospitalfield (½ m. W.), the ' Monkbarns ' of ' The Antiquary,' was once a hospice for pilgrims to the Abbey. The old house was fantastically enlarged by Patrick Allan, the painter (d. 1890).

About 1½ m. N., on a curious mound, is the over-restored church of *St. Vigeans* of 11th cent. foundation, but now of late-Gothic appearance, with a 19th cent. apse. Six Celtic sculptured stones are preserved in the church and two others have been used in the repair of the fabric. The inscription on the ' Drosten Stone ' is in Roman lettering but in the ancient Pictish language. *Colliston House*, 2½ m. farther on, was built in 1583, perhaps by Archbp. Beaton.

The bold red sandstone cliffs on the coast N. of Arbroath present some fine scenery. The cliff path running N.E. leads to (2 m.) the *Pint Stoup*, an isolated stack. We may go on hence by a rough path along the cliffs to (3½ m.) *Auchmithie*, the ' Mussel Crag ' of ' The Antiquary,' picturesquely placed high above its small harbour. Boats may be hired to visit the caves to the south. About 3½ m. N. of Auchmithie (road for 2 m.) is the grand *Red Head*, the scene of the escape of Sir Arthur and Miss Wardour in ' The Antiquary.' Farther on opens the wide sandy sweep of *Lunan Bay* (Lunan House, RB. 25/, P. 10 gs.), overlooked by the ruin of *Red Castle*.

To the S.E. of Arbroath, c. 11 m. out to sea, is the **Inchcape** or **Bell Rock**, with a lighthouse built in 1807–11 by Robert Stevenson, grandfather of R. L. Stevenson. The rock, covered by the sea at high tide, is said to take its name from a warning bell placed on it by an abbot of Aberbrothock. The legend of the removal of the bell by Sir Ralph the Rover and his subsequent shipwreck on the rock is romantically told by Southey.

Arbroath is connected by main roads with Forfar (15 m. ; A 932) and Brechin (14 m. ; A 933), the two roads diverging at (6 m.) *Friockheim* (pron. ' Freecum '). About 1 m. N.W. of Arbroath B 9127 diverges left for (2¾ m.) *Arbirlot*, in the pleasant glen of the Elliot, with the old tower of *Kelly Castle*, the ancient seat of the Auchterlonies, and for (6½ m.) *Carmyllie*, where there are extensive flagstone quarries and where the reaping machine was invented by Patrick Bell (1826).

MOTOR-BUSES run to *Forfar* viâ Carmyllie in 55 min. ; to *Montrose* (½ hr.) going on to Aberdeen ; to *Carnoustie* (28 min.) and *Dundee* (65 min.).

24 m. *Inverkeilor* (Chance Inn, RB. 18/6), with the 17th cent. Northesk pew-front in its church, is 2½ m. N.W. of Red Head and 2 m. S.W. of Lunan Bay (see above). We reach the S. Esk at *Ferryden* and cross it on a good 19th cent. bridge whose central piers rest on the island of *Inchbrayock*, or *Rossie*, where there is an old churchyard with monuments.

To the W. is *Montrose Basin*, a broad tidal lagoon about 2 m. square. An effort made to drain it in 1670, with the aid of Dutch workmen, was foiled by a violent storm. *Craig House*, on its S. shore, is a little 15th cent. tower with a house of 1639.

31 m. **MONTROSE** (*Central, Park*, at both RB. 21/6, P. 10 gs. ; *Star*, RB. 21/, P. 8 gs. ; *George*, RB. 21/6, P. 9 gs. ; *Corner House*, RB. 18/6, P. 9 gs. ; *Links House*, unlic., P. 9 gs.), an old but well-built royal burgh (10,750 inhab.) with quarries and brickworks and a fishing harbour, is adjoined by several excellent golf courses and is often crowded with visitors in summer.

History. Montrose is of great antiquity and possessed a strong castle which was occupied by Edward I in 1296 and destroyed by Wallace the year after. Here Balliol submitted to Edward I personally, after his formal abdication at Brechin. In 1330 Sir James Douglas, according to Froissart, embarked here with the heart of Bruce on his way to the Holy Land. John Erskine of Dun in 1534 established here the first school in Scotland for teaching the Greek language, which played an important part in the spread of Protestantism in Scotland. The first Greek teacher was the Frenchman Pierre de Marsiliers, and among his pupils were George Wishart and Andrew Melville. The rebellion of 1715 ended at Montrose with the secret embarkation of the Old Pretender and the Earl of Mar (Feb. 4th, 1716). James Graham (1612–50), the great Marquess of Montrose, was born at *Old Montrose*, on the S.W. side of the Basin ; Andrew Melville (1545–1622) at Baldovie, S. of the Basin ; and Joseph Hume (1777–1855), the Radical M.P., in the town.

In the wide High St. are statues of Hume and of Sir Robert Peel ; the *Old Church* (1791) has a graceful spire of 1834, by Gillespie Graham ; near it is the *Town Hall* (1763). The *Medicine Well*, N. of the town, was frequented as a spa in the 18th cent. To the E. are pleasant gardens, with the Links beyond, and finally the sandy beach (bus from High St.) and bathing station.

MOTOR-BUSES to *Forfar* (1 hr.) viâ Friockheim ; to *Fettercairn* (¾ hr.) viâ Laurencekirk or (1 hr.) viâ Brechin and Edzell ; to Johnshaven and *Inverbervie* (¾ hr.) ; etc.—On the Brechin road is (3¾ m.) *Dun House* (now a private hotel, RB. 21/, P. 9½ gs.), the birthplace of John Erskine (1509–91 ; see above), rebuilt by Wm. Adam (c. 1730) with a 14th cent. gateway.

The Aberdeen road follows the coast. At (34¼ m.) *North Water Bridge* the N. Esk is crossed below the Pounage Pool, where John o' Arnha' encountered the kelpie, as related in the ballad by George Beattie (1786–1823), who lies in the churchyard of (36 m.) *St. Cyrus* (Hotel, RB. 16/6). By the sea is the *Kaim of Mathers*, a refuge built by a Barclay (1421) to escape the vengeance of James I for having slain Sir John Melville, Sheriff of the Mearns.—About 1 m. beyond (37¼ m.) the *Bush Hotel* we cross the romantic *Den Finella*, with its waterfall.—Between the fishing villages of (39½ m.) *Johnshaven* (Anchor, RB. 16/6) and (42½ m.) *Gourdon* (Commercial, RB. 17/6), both lying below the road, the coast becomes rocky.—44 m. **Inverbervie** or *Bervie* (885 inhab. ; *Castle*, RB. 15/6 ; *Anchorage*, unlic., RB. 15/, both plain) was made a

royal burgh in 1342, the year after David II landed here from
his seven-year exile in France. Here was born John Coutts
(1699–1751), father of Thomas Coutts, the London banker.

Hallgreen Castle, ½ m. S., was probably the birthplace of Dr. Arbuthnot
(1667–1735), the friend of Pope.—A pleasant walk ascends the Bervie to (1¼ m.)
the charming little *Allardice Castle*. *Arbuthnott* church, 1½ m. farther, dates partly
from 1242 and has a two-storied 16th cent. chapel attached. *Arbuthnott House*
(1588 and 1754), succeeding an old tower, has been in the hands of the Arbuthnott
family since at least 1206. The fine 17th cent. plaster ceilings may be viewed on
written application to Lord Arbuthnott.

We cross the Bervie and, leaving on the right the road to
Kinneff church (2 m.), where the Scottish regalia lay hidden,
pass above (52½ m.) Dunnottar (comp. p. 288).—54 m.
Stonehaven and thence to (69 m.) **Aberdeen,** see Rte. 39.

39. FROM PERTH TO ABERDEEN VIÂ FORFAR

Road, 82 m. A 94. 13 m. *Coupar Angus.*—18 m. *Meigle.*—24 m. *Glamis.*—
30 m. **Forfar.**—43 m. *Brechin.*—54 m. *Laurencekirk.*—68 m. *Stonehaven.* A 92.
82 m. **Aberdeen** (Rte. 39).

Railway, 90 m. in 1¾–3½ hrs. Principal Stations : 15¾ m. *Coupar Angus.*—
20½ m. *Alyth Junc.* (for *Alyth*, 5½ m.).—32½ m. **Forfar** (for Kirriemuir, 6 m.;
Brechin, 15 m.).—48 m. *Bridge of Dun* (for **Montrose**, 5½ m.).—60 m. *Laurencekirk.*—73¾ m. **Stonehaven.**

Crossing Perth Bridge we turn left, but after ¼ m. bear right
on Strathmore St. for (2 m.) *New Scone* and (5½ m.) *Balbeggie*
(Macdonald Arms, RB. 13/6). To the right we enjoy a fine
view of the Sidlaw Hills, including *Dunsinane* (1012 ft.) at
the S.W. end, crowned with the remains of an ancient fort,
identified with 'Macbeth's Castle.'—13 m. **Coupar Angus**
(2175 inhab. ; *Royal, Moorfield*, RB. 15/6–17/6) is so called,
though in Perthshire, in order to distinguish it from Cupar
Fife. In the churchyard are vestiges of a once wealthy abbey,
founded for Cistercians in 1164 by Malcolm IV.

From Coupar Angus a road (frequent motor-buses) runs N.W. to (4¾ m.) *Blairgowrie*, crossing the Isla and passing *Stormont Loch.*
The Dundee road (A 923 ; motor-bus in ¾ hr.) runs S.E., viâ (2 m.) *Pitcur*,
where there is a remarkable earth-house (key at Hallyburton House).—3⅓ m.
Lundie, to the left, has a Norman window and chancel arch (at present concealed)
in its church. Adm. Lord Duncan (1731–1804), victor at Camperdown in 1797,
lies in the graveyard. Farther on we pass c. 1 m. N. of Fowlis Easter.—14 m.
Dundee, see Rte. 37c.

At (18 m.) *Meigle* we cross the Dundee–Alyth road (Rte.
37c) and 3 m. farther on we enter Angus.

Angus or **Forfarshire** lies N. of the Firth of Tay, between Perthshire and the
North Sea. In the N. is the *Mounth*, the great S.E. spur of the Grampian system,
and the *Braes of Angus*, with their picturesque glens ; towards the S. are the
Sidlaw Hills ; and between lies the *Howe of Angus*, an extension of Strathmore
(p. 231). Apart from the great textile industries of Dundee, Arbroath, Forfar,
and Brechin, the county is mainly agricultural and offers good angling. The Old
Steeple of Dundee, Arbroath Abbey, and the cathedral and round tower at
Brechin are important monuments. Glamis Castle figures in 'Macbeth'; and
Kirriemuir is the 'Thrums' of Barrie. The Bell Rock belongs to the county.

At (24½ m.) *Eassie* the ruined church (l.) contains a sculptured stone like those at Meigle.—26¾ m. *Glamis* (pron. 'Glahms') village lies 1 m. S. of ***Glamis Castle** (Earl of Strathmore), one of the finest and most picturesque of the Scottish castles now inhabited (adm. 2/6, grounds only 1/; Wed. & Thurs. 2–6 in May–Sept.; Sun. also 2–6 in July–Sept.; teas).

The castle owes its present aspect (1675–1687), with its clusters of turrets, bartizans, and extinguisher roofs, to the 1st Earl of Strathmore, but portions of the high square tower with walls 15 ft. thick are much older.

Malcolm II died (some accounts say was murdered) in this neighbourhood in 1034, so, as Macbeth (d. 1057) was Thane of Glamis and was said to have murdered a king, Shakespeare's 'Macbeth' was not unnaturally but quite unhistorically located in the later feudal castle that was built here. At the burning of Lady Glamis (1537) for witchcraft and for conspiring to poison James V the castle was forfeited to the Crown, but when her innocence had been established it was restored to her son, whose descendant, Patrick Lyon, became earl of Strathmore in 1677. In 1715 the Old Pretender lodged here for some time and held his apology for a court. In 1930, Princess Margaret, grand-daughter of the 14th Earl of Strathmore, was born in the castle.

The house is entered by a low door surmounted by the Lyon arms; the adjacent royal arms allude to James V's residence here during the forfeiture. A winding stair in a cylindrical corner-tower leads to a low vaulted hall hung with armour and with the buff coat of Claverhouse. The drawing-room (once the hall) has a fine cradle-vaulted ceiling, a noble fireplace, and portraits, cabinets, and tapestry. Opening off the drawing-room is a panelled chapel, consecrated shortly before 1688. Glamis, says Sir Walter Scott, "contains a curious monument of feudal times, being a secret chamber, the entrance of which by the law or custom of the family must only be known to three persons at once, the earl, his heir-apparent, and any third person they may take into confidence." The battlements command a splendid view over Strathmore and to the Grampians. In the castle is preserved the 'lion-cup' of Glamis, from which Scott took his idea of the 'Blessed Bear of Bradwardine' in 'Waverley.'

In the village of *Glamis* is a sculptured stone, called King Malcolm's gravestone; 'jougs' hang near the churchyard gate. Some old cottages in Kirk Wynd, adapted as an *Angus Folk Museum* (adm. 1/, 1–6 daily except Sat.), contain domestic and farming implements, Patrick Bell's workbench (1828), a handloom in use in 1830–1949, etc. A 928 leads N. to (5 m.) *Kirriemuir* (motor-bus). *St. Orland's Stone*, a symbol stone, 1½ m. N.E. of the railway-crossing, has hunting and boating scenes.

30 m. **Forfar** (*Royal*, RB. 18/6, P. 7½ gs.; *County*, RB. 17/6), the capital (9980 inhab.) of Angus, lies near the E. end of the small *Forfar Loch*, on whose shores one of the last battles between the Scots and Picts was fought. Forfar is a royal burgh of David I, with jute mills. In the *Town Hall* are some good portraits and the Forfar 'bridle,' used as a gag for witches who were mercilessly persecuted here. An octagon turret, formerly the Town Cross (temp. Charles I), marks the site of the Castle, a royal residence, where a parliament in 1057 under Malcolm Canmore is said to have first conferred surnames and titles on the Scottish nobility. The murderers of Malcolm II are said to have perished while trying to escape across the ice on the loch.

About 1¼ m. E., by the Montrose road, are the ruins of *Restennet Priory* (adm. 6d.), supposed to have been founded in the 7th cent. by St. Boniface, and refounded by Malcolm IV c. 1153 for Augustinians from Jedburgh. The tower may be as early as the 9th cent., but has a 12th cent. upper storey and a 15th cent. spire. The rest of the church is 12th cent. work.

To the left of the road from Forfar to Friockheim and Arbroath (A 932), beyond the lochs of Rescobie and Balgavies (pron. Be-gus), is (5 m.) *Balgavies*, a newer house grafted on an old castle.—7 m. *Guthrie* has a square castle-tower of 1468.

The direct hill-road (rising to 517 ft.) to (9½ m.) Brechin passes (4¼ m.) *Aberlemno* (Inn) where two 8th cent. stones show reliefs of combats. A road on the right, 1½ m. farther on, leads to (¾ m.) the ruined *Melgund Castle*, said to have been built by Card. Beaton.—7 m. *Auldbar Castle*, on the right, was partly built by Sir T. Lyon (d. 1608), son-in-law of Regent Morton.—9½ m. *Brechin*, see below.

Kirriemuir (*Airlie Arms*, RB. 17/6, P. 8 gs. ; *Ogilvy Arms*, RB. 19/6, P. 8 gs. ; *Thrums*, temperance, RB. 12/6), 6 m. N.W. of Forfar, is a jute-manufacturing town (3570 inhab.) situated on the S. slopes of the Braes of Angus, and celebrated as ' Thrums ' in the novels of Sir James Barrie. It was one of the last towns in Scotland to abandon the hand-loom. The streets are narrow except the Square, with the quaint *Old Town Hall*, or High St., off which runs Bank St. where the *Auld Licht Kirk* was situated. On the *New Town Hall* is a Polish shield of thanks for hospitality in 1940–41. Sir James Barrie was born in 1860 at No. 9 Brechin Road (N.T. ; adm. on application) ; the white house at the top of the street, almost opposite, is the ' Auld Licht Manse ' ; and the ' Window in Thrums ' is still to be seen on the right at the top of the hill leading to Southmuir on the opposite side of the valley. In the pavilion behind the cemetery (in which Barrie is buried) is a camera obscura (open on Sat. and Sun. afternoons, June–Sept.). Sir Charles Lyell (1797–1875), the geologist, was born at *Kinnordy*, 1 m. N.W., while in *Caldhame Wood*, 1¼ m. N. of the town, is the northernmost known road of the Roman Empire.

The road to GLEN CLOVA (by which walkers may reach Braemar or Ballater) ascends the hill N. of Kirriemuir, affording fine views. After 3 m. we leave some distance to the right the well-preserved four-storied fortalice of *Inverquharity* (15th cent.), for 400 years a seat of the Ogilvies, and ½ m. farther on we cross the Prosen and skirt the grounds of *Cortachy Castle*, where the Earl of Airlie has a famous herd of polled Angus cattle (adm. by order). Beyond the park (4½ m.) a road leads E. to (½ m.) *Cortachy*, whose church has a good Perp. window, and along the foothills of the Braes of Angus to (14 m.) *Brechin* (p. 286).—From (5½ m.) *Dykehead* (Royal Jubilee Arms, RB. 18/6, P. 8 gs.) the road to the left leads up the well-wooded *Glen Prosen*, past a memorial fountain to Scott and Wilson, the Antarctic explorers, " who knew this glen." The Airlie Monument, on the hill opposite, commemorates the 8th Earl of Airlie (1856–1900), who fell in the S. African War. Our road ascends the South Esk and at (8½ m.) a bridge we have a choice of roads, one on either side of the river, which, however, reunite at (15½ m.) **Milton of Clova** (*Ogilvy Arms*), a lonely village overlooked by a single fragment of *Clova Castle*. This was the scene of the so-called ' Start,' an abortive attempt of Charles II to escape from his Presbyterian supporters at Perth (1650). Having made a rendezvous with his Highland partisans at Clova, he escaped so far, but, when they failed to put in an appearance, he was obliged to return to Perth.

A steep ascent of ¾ hr., at the back of the inn, leads by a faint path to (1½ m. ; 2090 ft.) *Loch Brandy*, a cliff-bound tarn. To the W. is the *Snub of Clova*, a sharp ridge marked by a curious fissure which is gradually widening and must eventually precipitate a huge mass of rock into the loch. In the line of hills opposite is a depression known as the *Sneck of Barns*, by which lies the shortest way to Glen Prosen (see above).—The road goes on up the glen to (18½ m.) *Braedownie* (985 ft.), amidst fine surroundings, with a youth-hostel near by. *Dreish* (3105 ft.) is prominent to the S. The track on the right, the Capel Mounth, ascending the main glen, leads to Ballater (p. 300). That on the left, the Tolmounth track or 'Jock's Road,' up *Glen Doll*, leads to *Glen Callater* and Braemar (p. 302).

The main road beyond Forfar crosses the S. Esk beyond (36 m.) *Finavon* (Red Lion, RB. 18/, P. 6 gs.). Finavon Castle (r.) is a keep (c. 1500) of the Earls of Crawford, added to in 1593. It collapsed in 1712.—38½ m. *Careston Castle* (l.) is mainly 15th cent.

43 m. **BRECHIN** (*Northern*, RB. 19/6, P. 9½ gs.), noted for its cathedral and round tower and as the birthplace of Dr. Thomas Guthrie (1803–73), is a linen and paper making royal burgh (7250 inhab.) on and above the S. Esk.

It was at Brechin that John Balliol, on July 10th, 1296, solemnly handed over the realm of Scotland to Bp. Bek of Durham, Edward I's representative. The so-called 'Battle of Brechin' was fought in 1452 on the hill S. of Stracathro (see below), when 'Earl Beardie,' the 'Tiger' Earl of Crawford, a partisan of the Douglases, was defeated by the loyal clansmen under Huntly.—Sir Robert Watson Watt, pioneer of radiolocation, is a native of Brechin.

The *Cathedral founded by David I in 1150, now the parish church, is the successor of an early Culdee abbey. It was barbarously treated in 1807, when the transepts were demolished, but was judiciously restored in 1900–02 when the choir, a graceful example of pure lancet work, left in ruins at the Reformation, was roofed and reglazed and the transepts rebuilt. The fine old W. window and portal remain, and the broad projecting tower (good view), surmounted by a low spire, was built by Bp. Patrick c. 1360. The nave piers date from two periods in the 13th cent.; in the N. aisle is a fine cross-head (c. 900) in the Northumbrian style; and some good 11–13th cent. tombstones are preserved in the church.

The **Round Tower,** assigned to the 10th or 11th cent., is 87 ft. high, 15 ft. in diameter at the base and 12½ ft. at the top, and is surmounted by a conical roof of the 14th century. It differs from Abernethy tower in being attached to the church and in being of irregular but solid masonry. On the W. side is a narrow doorway 6 ft. above the ground, with jambs inclining inwards, surrounded by a beaded moulding and surmounted by a crucifix carved in low relief. The two figures at the sides are Celtic ecclesiastics.

In the Vennel near the cathedral is a fragment of wall supposed to have formed part of the bishop's palace; and in Maisondieu Lane (l. of Market St.) is the façade of the chapel of the hospital founded in 1256.

Brechin Castle, separated from the cathedral by its moat, is the seat of the Earl of Dalhousie, head of the Maule family.

It was rebuilt in 1711, but during the invasion by Edward I (1303) was strong enough to stand a siege of three weeks, only surrendering after its governor, Sir Thomas Maule, had been killed.

The **Caterthuns** (5½ m. N.W.), two prehistoric forts, lie on either side of the road to Lethnot Church. After crossing the Cruick Water we climb to (5½ m.; 795 ft.) the ridge on which the forts are. The *White Caterthun* (l.; 976 ft.) is an oval fortification whose inner wall, having been overthrown by violence, has poured down the hillside in a cataract of stones and become confounded with a lower wall defended by a trench. The *Brown Caterthun* (r.; 943 ft.) is a series of concentric entrenchments, nearly circular. There is a splendid view of the Grampians to the N. and W., and over Strathmore, the Hill of Wirren (5 m. N.; 2220 ft.) being conspicuous.

Kinnaird Castle (Earl of Southesk), 2½ m. S.E. of Brechin, is the 19th cent. successor of the ancestral seat of the Carnegies. Permits to drive through the lovely 1300-acre deer-park, from the Estate Office, Kinnaird, Brechin.

The road (B 966) to Edzell runs N. viâ (4½ m.) *Stracathro*, in whose churchyard John Balliol met Bp. Bek (p. 286) in 1296 and abandoned the French alliance. Near by is the most northerly Roman fort so far discovered.—6½ m. **Edzell** (*Glenesk*, RB. 27/6, P. 12 gs.; *Central*, RB. 22/6, P. 9½ gs.) is a neat village with a golf course, near the attractive valley of the N. Esk. The *Castle (adm. 1/, 10–4 or 7, Sun. from 2), c. 1 m. W., has preserved more or less intact its oldest part, the square Stirling Tower, with the bower used by Mary, Queen of Scots, on her visits to Edzell. The lower round tower is much damaged, and the connecting range built by the Lindsays, formerly the state apartments, is a mere shell.

The keep overlooks a square enclosure, once the flower garden or 'viridarium' of Sir David Lindsay, whose arms and the date 1604 appear over a doorway in the N.E. corner. The walls are decorated with bas-reliefs of the virtues, sciences, planets, etc., and are indented with large square holes, which, from a distance, are seen to form, in combination with the mullets surmounting them, the Lindsay arms. In the angle is a turreted garden house of the same date.

FROM EDZELL TO LOCHLEE, 14½ m., by road up the leafy Glen Esk. The road running N. from Edzell crosses the N. Esk (1 m.) at the picturesque *Gannochy Bridge*, and skirts the grounds of *The Burn*, now a students' hostel, through which (by applying at the lodge) visitors may obtain leave to follow the river in its deep sandstone gorge. Beyond (11½ m.) *Tarfside* (House of Mark, unlic., RB. 15/), the road ends at (14½ m.) *Lochlee Church*. A cart-road running W. from the church passes the ruins of *Invermark Castle*, the old residence of the Stirlings, and, beyond (1 m.) a ruined church on a Culdee site, reaches the wild *Loch Lee* (1¼ m. long).—Mountain paths lead from Tarfside to (19 m.) Banchory or (13 m.) Aboyne, and from Lochlee church to (16½ m.) Aboyne viâ *Glen Mark*, in which is the Queen's Well, a favourite halt of Queen Victoria (comp. Rte. 41).

Beyond Brechin, A 94 passes S. of Stracathro (see above). —A cottage at (49 m.) *Logie Pert*, by the North Esk bridge, was the birthplace of James Mill (1773–1836). Beyond the river we are in Kincardineshire.

Kincardineshire, or **The Mearns,** is a small maritime county with a bold and rocky coast. The Grampians invade its E. part, and S. of these the *Howe of the Mearns* prolongs the Howe of Angus towards the coast. The name Mearns has been derived from Mernia, brother of Kenneth II and Mormaer of this region. The 'men o' the Mearns' are proverbially noted for strength and efficiency.

54 m. Laurencekirk (1485 inhab.; *Gardenston Arms*, RB. 15/, P. 6 gs.; *Royal*, RB. 14/) is the chief town of the fertile Howe of the Mearns, with linen mills. It was founded by Lord Gardenston in 1779, united with the old village of Conveth, and once famous for its manufacture of snuff-boxes. James Beattie (1735–1803), author of 'The Minstrel,' was born near the town.

Fettercairn (*Ramsay Arms*, RB. 18/6, P. 8 gs.), 4½ m. N.W., is a picturesque village with the shaft of the town cross of Kincardine (see below), bearing marks indicating the length of the Scots ell. Boswell's journals, and many letters in his hand and Johnson's were discovered in 1930–31 in Fettercairn House, the home of his executor, Sir Wm. Forbes. About ¾ m. S.W., on the road to (4½ m.) *Gannochy Bridge* (see above), is *Balbegno Castle* (1569 and 18th cent.), with mural paintings. A hill road running N. from Fettercairn to Deeside passes (2¼ m.) a road on the right leading to the ruins of *Kincardine Castle*, ¾ m. S., the sole vestige of the ancient county town and royal residence, from which Balliol wrote to Edward I offering to abdicate. Tradition identifies it as the stronghold into which, in 994, Kenneth II was enticed by Finella, wife of the Mormaer of the Mearns, and there slain. To the left is *Fasque*, the country home of the Gladstones after 1838, where W. E. Gladstone spent his honeymoon.—The Deeside road goes on to (4 m.) *Clattering Bridge*, where it bears to the left, leaving the Slack Burn and its deep corrie on the right. After a steep climb to (6½ m.; 1488 ft.) *Cairn o' Mounth* (fine view) it begins the more gradual descent into *Glen Dye*, commanding good views of Deeside.—10 m. *Bridge of Dye* (1681). About 2½ m. farther on the road forks, the left branch leading to (23 m.) *Aboyne*, the right branch to (18 m.) *Banchory*, see R. 41.

From Fettercairn B 966 leads N.E. to (6½ m.) *Auchenblae* (Inn), opposite which, in *Fordoun* churchyard on the steep bank of the Luther Water, is a fragment of 'the mother church of the Mearns' or St. Palladius's Chapel. St. Palladius, an Irish bishop (d. c. 430), whose relics are supposed to have been buried here by his disciple Ternan, was until recently commemorated by the annual Paldy Fair in July. Fordoun is the supposed birthplace of John of Fordoun, the 14th cent. Scottish historian. Here also is a stone with a Pictish inscription.—*Drumtochty Castle* (now a school), 2½ m. higher up the Luther Water, was used as a school by the Norwegian government in 1942–45.

From Auchenblae we may regain the main road (2½ m. S.E.), passing (l.) *Monboddo*, a seat of the Burnetts from 1671 to 1958. The house has been enlarged since Johnson and Boswell dined there and esteemed it "a wretched place." Their host was Lord Monboddo (1714–99), a judge noted for his eccentric views on the possession of tails by men.

57½ m. Fordoun road-end (Redhall, to the left, RB. 15/6)

68 m. STONEHAVEN (*Bay*, RB. 21/, P. 11 gs.; *Heugh*, RB. 22/6, P. 10 gs.; *Mill Inn*, RB. 19/6, P. 8 gs.; *St. Leonard's*, RB. 17/6, P. 11 gs.; *Crown, Royal*, RB. 17/6–18/6, P. 8 gs.; *Queen's, Station*, RB. 16/6, P. 7 gs.), the county town (4430 inhab.) of Kincardineshire since 1607, is a cheerful fishing port and bathing resort within easy reach of fine cliff scenery. The old High St., at the S. end of the town, passing a tower of 1790, leads to the attractive harbour and the early-17th cent. *Tolbooth*, formerly a storehouse of the Earls Marischal, while to the N. beyond the new town is a fine open-air swimming pool.

*Dunnottar Castle, near the Montrose road, 1½ m. S. (adm. 6*d*. 9.30–6, Sun. 2–6; bus in summer in 5 min.), stands on a rock by the sea separated from the mainland by a deep chasm. The great square tower and the chapel, the oldest surviving buildings, are said to have been built by Sir William Keith, great Marischal of Scotland, c. 1392, but an earlier castle was taken from the English

by Wallace in 1297. The gatehouse (c. 1575) was the strongest in Scotland.—
In 1645 the 7th Earl Marischal, a staunch Covenanter, withstood a siege from
the victorious Montrose, who in revenge wasted the country for miles round
and burned the town of Stonehaven. During the wars of the Commonwealth
the Scottish regalia were kept here, and when the castle was besieged in 1652,
Ogilvy, the governor, did not surrender until the regalia had been conveyed
away, according to one story, through the midst of the besiegers by Mrs. Grainger,
wife of the minister of Kinneff, who held the crown in her lap and carried the
sceptre disguised as a distaff. The English commander is said to have helped
her into the saddle himself, quite unconscious of the treasure she had about her.
Until the Restoration the regalia lay buried behind the pulpit of *Kinneff Church*
(6½ m. S.; monument to Mrs. Grainger). The 'Whigs' Vault,' a dungeon with a
window open to the sea, was the prison of 167 Covenanters in 1685, and it was the
headstone of their graves that ' Old Mortality ' was cleaning when Scott visited
him in the churchyard, over 1 m. inland, where the 16th cent. Marischal Aisle has
been rebuilt.

From Stonehaven to *Montrose* and *Dundee*, see Rte. 38 ; by the Slug Road
to *Banchory*, see p. 298.—B 979, leading N. to (10 m.) *Maryculter*, is the *Elsick
Mounth* road, the approach route of the Romans to Deeside.

72 m. **Muchalls** (*Marine*, RB. 19/6, P. 9½ gs.) has spectacular
red sandstone cliffs. The 17th cent. *Castle* of the Burnetts of
Leys (adm. 2/, Tues. & Sun. in summer 3–5.30) is ½ m. inland
(poor road).—Beyond Muchalls several short lanes on the
right lead down to villages, such as *Skateraw* (Newton Arms,
RB. 15/; Cammachmore, RB. 16/6, both on A 92) and
Portlethen, where a little inshore fishing is carried on. About
1 m. N. of Portlethen is *Findon* or *Finnan*, a remote village
which gave its name to smoked haddocks.—At 77½ m. A 92
bears left for the direct approach to (82 m.) **Aberdeen**.

By following A 956, which leads to the harbour quarter of Aberdeen, we may
turn right to visit *Cove*, a seaside village with a view of the bold rocky coast of
Nigg Bay.

40. ABERDEEN AND ITS ENVIRONS

ABERDEEN (182,725 inhab.), surnamed for obvious reasons
' the Granite City,' is a well-built, prosperous, and bustling
place, with a good harbour at the mouth of the Dee, exporting
chiefly granite, fish, and cattle. It is a university town, with
a cathedral ; and it is, moreover, a sea-bathing place, with a
sandy beach offering ample bathing facilities. Before the
incorporating act of 1891 the city embraced two parts : Old
Aberdeen, representing the primitive ecclesiastical settlement
towards the mouth of the Don (whence the original name of the
city : Abberdeon or Aberdon), which became a burgh of
barony in 1498 ; and the present town of Aberdeen, the centre
of business, representing the royal burgh that sprang up round
the royal castle and was rebuilt and extended after its destruction by Edward III. The Aberdonians enjoy (in all
senses) the reputation (freely supported by humorous anec-
dotes, largely of home manufacture) of carrying Scottish
thrift to its utmost limits.

Hotels. Caledonian (b ; 8, 9), 10 Union Terrace, RB. 30/; **Station,** (c ; 15), RB. 28/6, P. 10–11 gs. ; **Imperial** (e ; 9), Stirling St., RB. 22/6, P. 10–11 gs. ; **Marcliffe,** Queen's Terr. (Albyn Pl., beyond Pl. 13), RB. 27/6–30/, P. 12 gs. ; **George,** Bon Accord Terr. and Union St. (Pl. 14), RB. 25/, P. 12 gs. ; **Douglas** (d ; 10), Market St., RB. 24/6–27/6 ; **Royal,** Bath St., RB.22/6–27/6, P. 10–11 gs., **Waverley,** 22 Guild St., RB. 21/, these two near the station ; **Bridge,** 4 Bridge St. (Pl. 15), RB. 20/, P. 9½ gs. ; **Northern,** 1 Gt. Northern Rd. (beyond Pl. 3), RB. 24/.—Unlic. : **Great Western,** 253 Gt. Western Rd., RB. 19/6–25/ ; **Osborne,** Queen's Gdns., RB. 19/6 ; and many others.

Restaurants. *Royal Athenæum, Palace, Victoria,* all in Union Street.

Post Office (Pl. 15), Crown Street.

Motor-Buses. 1. Bridge of Dee–Union St.–King St.–Bridge of Don ; 3. Castle St.–Beach ; 4. Castle St.–Union St.–Queen's Road.–Hazlehead ; 17. Hilton – Union St. – Torry ; 20. Broad St.–Old Aberdeen–Tillydrone ; 21. Broomhill–Pittodrie (football ground) and King's Links ; and many other services. Short tours daily in summer from Castle St. (1/–4/).—**Country Buses** from the Wallace

Statue, Blackfriars St., or Schoolhill to the surrounding villages (*Cove, Skene, Echt, Dyce, Cluny, Newburgh, Banchory,* etc.); also to *Edinburgh* (7 hrs.) viâ *Perth* (4 hrs.) and *Stirling* (5 hrs.); *Glasgow* (6¾ hrs.) viâ Forfar or Dundee ; *Inverness* (5 hrs.) viâ Elgin (3¼ hrs.) ; *Braemar* (c. 2¾ hrs.) ; *Strathdon* (c. 2¼ hrs.) viâ Alford (70 min.) ; *Brechin* (2 hrs.) viâ Stonehaven ; *Peterhead* (1½ hr.) ; *Banff* (c. 2¾ hrs.) ; etc.

Amusements. THEATRES. *Her Majesty's* (Pl. 8), Rosemount Viaduct ; *Tivoli* (Pl. 15), 32 Guild St.—CINEMAS, *Regal* and others in Union St. ; *Palace,* Bridge Pl.—DANCING, *Beach Ballroom.* —SWIMMING. *Beach Bathing Station,* with all kinds of baths and a swimming pool.—GOLF. Municipal courses at the *King's Links* beside the Beach Promenade, at *Hazlehead,* and at *Balnagask,* near Girdle Ness ; visitors are admitted to the *Murcar Club,* 1 m. beyond the Bridge of Don.

Steamers from Matthews' Quay to *Orkney* and *Shetland* (Rte. 65).

Air Services from *Dyce Airport* (6 m. N.W. ; bus from B.E.A. Office, 337 Union St.) to *Orkney* and *Shetland* (Rte. 65) ; to *Glasgow* and to *Edinburgh,* with connections to Manchester, Birmingham, and London.

History. Aberdeen, which has had its share in most of the historic struggles in Scotland, is an ancient royal burgh with charters dating back to c. 1179. Edward I visited this " good town upon the sea " in 1296. Bruce sought refuge in it after the battle of Methven (1306), though the legend that the city motto, ' Bon Accord ' (good fellowship), was first used as a watchword in a successful insurrection on his behalf against the English garrison, is now discredited (comp. p. 293). In 1337 Edward III burned the town, which, however, was rebuilt on a larger scale. In 1411 the Aberdonians, headed by Robert Davidson, their alderman (' provost ' is a title of later introduction), fought under the Earl of Mar at the red Harlaw (p. 310) ; but there is no evidence for the common story that, because Davidson was slain, all succeeding provosts were forbidden to quit the city during their term of office. In the wars of the Covenant Aberdeen was three times occupied by Montrose, twice when he was a covenanting leader and once (1644) after he had become a royalist. On that last occasion the Aberdonians were routed at the battle of the Crabstone, the most disastrous engagement they ever took part in. For some years after 1651 the town was held by the forces of the Commonwealth. Aberdeen was only slightly Jacobite in its sympathies, though James VIII was proclaimed there by the rebel forces in 1715 and in 1745. It was at Aberdeen that Sir John Cope embarked for Dunbar, just before the battle of Prestonpans, and Cumberland spent six weeks there in 1746, on his way to Culloden.—Among eminent natives of Aberdeen are : John Barbour (1316 ?–1395), author of ' Brus ' ; George Jameson (1586–1644), the " Scottish Vandyke " ; James Gibb or Gibbs (1682–1754), Archd. Simpson (1790–1847), and Sir Ninian Comper (b. 1864), architects ; Alexander Cruden (1701–70), of the ' Concordance ' ; William Dyce (1806–64), John Phillip (1817–67), and Sir George Reid (1841–1913), artists ; and Sir Arthur Keith (1866–1955), anthropologist. Lord Byron (1788–1824) spent eight years of his boyhood at Aberdeen and attended the grammar school.

University. Aberdeen University includes *King's College* (p. 294), founded in 1494, now devoted to Arts (including Mathematics), Divinity, and Law, with

Botany, Geography, Chemistry, and Psychology; and *Marischal College* (p. 294), founded in 1593, with the other branches of Science. Since 1938 the School of Medicine has been in the New Infirmary, Foresterhill, to the E. In 1641 Charles I granted a charter incorporating the colleges as a ' Caroline ' University, but after the Restoration they were disunited, and their present union dates only from 1860. In electing their rectors the students vote, as in Glasgow, by ' Nations,' here Mar, Buchan, Moray, and Angus.

Market St. (Pl. 16), coming from the harbour, leads N. passing the large *Market Hall*, to Union Street (see below). Here we turn to the right (E.) for the broad open space known as CASTLE STREET (Pl. 10). In the middle stands the *City Cross, a remarkable Jacobean structure of 1686, with a floreated column crowned by a marble unicorn rising from a hexagonal base on which are panels decorated with medallion heads of Scottish sovereigns from James I to James VII and the arms of Scotland and Aberdeen. Behind the massive *Salvation Army Citadel*, at the E. end of the street, is Castle Hill (Pl. 5, 11 ; view), the site of the old castle, now occupied by tenements.—On the N. side of Castle St. is the **Town House** (1886), with which is incorporated the tower and spire of the old *Tolbooth* (14th cent.) In the vestibule is a suit of armour at one time believed to be Alderman Davidson's (see above), and in the charter room are royal charters, from the reign of William the Lion (c. 1179) downward, and the Burgh Records, complete, with the exception of a single volume, from 1398 to the present day (adm. free 10–4, Sat. 10–1).

Broad St., the narrow street skirting the W. side of the Municipal Buildings, leads to *Marischal College* and *Old Aberdeen* (see below). Byron when a boy lived with his mother at No. 64 (demolished).—Marischal St., running S. from Castle St. to the harbour, occupies the site of the house of the Earl Marischal, from whose windows Mary, Queen of Scots, was forced to witness the execution of Sir John Gordon after the battle of Corrichie (p. 298).—In Shiprow, connecting Castle St. with Market St., is *Provost Ross's House* (adm. free Mon. & Fri. 2.30–4.30), the oldest house in Aberdeen, built in 1593 perhaps by Andrew Jamesone. Shiprow is part of the old road up Deeside, which (under the names Green Hadden, Windmill Brae, Langstane Place, and Hardgate) runs roughly parallel with Union Street.

UNION STREET (Pl. 10, 9, 14), which leads S.W. from Castle St., is the fine main street of Aberdeen, begun in 1800, the year of the union of the parliaments of Great Britain and Ireland. At the corner of St. Nicholas St. is a bronze statue of Queen Victoria (1893), and a little farther on, in front of the Town's Churchyard, is a Grecian colonnade (1830) built by John Smith in imitation of Burton's Hyde Park Corner, then just completed. Within the churchyard stands the church of **St. Nicholas,** once the largest parish church in Scotland, but divided at the Reformation into the **East and West Churches** (Pl. 9). Before the rebuilding St. Nicholas, dedicated to the patron saint of the city, was a structure of the 13–15th centuries. The *West Church*, however, was rebuilt in 1752–55, on Gibbs' design—by no means his best work; the *East Church*, rebuilt in 1837, lost its ancient spire by fire in 1874 but has been restored with a new spire (1887); between these is the ancient *Transept* (adm. free; 10–5), a vestibule to both churches. Carillon concert on Wed. in July–Aug. at 8 p.m.

In the S. transept, or *Drum's Aisle*, are effigies of Forbes of Drum and his wife (15th cent.) and the only medieval brass in Scotland (an unfinished inscription to Sir A. de Irwyn; d. 1457); also a tablet to Robert Gordon, founder of the college, and the defaced expiatory tabernacle of Provost Leith. The N. transept, or *Collison's Aisle*, an interesting little example of transitional work (1200–1520), contains the alleged effigy of Alderman Davidson (p. 290) and a tablet to the wife (d. 1568) of Canon Heriot, the first Protestant minister of Aberdeen.—In the *West Church*, with good contemporary woodwork, are shown four large *Embroidered Panels (Finding of Moses; Return of Jephthah; Esther; Susanna and the Elders) attributed to a daughter of George Jamesone. On the S. side are effigies of Menzies of Maryculter, a leader of the Aberdonians at Harlaw, and of his wife.

Below the E. church is the original *Crypt*, or **St. Mary's Chapel**, an interesting little structure vaulted in stone (restored), founded c. 1420 (shown on application to the church officer; entr. in Schoolhill). It contains fragments of Gothic stalls (16th cent.) and some fine panels and seats, dated 1613–1706. In the 17th cent. the chapel was used as a prison for witches, in the 18th cent. as a plumber's shop, and in the early 19th cent. as a soup-kitchen.

The massive *New Market*, on the left, is by Simpson (1842); while the *Trades Hall* or *Trinity Hall* (adm. free), a little farther on, contains some curiously carved chairs and portraits attributed to Jamesone.—*Union Bridge* (Pl. 9), widened since its erection in 1803 by Thomas Fletcher with some assistance from Telford, carries Union St. across the Denburn valley, through which the railway runs. On the right, at the corner of Union Terrace, stands a granite statue of Edward VII, by Alfred Drury, and a little farther on is the classical *Music Hall* (1820), used for concerts and meetings. Behind it, in Golden Sq., is a granite statue of the 5th Duke of Gordon (1770–1836), Scott's "Cock o' the North, my Huntly braw." The tall spire in Huntly St. is that of *St. Mary's Cathedral* (R.C.; 1860). In Crown St., diverging on the left, is the *Post Office* (Pl. 14), nearly opposite which is Crown Terrace, with *St. John's Church* (Episcopal) containing an early-16th cent. font from Kinkell, showing the Five Wounds of Christ.—Union St. ends on the W., at the Church of Scotland *Christ's College* (1851), a Tudor edifice entered from Alford Place (adm. free; 10–4, Sat. 10–1).

Albyn Place (bus No. 4), with its distinguished 19th cent. granite mansions, continues the line of Union St. W. to Queen's Cross, whence Queen's Road goes on to *Rubislaw Granite Quarries* (visitors usually admitted on application). Farther on is *Hazlehead*, a public park of 800 acres with golf courses, a maze, and a restaurant. To the S., in Countesswells Rd., is the *Macaulay Institute for Soil Research*.—From Queen's Cross we may return eastwards to the city (fine views) viâ Carden Terrace and Skene St., passing the *Grammar School* (Pl. 7; 1863), a foundation dating at least from 1418. In front stands a statue of Byron, but the old grammar school at which Byron was a pupil in 1795–98 stood in the Schoolhill.

Union Terrace (Pl. 8, 9), a row of fine buildings overlooking the attractive public gardens in the Denburn Valley, beside the railway, leads N. from the statue of Edward VII to

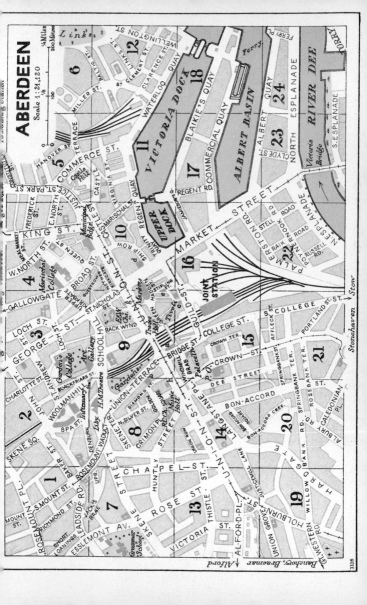

ABERDEEN

Scale 1:24,120

¼ Miles

⅛

200 Metres

Rosemount Viaduct. In Union Terrace is a statue of Burns, by Bain-Smith, and in the open space at the N. end are a poor seated figure of Prince Albert, by Marochetti, and a much more imposing *Statue of Wallace* (by W. G. Stevenson) in defiant mood. *Her Majesty's Theatre*, opposite, is separated by a church from the *Public Library*, while behind are the fine buildings of the *Old Infirmary*.

The infirmary stands in the Woolmanhill, the site of the ancient wool-market, which was also the scene of public revels managed by an official called the ' Abbot of Bon-Accord ' ; whence, states Mr. G. M. Fraser, late Librarian of Aberdeen, arises the motto which has figured on the town's coat-of-arms since 1430.

At the corner of Schoolhill and Blackfriars St. rises the city *War Memorial* (1925), a columned pavilion with a dome, immediately adjoining and incorporated with the **Art Gallery and Museum** (Pl. 3, 9 ; adm. free 10–5, Sat. 10–9, Sun. 2–5), a fine building of 1885. On the ground floor of the Art Gallery are a beautiful Hall of Memory and the Cowdray Hall (a lecture-room), besides an excellent collection of casts and a small museum of applied art. In the basement is a Regional Museum, illustrating many aspects of the life of Aberdeen and N.E. Scotland. The picture gallery on the upper floor has several fine portraits by *Raeburn*, a good conversation piece by *Zoffany*, and examples of *Romney, Alex. Nasmyth* and *David Cox*. It includes the unique *Macdonald Collection of ninety-two uniform portraits of contemporary British artists, nearly all painted by themselves, works by Scottish artists (*Sir G. Reid, Pryde, MacEvoy*), portraits by *Aug. John* (Lloyd George), *Orpen* (Lord Bryce), and *Toulouse-Lautrec* (Conder), and works by *Monet, Harpignies, Boudin, Forain, Vlaminck, Conder, Ginner, Meninsky, Connard*, and other recent painters.——The building to the E., beyond the archway leading to Gordon's College (in front of which is a statue of Gen. Gordon), is the *School of Art*, on the site of the former Grammar School. *Robert Gordon's College* (Pl. 3), an interesting old institution, founded in 1739 as a ' hospital ' for the board and education of the sons of burgesses, now includes a flourishing technical college, a secondary school, and the school of art.

The founder, Robert Gordon (1665–1732), was the grandson of Robert Gordon of Straloch (1580–1661), the geographer and first graduate of Marischal College.

From Schoolhill the old Upper Kirkgate (Pl. 3) leads E. to Broad St., passing the end of the narrow Guestrow (Pl. 3–10), anciently Ghaist Row (ghost row), as overlooking the churchyard of St. Nicholas. In Guestrow is *Provost Skene's House* (adm. free weekdays 10–1, 2.15–5), the turreted mansion occupied by the Duke of Cumberland in 1746. Built c. 1545, t was altered by Skene in 1669–85, and preserves some 16th ent. mural paintings and plaster ceilings. It contains a collection illustrating old Scottish town life. James Beattie, the poet (see below) and professor of Moral Philosophy at Marischal College, died in 1803 in Crown Court, on the N. side of Upper Kirkgate, and Samuel Rutherford lived in this street during his banishment to Aberdeen in 1638.

Conspicuous in Broad St. rises the magnificent grey granite façade of ***Marischal College** (Pl. 4), the buildings of which enclose a quadrangle. The wing next the street, in the Perp. Gothic style with its numerous pinnacles, was designed by Marshall Mackenzie and opened in 1906. In the quadrangle, entered by a fine archway, are the older buildings of 1836–44, with the graceful **Mitchell Tower* (233 ft.), named after the donor. The graduation *Hall*, 116 ft. long, has a magnificent E. window illustrating the history of the college. On application to the sacrist (to the left on entering) visitors are shown the hall and portrait gallery (3*d*.) or may ascend the tower (3*d*.); (adm. daily in July–Sept. and on all Sat. 11–12 and 2.30–3.30 ; other months 11–12 only).

Marischal College is an integral part of Aberdeen University and was originally founded by George Keith, Earl Marischal, in 1593 in the old buildings of the Greyfriars monastery (1469), which, partly rebuilt, remained in use until c. 1844. The Greyfriars church was pulled down in 1903.

From Marischal College Broad St. (bus 20) is continued by Gallowgate (Pl. 3), Mounthooly, the Spital, and High St., to (c. 1 m.) **Old Aberdeen,** the quiet academic quarter near the Don, with its detached houses and pleasant gardens.

Old Aberdeen may be reached also from Castle St. by the tramway running viâ King St. to the Brig o' Don (see below). In King St. (Pl. 4) is *St. Andrew's Episcopal Cathedral* (1817) which contains a statue of Bp. Skinner (d. 1816), by Flaxman. The interior was successfully altered by Comper, who added the double-aisled chancel (1941–42). Bp. Samuel Seabury (p. 50) was consecrated in Aberdeen in 1784.

In the High St. of Old Aberdeen is **King's College** (open 10–1, 2–5 ; adm. 3*d*.), founded by Bp. Elphinstone in 1495 as the College of St. Mary of the Nativity, but taking its present name from James IV.

Of the old buildings the chief relic is the *Chapel* (1500–05), with a fine lantern tower, the crown of which was rebuilt after a storm in 1633. The *Round Tower*, in the old quadrangle, is a defensive work of 1525 ; while E. of the chapel is the *Cromwell Tower* (1658), originally a hall of residence, to the cost of which Gen. Monk and some of Cromwell's officers in Scotland contributed. The other buildings range from 1825 (W. front) to 1957. On the lawn in front of the chapel is the over-elaborate cenotaph of Elphinstone (by H. Wilson ; 1931).

The ***Chapel** has seven windows with glass by D. Strachan, including a good round-headed Flamboyant W. window. The antechapel, arranged to form a University War Memorial, is separated from the chapel proper by the former rood-screen. Beyond is a double row of canopied stalls, some with misericords. The carving throughout is elaborate and delicate and the tracery differs in every panel. On Bp. Stewart's pulpit (1540 ; brought from the cathedral and much restored) are heads of Scottish kings from James I to James VII ; opposite is Bp. Forbes's chair (1627).

In the pavement are the tomb of Bp. Elphinstone and a slab commemorating Hector Boece (d. 1536), the historian and first principal ; both are of Tournai marble. Against the E. wall is an altar-table re-used as the tomb of Peter Udny (sub-principal ; d. 1601).—To the E. of the church is an ancient cross-slab from Balgownie ; and on Cromwell's Tower are memorials to Prof. Scougal (d. 1678) and to Alex. Forsyth of Belhelvie (d. 1843), inventor of the percussion lock.— The *Library* contains some fine old MSS. and missals, including the Salisbury Missal, bequeathed by Bp. Gilbert Burnet.—In the *Senatus Room* are interesting portraits and historical paintings.

The curious ' oriental ' gateway, almost opposite King's College, once the avenue-gate of Powis House, admits to an enclosure with professors' houses. About ½ m. N., viâ the Chanonry, the canons' quarter or cathedral precinct, rises the prettily situated *Cathedral of St. Machar, the only ancient granite cathedral in Britain (10 till dusk ; Sun. 2.30–4.30 ; services at 11 & 6).

The see was founded before 1157, but the earliest extant work (of Bp. Kininmunde ; 1356–62), which is of sandstone, finely carved, includes only two of the external piers at the crossing, a portion of the transepts, and a window in the E. bay of the S. nave aisle. A central tower, completed c. 1512, fell in 1688, owing, it is said, to the removal of stones from the choir by Cromwell's soldiers to build their fort on the Castle Hill of Aberdeen more than 30 years before. The sandstone steeples on the two W. towers were added by Bp. Gavin Dunbar (d. 1532), but otherwise the cathedral as it stands is mainly the work of Bp. Lichtoun (1424–40). The W. front contains an original seven-light window and a round-arched doorway. The nave has seven bays with pointed arches resting on round piers and a good regular clerestory, the choir was perhaps never completed, and the transepts exist only in ruins.

INTERIOR. About 1530 Bp. Dunbar added the flat ceiling of panelled oak (restored) with its 48 shields, glittering with the blazonries of Pope Leo X, the Emperor Charles V, St. Margaret, the kings and princes of Christendom, and the bishops and nobles of Scotland. Near the E. end of the S. aisle is an effigy of Canon Dodds (14th cent.), and in the N.W. corner are those of Bp. Lichtoun (reconstructed), Canon Idil (d. 1468 ; remarkable robes), and another canon. The font, with St. Machar baptizing in the Don, is by D. Strachan ; the E. window is by Wm. Wilson (1953). Off the W. gallery opens the small Charter Room, with interesting documents and seals.

In the ruined S. transept is the handsome canopied tomb of Bp. Dunbar ; in the N. transept is the mutilated recess of Lichtoun's tomb.

Don St. prolongs the Chanonry E. of the cathedral, past *Seaton Park* (l.), to (¾ m.) *Balgownie* (with some 17th cent. houses) and the *Auld Brig o' Don*, or **Bridge of Balgownie,** a pointed arch, 62 ft. wide, spanning a deep pool of the river and backed by fine woods. Built by Bp. Cheyne at the

M

beginning of the 14th cent., it became somehow connected with a curious superstition :

> " Brig o' Balgownie, wight's your wa' ;
> Wi' a wife's ae son an' a mear's ae foal
> Doun ye shall fa'."

Lord Byron alludes to it in ' Don Juan ' and adds in a note, " I still remember, though I may misquote, the awful proverb which made me pause to cross it, yet lean over with a childish delight, being an only son."

In 1605 Sir Alexander Hay endowed the bridge with a small property, which has so increased in value that it built the *New Bridge of Don* (1830) a little lower down at a cost of £26,000, bore most of the cost of the Victoria Bridge, and contributed to many other public works.

Market St. (Pl. 16, 23), leading S., is the direct approach to the extensive **Harbour** which was constructed by Smeaton, Telford, and others with great difficulty owing to the shifting nature of the soil. The S. or *Albert Basin* (Pl. 17, 18) represents part of the old channel of the Dee, diverted in 1872. Hundreds of tons of fish are exported from Aberdeen every day, and an early morning visit (c. 8 a.m.) to the *Fish Market* beside this basin reveals a most interesting scene of activity and bustle, while the fish is being landed and sold by auction. The fishermen's quarter is at *Footdee*, at the N. entrance to the harbour ; while northward extends the sandy beach (2 m. long), with 18-hole golf links and many popular attractions.

Victoria Bridge (Pl. 23), at the S. end of Market St., crosses the Dee to the residential and fishing suburb of **Torry** (Pl. 24). To the E. are a breakwater at the mouth of the harbour and *Girdle Ness* (fine sea-view), with a lighthouse and the small Walker Park. Greyhope Rd. leads W., past the *Torry (Marine Food) Research Station*, to the ruined church of *St. Fittack*, i.e. St. Fiacre, the original parish church of *Nigg*. The present church, 2½ m. S.W. on the main road, dates from 1829, with 17–18th cent. portions.

A fine esplanade skirts the N. bank of the Dee above the Victoria Bridge, passing under the *Wellington Suspension Bridge* and a railway bridge, just above which is *Duthie Park* (45 acres). Beyond the park is the *George VI Bridge* (1939) ; and about ½ m. farther on we reach the **Bridge of Dee,** built in 1520–27 by Bishop Gavin Dunbar, a remarkable structure of seven ribbed arches, decorated with inscriptions and coats-of-arms. When the bridge was widened in 1841–42 the W. face was carefully replaced so as to preserve the medieval appearance. In 1639 the passage of the bridge was won by Montrose, at that time a Covenanter, after a struggle of two days.

The bridge is reached direct by motor-bus viâ Holburn St. and the suburb of Ruthrieston, where a rebuilt pack-horse bridge crosses the Ruthrieston Burn.

FROM ABERDEEN TO TARLAND (Ballater, Aboyne), 31 m., motor-bus in 1 hr. 25 min. Leaving Aberdeen by Alford Place, we run W. on A 944, diverging left at 6 m. on A 974.—About 1 m. N.W. of (13 m.) *Echt* (Cowdray Arms, RB. 17/6, P. 7 gs.) is the *Barmekin of Echt*, an isolated conical hill, having on it five concentric circles of prehistoric fortification, two of which are still of some height. Close by are several cairns, and on the farm of Sunhoney (r.) between Echt and

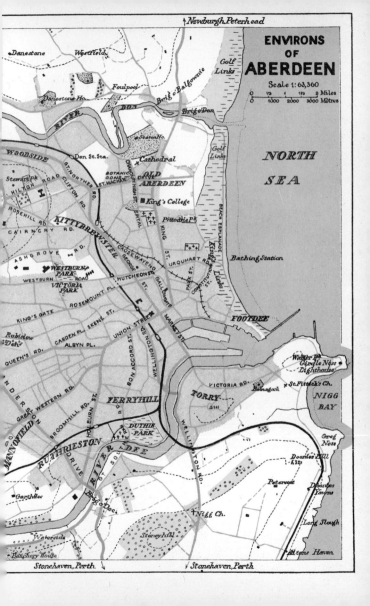

ENVIRONS
OF
ABERDEEN

Scale 1 : 63,360

0   ½   1   1½   2 Miles
0   1000   2000   3000 Mètres

NORTH

SEA

↑ Newburgh, Peterhead

Danestone   Westfield

Foulpool

Danestone Ho.   Brig o'Balgownie

RIVER   DON

Brig o'Don

Golf
Links

Seaton Ho.

WOODSIDE

Don St. Sta.

Cathedral

Golf
Links

Stewart Pk.   BOTANIC GDNS.   OLD
HILTON ROAD   ST. MACHAR   ABERDEEN

ROSEHILL RD.   CLIFTON RD.   GT. NORTHERN RD.   HIGH ST.   CRYPT

King's College

CAIRNCRY RD.   KITTYBREWSTER   HOSPITAL

Pittodrie Pk.

ASHGROVE RD.   KING ST.

WESTBURN   CAUSEWAYEND   GEORGE ST.   GALLOWGATE   URQUHART RD.   King's   Links   BEACH ESPLANADE

WESTBURN   ROAD   MUTCHEON ST.   PARK ST.   CONSTITUTION ST.

PARK

VICTORIA
PARK

ROSEMOUNT PL.   Bathing Station

KING'S GATE

Rubislaw   CARDEN PL.   SKENE ST.   UNION STREET   MARKET ST.   FOOTDEE

"Den"   ALBYN PL.   BON ACCORD ST.   WELLINGTON RD.

QUEEN'S RD.   GREAT WESTERN RD.   WELLINGTON ST.   Walker Pk.   Girdle Ness   Lighthouse

VICTORIA RD.   Balnagask   St. Fittick's Ch.

FERRYHILL   TORRY   NIGG

MANNOFIELD   BROOMHILL RD.   HOLBURN ST.   DUTHIE   △ 141   BAY

RUTHRIESTON   DRIVE   PARK   WELLINGTON RD.   Greg
Ness

RIVER   DEE   Doonies Hill
△ 159

GarthDee   Brig o'Dee   Peteroon   Doonies
Towns

Waterside   Nigg Ch.   Long Slough

Balgichay House   Stoneyhill   Altens Haven

← Stonehaven, Perth   ↓ Stonehaven, Perth →

Midmar, is a fine stone circle.—14½ m. *Midmar*, with a picturesque turreted castle on the left.—At (25 m.) *Camphill* we cross the road from Alford to Aboyne (A 980). About 1½ m. N. is **Craigievar Castle** (Lord Sempill ; adm. on written application to Mrs. Forbes-Anderson, the Mains, Craigievar), a seven-storied baronial hold of the latest type (1610–24), with turrets and high-pitched roofs. The fine hall has a magnificent Renaissance ceiling with pendants and retains its screens and a huge fireplace. Over the fireplace are a coat-of-arms and the inscription ' Doe not vaiken sleiping dogs.'

Lumphanan (Macbeth Arms, RB. 14/6, P. 6 gs.), 2½ m. S. of the cross-roads, has a station on the Ballater railway, and is served by direct motor-bus from Aberdeen (24½ m.) viâ (17 m.) *Raemoir* (see Banchory) and (21½ m.) *Torphins* (Learney Arms, RB. 21/, P. 8 gs. ; Bridge House, unlic., RB. 16/6, P. £7), a summer resort noted for its bracing air. *Macbeth's Cairn*, ½ m. N.W. of Lumphanan, is supposed to mark the place where Macbeth, fleeing from Dunsinane, was killed by Macduff, after making his last stand at the *Peel Bog* (¾ m. S.W., close to the line), a circular moated earthwork c. 120 ft. in diameter and 18 ft. high (really much later than Macbeth).

The Tarland road passes (26¼ m.) *Corse House* and the ruins of *Corse Castle* (1581), which belonged c. 1600 to Patrick Forbes, of Aberdeen. He is said to have been visited by the devil, who, being worsted in an argument, flew out in a rage, carrying with him the whole front of the house. After (27½ m.) *Tillylodge* a fine view opens on the left, and farther on, on the same side, is the well-preserved earth-house of *Culsh*. Beyond (31 m.) *Tarland* (Aberdeen Arms, RB. 17/6, P. 7 gs.) the road forks, the right branch (A 974) leading to (42 m.) *Cambus o' May.* The left branch (sharp turn) passes the remains of *Coull Castle* (33½ m.), on a rocky eminence near *Coull Church.* It belonged to the Durwards, a family of note in the time of Alexander II, and it is said that the church bell tolls of its own accord whenever one of the name dies.—*Aboyne* is 3¼ m. farther on.

From Aberdeen to *Alford* and *Strathdon*, see Rte. 42 ; to *Ballater* and *Braemar*, see Rte. 41 ; to *Dundee* (Edinburgh), see Rte. 38 ; to *Inverness*, see Rte. 43 ; to *Macduff* and *Banff*, see Rte. 44 ; to *Perth*, see Rte. 39 ; to *Peterhead* and *Fraserburgh*, see Rte. 45.

41. FROM ABERDEEN TO BALLATER AND BRAEMAR

Road, 58 m. A 93. We quit Aberdeen viâ Great Western Road (Pl. 19).—18 m. *Banchory.*—30½ m. *Aboyne.*—41¼ m. *Ballater.*—48¼ m. *Crathie.*—50 m. *Balmoral.*—58 m. **Braemar.**—Motor-Buses to *Braemar*, four times daily in 2¾–3 hrs. (6/2, ret. 11/2).—For the passing visitor to Deeside, however, it is better to go by road all the way by one of the numerous Motor Coaches that ply from Aberdeen in the season, with short halts at Banchory, Aboyne, Ballater, and Crathie.

Railway to Ballater, 43¼ m. in 1½–1¾ hr., 3–4 times daily. Principal Stations : 7½ m. *Culter.*—14½ m. *Crathes.*—17 m. *Banchory.*—24 m. *Torphins.*—27 m. *Lumphanan.*—32½ m. *Aboyne.*—37 m. *Dinnet.*—43½ m. **Ballater.**

Except between Banchory and Aboyne, where the railway describes a loop to the N., road and railway run side by side, close to the N. bank of the **Dee.** There are, however, alternative roads on the S. bank, between Aberdeen and Banchory and between Aboyne and Braemar. The Dee, issuing from the wild Cairngorms (p. 243), a true impetuous Highland stream, in its narrow, rocky, and impressive channel, flows down the widening valley through the forests of Mar and Invercauld, passing Balmoral Castle, and below Ballater gradually loses its Highland character. It is a famous salmon stream, but it used to be said " ae fit o' Don's worth twa o' Dee, unless it be for fish or tree." The range of hills to the S. of the lower Dee used to be called the Mounth ; the more isolated summits to the N. afford fine views.—Road on the S. bank, see below.

Aberdeen, see Rte. 40.—4 m. *Cults* (Hotel, RB. 19/6, P. 6–8 gs.) adjoins *Bieldside* (Hotel, RB. 18/, P. 8 gs.) with its golf course. On the right, farther on, is the large Tor-na-Dee **sanatorium.—8 m.** *Peterculter* (Gordon Arms, RB. 21/, P.

7½–8½ gs.), with paper-mills, enjoys a pleasant situation. The Roman camp of *Normandykes* lies S.W., beyond the railway. *Drum Castle*, 2 m. N.W., is a mansion of 1619 attached to a square tower built c. 1280 with walls 12–15 ft. thick. The Irvines of Drum (who still hold the estate) played a conspicuous part at Harlaw. On the other side of the Dee are Durris House and, beyond, a tower in honour of the last Duke of Gordon.

In a detached part of Kincardineshire is (15½ m.; right) ***Crathes Castle** (N.T.; adm. 2/6; Wed. & Thurs. 11–8, Sun. 2.30–8; gardens only Sat. 2.30–8; in winter Wed. & Sat. 11–4.30), a double square tower of 1533–96 with some remarkable paintings (1599) of the Muses, the Virtues, and the Nine Worthies, and an oak-panelled ceiling, unique in Scotland. In the main hall is preserved the Horn of Leys, a jewelled ivory horn said to have been presented by Robert Bruce to Alex. Burnett in 1323. The lovely garden dates from 1702, when the E. wing was added. Bp. Gilbert Burnet was a scion of the Burnetts of Crathes.—We enjoy a good view up Glen Dye (left) as we approach the neat village (1960 inhab.) and summer resort of (18 m.) **Banchory** (*Tor-na-Coille*, RB. 25/6, P. 11 gs.; *Banchory Lodge*, on the Dee, RB. 21/, P. 10 gs.; *Raemoir*, 2½ m. N., with fine grounds, similar charges; *Burnett Arms*, RB. 19/6, P. 9 gs.), or *Banchory Ternan*, where Andrew Lang died in 1912.

About ½ m. below Banchory the Dee is joined by the Feugh, on which is the charmingly situated *Bridge of Feugh*. *Tilquhillie Castle* (16th cent.), 2½ m. S.E., is now a farmhouse.—From the Bridge of Feugh we may return to *Aberdeen* (19 m.) by A 943, a fine road on the S. bank of the Dee. At 2¼ m. from the bridge, the picturesque so-called Slug Road strikes off on the right for (15 m.) *Stonehaven*, rising to 757 ft. and affording fine views of Deeside and the North Sea.—7½ m. *Durris Bridge*.—11 m. *Maryculter* (Mill Inn, RB. 17/6, P. 7–7½ gs.; Deeside, similar charges) is connected by a bridge with Peterculter. On the right is *Blairs College*, a Roman Catholic foundation of 1827, in fine buildings of 1908, which contains a noted portrait of Mary, Queen of Scots, found concealed at Douai after the French Revolution, and all that remains of the library of the Scots College at Paris, besides other treasures. We approach Aberdeen through (13½ m.) *Banchory Devenick* (Ardoe House, with fine grounds, RB. 21/, P. 10 gs.).

To the N. of Banchory viâ (2½ m.) *Raemoir*, where a quaint old mansion stands in the hotel grounds, rises the *Hill of Fare* (1545 ft.). On its S.E. slopes is the *Howe of Corrichie*, where the recalcitrant Earl of Huntly was defeated and slain in 1562 by the adherents of Mary, Queen of Scots, Sir John Gordon, son of the earl and an aspirant to Mary's hand, was captured and executed at Aberdeen.

A good but hilly road, crossing the Dee at Banchory, leads S. viâ (3 m.) *Strachan* (where we turn left), and over the hills by *Glen Dye* and the Cairn o' Mounth to (17½ m.) *Fettercairn* (p. 288).—By keeping straight on from Strachan and (5 m.) *Feughside Inn* (P. 10 gs., incl. fishing) we may follow the Feugh to its source in the Forest of Birse, whence strong walkers may cross the Mounth ridge to *Tarfside* in Glen Esk, 16 m. from Feughside. The road on the right, c. 1¼ m. beyond Feughside Inn, leads N.W. to (14½ m.) Aboyne viâ *Birse*.

Beyond Banchory the railway makes a detour viâ Torphins and Lumphanan; the road keeps nearer the wooded bank of the Dee. At (21 m.) *Bridge of Canny* we cross the Canny descending from the Hill of Fare, on the right.—At 24 m., on our left, the Dee is crossed by *Potarch Bridge* (Inn), picturesquely set, whence a road runs S.E. to Feughside Inn and another W. to Aboyne viâ Birse.—26 m. *Kincardine O'Neil* (Gordon Arms, plain, RB. 18/, P. 8 gs.) has a ruined 13th cent. church with a good N. doorway of several orders and E. and W. lancet windows.—We cut across a bend of the Dee and rejoin the railway.

30½ m. **Aboyne** (*Huntly Arms*, RB. 21/–24/6 ; *Birse Lodge*, RB. 25/6, P. 11 gs. ; *Charlestown*, RB. 18/6, P. 7 gs.) is an attractive village pleasantly built around a large green and surrounded by distant hills. It is a highly popular summer resort with a golf course, and its Highland Gathering in the first week of September is one of the great events in the Highland season. The bridge over the Dee, S.W. of the village, affords fine views up and down stream.

Aboyne Castle (Marquess of Huntly ; no adm.), N. of the town, dates from 1671–1869 and is the successor of the ruined 13th cent. *Coull Castle* (p. 297), 2 m. farther N.

Crossing the bridge at Aboyne we may ascend the picturesque *Glen Tanner* or *Tanar*, which runs S.W., passing the little chapel of St. Lesmo at (4 m.) *Glentanar Lodge*. From (10 m.) the end of the cart-road the track known as the *Mounth Road* ascends in 2 m. to 2500 ft. on the shoulder of the conical *Mount Keen* (3077 ft.) and descends to Glen Mark and (16½ m.) *Lochlee* (p. 287).

From the bridge of Aboyne a hill track, the *Fungle Road*, runs S. to join (at 4½ m.) the route from *Banchory* to *Glen Esk*, p. 287.—A third hill track, the *Fir Mounth Road*, runs S. from the church in Glen Tanner, ascends to 2363 ft. on the E. side of the *Hill of Cat* (2435 ft), then drops down into Glen Tennet to reach Glen Esk at Tarfside.

The road on the S. bank from Aboyne to (10½ m.) Ballater, runs near (7 m.) *Ballaterich* (2 m. S. of Cambus o' May), where Lord Byron spent some weeks of his boyhood and " roved a young highlander o'er the dark heath " ; and then passes (8½ m.) *Pannanich Wells Hotel* (RB. 12/6, P. 5½ gs.), a long white building.

From Aboyne to *Tarland*, etc., see Rte. 40.

From Aboyne the road and railway run across the bleak Moor of Dinnet to (36 m.) *Dinnet* (Profeit's, RB. 19/6, P. 8–9 gs.). To the N. are *Loch Kinord* and *Loch Davan*, pretty sheets of water fringed with wood and noted for aquatic plants as well as for their crannogs and other antiquities. In Loch Kinord is also an island with a castle, where Edward I rested on his return from Loch-in-Dorb.—38½ m. *Cambus o' May* (Hotel, RB. 24/, P. 10 gs.), to the N.E. of which is the fine hill of Culblean, backed by the grand mass of Morven (2862 ft.).

Below *Culblean* in 1335 the army of David II, under Sir Andrew de Moray, defeated Edward III's partisans led by Atholl, in a decisive battle which confirmed the results of Bannockburn (memorial on the Tarland road). The cairns in the neighbourhood are said to cover the slain.

About 2 m. from the station is the *Burn o' the Vat*, a singular fissure at the base of Culblean, whence a burn issues to flow into Loch Kinord. A motor road diverging to the N. from the main road, c. 1 m. W. of the station, leads to (2 m.) the burn, whose course we follow to the left for c. ¼ mile to a remarkable round cauldron and a waterfall behind which a fugitive of the '45 is said to have hidden.

41½ m. **Ballater** (*Invercauld Arms*, RB. 21/6, P. **12** gs. ;
Loirston, RB. 21/–27/6, P. 10–12 gs., unlic. ; *Craigendarroch*,
N. of the town, RB. 18/–22/6, P. 9–11 gs. ; *Craigard*, RB. 21/,
P. 8½–9 gs. ; *Towers*, *Tullich Lodge*, similar charges, these
three unlic. ; and many others), the terminus of the railway,
is a pleasant little town (1300 inhab.), much resorted to for its
fine air and beautiful surroundings of wood and moorland.
Mountain excursions are numerous, but towards the stalking
season freedom of access is restricted.

To the N. of the town is the wooded *Craig-an-Darach* (1250 ft. ; *View), easily
ascended by a path in c. ½ hr. Behind it is the precipitous and wooded *Pass of
Ballater*, near whose E. end is *Monaltrie House* (p. 301). In the distance behind
rises *Morven* (2862 ft.), remarkable for having scarcely any heather upon its
sides, though the lower portions are thickly clad with juniper.—Another view-
point, as easily reached, is *Craig Cailleach* (1896 ft.), S. of the Dee bridge.

To Loch Muick and Glen Clova. The Muick, which joins the Dee on the
S. ½ m. above Ballater Bridge, is for 8½ m. on both banks flanked by good roads,
but that on the left bank is sometimes closed. We follow the E. bank, then,
c. 2 m. from Ballater, cross the *Bridge of Muick* to the W. bank, on which appear
(3 m.) the beautiful woods of *Birkhall*, a three-storied mansion of 1715 bought
in 1885 by Edward VII when Prince of Wales. About ½ m. upstream a ford
joins the two roads, so that sometimes driving round is possible.—At (6 m.)
the *Linn of Muick* and its pretty cascade the scenery is very charming ; farther
up the glen is rather monotonous and bare. There is a ford at 8 m. and another
at 9½ m. near to *Allt-na-Giubhsaich* (' The Hut '), a shooting lodge 1 m. short
of the foot of **Loch Muick**—a beautiful sheet of water 2½ m. long and hemmed
in on all sides but one by steep mountains. Here Queen Victoria and Prince
Albert stayed in 1849, and it was again occupied by the court when the Queen
built the Glasallt Shiel (1868), 2¾ m. farther on, on the N. side of the loch.
From Glasallt a steep track goes on (2¼ m.) to the small *Dhu Loch* (2090 ft.),
between the precipices of Lochnagar (N.) and Cairn Bannoch (S.).—From the
ford over the Muick near The Hut the *Capel Mounth* track, marked by conspicuous
poles (marshes on both sides), leads S.W. over the moors, and after reaching
(12½ m.) the height of 2250 ft., descends steeply to (15 m.) *Braedownie* in Glen
Clova, see p. 286.

Lochnagar (p. 303) may be ascended from Allt-na-Giubhsaich whence there is a
good path to the summit, 12 m. from Ballater.

From Ballater viâ Glen Gairn to Cock Bridge (Strathdon), 15 m. A
hill-road (B 972), diverging N. from the Braemar road just beyond the Bridge of
Gairn, c. 1½ m. W. of Ballater, ascends the W. (r.) bank of the Gairn to (6½ m.)
Gairnshiel Lodge (p. 305), where, turning right on A 939, we cross the stream.
Striking N.E. we ascend for c. 10 m. and descend to (12½ m.) *Tornahaish Bridge*
on the Strathdon road, where we turn left (W.) for (15 m.) *Cock Bridge* (p. 308).
[Pedestrians save c. 2½ m. by ascending the road on the E. (l.) bank of the Gairn
to (3¾ m.) Lary, and thence taking the track through Glen Finzie, to strike
the mountain road c. 2 m. N.E. of Gairnshiel Lodge ; comp. the map.]—The
road to the left at Gairnshiel Lodge completes the circuit round Geallaig Hill
and rejoins the Braemar road at Monaltrie (Balmoral). About 1¼ m. from the
Lodge a fair road diverges on the right for (4 m.) *Daldownie* and (8 m.) *Loch
Builg*, on the hill route from Braemar to Tomintoul.

A 973, on the S. bank of the Dee, offers a pleasant alternative route to Crathie
(8 m.), passing (2 m. r.) *Knock Castle*, a charming little 16th cent. tower-house,
and the woods of Abergeldie.

　　The main road to Braemar (A 93) goes on by the left bank
of the Dee, winding round Craig-an-Darach and crossing
(43 m.) the Gairn. The district is pleasantly wooded. On the
left is Craig Giubhais (Craig Youzie ; ' Hill of Firs ').—44¾ m.
Coillecrioch Inn.—47½ m. *Abergeldie Castle*, a tower of c. 1550,

garrisoned by Mackay in 1689, is seen on the S. bank of the Dee, here crossed by a private suspension bridge. With its 19th cent. additions, it has been leased as a royal residence since 1848, and was the Highland abode of Edward VII when Prince of Wales after his marriage.—48½ m. **Crathie Church,** a neat little granite church (1895) just above the road, is attended by the Royal Family when in residence at Balmoral.

In the church are the royal pew and memorials to various members of the Royal Family.—In the churchyard beside the ruined old church, near the river, is the monument erected by Queen Victoria to her faithful attendant John Brown (d. 1883). John Brown's house, across the river, may be seen from the road near this point.—To Ballater by the S. bank, see above.

Lochnagar (p. 303) may be ascended from Crathie, but only at certain seasons. A good path leads to the foot of the mountain.

On the hills across the Dee are seen commemorative cairns to members of the Royal Family, the most conspicuous being that in memory of Prince Albert ; and at 49½ m. (1 m. beyond Crathie Church) we have a view of **Balmoral Castle,** the sovereign's Scottish residence, situated on a curve of the Dee at the foot of Craig Gowan. The mansion, of white Crathie granite in the Scottish ' baronial ' style, was begun in 1853 by William Smith of Aberdeen with modifications by Prince Albert, and was first occupied in 1855. It succeeds a 16th cent. tower of the Gordons, enlarged in 1830.

The estate of Balmoral (c. 11,000 acres) was purchased in 1852 from the trustees of the Earl of Fife for £31,500 by Prince Albert, who also planted the picturesque grounds with rare coniferous and forest trees. The property was left to Queen Victoria, who added Ballochbuie Forest and bequeathed it as a royal residence for her successors. The Bachnagairn estate, to the S., was added by George VI in 1947.—In the absence of the Court the public is admitted to the grounds on Tues., Wed., and Thurs. in May–July (10–5 ; adm. 1/6, devoted to local charities). The interior of the castle is not shown and no cars are allowed in the grounds.—Queen Mary's sunk garden, Queen Victoria's garden-cottage, and the sculptures on the castle are interesting.

Farther on we pass (r.) the end of A 939 leading N. to Strathdon (see above) and the remains of the old house of *Monaltrie*, burned in 1745 ; while on the left we have a view up Glen Gelder, beneath " the steep frowning beauties of dark Lochnagar."—At 51 m., beside the river, is a mound with a few fir trees known as the *Cairn-na-Cuimhne* or Cairn of Remembrance. The story goes that the Farquharsons, whose old castle occupied the site of Balmoral, used to assemble here before an expedition, and deposit each man a stone ; on their return they each picked one off the cairn so formed, the number left marking the loss of the clan.—Beyond (51½ m.) *Inver Hotel* (RB. 17/6) the hills begin to close in. On the S. of the river is the royal *Ballochbuie Deer Forest* (no adm.).

At (55½ m.) *Invercauld Bridge*, built when the *Old Bridge of Dee* (1752 ; l.) became royal property, the road crosses the Dee, while the approach to the magnificent domain of Invercauld continues along the left bank. The country here is

finely wooded, with abrupt bold hills, conspicuous among
which is Craig Clunie (l.), a towering cliff, fringed with pines,
and overhanging the road. About halfway up it is a recess
in the crags which goes by the name of the ' Laird of Clunie's
Charter Chest,' because in unsettled times the laird of Clunie
used to hide his title-deeds there. The valley here expands
and presently, across the Dee, we see *Invercauld House*, the
ancient seat of the Farquharsons, whence the Earl of Mar
dated his address, calling out the clans, whose chiefs assembled
here (1715). The mansion is of the 15th cent., but received
its tall baronial tower and a new wing in 1874.

The road passes (57 m.) under a crag (l.) called the ' Lion's
Face ' from a supposed resemblance, while between the road
and the river is *Braemar Castle*, a tall plain baronial building
of 1628, rebuilt c. 1748. After 1715 it was long garrisoned by
Hanoverians to keep the Highlanders in check. We round a
sharp turn.

58 m. **Braemar** (*Invercauld Arms*, RB. 25/–30/, P. 12–14 gs. ;
Fife Arms, RB. 17/6–21/, P. 9–11 gs. ; *Mayfield*, unlic.,
P. 7 gs.), or *Castleton of Braemar*, is a neat though scattered
double village (1100 ft.), the portion W. of the Clunie being
called *Auchindryne*. It is a highly popular resort near some of
the finest mountain scenery in Scotland, but the proximity of
deer forests and of the Royal Domain restricts the freedom of
rambling over the hills. Surrounded in winter by snow-clad
mountains, with slopes both easy and difficult, Braemar is one
of the best centres in Scotland for winter sports.

On the E. side of the bridge over the Clunie, which dashes
in leaps through the village to join the Dee, are the foundations of *Kindrochit Castle*, a hunting-lodge of Robert I rebuilt
after 1309, but already derelict in 1600 ; but the mound
on which the Earl of Mar raised the standard of rebellion in
1715 was removed to make room for the Invercauld Arms.
In 1881 R. L. Stevenson lived in a cottage at the S. end of
Castleton Terrace (tablet) and there wrote part of ' Treasure
Island ' ; opposite are the Invercauld Galleries, an exhibition
of handicrafts, etc. The famous Braemar Gathering held in
August in the Princess Royal Park, at the W. end of the village,
is usually attended by a royal party from Balmoral.

Morrone (2819 ft. ; c. 2½ hrs. up and down), the hill 2½ m. S.W., between the
Dee and the Clunie, commands an even better view than does Lochnagar.—
The ' Queen's Drive,' a grassy road (for walkers only) round the S. side of the
Lion's Face (see above), is an alternative to the first 1½ m. of the high road.

The picturesque **Linn of Quoich**, only 2½ m. W., in a direct line, is not easily
accessible (enquire as to route before starting). When the Dee is low cars may
cross at a ford, c. 1 m. above Invercauld Bridge, but usually they must make a detour
viâ Invercauld Bridge and thence by a road passing to the N. of Invercauld
House (8 m. in all). Pedestrians are sometimes permitted to cross the Victoria
private bridge (see below ; c. 6 m. to the Linn), otherwise they follow the road
route. The Quoich water rushes over a succession of rocky ledges and in its fretted
course, whirling loose stones along with it, has scooped out hollows in the mic-

aceous schist—hence the name Quoich or ' cup.' The upper reaches of the
Quoich, in the desolate E. corries of *Ben-a-Bhuird* (3924 ft.) are a good hunting-
ground for cairngorm crystals.

*Lochnagar (3786 ft. ; 4–5 hrs.), c. 12 m. S.E., commands a splendid panorama
of mountains. We follow the road up the Clunie for c. 2 m., then diverge to the
left by a rough road for (5 m.) the shooting-lodge at the N. end of *Loch Callater*,
whence a track, not easily missed except in mist or snow, ascends in 2½–3 hrs.
more to the central (3768 ft.) and the N. summit (*Cac Carn Beag* ; 3786 ft.). To
the N.E. we look down upon *Loch-na-Gar* (' Loch of goats ') at the desolate foot of
stupendous precipices. The descent may be made to Glen Muick (N.E.) or to
Glen Clova (S.E.).

FROM BRAEMAR TO BLAIR ATHOLL BY GLEN TILT

29 m. ROAD to *White Bridge*, 9½ m. ; thence BRIDLE PATH to Forest Lodge,
11½ m. ; thence ROAD to *Blair Atholl*, 8 m.—Ponies for the bridle-path and guides
(not necessary) should, if required, be ordered in advance from the hotels either
at Braemar or at Blair Atholl ; and cars may be ordered for the final road section
(either from Blair Atholl or from Braemar, according to the direction in which
the journey is made). Bicycles will be found a great encumbrance in the central
section. There is no inn en route and in the stalking season (mid-Aug.–mid-Oct.)
there may be restrictions on the use of cars.

The road running W. from Braemar, up the valley of the
Dee, is a beautiful terrace drive overlooking the river. On
the opposite bank is seen the opening of Glen Quoich, and as
we proceed we may discern, in clear weather, the successive
summits of the flat-topped Ben-a-Bhuird (3924 ft.), Cairngorm of Derry (3788 ft.), and Ben Macdhui (4296 ft.) away to
the north. The road crosses (3¾ m.) a small bridge just above
the *Linn of Corriemulzie*, where a stream descends over many
small waterfalls in a ravine (much obstructed by fallen
timber).—3¾ m. The private *Victoria Bridge* leads across the
Dee to *Mar Lodge* (1898), built by the late Duke of Fife to
replace his previous mansion on the S. bank, burned down in
1895.—4½ m. *Inverey* is a hamlet at the junction of the Ey
with the Dee.

A rough road leads thence up the valley of the Ey to (1½ m.) a deep chasm in
the rock with a shallow cave or groove, only a feet above the torrent, known
as the ' Colonel's Bed,' from a tradition that Colonel John Farquharson, who
had been out with Claverhouse at Killiecrankie (1689), there hid for some time.
It is a remarkable scene, the cliffs rising 50–60 ft. above the water and descending
20 ft. below its surface, forming a pool black as ink. We enjoy fine views of the
Ben Macdhui range as we return.

At (6½ m.) the ***Linn of Dee,** which is spanned by a bridge,
the river dashes through a rocky cleft between the rocks that
approach within 4 ft. of each other, fretting against the sharp
sides and plunging down small cascades. In spate the scene
is very impressive. Byron, while a boy, had a narrow escape
here. He tripped on a knot of heather and was barely saved
from rolling into the torrent by being seized by an attendant.

Above the Linn cultivation is left behind and we follow the
left or N. bank of the Dee, passing the point where the route

to Aviemore viâ the Larig Ghru strikes off to the N., immediately short of (9½ m.) *White Bridge* over the Dee. Just above
the bridge is the **Chest of Dee*, where the river flows through
a rock-bound channel in a series of deep pools. We cross the
bridge (often broken down), beyond which the road deteriorates, and quit the Dee, ascending a tributary to the S. We
cross (11 m.) the Geldie (up which a track runs viâ Glen
Feshie to Kingussie), and at (12 m.) *Bynack Lodge* (empty ;
a useful shelter) the track ends and becomes a bridle-path.
Looking back we see the whole of the Ben Macdhui range ;
in front are the precipices of Ben-y-Gloe.

The BRIDLE PATH crosses an open moor. At 14 m. (c.
1600 ft.) *Perthshire* is entered and soon afterwards the tiny
Tilt, coming down from Loch Tilt (½ m. W.), is crossed.
For the rest of our journey we follow **Glen Tilt,** which was
once inhabited by the clan Mackintosh, from whom it was
purchased by the Earl of Atholl in 1532. Its chief peculiarities
are its extreme straightness, giving it in places the appearance
of a gigantic canal cutting, and the uniform steepness of the
hills on both sides.—We cross (16 m.) the *Bedford Memorial
Bridge* over the Tarff (a larger stream than the Tilt), which
flows in from the W. in a succession of fine falls hemmed in
by cliffs.

About 1¾ m. up the right bank of the Tilt's first large tributary, on the left
½ m. before the bridge, is *Falar Lodge* (1750 ft. ; said to be the highest inhabited
house in Britain) whence a track climbs the hills to the S. and descends Glen
Fernait to (14½ m.) *Straloch*. Higher up is the great corrie in *Ben Uarn* (3424 ft.).

At 17 m. the Tilt is joined by a stream from Loch Loch
(2 m. S.E.), and at 18 m. a cairn (view) above the path commemorates a visit of Queen Victoria. About 2 m. farther on
we reach one of the grandest parts of the glen. The Tilt
flows through a granite dyke, rushing burns descend on both
sides, and we can enjoy glimpses into the recesses of Ben-y-
Gloe (3671 ft.), which may be ascended from the footbridge
c. 3 m. downstream. The old lake-terraces on the E. side are
very marked.

Beyond (21 m.) *Forest Lodge*, the principal shooting
quarters of the Duke of Atholl, the owner of the Forest of
Atholl, one of the largest deer-forests in Scotland, the bridle-
path once more becomes a ROAD, and the glen becomes less
wild. At (22¼ m.) a picturesque foot-bridge the river flows in
a bed of rose-coloured granite. Backwards there is a fine
view of the white quartzite peak of Cairn Bhac, 12 m. distant
and 3 m. E. of Loch Tilt. At 24 m., just after crossing the
river, a keeper's cottage, ' *Marble Lodge*,' is passed. Lower
down, the river offers at every turn beautiful combinations of
rock and water. At 25 m. the public right-of-way keeps to the
left behind a wood, leaves the glen, ascends, keeps along the

brow of the hill, and comes down to Blair Atholl by the side of the Fender. The road keeps straight on, crossing (26½ m.) the Tilt again. The river, much more rapid and very thickly wooded, becomes exceedingly fine, but to see it the road must be left and paths (l.) taken at intervals to view-points. At 28 m. the *Old Bridge of Tilt* is crossed, not far from the *Falls of Fender*.—29 m. **Blair Atholl,** see p. 236.

FROM BRAEMAR TO LOCH BUILG (Tomintoul), 13 m., hill road. Crossing (2¼ m. E.) Invercauld Bridge, we take the second turning on the left, and at 5 m. diverge again to the left. The road ascends in very steep zigzags to (2½ m.) 2390 ft. affording magnificent mountain views behind us and on the W. (l.). We begin to descend after c. 10 m. and crossing the Gairn, reach (13 m.) the somewhat uninteresting **Loch Builg,** which drains into the Spey.—A track skirts the E. side of the loch and goes on to (16¾ m.) *Inchrory,* a lonely shooting-lodge near the Avon, which flows from the desolate Forest of Glenavon on the W., and thence a cart-road descends close to the Avon to (24 m.) *Tomintoul* (p. 250).— From Loch Builg a fair road leads S.E. down the bank of the Gairn to (4 m.) *Daldownie* (p. 299 ; to the right for Balmoral, 4½ m.) and (8 m.) *Gairnshiel Lodge* whence the return may be made to Ballater (6½ m. more).

ASCENT OF BEN MACDHUI (4296 ft.), c. 18 m., a day's excursion. Crossing the Dee at (6½ m.) the *Linn of Dee* (p. 303) a road strikes N. up *Glen Lui* to (10 m.) *Derry Lodge* (now a shelter of the Cairngorm Club), where it ends at the confluence of the Lui Beg burn (W.) and the Derry (E.). Thence there is a choice of routes. A. The recognised bridle-path (wet in places) climbs along the bank of the Derry, crossing and recrossing the stream, to (15½ m.) the *Hutchison Memorial Shelter* in Corrie Etchachan. *Loch Etchachan* (3058 ft.), which we leave on our r., lies " like a drop of ink at the base of a huge, dark, mural precipice." During the following long and steep ascent of the E. slope of Ben Macdhui we have fine views over Glen Derry to the long ridge of Ben-a-Bhuird. The final half-mile or so is over comparatively level ground.—B. A shorter and finer route (6 m.) ascends the right bank of the Lui Beg to (3 m.) a fork of the stream. We cross the E. arm and climb the dividing ridge, skirting the precipices W. of Lochan Uaine (very rough going) and making straight for the summit. This ascent affords magnificent views. Prominent to the S.W. are the ridge of Cairn-a-Mhaim (3328 ft.) and the Devil's Point (3303 ft.).—For the *View from Ben Macdhui, and the descent to *Aviemore,* see p. 243.

A visit to the wild **Loch A'an** or *Avon* (p. 243) may be combined with this ascent. By keeping to the E. side of Loch Etchachan and due N. till a stream is reached and then following down the left bank of the latter, a steep descent may be made to Loch A'an in ¾ hr.—An easier but longer route to Loch A'an from Braemar passes the entrance of Corrie Etchachan, 3½ m. from Derry Lodge, keeps straight on N., to the E. of Ben Vain, and descends by the Dhu Lochan to (6 m. ; l.) the N.E. end of Loch A'an. From the Dhu Lochan a track goes on N., past Ben Bynack (3574 ft.), to join the road through Glenmore Forest at the Pass of Revoan (p. 243), 24 m. from Braemar.

From Braemar to *Aviemore,* see p. 244; to *Perth* viâ Glenshee and Blairgowrie, see Rte. 29 ; to *Kingussie,* see p. 241.

42. FROM ABERDEEN TO ALFORD AND STRATHDON

ROAD, 53 m. A 944. 9 m. *Skene.*—21 m. *Tillyfourie.*—26 m. *Alford.*—33 m. *Mossat Toll.*—A 97. 44½ m. *Strathdon.*—B 973. 53 m. *Cock Bridge.*—MOTOR-BUS 2 or 3 times daily to *Strathdon* in c. 2 hrs. ; to *Alford,* 3 or 4 times daily in 70 min.—Another bus runs to Alford in 1¼ hr. viâ Buicksburn, Kemnay, and Monymusk ; another on Mon., Fri., and Sat. to Mossat Toll and Lumsden.

This route runs from E. to W. through the heart of **Aberdeenshire,** which is the most easterly county of Scotland and the fifth in point of size. The stern mountain grandeur of the Cairngorms in the extreme S.W. (Ben Macdhui,

Lochnagar, Ben-a-Bhuird), the beautiful long valleys of the Dee and Don, and the fine coast scenery, combine to make it one of the most attractive areas in Scotland. It comprises five principal districts. *Mar*, between the Dee and Don, occupies practically the S. half of the county, including Aberdeen, the royal domain about Balmoral, and the above-mentioned mountains. Between the Don and the Ythan is *Formartine*, with its sandy coast, and farther N. is *Buchan*, scant of trees but well cultivated, including Peterhead and Fraserburgh. *Garioch* (pron. ' Gherrie '), inland from Formartine, is a fertile region called the ' girnel ' or granary of Aberdeenshire ; and towards the N.W. of the county is the hilly *Strathbogie*. The historic sites in the county include the important battlefield of Harlaw, while antiquities both prehistoric and medieval have survived in greater quantity than anywhere else in the country. Frequent family names are Farquharson, Forbes, Gordon, Grant, Fraser, and Duff. The famous Aberdeen-Angus cattle were originally bred at Keillor in Angus (1829) and at Tillyfourie in Aberdeenshire (1864).

Leaving Aberdeen by Alford Place, Queen's Rd., and Hazlehead, we bear right after 6 m.—9 m. *Skene* (r.) is a village giving name to a small loch (9¾ m. ; l.).—12 m. *Dunecht*. To the left is the mansion of *Dunecht* (1820), once famous for its observatory ; the road on the right leads in 3 m. to *Castle Fraser* (1454–1618 ; no adm.), an imposing baronial mansion with characteristic 17th cent. turrets. To the left of (21 m.) *Tillyfourie* is the wooded Corrennie Hill, with pink granite quarries.—26 m. **Alford** (450 ft. ; *Forbes Arms*, at Bridge of Alford, 1¾ m. N.W., RB. 15/, P. 7 gs. ; *Haughton Arms*, P. 7 gs. with fishing ; *Haughton House*, RB. 15/, P. 6 gs. ; *Whitehaugh*, unlic., RB. 21/, P. 9 gs.) stands in the centre of the hill-girt Howe of Alford. The decayed *Balfluig Castle* (1556), ¾ m. S.E., belonged to the Lords Forbes, who now occupy *Castle Forbes* (19th cent.), 4 m. N.E. Montrose defeated the Covenanters under Baillie and Urry between the village and the Don bridge in 1645.

Terpersie Castle (4 m. N.W.), now a ruin, has three stories each of one room. On one of the window-sills is the date 1561, and above is a beautifully cut boar's head, the Gordon crest.

The return to Aberdeen may be made by B 993 and B 994, bearing left at (5 m.) *Tillyfourie* (see above).—8½ m. *Monymusk* rose beside a Culdee priory which was transformed in 1245 into a house of Austin canons. Bruce, on his way to the battle of Barra, encamped on Crichie Hill, near Kintore, and is said to have bivouacked in the Camp Field, ½ m. E. of the 15th cent. Monymusk House. The church is partly Romanesque. About 1 m. up the Don (r.) are the ruins of *Pitfichie*, once the property of the family of General Sir John Urry, who began as a Royalist, fought as a Covenanter against Montrose and finally, having joined Montrose in his last hapless attempt, was made prisoner and beheaded in Edinburgh (1650). To the S. (1½ m.) is *Cluny Castle*, a mansion of 1836 on the site of a Gordon stronghold.—To the N. (11½ m.) *Kemnay* (Burnett Arms, RB. 17/6, P. 8–10 gs.) is *Fetternear House*, once the country seat of the bishops of Aberdeen, which was made over to Wm. Leslie, Baron of Balquhain, in 1566 for his part in saving Aberdeen cathedral from destruction. The large Kemnay quarries supplied stone for the Thames Embankment and the piers of the Forth Bridge.— We bear right on B 994, and join A 96 1 m. S. of Kintore and 12 m. N.W. of (26½ m.) Aberdeen.

The ROAD up Strath Don (A 944) passes the site of the above-mentioned battle, crosses the Don at (2 m.) *Bridge of*

Alford (Hotel, see above), and keeps up its left bank for 3½ miles.

The woods of *Brux*, across the river, once belonged to the Camerons. The story goes that the Camerons agreed with the Mowatts of Abergeldie to settle their feuds at a conference between twelve horsemen from either side. The Mowatts appeared at Drumgowdrum, the rendezvous, with twelve horses, but with two men on each horse, and promptly massacred the Camerons, whose property devolved on an only daughter. A cadet of the house of Forbes challenged and slew Mowatt in single combat, married the heiress, and founded the family of Forbes of Brux. The last of his line was proscribed in 1715, but concealed himself in the neighbourhood by working as a labourer. A wall built by his own hands is still pointed out.

At (33 m.) *Mossat Toll* we join the road coming S. from Lumsden (see p. 311) and turn to the left.—34½ m. *Kildrummy* (Castle, RB. 27/6, P. 12 gs., adjoining the castle ; Kildrummy, nearer Mossat). Off the road to the left is the church (1805) with a semicircular porch, and, on a mound, some fragments of the medieval church, including an Elphinstone vault (1605) and the tomb of a Forbes of Brux (14th cent.) ; farther on is the large and imposing ruin of ***Kildrummy Castle** (adm. free), the most striking object in Strath Don.

The castle, once a seat of the kings of the Scots, was built in the reign of Alexander II by Gilbert, Bp. of Caithness, and rebuilt in 1303 for Edward I of England. Bruce sent his wife and children hither for safety when he fled to Rathlin (1306), but when the castle was besieged by the Earls of Lancaster and Hereford they fled to Tain. Kildrummy fell by treachery into the hands of the English, and the garrison " were all hangyt and drawyn." It later became a seat of the Erskines of Mar but was forfeited after the '15 rebellion. The important *Chapel, usually an inconspicuous feature in Scottish castles, has a triple lancet window, in imitation apparently of Elgin. Of the six towers which once rose above its walls two are fairly well preserved.

The road now enters the *Den of Kildrummy*, a narrow winding pass, beyond which Morven (2862 ft.) appears to the S., and we descend to (36½ m.) the plain little *Glenkindie Arms Hotel*. On the other side of the Don are the church and ruined castle of *Towie*. In the second field on the right beyond (38½ m.) *Glenkindie House* (766 ft.) is a remarkable earth-house with two communicating chambers.—Crossing (39 m.) the *Bridge of Buchat* (797 ft.) we reach the majestic ruin of *Glenbuchat Castle* (c. 1590), the seat of John Gordon ' old Glenbucket ' (d. 1750), who sacrificed his lands for the Stewart cause. An inscription over the door reads ' No thing on arth remanis bot fame.'

About 3 m. along the road running N.W. to (6 m.) *Glenbuchat Lodge* a hill track diverges on the right for (2 m.) the *Sources of the Deveron* and (7½ m.) *Cabrach*.

The Don curves around Ben Newe, and we cross and recross the river to avoid the grounds of *Castle Newe*, demolished. The road to Cambus o' May diverges on the left. Near (43½ m.) *Colquhonnie Hotel* (RB. 16/6, P. 7–7½ gs.) are the scanty ruins of *Colquhonnie Castle* (16th cent.), begun by the Forbeses of Towie, but never finished, because, it is said, three lairds fell from the top and were killed.—From *Bellabeg* the church spire of (44½ m.) **Strathdon** (990 ft.) is conspicuous across the river.

A road hence ascends the Water of Nochty to (5 m.) Glenbuchat Lodge (see above). A hill track diverges on the left 2¼ m. along this road and crosses the *Ladder Hills* (c. 2400 ft.) for (12 m.) *Knockandhu* in Glen Livet.

We cross the Nochty, and pass (r.) the *Dun of Invernochty* (40 ft. high), the site of the chief castle of Mar before Kildrummy. On the left is *Poldullie Bridge*, built by Black Jock Forbes of Inverernan in 1715.—Beyond (46½ m.) the hamlet of *Parkvilla* we cross the Ernan, and a little farther on *Glen Conrie* (l.), where the Earls of Mar are said to have kept their hounds, is seen across the river. Our road ascends through beautiful country, passing (50½ m.) *Tornahaish Bridge*, where a road diverges to the S. for Glen Gairn and Deeside (A 939; the Glaschoille road).—We cross the Don a little short of (53 m.) **Cock Bridge** (1330 ft.; *Allargue Arms*, RB. 15/, P. 6 gs.), with a youth hostel on the old road leading S.E. to the Glaschoille road.

To the S. stands **Corgarff Castle**, probably built c. 1550 by the Elphinstones. Its siege in 1571 by Adam Gordon, brother of the Earl of Huntly, is commemorated in the ballad of 'Edom o' Gordon,' though the scene is there transferred to Berwickshire. It was defended by the wife of Alexander Forbes, the absent master, who, rather than surrender, suffered Gordon to set fire to the tower and perished in the flames with her children and the entire household. The castle was garrisoned in 1745 and was kept up as a small military station for the repression of smuggling until c. 1830, but is now ruinous.

A fine wild moorland road, the *Lecht*, part of the military road of 1752, ascending in 2½ m. to 2090 ft., runs N.W. to (9½ m.) *Tomintoul* (p. 250).

A track leads W. by the *Sources of the Don* to (6 m.) *Inchrory Lodge* (p. 305), on the route from Braemar to Tomintoul.

43. FROM ABERDEEN TO INVERNESS

On the three Railway Routes to Inverness the sections between Aberdeen and Cairnie and between Elgin and Inverness are identical. Picturesque highland scenery is traversed by the route viâ Craigellachie; while the devious route viâ Portsoy and Buckie follows the fine coast-line of Banffshire.

(A) Viâ Orbliston, 108¼ m. in 4–5 hrs. Principal Stations: 6¼ m. *Dyce.*—13¼ m. *Kintore.*—16¾ m. *Inverurie.*—27½ m. *Insch.*—36 m. *Gartly.*—41 m. **Huntly.**—48¼ m. *Cairnie* (exchange station only).—53¼ m. **Keith Junction.**—65 m. *Orbliston* (for Fochabers).—71¼ m. **Elgin,** junction for *Lossiemouth,* 5¾ m.—80½ m. *Kinloss.*—83 m. **Forres.**—92½ m. **Nairn.**—98½ m. *Gollanfield.*—108¼ m. **Inverness.**

(B) Viâ Craigellachie, 117¾ m. in 4–5 hrs. Principal Stations: to (53¼ m.) **Keith,** see above.—54 m. *Keith Town.*—64 m. *Dufftown.*—68 m. **Craigellachie,** junction with the main line from Perth.—71 m. *Rothes.*—80¾ m. **Elgin** and thence to Inverness, see above.

(C) Viâ Portsoy, 124½ m. in 7–8 hrs. (no through carriages beyond Elgin). Principal Stations: to (48¼ m.) *Cairnie,* see above.—58½ m. *Tillynaught* (junction for **Banff,** 6 m.).—61 m. *Portsoy.*—66½ m. *Cullen.*—72½ m. **Buckie.**—77½ m. *Spey Bay.*—87½ m. **Elgin** and thence to Inverness, see above.

A. By Road viâ Huntly

ROAD, 105 or 107 m.—A 96. We quit Aberdeen by George St. (Pl. C 1).—
13 m. *Kintore.*—17 m. *Inverurie.*—24¼ m. *Oyne.*—39 m. *Huntly.*—50 m. *Keith.*—
58 m. *Fochabers.*—67 m. **Elgin.**—79 m. *Forres.*—89 m. *Nairn.*—105 m. **Inverness,**
entered by Eastgate (Pl. C 1).—The road viâ Gartly is 2 m. longer.—MOTOR-BUS
every 2 hrs. in c. 5 hrs. ; to *Elgin* in 3¼ hrs.

Quitting Aberdeen, A 96 ascends the vale of the Don, with
its paper-mills and granite-quarries.—At (4 m.) *Bucksburn*,
with the Rowett Research Institute for Animal Nutrition,
we leave the valley on the right. A descent to (12 m.) the
junction of B 994 (for Kemnay, r. ; see above) brings us back
to the Don valley at (13 m.) **Kintore** (*Torryburn*, RB. 15/–17/6,
P. 6–8 gs. ; *Kintore Arms*, RB. 14/6), a royal burgh since
1506, though its population is only 900. The quaint *Town
House* dates from 1727–37 ; the church contains a 16th cent.
' sacrament house ', and in the churchyard is a sculptured
stone combining pagan and Christian emblems. *Balbithan
House* (late 17th cent.) is 1 m. N.E. beyond the Don.

About 1½ m. S.W. are the ruins of *Hallforest Castle*, an early-14th cent. hunting-
lodge granted to Sir Robert de Keith, Earl Marischal, for services rendered at
Bannockburn.

Beyond Port Elphinstone, a suburb of Inverurie, we cross
the Don above the confluence of the Urie.—17 m. **Inverurie**
(5050 inhab. ; *Kintore Arms*, RB. 15/6–17/6, P. 8 gs. ; *Gordon
Arms*, RB. 13/6–15/6) is said to have been made a royal burgh
by Bruce but its status dates more probably from Queen
Mary's charter of 1558. A tablet in North St. marks the house
of William Thom (1798–1848), the weaver poet. The road
crossing the Urie S. of the town leads in ½ m. to *The Bass*, a
natural double mound, partly hand-dressed, which was the
site of a feudal stronghold visited by Mary, Queen of Scots,
in 1562. In the cemetery, to the left, are three Pictish
sculptured stones, one with a lively incised figure of a pony,
another with a clear ' spectacle-mark '.

The riverside road goes on, passing an entrance to *Keith Hall*, a 16th cent.
house with a Renaissance front (1697–99), in which Arthur Johnston (1587–1641),
the Latin poet, was born.—2 m. The ruined church of **Kinkell** (early 16th cent.)
contains a fine ' sacrament house ' (1524) and the tombstone (re-used by a
Forbes) of Gilbert de Greenlaw, slain at Harlaw (see below) ; also a replica of the
carved Crucifixion now in Aberdeen museum.

The neighbourhood of Inverurie abounds in ancient monuments: most interesting are the *Brandsbutt Stone* (½ m. N.W.), with ogams and Pictish symbols ; the
Loanhead Stone Circle (c. 1800 B.C.), 5 m. N., near *Daviot* ; and the *Maiden Stone*,
a Christian sculptured stone (10 ft. high), 4½ m. N.W. on the roadside beyond
(3½ m.) *Chapel of Garioch*. It takes its name from the comb and mirror carved in
the lowest compartment on the E. side. The road to it passes (2¼ m. ; r.) the
ruined tower of *Balquhain* (1530), an ancient seat of the Leslies. Cumberland
ordered it to be burnt in 1746, but his soldiers, bribed by a tenant of the Leslies,
used damp straw.

We now ascend the Urie, with Bennachie conspicuous on
the left. To the right, beyond the river, are *Harlaw House*

and the tall monument marking the ' sair field ' of **Harlaw,** where, on July 24th, 1411, the Earl of Mar checked the advance of the Highlanders under Donald, Lord of the Isles, who, with a force probably more numerous than that which opposed him, was marching on Aberdeen.

"The great Battle of Harlaw," says Scott, "might be said to determine whether the Gaelic or the Saxon race should be predominant in Scotland." A fine ballad referring to the battle is introduced into ' The Antiquary.'

At (21½ m.) *Pitcaple* Montrose, on his way S. as a prisoner in 1650, rested for a night in the castle (c. 1570, with additions of 1830), the lady of the house being his cousin.

A 96 crosses the Gadie and mounts the Urie to the right, passing (28 m. ; r.) *Williamston*, the gardens of which are open daily Apr.–Oct. (10–6 ; adm. 1/). Farther on it crosses the *Foudland Hills* (1529 ft.), which, although of no great height, were in winter the terror of travellers on account of the snow, and joins A 979 at Huntly.

About 3 m. N. of this road is *Glenmailen*, the site of a camp of the Romans on their northward drive into Scotland. The road goes on beyond it to (5 m.) the old mansion of *Frendraught*, the scene of the tragedy ' The Burning of Frendraught ' in 1630, when Sir James Crichton is said to have caused the death of Lord Aboyne, heir of the Marquess of Huntly, and Gordon of Rothiemay, by wilfully setting fire to the tower in which they were lodged. The church of (7½ m.) *Forgue* possesses the oldest silver communion cup in Scotland (1629), presented by Crichton after he had been absolved of the charge in 1653. A mile W. of Forgue we join A 97, the Huntly-Banff road.

We take A 979 (l.). On the left is the ruin of *Harthill Castle*, built in 1600 by Patrick Leith, and burnt soon after by the Covenanters.—24½ m. *Oyne*, on the Gadie burn, is the usual starting-point for the ascent of BENNACHIE, 2½–3 m. S., a beautiful ridge whose highest summit is *Oxen Craig* (1733 ft.). On *Mither Tap* (1698 ft.), the E. summit, are the remains of a remarkable hill fort. The praises of the country are sung in the charming lyric ' Where Gadie rins.' For the road ascending its upper vale, see Rte. 43B.—27½ m. *Insch* (Commercial, RB. 15/, P. 7 gs. ; Station, RB. 15/, P. 6 gs.) is a village of some importance, on the right. At Newton House, 2½ m. N.E. (on A 96), are two inscribed stones, one bearing two inscriptions, one in ogams, the other perhaps in an ancient form of Gaelic.—Road and railway now ascend between (r.) *Dunnideer*, a conical hill surmounted by a ruined castle (16th cent.) built partly on the site of a vitrified fort, and (l.) the hill of *Christ's Kirk*, named after a suppressed parish, where a fair, called ' The Sleepy Market,' was at one time held during the night.

Of Dunnideer Boece says that " the sheep that gangs on this mountain are yellow, their teeth hewit like gold." Christ's Kirk is said by some to be the scene of James I's poem, ' Christ's Kirk on the Green ' (comp. p. 261).

Between (31 m.) *Wardhouse* and (32½ m.) *Kennethmont* we cross the watershed and enter the more varied country of Strathbogie. Just N. of Kennethmont is *Leith Hall* (N.T. ; adm. free Thurs. & Sat. 10–6), the home of the Leith family since 1650, with Leith and Hay family relics and attractive gardens. The N. wing dates from the mid-17th cent., while additions of 1750 and 1850 enclose a courtyard.—At 33½ m., S. of *Gartly*, we join A 97.

This road, running S., leads to Strathdon and Deeside, crossing Rte. 43B at (3½ m.) *Rhynie.* The summit prominent to the S.W. as we proceed is the *Buck of Cabrach* (2368 ft.).—From (5½ m.) *Auchindoir*, where the old church contains a fine sacrament-house, a steep but beautiful road leads to (½ m. r.) *Craig Castle* (16th cent.), with a fine portal of 1720 and an 18th cent. wing, overlooking a deep wooded glen.—7½ m. *Lumsden* (Lumsden Arms, RB. 16/, P. 5–6 gs.) is a winter home of the wandering tinkers of Scotland. Here was born Sir W. Robertson Nicoll (1851–1923), founder of 'The British Weekly'.—At (9½ m.) *Mossat Toll* we strike the road from Alford to Strathdon (Rte. 42).

41 m. **Huntly** (*Huntly Castle*, ¾ m. N. in Huntly Lodge dower-house, RB. 17/6–20/, P. 7–10 gs. ; *Huntly*, RB. 17/6, P. 8 gs. ; *Gordon Arms*, RB. 15/, P. 7 gs. ; *Hill*, RB. 15/6– 17/6, P. 6–8 gs.), built on a rectangular plan, is the chief town (4200 inhab.) of the district of *Strathbogie* and stands a little above the confluence of the Bogie and the Deveron. It is a favourite summer station and angler's resort, 20 miles of water on the Deveron and its tributaries being owned by the town. Castle St. leads N. from the square to the Gordon Schools and (½ m. ; fine double avenue) the castle in a charming site above the Deveron.

*Huntly Castle (known as *Strathbogie Castle* until 1544), now an imposing ruin (adm. 6*d.*, 10–4 or 7, Sun. from 2), was the cradle of the earls of Huntly, the most powerful lords in the N. until c. 1550. Before the mad attempt of the 4th Earl to kidnap Queen Mary, they held three earldoms and ruled like kings in the whole region. In 1307 Robert Bruce, though sick from much exposure, defeated the Comyn's forces at *Slioch*, 2 m. S.E., and granted an old fortress of the Comyns on this site to his lieutenant Sir Adam Gordon of Gordon in Berwickshire, founder of the Huntly family. The castle, burned in 1594, was rebuilt (1602) by the 1st Marquess in a more ornamental style, with lettered parapets giving his name and that of his marchioness, Henriette Stewart; but this castle likewise fell into disrepair c. 1760. Much of the material was used to enlarge *Huntly Lodge* (½ m. N.).

George MacDonald (1824–1905) describes his native town of Huntly in 'Alec Forbes of Howglen.' The house in which he was born stands (altered) in Duke St., and 'The Farm,' S.E. of the town in which he spent part of his boyhood, is identified with ' Howglen.'

MOTOR-BUSES run from Huntly to *Banff* (21 m. in 1½ hr.) viâ the large village of (11¾ m.) *Aberchirder*, crossing the Deveron near the tall tower of *Kinairdy*, a Crichton stronghold ; to *Cullen* (26 m. in 1½ hr.) viâ (4½ m.) *Rothiemay* (Forbes Arms), with an old bridge on the Deveron. For Forgue, etc., see p. 310.

Beyond Huntly A 96 crosses the Deveron and soon ascends above its valley, then enters Banffshire.—52 m. **Keith** (*Royal*, RB. 19/6, P. 8 gs. ; *Commercial*, RB. 17/6, P. 6 gs. ; *Queen's*, unlic., RB. 16/6) is another regularly planned town (4350 inhab.). In the angle between the railway and the road to the upper town are the ruins of *Milton Tower*, a castle of the Oliphants. The Roman Catholic church, with large statues of SS. Peter and Paul on its façade, contains a noteworthy altarpiece presented by Charles X of France. ·

Fife Keith, on the opposite bank of the Isla, once a separate town, is connected with Keith by two bridges, the older dating from 1609. *Newmill*, 1½ m. N., beyond the main station, was the birthplace of James Gordon Bennett (c. 1800– 72), founder of the ' New York Herald.' *The Balloch* (1199 ft.), a prominent hill 2¼ m. E., commands a fine view.—At *Auchinhove*, in the Pass of Grange, near the Isla c. 4 m. E. of Keith, is the northernmost unmistakable trace of Roman occupation in Britain.

The road from Keith to *Dufftown* (10 m. ; A 920) ascends Strath Isla above and alongside the railway, passing (r.) the park and gardens of *Drummuir* and the beautiful *Loch Park*, with steep sides.—The road to *Craigellachie* (11 m. ; A 95) follows the Elgin railway to (5 m.) *Mulben*, there turning left. B 9013, keeping straight on at Mulben, descends a wooded defile and crosses the Spey (7½ m.) beside a large railway viaduct. The road bridge superseded the 'Boat o' Brig,' the ferry here on the old Inverness road. St. Mary's Well, at *Orton*, on the Moray bank of the Spey, 2 m. N., was the scene of a medieval pilgrimage on the last Sunday in May (revived in 1936).

A 96, the modern Inverness road, rises to 617 ft. on the border of Moray, then descends through a pine-wood intersected by three deep ravines called *The Dramlechs*.

Moray or **Elginshire** is a small maritime county on the Moray Firth. The fertile 'Laigh of Moray' occupies the lowlands in the N. ; to the S. the country rises in uplands to over 2000 ft. The rapid Spey separates Moray from Banffshire, on the E. ; the Findhorn, which enters from Nairn on the W., is noted for its lovely scenery. "There are salmons in both." On the coast, W. of the Findhorn, are the shifting Culbin Sands, which c. 1694 overwhelmed a fertile barony of many thousand acres. Elgin cathedral, Pluscarden priory, Kinloss abbey, and Sweno's Stone at Forres are among the antiquities of the county. The ancient province of *Moray*, much larger than the modern county, extended from the Spey W. to the Beauly and from the sea S. to the Grampians.

50 m. **Fochabers** (*Gordon Arms*, RB. 18/6, P. 12 gs. ; *Speybank*, RB. 18/6, P. 10 gs. ; *Grant Arms*), on the E. bank of the Spey, is a regularly planned little place, having been removed bodily in 1798 from its original site close to Gordon Castle. The town, with the classical church of Bellie parish, was designed by John Baxter. The market cross remains on the old site.

Gordon Castle (no adm.) stands N. of the town in a wooded park of 1300 acres. Formerly a marsh, the estate was called the Bog of Gight (windy bog) and its lord the 'Guidman o' the Bog' until the time of the first Duke of Gordon (1684). This was the first halting-place of Charles II after his landing (see below). The mansion, rebuilt by Baxter (comp. above), had a battlemented front nearly 600 ft. long, and incorporated the 15th cent. tower of Gight, but most of it has been demolished since 1950. The house and policies are still in possession of the family of the Duke of Richmond and Gordon, to whom the estate passed in 1836 on the death of the last Duke of Gordon ; but some 90,000 acres were sold to the Crown in 1937.

On the W. bank of the Spey, 1¾ m. from Fochabers, B 9015 turns N. for (3½ m.) *Garmouth*, a quaint village, whose harbour shifts constantly with the flooding of the Spey. Charles II landed here in June 1650, after signing the two Covenants. In 1784 two Yorkshiremen who came to purchase timber from the Duke of Gordon established (1 m. farther down the river) a shipbuilding village which they named *Kingston*, after their native town, Kingston-upon-Hull.

From Fochabers to *Banff*, see Rte. 44.

Beyond (66½ m.) *Lhanbryde* (Tennant Arms, RB. 15/6) we have, on a clear day, a distant view across the Moray Firth of the Sutherland and Caithness mountains. On the left is *Coxton*, a well-preserved tower.

Urquhart, 1 m. N., was the site of a Benedictine priory founded by David I in 1136. There is a well-preserved stone circle at Viewfield farm, 1 m. farther N., a little beyond which is the 17th cent. *Innes House*.

69 m. **ELGIN,** a pleasant royal burgh (10,625 inhab.) and county town on the S. bank of the deep but sluggish Lossie, boasts of one of the finest ruined cathedrals in Scotland.

Hotels. Gordon Arms, 122 High St., RB. 24/6, P. 11½ gs.; **Station,** RB. 22/6, P. 9 gs.; **Tower,** High St., RB. 18/, P. 8 gs.; **Grand,** South St., RB. 17/6, P. 7 gs.; **Royal,** unlic., RB. 19/6, P. 11 gs.; **Oakwood Rustic Motel,** 2 m. W., RB. 16/.

Post Office, Commercial St.

Motor-Buses to *Lossiemouth* (24 min.); *Burghead* (32 min.); *Inverness* (1¾ hr.) viâ Forres and Nairn; *Knockando* (1 hr.) viâ Rothes; *Carrbridge* (2½ hrs.) viâ Craigellachie and Strathspey; *Dufftown* (1½ hr.) viâ Craigellachie; *Aberdeen* (3 hrs.) viâ Keith and Huntly; *Banff* (2 hrs.) viâ Fochabers, Buckie, and Cullen.

History. Elgin, of ancient but uncertain foundation, is first mentioned in 1190 and in the Middle Ages was favoured as a royal residence, especially by James II. It marked the northern limit of Edward I's progress through Scotland in 1296. Part of the town was burned by the Wolf of Badenoch in 1390, and half of it was again destroyed in the struggle between Huntly and Douglas (1452). Prince Charles Edward spent 11 days before Culloden at Thunderton House, while Johnson and Boswell ate "a vile dinner" in 1773 at the old Red Lion, still standing at No. 46 High St. In 1778, at the Cross, the Highland Light Infantry were first embodied (as the Macleod Highlanders) by Lord Macleod. More recently Elgin has been noted as a centre of education : the Academy is the successor of an old grammar school, recorded in 1489 ; Graham Bell, pioneer of the telephone, was a pupil teacher (1863–4) and resident master (1865–7) at Weston House Academy ; and George Saintsbury was the not very successful headmaster of Elgin Educational Institute in 1872–4.

The long and broad High Street still retains a few old arcaded houses (notably No. 46). In the middle of the street stands *St. Giles's Church* (1828), by Archd. Simpson ; near it is the old Tower Hotel. At the E. end of the church stands the *Muckle Cross* of Elgin, originally erected c. 1650, destroyed c. 1792, and rebuilt in 1888 ; and at the W. end is a fountain marking the site of the old tolbooth. The *County Buildings* (1939–52) and the *Town Hall,* burned in 1939 and rebuilt in 1952–58, are good modern works. Gordon's Hotel, on the S. side of the street, occupies *Thunderton House* (1650 ; see above). Near the W. end of High St. rises *Lady Hill,* an eminence so called from the chapel (St. Mary's) of the old castle which once stood here and was visited by Edward I in 1303. It now bears a tall column in honour of the last Duke of Gordon (d. 1836), which visitors may ascend (view). Farther W. is the admirable building of *Gray's Hospital* (1815).

At the other (E.) end of the High St. is the *Little Cross* (17th cent. ; restored), marking the old boundary between the burgh and cathedral lands. Opposite is the *Museum* (adm. 6d.) founded in 1842 by the Elgin Literary and Scientific Society, noted for its fossils from the Old Red sandstone and for two incised figures of bulls (8th cent.) from Burghead. Farther on is *Cooper Park* (40 acres), with the fine Georgian mansion of *Grant Lodge,* housing the public library.

The ***Cathedral,** now a beautiful ruin, was one of the finest churches in Scotland, known as the ' Lanthorn of the North ' and described by Bp. Barr in the 14th cent. as " the ornament of the district, the glory of the Kingdom, and the admiration of foreigners." Adm. 1/ (10-4 or 7 ; Sun. from 2).

History. The see of Moray was in existence before 1124, but for the next century the bishop's seat alternated between Birnie, Spynie, and Kinneddar. The present cathedral was founded in 1224 but does not appear to have been completed when, in 1270, it was seriously damaged by fire. In 1390 the ' Wolf of Badenoch,' brother of Robert III, having quarrelled with the bishop and been excommunicated, descended upon the cathedral with his ' wyld, wykked Heland-men ' and again gave it to the flames. It was rebuilt with a central tower, which fell in 1506, was raised again in 1538, and again collapsed in 1711. In 1555 the church was desecrated by the ' Bloody Vespers,' a murderous brawl between the Dunbar and the Innes families. A considerable part of the building fell into decay after 1567, when, by order of the Privy Council, the roof was stripped of its lead in order to raise funds for paying the troops, an object that is said to have been defeated by the foundering of the plunder-laden ship on its voyage to Holland. In 1640 a beautiful rood-loft, richly adorned and painted with biblical subjects, was torn down, and the tracery of the W. window was smashed by Cromwell's troops in 1650. The church gradually became a complete ruin, but the remains were carefully tended by John Shanks, a poor souter, for many years before the Government appointed him keeper in 1825.

In 1748 Gilzean Anderson, the half-crazed widow of a soldier, returned to her native town and took up her abode in the lavatory of the cathedral, using the piscina as a cradle for her infant son. The boy enlisted as a private in the service of the Hon. East India Company, rose to the rank of Lieutenant-General, and acquired a fortune, part of which he bequeathed to the town.

The total length of the cathedral was c. 290 ft., the length of the transepts, c. 120 ft. Two stately *W. Towers* (before 1390 ; 90 ft. high) flank a very handsome portal, deeply recessed with vigorous mouldings, now much defaced, like all the carving in the cathedral. Above is the great Alpha window, surmounting an interior arcade of four bays. Of the *Nave* of six bays with double aisles nothing remains but the stumps of some of the piers. The transepts are known as the Innes Aisle (S.) and the Dunbar Aisle (N.). The finest parts of the church (13–14th cent.) are those which escaped the fire of 1390. These include the façade of the S. transept, pierced by a fine doorway with toothed moulding surmounted by a pointed oval, the round arch appearing in the upper range of windows above the pointed ; and the E. end of the choir. The *Choir,* flanked by side chapels, has a graceful clerestory of double and triple lancet windows. The raised chancel is lighted from the E. by two rows of five lancets with piers instead of mullions between the compartments and surmounted by a rose-window (the Omega window), from which the tracery has vanished.

On the N. side of the central space is a cross-slab (9–10th cent.), carved on one side with a Runic cross, on the arms of which are the symbols of four priests (or the Evangelists ?) ; on the other side are figures of a knight carrying his hawk, the spectacle ornament, the broken mace, and the half-moon.

Between the N. aisle of the choir (St. Columba's Aisle) and the octagonal chapter house is the small *Lavatory,* with the piscina in which Gen. Anderson was cradled (comp. above).

The *Chapter House* (early 15th cent.), better preserved than the other buildings, having been used as a court-house until 1731, retains its elegant central pier and finely groined roof. The S. choir aisle (St. Mary's Aisle), which has kept its stone vault, was the former burial-place of the Gordon family. The fine tomb at the E. end is that of Bp. Winchester (d. 1460) ; in the centre is the tomb of the 1st Earl of Huntly (d. 1470), and farther W. is an armed effigy of Hay of Lochloy (d. 1422).

The burial-ground S. of the cathedral contains many quaintly inscribed tombstones.—Of the four gateways in the cathedral precinct wall the only survivor is *Panns Port* or E. gate.—A wing (1406) of the *Bishop's House* stands to the N.W. of the cathedral.

A little farther to the E. is *Anderson's Institution* for the maintenance of 10 old people and the education of c. 300 children, founded by Gen. Anderson (1746–1824 ; see above), in a fine building of 1832.

To the S. of the Little Cross (p. 313) and entered from Abbey St. are the remains of a Franciscan friary, founded by John Innes in 1479, incorporated in a modern convent. The charming little *Greyfriars Chapel* (15th cent.) was well restored by the 3rd Marquess of Bute.

A road leads S.W. from Elgin, crossing the Lossie at *Palmer's Bridge*, a reminder of the passage of pilgrims, to (7 m.) **Pluscarden Abbey**, which, protected from sea-winds by a range of fir-clad hills, stands at the narrowest point of a valley which expands W. in a long vista of luxuriant fertility. The well-preserved remains were purchased and partly restored by the Marquess of Bute. They have now been presented to the Benedictines, and the abbey is being rebuilt and is open at all reasonable hours except Sun. morning. This monastery, dedicated to St. Andrew, was founded by Alexander II in 1230 for Valliscaulians, but became Benedictine in 1454. Its *Church*, transitional in style between Romanesque and E.E., was cruciform, with a square central tower. The nave was never completed ; the aisleless choir of three bays is 56 ft. long. The N. transept had a large round window in the gable. The old groined roof is still extant in the aisles of the transepts and in the Dunbar Vestry (c. 1550), N. of the choir. On the N. wall of the choir is a 16th cent. tabernacle from Flanders, with two angels supporting the monstrance. The E. end has a four-light lancet window, surmounted by a traceried window and a vesica above ; two small chapels on the S. side retain their vaults. The *Chapter House*, about 30 ft. square, shows remarkably delicate mouldings, and, like that of Elgin, is supported by a single central pier. This, with the rebuilt *Refectory*, is shown to male visitors on request.

The church of *Birnie*, near the Lossie, 3 m. S. of Elgin, was the original seat of the see of Moray (before 1184) and still preserves its nave and chancel entire. There is no E. window, the church being lighted by round-headed windows of Norman date. In the interior is the ' Ronnel Bell,' said to have been made of silver and copper at Rome but probably of Celtic origin. To be thrice prayed for in Birnie kirk will ' either mend ye or end ye,' and to be buried in Birnie kirkyard is the ambition of many of the country people.

FROM ELGIN TO LOSSIEMOUTH, 5½ m., railway in 15 min. The road (A 941) passes (2¾ m. ; r.) the ruins of *Spynie Palace*, the castle of the bishops of Moray from c. 1205 to 1686. The most prominent feature is the huge square tower (c. 1470), originally of six stories, built as a protection from the turbulent Gordons. A court with three angle towers was added later, protected on the S. and E. sides by a moat. Over the main entrance the arms of Bishop John Innes (1406–14) are still visible, and on the S. side the chapel can be identified. In the old churchyard to the S.W. stood until 1736 the church of Spynie, the Cathedral of Moray in 1203–24.

5½ m. **Lossiemouth** (4950 inhab. ; *Stotfield & Marine*, RB. 27/6) has a good harbour and serves as the port of Elgin. The life of the fisher-folk is well described by George MacDonald in ' Malcolm ' and other novels. There is an excellent bathing beach and a very fine golf course, but the countryside is wind-swept.

J. Ramsay MacDonald (1866–1937), the first Labour prime minister, was a native of Lossiemouth.—The bishops of Moray had a castle at *Kinneddar*, 1 m. S.W., while the chapel of *Michaelkirk* (1705), farther on, is perhaps the latest example of ' survival ' Gothic.

FROM ELGIN TO BURGHEAD, 8 m. N.W. by road (bus hourly in 32 min.).— **Burghead** is a large fishing village of 1370 inhab., built on a point whose extremity commands a fine sea view. The headland has been fortified from before Pictish times and the Danes also had a fort here. The so-called ' Roman Well,' within an Iron-Age fort, is probably an early Christian baptistery. The curious custom of ' burning the clavie,' when a lighted tar-barrel is carried through the streets, traditionally to scare away evil spirits, still takes place annually in January.—We may return E. along the coast to (2 m.) *Hopeman*, another fishing village. Thence B 9012 leads back S.E. to Elgin (7 m.) viâ (3½ m.) *Duffus*, where the church has a fine 16th cent. porch and the shaft of a good 14th cent. churchyard cross. The ruined moated *Duffus Castle*, where David I stayed during the erection of Kinloss Abbey, is 1¼ m. S.E., on the Lossiemouth road (B 9135). It has a fine 14th cent. tower crowning a Norman motte. *Gordonstoun School*, 1 m. E. of Duffus, occupies the 17th cent. mansion built by Sir Robert Gordon (1647–1704), the ' warlock of Gordonstoun.' It was founded in 1934 by English friends of Salem, in Germany, whose headmaster, Kurt Hahn, had escaped to Britain after imprisonment by the Nazis. The Duke of Edinburgh is a former pupil. The school also occupies the neighbouring mansions of Duffus House and Hopeman Lodge.—Robert Barclay of Ury (1648–90), the Quaker, a friend of Penn and Fox, was born at Gordonstoun.

From Elgin to *Aberdeen* viâ Craigellachie, see Rte. 43B.

On the left, as we leave the Burghead road on the right, is the **York Tower**, on the **Knock of Alves**, commemorating Frederick, Duke of York (d. 1827), son of George III.—About 1 m. to the right beyond (77 m.) *Newmill*, is **Kinloss**, celebrated for its ABBEY, one of the important Cistercian foundations of David I (1151), who chose as its site a clearing whither he was miraculously guided by a white dove when he had lost his way in the forest. Among the powerful abbots was Robert Reid who became Bp. of Orkney in 1541. After the Reformation the buildings served as a quarry, and little survives beyond a fine round-headed archway, the vaulted E. end of the church (fitted up as a chapel), and part of the abbot's lodging.

Findhorn (Crown, RB. 17/6, P. 7 gs. ; Culbin Sands, P. 5–7 gs.), a fishing village and summer resort 3 m. N.W., at the entrance to Findhorn Bay, the estuary of the Findhorn, commands a charming view of Forres. It is the third village of its name, its two predecessors, which were built more to the N.W., having been swept away, the first by the encroachment of Culbin Sands, the second by the great flood of 1701.

80½ m. **FORRES,** c. 2 m. from the mouth of the Findhorn, is a clean little royal burgh (4460 inhab.), priding itself on its genial climate and its mention in ' Macbeth '.

Hotels. Cluny Hill, S.E. of the town, RB. 30/, P. 13–15 gs. ; **Royal Station,** RB. 17/6, P. 7–8 gs. ; **Carlton,** RB. 18/6, P. 7–8 gs. ; **Victoria,** RB. 19/6, P. 7½–9 gs. ; **Queen's,** RB. 20/, P. 8–9 gs. ; **Park,** E. of the town, similar charges.

Motor-Buses several times daily to *Findhorn Bay* (boating, bathing, and fishing), and to *Findhorn* and *Burghead* ; to *Elgin* viâ Kinloss ; and to *Nairn* and *Inverness.*

History. Donald II was killed at Forres and his son, Malcolm I, is said to have lived in the neighbourhood and was perhaps murdered at Blervie Castle, 4 m. S.E., in 954. Malcolm's son Duffus was, in turn, slain by the governor of Forres in 967 ;

his body was hidden in a river-pool, upon which the sun refused to shine until it was found. The gentle Duncan held his court at Forres, and it was on their way thither that Macbeth and Banquo met, on the 'blasted heath' (see below), the 'weird sisters,' three of the witches for whom Forres was notorious. After the foundation of the bishopric at Elgin the importance of Forres declined. Lord Strathcona (1820–1914) was a native of Forres.

The obelisk to a Crimean hero at the W. end of High St. stands on the site of the royal castle, long since vanished. The *Falconer Museum*, likewise in High St., contains interesting fossils. *Forres House*, at the E. end, with the library, has a fine public park. But the most interesting object near Forres is *Sweno's Stone*, beyond the E. end of the town on the left of the Kinloss road, a slim shaft of sandstone 23 ft. high, carved with figures of warriors, animals, and knots.

It has been conjectured to commemorate a victory of Sweyn, son of Harald, over Malcolm II in 1008. On the S. side of the road, a little farther on, is the granite *Witches' Stone*, marking the spot where the Forres witches used to be burnt.

The ascent of the *RIVER FINDHORN leads through scenery unsurpassed in Scotland and should certainly be made as far as Randolph's Leap (8 m.).—We follow the Grantown road to (5 m.) *Sluie* in the Altyre woods, where walkers should take a path that ascends the right bank of the Findhorn for 2½ m. passing Logie House. The river has cut a sinuous course through a deep gorge in the sandstone, and the path offers a changing view every 100 yards of the clear brown water swirling over rocks or still in dark pools. We rejoin the road just before crossing the tributary Divie near *Relugas House*. A path at a gate, 200 yds. farther on, leads to *Randolph's Leap*, the most striking part of the Findhorn valley, a little above the inflow of the Divie. Hence we may return to the road and follow the river up past *Relugas* village to (1 m.) *Daltulich Bridge*, whence a road returns to Forres (9 m.) through Darnaway Forest, encircling *Darnaway Castle* (Earl of Moray ; no adm.), a mansion of 1810 with a fine 15th cent. hall. It was often visited by James IV, who had gifted it to his mistress, Lady Janet Kennedy.

The road on the left at Daltulich Bridge ascends the left side of the valley to the road from Nairn to Grantown (11 m. from Forres), just N. of Logie Bridge.

From Forres to *Aviemore*, see Rte. 32.

Beyond Forres the road crosses the Findhorn, 3 m. above its mouth in *Findhorn Bay*, which is bounded on the N.W. by the *Culbin Sands* (3600 acres ; 100 ft. high), a waste of moving sand, now largely afforested. Before the extraordinary sandstorm of 1694 this tract was famed as the 'girnel' or granary of Moray, and occasionally after storms the lofty dunes reveal parts of the old buildings.—About ¼ m. beyond (84¼ m.) *Brodie* we may catch a glimpse (r.) of the stately Brodie House, seat of the ancient family of the same name. The *View northward across the Moray Firth extends to Morven in Caithness. On the right farther on is *Hardmuir*, now cultivated and wooded, but supposed to have been the heath on which Macbeth and Banquo encountered the witches. We enter Nairnshire.

Nairnshire is a small maritime county, across which lies the middle course of the Findhorn. Cawdor Castle is in this county, which shares the history and the reputation for witches of Moray.

87 m. *Auldearn* was the scene of one of Montrose's most brilliant victories (May 9th, 1645), in which, with 1500 foot

and 200 horse, he routed a Covenanting force, more than twice as numerous, under General Urry.

Montrose raised his standard on *Castle Hill* (now crowned by a 17th cent. dovecot ; N.T.), N.W. of the village. *Boath House*, adjoining, is an attractive work by Archd. Simpson (1827).—The ruined *Inshoch Tower*, once the seat of the Hays of Lochloy, is 1¼ m. N.E.

91 m. **NAIRN** (4700 inhab.), at the mouth of the river Nairn, a favourite resort with good sands and three golf courses, is surrounded by delightful country.

Hotels. Golf View, open May–Oct., RB. 35/; **Newton,** RB. 35/; RB. 15–18 gs.; **Royal Marine,** RB. 27/6; **Windsor,** comfortable, RB. 21/, P. 10 gs.; **Clifton,** RB. 19/6, P. 9 gs.; **Alton Burn,** 1½ m. W., RB. 25/, P. 10 gs.; **Highland,** in the town, RB. 21/, P. 10 gs.; **Lovat Lodge,** RB. 25/; **Washington,** RB. 17/6, and many other unlic. houses.

History. Nairn, formerly Invernairn, was created a royal burgh by William the Lion. The town stands on the division between the Highlands and Lowlands, and James VI used to boast that he had a town so long that the people of one end did not understand the language of the other. Dr. Johnson, who found the same state of affairs prevailing, described the town as "in a state of miserable decay," but it is many years since Gaelic was spoken here. The Duke of Cumberland celebrated his birthday here on the day before Culloden.

In the High St. are an old cross, the *Post Office*, and the *Town House* of 1818. The N.E. part of the town, or Fishertown, towards the harbour, was the quarter of the fisher-folk, now much reduced in number. Many bear the surname Main, and are distinguished by curious nicknames.

The moated **Cawdor Castle** (Earl Cawdor ; no adm.), 5¾ m. S.W., has an old central tower (1454) surrounded by 16th cent. buildings, remodelled c. 1650 ; Shakespeare followed tradition in making it the scene of the murder of Duncan by Macbeth. A carving over the chimney-piece in the dining-room, dating from before Sir Walter Raleigh's time, depicts monkeys smoking pipes. *Cawdor* village is attractive, with a church mainly of 1619 and a mill of 1635.

Just beyond a bridge across the Nairn (1½ m. W. of Cawdor) is the entrance to *Kilravock Castle* (pron. Kilrock), built in 1460 and ever since occupied by the Rose family. In 1746 the laird, although not a Jacobite, entertained Prince Charlie to dinner and showed him the gardens, while the Duke of Cumberland slept at his town house in Nairn. *Dalcross Castle*, in Inverness-shire, 1½ m. W. of Kilravock, consists of two blocks of corbie-stepped buildings at right angles, built by Lord Lovat in 1621. It was completely restored in 1896 and retains many old features including spiral stair and secret stair.

The Grantown road (A 939) leads S.E. from Nairn to (9½ m.) *Logie Bridge*, on the Findhorn, and joins the road from Forres at (23 m.) *Dava* (Rte. 32). Just short of Logie Bridge by-roads on the right lead to (1 m.) *Ardclach*, where a lane on the left descends to a curious detached and fortified belfry (1655) on a promontory above the Findhorn. The by-road goes on to (4½ m.) *Dulsie Bridge*, where the river is confined in a narrow chasm, praised by Charles St. John. Farther up, the narrow valley, its upper part traversed only by farm-tracks, is known as *The Streens*.

The seaside village of *Ardersier*, 7 m. W. of Nairn, is connected by a shore road with (1¾ m. more) *Fort George*. The fort, in an imposing position on a promontory opposite Chanonry Point, is an irregular polygon with six bastions. Built in 1784 to accommodate 2500 men, it was until 1958 the depôt of the Seaforth Highlanders.—Motor-bus to *Inverness*.

On the right, beyond (98½ m.) the Inverness airport of *Dalcross* (the castle lies to the S., viâ Croy), is *Castle Stewart*,

a fine turreted house probably built by the Earl of Moray early
in the 17th century. In 1624 it was despoiled by the Mackintoshes, but it has since been repaired.—103½ m. *Allanfearn*.
—107 m. **Inverness**, see Rte. 54.

B. By Road viâ Craigellachie

ROAD, 111 m. To (24½ m.) *Oyne*, see Rte. 43A.—B 9002. 37½ m. *Rhynie*.—
45¾ m. *Cabrach*.—A 941. 55 m. *Dufftown*.—60 m. *Craigellachie*.—73 m. **Elgin.**
Thence to *Inverness*, see Rte. 43A.

From Aberdeen to *Oyne*, see Rte. 43A. Our road bears left
from the Huntly road, and ascends the Gadie valley.—28¾ m.
Auchleven (Premnay, RB. 15/, P. 110/).—30½ m. *Leslie
Castle* (r.), a substantial ruin, was built by William Forbes
in 1660–64, and is still almost entirely medieval in style.

The Suie Road, running S. to Alford, crosses the *Correen Hills* at 1281 ft. ; on
their N. slope, S. of Clatt, was fought the battle of *Tillyangus* (1571), when Edom
o' Gordon defeated 'Black Arthur' Forbes, in their bitter family feud. Forbes
was slain, and his body is said to have rested on *Lord Arthur's Cairn* (1699 ft.),
highest of the Correens, on its way to Forbes kirkyard.

We quit the Gadie and descend into Strathbogie.—36 m.
Druminnor, a mansion of 1577, incorporates the original
15th cent. tower of the Lords Forbes (adm. on written application to Miss Forbes-Sempill).—37½ m. *Rhynie* (Richmond
Arms, RB. 14/6, P. 6 gs.), also on the road (A 97) from Huntly
to Strathdon, is dominated on the N.W. by *Tap o' Noth* (1851
ft.), whose conical summit is crowned by an important
vitrified fort with a rampart 15 ft. high. A 941, which we
follow, passes *Lesmore Castle*, a ruined Gordon stronghold,
and ascends to 1370 ft. ; at the summit we enter Banffshire.—
About 2 m. W. of (45¾ m.) *Cabrach* is *Aldivalloch*, the house of
" Roy's wife " in the well-known song by Elizabeth Grant of
Carron. The road descends and crosses the Deveron then
traverses a high moorland (1130 ft.) before dropping down to
Glen Fiddich.—A track on the right, 1½ m. from Dufftown,
leads to (¾ m.) *Auchindoun Castle*, the stronghold of 'Edom
o' Gordon' in the mid-16th cent., with a central tower erected
by Robert Cochrane, the favourite of James III. The ruins,
which include a fine Gothic hall, are surrounded by prehistoric earthworks.

55 m. **Dufftown** (*Elms*, unlic., P. 5 gs.), above the confluence
of the Dullan and the Fiddich, was founded in 1817 by James
Duff, 4th Earl of Fife, and is a centre of the distilling industry,
with 1460 inhab. About ⅛ m. S., on the steep bank of the
Dullan, is *Mortlach Church*, a 12th cent. building containing
some ancient tombstones. To the N. is the massive ruin of
Balvenie Castle, the 14th cent. stronghold of the Comyns,
later of the Douglases and from 1460 the property of the

Atholl family, whose motto is on the front (adm. 6*d*., 10–4 or 7, Sun. from 2). The buildings are mainly 15–16th cent. and include a notable iron yett.

A road (B 9009 ; bus to Tomintoul) runs S.W. up *Glen Rinnes*, the valley of the Dullan, the limestone scenery of which contrasts pleasingly with the granite peaks of the *Convals* (1810 and 1867 ft.) and of *Ben Rinnes* (2755 ft.) to the W. Beyond (7 m.) the watershed (1022 ft.) we descend into *Glen Livet* (c. 12 m.). Thence to *Tomintoul*, see p. 250.

The road runs N.W. above Glen Fiddich on the other side of which is the old turreted mansion of *Kininvie*—60 m. **Craigellachie** (*Craigellachie*, RB. 25/, P. 11 gs.), where the Fiddich falls into the Spey, is sometimes called Lower Craigellachie to distinguish it from the rock at Aviemore.

FROM CRAIGELLACHIE TO KNOCKANDO, 8½ m. (B 9102).—Crossing the Spey, we turn sharp left on B 9102.—5 m. *Archiestown* (Hotel, RB. 21/, P. 10 gs.).—8½ m. *Knockando* stands above an especially beautiful stretch of the Spey, which here follows a winding course. To the N. is the parish church on a hill, with three worn sculptured slabs in the churchyard. The brothers Grant, supposed to have been drawn by Dickens as the ' Cheeryble Brothers,' were natives of the parish. B 9102 goes on up Speyside to Blacksboat bridge and Grantown (16 m.), while a moorland road runs N.W. to Dallas (7½ m.).

From Craigellachie to *Keith*, see Rte. 43A ; to *Grantown* by A 95, see p. 249.

Quitting Craigellachie, we cross the Spey into Moray, traversing Telford's graceful iron bridge of a single span (150 ft. ; 1812–15).—63½ m. *Rothes* (Station, RB. 16/6, P. 7–9 gs.) is picturesquely situated on the left bank of the Spey in full view of Ben Aigan (1544 ft.). The village (1210 inhab.) gives the title of earl to the Leslie family, who, however, sold their old castle and estates to the Earl of Seafield c. 1700 and migrated to Fife. The wooded *Conerock Hill* (1 m. S.W.) affords a fine view.—We quit the Spey and traverse the Glen of Rothes. 66½ m. *Rothes Glen Hotel* (RB. 18/6–22/6, P. 8–10½ gs.).—73 m. **Elgin,** and thence to (111 m.) **Inverness,** see Rte. 43A.

44. FROM ABERDEEN TO MACDUFF AND BANFF

ROAD, 46 m.—4 m. *Bucksburn.*—A 947. 6½ m. *Dyce.*—18 m. *Old Meldrum.*—27 m. *Fyvie.*—35 m. *Turriff.*—46 m. **Banff Bridge.**—MOTOR-BUSES to *Banff* in 2½ hrs. viâ Turriff and Macduff ; to *Macduff* in 2¾ hrs. viâ Inverurie, Aberchirder, and Banff.

RAILWAY. *Banff* is the terminus of a branch (6 m.) from Tillynaught, on the line from Aberdeen to Elgin viâ Portsoy.

From Aberdeen to (4 m.) Bucksburn, see Rte. 43A. A 947 keeps right, crossing the railway, for (6½ m.) *Dyce*, with the Aberdeen airport. At the old churchyard in a bend of the Don, 1¼ m. N.W. are two important sculptured stones, and 2 m. W. is a remarkable stone circle.—18 m. *Old Meldrum* (980 inhab. ; Meldrum House, in an old mansion, 1 m. N., RB. 21/–25/, P. 8–10 gs. ; Meldrum Arms, RB. 12/6, P. 6 gs.) was the birthplace of Sir Patrick Manson (1844–1922), ' father of tropical medicine.' About ¾ m. S. rises *Barra Hill*

(634 ft.), with a prehistoric fort, the site of the battle in which Bruce defeated Comyn, Earl of Buchan (1307).

B 9000 leads E. towards the coast viâ (4½ m.) *Pitmedden*. About 1 m. S. is *Udny Castle*, incorporating an old four-storied tower, and just to the N., on B 9004, is *Pitmedden House*, with gardens laid out by Sir Alex. Seton c. 1675 (N.T.; adm. daily). Less than 1 m. E. of this is the splendid ruin of *Tolquhon Castle* (adm. 6*d.*; 10–4 or 7, Sun. from 2), the chief mansion of Formartine. An inscription over the entrance states that " Al this warke, excep the auld tor, was begon by William Forbes, 15 Aprile 1584, and endit be him 20 Oct. 1589." The " auld tor," though called Preston's Tower after the original owners, was built by Sir John Forbes after 1420. In the opposite corner of the quadrangle is the spacious hall, preserving most of its original paving ; and to the W. are the pleasant grounds.—B 999 leads N. from Pitmedden to (2¾ m.) *Tarves*, where Wm. Forbes's monument (1589), by Thos. Leiper, master mason at Tolquhon, with lively Renaissance detail, survives from the old church.

27 m. *Fyvie*, once a royal burgh. On the right beyond the village, overlooking the river Ythan, is *Fyvie Castle* (no adm.), one of the stateliest and best preserved castellated mansions in Scotland.

The four older towers (15–18th cent.) are named after their builders : Preston, Meldrum, Gordon, and Seton. To these has been added the 19th cent. Leith Tower. On the Preston Tower is a figure of the Trumpeter of Fyvie, the subject of a charming love-ballad. In the garden are traces of the entrenchments made by Montrose when he was nearly captured by Argyll (1644).

From Fyvie to *Methlick* and *Ellon*, see Rte. 45.

On the left, before (30½ m.) *Auchterless*, is the farmhouse of *Towie-Barclay*, with the fine ruined tower (c. 1510 ; adm. on application) of *Tolly Castle*, the residence of the Barclays, a family to which Prince Michael Barclay de Tolly (1759–1818), marshal in the Russian army during the Napoleonic wars, belonged.—On the right, 2 m. farther, is *Hatton Castle*, preserving part of the old tower of Balquholly, the seat of the Mowatts.

35 m. Turriff (3000 inhab. ; *Commercial, Union*, at both RB. 18/6) is pleasantly situated on a hillside above the Idoch Water. The church, approached by an early 18th cent. gateway, preserves a belfry of 1636 and Lindsay and Leslie tombs. In 1639 the Master of Forbes, who had collected a body of Covenanters, was routed here by a party of royalist Gordons. The skirmish, in which the first blood in the Civil War was shed, is known as the ' Trot of Turriff.'

Delgatie Castle (adm. 2/, Wed. & Sat. 2–6 in May–Sept. ; other times 5/, minimum 4 pers.), the tower-house of the Hays of Errol, has good painted ceilings of 1590 ; *Gask House*, 1½ m. S., now a farmhouse, was an old seat of the Forbeses ; while *Craigston Castle*, 3¾ m. N.E., was built in 1604–7 in imitation of the principal tower of Fyvie.

We quit the Deveron, the lower course of which is followed by a by-road. On a rocky eminence to the left farther on are remains of *Kinedart Castle*, one of the Comyns' strongholds.—**41 m.** *King Edward* (pron. ' Kinedart ') ; the name is a corruption through Kinedart of Ceann-eadar.—**46 m.** *Banff Bridge*, built by Smeaton in 1779, crosses the Deveron near its mouth, with Macduff on the right and Banff on the left.

Macduff (*Fife Arms*, RB. 17/6, P. 8 gs. ; *Bayview*, similar charges ; *Shore*, unlic., RB. 13/6) is a plain but cheerful town (3320 inhab.) with a large harbour, devoted to herring-fishing. Known as *Down* until 1783, it was given its present name by the Earl of Fife, the owner of the harbour, whose family name was Duff. There is a fine sea view from the *Hill of Down*, with its War Memorial Tower 70 ft. high. To the E. is *Tarlair* (bus) with a fine bathing-pool (adm. 9*d*.) in a rocky bay.

BANFF (*Fife Arms*, RB. 20/–25/, P. 11–13 gs. ; *Seafield*, unlic., RB. 17/6, P. 7 gs. ; *Crown*, RB. 17/6, P. 7½–8 gs.), a small but ancient seaport and royal burgh (3350 inhab.), rises above the S.W. shore of Banff Bay at the mouth of the Deveron. It retains some 17–18th cent. burghers' houses in and near High Shore ; while opposite the Post Office is the old cemetery, with an aisle of the pre-Reformation church, and Leslie, Ogilvy and Sharp tombs (key at Police Station).

Only a few walls and a ditch, on the shoulder of the hill next the sea, represent the old *Castle*, once a royal residence occupied for a day or two by Edward I in 1296 and 1298. The wing in which Archbp. Sharp was born (1618) has been demolished and the present castle (1750), with 7 acres, is in use as a community centre. In Low St., the chief street, once stood the Black Bull Inn, visited by Dr. Johnson in 1773, and a house occasionally occupied by Byron and his mother ; the *Town House* retains a steeple of c. 1650. The Biggar Fountain, in this street, occupies the site of the gallows where, in 1701, James Macpherson, the half-gipsy fiddler and free-booter, met his death " sae rantin'ly, sae wantonly," vainly offering his fiddle as a gift to the cautious onlookers. The *Mercat Cross* is now at the Plainstanes, adjoining.—José de San Martín, the Argentine patriot, lived in exile at Banff, and was given the freedom of the burgh in 1824.

At the end of Low St., close to the church, is the entrance lodge of *Duff House* (by Wm. Adam ; 1745), formerly the seat of the Duke of Fife, an unfinished copy of the Villa Borghese. The duke presented the estate to the town in 1906. The house is at present untenanted ; the grounds (a public park) include a golf course. At the other end of the park (2 m. S.) is *Alvah Bridge*, where rocks rise steeply from a deep pool of the Deveron. At *Inchdrewer Castle* (1¼ m. W. of the bridge) George Ogilvy, Lord Banff, was burnt in 1713 in a fire perhaps kindled by his servants in order to conceal their thefts.

Motor-Buses at frequent intervals to Macduff (5 min.), going on in summer to *Tarlair* (10 min.) ; to *Gardenstown* (1 hr.) ; to *Aberdeen* (see above) ; to *White-hills* (17 min.) ; to *Buckie* (70 min.), *Elgin* (2 hrs.), and *Inverness* (3¾ hrs.) ; to *Huntly* (1⅓ hr.) ; to *Fraserburgh* viâ New Pitsligo and Strichen (1½ hr.) ; etc.

From Macduff to Fraserburgh, 21 m. by the coast road, offering fine cliff scenery.—7 m. *Gardenstown* (Garden Arms, RB. 20/, P. 10 gs.), on Gamrie Bay, 1 m. N. of the road, is a quaint cliff-side fishing village, connected by coast-path with the smaller village of *Crovie* (1 m.). *Troup Head* (366 ft.), with its rock-chimney called Hell's Linn, is 1½ m. farther N.E.—We enter Aberdeenshire.—10 m. *Pennan Bay* (Inn at the tile-roofed fishing village).—13 m. *New Aberdour*. On a rock 65 ft. above Aberdour Bay is *Dundarg Castle*, a stump of a tower joined by a narrow neck to the shore. In the *Cave of Cowshaven* (1½ m. W.) Alexander Forbes, last Lord Pitsligo, outlawed for his share in the '45, was concealed by his neighbours despite the large rewards offered.—17¼ m. *Rosehearty* (Forbes Arms, RB. 18/6, P. 8 gs.) is a fishing village connected by a frequent service of motor-buses with Fraserburgh. The ruins of *Pitsligo Castle* (1577) are ½ m. inland, on the road to (1 m.) Pitsligo church. The late 19th cent. church contains the Forbes loft and other rich wood-carving from the adjoining disused church of 1634. Farther E. is the ruined *Pitullie Castle* (17th cent.) above the village of (19 m.) *Sandhaven*.—21 m. *Fraserburgh*, see p. 326.

FROM BANFF TO ELGIN viâ the coast road and Fochabers, 37 m. The direct road (A 98; 36 m.) runs inland between Banff and Portsoy and between Cullen and Fochabers. The bus service (hourly) follows the coast.

RAILWAY, 35¼ m. in c. 2 hrs. Principal Stations : 6 m. *Tillynaught*, where trains are changed.—8¾ m. *Portsoy*.—14¼ m. *Cullen*.—20¼ m. **Buckie**.—22¾ m. *Portgordon*.—25¼ m. *Spey Bay*.—26½ m. *Garmouth*.—35¼ m. **Elgin**.

The E. portion of this route lies in **Banffshire**, a long narrow county that stretches N. along the N.W. border of Aberdeenshire from the remote mountain valleys at the N. base of the Cairngorm group to the shores of the Moray Firth. Banff is wholly agricultural and pastoral, except for the row of busy fishing villages and little towns on its N. seaboard—Macduff, Banff, Portsoy, Buckie, and the rest—and its distilleries, of which perhaps Glenlivet is best known. Though not reckoned a Highland county it contains the highest village N. of the Forth, viz. Tomintoul. Many of the remoter districts escaped the Reformation and have remained Roman Catholic strongholds. For some unexplained reason the phrase ' Go to Banff ' used to be a somewhat colloquial expression of contempt.

Proceeding due W. from Banff, we diverge to the right on B 9139, leaving on the right the small seaside village of *Whitehills*.—5¼ m. We cross the wooded glen of the Burn of Boyne, which is overlooked by the ruined *Boyne Castle* (1485), a stronghold of the Ogilvies.—7 m. **Portsoy** (*Station*, RB. 20/, P. 7 gs.), a plain little fishing port (1790 inhab.), is noted for the beauty and variety of the rock-formations along the coast. Portsoy marble is a beautiful variety of serpentine ; a peculiar flesh-coloured granite is likewise quarried here.

A pleasant detour may be made inland viâ *Fordyce* (2¾ m. S.W.), an agreeable village built round a small 16th cent. castle (adm. on request) and church with a good belfry. On the road to Cullen is the old house of *Birkenbog*, birthplace of Thomas Nicholson (1645–1718), first vicar-apostolic of Scotland.

13 m. **Cullen** (*Cullen Bay*, RB. 21/, P. 10½ gs. ; *Waverley*, RB. 18/6, P. 8 gs. ; *Seafield Arms*, RB. 19/, P. 8 gs. ; *Royal Oak*, RB. 19/6, P. 9 gs. ; *Grant Arms*, RB. 17/6, P. £7), a small fishing town (1560 inhab.), seaside resort, and royal burgh. The old town was demolished in 1822 to make room for improvements at Cullen House (see below) ; but the fine *Mercat Cross*, with a plaque of the Madonna, stands in the square. The streets slope down to the fishertown and bay, on the shore of which are the rocks called the ' Three Kings of Cullen.' Elizabeth de Burgh, second wife of Robert Bruce, died in 1327 in the castle, whose site is now doubtful. George Macdonald lived in a house in Grant St., now a tea-room.

The castellated *Cullen House* (½ m. S. ; grounds open Tues. & Fri. in summer 10–6) contains a portrait of Geo. Jamesone by himself and fine painted ceilings. The neighbouring church (adm. 2–5 on Tues. in summer, or by appointment with the minister), founded by Bruce, was made collegiate in 1543 by Alexander Ogilvy of Findlater, whose *Tomb, with that of his wife Margaret Gordon, is adorned with monastic ' weepers.' In the N. wall of the chancel is a tabernacle, one of the few remaining in Scotland. The elaborately carved Seafield pew dates from 1602 ; and there is a good memorial to James, Earl of Findlater and Seafield (d. 1730).—*Findlater Castle*, whose ruins are 2 m. E. on a rock jutting into the sea, was a stronghold of the Ogilvies.

The *Bin of Cullen* (1050 ft.), which rises 2½ m. S.W. of the town, commands a fine view across the Moray Firth to Morven in Caithness.—The ruined church of *Deskford*, 4 m. S. on the Keith road, contains a fine sacrament-house of 1551.

Leaving Cullen our road (A 942) keeps along a magnificent rocky stretch of coast, passing the fishing villages of *Port-knockie* (Victoria, RB. 15/), *Findochty*, and *Portessie*.—21 m. **Buckie** (*St. Andrews*, RB. 21/, P. 8½ gs. ; *Marine*, RB. 18/6, P. 8 gs. ; *Reapers*, unlic., RB. 16/, P. 6 gs. ; *Commercial*, RB. 15/6, P. 8 gs.) is the largest fishing village in Scotland (7700 inhab.) and has a good harbour.—Passing (22 m.) *Buckpool* and (23½ m.) *Portgordon* (Richmond Arms, RB. 14/6), where the harbour was built by the Duke of Richmond and Gordon in 1874, we turn inland (B 9014), cross the Burn of Tyret and enter Moray.

Spey Bay (Gordon-Richmond, RB. 22/6, P. 12 gs.), 3½ m. N. of Fochabers, is a small golfing and bathing resort, 1½ m. right of our road.

28½ m. *Fochabers Bridge*, and thence to (37 m.) **Elgin**, see Rte. 43A.

45. FROM ABERDEEN TO PETERHEAD AND FRASERBURGH

ROADS. To Peterhead, 32½ m. A 92. 12 m. *Foveran* church.—A 975. 14½ m. *Newburgh*.—23½ m. *Cruden Bay*.—A 952, 29½ m. *Boddam*.—32½ m. **Peterhead.** MOTOR-BUS viâ Ellon in 1½ hr. ; viâ Cruden Bay in 1 hr. 40 min.

To Fraserburgh, 43 m. A 92. 12 m. *Foveran* church.—17 m. *Ellon*.—21½ m. *Birness Toll* (r. for Cruden Bay).—31 m. *Mintlaw*.—43 m. **Fraserburgh.**— MOTOR-BUS direct in c. 1¾ hr. ; viâ New Pitsligo and Methlick in 2½ hrs.

RAILWAY to Peterhead, 44 m. in 1¾–2 hrs. ; to Fraserburgh, 47 m. in c 2 hrs. Principal Stations : 6¼ m. *Dyce*.—11½ m. *New Machar*.—14½ m. *Udny*.—19¼ m. *Ellon*.—31 m. **Maud Junction.** Thence viâ (35 m.) *Mintlaw* and (42 m.) *Inverugie* to (44 m.) **Peterhead** ; or viâ (32¾ m.) *Brucklay*, for New Pitsligo, (36¾ m.) *Strichen* and (41¾ m.) *Lonmay* to (47 m.) **Fraserburgh**.

We leave Aberdeen by Old Aberdeen and the Bridge of Don, and traverse the rather uninteresting coastal lowlands. 7 m. *Balmedie*. The old church of *Belhelvie*, a little farther on, preserves a Carolean tomb, to an Innes of Blairton, in its churchyard.—At (12 m.) *Foveran* church we bear right, on A 975.—14½ m. *Newburgh* (Udny Arms, RB. 30/, P. 14 gs. ; Ythan, RB. 17/6, P. 8 gs.) is a little port at the mouth of the Ythan. On the other side of the river are the sands of *Forvie*, covering a buried village.—We cross the estuary of the Ythan, a good fishing stream celebrated for its mussel-pearls, and (19½ m.) leave on the right the road to the scanty ruins of *Old Slains Castle*, destroyed by James VI in 1594.

The coast now becomes cliff-bound.—23½ m. **Cruden Bay**
(*Kilmarnock Arms*, RB. 17/6, P. 9 gs. ; *Red House*, RB. 17/6,
P. 8 gs.) is a golfing resort with fine sandy links, called the
Ward of Cruden. Slains Castle, ½ m. N., now dismantled,
was the seat of the Earls of Erroll, hereditary High Constables
of Scotland. Its situation on the cliff-edge was declared by
Dr. Johnson to be " the noblest he had ever seen."

About 2 m. N. of Cruden Bay are the **Bullers of Buchan** (perhaps a corruption
of Boilers), a tremendous hollow in the rock, 200 ft. deep and 50 ft. wide, probably
a cave whose roof has collapsed. In rough weather the waves rush in with
immense violence through the natural archway at the bottom, though in calm
weather it may be approached by sea. Dr. Johnson, who insisted on being rowed
into the ' Pot,' called it " a rock perpendicularly tubulated," and described the
Dunbuy Rock, to the S., as " a yellow protuberance of stone, open to the main
sea on one side, and parted from the land by a very narrow channel on the other,
covered with sea birds."

The road passes (27½ m.) *Longhaven* and (29½ m.) *Boddam*
(Seaview, RB. 17/6, P. 7 gs.), a fishing village connected by
bus with Peterhead. The houses are squarely built of the
local granite. The 14th cent. castle, ½ m. S., was built by the
Keiths on the end of a rocky promontory. *Buchan Ness*,
to the E., is the easternmost point of Scotland, and ¾ m.
inland are the famous quarries of pink Peterhead granite.—
31 m. *Burnhaven*, a creation of the 19th cent., adjoins the
convict prison.

32½ m. **Peterhead** (*Palace*, RB. 19/6, P. 9 gs. ; *North
Eastern*, RB. 18/, P. 7 gs. ; *Royal*, similar charges.—*Post
Office*, Marischal St.), founded in 1593 by George Keith, 5th
Earl Marischal, is the chief town (12,750 inhab.) of Buchan
and a grim grey seaport with shipbuilding yards and a large
and busy harbour. In front of the *Town House* (1788), in
Broad St., is a statue of Marshal James Keith (1696–1758),
presented in 1868 by William I, King of Prussia, in commemoration of the marshal's services to his ancestor, Frederick
the Great. Both the marshal and his brother George, 10th
and last Earl Marischal, were exiled after the defeat of the
Old Pretender in 1716, as a punishment for permitting his
clandestine landing at Peterhead in Dec. 1715. *Arbuthnot House*
(1805), at the other end of Broad St., is now council offices.

The breakwater on the S. side of Peterhead Bay was constructed in 1886–1912
by convicts from the prison near the shore; the N. arm, still incomplete, was
begun in 1912. The harbour of refuge thus enclosed is sorely needed on this
exposed and stormy coast.

From Peterhead to Fraserburgh, 18 m. (A 952, 92), motor-bus in 50 min.
2½ m. *Inverugie Castle*, in ruins, was the birthplace of Marshal Keith (see above).—
8½ m. *Crimond* was the home of Jessie Irvine (1836–87) to whom the famous
psalm-tune so named is ascribed, and is the scene of the ballad ' Logie o' Buchan,'
by Geo. Halket, schoolmaster at Rathen in 1714–25. Between Crimond and the
sea is the shallow *Loch of Strathbeg* (2½ m. long), at whose E. end are the ruins
of *Rattray Castle* and the 13th cent. *St. Mary's Chapel*.—At (12 m.) *Lonmay* we
join the main road from Aberdeen (see below).

From Peterhead to Banff, 33 m. (A 950, 98). We cross the Aberdeen–
Fraserburgh road at (8 m.) *Mintlaw*. To the left, 1½ m. farther, is the village of

Old Deer, the seat of a monastery founded by St. Drostan (7th cent.), whose sole relic is the 'Book of Deer,' now in the University Library at Cambridge, a 9th cent. Latin MS. of parts of the New Testament, with Gaelic marginal notes of the 11th or 12th cent., referring to historical events and grants of land to the monastery, the earliest specimen known of Scottish Gaelic writing.—10 m. **Deer Abbey** (adm. 6*d.* ; 10–4 or 7 ; Sun. from 2) was founded by Wm. Comyn, Earl of Buchan, in 1219 for Cistercians from Kinloss in a pleasant site on the S. Ugie Water. The chief remains are the 14th cent. refectory and abbot's lodge ; the church was swept away by Ferguson of Pitfour in 1854. Beyond the railway is *Aikey Brae*, the scene of a fair on the 3rd Sun. in July, once famous for its horse-sales. Here in 1308 the Comyns were finally defeated by Edward Bruce.—Beyond (18 m.) *New Pitsligo*, once a centre of illicit distillery, we join A 98, coming from Fraserburgh.—31¼ m. *Macduff* and (33 m.) *Banff*, see Rte. 44.

The FRASERBURGH ROAD (A 92) runs N. from (12 m.) *Foveran* church. At (17 m.) **Ellon** (*Buchan*, RB. 17/6, P. 7 gs. ; *New Inn*, RB. 16/6, P. 7 gs. ; *Station*, RB. 14/6), a large village (1500 inhab.), is the *Earl's Mount*, an ancient mote-hill where justice was administered by the earls of Buchan.

The road to Fyvie (B 9005) runs up the Ythan to (7 m.) *Haddo House* (Marquess of Aberdeen), an 18th cent. house by Adam (no adm.), and to (11 m.), beyond *Methlick* (Ythanview, RB. 17/6, P. 6 gs.), the ruins of the tower-house of *Gight*, occupied by the Gordons from 1479 until Lady Catherine Gordon, Byron's mother, was forced to sell it to pay her husband's debts (1787).

At (21½ m.) *Birness Toll* A 952 diverges right for Peterhead viâ Hatton, and at (31 m.) *Mintlaw* (Pitfour Arms) the Peterhead–Banff road is crossed. The country becomes very bare as we approach *Mormond Hill* (769 ft. ; wide view). The large village of *Strichen* (Freemasons', RB. 16/6 ; Mormond, RB. 15/) lies S.W. of the hill.—41 m. *Philorth House* (r.) has wooded grounds that contrast strongly with their bleak surroundings.

47¼ m. **Fraserburgh** (*Royal, Station, Saltoun Arms, Alexandra*, at all RB. 17/6–18/6), an important centre (10,450 inhab.) of the herring fishing and timber trades, with a fine harbour, was founded in 1546, on the site of the old village of *Faithlie*, by Sir Alex. Fraser, an ancestor of the 16th Lord Saltoun (d. 1853), whose statue surmounts the entrance to the *Town Hall* (1855) in Saltoun Square. Here are also the *Cross* (1736) and the *Parish Church* (rebuilt in 1899). Under James VI an attempt was made to found a university here.

On *Kinnaird's Head*, the Taezalorum Promontorium of Ptolemy, a slate rock rising 60 ft. above the sea to the N. of the town, is a square machicolated tower of four stories built by Sir Alex. Fraser in 1574 and since 1787 surmounted by a lighthouse. Below it is the *Wine Tower* (probably 15th cent.), 25 ft. high, built over a cave called the *Sealch's Hole* (100 ft. long).

A road (and light railway) runs S.E. around Fraserburgh Bay, behind whose fine sands is a golf course, to (3¼ m.) *Inverallochy*, with quaint fishermen's cottages, and (4½ m.) *St. Combs*. On the right of the road to St. Combs are *Cairnbulg Castl* (restored c. 1897), a stronghold of the Comyns and their successors in the earldom of Buchan, and, farther on, *Inverallochy Castle*, a fragmentary ruin.

Motor-buses run from Fraserburgh to *Peterhead* ; to *Rosehearty* and *New Aberdour* ; and to *New Pitsligo* and *Macduff*.

IV. OBAN AND WESTERN SCOTLAND

46. FROM EDINBURGH TO OBAN VIÂ CALLANDER

ROAD, 126 m. From Edinburgh to (54 m.) **Callander,** see Rte. 23B. A 84.
68 m. *Lochearnhead.*—A 85. 73 m. *Lix Toll* (to the right for *Killin,* 3 m.).—
84 m. **Crianlarich.**—89 m. *Tyndrum.*—101 m. *Dalmally.*—114 m. *Taynuilt.*—
121 m. **Connel Ferry.**—126 m. **Oban.**

RAILWAY from Princes St. Station, 123 m. in 5–5¾ hrs. Principal Stations :
to (52¼ m.) *Callander,* see Rte. 23B.—61 m. *Strathyre.*—64 m. *Balquhidder*
(bus to Lochearnhead).—71½ m. *Killin Junc.* (for **Killin,** 4¼ m.).—81½ m. *Crianlarich.*—86¼ m. *Tyndrum.*—98½ m. **Dalmally.**—101 m. *Loch Awe.*—110 m.
Taynuilt.—116¾ m. **Connel Ferry** (junction for *Ballachulish,* Rte. 51B.).—123 m.
Oban.

This railway runs through some of the most beautiful scenery in Scotland,
rivalled for variety only by that on the West Highland Railway (Rte. 48). Except
near Loch Awe the finest views are to the right. Dining cars and observation
cars (from Glasgow) or sleeping cars (from London) accompany the principal
expresses.

From Edinburgh to (54 m.) *Callander,* see Rte. 23.—Leaving
Callander the road keeps to the N. bank of the Leny, and in
about 2 m., between Ben Ledi (2875 ft.) on the left, and a
lower range of hills on the right, it enters the finely wooded
*Pass of Leny (p. 205), beyond which the road and railway
separate to meet again at Strathyre. The road skirts the E.
shore of *Loch Lubnaig,* the ' bent loch,' for the whole of its
4 miles, and passes (58¾ m.) the tiny churchyard marking the
site of *St. Bride's Chapel* (p. 205).—From (59 m.) *Ardchullarie,*
a farmhouse where Bruce the Abyssinian explorer (p. 201),
wrote part of his ' Travels,' a delightful path leads up the glen
to the N.E. and then down *Glen Ample,* with Ben Each
(2660 ft.), Stuc-a-Chroin (3189 ft.), and Ben Vorlich (3224 ft.)
on the right, to (8 m.) Lochearnhead. At the head of Loch
Lubnaig is a curious long and narrow alluvial peninsula,
formed by the deposits of the Balvaig, which here flows into
the lake.—63 m. **Strathyre** (*Station,* RB. 18/6, P. 8 gs. ;
Munro's, Rosebank, unlic., RB. 17/6, P. 7 gs.), a quiet village
and summer-resort, is a good centre for walks.

A picturesque road, crossing the Balvaig and ascending its valley, known as
Strathyre, passes the farm of *Ardoch,* birthplace of Dugald Buchanan (1716–68),
the Gaelic poet and evangelist, and leads to Balquhidder (4 m. ; see below). The
district is described in the ' Legend of Montrose ' and, in ' The Lady of the Lake,'
the fiery cross " glanced like lightning up Strathyre."

65¼ m. *Kingshouse Platform* (Kingshouse, RB. 18/6), where
trains stop only on previous arrangement with the stationmaster at Strathyre, is 2 m. E. of the neat village of
Balquhidder, the burial-place of Rob Roy, which lies at the
E. end of Loch Voil. Balquhidder Station is 1 m. farther along
the main road ; and there is a large youth hostel on the S.
side of the loch. The ' Braes of Balquhidder,' celebrated in

N

Tannahill's pretty song, rise above the N. bank of the loch, and are well seen from beside the present church (1855). Robert MacGregor (' Rob Roy,' d. 1734) no doubt lies in the churchyard, but the three uninscribed tombstones within an iron railing in front of the ruined *Old Church* (1631), date from centuries before his time.

The central tombstone, said to be Rob Roy's, is a rough slab of slate, carved with a cross, with a sword on one side and a kilted man with a dog or other animal at his feet on the other. The stone on the left, " only distinguished by a rude attempt at the figure of a broadsword," is reputed that of Helen (more correctly Mary), his widow. The right-hand stone, supposed to commemorate his sons Coll (d. 1735) and Robert (' Robin Oig '; executed 1754), bears the MacGregor arms—a pine-tree torn up by the roots and crossed by a sword piercing a crown, in allusion to the claim of royalty made by the chiefs of the clan.—It was in the old church that the Clan MacGregor gathered in 1589 round the head of the King's forester, which had been cut off, and swore to protect the murderers; the new church contains a 17th cent. sessions chest and a curious effigy of the local apostle, St. Angus (8th cent.). A cottage in the village. was the scene of the piping contest between Robin Oig and Alan Breck (in ' Kidnapped '), which ended in the unquestioned victory of MacGregor.

FROM BALQUHIDDER TO INVERLOCHLARAIG, 7 m., by a charming road (rough after the first 3½ m.) along the N. shores of *Loch Voil* and the smaller *Loch Doine.* —From (7 m.) *Inverlochlaraig,* where Rob Roy died in 1734, ' a peaceful subject ' after his life of violence, walkers may proceed through the hills (no paths), N.W. to (8 m.) *Crianlarich* (see below) or S.W. to (5 or 6 m.) *Glengyle,* at the head of Loch Katrine.

A by-road starting between the village and the youth hostel runs S. up *Glen Buckie* to (2½ m.) *Bailemore,* whence a path goes on to *Glen Finglas* and (11 m.) *Brig o' Turk* (p. 214). This is a beautiful walk of c. 4 hrs. in dry weather, but at other times had better not be attempted.

Beyond Balquhidder station the railway winds up the hillside, commanding fine views (r.) of Stuc-a-Chroin and Ben Vorlich, at whose base stretches Loch Earn. At the far end of the loch appears St. Fillans, with the Melville Monument above Comrie in the distance. High above the river and road, the railway climbs the wild *Glen Ogle* to the watershed (950 ft.), on which lies a lonely tarn. As we begin to descend we come into sight of Loch Tay, with Killin at its head and Ben Lawers rising from its N. bank. The line curves to the west for (71½ m.) *Killin Junction;* then, running W. high up on the S. side of Glen Dochart, affords a good view of the twin peaks of Ben More and Stobinian on the left, and rejoins the road at (75¼ m.) *Luib* (see below).

The road descends through the village of (68 m.) *Lochearn-head,* with pleasant views down Loch Earn (see Rte. 28), and joins A 85. A steady ascent follows, up the wild and rocky *Glen Ogle,* to (70¾ m.) the watershed (948 ft.) beside the little Loch Lairig Eala. The descent on the N. side is steeper, and we reach the valley road at (73 m.) *Lix Toll* (605 ft. ; teas), in Glen Dochart, where the Killin road turns to the right.

———————

ROAD TO KILLIN AND KENMORE (A 827), 19 m. The road descends the Dochart, crossing the rushing stream by the old bridge where the river, studded with boulders, is divided by two islands.

On Inch Buie, the lower of these, was the burial-place of Clan MacNab, the most powerful family in the district until their emigration to Canada in 1823. The key to the burial-ground may be obtained from *Kinnell House* (c. 1654), an ancient abode of the MacNabs on the S. bank below the bridge, in the vinery of which is a huge vine planted in 1832.

3 m. **Killin** (*Killin Hotel*, RB. 25/, P. 14 gs.; *Bridge of Lochay*, RB. 23/6, P. 11 gs.; *Queen's Court*, unlic., RB. 19/6, P. 9 gs.; *Clachaig*, unlic., RB. 17/6, P. 8 gs.), a charming village and winter sports centre, lies between the Dochart and the Lochay, ½ m. above the point where they unite before flowing into Loch Tay. The name (Cille fhionn) signifies 'white church' and has nothing to do with Fingal. The monument in front of the church commemorates the Rev. James Stewart, the first translator of the New Testament into Scottish Gaelic (1767).

The beauty of the surrounding country is well surveyed from *Stronachlachan* (1708 ft.), easily ascended in 1 hr. by a path starting beside the school.—*Finlarig Castle*, a picturesque ruin c. ½ m. N. of the village beyond the Lochay (r.), was anciently a seat of the earls of Breadalbane; close by is a neglected mausoleum where 14 Campbell chiefs are buried.—From *Bridge of Lochay*, ¾ m. N. of the village, a pleasant road ascends *Glen Lochay*; it passes the new power station and the waterfall (1½ m.; fish-pass) and continues beyond *Kenknock* (6½ m.), connected by a rough track with Glen Lyon.

Loch Tay (355 ft.), 14½ m. long, c. ¾ m. broad, and in places over 500 ft. deep, is finely set between high hills on both banks, and is famous for its salmon. Its chief feeders are the Dochart and the Lochay at its W. end; from its E. end issues the full-grown Tay. Roads skirt both banks; that on the N. bank is the shorter (16 m.), but that on the S. bank (17 m.; see p. 248) keeps near the loch and commands finer views, especially of Ben Lawers.

Killin is connected with *Killin Junction* by a branch railway (4¼ m.); and motor-buses in summer run to Kenmore and Aberfeldy (see Rte. 31).

The ROAD ON THE N. BANK crosses the Bridge of Lochay and, ascending past the golf course and above the Finlarig power station, keeps high above the loch, with splendid views. After c. 4 m. a good hill-road diverges on the left for Bridge of Balgie in Glen Lyon (9 m.). From the top of the rise farther on the twin peaks of Ben More and Stobinian are visible behind us.—11 m. *Lawers* (600 ft.; Ben Lawers, unlic., RB. 17/6, P. 7½ gs.) is the most convenient base for the ascent of Ben Lawers (5 hrs. up and down).

Ben Lawers (3984 ft.), the 'echoing mountain,' is very easy to climb and is well worth while ascending. The ascent leads up the farther side of the first burn E. of the hotel and avoids the steep slope S.E. of the summit by a short detour to the crest of the N.E. ridge. The summit, artificially raised to 4000 ft. by means of a cairn, commands a glorious *View, including Ben Nevis (N.W.), Ben Cruachan (W.), and the Cairngorms (N.E.), while to the S.E. it sometimes extends as far as the Fife hills, the Bass Rock, and North Berwick Law. An alternative descent leads viâ the S. ridge and then E. to the wooded crest of *Meiller* (Meall Odhar; 1794 ft.), though the intervening depression is apt to be boggy. Ben Lawers and its S.W. spur *Ben Ghlas* (3657 ft.) are N.T. property (8000 acres); their slopes are noted for their remarkable variety of alpine plants which visitors are specially urged not to collect. In *Coire Odhar*, W. of Ben Ghlas, are the headquarters of the Scottish Ski Club.

The road descends gradually to the level of the loch, reaching it at (15 m.) *Fearnan* (Tigh-an-loan, RB. 18/6, P. 8½ gs.), where an alternative road to Aberfeldy (10 m.)

viâ Fortingall (2 m.) in Glen Lyon diverges on the left.—We
skirt *Drummond Hill* and turn abruptly to the right at the
end of the loch, crossing the Tay by a narrow bridge for
(19 m.) *Kenmore* (see Rte. 31).

From Lix Toll the Oban road ascends *Glen Dochart,* the
scene of Hogg's ' Spectre of the Glen.'—76 m. *Luib* (Hotel
RB. 20/, P. 8 gs.), a hamlet 1¼ m. E. of its station, is
a favourite anglers' resort. When William and Dorothy
Wordsworth spent a night here in 1803 " the servant was
uncivil, because, forsooth, we had no wine."

The ascent of **Ben More** (3843 ft. ; c. 2 hrs.), which from its central position
commands one of the finest views in Scotland, may be made from a point on
the road 1½ m. W. of Luib station, or (very steep) from a point 3 m. farther on
(c. 2 m. short of Crianlarich). To the S. of Ben More, beyond a great dip, rises
Stobinian (3827 ft.).

The road skirts the base of Ben More and passes *Loch
Iubhair* (the ' juniper loch ') and *Loch Dochart,* ½ m. apart.
In the latter is " one grove-like island," with a ruined castle.
—84 m. **Crianlarich** (*Hotel*, RB. 22/, P. 9 gs.) is a small village
with beautiful environs, most of whose inhabitants are employed by the railway which has two stations here (220 yds.
apart).

For the West Highland Railway from *Glasgow* to *Fort William* and *Mallaig,*
see Rte. 48.—A motor-bus leaves Crianlarich twice daily for (20 min.) *Ardlui,*
at the head of Loch Lomond, going on to Glasgow viâ Arrochar (see Rte. 12).

We pass under the lofty viaduct of the West Highland
railway and ascend Strathfillan, close to the railway on the S.
side of the Fillan Water.

In the stream, c. 3 m. from Crianlarich, is *St. Fillan's Pool,* a ' holy pool ' to
which lunatics were brought to be cured. After being plunged into its waters they
were bound and left on its banks all night. If the knots were still tied next
morning a cure was considered hopeless. On the farther bank are the ruins of
Strathfillan Priory (Augustinian ; 1318), dedicated by Bruce to St. Fillan as a
thank-offering for Bannockburn.

As the valley becomes bleaker the railway makes a wide
curve towards *Ben Lui* (3708 ft.), on whose slopes the Tay
rises. Between road and railway lies *Dalry* (' the King's
field '), memorable for an adventure of Robert Bruce.

Fleeing after his defeat at Methven in 1306, Bruce was attacked here by
John MacDougall of Lorn, a kinsman of the Red Comyn, at the head of a swarm
of Highlanders. One of these seized Bruce's mantle and, though mortally
wounded, held it so fast that Bruce was compelled to abandon it with the brooch
that fastened it. This ' Brooch of Lorn ' is still treasured at Dunollie.

89 m. **Tyndrum** (*Royal*, RB. 27/), a fishing and mountaineering resort, has two stations, ½ m. apart, one on each side of the
road. To Bridge of Orchy and Fort William, see Rte. 48.—
About ¾ m. farther on we cross the Perthshire border and enter
Argyllshire.

Argyllshire, a great W. maritime county containing some of the most impressive mountain and loch scenery in Scotland, comprises a mainland portion stretching from the Firth of Clyde to Inverness-shire, with a coast-line broken into a fringe of peninsulas, large and small, by narrow sea-lochs running deep into the land ; and a large number of islands, of which the chief are Mull, Islay, Jura, Tiree, Coll, Iona, and Staffa. The name Argyll signifies ' boundary of the Gael,' in reference to the Dalriadic conquest of the West in 498 ; and the old district names are famous in the romantic and savage annals of the Highlands. N. of Loch Linnhe and the Sound of Mull are *Morvern, Ardnamurchan, Sunart,* and *Ardgour* ; E. of Loch Linnhe lies *Appin,* with *Benderloch* between Loch Creran and Loch Etive ; Loch Awe, farther S., separates *Lorn* from *Argyll* proper, with Inveraray the ancient capital ; and E. of Loch Fyne *Cowal* stretches its peninsulas, fringed with seaside resorts, to the Firth of Clyde. *Knapdale,* between the Crinan Canal and West Loch Tarbert, is the N. portion of the long narrow peninsula that is continued S. by *Kintyre* to the famous Mull. Argyllshire is the country of the Campbells ; other famous families are the MacLeans, the Stewarts of Appin, the MacDougalls of Lorn, the Macdonalds of Glencoe, and the Macfarlanes of Glen Croe.

Passing *Lochan Bhith* (822 ft. ; l.) the road hastens down Glen Lochy, a bare green valley with the river on the left. The giant steps on Ben Lui are presently seen on the left ; on the right we have a view up Glen Orchy ; and in front is the ' horseshoe ' of Ben Cruachan. The descent ends in the broad Strath Orchy with its oak groves.—101 m. **Dalmally** (*Hotel,* RB. 19/6, P. 9½ gs. ; *Rfmts.* at station) is an excellent centre for excursions. The hotel and the church are picturesquely situated beside the river, ¾ m. E. of the station and shops. About 1¾ m. S.W., on the old Inveraray road, stands a monument to Duncan Ban MacIntyre (p. 335), on a hill commanding a grand view.

Ben Lui (3708 ft.), or *Ben Laoigh,* is easily ascended from Dalmally in 3½–4½ hrs. A farm-road diverging from the Tyndrum road, c. 1½ m. E., leads S. under the railway to (4 m.) the farm of *Socach,* whence we mount S.E. over Ben-a-Clee (3008 ft.). The view from the top is not easily surpassed in Scotland : N. over the Black Mount to Ben Nevis and the Cairngorms ; W. to the Paps of Jura and Mull ; S. to Ben Lomond, the Clyde, and Arran ; E. to Ben More and Ben Lawers. The descent to Tyndrum is very steep.

From Dalmally to Bridge of Orchy, 12 m., a beautiful but hilly road ascends N.E. through the lonely *Glen Orchy,* which, like many of the neighbouring glens, was property of the MacGregors until they were dispossessed by the Campbells. 7 m. *Falls of Orchy.*—12 m. *Bridge of Orchy,* see Rte. 48.

Motor-coaches in summer to Inveraray (see p. 158).

Beyond Dalmally the road descends to the head of Loch Awe, where it crosses the united stream of the Orchy and the Strae. On the left we have a fine view of Kilchurn Castle on a peninsula in the loch.

104½ m. **Loch Awe** (*Loch Awe,* RB. 32/, P. 10½ gs. ; RB. 21/, P. 9 gs.) is a station beside a pier on the loch (motor-launch cruise twice daily in June–Sept.) ; see also p. 341.

*Kilchurn Castle, best visited by boat from Loch Awe, is an oblong structure with a square keep flanked by bartizans. The keep was built in 1440 by Sir Colin Campbell, Knight of Rhodes, ancestor of the Breadalbane family, or, according to legend, by his wife during his absence in the East. The remainder was built in 1693 by Ian, Earl of Breadalbane, and over the gateway are his arms and those of his wife. Until 1740 it was occupied by the family, and in 1746 it was garrisoned by Hanoverian troops. The top of one of the towers was blown down in ' the Tay Bridge gale ' in 1879 and turned completely over without being broken.

St. Conan's Church (l.), an unexpectedly elaborate memorial (1881–1930), contains relics from Greyfriars, Edinburgh, and other churches. We enjoy a good view of the islands in the lake and at 108 m. we pass the beautiful *Falls of Cruachan.*

Ben Cruachan (3689 ft.), one of the most conspicuous mountains in Scotland, thanks to its semi-isolated position, is ascended hence in 3 hrs., a laborious climb well rewarded by a magnificent view. The route leads up the W. side of the Cruachan Burn, not quitting it until the saddle between the main peak and *Meall Cuanail* (3004 ft.), the S. spur, is quite open on the left. It then makes for the saddle (2750 ft.) and ascends thence by an extremely rough rock staircase to the top. The *View includes Goat Fell in Arran on the S., the islands from Jura to Rum on the W., while to the N. and E. is a succession of giant peaks : Ben Nevis, the Glencoe mountains, Ben Alder, Ben Lawers, and Ben More, descending on the S.E. to Ben Lomond and the hills above Loch Long. Loch Awe, Loch Etive, and Loch Linnhe are all visible, and the crags and corries on the N. face of the mountain itself are exceptionally grand.

The descent may be made to *Dalmally* (3¾ hrs.) by following the main ridge E. and descending the N. arm of the ' horseshoe '; or (better) to *Taynuilt* (3¼ hrs.) viâ the W. peak (3611 ft. ; fine view) and the steep slopes leading W. and S. to Bridge of Awe.

The road and railway now enter the ***Pass of Brander,** the grand defile through which the Awe reaches the sea. " The tremendous mountain, Ben Cruachan, rushes down in all the majesty of rocks and wilderness to the lake, leaving only a pass in which the warlike clan of MacDougal of Lorn was almost destroyed by the sagacious Robert Bruce (1308)."

We cross the foaming river at *Bridge of Awe*, leave on the right Inverawe House, an old Campbell lordship, and reach (114 m.) **Taynuilt** (*Hotel*, RB. 21/, P. 11 gs.), an attractive village, ½ m. S. of *Bonawe*, where the Awe enters Loch Etive (ferry to the granite quarries opposite 6*d.*, cycle 1/3).

On a hill to the S. is a monument to Nelson (1805) erected by the workmen of the charcoal furnace of Bonawe, in which ore brought from Furness was smelted (1753–1876). This was Nelson's first monument, raised before his remains reached England.

FROM TAYNUILT TO TAYCHREGGAN, 8 m., a charming short drive. The road leads S. through the narrow wooded *Glen Nant*, close by the stream, and farther on undulates across the moors. From (5½ m.) the highest point (515 ft.) we have a good view of Ben Cruachan and a distant peep of Ben Lui.—On the left lies Loch Tromlee.—6½ m. *Kilchrenan* churchyard contains a block of red granite with a claymore in relief upon it, a monument set up by the Duke of Argyll in 1866 to his ancestor Cailean Mor (comp. p. 157).—The road ends on the shore of Loch Awe at (8 m.) *Taychreggan* (Hotel, RB. 27/, P. 9 gs.). The narrow road on the r. at Kilchrenan leads viâ Loch Avich (9 m.) to the coast (p. 340).

From Bonawe a track ascending the wild S.E. shore of Loch Etive affords access to (3 m.) *Glen Noe*, the ancestral home of the MacIntyres, at the back of Ben Cruachan, and to (6 m.) the long *Glen Kinglass*, whose headwaters merge in thcse of Glen Orchy.

A road descending the N. side of Loch Etive to North Connel from the quarries leads to (3½ m.) *Ardchattan Priory*, named after St. Cathan, a companion of St. Columba. This Valliscaulian house was founded by the MacDougalls in 1231 and was the meeting-place of one of Bruce's parliaments, among the last in which business was conducted in Gaelic. The plain church contains the curiously sculptured tombs of two former priors.

The road reaches the shore of *Loch Etive* at 118¼ m., just

beyond the turning for (1 m. r.) *Achnacloich*, the terminus of the motor-boat service from Lochetivehead.—The great cantilever bridge across Loch Etive (the largest in Europe after the Forth Bridge) comes into view as we approach (121 m.) **Connel Ferry** (*Falls of Lora*, RB. 25/6, P. 12 gs., closed Nov.–March ; *Dunstaffnage Arms*, RB. 21/, P. 8½ gs. ; *Loch Etive*, unlic., RB. 16/6, P. 7 gs.), important mainly as the junction of our road with the Ballachulish road (A 828 ; Rte. 51D). The *Falls of Lora*, whose music lingered in the ears of Ossian, are a sea-cataract formed by a reef of rocks stretching two-thirds of the way across the mouth of Loch Etive, over which the tide pours with a tremendous roar at low spring tides. The road turns S., passing the new village of Dunbeg (r.),—126 m. **Oban**, see Rte. 49.

47. FROM GLASGOW TO OBAN

From Glasgow to Oban the traveller may go throughout by railway ; the motorist will find an interesting road all the way, on which tourist coaches ply in summer. The favourite tourist route, however, is perhaps that by steamer to *Ardrishaig*, and thence by coach.

A. By Road

The shortest route (97 m.) is viâ **Loch Lomond** and (55 m.) **Crianlarich** (see Rtes. 12B and 46).

A less rapid route (121 m.), affording magnificent views of the western sea-lochs, strikes W. at (38 m.) **Arrochar** (p. 143). A 83.—44½ m. *Rest and be Thankful.*—50 m. *Cairndow*.—60 m. **Inveraray**.—68 m. *Furnace*.—84 m. **Lochgilphead**, and thence to (121 m.) **Oban**, see below.

In summer MOTOR COACHES (MacBrayne's) leave 46 Parliamentary Rd., Glasgow, at c. 9 a.m. and 3 p.m. for (3¾ hrs.) *Ardrishaig* by the latter route (11/, return 21/). The morning coach connects at Lochgilphead on weekdays with the coach from Ardrishaig to *Oban*.

B. By Railway

I. VIÂ STIRLING AND CALLANDER, 116¾ m., from *Buchanan St.* in 3¾–4¼ hrs.— From Glasgow viâ (22 m.) *Larbert* and (30 m.) *Stirling* to (46 m.) *Callander*, see Rte. 23. Thence to (116¾ m.) **Oban**, see Rte. 46.

II. VIÂ ARROCHAR AND CRIANLARICH, 101 m., from *Queen St.* in 4–6 hrs. No through fares. Connections poor.—From Glasgow to (59 m.) *Crianlarich*, where we change stations, going downhill and to the right to (½ m.) the lower station, see Rte. 12B. Thence to (101 m.) **Oban**, see Rte. 46.

C. By Clyde Steamer to Ardrishaig and thence by Road

The voyage 'down the Clyde' to *Ardrishaig*, a delightful trip through land-locked waters, is described in Rte. 13H. MOTOR COACH every weekday in connection from Ardrishaig to *Oban* in 2¼ hrs. (9/8, return 14/3).

At Ardrishaig the Oban motor coach starts from the pier. The road at first keeps alongside the Crinan Canal viâ (2 m.) **Lochgilphead** (*Stag, Argyll*, at both RB. 19/), the little county-town (1230 inhab.) of Argyll, where we connect with the motor coach from Glasgow viâ Inveraray.

The **Crinan Canal,** which permits small boats to pass from Loch Gilp to the W. coast (9 m.), was cut in 1793–1801 to obviate the necessity of the long and often tempestuous voyage round the Mull of Kintyre. With 15 locks in 9 m. it is now used mainly by pleasure-boats (open 6.30 a.m.–8.30 p.m.). Skirted by a narrow road from Cairnbaan (see below), it has on the right a wide expanse of moor and marsh, reclaimed by Malcolm of Poltalloch (see below). The left bank rises steeply to the hills of *North Knapdale*, the country of the Macmillans. The canal ends at (9 m.) *Crinan* (Hotel, RB. 23/6, P. 11 gs.), on Loch Crinan, a bay of the Sound of Jura.—From *Bellanoch*, 1½ m. short of Crinan, a road runs S., dividing after 1½ m. The left branch reaches (3 m.) *Loch Sween*, a fine sea-loch, known for a successful scheme (initiated in the Second World War) to accelerate the growth of fish-food and thereby of fish. Near its mouth is (10 m.) *Castle Sween*, a ruin associated by some with Sweyn of Denmark.—At (12½ m.) *Kilmory* chapel, where the good road ends, are many sculptured monuments, including the fine Macmillan's Cross.—The right branch leads to (5½ m.) *Tayvallich* (Dunbhronaig, unlic.), RB. 17/6, P. 7 gs.), on the W. shore of Loch Sween, and (10 m.) *Keills*, with a ruined church and a notable sculptured cross, looking across to Jura.

At (3¾ m.) *Cairnbaan* (Hotel, RB. 17/6, P. 8 gs.) the main road strikes N. for (5 m.) *Kilmichael Glassary*. A mile farther on, to the left, rises the isolated hillock of *Dunadd*, once fortified. This was the 'capital' of the kingdom of Dalriada, c. 500–850 ; and on its highest rock are carved a fine figure of a *Boar, and a footprint, the probable site of inauguration of the kings of the Scots. The wide view of Jura over the reclaimed marsh is impressive.

On the left farther on are the woods of *Poltalloch*, W. of which, on the N. shore of Loch Crinan, is *Duntroon Castle* (13th cent.), a Campbell stronghold until 1792.

9 m. *Kilmartin* (Inn) is a pretty village with a fine but mutilated Celtic Crucifixion and several medieval sculptured stones, now in an enclosure in the churchyard. About 1½ m. farther on, near the ruins of *Carnassary Castle*, built in the 16th cent. by a Bishop of the Isles, we reach (10½ m.) *Ford Road End*. Thence viâ the Pass of Melfort to (38½ m.) **Oban**, see Rte. 49.

48. FROM GLASGOW TO FORT WILLIAM AND MALLAIG

ROAD, 149 m. (A 82). From Glasgow to (53 m.) *Crianlarich*, see Rte. 12 ; thence to (58 m.) *Tyndrum*, see Rte. 46.—64 m. *Bridge of Orchy*.—92 m. **Ballachulish**. We ferry ¼ m. (or go around Loch Leven, 19 m.) to N. Ballachulish.—104 m. **Fort William.**—Thence to (149 m.) *Mallaig*, see Rte 53A. This fine road traverses some of the most magnificent country in Scotland.

RAILWAY from Queen St. Station ('West Highland Railway'), 164¾ m. in 6¼–6½ hrs. ; to *Fort William*, 123 m. in 4¼–4½ hrs. Restaurant and buffet cars from Glasgow ; sleeping cars from London (King's Cross).—To (59 m.) *Crianlarich*, see Rte. 12. Between Crianlarich and (104¾ m.) *Tulloch* the railway follows an independent course, far from any road after the first few miles, and is described in Rte. 48B.—113¾ m. *Spean Bridge*.—123 m. **Fort William.**—Thence to (164¾ m.) **Mallaig**, see Rte. 53A.

A. By Road

From Glasgow to (58 m.) *Tyndrum*, see Rtes. 12 and 46. A 82 diverges right from the Oban road and ascends to the watershed (1045 ft.) between the North Sea and the Atlantic, where we enter Argyllshire and descend with the railway on the right.   *Ben Douran* (3524 ft. ; 'stormy mountain'), celebrated in the poems of Duncan Ban MacIntyre, dominates the view on the right.   A path for Glen Lyon ascends the glen on its S.E. side.—64 m. *Bridge of Orchy* (Hotel, RB. 35/) is a fishing resort.

The hilly and winding old road to (12½ m.) the Kingshouse Hotel crosses the Orchy and, passing a beautiful pine-wood, descends to (3 m.) *Inveroran* (Hotel, RB. 21/, P. 9 gs.), at the S.W. end of *Loch Tulla*, near which Duncan Ban MacIntyre (1724–1812), the 'Burns of the Highlands' was born. Thence, ascending to 1449 ft., it strikes across the Marquess of Breadalbane's deer-forest of Black Mount, with dark and glistening corries on the W., and on the E. the vast expanse of Rannoch Moor, with the cone of Schiehallion in the distance.

From Bridge of Orchy S.W. down *Glen Orchy* to (12 m.) *Dalmally*, see p. 331.

The new road skirts the E. bank of the Orchy and the S.E. shore of Loch Tulla (see above) ; then, crossing the Tulla, it curves round the W. flank of Glas Bheinn (1639 ft.).

A rough road ascends Glen Tulla for 5½ m., passing (1 m.) the ruins of *Achallader Castle*, an old stronghold of the Fletchers and later of the Glenlyon Campbells, in which the plot for the massacre of Glencoe is said to have been hatched. At (2¾ m.) *Crannach* may be seen some of the finest remnants of the old Caledonian Forest.

Traversing the flat isthmus between *Loch Bà* (r.) and two smaller lochans, we skirt the S.W. side of the Moor of Rannoch, and rejoin the old road. A spur-road on the right (part of the old road) leads to (76 m.) the *Kingshouse Hotel* (RB. 15/6 ; P. 7 gs.), the scene of a dramatic episode in ' John Splendid.' This is a base for the ascent of *Clachlet* (Clach Leathad, 3602 ft.), the chief summit of the Black Mount, which has long been prominent on the left.

Where the Kingshouse road rejoins the main road (77 m.), we reach the head of Glen Etive, which is traversed by a rather narrow road to Lochetivehead. This road, as well as our own route, which now begins the descent of *Glen Coe*, is described in Rte. 51c, as far as the foot of the glen.—Thence either viâ (92 m.) *Ballachulish* or viâ (97 m.) *Kinlochleven* to (104 m.) **Fort William,** see Rte. 51B ; for the continuation of the road to (149 m.) **Mallaig,** see Rte. 53A.

B. By Railway

MOTOR-BUS also (coming from Kingussie) on the section between Tulloch and Fort William.

From Glasgow to (59½ m.) *Crianlarich*, see Rte. 12.—We cross the Oban railway and the Fillan and turn W. along the N. side of Strathfillan, enjoying fine retrospective views of the twin peaks of Ben More (3843 ft.) and Stobinian (3827 ft.) and of the Glen Falloch mountains, while on the left front is Ben Lui (3708 ft.), with the headwaters of the

Tay. In spring excellent mountaineering and ski-ing may be enjoyed among the many fine peaks of this district.—64¼ m. **Tyndrum** has another station on the line from Callander to Oban (Rte. 46).

We turn N. and climb to the watershed (1043 ft.) between the Atlantic and the North Sea, where we enter Argyllshire. On the left, in the distance, the peaks of the Black Mount come into view ; and on the right rises Ben Douran (3524 ft.). Before reaching the base of Ben Douran the railway makes a horseshoe sweep round the foot of Ben Odhar and Ben-a-Chaisteil, crossing two glens. We pass a large boulder known as ' Rob Roy's Putting Stone ' (left) before reaching (71¾ m.) *Bridge of Orchy* (see above).

The railway skirts *Loch Tulla* (2 m. long), and then, with a view of the precipitous sides of Clachlet (3602 ft.) on the left, ascends the valley of the Tulla, passing the ruins of *Achallader Castle*, and some of the finest remains of the old Caledonian Forest, and entering roadless country. In c. 4 m. more, on the watershed of the Tulla (1127 ft.), we re-enter Perthshire and begin to traverse the **Moor of Rannoch** (20 m. square ; average level, 1000 ft.), the largest and most desolate moor south of Sutherland.

The moor, which occupies the W. portion of the district of Rannoch, and includes the long dark Loch Lydoch (see below), is for the most part a bleak and exposed expanse of bog, moor, and rock, but is not without an attractiveness of its own. In this desolate region, almost destitute of cover, David Balfour and Alan Breck (in ' Kidnapped ') had some of their most trying adventures. On a clear day the panorama of the surrounding mountains is very fine. As we look back from the watershed Ben Cruachan may be seen to the S.W. ; N.W. is Ben Nevis, and in front Ben Alder. As we proceed the Glencoe mountains become visible on the left ; Ben Lawers is on our right, and as we approach Rannoch Schiehallion stands out conspicuously to the E. On the left are traces of the 'Soldiers' Trenches,' a series of earthworks constructed to give employment to the English garrison after the '45.

For the foundations of the railway across the boggy stretches of the moor, the engineers employed huge bundles of faggots, which have become ' pickled ' against rot by the action of the peaty water.

We cross the Gaur, which has been dammed at Loch Eigheach, c. 2 m. below Rannoch, to provide electric power.— 87½ m. *Rannoch* station (Inn, small) lies 6 m. W. of Loch Rannoch. A motor-bus runs to Kinloch Rannoch (17 m.) in connection with the trains (comp. p. 236).

A track, difficult to follow, leads W. from Rannoch station to (15 m.) *Kingshouse Inn* (p. 335), keeping well up on the high ground N. of the narrow *Loch Lydoch* or *Laidon* and the smaller lochs to the W. of it. Keeping the conical Buchaille Etive (p. 353) as a landmark ahead of us, we pass (c. 7–8 m.) a shepherd's hut and (11½ m.) a shooting lodge, whence a rough road leads to the inn.

About 1 m. N. of Rannoch we traverse the Cruach Cutting snow-tunnel and c. 1 m. farther on pass (l.) the little *Loch Chlaidheimh* or *Cly*, where the three counties of Perth, Argyll, and Inverness meet. We enter Inverness-shire.

This loch is said to derive its Gaelic name Chlaidheimh (sword) from the story of Lochiel and an Atholl chief who agreed to meet here in conference, unarmed. One of them, growing angry, drew a sword which he had concealed about his person, when the other promptly produced his. Finding that each had failed to outwit the other, they, by mutual consent, hurled their weapons into the loch.— The Black Water, descending W. from Loch Cly to Loch Leven, has been damned to form a power-reservoir 8 m. long for the Kinlochleven works.

Just beyond (94¾ m.) *Corrour,* beside little Loch Siolaig, the line attains its summit level (1354 ft.).

Loch Ossian, with its lonely youth hostel (closed Oct. 1st–March 29th) lies 1 m. right. The mountain on the N. side of the loch is a deer-sanctuary and should be avoided.

We skirt *Loch Treig* (5½ m. long, ½ m. wide), with grassy and almost treeless sides so furrowed by burns that the line crosses over 150 large and small bridges as it skirts its E. bank. Loch Treig is included in the Lochaber Power Scheme, as is indicated by the great dam (440 ft. long, 40 ft. high) at its N. end, whence the Treig issues to join the Spean.

The waters of Loch Treig, raised 40 ft. and combined with those of Loch Laggan (piped from the Spean dam, p. 241), are conducted by a tunnel beneath Ben Nevis to the aluminium works at Inverlochy.

Just before (104¾ m.) *Tulloch* we cross the course of the Spean, a river once famous for its salmon, and thenceforward keep parallel with the road from Kingussie to Fort William. The line descends Glen Spean, with one of the famous parallel roads (see below) well marked on the right, and enters the grand gorge of *Achluachrach,* the waterfall in which is an insurmountable barrier to salmon.—110½ m. **Roy Bridge** (*Roy Bridge, Glenspean Lodge,* 1½ m. upstream, at both RB. 21/, P. 10 gs.) is the station for the famous *Parallel Roads of Glen Roy,* shelves or terraces made on the hill-sides by the shore-waters of a lake that once filled the glen.

A rough road leads N. up Glen Roy to (9 m.) a shooting lodge of The Mackintosh, but an excellent view of the roads may be obtained from a point c. 4 m. from the station, where three distinct terraces are seen extending along both sides of the valley. " The highest is, of course, the oldest, and those beneath it were formed in succession as the waters of the lake sank. Until Agassiz suggested the idea of a dam of glacier-ice the great difficulty in the way of understanding how a lake could ever have filled these valleys was the entire absence of any relic of the barrier that must have kept back the water " (Geikie).—From the head of the glen a path leads W. over a pass (1150 ft.) to Loch Spey and the headwaters of the Spey (p. 240).

As we quit Roy Bridge we cross the Roy, with *Keppoch House* on the left, the name of which recalls the murder avenged at Invergarry (p. 357). The last clan battle in Scotland is said to have been fought here in 1688, between the Mackintoshes and Clan Ranald.—Beyond (113¾ m.) *Spean Bridge* (p. 356) the railway (view of Ben Nevis on the left) runs parallel with the road to (123 m.) **Fort William,** see Rte. 52.

49. OBAN

OBAN (6225 inhab.), finely situated on the shore and slopes of a picturesque bay landlocked by the island of Kerrera, is not only a bracing summer resort, but, as a focal point of numerous excursions by road, rail, or steamer, fairly earns its sobriquet of ' Charing Cross of the Highlands.' In summer it is a busy place and its ample hotel accommodation is frequently overtaxed. The sheltered bay, famous for its views of sunset amid the mountains of Mull, is a favourite yachting station, especially during the Argyllshire Highland Gathering in the second week of September.

Hotels (prices lower in Oct.–June). **Station,** George St., RB. 26/, P. 17 gs. ; **Park,** RB. 32/6, P. 13 gs. ; **Great Western,** RB 27/6, P. 13½ gs. ; **Alexandra,** RB. 33/, P. 14 gs. ; **Marine,** RB. 30/, P. 16 gs., four large houses on the Esplanade (closed Nov.–March) ; **Regent,** RB. 32/ P. 11 gs. (closed Oct.–Apr.) ; **Esplanade,** RB. 27/, P. 11 gs., open always ; **Royal,** Argyll Sq., RB. 27/6 ; **Argyll** (Apr.–Oct.),**Columba, King's Arms,** at these three P. from 9 gs. ; **Burnbank, Palace, King's Knoll,** P. 9 gs. ; these three unlic. ; many other unlicensed hotels and boarding-houses.

Post Office, Albany St., at the S. end of the town.

Motor-Buses at frequent intervals to *Ganavan.*—MOTOR-BUSES also to *Easdale* and *Cuan Ferry* (for Luing) in 1 hr. ; to *Connel Ferry* (¼ hr.) and

Taynuilt (¾ hr.) ; *vià* Kilmelfort to *Ardrishaig* (in c. 2¼ hrs.), connecting with the Glasgow steamer ; Glencoe circular tour, see Rte. 51c.

Steamers to *Lismore* and *Fort William* (Rte. 51A), the *Hebrides* (Rte. 59), *Staffa* and *Iona,* Tobermory (Rte. 50), etc.—Short cruises (5/–10/) to Mull, Loch Melfort, etc., daily in the season.

Amusements. GOLF at *Glencruitten,* ½ m. E. of the railway station.— BATHING at *Ganavan,* 2 m. N., with tea-room.— ROWING, SAILING, and MOTOR BOATS for hire. TENNIS COURTS ; BOWLING GREEN ; PUTTING COURSES.—FISHING in the Burgh Reservoir (off the Ardrishaig road, 1½ m. S.).—DANCING in the Corran Park pavilion ; also PIPE BAND on summer evenings.

A Renfrew trading company erected a storehouse at Oban in 1713, and in 1786 an unsuccessful attempt was made to establish a fishing-station here ; but Oban's rise and prosperity coincide with the rise and progress of the 'tourist industry' in Scotland in the 19th cent. though it is again an important fishing-port to-day. Dr. Johnson and Boswell found a " tolerable inn " at Oban in 1773, and in 1814, the year of the publication of ' The Lord of the Isles,' Sir Walter Scott paid a visit.

Between the Railway Station and Quay, animated with steamers, fishing-boats, and the evening fish-auctions, and the North Pier the open sea-front of Oban is flanked by George St., the principal street, with excellent shops. Its line is continued round the bay by the Esplanade, with its small public park and attractive hotels. The granite *Cathedral* (1932) of the Catholic diocese of Argyll and the Isles is by Sir Giles Scott. Next to the war memorial, a little farther on, is the *Clach-a-Choin,* or *Dog Stone,* an isolated block of rock, to which Fingal used to tie his dog Bran. Beyond the next point a zigzag path ascends to the ruins of **Dunollie Castle** (key at Dunollie House ; closed at dusk and 2–5 on Sun.).

This ancient stronghold (12th or 13th cent.), now reduced to an ivied keep and some fragments, is finely situated on a bluff overlooking Loch Linnhe, and was originally protected landward by a moat. It belonged to the MacDougalls, Lords of Lorn, whose descendant preserves the ' Brooch of Lorn ' (p. 330) in *Dunollie House* (1746 and later) among the trees at the base of the castle. The brooch was taken from the MacDougalls at the burning of Gylen (see below), but was returned by Campbell of Lochnell in 1826.

In the opposite direction (S.) Shore St. leads to the pleasant coast-road, passing Gallanach park (sea bathing) and (1½ m.) a ferry for Kerrera (2/ ret.).

On the hill (view) behind the town two uncompleted buildings attract the visitor's attention. *McCaigs Folly*, the curious circular structure, was intended to be a view tower, museum, and art gallery. The other is a hydropathic establishment which for lack of funds was never completed.—*Pulpit Hill*, to the S., commands a splendid view (mountain indicator).

The island of **Kerrera** is a natural breakwater, protecting the harbour of Oban. Here Alexander II died in 1249, during an attempt to subjugate the Norsemen of the Hebrides. At the S. end of the island is *Gylen Castle*, long a stronghold of the MacDougalls, burned by Cromwellians under Robert Montgomery in 1645. An obelisk on the N. end commemorates David Hutcheson, founder of the West Coast steamer services.

Excursions from Oban

Excursions from Oban are somewhat bewildering from their number and from the various ways in which many of them can be made—with different combinations of road, rail, and steamer. Visitors will do well to provide themselves with the summer programmes of the British Railways and of MacBrayne's steamers (office at the N. Pier) as well as with those of the motor coaches plying from the town.

Dunstaffnage and Connel Ferry may be reached by road (7 m., incl. the visit to the castle) or railway (see p. 333).—The road ascends N. from the end of George St. and at 3 m. reaches the end of a side road which turns sharp left through the new village of Dunbeg.—4 m. The ruined **Dunstaffnage Castle,** built upon a natural pedestal of rock, commands the entrance to Loch Etive (adm. daily 2/6, 10–12.30, 2–6).

The castle, an irregular four-sided structure with three round towers, has been ascribed to the 13th cent., but as it now stands shows slight evidence of being older than the 15th century. It is c. 400 ft. round ; the walls in some places are 66 ft. high and 10 ft. thick. In the ruins is a brass gun from a ship of the Spanish Armada sunk at Tobermory. The castle passed to the Lords of Lorn and was taken by Bruce after his victory in the Pass of Awe. It was garrisoned in 1715 and 1745, and Flora Macdonald was a prisoner here for some days in 1746. Dunstaffnage plays a part in Scott's ' Lord of the Isles ' and, under the name ' Ardenvohr,' in the ' Legend of Montrose.' The chapel adjoining (16th cent.) is the burial-place of the Campbells of Dunstaffnage, the hereditary captains of Dunstaffnage.

We return to the main road and proceed, passing Dunstaffnage House, to (7 m. ; 5 m. direct) *Connel Ferry* (p. 333), whence we may return by railway.

FROM OBAN TO FORD AND LOCH AWE, returning viâ
Taynuilt, a fine round of 78½ m., with some narrow roads.
The road quits Oban viâ Combie St., at the S. end of the town,
and begins a long climb. High up, on our right, appears
Soroba Lodge, the "white house on the hill," where Robert
Buchanan (1841–1901), novelist and poet, lived in 1866–74.
From (2½–3 m.) the top of our ascent, whence we have a wide
view, including the top of Ben Cruachan, on the left, we drop
to (4½ m.) the head of *Loch Feochan*.

At 3¾ m. a road strikes abruptly left for (½ m.) *Cleigh*, and (1¼ m.) *Loch Nell*, a
beautiful sheet of water with crannogs, at the S.W. angle of which is the *Serpent
Mound*, a curious heap of boulders about 80 yds. long, so called from its serpentine
shape. From Loch Nell this old road, now very rough, goes on N. to (6½ m.)
Connel Ferry, giving off (r. at 3 m.) a branch leading viâ *Glen Lonan*, with its
pretty little fishing-loch, to (10 m.) *Taynuilt*.

We follow the S. side of Loch Feochan to (8 m.) *Kilninver*,
where we turn left to ascend Glen Euchar, leaving the road
to Seil on the right.

Farther on to the left, upper Glen Euchar is traversed by the old main road to
Loch Awe viâ (2½ m.) *Loch Scamadale*. Beyond the head of the loch is (4 m.)
Braglenbeg, an old Campbell house where the Brooch of Lorn was kept hidden for
nearly 200 years after the burning of Gylen (see above).

Traversing Glen Callan, with its lofty wooded sides, we
descend above (13½ m.) the *Pass of Melfort*, of which at one
point we have a tolerably good view. The romantic but
dangerous old road, in the ravine, is now interrupted by a
small reservoir.—15½ m. *Kilmelfort* (Cuilfail, RB. 24/, P. 12 gs.),
near Loch Melfort, is an angler's resort, with loch and sea-
fishing.

Here a road diverges on the left for (5 m.) *Loch Avich* (3 m. long), the ' Loch
Launa ' of Ossian, which drains into Loch Awe by the Avich, a river with fine
falls and deep pools.—Thence to (17 m.) Kilchrenan, see p. 332.

Our road now keeps round the coast, with fine views
seawards to the islands of Shuna, Luing, and Scarba. On the
right, at 21 m., is the road to *Lunga House Hotel* (P. 9 gs.).
We cross to (23 m.) the head of *Loch Craignish*, with its wooded
islands. A zigzag climb, overlooking the beautiful loch, with
the Paps of Jura conspicuous to the W., is quickly followed
by a steep descent. At (28 m.) *Ford Road End*, in sight of
Carnassary Castle, we leave the Ardrishaig road (Rte. 47c),
and, turning sharp to the left, begin to ascend to the pretty
Pass of Craigenterive. We skirt *Loch Ederline* just before
reaching (31 m.) *Ford* (Hotel, P. £10), a tiny hamlet lying
c. ¾ m. from Loch Awe.

*Loch Awe, 23 m. long with an average width of c. 1 m., is one of the largest
and most beautiful of Scottish lochs. The head or S. end is comparatively
tame, while the foot is magnificently grand, but this is no real exception to the
rule obtaining in most lochs, for in geologic times it discharged to the S., towards
Loch Crinan, and not as at present to the N., by the Awe into Loch Etive. The
Campbells, the Macarthurs, and the MacGregors were the principal clans on its

OBAN DISTRICT

John Bartholomew & Son Ltd Edinburgh

Height of Land in Feet

0   500   1000   1500   2000   3000

Natural Scale 1:253,440

Miles
0   1   2   3   4   5   6

Kilometres
0   2   4   6   8   10

banks in the Middle Ages ; and the slogan of the Campbells, ' It's a far cry to Lochow,' was a defiant boast of the inaccessibility of their remote fastnesses.

A fair but hilly and often narrow road keeping close to the S.E. shore of Loch Awe passes (32½ m. ; r.) the ruined church of *Kilneuair* (13–16th cent.), with some late-medieval tombs and 'penitential' cell. The footpath by the church is an old road to Furnace on Loch Fyne.—33 m. (l.) *Fincharn Castle* is a ruined stronghold of the Macdonalds. In front of (39 m.) *Port-in-Sherrich* lies *Innis Sherrich*, with an old chapel and cemetery. A little farther on is *Innis Chonell*, with the ruins of *Ardchonell Castle*, a stronghold of the Campbells. On the left (40½ m.) the river Avich enters the loch, and on the right are two charming waterfalls.—47 m. *Portsonachan Hotel* (DRB. 45/, P. 14½ gs.), well situated.—48¼ m. *Ardbrecknish House Hotel* (RB. 25/, P. 11 gs.). We quit the shore and join the Inveraray road at (50½ m.) *Cladich*, but soon descend again to the tiny Innishail church.

The loch widens, and the view to the N., with the islands in the foreground and the enormous mass of Ben Cruachan in the background, is one of the most striking in the Highlands. In the loch lies *Innishail*, the 'isle of rest,' on which are the ruins of the church of St. Pindoca and a burial-ground of the Macarthurs, with the carved tombstones of warriors. Between Innishail and *Innis Fraoch*, with its ruined castle of the Macnaughtons, we have a view (l.) into the gloomy Pass of Brander. Off the opposite bank is the large island of *Innis Chonain*, approached by a bridge. We join (54¾ m.) A 85, 1¼ m. W. of Dalmally station.—For the return to (78½ m.) *Oban* viâ Taynuilt and Connel Ferry, see Rte. 46.

FROM OBAN TO SEIL AND EASDALE, c. 15 m., motor-bus tour every afternoon in c. 3½ hrs. (including tea).—To (8 m.) *Kilninver*, see above. The Seil road (B 844) skirts the little Loch Seil then crosses (12 m.) the beautiful *Clachan Sound* (Tigh-an-Truish Hotel) by the attractive humpbacked ' Atlantic Bridge ' (1872) on to the island of **Seil**.—14 m. *Balvicar*, with slate quarries. The bus calls at (16 m.) *Cuan Ferry*, at the S. end of Seil (see below), then returns to Balvicar, affording a fine view of *Ardmaddy Castle* (on the mainland), the ancient seat of the Marquess of Breadalbane. The terminus of the bus is at (16 m.) *Easdale Sound* (Inshaig Park, RB. 21/, P. 10 gs.), opposite the much-quarried islet of *Easdale* (ferry daily), once famous for slates. The sound is a haunt of trippers from Oban (tea-rooms) ; motor-launch from the Inshaig Park hotel.—*Cuan Ferry* (see above ; free ; hours at Kilninver P.O.) takes passengers and cars to **Luing**, another slate-quarrying island, 6 m. long.

From Oban to *Ballachulish* and *Fort William*, see Rte. 51 ; to *Edinburgh* viâ Callander, see Rte. 46 ; to *Glasgow*, see Rte. 47 ; to the *Hebrides* (Skye, Lewis, etc.), see Rtes. 58, 59 ; to *Staffa* and *Iona* (Mull), see Rte. 50.

50. FROM OBAN TO MULL AND TO IONA

To TOBERMORY. Mail Steamer (10/9, 6/) every weekday afternoon viâ *Craignure*, *Lochaline*, *Salen* (8/, 4/3), and *Drimnin* in 3–3½ hrs., returning the following morning. The steamer calls at Lismore on Wed. ; there is a daily connection in summer to *Kilchoan* (comp. p. 344).—On Tues., Thurs., and Sat. in summer the Iona steamer (see below) sails direct to Tobermory in 1½ hr. ; and on Mon., Wed., and Fri. (all the year) there is an early morning 'Inner Islands' steamer to Tobermory (2¼ hrs.), returning the following morning.

To IONA. Steamer direct on Mon., Wed., Fri., June 9th–Sept. 14th at 9 a.m. in 2¼ hrs. A halt of c. 1¾ hr. is made at Iona, and the steamers return viâ Tobermory, passing near Staffa and rounding the N. of Mull, to reach Oban c. 6 p.m. (day trip 37/6). On Tues., Thurs., and Sat. the route is reversed. Iona is visited also by a steamer on Mon. & Wed. in summer from Fort William (day return 42/6).—The voyage should not be undertaken when the weather is at all bad, for with a rough sea one is sure to get a good tossing off the Mull coast. In fine weather nothing can be more delightful.

To see Iona with the passengers of an excursion steamer is not to see it at its best, and for an adequate visit a night should be spent on the island. Staffa may be visited by motor boat from the steamer or from Iona in good weather.

A. To Tobermory

Leaving Oban Bay by the N. channel we see on our right Dunollie Castle. On Kerrera (l.) is the monument to David Hutcheson (p. 339). As the steamer crosses the mouth of Loch Linnhe a grand view is obtained to the N. and E. of mountain ranges from Ben Nevis to Ben Cruachan, while in the centre of the loch lies Lismore, at which the outward steamer calls on Wed. On the left, visible at low water and marked by a beacon, is the *Lady Rock*, on which one of the Macleans of Duart marooned an uncongenial wife, who, however, was rescued by fishermen. The story is related in Joanna Baillie's 'Family Legend' and in Campbell's 'Glenara.' Ahead rises the mountainous contour of Mull.

The island of **MULL**, a 'mass of hill,' round which the steamer coasts, is roughly triangular in shape and c. 30 m. long. Its coasts, especially on the W. side, are so indented with sea-lochs and creeks that, while the coast-line measures about 300 m., it is only 3 m. from sea to sea between the Sound of Mull at Salen, and the Atlantic at *Loch-na-Keal*, the 'Loch Gyle' of 'Lord Ullin's Daughter,' a long and broad fiord that nearly cuts the island in two. To the S. of Loch-na-Keal is *Loch Scridain*, beyond which projects a long granitic promontory, with grand cliff scenery, known as the *Ross of Mull*. The S. half of Mull is occupied by a lofty mountain mass culminating in *Ben More* (3169 ft. ; see below). The stern scenery has a charm of its own, though to Dr. Johnson, affected by its rainy climate, it was 'worse than Skye.' It was through this wild island that David Balfour (in 'Kidnapped') found his way from Erraid (p. 348) to the coast opposite Loch Aline in Morvern.

On the mainland of Mull (l.) is a lighthouse in memory of William Black (1841–98), many of whose novels are set in the West Highlands and Islands, and conspicuous on a headland is the ancient *Duart Castle*, confiscated after Culloden, but repurchased and restored in 1912, and now again, after nearly 150 years of alienation, the seat of the chief of the Macleans. Passing on the left the 19th cent. *Torosay Castle*, we call at *Craignure* (Inn, RB. 15/, P. 6½ gs.) and enter the *Sound of Mull* (c. 2 m. wide), which separates the high hills and cliffs of *Morvern* (r.) from the still more striking mountains of Mull.—Motor-bus (in connection with steamer) to Bunessan and Fionphort (for Iona ferry).

We cross the sound to the Morvern coast, on which appear

the ruins of **Ardtornish Castle,** in a wild and picturesque situation on a chain of rocks overhanging the sea, backed by basaltic cliffs over which pour two graceful waterfalls.

ARDTORNISH, built c. 1340, was, during the latter part of the 14th and the whole of the 15th cent., the headquarters of the 'Lords of the Isles'; but at the date of Sir Walter Scott's poem (early 14th cent.) their main residence was in Islay. The ruins are not large: the square keep, with its thick walls, and the broken rampart of the courtyard, giving but a faint notion of the grandeur of the 'Ardtornish Halls' as described by Scott. The Lord of the Isles, in the time of Robert Bruce, was in reality Angus Og, but for poetical purposes Scott conferred on him the more euphonious name of Ronald.

Beyond Ardtornish, at the narrow entrance to *Loch Aline,* is the village of **Lochaline,** with a cross brought from Iona. The former inhabitants of St. Kilda were settled in this region.

For nearly 3 m. along the W. bank of Loch Aline stretch the notable deposits of silica sand, which since 1940 have been mined by Charles Tennant & Co., with a yearly output of c. 45,000 tons suitable for the manufacture of optical glass. The crushing plant is connected with the mines by a light railway, and a small hotel is available for business and private customers.—A road runs along the shore of the loch to (3½ m.) the square turreted tower of *Kinlochaline Castle,* and goes on to (20 m.) Strontian or (32 m.) Ardgour.—Another road skirts the sound, passing (4 m.) *Fiunary,* the home of Norman Macleod (1783–1862), author of the lovely lament 'Farewell to Fiunary,' and ends at (10½ m.) *Drimnin.*

There are fine views of Ben More and Ben Talla as we approach **Salen** (*Hotel,* RB. 18/, P. 9 gs.; *Glenforsa House,* 1½ m. E., unlic., RB. 12/6, P. 7 gs.), a convenient central point for the exploration of Mull and a good starting point for the ascent of Ben More.

In the ruined chapel of *Pennygowan* (1 m. beyond the Glenforsa hotel) is a broken cross-shaft with a Virgin and Child.
Ben More (3169 ft.) is approached by the road across the isthmus to (3 m.) *Loch-na-Keal,* to whose S. shore we keep until nearly abreast of the island of *Eorsa.* From this point the ascent presents no difficulties. The *View from the summit extends from Islay to the Outer Hebrides.—The descent may be made to the head of *Loch Scridain,* seen to the S. Thence it is 12 m. to *Bunessan* or 18½ m. to *Iona* (p. 346). A path leads from the head of Loch Scridain over a pass to the E. of Ben More past beautiful *Loch Ba* and joins the highroad 4 m. from (13 m.) *Salen.*

To the N.W. of *Salen Bay,* on a high rocky peninsula at the mouth of the Aros, are the ruins of *Aros Castle.* Rugged Ben Hiant and the other Ardnamurchan hills now form a magnificent background as we cross the sound to call at *Drimnin,* on the Morvern shore. The words " God is Love," conspicuous on the low cliff as we enter Tobermory harbour, were first painted c. 50 years ago.

Tobermory (*Western Isles,* RB. 25/, P. 11 gs., summer only; *MacDonald Arms,* RB. 20/, P. 10 gs.; *Mishnish,* RB. 17/, P. 10 gs.; *Strongarbh,* unlic., P. 8 gs.), whose name means ' Well of Mary ' or ' St. Mary's Well," is the chief place (693 inhab.) in Mull and is favoured as a summer resort. With attractive houses on the quay, it stands on the shore and slopes of a small bay with thick woods, sheltered by the islet of

Calve. In the neighbourhood are several picturesque waterfalls. On the S. side of the bay are the beautiful grounds of
Aros House (adm. on application at the lodge). There is a
9-hole golf course.

In 1588 the ' Florencia ' or ' Florida,' a galleon of the Spanish Armada, was
blown up and sunk in Tobermory Bay by a Scottish hostage, unjustly detained,
who found his way to the powder magazine. Attempts to retrieve treasure from
the wreck have been made at intervals since the 17th cent. and, more systematic-
ally, since 1904 ; but beyond some cannon, a few coins, etc., nothing of value
has been raised. Dr. Johnson visited Tobermory in 1773, and Miss Isabella
Bird (Mrs. Bishop, 1831–1904), the traveller, first woman fellow of the Royal
Geographical Society, occupied a house here (' The Cottage ') for some years.

MOTOR-BUS every weekday to *Salen* and *Gruline*.—BUS TOURS daily exc.
Mon. & Sat. to *Calgary Sands*, going on to *Torloisk* on Tues. & Fri. ; on Mon. to
Gribun Cliffs ; on Sun., Wed. & Fri. to *Iona*, viâ Salen, Gribun or Craignure and
Bunessan, with tea at Killunaig Farm, Pennyghael (20/), on return ; on Thurs.
to *Lochbuie* viâ Salen and Gribun returning viâ Craignure.

FROM TOBERMORY TO KILCHOAN, motor-launch 2 or 3 times
daily throughout the year. Leaving Tobermory we pass
Rudha-nan-Gall lighthouse and cross the mouth of Loch
Sunart. On the N. shore are the imposing ruins of **Mingary
Castle,** which belonged to the MacIans, a younger branch of
the Macdonalds, Lords of the Isles. Here, in 1495, James IV
held his court to receive the submission of the insular chieftains. In 1644 it was taken for Montrose by Alastair Macdonald, the ' Colkitto ' of Milton's sarcastic sonnet, and
subsequently besieged by Argyll, but was relieved. To the
W. is **Kilchoan** (*Hotel*, RB. 25/, P. 9½ gs. ; motor-bus on weekdays to Acharacle, p. 360), on the S. side of Ardnamurchan,
at the mouth of Loch Sunart.

In the extreme W. a lighthouse marks *Ardnamurchan Point*, the most W. point
on the mainland of Scotland, 5 m. from Kilchoan by road ; while another road
runs N. from Kilchoan to (5 m.) *Sanna Bay*, facing W. among high dunes.

FROM TOBERMORY TO THE W. COAST AND FIONPHORT BY ROAD (motor-bus
tours in summer, see above). Cutting across the N. point of Mull, the road
momentarily regains the sea at (8 m.) *Dervaig* (Inn), on the narrow Loch Cuan.
—Emigrants from (13 m.) *Calgary Bay*, with a fine sandy beach, on the W. coast
gave its name to Calgary in Alberta. At Sunipol the poet Campbell lived as a
private tutor in 1795 and composed ' The Exile of Erin ' and much of ' The
Pleasures of Hope.'—19½ m. *Torloisk* is on Loch Tuath, which is bounded on the
S. by the islands of *Gometra* (with basaltic columns) and *Ulva*, with lofty cliffs
also of basalt. Ulva was the birthplace of Gen. Lachlan Macquarrie (d. 1824),
first governor of New South Wales ; but old Ulva House, where the Macquarrie
entertained Johnson and Boswell, was burned down in 1954.—Beyond (24 m.)
Ulva Ferry we skirt the shore of the deep-cut *Loch-na-Keal*, the ' Loch Gyle ' of
Campbell's ballad.—31 m. *Gruline*, at the head of the loch, is only 2½ m. by road
from Salen. The S. shore of Loch-na-Keal lies below the slopes of Ben More
(ascent, see above), and at its mouth lies the small green islet of *Inch Kenneth*,
where Johnson and Boswell were hospitably entertained by Sir Alan Maclean.
It contains the ruins of a 19th cent. mansion and of an old church 60 ft. long.
The road next passes below the *Gribun Rocks*, an impressive range of overhanging cliffs, and then crosses the peninsula of *Ardmeanach*, with its splendid
cliffs and caves, to (44 m.) *Killiemore*. On the S. shore of Ardmeanach is the
experimental farm of *Burg* (N.T.) We now round the beautiful *Loch Scridain*,
from the head of which (48½ m.) a fine road crosses the island viâ *Glen More* to
Craignure (16 m.). At the E. end of this glen, at Strathcoil, is a memorial (built
with the stones of the bard's house) to Dugald Macphail (1818–87), author of

'An t'Eilean Muileach,' an exile's song in praise of Mull, written at Newcastle-on-Tyne.—The final stretch of the Fionphort road traverses the *Ross of Mull*, famous for its granite quarries, viâ (51 m.) *Pennyghael* and (60½ m.) **Bunessan** (*Ardfenaig House*, half-way to Fionphort, RB. 25/, P. 11 gs.; *Argyll Arms*, RB. 18/6, P. 8 gs.).—66½ m. *Fionphort* is connected by ferry (2/, cycle 1/6, motor-cycle 3/) with Iona (bus to Craignure in connection with steamer). *Erraid* (see p. 348) is 2 m. S.; *Carsaig* (see p. 349) is on the S. shore, 3 m. S. of Pennyghael.

B. To Staffa and to Iona

The route described here, viâ Tobermory, follows the N. and W. coast of Mull, calling later at *Iona*; for the direct route from Oban to Iona, by the S. shore of Mull, see p. 349.

From Oban to *Tobermory* by the Sound of Mull, see Rte. 50A. Leaving Tobermory we round Ardmore Point into the open Atlantic. Beyond the Ardnamurchan lighthouse, on the right, the precipitous Sgurr of Eigg is seen, together with the lofty peaks of Rum, and, if the day be clear, the magnificent outline of the Coolins in Skye. In the distance, straight in front, are Coll and Tiree.—On Mull is *Glengorm Castle,* built in 1860 to supersede Quinish House, and ahead, as we round *Caliach Point,* we see before us the *Treshnish Isles,* a pictur-esque group of basaltic trap rocks rising in terraces.

The isle seen farthest W. is, from its curious shape, called *The Dutchman's Cap.* On the most N., *Cairn a' Burgh Beg,* pierced by a natural arch, are the remains of a castle besieged in James IV's campaign against the Lord of the Isles. Later the Macleans defended the island against Cromwell.

Soon *Loch Tuath* is seen on the left, bounded on the S. by the basalt islands of *Gometra* and *Ulva.* To the S. of them lies *Little Colonsay,* over which we have a good view of Ben More as we approach Staffa.

**Staffa, a small uninhabited island, is famous for its wonderful caves and remarkable basaltic formations. It is little more than 1½ m. round, with a perpendicular face (140 ft.) towards the S. and W. and a more gradual slope to the sea on the N.E. When the sea is calm passengers who desire to land are taken ashore by boat.

STAFFA (Norse, Staphi-ey, 'the island of pillars') was unknown to the outer world before a visit paid to it in 1772 by Sir Joseph Banks, who, on his way to Iceland, had been driven into the Sound of Mull and heard of this extraordinary place from a Mr. Leach, an Irish visitor, who had landed there a few days before. The earliest account of it is to be found in Pennant's 'Tour in Scotland' (1774).

The N.W. coast of Scotland was once the scene of violent volcanic action, and the subterranean disturbances found a vent along a line from Skye to Ireland, the effects of which may be traced through Staffa, Mull, Islay, Rathlin and the Giant's Causeway. A great quantity of liquid basalt was ejected to the surface, which, when beginning to cool, formed a number of nuclei, equi-distant from each other, which gradually absorbed the intervening mass into as many equal spheres. The pressure of the spheres one upon the other caused them to assume a prismatic shape.

The normal landing-place is at the mouth of *Clam Shell Cave,* of no great dimensions, but interesting from the curious curvature of the basaltic columns, which gives it its name. This cave cannot be entered ; the best view of it is from the boat on landing. We follow to the W. the *Great Causeway*, similar to the Giant's Causeway in Ireland. On the left is an islet, about 30 ft. high, called *Buchaille* ('Herdsman '), with the basalt columns, visible only at low water, distorted so as in many cases to become horizontal or even inverted ; on the right the superincumbent weight has given a convex curvature to the columns. ***Fingal's Cave,** the most famous of all the caverns, is 227 ft. long, and the height from the water at mean tide is 66 ft., the depth of the sea within being about the same. The sides of the aperture are vertical and nearly parallel. The whole of the sides, ground, and roof is composed of black pentagonal or hexagonal pillars divided transversely by joints at nearly uniform distances of 2 feet. A good path with a stout handrail has been made along the interior. It is difficult to exaggerate the impressiveness of this marvellous place, which inspired Mendelssohn's ' Die Fingalshöhle ' or ' Hebrides ' overture.

Beyond Fingal's Cave, not visited but seen as the steamer sails S., is the *Boat Cave* (12 ft. by 16 ft., 150 ft. long), accessible only by boat, and cut out of the volcanic tuff below the columnar stratum. Farther W. is *Mackinnon's*, the *Cormorant's*, or *Scart's Cave* (48 ft. by 50 ft., 220 ft. long).

About 6 m. S. of Staffa is the island of ***Iona** (*St. Columba*, P. 9 gs. ; *Traighmhor, Argyll*, P. 7 gs., all unlic. ; 175 inhab.), separated from Mull by a strait only 1 m. broad (ferry). It is a treeless but not unfertile island, 3 m. long by 1½ m. broad, and it is rich in venerable associations. Boats convey passengers from the steamer to a stone jetty on the E. side of the island ; day-passengers are allowed c. 1 hr. ashore.

Iona, originally known simply as ' Ia ' or ' Hy,' was called *Ioua Insula* by Adamnan in his ' Life of Columba,' a form transcribed by a careless copyist into Iona. Later it was named *Icolmkill*, the ' island of Columba of the church.'

In 563 St. Columba, for some reason not fully known, left Ireland, where he was born in 521, and with twelve companions, perhaps after a preliminary halt in Kintyre, landed at Iona, the nearest land from which he could no longer see his native shores. There he founded a monastery of which nothing now remains, and thence he set out on those journeys which resulted in the conversion of the Northern Picts and in the extension of Christianity far and wide over Scotland and even over Orkney, Shetland, and Iceland. Here too he died in 597, shortly after St. Augustine had landed in Kent to convert the English, and here he was buried. Two hundred years later his remains were taken to Ireland, but all subsequent trace of them has disappeared. Iona, thus hallowed, early became a pilgrim resort, and it was the burial-place of Scottish kings and chiefs until it was superseded by Dunfermline in the 11th century.

Danish and Norwegian pirates pillaged the island over and over again : in 807 they burnt and destroyed the monastery and all belonging to it. In 1203 Reginald, son of Somerled, Lord of the Isles, founded a new monastery for Benedictines, and a few years later on an Augustinian nunnery. The Benedictine church served as the cathedral of the see of Sodor from 1499 until the dissolution in 1578, and in 1615 it was annexed to the Protestant bishopric of the Isles. Wordsworth wrote three sonnets upon Iona, but it is Dr. Johnson's words that recur most readily to the memory: "That man is little to be envied whose patriotism would not gain force upon the plain of Marathon, or whose piety would not grow warmer among the ruins of Iona." In 1899 the 8th Duke of Argyll presented the cathedral to the Church of Scotland and restoration was soon after begun. In 1938 the Iona Community, a religious brotherhood for the training of students, was founded by Dr. George Macleod. The Community has undertaken restoration and excavation work in and about the cathedral.

Beyond the village we reach the ruins of the Romanesque *Church* of the Priory for Austin nuns (before 1208). It measures 58 ft. by 20 ft., and comprises a nave, with an aisle, adjoining which is a little chapel still retaining some of its vaulting. In a neighbouring building can be seen (through a glass panel) the tomb of the last prioress (d. 1543), whose effigy in hood and cloak occupies one half of the slab, the remainder being broken away. To the S. of the church are the remains of the cloister court and dormitory.

Following the lane we pass the 15th cent. *Maclean's Cross*, 11 ft. high and carved with great force and excellence of design.

In *St. Oran's Cemetery* or Reilig Odhrain, the oldest Christian burial-place in Scotland, 48 Scottish, 8 Norwegian, 4 Irish and 2 French kings are said to rest. They were originally buried in three chapels, which have entirely disappeared, and the carved slabs now ranged into rows of kings, chiefs, and others, are all of the later Middle Ages. The last king buried here was Duncan (1040), murdered, according to Shakespeare, by Macbeth and "carried to Colmekill, the sacred storehouse of his predecessors and guardian of their bones." The ashes of Marjory Kennedy-Fraser (1857–1930), collector and transcriber of Gaelic songs, were buried here in 1932. Another enclosure contains tombs of the Macleans of Mull, the last four priors of Iona, and of Dr. John Beaton of Mull (d. 1657), physician to James VI. Here is *St. Oran's Chapel*, a small chamber of Romanesque architecture now restored, said to stand on the site of St. Columba's church and to have been built by Queen Margaret (1080), thus being the oldest building on the island. It is entered by a low doorway, deeply recessed, with chevron mouldings. Within is the tomb of Scott's 'Lord of the Isles' (p. 343), and a trefoil arch, beneath which St. Oran's tomb is supposed to have stood. Leaving "this awful ground," to use Johnson's words, we proceed N. to the Cathedral, the principal building on the island. Opposite its W. façade stands *St. Martin's Cross* (10th cent.), of granite, 14 ft. high and boldly carved with Runic ornaments and figures; while to the left is the graceful 10th cent. *St. John's Cross*, restored from fragments in 1926 but blown down twice since 1954. St. Martin's Cross and Maclean's Cross (see above), alone remain upright (in 1958) of the 360 crosses said to have been on the island before

the Reformation. Near the *Well* a broken shaft is all that
remains of *St. Matthew's Cross*. The restored cell or chapel
at the N.W. angle of the nave almost certainly covered the
tomb of St. Columba.

The **Cathedral** (St. Mary's), dating mainly from the early
16th cent., has undergone many later additions and restorations. Cruciform in plan, its interior length is c. 150 ft, and
its breadth across the transepts 70 ft. Its chief external
feature is the low square tower (70 ft. high) above the crossing,
with four windows, filled with late tracery of elegant design,
differing in each case. Within the church the arches supporting the tower and the carved capitals of the columns in the
choir should be noticed. In the chancel are tombs of Abbot
Mackinnon (d. 1500) on the N., and Abbot Mackenzie on the
S.; on the S. side are three sedilia in the Gothic style of the
14th cent. The elaborate Sacristy doorway (N.) dates from
1500. The S. transept contains a monument (1912) to the
8th Duke of Argyll (d. 1900) and the tomb of his third duchess
(d. 1925), with a marble effigy by Sir George Frampton.

Adjoining the cathedral on the N. are the restored monastic
buildings: the *Chapter House* (completed 1955) retains its
Norman doorway and its vault; the *Refectory* (1949) preserves a stone regarded as Columba's pillow. The *Undercroft*, on the W. side of the *Cloister* (1959), contains a collection
of tombstones from Reilig Odhrain and the shaft of a cross of
Abbot Mackinnon (1489). To the N.E. is a small quadrangular
chapel, of which the dedication is unknown; also a single
gable of the Bishops' House. The *Infirmary* may be restored
as a Museum.

In 1957 excavations on *Tor Abb*, a hillock W. of the cathedral, revealed the
remains of a cell, in all probability that of St. Columba's.

There are several other interesting spots on Iona, the
highest ground in which, *Dun-I* (332 ft.), at the N. end,
commands a fine panorama. On the S. coast is *Port-na-
Churaich*, on whose beautiful beach St. Columba is supposed
to have landed in his coracle. Near the extreme S.E. point is
a marble quarry; and on the W. coast, 1½ m. S.W. of the
cathedral, is a ' spouting cave.'

Ferry to *Fionphort* and bus thence to *Craignure*, see Rte. 50A.

Quitting Iona the steamer steers S. to double the Ross of
Mull. A position near the bow should be taken to watch the
steamer being conned through the *Torrans*, an archipelago of
granite rocks off the Ross, amid which the ' Covenant ' (in
' Kidnapped ') was wrecked. On the left is the tidal islet of
Erraid or *Earraid* on which David Balfour was cast up.

About 15 m. S.W. of Iona *Dhu Heartach Lighthouse*, on St. John's Rock, is
visible in exceptionally clear weather. This solitary trap rock rises out of deep

water, in the midst of reefs extending over some stormy square miles, and the construction of the lighthouse (1867–72), which rises 143 ft. above sea-level, was attended with great difficulties.

We now steer E. along the S. coast of Mull, and the stern and fissured cliff scenery, where the granite has given place to freestone capped with basalt, is extraordinarily fine. There is no coast-road. Farther on the cliffs are c. 1000 ft. high, higher than all others in Scotland, except those of St. Kilda, Foula, and Hoy. Close to the margin of the sea are seen the remarkable *Carsaig Arches*, huge tunnels formed by the sea in the basaltic rock, and a little farther E. is the *Nun's Cave*, with curious carvings. *Carsaig Bay*, with its pink cottages and conspicious church, has become well known as the scene of the film ' I Know Where I'm Going.' We cross the mouth of *Loch Buie*, at the head of which are the ruins of *Moy Castle*, for centuries a stronghold of the Maclaines of Lochbuie, and the old mansion where Dr. Johnson stayed and was offended at being offered cold sheep's head for supper. A little N. of the castle is a stone circle. There are grand basaltic cliffs along the sea-coast as well as inland between Loch Buie and *Loch Spelve*, a sea-loch with a narrow entrance : to the N. rise Ben Buie (2354 ft.) and Ben Creach (2289 ft.).

As we cross to the mainland we enjoy grand views to the right of the *Garvelloch Isles* ('rough isles '), or *Isles of the Sea*, with ' beehive ' cells and other early monastic remains (boat from Easdale, p. 341), of Scarba, and, in the distance, of the Paps of Jura, Islay, and Colonsay. Crossing the *Firth of Lorn* we have a splendid view of Ben Cruachan (N.W.) before reaching the Sound of Kerrera and *Oban*.

51. FROM OBAN TO BALLACHULISH AND FORT WILLIAM. GLEN COE

STEAMERS leave Oban for (2¼ hrs.) *Fort William* on Mon. and Fri. (mid-May-Sept.), also on Wed. (from mid-June), at 10 a.m. and 6 p.m. ; on Tues. and Sat. (early June-Sept.) at 5.30 p.m. The return journey from Fort William starts at 2 and 8 p.m. (Mon. & Wed. also at 7 a.m. from early June).—Fares : 13/, return 19/5.—The steamer usually calls at *Appin* by arrangement ; and there is a twice-daily service (3 times on Wed.) between Oban and Lismore throughout the year (Sun. excepted) in 1 hr.

RAILWAY from Oban to *Ballachulish*, 33¾ m. in 1½ hr. Carriages are changed at Connel Ferry. An admirable circular tour, 7 hrs. in all, may be arranged (June-Sept.) by taking the morning train to Ballachulish, and returning to Oban by the Glencoe motor coach to Lochetivehead, motor boat thence to Achnacloich, and train thence to Oban. Fares 19/6, 16/6. The route may be reversed (8¼ hrs.).

The ROAD ROUTE is roundabout, though pleasant.—A 85. 5 m. *Connel Ferry*.—A 828. 24 m. *Appin*.—37 m. *Ballachulish Ferry* to *North Ballachulish*.—A 82. 49 m. **Fort William**.—The ferry at Ballachulish (which is not available for cars after dark) may be avoided by following the fine road round Loch Leven, adding 19 interesting miles to the journey.

A. From Oban to Fort William by Steamer

The sail up Loch Linnhe is very beautiful. Leaving *Oban* by the N. channel we pass (r.) Dunollie Castle and, just before we enter the *Linn of Lorn*, Ben Cruachan is conspicuous on our right. We have on the left, backed by the hills of Morvern, the verdant Lismore, a long, low, narrow, island in the mouth of Loch Linnhe.

Lismore (' great enclosure ') was once the seat of the diocese of Argyll (separated from Dunkeld c. 1200), from which the bishops acquired the title ' Episcopi Lismorenses.' The humble parish church (1749) incorporates the choir of the tiny cathedral of which only the medieval doorways, sedilia, and a piscina survive. In 1952, however, excavations revealed some walls of the nave and the W. tower ; and the Bachull Mor, pastoral staff of St. Moluag (d. 592), was returned to Lismore. On the W. coast, on a high rock, are the ruins of the ancient episcopal castle of *Achnadun*. At the S. end of the island is a lighthouse.—The ' Book of the Dean of Lismore ' is a MS. collection of Gaelic and English poems made in the 16th cent., of especial interest for the light it throws upon the Ossianic problem.— Motor launch from Achnacroish to *Oban*, see above ; ferry to Port Appin, see p. 351.

On the right we see *Eriska*, at the mouth of *Loch Crevan*. Just beyond *Airds Bay*, on which is the mansion of *Airds* (before 1745), lies *Port Appin* (p. 351), behind which the mountains of Appin tower to the E. The steamer calls here on request. On an islet at the mouth of Loch Laich is *Castle Stalker*, built to receive James IV and long the residence of the Stewarts of Appin. Except at high tide we keep outside the island of *Shuna*, on which is a ruined castle. Ben Nevis comes into view ahead, and to the N.W. are the mountains of Ardgour with Glen Tarbert running through to Loch Sunart. On the E. coast, beyond a promontory, is *Ardsheal House*, near the scene of the Appin murder. The steamer crosses the mouth of Loch Leven between Corran (r.) and Ardgour (l.) to enter the *Corran Narrows* (less than ¼ m. broad), in which there is a strong tide-race. We pass the entrance to Cona Glen and Glen Scaddle and gain a not particularly impressive view of Ben Nevis. 2¼ hrs. **Fort William** (see Rte. 52).

B. From Oban to Ballachulish and Fort William by Road

The RAILWAY from North Connel to Ballachulish keeps close to the road except for the road-detour round Loch Crevan.

The railway bridge at Connel (no ferry) may be used by pedestrians (2*d.*), cycles (4*d.*), motor cycles (1/3) and motor cars (4/–6/).

To (5 m.) *Connel Ferry*, see Rte. 47. Crossing the bridge to North Connel (Lochnell Arms) the road runs between the shore and the *Moss of Achnacree*, a raised beach, and enters a cutting at the foot of a great precipice of conglomerate. Near the station of (7½ m.) *Benderloch* is a twin-peaked hill, sup-

posed to be the site of *Beregonium,* the name assigned by
Boece to the capital of the Fingalian kings.

There is only the slightest evidence to suggest that the vitrified fort on the
top of this little hill (fine view) was the Fort of the Sons of Uisneach and a Pictish
capital (the ' Selma ' of Ossian). There are traces of a raised way between the two
peaks which was more probably the work of Christian times.

To the left is the road to (13½ m.) the tidal island of *Eriska* (Hotel).

Crossing another raised beach we see *Barcaldine Castle*
(15th cent.) on the left as we approach *Loch Creran,* whose
wooded S. shore is followed for 5 miles. At the Narrows the
loch is crossed by a long railway bridge affording fine views,
while the road makes a circuit round the head of the loch.
From (19 m.) *Glasdrum* a track leads up *Glen Creran,* amidst
fine river and mountain scenery, to *Ballachulish* (12 m.)

We now traverse the *Strath of Appin* to (24 m.) *Appin,* on
the left of which a road leads to *Port Appin* (2 m. ; Airds,
RB. 18/6, P. 9 gs.), a quiet little place. Thence a ferry plies
6 or 7 times daily to *Lismore* (passenger or cycle 1/3, ret. 2/ ;
motor cycle 2/9). The Oban–Fort William steamer calls here
by arrangement.

Appin, a corruption of Abthain, or ' abbey lands,' is the district between Loch
Linnhe and Glen Creran. The ' Appin Murder ' (1752), when Campbell of Glenure
was shot by an unknown hand though James Stewart ' of the Glens ' was hanged
for the crime, plays a great part in ' Kidnapped ' and ' Catriona.'

Beyond (25½ m.) *Portnacroish* the road ascends with a
splendid retrospect of Castle Stalker, of Lismore, and of the
Morvern mountains. We follow the coast, with Shuna on
our left, and soon cross the beautiful Salachan Burn, a
mountain torrent. Between (30 m.) *Duror* (Hotel, RB. 18/6,
P. 7 gs. ; Inshaig Farm) and the coast is the promontory of
Ardsheal ; here, on the old Lettermore road, the Appin
murder (inscription) took place.—37 m. **Ballachulish Ferry**
(*Ballachulish Hotel,* RB. 25/, P. 10 gs. ; *Craigrannoch,* unlic.
RB. 18/, P. 7 gs.), for the direct Fort William road. On a
hill, above the ferry, a monument (much overgrown) marks
the spot where James of the Glens was hanged. At the village
(Laroch House, unlic., RB. 17/6, P. 6½ gs.), 1½ m. W., are huge
slate quarries. The hills behind afford splendid views of the
lochs and of Ben Nevis.

In the isle of *St. Munda,* in Loch Leven, are ancient burial-places, paved with
grave-stones including those of the Macdonalds of Glencoe (with a stone from
the house of John Macdonald, son of the chief, who was shot in the massacre).

FROM BALLACHULISH AROUND LOCH LEVEN, a remarkably fine drive. Diverging to the left from the Glen Coe road at (2½ m.) *Glencoe* (see below), an excellent
road skirts the S. bank of Loch Leven (views) to (10 m.) **Kinlochleven** (*Tartan,*
RB. 25/, P. 10½ gs.), a small town (1750 inhab.) with large aluminium works and
red-roofed houses, presenting a curiously industrial aspect amid its Highland
surroundings. The tramp of two navvies, bound for these works from Glasgow
viâ the Devil's Staircase, is realistically described in *Patrick MacGill's* ' Children
of the Dead End.'—The attractive road returning by the N. bank of the loch
(motor-buses) crosses (11½ m.) a burn, which has formed a fine series of pot-holes
(l.) , and at 19 m. joins the direct road at North Ballachulish (see below.)

A ferry (3*d*., cycle, 6*d*., motor cycle 2/, motor car 4/–6/) crosses the mouth of Loch Leven to *North Ballachulish* (Loch Leven, RB. 22/6, P. 9½ gs.), in Inverness-shire, whence a road ascends the shore of upper Loch Linnhe.—At (40 m.) *Onich* (Creagdhu, RB. 33/, P. 12 gs.; Allt-nan-Ros, RB. 21/6, P. 10 gs.; Onich, RB. 25/, P. 11 gs., all closed in winter), a straggling village, we leave the shore, but soon regain it beyond (41½ m.) *Corran Ferry* (Nether Lochaber, RB. 22/6, P. 8 gs.) on the Narrows of Loch Linnhe. A ferry (4*d*., cycle 6*d*. motor cycle 2/, car 6/) crosses the Narrows to Ardgour for the roads to Loch Eil and to Salen (p. 360) or Lochaline (p. 343).—Our road keeps close to the Loch Linnhe shore.— 49 m. **Fort William,** see Rte. 52.

C. From Ballachulish to Glen Coe, Glen Etive, and Oban

A motor leaves Ballachulish Ferry Station at 11.15, reaching Lochetivehead at 1.15 p.m., in connection with a motor yacht down Loch Etive to *Achnacloich*, where we rejoin the railway, arriving at Oban at 4.37 p.m. Fares from Ballachulish 16/9, 15/. A halt for light refreshments is made at the Glencoe Hotel; luncheons and teas are obtainable on the yacht.

The narrow and winding old road through Glen Coe has been superseded by a straight new road, generally at a lower level, which, though it provides an easier passage, is less in keeping than the old road with the character of the glen and has less effective views.

Ballachulish, see above. Leaving the station we pass great heaps of quarry refuse. We turn inland at *Glencoe* (Hotel, RB. 20/, P. 9 gs.), leaving on the left the *Bridge of Coe*, near which was fired the first shot of the massacre. The strange *Pap of Glencoe* (2430 ft.), a bare peak with steep rifted gullies dangerous to ascend, is conspicuous on the left. A monument marks the site of the destroyed clachan (see below). As far as (3½ m.) *Clachaig Hotel* (RB. 18/6, P. 8 gs.) on the old road, the glen is green, but as we cross the stream and ascend to *Loch Triochatan*, beside whose kelpie-haunted waters Ossian is said to have been born, its character changes completely. On the left is a vast wall of rock (Aonach Eagach) and on the right, " where naked crests fight to achieve the skies," the ' Three Sisters of Glencoe '—*Aonach Dubh*, *Gearr Aonach*, and *Ben Fhada*—appear in succession. Behind Aonach Dubh, in which a great cleft has been named Ossian's Cave, rises *Bidean-nam-Bian* (3766 ft.), the highest peak in Argyll.

Glen Coe was the scene, on Feb. 13th, 1692, of a massacre, carried out, ostensibly under the orders of William III, by Campbell of Glenlyon and 128 soldiers who had lived for some days upon friendly terms with the inhabitants. The reason alleged for the slaughter was the failure of Macdonald of Glencoe to take the oath of allegiance to the king. He had delayed until the last and, when at length he went to Fort William, he found no magistrate there competent to receive his oath and was forced to go to Inveraray. When the papers arrived at Edinburgh, a few days late, they were suppressed by the Secretary of State,

Sir John Dalrymple, Master of Stair, and the extirpation of the clan was decreed at the instigation of the Earl of Breadalbane, whose lands the Glencoe men had plundered. The massacre began suddenly at dawn ; the order for it is said to have been written on the nine of diamonds, known since then as ' the curse of Scotland.' Of the 200 occupants of the glen more than 40 were slain, several died from exposure, and more would have perished had not the severity of the weather prevented the royal troops from occupying the passes in time.

It is hard to say under what aspect Glen Coe is finest—whether with the shifting lights of cloud or sunshine, or when the storm is breaking over its precipitous black jagged rocks. In the latter case the innumerable torrents that whiten the rifted walls are not the least remarkable feature of the scene. Much of the upper glen, including the two ' Shepherds of Etive,' and Bidean-nam-Bian (12,800 acres), now belongs to the Nat. Trust.

" Up the glen did Alan Breck and David Balfour escape after the Appin murder. But you will look in vain for the big stone on the top of which they ' birstled ' or toasted in the sun. As to their famous leap over the linn, it was quite needless ; they could easily have forded the burn at a hundred places. Otherwise the scene is very like the description in ' Kidnapped,' the big, steep, weather-worn stumps of hills frowning all around " (Andrew Lang).

Above the road, to the left (c. 7½ m.), is the so-called *Study* (Scot. ' studdie,' anvil), a terrace which commands perhaps the finest view of the glen with its charming waterfall. The steep path (r.) leads in 4 m. to Dalness in Glen Etive.

Crossing (8½ m.) the watershed (1011 ft.) we reach (9½ m.) *Altnafeadh*, whence the *Devil's Staircase*, part of an old military road now in disrepair, crosses the range of hills on the N. (1754 ft.) and descends to (6 m.) *Kinlochleven* (p. 351). Opposite is the lonely cottage of Lagangarbh, now a climbers' hut.—At (11½ m.) a road-fork we diverge to the right for Loch Etive.

The main road, for Bridge of Orchy and Tyndrum, etc., keeps straight on, while the old road bears left for (1 m. from the fork) *Kingshouse Hotel* (p. 335).

Our road, skirting the great mass of *Buchaille Etive Mor* (3345 ft.), ' the Shepherd of Etive,' descends the desolate and impressive *Glen Etive*. On the left rises *Clachlet* (3602 ft.), the chief peak of the Black Mount (p. 335). Near (17½ m.) *Dalness* the river forms fine rapids, and, as we near (24 m.) *Lochetivehead* (no inn), where the road ends, *Ben Staraṽ* (3541 ft.) rises grandly on the E. bank of the loch.

A motor yacht starting c. 2 p.m. descends **Loch Etive,** which has a very wild aspect in its upper reaches. Ahead, the steep and rocky sides of Ben Cruachan cast a gloom over the loch before we call at (34 m.) *Taynuilt* pier, and round the wooded Airds Point (fine views to the mountains of Mull) to (38 m.) *Achnacloich.*—Railway thence to (47½ m.) **Oban,** see Rte. 46.

52. FORT WILLIAM TO INVERNESS. THE GREAT GLEN

ROAD (A 82), 66½ m. Motor-Bus twice daily in 2¾ hrs. (10/2, ret. 17/8.)—25½ m. *Invergarry.*—32½ m. **Fort Augustus.**—39¼ m. *Invermoriston.*—52 m. *Drumnadrochit.*—66½ m. **Inverness,** entered viâ Tomnahurich St. (Pl. A 2).

The **Caledonian Canal** extends in an almost straight line for 60½ m. between Loch Linnhe and the Moray Firth, following the 'great glen' of GLENMORE, which cuts a deep rift from S.W. to N.E. through the main watershed of Scotland. About 22 m. of its course are artificial, but the rest takes advantage of the natural Lochs Lochy, Oich, and Ness, which lie strung out along the valley. The route of the canal (which is government property) was surveyed by James Watt in 1773 and its construction was begun by Telford in 1803. It was opened for traffic in 1822, but proved too shallow and was not finally completed until 1847, having cost £1,256,000 in all. For many years it was much used, particularly by sailing boats, which thus avoided the long voyage round Cape Wrath. Now, however, owing to the small capacity of the 29 locks, and to the greater seaworthiness of the steam trawlers, the canal is little used. The scenery throughout is very fine.

FORT WILLIAM (2675 inhab.), on Loch Linnhe, is a favourite starting-point for the ascent of Ben Nevis and for other interesting excursions. The summit of Ben Nevis is not visible from the town.

Hotels. Alexandra, RB. 30/, P. 13½ gs.; **Grand,** RB. 27/, P. 12 gs.; **Imperial,** RB. 25/6, P. 12 gs.; **Station,** RB. 23/, P. 12 gs., open May–Oct.; **Highland,** P. 9½ gs.; **Palace,** RB. 22/6; **West End,** RB. 21/, P. 11 gs.; **Cruachan,** RB. 20/, P. 10 gs., small.

Steamer Quay close to the station for steamers to Oban (see Rte. 51A). A steamer in summer leaves at 7 a.m. on Mon. and Wed. for *Iona*, passing close to Staffa, and arriving back c. 8 p.m. (42/6).

Motor-Buses to *Corpach* (⅓ hr.); to *North Ballachulish* and *Kinlochleven* (1 hr.); to *Glenfinnan* (1¼ hr.; weekdays); to *Roy Bridge* (35 min.); to *Fort Augustus* (80 min.) and *Inverness* (2¾ hrs.); to *Glencoe* (1½ hr.) and *Tyndrum* (2¾ hrs.), daily, going on to *Glasgow* (6 hrs.); to *Loch Laggan* (1¼ hr.) and *Kingussie* (2¼ hrs.) on Fri.; to *Achnacarry* (1 hr.) on Tues. Fri., and Sat.—NIGHT-BUS to *Kingussie* (2¼ hrs.) connecting with the London train (also Edinburgh & Glasgow).

The fort from which Fort William takes its name stood at the N. end of the present town, but has been entirely pulled down to make way for the railway. It was originally built of earth by General Monk in 1655 and was rebuilt of stone under William III, with the view of keeping in check the turbulent Highlanders. The town, for a brief period known as Maryborough, after William III's queen, has considerably developed since the advent of the railway in 1894. In the *Town Hall* is the Union Jack hauled down in 1947 at Fort William, Calcutta, when India became a Dominion. The flag had flown there since the establishment of the fort in the 17th cent. The *West Highland Museum* (adm. 1/), in Cameron Square, has an interesting collection including a crofter's kitchen, early farm implements, brooches, dirks, and jougs, as well as a helmet of Montrose and a surveying level of Telford's. Among the Jacobite relics are the bed in which Prince Charles slept at Fassifern House, a ' secret ' portrait of the Prince, and Flora McDonald's fan. Here also is the pine panelling (1707) from the Governor's House.

The ASCENT OF ***Ben Nevis** (4406 ft.; 4 hrs. up, 3 hrs. down; guide not necessary), the highest mountain in the British Isles (Snowdon 3560 ft.), which lies c. 2 m. S.E., is the favourite excursion from Fort William. Ben Nevis is not a graceful mountain, and owing to the absence of a cone or peak, its great height and gigantic mass are not immediately realised. Its leading features are the deep Glen Nevis (see below), on the S., the imposing buttresses and gullies, on the N., and the grand corrie, on the N.E., at the head of which a narrow arête connects the summit with the spur of *Cairn Mor Dearg* (4012 ft.).

From the bridge over the Nevis, ½ m. N. of Fort William, a road ascends the right bank of the stream to (1½ m.) *Achintee Farm*, whence a well-marked pony-track (5 m. long) ascends to the summit. From a small tarn (2200 ft.) where we join the path from Lochy Bridge, the track, steeper and rougher, reaches the top in six long zigzags. On the summit are the ruins of an observatory (1881–1905) and of an inn.

The not very interesting route from Lochy Bridge, on the Inverness road, ascends the Allt Coire-an-Lochan to the tarn at 2200 ft. An alternative and much harder route (not recommended for the descent and not for the inexperienced) leaves the regular Lochy Bridge track just short of the tarn (see above) and strikes off to the left along the mountain side (no track). Beyond a deer fence we descend towards the Allt-a-Mhuilinn (Voolin), hold S.E. up the corrie, and mount the arête between Cairn Mor Dearg (left) and the summit (right). A club-hut was opened in 1929 at the head of the Allt-a-Mhuilinn glen, a little aside from the usual track.

The *VIEW on a clear day is very extensive, but not so pleasing as from many other more isolated mountains. It commands a radius of nearly 100 m., except to the N.E., where the Cairngorm mountains bound the horizon, but it is rarely clear in all directions at the same time. To the S. Loch Linnhe, the Glencoe mountains, Ben More (Mull), Ben Cruachan, and the Paps of Jura are visible, and, in exceptionally clear weather, the N.E. coast of Ireland ; the the S.E. Ben More, Ben Vorlich, Ben Lawers, and (very marked) Schiehallion ; N.E. a glimpse is caught of Loch Laggan and (occasionally) of Ben Macdhui ; the Caledonian Canal runs N., visible sometimes as far as Inverness ; amid the sea of mountains to the N.W. Mam Soul and Scour Ouran may be identified, and farther W. are the ragged peaks of the Coolins (Skye), the hills of Rum, and the Sgurr of Eigg. Loch Eil runs W. from the mountain-foot towards Glenfinnan.

Glen Nevis ranks among the finest glens in Scotland. From Fort William a road ascends the left bank of the Nevis, passing (3 m.) a log-built youth hostel, at the foot of a wooded hill, the site of the medieval fort of *Dun Dige*; (5 m.) *Dunjardil* (Dundbhairdghal), a good vitrified fort (magnificent view) 1500 ft. above the road; and (8 m.) *Achriach*, 2½ m. beyond which it comes to an end. The stream forms a fine waterfall at Achriach and a still finer one c. 4 m. farther up in a magnificent gorge.

From the upper fall good walkers may push on by a track leading over the pass (1320 ft.) to (8 m.) *Loch Treig* and (15 m.) *Tulloch* station (p. 337).

From Fort William to *Ballachulish* and *Oban* by road, see Rte. 51B ; to *Oban* by steamer, see Rte. 51A ; to *Glasgow* by railway viâ the Moor of Rannoch, see Rte. 48B ; to *Mallaig*, by road and railway, and to *Ardgour*, see Rte. 53A ; to *Inverie* (Loch Nevis), see Rte. 53B.

Leaving Fort William we pass the Glen Nevis road on the right. On our left is the village of *Inverlochy*, with the long pier of the British Aluminium Co. ; their huge factory and pipe-lines are seen on the right farther on. A little short of *Lochy Bridge* (comp. Rte. 53), on the left, are the ruins of old *Inverlochy Castle*, a square building with round corner-towers.

This castle dates probably from the late 15th cent., and in the time of Charles II it was still unfinished. Under its walls, in 1645, the Covenanters under Argyll were defeated by Montrose, with a loss of 1500 men, in a battle described by Scott in the 'Legend of Montrose,' and by Neil Munro in 'John Splendid.' Argyll himself retired to his galley at the beginning of the action. The victory encouraged Charles I to break off the negotiations at Uxbridge, with disastrous consequences to himself.—A curious old legend places an ancient Pictish city on this site, where King Achaius is said to have signed a treaty with Charlemagne in 790.

On the left appear the Glenfinnan mountains at the head of Loch Eil. We pass (3 m. ; l.) the 19th cent. Inverlochy Castle, now the centre of a cattle ranch. To our right is a magnificent view of the N. precipices of Ben Nevis, where some snow usually lingers in the gullies all the year round.—9½ m. **Spean Bridge** (*Hotel*, RB. 22/6, P. 9–11 gs. ; *Druimandarrich*, unlic., RB. 16/6, plain), at a lovely stretch of the river.

In the beautiful valley of the Spean, near (1 m.) High Bridge, now a mere ruin, a skirmish on Aug 16th., three days before the standard was raised at Glenfinnan, began the rising of 1745. Gen. Wade's road crossed the Spean by the Low Bridge (1736), 1 m. farther down, and joined the Inverness road at the farm of Stronenaba, c. 2 m. N.W. of Spean Bridge.

From Spean Bridge to *Roy Bridge* and *Tulloch*, see p. 337 ; thence to *Kingussie*, see p. 241.

Our road sweeps round to the left and ascends to the *Commando Memorial* (1952; by Scott Sutherland), standing watch over the wild country in which the Commandos trained in the Second World War. Thence a road (B 8004 ; l.) descends to Gairlochy, passing the *Falls of Mucomir* where the Spean cascades into the Lochy.—We soon descend to **Loch Lochy,** 10 m. long and never more than 1 m. broad. The sides of the loch become steep and are wooded in places. The sharp Ben Tee (2956 ft.) is conspicuous on the left as we quit the loch beside (22 m.) *Laggan Locks*, near which is an old burying-ground of the MacDonells of Glengarry. A sanguinary clan affray, between the Frasers and the Macdonalds, fought at Laggan in July, 1544, is known as the 'Battle of Shirts,' because the combatants discarded their plaids in the hot summer weather.

There is a good path on the N.W. shore from Laggan Locks to the 'Dark Mile,' comp. p. 362.

The canal passes through a beautiful avenue of larch and the road crosses it just before reaching the narrow *Loch Oich* (4 m. long). On the W. shore of the loch, c. 1 m. from its foot, is a singular monument known as *Tober-nan-ceann* (' well of the heads ').

Crowning it are seven men's heads carved in stone ; beneath is a spring. In the 17th cent. Keppoch, head of a branch of the MacDonells, sent his two sons to

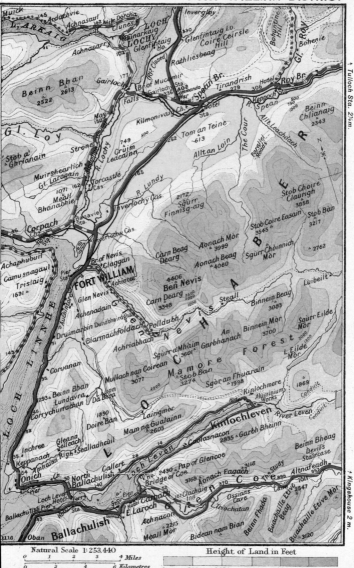

Natural Scale 1:253,440

0 1 2 3 4 Miles

0 2 4 6 Kilometers

Height of Land in Feet

0   500   1000   1500   2000   3000

be educated in France and died in their absence, leaving his affairs to the management of his seven brothers, who murdered the boys on their return. The family bard had the murderers put to death and presented their heads to the chief of the clan at Glengarry, after washing them in this well. An inscription in Gaelic, English, French, and Latin records this " ample and summary vengeance."—The monument was erected by Col. MacDonell of Glengarry (d. 1828), who was a thorough Highlander, admiring everything Celtic with a dogged enthusiasm, and supposed to have been the original of Fergus MacIvor in ' Waverley.'

Half-way up the W. side of the loch, on a rock called *Craig-an-Fhithich* (the clan's slogan, meaning ' rock of the raven '), are the ruins of *Invergarry Castle*, the ancient seat of the MacDonells of Glengarry. Prince Charles lodged here before and after Culloden shortly before the castle was burnt by the Duke of Cumberland.—25½ m. **Invergarry** (*Hotel*, RB. 30/, P. 12 gs.), with a new power station on Loch Oich, is the starting-point of the fine route through Glen Garry to the W. coast (Rte. 53c). At the N. end of the loch a swing-bridge takes the road over the canal, near *Aberchalder Lodge*, at the foot of a grand ravine. Here Prince Charles's forces began their march S. on Aug. 27th, 1745. The road parts company with the canal, which descends through several locks.

32½ m. **Fort Augustus** (*Lovat Arms*, RB. 22/, P. 13 gs. ; *Caledonian*, May–Sept. only, same charges ; *Inchnacardoch*, RB. 20/, P. 9½ gs.), formerly called *Kilchumein*, at the head of Loch Ness, is a quiet place and a convenient centre for visiting many beautiful glens. It is also an anglers' resort. Here the canal passes through six locks.

The fort, commanding Glen Tarff and the wild pass of Corrieyarrick (see below) and named after William Augustus, Duke of Cumberland, was erected after the rebellion of 1715, and was enlarged by General Wade in 1730. Captured by the Highlanders in the '45, it was reoccupied by the Royal troops after Culloden, and here Cumberland was presented with the bleeding head of Roderick Mackenzie, a young Edinburgh lawyer, purporting to be that of Prince Charlie (comp. p. 364).—Dr. Johnson declared in 1778 (five years after his Highland tour) that " The best night I have had these 20 years was at Fort Augustus."

The remains of the fort were sold in 1867 by the Government to Lord Lovat, who in 1876 presented them to the Benedictine Order for the erection of an *Abbey* (adm. 10.30–12 and 2.30–5). The buildings include a cloister and tower by P. P. Pugin (1893) and the Romanesque church by R. Fairlie begun in 1914.

The abbey was colonised by monks from the Schottenkloster at Ratisbon (founded by St. Marianus, or Muiredach, of Dunkeld in 1074 and dissolved in 1862), and a Latin and Gaelic MS. by the founder is preserved in the library.

In the far corner of the churchyard, between the Tarff and A 82, rest the ashes of " John Anderson, my jo."—To the S.E. of Fort Augustus is the wild *Pass of Corrieyarrick*, crossed by Gen. Wade's derelict road to Speyside, which gave passage to the Jacobites in 1745 (see p. 240).

FROM FORT AUGUSTUS TO INVERNESS VIÂ FOYERS, 32 m., by another of Wade's roads (A 862 ; steep, up to 1:4). We ascend Glen Doe to the E., then skirt (4 m.) *Loch Tarff* and, beyond the summit-level (1162 ft.), descend into the Foyers valley, crossing the stream at (9 m.) *Whitebridge Hotel* (RB. 22/6, P. 10 gs.) at the foot of the charming glen of the Fechlin, leading up to *Loch Killin*

(5 m.).—At (10½ m.) the fork A 862 keeps right for *Gorthlick* (3 m.), on the shore of *Loch Mhor*, a sheet of water 5 m. long formed by the union of Loch Garth and Loch Farraline when the Foyers was dammed for the aluminium works (see below). Roads go on through the little-visited Strath Errick to Strath Nairn (Daviot ; r.) or Inverness (l.).

From here we follow the left branch (B 852) down the right bank of the Foyers to (14 m.) *Foyers Hotel* (RB. 25/, P. 11 gs.) on Loch Ness. As we descend the narrow and tortuous gorge we pass the two *Falls of Foyers*, now of no great volume. At the mouth of the river are the penstocks and factories of the aluminium works. The road skirts Loch Ness, passing (15¾ m.) *Inverfarigaig*. where a side-road and the river approach the loch by a romantic gorge.—At (24 m.) *Dores* (Inn) we quit the loch and, leaving on the left the grounds of the 18th cent. *Aldourie Castle*, we approach (32 m.) *Inverness* by the riverside Island-bank Road.

Loch Ness, which the road now skirts, is 24 m. long and, in places, 900 ft. deep, and has never been known to freeze. It is a beautiful stretch of water, with grassy banks framed by wooded hills. We cross the river Moriston alongside the attractive old bridge.—39½ m. **Invermoriston** (*Glenmoriston*, RB. 24/, P. 12 gs. ; *Tigh-na-Bruaich*, unlic., RB. 18/6, P. 8 gs.) is situated at the foot of *Glen Moriston* (see Rte 53D). Beyond (42 m.) *Alltsaigh* youth hostel we pass beneath *Mealfourvonie* (2284 ft.), a mountain very conspicuous from the N. Farther on (r.) a memorial commemorates John Cobb, who lost his life in the loch while attempting to break the water speed record in 1952.

Just before turning W. to cross the mouth of Glen Urquhart we pass the imposing ruin of *Castle Urquhart* (adm. 6d. ; 10–4 or 7, Sun. from 2), picturesquely situated on a bluff above the loch. This strong castle, reinforced by Edward I, passed through several hands ; in 1509 James IV gifted the castle to the Seafield Grants, who built much of the existing ruins and held it for four centuries. The arrangements at the windows for pouring molten lead upon assailants are noteworthy.— We cross the Coiltie, leaving the *Lewiston Arms Hotel* (RB. 25/, P. 11 gs.) on our left, and then the Enrick, to reach (52 m.) **Drumnadrochit** (*Hotel*, RB. 27/6, P. 12 gs.), a pleasant little hamlet.

About ½ m. S.W. of the Lewiston Arms is Balmacaan House, and c. 1 m. farther S.W., on a tributary of the Coiltie, are the pretty *Falls of Divach*.

From Drumnadrochit a road amid beautiful woods runs by the side of the Enrick up Glen Urquhart to (12 m.) Cannich (p. 369) in Strath Glass, passing (5 m.) the little *Loch Meiklie* and (7½ m.) *Corriemony* (motor-bus, coming from Inverness). From this road, c. 1 m. W. of the hotel, a good road runs N. to (13 m.) *Beauly* (p. 368), joining the Inverness road c. 1 m. S. of Lovat Bridge.

Farther on the hills sink, the loch narrows, and, passing (l.) the Italianate *Dochfour*, we skirt for a while the wood-fringed canal running alongside the River Ness. We cross the canal shortly before reaching (66½ m.) **Inverness**, see Rte. 54.

53. BETWEEN THE CALEDONIAN CANAL AND THE WEST COAST

The present route deals with the approach from Fort William to the west coast at Arisaig and Mallaig, and also with the parallel valleys farther north, traversing wild and magnificent country in S.W. Inverness-shire, through which the fugitive Prince Charlie wandered after Culloden. Loch Hourn and Loch Nevis, both opening upon the Sound of Sleat, are among the chief attractions of this region. Sir A. Geikie points out that " the height and the angular form of the mountain ridges, the steep and deeply rifted slopes, and the ruggedness and sterility of the whole landscape, distinguish these two sea-lochs from the rest of the fiords on the W. coast." Both may be visited by motor launch from Mallaig.

Hydro-electric operations in Glen Garry and in Glen Moriston have made considerable alterations to the landscape—enlarging lochs, submerging familiar valleys and hamlets, and even diverting well-established roads. Care, however, has been taken, as usual, to preserve the scenic amenities, e.g. in the architecture of the power stations, and special attention has been paid to the interests of salmon-fishing.

A. From Fort William to Mallaig

ROAD (A 830; road recently widened), 44½ m.—3½ m. *Corpach.*—18¼ m. *Glenfinnan.*—35½ m. *Arisaig.*—44½ m. **Mallaig.**—Cyclists may vary this route by taking the ferry from Fort William to Camus-nan-Gall and following A 861 along the S. bank of Loch Eil, which commands fine views of Locheil Forest to the N.— MOTOR-BUS twice daily (not Sun.) to *Glenfinnan* in 1–1¼ hr. in summer ; on Tues., Thurs., and Sat. from Oct. to mid-May.

RAILWAY, 41½ m. in c. 1½ hr. This is part of the ' West Highland Route,' with through carriages from Edinburgh (Waverley), Glasgow (Queen St.), and London (King's Cross) and observation cars from Fort William.—Principal Stations : 2½ m. *Banavie.*—3½ m. *Corpach.*—10¼ m. *Locheilside.*—17 m. *Glenfinnan* (c. 1 m. from pier ; bus).—26 m. *Lochailort.*—34¼ m. **Arisaig.**—39 m. *Morar.*—41¾ m. **Mallaig.**

We soon diverge left from the Inverness road at Lochy Bridge and then cross the Caledonian Canal, leaving Banavie on the right.—Beyond (3½ m.) *Corpach* (Hotel, RB. 18/6, P. 8 gs. ; *Achdalieu*, 3 m. W., RB. 27/6, P. 12 gs., May–Sept.), above the S. entrance of the canal, are (r.) the church of *Kilmallie*, and an obelisk commemorating Col. John Cameron of Fassifern who fell at Quatre Bras (1815). For the next nine miles the railway and road closely skirt the N. bank of **Loch Eil,** the N.W. arm of Loch Linnhe, 8 m. long and ¾ m. broad. We pass (8 m.) the foot of Glen Suileag, with *Fassifern House* among the trees, where Prince Charles Stewart spent a night, four days after raising his standard at Glenfinnan. At the foot of (12 m.) Glen Fionnlighe we are joined by the road from Ardgour (see below), and soon lose sight of Ben Nevis.— 18½ m. **Glenfinnan** (*Stage House,* RB. 20/, P. 10 gs. or 11 gs. with fishing) is an angling resort at the head of Loch Shiel, which forms the county boundary between Inverness and Argyll.

About ¾ m. E., close to the loch, the conspicuous **Prince Charlie's Monument** marks the spot where Prince Charles Stewart unfurled his standard on Aug. 19th, 1745, on his " daring and romantic attempt to recover a throne lost by the imprudence of his ancestors." The monument, with a statue by Greenshields,

O

was erected in 1815 by Alexander Macdonald of Glenaladale (see below), a descendant of one of the prince's most devoted followers (N.T.; adm. 6d. 10–6 weekdays, Sun. in summer 2–5). A tablet (1923) in the large Roman Catholic church in the grounds of the neighbouring Glenfinnan House likewise commemorates the prince.

FROM GLENFINNAN TO ACHARACLE, small steamer daily (not Sun.) at 1 p.m. in 2 hrs.; also at 6.30 p.m. in 1½ hr. (non-stop) in June–Sept. The steamer traverses the whole length of **Loch Shiel**, a fresh-water loch 18 m. long but nowhere more than 1 m. broad. At its head and for two-thirds of its length the loch is wild, with rocky sides clothed with Scots firs and birches and bounded by mountains of considerable height, but for the remaining third the banks are covered with enormous peat mosses. On the W. side c. 6 m. down, opens *Glenaladale*. About 6 m. farther on the steamer passes the 'Narrows,' in which lies *Eilean Fhionain*, an islet containing a ruined chapel. On the S. rises *Ben Resipol* (2774 ft.). After touching at *Achnanellan* (14 m.; S. bank) and *Dalilea* (15 m.; N. bank) the steamer goes on to (18 m.) **Acharacle** (*Loch Shiel*, unlic., RB. 19/6, P. 10 gs.; *Ardshealach Lodge*, RB. 17/6, P. 8 gs., unlic.), a favourite angling resort. A stream (2 m. long) issuing from the loch at *Shiel Bridge* (½ m. N. of Acharacle) connects it with the sea at *Dorlin*, with *Castle Tirrim*, or *Tioram*, a ruined 14th cent. hold of John of Moidart. A road with fine views runs N.E. from Shiel Bridge to (5 m.) *Kinlochmoidart*, where Prince Charlie stayed during the rally of the clans at Glenfinnan (Aug. 6th–19th, 1745). Seven beeches commemorate the 'Seven Men of Moidart,' who were his first adherents.

FROM ACHARACLE TO ARDGOUR AND FORT WILLIAM, 38½ m., motor-bus all the year to Ardgour and to Kilchoan (not Sun). The narrow road leads S. to (3½ m.) *Salen* (*Hotel*, RB. 17/6, P. 8 gs.), on the N. shore of the beautiful *Loch Sunart* (20 m. long). A difficult road runs W. to *Kilchoan* (19 m.), passing (c. 7 m.) *Glenborrodale House Hotel* (RB. 17/6, unlic., small). Our road runs E. along Loch Sunart to (12½ m.) *Strontian* (Horsley Hall, unlic., RB. 23/, P. 10 gs.; Strontian, similar charges), pronounced Stronteean. In the lead mines here the element strontium was discovered. From the head of the loch a road runs S. to Lochaline (p. 343), but we go on E. and reach the shore of Loch Linnhe at (20½ m.) *Inversanda*. Special care should be taken on this stretch of road.— 27½ m. **Ardgour** (*Hotel*, RB. 21/, P. 9½ gs.) is connected with the main Fort William road by Corran Ferry (p. 352), across the Narrows of Loch Linnhe. Or, from Ardgour, we may skirt the N.W. shore of the loch to (38 m.) *Camus-nan-Gall*, opposite Fort William, and then the S. side of Loch Eil to join (48½ m.) the Glenfinnan road (see above).

Leaving Glenfinnan the road mounts a bare glen and then descends in wide curves to skirt the N. bank of *Loch Eilt* (3½ m. long), at the W. end of which are several little islets. —25½ m. *Lochailort Inn* (RB. 18/6, P. 8 gs.) stands at the head of the sea-loch of that name.

To the S. a road leads to (1 m.) *Inverailort House*, whence an attractive path goes on alongside Loch Ailort and up (8½ m.) *Glen Uig* to (15 m.) *Kinlochmoidart*.

We skirt the head of Loch Ailort (view on the left) and, after passing the little *Loch Dhu*, we come into view of *Loch-nan-Úamha* (loch of the caves), on whose shore, at Borrodale, Prince Charles landed (Aug. 5th, 1745) from the French frigate 'La Doutelle.' Hence too he sailed in the following year, a disappointed and defeated man. The road follows the loch-shore, passing through several woods between which delightful glimpses of the sea are caught. We cross the Borrodale Burn (see above), and a little farther on we have a charming view across Arisaig Bay to the Sgurr of Eigg, 12 m. out at sea, backed by the mountains of Rum.—35½ m. **Arisaig** (*Hotel*, P. 9 gs.; motor-bus to Mallaig), a hamlet with

three churches, overlooking Loch-nan-Cilltean, which is
sheltered by seal-haunted islets.—The road now crosses a
wide moor, keeping close to the sea, and the peaks of Rum and
then those of Skye are conspicuous. The short river Morar,
with rapids on both sides of the road, is crossed beside an
underground power-station (1948).—41¼ m. *Morar* (Hotel,
RB. 22/6, P. 9 gs. ; good view), with the workshops of the
Highland Home Industries, overlooks the beautiful white
sands at the mouth of the river.

Loch Morar (12 m. long and 1 m. broad), though only ¾ m. to the right, is not
visible from the road. This loch, only 30 ft. above the sea, is remarkable for
its extraordinary depth, 180 fathoms, "the deepest known hollow on any
part of the European plateau except the submarine valley which skirts the S.
part of Scandinavia" (Geikie). On the largest of a group of islands near the
W. end Lord Lovat (1667–1747) was captured two months after Culloden.

44½ m. **Mallaig** (*West Highland*, RB. 22/6, P. 12 gs. ;
Marine, unlic., RB. 20/, P. 9½ gs.), the terminus of the
railway, is also a port of call for herring-boats and for steamers
to the Western Isles (comp. Rtes. 58, 59).

Passenger ferry service in ½ hr. to *Skye* (Armadale) 4 times daily in summer.
Mail boat twice daily to *Loch Nevis* (Inverie) in ¾ hr. on Mon., Wed., Fri. & Sat. ;
also to *Tarbet* and *Kinlochnevis* on Mon. & Fri. Day cruises with 1–2 hrs. ashore
to *Loch Scavaig* and *Loch Coruisk* on Mon. & Wed. ; to *Loch Hourn* (Kinlochhourn) on Tues. ; to *Rum* or *Loch Duich* on Thurs. ; to *Loch Moidart* on Fri. ;
to *Eigg* on Sat.

B. From Fort William to Inverie (Loch Nevis)

36 m. Road to (7 m.) *Achnasaul*, thence bridle-path. There is no inn on the
route. MOTOR-BUS from Fort William to *Achnacarry* on Tues., Fri., and Sat.

We leave Fort William as for Mallaig (see Rte. 53A) but
beyond the Canal at (3 m.) *Banavie* (Lochiel Arms, unlic.,
RB. 19/6, P. 9 gs.) we diverge right on B 8004. The road
junction here lies at the head of *Neptune's Staircase*, a series
of eight locks on the canal which ascends through three more
locks from Corpach on Loch Linnhe. This rise of 80 ft. was
Telford's greatest difficulty.—As we quit Banavie we have
a view over a great part of the mountains of LOCHABER
(the district at the 'mouth of the lochs'), keeping above the
canal and Lochy on the bank of which is the old Mackintosh
stronghold of *Tor Castle*.—We cross (6¼ m.) the mouth of
Glen Loy, down which Prince Charles marched in 1745.—At
(8 m.) *Gairlochy* we are joined by the road from Spean Bridge
(3½ m.), see p. 356. The road skirts *Loch Lochy* for 2½ m.
and crosses the Arkaig, having on the left the magnificently
timbered grounds (adm. occasionally on application to the
factor) of *Achnacarry House*, near the remains of the ancient
castle burnt by the Duke of Cumberland in 1746. The estates
belonged in 1664 to Sir Ewen Cameron (1627–1718), the
Ulysses of the Highlands' and the Lochiel of Killiecrankie ;

they were forfeited by his grandson Donald, 'the gentle Lochiel,' in 1745, but were restored to the family in 1784. For some years after the '45 the tenants, besides paying their rents to the Crown, subscribed to support their exiled lord. In the park, S. of the Arkaig, is a famous long beech avenue, planted by Lochiel. Commandos were based here in the Second World War (comp. p. 356).

The road soon turns W. and approaches *Loch Arkaig* by the 'Dark Mile,' a fine avenue no longer dark, on the left bank of the river. We follow the N. bank of the loch for its whole length (13 m.) and pass the islet burying-place of the Lochiels. Beyond (7 m.) *Achnasaul* the road deteriorates into a mere bridle track.—At (17 m.) *Murlaggan* treasure is said to have been thrown into the loch at the time of the last Jacobite rally (1746).—19 m. We quit the loch and begin to ascend *Glen Desseray*, described with its Jacobite associations in Principal Shairp's poem 'Glen Desseray.' The three cairns at its head (24 m., 1000 ft.) mark the meeting-point of Lochiel, Lovat, and Knoidart; and before us is the magnificent *Mamna-Cloich Airde Pass*, descending steeply to (27 m.) *Sourlies*, a farm at the head of Loch Nevis.

*Loch Nevis (' Loch of Heaven '), surrounded by stern bare hills, separates the districts of Knoidart (N.) and Morar (S.). The chief features here are the outlines and grandeur of the hills, which rise immediately from the shore. Like Loch Hourn (see below), Loch Nevis has a narrow upper reach, connected by a strait with its lower expansion.

A rough track follows the S. shore of the upper loch to (32 m.) *Tarbet*, which is only c. 1 m. N. of South Tarbet on Loch Morar (see above). The main track, however, runs inland and, with a fine view of *Sgurr-na-Ciche* (3410 ft.) on the right, ascends steeply to (30 m.; 1709 ft.) the head of *Glen Meadail*, whence it descends to (36 m.) *Inverie*, near the mouth of Loch Nevis. For the boat to Mallaig, see p. 361.

From Inverie the delightful bridle path up *Glen Dulochan* leads to (10 m.) *Barrisdale*, on Loch Hourn, and thence to (16 m.) *Kinlochhourn* (see below).

C. From Invergarry to Loch Hourn or Loch Duich viâ Glen Garry

27½ m. (34 m. to Loch Duich; A 87). The road to Loch Hourn is a dead end, but that to Loch Duich is one of the main approaches to Skye and the far N.W.—MOTOR-BUS to *Glenquoich* on Mon., Wed., and Fri. throughout the year.

From *Invergarry* (p. 357) the road ascends the valley of the Garry, which in recent years has borne the scars of hydro-electric construction work. A salmon hatchery has been built here to help combat the interference with their spawning-ground. 3 m. *Loch Garry* has been doubled in length.

At 5 m. a new road on the right crosses the hills into *Glen Loyne,* reaching it at the foot of Loch Loyne (also greatly extended by a dam), then descends the river Loyne to join (8½ m.) the road from Invermoriston to *Loch Duich.*

11 m. *Tomdoun* (Hotel, RB. 25/, P. 12 gs.), an angling centre. The old road going N. across the hills to Glen Loyne has been submerged at its N. end. At the upper end of Loch Garry (formerly the separate Loch Poulary) are the salmon traps worked in connection with the hatchery (see above). The road skirts *Loch Quoich,* now 9 m. long, the level of its waters having been raised 100 ft. by a dam at the E. end (122 ft. high, 1000 ft. long), the largest ' rock-filled ' dam in Britain. After rounding *Gleourach* (3395 ft.) the road crosses (21 m.) Glenquoich Bridge, at the foot of *Glen Quoich,* now partly submerged.

An old route, crossed by Gen. Monk in 1654 and much used in the days of the military patrols (1746–50), still ascends Glen Quoich and crosses the *Bealach Dubh Leac* (c. 2300 ft.) into Glen Shiel (8 m.), 3½ m. above Shiel Bridge.

Our road strikes N.W., with *Sgurr Mhoraire* (3365 ft.) on the right, where Prince Charlie had to run the gauntlet of the sentries (July 21st, 1746), and descends (steep and rough) to (27¼ m.) the head of ***Loch Hourn*** (' Loch of Hell ') near *Kinlochhourn Lodge.* No hotel accommodation can be had nearer than Invershiel or Tomdoun. The loch (c. 11 m. long), which separates the district of Knoidart (S.) from that of Glenelg (N.), consists, like Loch Nevis, of a narrow upper reach and of a wider lower loch. The upper loch is particularly grand, with bare and savage scenery. Above the N. shore of the lower loch rises the singular peak of *Ben Screel* (3196 ft.) and on the S. is *Ladhar Bheinn* (Lairven ; 3343 ft.).—The road ends at Kinlochhourn, but a delightful hilly path leads along the S. side of the upper loch to (6 m.) *Barrisdale,* where it turns inland to descend through Glen Dulochan to (16 m.) *Inverie* (see above), on the N. shore of Loch Nevis.

The path climbing N.W. from behind Kinlochhourn lodge leads across the *Uiedalan Pass* (c. 1600 ft.) to Glen Beg and (16 m.) *Glenelg.* At 2 m. a very rough path, crossing the *Bealach Coire Mhalagain* (2500 ft.), S.E. of the fine rocky peak called *The Saddle* (3317 ft.), strikes N. for (13 m.) *Invershiel* (see below) ; and at 4 m. a better path descends W. down *Glen Arnisdale,* for (9 m.) *Arnisdale.*

D. From Invermoriston to Loch Duich viâ Glen Moriston and Glen Shiel

36 m. This road was the chief approach to Skye until the construction of the railway to Kyle of Lochalsh. Motor-Bus daily in summer to *Cluanie Bridge*; through service on Sat. only from Inverness to Glenelg (3½ hrs.).

Invermoriston, see p. 358.—The first stretch of *Glen Moriston* still bears the mark of the hydro-electric scheme, recently completed. Beyond Dundreggan dam and (8¼ m.) *Torgyle* the country begins to grow bleaker. Opposite (10¼ m.) *Achlean* is an old graveyard of the Grants, and below (13½ m.) *Ceannacroc*

Bridge, with a new generating station, the Moriston is joined by the Doe (r.). About 2½ m. up this river, in a remarkable cave called *Corriedoe*, Prince Charles lay from Aug. 24th to 28th, 1746, " as comfortably lodged as if he had been in a royal palace." Near the mouth of the Doe is a monument to Roderick Mackenzie, who allowed his captors to imagine him to be Prince Charles (comp. p. 357).—We pass (15 m.) the mouth of Glen Loyne, where the new road to Invergarry diverges. We soon reach (17 m.) *Loch Cluanie* (7½ m. long), recently extended by 3 m. at its W. end by the inclusion of the small Loch Beag ; while on its N. shore the road has been rebuilt higher up the hillside on the N. side of the former Loch Lundie, now a bay of the main loch. After about 3 m. we enter Ross-shire. Near the end of the loch is (24 m.) *Cluanie Bridge* (Inn), at the N. end of the old Tomdoun road (p. 363).

A track running N. from the Invermoriston road nearly 1 m. E. of Cluanie Bridge leads to (7 m.) *Alltbeath Youth Hostel* (p. 370).

After another 2½ m. of ascent we reach the summit-level (889 ft.) and begin the descent into lonely **Glen Shiel,** through the *Pass of Strachel*, a magnificent defile, overhung by peaked and serrated mountains cleft by mysterious corries. It was this glen that inspired Dr. Johnson with the idea of writing the ' Journey to the Western Isles.'

In 1719 the pass was the scene of a skirmish between a small force of regular troops under Gen. Wightman and a body of insurgent Highlanders, chiefly Macraes and Mackenzies, under the Earl of Seaforth, a supporter of the Earl of Mar (p. 203). A Spanish fleet of 30 vessels had been despatched from Cadiz in support of the Stewart case, but only two ships reached Loch Duich, where they landed 300 Spaniards and 2000 stand of arms. The Highlanders fought fiercely but in vain ; the Spaniards laid down their arms ; and Lord Seaforth was badly wounded.

35 m. Shiel Bridge (*Kintail*, at Invershiel ; *Ratagan House*, 1 m. N.W., unlic., RB. 17/6, P. 6½ gs.) stands just short of *Loch Duich* at the mouth of the glen. A bus service runs viâ the N. shore of Loch Duich to Dornie and Kyle of Lochalsh ; and Glenelg lies 9 m. W. by hill-road. *Ratagan* youth-hostel is 1 m. N.W. of the bridge (comp. Rte. 55).

If time can be found, it is worth while to climb *Scour Ouran* (3505 ft. ; 2–3 hrs. ; steep but easy), highest of the ' Five Sisters of Kintail.' A boggy path ascends the right bank of the Shiel, from which, beyond (2 m.) the mouth of a ravine, we strike straight up the nose of the mountain. The N.T. own 15,000 acres here.

The splendid *View includes the Outer Hebrides from Harris to Barra, the Coolins, and the Sgurr of Eigg ; to the N. the mountains around Loch Maree ; to the S. Ben Nevis, the Glencoe mountains, and Ben Alder, with Ben More in Mull farther off, and sometimes the Paps of Jura ; to the E. and N.E. the view is more restricted, and the long ridges of Ben Attow and Mam Soul are prominent, with Loch Affric visible to the right.—The descent may be made by the N. ridge to Glenlichd House in *Glen Lichd* (see p. 370), which falls into Loch Duich at (3½ m.) Croe Bridge.—For the ascent of *Ben Attow*, see p. 370.

V. NORTHERN SCOTLAND AND ITS ISLANDS

54. INVERNESS. INVERNESS TO LOCH DUICH

A. Inverness and its Environs

INVERNESS (28,100 inhab.), known as the capital of the Highlands, is a modern-looking town in a fine situation commanding lovely views over a varied and beautiful country. In the tourist season it is always busy and often full, and during the fashionable Northern Meeting (3rd week in Aug.), when the Highland dress is much in evidence, it is over-crowded. The Ness (whose whole course is but 6 m. from Loch Ness to the sea) flows through the town in a limpid stream. The air of Inverness, as in the days of King Duncan, "nimbly and sweetly recommends itself unto our gentle senses." The English spoken in Inverness is of old repute. Defoe, writing in 1723, says, "They speak as good English here as in London"; the usual explanation being that the people (whose native tongue was Gaelic) learned their English from Cromwell's garrison.

Hotels (charges lower in Oct.–June). **Station** (a; C 1), RB. 35/, P. 55/; **Royal** (d; B 1), T.H., Academy St., RB. 24/; **Caledonian** (b; B 1), 31 Church St., RB. 27/6; **Douglas** (f; B 1), Union St., RB. 27/6; **Cumming's**, Church St. (B 1), RB. 25/6, P. 11 gs.; **Columba** (h; B 2), 7 Ness Walk, unlic.; **Queensgate** (B 1), RB. 20/; **Lochardil**, Stratherrick Rd., RB. 21/, P. 10 gs.; **MacDougall's**, Church St., and many other unlic. houses.—**Drumossie**, 2 m. S.E. at Inshes, RB. 25/, P. 14 gs.

Post Office (B 1), Queensgate.

Motor-Buses. Frequent service from Academy St. to *South Kessock* (10 min.) with ferry connection for Rosemarkie and Cromarty (1¼–1¼ hr.); also from the Bus Station, Margaret St. (C 1) to *Fort George* (36 min.); *Culloden* (18 min.) and *Nairn* (65 min.); *Banff* and *Macduff* (3¾ hrs.) viâ Forres, Elgin, and Fochabers; *Aberdeen* (5 hrs.) viâ Forres, Elgin, and Huntly; *Aviemore, Kingussie,* and *Newtonmore* (2 hrs.; summer only); *Tomatin* (50 min.); viâ Gorthlick to *Whitebridge* (1½ hr.);

Foyers (1¼ hr.); viâ Glenurquhart to *Corriemony* (1¼–1½ hr.); *Fort Augustus* (1½ hr.) and *Fort William* (2¾ hrs.); *Ullapool* (3 hrs.); viâ Dingwall (65 min.) and Dornoch (4 hrs.) to *Helmsdale* (5½ hrs.; with connection to Wick and Thurso); viâ Conon Bridge to *Cromarty* (2 hrs.); *Fortrose* and *Rosemarkie* (c. 1½ hr.). Also express service in summer to *Glasgow* (8 hrs.) viâ Kingussie, Pitlochry, Perth, and Stirling.

Air Services from Dalcross Airport (8 m. S.E.) to *Glasgow* in 70 min.; to *Stornoway* in 55 min.; viâ Wick (¾ hr.) to *Orkney* (1 hr. 20 min.) and *Shetland* (3 hrs.). Motor service from 13 Queensgate ¾ hr. before departure of plane.

Amusements, *Empire* (also theatre) and other cinemas, Academy St.—*Tennis Courts,* Bellfield Park.—*Golf Course,* at Culcabock, 1 m. S.E.—*Swimming Pool* (indoor), Albert Place.

Northern Meeting, 3rd week in Aug., with Highland games in the ground beside St. Andrew's Cathedral, and dancing in the Northern Meeting Rooms, Church St.

History. St. Columba is said to have visited King Brude c. 565 at a castle 'near the Ness,' probably the predecessor of the stronghold of Macbeth, Mormaer of Ross and Moray (11th cent.). Macbeth's castle, the site of which is located S. of the railway, c. ¼ m. E. of the station, was razed by King Duncan's avenger, Malcolm Canmore, by whom (in 1057) or by David I (c. 1140) a new castle was founded on the present Castle Hill. In the Scottish War of Independence Inverness was thrice occupied by the English, and when Bruce recaptured it in 1307 he destroyed the castle. In later reigns town and castle alike suffered from the savagery of the Highlandmen, and were the scene of many assemblies called by the kings in their attempts to control the wild chieftains. When Mary, Queen of Scots, visited the town in 1562 she was refused admission to the castle by the governor, but the castle surrendered the next day and the governor was hanged. Oliver Cromwell appreciated the town's strategic importance, and in 1652–57 built a strong fort, known as 'The Sconce,' on the right bank of the Ness downstream, using for this purpose stones from the abbey of Kinloss (p. 316). This, however, was pulled down at the Restoration to please the clans. Inverness Castle was occupied by the Jacobites in 1715, and again in 1745 by Prince Charlie, who blew it up, leaving little remaining. The site was finally cleared in 1834 to make way for the present buildings.

Academy St., in which is the *Railway Station* (B, C 1), and Union St. and Queensgate, connecting it with Church St. (B 1) on the S.W., are the chief shopping streets. In Church St., near its S. end, is *Abertarff House* (No. 71) of the late 16th cent., long the town residence of the Lovats ; No. 43 stands on the site of Lady Drummuir's house, occupied in 1746 successively by Prince Charlie and the Duke of Cumberland ; and at the N. end of the street is the *High Church* (1769–72), nearly opposite which *Dunbar's Hospital* (1668 ; now dwellings) offers an interesting example of 17th cent. domestic architecture. Just beyond the church Friars Lane leads (l.) towards the Ness, passing the narrow Friars St. (B 1 ; r.), near the corner of which is the tiny burial ground in which is preserved a pillar of the Dominican friary founded by Alexander II before 1240.

Church St. is continued by Chapel St. and Shore St. to the site of *Cromwell's Fort*, where only a clock-tower and some traces of barracks and ramparts remain.

Close against the façade of the *Town Hall* (B 2 ; 1880), in High St. (at the S. end of Church St.), stands the restored *Mercat Cross*, on a base enclosing the famous *Clach-na-Cudainn* (' stone of the tubs '), a rude unhewn block on which women carrying water from the river used to rest their tubs or pitchers, which has long been the palladium of the town or, as Scott puts it, " the charter stone of the burgh," though its origin is unknown.

In the vestibule of the town hall is a beam from Cromwell's fort (to the right of the staircase), and in the Assembly Room, on the upper floor, are good decorations and some portraits, including one of Flora Macdonald.

Castle Wynd, by the town hall, ascends towards the *Castle Hill*, passing the *Public Library and Museum* (adm. free ; 10–4 or 5; closed Tues. and Thurs. from 1 p.m. and Sun.), especially notable for its collection of Jacobite relics. Within the large gateway at the top of the hill, which overlooks the river, is the old *Castle Well*, rediscovered in 1909. The present

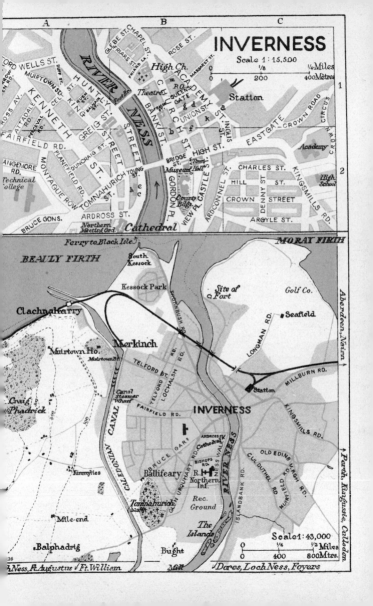

Castle, a 19th cent. structure on part of the site of the ancient stronghold, accommodates the county offices and law-courts. In the council room is a good portrait of Sir Charles Grant by Raeburn. On the terrace, S. of the castle, is a bronze statue of Flora Macdonald, from beside which we command a lovely *View.

At the corner of Bridge St. is the *Town Steeple* of 1791, once the jail, with the town clock and bells. At the last house (No. 32) on the right in Bridge St. Queen Mary is said to have lodged when refused admission to the castle in 1562.

On the opposite bank of the Ness, a short distance above the suspension bridge, is *St. Andrew's Cathedral* (B 2) for the episcopal see of Moray, Ross, and Caithness (open 9–9, Sun. services 11 and 6.30), a handsome building (1866–69) of rose-coloured stone from Conon, with an octagonal chapter house and an angel font copied from Thorvaldsen's in Copenhagen cathedral. The tablet to Bp. William Hay (d. 1707), in the Lady Chapel, was originally in the High Church.

Ardross St., leading W. from St. Andrew's Cathedral, passes the *Northern Meeting Park* and is continued by Bruce Gardens, skirting a public park, to (⅜ m) **Tomnahurich** ('hill of the fairies'), a wooded oval hill (220 ft.), now attractively laid out as a *Cemetery*. Cars can drive to the top. Many fairy legends cling to this spot, with tales of local Rip van Winkles, etc., and even Thomas the Rhymer has found his way hither in story.

About a mile above the town the Ness is divided by several tree-clad *Islands*, joined to each other and to the banks by footbridges and forming an attractive public park. Here in the 17th cent. the burgh magistrates used to give open-air entertainments to the judges of assize. From the Islands a road viâ Bught Mill leads to (¾ m.) Tomnahurich (see above).

Craig Phadrick ('Patrick's Rock'; 550 ft.), the northernmost of the line of hills on the W. side of the Caledonian Canal, lies 2 m. W. of Inverness viâ Telford St. and Muirtown Bridge on the canal. On the wooded summit, which affords a good view, are two ramparts of partially vitrified stones. Some authorities locate King Brude's castle on this hill.

From Inverness to the Field of Culloden (pron. Cullodden), 5 m. E. by road (motor-bus). The return may be made viâ the Clava Stones.—The direct road, quitting Inverness by the Perth road (Kingsmills Road, Pl. C 2), passes (1 m.) *Culcabock* and (2 m.) diverges to the left, nearly opposite the avenue gates of Inshes. We ascend and traverse a wood and reach (c. 5 m.) *Culloden Moor* or *Drummossie Moor*, the scene of the **Battle of Culloden,** where the last hopes of the return of the house of Stewart to the throne of Britain were for ever crushed on April 16th, 1746. A tall cairn (1881) on the N. (l.) side of the road (made since the battle) commemorates the fallen, and on both sides are the scattered stones, marked with the names of the clans, that show the graves of the Highlanders and the English. At the cross roads c. 300 yds.

farther on a boulder, called the *Cumberland Stone,* marks the position taken up by the royal commander before the battle. The N.T. owns 11 acres, including the above monument, and *Leanach* farmhouse, reputedly the Jacobite battle-head-quarters.

Prince Charlie's army, covering Inverness, consisted of c. 5000 Highlanders ill-armed, ill-fed, and exhausted by an abortive attempt to surprise the enemy the night before. The Duke of Cumberland advanced from Nairn at the head of 9000 men. The action began at 1 o'clock with an artillery duel, and in spite of the fearless impetuosity of the clans, who broke the first line of their opponents, resulted in the absolute rout of the Jacobites. Of the royal troops only 50 men were slain, while 1200 Highlanders fell. The carnage was enormously increased by the brutal order of the Duke of Cumberland to spare none of the wounded. For several days after the battle search parties devoted their energies to massacring the wounded clansmen who had crawled for refuge into the neighbouring woods and farms. During the pursuit of the vanquished Jacobites by the English cavalry even spectators from Inverness were massacred ; and the Provost of Inverness, after the capitulation of the city, was kicked downstairs, at the orders of Cumberland's general, for venturing a protest against the inhumanity of the English soldiery.

About 1 m. beyond the railway is *Culloden House,* built in 1772–83 on the site of the old mansion which in 1746 belonged to Duncan Forbes, President of the Court of Session, a staunch supporter of the Hanoverian cause. Here Prince Charlie slept on April 14th, 1746, two days before the battle.

A good road descends S.E. (r.) from the Cumberland Stone to the river Nairn, which it crosses. About ¼ m. beyond the bridge a narrow road diverges on the right for (¼ m.) the **Stones of Clava,** one of the most extensive remains of the kind in Britain, of the Bronze Age. Of the three large cairns ringed by circles of standing stones varying from 36 to 420 ft. in circumference, two contain chambers with an entrance-passage, the third a chamber with no entrance. Beyond the Stones our road strikes a road leading from Fort Augustus to Cawdor and Nairn.

From Inverness to *Aberdeen,* see Rte. 43 ; to the *Black Isle* and *Cromarty,* see Rte. 60 ; to *Fort William,* see Rte. 52 ; to *Kyle of Lochalsh* and *Strathpeffer,* see Rte. 55 ; to *Perth* viâ Aviemore and Pitlochry, see Rte. 30 ; to *Wick* and *Thurso,* see Rte. 61.

From INVERNESS TO BEAULY, 13 m. (bus in 40 min.). Our road (A 9) leaves Inverness viâ Telford St., and crosses the Caledonian Canal which descends six locks to reach the sea at (1¾ m.) *Clachnaharry* ('the watchman's stone' whence the citizens looked out for predatory Highlanders). We skirt the S. side of Beauly Firth.—3½ m. *Bunchrew House,* built by the Frasers in 1621, later belonged to Lord-President Forbes (see above). We quit the shore and at *Kirkhill* see the chapel of *Wardlaw,* the burial-place of the Fraser chieftains until 1815.— 9 m. *Moniack Tower* (l.) was a stronghold of Simon, Lord Lovat.—At (12 m.) *Lovat Bridge* we cross the Beauly River and turn right.—13 m. **Beauly** (pron. 'Bewley'; *Lovat Arms,* RB. 21/, P. 10 gs.) derives its name from the *Priory* 'de bello loco,' the ruins of which stand in a churchyard with some venerable trees, at the end of the broad street with the shaft of the old market cross at the entrance.

The priory (adm. free, 10–4 or 7, Sun. from 2) was founded c. 1230 by Sir John Bisset of the Aird for French Valliscaulian monks. The façade, pierced by three lancets, was built after 1530 by Abbot Reid, later bishop of Orkney. In the S. wall are three rare and beautiful triangular windows, with cusped trefoils, of the 13th cent. (recalling those in the triforium at Westminster). Other notable features are the window-arcading in the chancel and the 13th cent. W. doorway of the S. transept. The N. transept (restored 1901) is the burial-place of the Mackenzies of Kintail with a monument of Sir Kenneth (d. 1391), opposite which is the restored tomb of Prior Mackenzie (d. 1479).—*Taradale House* (p. 371) s 2 m. N.E.

From Beauly to the N., see Rte. 61 ; to *Drumnadrochit*, see p. 358.

B. From Beauly to Loch Duich via Strath Glass and Glen Affric

45½ m. This route leads through magnificent Highland scenery ; the road ends after about 30 miles.—Motor-Bus runs twice daily (all the year round) from Beauly to *Cannich* and *Tomich*.

The Glen Affric hydro-electric scheme has made some changes in the landscape but the great care expended in an effort not to mar the general aspect of an unspoilt highland glen has been remarkably successful ; construction work is now in progress along the Beauly river, at the beginning of this route, for harnessing these waters.

From *Beauly* (p. 368) we follow the Inverness road and turn right on to A 831, just short of (1 m.) *Lovat Bridge*.— By crossing the field beyond the churchyard (l.) of (2¼ m.) *Kilmorack* we may obtain a view of the beginning of *Kilmorack Gorge* ; the waters of the Beauly in the more striking part of the gorge higher up are to be utilised in another hydro-electric scheme.

The charming by-road crossing the river passes *Beaufort Castle* (19th cent.; Lord Lovat), and ascends the right bank of the river to join the main road at Cannich.

About 1 m. farther on the road enters the grand defile of *The Dhruim* (pron. Dream). Extraordinary ' stacks ' of Old Red Sandstone rise in mid-stream and the beauty of the scene is enhanced by fine woods. At the upper end of the gorge (5¼ m.) a path leads to the river, here divided by *Eilean Aigas*, a small house on which (approached from the other side) was a refuge of Lord Lovat in 1697 and was occupied as a summer retreat by Sir Robert Peel before his death.—9 m. *Erchless Castle*, now modernised, was formerly the seat of The Chisholm, chief of the clan that has owned Strath Glass since the 14th century.—10 m. *Struy Bridge*, on the Farrar.

A road runs hence up Strath Farrar for some 12 m. to the E. end of *Loch Monar* (5 m. long), passing two smaller lochs and much fine woodland. From the W. end of Loch Monar we may find our way W. by moorland tracks to (15 m. W.) *Attadale* (p. 373) or (10 m. S.W.) *Carnach* (p. 374).

Near the pretty hamlet of *Struy* (10½ m.) a bridge crosses to the road on the S. side of the Glass, as the Beauly river is now called. We pass (14 m. ; r.) the *Well of St. Ignatius*, with Roman Catholic inscriptions, and reach (17 m.) **Cannich** (*Glen Affaric*, RB. 19/6, P. 10 gs. ; fishing permits), at the confluence of the Cannich and the Glass. Here A 831 (for Glen Urquhart) crosses the Glass, up the right bank of which a road leads to the model village of *Tomich* (3½ m. ; Hotel, unlic., RB. 15/, P. 7 gs.).

The scenery to the N.W. up GLEN CANNICH (' the glen of the cotton-grass '), beginning with a pretty waterfall (1½ m.), is very striking. Farther up, the glen is wilder and the S. side is densely wooded with Scots fir and birch. The road passing (10 m.) *Mullardoch Hotel* (RB. 21/, P. £10) and a succession of lochs ends at (12 m.) the huge dam (2385 ft. long) of *Loch Mullardoch* which has been combined with *Loch Lungard* in a single sheet 9 m. long. A new path goes along the N. side of the loch, leading to *Carnach* (14 m. ; p. 374).

From Cannich to *Drumnadrochit* viâ *Glen Urquhart*, see p. 358.

Beyond (19 m.) Fasnakyle power station (1952), built of Greenbrae sandstone, we soon pass *Fasnakyle House*, where fishing permits are obtainable. Thence the road, narrow and winding (with passing places), goes through delightful scenery, a combination of sylvan beauty and mountain grandeur. We ascend the Affric through *Chisholm's Pass*, at the far end of which is the Beneveian dam. We then skirt the N. shore of (23 m.) *Loch Beneveian* (5 m. long), a lovely stretch of water dotted with islets, until we reach (27 m.) the end of this new road. Walkers go on past (29 m.) *Affric Lodge*, picturesquely placed on a promontory on the N. bank of the beautiful *Loch Affric* (744 ft. ; 3½ m. long), overlooked on the right by *Sgurr-na-Lapaich* (3401 ft.), with *Mam Soul* (see below) towering ahead.—A track goes on along the N. side of the loch to (33½ m.) the little *Loch Coulavie*, whence it is continued by a wild path leading up the *Pass of Athnamulloch*, defended by Col. Donald Murchison (an ancestor of the geologist) for his chief, the Earl of Seaforth, against the soldiers of George II.—Our path is continued up the Affric to (36 m.) *Alltbeath Youth Hostel*, 8 m. N. of Cluanie Bridge (Rte. 53D) by a rough track.

Ben Attow (3383 ft.), in Gaelic *Beinn Fhada* (' long mountain '), is ascended from Alltbeath (c. 2 hrs.) ; an alternative route starts at Cluanie Bridge (p. 364). *Mam Soul* (3862 ft.) and its twin peak *Cairn Eige* (3877 ft.), N.W. of Loch Affric, are climbed from Affric Lodge by a path on the right about the middle of Loch Affric (c. 3½ hrs.). The ascents present no difficulty, but the views, though extensive, are confused. *Sgurr nan Ceathreamhnan* (' Keernan ' ; 3771 ft.) on the N. is best climbed from Glomach (p. 375).

Henceforth the track keeps to the right of Ben Attow and ascends *Glen Grivie* to (40m.) *Loch a' Bhealaich*, the source of the river Glomach. Leaving the loch on the right we cross boggy ground to reach (41½ m.) the *Bealach-an-Sgairne* or *Pass of Kintail* (c. 1700 ft.), whence there is a sudden and very impressive descent to (45½ m.) **Croe Bridge** (p. 375), on the sea at Loch Duich, where we join the high-road between Dornie and Shiel Bridge. There is a slightly longer alternative route from Alltbeath to Croe Bridge traversing *Glen Fionn* and *Glen Lichd* on the S. side of Ben Attow.

55. FROM INVERNESS TO KYLE OF LOCHALSH

ROAD, 89 m. We quit Inverness viâ Telford St. (Pl. A 1).—A 9. 13 m. *Beauly.*—
15 m. *Muir of Ord.*—21 m. **Dingwall.**—A 834. 25 m. **Strathpeffer.**—34 m. *Garve.*—
A 832. 50 m. *Achnasheen.*—A 890. 70 m. *Jeantown.* At (75 m.) **Strome Ferry** a
ferry crosses Loch Carron.—89 m. **Kyle of Lochalsh.**—Motorists may avoid the
ferry by entraining their cars at Strathcarron station for Kyle (or vice versa ;
33/10–40/6 ; two days' notice desired). A 832 leads direct from Muir of Ord to
Contin, saving 6 m. but missing Dingwall and Strathpeffer.

RAILWAY, 82¼ m. in 3¼–3½ hrs. Principal Stations : 10 m. *Beauly.*—18¾ m.
Dingwall.—23½ m. *Achterneed* (for Strathpeffer, 1 m. S.).—30½ m. *Garve.*—46½ m.
Achnasheen.—59 m. *Achnashellach.*—64½ m. *Strathcarron.*—72 m. *Strome Ferry.*
—82¼ m. **Kyle of Lochalsh.**

From Inverness to (13 m.) *Beauly,* see Rte. 54A.

The county of **Ross and Cromarty,** which the road now enters, extends across
country from the North Sea to the Atlantic, and includes the half-island of
Lewis. Outside the comparatively fertile E. coast strip it is a land of brown
moorland and bare rock, and except among the fiord-like lochs of the W. coast
the scenery cannot compare with that of Inverness. The county of Cromarty,
now entirely incorporated with Ross-shire, consisted of a small hereditary
sheriffdom near the town of Cromarty and eight or ten detached portions in N.
Ross-shire, annexed in the late 17th cent. at the request of Viscount Tarbat,
later Earl of Cromartie, who desired to have all his lands in one county. The
Mackenzies, Munroes, and Rosses were the chief clans, and the history is little
more than a recital of their feuds. Lewis is the country of the MacLeods. An
enormous hydro-electric scheme is in progress, involving the Conon river and its
tributaries Bran, Meig, and Orrin.

At (15 m.) *Muir of Ord* (Tarradale, RB. 22/6, P. 10 gs. ;
Station, RB. 18/6 ; Ord Arms, 1 m. N., RB. 24/), the centre of
a crofting district where large live-stock fairs were formerly
held, we cross A 823 which runs E. through the Black Isle to
Fortrose (13½ m. ; Rte. 60) and N.W. to *Contin* (6 m.).

Just N. was the old church of *Kilchrist,* burnt with all its Mackenzie congregation in 1603 by the Macdonalds, whose piper marched round it until the
flames died down.

About 1½ m. along the Fortrose road we turn right for (⅓ m.) *Taradale House,*
birthplace of Sir Roderick Murchison (1792–1871), the geologist, close to the
Beauly Firth. It contains an extensive library and museum available to students
(adm. on application). On the shore of the firth c. 2 m. farther on stands the
church of *Killearnan,* dating from 1450, c. ½ m. E. of which is *Redcastle,* an old
fort of the Mackenzies, still inhabited.

As we approach (18 m.) *Conon Bridge* (Hotel, RB. 21/6,
P. 10 gs.), a village frequented by anglers, we have on our
left a good view of *Strath Conon* (see below) surrounded by
fine hills, conspicuous among which is Ben Wyvis (N.W. ;
3429 ft.). Beyond the Conon was *Brahan Castle,* built by the
1st Earl of Seaforth in 1621 but now demolished, where the
Mackenzies submitted to Gen. Wade in 1725.

Ferintosh, 3 m. N.E. of Conon, was celebrated for its whisky and was the scene
of the first Communion of the Free Church of Scotland in 1843.

We cross the Conon 1 m. above its outflow into Cromarty
Firth and soon reach (21 m.) **Dingwall** (*National,* RB. 21/6,
P. 10 gs. ; *Royal,* RB. 20/6, P. £10 ; *Lisliard,* unlic., P. 8 gs. ;
Caledonian, plain, RB. 15/, P. 7 gs.), the county town (3370

inhab.) of Ross, which stands at the head of the Firth. The town, created a royal burgh by Alexander II in 1226, derives its name from the Norse 'Thingvollr,' i.e. 'field of the thing' or Parliament (comp. p. 398). In the main street is a quaint *Town House* bearing the date 1730 and the town arms (a 'sun in splendour'). Church St. leads hence to the *Church*, near which is an obelisk. "Erected by George, 1st Earl of Cromartie . . . who d. 1714, and is buried 3 ft. 6 in. to the S. thereof." The earl is said to have chosen this sepulchral arrangement in order to frustrate his wife's declared intention of dancing on his grave. A tower on the hill S. of the town commemorates the birth at Urquhart, near Dingwall, of Gen. Sir Hector Macdonald (1853–1903).

From Dingwall to *Wick* and *Thurso*, see Rte. 61 ; frequent motor-buses to *Strathpeffer*.

The road to the W. (A 834) turns away from the Firth and runs up the right bank of the Peffery, having on the left the ridge of *Druim Chat* ('cat's back'), on which is the large and very perfect vitrified fort of *Knockfarrel* (720 ft. ; view).

25 m. **Strathpeffer** (*Ben Wyvis*, RB. 28/6, P. 14 gs. ; *Strath-peffer*, RB. 22/6, P. 9 gs. ; *Richmond, Holly Lodge, Mackay's*, all three unlic. with P. 9½ gs.) is a spa of old repute situated near the foot of Ben Wyvis in a sheltered valley, whose trees and other vegetation exhibit an unexpected 'Lowland' luxuriance in this region of Highland moors. The bath establishment and pump room have not re-opened since the war, but the village is a good centre for excursions and for fishing. The golf course (view) is high above the village to the N.

In a field on the left of the Dingwall road (path beyond last house) a stone pillar with the rude figure of an eagle is said to mark the place where the Mackenzies defeated the Munroes in 1478, after previously vanquishing the Macdonalds.

The huge bulk of **Ben Wyvis** (3429 ft.), whose summit is c. 10 m. N. of Strath-peffer, dominates all the country around. The ascent (8–10 hrs. there and back), easy all the way, but somewhat tedious, requires an early start. We follow the road N.E., and beyond (½ m. ; l.) the entrance (no adm.) to *Castle Leod* (built after 1616), the property of the Countess of Cromartie, turn left for (1 m.) *Achterneed* station. We pass under the railway and follow a cart road, which ends c. 2½ m. farther on. Thence the ascent, somewhat boggy in places, is over grass and heather. The view from the top is varied and extensive on the S. and E.; on the N. and W. rise other mountain ranges. The most W. of the three summits (An Cabar, 3106 ft.) commands the finest view of the Strathpeffer district.

Short walks may be taken from Strathpeffer to *Knockfarrel* (2 m. ; comp. above) ; or to the *Falls of Rogie* (2½ m.), viâ the tiny Loch Kinellan, and thence to the pretty little *Loch Achilty*, c. 1½ m. S.W., reached by crossing the Blackwater.

Our road (A 834) joins the direct road from Muir of Ord at (28 m.) *Contin* (Achilty Hotel, 1 m. N.W., RB. 17/6, P. 8 gs.). Beyond *Tor Achilty* (650 ft.), on the left, lies Strath Conon, the river in which has been dammed and special salmon lifts are provided. We ascend the Blackwater, passing near the

Falls of Rogie (see above) and joining the railway at the E. end of *Loch Garve* (1¾ m. long).—From (34 m.) **Garve** (*Hotel*, RB. 25/, P. 12 gs.) a road runs N.W. to Ullapool (Rte. 56) up Strath Garve (r. ; fine view of Ben Wyvis). Our road goes W., touching (40 m.) the tip of the crescent-shaped *Loch Luichart* (now c. 6 m. long) by the Grudie Bridge power station. Thence a cart-road ascends the Fannich to (4½ m. N.W.) the wild *Loch Fannich* (7 m. long).—The road skirts *Loch Culen*, now united with Loch Achanalt, in Strath Bran and then follows the river, with a fine view (l.) of the three grand peaks of *Scuir Vuillin* (2845 ft.). As we leave (50 m.) **Achnasheen** (*Station*, RB. 18/6, P. 8 gs. ; bus to Loch Maree and Gairloch), we have an excellent but brief glimpse (r.) of the grand peaks of Sgurr Dubh, Liathach, and Ben Eay, all above Glen Torridon.—Our road follows the railway and keeps close to *Loch Gowan*, attaining its summit-level (634 ft.) in the wild and broken country between this loch and *Loch Scaven* ; the scenery increases in grandeur, and beyond a fine gorge on the left are the magnificent corries of *Moruisg* (3026 ft.).—58¾ m. *Achnashellach*, in the lower part of Glen Carron, has a youth hostel.

A hill-road runs N. over the *Coulin Pass* (900 ft.) to (9½ m.) *Loch Clair*, on the road from Glen Torridon to Kinlochewe (p. 377).

Passing *Loch Doule*, which is shadowed by cliffs and screes and has on its N. side the wild mountains of *Sgurr Ruadh* (3142 ft.), the railway and road separate, the road keeping to the N. side of the Carron and the grand sea-loch into which it flows, while the railway crosses to the S. side of the river and reaches Strome Ferry viâ *Attadale*, with fine views N.— 68 m. *Strathcarron* (Hotel, RB. 22/6, P. 10½ gs., at the station 1 m. S. of the main road).—71 m. **Lochcarron** or *Jeantown* (*Hotel*, RB. 22/6, P. 11 gs. ; *Rock Villa*, unlic., P. 7½ gs.), a fishing village on the N. shore of Loch Carron with a Scandinavian 'dun' behind it, is the junction for the Shieldaig and Applecross road.

The ROAD TO SHIELDAIG (motor-bus daily from Strathcarron in 2 hrs.) ascends steeply to the right, crossing the romantic *Pass of Kishorn* (400 ft.). The fine view thence extends W. over the mouth of Loch Carron to Skye and N. to Ben Bhan (2936 ft.), on which the Torridon sandstone formation is well seen.—4 m. *Kishorn* stands on the sea-loch of the same name. The road from (5½ m.) the head of the loch (branch road to Applecross, below) up the River Kishorn and down Glen Shieldaig is wild and beautiful.—14 m. **Shieldaig** (*Inn*, plain) is a fishing village in a secluded situation on the shore of Loch Shieldaig, the middle portion of **Loch Torridon**, backed by Ben Shieldaig.—An excellent track, skirting a succession of delightful little bays opening on Upper Loch Torridon, crosses the short stream (with falls) which issues from Loch Damph and skirts Ben Damph forest before joining the high road at (9 m.) the head of Loch Torridon, whence a road leads E. to (10½ m.) *Kinlochewe*. From *Inverbain*, on the W. shore of Loch Shieldaig, a track leads S.W. across the hill (1213 ft.) to (c. 3¼ hrs.) *Applecross* (see below) ; and from Shieldaig a passenger ferry crosses Loch Torridon to *Inveralligin*.

The Road to Applecross from Strathcarron leaves the Shieldaig route at the head of *Loch Kishorn* (see above), whence, turning W., it zigzags up the alpine *Pass of *Bealach-nam-Bo* (2054 ft.; comp. p. 215), one of the highest roads in Scotland. Splendid views are obtained to the S. over Loch Carron to the mountains between Loch Duich and Loch Hourn, to the S.W. of the Coolins in Skye, and to the N.W. of the Quiraing in Skye and of the Outer Hebrides. A steep descent brings us to (22 m.) **Applecross** (*Hotel*, unlic., RB. 19/6), in Gaelic '*A Chomraich*,' i.e. the Sanctuary. A slab carved with a cross still standing near the abandoned church is a relic of *St. Malrube's Church*, founded in 673 by Maelrubha (d. 721), a monk of Bangor in Ireland. *Toscaig*, 4 m. S., is connected by steamer with Kyle of Lochalsh (every weekday in 1 hr.).

At (75 m.) **Strome Ferry** (*Hotel*, RB. 25/6, P. 10½ gs.) the Kyle of Lochalsh road crosses Loch Carron by ferry. The remains of *Strome Castle*, and North Strome youth-hostel are near by. The S. bank is reached by ferry (1/, cycle 1/, motor cycle 2/, car 10/, day return 15/; not on Sun.). The road crosses Strath Ascaig to the S., rising steeply to the crest of the ridge (683 ft.) between Loch Carron and Loch Alsh, and descends Glen Udalain, passing a power reservoir.—At (81½ m.) *Auchtertyre* school we are joined by the road from Dornie on Loch Duich.—Beyond (82½ m.) *Balmacara Hotel* (RB. 23/6, P. £12), the road ascends inland (fine views) and finally approaches Kyle of Lochalsh from the N.

82 m. Kyle of Lochalsh (*Lochalsh*, RB. 42/, P. 64/ or 18 gs.; *Kyle*, RB. 18/6, P. 9 gs.), the terminus of the railway and of the principal road-approach to Skye, is the centre of a district famed for the beauty of its sea-lochs. There is a frequent ferry service to Kyleakin in Skye (p. 380) ; the jetty is 10 min. walk from the station ; accompanied luggage is conveyed free to and from services connecting with the trains.

Steamers to *Mallaig, Glenelg, Eigg, Canna, Stornoway*, and the *Outer Hebrides*, see Rte. 59 ; to *Portree*, see Rte. 58 ; to *Toscaig*, see above.

The estate of **Balmacara** (Hotel, see above), which comprises a large part of the peninsula on which Kyle stands, was bequeathed to the Nat. Trust by Lady D. Hamilton in 1946. On the shore between Kyle and Balmacara is a monument to Col. Murchison (p. 370), erected by his descendant Sir Roderick. *Balmacara House*, overlooking Loch Alsh, is a boys' school specialising in crofting agriculture, while to the N. the estate extends to *Plockton* (Hotel, RB. 21/, P. £10), a large crofting village on Loch Carron, 5½ m. N. of Kyle by road or rail. The modern *Duncraig Castle*, on a by-road from Plockton to Strome Ferry, is now a school.

From Kyle of Lochalsh to Dornie, Glen Shiel, and Glenelg, 29 m. by road (motor-bus to Glenshiel daily).—We follow the Strome Ferry road as far as (6½ m.) *Auchtertyre* school, where we diverge to the right.—Beyond (9½ m.) *Ardelve* (for Loch Long, see below) we reach the mouth of Loch Long at (10½ m.) *Dornie Ferry* (Loch Duich, RB. 25/6, P. 10 gs.), where a bridge across Loch Long replaces the old ferry.

From Ardelve a good road ascends Loch Long to (6 m.) *Killilan*, and is continued thence up Glen Elchaig to (12½ m.) *Carnach* (300 ft.) at the head of the little Loch-na-Leitreach and (14 m.) *Iron Lodge*. A path leaving the cart-road at (c. 11¼ m.) the foot of Loch-na-Leitreach and crossing the end of the lake and the Glomach (no bridges) leads up the left bank of the stream to (c. 1¼ m.) the *Falls of Glomach* (see below), whence Carnach may be reached by c. 1 hr.'s rough walk across the hill to the N.E.—Above Iron Lodge the track, becoming less distinct, crosses desolate moors (c. 1400 ft.) and finally descends to (c. 8 m. N.E.) *Loch Monar* (p. 369). From Iron Lodge a rough track diverging on the right ascends to 1096 ft. and then drops down to *Loch Lungard* (4 m. ; p. 370).

From Dornie Ferry a passenger ferry (½ m. ; return 2/6, cycle 6*d.*; not Sun.) crosses Loch Duich to *Totaig*, whence a level road follows the S. side of the loch to (6 m.) *Shiel Bridge* (p. 364), while a path leads S.W. viâ Ardintoul to (6 m.) *Bernera* and (8 m.) *Glenelg* (see below). A short cut to Glenelg strikes inland c. 3 m. along this path.

10¾ m. *Dornie* (Hotel, RB. 22/6, P. 10 gs.) is a neat village standing at the foot of the savagely grand *LOCH DUICH*, whose fine N.E. shore we follow. On the little *Eilean Donan,* connected with the shore by a bridge (adm. 2/6 weekdays 10–12.30, 2–6 ; tea-room), is a stronghold of the Mackenzies, earls of Seaforth. .Battered by an English warship in 1719, it was well restored in 1932, when a war memorial to the Clan MacRae was unveiled. The road mounts to 506 ft., commanding a fine view of the head of the loch, where Scour Ouran stands out conspicuously. After the descent to *Inverinate* and (16 m.) *Kintail* church, Ben Attow (3383 ft.) becomes prominent ahead as we make a wide circuit to cross (18 m.) *Croe Bridge* at the head of the loch (see Rte. 54B).

About 7½ m. N.E. by road to (1¾ m.) *Dorusduain Lodge* and a rough walk over the ' coffin road ' (Bealach na Sroine ; 2000 ft.), N. of Glasven (3006 ft.), are the ***Falls of Glomach** (N.T.). Descending 900 ft. we strike the Glomach near the *Falls,* amid a scene of perfect solitude. They are amongst the finest in Great Britain and have a drop of 370 ft. ; the volume of water is not large, except after rain, but the pure white foaming cascade falling over black precipices of inverted strata and the depth of the chasm are very impressive. The return may be made viâ Glen Elchaig (see above). *Sgurr nan Ceathreamhnan* (' Keernan ' ; 3771 ft.), a laborious but easy climb of 2¼ hrs. from the falls by its N.W. shoulder, commands a splendid view of Ben Attow and Mam Soul.—Ascent of *Ben Attow*, see p. 370.

From Croe Bridge the road skirts the head of Loch Duich to (20¾ m.) the mouth of *Glen Shiel*, with its hotel and youth-hostel (Rte. 53D).—The road westwards over (23½ m.) the *Pass of Mam Ratagan* (1116 ft.) is much improved since Johnson and Boswell found it " a terrible steep to climb, nothwithstanding the road is formed slanting along it." The retrospective view of Loch Duich and its surrounding mountains is succeeded by a good view S., in which the singular peak of *Ben Screel* (3196 ft.) is conspicuous. As the road falls to the coast at (29 m.) **Glenelg,** we have a fine view over the Sound of Sleat to Skye and see ruins of barracks erected in 1722 at *Bernera* (2 m. N.).

About 1 m. S. of Glenelg, in the country of the MacRaes, is *Glen Beg*, 2 m. up which are two ruined brochs, c. 25 ft. high and 30 ft. in diameter. About 1½ m. farther up the glen (½ m. beyond the end of the road) is the semi-circular broch-like *Dun Grugaig*, overhanging a waterfall. The track goes on to (16 m.) *Kinloch-hourn.*

A bus runs S. and E. every evening to *Arnisdale* (1¼ hr.) on Loch Hourn by a poor road. continued by a track to (7½ m. farther) *Kinlochhourn.*

For the steamer from Glenelg to *Mallaig, Kyle of Lochalsh*, etc., see p. 379 ; footpath to *Totaig*, see above. Motor-bus on Sat. to *Inverness.*

56. FROM GARVE TO ULLAPOOL

33 m. Motor-Bus daily in connection with mid-day train in 2¼ hrs., going on to *Achiltibuie* in 4½ hrs., also (coming from Inverness), in connection with the evening train, to *Ullapool* only in 1½ hr.; mail-car between Braemore and *Dundonnell*.

Garve, see Rte. 55. Our road (A 835) soon leaves the main road and, turning N., ascends *Strath Garve*, by the side of the Blackwater with Ben Wyvis (3429 ft.; p. 372) on our right, through country growing ever bleaker.—10 m. *Altguish Inn* (RB. 21/, P. 8½ gs.). The Glascarnoch river has been dammed here, and a new loch, 3¾ m. long, has been created, connected by tunnels with another loch in Strath Vaich, to the N., and with a power-station on Loch Luichart, to the S.—We cross (15¼ m.) the watershed (915 ft.) and skirt the N. bank of *Loch Droma* (1¼ m. long) before descending the now treeless *Dirrie More* ('the big oak-forest'), a dreary foreground, but with a fine view ahead of An Teallach (see below). After 20 m. the scenery completely changes and for some miles we skirt the fine woods of *Braemore*.

Just before the lodge gate a fine road (A 832), called 'Destitution Road' because made during the famine of 1851, strikes off to the left for (13½ m.) *Dundonnell* (see below). From 615 ft. it climbs to 1110 ft. within 6 m., affording magnificent views of *An Teallach* ('the Forge'; 3483 ft.), one of the most picturesque mountain ranges in Scotland, with a fine prospect of sea-lochs beyond. The latter part of the descent leads through a deep and narrow ravine.

We descend rapidly, keeping alongside the extraordinary deep gorge of *Corrieshalloch* (N.T.), with the *Falls of Measach* (150 ft.), well seen from the suspension bridge to which a path descends from the road. The corrie is one of the finest cañons in Scotland, and, unlike the majority, is eroded in schist instead of in sandstone. The bridge on the left (25¼ m.) leads to *Lochbroom Church*, at (26 m.) the S. end of **Loch Broom,** a deep inlet of the sea, to whose E. shore we keep. Up Glen Lael to the E. we have a good view of Ben Derg (3547 ft.); in the distance ahead appears Ben More Coigach (2438 ft.).—33 m. **Ullapool** (*Royal*, RB. 25/, P. 13 gs.; *Caledonian*, RB. 21/6, P. 10 gs.; *Morefield*, ½ m. W., RB. 24/6, P. 10 gs.; many guest-houses), an attractive little fishing town of well-built whitewashed houses, was established by the British Fishery Society in 1788. It has a good harbour and bathing, and commands fine views. On the hill opposite the town is a broch.

From Ullapool to Poolewe, 31 m., an interesting route. A ferry across Loch Broom to (½ m.) *Altnaharrie* (2/, bicycle 1/) saves the long though picturesque round viâ Braemore (comp. above). From the ferry the track ascends 700 ft. in 1 m.; we have a magnificent view of the wild An Teallach (3483 ft.) as we descend to join the road at (6 m.) *Dundonnell* (Hotel, RB. 18/6, P. 8½ gs.), at the head of *Little Loch Broom*. The road goes on along the S. side of the loch passing (8 m.) the fine *Ardessie Falls* and (11½ m.) *Badcaul* (Glenorchy, unlic., RB. 15/6), crosses a promontory (530 ft.), and descends to (15½ m.) *Gruinard*

Bay. We traverse (16 m.) a grand defile, cross the Gruinard River, skirt the head of the bay, and ascend the steep Gruinard Hill (1 in 8), a road cut in the face of the cliff. Beyond (21½ m.) *Laide* we cross another ridge (*Views).—24½ m. *Aultbea* and thence to (31 m.) *Poolewe*, see Rte. 57.

From Ullapool to Lochinver. A. Vià Loch Lurgain, 31 m., a poor road with magnificent scenery. We go N., crossing (7½ m.) *Strathkanaird Bridge*, to (10 m.) *Drumrunie Lodge Hotel* (RB. 22/6, P. 10 gs., with fishing rights) beyond which we turn W. (l.), and, with *Coulbeg* (2523 ft.) on our right and *Ben More Coigach* (2438 ft.) on our left, reach (12 m.) *Loch Lurgain*. On the N. rises *Stack Polly* (2009 ft.). These strange isolated peaks of Torridon sandstone, with *Coulmore* (2786 ft.) farther N.E., may be ascended (not in the stalking season) from the climbers' hut on the N. bank of Loch Lurgain. From (18 m.) the W. end of *Loch Baddagyle* the road straight on leads to *Achiltibuie* (6½ m.; Summer Isles, RB. 19/6, P. 9½ gs.), near the mouth of Loch Broom, and *Achininver* youth hostel (8½ m. ; connected by a rough wet path with Strathkanaird Bridge, see above). Our road turns N.E. and winds between land and sea lochs through some of the wildest country in Scotland.—31 m. *Lochinver*, see p. 405.—B. Vià Ledmore, 37 m. Keeping straight on at (10 m.) *Drumrunie Lodge* (see above) we cross a pass (757 ft.), and descend through *Elphin* to (18 m.) *Ledmore*. Thence to (37 m.) *Lochinver*, see Rte. 62A.

Off the mouth of Loch Broom are the *Summer Isles*, of which the largest is *Tanera More*, where Dr. Fraser Darling, the naturalist, transformed an uninhabited ruin into a comfortable home surrounded by productive farmland.

57. FROM ACHNASHEEN TO LOCH MAREE, GAIRLOCH, AND AULTBEA

42½ m. Motor-Bus daily (3 hrs.) in connection with the morning trains to and from the South. This beautiful route traverses perhaps the finest and most characteristic part of Ross-shire.

Leaving *Achnasheen* (p. 373) the road (A 832) runs W. along (1 m.) the N. bank of *Loch Rosque,* or *Loch-a-Chroisg* (3½ m. long), at the E. end of which the river Bran has cut its way through some interesting lake-terraces (comp. p. 337). Beyond the W. end of the loch Sgurr Dubh (2566 ft.), Liathach (3456 ft.), and Ben Eay (see below) are well seen on the left. The short ascent to the watershed (815 ft.) is succeeded by the descent of the narrow *Glen Docharty*, during which Loch Maree suddenly comes into view, flanked on the N. by the grand mass of Slioch (see below). The scattered hamlet of (10 m.) **Kinlochewe** (*Kinlochewe*, RB. 23/, P. 10 gs.) lies two miles short of the head of Loch Maree amidst grand scenery, notable for the view of the white quartzite and red sandstone peaks of *Ben Eay* or *Beinn Eighe* (' the file mountain ' ; 3309 ft.) 4 or 5 m. W., ' literally powdered with its own dust,' says Lord Cockburn. The ascent is for the experienced climber.

Over 10,000 acres of its W. slopes, extending from Loch Maree to Loch Clair, were created a ' nature reserve ' in 1951. This is the haunt of the golden eagle, the wild cat, and the pine marten, and on the shore of Loch Maree is a large remnant of the ancient Caledonian pine forest. On the N. side, outside the reserve, is Coire Mhic Fhearchair, one of the wildest corries in Scotland.

Slioch (3260 ft. ; 4½ m. N.N.W.) is reached by the track down the right bank of the river to Loch Maree. We cross (3 m.) the stream of Glen Bannisdale just below a fine dark rocky pool and turn up the glen. The ascent soon becomes steep and rough. After another 1½ m. we make our way up the course of a large tributary with many cataracts which descends practically from the summit. The view is extensive but the mountain has a reputation for cloudiness.—A comparatively easy route from Furnace (boat from Loch Maree hotel) ascends half-way to *Loch Garvaig* and strikes up the W. face of the mountain.

The road from Kinlochewe to (10½ m.) *Torridon* (motor-bus daily, 65 min.) runs up the valley to the S. At (3¼ m.) *Loch Clair* it is joined by the track from Achnashellach (p. 373) and it soon after reaches the head of Glen Torridon, from which *Liathach* (3456 ft.), a typical mountain of 'Torridonian' sandstone, is finely seen. Its sandstone strata at a height of 3000 ft. are strangely capped with quartzite.—From (10½ m.) *Torridon* to Gairloch by the coast, see below ; to Shieldaig, see p. 373.

11¾ m. The road reaches the S.E. extremity of ***Loch Maree** (12 m. long by ¾–2½ m. broad), one of the largest and finest lochs in the Highlands, once perhaps an arm of the sea in continuation of Loch Ewe.

Loch Maree is notable for the variety and individuality of its scenery. Above its S. arm the mass of Slioch (3260 ft.) rises so abruptly that the rifts and gullies which scar it can be seen from base to summit at a glance. Farther N.W. the striking contour of *Ben Lair* (2817 ft.) is the dominant feature, while the rocks on the opposite shore are remarkable for the beautiful vegetation which festoons them. The broader N. half of the loch embraces a cluster of islets clad with fir and heather. Of these the little *Isle Maree*, the nearest to the N.E. shore, bears the ruins of a chapel, some ancient graves, and a well whose waters were held a cure for madness. This isle is said to have been the hermitage of St. Maree or Maelrubha (p. 374).

Just before (15¾ m.) *Bridge of Grudie* we enjoy a magnificent view (l.) of Ben Eay up *Glen Grudie* and (r.) of Slioch and Ben Lair. At (20 m.) *Talladale* is the *Loch Maree Hotel* (P. 14 gs.), where boats may be hired. The road now passes through thick hanging woods of birch and pine to (22 m.) *Slatadale*, at the widest part of the loch.

A path runs hence along the N.W. shore to Poolewe (7 m.), but the road leaves the loch, ascending 200 ft. in 1 m. (magnificent retrospect), and descends the narrow *Kerrysdale*, where a dam has formed a new loch on the left, with the Kerry Falls below it.—29 m. **Gairloch** (*Gairloch*, RB. 33/, P. 14 gs.; *Millcroft*, unlic., RB. 18/6, at Strath, 1 m. N.W.) is a scattered hamlet at the head of a sea-loch and at the mouth of the picturesque *Flowerdale* with a magnificent retrospective view to the S. of Ben Alligin (3232 ft.) and Baeishven (2869 ft.).

Walkers may reach Torridon (26½ m.) by a coast road and path affording magnificent views, with a number of crofts offering summer accommodation.—We follow B 8050 (bus to Opinan) to (3½ m.) *Shieldaig Gairloch* (Shieldaig Lodge, RB. 27/6, P. 10½ gs.) and (4½ m.) *Badachro* (Badachro Inn, RB. 16/, P. 7 gs.). From (5½ m.) *Opinan* a by-road to (11 m.) *Red Point*, at the mouth of *Loch Torridon*, is continued by a rough path along the desolate shore past (15½ m.) *Craig* (Y.H. and foot-bridge) to (18½ m.) *Diabaig*, a charmingly placed hamlet. Here a rough and hilly road begins, soon passing two small lochs. From (22½ m.) *Inveralligin* (Y.H. ; boat to Shieldaig, p. 373) we follow the N. shore of *Upper Loch Torridon* to reach (26½ m.) *Torridon*, at the head of the loch (see above).

The road N.E. from Gairloch to Poolewe commands fine views over a wide expanse of sea to the N. point of Skye and the mountains of Harris. It soon turns E., crossing a ridge

(456 ft.), and descends past *Loch Tollie*. There is a magnificent view of mountains in front and (r.) of Loch Maree.
The road then runs beside the short river Ewe, famous for
its salmon.—36 m. **Poolewe** (*Poolewe*, RB. 25/6, P. 12 gs. ;
Pool House, RB. 25/, P. 10½ gs., with lake and sea fishing)
stands on the sea-shore at the head of *Loch Ewe*, with a
curious 'pool' where the river enters the sea. *Inverewe*, just
to the N., is noted for its sub-tropical *Garden (N.T., with
2125 acres ; adm. 2/6 daily 10–dusk, Sun. 2–dusk), created
by Osgood Mackenzie from 1862, and best seen in April–June
(tea-room).

Fionn Loch ('white loch' ; 7 m. long), 6 m. E. of Poolewe across desolate
country, is overshadowed at its S. end by the precipices of *Ben Lair* (2817 ft.;
S.E.).

The road to (42½ m.) **Aultbea** (*Hotel*, R.B 20/, P. 9½ gs.)
runs N. above the E. side of Loch Ewe.—For the continuation
of the road to *Ullapool*, see Rte. 56 ; the bus goes on as far as
Laide, 3 m. N. on Gruinard Bay.

58. SKYE

Approaches (not on Sunday and less frequently in Oct.–April). A. FROM KYLE
OF LOCHALSH. (1) Ferry to *Kyleakin*, frequent service (6*d.* ; cycle 1/ ; motor-
cycle 3/2 ; car 9/).—(2) Steamer at 2.45 p.m. (coming from Mallaig) to *Raasay*
(8/, 4/3) and *Portree* (8/9, 4/9).—(3) Steamer (10 a.m.; also on Mon. at 8.30)
to (1½ hr.) *Armadale* (10/2, 5/2), going on to Mallaig.—B. FROM MALLAIG. (1)
Steamer at 12.30 p.m. for *Kyle of Lochalsh* (1¾ hr. ; 12/, 6/2), *Raasay* (3½ hrs. ;
18/11, 9/7), and *Portree* (4½ hrs. ; 20/11, 10/10), returning from Portree at 8 a.m.
On the outward journey calls are made at *Armadale* (2/2, 1/2) daily in summer,
and *Glenelg* (8/11, 4/6) on Mon., Thurs., and Sat. ; on the inward journey at
Armadale and at *Glenelg* on Wed. and Fri. (2) Motor-vessel 4 times every weekday
in summer to *Armadale* in ½ hr. (4/ ; in connection with bus to Portree).—C. FROM
GLENELG. Steamer services, see above ; the ferry from Bernera to *Kylerhea* is
suspended.
EXCURSIONS. On Thurs. in summer a steamer leaves Kyle of Lochalsh at
10 a.m. and Mallaig at noon for *Loch Scavaig*, allowing time for a visit to *Loch
Coruisk*, and returning to Kyle c. 7.30 p.m. Return fares (including boats), from
Kyle 25/, from Mallaig 20/.

SKYE (possibly from 'sgiath,' a wing, suggested by the
shape of the island) is, after Lewis, the largest (c. 600 sq. m.)
of the Hebrides and is included in Inverness-shire (p. 238).
This beautiful island, wild, lonely, and still primitive, amply
repays a visit by its striking scenery. It boasts the most
awe-inspiring mountains in Britain ; its coasts, broken by
impressive sea-lochs, present fine and often strange cliff
scenery ; and its mild and misty climate is more than out-
weighed by wonderful atmospheric effects of weird and
romantic beauty. The population (8250) is scattered and
poor, and the croft system of farming is still general.

The Norsemen, though masters of Skye until the 13th cent., appear to have made few settlements in the island, and its history until the 18th cent., apart from its participation in the struggles of the Lords of the Isles with the Crown, is mainly one of disputes between the Macdonalds (of Trotternish, Sleat, etc.), the Mackinnons (of the E. coast), the MacLeods of Lewis (Vaternish and Dunvegan), and the MacLeods of Harris (Duirinish and Minginish). The name of Ossian is connected with various places in the island. Prince Charlie spent some time in Skye in 1746, after Culloden, and in 1773 the island was visited by Dr. Johnson. In 1881–5, after a succession of bad harvests and unsuccessful fishing seasons, Skye was the scene of serious riots amongst the crofters.

A. From Kyleakin to Broadford

8 m. MOTOR-BUS 2 or 3 times every weekday (25 min.), going on to Portree, Sligachan, and Dunvegan.—The straits of KYLE AKIN, ½ m. wide, separating Skye from the mainland (ferry, see p. 374), are named after Hakon, King of Norway, who sailed through them in 1263 on his way to the Battle of Largs. On the Skye shore is the straggling village of **Kyleakin** (*King's Arms*, RB. 26/, P. from 10 gs. ; *Marine, Heathmount*, RB. 23/6, P. 12 gs.), E. of which, on a promontory, are the picturesque ruins of *Castle Moil*, a small keep said to have been built by the daughter of a Norwegian king. This lady, wife of a Macdonald and usually called 'Saucy Mary,' stretched a chain across the Kyle and endeavoured to levy a toll from passing ships.—The Broadford road runs S.W., keeping near the shore (fine sea views).—4 m. *Lusa*, whence a road runs S., viâ the head of Glen Arroch (911 ft.) and a steep descent, to *Kylerhea* (7 m.).—Offshore is the curiously green island of *Pabay* (1½ m. N.), rich in fossils of the Upper Lias formation.—We are joined (6½ m.) by the road from Sleat (see below) and traverse a crofting district to (8 m.) **Broadford** (*Broadford*, RB. 23/6, P. 11 gs. ; *Dunollie*, unlic., RB. 23/, P. 10 gs.), a scattered township and a tourist centre, behind which rises the red granite *Ben-na-Cailleach* (2403 ft.).

B. From Kyleakin to Armadale

20 m. MOTOR-BUS twice every weekday in summer (1½ hr. ; once in winter).—After following the Broadford road for 6½ m. we diverge to the S.W. (r.) and cross the neck of the peninsula of SLEAT (pron. ' slate '), the S.W. arm of Skye. We reach the sea beyond (11 m.) *Kinloch Lodge* (Hotel, RB. 26/, P. 12 gs.) and command a fine view across the *Sound of Sleat* to the grand Loch Hourn on the mainland.—14 m. **Isleornsay** (*Duisdale*, unlic., RB. 26/, P. 11 gs., May–Sept. only ; *Isleornsay*, RB. 25/, P. 11½ gs.) with good bathing and fishing, takes its name from an island close inshore, on which are a lighthouse and ruins of a chapel. We strike inland again to (16½ m.) *Loch-nan-Dubhrachan*.

From the loch a road runs N.W. to (4 m.) *Ord* (Ord House, unlic., RB. 19/6, P. 8½ gs.), a lonely spot where Alex. Smith, author of 'A Summer in Skye,' spent three summers. Thence the return may be made by a rough road running S.W. near the shore for 3½ m. and then turning W. inland viâ (5½ m.) *Loch Dhugaill*, commanding a *View of the Coolins. The main road is rejoined at Ostaig House, half-way between Knock and Armadale (8 m. from Ord).

We regain the coast at (16½ m.) *Teangue*, near the ruined Knock Castle.—At (20 m.) **Armadale** (*Ardvasar*, RB. 19/6, P. 9 gs. ; steamers, see above) is the Gothic *Armadale Castle* (Lord Macdonald), in fine grounds. The present castle was built c. 1815 and is not, therefore, " the small house on the shore " of which Boswell wrote : " instead of finding the Lord of the Macdonalds surrounded with his clan and a festive entertainment, we found a small company, and cannot boast of our cheer."—The *Point of Sleat*, the S. extremity of Skye, is 5 m. S.W. by road and footpath.

C. From Broadford to Loch Coruisk and the Coolins

Loch Coruisk and Loch Scavaig lie at the foot of the famous Coolins, in the wildest and most characteristic setting in the island. They are most usually visited by excursion steamer from Mallaig or Kyle of Lochalsh, but the land routes from Broadford, though fatiguing and missing the impressive entrance to Loch Scavaig from the sea, will reward the traveller by their striking scenery.

I. Viâ Torrin

14½ m. ROAD to Strathaird House 9¾ m., thence by rough footpath. The return to Sligachan adds 8–8½ m. making a stiff day's tramp of c. 23 m. Motor-bus daily to Elgol, in connection with motor-boat for Loch Coruisk.

A good road runs S.W. past (3 m.) the loch and ruined church of *Kilchrist* to (5 m.) the hamlet of *Torrin* on *Loch Slapin*. Above Torrin are the *Red Hills* (2403 and 2323 ft.) and beyond the fine sea-loch rises the extraordinary *Blaven* (3042 ft.), a mass of serrated hypersthene rock which in dry weather has a curious resemblance to hot coke.

A boat may be hired at Torrin to visit (c. 5 m.) *Spar Cave* with its fine stalag-mitic interior (accessible at low tide in fair weather).

The hilly road rounds the head of Loch Slapin and leaving the shore reaches (9¾ m.) *Strathaird House*, where the foot-path to Loch Coruisk (2½ hrs. ; for hardy walkers only and unpleasant after rain) diverges on the right. The road goes on to (14 m.) *Elgol* (Grand View, RB. 16/, P. 130/), a village with a post office. From its harbour far below motor-boats may be hired to cross Loch Scavaig to Loch Coruisk (the motor-bus awaits the boats' return).

Off the mouth of Loch Scavaig is the isle of *Soay* (3 m. by 1¾ m.), the site of an unsuccessful factory for extracting the oil and processing the skins of basking sharks. Most of the inhabitants were removed to Mull in 1953, but some farmers from the south reoccupied the isle in 1954 (guest-house at Sandys, P. 5–6 gs.). Boat from Elgol 30/–35/ ; or by telegram from Sandys, 20/ ; mail-service also from Mallaig (apply at Marine Hotel).

The path from Strathaird leads due W. and soon ascends to a crest from which a fine view of the Coolins to the W. is obtained, while S.W., over Soay, appear the distant Canna, flat and fertile, Rum, towering and mountainous, and Eigg, distinguished by its lofty Sgurr.—At (12 m.) the shooting-lodge and farm of *Camasunary* we reach the shore of ***Loch Scavaig,** a sea-loch whose dark head, overshadowed by an amphitheatre of stern and jagged peaks, is magnificently impressive to those approaching by sea.

An easy path ascending the valley to the right leads viâ (1 m.) Loch-na-Creitheach to (8 m.) Sligachan (see below).

We follow the track leading W. along the shore, which is poor and awkward in places. At (13¾ m.) the ' *Bad Step* ' it follows a very narrow ledge (c. 15 ft. above high-water mark) on a rock shelving down to the sea, which presents no real difficulty but requires a steady head. We emerge at the head of Loch Scavaig, beneath *Trodhu* or *Sgurr-na-Strigh* (' Peak of Strife ' ; 1623 ft.) ; opposite is *Garsbheinn* (2934 ft.) with its roaring cataract. A short ascent up the left bank of the Scavaig brings us to (14½ m.) a rocky dam whence we view the extraordinary wilderness surrounding ***Loch Coruisk** (*Coire Uisg*, i.e. ' cauldron of water ' ; 1½ m. long), a gloomy lake at the foot of the black and savage Coolins (see p. 383), " black waves, bare crags, and banks of stone." Bruce (in Scott's ' Lord of the Isles '), fleeing from Ardtornish, landed in Loch Scavaig and on the banks of Loch Coruisk encountered the murderous Cormac Doil and his ' down-look'd ' men.

II. Viâ Sligachan

25 m. ROAD to *Sligachan*, 18 m. Rough walk thence to Loch Coruisk in 6 hrs. Bus from Broadford to Sligachan 2 or 3 times on weekdays in summer (55 min.), less often in winter.

The road, running W. from Broadford across a promontory, reaches the coast in 2 m. and follows it all the way to Sligachan. The island of *Scalpay* (1298 ft.), ½ m. offshore, has a chapel on the site of a Culdee cell. At (3½ m.) *Strollamus* the old hill-road diverges on the left, saving pedestrians a mile.—We round the sheltered *Loch Ainort*, whose shores are the haunt of heron and red deer. The hill-road on the left beyond the head of the loch saves 2 m. but commands no view of any interest. The main road rounds another point and follows the S. shore of Loch Sligachan.—14½ m. *Sconser Lodge*, incorporating a historic 18th cent. inn, faces Raasay (see below) ; above us to the left is the grand syenite pyramid of *Glamaig* (2537 ft.), and the Coolins are seen beyond the head of the loch.—18 m. **Sligachan** (*Hotel*, RB. 28/, P. 14½ gs.), at the junction of the roads to Portree and Dunvegan, is a favourite resort for mountaineers and anglers.   Ascents in the Coolins and road to Portree, see below.

Off the mouth of Loch Sligachan, separated from Skye by the Sound of Raasay, is the island of **Raasay**, 15 m. long but of very uneven width. Facing the narrowest part of the sound is *Raasay House* (now a hotel, RB. 19/, P. 12 gs.), where Johnson and Boswell were hospitably entertained by the MacLeod of Raasay. On the E. shore, 10 m. N., is *Brochel Castle*, a ruined stronghold of the MacLeods, and at the S. end of the island is an iron mine. Steamers, see p. 379.

The direct track for Loch Coruisk (ill-marked) ascends the right bank of the Sligachan burn.   On the left are the mountains of Lord Macdonald's Forest, ahead is the conical Marsco (2414 ft.), with Sgurr-nan-Gillean (see below) on the other side of the glen.   As we approach (3½ m.) the head of the glen the impressive *Harta Corrie*, offering an alternative approach to the N.W. end of Loch Coruisk, diverges to the right.   The 'Bloody Stone,' ¾ m. up this corrie, marks the site of the last clan battle between the Macdonalds and the MacLeods (1601).—Keeping well up the right side of Strath-na-Creitheach (which descends to Camasunary, see above), we cross the ridge of *Drumhain* (1038 ft. ; 5¾ m. ; *View*). Across the head of Loch Coruisk is seen the 'inaccessible pinnacle' of *Sgurr Dearg* (3254 ft.), resembling a slate stuck vertically into a wall.   The steep descent to (7 m.) **Loch Coruisk** (see above) follows the left bank of a burn.

III. THE COOLINS

The ***Coolins** or *Cuillin* (2934–3309 ft.), barest and most precipitous of British mountains, are a tumbled irregular mass of rough gabbro on basalt, a fine firm rock affording some of the best rock-climbing in Britain and interesting to geologists on account of the frequent glacial striations and perched boulders.   The greatest danger to the inexperienced climber is the mist which shrouds them at almost every season.   Even in fine weather a peculiar blue haze hovers in the corries.

Sgurr-nan-Gillean (3167 ft.), the northern buttress of the group, is the favourite climb.   The easiest route, ascending the S.E. side from the head of Glen Sligachan (6–9 hrs. from Sligachan and back), is difficult enough and a guide is desirable. The 'Pinnacle Route' (9 hrs.), which surmounts the four pinnacles at the N.E. corner, is for expert climbers only, who may continue the climb by a traverse W. along the narrow ridge to the summit of *Bruach-na-Frithe* (3143 ft.), going on thence by an easy descent to Bealach-a-Mhaim (see below).

An interesting route across the main ridge of the Coolins (c. 10 m.) leaves Sligachan by the Dunvegan road, quitting it after ½ m. and ascending the left bank of the stream beyond Cuillin Lodge.   Beyond (3¼ m.) the pass of *Bealach-a-Mhaim* (1030 ft.)

we keep to the left, up the right bank of the rough Coire-a-
Mhadaidh, and cross the main ridge by *Bealach-na-Glaice
Moire* (2510 ft.), between Bidein (l.) and Sgurr-a-Mhadaidh.
The steep descent leads down the desolate valley of Coire
Uisg to (10 m.) *Loch Coruisk* (p. 382).—After crossing Bealach-
a-Mhaim (see above) we may keep straight on and descend
Glen Brittle, soon joining a road from Carbost (r. ; see below).
—9 m. *Glenbrittle* (Glenbrittle House, unlic., pens. 6 gs.), with
a youth hostel, is the usual starting-point for the ascent of
Sgurr Alasdair (3309 ft. ; c. 6 hrs.), the highest of the Coolins.
It is connected with Sligachan by motor-bus twice daily.

D. From Sligachan to Dunvegan

24 m. MOTOR-BUS every weekday in summer in 1½ hr., by a
good road (A 863) affording fine views of the Coolins.—After
a short ascent to a group of moorland lochs the road descends
to (6 m.) *Drynoch* on Loch Harport, a deep narrow sea-loch,
6 m. long. At the hamlet of *Carbost* (Old Inn, unlic., RB. 12/6),
2½ m. down the S. side, is the celebrated Talisker distillery.—
We follow the hilly road N.W. to (10½ m.) *Dun Taimh* (l.),
a well-preserved fortified mound, and (14 m.) *Struan* (Ullinish
Lodge, 2 m. W., RB. 21/, P. 9 gs.; Balgowan House, unlic.,
summer only, RB. 16/6, P. 7½ gs.), connected by a hill-road with
Portree.   Thence after passing (17½ m.) *Ose* (Ose Farm Hotel,
unlic., RB. 19/, P. 8 gs.), on the island-studded Loch
Bracadale, we cross the narrow neck of the peninsula of
Duirinish, whose two chief hills are *MacLeod's Tables*.

A road on the left (B 884) as we approach Dunvegan leads to (7 m.) *Glendale*, on
Loch Pooltiel, the centre of the crofters' riots of 1882. *Dunvegan Head*, the
N. extremity of Duirinish, has sheer black cliffs 100 ft. high, and off *Idrigill
Point*, at the S. end, are three basaltic stacks called *MacLeod's Maidens*. The
MacCrimmons of Duirinish were far-famed as pipers and established a piping
college at *Boreraig*, on the road to Dunvegan Head. The last MacCrimmon, Ian
Dubh, died here c. 1824. A cairn has been built above the hollow in the cliff
used for the school, and a proposal is afoot to establish a ' piping college ' here.

Passing (r.) the ruins of old Duirinish church we reach
(24 m.) **Dunvegan** (*Hotel*, RB. 21/, P. 8½ gs. ; *Atholl*, unlic.,
P. 7 gs.), a village at the head of Loch Dunvegan. About
1 m. N. is *DUNVEGAN CASTLE (adm. 2/ in summer Mon.–Fri.
2–5), formerly accessible only from the sea by a small gateway
with a portcullis opening on the rocks. The present entrance
is by a bridge thrown across a ravine which formerly served as
moat. This castle, the seat from time immemorial of the
MacLeod of MacLeod, is a massive pile showing every style
from the 15th cent. to the 19th.

In the *Tower* (probably 15th cent.), whose walls are 10 ft. thick, is the dungeon
(shown to visitors), entered from the second floor near the drawing-room. The
S. tower, containing the Fairy Room, was built in the early 16th cent., and the
connecting wing, including the dining-room, about a century later. Among the

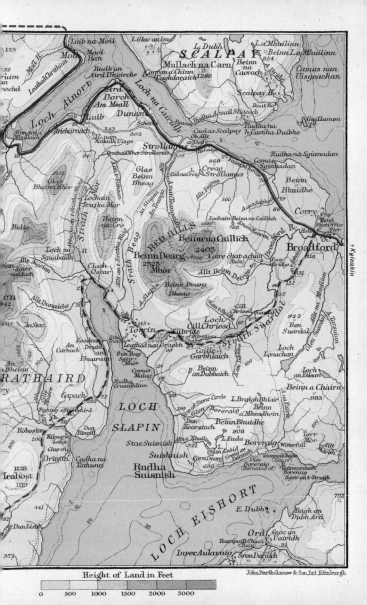

Height of Land in Feet

John Bartholomew & Son, Ltd. Edinburgh.

0   500   1000   1500   2000   3000

interesting objects preserved in the castle are an ancient Irish cup of bog-oak, the drinking-horn of Rory More (Sir Roderick MacLeod, the 12th chief, knighted by James VI), and the Fairy Flag of mysterious origin ; also relics of Prince Charlie, and letters from Dr. Johnson (1773) and Scott (1815), referring to their visits.—The castle stands in an old-fashioned garden, in charming contrast to the wilderness around. The waterfall in the woods behind is known as *Rory More's Nurse.*

E. Portree and North Skye

Portree, 9½ m. N. of Sligachan by road viâ Glen Varragill or reached by steamer from Kyle of Lochalsh, is the only town (1100 inhab.) in Skye, and in the tourist season is a place of some little bustle. Its name (' king's haven ') dates from a visit paid by James V, before whose time it was called *Kiltaragleann* (' the church at the bottom of the glen ').

Hotels. Royal, RB. 25/, P. 12 gs. ; **Portree,** RB. 22/6, P. 11 gs. ; **Rosedale** RB. 17/6, P. 9 gs., May–Sept. ; **Beaton's, Nicolson's,** small temperance houses.

Motor-Buses on weekdays to *Sligachan, Broadford,* and *Kyleakin* or *Armadale* ; to *Dunvegan* viâ Fairy Bridge (going on to *Glendale*) ; to *Glenbrittle* (1 hr.) viâ Carbost ; to *Kilmaluag* viâ Uig or viâ Staffin ; *Fiskavaig* ; *Vaternish* ; etc.

Steamers to *Raasay, Kyle of Lochalsh, Armadale,* and *Mallaig.*

Golf Course (1 m. W.) on the road to Struan.

The quaint little town, headquarters of a fishing fleet, is built partly on a platform of rock which presents towards the harbour a cliff-face 60–80 ft. high. Though an excellent centre for exploring the island, Portree contains little of general interest beyond the room (at the Royal Hotel) where Prince Charlie bade farewell to Flora Macdonald on June 30th, 1746 : " For all that has happened I hope, Madam, we shall meet in St. James's yet."

From Portree to the Storr and Staffin. Energetic walkers may follow the main ridge of *Trotternish,* the N. peninsula of Skye, and descend to Staffin or Uig (9–10 hrs.). The hilly road (A 855) affords magnificent views.—We ascend due N. up the valley of the Chracaig, and pass *Loch Fada* and (6 m.) *Loch Leathan,* united in 1952 to form a reservoir for a hydro-electric scheme with a power-house on Bearreraig Bay, below. A cave on the seashore E. of Loch Fada (4 m. from Portree ; best approached by boat) is associated with Prince Charlie, but actually he spent the night of July 2nd, 1746, in a byre 2 m. farther S. To the N.W. of Loch Leathan rises the **Storr** (2360 ft.), described by Geikie as ' a series of pinnacles and crags which have been split off from the main mass of the plateau basalts.' The summit (3–4 hrs.) commands a fine view of the Outer Hebrides and the Ross-shire mountains. The *Old Man of Storr,* at the E. foot of the mountain, is a black obelisk of trap, 160 ft. high.—The road rises again to 639 ft., with the basalt precipices of the Trotternish mountains on the left, and a fine range of cliffs facing the

long isles of Raasay and *South Rona* on the right.—11 m.
Invertote, at the mouth of the Lealt, with the quay serving
the diatomite beds (see below).—15 m. *Loch Mealt* pours its
waters into the sea in a fine cascade. This, like the imposing
Kilt Rock, a cliff so called from the form and colour of the
strata, is best seen from a boat, which may be hired at (17 m.)
Staffin.

High up on the ridge, 5 m. S. of Staffin, in the dry bed of *Loch Cuithir*, is a
deposit of diatomite (absorbent clay), which is intermittently worked.

About 1½ m. beyond Staffin the road forks. The left branch leads direct, past
the Quiraing, to (7 m. from Staffin) *Uig* (see below). The right branch describes a
curve round the extreme N. of the island viâ (5 m.) Flodigarry, etc., before
reaching (15 m.) Uig.

FROM PORTREE TO UIG AND THE QUIRAING, 20½ m. by a fair
road (A 850, A 856), then 1½ m. by footpath. Ascending N.E.
across undulating moorland, with views of the Coolins (S.)
and of Harris (N.), we leave (4 m.) the Dunvegan road on the
left and descend to (6½ m.) *Kensaleyre* on an arm of Loch
Snizort Beag.—9½ m. *Kingsburgh* (on the left, not seen from
the road) is the successor of the house in which Prince Charlie
found refuge in 1746, and where Johnson and Boswell were
entertained by the laird and his wife, Flora Macdonald.
Johnson slept in the prince's bed but " had no ambitious
thoughts about it." A long ascent beyond Glen Hinnisdal
brings us into view of the cheerful Uig Bay with the imposing
Ru Idrigil jutting out on the N.—15 m. **Uig** (*Hotel*, RB. 21/6,
P. 10½ gs., unlic.), whose name signifies ' nook ' or ' corner,'
is a neat village noted for its mild climate.

A fair road leads hence round the N. end of Trotternish to (15 m.) *Staffin*.
Near (3½ m.) *Kilbride*, in a bay below Monkstadt or Mugstot House, the Young
Pretender landed on June 29th, 1746, when, disguised as ' Betty Burke,' a
female servant, he accompanied Flora Macdonald from Benbecula (comp.
p. 394).—The grave of Flora Macdonald (1722–90) is in the graveyard of (5½ m.)
Kilmuir, to the right of the road. On the gravestone is inscribed Dr. Johnson's
tribute.—8 m. *Duntulm* (Duntulm Lodge, RB. 35/, P. 12½ gs.) ; the castle (l.),
now in ruins, was long the seat of the Macdonalds of the Isles. From the crofts
of *Kilmaluag*, farther E., we enjoy a wide prospect of the Minch, and at (11½ m.)
Flodigarry (Hotel, RB. 35/, P. 12 gs.) we reach the first married home of Flora
Macdonald, who married Allan Macdonald of Kingsburgh in 1750.—15 m.
Staffin, see above.

The road to the Quiraing climbs above Uig in sweeping
zigzags (short cut for walkers up the right bank of the river
Rha). At (20½ m.) the road-summit (852 ft.), the path to the
Quiraing diverges to the left along the foot of a cliff. We
follow this for c. 1½ m. and soon reach the **Quiraing,** an extraordinary mass of towers and pinnacles into which cattle were
driven during forays. The ascent into the inner recesses of
this labyrinth (c. ¾ hr. from the road) is a hand-and-foot
business, but a rough track zigzags up the slope of the gully
on the right of which stands *The Needle*, an imposing obelisk
120 ft. high. Beyond the Needle is a large amphitheatre

in whose centre stands the *Table,* a huge grass-covered rock-mass. The view thence of the sea and the mountains of Ross through the splintered rocks is most impressive.

From Portree to Vaternish, 27 m., a long and somewhat wearisome road. We leave (4 m.) the Uig road on A 850, and descend to (6½ m.) *Skeabost* (Hotel, RB. 35/, P. 17 gs.) with its picturesque old churchyard (r.).—13 m. *Edinbane* (Hotel, RB. 18/, P. 9½ gs.), at the head of Loch Greshornish.—Our *Fairy Bridge* the road on the left leads in 4 m. to Dunvegan, with fine views S.—Our road leading N. up the W. side of the peninsula of *Vaternish* passes (23 m.) *Stein* (Hotel, RB. 16/6, P. 8 gs.) and ends at (27 m.) *Trumpan,* the burial-place of Lady Grange (p. 395). Trumpan old church with its congregation of MacLeods was burnt by the Macdonalds in the savage old manner, but the rest of the MacLeods, arriving with the fairy flag, succeeded in turning the tables.

59. THE WESTERN ISLES

The **WESTERN ISLES,** or **HEBRIDES,** known to Ptolemy and Pliny as *Hebudæ* or *Hebudes,* were called *Sudreyjar,* or Southern Islands, by the Norsemen, a form which has been preserved in the title of the bishop of Sodor and Man, though the bishop's jurisdiction over the Hebrides ended in the 14th century. They include between 40 and 50 inhabited islands and innumerable barren islets and reefs. The islands were under Norse domination from the 8th cent. until 1266, when Magnus, Earl of Orkney, abandoned all claim to them. The lordship of the isles was afterwards claimed by Somerled, who had married a daughter of one of the Norse kings (c. 1110), but the title ' Lord of the Isles ' was first adopted by John Macdonald of Islay (d. 1386). The power of the Lords of the Isles was gradually undermined by the Scottish kings, and the title was annexed to the Crown by James IV ; and even the shadow of it vanished in 1748, with the abolition of heritable jurisdictions. The *Inner Hebrides* (Skye, Mull, etc.) are divided from the *Outer Hebrides* by the Minch. Gaelic is almost universally spoken ; accommodation is limited and should be booked in advance.

Steamers. The steamers to the Western Isles are managed by David MacBrayne, Ltd., 44 Robertson St., Glasgow, C.2. Travellers should procure their time-tables as the hours of sailing and the order of ports of call are frequently varied. Extra sailings are usually advertised in the ' Glasgow Herald ' newspaper. Meals (either in the first-class saloon or second-class fore-cabin) ; B. 5/6, L. 6/6, T. 2/6 or 5/6. Bicycles, 25 m., 4/, 50 m. 6/3, 100 m. 9/2, etc. Berths in staterooms (12/6–20/) or in cubicles (5/–10) are reserved at MacBrayne's offices (North Pier, Oban ; Steam Packet Office, Kyle of Lochalsh ; Maritime Buildings, Stornoway ; no telephone bookings).

From Gourock (see Rte. 13H). A steamer sails every weekday at 9.30, calling at Dunoon, Innellan, Rothesay, and Tighnabruaich, for *East Tarbert* (12 noon), whence a bus in connection crosses Kintyre to (5 min.) *West Tarbert.* Steamer thence on Mon., Wed., & Fri. viâ *Jura* to *Port Askaig* (4.40 p.m.) in Islay, going on on Mon. & Fri. to Colonsay (6 p.m.). On Tues., Thurs., & Sat. the steamer goes viâ *Gigha* to *Port Ellen* (4.25 p.m.) in Islay. Return on the following weekday.

From Oban. Steamer at 6.30 a.m. on Mon., Wed., and Fri., for *Tobermory, Coll, Tiree, Castlebay* (Barra), *Lochboisdale* (S. Uist), and *Castlebay* ; returning on Tues., Thurs., and Saturday.—On Mon. only passengers may tranship at Lochboisdale for *Lochmaddy, Rodil, Tarbert, Scalpay,* and *Kyle of Lochalsh,* and back to Lochboisdale, whence they may return to Oban by the Wed. evening boat.

From Kyle of Lochalsh and Mallaig. The steamer leaves Kyle of Lochalsh on Mon. c. 8.30 a.m. for *Glenelg* or *Armadale, Mallaig* (c. 1 p.m.), *Eigg, Rum, Canna, Lochboisdale* (c. 8 p.m.) and *Lochmaddy* (N. Uist ; c. 12.30 a.m.). Lochmaddy is left c. 5.30 a.m. on Tues., calls are made at *Rodil, Tarbert,* and *Scalpay* (all in Harris), and *Kyle of Lochalsh* is again reached c. 2.45 p.m. On Wed. and Fri. a boat leaves Kyle c. 6 a.m. and follows the above route reversed, *Lochboisdale* being reached c. 7 p.m. The return journey starts at 2 a.m. on Thurs., *Mallaig* being reached c. 9.45 a.m. and *Kyle* c. 2.45 p.m.—The Fri. boat on its return journey sails direct from Lochboisdale to *Mallaig* (6.15 a.m. Sat.), then goes on to Eigg, Rum, and Canna ; passengers for *Kyle* should tranship at Mallaig and proceed by the next direct steamer.—STORNOWAY is reached from *Kyle of Lochalsh* by a daily steamer leaving c. 2.30 p.m. and arriving c. 7 p.m. A steamer in connection leaves *Mallaig* c. 12.30 p.m. for Kyle of Lochalsh (2.15 p.m.), where passengers change steamers.

From Kyle of Lochalsh and from Mallaig to *Skye*, see Rte. 58 ; from Oban to *Mull* and *Iona*, see Rte. 50.

Air Services. From *Glasgow* (Renfrew Airport) once or twice on weekdays viâ Campbeltown to *Islay* (Glenegedale Airport ; 70 min.) ; every weekday in summer (Mon., Wed., Fri. in winter) to *Tiree* (Reef Airport ; 1 hr.), going on to *Barra* (Northbay ; 1¾ hr.) 3 or 4 times weekly ; every weekday viâ *Benbecula* (Balivanich Airport ; 80 min.) to *Stornoway* (2 hrs. 10 min.). From *Inverness* (Dalcross Airport) every weekday (in connection with plane from Glasgow) to *Stornoway* (50 min.). Transport to the airports is provided at Glasgow (St. Enoch Station ; 3/), Inverness (Station Square ; 3/), and Stornoway (Town Hall ; 1/6). The call at Barra is made subject to tidal conditions.

A. Islay, Jura, Colonsay

STEAMER from West Tarbert, see above.—Airport at *Glenegedale*, Islay, 4½ m. N.W. of Port Ellen, beyond the golf course (bus service to Port Ellen, Bowmore, and Port Charlotte).

From West Tarbert (Rte. 13H) the steamers traverse the wooded length of *West Loch Tarbert* (10 m.), between the Knapdale hills (r.) and those of Kintyre. The Port Ellen steamer enters the Sound of Gigha and calls (1 hr. 25 min.) at **Gigha,** a low island 6 m. long with an indented rocky coast.

To the S. of the inn at *Ardminish Bay* (tea on request) is (½ m.) *Achamore* (Sir J. Horlick, Bart.), noted for its lovely gardens (adm. 1/ daily Apr.–Sept.). The house (adm. 5/ by written appointment) contains fine furniture and needle-work. Ferry to Tayinloan, see p. 156.

Passing between Gigha and *Cara*, the steamer proceeds due W. to Port Ellen in Islay.—The Port Askaig steamer halts for the mail off the lonely N. end of Gigha, then calls at (2¼ hrs.) *Craighouse*, in a landlocked bay near the S. end of Jura, before entering the Sound of Islay.—**Jura** (28 m. long, 8 m. broad ; 250 inhab.), which boasts magnificent scenery but is seldom visited on account of the lack of accommodation, is remarkable for the exceptionally slight traces of Norse occupation in its place-names.

The scattered crofts along the S. and E. coasts are linked by a road from *Feolin Ferry* (see below) viâ (5 m.) *Jura House* and (8 m.) *Craighouse* (Keills, unlic., RB. 20/, P. 7 gs.), to (17 m.) *Lagg* and (24 m.) *Ardlussa*. Jura is nearly cut in two by *Loch Tarbert*, a deep inlet on the W., which practically divides it into two deer forests, Ardlussa forest to the N. and Jura forest to the S.. In the latter are the **Paps of Jura** (*Beinn-an-Oir*, ‘ mountain of gold,’ 2571 ft. ; *Beinn Siantaidh* ‘ hallowed mountain,’ 2477 ft. ; *Beinn-a-Chaolais*, ‘ mountain of the strait,’ 2407 ft.), three breast-like eminences, conspicuous from afar and commanding magnificent views. Off the N. end of Jura are the whirlpool of *Corrievreckan*, a tide-race dangerous to small craft, and the island of *Scarba*.

ISLAY, the most southerly of the Hebridean isles, is one of the largest, being c. 25 m. long by 20 m. broad. The W. side is, however, deeply indented by Lochs Gruinart and Indaal, which almost sever the *Rhinns* district (fine coast scenery) from the remainder. To the S.W. is the *Oa*, another peninsula noted for its bold cliffs. The inhabitants (4250) are mainly employed in farming and fishing, or in whisky distilleries.

Port Askaig (*Hotel*, RB. 20/, P. 8 gs.) is a tiny wooded hamlet charmingly situated on the Sound of Islay, here only ½ m. wide. A passenger ferry crosses to Feolin in Jura, while the road (A 846) climbs S.W. After 2 m. we leave on the right the track to (¾ m.) *Loch Finlaggan*, with an island on which are remains of a castle of the Macdonalds, Lords of the Isles.—8 m. *Bridgend* (Hotel, RB. 20/, P. 11 gs.), near the head of Loch Indaal.—10½ m. **Bowmore** (*Seaview*, RB. 15/6, P. 8 gs. ; *Lochside*, RB. 15/6, P. 7 gs. ; *Imperial*, RB. 14/6, P. 140/), a large fishing village on *Loch Indaal*, was the scene of the rifling exploits of an American privateer in 1813. The curious round church of Kilarrow parish, at the top of the street, dates from 1769. The road (A 847) running round Loch Indaal from Bowmore and Bridgend leads viâ (5 m. from Bowmore) *Uiskentui* and the fishing and distilling hamlet of (8 m.) *Bruichladdich* to (10 m.) *Port Charlotte* (Port Charlotte, RB. 19/6, P. 8½ gs. ; *Lorgha*, P. 10 gs.), near which are the graves of many American soldiers drowned when the S.S. ' Tuscania ' was torpedoed offshore on Feb. 5th, 1918. Farther on, at the extreme S. end of the Rhinns (see above) is (17 m.) *Portnahaven* (Hotel, RB. 21/, P. 7 gs.), sheltered from the S.W. by *Orsay*, a small island with a lighthouse. The currents off this coast are noted for their violence and rapidity.

From *Uiskentui* (see above) a road runs N.W. to (3 m.) the head of *Loch Gruinart*, where the Macdonalds, after a fierce battle, drove back the invading MacLeans of Mull (1598). On hearing of the MacLean's death James VI granted the island to Sir John Campbell of Calder. The road soon trends S.W. and, just before we reach (6 m.) *Loch Gorm*, in which are the ruins of an island stronghold of the Macdonalds, a by-road strikes N. for (3 m.) *Sanaigmore*, near one of the finest caves in the rocky W. coast of the Rhinns. In 1847 the emigrant ship *Exmouth* ' foundered here with all hands. Beyond Loch Gorm is (9 m.) *Kilchoman Church*, with a very fine sculptured Celtic cross. Between the church and (⅓ m. W.) *Machar Bay* are the graves of those drowned when the S.S. ' Otranto,' carrying American troops, was lost after a collision (Oct. 6th, 1918). Of the 400 American dead, however, all but two have been removed.

From Bowmore (see above) a road (A 846) runs S. past Glenegedale airport to (10 m.) **Port Ellen** (*Machrie*, on the golf course, RB. 20/, P. 12 gs. ; *White Hart*, *Islay*, at both, RB. 17/, P. 8–8½ gs.), the principal village in Islay, with first-class golf links at Machrie, 3 m. N.W. From Port Ellen another road goes S.W. past (1½ m.) *Kilnaughton Bay*, with a graveyard of the ' Tuscania ' victims (see above), and across the hilly *Oa* peninsula to (6½ m.) the W. coast, where there is another large cemetery. In the rocky N.W. coast of the Oa are many caves, accessible only by boat. The *Mull of Oa* lies c. 1 m. S.W. of the road-end ; on another point 1¾ m. S.E. are the remains of the entrenched camp of *Dun Aidh*.—The road leading E. from Port Ellen winds under the hill of *Cnoc*, where two upright stones mark the supposed resting-place of the Danish princess Yula, to whom some trace the name of Islay. *Dun Naomhaig*, a strongly built round tower overlooking (2½ m.) *Lagavulin*, is supposed to have been a fortress of the Macdonalds. At (7¼ m. ; r.) *Kildalton* burying-place are two fine Celtic crosses and sculptured grave-slabs. From (9½ m.) *Ardtalla* a path leads N. to (4 m. more) *McArthur's Head* (lighthouse) at the entrance to the Sound of Islay. *Ben Bheigeir* (1609 ft. ; c. 2 m. inland) is Islay's highest hill.

The steamer goes on from Port Askaig through the Sound of Islay to (1 hr.) **Colonsay** (8 m. long by c. 2½ m. broad), noted for its rich pasture (*Hotel*, at *Scalasaig* pier, RB. 18/6, P. 10 gs.) and separated at its S. end from the smaller **Oronsay** by a narrow sound which is dry for 3 hrs. at low tide. The islands (230 inhab.) are named after St. Columba and St. Oran, his companion.

The gardens of *Kiloran* (Lord and Lady Strathcona), 2 m. N. of the pier, are noted for azaleas, rhododendrons, etc. (adm. 1/ daily Apr.–Sept.).

In the W. arm of Oronsay are the interesting ruins of an Augustinian priory of obscure history, but probably on a Celtic site. The roofless *Church*, c. 60 ft. long, is almost entirely undecorated. Adjoining it is a cloister, whose arches, resting on square wall piers, are straight-sided, like those of Saxon buildings in England. In the churchyard is a fine sculptured *Cross*, its head adorned with a relief of the Crucifixion, and bearing an inscription in memory of Prior Colin (d. 1510). Another smaller cross is made up of parts of two crosses ; and the prior's house re-roofed in 1927, contains good 16th cent. tomb-slabs.

B. Coll and Tiree, and the Outer Isles

STEAMERS from Oban, from Kyle of Lochalsh, and from Mallaig, see p. 387.—AIRPORTS on Tiree, Barra, Benbecula, and Lewis ; comp. p. 388.

FROM OBAN TO LOCHBOISDALE

Leaving Oban, the steamer steers through the Sound of Mull, calls at Tobermory, then proceeds due W. to (4 hrs.) Coll. After Coll, it calls at (5½ hrs.) Tiree, then passes between the islands.

Coll (12 m. by c. 3 m. ; 210 inhab. ; *Coll Hotel*, RB. 20/, P. 130/) is a crofting island (340 ft.), visited by Johnson in 1773. Near the S. end are the ruins of the 14th cent. castle of the MacLeans of Coll. To the S.W., separated from Coll by the Sound of Gunna, is **Tiree** (11 m. by c. 3 m. ; 1200 inhab. ; *Scarinish Hotel*, RB. 15/, P. 8 gs.), a low wind-swept island (460 ft.), known in Gaelic legend as ' the kingdom whose summits are lower than the waves '. It is noted for a beautiful pink marble spotted with green, and for its bulb-growing industry started in 1954. There are several fine sandy beaches, notably at Traigh Mor, E. of the pier, with a small golf course. The airfield is 2 m. W. of the hotel and pier. *Skerryvore* lifts its lonely light (unmanned since 1954) 10 m. S.W., while the *Treshnish Isles* lie 10 m. E.

The steamer now steers N.W. for *Castlebay* in Barra (as we approach, the conical islet of *Muldoanich*, 505 ft. high, is prominent) then goes on to its terminus at *Lochboisdale* in South Uist.

FROM KYLE OF LOCHALSH TO THE SMALL ISLES AND THE OUTER HEBRIDES

The steamer leaving Kyle on Monday (see p. 387) traverses the Sound of Sleat and calls at Glenelg or Armadale before reaching *Mallaig*, where it halts for 2½ hrs. It then serves the Small Isles, a group of islands (no hotels) lying S. of Skye. About 6 m. S.W. of the Point of Sleat is **Eigg** (pron. ' egg ' ; 5 m. by 2½ m.), an isle distinguished by a peculiarly-shaped hill at the S. end terminating in the remarkable *Sgurr of Eigg* (1289 ft.), a mass of black glassy ' pitchstone ' towering to a height of 400 ft. above its high-lying base. The rock of which it is made was poured forth in a molten state and has for the most part assumed columnar forms. A cave near the S.E. shore was the scene of a terrible tragedy (late 16th cent.), referred to in ' The Lord of the Isles,' when the MacLeods of Skye having landed to avenge a supposed wrong lit a fire at the entrance to the cave and suffocated 200 Macdonalds who were hiding within. Scott says that in 1814 he ' brought off a skull from among the numerous specimens of mortality which the cavern afforded." A Celtic cross-slab has been erected in *Kildonnan* churchyard ; the ' musical sands ' are in the bay of Camas Sgiotaig, on the W. side, 4 m. N. of Glamisdale pier.—*Muck* (not called at), the most southerly of the group, lies 3 m. S.W. of Eigg and 7 m. N. of Ardnamurchan.—**Rum**, 4 m. N.W. of Eigg, is the largest of the group (8 m. square) and rises steeply from the coast to a magnificent group of peaks, culminating in *Askival* (2659 ft.). In 1826 the whole population save one family was forced to emigrate ; and the island is now a nature reserve and casual landing is discouraged (as it has been for over a century), but the half-wild ponies are free to remain. In 1888–1957 it was owned by the Bulloughs of Lancashire, and Kinloch Castle (1901) and a small ' classical ' mausoleum are reminders of their occupancy.—**Canna** (4½ m. by ¾ m.), 3 m. W of Rum, is celebrated for its *Compass Hill*, (458 ft.), ½ m. N. of the harbour at the E. end of the island. The rich iron deposits in the basalt cliffs frequently affect the compasses of passing vessels. On the summit of a lofty and slender stack near the harbour are ruins of a tower where a jealous Lord of the Isles is said to have confined his beautiful foreign wife. Canna church, with a round tower, was built in 1914. A finely sculptured, though mutilated, cross, ¼ m. N. of the post office, marks the site of St. Columba's chapel.

From Canna the steamer steers due W. to *Lochboisdale* in S. Uist, and reaches *Lochmaddy* in N. Uist shortly after midnight. On Tues. morning it calls at *Rodil* and *Tarbert* in Harris, then, after a call at *Scalpay*, sails direct across the Minch to *Kyle of Lochalsh*.

The steamer leaving Kyle on Wed. morning follows the route of the Mon. boat in reverse ; the Fri. morning steamer takes the same route as the Wed. boat as far as Lochboisdale, then returns direct to *Mallaig*, afterwards serving the Small Isles on Sat. forenoon.

From Kyle of Lochalsh to Stornoway

The daily steamer (comp. p. 388) crosses the mouth of Loch Carron, passes between the mainland and the *Crowlin Islands* (l.), then leaves Applecross on the right and Raasay and South Rona on the left with the Trotternish hills behind. On the left, at the entrance to the Little Minch are seen the *Shiant Islands*, backed by the distant mountains of Harris; and, as we approach *Stornoway*, the Eye peninsula extends away to the right.

The **OUTER HEBRIDES** (comp. p. 387), known collectively as the Long Island, extend from the Butt of Lewis to Barra Head (130 m.), and are separated from Skye by the *Little Minch* and from the mainland by the *Minch* (15–40 m. wide). Their scenery is unique. For the most part the long sandy shores, which on the W. receive the full force of the Atlantic, are broken by innumerable sea-lochs and girdled by islets. The moors are likewise broken up by an infinite number of lochs, the proportion of water to land being unusually high. Trees are few, and the scanty soil is poor and often difficult to drain. Pasture is limited, but lobster-fishing, the manufacture of tweed, and the harvesting of seaweed for the extraction of alginates have recently developed in importance. The herring, which deserted the Minch in 1912, ruining the fishing-ports on its coasts, returned unaccountably in 1950.

Relics of the Stone and Bronze Ages are striking rather than numerous ; increasing evidence of populousness in the Iron Age has resulted from recent excavations in Uist. The ' black houses,' built mainly of turf, without window or chimney, and with the fire in the centre of the bare clay floor, once common in the remoter districts, are fast disappearing, though some survive as byres. Gaelic is spoken throughout the isles and the people in the more southern islands are almost all Roman Catholic.

LEWIS (called ' *The Lews* ') is the largest of all the Hebrides (23,350 inhab.), and is the only one of any importance in Ross-shire. With its S. extension Harris, which is in Inverness-shire, it forms a single island, 59 m. long and 18–20 m. broad. In the reign of James VI the Fife Adventurers made an unsuccessful attempt to colonise Lewis, and an effort by Lord Leverhulme (1851–1925), who purchased Lewis and Harris in 1918, to modernise the methods of farming and fishing was equally fruitless, largely owing to the conservative indifference of the islanders.

Stornoway, on the E. coast of Lewis (4950 inhab.), is the largest town in Ross-shire. It was founded by James VI and stands at the head of a good harbour which in May and June is thronged with herring boats from all parts.

Hotels. Caledonian, RB. 19/6, P. 9½ gs. ; **County,** RB. 22/6, P. 11½ gs. ; **Royal,** RB. 23/6, P. 9 gs. ; **Park Guest House,** unlic., RB. 17/6, P. 7 gs.

Motor-Buses daily or oftener (Mon.–Sat.) to *Tarbert* and *Rodil*; to *North Tolsta* (E. coast) ; and to *Barvas* and *Ness*. Circular tour on Mon.–Fri. in summer to *Callanish, Carloway,* and *Bragar* ; on Wed. to *Uig*.

Steamers to *Kyle of Lochalsh*.—AIR SERVICES from the airport, 2 m. E. (motor service from Town Hall), to *Inverness*, and to *Glasgow* viâ Benbecula.

Amusements. *Golf Course* within the Lochs Rd. entrance to the castle grounds.—*Pipe Band* on Mon. and alternate Sat. evenings on the quay.

Famous sons of Lewis are commemorated in the *Town Hall*, while on *Martin's Memorial Church*, in Francis St., a tablet marks the site of the birthplace of Alexander Mackenzie of Luskentyre (1755–1820), discoverer of the Mackenzie River. *St. Peter's Church* (Episcopalian) farther up (r.) contains Livingstone's prayer-book and a red granite font (within the modern font) brought from the Flannan Isles and perhaps the oldest in Scotland. At the top of the street is the main building of the *Nicolson Institute*, a well-known school. On the W. side of the harbour is *Lewis Castle* (1856–63), presented by Lord Leverhulme to the town, and occupied since 1953 as a technical college. The grounds are noted for their rhododendrons.

A walk of 3½ m. past the castle and across the pretty river Creed (or a boat from the quay) will bring us to Arnish lighthouse, at the harbour mouth, on the edge of *Arnish Moor*, where Prince Charlie's Cairn and Loch commemorate the night spent by the Prince in a farmhouse near by on his retreat from Culloden.— To the E. of the town, between Broad Bay and the Harbour, the land runs out past the airfield to (3 m.) the Braighe, a narrow causeway leading to the croftdotted Eye Peninsula. The roofless church of *Eye* (Little Steading, at Aignish, unlic., RB. 20/, P. 7 gs.), at the end of the causeway, contains the armed effigy of Roderick MacLeod (15th cent.) and a cross-slab to his daughter Margaret MacFingone, mother of the last abbot of Iona.

The right branch of the Lochs road (A 858) running W. from Stornoway leads to (13½ m.) *Garynahine* and (15 m.) **Callanish**, noted for a remarkable group of *Standing Stones*. This great setting includes a circle of stones, 40 ft. in diameter, within which is a small annular cairn in three divisions, one with a monolith, 18 ft. high, at one end. From this circle radiate single rows of stones, E. and W. and a double but incomplete row to the S., while a long double row runs N. The total number of stones is 47 and the full length N. and S. is 400 ft. About ½ m. E., within ¼ m. of each other, are two more circles.—Callanish lies near the head of *Loch Roag*, a jagged sea-loch containing the large island of *Bernera* (bridge built in 1953) and other islets. From Garynahine (see above) B 8011 rounds Loch Roag and ends (20 m.) c. 1 m. from *Gallan Head*, at its mouth, 2½ m. beyond *Uig*. The whole of this remote district repays detailed exploration. Nearly 20 m. W. are the **Flannan Islands**, or ' *Seven Hunters*.' The largest of this lonely group bears remains of hermits' cells. They are visited by a half-yearly boat from Callanish (Breasclett).

From Callanish A 858 goes on through a crofting district to (22 m.) *Carloway* (Park House, unlic., RB. 15/), just short of which is a well-preserved broch,

30 ft. high (l.). Thence it continues parallel with the N.W. coast (many fine beaches, notably at *Dalmore*) to (29 m.) *Bragar* and (34 m.) *Barvas*. It is continued by A 857 which passes (33½ m.) *Upper Shader*, with the Thrushel Stone, a monolith 20 ft. tall (in the village, l.) and, on the moor to the E., the stone circle and cairn of Steinacleitt.—49½ m. **Ness**, with its long one-storied street, is connected by road with the **Butt of Lewis** (2 m. N.W.; 142 ft.), a wild cape surmounted by a lighthouse (adm. 11–3, Mon.–Fri) and surrounded by impressive cliffs and rock pinnacles, the haunt of seafowl. Amid barley-fields near by stands the church of *Eorropaidh*, or *Teampull Molua* (13th cent.; restored; key at Eoropie store), where a yearly episcopal service is held. On the E. side is the little harbour of *Port of Ness*, whence the Nessmen sail in Aug.–Sept. to fetch the 'guga', or young gannet, a favourite local dainty, from *Sula Sgeir*, a lonely islet 49 m. N.—From Barvas (see above) A 857 returns direct to (12 m.) Stornoway.

A 859 from Stornoway leads S.W. amidst a multitude of small lochs and past *Loch Erisort* (11 m.) and *Loch Seaforth* (18 m.), two long and beautiful sea-lochs (Valtos House, on Loch Erisort, unlic., RB. 20/, P. 6 gs.).

The Seaforth Highlanders are named after Loch Seaforth, which penetrates the district of Park, once a favourite hunting-ground of the Mackenzie, who first raised the regiment.

At (23 m.) the county boundary at Aline we enter **Harris** (3120 inhab.), the S. part of Lewis. Harris consists mainly of rock-strewn hills with but a slight sprinkling of stunted heather. The best qualities of its famous tweed are spun in Stornoway and hand-woven in the island.—At (26 m.) the summit-level (685 ft.), with marvellous views on both ascent and descent, we skirt *Clisham* (2622 ft.) the highest mountain of the Outer Hebrides, frequented by rock-climbers. Beyond (31 m.) *Ardhasaig Bridge* we reach *West Loch Tarbert*, which we skirt as far as (35 m.) **Tarbert** (*Harris*, RB. 20/), a village on an isthmus ⅛ m. wide. The steamer pier is on *East Loch Tarbert*.

An interesting road runs S. from Tarbert, at first along the E. coast, then crossing to the W. coast by (7 m.) *Glen Laxdale*, in which are the best examples in Scotland of 'funeral cairns,' built where coffin-bearers rested their burden on their way west to the graveyard at *Luskentyre*. To the W. of (15 m.) *Scarista* lies *Toe Head*, a curiously shaped peninsula beyond a vast stretch of sand. We ascend thence S.W. and enter the wild *Glen Coishletter*, at the foot of which is (20 m.) *Leverburgh*, or *Obbe*, on the beautiful *Sound of Harris*, where Lord Leverhulme attempted to establish a fishing station. The road ends at (23 m.) **Rodil** (*Hotel*, good, RB. 18/, P. 10 gs.; steamer, see p. 387), above which is the singular cruciform church of *St. Clement* (c. 1500; restored). On its sturdy square tower is sculpture " of a kind the last which one would have expected to find on a building dedicated to religious purposes." Within, in a remarkably fine recessed tomb, is an effigy in armour of Alastair 'Crotach' (1528), one of the MacLeods of Dunvegan; there are two other similar monuments, and in an enclosure in the churchyard is the tomb of Donald MacLeod of Berneray (1693–1783), who fought for Prince Charlie at Falkirk and had nine children after his third marriage at the age of 75.—The return to Tarbert may be made by a fine road on the E. coast (view of Skye), passing the small lobster-port of *Finsbay*, and the village of *Geocrab*, with a tweed-mill.

From Ardhasaig Bridge (see above) a winding road leads W. At 4½ m. a track diverges N. for 4 m. to *Loch Voshimid*, in which is said to be " the island that likes to be visited."—At (8½ m.) *Amhuinnsuidhe Castle*, on the coast road, Barrie wrote much of 'Mary Rose.' Thence a narrow road goes on to (13 m.) the lovely *Husinish Bay*, where a ferry-boat for *Scarp* may be summoned by telephone.

The steamer crosses the island-studded *Sound of Harris* with numerous beacons (for Lord Leverhulme's fishing station) to *Lochmaddy* in **North Uist,** an island 17 m. long and 13 m. wide (1900 inhab.) nearly half covered by water.

Lochmaddy (*Hotel*, RB. 21/, P. 12 gs.), the chief village, stands on the sea-loch of the same name, which, though only 5 m. long with an entrance 1 m. wide, has a coastline so tortuous that its length has been computed at 360 miles. The name ('madadh' a hound) comes from three basaltic islets at the entrance. On the S. side is *Ben Lee* (920 ft. ; best reached by boat from the hotel), commanding a unique view of the waterlogged island. In clear weather the *Monach Isles* (17 m. W.), St. Kilda (53 m. N.W.), and the Coolins (40 m. S.E.) may be seen.—The road encircling the island (33 m.) is served by two motor-buses (not Thurs., Sat., or Sun.) from Lochmaddy to *Baleloch* on the W. coast. That on the N. side calls at (7½ m.) *Newton Ferry* (Newton House, RB. 20/, P. 10 gs.) on the Sound of Berneray and (11 m.) *Sollas*, with an airstrip. The southern service makes a divergence at 8½ m. (beyond the deep inlet of *Loch Eport*) for (11 m.) *Carinish*, on the S. shore, and serves (11 m.) *Claddach* (Westford Inn, good, RB. 16/, P. 6 gs.), opposite Kirkibost island.

From Carinish we may cross the *North Ford* (4¼ m.) by boat or cart according to the tide (causeway in construction 1959) to *Grimsay* and **Benbecula,** an island 7–8 m. square with a road from *Gramisdale* at the N. end to (5½ m.) *Creagorry* (*Hotel*, RB. 18/6, P. 10 gs.). On June 28th, 1746, Prince Charlie sailed hence to Skye (Kilbride) with Flora Macdonald. As a result of the construction of an airfield at *Balivanich*, 2 m. W. of Gramisdale, a bridge has been built to replace the *South Ford* between Creagorry and Carnan in South Uist. Motor-buses run every weekday between Gramisdale, the airport, Creagorry, and Lochboisdale.

The Outer Islands steamer goes direct from Lochmaddy to *Lochboisdale* in **South Uist,** an island (20 m. by 7 m. ; 2450 inhab.) where the crofter's lot is perhaps hardest. Between its mountains, *Hekla* (1988 ft.) and *Ben More* (2034 ft.), Prince Charlie lodged in a forester's hut from May 14th to June 5th, 1746.

At **Lochboisdale**, near the S. end of the island, are an excellent *Hotel* (RB. 22/, P. 9 gs.) and a tea-room, and there is an unlicensed inn (RB. 15/) at *Carnan* (at the extreme N.). Carnan is connected with *Polochar* (at the extreme S.) by a road (21½ m.) with a branch to Lochboisdale (3 m.). About 8 m. N. of Polochar, just after a cross-roads, are (l.) the ruins of Flora Macdonald's home, at *Milton*. Her first meeting with Prince Charlie was at her brother's shieling of Alisary, on the E. side of the main road. Near the N. end of the island the road crosses the shallow *Loch Bee*. On the machar between this and the W. coast a rocket range was constructed in 1955–58 ; overlooking it, on the height of *Rueval* (286 ft.), 4 m. S. of Carnan, is a granite statue, 125 ft. high, of Our Lady of the Isles, designed in 1954 by Hew Lorimer. *Eriskay*, S. of South Uist, is a small island where Prince Charlie first landed on Scottish soil (July 23rd, 1745). Its charming folk songs have been gathered by the Kennedy-Frasers.

Barra, a singularly barren island c. 5 m. by 4 m., has the southernmost port of the Outer Islands, approached by the Inner Islands steamer. The harbour, **Castlebay** (*Castlebay*, RB. 17/6, P. 8 gs. ; *Craigard*, RB. 17/6, P. 7 gs.), has in its midst *Kisimul Castle* (12th cent. ; restored 1956–57), the seat of the Macneil of Barra, an ancestor of whom is said to have refused the hospitality of Noah as ' the Macneil had a boat of his own.' The island is encircled by a road (12½ m.) which affords access to *Traigh Mor*, a sandy expanse near the N. of the island, connected by air service with Tiree and Glasgow 3–4 times weekly (tide permitting).

South of Barra is a group of smaller islands, one of which, **Mingulay** (10 m. S.), has cliffs 700–900 ft. high. The rocks are fissured by whin dykes, which the sea has in part washed out, so that boats may pass between their vertical walls. On the W. side is a natural bridge 550 ft. above the water. *Sandray*, between Barra and Mingulay, is noted for its flowers. Beyond Mingulay is *Berneray*, with a lighthouse (visible for 33 m.) on **Barra Head** (580 ft.), the S. extremity of the Outer Hebrides.

St. Kilda, a lonely group of four islets (c. 3 sq. m.), 45 m. W. of N. Uist, is visited by occasional steamers. The largest island (c. 3 m. long) rises to a height of 1397 ft. and is girdled by magnificent cliffs, the highest being over 1300 ft. In Aug. 1930 the entire population (35 in number), interesting for their isolation and primitive ways, were removed from the island with their goods and chattels, and settled for the most part near Lochaline. St. Kilda, abandoned to its half-wild mouflon sheep, called *Soay* sheep from the second island, on which they pasture, and to the sea-fowl, which breed here in amazing numbers, is now a bird sanctuary and belongs to the National Trust. In 1957 a ' plotting station ' was established here, in connection with the South Uist rocket range, among the old crofts of Village Bay. The Gaelic name of the main island is Hirt or Hirta ; ' St. Kilda ' (there is no such saint) is probably a sailors' corruption of that, by way of the island dialect which, it is said, replaced the 'r ' sound by ' l '.—It was to this lonely islet that Lord Grange, a judge of the Court of Session, sent his wife when she became privy to certain incriminating Jacobite secrets (1734). He then celebrated her funeral, though the unfortunate lady lived for 3 years after her removal from the island in 1742.—*Soay* (see above) is to the N.W. ; while the cliff-bound *Boreray* (1245 ft.) is 4 m. N.E.

60. FROM INVERNESS TO CROMARTY ACROSS THE BLACK ISLE

22 m. in c. 1¾ hr. MOTOR-BUS from Inverness to *South Kessock*, 1¼ m. ; thence FERRY to *North Kessock*, ½ m. (6d., cycle 3d., motor-cycle 1/3, motor car 3/) ; thence MOTOR-BUS to *Cromarty*, 20 m. in 70–80 min.

Cromarty may be reached also in c. 2 hrs. by taking bus or train to Conon Bridge and bus thence along the N. side of the Black Isle.—*Fortrose* and *Rosemarkie* may also be reached by motor-bus or rail viâ Muir of Ord (1½ hr.).

The **Black Isle** is the broad promontory between the Moray Firth and Beauly Firth (S.) and the Cromarty Firth (N.). The name is probably a translation from the Gaelic Eilean Dubh, itself a corruption of Eilean Dubhthaich (' St. Duthac's Isle '). The lordship of the central ridge, known as *Mulbuie* or *Ardmeanach* (' the monk's height '), was granted by Mary, Queen of Scots, to Darnley on their marriage.

From *South Kessock*, 1¼ m. N. of Inverness by road, we cross the Beauly Firth by ferry (see above) to (½ m.) *North Kessock* (Inn), beneath the wooded Ord Hill (c. 550 ft.). The Cromarty road runs W. then N. to (4½ m.) *Munlochy* (Hotel, RB. 18/6), where we join A 332 from Muir of Ord. *Rosehaugh*, ½ m. left farther on, was the estate of Sir George Mackenzie (d. 1691).— 8 m. *Avoch* (pron. ' Auch ' ; Central, Station, both plain, RB. 15/–17/6) is the last of the fishing ports of the Moray Firth. Its people are said to be descendants of a Danish colony, whose local speech has preserved many Norse words and expressions.—10 m. **Fortrose** (*Royal Station*, RB. 17/6, P. 7 gs.) is a decayed port, made a royal burgh in 1592 by the union of the towns of Chanonry and Rosemarkie.

The lane running S. from the broken shaft of the old *Cross* leads to the green close in which stands the ruined red-sandstone *Cathedral*, a mere fragment of the church founded by David I for the see of Ross. Cromwell is said to have used many of its stones to build the fort at Inverness. The existing remains are partly in a late-14th cent. Dec. style (S. nave aisle) and partly in the Perp. style of

Melrose, the church having been completed in 1485 by Abbot Fraser, a monk of that abbey. On the N. wall is the canopied tomb, much mutilated, of Euphemia, Countess of Ross, builder of this aisle (c. 1395), and there is a later and poorer monument of a bishop. An arched compartment at the W. end is walled off as the burial-place of the Mackenzies of Seaforth. A 15th cent. bell in the clock-tower is rung daily for curfew. To the N.E. is the detached 13th cent. *Chapter House* which preserves some sedilia in its lower chamber.

10¾ m. **Rosemarkie** (*Marine*, RB. 21/, P. 9 gs., May–Oct. ; *Marita*, unlic., RB. 15/6, P. 6½ gs.), frequented for golf and bathing, has an interesting sculptured stone in the parish churchyard. This recalls the foundation here, in 716, of the church of St. Peter, by St. Boniface (Curitan), who died at Rosemarkie. The walk N.E. along the edge of the fulmar-haunted cliffs has been rendered classic to geologists by the writings of Hugh Miller (see below). Chanonry Point, 1½ m. long, extends past the golf course into the firth opposite (1 m.) Fort George.—At 12½ m. the road forks, the left branch leading to *Balblair* (5¾ m. ; ferry to Invergordon).

20 m. **Cromarty** (*Royal*, RB. 18/6) is a small town (725 inhab.) whose importance departed with the failure of its herring-fishery. The church is a typical work of c. 1700, with three 18th cent. lofts. *Cromartie House*, S.E. of the town, stands on the site of the castle of the Urquharts (destroyed in 1772), the birthplace of Sir Thomas Urquhart (1611–60), translator of Rabelais. The statue of Hugh Miller (1802–56), the geologist, on a hill above the town, is close to the churchyard which contains several tombstones cut by him while a mason. He was born in a thatched cottage (1711) in the main street, now well arranged as a museum (N.T. ; open weekdays 10–12, 2–5).

The entrance to **Cromarty Firth,** which extends like a sickle for c. 18 m. S.W. of the town, is " cut through a long lofty range of gneiss precipices " and is " an abnormal opening, and not the original mouth of the firth." Charles II landed in the firth in 1650 on his way to be crowned at Scone. On either side rise the *Sutors*. The South Sutor (463 ft.), 1½ m. E. of Cromarty, affords a splendid view southward. There is a ferry (by arrangement ; 5/ per 5 pers. or 1/6 ret. per pers. for more than 5) from Cromarty to (¾ m.) *Nigg* (p. 397), near the North Sutor (486 ft.), and a steam launch plies thrice every weekday to *Invergordon* (1/3). The firth was a fleet base during both World Wars.

61. FROM INVERNESS TO WICK AND THURSO

ROAD ROUTES. As far as (101 m.) *Helmsdale* the route follows A 9. Thence the best road to (155 m.) **Thurso** is the inland route (A 897) viâ Kinbrace, continued along the N. coast by A 836. The picturesque direct road (A 9), with violent hills, from Helmsdale to (137 m.) **Wick** is being 'improved' to take the heavy traffic proceeding to Dounreay. Wick and Thurso are connected by A 882 (21 m.), as well as by the longer but more interesting coast-road viâ John o' Groats. The shortest road to Thurso (144½ m.) diverging from A 9 at Latheron is not recommended.—MOTOR-BUS every 2 hrs. to Invergordon (2 hrs.), Tain (2½ hrs.), Dornoch (4 hrs.), and Helmsdale (5½–6 hrs.), with connection thence to Wick (2–2¼ hrs.) and Thurso (3–3½ hrs.), 3 times daily. On Sun. 4 times to Tain, going on once to Helmsdale (4¾ hrs.) and Wick (6¼ hrs.).

RAILWAY to Wick, 161¼ m. in 5¾–6¼ hrs. ; to *Tain*, 44 m. in 1¾ hr. ; to *Lairg*, 66½ m. in 2¾ hrs. ; to *Dornoch*, 88½ m. viâ The Mound, in 4 hrs. ; to *Helmsdale*, 101¼ m. in 4 hrs. ; to *Thurso*, 153¾ m. in 5¾–6½ hrs. viâ Georgemas.—The best views are on the right, except between Invershin and Lairg. The railway route coincides fairly closely with the road, except between Bonar Bridge and The Mound, and beyond Forsinard.

AIR SERVICES every weekday from Inverness to *Wick* (45 min.), and from Aberdeen to *Wick* (1 hr.).

From Inverness to (21 m.) *Dingwall*, see Rte. 55. Thence railway and road run close beside the Cromarty Firth, which extends N.E. for c. 18 m. ; on the left are the hill and woods of *Tulloch Castle*. To the left farther on is *Foulis Castle* (rebuilt 1754–72), long held by the Munros on the tenure of furnishing a snowball, if required, at midsummer.—27½ m. *Evanton* (Novar Arms, RB. 20/, P. 200/). To the right is *Balconie House*, on the site of a fortress of the earls of Ross ; *Castlecraig*, once a residence of the bishops of Ross, is seen across the firth. Overlooking Alness Bay (N.E.) was the war-time naval air base H.M.S. ' Fieldfare.'

By following the road up the left bank of the River Glass, to the N.W., for ¾ m. we reach the path leading to the **Black Rock of Novar**, an extraordinary ravine (c. 2 m. long) cut by the *Allt Graat* (' ugly burn '), which flows out of *Loch Glass* (4 m. long) on the northern flanks of Ben Wyvis. At one place the gorge is only 17 ft. wide, between verdant cliffs 110 ft. high. The finest view is from (c. 1¾ m.) the second bridge over the main stream.

A road on the left (A 836), 2 m. beyond Evanton, leads due N. to (20 m.) Bonar Bridge (see below), passing (8½ m.) *Aultnamain Hotel* (RB. 17/6, P. 7 gs.), and commanding splendid views.—The ' Indian temple ' crowning Knock Fyrish (1483 ft.) to the left above Evanton was put up by Gen. Sir Hector Munro (1726–1805), of *Novar House*, as an unemployment relief work.

At (31 m.) *Alness* (Station, Commercial, RB. 20/, P. 9½ gs.), where the disused 18th cent. kirk contains the Novar loft, the road crosses the River Alness, which descends from Loch Morie, 8 m. N.W.—34½ m. **Invergordon** (1510 inhab. ; *Royal*, RB. 21/6, P. 10 gs.), with a good harbour and a wide main street, is a sleepy place except when the Fleet sails north.

Ferry to the *Black Isle*, 6d., motor cycle, 1/6 ; motor-launch to *Cromarty*, thrice on weekdays, 1/3.

39 m. We pass the small round church-tower (1616) of *Kilmuir*, 1 m. E. of which is *Tarbat House* (Countess of Cromartie), built in 1787 on the site of one of the old castles of the Mackenzies, earls of Cromartie, a title forfeited after the rebellion of 1745 but restored in 1861. About ½ m. N.W. of (40 m.) *Kildary* is *Balnagown Castle*, in the 19th cent. baronial style, with a 16th cent. tower.

The road to the right just beyond the bridge leads to (5¾ m. S.E.) *Nigg* on the E. side of the sandy Nigg Bay. At the W. end of the parish church is a fine sculptured stone, representing two suppliant figures with dog-like animals beneath their outstretched hands. Above a chalice is the Dove bearing the wafer (scarcely discernible), and beneath is a typical cross—The ferry to Cromarty is at *Nigg Ferry* (Hotel, RB. 15/, plain), 2 m. S. (see p. 396).

Fearn, the centre of the farming district of Easter Ross, lies c. 5 m. N. of Nigg. The Premonstratensian *Abbey*, founded in 1221 by Farquhar, 1st earl of Ross, at

Edderton (10 m. N.W.), was removed hither in 1238 on account of the fertility of the soil. The young Patrick Hamilton, the earliest martyr of the Scottish Reformation (burnt at St. Andrews in 1528), was titular abbot, and at his death the abbey was annexed to the bishopric of Ross. The *Church* was used till 1742, when the roof fell in one Sunday, killing 44 persons. Subsequent repairs have been made without the slightest regard to architectural propriety. On the N. and S. are the ruined remains of small transeptal chapels. In the former S. chapel under a carved canopy is a much worn recumbent figure representing a lady of Clan Mackenzie. The E. end of the chancel is the burial-place of the Ross family. At *Hill of Fearn* (Inn), the village ½ m. W., Peter Fraser (1884–1950), Prime Minister of New Zealand from 1940 to 1949, was born and educated.

On the coast 2 m. E. is *Balintore* (Hotel, RB. 16/6, P. £7, plain) with a little harbour (salmon and herring fishing). Beyond *Shandwick*, ½ m. S., to the right of the road, stands an ancient and battered cross-slab, c. 9 ft. high, adorned with bosses and almost indistinguishable figures. A more famous stone (now in the Museum of Antiquities in Edinburgh) was found at *Hilton of Cadboll*, just N. of Balintore. Thence a path runs N. along the coast to (c. 8½ m.) *Tarbat Ness Lighthouse*. The road from Tarbat Ness to (13 m.) *Tain* passes (3 m. ; r.) the fishing village of *Portmahomack* (Caledonian, RB. 15/, P. 7 gs.).

The road soon turns N.W. and descends to *Dornoch Firth*, an arm of the sea running inland for c. 15 miles. Its entrance is impeded by a sandbank called the *Gizzen* or *Geysen Briggs*— a name of Norse origin—and in stormy weather the breaking of the waves may be heard at a considerable distance.

46½ m. **Tain** (*Royal*, RB. 22/6, P. 10 gs. ; *Mansefield House*, RB. 18/, P. 9 gs. ; *St. Duthus, Balnagown*, RB. 18/, P. 7 gs.) is a solidly built little town (1600 inhab.) whose importance has dwindled since it was made a royal burgh by James VI (1587). Its name is a corruption of the Norse ' Thing ' (assembly place). In the main street is the sturdy *Tolbooth* (rebuilt 1707–c. 27) with a conical spire and small pointed angle-turrets. Near it is the church of *St. Duthus* (1371), a fine Dec. building with beautiful E. window and good sedilia, made collegiate in 1487 under James III. The pulpit was presented by the Regent Moray. There is an excellent golf course on Morrich More, the expanse of sandy links to the N.E. of the town.

Between the town and the golf course, in the cemetery, stands a ruined ivy-clad *Chapel*, dedicated in the 13th cent. to St. Duthus or Dubhthaich (1000–65), bishop of Ross, a native of Tain, whose remains were translated from Armagh to this site in 1253. The queen and daughter of Robert Bruce, who had fled from Kildrummy Castle, were taken here by the Earl of Ross and handed over to Edward I (1307). James IV made a yearly pilgrimage hither from 1493 to 1513 as a penance for his treatment of his father (comp. p. 201), and in 1527 James V followed in his footsteps, at the instigation of Archbp. Beaton who wished him out of the way during the condemnation of Patrick Hamilton, a connection of the royal famliy.

Dornoch Cathedral now comes into view across the firth, only c. 5 m. from Tain as the crow flies ; but the road makes a detour of 26½ m. round the Dornoch Firth. Skibo Castle (see below) is likewise seen on the opposite shore.—Next is (52 m.) *Edderton* with an 18th cent. church and pulpit.— Skirting Struie Hill (1082 ft.), we are joined at 57 m. by the

direct road from Evanton viâ Aultnamain (see above).—
60½ m. *Ardgay* (pron. Ardguy), wth Bonar Bridge Station,
stands at the foot of *Strath Carron* (Braelangwell Lodge, 6 m.
W., P. from 35 gs. with fishing), which is ascended by pleasant
riverside roads.—61½ m. **Bonar Bridge** (*Bridge, Caledonian,*
RB. 20/, P. 9 gs. ; *Dunroamin,* RB. 16/6, P. 7 gs.) lies at the
head of the firth, in Sutherland. The bridge, built by Telford
in 1812 and rebuilt after a flood in 1892, spans the channel
between Dornoch Firth and the Kyle of Sutherland.

From Ardgay a road, and the railway, lead to (3 m.) *Culrain* station and (3½ m.)
the 'baronial' *Carbisdale Castle* (now a youth hostel), high above the Oykell.
Here Montrose made his final stand for Charles II in 1650. The road, now
narrower, goes on for 14 m. up the S. side of Strath Oykell, and pedestrians and
cyclists may cross the river to Rosehall, on the main road on the N. bank
(comp. Rte. 62A).—A mountain road (fine views) runs from Bonar Bridge past
(6 m.) *Loch Buidhe* (528 ft.) to (14 m.) The Mound (see below).

From Bonar Bridge to Lairg, 10 m., by road or railway.—
3½ m. *Invershin* (Hotel, at the station, RB. 19/6, P. 8½ gs.) is
picturesquely situated at the junction of the Shin and the
Oykell. To Lochinver by Strath Oykell, see Rte. 62A.
Carbisdale Castle is prominent opposite, and may be reached
by a private ferry. Road and railway (fine views) ascend the
left bank of the Shin, a good and early salmon river. There
is a power station at Inveran, 1 m. N., near the Strath Oykell
road.

10 m. **Lairg** (*Sutherland Arms,* RB. 25/, P. 12 gs.), situated
at the foot of *Loch Shin*, 2 m. N. of its station (motor-bus),
is a favourite and frequented centre for anglers, and is
important as the starting-point of the motor services to N.W.
Sutherland (see Rte. 62).

The river Shin is dammed c. ½ m. below the natural outlet of the loch ; but
the main dam of the Loch Shin hydro-electric scheme crosses the 'narrows' of
the loch c. 1 m. N.W., near the 'Little Loch' between the dams serving as a reservoir.
Beyond Lairg the railway rises steeply to the E. and crosses the watershed into
Strath Fleet. The road which follows it is served by a motor-bus to Golspie (1 hr.).
Beyond (10 m.) *Rogart* (whence a moorland road runs N. and E. to Brora) we
enjoy a view of Loch Fleet, and regain the coast at (14 m.) *The Mound.* Near
Rogart the gardens of *Blarich* and of *Rovie Lodge* are open 2–6 on Sun. in August.

From Bonar Bridge the main road skirts the N. shore of
the firth to (64½ m.) *Creich* ; on the promontory (r.) is *Dun
Creich,* a vitrified fort. The road goes on through beautiful
oak woods and as we pass a ruined old mill at (67 m.) *Spin-
ningdale* (Inn) we have a fine view across the firth.—On the
roadside (r.), opposite (69 m.) *Ospisdale House,* a large stone
column is said to commemorate the death in battle of a
Danish chief named Ospis.—70½ m. *Skibo Castle,* on the right,
belonged successively to the bishops of Caithness, the Mackays, the Dempsters, and to Andrew Carnegie (p. 252), who

spent large sums on the property. At (73 m.) *Milltown of Evelix* the Dornoch road bears to the right.

---

75 m. **DORNOCH** (*Dornoch*, June–Sept., RB. 29/–48/, P. 14½–19 gs. ; *Royal Golf, Burghfield House*, at both, RB. from 24/, P. 10–14 gs. ; *Dornoch Castle*, RB. 21/6–27/6, P. 8–13 gs., Apr.–Oct., in the former episcopal castle), notwithstanding its small population (800), is the county town of Sutherland and a royal burgh with spacious squares. Once the seat of the bishop of Caithness, it still has the prim look of a small cathedral town. The magnificent golf course, reputed in the 17th cent. to surpass even that of St. Andrews, and the wide bathing-sands attract many visitors. Dornoch is distinguished as the scene of the last judicial execution for witchcraft in Scotland (1722), when an old woman was burnt for transforming her daughter into a pony and having her shod by the devil. A plaque in the cathedral commemorates the Norwegian Brigade, who trained at Dornoch in 1942.

The once formidable Castle of the bishops, of which the high tower alone remains, was destroyed in 1570 by the Master of Caithness and Mackay of Strathnaver, who, taking advantage of the minority of Alexander, Earl of Sutherland, plundered the city at the same time. It now serves as a hotel.

The **Cathedral,** conspicuous by its high roof, low tower, and stunted spire, was begun c. 1224 by Bp. Gilbert de Moravia, though established c. 1150 on the probable site of a Celtic foundation. Much damaged in 1570 and neglected afterwards, the church was too drastically refashioned and the nave rebuilt by Wm. Burn in 1835–37 for the Duchess of Sutherland. A happier restoration took place in 1924 when the removal of plaster revealed the 13th cent. stonework of the crossing, the choir, and the E. sides of the transepts. The windows are single lancets except at the W. end, where the five-light window is a good copy of a type common in this part of Scotland. Sixteen earls of Sutherland are said to lie in the cathedral. At the W. end are a statue of the 1st Duke of Sutherland (d. 1833), by Chantrey, and the mutilated effigy of Sir Richard de Moravia, brother of the founder, killed in battle against the Danes at *Embo*, 2 m. N., where a large stone is supposed to commemorate the event.

A 9 runs N., through woods, to Loch Fleet, a landlocked arm of the sea. At its head is (80 m.) *The Mound,* named after an embankment 1000 yds. long by which a part of Loch Fleet was reclaimed. It was raised by Telford in 1815 at a cost of £9600 and carries the road and the railway to Dornoch.

Beyond The Mound railway and road approach the sea beneath the slopes of Ben Lundie (1462 ft.) and Ben Vraggie (1256 ft.). On the latter stands a colossal statue, by Chantrey, of the 1st Duke of Sutherland.—85 m. **Golspie** (*Sutherland Arms*, RB. 23/, P. 10 gs. ; *Stag's Head*, RB. 18/6, P. 9 gs. ; *Ben Bh'Raggie*, RB. 16/6, P. 8 gs.), an attractive village of one long street, partly built of red sandstone, has a good golf course and fine sands. The 18th cent. *Church* contains the splendid Sutherland loft and canopied pulpit of 1738.

To the N.E. (c. 1 m.), by a pleasant walk crossing the Golspie Burn, whose old bridge bears an inscription concerning ' Morfhear Chatt,' i.e. the head of the Sutherlands, is **Dunrobin Castle,** the magnificent seat of the Duke of Sutherland (adm. 2/6 ; weekdays 2–5 in July & Aug.). The castle, on a natural terrace close to the sea, consisted originally of a square keep with angle-turrets, built by Robert, 2nd Earl of Sutherland, c. 1275, and called Dun Robin after him. Enlarged in the Scottish baronial style by Sir Chas. Barry in 1844–48, it was altered in 1921 by Sir Robt. Lorimer ; among the contents are pictures by Canaletto, Romney, Lawrence, and Ramsay, as well as Mortlake tapestries.

Motor-Bus on weekdays from Golspie to *Lairg* (1 hr.) and *Bettyhill* (4 hrs.).

The road between Golspie and Helmsdale never strays far from the sea, over which we have magnificent views to the Moray coast. On the left is the private station for *Dunrobin*, opposite the castle, with a statue of the 2nd Duke of Sutherland. About a mile farther on we pass a ruined broch, on the right.—90 m. **Brora** (*Links*, *Royal Marine*, RB. from 25/, P. 12 gs. ; *Sutherland Arms*, RB. 21/, P. 10 gs.), on the salmon river of the same name, is a large and scattered village (1075 inhab.). It attracts sea-bathers in summer and offers also good angling and good golf. A small coal deposit here has been worked at intervals since the 16th century.

In the wild upper part of *Strath Brora* is *Loch Brora*, 4 m. long, skirted by a road to Rogart. On the W. side of the loch rises the picturesque *Carrol Rock*, a cliff 684 ft. high (5 m. from Brora), and the neighbourhood abounds in ruined brochs.

93 m. On the right is a large *Broch, 31 ft. in diameter inside, with domed chambers in the wall and outworks covering an entrance-passage, and c. 2 m. farther on is Glen Loth, where the last Scottish wolf was killed c. 1700 (memorial).—Passing (99 m.) the village of *Portgower* we reach (101 m.) **Helmsdale** (*Bridge*, RB. 20/, P. 10 gs. ; *Navidale House*, 1 m. N.E., RB. 15/–20/, P. 10 gs. ; *Belgrave Arms*, RB. 17/6, P. 9 gs.), a grey-built fishing village with a tiny harbour, at the foot of Strath Ullie. The ruined castle, built by the 7th Countess of Sutherland in 1488, was the scene of the murder of the 11th earl and his countess in 1567 at the instigation of George Sinclair, Earl of Caithness. The main coast road onward affords splendid views, but is very severe for the first 20 miles.

From Helmsdale to Thurso by Road, 54 m. The road (A 897), following the railway for 24 m., ascends *Strath Ullie*, where cultivation gradually gives place to moor. Beyond (9 m.) *Kildonan* we pass Suisgill Lodge, with its beautiful flower-garden bordering the road, and then (11½ m.) the *Suisgill Burn*, the principal scene of the 'Sutherland gold-diggings' of 1868–69. Remains of brochs are seen on both sides of the road as we proceed, and ahead, in the distance, appear the twin peaks of Ben Griam (1936 and 1903 ft.) with Ben Loyal (2504 ft.) behind.—17 m. **Kinbrace** (*Garvault*, RB. 16/, P. 8 gs.) is the junction of a road to Bettyhill (see below).—20 m. *Loch-an-Ruar*.—At (24 m.) Forsinard road and railway part, the railway traversing some 20 m. of boggy moorland to the N.E. We begin to descend the green and well-cultivated *Strath Halladale*, the former boundary between the Mackay's territory and that of the Earl of Sutherland. On the right, by an old mill beyond the bold rock called Craigtown, diverges the pretty gorge of the Smigel Burn.—At 38 m. we join the road from Thurso to Tongue (r. for Thurso l. for Tongue).—54 m. *Thurso*, p. 410.

From Kinbrace a motor-bus (in connection with trains) runs to Bettyhill (29 m. in 2 hrs.), first crossing an uninhabitated moorland with fine views (l.) of the lochs that feed the Helmsdale river, with Ben Armin and Ben Clibreck behind them.—At (16½ m.) Syre Bridge we reach the beautiful *Strath Naver*, a valley largely depopulated in 1810–20, and join the road from Altnaharra—18½ m. *Skail Hotel* (unlic., RB. 12/6, P. 110/). About 2 m. farther is a large stone circle, and in 1½ m. more, near the mouth of a burn, is a well-preserved broch.—23 m. Beyond the river (r.) is the small *Loch-ma-Naire*, believed to possess marvellous healing powers.—26 m. We join the main Thurso–Tongue road 3 m. S. of Betty-hill (see Rte. 64).

Leaving Helmsdale we enter *Navidale* and ascend a long hill, winding round ravine after ravine. We reach (105 m.) a plateau (750 ft.) which ends towards the sea in the bold and rocky *Ord of Caithness*, the S. boundary of the Caithness coast, commanding a magnificent view. It has been considered unlucky for a Sinclair to cross the Ord on a Monday ever since a large party of the clan passed it on that day on their way to Flodden, whence none of them returned.

Caithness, though the most northerly county of the Scottish mainland, with the famous John o' Groats House at its N. end, is not a Highland county, but is ' lowland ' both in natural features and customs, and Gaelic is scarcely spoken at all within it. One-third of the surface is bog, but there is a wide strip of fertile ground bordering the bold and rocky coast. The Norse invasion of the 10th cent. is recalled by many place names ending in -ster, -dale, or -goe, and by numerous Danish barrows and other antiquities. Wick, with its fishing industry, and Thurso are the chief towns. Most of Caithness has since the 15th cent. been in the hands of the family of Sinclair, and the Gunns, Keiths, and Sutherlands have likewise played a part in the restless annals of the county. Characteristic features are the neat cottages and the field-boundaries of Caithness flags.

An abrupt descent brings us to (111 m.) *Berriedale*, where two wooded valleys, a rare sight in Caithness, unite before their waters fall into the sea beside the ruins of Berriedale Castle, an old fortress of the Earls of Caithness. On the left rise the steep conical mountains of *Scaraben* (2054 ft. ; 4 m. N.W.) and *Morven* (2313 ft. ; 8 m. N.W.), the latter a familiar landmark all over Caithness.—Beyond Berriedale, we ascend a long hill and command a fine view of the bare table-land, which, with the peaks mentioned above, characterises S. Caithness. About 1 m. short of (117 m.) **Dunbeath** (*Dunbeath*, RB. 17/6, P. 7 gs. ; *Inver Guest House*, unlic., RB. 17/6, P. 100/) we pass *Dunbeath Castle*, whose 15th cent. keep (enlarged c. 1870) was captured for Montrose in 1650. The Duke of Kent (1902–42) lost his life in an air accident on Aug. 25th, 1942, at the Eagle's Rock, above *Braemore*, 6½ m. W. of Dunbeath by hill-road (monument).—120 m. *Latheronwheel*, with a picturesque harbour (r.).—At (121 m.) *Latheron* is an old tower, in which the church bells formerly hung.

A road runs hence viâ (18 m.) *Georgemas* to (23½ m.) Thurso, passing (c. 5 m.) near a stone circle (1 m. along the by-road, r., at *Achavanich*).

Beyond (121¼ m.) *Forse*, where a strongly-built village of the 1st–2nd cent. A.D., called ' The Wag,' has been excavated, we reach (124 m.) **Lybster** (*Portland Arms*, RB. 21/, P. 8 gs.), a fishing village of some importance. The road keeps a little distance from the rocky coast, traversing a crofting district with one or two highly cultivated farms. At (130 m.) *Whaligoe* is a fine example of the inlets in the Old Red Sandstone so numerous on this coast.—From (134½ m.) *Hempriggs Loch* we may discern Duncansby Head to the N. and the distant Orkneys, with the lofty cliffs of Hoy.

137 m. **WICK**, from the Norse *Vik*, a bay, an important fishing town (7160 inhab.) at the head of Wick Bay, is the county town of Caithness and is mentioned in the Sagas as early as 1140. It became a royal burgh in 1589.

Hotels. Mackay's, RB. 18/6, P. 8 gs.; **Rosebank,** RB. 17/6, P. 7 gs. ; **Nethercliffe,** RB. 18/6, P. 8 gs.

Motor-Buses to *Thurso* viâ Castletown (1 hr.) and viâ Halkirk (65 min.) ; to *John o' Groats* (¾ hr.) and *Dunnet* (1½ hr.) ; to *Lybster* (40 min.) and

Helmsdale (2 hrs.).—AIR SERVICES to *Orkney, Shetland, Aberdeen,* and *Inverness* from the airport, 1 m. N.

Golf Course at Reiss, 3 m. N.— *Swimming Pools* on both the N. and S. sides of the bay.

At the season of the HERRING FISHERY (mid July–mid Sept.) Wick is crowded by a large influx of fishermen, fish-curers, and gutters. The harbour is then surrounded by wooden erections containing troughs where the herring are gutted before being thrown into the salting boxes. The rapidity with which the rows of women perform this task is almost incredible. At the close of the Northern curing season large numbers of the women migrate temporarily to the English E. coast fishing ports.

The *Harbour*, on which enormous sums have been spent without conspicuous success, can be entered by large steamers at high water only. R. L. Stevenson was employed on its improvement in 1868, but found the life of an engineer too strenuous for his health.

The old town of Wick, N. of the river, with the narrow winding High Street, and the wider Bridge Street, is the chief shopping centre. The Parish Church (1830), at the W. end of High Street, is adjoined by the *Sinclair Aisle*, the burial-place of the earls of Caithness, a relic of an older building. In Bridge St. is the quaint *Town Hall* with its cupola ; and in the *Library and Museum* is preserved the tomb of a Benedictine (late 15th cent.) from the old church. To the S.E., across the bridge, lies *Pulteneytown*, a harbour suburb laid out by Telford in 1808 for the British Fisheries Society.

There is fine CLIFF SCENERY both N. and S. of Wick. To the S. " the waves have quarried out masses of flagstone and piled them up in huge heaps on the top of the cliffs, 60 or 100 ft. above high water " ; these ridges once extended far into the fields above the cliffs.—About 1½ m. S. is a windowless square tower (14th cent.) of the Cheynes, named *The Castle of Old Wick*. It was taken by the Master of Caithness in 1569. Beyond is a stack connected with the mainland by a natural arch called the *Brig o' Tram*, and farther S. is a large flat-topped stack called *The Brough*, with a tunnel through it.

On the cliffs of *Noss Head* (3 m. N.) is a lighthouse, and ½ m. W., on the shore of *Sinclair's Bay*, are the ruins of *Castle Girnigoe*, with those of *Castle Sinclair* beside it. In 1672 the Earl of Caithness sold his estates to Campbell of Glenorchy, but Sinclair of Keiss disputed the sale. Glenorchy then invaded the territory and laid siege to Girnigoe, an expedition to which the song ' The Campbells are coming ' is said to refer.—Still farther W. (2½ m. from Wick) is *Ackergill Tower*, 65 ft. high, with square turrets at the angles, formerly a seat of the Earls Marischal. Beyond lie the golf-links and bathing-beach of *Reiss*.

FROM WICK TO THURSO (21 m.) there are several routes. The most direct road (A 882) follows the S. side of the Wick Water to (8½ m.) **Watten** (*Guest House*, unlic., RB. 15/, P. 7 gs., with fishing), a particularly neat Caithness village with an ancient meal-mill. *Loch Watten* (r.), 3½ m. long by ½ m. broad, is noted for its trout. We cross the railway (13¾ m.) a little N.E. of *Georgemas Junction* where the Wick and Thurso lines separate ; then join the road from Latheron (see above), and (15 m.) pass 1½ m. E. of *Halkirk* (Ulbster Arms, RB. 20/, P. 10 gs.), a village laid out in squares. On the opposite bank of the Thurso River is *Braal Castle*, a three-storied tower, once moated, with a modern house adjoining.—21 m. *Thurso*, see Rte. 63.

A more northerly route (B 876), viâ Reiss and Castletown, traverses the parish of *Bower*, a typically well-tilled area, and passes (12 m.) *Thura Inn*, an old coaching-house.—16 m. *Castletown* and thence to (21 m.) *Thurso*, see Rte. 63.

From Wick to *John o' Groats* and *Dunnet*, see Rte. 63.

62. SUTHERLAND

Sutherland, the 'south land,' a county occupying the N.W. angle of Scotland and extending from Dornoch to Cape Wrath, is named from the point of view of the Norsemen of Caithness, who overran it in the 11th cent. and held it for about a hundred years. Apart from a certain number of more or less fertile straths and glens, it is mainly a stern and mountainous land of heath and bog, of treeless deer forests and barren grouse-moors, and it has a larger proportion of its surfaced covered by water than any other Scottish county. It is also the most sparsely peopled county. At the 'Sutherland Clearances' of 1810–20, denounced by Hugh Miller but not entirely indefensible, about 15,000 peasants were removed from the interior to crofts and allotments on the coast, with the alternative of emigration. Since then much has been done for the crofters by the dukes of Sutherland, the principal landowners (earls since 1228, dukes since 1833). The county gave name to the Sutherland Highlanders or 93rd Foot (a regiment now united with the Argylls), who won fame as the 'Thin Red Line' at Balaclava.

A. From Lairg or Invershin to Lochinver via Loch Assynt

From Lairg, 46 m. MOTOR-BUS every weekday in 2¾ hrs. leaving Lairg at 1.45 p.m. and Lochinver at 8.15 a.m.

From Lairg the road (A 839) runs S.W. over a high dreary moor to (9 m.) *Rosehall* (Achness House, RB. 19/, P. 9 gs.), before which we are joined by the road (A 837) coming from Invershin up the N. bank of the Oykell. We cross the Cassley 1 m. above its junction with the Oykell, the boundary between Ross and Sutherland.—11½ m. *Tutim* or *Tuiteam-Tarbhach* ('fertile fall of slaughter') was the scene (c. 1397) of a battle between the MacLeods of Assynt and Lewis and the Mackays of Sutherland. Only one of the MacLeods returned to Lewis, and he died of his wounds.—We traverse the most charming part of *Strath Oykell*, whose slopes are wooded with birch, oak, and wych elm. The river is crossed at (15 m.) *Oykell Bridge* (Balnagown Arms, for fishing and deer-stalking).

As we ascend the glen, gradually rising higher above the Oykell, Canisp (see below) comes into view in front; and to the right of it is Breabag (2670 ft.), one of the outliers of Ben More Assynt (see below), itself seen still farther to the right. Beyond (21 m.) *Loch Craggie* a group of singular isolated peaks of Torridon sandstone rising above a platform of pre-Cambrian gneiss stands out in most impressive grandeur:—*Coulbeg* (2523 ft. ; l.), *Stack Polly* (2009 ft.), *Coulmore* (2786 ft.), *Suilven* (2399 ft.), known to sailors as the 'Sugar-loaf,' and *Canisp* (2779 ft. ; r.). At 23 m. just beyond the water-shed (536 ft.) a road diverging r. crosses the Oykell below *Loch Ailsh,* at the N. end of which is *Benmore Lodge Hotel* (May–Oct. ; P. 20 gs. incl. shooting and fishing).—25 m. *Altnacealgach Hotel* (RB. 20/, P. 10 gs.) is on the N.E. side of *Loch Borrolan.*

The name, signifying ' the cheat's burn,' is said to have arisen from a dispute which took place here about the boundary of the two counties (Sutherland, W. ; Ross, E.), some witnesses having sworn that they were standing on Ross-shire ground because they had filled their shoes with earth from the Balnagown estate in that county.

The country around (27 m.) *Ledmore,* whence a road runs S.W. to Ullapool (p. 376), is a network of lochs and rivers.—The little *Loch Awe* (29½ m. ; l.) has a number of small wooded islets, one with ruins of a fort. The road descends by the side of the Loanan, leaving on the right *Allt-nan-Uamh,* with its curious caves, and then the prominent limestone cliffs of Stronchrubie.—33 m. *Inchnadamph* (Hotel, RB. 21/, P. 11 gs.), in a sheltered corner at the E. end of **Loch Assynt,** is noted for rare plants and ferns, and the fine loch, c. 7 m. long, owes much of the diversity of its scenery to the variety of the rocks which surround it.

34¼ m. *Ardvreck Castle* is a ruin of three stories built c. 1490 by the MacLeods, who in the mid-13th cent. obtained Assynt by marriage. The Marquess of Montrose, who after his defeat at Culrain in 1650 had fled to the wilds of Assynt but was soon captured, was confined at Ardvreck for a short time, before being sent to Skibo and thence to Edinburgh. Near Ardvreck are the ruins of *Calda* or *Edderchalder House,* a 17th cent. mansion built by the Mackenzies, destroyed by fire.—From (35 m.) *Skiag Bridge* a road runs N. to (6¾ m.) Kylesku Ferry and (19 m.) *Scourie* (see below).—We now come into full view of the saw-like edge of Quinaig, before curving round the W. end of Loch Assynt. After passing (39½ m.) the beautiful little *Loch Letteressie,* on the right, we follow the turbulent River Inver in its rapid descent to the sea.—46 m. **Lochinver** (*Culag,* RB. 25/, P. 11 gs.), a village lying around the head of the sea-loch of the same name, commands fine views over the Minch (here c. 35 m. wide) to Lewis.

Ascent of Suilven. The road running S. from Lochinver towards *Ullapool* (see p. 376) passes (½ m.) the charming little *Loch Culag.* From (2½ m.) *Inver-kirkaig* a path leads for c. 2 m. up the right bank of the Kirkaig to a point where the river plunges down 60 ft. into a dark abyss. Another ½ m. brings us to *Loch Fewin,* skirting whose W. and N. sides we arrive at the S. slopes of **Suilven** (2399 ft.), which by reason of its sugar-loaf form affords a most remarkable *View. In the distance out at sea are Lewis and Harris, and at the foot of the mountain are innumerable lochs, large and small.—For an alternative ascent, equally steep, we follow the road running E. from Lochinver to (1½ m.) *Glencanisp Lodge,* whence a path goes on up the N. bank of a stream, crossing it at (3 m.) a foot-bridge. The ascent thence of the N.E. slopes of Suilven leads through a labyrinth of small lochs.

From Lochinver to Scourie. A. Viâ Loch Assynt and the Skiag Burn,

30 m., see below.—B. The coast route (34 m. ; motor daily as far as Drumbeg) strikes N.W. from the Loch Assynt road ½ m. after crossing the Inver and leaves on the left the road to *Achmelvich* youth hostel.—4½ m. *Loch-an-Ordain* (' the hammer loch '), on the right, has a curious echo. Shortly afterwards we cross a stream which has on its right bank, not far from the sea, a very primitive corn-mill.—Beyond (7 m.) *Stoer* church *Cnoc Poll* (352 ft.), a hill commanding a very fine panoramic view, rises between us and the sea. We cut across the base of the promontory ending in the Point of Stoer, and regain the coast at (9 m.) *Clashnessie Bay*, whence the road runs E. along the S. side of *Eddrachillis Bay* to (14 m.) *Drumbeg* (Hotel, RB. 18/6, P. 8½ gs.), with fine views N. towards Handa. The road, after skirting the heads of Loch Nedd and Loch Ardvar and the S. shore of *Loch Cairnbawn*, which served as a submarine base in 1939–45, joins the Loch Assynt road 1½ m. short of (23 m.) *Kylesku Inn* at the ferry. Thence to (34 m.) *Scourie*, see below.

B. From Lairg to Scourie and Durness

56 m. MOTOR-BUS to (44 m.) *Scourie* on weekdays in 2¾ hrs., leaving Lairg at 1.45 and returning from Scourie at 8 a.m. A bus in connection runs between (37 m.) *Laxford Bridge* (see below) and (56 m.) *Durness* (3½ hrs. from Lairg) ; another runs from (41½ m.) *Rhiconich* to (45¼ m.) *Kinlochbervie* (3 hrs. from Lairg), and (48½ m.) *Balchrick*.

From Lairg the road (A 838) runs N.W. by the side of **Loch Shin** (16½ m. long by c. ½ m. broad), now a hydro-electric reservoir. This, the largest loch in Sutherland, offers good angling, but the surrounding moors are not very interesting. Towards the upper end, however, the landscape is commanded by *Ben More Assynt* (W. ; 3273 ft.), *Ben Leod* (ahead ; 2597 ft.), and *Ben Hee* (N. ; 2864 ft.).—16 m. *Overscaig* (Hotel, RB. 20/, P. 10 gs.) is opposite the Cassley power-station. Beyond (17 m.) the head of the loch the road, fringed with pleasant woods of dwarf birch, is carried along the banks of *Loch Griam* (now united with Loch Shin), *Loch Merkland*, and *Loch More*, beneath *Meallan Liath* (2625 ft.), where draining and afforestation are in progress.—On the W. side of (32 m.) *Loch Stack*, in which sea-trout abound, is *Ben Stack* (2364 ft.), which rears an abrupt peak of pre-Cambrian gneiss capped with Cambrian quartzite. To the N. rise *Arkle* (2580 ft.) and beyond it *Foinaven* (2980 ft.), in the great Reay Deer Forest. The road runs beside the Laxford, a noted salmon river whose name signifies ' salmon river ' in the Norse tongue. At (37 m.) *Laxford Bridge* our road strikes S.W. for (44 m.) **Scourie** (*Hotel*, good, RB. 25/, P. 12 gs., with fishing ; *Sea View*, unlic., P. 8 gs.), a small village between Loch Baddidarroch and Scourie Bay (*View from the rising ground, 1 m. S.).

About 2 m. N.W. and ½ m. from the shore is the island of **Handa**, 4½ m. round, whose N.W. side rises in a range of indented and irregular cliffs 400 feet high. The emerald water in the caves contrasts beautifully with the warm red Torridonian sandstone. When the sea is smooth a small boat from the lobster-fishing hamlet of Tarbet (round the island c. 30/ ; motor-boat excursions often arranged at lower rates) may be taken close in (landing on the S. side). On the narrow ledges of the cliffs during the breeding season (May to July), myriads of guillemots, puffins, and razorbills sit on their eggs ; they are remarkably tame and the island is preserved as a sanctuary for sea-fowl.—Handa is sufficiently far from the coast to command magnificent views of the mountains. " To the S. a detached pillar or rock, from 200 to 300 ft. high, at the point of Rhu Stoer, looks in the distance exactly like a large ship under studding-sails."

FROM SCOURIE TO LOCHINVER viâ LOCH ASSYNT, 30 m. S.E. As the road approaches (2½ m.) *Badcall Bay* (Caladh House, unlic., P. 150/; youth hostel), we see Ben Stack to the E. and soon have a charming view (r.) over *Eddrachillis Bay* and its 24 islets, bounded on the S.W. by the distant line of coast ending in the Point of Stoer. We cross several steep hills and pass numerous small lochs, whose dark still waters give an appearance of great depth.—11 m. *Kyle Strome* is at the N. end of **Kylesku Ferry** (¼ m.; free) across the upper part of *Loch Cairnbawn*, which above the ferry divides into two branches :—*Loch Glendhu* (E.) and *Loch Glencoul* (S.E.). The scenery around both lochs is wild and gloomy and 1½ m. above the head of Loch Glencoul (S. side) is *Eas Coul Aulin*, a waterfall c. 600 ft. high, the highest in Britain. Near the ferry, on a tidal island, are the remains of a broch, c. 8 ft. high.

At the S. end of the ferry is *Kylesku Inn* (RB. 15/, P. 140/, simple), ½ m. from the crofts of *Unapool*. The road climbs steeply and after 1 m. leaves the coast road to Lochinver on the right. We cross (16¾ m.) the pass (813 ft.; *View) between the pointed *Quinaig* (2653 ft.) and *Glasven* (2541 ft.) and descend steeply to (19 m.) *Skiag Bridge* on Loch Assynt, 2 m. N.W. of Inchnadamph. Thence to (30 m.) *Lochinver*, see above.

The ROAD TO DURNESS from Laxford Bridge crosses the bridge, ascends steeply to the head of *Loch Laxford*, and turns N. through rough country, too much encumbered by ponderous masses of gneiss to afford many distant views, though at every turn the winding road discloses some fresh feature. Perched boulders left by ancient glaciers are very numerous. At the head of the croft-surrounded *Loch Inchard* is (41½ m.) *Rhiconich* (Hotel, RB, 21/, P. 8 gs.), and at the head of the glen to the right we see the finely curved outline of the isolated *Arkle* (Arcuil; 2580 ft.), with *Foinaven* (Foinne Bheinn; 2980 ft.) to the left.

At Rhiconich passengers change buses for **Kinlochbervie** (Garbet, RB. 22/6, P. 12 gs.), 3¾ m. N.W. at the mouth of Loch Inchard, developed since 1947 as a landing-port for herring and whitefish. The bus goes on to (7 m.) *Balchrick*, whence walkers may follow the uninhabited coast for 4½ m. N. to the beautiful *Sandwood Bay* off which are the islet of *Bulgach* and, near inshore, the solitary stack called *Am Buachaille* (' The Shepherd ').

The Durness road ascends the Achriesgill Water, crossing it after 2½ m. by a bridge from which we gain a good view backward.—46 m. *Gualan House*, near the road-summit (596 ft.), once a travellers' refuge, is now a shooting-lodge. The ' Gualan ' (' shoulder '), over which the road is carried, sinks into the wide and desolate Strath Dionard, bounded on the E. by the twin peaks of *Cranstackie* (Grann Stacach; 2630 ft.) and *Ben Spionnaidh* (2537 ft.). The road crosses (50½ m.) the Dionard and descends beside it to the E. shore of the shallow Kyle of Durness, a sea-loch.—From (54 m.) *Keoldale* we trend N.E.—56 m. **Durness**, see Rte. 64.

C. From Lairg to Tongue and Bettyhill

MOTOR-BUS every weekday, leaving Lairg at 1.45 p.m., to (37 m.) *Tongue*, in 2¼ hrs., going on viâ (45 m.) *Skerray* to (55 m. in 3½ hrs.) *Bettyhill*.

Lairg, see p. 399. The road (A 836) runs N. for 2 m. near *Loch Shin* (p. 406) and then diverges to the right from the Scourie road, up the desolate *Strath Tirry*. At (12 m.) *Crask Inn* (RB. 13/6, P. 6½ gs.) we cross the Tirry. The flat-topped hill on the left is named Lord Reay's Green Table. At (13 m.) *The Crask* (828 ft.) we cross the watershed, and thence descend *Strath Bagastie*. *Ben Clibreck* (Cleith Bric; 3154 ft.) stands up boldly on our right.—21 m. *Altnaharra* (Hotel, RB. 25/, P. 12 gs.), at the head of *Loch Naver* (6 m. long), is a bleak spot much frequented by anglers.

The direct road hence to (24½ m.) Bettyhill skirts the attractive N. shore of Loch Naver, and from its E. end descends the sombre *Strath Naver*, the lower part of which is traversed by the bus from Kinbrace to Bettyhill.

The rough road running W. from Altnaharra ascends Mudale to the watershed at (6 m.) *Loch-na-Meadie*, then descends, with views of Ben Hope, into *Strath More*, a steep-sided valley, with a lawn of smooth velvety turf at the bottom, running S. from the conical *Ben Hee* (2864 ft.). Beyond (11 m.) *Dun Dornadilla*, a well-preserved broch c. 150 ft. round, we reach *Allt-na-Cailleach* (the old woman's burn) with a magnificent waterfall, at the foot of which was born Robert Mackay, known as Rob Donn (1740–78), the Reay Forest bard. At the derelict farm of *Muiseal*, 1¼ m. farther, begins the best ascent of *Ben Hope* (3040 ft.), the most northerly 3000-ft. peak in Scotland, noted for alpine flowers and ptarmigan. Leaving a hill-track to Eriboll on the left, we skirt the E. shore of *Loch Hope* (6 m. long) and join A 838 at (20 m.) *Hope Lodge* (p. 412).

Beyond Altnaharra the road traverses a dreary moorland (732 ft.) and then descends to (27 m.) the W. shore of *Loch Loyal*, a beautiful sheet of water, which, with its continuation *Loch Creagach*, is 7 m. long. To the W. is the huge granite mass of *Ben Loyal* (2504 ft.), terminating in four colossal splintered peaks.—After another rise we descend (*View) to (37 m.) **Tongue,** on the E. slopes of the shallow Kyle of Tongue, which runs in from the sea. Thence to *Bettyhill*, see Rte. 64.

63. FROM WICK TO THURSO VIA JOHN O' GROATS

36 m. MOTOR-BUS twice on Tues., Thurs., and Sat. in c. 2 hrs. ; to *John o' Groats* in ¾ hr. Also on Sun. afternoon from Wick and from Thurso to John o' Groats.

The road (A 9) runs N. from Wick keeping some distance from the shore of *Sinclair's Bay* and traversing a district that in former days was the scene of much strife among the Sinclairs, the Sutherlands, the Keiths, and the Gunns.—At (3 m.) *Reiss* we diverge (r.) from the road to Castletown and Thurso.—5½ m. We cross the Wester Water as it issues from the *Loch of Wester*, and traverse the wide links of Keiss.— 8 m. *Keiss Castle* is near the ruins of its predecessor, which stood on a rock jutting out into the sea. To the left of the road farther on is a Baptist chapel erected in memory of Sir Wm. Sinclair, founder and pastor of the first Baptist Church in Scotland (1750).—We pass on the right (11 m.) the ruins of *Bucholy Castle* (c. 1155), which belonged to the Mowats.— Beyond (13 m.) *Freswick* and (13½ m.) a road diverging on the left for Mey (6 m.), our road crosses *Warth Hill* (412 ft. ; *View of the Orkneys).

17 m. **John o' Groats** (*John o' Groats House*, RB. 20/, P. 8 gs. ; *Seaview*, RB. 17/6, P. 7 gs.), on a sandy shore, though not the northernmost point of the mainland (Dunnet Head, see below, is that) is the usual terminus of ' end to end ' races, etc., either within Scotland (Maiden Kirk to John o' Groats, 280 m.) or including the whole length of Great Britain (Land's End to John o' Groats, 876 m.). Several houses (including a tea-house) have latterly been built, and it is a resort of excursionists (especially on Sun.) from the surrounding country. Small shells, known as ' groatie buckies,' are found on the beach.

A mound marked by a flagstaff close to the hotel occupies the site of the original house, which is said to have been built for an annual family meeting in memory of John de Groot, a Dutchman who settled in Scotland in the reign of James IV. Legend relates that to avoid disputes as to precedence among John's eight descendants, who were joint owners of the land, the house was octagonal, with eight doors, and contained an octagonal table ; so that each man entered by his own door and sat at the head of the table. An ingenious explanation of the story suggests that John worked a ferry to Orkney and built a shelter for his customers, with eight recesses to protect them from the wind at any angle.

The *View hence of *Stroma*, a small island which was swept by the sea in a storm in 1862, and of South Ronaldsay and the cliffs of Hoy is magnificent.

A road runs E. and ascends to the lighthouse on (2 m.) **Duncansby Head** (210 ft.), the *Virvedrum* of Ptolemy, the N.E. promontory of Scotland, which commands a fine view of the Orkneys, the Pentland Skerries, and the headlands of the E. coast. To the N., at the entrance to the Pentland Firth, are the *Boars of Duncansby*, a reef whose name suggests the force and fierceness of the sea (comp. below). A little to the S. of the cape the three *Stacks of Duncansby* stand like obelisks in the sea, and the sandstone cliffs are severed by tremendous gashes running up into the land and exhibiting on each side a clean fracture of the horizontal strata. One of these ' goes ' is bridged by a natural arch.

The road (B 876) from John o' Groats, running W. to Thurso, passes (19 m.) *Huna*, the boat-station for the island of Stroma (2 m. ; see above), and (20 m.) the large white church of *Canisbay* (16th–17th cent.), the most northerly on the Scottish mainland. On its S. end is a tombstone with a large cross recording the death of Donald Grot, son of John Grot, in 1568.—The road ascends Mey Hill (212 ft.) to the N. of which a line of breakers marks the deadly reef called the *Merry Men of Mey* ; when the ebb tide meets a W. wind the surface is covered with foam, though all around is still and clear. To the N. of (24 m.) *Mey* is *Barrogill Castle* (c. 1570 ; restored), once a seat of the earls of Caithness, but purchased in 1952 by Queen Elizabeth, the Queen Mother, and named *Castle of Mey*.—We pass *St. John's Loch* (r.) as we approach (28 m.) **Dunnet** (*Northern Sands*, RB. 23/, **P.** from 9 gs.), with its fine sandy beach. Here Timothy Pont, the topographer, was minister in 1601–8 in the characteristic old church with its saddleback tower.

Dunnet Head (4 m. N.E. by a good road), a bold promontory of sandstone, is the northernmost point of the Scottish mainland, and affords a magnificent *View across the Pentland Firth of the Orkneys and of a great part of the N. coast, and, inland, of Ben Loyal, Ben Hope, etc. The windows of the lighthouse (346 ft. high) are said to be sometimes broken by stones hurled up by the sea.

The **Pentland Firth** (properly *Petland* or *Pictland*), the channel 6½–8 m. wide separating Scotland from the Orkneys, is celebrated for its fast-flowing tides (6–10 knots) and its treacherous currents. When the tide is flowing the main current sets from W. to E., changing direction at the ebb, but the coast currents run in opposition to this, forming the well-known ' roosts ' or races. The isle of *Swona*, a S. outlier of the Orkneys, set in the full stream of one of these currents gives rise to a dangerous whirlpool (the Well of Swona), and there is another called the Swelkie, at the N. end of Stroma.

The road crosses the Links of Dunnet, the sandhills at the head of Dunnet Bay, and at (32 m.) *Castletown* (St. Clair Arms, RB. 18/6, P. 8 gs.), once the centre of the flagstone industry, is joined by the direct road from Wick. Going on W. we pass (35¼ m.) the shell of *Thurso Castle*, the home of Sir John Sinclair, and of his daughter Catherine Sinclair (1800–64), the story-writer.

36 m. **THURSO** (Norse, *Thors-a*, Thor's river) is a grey little town (3200 inhab.) on the Thurso river with a small harbour and a pleasant paved promenade overlooking Thurso Bay.

Hotels. Royal, RB. 22/6, P. 12½ gs.; **Pentland.** RB. 21/, P. 10 gs.; **St. Clair,** RB. 19/6, P. 8½ gs.; **Holborn,** P. 7 gs.

Motor-Buses. To *Wick* in 60–70 min. viâ Castletown, or viâ Halkirk and Watten, or viâ Gillock ; to *John o' Groats* viâ Dunnet and Scarfskerry

in 1–1½ hr., going on to Wick ; to *Reay* in 40 min. ; to *Scrabster*, for the Orkney boats.

Steamer from Scrabster pier (2 m. N.W.) every weekday at 10.15 a.m. to *Stromness* in c. 2¼ hrs. (13/6, ret. 27/ ; car from 77/6, plus 6/dues, must be ready 1 hr. in advance ; cycle 4/6).

History. Thurso was the chief port for the trade between Scotland and Scandinavia, and in the 14th cent. was of such importance that its weights and measures were adopted for the whole country. The chief industries are fishing and catering for summer visitors, but an attempt is being made to revive the preparation of ' Caithness flags,' the paving-stones which have furnished sidewalks for Paris and for many other cities. They are quarried in the unusually fissile variety of red sandstone which abounds locally. Here Hawker and Grieve, the first airmen to attempt the Atlantic flight (May 1919), landed from the Danish steamer which picked them up in mid-ocean. Renewed activity was brought to the town by the establishment of the industrial atomic power-station at Dounreay (see below) in 1954.

The *Town Hall* (1872) adjoins the *Museum* (adm. 10–12, 2–5, 6–8 ; closed on Sun. & at 12 on Thurs.) with a fine collection of plants and coral fossils bequeathed by Robert Dick (1811–66 ; monument in the new cemetery), a local baker who acquired a remarkable knowledge of botany and geology. Opposite the parish church (by Burn, 1833) are a war memorial and a statue, perhaps by Chantrey, of Sir John Sinclair (1754–1835), the agriculturist. In the *Fisherbiggins*, close to the harbour, are the ruins of the medieval church of St. *Peter*, reconstructed in the 17th century.   Near by is a small Runic cross.

A favourite walk leads N.E. to (1½ m.) *Harold's Tower* (now the burial-place of the Sinclairs), erected by Sir John Sinclair over the grave of Harald, Earl of Caithness, slain here in 1196.

About 1 m. N.W. on the shore of Thurso Bay, beyond *Pennyland*, the birthplace of Sir Wm. Smith (1854–1914), founder of the Boys' Brigade, are the scanty ruins of the old *Bishop's Palace.* Here in 1202, Adam, Bp. of Caithness, had his tongue cut out by Harald, Earl of Orkney, on account of his attempt to levy ' Peter's Pence.'—A mile farther along the fine sandy beach is **Scrabster Pier**, with a large oil depôt, whence the mail-steamers sail to Orkney. The estate of Scrabster used to belong to the Crown and the Sovereign was locally known as the ' Laird of Scrabster.'

Holborn Head, c. 20 min. N. of Scrabster by coast path, appears in many places to be split from top to bottom. The largest of the chasms is open to the sea on one side and is spanned by two natural arches. A short distance N.W. is the *Clett,* a sea-girt rock (c. 150 ft.), covered with sea-birds during the breeding season.

64. FROM THURSO TO TONGUE, DURNESS, AND CAPE WRATH

80 m. ROAD to Durness round the Kyle of Tongue and Loch Eriboll, through varied and magnificent scenery, but requiring careful driving. MOTOR-BUS every weekday from Thurso at 2.45 p.m. for *Melvich, Bettyhill, Skerray,* and (44 m.) *Tongue* (3½ hrs.), returning at 7.20 a.m. Between Thurso and Reay the buses follow the inland road, viâ Shebster.

Leaving Thurso (Rte. 63) the coast road (A 836) climbs (3½ m.) *Scrabster Hill* (321 ft.) ; to the right across the Pentland Firth the cliffs of Hoy are seen.—5½ m. *Bridge of Forss.* At *Crosskirk*, on the coast 1 m. N., is the small ruined chapel of St. Mary (? 12th cent.).—At (9½ m.) *Dounreay* are the buildings of an industrial atomic energy plant, begun in 1954, with its conspicuous 135 ft. sphere.—11 m. *Reay*, from which Lord Reay, chief of the Clan Mackay, takes his title, lies near the head of Sandside Bay. The church (1739) is of the old Caithness pattern, with an external tower-stair and contemporary loft and pulpit.—13½ m. We enter Sutherland and cross (15½ m.) Strath Halladale, joining A 897. —17 m. *Melvich* (Hotel, RB. 22/6, P. 9½ gs.) is near the fine cliffs of Portskerra and Bighouse.—We traverse a dull moor to (21 m.) *Strathy*, lying 3 m. S. of Strathy Point, with a lighthouse finished in 1957. A steep ascent brings us to (24½ m.) *Armadale* (Armadale House, unlic., P. 6½ gs.), in a pleasant valley, noted for its sheep, beyond which the scenery becomes more varied, with glimpses of the sea.—At *Kirtomy Point*, 2 m. N. of (28 m.) *Kirtomy Bridge*, is a long tunnel by which boats may pass under the rocks, and which Pennant describes as the most curious cavern in the world.—There is a fine sculptured stone outside the W. end of (30 m.) *Farr Church* (1774 ; with contemporary pulpit).—31 m. **Bettyhill** (*Hotel*, good, RB. 22/6, P. 10 gs.) stands at the foot of *Strath Naver.*

Motor-Buses from Bettyhill viâ Skerray to *Tongue* and *Lairg* (Rte. 62c), and up Strath Naver to Kinbrace (p. 401).—Another service runs to (10 m.) *Skerray* only, diverging from the Tongue road at Borgie Bridge (see below) and passing (7½ m.) *Borgie Hotel* (RB. 24/, P. 10 gs.).

The main road runs W. to (37½ m.) *Borgie Bridge* (r. for Skerray, see above). From the top of the next ascent we may see the distant Ben Clibreck, with Ben Loyal and Ben Hope nearer at hand ; to the N., at the mouth of the shallow *Kyle of Tongue*, are *Roan Island*, whose S. face rises perpendicularly from the water, and the *Rabbit Islands* farther W.—We trend S. (view) and reach (44 m.) **Tongue** (*Bungalow*, RB. 17/6, P. 8½ gs., mid-May–Sept.), a charming place with good fishing, dominated by the remains of *Castle Varrich*, of unknown history. *Tongue House*, a nondescript building near the ferry, was the ancient seat of the Lords Reay, the country around as far as Cape Wrath and Scourie being known as ' Lord Reay's Country ' or ' Mackay's Country ' before it was sold to the Duke of Sutherland.—For the road to *Lairg*, see Rte. 62c.

A somewhat rough road leads S. from Tongue on the E. side of the Kyle (not seen), with views ahead of Ben Loyal (l.) and Ben Hope (r.), and as we follow the W. bank, after doubling (c. 48 m.) the S. end of the Kyle, we have a fine view of the line of crags on the opposite side, with Castle Varrich conspicuous.—At 53 m. we turn inland and the moorland road (*Views) rises steadily, passing (56½ m.) *Moin House*, built (1830 ; inscription) as a travellers' refuge and to commemorate the construction of the road across the morass of the Moin. At (59 m.) *Hope Lodge* (road to Altnaharra, p. 408) we cross the Hope river, which has a short but attractive course between Loch Hope and Loch Eriboll, of which a fine view is soon obtained. About 6 m. N.E. is *Kennageall* or *Whiten Head*, a splendid perpendicular cliff, on the N.E. side of which is a fine series of caves.—At 61 m. the road begins the circuit of **Loch Eriboll**, a beautiful fjord c. 10 m. long, whose calm clear waters afford an excellent harbour of refuge on this stormy coast. At its head, beyond (64 m.) *Eriboll*, is *Craig-na-Faoilinn* (934 ft.) with a rolling echo, beyond which rise the peaks of Ben Spionnaidh and Cranstackie and the ridge of Foinaven.—We regain the N. coast at (75 m.) *Rispond*.—At (78 m.) *Lerin* (Smoo Cave Hotel, unlic., RB. 16/6, P. 7 gs.) we pass above the ***Cave of Smoo,** entered from the shore below.

The cave, much admired by Scott, opens at the extremity of a deep cove in the limestone cliffs. Of the three chambers the outermost is 33 ft. high, 203 ft. long, and 120 ft. broad. The inaccessible second cavern (70 ft. by 30 ft.), into which a burn descends from the roadside through a natural opening, may be seen with difficulty from the separating barrier. Beyond it is yet a third chamber. A rubber dinghy for exploring the cave can be hired at the Cape Wrath hotel.

80 m. **Durness** (*Cape Wrath*, RB, 22/6, P. 10 gs., at Keoldale, 2 m. S.W. ; *Parkhill*, unlic., RB. 19/6, P. 8 gs.) is a straggling little community 2½ m. S. of *Faraid* or *Far-Out Head*.

Balnakill (1 m. N.W.) was once the summer abode of the Bishops of Caithness, afterwards of the Lords Reay. The present house (early 18th cent.) is now a farmhouse. Beside it, close to a bay of lovely white sand, is the roofless *Church* of Durness, formerly a cell of the monastery at Dornoch. Within are an old font and a monument with quaint carvings and the inscription : " Donald Mackmurchov hier lyis lo : vas il to his freind var to his fo : true to his maister in veird and vo. 1623." In the churchyard is an obelisk in memory of Rob Donn (p. 408).

From Durness to Cape Wrath, 13½ m. Pedestrians and cyclists may ferry the *Kyle of Durness* (1/3 ; cycle 2/6 ; motor cycle 7/6) at (2 m. S.W.) *Keoldale* (Hotel, see above) ; cars can cross at low water c. 2 m. farther up by previous arrangement with the Commissioners of Northern Lights, 84 George St., Edinburgh, 2.

The road beyond the ferry crosses the bleak and absolutely uncultivated moor known as the *Parph*, once a notorious haunt of wolves, and later famous for its red deer. From (4½ m.) *Loch-in-Shore* (good fishing) we ascend, with fine retrospective views, to 551 ft., having on the right the S.W. face of Scrishven (1216 ft.), a bare wall of red granite. Soon the Minch appears on the W., with Lewis in the distance, as we make a final ascent to (11 m. ; 378 ft.) the fort-like *Lighthouse*, built in 1828 at a cost of £14,000 (no adm. on Sun. ; permission to sleep there only from the Commissioners of Northern Lights in Edinburgh, the keepers being forbidden to harbour any but storm-bound travellers). The coast near **Cape Wrath** (523 ft.), the N.W. extremity of Scotland, is very precipitous and affords striking examples of the action of waves. The cliffs of gneiss have so many veins of rich pink pegmatite that they glow with a roseate hue. Primula scotica grows here abundantly. The *View extends E. past Far-Out Head (9 m.), at the mouth of the Kyle of Durness, to Strathy Point (36 m.), far beyond which, to the left, the cliffs of Hoy (60 m.) may be seen. On a clear day Stack Skerry and Sule Skerry (37 and 42 m. N.E.), the lonely island of North Rona (40 m. N.W.), the Butt of Lewis (45 m. W.), and the mountains of Harris (80 m. S.W.) are visible.

From Durness to *Laxford Bridge* (for Lairg or Scourie), see Rte. 62B.

65. ORKNEY AND SHETLAND

Approaches. I. By Sea. The North of Scotland and Orkney and Shetland Shipping Co., Ltd. (Matthews' Quay, Aberdeen) run regular services to Orkney and Shetland. (A) The ' St. Magnus ' or ' St. Ninian ' leaves Leith (Victoria Wharf) Mon. & Thurs. and Aberdeen (Matthews' Quay) Tues. & Fri. for *Kirkwall* (11 or 18 hrs.) and *Lerwick* (28 or 35 hrs.), returning from Lerwick Thurs. & Sun., from Kirkwall Fri. & Mon. (B) The ' St. Clair ' leaves Aberdeen Mon. & Thurs. for *Lerwick* direct (14 hrs.), returning Tues. & Sat. (C) The ' St. Rognvald ' or ' St. Clement ' leaves Leith Sun. and Aberdeen Mon. for *Kirkwall* (11 hrs.) and *Stromness*, calling at *St. Margaret's Hope* fortnightly, and returning Wed. (D) Special cruises are run throughout the year (most frequently in summer) from Leith and Aberdeen (4–14 days), the longer trips including a week or more at an island hotel.—Fares. To *Kirkwall* : from Leith 58/6, 46/, ret. 110/, 80/ ; from Aberdeen 50/, 37/6, ret. 95/, 67/6. To *Lerwick* : from Leith 70/, 47/6, ret. 127/6, 85/ ; from Aberdeen 60/, 42/6, ret. 110/, 76/. Meals : B., T., or S. 5/, L. 6/6, D. 7/6. Cruises, inclusive charges from c. £10 to £32. Cycles, 7/. Cars : return fare between any two ports, from £5 10/ (for 10 cwt.) upwards, plus loading and unloading charges of 5/–13/6 ; reservations should be made well in advance.

Lerwick is served also by the Faroe steamer, 'Tjaldur,' from *Copenhagen* (2 days) and *Kristiansand* (1 day). Fares. To Copenhagen £12 10/, Kristiansand £10 (ret. double).

For the service between Thurso (Scrabster) and *Stromness*, see Rte. 63 ; for services to the *Outer Isles*, see p. 422.

II. BY AIR. (A) From Glasgow viâ Inverness and Wick to *Orkney* (2 hrs. 40 min.) and *Shetland* (4 hrs. 20 min.) every weekday. (B) From Glasgow and Edinburgh viâ Aberdeen and Wick to *Orkney* (3 hrs. 10 min. from Edinburgh ; ¾ hr. more from Glasgow) ; connection at Aberdeen for *Shetland* direct (4 hrs. 10 min. from Edinburgh) every weekday. (C) Supplementary service between Glasgow and *Orkney* (Mon.–Fri. in summer) with change at Wick. Fares. To *Orkney* from Edinburgh 132/, ret. 197/ ; from Glasgow 136/, 206/ ; from Aberdeen 84/, 121/ ; from Inverness 75/, 125/. To *Shetland* from Edinburgh 178/, 233/, from Glasgow 187/, 243/, from Aberdeen 121/, 165/, from Inverness 132/, 212/, from Orkney 72/, 87/. Transport is provided between Orkney Airport (Grimsetter) and Kirkwall (3 m. ; 1/6), and between Shetland Airport (Sumburgh) and Lerwick (25 m. ; 3/6).

The isles of **Orkney** are separated from Caithness by the Pentland Firth. *Mainland*, the largest island, called *Pomona* by geographers through a mistranslation of Solinus, lies c. 18 m. N. of Caithness. It is 24 m. long and of very irregular shape, varying in width from 1½ to 14 m. Around its marvellously indented shores are scattered some 70 islands, 24 of which are inhabited (21,250 inhab.), the remainder being pasture 'holms' or mere 'skerries' almost awash at high water. *Hoy*, with its fine cliffs, is the only island that rises to any considerable height. Prehistoric chambered cairns, earth-houses and brochs are abundant and often well preserved, but the great charm of the group is in the wonderful seascapes, seen to great advantage from the steamers in the practically nightless midsummer. On the longest day the sun rises at 3.2 a.m. and sets at 9.23 p.m., but on the shortest day it does not rise till 9.10 a.m. and sets at 3.17 p.m. The climate is mild and equable and at the end of October or beginning of November is often marked by what is locally called the 'peerie' (or little) summer. The islands, though strikingly treeless, are well cultivated and poultry farming, with a notable output of eggs, has latterly become important. Fishing has greatly diminished in recent years. Unlike the rest of Scotland, many of the landowners acknowledge no feudal superior but hold land on udal or allodial tenure, which, like the local dialect, is a relic of the Norse colonisation.

The isles of **Shetland**, a group lying 60 or 70 m. N.E. of Orkney and extending farther N. than Cape Farewell in Greenland, present the same bleak and treeless appearance, but the cliff scenery is even more remarkable, and the long sea lochs or 'voes' have a desolate charm that is all their own. The name Shetland or Zetland is a corruption of the old Norse *Hjaltland*. In all the 100 islands (19 of which are inhabited) there is no place more than 3 m. from the sea. The inhabitants (19,350) are mostly fishermen or crofters, very often both. Shetland ponies are bred and exported and there is a peculiar breed of sheep, said to be identical with the wild sheep of Siberia. The finest Shetland wool, knitted into beautiful soft shawls, etc., comes from Unst, and is not shorn, but is plucked or 'roo'd' from the sheep's neck. Seals are often seen and frequently killed, and there is good sea and loch fishing. The climate is variable, damp and stormy, but seldom really cold ; though summer is very short. At midsummer one may read outdoors at midnight, and frequently the northern heavens remain so bright that the rosy tints of the sunset lose themselves only in the dawn. As in Orkney, much of the land is held on udal tenure.

History. The broch-building Picts who colonised Orkney and Shetland c. 200 B.C. had been evangelised by Celtic missionaries long before the first incursion of the Northmen in the 8th century. In 875 the isles were conquered by Harald Haarfagr, first king of all Norway. Given by him, traditionally, to Sigurd, brother of Rognvald, the father of Rollo of Normandy, they were governed by their own earls, more or less in dependence on the crown of Norway, until 1468, when they were mortgaged by Christian I, king of Norway and Denmark, to James III of Scotland as a surety for 60,000 florins, the dowry of his wife Margaret, Princess of Norway. Of the 10,000 florins to be paid before the princess left Copenhagen Christian could raise only 2000, and Orkney and Shetland have remained in 'wadset' or pledge ever since. In 1472 they were annexed to the Scottish crown, but theoretically might be reclaimed by the king of Norway on payment of the dowry. Shetland was entrusted to stewards appointed by the crown, but as they farmed out the revenues the islanders suffered greatly from the exactions of their bailiffs. The memory of Earl Patrick Stewart, whose father, Robert Stewart, received the lands of the last Orkney earl from his half-sister Queen Mary, is still recalled with execration ; his abuses, which included attempts to tamper with the weights and measures, led to his downfall. Bishop Law, who was largely instrumental in securing his execution in 1615, annexed 7¼ parishes, and the remainder of the ' Earldom Estate' passed through James, Earl of Morton (1707), to Sir Lawrence Dundas (1765), whose descendant, the Marquess of Zetland, still owns much land in Orkney, but little in Shetland. In both World Wars the waters of Orkney and Shetland, notably Scapa Flow and the northern voes, played a prominent part in the affairs of the Royal Navy and (later) of the Royal Air Force, while in 1940–45 Shetland served as headquarters of the clandestine service between Britain and Norway. The islands, especially Shetland, were harassed, rather than seriously attacked, by the Luftwaffe in the Second World War.

Norse is the source of all the place-names in Orkney and Shetland, and to some extent in Caithness. The old Norn language, a Norse tongue similar to Faröese, was last spoken in Shetland, it is believed, by Walter Sutherland of Unst (d. c. 1850).

A. Orkney

KIRKWALL, a little royal burgh (4350 inhab.) turning the gables of many of its houses towards the long, irregular, narrow flag-paved main street, stands at the head of Kirkwall Bay, one of the numerous deep indentations of the N. coast of Mainland. On New Year's Day a football match is played in the streets ('Up-the-Gates' v. 'Down-the-Gates').

Hotels. Kirkwall, RB. 21/, P. 11 gs.; **Royal,** RB. 20/, P. 8 gs.; **Queen's,** RB. 17/6, P. 8 gs.; **Ayre,** RB. 18/6, P. 7 gs.

Motor-Buses on weekdays to *Stromness* direct (frequent service) or viâ Orphir or viâ Harray and Sandwick (for Skara Brae). To *Dounby, Birsay,* etc. To *St. Margaret's Hope,* 2 or 3 times daily. To *Evie,* to *Deerness,* etc. Also round tours daily.

Steamers (all with 1st and 2nd cl. cabins) of the Orkney Steam Navigation Co. make the round of the North Isles every Tues. and Fri. in summer; for steamers to the other islands, see below; to Shetland, see Rte. 65B.

History. Owing to its harbour and the foundation of the cathedral in the 12th cent., Kirkwall became a place of local importance at an early date. In 1486 it was made a royal burgh by James III. James V lodged in the Bishop's House and held various meetings with the island magnates in Parliament Close, whose site is now occupied by the Commercial Bank. The old castle (14th cent.) was so strong that its builder, Earl Henry Sinclair, was suspected of having been helped by the devil. Held by Balfour, Governor of Orkney (1567), against the fugitive Earl of Bothwell, it was demolished at the suppression of the Orkney Rebellion (1614), and the last fragments were removed when Castle St. was built. In 1650 Montrose mustered 2000 Orkneymen at Kirkwall for his expedition against the Covenanters, which ended in the disaster of Culrain.

The ***Cathedral of St. Magnus** is a cruciform building of grey flagstone and red and yellow sandstone, with a central tower and spire. The preponderant style is a severe and massive Romanesque. The church is open on weekdays 10–1, 2–5 or 6; closed on Tues. from 12; tower closed also on Sat. from 12.

History. The good Earl Magnus of Orkney having been murdered in Egilsay in 1115, his nephew and heir, Rognvald III, founded (1137) this church in his honour. The skeletons of St. Magnus and St. Rognvald were rediscovered in 1926 hidden in pinewood chests within two pillars, the former with his skull pierced by the blow which caused his death. The body of Hakon, who died at Kirkwall after the Battle of Largs, rested here on its passage to Trondhjem. The see was suffragan to Nidaros (Trondhjem) from 1154 to 1472, when it came under the jurisdiction of St. Andrews. The building of Rognvald's church, which had a semicircular E. apse, apparently went on until well into the 13th cent., the transepts, with the three W. bays of the choir and two E. bays of the nave, with interlacing wall-arcades, being the oldest part of the church; the pointed arches supporting the tower are later. After 1250 the three E. bays of the choir were added; though the round arch is retained, the mouldings are of Early English character; finally the church was completed in the 14–15th cent. by the W. extension of the nave, probably in two stages. At the Reformation the cathedral was saved by the townsmen, and Kirkwall continued to be an episcopal see under a succession of seven Protestant bishops till the Revolution. Cromwell's soldiers used the steeple as a prison and as a fortress and turned the nave partly into a barrack and partly into a stable. The building fell into neglect, and the choir, used as a parish church, was cumbered with galleries, removed in the restoration of 1912–20.

EXTERIOR. The cathedral is 234 ft. long and 101 ft. across the transepts. The use of red and yellow sandstone, in varied patterns, throughout the church is highly effective, notably in the W. front, where the colour compensates for the weathering of the carvings in the triple portal, and in the S. transeptal doorway. Bishop Reid's doorway, with its segmental head, one of the latest additions to the church (c. 1550), is on the S. of the nave, while the N. doorway, with its high peaked canopy, is likewise interesting. The central tower (133 ft.; view), entered from the S. transept, was probably completed at the same time as the choir; the steeple replaces a 17th cent. one destroyed by fire in 1671.

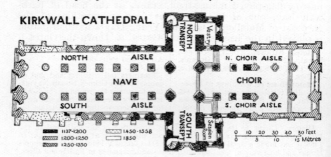

Lining the INTERIOR of the cathedral is a series of interesting sculptured tombstones, mainly of the 16th and 17th cent.; the earliest (c. 1300) is in the N. choir aisle. In the S. nave aisle is the canopied Paplay tomb (14th cent.), in the S. choir aisle that of Lord Adam Stewart (d. 1575), son of James V. Hanging in the N. nave aisle is the ' mort-brod ' of Robert Nicolsone (c. 1690), adorned with emblems of mortality, the sole remaining example of this old Orcadian type of memorial. A plaque here commemorates the 833 men lost in the ' Royal Oak ' in 1939; and in the 5th bay is a fragment of vault-painting. A beautiful interlaced blind arcade lines the walls near the crossing (the oldest part of the church), while the keeled shafts of the clustered piers supporting the tower and the bold mouldings of the tower arches (late 12th cent.) are noteworthy. The transepts, unlike the nave and choir, are not vaulted; the S. rose window is a 19th cent. reconstruction.

The two transeptal chapels (late 12th cent. : shown on request) are now used as vestries ; they contain two brazen alms-dishes (Dutch : 1630) and some 17–18th cent. Communion plate. A dark archway in the S. choir wall, above the main arcade, is the entrance to ' Marwick's Hole ', a vaulted chamber once used as a prison.

In the raised choir the massive piers of the central bay contain the remains of St. Magnus (S.) and St. Rognvald (N.) ; the cathedral is thus unique in Britain in enshrining the relics of both patron saint and founder. The contrast between the Romanesque work to the W. and the later work of the E. bays is most striking ; the fine and unusual E. window is ascribed to Bp. Stewart (c. 1511), but is probably earlier ; the decoration of the three arched recesses below it is notable. At the E. end of the aisles are monuments to the explorers John Rae (1819–93) and W. B. Baikie (1825–64) ; the statue of St. Olaf in the N. aisle is a replica (1937) of one in Trondhjem cathedral.

The ruined **Bishop's Palace** (founded c. 1500), S. of the cathedral, is open free 10–4 or 7 (Sun. from 2). The massive tower (1550), round without and square within, bears a statue, probably of St. Olaf, but said to represent Bp. Robert Reid, the distinguished scholar, lawyer, and diplomatist (d. 1558), who rebuilt the upper floors ; the three great W. buttresses were added c. 1600. Hakon, king of Norway, defeated at Largs, died in 1263 in a previous building on the site.

To the E. of the Bishops' Palace stands the ruined **Earl's Palace** (same hours), built by Earl Patrick Stewart (1600–07), a good specimen of the baronial style at a period when castellation was beginning to be used more for ornament than defence.

The building is L-shaped with angle-turrets. On the ground floor are kitchens and storerooms. The handsome dining-hall on the first floor, in which Sir Walter Scott places the interview of Cleveland and Bunce in ' The Pirate,' has a three-light window on the S., two bays on the E., and one on the W. Its huge fireplace, a fine flat arch, bears the initials P. E. O. (Patrick, Earl of Orkney) on its pillars. Beyond are two more rooms, one with a bay and an oriel, the other with ' studies ' in the corner turrets.

Outside the W. front of the cathedral is the *Town Cross* (rebuilt 1956 ; steps original) and facing it is the *Town Hall and Post Office*, adjoined by *Tankerness House*, the 16th cent. mansion of the Baikies, with a picturesque courtyard. In St. Ola's Wynd, at 24 Bridge St., is an arched doorway, a remnant of the church of *St. Ola* (1544), the successor of the original parish church of Kirkwall, which was burnt by the English fleet of Henry VIII during his rude courtship of the infant Queen Mary as a bride for his son (1502).

Just N.W. of Kirkwall, on the Hatston road, is the earth-house of *Grain* ; and at *Rennibister*, 4 m. along the Stromness road, is another earth-house. These souterrains, probably of the Bronze Age, are oval chambers 5–6 ft. in height approached by a sloping passage. At Rennibister the entrance is now from the top. On *Wideford Hill* (741 ft. ; 2½ m. W.), halfway up is a chambered cairn approached by a passage 2 ft. wide, 2 ft. high, and 17½ ft. long. The top of the hill is occupied by a P.O. radar station.

Shapinsay, 5 m. N.E. of Kirkwall and only 1 m. from the nearest point on Mainland, is reached by motor-boat several times every weekday. The landing-place, near the S.W. corner, is at *Ell Wick*, the fine harbour in which Hakon assembled his fleet before the fatal expedition to Largs in 1263. Overlooking it is *Balfour Castle*, a baronial mansion of 1847 (grounds open occasionally in summer). Near the N.E. point is *Quholm*, the croft occupied by the ancestors of Washington Irving, who was born on an American ship bound hence to New York.

The New Scapa Road runs nearly due S. from Kirkwall to (1¾ m.) *Scapa Bay* (cafés), with fair sands, to the S. and W. of which lies the island-surrounded **Scapa Flow** (50–60 sq. m.), which, after its naval activity during two great wars, has reverted to its normal appearance of its solitude.

In 1912 it was decided that Scapa Flow should be the main base of the British Grand Fleet in case of a European war, but no fortification was undertaken. In July 1914 the fleet moved to these waters. The defences were first penetrated by German submarines in Oct. 1914. On July 9th, 1917, the ' Vanguard ' was torpedoed in the Flow, all the crew being drowned save two.

The greater part of the German fleet, 70 vessels in all, including 10 battleships, which surrendered to Great Britain at the Armistice, lay in Scapa Flow from Nov. 1918 to June 21st, 1919, when almost all of the vessels were scuttled or beached by their crews who had been permitted to remain on board. The battleships lay between Cava and Houton Head, the destroyers between Risa and Fara and Hoy. From 1924 to 1933, 33 vessels were raised from comparatively shallow water, including 3 battleships, 4 battle-cruisers, 1 mine-laying cruiser, and 25 destroyers. In 1935 to 1939, one battle-cruiser and 5 more battleships were raised from water up to 26 fathoms. Salvage concluded in 1947, when the work-shops were removed to Faslane Bay, on the Clyde.

In 1939 the roadstead again became a naval base (with headquarters at Lyness in Hoy) and was soon subjected to German air attacks. In Oct., 1939, the defences were again penetrated by a submarine, when the ' Royal Oak ' was torpedoed with a loss of 833 lives. As a result, causeways were built, linking Mainland with South Ronaldsay and preventing access by sea from the E. In 1942–44 (see below) the causeways were surfaced to form a road.

From Kirkwall to St. Margaret's Hope, 13½ m. (A 961). Running a little E. of S., the road commands good views of Scapa Flow, and reaches the S. coast of Mainland at (6 m.) *St. Mary's Holm.* Just beyond begins the first part of the *Churchill Causeway* (see above), crossing Holm Sound and traversing the islets of *Lamb Holm* and *Glimps Holm.* On Lamb Holm is a chapel built by Italian prisoners-of-war who were employed in the construction of the road. On the sandy island of (c. 10 m.) *Burray* is a broch with walls now c. 15 ft. high. Another causeway across Water Sound brings us to (11½ m.) the fertile island of **South Ronaldsay** (c. 7 m. by 2 m.) and (13½ m.) the village of *St. Margaret's Hope*, where the ship on which Queen Margaret, the Maid of Norway, had died while on her way to Scotland, put in and received Bp. Dolgfimur on board before returning to Norway (1290). This was the sad prelude of the long wars for Scottish independence. Hoxa Head, the W. point of the island, on which there is a broch, commands a view, across Hoxa Sound, of Hoy, behind the low island of *Flotta.* The S. end of S. Ronaldsay is within 6 m. of Duncansby Head, in Caithness.

From Kirkwall to the S.E. Coast, 11½ m. A 960, running S.E., skirts the heads of two large bays : *Inganess Bay* (2½ m. ; good bathing) and *Deer Sound* (6½ m.). To the S. of the former is *Grimsetter* airfield, and between the two bays is *Tankerness* peninsula, on the S.E. side of which, 2½ m. from the high road, is *Tankerness Hall*, whence the daughter of Sir John Sinclair, the greatest heiress of Orkney, eloped on her bridal morning with young Halcro of Brough, to escape a forced marriage with the old and ugly Tulloch of Sound. Tradition affirms that Mary of Guise dismissed Tulloch's appeal with sympathetic approval of the bride's choice. In *Deer Sound* (the ancient Rörvaag) Olaf Tryggveson of Norway surprised Earl Sigurd II, and forced on him Christian baptism (995). The inmost recess of the sound approaches to within a furlong of the S.E. coast. On the isthmus is (8 m.) the sepulchral barrow called *Dingy's* (Ninian's) *Howe*, where

St. Ninian drove out the evil spirit which had for weeks reanimated the corpse of Amund to unnatural strife with his devoted brother, who had in his love entered and shared his grave. Beyond the isthmus is the Deerness peninsula, traversed by the road to its terminus at (11½ m.) *Sandside Bay*, where Earl Thorfinn defeated ' the gracious Duncan,' nicknamed by the Norsemen Carol-King. In its ruined broch Thorkel Foster executed wild justice on the tyrant Earl Einar II. About ¾ m. farther N. is the *Gloup of Deerness*, a remarkable chasm in the cliffs, and ¾ m. beyond is the *Brough of Deerness*, a stack-rock with the remains of a chapel on the cliff-top near by. To the S.E., 1½ m. offshore, is *Copinsay*, whose green W. slopes contrast strongly with its E. precipice. The curious islet off its N. end is called the *Horse of Copinsay*.

From Kirkwall to Stromness, 15 m. This road (A 965) runs W. between the bay and the *Peerie Sea* (a salt-water lagoon) by one of the natural causeways called ' ayres ' which are common in Orkney. On the right is Rennibister earth-house (p. 417), while farther on the *Bay of Firth* contains the pretty green islet of *Damsay* (St. Adamnan's-ey) with remains of a castle often mentioned in the sagas. To the left is the roofless old mansion of Cursiter. At the W. corner of the bay is the village of (6½ m.) *Finstown* (Inn), with its many churches.

From here A 966 runs N. to Birsay (17 m.) viâ (9 m.) *Evie*, with the large *Broch of Gurness* (adm. 6*d.*), partly ruined, at Aikerness, 1 m. N.E. on the shore of Eynhallow Sound.—A 986 also leads from our road c. 1½ m. farther on, to Birsay (11 m.) viâ (5½ m.) *Dounby* (Smithfield Hot.). On a side road connecting Dounby with Evie is *Klick Mill* (adm. 6*d.*), a surviving example of the traditional horizontal water-mill of Orkney (3 m. from Dounby).

9½ m. ***Maeshowe** (' mestr,' greatest, ' haugr,' mound or cairn), on the right of the road, is a huge chambered cairn dating probably from the time of the first settlers in Orkney (c. 1500 B.C.). Adm. 6*d.*; guide at the farm of Tormiston, on the left of the road.

Legends still linger round Maeshowe and its strong but stupid ' hog-boy ' (haug bui—dweller in the mound), the guardian of its long-stolen treasures and its secrets. The chamber is now artificially lit.

The tumulus, a great cone of earth 115 ft. in diameter, 24 ft. high, and over 300 ft. in circumference, is surrounded by a trench 45 ft. wide and c. 6 ft. deep. It was rifled by treasure-seekers in the 12th cent., but whether they found it a ruin or not, it is evident that the runes (see below) were not inscribed till the roof was uncovered, and probably not until ages of exposure had decayed the surface of the stone. The robbers showed little respect to the dead ; for the stones which once closed the cells were torn out and buried in the ruins of the fallen roof. A passage, opening from the W., 36 ft. long, 3¼ ft. wide, and 4½ ft. high, leads to the central chamber 15 ft. square with sepulchral cells 5½–7 ft. in length on three of its sides. The roof and floor of each cell are of single stones, and the stones that formed the doors were found on the ground in front of them. The four walls of the central chamber are built of slabs 15 ft. long ; from a height of c. 6 ft. above the floor they converge towards the centre. The present roof is a light structure of brick, the original material having proved too heavy for the decaying walls. At the angles are large projecting piers, with supporting monoliths c. 10 ft. high. The whole structure shows extraordinary skill in the art of building without mortar and is covered by an immense cone of earth. Of the 24 runic inscriptions in various parts of the chamber some are dated to the Crusade of 1151 ; others appear to be later in the 12th cent. ; while the animated dragon, the walrus, and the knot of serpents may be rather earlier.

Beyond the Kirk of Stenness (r.) are the ruins of the *House of Stenness*, where Earl Havard was murdered by his wicked wife Ragnhild (c. 980), and the imaginary scene of some of the most stirring scenes of 'The Pirate.' At 10¼ m. a by-road (r.) passing between the tidal *Loch of Stenness* (l.; 4 m. long) and the fresh-water *Loch of Harray* (r.; 5 m. long) leads to the ***Standing Stones of Stenness*** (*Leigh*, private, RB. 15/6, P. 6 gs.), the Stonehenge of Orkney.

A few hundred yards along this road, on the right, is the small CIRCLE OF STENNESS, of whose original stones only four are upright. The 'dolmen' is a spurious erection of 1906, while the Stone of Odin, which stood, till 1814, 150 yds. N. has vanished. The latter stone is recorded in 'The Pirate' as having been pierced by a hole, and an oath taken with hands joined through this hole was deemed more binding than any other.—A little farther on stands the *Watch Stone* (18½ ft. high), just before the Bridge of Brogar, a narrow causeway separating the two lochs. A short distance beyond the Bridge is the beautifully situated **Ring of Brogar** (view), a circle of unhewn sandstone monoliths occupying a space of c. 2½ acres (366 ft. across) surrounded by a trench 29 ft. broad and 6 ft. deep and crossed by two narrow banks of earth. The stones stand c. 18 ft. apart and c. 13 ft. from the trench and range from 6 to 13 ft. in height. When complete there were probably c. 60 ; 27 remain standing. There are scores of sepulchral tumuli in the immediate neighbourhood, which, when excavated, are often found to contain a small slabbed cist.—By going for 3 m. beyond the Ring of Brogar we may strike the road from Stromness to Birsay.

Returning to the main road we pass (11 m.) the *Standing Stones Hotel* (for cruise-parties only), and (12¼ m.) reach *Bridge of Waith* at the shallow entrance of the Loch of Steenness. On a point in the loch, a little N. of the bridge, is the fine chambered cairn of *Unston*, from which was unearthed the largest collection of Neolithic pottery found in Scotland.

15 m. **Stromness** (*Stromness*, RB. 17/6–21/, P. 10–12 gs. ; *Scott's Temperance*, RB. 14/, P. 110/), a town of 1500 inhab., consists of one narrow street with steep wynds (one called Khyber Pass) running up the granite hill which shelters it from the Atlantic, and down to the jetties of its sheltered harbour. Stromness used to be the N. port of call for rice-ships from America, and later of the Hudson's Bay whaling fleets. Sir John Franklin put in here in 1819 to collect crew for his first Arctic expedition. It contains an interesting little museum (S. end ; adm. 6*d*.) and has a golf course. From the cemetery, in a situation of lonely grandeur 1 m. W., there is a fine view of the opposite cliff of Hoy.

FROM STROMNESS TO KIRKWALL viâ Orphir, 16 m. by A 964. Beyond (2¾ m.) the *Bridge of Waith* (see above) we strike off to the S., passing (3¾ m.) *Mill of Ireland* and (5¼ m. r.) *Hall of Clestran*, the home of John Rae (p. 417). On the right at 8 m. are *Houton* bay and holm. A few minutes S. of (9 m.) the church of **Orphir** are remains of a circular church, unique in Scotland, built after 1120 by Earl Hakon after a pilgrimage to Jerusalem undertaken as a penance for the murder of St. Magnus (p. 422) and dedicated to St. Nicholas. Passing (11½ m.) between the *Loch of Kirbister* (trout fishing) and *Waulkmill Bay* (r.), with the best bathing in Orkney, we have Scapa Bay on our right.—14 m. *Kirkwall*.

FROM STROMNESS TO SKARA BRAE AND BIRSAY, 14 m. Passing the N.W. end of the Loch of Stenness, we reach, at

(5 m.) *Loch Clumly,* an overthrown cromlech called the *Stones of Via* (r.). At 5¼ m. we turn left on B 9055, skirt the Loch of Skaill, and then reach the shore at the Bay of Skaill (good bathing). On the left is the old farmhouse-mansion of *Skaill,* and beyond it, at the water's edge, is the prehistoric village of (7 m.) ***Skara Brae** (adm. 1/ ; 10–4 or 7, Sun. from 2), a late-Neolithic settlement dating from c. 1500 B.C., remarkable for the completeness of its preservation. The huts, with their low entrances and curious stone bed-steads, floor-boxes, and ' dressers,' open on to ' streets ' (c. 4 ft. high, 2 ft. wide) roofed with slabs and cutting through a huge midden. The smaller remains—tools, beads, vessels of pottery, stone and whalebone, and animal bones (now mostly at Edinburgh)—indicate two or three periods of occupation. The village was apparently abandoned because of encroaching sand and was uncovered in a storm in 1850.

Good walkers may return to Stromness by the cliffs (c. 9 m.) to enjoy the fine rock scenery, including several isolated stacks.

The road thence to Birsay affords a curious backward glimpse through the *Hole of Row,* a natural arch formed by the sea ; it then crosses high ground and leaves (12 m.) a track to Marwick Head on the left. On *Marwick Head* (280 ft. ; 1 m. W.) is the *Kitchener Memorial Tower,* unveiled in 1925, " on that corner of his country, which he served so faithfully, nearest to the place where he died on duty." On June 5th, 1916, H.M.S. ' Hampshire,' in which Lord Kitchener had set sail from Thurso for Archangel, struck a mine c. 1½ m. off the coast and sank rapidly. There were few survivors and Kitchener's body was never recovered.—We rejoin the main road shortly before (14 m.) **Birsay** (*Barony,* RB. 16/6–21/, P. 6–9 gs.). The *Palace,* the residence of the earls of Orkney before the rise of Kirkwall in the 12th cent., was rebuilt by Earl Robert Stewart (c. 1580) in imitation of Falkland Palace, but is now a grey old ruin. Over its entrance was the famous inscription ' Dominus Robertus Stuartus, filius Jacobi Quinti, Rex Scotorum,' the bad grammar of which was taken for treason.

On the *Brough of Birsay,* an island joined to Mainland except at high tide, are the excavated ruins of the *Church of St. Peter,* the first cathedral of Orkney, an early-11th cent. building on an older Celtic site, with a nave, chancel, and apse. To the N. of the church is the bishop's palace, with a cloister ; to the S. the graveyard, with Celtic tombs ; while to the E., lower down, are extensive ruins of Earl Thorfinn's palace, with elaborate heating arrangements.

From Birsay to *Finstown* and *Kirkwall,* see p. 419 ; the route viâ (8 m.) *Evie* (p. 419) round the N. coast has splendid cliff scenery for the first few miles and passes (4 m.) *Costa Head* (478 ft.), crowned by an experimental wind-operated generator (1950).

Hoy (*Royal*, at Longhope, RB. 16/6, P. 7 gs. ; car for hire), the second largest (14 m. by 6 m. ; 950 inhab.) and loftiest of the islands, is reached from Mainland by steamer daily exc. Sun. & Thurs. in summer (Sat. only in winter). The steamer leaves Longhope (see below) at 7.30 or 8 a.m. : on Mon. & Fri. it runs viâ *Lyness* and *Flotta* to (2¾ hrs.) *Scapa*, returning by the same route (2¼ hrs.) at 4 p.m. ; on Tues., Wed., and Sat. it runs to *Stromness* (3½ hrs.) viâ *Lyness, Flotta, Fara* (not. Wed.), *Linksness* (Hoy Pier), and *Graemsay*, returning by the same route (omitting Fara) at 3.30 or 4 p.m. The ferry between Houton and Lyness is closed. Motor-boats can be hired at Stromness for Graemsay and Hoy pier (c. 1 hr.).—*Longhope*, where the night should be spent, is in *South Walls*, the S.E. arm of the island, almost separated from the rest by the landlocked inlet of *Long Hope*, c. 4 m. long. Thence a road skirts the inlet, above the inner end of which, in the most fertile part of the island, is *Melsetter*, a mansion built by W. R. Lethaby in 1898, but now standing empty with its once-famous gardens neglected. The road, keeping near the indented E. coast, with the isles of *Flotta* and *Fara* offshore, passes above (7 m.) the former naval base of *Lyness*, and runs, in view of *Risa* and *Cava* islets, to (15 m.) *Linksness*, with Hoy church and pier, facing Graemsay (good bathing). From Linksness a road, rounding the S. side of *Ward Hill* (1565 ft. ; noted for rare plants ; *View), runs to (5½ m.) the lovely bay of *Rackwick*, on the W. coast. Above the road, 2½ m. from the pier, is the **Dwarfie Stone,** a mass of rock 28 ft. long by 14 ft. wide, hollowed out to form a corridor and two chambers, one with a stone shelf. It has been identified as a late-Neolithic burial chamber. It plays an important part in ' The Pirate ', and Hugh Miller has left his initials chiselled on it. The finest coast scenery is accessible only to walkers. Striking N.W. from Linksness pier, they reach the N. coast at (3½ m.) *The Kame* and thence go S. along the magnificent W. cliffs viâ (5 m.) *St. John's Head* (1140 ft.) to (7½ m.) the *Old Man of Hoy*, an isolated column 450 ft. high of shale capped with red sandstone, which is conspicuous from most of the N. coast of Caithness and Sutherland. *Rora Head* (1 m. S.) is 337 ft. high and 1 m. E. of it the cliffs rise to 500 ft., on the way to (¾ m. more) Rackwick (see above).

From Kirkwall to the North Isles

A steamer sails on Thurs. & Sat. (returning Mon. & Thurs.) to Egilsay, Wyre, and **Rousay** (10 m. N.N.E.), an island (5 m. by 3½ m.) with a notable broch and stalled cairn at *Midhowe* (W. end) near the old ruined church. Rousay is reached also by bus to Evie and mail-boat thence ; there are three other stalled cairns near the post-office pier. Above the steamer-pier (at the S.E. corner) is *Taiverso Tuick*, a two-storied chambered *Cairn. In *Eynhallow Sound*, between Rousay and Mainland, lies the small and uninhabited *Eynhallow*, with ruins of the church of a monastery, probably a Benedictine house of c. 1100.—To the E. of Rousay is **Egilsay,** 3 m. long. Near the pier is a 12th cent. church dedicated to St. Magnus, and said to be built upon the spot where he was murdered in 1115 by Earl Hakon, his cousin. Its remarkable *Round Tower*, now 48 ft. high, was probably about 60 feet. On *Wyre* (2¼ m. long), S. of Rousay and S.W. of Egilsay, is another 12th cent. church, probably built by Bp. Bjarni (c. 1190), son of Kolbein Hruga, a Norwegian robber-baron, whose stronghold (now called *Cubbie Roo's Castle*), with its little keep and later outworks, has been cleared by the Ministry of Works. —The Saturday boat goes on to Papa Westray and Westray.

On every weekday except Mon. (round trip on Fri. & Tues. 16/) a steamer serves the North Isles proper. Passing between Shapinsay and *Gairsay* (l.) the boats follow varying courses. About 4 m. N.E. of Shapinsay is **Stronsay** (*Mitchell's Hotel* and pier on the N.E.), a very irregular island 7 m. long. The Moncur Memorial Church (1955) is a good work.—To the N. of Stronsay is **Sanday** (14 m. long ; *Kettletoft Hotel*, RB. 13/, P. 110/, and pier on the S.), with a chambered cairn at Quoyness on the W. side of Kettletoft bay. To the W. lies **Eday** (8 m. long), with a pier at each end. Its N.E. coast (Calfsound Pier) is separated from the small *Calf of Eday* by the narrow *Calf Sound, the most picturesque part of the steamer-route, where John Gow, the pirate, was wrecked and captured in 1725. A little W. of the pier is another two-storied cairn (at Huntersquoy). From the N. entrance of the sound, between the grand promontories of Grey Head (E.) and Red Head, we strike N.W. to **Papa Westray** (4 m. by c. ¾ m.).

This island, called ' Papa ' like many others from the hermits' cells which once abounded on them, preserves on the E. shore of its small loch (S.) the remains of a chapel of St. Tredwall, the mysterious Triduana, resorted to for affections of the eyes (comp. p. 74). Near the chapel is a broch, and on the tiny *Holm of Papa*, to the E., is a huge cairn (104 ft. long) with no less than 14 chambers opening off its central passage.—**Westray** (10 m. long), to the W., has a hotel (Pierowall, RB. 14/6, P. 6 gs.) at *Pierowall Bay*, the deepest indentation of the E. shore. *Noltland Castle*, whose extensive ruins lie 1 m. W., was founded c. 1560 by Gilbert Balfour of Westray. In 1650 his descendant sided with Montrose, and Covenanting troops burned the castle. It is notable for its stately hall and vaulted kitchen, and for the magnificent winding staircase with its elaborately carved newel. One of the grandest capes in Orkney is *Noup Head* (2¼ m. farther W.), where the overhanging cliffs, swarming with sea-fowl, are as impressive, though not so high (the lighthouse stands 200 ft. high), as those of Hoy. On the W. coast 1 m. S. is the *Gentlemen's Cave*, where several Jacobite gentlemen hid for a whole winter after Culloden. There are remains of two old churches : *St. Mary's* (? 13th cent.), at Pierowall, and *Cross Church* (? 12th cent.), 3 m. S. It was in a predecessor of the former that St. Rognvald heard Mass on his first arrival in Orkney in 1136.—To the N.E. of Sanday is *North Ronaldsay* (3 m. by c. 1 m.), northernmost of the Orkneys, notable for the 12-mile stone wall that surrounds it, to keep the small native sheep off the cultivated land (mail-boat Wed., Fri., Sat. from Sanday ; fortnightly steamer from Kirkwall ; ret. 32/).

B. Shetland

For steamer and air services, see p. 413. The sea passage from Kirkwall to Lerwick takes 8 hrs. (33/6, 26/ ; ret. 63/, 47/6).

From the Bay of Kirkwall the course (116 m.) lies E. and N.E., passing Shapinsay (l.), the flat islet of *Auskerry* (r.), and Stronsay (l.), beyond which we catch distant views of Sanday and of North Ronaldsay. Halfway between Orkney and Shetland is the isolated **Fair Isle** (sheep island ; 3 m. by 1½ m. ; 73 inhab.), with its two lighthouses. In 1588, during the northward retreat of the Spanish Armada, one of the ships, perhaps the flagship of the Duke of Medina Sidonia, was wrecked here. It is not now believed that the Spaniards taught the islanders the elaborate patterns which decorate their knitted hosiery and jerseys. A bird-watching station of the Scottish Ornithological Club was set up here in 1946, and a hostel (P. 6 gs. ; apply to S.O.C., 5 Charlotte Sq., Edinburgh) was opened in 1948. A motor vessel sails on Wed. morning (ret. 21/) to the island from Grutness Pier, Sumburgh.

When Fair Isle is lost to sight the bare *Sumburgh Head* (300 ft. ; lighthouse), the S. point of Shetland, comes into view. Past it rush furious currents called the Roost of Sumburgh. We skirt the E. side of the long S. arm of Shetland's *Mainland* and, 10 m. from Sumburgh Head, pass Mousa. A further 10 m. brings us abreast of Bressay, which forms one of the finest natural harbours in the world for Lerwick.

LERWICK (pron. Ler-wick), of 17th cent. origin, is the county town (5540 inhab.) of Shetland and the most northerly town in Britain, deriving its name from the Norse *Leir-vik*, i.e. ' clay creek.' It occupies a pleasant site on the E. coast of Mainland, sheltered from the E. by the island of Bressay.

Hotels. Queen's, RB. 17/6, P. 8½ gs. ; **Grand,** RB. 21/, P. 10 gs. ; **Hayfield,** unlic., RB. 20/, P. 9 gs.

Motor-Buses to *Scalloway* (frequent service) ; to *Sandwick* daily, going on to *Dunrossness, Spiggie,* and *Sumburgh* (not Mon.) ; to *Mossbank* daily (for Yell and Unst ; day-return Fri. only) ; to *Walls, Sandness, Hillswick, North Roe,* etc., daily exc. Mon. Cir-

cular tours on Thurs. morning and Sun. afternoon (6/–8/) ; other tours daily.

Steamers. To *Orkney* and the South, see p. 413. Motor Launch daily to *Bressay.* To the North Isles, M.V. ' Earl of Zetland ', on Mon., Wed., and Fri. to *Whalsay, Fetlar, Yell,* and *Unst,* returning on Tues., Wed., and Sat. The Tues. boat calls at the *Out*

Skerries between Yell and Whalsay. | times in summer in 1 day, coming from
Fare 15/, return 30/ ; inter-island 7/6, | Copenhagen and Kristiansand. Ordin-
15/. On Thurs. trip round *Bressay*. To | ary return Lerwick–Thorshavn £18,
the *Faroe Islands*, M.V. 'Tjaldur' 6–7 | 6-day trip £22 (meals included).

History. King Hakon and his 200 galleys anchored here on their way to Largs in 1263, and the harbour has since been the theatre of many maritime events. The Dutch fishing-fleet used to anchor here every summer, and in June 1640 their armed escort was attacked and sunk by French ships of war. Some cannon dredged up from the harbour in 1922 are believed to be from the sunken vessel. Lerwick town itself does not appear to be older than the 17th cent. ; part of it was burned by the Dutch in 1673. The destroyers that patrolled northern waters in the Second World War were the latest of the many naval forces that have found shelter in the roadstead.

The Up Helly A' festival, on the last Tues. in Jan., welcomes the return of the sun, and is doubtless a survival of pagan sun-worship. Some 300 men in fancy dress, each bearing a lighted torch, follow the Guizer Jarl (dressed as a Viking chieftain) behind a replica of a Norse galley. At the last, the torches are thrown on to it to make a bonfire, and the guizers are entertained in the town. Next day, a holiday, the guizers, still in fancy dress, collect money for local charities.

Fishing is the main industry, and in summer the *Harbour* is crowded with boats of various nationalities ; but weaving is also important. The old town is irregularly built, some of its houses being pushed out into the water, an arrangement which facilitated the landing of contraband from the Dutch 'busses.' Parallel with the shore runs *Commercial St.*, a flagged causeway of varying width antedating the appearance of wheeled vehicles in Shetland. Thence steep and narrow lanes run up the hillside, to Hillhead, with the churches and public buildings. The *Town Hall* (1881 ; adm. 6*d.* ; 10.30–12.30, Tues.-Fri. also 2.30–4.30) has windows illustrative of Shetland history and commands a fine view. In the vestibule of the *County Buildings*, opposite, is the *Papil Stone (found on W. Burra in 1943), a sculptured stone, probably of the late 7th cent., with a procession of 'papas,' or missionary priests, one on horseback. Below is *Fort Charlotte*, built by Cromwell and repaired under Charles II. Destroyed by the Dutch in 1673, it was repaired and garrisoned during the Napoleonic War.

The best short walk is round *The Knab*, a bold headland ½ m. S., with views of Bressay and Brei Wick.—Beside the Scalloway road, 1 m. W. of the town, is *Clickimin Loch*, which is separated from the sea only by a narrow strip of shingle and encloses a peninsula (once an island) approached by a causeway. On this is a large *Broch, guarded by a gateway, an enclosure, and an unusual forework. The broch itself, 65 ft. in diameter, with walls 18 ft. thick and c. 15 ft. high, stands on a stone platform perhaps added later (adm. 6*d.*).

FROM LERWICK TO SCALLOWAY. The main road, or North Road (bus in 20 min.) is 7 m. long ; the South Road is 6½ m. An interesting round is to go by the S. road and return viâ Tingwall.—Passing Clickimin Loch, we turn right off the Sumburgh road at (4 m.) *Hollanders' Knowe*, where the Dutch fishermen used to chaffer with the Scalloway market-wives before the rise of Lerwick, cross the watershed and descend in curves (*View).

6¼ m. **Scalloway** (*Royal*, RB. 16/6, P. 8 gs.; *Scalloway*, RB. 17/6, P. 8½ gs.), the former capital of Shetland, stands at the end of the road on a charming bay sheltered by islands. A tablet on a slipway in the village recalls its inspection in 1942 by Prince Olaf (now King of Norway), when it was the main Norwegian naval base. Overlooking the harbour from the E. is the *Castle* (key at the house above), built in 1600 by 'the wicked Earl' Patrick Stewart in the old-fashioned medieval style. It fell into disuse after Patrick's fall in 1615.

A motor-launch sails 2–3 times daily (once on Sun.) to (½ hr.) *Hamnavoe*, a cheerful-looking fishing village on the island of *West Burra* (5 m. long), which is concealed from Mainland by the parallel islands of *Trondra* and *East Burra*. The site of Papil church (comp. above) is 3½ m. S. of Hamnavoe, a mile past the bridge to E. Burra.

On Wed. (weather permitting) a motor vessel sails to (27 m. W.) **Foula**, a solitary island with 75 inhab., 16 m. from the nearest land. It has magnificent cliffs (1220 ft.) well depicted in the film 'The Edge of the World' (1936). It is served also in summer by motor-vessel excursions from Hillswick; but landing is by no means a certainty. Sea-fowl are abundant, and it is a favourite breeding-place of the bonxie, or great skua, the robber of the seas. The old Norse language was in common use until c. 1800.

Leaving Scalloway we retrace our steps for 1 m. and ascend the beautiful Tingwall valley, passing (7½ m.) *Asta Loch* and (8½ m.) *Tingwall Loch*. In this valley was held the annual Althing, or open-air parliament of the Shetlanders in Norse times, where public justice was meted out.

On an islet (now a peninsula) in Tingwall Loch disputed cases were settled by trial of battle, which was decided when one of the contestants had killed his opponent.

At (10½ m.) a cross-roads we turn sharp right, and at (12¼ m.) *Fitch Bridge*, above the head of the picturesque Dales Voe, we join the main road from Scalloway to (15 m.) *Lerwick*.

The excursion from Lerwick to Bressay and Noss can be managed in an afternoon, but a whole day should be devoted to it. It is made by ferry to Bressay; car, in connection, across the island to Noss Ferry; row-boat thence to Noss (each section 2/ return, including permit to land on Noss, on Sun., Mon., and Thurs. in good weather). Across Bressay Sound (½ m. wide) lies **Bressay** (5 m. by 2 m.), an island with a golf course and a fine coast, with a Ward Hill (742 ft.) commanding a good view. Separated from the E. coast of Bressay by Noss Sound (200 yds.; strong current) is the *Isle of Noss, now a bird sanctuary. The ferry-boat on the Bressay side is reached by a rough scramble. The E. side of the isle, especially the magnificent headland, the *Noup of Noss* (592 ft.), is frequented by myriads of sea birds in the breeding season, including bonxies, puffins, and a small colony of gannets. To the S. is a stack, the *Holm of Noss*, formerly reached by a cradle swung on ropes across the fine chasm (60 ft. wide) which separates it from Noss. The *Cave of the Bard*, a stalactite cave on the W. side of *Bard Head* (264 ft.), the S. extremity of Bressay, is noted for its remarkable echo, and off the head is a natural arch called *The Giant's Leg*.

FROM LERWICK TO SUMBURGH (Jarlshof and the Airport), 26½ m. by a beautiful winding road.—Leaving the old Scalloway road at the Hollanders' Knowe (see above), we enjoy fine views of the S. heads of Bressay, then (8½ m.) cross the depression of *Quarff*, where boats used to be dragged across the isthmus to the W. shore. Beyond is the peninsula of Dunrossness.   14½ m.   We pass above the village of *Sandwick* and command a view of Mousa and its broch.

From Sandwick we may cross by boat to (1 m.) the island of **Mousa,** on which is a well-preserved **Broch*, 45 ft. high and 50 ft. in diameter at the base. To this fortress Erland, son of Harald the Fair-spoken, is said to have carried off (c. 1150) the mother of Harald, Earl of Orkney, a famous beauty ; the earl, unable to take it by force or famine, was glad to assent to the terms by which the lady became the wife of her captor.

Leaving on the right the road to Bigton and Spiggie, we soon obtain a distant view of Foula, far off to the W.   From (21½ m.) *Dunrossness* church a road bears right for *Quendale* (3 m.), with its sands, beneath the imposing *Fitful Head* (928 ft.).   On the pearly cliffs of this grand promontory (Old Norse, hvitfugla hövdi, ' white birds' head ') was the home of Norna, the Shetland prophetess in Scott's ' Pirate.'— 25½ m. **Sumburgh** (*Sumburgh Hotel*, RB. 17/6, P. 8 gs.) adjoins the airport and has two fine beaches, one on each side of the peninsula.   Beyond the airfield (r.) lies the series of ruins of many ages known as ***Jarlshof** (adm. 1/ daily 10–4 or 7, Sun. from 2), perhaps the most interesting ancient site in Britain.

This site, with fertile soil and a good harbour, has been continuously occupied since the Bronze Age at least ; its systematic excavation by the Ministry of Works dates from 1925–52.   Rising in the centre is a late-16th cent. laird's house, the ' Jarlshof ' assigned by Scott as a residence to Magnus Troil (in ' The Pirate '). Extended by Earl Patrick Stewart in 1604–05, it was already roofless in 1700. To the W. (next the little museum) are Bronze Age huts recalling the earlier huts of the Skara Brae type, while to the S.E. is an Iron Age broch (1st cent. A.D.), half eroded by the sea, with later Iron Age ' wheel houses ' (? 3rd–8th cent.) built within its walls.   Inland is a confused group of Viking ' long houses ' of two periods (9th–14th cent.) ; and between them and the Bronze Age huts are foundations of a medieval farmstead (14–16th cent.).   As well as finds from the excavations, the museum contains three grave-slabs from Quendale church, now lost beneath the sea.

The road ends at (26½ m.) *Grutness* pier, while to the S. rises *Sumburgh Head*, with its lighthouse (view of Fair Isle, for which Grutness is the usual sailing-point).

The return may be made by taking the attractive W. road at Dunrossness church, passing the *Spiggie Hotel* (RB. 14/, P. 6 gs.) and *Henderson's Hotel* (RB. 12/6, P. 5 gs.) at *Scousburgh*, and leaving on the left, at Bigton, *St. Ninian's Isle*, with the saint's holy well and the foundations of a medieval church, 50 ft. long, with an apse, surrounded by an earlier burial-ground.   In 1958 excavations here yielded a remarkable hoard of silver ornaments (8th cent.) of Scottish Celtic manufacture.   The view of Foula is outstanding, and seals are often to be seen from the road.

FROM LERWICK TO THE NORTH ISLES. (a) BY SEA. All the main islands may be reached by the motor-vessel ' Earl of Zetland ' on Mon., Wed., & Fri. (p. 423). All services call at (13 m.) *Whalsay* (5½ m. by 2 m.), a famous fishing station ; at *Fetlar*, a fertile island noted for its ponies, its cliffs, and the treacherous currents around it (anchorage at Brough Lodge, at the W. end, or occasionally at Houbie, on the S. side) ; at *Mid Yell* (see below) ; and at *Uyeasound* (S. end of Unst ; see below). The Mon. boat serves also *Baltasound* (N. Unst), and the *Out Skerries* (N.E. of Whalsay) ; the Fri. boat calls at *Baltasound* and *Cullivoe* (N. Yell). Owing to the lack of piers, passengers for the smaller isles are landed and embarked by ' flit-boat '.

(b) THE ' OVERLAND ' ROUTE (bus and ferry daily exc. Sun. to Haroldswick ; return trip on Fri. only, 12½ hrs.) diverges from the north Scalloway road at (3½ m.) *Fitch Bridge* and keeps to the right above the head of the Tingwall valley. —Beyond (9½ m.) the large *Loch of Girlsta* we leave on the r. the road to *Nesting* parish, noted for its numerous brochs, then, traversing the utterly desolate Pettadale, we descend towards the pretty village of (19 m.) *Voe*, at the head of the W. coast inlet of *Olna Firth*, a cruiser base in 1914–18. Eastward from Voe lies the district of *Lunnasting*, with the 17th cent. Lunna House. Our road soon bears right to skirt the long fiord of *Dales Voe*, and reaches the E. coast at (28¼ m. ; 1¼ hr.) *Mossbank* (rfmts.).—Here the ferry (½ hr. ; 2/6) crosses Yell Sound (frequented by eider duck) to *Ulsta* at the S. end of the peaty island of **Yell** (17 m. by 6 m.). A bus traverses either the E. or the W. side of the island to *Mid Yell*, where voes cut the island nearly in half, and to *Gutcher* on the N.E. coast. *Hascosay*, off the mouth of Mid Yell Voe, has some caves still virtually unexplored ; while beyond *Cullivoe*, N. of Gutcher, is the best coastal scenery.— Another ferry (¼ hr. ; 2/6) crosses Bluemull Sound to *Belmont* in **Unst** (12 m. by 3–4 m.), the grandest and most fertile of the islands, noted for its knitted lace shawls. We call at the port of *Uyeasound*, 2 m. E. of which is *Muness Castle* built by Lawrence Bruce in 1598, and thence go N. to **Baltasound** (*Springfield*, RB. 16/6, P. 8 gs.), a scattered village with chromate deposits. *Haroldswick*, c. 2 m. N., the ordinary bus terminus, has the most northerly post office in Britain. Thence the Fri. bus goes on past an airfield to a point on the flank of *Saxa Vord* (934 ft.), a prominent seamark for 40 m. round, now crowned by a radar station. From the bus-stop a view is obtained, across the deep inlet of *Burra Firth*, to *Muckle Flugga Lighthouse*, the most northerly habitation of Britain (60° 51′ 22″ N. lat.), on a rock 1 m. N.W. of the entrance to the firth. In fine weather a boat may be hired at Burrafirth to view the lighthouse and the stacks of *Hermaness*, the magnificent promontory W. of the firth, now a sea-birds' sanctuary.

FROM LERWICK TO HILLSWICK, 36½ m., motor-bus. From (19 m.) *Voe* (see above) the road follows the shore of Olna Firth, past the slight remains of the last whaling station in Shetland, to (24 m.) *Brae*, where the mansion of *Busta* (l., above the voe) occupies one of the most favoured positions in Shetland. A road on the right (leading to Mossbank) skirts *Sullom Voe*, an important naval and air base in 1939–45, the target of the first German air-raid in 1939. The Sullom Voe Hotel (RB. 16/, P. 7 gs.), 4¼ m. from Brae, occupies the former officers' quarters.—We cross (25½ m.) the narrow isthmus of *Mavis Grind*, less than 50 yds. wide and often swept by the waves. *Northmaven*, the peninsula to the N., is indented with fine sea-lochs and, in *Ronas Hill* (1475 ft. ; *View), includes the highest point in the Shetlands. At 30 m. we diverge to the left from the road which goes on to the crofts of the extreme N. (9 m.) and reach (36 m.) **Hillswick** (*St. Magnus*, for cruise-parties only), a centre for fishing and for exploring the coast.—Off the W. coast of the peninsula on which Hillswick stands are the *Drongs*, stacks which have taken various fantastic shapes, and 3 m. W. is *Dore Holm*, with a huge natural arch. On the W. shore of Esha Ness (lighthouse of 1929), the promontory W. of Hillswick, is (5 m.) the **Grind of the Navir* (' gate of the giants '), where the porphyry cliffs have been strangely eroded by the sea. The water from *Houland Loch*, a little S., falls from a height of 60 ft. into the *Holes of Scraada*, an enormous cauldron communicating with the sea by a passage 100 ft. long. A blow-hole called the Cannon, close at hand, demonstrates an earlier stage in the formation of these cavities.

FROM LERWICK TO WALLS AND SANDNESS, motor-bus. Leaving the N. road above Tingwall, A 971 (*View on the descent) passes (12 m.) *Whiteness* (Taing House, summer only, P. 3 gs.), on the isthmus between Stromness Voe and Strom Loch (r.), on an island in which are the foundations of *Strom Castle*, perhaps the residence of the lords of Shetland before the building of Scalloway castle.— 12¾ m. We round the head of the long Weisdale Voe ; *Kergord*, in the valley to the right, has the largest group of trees in Shetland. The road goes on to (22¼ m.) *Bridge of Walls* and (24¼ m.) *Walls*, the nearest port to Foula ; by-roads on both sides serve the crofts and voes of this western peninsula. At Stanydale in *Sandsting*, 1½ m. E. of Bridge of Walls, an oval Neolithic temple of Mediterranean type, unique in Britain, was excavated in 1950. From the bridge the main road leads r. to (30 m.) *Sandness*, where a mail boat crosses the boisterous Sound of Papa to the island of *Papa Stour*, noted for its magnificent caves. There was a leper colony on the islet of *Brei Holm*, off its E. coast, as late as the 18th cent. ; while 4 m. N.W. are the dangerous seal-haunted *Ve Skerries*.

INDEX

Topographical names are printed in black type, names of persons in italics, other entries, including the subordinate indexes of Edinburgh and Glasgow, in Roman type. *Bens, Glens, Lochs,* and *Saints* are indexed in alphabetical sub-groups under these headings.—Place names are followed by their counties (in brackets), but for villages, lochs, etc., in the Hebrides islands are named instead of counties. The following abbreviations are used in the index :

Aber	= Aberdeen.	Inv	= Inverness.
Arg	= Argyll.	Kinc	= Kincardine.
Berw	= Berwickshire.	Kinr	= Kinross.
Caith	= Caithness.	Kirk	= Kirkcudbright.
Cla	= Clackmannan.	Lnrk	= Lanark.
Cumb	= Cumberland.	Midl	= Midlothian.
Dumf	= Dumfries.	Nthb	= Northumber-
Dunb	= Dunbarton.		land.
Eastl	= East Lothian.	Ork	= Orkney.
Peeb	= Peebles.		
Renf	= Renfrew.		
Rox	= Roxburgh.		
Selk	= Selkirk.		
Shet	= Shetland.		
Stir	= Stirling.		
Suth	= Sutherland.		
Westl	= West Lothian.		
Wig	= Wigtown.		

PRINTED IN GREAT BRITAIN BY J. & J. GRAY, ANNANDALE STREET, EDINBURGH

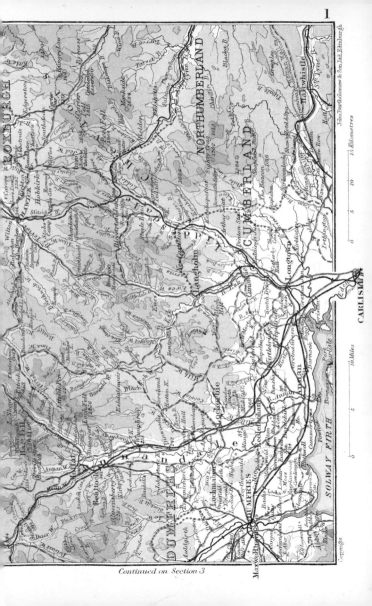

CARLISLE

SOLWAY FIRTH

NORTHUMBERLAND

CUMBERLAND

ROXBURGH

DUMFRIESSHIRE

DUMFRIES

John Bartholomew & Son, Ltd. Edinburgh

0   5   10 Miles

0   5   10   15 Kilometres

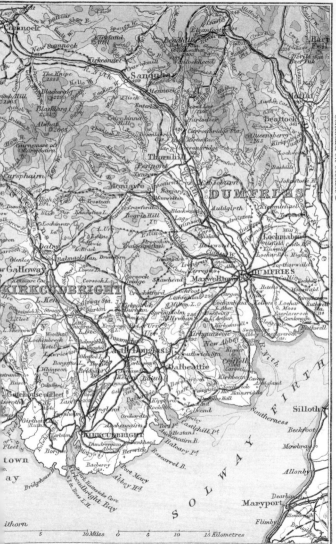

5   10 Miles 0   5   10   15 Kilometres

Strait of Corri

Dhu Heartearch
L. Ho.

Maol na Cala

Killoran
L. Spotar
Kilchatt
Colonsay Ho.
Colonsay
Dungallan
Ardskinish Pt.
Balaruminmore

Oronsay

Glengarrisdale B.
Glendebadel B.

Ben Bro.

JURA

Loch Tarbert

Rudha Mhail

Sgarbhnairrac

Nave I.
Ardnave

Garbhsiann

Paps of
Jura

Ardmenish

Ton Mor Pt.
Sanaig Pt.
Sanaigmore
L. Corr

Distillery
Milassdean

Port Askaig

Saligou B.

Cul Pt.
Kilchoman
Machir
Kilchiaran B.
Ben Tartabhaila

Bridgend
Inn
ISLAY
Bowmore

Small Isles
Bay

Small Isles Pt.

Proaig B.

Ben Bhan

Cladville
Port Wemyss
Orsay
Rhinns L. Ho.

Loggan
Bay

Bealloch a Gaoch Pt.
Claggain Bay
Kintour B.
Ardmore Pt.

W. Tarbert

Gigha I.
(Ghia)
Gighie

Slochd Mhaol Doraidh
Glen Astle
Port Ellen

The Oa

Mull of Oa

Ballychatrigan

Otter Rk.

Cara I.

Campbeltown
Machrihanish
Losset Park
Davarr I.
Kildalloig
KINTYRE

Earadale Pt.
Killellan

Achinhoan Hd.

Dun Ban

Polliwilline B.
Macharioch
Southend
Keil
Carskey
Mull
of Kintyre
L.Ho.

Sheep I.
Sanda I.
L. Ho.

BUTE County, includes
the Islands of Bute, Arran
& the Cumbraes.

Machri

Machriha

0   5   10 Miles   0   5   10   15 Kilom

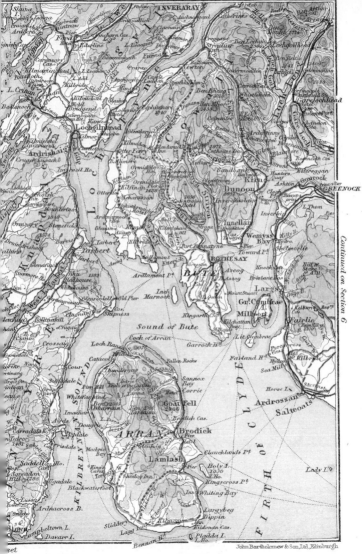

John Bartholomew & Son, Ltd. Edinburgh

INVERARAY

Lochgilphead

Ardrishaig

Otter Ferry

Tarbert

DUNOON

Innellan

ROTHESAY

Wemyss
Bay

Largs

Millport

Sound of Bute

Goat Fell

ARRAN

Brodick

Lamlash

Whiting Bay

FIRTH OF CLYDE

KILBRENNAN SOUND OF KINTYRE

Ardrossan

Saltcoats

Troon

Prestwick

AYR

0   5   10 Miles   0   5   10   15 Kilometr

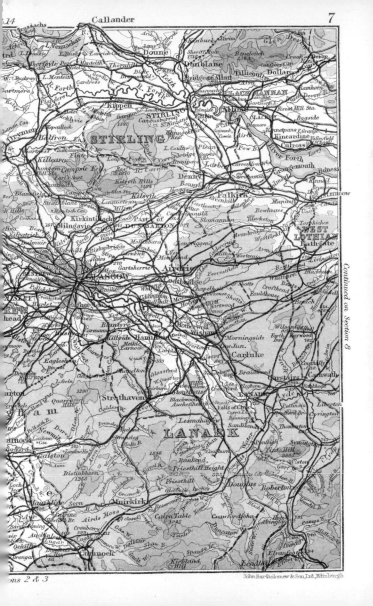

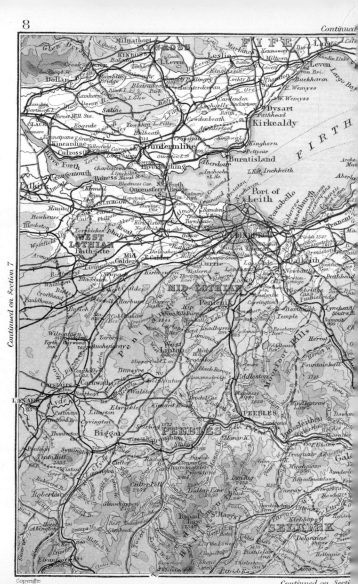

Copyright

0   5   10 Miles   0   5   10   15 Kilometres

0   5   10 Miles   0   5   10   15 Kilometre

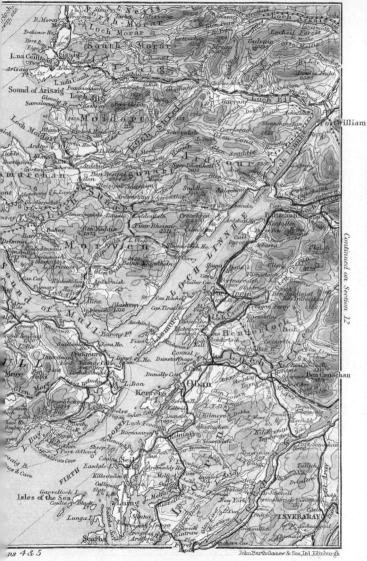

Continued on Section 12

Continued on Section II

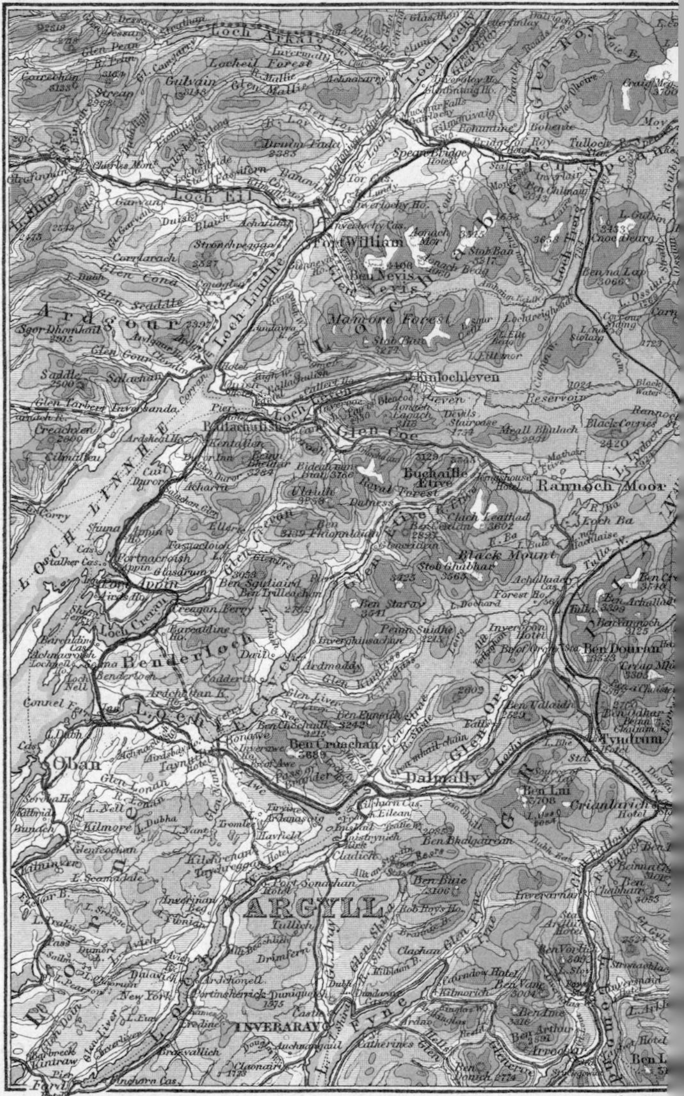

Loch Arkaig
Locheil Forest
Glen Roy
Glen Mallie
Loch Eil
Fort William
Ben Nevis 4406
Mamore Forest
Kinlochleven
Ardgour
Sgor Dhonuill
Loch Linnhe
Glen Coe
Buchaille
Etive
Rannoch Moor
Ballachulish
Black Mount
Stob Ghabhar
Glencreran
Loch Creran
Appin
Ben Starav
Benderloch
Ben Cruachan
Dalmally
Connel F.
Oban
ARGYLL
Loch Awe
Ben Lui
Crianlarich
Ben Vorlich
Glen Orchy
Loch Etive
INVERARAY
Loch Fyne
Ben Arthur
Arrochar
Ben L.

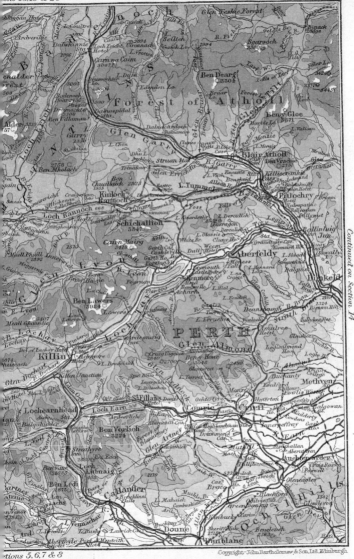

Continued on Section 14

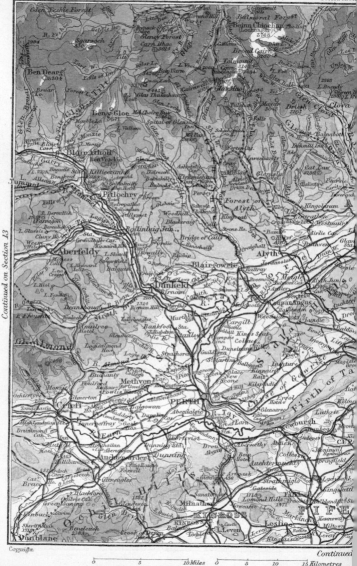

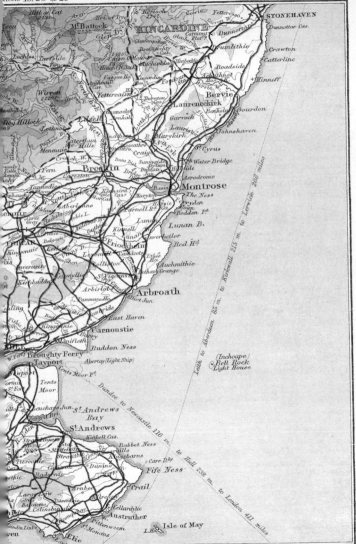

STONEHAVEN

KINCARDINE

Dunnottar

Dunnottar Cas.

Crawton

Catterline

Roadside

Redcliff

Bervie

Laurencekirk

Johnshaven

Gourdon

Bervie Ho.

Garvock

Marykirk

St Cyrus

North Water Bridge

Aerodrome

Brechin

Montrose

The Ness

Pryden

Boddon Pt.

Lunan B.

Inverkeilor

Red Hd.

Auchmithie

Arbroath

Eliot Jun.

East Haven

Carnoustie

Buddon Ness

Broughty Ferry

Tayport

Abertay (Light Ship)

Tents Moor Pt.

Tents Moor

Dundee to Newcastle 118 m.

St Andrews Bay

St Andrews

Kinkell Cas.

Babbet Ness

Kingsbarns

Carr Brs.

Fife Ness

Crail

Isle of May

Anstruther

Cellardyke

St Monans

Elie

Leith to Aberdeen 82 m. to Kirkwall 215 m. to Lerwick 265 miles

to Hull 298 m. to London 411 miles

(Inchcape)
Bell Rock
Light House

Boreray

Valley

Griminish Pt.

Scalpsey

Hougar

Tighary

Balranald

Paible

Claddach

Sollas

Portan Long

Trumpan

Newton Ho.

L. Fada

North Uist

L. Scatavagh

Inver Loch Maddy

L. nan-Ian

Harmetray

Ben Lee

Loch Eport

Baleshare

Gramisdale

Benbecula

Balivanich

Benbecula Sound

Ben Eaval 1133

Grimiuish

Oban

Ronay

Wiay I.

Langrat L.

Carnan

L. Uskevagh

L. Druidibeg

L. Skiport

Howmore

L. Aultibride

Hecla 1988

Ru Ushinish

Ardvula Pt.

Rothay

Caradale

Ben More 2035

L. Kildonan

Milton

Arnaval

South Uist

L. Naserable

Loch Eynort

L. Leanamore

Hecla 1227

Askernish Ho.

Stuiley

Daliburgh

Usinish

L. Allan

Hoibnebreteann

Loch boisdale

L. Duine Kettle

Calvay

Loch Boisdale

Pollachar Inn

Sound of Barra

Lingay's

Ben Scrien 609

Eriskay

Flaray

Scurrival Pt.

Fuday

Stack Is.

Eoligarry

Gighay

Hellisay

Barra Ch.

Inn.

Bervagh

Barra I.

Ersary

Castlebay

Kisimul Cas.

Vatersay

Muldoanich

LITTLE

MINCH

Vaternish

Unis

Trumpan

Ardmore

Hali

Isa

Dunvegan Hd.

Biodan Athair 1025

Galtrigill

Beravaig

Milovaig

Bloshorm

Oisgill B.

Colbost

Eist

Skin

Moonen B.

Ramasaig

Hoe Pt.

Olisdale

McLeods Mai

Idr

I S L

S

Can

Garrisdale F

Hyske

Mills Rk.

0   5   10 Miles   0   5   10   15 Kilometres

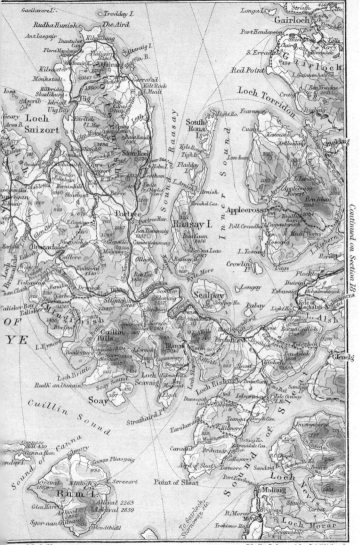

Continued on Section 17

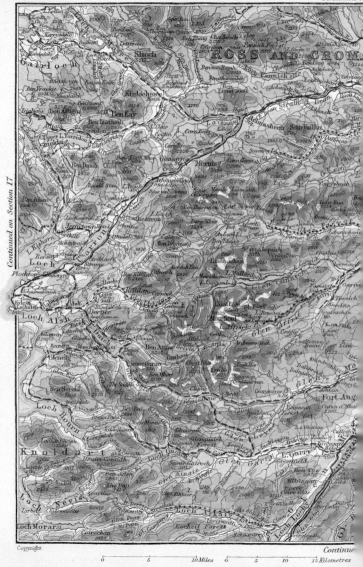

ROSS AND CROM

Gairloch

Knoidart

Fort Aug

Continue

0   5   10 Miles   0   5   10   15 Kilometres

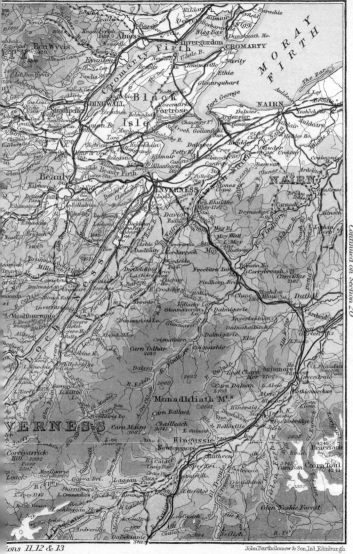

Continued on Section 20

Copyright

Continued

Continued on Section 19

0   5   10 Miles   0   5   10   15 Kilometres

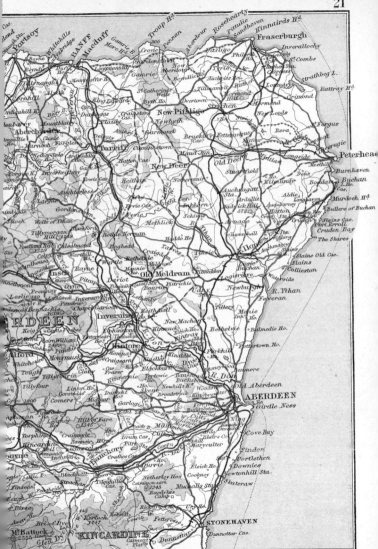

John Bartholomew & Son, Ltd, Edinburgh.

Gallon Hd.

Uig B.
Valtos
Uig
Miavaig
Suainashal
1250

L.
Roag
LEW
Callernish
Garynahine
Stone
Circles

Aird Bhreidhuis
Mealasbhal
1750

L.
Langabhat
Garynahine
L. Morsgail

Treitasbhal
Roinebhal
Achmore
Balallan

Crionabhal
1300
L. Beag

Malista

L. Hamanaway

Scallabhal
Resort
Luachair

Laxdale

P

Scarpay

Gas Koir

Forest
Harris

Ben M
1750
Fi

W. L. Tarbert

Loch Seaforth

Taransay

W. L. Tarbert
Tarbert

Yarnach

Aird Vanish

Lusboost

E. L. Tarbert

Scalpa

Toe Hd.
Borve Lo.
L. Ho.

Sound of Harris

C. Dirncuity

St. Kilda 57 miles
Skillay

Pabbay

Ensay

L. Stromas

Langavat

L. Chreosabhaigh

Killegray

Leverburgh
Rodel

Fiusbay

Flodavagh

Berneray

Groay
or Bernera

Lingay

Gilsay

Renish

Boreray

Portnan Longa
Newton
Farm

Phir
or Bernera

Harmetray

Vallay
Trumisgarry

Scalpay
Hougary

L. Fada

North Uist
L. Scatavagh

Loch Maddy

Vaternish Pt.

Unish

Balranald

Paible
Claddach

L. nan Ian

Loch Eport

LITTLE

Baleshare

Carinish
Inn

Ben Eaval 1133

Ronay

MINCH

Loch Dunvegan

Dunvegan Hd.

Gramisdale Inn

Benbecula

L. Rules Way

L. Uskevagh

Biodan Athan
L. Pooltiel

Oisgill B.

Eist

Mooren B.

Copyright

Continued

0   5   10 Miles
0   5   10   15 Kilometres

N O R T H

M I N C H

Shiant
East
Bank

37 miles

Stornoway to Kyle of Lochalsh

51 miles

62 mi

Stornoway Harb.

Stornoway

Sandwick

Knock Bayble

Suordel

Chicken Rock

Arnish

Luirbost

Ranish

Crossbost

Cromore

L.Odairn

Kebock Hd.

Lemreway

Jubhard

L.Shell

Eilean Mhuire

Shiant I?

Skeir Graitich

Skeir na Mule

Trodday I.

The Aird

Rudha Hunish

Iasgair

Duntulm Cas.

Flora Macdonald's

Kilmaluag

Kilmuir

Cuinag

Balmacara

Quiraing

Staffin B.

Kilvaxter

Monkstadt

Kilbride

Skudiburgh

Uig Bay

Uig

Earlish

Greshornish Pt

Greenstone Pt

Rudha Mor

Slaggan

Aultbea

Laid

Charles

Rudh Re

Cove

Inverasdale

Midtown

Naast

Poolewe

Loch Ewe

L.Luie

Rudha na

Melvaig

Altgreshan

Enoc Breac

N.Erradale

Sand

Strath

Longa I.

Gairloch

Port Henderson

Shieldaig

Kerrysdale

Kerry

S.Erradale

Gairloch

Red Point

L.Gaineamhach

Ben Vrackie

Bealach

Loch Torridon

Fearnmore

Craig

Diabaig

Bad Allan

Cuaig

Kenmore

Ardhesaig

Upper L.Torridon

Shieldaig

Ben Damh

Applecross
Forest

Ben Bhan

Applecross

Lightho.

South
Rona I.

Kyle Rona

Tigh I.

Fladday
I.

Lon ban

Amish

Arnish

Brochel Cas.

Kyleakin

Storr Rock

Holm I.

Kealtham

Py.Charles

Berry

Portree

Kingsburgh

Bracadale

Drynoch

Dunvegan

Loch
Eizort

S K Y E

Inner Sound

South Rona

Kyle of Raasay

John Bartholomew & Son, Ltd. Edinburgh

Continued on Sections 17 & 23

SU...

Clashmore L.
Balloladdich
Stoer
Clachtoll
Achmelvich
Loch Roe
Soya I.
Rhu Coigach
Enard Bay
Reiff
Rhu More
Altandhu
Mullagrach I.
Ristol I.
Summer Is.
Tanera Beg
Tanera More
Glas-leac Mor
Glas-leac Beg
Priest I.
Dubh I.
Bottle I.
Cailleach Hd.
Achnahaird
Achiltibuie

Lochinver
Inverkirkaig
L. Kirkaig
Canisp
3785
Suilven
Stronchrubie
Cam Loch
L. Urigill

Quinag
Ben Leod
Loch Assynt
Inchnadamph
Ben More
3273

Coigach
Ben More
Achduart
Achlunachan

Loch Broom
Ullapool
Ardmair
Scoraig
Annat

Little Loch Broom
Badcaul
Gruinard Bay
Gruinard
Badluarach
Laide
Sail Mhor
Dundonnell Ho.
An Teallach
3483
Toll Lochan

Ben Dearg
3547

Poolewe
Hotel
Tournaig
Inverewe
Loch Maree
Slioch
3217

Kinlochewe
Hotel
Ben Eay
Ben Alligin
Ben Lair
Beinn Eighe
Torridon
Upper L. Torridon
Shieldaig
Ben Damph
Ben Damh
Lochcarron
Strathcarron

ROSS AND CROMARTY

Achnasheen
Loch Fannich
Strathconon
Ben Wyvis

Strathcarron

0   5   10 Miles   0   5   10   15 Kilometres

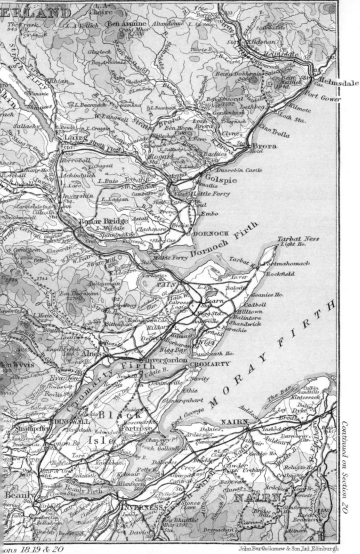

John Bartholomew & Son, Ltd, Edinburgh

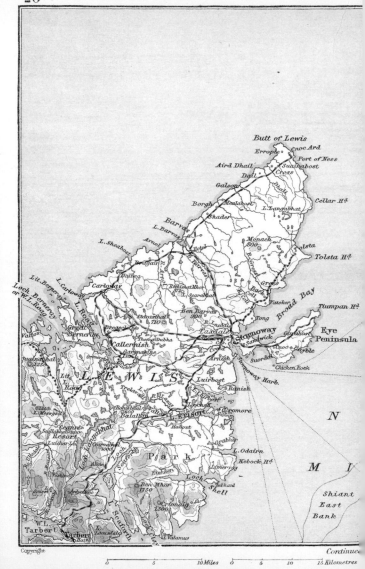

0 5 10 Miles 0 5 10 15 Kilometres

Copyright

Cape Wrath
Light Ho. 270
Clash Carnoch
Cnoc-a-chaoish 563
Keisgog B.
Ben Dearg 1283
Eilean Bulgac
The Shepherd
Sandybod
Sheigra 397
Oldshoremore
Roan I.
Loch Inchard
Kinlochbervie
Badcall
Kinloch
L. Doine
Sallachness
Loch Laxford
Handa 406
Scourie B.
Scourie
Badcall
Eddrachillis F.
Ben Stack 2367
Badcall
Ben Auskaird
Eddrachillis
Bay
Ben Strome
L. Cairnbawn
Pt. of Stoer
Oldany
Drumbeg
Rhu Stoer
L. Culfraichie
Oldany I.
Enspoio
Clashmore I.
Clashnessie
Ballchladdich
Culkein
Quinag
Stoer
Clashtoll
Lettergie
Achmelvich
ASSYNT
Loch Inver
Lochinver
Seya I.
Inver
Camisp 2386
L. Kirkaig
Sullven
Inverkirkaig
Rhu Coigach
Enard
Bay
Canl.
Reiff
Kilmore
Altandove
Midlagreach I.
Ristol I.
Polbain
Glas-leac Mor
Coulbeg
Summer Is.
Tanera Beg
Horse I.
Glas-leac Beg
Priest I.
Dubh I.
Bottle I.
Martin
Ben More
Greenstone Pt.
Cailleach
Ho.
Ardmair
Rhidorroch

Stornoway to Thurso 103 miles

Continued on Sections 24 & 28

ions 22 23 & 24

Continued on Section 27

Continued

0   5   10 Miles   0   5   10   15 Kilometres

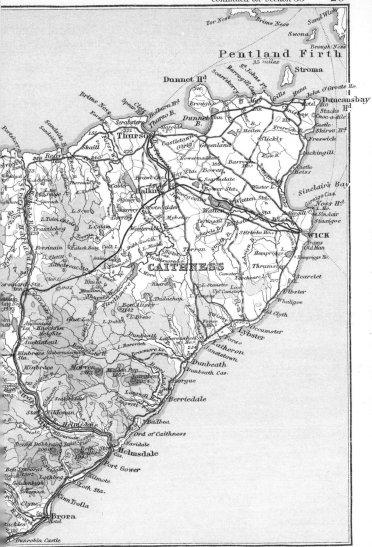

Tor Ness   Brims Ness   Sand Wick
Swona
Brough Ness

Pentland Firth
35 miles   Stroma

Dunnet Hd   Barrock Ho   St Johns Pt   Scarskerry   Gills   John O'Groats Ho.
Brims Ness   Clett   Holburn Hd   Brough   Mey   Hotel   Duncansbay Hd
Fors Ho   Spear Hd   Thurso B.   Dunnet   Inn   Canisbay   Stacks   Cnoc-a-dile
Sandside B.   Scrabster   356   Thurso B.   B.   L. B.   Freswick B.   Castle   Skirsa Hd
Portskerra   155   321   Skaill   Harold's   Dunnet   Inn   L. Heilen   Freswick
Sandside B.   Reay   386   340   Castletown   Stickly   Kirk B.   Auchingill
173   Olrig   Greenland   Barrogill   I. Ho.
Skaill   Thurman   Bowermaddens   189   Heiss
L. Scye   Brawl Cas.   Hoy Std   Bower   Barrock   Wester L.   Sinclair's Bay
Calder   Olrig   Scarmclate   Craigo Cas.   Noss Hd
L. Calum   L. Watten   Sinclair
Tradlebeg   Halkirk   Georgemas   Bower Sta.   Watten Sta.   Staxigoe
Forsinain   Shurrey   Scotscalder   Myhster   Strokes Ho.   Wick
 Achena Bea   Westerdale   Watten   Tartingell   sta   Trams   Old Man
L. More   Torran   Acharole B.   Strokes Ho.
CAITHNESS   Hemprigs   Thrumster   Scarlet
Dunbeath   Latheronwheel   Camster   Thurso   Ubster
Inver   L. Rangag   Loch Watenan   Whaligoe
Ben Alisky   Thulachan   Swiny   Occumster   Ld Clyth
L. Dubh   L. Breac   Forse   Lybster
L. Rangag   Latheron
Kinbrace Sta.   Dunbeath   Latheronwheel   254   Janetstown
Kinbrace   Braemore Lo.   Inn   Dunbeath Cas.
Morven   2313   Maiden Pap   1587   Scaraben   2054   Gorgue
Langwell Ho.   Berriedale
Langwell wr   Badbea
Helmsdale   Ord of Caithness
Beinn Dobhraidh   2060   Navidale
Helmsdale   Port Gower
Ben Sphurat   1940   Loth Sta.
Gordonbush   Kilmote
Brora   Hotel
Clyne   Cinn Trolla
Dunrobin Castle

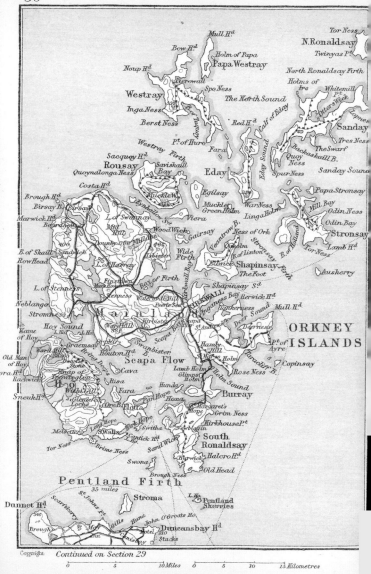

ORKNEY ISLANDS

Tor Ness
N. Ronaldsay
Twinyas Pt.

Mull Hd.
Bow Hd.
Holm of Papa
Papa Westray
Noup Hd.
North Ronaldsay Firth
Holms of Ire
Whitemill Pt.
Pierowall
Spo Ness
Otters Wick
Westray
Inga Ness
The North Sound
Sanday
Berst Ness
Red Hd.
Calf of Eday
Backaskaill B.
Tres Ness
Pt. of Huro
Fara
Eday Sound
Quoy Ness
Spur Ness
Sanday Sound
Westray Firth
Sacquoy Hd.
Saviskaill Bay
Papa Stronsay
Rousay
Egilsay
War Ness
Mill Bay
Odin Ness
Quoyndalonga Ness
Eday
Linga Holm
Odin Bay
Costa Hd.
Muckle Green Holm
Stronsay
Brough Hd.
Birsay B.
Muckle Wevie
Viera
Lamb Hd.
Birsay
Byrholm B.
Wood Wick
Gairsay
Ness of Ork
Tor Ness
Marwick Hd.
L. of Swannay
Mid Hill
Wide Firth
Auskerry
Boardhouse
Dounby
Millhouse
Shapinsay
B. of Skaill
Sandwick
Isbister
The Foot
Row Head
L. of Harray
Shapinsay Sd.
Ness
Kirkwall
Berwick Hd.
L. of Stenness
Mainland
KIRKWALL
Inganess Bay
Neblango
Stenness
Bankerness
Stromness
Bay of Firth
Deer Sound
Mull Hd.
Hoy Sound
Wardhill
Kirbister
Scapa Bay
St Andrews
Deerness
Kane of Hoy
Graemsay
Houton Hd.
Swanbister
Pt. of Ayre
Old Man of Hoy
Rora Hd.
Brims Ders
Cava
Scapa Flow
Hamly Hill
Taracliff B.
Copinsay
Radwick
Snap of Trowieglen
Risa
Fara
Lamb Holm
Holm Sound
Rose Ness
Sneuk Hd.
HOY
Withi Hill
Glenels Lochs
Flotta
Hunda
Hoxa
Burray
Pan Hope
Margaret's Hope
Melsetter
Long Hope
Switha
Newbigging
Grim Ness
S. Walls
Kirk Hope
Cantick Hd.
Sand Wick
South Ronaldsay
Kirkhouse Pt.
Tor Ness
Brims Ness
Swona
Barwick
Halcro Hd.
Old Head
Pentland Firth
35 miles
Brough Ness
Dunnet Hd.
Scarsberry
St Johns Pt.
Stroma
Pentland Skerries
Brough
May
Gills
Huna
John O'Groats Ho.
Duncansbay Hd.
Finstry
Hotel
Stacks

Continued on Section 29

Copyright

0   5   10 Miles   0   5   10   15 Kilometres

SHETLAND

ISLANDS

West Burra — Norbister, Gladdabister, Canningsburgh, Belli Ness

Cliff Hills, S. Havra, Hoswick, Ireland, Sandwick, Mousa, No Ness, St Ninian's, Rerwick, Levenwick, Sel of Shuna, L. of Spiggie, Boddam, Dunrossness Ch., al Head, Garthbanks, Quendale, Virkie, N. Grutness, Quendale R., V. of Sumburgh, Sumburgh Head

Muckla Flugga, Herma Ness, Burra Firth, Nor Wick, Setland, Norwick, L. of Cliff, Haroldswick, Harolds Wick, Baltasound, Balta, Westing, Keolta, Balta, Huney, Sandwick, Crossound, Mu Ness, Uness Cas.

Uyea, Kess of Bratland, Gloup Voe, Cullivoe, Gossa W., Dalsetter, Belmont, Uyea

Nev of Stuis, Pt of Fethaland, Hara, Colvister, Mid Yell, Hascosay, Sellar Ch., Vindra, Funzie, Fetlar

Yell Sound, Islister, Burra Voe, Uyea, Lang Clodie Wick, The Faither, W. Sandwick, Otterswick, Otters Wick, Colgrave Sd., Wick of Gruting, Rick of Tresta

Hamna Voe, Collafirth, Colla Fm., Romas H., Ollaberry, Cuss, Ulsta Bay, Kirmaboe, Burravoe, Neoga Ness, Esha Ness, Stenness, Heylor, Lela W., Bigga, Samphrey, Hamna Voe, Hillswick, Bardister, Mossbank, Baa Taing, Sullom, Sullom Voe, Urana Holm

St Magnus, Mangaster, Ch., Bay, Voe, Lunna, Lunn Ness, Out Skerries

Muckle Roe, Swarbacks Minn, Olna Fm., Skotberry, Laxo, W. Linga, Whalsey

Papa Stour, Vementry, Dale, Dury Voe, Stava Ness, Neap, SHETLAND

Sd. of Papa, Sandness, Melby, Burrafirth, Clousta, Aith, Sandwater, Skellister, S. Nesting Bay, Moul of Eswick, ISLANDS

Sandness Hill, Mu Ness, Linga W., Effirths Hotel, Tresta, Vidlin, Walls, Setter, Gruting, Breakon, Weisdale Voe, Whiteness, Walbister

Braga Ness, Reawick, Tingwall, Kebister Ness, Vaila, Gruting Voe, The Deeps, Whiteness Voe, Maryfield, LERWICK, Bressay, L. of Noss, Scalloway, Sound, Trondra, Ward of Bressay 742, Bard Hd.

West Burra, Norbister, Gladdabister

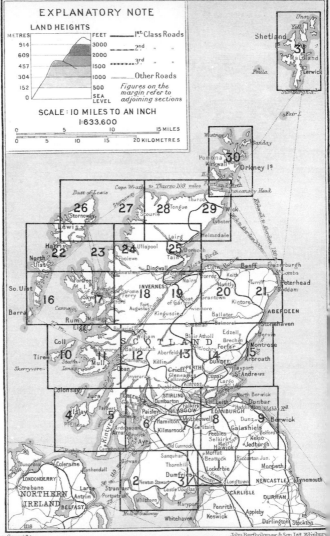

EXPLANATORY NOTE

LAND HEIGHTS

METRES		FEET	
914		3000	1st. Class Roads
609		2000	2nd "
457		1500	3rd "
304		1000	Other Roads
152		500	Figures on the margin refer to adjoining sections
0	SEA LEVEL	0	

SCALE : 10 MILES TO AN INCH
1:633.600

0   5   10   15 MILES
0   5   10   15   20 KILOMETRES